Who Offers Part-Time Degree Programs?

SECOND EDITION

Karen C. Hegener, Editor
Andrew T. Rowan, Data Editor
Amy J. Goldstein, Assistant Editor

With an Introduction by
Kay Kohl
Executive Director of the National
University Continuing Education Association

ADULT LEARNING CENTER

Peterson's Guides
Princeton, New Jersey

Copyright © 1985 by Peterson's Guides, Inc.

All rights reserved. No part of this book may be reproduced, stored in a retrieval system, or transmitted, in any form or by any means, electronic, mechanical, photocopying, recording, or otherwise, without the written permission of Peterson's Guides, Inc.

Library of Congress Cataloging in Publication Data

Main entry under title:

Who offers part-time degree programs?

Includes index.
1. Degrees, Academic—United States. 2. Students, Part-time—United States. 3. Universities and colleges—United States—Directories. 4. Evening and continuation schools—United States—Directories. I. Hegener, Karen C. II. Rowan, Andrew T., 1962- . III. Goldstein, Amy J.
LB2381.W53 1984   378'.24'02573   84-22744
ISBN 0-87866-285-5

Printed in the United States of America

10 9 8 7 6 5 4 3 2 1

For information about other Peterson's publications, please see the listing at the back of this volume.

Contents

Introduction	v
Section 1: Colleges Offering Part-Time Degree Programs	1
Section 2: Directories of Specialized Information	364
Colleges Offering Part-Time Evening Programs	365
Colleges Offering Part-Time Weekend Programs	379
Colleges Offering Part-Time Summer Programs	382
Colleges Offering External Degree Programs	393
Index to Colleges	397

Introduction

American adults are seeking university diplomas in increasing numbers. In part, the surge of adults campusward can be explained by the fact that they constitute a larger proportion of the population than ever before. But also, the need and desire among adults to obtain degrees is more acute today.

Most adults are drawn to enroll in part-time degree programs by the prospect of enhancing their career opportunities. The rapid introduction of new technologies has rendered even accomplished workers' skills obsolete and effectively prevented the reentry of still others, especially women who may have elected to remain out of the full-time work force for a few years to raise a family. In a nation where one quarter of the adult population between 25 and 34 years of age possesses a college degree, it is perhaps inevitable that credentials tend to strongly influence how employers categorize and remunerate their employees.

Farsighted businesses and industries recognize that an educated work force can be expected to maintain and contribute to productivity and accordingly offer their employees educational benefits. A substantial number of the students enrolled in part-time degree programs are there with tuition assistance from their employers. The best part-time degree programs enable a student to acquire highly specialized job-related skills together with a broad foundation in the liberal arts. The effective combination of the two is what prepares individuals to become creative problem solvers and critical thinkers who can relate narrow professional concerns to a broader societal context.

New family patterns also are responsible for promoting increased interest in part-time degree programs. More than half the married women in the United States now hold full-time jobs; this reveals that a full-time job outside the home is now an essential aspect of life for a majority of adults in this country—both men and women. With work playing a more critical role in more people's lives, interest in part-time degree programs has grown because education offers adults the means to enrich the career aspect of life's experience.

The academic institutions described in this book are among those that have responded to the demand for part-time degree programs. *Who Offers Part-Time Degree Programs?* provides a comprehensive survey of available opportunities at accredited colleges and universities in the United States. As such, the volume constitutes an excellent resource for educational professionals—counselors, librarians, and researchers. It also can introduce the prospective part-time degree student to the range of undergraduate and graduate educational opportunities.

This book shows that many colleges and universities are committed to creating new educational options for part-time degree students. Institutions across the country have demonstrated a flexibility in organizing courses for credit on a part-time basis through evening, daytime, weekend, summer, and external degree programs. Students are not required to take a prescribed number of courses, but depending upon their readiness they may enroll in a single course or begin immediately with a more extensive schedule.

Institutions of higher education have embraced new delivery systems. By pooling their course development resources, colleges and universities have been able to improve the quality and diversity of their course offerings. For the highly motivated part-time degree student, television or computer-assisted instruction may offer greater flexibility and the opportunity to take a heavier load.

Beyond adapting schedules and utilizing new delivery systems, colleges and universities are taking seriously their responsibility to serve the part-time degree student. They are developing financial aid programs to assist qualified part-time students. They are offering special seminars to help those who have been away from school for some time to sharpen their academic skills and develop strategies that will enable them to make the most of their college experience. They are granting college credits for skills and knowledge acquired outside the academic setting. They are offering career planning and placement counseling to part-time students interested in career advisement and job opportunities.

Part-time students now account for nearly half of the enrollment in America's colleges and universities. The individual who decides to pursue a degree on a part-time basis, therefore, joins one of the fastest-growing populations in higher education.

Kay Kohl
Executive Director of the
National University Continuing
Education Association

SECTION 1
Colleges Offering Part-Time Degree Programs

The colleges and universities included in this book are those that reported offering part-time degree programs on Peterson's 1984 Annual Surveys of Undergraduate and Graduate Institutions. A part-time degree program is one that allows a student to earn a degree by attending classes *exclusively* part-time. All the colleges and universities in this book are located in the United States or in a U.S. territory, grant recognized postsecondary degrees, and meet the accreditation criteria of the U.S. Department of Education or the Council on Postsecondary Accreditation.

Each profile consists of a general information paragraph followed by specific data about undergraduate and/or graduate part-time programs.

General Information

This paragraph gives a brief introduction to the college, covering the following elements.

Institutional control: A *public* college receives its funding wholly or primarily from the federal, state, and/or local government. A private college is supported primarily by tuition, gifts, and endowment. This category includes *independent* (nonprofit), *independent-religious* (sponsored by or affiliated with a certain religious group or having a nondenominational or interdenominational religious orientation), and *proprietary* (profit-making) institutions.

Campus setting: The categories are *metropolitan* (located in a major metropolitan area with a population of over 500,000), *city* (population 50,000 to 500,000), *small-town* (population under 50,000), and *rural*.

Degrees awarded: An associate degree program (designated by *A*) may be either a college-transfer program, equivalent to the first half of a bachelor's degree, or a terminal program providing training for a specific occupation. A bachelor's degree program (*B*) is a complete undergraduate program in a liberal arts, science, professional, or preprofessional field. A master's degree (*M*) is the first graduate degree in the liberal arts and sciences and certain professional fields. A doctoral degree (*D*) is the highest degree awarded in research-oriented academic disciplines; the first professional degrees in such fields as law and medicine are also at the doctoral level.

Accessibility: A campus that meets federal standards for access to buildings and facilities by the physically handicapped is designated a *barrier-free campus*.

Enrollment: *Total enrollment* is the number of matriculated students, both full-time and part-time, in 1983–84. If the institution has both graduate and undergraduate students, generally an *undergraduate enrollment* figure is also given. This is then further broken down into percentages of *part-time* students, *women*, and students *over 25*.

Faculty: The total number of full-time and part-time faculty members teaching undergraduate and/or graduate courses in 1983–84 is given.

Library holdings: Numbers of *bound volumes*, *titles on microform*, *periodical subscriptions*, and *records/tapes* are listed.

Undergraduate Information

This paragraph provides information specifically about part-time programs and services at the undergraduate level.

Schedule: *Courses* and *complete degree programs* for part-time students may be offered during the *daytime, evenings, weekends,* or *summer,* as indicated.

Special programs: *External degree programs* emphasize off-campus, self-directed study. They usually require no more than 25 percent of degree credit to be earned through traditional class attendance and grant credit for documented on-the-job and other training and for experiential learning. *Adult/continuing education programs* are specially designed for "nontraditional" students—usually older students who are starting college for the first time or returning after some time off.

Career services: The services available to part-time students may include *individual career counseling, group career counseling, individual job placement,* and *employer recruitment on campus*.

Tuition: Costs are given for the 1984–85 academic year. *Part-time tuition* is expressed in terms of a per-unit rate (per credit, per semester hour, etc.) as specified by the institution. For public institutions at which tuition varies according to residence, separate figures are given for area and/or state residents and for nonresidents.

Colleges Offering Part-Time Degree Programs

Graduate Information

If an institution offers any part-time graduate programs, this paragraph focuses on the units within the institution that permit part-time study. The names of the units in which *part-time study is available* and those in which a *degree can be earned exclusively through evening/weekend study* are listed. Expenses are given as *tuition* and/or *fees,* expressed in the same manner as undergraduate tuition. Finally, the names of units in which *institutional financial aid* is available to part-time students are listed; this aid is distinct from federal or state money that would be available to qualified graduate students at any approved institution.

Alabama / **Colleges Offering Part-Time Degree Programs**

ALABAMA

Alabama Agricultural and Mechanical University
Normal 35762

Public institution; city setting. Awards A, B, M. Total enrollment: 4,310. Undergraduate enrollment: 3,465; 5% part-time, 49% women. Total faculty: 500. Library holdings: 350,000 bound volumes, 1,056 periodical subscriptions, 3,289 records/tapes.

Undergraduate Courses offered for part-time students during daytime, evenings, summer. Complete part-time degree programs offered during daytime, evenings, summer. Adult/continuing education programs available. Part-time tuition: $60 per semester hour for state residents, $70 per semester hour for nonresidents.

Graduate Part-time study available in School of Graduate Studies. Degree can be earned exclusively through evening/weekend study in School of Graduate Studies. Basic part-time expenses: $60 per credit tuition for state residents, $70 per credit tuition for nonresidents.

Alabama Aviation and Technical College
Ozark 36360

Public institution; small-town setting. Awards A. Barrier-free campus. Total enrollment: 409 (all undergraduates); 31% part-time, 4% women, 33% over 25. Total faculty: 40.

Undergraduate Courses offered for part-time students during daytime, evenings, weekends, summer. Complete part-time degree programs offered during daytime, evenings, weekends, summer. Career services available to part-time students: individual career counseling, individual job placement, employer recruitment on campus. Part-time tuition: $340 per year for state residents, $680 per year for nonresidents.

Alabama Christian College
Montgomery 36193

Independent-religious instutition; city setting. Awards A, B. Barrier-free campus. Total enrollment: 1,635 (all undergraduates); 10% part-time, 31% women, 33% over 25. Total faculty: 93. Library holdings: 25,000 bound volumes, 50 periodical subscriptions.

Undergraduate Courses offered for part-time students during daytime, evenings. Complete part-time degree programs offered during daytime, evenings. Adult/continuing education programs available. Career services available to part-time students: individual career counseling, individual job placement, employer recruitment on campus. Part-time tuition: $95 per semester hour.

Alabama State University
Montgomery 36195

Public institution; city setting. Awards A, B, M. Total enrollment: 4,050. Undergraduate enrollment: 3,790; 12% part-time, 57% women. Total faculty: 247. Library holdings: 247,000 bound volumes, 10,708 titles on microform, 1,016 periodical subscriptions, 6,000 records/tapes.

Undergraduate Courses offered for part-time students during daytime, evenings, weekends, summer. Complete part-time degree programs offered during daytime, evenings, weekends, summer. Adult/continuing education programs available. Career services available to part-time students: individual and group career counseling, individual job placement, employer recruitment on campus. Part-time tuition: $22 per quarter hour for state residents, $44 per quarter hour for nonresidents.

Graduate Part-time study available in School of Graduate Studies.Basic part-time expenses: $30 per credit tuition for state residents, $60 per credit tuition for nonresidents. Institutional financial aid available to part-time graduate students in School of Graduate Studies.

Alabama Technical College
East Gadsden 35999

Public institution; city setting. Awards A. Total enrollment: 825 (all undergraduates); 32% part-time, 15% women, 25% over 25. Total faculty: 45. Library holdings: 5,368 bound volumes, 65 titles on microform, 426 periodical subscriptions, 194 records/tapes.

Undergraduate Courses offered for part-time students during daytime, evenings. Complete part-time degree programs offered during daytime. Career services available to part-time students: individual career counseling, employer recruitment on campus. Part-time tuition: $255 per year.

Alexander City State Junior College
Alexander City 35010

Public institution; small-town setting. Awards A. Barrier-free campus. Total enrollment: 1,174 (all undergraduates); 33% part-time, 51% women, 20% over 25. Total faculty: 88. Library holdings: 32,063 bound volumes, 455 periodical subscriptions, 1,155 records/tapes.

Undergraduate Courses offered for part-time students during daytime, evenings, summer. Complete part-time degree programs offered during daytime, evenings, summer. Adult/continuing education programs available. Career services available to part-time students: individual career counseling, employer recruitment on campus. Part-time tuition: $15 per quarter hour for state residents, $30 per quarter hour for nonresidents.

Athens State College
Athens 35611

Public institution; small-town setting. Awards B. Total enrollment: 1,110 (all undergraduates); 48% part-time, 52% women. Total faculty: 78. Library holdings: 62,000 bound volumes, 400 periodical subscriptions, 1,000 records/tapes.

Undergraduate Courses offered for part-time students during daytime, evenings, weekends, summer. Complete part-time degree programs offered during daytime, evenings, weekends, summer. External degree and adult/continuing education programs available. Career services available to part-time students: individual career counseling, individual job placement, employer recruitment on campus. Part-time tuition: $20 per quarter hour for state residents, $40 per quarter hour for nonresidents.

Auburn University
Auburn University 36849

Public institution; small-town setting. Awards B, M, D. Total enrollment: 18,426. Undergraduate enrollment: 16,726; 8% part-time, 41% women, 7% over 25. Total faculty: 1,105. Library holdings: 1.2 million bound volumes, 1.6 million titles on microform, 15,000 periodical subscriptions, 4,253 records/tapes.

Undergraduate Courses offered for part-time students during daytime, evenings, summer. Complete part-time degree programs offered during daytime, summer. Adult/continuing education programs available. Career services available to

Colleges Offering Part-Time Degree Programs / Alabama

Auburn University (continued)
part-time students: individual and group career counseling, individual job placement, employer recruitment on campus. Part-time tuition and fees per quarter (1 to 9 quarter hours) range from $81 to $329 for state residents, $186 to $754 for nonresidents.

Graduate Part-time study available in Graduate School, School of Pharmacy, School of Veterinary Medicine. Basic part-time expenses: $31 per credit hour tuition plus $50 per quarter fees for state residents, $71 per credit hour tuition plus $50 per quarter fees for nonresidents. Institutional financial aid available to part-time graduate students in Graduate School, School of Pharmacy, School of Veterinary Medicine.

Auburn University at Montgomery
Montgomery 36193

Public institution; city setting. Awards B, M. Barrier-free campus. Total enrollment: 5,366. Undergraduate enrollment: 4,830; 31% part-time, 52% women, 15% over 25. Total faculty: 350.

Undergraduate Courses offered for part-time students during daytime, evenings, weekends, summer. Complete part-time degree programs offered during daytime, evenings, weekends, summer. Adult/continuing education programs available. Career services available to part-time students: individual career counseling, individual job placement, employer recruitment on campus. Part-time tuition: $26 per quarter hour for state residents, $66 per quarter hour for nonresidents.

Graduate Part-time study available in School of Business, School of Education, School of Sciences. Degree can be earned exclusively through evening/weekend study in School of Business, School of Education. Basic part-time expenses: $26 per quarter hour tuition plus $10 per quarter fees for state residents, $60 per quarter hour tuition plus $10 per quarter fees for nonresidents. Institutional financial aid available to part-time graduate students in School of Business, School of Education.

Birmingham-Southern College
Birmingham 35254

Independent-religious instutition; metropolitan setting. Awards B, M. Total enrollment: 1,587. Undergraduate enrollment: 1,550; 2% part-time, 51% women, 12% over 25. Total faculty: 135. Library holdings: 138,500 bound volumes, 750 periodical subscriptions, 2,000 records/tapes.

Undergraduate Courses offered for part-time students during daytime, evenings, summer. Complete part-time degree programs offered during daytime, evenings. Adult/continuing education programs available. Career services available to part-time students: individual and group career counseling, individual job placement, employer recruitment on campus. Part-time tuition: $855 per unit.

Graduate Part-time study available in Graduate Program in Public and Private Management. Degree can be earned exclusively through evening/weekend study in Graduate Program in Public and Private Management. Basic part-time expenses: $570 per course tuition.

Brewer State Junior College
Fayette 35555

Public institution; rural setting. Awards A. Barrier-free campus. Total enrollment: 731 (all undergraduates); 55% part-time, 52% women, 12% over 25. Total faculty: 29. Library holdings: 23,971 bound volumes, 220 periodical subscriptions, 1,300 records/tapes.

Undergraduate Courses offered for part-time students during daytime, evenings, summer. Complete part-time degree programs offered during daytime, evenings, summer. Adult/continuing education programs available. Career services available to part-time students: individual and group career counseling, individual job placement. Part-time tuition: $15 per quarter hour for state residents, $30 per quarter hour for nonresidents.

Chattahoochee Valley State Community College
Phenix City 36867

Public institution; small-town setting. Awards A. Barrier-free campus. Total enrollment: 1,548 (all undergraduates); 35% part-time, 54% women. Total faculty: 54. Library holdings: 50,000 bound volumes, 325 periodical subscriptions, 3,000 records/tapes.

Undergraduate Courses offered for part-time students during daytime, evenings, weekends, summer. Complete part-time degree programs offered during daytime, evenings, weekends, summer. Adult/continuing education programs available. Career services available to part-time students: individual and group career counseling, individual job placement, employer recruitment on campus. Part-time tuition: $12.50 per quarter hour for state residents, $25 per quarter hour for nonresidents.

Community College of the Air Force
Maxwell Air Force Base 36112

Public institution. Awards A. Total enrollment: 217,741 (all undergraduates); 84% part-time, 10% women, 48% over 25. Total faculty: 10,000.

Undergraduate Courses offered for part-time students during daytime, evenings. Complete part-time degree programs offered during daytime, evenings. Adult/continuing education programs available. Career services available to part-time students: individual career counseling.

Concordia College
Selma 36701

Independent-religious instutition; small-town setting. Awards A. Total enrollment: 303 (all undergraduates); 1% part-time, 65% women, 20% over 25. Total faculty: 21. Library holdings: 19,085 bound volumes, 97 periodical subscriptions, 584 records/tapes.

Undergraduate Courses offered for part-time students during daytime, evenings. Complete part-time degree programs offered during daytime, evenings. Adult/continuing education programs available. Career services available to part-time students: individual and group career counseling, individual job placement, employer recruitment on campus. Part-time tuition: $88 per credit hour.

Ed E Reid State Technical College
Evergreen 36401

Public institution; rural setting. Awards A. Barrier-free campus. Total enrollment: 395 (all undergraduates); 12% part-time, 35% women. Total faculty: 23.

Undergraduate Courses offered for part-time students during daytime, evenings, summer. Complete part-time degree programs offered during daytime, evenings, summer. Adult/continuing education programs available. Career services available to part-time students: individual career counseling, individual job placement. Part-time tuition per quarter (1 to 11 quarter

Alabama / **Colleges Offering Part-Time Degree Programs**

credits) ranges from $15 to $65 for state residents, $30 to $130 for nonresidents.

Enterprise State Junior College
Enterprise 36331

Public institution; small-town setting. Awards A. Barrier-free campus. Total enrollment: 1,864 (all undergraduates); 30% part-time, 58% women. Total faculty: 84. Library holdings: 30,000 bound volumes, 35 periodical subscriptions, 300 records/tapes.

Undergraduate Courses offered for part-time students during daytime, evenings, summer. Complete part-time degree programs offered during daytime, evenings, summer. Adult/continuing education programs available. Career services available to part-time students: individual and group career counseling, individual job placement, employer recruitment on campus. Part-time tuition: $15 per quarter hour for state residents, $30 per quarter hour for nonresidents.

Gadsden State Junior College
Gadsden 35999

Public institution; small-town setting. Awards A. Barrier-free campus. Total enrollment: 3,476 (all undergraduates); 34% part-time, 55% women, 43% over 25. Total faculty: 189. Library holdings: 74,694 bound volumes, 666 periodical subscriptions, 461 records/tapes.

Undergraduate Courses offered for part-time students during daytime, evenings, summer. Complete part-time degree programs offered during daytime, evenings, summer. Adult/continuing education programs available. Career services available to part-time students: individual and group career counseling, individual job placement, employer recruitment on campus. Part-time tuition: $15 per quarter hour for state residents, $30 per quarter hour for nonresidents.

George Corley Wallace State Community College
Selma 36701

Public institution; small-town setting. Awards A. Barrier-free campus. Total enrollment: 1,466 (all undergraduates); 33% part-time, 18% women, 25% over 25. Total faculty: 63. Library holdings: 28,000 bound volumes, 200 titles on microform, 50 periodical subscriptions, 800 records/tapes.

Undergraduate Courses offered for part-time students during daytime, evenings. Complete part-time degree programs offered during daytime, evenings. Adult/continuing education programs available. Career services available to part-time students: individual career counseling, employer recruitment on campus. Part-time tuition: $15 per quarter hour for state residents, $30 per quarter hour for nonresidents.

George C Wallace State Community College
Dothan 36303

Public institution; rural setting. Awards A. Total enrollment: 3,200 (all undergraduates); 35% part-time, 48% women. Total faculty: 130. Library holdings: 33,119 bound volumes, 459 periodical subscriptions, 3,200 records/tapes.

Undergraduate Courses offered for part-time students during daytime, evenings, summer. Complete part-time degree programs offered during daytime, evenings, summer. Adult/continuing education programs available. Career services available to part-time students: individual and group career counseling, individual job placement, employer recruitment on campus. Part-time tuition: $15 per quarter hour for state residents, $30 per quarter hour for nonresidents.

Huntingdon College
Montgomery 36194

Independent-religious instutition; city setting. Awards A, B. Total enrollment: 742 (all undergraduates); 16% part-time, 55% women. Total faculty: 51. Library holdings: 95,000 bound volumes, 350 periodical subscriptions, 1,000 records/tapes.

Undergraduate Courses offered for part-time students during daytime, evenings, summer. Complete part-time degree programs offered during daytime, evenings, summer. Adult/continuing education programs available. Career services available to part-time students: individual and group career counseling, employer recruitment on campus. Part-time tuition: $110 per semester hour.

International Bible College
Florence 35630

Independent-religious instutition; small-town setting. Awards A, B. Barrier-free campus. Total enrollment: 207 (all undergraduates); 35% part-time, 26% women, 60% over 25. Total faculty: 19. Library holdings: 9,506 bound volumes, 103 titles on microform, 94 periodical subscriptions, 998 records/tapes.

Undergraduate Courses offered for part-time students during daytime, evenings, summer. Complete part-time degree programs offered during daytime. Adult/continuing education programs available. Career services available to part-time students: individual career counseling. Part-time tuition: $60 per semester hour.

Jacksonville State University
Jacksonville 36265

Public institution; small-town setting. Awards B, M. Total enrollment: 6,522. Undergraduate enrollment: 5,886; 21% part-time, 53% women. Total faculty: 529. Library holdings: 345,000 bound volumes, 520,142 titles on microform, 18,645 periodical subscriptions.

Undergraduate Courses offered for part-time students during daytime, evenings, summer. Complete part-time degree programs offered during daytime, evenings, summer. Adult/continuing education programs available. Career services available to part-time students: individual career counseling, individual job placement, employer recruitment on campus. Part-time tuition: $35 per semester hour for state residents, $45 per semester hour for nonresidents.

Graduate Part-time study available in College of Graduate Studies and Continuing Education. Degree can be earned exclusively through evening/weekend study in College of Graduate Studies and Continuing Education. Basic part-time expenses: $43 per hour tuition for state residents, $57 per hour tuition for nonresidents. Institutional financial aid available to part-time graduate students in College of Graduate Studies and Continuing Education.

James H Faulkner State Junior College
Bay Minette 36507

Public institution; small-town setting. Awards A. Barrier-free campus. Total enrollment: 1,665 (all undergraduates); 33% part-time, 60% women, 33% over 25. Total faculty: 85. Library holdings: 36,000 bound volumes, 125 titles on microform, 150 periodical subscriptions, 1,000 records/tapes.

Colleges Offering Part-Time Degree Programs / *Alabama*

James H Faulkner State Junior College (continued)

Undergraduate Courses offered for part-time students during daytime, evenings, summer. Complete part-time degree programs offered during daytime, evenings, summer. External degree and adult/continuing education programs available. Career services available to part-time students: individual career counseling, employer recruitment on campus. Part-time tuition: $15 per quarter hour for state residents, $30 per quarter hour for nonresidents.

Jefferson Davis State Junior College
Brewton 36427

Public institution; small-town setting. Awards A. Barrier-free campus. Total enrollment: 846 (all undergraduates); 30% part-time, 50% women. Total faculty: 47. Library holdings: 926 bound volumes, 330 periodical subscriptions, 1,204 records/tapes.

Undergraduate Courses offered for part-time students during daytime, evenings, summer. Complete part-time degree programs offered during daytime, evenings, summer. Adult/continuing education programs available. Career services available to part-time students: individual and group career counseling. Part-time tuition: $15 per quarter hour for state residents, $30 per quarter hour for nonresidents.

Jefferson State Junior College
Birmingham 35215

Public institution; metropolitan setting. Awards A. Barrier-free campus. Total enrollment: 6,587 (all undergraduates); 57% part-time, 52% women, 23% over 25. Total faculty: 305. Library holdings: 53,560 bound volumes, 191 titles on microform, 323 periodical subscriptions, 1,689 records/tapes.

Undergraduate Courses offered for part-time students during daytime, evenings, summer. Complete part-time degree programs offered during daytime, evenings, summer. Adult/continuing education programs available. Career services available to part-time students: individual career counseling, individual job placement, employer recruitment on campus. Part-time tuition: $15 per quarter hour for state residents, $30 per quarter hour for nonresidents.

John C Calhoun State Community College
Decatur 35602

Public institution; rural setting. Awards A. Barrier-free campus. Total enrollment: 6,111 (all undergraduates); 53% part-time, 51% women, 38% over 25. Total faculty: 296. Library holdings: 40,660 bound volumes, 1,036 titles on microform, 321 periodical subscriptions, 1,877 records/tapes.

Undergraduate Courses offered for part-time students during daytime, evenings, weekends, summer. Complete part-time degree programs offered during daytime, evenings, summer. Adult/continuing education programs available. Career services available to part-time students: individual and group career counseling, individual job placement, employer recruitment on campus. Part-time tuition: $15 per quarter hour for state residents, $30 per quarter hour for nonresidents.

Judson College
Marion 36756

Independent-religious instutition; rural setting. Awards B. Total enrollment: 409 (all undergraduates); 5% part-time, 100% women. Total faculty: 35. Library holdings: 53,500 bound volumes, 325 periodical subscriptions, 2,170 records/tapes.

Undergraduate Courses offered for part-time students during daytime. Complete part-time degree programs offered during daytime. Adult/continuing education programs available. Career services available to part-time students: individual and group career counseling, individual job placement, employer recruitment on campus. Part-time tuition: $96 per semester hour.

Livingston University
Livingston 35470

Public institution; small-town setting. Awards A, B, M. Barrier-free campus. Total enrollment: 1,517. Undergraduate enrollment: 1,316; 14% part-time, 56% women, 20% over 25. Total faculty: 83. Library holdings: 108,000 bound volumes, 250,000 titles on microform, 530 periodical subscriptions.

Undergraduate Courses offered for part-time students during daytime, summer. Complete part-time degree programs offered during daytime, summer. Career services available to part-time students: individual career counseling, individual job placement, employer recruitment on campus. Part-time tuition: $22 per quarter hour.

Graduate Part-time study available in School of Graduate Studies. Basic part-time expenses: $23 per quarter hour tuition. Institutional financial aid available to part-time graduate students in School of Graduate Studies.

Lurleen B Wallace State Junior College
Andalusia 36420

Public institution; small-town setting. Awards A. Barrier-free campus. Total enrollment: 860 (all undergraduates); 30% part-time, 57% women. Total faculty: 49. Library holdings: 11,000 bound volumes, 25 periodical subscriptions, 1,100 records/tapes.

Undergraduate Courses offered for part-time students during daytime, evenings, summer. Complete part-time degree programs offered during daytime, evenings, summer. Adult/continuing education programs available. Career services available to part-time students: individual and group career counseling, individual job placement. Part-time tuition: $15 per quarter hour for state residents, $30 per quarter hour for nonresidents.

Miles College
Birmingham 35208

Independent-religious instutition; metropolitan setting. Awards B, D. Total enrollment: 687. Undergraduate enrollment: 625; 7% part-time, 52% women. Total faculty: 80. Library holdings: 80,783 bound volumes.

Undergraduate Courses offered for part-time students during daytime, evenings, summer. Complete part-time degree programs offered during daytime, evenings, summer. Adult/continuing education programs available. Career services available to part-time students: individual career counseling. Part-time tuition: $120 per semester hour.

Mobile College
Mobile 36613

Independent-religious instutition; city setting. Awards A, B, M. Barrier-free campus. Total enrollment: 1,002 (all undergraduates); 27% part-time, 68% women. Total faculty: 74. Library holdings: 86,538 bound volumes, 359 periodical subscriptions, 2,546 records/tapes.

Alabama / **Colleges Offering Part-Time Degree Programs**

Undergraduate Courses offered for part-time students during daytime, evenings, summer. Complete part-time degree programs offered during daytime, evenings, summer. Adult/continuing education programs available. Career services available to part-time students: individual career counseling, individual job placement, employer recruitment on campus. Part-time tuition: $95 per semester hour.

Northeast Alabama State Junior College
Rainsville 35986

Public institution; rural setting. Awards A. Barrier-free campus. Total enrollment: 998 (all undergraduates); 41% part-time, 56% women. Total faculty: 63. Library holdings: 40,000 bound volumes, 240 periodical subscriptions, 434 records/tapes.

Undergraduate Courses offered for part-time students during daytime, evenings, weekends, summer. Complete part-time degree programs offered during daytime, evenings, weekends, summer. Adult/continuing education programs available. Career services available to part-time students: individual career counseling, individual job placement. Part-time tuition: $15 per quarter hour for state residents, $30 per quarter hour for nonresidents.

Oakwood College
Huntsville 35896

Independent-religious instutition; rural setting. Awards A, B. Total enrollment: 1,465 (all undergraduates); 8% part-time, 52% women, 21% over 25. Total faculty: 106. Library holdings: 93,837 bound volumes, 7,222 titles on microform, 500 periodical subscriptions, 4,820 records/tapes.

Undergraduate Courses offered for part-time students during daytime. Complete part-time degree programs offered during daytime. Career services available to part-time students: individual and group career counseling, individual job placement, employer recruitment on campus. Part-time tuition: $120 per hour.

Opelika State Technical College
Opelika 36801

Public institution; small-town setting. Awards A. Barrier-free campus. Total enrollment: 525 (all undergraduates); 18% part-time, 35% women, 26% over 25. Total faculty: 32.

Undergraduate Courses offered for part-time students during daytime, evenings. Complete part-time degree programs offered during daytime, evenings. Adult/continuing education programs available. Career services available to part-time students: individual and group career counseling, individual job placement, employer recruitment on campus. State resident part-time tuition per quarter ranges from $47.50 for evening students to $85 for half-time day students. Nonresident part-time tuition per quarter ranges from $95 for evening students to $170 for half-time day students.

Samford University
Birmingham 35229

Independent-religious instutition; metropolitan setting. Awards A, B, M. Total enrollment: 4,121. Undergraduate enrollment: 2,970; 34% part-time, 60% women. Total faculty: 291. Library holdings: 418,290 bound volumes, 322,534 titles on microform, 2,533 periodical subscriptions, 3,200 records/tapes.

Undergraduate Courses offered for part-time students during daytime, evenings, summer. Complete part-time degree programs offered during daytime, evenings, summer. External degree and adult/continuing education programs available. Career services available to part-time students: individual career counseling, individual job placement, employer recruitment on campus. Part-time tuition: $113 per semester hour.

Graduate Part-time study available in School of Graduate Studies. Degree can be earned exclusively through evening/weekend study in School of Graduate Studies. Basic part-time expenses: $119 per semester hour tuition. Institutional financial aid available to part-time graduate students in School of Graduate Studies.

S D Bishop State Junior College
Mobile 36690

Public institution; city setting. Awards A. Total enrollment: 1,629 (all undergraduates); 30% part-time, 67% women, 22% over 25. Total faculty: 51. Library holdings: 32,865 bound volumes, 2,616 titles on microform, 277 periodical subscriptions, 1,525 records/tapes.

Undergraduate Courses offered for part-time students during daytime, evenings. Complete part-time degree programs offered during daytime, evenings. Adult/continuing education programs available. Career services available to part-time students: individual and group career counseling, individual job placement, employer recruitment on campus. Part-time tuition: $15 per quarter hour for state residents, $30 per quarter hour for nonresidents.

Selma University
Selma 36701

Independent-religious instutition; small-town setting. Awards A, B. Total enrollment: 342 (all undergraduates); 14% part-time, 50% women. Total faculty: 32. Library holdings: 42,000 bound volumes, 25 periodical subscriptions, 250 records/tapes.

Undergraduate Courses offered for part-time students during daytime, evenings. Complete part-time degree programs offered during daytime, evenings. Career services available to part-time students: individual career counseling. Part-time tuition: $55 per credit.

Shelton State Community College
Tuscaloosa 35404

Public institution; small-town setting. Awards A. Total enrollment: 2,898 (all undergraduates); 35% part-time, 54% women, 32% over 25. Total faculty: 31. Library holdings: 17,031 bound volumes, 1,030 titles on microform, 1,170 records/tapes.

Undergraduate Courses offered for part-time students during daytime. Complete part-time degree programs offered during daytime. Adult/continuing education programs available. Career services available to part-time students: individual career counseling, individual job placement, employer recruitment on campus. Part-time tuition: $15 per quarter hour for state residents, $30 per quarter hour for nonresidents.

Snead State Junior College
Boaz 35957

Public institution; small-town setting. Awards A. Total enrollment: 1,104 (all undergraduates); 31% part-time, 57% women. Total faculty: 49. Library holdings: 3,400 bound volumes, 132 periodical subscriptions.

Undergraduate Courses offered for part-time students during daytime, evenings, summer. Complete part-time degree programs offered during daytime, evenings. Adult/continuing edu-

Colleges Offering Part-Time Degree Programs / Alabama

Snead State Junior College (continued)

cation programs available. Part-time tuition: $15 per quarter hour for state residents, $30 per quarter hour for nonresidents. Students taking 10 or more credits per quarter pay the full-time rate for tuition.

Southeastern Bible College
Birmingham 35256

Independent institution; metropolitan setting. Awards A, B, M. Total enrollment: 180. Undergraduate enrollment: 171; 25% part-time, 45% women, 25% over 25. Total faculty: 21. Library holdings: 30,000 bound volumes, 80 periodical subscriptions, 200 records/tapes.

Undergraduate Courses offered for part-time students during daytime, evenings, summer. Complete part-time degree programs offered during daytime. Adult/continuing education programs available. Career services available to part-time students: individual job placement, employer recruitment on campus. Part-time tuition: $85 per semester hour.

Graduate Part-time study available in Graduate School. Basic part-time expenses: $60 per semester hour tuition plus $10 per summer fees.

Southern Institute
Birmingham 35205

Proprietary institution; metropolitan setting. Awards A. Total enrollment: 415 (all undergraduates); 35% part-time, 85% women. Total faculty: 25. Library holdings: 35,000 bound volumes, 80 periodical subscriptions.

Undergraduate Courses offered for part-time students during daytime, evenings, summer. Complete part-time degree programs offered during daytime, evenings. Adult/continuing education programs available. Career services available to part-time students: individual and group career counseling, individual job placement, employer recruitment on campus. Part-time tuition: $65 per hour.

Southern Union State Junior College
Wadley 36276

Public institution; rural setting. Awards A. Barrier-free campus. Total enrollment: 1,691 (all undergraduates); 30% part-time, 53% women. Total faculty: 106.

Undergraduate Courses offered for part-time students during daytime, evenings, summer. Complete part-time degree programs offered during daytime, evenings, summer. Adult/continuing education programs available. Career services available to part-time students: individual career counseling. Part-time tuition: $15 per quarter hour for state residents, $30 per quarter hour for nonresidents.

Southwest State Technical College
Mobile 36690

Public institution; city setting. Awards A. Barrier-free campus. Total enrollment: 942 (all undergraduates); 15% part-time, 46% women. Total faculty: 43.

Undergraduate Courses offered for part-time students during evenings, summer. Complete part-time degree programs offered during evenings. Career services available to part-time students: individual career counseling. Part-time tuition: $337.50 per year for state residents, $675 per year for nonresidents.

Spring Hill College
Mobile 36608

Independent-religious instutition; city setting. Awards B, M. Barrier-free campus. Total enrollment: 1,200. Undergraduate enrollment: 1,100; 14% part-time, 49% women, 10% over 25. Total faculty: 77. Library holdings: 126,645 bound volumes, 9,000 titles on microform, 470 periodical subscriptions.

Undergraduate Courses offered for part-time students during daytime, evenings, weekends, summer. Complete part-time degree programs offered during daytime, evenings. External degree and adult/continuing education programs available. Career services available to part-time students: individual and group career counseling, individual job placement, employer recruitment on campus. Part-time tuition: $89 per semester hour.

Talladega College
Talladega 35160

Independent-religious instutition; small-town setting. Awards B. Total enrollment: 525 (all undergraduates); 6% part-time, 58% women, 2% over 25. Total faculty: 58. Library holdings: 73,000 bound volumes, 2,480 titles on microform, 416 periodical subscriptions, 12,034 records/tapes.

Undergraduate Courses offered for part-time students during daytime, summer. Complete part-time degree programs offered during daytime. Adult/continuing education programs available. Career services available to part-time students: individual and group career counseling, individual job placement, employer recruitment on campus. Part-time tuition: $113 per credit hour.

Trenholm State Technical College
Montgomery 36108

Public institution; city setting. Awards A. Barrier-free campus. Total enrollment: 891 (all undergraduates); 42% part-time, 52% women, 60% over 25. Total faculty: 60. Library holdings: 477 bound volumes, 14 periodical subscriptions, 188 records/tapes.

Undergraduate Courses offered for part-time students during daytime, evenings. Complete part-time degree programs offered during daytime, evenings. Adult/continuing education programs available. Career services available to part-time students: individual job placement. Part-time tuition: $7.50 per contact hour for state residents, $15 per contact hour for nonresidents.

Troy State University
Troy 36082

Public institution; small-town setting. Awards A, B, M. Barrier-free campus. Total enrollment: 7,019. Undergraduate enrollment: 6,130; 37% part-time, 46% women, 10% over 25. Total faculty: 388. Library holdings: 200,201 bound volumes, 20,209 titles on microform.

Undergraduate Courses offered for part-time students during daytime, evenings, weekends, summer. Complete part-time degree programs offered during daytime, evenings, summer. Adult/continuing education programs available. Career services available to part-time students: individual and group career counseling, individual job placement, employer recruitment on campus. Part-time tuition: $27.30 per quarter hour for state residents, $39.70 per quarter hour for nonresidents.

Graduate Part-time study available in Graduate School, School of Nursing. Basic part-time expenses: $33 per credit hour tuition for state residents, $42 per credit hour tuition for nonresidents.

Alabama / **Colleges Offering Part-Time Degree Programs**

Troy State University at Dothan/Fort Rucker
Dothan 36301

Public institution; small-town setting. Awards A, B, M. Barrier-free campus. Total enrollment: 1,631. Undergraduate enrollment: 1,135; 76% part-time, 50% women. Total faculty: 73. Library holdings: 33,863 bound volumes, 1,618 titles on microform, 607 periodical subscriptions, 1,126 records/tapes.

Undergraduate Courses offered for part-time students during daytime, evenings, summer. Complete part-time degree programs offered during daytime, evenings, summer. Career services available to part-time students: individual and group career counseling, individual job placement, employer recruitment on campus. Part-time tuition: $26 per quarter hour for state residents, $28 per quarter hour for nonresidents.

Graduate Part-time study available in Graduate School. Basic part-time expenses: $31 per quarter hour tuition.

Troy State University in Montgomery
Montgomery 36195

Public institution; city setting. Awards A, B, M. Barrier-free campus. Total enrollment: 2,004. Undergraduate enrollment: 1,546; 77% part-time, 47% women, 65% over 25. Total faculty: 142. Library holdings: 13,373 bound volumes, 1,154 titles on microform, 278 periodical subscriptions, 452 records/tapes.

Undergraduate Courses offered for part-time students during daytime, evenings, weekends, summer. Complete part-time degree programs offered during daytime, evenings, weekends, summer. Adult/continuing education programs available. Career services available to part-time students: individual and group career counseling, individual job placement, employer recruitment on campus. Part-time tuition: $24 per quarter hour.

Graduate Part-time study available in Graduate Programs. Degree can be earned exclusively through evening/weekend study in Graduate Programs. Basic part-time expenses: $27 per credit hour (minimum) tuition.

Tuskegee Institute
Tuskegee Institute 36088

Independent institution; small-town setting. Awards B, M. Total enrollment: 3,400. Undergraduate enrollment: 3,182; 3% part-time, 50% women, 1% over 25. Total faculty: 337. Library holdings: 258,000 bound volumes, 1,184 periodical subscriptions, 3,182 records/tapes.

Undergraduate Courses offered for part-time students during daytime. Complete part-time degree programs offered during daytime. Adult/continuing education programs available. Career services available to part-time students: individual and group career counseling, individual job placement, employer recruitment on campus. Part-time tuition per semester (1 to 9 credits) ranges from $425 to $1685.

United States Sports Academy
Mobile 36608

Independent institution (graduate only). Total enrollment: 60 (coed; 11% part-time). Total faculty: 18. Library holdings: 1,163 bound volumes, 2,702 microforms.

Graduate Part-time study available in Graduate Programs. Basic part-time expenses: $60 per quarter hour tuition plus $15 per quarter fees.

University of Alabama
University 35486

Public institution; city setting. Awards B, M, D. Total enrollment: 15,497. Undergraduate enrollment: 12,870; 6% part-time, 48% women. Total faculty: 919. Library holdings: 1.2 million bound volumes, 12,990 periodical subscriptions, 13,380 records/tapes.

Undergraduate Courses offered for part-time students during daytime, evenings, weekends, summer. Complete part-time degree programs offered during daytime, evenings, weekends, summer. External degree and adult/continuing education programs available. Career services available to part-time students: individual and group career counseling, individual job placement, employer recruitment on campus. Part-time tuition and fees per semester (1 to 11 semester hours) range from $155.50 to $630.50 for state residents, $213.50 to $1268.50 for nonresidents.

Graduate Part-time study available in Graduate School. Basic part-time expenses: $50 per hour tuition plus $114 per semester (minimum) fees for state residents, $114 per hour tuition plus $114 per semester (minimum) fees for nonresidents.

University of Alabama in Birmingham
Birmingham 35294

Public institution; metropolitan setting. Awards B, M, D. Total enrollment: 14,679. Undergraduate enrollment: 10,426; 57% part-time, 54% women, 30% over 25. Total faculty: 1,654. Library holdings: 591,407 bound volumes, 728,402 titles on microform, 8,041 periodical subscriptions, 25,923 records/tapes.

Undergraduate Courses offered for part-time students during daytime, evenings, weekends, summer. Complete part-time degree programs offered during daytime, evenings, weekends, summer. Adult/continuing education programs available. Career services available to part-time students: individual and group career counseling, individual job placement, employer recruitment on campus. Part-time tuition: $42 per semester hour for state residents, $84 per semester hour for nonresidents.

Graduate Part-time study available in Graduate School, School of Optometry. Degree can be earned exclusively through evening/weekend study in Graduate School. Basic part-time expenses: $49 per credit hour tuition plus $30 per quarter fees for state residents, $98 per credit hour tuition plus $30 per quarter fees for nonresidents. Institutional financial aid available to part-time graduate students in Graduate School, School of Optometry.

University of Alabama in Huntsville
Huntsville 35899

Public institution; city setting. Awards B, M, D. Barrier-free campus. Total enrollment: 6,116. Undergraduate enrollment: 5,172; 45% part-time, 52% women. Total faculty: 351. Library holdings: 253,673 bound volumes, 2,734 periodical subscriptions.

Undergraduate Courses offered for part-time students during daytime, evenings, weekends, summer. Complete part-time degree programs offered during daytime. Adult/continuing education programs available. Career services available to part-time students: individual career counseling. Part-time tuition and fees per semester (1 to 12 semester hours) range from $55 to $420 for state residents, $110 to $840 for nonresidents.

Graduate Part-time study available in School of Graduate Studies. Basic part-time expenses: $50 per hour tuition. Institutional financial aid available to part-time graduate students in School of Graduate Studies.

Colleges Offering Part-Time Degree Programs / Alabama

University of Montevallo
Montevallo 35115

Public institution; small-town setting. Awards B, M. Barrier-free campus. Total enrollment: 2,461. Undergraduate enrollment: 2,225; 10% part-time, 58% women. Total faculty: 173. Library holdings: 165,000 bound volumes, 265,000 titles on microform, 1,450 periodical subscriptions.

Undergraduate Courses offered for part-time students during daytime, evenings, weekends, summer. Complete part-time degree programs offered during daytime, summer. Adult/continuing education programs available. Career services available to part-time students: individual and group career counseling, individual job placement, employer recruitment on campus. Part-time tuition: $35 per semester hour for state residents, $60 per semester hour for nonresidents.

Graduate Part-time study available in College of Arts and Sciences, College of Education, College of Fine Arts.

University of North Alabama
Florence 35632

Public institution; small-town setting. Awards B, M. Barrier-free campus. Total enrollment: 5,323. Undergraduate enrollment: 4,825; 17% part-time, 55% women. Total faculty: 222. Library holdings: 196,553 bound volumes, 64,869 titles on microform, 1,429 periodical subscriptions, 1,400 records/tapes.

Undergraduate Courses offered for part-time students during daytime, evenings, summer. Complete part-time degree programs offered during daytime, evenings. Adult/continuing education programs available. Career services available to part-time students: individual and group career counseling, individual job placement, employer recruitment on campus. Part-time tuition: $40 per semester hour for state residents, $58 per semester hour for nonresidents.

Graduate Part-time study available in School of Business, School of Education. Degree can be earned exclusively through evening/weekend study in School of Business, School of Education. Basic part-time expenses: $43 per credit hour tuition for state residents, $61 per credit hour tuition for nonresidents. Institutional financial aid available to part-time graduate students in School of Business, School of Education.

University of South Alabama
Mobile 36688

Public institution; city setting. Awards B, M, D. Total enrollment: 9,380. Undergraduate enrollment: 8,003; 25% part-time, 51% women, 25% over 25. Total faculty: 583. Library holdings: 267,383 bound volumes, 674,899 titles on microform, 5,279 periodical subscriptions, 2,675 records/tapes.

Undergraduate Courses offered for part-time students during daytime, evenings, weekends, summer. Complete part-time degree programs offered during daytime, evenings, summer. Adult/continuing education programs available. Career services available to part-time students: individual and group career counseling, employer recruitment on campus. Part-time tuition and fees per quarter (1 to 11 quarter hours) range from $59 to $339 for state residents, $193 to $473 for nonresidents.

Graduate Part-time study available in Graduate School. Degree can be earned exclusively through evening/weekend study in Graduate School. Basic part-time expenses: $34 per quarter hour tuition plus $31 per quarter fees for state residents, $203 per quarter (minimum) tuition plus $31 per quarter fees for nonresidents. Institutional financial aid available to part-time graduate students in Graduate School.

Walker College
Jasper 35501

Independent institution; small-town setting. Awards A. Total enrollment: 789 (all undergraduates); 40% part-time, 61% women. Total faculty: 36. Library holdings: 22,043 bound volumes, 577 titles on microform, 185 periodical subscriptions, 425 records/tapes.

Undergraduate Courses offered for part-time students during daytime, evenings, summer. Complete part-time degree programs offered during daytime, evenings, summer. Adult/continuing education programs available. Career services available to part-time students: individual career counseling. Part-time tuition: $54 per credit.

Wallace State Community College
Hanceville 35077

Public institution; rural setting. Awards A. Total enrollment: 2,761 (all undergraduates); 32% part-time, 53% women, 30% over 25. Total faculty: 133. Library holdings: 16,000 bound volumes, 150 periodical subscriptions, 250 records/tapes.

Undergraduate Courses offered for part-time students during daytime, evenings, summer. Complete part-time degree programs offered during daytime, evenings, summer. Adult/continuing education programs available. Career services available to part-time students: individual and group career counseling, individual job placement, employer recruitment on campus. Part-time tuition: $15 per quarter hour for state residents, $30 per quarter hour for nonresidents.

ALASKA

Alaska Bible College
Glennallen 99588

Independent-religious instutition; rural setting. Awards A, B. Total enrollment: 34 (all undergraduates); 3% part-time, 30% women. Total faculty: 11. Library holdings: 18,813 bound volumes, 45 titles on microform, 152 periodical subscriptions, 1,603 records/tapes.

Undergraduate Courses offered for part-time students during daytime, evenings. Complete part-time degree programs offered during daytime, evenings. Career services available to part-time students: individual career counseling. Part-time tuition: $50 per credit.

Alaska Pacific University
Anchorage 99508

Independent-religious instutition; city setting. Awards A, B, M. Total enrollment: 668. Undergraduate enrollment: 380; 57% part-time, 74% women, 54% over 25. Total faculty: 65. Library holdings: 300,000 bound volumes, 3,830 periodical subscriptions, 6,654 records/tapes.

Undergraduate Courses offered for part-time students during daytime, evenings, weekends, summer. Complete part-time degree programs offered during daytime, evenings, summer. Adult/continuing education programs available. Career services available to part-time students: individual career counseling, individual job placement, employer recruitment on campus. Part-time tuition: $140 per credit.

Alaska / **Colleges Offering Part-Time Degree Programs**

Sheldon Jackson College
Sitka 99835

Independent-religious instutition; small-town setting. Awards A, B. Total enrollment: 245 (all undergraduates); 23% part-time, 52% women. Total faculty: 32. Library holdings: 63,000 bound volumes, 20 titles on microform, 396 periodical subscriptions, 3,000 records/tapes.

Undergraduate Courses offered for part-time students during daytime, evenings. Complete part-time degree programs offered during daytime, evenings. External degree and adult/continuing education programs available. Career services available to part-time students: individual and group career counseling. Part-time tuition: $122 per credit.

University of Alaska, Anchorage
Anchorage 99508

Public institution; city setting. Awards B, M. Barrier-free campus. Total enrollment: 4,088. Undergraduate enrollment: 4,012; 58% part-time, 61% women, 63% over 25. Total faculty: 224. Library holdings: 297,530 bound volumes, 28,211 titles on microform, 3,830 periodical subscriptions, 6,276 records/tapes.

Undergraduate Courses offered for part-time students during daytime, evenings, weekends, summer. Complete part-time degree programs offered during daytime, evenings, weekends, summer. Adult/continuing education programs available. Career services available to part-time students: individual and group career counseling, individual job placement, employer recruitment on campus. Part-time tuition: $30 per credit for state residents, $80 per credit for nonresidents.

Graduate Part-time study available in College of Arts and Sciences, College of Nursing and Health Sciences, School of Business and Public Affairs, School of Education, School of Engineering.Basic part-time expenses: $60 per credit tuition for state residents, $120 per credit tuition for nonresidents.

University of Alaska, Anchorage Community College
Anchorage 99508

Public institution; city setting. Awards A. Barrier-free campus. Total enrollment: 9,352 (all undergraduates); 72% part-time, 62% women, 66% over 25. Total faculty: 543. Library holdings: 279,415 bound volumes, 30,734 titles on microform, 3,843 periodical subscriptions, 9,182 records/tapes.

Undergraduate Courses offered for part-time students during daytime, evenings, weekends, summer. Complete part-time degree programs offered during daytime, evenings, summer. Adult/continuing education programs available. Part-time tuition: $25 per credit for state residents, $65 per credit for nonresidents.

University of Alaska, Fairbanks
Fairbanks 99701

Public institution; small-town setting. Awards B, M, D. Total enrollment: 4,622. Undergraduate enrollment: 4,096; 31% part-time, 50% women. Total faculty: 427. Library holdings: 500,000 bound volumes, 300,000 titles on microform, 3,179 periodical subscriptions, 12,616 records/tapes.

Undergraduate Courses offered for part-time students during daytime, evenings, summer. Complete part-time degree programs offered during daytime, evenings, summer. Adult/continuing education programs available. Career services available to part-time students: individual and group career counseling, individual job placement, employer recruitment on campus. Part-time tuition: $30 per credit for state residents, $80 per credit for nonresidents.

Graduate Part-time study available in College of Arts and Sciences, College of Environmental Sciences, College of Human and Rural Development, School of Agriculture and Land Resources Management, School of Engineering, School of Management, School of Mineral Industry, Interdisciplinary Programs. Degree can be earned exclusively through evening/weekend study in College of Human and Rural Development.Basic part-time expenses: $60 per credit tuition plus $3 per credit fees for state residents, $120 per credit tuition plus $3 per credit fees for nonresidents.

University of Alaska, Islands Community College
Sitka 99835

Public institution; small-town setting. Awards A. Barrier-free campus. Total enrollment: 762 (all undergraduates); 95% part-time, 62% women. Total faculty: 61. Library holdings: 50,600 bound volumes, 300 periodical subscriptions, 1,640 records/tapes.

Undergraduate Courses offered for part-time students during daytime, evenings, weekends, summer. Complete part-time degree programs offered during daytime, evenings. Adult/continuing education programs available. Career services available to part-time students: individual and group career counseling, employer recruitment on campus. Part-time tuition: $25 per credit for state residents, $65 per credit for nonresidents.

University of Alaska, Juneau
Juneau 99801

Public institution; small-town setting. Awards A, B, M. Barrier-free campus. Total enrollment: 2,361. Undergraduate enrollment: 2,059; 87% part-time, 58% women, 80% over 25. Total faculty: 130. Library holdings: 46,000 bound volumes, 213,000 titles on microform, 782 periodical subscriptions, 1,500 records/tapes.

Undergraduate Courses offered for part-time students during daytime, evenings, weekends, summer. Complete part-time degree programs offered during daytime, evenings, summer. Adult/continuing education programs available. Career services available to part-time students: individual and group career counseling, individual job placement, employer recruitment on campus. Part-time tuition: $30 per credit for state residents, $80 per credit for nonresidents.

Graduate Part-time study available in School of Business, School of Education and Liberal Arts, School of Fisheries and Science.Basic part-time expenses: $60 per credit tuition plus $2 per credit fees for state residents, $120 per credit tuition plus $2 per credit fees for nonresidents. Institutional financial aid available to part-time graduate students in School of Business, School of Education and Liberal Arts, School of Fisheries and Science.

University of Alaska, Ketchikan Community College
Ketchikan 99901

Public institution; small-town setting. Awards A. Total enrollment: 860 (all undergraduates); 90% part-time, 55% women, 80% over 25. Total faculty: 77. Library holdings: 36,000 bound volumes, 200 periodical subscriptions, 620 records/tapes.

Undergraduate Courses offered for part-time students during daytime, evenings, weekends, summer. Complete part-time degree programs offered during daytime, evenings, weekends,

Colleges Offering Part-Time Degree Programs / Alaska

University of Alaska, Ketchikan Community College (continued)

summer. External degree and adult/continuing education programs available. Career services available to part-time students: individual career counseling. Part-time tuition: $25 per credit for state residents, $65 per credit for nonresidents.

University of Alaska, Matanuska-Susitna Community College
Palmer 99645

Public institution; rural setting. Awards A. Barrier-free campus. Total enrollment: 938 (all undergraduates); 65% part-time, 42% women, 90% over 25. Total faculty: 93. Library holdings: 13,500 bound volumes, 95 periodical subscriptions, 356 records/tapes.

Undergraduate Courses offered for part-time students during daytime, evenings, summer. Complete part-time degree programs offered during daytime, evenings, summer. Adult/continuing education programs available. Career services available to part-time students: individual career counseling. Part-time tuition: $25 per credit for state residents, $65 per credit for nonresidents.

University of Alaska, Tanana Valley Community College
Fairbanks 99701

Public institution; small-town setting. Awards A. Total enrollment: 2,534 (all undergraduates); 91% part-time, 62% women. Total faculty: 136. Library holdings: 359,893 bound volumes, 640 periodical subscriptions.

Undergraduate Courses offered for part-time students during daytime, evenings. Complete part-time degree programs offered during daytime, evenings. Adult/continuing education programs available. Career services available to part-time students: individual career counseling. Part-time tuition: $25 per credit for state residents, $65 per credit for nonresidents.

AMERICAN SAMOA

American Samoa Community College
Pago Pago 96799

Public institution; rural setting. Awards A. Barrier-free campus. Total enrollment: 845 (all undergraduates); 20% part-time, 50% women. Total faculty: 65. Library holdings: 18,000 bound volumes, 50 periodical subscriptions, 300 records/tapes.

Undergraduate Courses offered for part-time students during daytime, summer. Complete part-time degree programs offered during daytime, summer. Adult/continuing education programs available. Career services available to part-time students: individual and group career counseling, individual job placement, employer recruitment on campus. Part-time tuition: $2 per credit (minimum).

ARIZONA

American Graduate School of International Management
Glendale 85306

Independent institution (graduate only). Total enrollment: 964 (coed; 5% part-time). Total faculty: 97.

Graduate Part-time study available in Graduate Program. Basic part-time expenses: $250 per credit tuition.

American Indian Bible College
Phoenix 85021

Independent-religious instutition; metropolitan setting. Awards A, B. Barrier-free campus. Total enrollment: 76 (all undergraduates); 1% part-time, 67% women, 30% over 25. Total faculty: 20.

Undergraduate Courses offered for part-time students during daytime, evenings. Complete part-time degree programs offered during daytime, evenings. Career services available to part-time students: individual career counseling, individual job placement. Part-time tuition: $81 per semester hour.

Arizona College of the Bible
Phoenix 85021

Independent-religious instutition; metropolitan setting. Awards B. Barrier-free campus. Total enrollment: 134 (all undergraduates); 47% part-time, 38% women. Total faculty: 14. Library holdings: 16,500 bound volumes, 137 periodical subscriptions, 45 records/tapes.

Undergraduate Courses offered for part-time students during daytime, evenings, summer. Complete part-time degree programs offered during daytime, evenings, summer. Adult/continuing education programs available. Career services available to part-time students: individual career counseling, employer recruitment on campus. Part-time tuition: $110 per credit hour.

Arizona State University
Tempe 85287

Public institution; city setting. Awards B, M, D. Barrier-free campus. Total enrollment: 40,239. Undergraduate enrollment: 30,255; 17% part-time, 45% women, 24% over 25. Total faculty: 1,687. Library holdings: 1.7 million bound volumes, 1.5 million titles on microform, 19,900 periodical subscriptions, 13,500 records/tapes.

Undergraduate Courses offered for part-time students during daytime, evenings, summer. Complete part-time degree programs offered during daytime, evenings, summer. Adult/continuing education programs available. Career services available to part-time students: group career counseling, individual job placement, employer recruitment on campus. Part-time tuition: $51 per semester hour for state residents, $51 per semester hour for nonresidents.

Graduate Part-time study available in College of Business Administration, College of Education, College of Engineering and Applied Sciences. Basic part-time expenses: $51 per hour tuition.

Arizona Western College
Yuma 85364

Public institution; rural setting. Awards A. Barrier-free campus. Total enrollment: 4,333 (all undergraduates); 70% part-time, 50% women, 62% over 25. Total faculty: 208. Library holdings: 34,437 bound volumes, 210 periodical subscriptions, 1,272 records/tapes.

Undergraduate Courses offered for part-time students during daytime, evenings, summer. Complete part-time degree programs offered during daytime, evenings. Adult/continuing education programs available. Career services available to part-time students: individual and group career counseling, individual job placement. Part-time tuition: $16 per credit hour

Arizona / **Colleges Offering Part-Time Degree Programs**

for state residents. Nonresident part-time tuition and fees per semester (1 to 11 credit hours) range from $16 to $1455.

Central Arizona College
Coolidge 85228

Public institution; rural setting. Awards A. Barrier-free campus. Total enrollment: 4,906 (all undergraduates); 78% part-time, 60% women. Total faculty: 261.

Undergraduate Courses offered for part-time students during daytime, evenings. Complete part-time degree programs offered during daytime, evenings. Adult/continuing education programs available. Career services available to part-time students: individual and group career counseling, individual job placement, employer recruitment on campus. Part-time tuition: $15 per credit hour for state residents. Nonresident part-time tuition per credit hour ranges from $25 (for students taking 1 to 7 credit hours) to $120 (for students taking 8 to 14 credit hours).

Cochise College
Douglas 85607

Public institution; small-town setting. Awards A. Barrier-free campus. Total enrollment: 4,103 (all undergraduates); 72% part-time, 54% women, 49% over 25. Total faculty: 299. Library holdings: 53,239 bound volumes, 3,165 titles on microform, 351 periodical subscriptions, 5,273 records/tapes.

Undergraduate Courses offered for part-time students during daytime, evenings, weekends, summer. Complete part-time degree programs offered during daytime, evenings, weekends, summer. Adult/continuing education programs available. Career services available to part-time students: individual and group career counseling. Part-time tuition: $16 per credit hour for area residents. Part-time tuition per credit hour ranges from $21 (for students taking 1 to 5 credit hours) to $89 (for students taking 6 to 11 credit hours).

College of Ganado
Ganado 86505

Independent institution; rural setting. Awards A. Total enrollment: 223 (all undergraduates); 58% part-time, 76% women, 10% over 25. Total faculty: 26. Library holdings: 16,000 bound volumes, 100 periodical subscriptions, 550 records/tapes.

Undergraduate Courses offered for part-time students during daytime, evenings, summer. Complete part-time degree programs offered during daytime, evenings, summer. Adult/continuing education programs available. Career services available to part-time students: individual and group career counseling, individual job placement. Part-time tuition: $18 per credit hour.

Eastern Arizona College
Thatcher 85552

Public institution; rural setting. Awards A. Total enrollment: 1,419 (all undergraduates); 40% part-time, 52% women. Total faculty: 290. Library holdings: 33,000 bound volumes, 40 titles on microform, 250 periodical subscriptions, 1,200 records/tapes.

Undergraduate Courses offered for part-time students during daytime, evenings. Complete part-time degree programs offered during daytime, evenings. Adult/continuing education programs available. Career services available to part-time students: individual and group career counseling. Part-time tuition: $13 per credit for state residents, $101 per credit for nonresidents.

Embry-Riddle Aeronautical University, Prescott Campus
Prescott 86302

Independent institution; small-town setting. Awards A, B. Total enrollment: 884 (all undergraduates); 4% part-time, 10% women. Total faculty: 53. Library holdings: 25,606 bound volumes, 2,263 titles on microform, 137 periodical subscriptions, 206 records/tapes.

Undergraduate Courses offered for part-time students during daytime, summer. Complete part-time degree programs offered during daytime. Career services available to part-time students: individual career counseling, individual job placement, employer recruitment on campus. Part-time tuition: $115 per credit hour.

Glendale Community College
Glendale 85302

Public institution; city setting. Awards A. Barrier-free campus. Total enrollment: 13,690 (all undergraduates); 28% part-time, 2% women, 53% over 25. Total faculty: 374.

Undergraduate Courses offered for part-time students during daytime, evenings, summer. Complete part-time degree programs offered during daytime, evenings, summer. Adult/continuing education programs available. Part-time tuition: $14 per semester hour for area residents, $65 per semester hour for state residents, $90 per semester hour for nonresidents.

Grand Canyon College
Phoenix 85061

Independent-religious institution; metropolitan setting. Awards B. Total enrollment: 1,305 (all undergraduates); 26% part-time, 53% women. Total faculty: 90. Library holdings: 134,403 bound volumes, 48 titles on microform, 718 periodical subscriptions, 6,135 records/tapes.

Undergraduate Courses offered for part-time students during daytime, evenings, summer. Complete part-time degree programs offered during daytime, evenings, summer. Career services available to part-time students: individual job placement, employer recruitment on campus. Part-time tuition: $83 per semester hour.

Maricopa Technical Community College
Phoenix 85034

Public institution; metropolitan setting. Awards A. Barrier-free campus. Total enrollment: 3,414 (all undergraduates); 71% part-time, 45% women. Total faculty: 181. Library holdings: 35,000 bound volumes, 300 periodical subscriptions.

Undergraduate Courses offered for part-time students during daytime, evenings, summer. Complete part-time degree programs offered during daytime, evenings, summer. Adult/continuing education programs available. Career services available to part-time students: individual and group career counseling, individual job placement. Part-time tuition: $14 per semester hour for area residents, $74 per semester hour for state residents, $104 per semester hour for nonresidents.

Mohave Community College
Kingman 86401

Public institution; small-town setting. Awards A. Barrier-free campus. Total enrollment: 3,137 (all undergraduates); 92% part-time, 59% women, 75% over 25. Total faculty: 188. Library

Colleges Offering Part-Time Degree Programs / *Arizona*

Mohave Community College (continued)

holdings: 29,262 bound volumes, 349 periodical subscriptions, 300 records/tapes.

Undergraduate Courses offered for part-time students during daytime, evenings, weekends, summer. Complete part-time degree programs offered during daytime, evenings, weekends, summer. Adult/continuing education programs available. Career services available to part-time students: individual and group career counseling, individual job placement, employer recruitment on campus. Part-time tuition per semester (1 to 11 credit hours) ranges from $15 to $105 for county residents, $17 to $1216 for nonresidents.

Navajo Community College
Tsaile 86556

Public institution; rural setting. Awards A. Barrier-free campus. Total enrollment: 1,457 (all undergraduates); 82% part-time, 79% women, 47% over 25. Total faculty: 117. Library holdings: 67,000 bound volumes, 408 periodical subscriptions, 2,702 records/tapes.

Undergraduate Courses offered for part-time students during daytime, evenings, summer. Complete part-time degree programs offered during daytime, evenings, summer. Adult/continuing education programs available. Part-time tuition: $30 per credit.

Northern Arizona University
Flagstaff 86011

Public institution; small-town setting. Awards B, M, D. Barrier-free campus. Total enrollment: 11,501. Undergraduate enrollment: 9,552; 14% part-time, 51% women. Total faculty: 652. Library holdings: 710,703 bound volumes, 917,378 titles on microform, 4,917 periodical subscriptions, 21,878 records/tapes.

Undergraduate Courses offered for part-time students during daytime, evenings, summer. Complete part-time degree programs offered during daytime, evenings, summer. External degree and adult/continuing education programs available. Career services available to part-time students: individual and group career counseling, employer recruitment on campus. Part-time tuition: $51 per semester hour for state residents, $51 per semester hour for nonresidents.

Graduate Part-time study available in Graduate College. Basic part-time expenses: $51 per credit tuition.

Northland Pioneer College
Holbrook 86025

Public institution; rural setting. Awards A. Total enrollment: 5,274 (all undergraduates); 92% part-time, 62% women, 80% over 25. Total faculty: 492. Library holdings: 36,000 bound volumes, 90,000 titles on microform, 500 periodical subscriptions, 1,250 records/tapes.

Undergraduate Courses offered for part-time students during daytime, evenings. Complete part-time degree programs offered during daytime, evenings. Career services available to part-time students: individual and group career counseling, individual job placement, employer recruitment on campus. Part-time tuition: $5 per semester hour for area residents, $71 per semester hour for state residents, $75 per semester hour for nonresidents.

Phoenix College
Phoenix 85013

Public institution; metropolitan setting. Awards A. Barrier-free campus. Total enrollment: 13,000 (all undergraduates); 75% part-time, 58% women, 46% over 25. Total faculty: 503. Library holdings: 80,000 bound volumes, 2,800 titles on microform, 400 periodical subscriptions, 1,000 records/tapes.

Undergraduate Courses offered for part-time students during daytime, evenings, summer. Complete part-time degree programs offered during daytime, evenings, summer. Adult/continuing education programs available. Career services available to part-time students: individual and group career counseling, individual job placement. Part-time tuition: $14 per credit hour for area residents, $74 per credit hour for state residents, $104 per credit hour for nonresidents. State residents from counties in which there are community colleges pay area-resident tuition.

Pima Community College
Tucson 85702

Public institution; metropolitan setting. Awards A. Barrier-free campus. Total enrollment: 20,902 (all undergraduates); 73% part-time, 52% women, 48% over 25. Total faculty: 859. Library holdings: 185,514 bound volumes, 1,073 titles on microform, 1,000 periodical subscriptions, 24,171 records/tapes.

Undergraduate Courses offered for part-time students during daytime, evenings, weekends, summer. Complete part-time degree programs offered during daytime, evenings, summer. Adult/continuing education programs available. Career services available to part-time students: individual and group career counseling, individual job placement, employer recruitment on campus. Part-time tuition: $15 per credit hour for state residents, $85 per credit hour for nonresidents.

South Mountain Community College
Phoenix 85040

Public institution; metropolitan setting. Awards A. Barrier-free campus. Total enrollment: 1,481 (all undergraduates); 52% part-time, 67% women. Total faculty: 120. Library holdings: 5,400 bound volumes, 46 titles on microform, 410 records/tapes.

Undergraduate Courses offered for part-time students during daytime, evenings, summer. Complete part-time degree programs offered during daytime, evenings. Adult/continuing education programs available. Career services available to part-time students: individual and group career counseling, individual job placement. Part-time tuition: $14 per credit for area residents, $60 per credit for state residents, $90 per credit for nonresidents.

University of Arizona
Tucson 85721

Public institution; metropolitan setting. Awards B, M, D. Barrier-free campus. Total enrollment: 33,006. Undergraduate enrollment: 25,071; 29% part-time, 47% women, 33% over 25. Total faculty: 1,678. Library holdings: 1.6 million bound volumes, 2.1 million titles on microform, 39,982 periodical subscriptions, 132,318 records/tapes.

Undergraduate Courses offered for part-time students during daytime, evenings, summer. Complete part-time degree programs offered during daytime, evenings, summer. Adult/continuing education programs available. Career services available to part-time students: individual and group career counseling, individual job placement, employer recruitment on campus.

Part-time tuition: $51 per semester hour for state residents, $166 per semester hour for nonresidents.
Graduate Part-time study available in Graduate College. Basic part-time expenses: $51 per credit (minimum) fees. Institutional financial aid available to part-time graduate students in Graduate College.

University of Phoenix
Phoenix 85004

Proprietary institution; metropolitan setting. Awards B, M. Total enrollment: 4,997. Undergraduate enrollment: 2,746; 0% part-time, 39% women. Total faculty: 537.
Graduate Part-time study available in Graduate Programs. Degree can be earned exclusively through evening/weekend study in Graduate Programs. Basic part-time expenses: $130 per semester hour tuition.

Western International University
Phoenix 85021

Independent institution; metropolitan setting. Awards B, M. Barrier-free campus. Total enrollment: 850. Undergraduate enrollment: 480; 0% part-time, 63% women. Total faculty: 50. Library holdings: 5,000 bound volumes, 50 titles on microform, 65 periodical subscriptions, 10 records/tapes.
Undergraduate Courses offered for part-time students during daytime, evenings, summer. Complete part-time degree programs offered during daytime, evenings, summer. External degree and adult/continuing education programs available. Career services available to part-time students: individual career counseling. Part-time tuition: $1440 per year.
Graduate Part-time study available in Graduate Programs. Basic part-time expenses: $95 per credit hour tuition.

Yavapai College
Prescott 86301

Public institution; small-town setting. Awards A. Barrier-free campus. Total enrollment: 5,343 (all undergraduates); 86% part-time, 60% women, 72% over 25. Total faculty: 363. Library holdings: 48,867 bound volumes, 4,030 titles on microform, 441 periodical subscriptions, 3,150 records/tapes.
Undergraduate Courses offered for part-time students during daytime, evenings, summer. Complete part-time degree programs offered during daytime, evenings, summer. Adult/continuing education programs available. Career services available to part-time students: individual and group career counseling, employer recruitment on campus. Part-time tuition: $18 per credit hour for state residents. Nonresident part-time tuition per credit hour ranges from $20 (for students taking 1 to 6 credit hours) to $136 (for students taking 7 to 11 credit hours).

ARKANSAS

Arkansas College
Batesville 72501

Independent-religious instutition; small-town setting. Awards B. Barrier-free campus. Total enrollment: 653 (all undergraduates); 20% part-time, 60% women. Total faculty: 59. Library holdings: 72,000 bound volumes, 500 periodical subscriptions, 2,000 records/tapes.
Undergraduate Courses offered for part-time students during daytime, summer. Complete part-time degree programs offered during daytime. Adult/continuing education programs available. Career services available to part-time students: individual and group career counseling, individual job placement, employer recruitment on campus. Part-time tuition: $95 per credit hour.

Arkansas State University
State University 72467

Public institution; small-town setting. Awards A, B, M. Barrier-free campus. Total enrollment: 8,358. Undergraduate enrollment: 7,083; 24% part-time, 53% women, 29% over 25. Total faculty: 310. Library holdings: 818,637 bound volumes, 200,000 titles on microform, 2,200 periodical subscriptions, 8,308 records/tapes.
Undergraduate Courses offered for part-time students during daytime, evenings. Complete part-time degree programs offered during daytime, evenings. Adult/continuing education programs available. Career services available to part-time students: individual and group career counseling, individual job placement, employer recruitment on campus. Part-time tuition: $33 per credit hour for state residents, $71 per credit hour (minimum) for nonresidents.
Graduate Part-time study available in Graduate School. Degree can be earned exclusively through evening/weekend study in Graduate School. Basic part-time expenses: $33 per credit tuition for state residents, $81 per credit tuition for nonresidents. Institutional financial aid available to part-time graduate students in Graduate School.

Arkansas State University–Beebe Branch
Beebe 72012

Public institution; rural setting. Awards A. Barrier-free campus. Total enrollment: 1,010 (all undergraduates); 31% part-time, 42% women, 25% over 25. Total faculty: 32. Library holdings: 35,500 bound volumes, 125 periodical subscriptions, 1,022 records/tapes.
Undergraduate Courses offered for part-time students during daytime, evenings, weekends, summer. Complete part-time degree programs offered during daytime, evenings, weekends, summer. Adult/continuing education programs available. Career services available to part-time students: individual and group career counseling. Part-time tuition: $26 per credit hour for state residents, $36 per credit hour for nonresidents.

Arkansas Tech University
Russellville 72801

Public institution; small-town setting. Awards A, B, M. Total enrollment: 3,362. Undergraduate enrollment: 3,219; 10% part-time, 50% women. Total faculty: 150. Library holdings: 156,490 bound volumes, 364,302 titles on microform, 959 periodical subscriptions.
Undergraduate Courses offered for part-time students during daytime, evenings, summer. Complete part-time degree programs offered during daytime, evenings, summer. Adult/continuing education programs available. Career services available to part-time students: individual career counseling, individual job placement, employer recruitment on campus. Part-time tuition: $35 per credit for state residents, $69 per credit for nonresidents.
Graduate Part-time study available in Graduate Program in Education. Degree can be earned exclusively through evening/weekend study in Graduate Program in Education. Basic part-time expenses: $40 per credit hour tuition for state residents, $82 per credit hour tuition for nonresidents. Institutional financial aid available to part-time graduate students in Graduate Program in Education.

Colleges Offering Part-Time Degree Programs / Arkansas

Central Baptist College
Conway 72032

Independent-religious instutition; small-town setting. Awards A, B, M. Total enrollment: 232. Undergraduate enrollment: 223; 9% part-time, 42% women, 16% over 25. Total faculty: 21. Library holdings: 26,083 bound volumes, 822 titles on microform, 189 periodical subscriptions, 600 records/tapes.

Undergraduate Courses offered for part-time students during daytime. Complete part-time degree programs offered during daytime. Career services available to part-time students: individual career counseling, individual job placement, employer recruitment on campus. Part-time tuition: $100 per course.

Graduate Part-time study available in Graduate School. Basic part-time expenses: $40 per credit tuition.

College of the Ozarks
Clarksville 72830

Independent-religious instutition; small-town setting. Awards A, B. Total enrollment: 708 (all undergraduates); 17% part-time, 52% women. Total faculty: 40. Library holdings: 15,129 bound volumes, 3,056 titles on microform, 450 periodical subscriptions, 1,876 records/tapes.

Undergraduate Courses offered for part-time students during daytime, evenings, summer. Complete part-time degree programs offered during daytime, evenings, summer. External degree programs available. Career services available to part-time students: individual and group career counseling, individual job placement, employer recruitment on campus. Part-time tuition: $70 per semester hour.

Crowley's Ridge College
Paragould 72450

Independent-religious instutition; rural setting. Awards A. Total enrollment: 107 (all undergraduates); 29% part-time, 62% women, 5% over 25. Total faculty: 12. Library holdings: 12,500 bound volumes, 75 periodical subscriptions, 300 records/tapes.

Undergraduate Courses offered for part-time students during daytime, summer. Complete part-time degree programs offered during daytime, summer. Career services available to part-time students: individual and group career counseling. Part-time tuition: $60 per semester hour.

East Arkansas Community College
Forrest City 72335

Public institution; rural setting. Awards A. Barrier-free campus. Total enrollment: 1,322 (all undergraduates); 54% part-time, 70% women, 47% over 25. Total faculty: 69.

Undergraduate Courses offered for part-time students during daytime, evenings. Complete part-time degree programs offered during daytime, evenings. Adult/continuing education programs available. Career services available to part-time students: individual and group career counseling, individual job placement. Part-time tuition: $18 per semester hour for area residents, $25 per semester hour for state residents, $32 per semester hour for nonresidents.

Garland County Community College
Hot Springs 71913

Public institution; small-town setting. Awards A. Barrier-free campus. Total enrollment: 1,809 (all undergraduates); 70% part-time, 63% women, 60% over 25. Total faculty: 90.

Undergraduate Courses offered for part-time students during daytime, evenings, summer. Complete part-time degree programs offered during daytime, evenings, summer. Adult/continuing education programs available. Career services available to part-time students: individual and group career counseling, employer recruitment on campus. Part-time tuition: $20 per semester hour for area residents, $26 per semester hour for state residents, $63 per semester hour for nonresidents.

Harding University
Searcy 72143

Independent-religious instutition; small-town setting. Awards A, B, M. Total enrollment: 2,885. Undergraduate enrollment: 2,822; 8% part-time, 53% women, 2% over 25. Total faculty: 168. Library holdings: 161,022 bound volumes, 450,920 titles on microform, 1,473 periodical subscriptions, 3,424 records/tapes.

Undergraduate Courses offered for part-time students during daytime, evenings, summer. Complete part-time degree programs offered during daytime, summer. Career services available to part-time students: individual and group career counseling. Part-time tuition: $96.50 per semester hour.

Graduate Part-time study available in Graduate Studies. Basic part-time expenses: $104 per credit tuition plus $0 fees.

Henderson State University
Arkadelphia 71923

Public institution; small-town setting. Awards A, B, M. Barrier-free campus. Total enrollment: 2,824. Undergraduate enrollment: 2,651; 20% part-time, 53% women, 5% over 25. Total faculty: 122. Library holdings: 180,000 bound volumes, 1,564 periodical subscriptions, 4,548 records/tapes.

Undergraduate Courses offered for part-time students during daytime, evenings, summer. Complete part-time degree programs offered during daytime, evenings, summer. Career services available to part-time students: individual and group career counseling, individual job placement, employer recruitment on campus. Part-time tuition: $33 per semester hour for state residents, $66 per semester hour for nonresidents.

Graduate Part-time study available in Graduate Studies. Basic part-time expenses: $40 per hour tuition for state residents, $80 per hour tuition for nonresidents.

John Brown University
Siloam Springs 72761

Independent-religious instutition; rural setting. Awards A, B. Total enrollment: 768 (all undergraduates); 5% part-time, 52% women. Total faculty: 51. Library holdings: 80,000 bound volumes, 393 periodical subscriptions, 1,605 records/tapes.

Undergraduate Courses offered for part-time students during daytime. Complete part-time degree programs offered during daytime. Career services available to part-time students: individual career counseling, individual job placement, employer recruitment on campus. Part-time tuition: $120.83 per credit hour.

Mississippi County Community College
Blytheville 72315

Public institution; rural setting. Awards A. Barrier-free campus. Total enrollment: 1,180 (all undergraduates); 54% part-time, 66% women, 49% over 25. Total faculty: 65. Library holdings: 40,000 bound volumes, 200 periodical subscriptions.

Arkansas / **Colleges Offering Part-Time Degree Programs**

Undergraduate Courses offered for part-time students during daytime, evenings, summer. Complete part-time degree programs offered during daytime, evenings, summer. Adult/continuing education programs available. Career services available to part-time students: individual and group career counseling. Part-time tuition: $20 per semester hour for area residents, $30 per semester hour for state residents, $60 per semester hour for nonresidents.

North Arkansas Community College
Harrison 72601

Public institution; small-town setting. Awards A. Barrier-free campus. Total enrollment: 881 (all undergraduates); 48% part-time, 35% women. Total faculty: 75.

Undergraduate Courses offered for part-time students during daytime, evenings, summer. Complete part-time degree programs offered during daytime, evenings, summer. External degree and adult/continuing education programs available. Career services available to part-time students: individual career counseling, individual job placement, employer recruitment on campus. Part-time tuition: $20 per credit hour for area residents, $25 per credit hour for state residents, $38 per credit hour for nonresidents.

Phillips County Community College
Helena 72342

Public institution; small-town setting. Awards A. Total enrollment: 1,562 (all undergraduates); 50% part-time, 52% women, 35% over 25. Total faculty: 90. Library holdings: 50,000 bound volumes, 75 periodical subscriptions, 764 records/tapes.

Undergraduate Courses offered for part-time students during daytime, evenings, weekends. Complete part-time degree programs offered during daytime, evenings. Adult/continuing education programs available. Career services available to part-time students: individual career counseling, individual job placement. Part-time tuition: $19 per credit hour for area residents, $25 per credit hour for state residents, $37 per credit hour for nonresidents.

Shorter College
North Little Rock 72114

Independent-religious instutition; city setting. Awards A. Barrier-free campus. Total enrollment: 103 (all undergraduates); 27% part-time, 50% women. Total faculty: 17.

Undergraduate Courses offered for part-time students during daytime, evenings, weekends, summer. Complete part-time degree programs offered during daytime, evenings, summer. Part-time tuition: $60 per semester hour.

Southern Arkansas University
Magnolia 71753

Public institution; small-town setting. Awards A, B, M. Total enrollment: 2,165. Undergraduate enrollment: 2,043; 13% part-time, 60% women, 10% over 25. Total faculty: 112. Library holdings: 103,416 bound volumes, 992 periodical subscriptions, 300 records/tapes.

Undergraduate Courses offered for part-time students during daytime, evenings. Complete part-time degree programs offered during daytime, evenings. Adult/continuing education programs available. Career services available to part-time students: individual and group career counseling, individual job placement, employer recruitment on campus. Part-time tuition: $37 per semester hour for state residents, $57 per semester hour for nonresidents.

Graduate Part-time study available in Graduate Program in Education.

Southern Arkansas University–El Dorado Branch
El Dorado 71730

Public institution; small-town setting. Awards A. Total enrollment: 573 (all undergraduates); 62% part-time, 68% women, 44% over 25. Total faculty: 41. Library holdings: 15,024 bound volumes, 90 titles on microform, 252 periodical subscriptions, 1,740 records/tapes.

Undergraduate Courses offered for part-time students during daytime, evenings, summer. Complete part-time degree programs offered during daytime, evenings. Career services available to part-time students: individual career counseling, individual job placement, employer recruitment on campus. Part-time tuition: $26 per semester hour for state residents, $38 per semester hour for nonresidents.

Southern Arkansas University Tech
East Camden 71701

Public institution; rural setting. Awards A. Total enrollment: 805 (all undergraduates); 53% part-time, 23% women, 20% over 25. Total faculty: 43. Library holdings: 770 bound volumes, 135 periodical subscriptions, 450 records/tapes.

Undergraduate Courses offered for part-time students during daytime, evenings, summer. Complete part-time degree programs offered during daytime, evenings, summer. Adult/continuing education programs available. Career services available to part-time students: individual career counseling. Part-time tuition: $25 per semester hour for state residents, $37.50 per semester hour for nonresidents.

Southern Baptist College
Walnut Ridge 72476

Independent-religious instutition; rural setting. Awards A. Total enrollment: 459 (all undergraduates); 16% part-time, 51% women. Total faculty: 25. Library holdings: 140,000 bound volumes, 12,000 periodical subscriptions.

Undergraduate Courses offered for part-time students during daytime, evenings. Complete part-time degree programs offered during daytime, evenings. Career services available to part-time students: individual and group career counseling. Part-time tuition: $63 per hour.

University of Arkansas
Fayetteville 72701

Public institution; small-town setting. Awards A, B, M, D. Total enrollment: 13,483. Undergraduate enrollment: 11,462; 2% part-time, 42% women. Total faculty: 843. Library holdings: 1 million bound volumes, 916,152 titles on microform, 12,303 periodical subscriptions, 10,000 records/tapes.

Graduate Part-time study available in Graduate School. Basic part-time expenses: $56.50 per credit tuition for state residents, $119.50 per credit tuition for nonresidents. Institutional financial aid available to part-time graduate students in Graduate School.

Colleges Offering Part-Time Degree Programs / Arkansas

University of Arkansas at Little Rock
Little Rock 72204

Public institution; city setting. Awards A, B, M. Total enrollment: 10,091. Undergraduate enrollment: 8,898; 45% part-time, 54% women. Total faculty: 643. Library holdings: 330,162 bound volumes, 15,500 titles on microform, 5,185 periodical subscriptions.
Undergraduate Courses offered for part-time students during daytime, evenings, weekends, summer. Complete part-time degree programs offered during daytime, evenings, summer. Adult/continuing education programs available. Career services available to part-time students: individual and group career counseling, individual job placement, employer recruitment on campus. Part-time tuition: $45 per credit hour for state residents, $108 per credit hour for nonresidents.
Graduate Part-time study available in Graduate School, School of Law. Degree can be earned exclusively through evening/weekend study in Graduate School, School of Law.Basic part-time expenses: $55 per credit hour tuition for state residents, $118 per credit hour tuition for nonresidents. Institutional financial aid available to part-time graduate students in Graduate School, School of Law.

University of Arkansas at Monticello
Monticello 71655

Public institution; small-town setting. Awards A, B. Total enrollment: 1,915 (all undergraduates); 21% part-time, 55% women, 26% over 25. Total faculty: 107. Library holdings: 75,045 bound volumes, 768 periodical subscriptions, 957 records/tapes.
Undergraduate Courses offered for part-time students during daytime, evenings, summer. Complete part-time degree programs offered during daytime, evenings, summer. Adult/continuing education programs available. Career services available to part-time students: individual and group career counseling, individual job placement, employer recruitment on campus. Part-time tuition: $42.52 per hour for state residents, $92.50 per hour for nonresidents.

University of Arkansas at Pine Bluff
Pine Bluff 71601

Public institution; city setting. Awards A, B. Barrier-free campus. Total enrollment: 2,545 (all undergraduates); 17% part-time, 58% women, 24% over 25. Total faculty: 151. Library holdings: 170,345 bound volumes, 30,415 titles on microform, 829 periodical subscriptions, 450 records/tapes.
Undergraduate Courses offered for part-time students during daytime, evenings, weekends. Complete part-time degree programs offered during daytime, evenings, weekends. Adult/continuing education programs available. Career services available to part-time students: individual and group career counseling, individual job placement, employer recruitment on campus. Part-time tuition: $39 per credit hour for state residents, $102 per credit hour for nonresidents.

University of Arkansas for Medical Sciences
Little Rock 72205

Public institution; city setting. Awards A, B, M, D. Barrier-free campus. Total enrollment: 1,421. Undergraduate enrollment: 672; 50% part-time, 50% women, 32% over 25. Total faculty: 555. Library holdings: 128,005 bound volumes, 9,416 titles on microform, 2,688 periodical subscriptions, 1,900 records/tapes.
Undergraduate Courses offered for part-time students during daytime. Complete part-time degree programs offered during daytime. Part-time tuition: $55 per hour for state residents, $118 per hour for nonresidents.

University of Central Arkansas
Conway 72032

Public institution; small-town setting. Awards A, B, M. Total enrollment: 5,992. Undergraduate enrollment: 5,417; 25% part-time, 60% women, 10% over 25. Total faculty: 318. Library holdings: 365,000 bound volumes, 500,000 titles on microform, 2,600 periodical subscriptions.
Undergraduate Courses offered for part-time students during daytime, evenings, summer. Complete part-time degree programs offered during daytime, summer. Adult/continuing education programs available. Career services available to part-time students: individual and group career counseling, individual job placement, employer recruitment on campus. Part-time tuition: $35 per hour for state residents, $70 per hour for nonresidents.
Graduate Part-time study available in Graduate School.Basic part-time expenses: $35 per credit hour tuition plus $15 per semester fees for state residents, $70 per credit hour tuition plus $15 per semester fees for nonresidents.

Westark Community College
Fort Smith 72913

Public institution; city setting. Awards A. Total enrollment: 3,597 (all undergraduates); 54% part-time, 56% women, 40% over 25. Total faculty: 140. Library holdings: 37,837 bound volumes, 60 periodical subscriptions, 2,693 records/tapes.
Undergraduate Courses offered for part-time students during daytime, evenings, weekends, summer. Complete part-time degree programs offered during daytime, evenings, summer. Adult/continuing education programs available. Career services available to part-time students: individual and group career counseling, individual job placement, employer recruitment on campus. Part-time tuition: $19 per credit hour for area residents, $25 per credit hour for state residents, $49 per credit hour for nonresidents.

CALIFORNIA

Academy of Art College
San Francisco 94102

Proprietary institution; metropolitan setting. Awards B, M. Barrier-free campus. Total enrollment: 1,800. Undergraduate enrollment profile: 40% part-time, 65% women, 50% over 25. Total faculty: 120. Library holdings: 10,000 bound volumes, 100 periodical subscriptions.
Undergraduate Courses offered for part-time students during daytime, evenings, weekends, summer. Complete part-time degree programs offered during daytime, evenings, summer. Part-time tuition: $130 per unit.
Graduate Part-time study available in Graduate Program.Basic part-time expenses: $160 per unit tuition.

Allan Hancock College
Santa Maria 93454

Public institution; city setting. Awards A. Barrier-free campus. Total enrollment: 7,025 (all undergraduates); 93% part-time, 52% women, 60% over 25. Total faculty: 290. Library holdings: 55,000 bound volumes, 450 periodical subscriptions, 4,000 records/tapes.

California / **Colleges Offering Part-Time Degree Programs**

Undergraduate Courses offered for part-time students during daytime, evenings, summer. Complete part-time degree programs offered during daytime, evenings, summer. Adult/continuing education programs available. Career services available to part-time students: individual and group career counseling, individual job placement, employer recruitment on campus. Part-time tuition: $5 per unit for state residents, $77 per unit for nonresidents. State residents taking 6 or more units are charged the full-time rate for tuition.

American Baptist Seminary of the West
Berkeley 94704

Independent-religious institution (graduate only). Total enrollment: 100 (coed).

Graduate Part-time study available in Graduate and Professional Programs. Degree can be earned exclusively through evening/weekend study in Graduate and Professional Programs. Basic part-time expenses: $400 per course tuition plus $11.25 per semester fees.

American River College
Sacramento 95841

Public institution; metropolitan setting. Awards A. Barrier-free campus. Total enrollment: 21,410 (all undergraduates); 74% part-time, 56% women, 47% over 25. Total faculty: 523. Library holdings: 78,400 bound volumes, 450 titles on microform, 75 periodical subscriptions, 6,350 records/tapes.

Undergraduate Courses offered for part-time students during daytime, evenings, summer. Complete part-time degree programs offered during daytime, evenings, summer. Adult/continuing education programs available. Career services available to part-time students: individual and group career counseling, individual job placement, employer recruitment on campus. Part-time tuition: $5 per unit for state residents, $75 per unit for nonresidents. State residents taking 6 or more units are charged the full-time rate for tuition.

Antelope Valley College
Lancaster 93534

Public institution; city setting. Awards A. Barrier-free campus. Total enrollment: 6,888 (all undergraduates); 78% part-time, 57% women, 53% over 25. Total faculty: 250. Library holdings: 41,000 bound volumes, 4,184 titles on microform, 250 periodical subscriptions, 3,400 records/tapes.

Undergraduate Courses offered for part-time students during daytime, evenings, summer. Complete part-time degree programs offered during daytime, evenings, summer. Adult/continuing education programs available. Career services available to part-time students: individual and group career counseling, individual job placement, employer recruitment on campus. Part-time tuition: $5 per unit for state residents, $66 per unit for nonresidents. State residents taking 6 or more units are charged the full-time rate for tuition.

Antioch University West
San Francisco 94118

Independent institution; metropolitan setting. Awards B, M. Total enrollment: 982. Undergraduate enrollment: 390; 4% part-time, 78% women, 88% over 25. Total faculty: 151.

Undergraduate Courses offered for part-time students during daytime, evenings, weekends, summer. Complete part-time degree programs offered during daytime, evenings, summer. External degree and adult/continuing education programs available. Career services available to part-time students: individual career counseling. Part-time tuition: $160 per credit.

Graduate Part-time study available in Graduate Programs. Degree can be earned exclusively through evening/weekend study in Graduate Programs. Basic part-time expenses: $160 per credit tuition. Institutional financial aid available to part-time graduate students in Graduate Programs.

Armstrong College
Berkeley 94704

Proprietary institution; city setting. Awards A, B, M. Barrier-free campus. Total enrollment: 475. Undergraduate enrollment: 325; 28% part-time, 30% women. Total faculty: 34. Library holdings: 21,000 bound volumes, 200 periodical subscriptions.

Undergraduate Courses offered for part-time students during daytime, evenings, summer. Complete part-time degree programs offered during daytime, evenings, summer. Career services available to part-time students: individual career counseling. Part-time tuition: $66 per quarter hour.

Graduate Part-time study available in Graduate School of Accounting, Graduate School of Business Administration, School of Law. Degree can be earned exclusively through evening/weekend study in Graduate School of Accounting, Graduate School of Business Administration. Basic part-time expenses: $75 per unit tuition plus $6 per quarter fees.

Azusa Pacific University
Azusa 91702

Independent-religious instutition; small-town setting. Awards A, B, M (A through correspondence only). Barrier-free campus. Total enrollment: 2,425. Undergraduate enrollment: 1,450; 7% part-time, 51% women, 2% over 25. Total faculty: 128. Library holdings: 110,000 bound volumes, 2,000 periodical subscriptions.

Undergraduate Courses offered for part-time students during daytime. Complete part-time degree programs offered during daytime. Adult/continuing education programs available. Career services available to part-time students: individual and group career counseling, employer recruitment on campus. Part-time tuition: $216 per unit.

Graduate Part-time study available in Graduate Studies. Basic part-time expenses: $140 per unit tuition.

Bakersfield College
Bakersfield 93305

Public institution; city setting. Awards A. Barrier-free campus. Total enrollment: 10,319 (all undergraduates); 70% part-time, 54% women. Total faculty: 378. Library holdings: 54,886 bound volumes, 3,726 titles on microform, 221 periodical subscriptions.

Undergraduate Courses offered for part-time students during daytime, evenings, summer. Complete part-time degree programs offered during daytime, evenings, summer. Adult/continuing education programs available. Career services available to part-time students: individual and group career counseling, individual job placement. Part-time tuition: $5 per unit for state residents, $73 per unit for nonresidents. State residents taking 6 or more units are charged the full-time rate for tuition.

Barstow College
Barstow 92311

Public institution; small-town setting. Awards A. Barrier-free campus. Total enrollment: 2,021 (all undergraduates); 40% part-

Colleges Offering Part-Time Degree Programs / California

Barstow College (continued)

time, 47% women. Total faculty: 75. Library holdings: 34,000 bound volumes, 150 periodical subscriptions, 2,200 records/tapes.

Undergraduate Courses offered for part-time students during daytime, evenings, weekends, summer. Complete part-time degree programs offered during daytime, evenings, weekends, summer. Adult/continuing education programs available. Career services available to part-time students: individual and group career counseling, individual job placement, employer recruitment on campus. Part-time tuition: $3.45 per unit for state residents, $50 per unit for nonresidents. State residents taking 6 or more units are charged the full-time rate for tuition.

Bay-Valley Tech
Santa Clara 95050

Proprietary institution; city setting. Awards A. Barrier-free campus. Total enrollment: 519 (all undergraduates); 30% part-time, 30% women, 70% over 25. Total faculty: 29.

Undergraduate Courses offered for part-time students during evenings. Complete part-time degree programs offered during evenings. Career services available to part-time students: individual and group career counseling, individual job placement, employer recruitment on campus.

Biola University
La Mirada 90639

Independent-religious instutition; small-town setting. Awards B, M, D. Total enrollment: 3,083. Undergraduate enrollment: 2,067; 12% part-time, 58% women. Total faculty: 253. Library holdings: 180,000 bound volumes, 1,076 periodical subscriptions, 4,200 records/tapes.

Undergraduate Courses offered for part-time students during daytime, evenings, summer. Complete part-time degree programs offered during daytime. Adult/continuing education programs available. Career services available to part-time students: individual and group career counseling, individual job placement, employer recruitment on campus. Part-time tuition: $204 per unit.

Graduate Part-time study available in School of Arts, Sciences, and Professions, School of Intercultural Studies and World Missions, Talbot Theological Seminary. Degree can be earned exclusively through evening/weekend study in School of Arts, Sciences, and Professions. Basic part-time expenses: $176 per unit tuition. Institutional financial aid available to part-time graduate students in School of Arts, Sciences, and Professions, Talbot Theological Seminary.

Butte College
Oroville 95965

Public institution; rural setting. Awards A. Barrier-free campus. Total enrollment: 1,000 (all undergraduates); 59% part-time, 58% women, 47% over 25. Total faculty: 330. Library holdings: 50,000 bound volumes, 300 periodical subscriptions, 2,600 records/tapes.

Undergraduate Courses offered for part-time students during daytime, evenings, summer. Complete part-time degree programs offered during daytime, evenings, summer. External degree and adult/continuing education programs available. Career services available to part-time students: individual and group career counseling, individual job placement, employer recruitment on campus. Part-time tuition: $3.50 per unit for state residents, $53 per unit for nonresidents. State residents taking 6 or more units are charged the full-time rate for tuition.

Cabrillo College
Aptos 95003

Public institution; small-town setting. Awards A. Barrier-free campus. Total enrollment: 10,673 (all undergraduates); 72% part-time, 58% women, 50% over 25. Total faculty: 300. Library holdings: 60,000 bound volumes, 300 periodical subscriptions, 1,000 records/tapes.

Undergraduate Courses offered for part-time students during daytime, evenings, weekends, summer. Complete part-time degree programs offered during daytime, evenings, summer. Adult/continuing education programs available. Career services available to part-time students: individual and group career counseling, individual job placement, employer recruitment on campus. Part-time tuition: $5 per unit for state residents, $83 per unit for nonresidents. State residents taking 6 or more units are charged the full-time rate for tuition.

California Baptist College
Riverside 92504

Independent-religious instutition; city setting. Awards B, M. Barrier-free campus. Total enrollment: 678. Undergraduate enrollment: 644; 16% part-time, 52% women, 10% over 25. Total faculty: 70. Library holdings: 100,000 bound volumes.

Undergraduate Courses offered for part-time students during daytime, evenings, summer. Complete part-time degree programs offered during daytime, evenings, summer. External degree and adult/continuing education programs available. Career services available to part-time students: individual career counseling, individual job placement, employer recruitment on campus. Part-time tuition: $129 per unit.

California College of Arts and Crafts
Oakland 94618

Independent institution; city setting. Awards B, M. Total enrollment: 1,001. Undergraduate enrollment: 860; 19% part-time, 66% women, 30% over 25. Total faculty: 143. Library holdings: 29,132 bound volumes, 303 titles on microform, 364 periodical subscriptions, 3,300 records/tapes.

Undergraduate Courses offered for part-time students during daytime, summer. Complete part-time degree programs offered during daytime, summer. Career services available to part-time students: individual career counseling, individual job placement, employer recruitment on campus. Part-time tuition: $249 per credit.

Graduate Part-time study available in Graduate Programs. Basic part-time expenses: $249 per unit tuition. Institutional financial aid available to part-time graduate students in Graduate Programs.

California Institute of Integral Studies
San Francisco 94110

Independent institution (graduate only). Total enrollment: 214 (coed; 42% part-time). Total faculty: 55. Library holdings: 24,000 bound volumes.

Graduate Part-time study available in Graduate Programs. Basic part-time expenses: $127 per unit (minimum) tuition plus $30 per quarter fees. Institutional financial aid available to part-time graduate students in Graduate Programs.

California / Colleges Offering Part-Time Degree Programs

California Institute of the Arts
Valencia 91355

Independent institution; small-town setting. Awards B, M. Barrier-free campus. Total enrollment: 866. Undergraduate enrollment: 650; 2% part-time, 45% women, 3% over 25. Total faculty: 168. Library holdings: 59,921 bound volumes, 6,600 periodical subscriptions, 11,194 records/tapes.

Graduate Part-time study available in School of Art, School of Music. Basic part-time expenses: $6800 per year tuition. Institutional financial aid available to part-time graduate students in School of Art.

California Lutheran College
Thousand Oaks 91360

Independent-religious instutition; rural setting. Awards B, M. Total enrollment: 2,467. Undergraduate enrollment: 1,322; 8% part-time, 54% women. Total faculty: 166. Library holdings: 95,000 bound volumes.

Undergraduate Courses offered for part-time students during daytime, evenings, summer. Complete part-time degree programs offered during daytime, evenings, summer. Adult/continuing education programs available. Career services available to part-time students: individual and group career counseling, individual job placement, employer recruitment on campus. Part-time tuition: $190 per credit.

California Polytechnic State University, San Luis Obispo
San Luis Obispo 93407

Public institution; small-town setting. Awards B, M. Barrier-free campus. Total enrollment: 15,623. Undergraduate enrollment: 14,768; 15% part-time, 44% women. Total faculty: 958. Library holdings: 555,000 bound volumes, 3,900 periodical subscriptions.

Undergraduate Courses offered for part-time students during daytime, summer. Complete part-time degree programs offered during daytime, summer. Adult/continuing education programs available. Career services available to part-time students: individual and group career counseling, individual job placement, employer recruitment on campus. Part-time tuition and fees per quarter (1 to 11 units) range from $144 to $234 for state residents, $222 to $1092 for nonresidents.

California School of Professional Psychology
Berkeley 94704

Independent institution (graduate only). Total enrollment: 332 (coed; 27% part-time). Total faculty: 102. Library holdings: 15,000 bound volumes.

Graduate Part-time study available in Graduate Programs. Degree can be earned exclusively through evening/weekend study in Graduate Programs. Basic part-time expenses: $265 per semester hour tuition. Institutional financial aid available to part-time graduate students in Graduate Programs.

California State College, Bakersfield
Bakersfield 93309

Public institution; city setting. Awards B, M. Barrier-free campus. Total enrollment: 3,380. Undergraduate enrollment: 2,380; 33% part-time, 59% women. Total faculty: 205. Library holdings: 248,000 bound volumes, 300,000 titles on microform, 2,645 periodical subscriptions.

Undergraduate Courses offered for part-time students during daytime, evenings, weekends. Complete part-time degree programs offered during daytime, evenings. Adult/continuing education programs available. Career services available to part-time students: individual and group career counseling, individual job placement, employer recruitment on campus. Part-time tuition: $384 per year for state residents. State residents taking 6 or more units pay the full-time rate for tuition. Nonresident part-time tuition per quarter (1 to 11 units) ranges from $203 to $1063.

California State College, San Bernardino
San Bernardino 92407

Public institution; city setting. Awards B, M. Barrier-free campus. Total enrollment: 5,450. Undergraduate enrollment: 3,918; 39% part-time, 52% women. Total faculty: 272. Library holdings: 340,000 bound volumes, 1,800 periodical subscriptions.

Undergraduate Courses offered for part-time students during daytime, evenings, summer. Complete part-time degree programs offered during daytime, evenings, summer. External degree and adult/continuing education programs available. Career services available to part-time students: individual career counseling, individual job placement, employer recruitment on campus. Part-time tuition and fees per quarter (1 to 6 units) range from $143 to $237 for state residents, $221 to $1701 for nonresidents.

Graduate Part-time study available in School of Administration, School of Education, School of Humanities, School of Natural Sciences, School of Social and Behavioral Sciences, Interdisciplinary Programs. Degree can be earned exclusively through evening/weekend study in School of Administration, School of Education. Basic part-time expenses: $0 tuition plus $152 per quarter (minimum) fees for state residents, $78 per unit tuition plus $152 per quarter (minimum) fees for nonresidents.

California State College, Stanislaus
Turlock 95380

Public institution; small-town setting. Awards B, M. Barrier-free campus. Total enrollment: 4,448. Undergraduate enrollment: 3,121; 20% part-time, 56% women. Total faculty: 232. Library holdings: 237,000 bound volumes, 230,000 titles on microform, 2,500 periodical subscriptions, 2,500 records/tapes.

Undergraduate Courses offered for part-time students during daytime, evenings. Complete part-time degree programs offered during daytime, evenings. Adult/continuing education programs available. Career services available to part-time students: individual and group career counseling, individual job placement, employer recruitment on campus. Part-time tuition per semester for state residents (1 to 6 units) ranges from $175.50 to $295.50. Part-time tuition per semester for nonresidents (1 to 11 units) ranges from $292.50 to $1602.

Graduate Part-time study available in Graduate Programs. Basic part-time expenses: $0 tuition plus $193.50 per semester (minimum) fees for state residents, $117 per unit tuition plus $193.50 per semester (minimum) fees for nonresidents. Institutional financial aid available to part-time graduate students in Graduate Programs.

Colleges Offering Part-Time Degree Programs / California

California State Polytechnic University, Pomona
Pomona 91768
Public institution; city setting. Awards B, M. Barrier-free campus. Total enrollment: 16,701. Undergraduate enrollment: 15,210; 23% part-time, 40% women, 37% over 25. Total faculty: 989. Library holdings: 393,096 bound volumes, 1.1 million titles on microform, 3,055 periodical subscriptions, 3,032 records/tapes.

Undergraduate Courses offered for part-time students during daytime, evenings, summer. Complete part-time degree programs offered during daytime, evenings, summer. Adult/continuing education programs available. Career services available to part-time students: individual and group career counseling, individual job placement, employer recruitment on campus. Part-time tuition and fees per quarter (1 to 14 units) range from $134 to $224 for state residents, $206 to $1232 for nonresidents.

Graduate Part-time study available in Graduate Studies and Research. Basic part-time expenses: $0 tuition plus $140 per quarter fees for state residents, $78 per unit tuition plus $140 per quarter fees for nonresidents. Institutional financial aid available to part-time graduate students in Graduate Studies and Research.

California State University, Chico
Chico 95929
Public institution; small-town setting. Awards B, M. Barrier-free campus. Total enrollment: 14,129. Undergraduate enrollment: 12,670; 11% part-time, 50% women, 12% over 25. Total faculty: 944. Library holdings: 575,000 bound volumes, 4,025 periodical subscriptions, 9,200 records/tapes.

Undergraduate Courses offered for part-time students during daytime, evenings, weekends, summer. Complete part-time degree programs offered during daytime, evenings, weekends, summer. External degree and adult/continuing education programs available. Career services available to part-time students: individual and group career counseling, individual job placement, employer recruitment on campus. State resident part-time tuition and fees per semester (1 to 5 units): $223.50. Nonresident part-time tuition and fees per semester (1 to 11 units) range from $340.50 to $1630.50.

Graduate Part-time study available in Graduate School. Basic part-time expenses: $0 tuition plus $241.50 per semester fees for state residents, $117 per unit tuition plus $241.50 per semester fees for nonresidents. Institutional financial aid available to part-time graduate students in Graduate School.

California State University, Dominguez Hills
Carson 90747
Public institution; city setting. Awards B, M. Barrier-free campus. Total enrollment: 8,271. Undergraduate enrollment: 6,114; 31% part-time, 57% women. Total faculty: 489. Library holdings: 300,000 bound volumes, 3,000 periodical subscriptions, 3,000 records/tapes.

Undergraduate Courses offered for part-time students during daytime, evenings, weekends, summer. Complete part-time degree programs offered during daytime, evenings. External degree and adult/continuing education programs available. Career services available to part-time students: individual and group career counseling, individual job placement, employer recruitment on campus. Part-time tuition: $138 per unit for state residents. State residents taking 6 or more units per quarter pay the full-time rate for tuition. Nonresident part-time tuition per quarter (1 to 11 units) ranges from $216 to $996.

Graduate Part-time study available in School of Education, School of Humanities and Fine Arts, School of Management, School of Science, Mathematics and Technology, School of Social and Behavioral Science, University College. Basic part-time expenses: $0 tuition plus $150 per quarter fees for state residents, $78 per unit tuition plus $150 per quarter fees for nonresidents.

California State University, Fresno
Fresno 93740
Public institution; city setting. Awards B, M. Barrier-free campus. Total enrollment: 16,293. Undergraduate enrollment: 13,667; 19% part-time, 51% women, 31% over 25. Total faculty: 1,090. Library holdings: 666,870 bound volumes, 783,758 titles on microform, 4,000 periodical subscriptions, 44,488 records/tapes.

Undergraduate Courses offered for part-time students during daytime, evenings, weekends, summer. Complete part-time degree programs offered during daytime, evenings, summer. Adult/continuing education programs available. Career services available to part-time students: individual and group career counseling, individual job placement, employer recruitment on campus. Part-time tuition and fees per semester (1 to 11 units) range from $233 to $368 for state residents, $350 to $1655 for nonresidents.

Graduate Part-time study available in Division of Graduate Studies and Research. Basic part-time expenses: $0 tuition plus $242.50 per semester fees for state residents, $117 per unit tuition plus $242.50 per semester fees for nonresidents.

California State University, Fullerton
Fullerton 92634
Public institution; city setting. Awards B, M. Barrier-free campus. Total enrollment: 23,234. Undergraduate enrollment: 18,872; 35% part-time, 52% women, 39% over 25. Total faculty: 1,388. Library holdings: 500,000 bound volumes, 632,000 titles on microform, 4,000 periodical subscriptions.

Undergraduate Courses offered for part-time students during daytime, evenings. Complete part-time degree programs offered during daytime, evenings. Adult/continuing education programs available. Career services available to part-time students: individual and group career counseling, individual job placement, employer recruitment on campus. Part-time tuition: $426 per year for state residents, $117 per unit for nonresidents. State residents taking 6 or more units are charged the full-time rate for tuition.

Graduate Part-time study available in School of Business Administration and Economics, School of Human Development and Community Service, School of Humanities and Social Sciences, School of Mathematics, Science and Engineering, School of the Arts. Basic part-time expenses: $0 tuition plus $226.50 per semester fees for state residents, $117 per unit tuition plus $226.50 per semester fees for nonresidents. Institutional financial aid available to part-time graduate students in School of Business Administration and Economics, School of Human Development and Community Service, School of Humanities and Social Sciences, School of Mathematics, Science and Engineering, School of the Arts.

California State University, Hayward
Hayward 94542
Public institution; city setting. Awards B, M. Barrier-free campus. Total enrollment: 11,978. Undergraduate enrollment: 9,019; 39% part-time, 55% women, 50% over 25. Total faculty: 615. Library holdings: 655,855 bound volumes, 437,265 titles on microform, 2,529 periodical subscriptions, 15,499 records/tapes.

California / Colleges Offering Part-Time Degree Programs

Undergraduate Courses offered for part-time students during daytime, evenings, summer. Complete part-time degree programs offered during daytime, evenings, summer. Adult/continuing education programs available. Career services available to part-time students: individual and group career counseling, individual job placement, employer recruitment on campus. Part-time tuition: $390 per year for state residents. State residents taking 6 or more units are charged the full-time rate for tuition. Nonresident part-time tuition per quarter (1 to 11 units) ranges from $208 to $1068.

Graduate Part-time study available in Graduate Programs. Degree can be earned exclusively through evening/weekend study in Graduate Programs.Basic part-time expenses: $0 tuition plus $143 per quarter fees for state residents, $78 per unit tuition plus $143 per quarter fees for nonresidents. Institutional financial aid available to part-time graduate students in Graduate Programs.

California State University, Long Beach
Long Beach 90840

Public institution; city setting. Awards B, M. Barrier-free campus. Total enrollment: 31,492. Undergraduate enrollment: 25,817; 28% part-time, 52% women. Total faculty: 1,686. Library holdings: 815,894 bound volumes, 870,704 titles on microform, 5,000 periodical subscriptions, 151,713 records/tapes.

Undergraduate Courses offered for part-time students during daytime, evenings, weekends, summer. Complete part-time degree programs offered during daytime, evenings, weekends, summer. Adult/continuing education programs available. Career services available to part-time students: individual and group career counseling, individual job placement, employer recruitment on campus. State resident part-time tuition and fees per semester (1 to 5 units): $207. Nonresident part-time tuition and fees per semester (1 to 11 units) range from $324 to $1626.

Graduate Part-time study available in School of Applied Arts and Sciences, School of Business Administration, School of Education, School of Engineering, School of Fine Arts, School of Humanities, School of Natural Sciences, School of Social and Behavioral Sciences, Center for Public Policy and Administration.Basic part-time expenses: $0 tuition plus $225 per semester fees for state residents, $117 per unit tuition plus $225 per semester fees for nonresidents.

California State University, Los Angeles
Los Angeles 90032

Public institution; metropolitan setting. Awards B, M, D. Barrier-free campus. Total enrollment: 21,000. Undergraduate enrollment: 15,000; 43% part-time, 55% women, 40% over 25. Total faculty: 1,150. Library holdings: 820,000 bound volumes, 5,000 periodical subscriptions.

Undergraduate Courses offered for part-time students during daytime, evenings, summer. Complete part-time degree programs offered during daytime, evenings, summer. Adult/continuing education programs available. Career services available to part-time students: individual and group career counseling, individual job placement, employer recruitment on campus. Part-time tuition and fees per quarter (1 to 14 units) range from $140 to $230 for state residents, $214 to $1266 for nonresidents.

Graduate Part-time study available in School of Arts and Letters, School of Business and Economics, School of Education, School of Engineering and Technology, School of Health and Human Services, School of Natural, Behavioral and Social Sciences. Degree can be earned exclusively through evening/weekend study in School of Arts and Letters, School of Business and Economics, School of Education, School of Engineering and Technology, School of Health and Human Services.Basic part-time expenses: $0 tuition plus $155 per quarter fees for state residents, $78 per unit tuition plus $155 per quarter fees for nonresidents.

California State University, Northridge
Northridge 91330

Public institution; metropolitan setting. Awards B, M. Total enrollment: 27,736. Undergraduate enrollment: 22,828; 21% part-time, 54% women. Total faculty: 1,500. Library holdings: 600,000 bound volumes, 1.5 million titles on microform, 4,500 periodical subscriptions, 16,000 records/tapes.

Undergraduate Courses offered for part-time students during daytime, evenings, summer. Complete part-time degree programs offered during daytime, evenings, summer. External degree and adult/continuing education programs available. Career services available to part-time students: individual and group career counseling, individual job placement, employer recruitment on campus. Part-time tuition: $450 per year for state residents, $117 per unit for nonresidents. State residents taking 6 or more units are charged the full-time rate for tuition.

Graduate Part-time study available in Graduate Studies.Basic part-time expenses: $0 tuition plus $237 per semester fees for state residents, $117 per unit tuition plus $237 per semester fees for nonresidents. Institutional financial aid available to part-time graduate students in Graduate Studies.

California State University, Sacramento
Sacramento 95819

Public institution; metropolitan setting. Awards B, M. Barrier-free campus. Total enrollment: 21,636. Undergraduate enrollment: 17,262; 22% part-time, 51% women. Total faculty: 1,163. Library holdings: 780,000 bound volumes, 872,005 titles on microform, 51,000 periodical subscriptions, 3,868 records/tapes.

Undergraduate Courses offered for part-time students during daytime, evenings, weekends, summer. Complete part-time degree programs offered during daytime, evenings, weekends, summer. External degree and adult/continuing education programs available. Career services available to part-time students: individual and group career counseling, individual job placement, employer recruitment on campus. Part-time tuition and fees per semester (1 to 11 units) range from $209.50 to $344.50 for state residents, $326.50 to $1631.50 for nonresidents.

Graduate Part-time study available in Graduate Studies.Basic part-time expenses: $0 tuition plus $223 per semester fees for state residents, $117 per unit tuition plus $223 per semester fees for nonresidents.

Cerritos College
Norwalk 90650

Public institution; city setting. Awards A. Barrier-free campus. Total enrollment: 19,935 (all undergraduates); 76% part-time, 54% women, 23% over 25. Total faculty: 600. Library holdings: 72,817 bound volumes, 150 titles on microform, 403 periodical subscriptions, 11,763 records/tapes.

Undergraduate Courses offered for part-time students during daytime, evenings, summer. Complete part-time degree programs offered during daytime, evenings, summer. Adult/continuing education programs available. Career services available to part-time students: individual and group career counseling, individual job placement. Part-time tuition: $5 per unit for state residents, $73 per unit for nonresidents. State residents taking 6 or more units are charged the full-time rate for tuition.

Colleges Offering Part-Time Degree Programs / *California*

Cerro Coso Community College
Ridgecrest 93555

Public institution; small-town setting. Awards A. Barrier-free campus. Total enrollment: 3,535 (all undergraduates); 88% part-time, 54% women, 37% over 25. Total faculty: 125. Library holdings: 17,000 bound volumes, 13,500 titles on microform, 105 periodical subscriptions, 7,000 records/tapes.

Undergraduate Courses offered for part-time students during daytime, evenings, weekends, summer. Complete part-time degree programs offered during daytime, evenings. Adult/continuing education programs available. Career services available to part-time students: individual and group career counseling, individual job placement. Part-time tuition: $5 per unit for state residents, $73 per unit for nonresidents. State residents taking 6 or more units are charged the full-time rate for tuition.

Chabot College
Hayward 94545

Public institution; city setting. Awards A. Barrier-free campus. Total enrollment: 18,986 (all undergraduates); 80% part-time, 55% women. Total faculty: 1,060. Library holdings: 100,000 bound volumes, 450 titles on microform, 160 periodical subscriptions, 6,500 records/tapes.

Undergraduate Courses offered for part-time students during daytime, evenings, weekends, summer. Complete part-time degree programs offered during daytime, evenings, weekends, summer. Adult/continuing education programs available. Career services available to part-time students: individual and group career counseling, individual job placement, employer recruitment on campus. Part-time tuition: $3.50 per unit for state residents, $52.50 per unit for nonresidents. State residents taking 6 or more units are charged the full-time rate for tuition.

Chaffey College
Alta Loma 91701

Public institution; small-town setting. Awards A. Barrier-free campus. Total enrollment: 10,000 (all undergraduates); 50% part-time, 50% women, 55% over 25. Total faculty: 400.

Undergraduate Courses offered for part-time students during daytime, evenings, summer. Complete part-time degree programs offered during daytime, evenings, summer. Adult/continuing education programs available. Career services available to part-time students: individual and group career counseling, individual job placement, employer recruitment on campus. Part-time tuition: $3.50 per unit for state residents, $57 per unit for nonresidents. State residents taking 6 or more units are charged the full-time rate for tuition.

Chapman College
Orange 92666

Independent-religious instutition; city setting. Awards B, M. Total enrollment: 1,699. Undergraduate enrollment: 1,302; 14% part-time, 53% women. Total faculty: 193. Library holdings: 150,000 bound volumes, 1,000 periodical subscriptions, 4,000 records/tapes.

Undergraduate Courses offered for part-time students during daytime, evenings, summer. Complete part-time degree programs offered during daytime, evenings, summer. Adult/continuing education programs available. Career services available to part-time students: individual and group career counseling, individual job placement, employer recruitment on campus. Part-time tuition: $210 per credit.

Graduate Part-time study available in Graduate Studies. Degree can be earned exclusively through evening/weekend study in Graduate Studies. Basic part-time expenses: $210 per credit tuition. Institutional financial aid available to part-time graduate students in Graduate Studies.

Christ College Irvine
Irvine 92715

Independent-religious instutition; city setting. Awards A, B. Total enrollment: 327 (all undergraduates); 6% part-time, 54% women. Total faculty: 43. Library holdings: 56,312 bound volumes, 23 titles on microform, 350 periodical subscriptions, 1,452 records/tapes.

Undergraduate Courses offered for part-time students during daytime, evenings, weekends, summer. Complete part-time degree programs offered during daytime. Adult/continuing education programs available. Career services available to part-time students: individual and group career counseling, individual job placement. Part-time tuition: $75 per credit.

Church Divinity School of the Pacific
Berkeley 94709

Independent-religious institution (graduate only). Total enrollment: 100 (coed; 16% part-time). Total faculty: 17.

Graduate Part-time study available in Graduate and Professional Programs. Basic part-time expenses: $3500 per year tuition. Institutional financial aid available to part-time graduate students in Graduate and Professional Programs.

Citrus College
Azusa 91702

Public institution; small-town setting. Awards A. Barrier-free campus. Total enrollment: 9,684 (all undergraduates); 73% part-time, 53% women. Total faculty: 333. Library holdings: 67,613 bound volumes, 389 periodical subscriptions, 2,300 records/tapes.

Undergraduate Courses offered for part-time students during daytime, evenings, weekends, summer. Complete part-time degree programs offered during daytime, evenings, weekends, summer. Adult/continuing education programs available. Career services available to part-time students: individual and group career counseling, individual job placement. Part-time tuition: $5 per unit for state residents, $95 per unit for nonresidents. State residents taking 6 or more units are charged the full-time rate for tuition.

City College of San Francisco
San Francisco 94112

Public institution; metropolitan setting. Awards A. Barrier-free campus. Total enrollment: 23,212 (all undergraduates); 68% part-time, 52% women. Total faculty: 1,087. Library holdings: 76,000 bound volumes, 477 titles on microform.

Undergraduate Courses offered for part-time students during daytime, evenings, summer. Complete part-time degree programs offered during daytime, evenings, summer. Career services available to part-time students: individual and group career counseling, individual job placement, employer recruitment on campus. Part-time tuition: $5 per unit for state residents, $85 per unit for nonresidents. State residents taking 6 or more units are charged the full-time rate for tuition.

California / **Colleges Offering Part-Time Degree Programs**

Claremont Graduate School
Claremont 91711
Independent institution (graduate only). Total enrollment: 1,741 (coed; 78% part-time). Total faculty: 109.
Graduate Part-time study available in Graduate Programs. Basic part-time expenses: $315 per credit tuition plus $100 per semester fees. Institutional financial aid available to part-time graduate students in Graduate Programs.

Coastline Community College
Fountain Valley 92708
Public institution; city setting. Awards A. Total enrollment: 15,283 (all undergraduates); 95% part-time, 68% women, 75% over 25. Total faculty: 634.
Undergraduate Courses offered for part-time students during daytime, evenings, summer. Complete part-time degree programs offered during daytime, evenings, summer. External degree and adult/continuing education programs available. Career services available to part-time students: individual and group career counseling. Part-time tuition: $5 per unit for state residents, $77 per unit for nonresidents. State residents taking 6 or more units are charged the full-time rate for tuition.

Cogswell College
San Francisco 94108
Independent institution; metropolitan setting. Awards A, B. Barrier-free campus. Total enrollment: 456 (all undergraduates); 13% part-time, 15% women. Total faculty: 61. Library holdings: 9,600 bound volumes, 25 titles on microform, 325 periodical subscriptions.
Undergraduate Courses offered for part-time students during daytime, evenings, summer. Complete part-time degree programs offered during daytime, evenings, summer. External degree and adult/continuing education programs available. Career services available to part-time students: individual and group career counseling, individual job placement, employer recruitment on campus. Part-time tuition: $100 per unit.

Cogswell College Silicon Valley
Santa Clara 95051
Independent institution; city setting. Awards B (part-time evening programs only). Barrier-free campus. Total enrollment: 97 (all undergraduates); 100% part-time, 6% women, 95% over 25. Total faculty: 10.
Undergraduate Courses offered for part-time students during evenings, summer. Complete part-time degree programs offered during evenings. Adult/continuing education programs available. Career services available to part-time students: individual and group career counseling, individual job placement, employer recruitment on campus. Part-time tuition: $120 per quarter hour.

College of Alameda
Alameda 94501
Public institution; city setting. Awards A. Barrier-free campus. Total enrollment: 6,000 (all undergraduates); 70% part-time, 55% women, 53% over 25. Total faculty: 125.
Undergraduate Courses offered for part-time students during daytime, evenings, weekends, summer. Complete part-time degree programs offered during daytime. Adult/continuing education programs available. Career services available to part-time students: individual and group career counseling, individual job placement, employer recruitment on campus. Part-time tuition: $3.50 per unit for state residents, $49 per unit for nonresidents. State residents taking 6 or more units are charged the full-time rate for tuition.

College of Notre Dame
Belmont 94002
Independent-religious instutition; small-town setting. Awards A, B, M. Total enrollment: 1,254. Undergraduate enrollment: 739; 47% part-time, 61% women. Total faculty: 141. Library holdings: 92,897 bound volumes, 575 periodical subscriptions.
Undergraduate Courses offered for part-time students during daytime, evenings, weekends, summer. Complete part-time degree programs offered during daytime, evenings, summer. Adult/continuing education programs available. Career services available to part-time students: individual and group career counseling, individual job placement. Part-time tuition is $110 for 1 to 6 credit hours, $190 for 7 to 11 credit hours.
Graduate Part-time study available in Graduate Studies. Degree can be earned exclusively through evening/weekend study in Graduate Studies. Basic part-time expenses: $165 per unit tuition. Institutional financial aid available to part-time graduate students in Graduate Studies.

College of the Canyons
Valencia 91355
Public institution; small-town setting. Awards A. Barrier-free campus. Total enrollment: 3,685 (all undergraduates); 67% part-time, 55% women, 50% over 25. Total faculty: 95. Library holdings: 36,000 bound volumes, 180 periodical subscriptions, 2,300 records/tapes.
Undergraduate Courses offered for part-time students during daytime, evenings, summer. Complete part-time degree programs offered during daytime, evenings, summer. Adult/continuing education programs available. Career services available to part-time students: individual and group career counseling. Part-time tuition: $5 per unit for state residents, $95 per unit for nonresidents. State residents taking 6 or more units are charged the full-time rate for tuition.

College of the Center for Early Education
Los Angeles 90048
Independent institution; metropolitan setting. Awards A, M. Barrier-free campus. Total enrollment: 36. Undergraduate enrollment: 7; 0% part-time, 100% women. Total faculty: 14. Library holdings: 7,190 bound volumes, 125 periodical subscriptions, 430 records/tapes.
Undergraduate Courses offered for part-time students during daytime, evenings, summer. Complete part-time degree programs offered during daytime, evenings, summer. Adult/continuing education programs available. Career services available to part-time students: individual career counseling, individual job placement. Part-time tuition: $100 per unit.
Graduate Part-time study available in Graduate Program. Basic part-time expenses: $120 per credit fees.

College of the Desert
Palm Desert 92260
Public institution; small-town setting. Awards A. Barrier-free campus. Total enrollment: 11,200 (all undergraduates); 80%

Colleges Offering Part-Time Degree Programs / *California*

College of the Desert (continued)

part-time, 50% women, 60% over 25. Total faculty: 270. Library holdings: 40,000 bound volumes, 2,000 periodical subscriptions.

Undergraduate Courses offered for part-time students during daytime, evenings. Complete part-time degree programs offered during daytime, evenings. Adult/continuing education programs available. Part-time tuition: $5 per unit for state residents, $101 per unit for nonresidents. State residents taking 6 or more units are charged the full-time rate for tuition.

College of the Redwoods
Eureka 95501

Public institution; rural setting. Awards A. Barrier-free campus. Total enrollment: 10,964 (all undergraduates); 78% part-time, 59% women. Total faculty: 720. Library holdings: 50,000 bound volumes, 200 titles on microform, 300 periodical subscriptions, 2,000 records/tapes.

Undergraduate Courses offered for part-time students during daytime, evenings, summer. Complete part-time degree programs offered during daytime, evenings, summer. Adult/continuing education programs available. Career services available to part-time students: individual and group career counseling, individual job placement, employer recruitment on campus. Part-time tuition: $3.50 per unit for state residents, $53 per unit for nonresidents. State residents taking 6 or more units are charged the full-time rate for tuition.

College of the Sequoias
Visalia 93277

Public institution; city setting. Awards A. Barrier-free campus. Total enrollment: 7,288 (all undergraduates); 62% part-time, 55% women, 46% over 25. Total faculty: 160. Library holdings: 67,038 bound volumes, 5,616 titles on microform, 553 periodical subscriptions, 1,597 records/tapes.

Undergraduate Courses offered for part-time students during daytime, evenings, weekends, summer. Complete part-time degree programs offered during daytime, evenings, weekends, summer. Adult/continuing education programs available. Career services available to part-time students: individual career counseling, individual job placement, employer recruitment on campus. Part-time tuition: $5 per unit for state residents, $89 per unit for nonresidents. State residents taking 6 or more units are charged the full-time rate for tuition.

College of the Siskiyous
Weed 96094

Public institution; rural setting. Awards A. Barrier-free campus. Total enrollment: 1,889 (all undergraduates); 66% part-time, 54% women, 32% over 25. Total faculty: 141. Library holdings: 33,300 bound volumes, 174 periodical subscriptions, 5,831 records/tapes.

Undergraduate Courses offered for part-time students during daytime, evenings, weekends, summer. Complete part-time degree programs offered during daytime, evenings, weekends, summer. Adult/continuing education programs available. Career services available to part-time students: individual and group career counseling, individual job placement, employer recruitment on campus. Part-time tuition: $5 per unit for state residents, $78 per unit for nonresidents. State residents taking 6 or more units are charged the full-time rate for tuition.

Columbia College
Columbia 95310

Public institution; rural setting. Awards A. Barrier-free campus. Total enrollment: 2,714 (all undergraduates); 80% part-time, 60% women, 70% over 25. Total faculty: 91. Library holdings: 31,000 bound volumes, 310 periodical subscriptions, 4,150 records/tapes.

Undergraduate Courses offered for part-time students during daytime, evenings, weekends. Complete part-time degree programs offered during daytime, evenings. Adult/continuing education programs available. Career services available to part-time students: individual and group career counseling, individual job placement. Part-time tuition: $5 per unit for state residents, $81 per unit for nonresidents. State residents taking 6 or more units are charged the full-time rate for tuition.

Columbia College
Hollywood 90038

Independent institution; metropolitan setting. Awards A, B. Total enrollment: 360 (all undergraduates); 5% part-time, 5% women, 8% over 25. Total faculty: 38. Library holdings: 2,150 bound volumes, 12 periodical subscriptions, 2,000 records/tapes.

Undergraduate Courses offered for part-time students during daytime, evenings, summer. Complete part-time degree programs offered during evenings, summer. Adult/continuing education programs available. Career services available to part-time students: individual career counseling. Part-time tuition per quarter (8 to 14 units) ranges from $650 to $912.50.

Compton Community College
Compton 90221

Public institution; metropolitan setting. Awards A. Barrier-free campus. Total enrollment: 6,500 (all undergraduates); 56% part-time, 56% women, 44% over 25. Total faculty: 338. Library holdings: 41,985 bound volumes, 400 periodical subscriptions, 1,862 records/tapes.

Undergraduate Courses offered for part-time students during daytime, evenings, summer. Complete part-time degree programs offered during daytime, evenings, summer. Adult/continuing education programs available. Career services available to part-time students: individual and group career counseling, individual job placement, employer recruitment on campus. Part-time tuition: $5 per unit for state residents, $78 per unit for nonresidents. State residents taking 6 or more units are charged the full-time rate for tuition.

Condie Junior College of Business and Technology
Campbell 95008

Proprietary institution; small-town setting. Awards A. Total enrollment: 400 (all undergraduates); 25% part-time, 40% women, 50% over 25. Total faculty: 25. Library holdings: 1,500 bound volumes, 56 periodical subscriptions, 20 records/tapes.

Undergraduate Courses offered for part-time students during daytime, evenings, summer. Complete part-time degree programs offered during evenings, summer. Career services available to part-time students: individual and group career counseling, individual job placement, employer recruitment on campus. Part-time tuition: $70 per quarter hour.

California / **Colleges Offering Part-Time Degree Programs**

Consortium of the California State University
Long Beach 90802
Public institution (undergraduate and graduate). Total enrollment: 2,500. Graduate enrollment: 375 (coed; 100% part-time).
Graduate Part-time study available in Graduate Programs. Degree can be earned exclusively through evening/weekend study in Graduate Programs. Basic part-time expenses: $100 per unit fees.

Contra Costa College
San Pablo 94806
Public institution; small-town setting. Awards A. Total enrollment: 7,656 (all undergraduates); 71% part-time, 56% women, 55% over 25. Total faculty: 301. Library holdings: 58,660 bound volumes, 16,353 titles on microform, 324 periodical subscriptions, 826 records/tapes.
Undergraduate Courses offered for part-time students during daytime, evenings, weekends, summer. Complete part-time degree programs offered during daytime, evenings, weekends, summer. Adult/continuing education programs available. Career services available to part-time students: individual and group career counseling, individual job placement. Part-time tuition: $5 per unit for state residents, $80 per unit for nonresidents. State residents taking 6 or more units are charged the full-time rate for tuition.

Cosumnes River College
Sacramento 95823
Public institution; metropolitan setting. Awards A. Barrier-free campus. Total enrollment: 6,105 (all undergraduates); 78% part-time, 60% women, 51% over 25. Total faculty: 194.
Undergraduate Courses offered for part-time students during daytime, evenings, summer. Complete part-time degree programs offered during daytime, evenings, summer. Adult/continuing education programs available. Career services available to part-time students: individual and group career counseling, individual job placement. Part-time tuition: $5 per unit for state residents, $80 per unit for nonresidents.

Crafton Hills College
Yucaipa 92399
Public institution; rural setting. Awards A. Barrier-free campus. Total enrollment: 4,296 (all undergraduates); 25% part-time, 57% women, 41% over 25. Total faculty: 155.
Undergraduate Courses offered for part-time students during daytime, evenings, summer. Complete part-time degree programs offered during daytime, evenings, summer. External degree and adult/continuing education programs available. Career services available to part-time students: individual and group career counseling, individual job placement. Part-time tuition: $5 per unit for state residents, $73 per unit for nonresidents. State residents taking 6 or more units are charged the full-time rate for tuition.

Cuesta College
San Luis Obispo 93403
Public institution; rural setting. Awards A. Barrier-free campus. Total enrollment: 5,575 (all undergraduates); 60% part-time, 52% women, 24% over 25. Total faculty: 200. Library holdings: 41,300 bound volumes, 300 periodical subscriptions, 1,400 records/tapes.

Undergraduate Courses offered for part-time students during daytime, evenings, summer. Complete part-time degree programs offered during daytime, evenings, summer. Adult/continuing education programs available. Career services available to part-time students: individual and group career counseling, individual job placement. Part-time tuition: $5 per unit for state residents, $78 per unit for nonresidents. State residents taking 6 or more units are charged the full-time rate for tuition.

Cuyamaca College
El Cajon 92020
Public institution; city setting. Awards A. Total enrollment: 3,041 (all undergraduates); 83% part-time, 41% women. Total faculty: 136.
Undergraduate Courses offered for part-time students during daytime, evenings, weekends, summer. Complete part-time degree programs offered during daytime, evenings. Adult/continuing education programs available. Career services available to part-time students: individual and group career counseling, individual job placement, employer recruitment on campus. Part-time tuition: $5 per unit for state residents, $78 per unit for nonresidents. State residents taking 6 or more units are charged the full-time rate for tuition.

Cypress College
Cypress 90630
Public institution; city setting. Awards A. Barrier-free campus. Total enrollment: 13,987 (all undergraduates); 68% part-time, 59% women, 40% over 25. Total faculty: 390. Library holdings: 58,000 bound volumes, 450 periodical subscriptions.
Undergraduate Courses offered for part-time students during daytime, evenings, weekends, summer. Complete part-time degree programs offered during daytime, evenings, weekends, summer. Adult/continuing education programs available. Career services available to part-time students: individual and group career counseling, individual job placement, employer recruitment on campus. Part-time tuition: $5 per unit for state residents, $76 per unit for nonresidents. State residents taking 6 or more units are charged the full-time rate for tuition.

De Anza College
Cupertino 95014
Public institution; small-town setting. Awards A. Barrier-free campus. Total enrollment: 22,648 (all undergraduates); 78% part-time, 56% women, 60% over 25. Total faculty: 855. Library holdings: 77,000 bound volumes, 5,000 titles on microform, 580 periodical subscriptions, 27,500 records/tapes.
Undergraduate Courses offered for part-time students during daytime, evenings, summer. Complete part-time degree programs offered during daytime, evenings, summer. External degree and adult/continuing education programs available. Career services available to part-time students: individual and group career counseling, individual job placement, employer recruitment on campus. Part-time tuition: $3.50 per unit for state residents, $58.50 per unit for nonresidents. State residents taking 6 or more units are charged the full-time rate for tuition.

Dominican College of San Rafael
San Rafael 94901
Independent-religious instutition; small-town setting. Awards B, M. Total enrollment: 710. Undergraduate enrollment: 486; 35% part-time, 76% women, 26% over 25. Total faculty: 139.

Colleges Offering Part-Time Degree Programs / California

Dominican College of San Rafael (continued)
Library holdings: 85,000 bound volumes, 400 periodical subscriptions.

Undergraduate Courses offered for part-time students during daytime, evenings, summer. Complete part-time degree programs offered during daytime. Adult/continuing education programs available. Career services available to part-time students: individual and group career counseling, individual job placement, employer recruitment on campus. Part-time tuition: $200 per unit.

Graduate Part-time study available in Graduate Division. Basic part-time expenses: $205 per credit tuition.

D-Q University
Davis 95617

Independent institution; rural setting. Awards A. Total enrollment: 190 (all undergraduates); 60% part-time, 59% women, 50% over 25. Total faculty: 32. Library holdings: 26,400 bound volumes, 10 periodical subscriptions.

Undergraduate Courses offered for part-time students during daytime, evenings, weekends, summer. Complete part-time degree programs offered during daytime, evenings. Adult/continuing education programs available. Career services available to part-time students: individual career counseling. Part-time tuition: $122.50 per unit.

Evergreen Valley College
San Jose 95135

Public institution; metropolitan setting. Awards A. Barrier-free campus. Total enrollment: 7,628 (all undergraduates); 74% part-time, 55% women, 44% over 25. Total faculty: 177. Library holdings: 34,352 bound volumes, 107 titles on microform, 408 periodical subscriptions, 4,000 records/tapes.

Undergraduate Courses offered for part-time students during daytime, evenings, weekends, summer. Complete part-time degree programs offered during daytime, evenings, weekends, summer. Adult/continuing education programs available. Career services available to part-time students: individual and group career counseling, individual job placement, employer recruitment on campus. Part-time tuition: $5 per unit for state residents, $83 per unit for nonresidents. State residents taking 6 or more units are charged the full-time rate for tuition.

Fashion Institute of Design and Merchandising, Los Angeles Campus
Los Angeles 90017

Proprietary institution; metropolitan setting. Awards A. Barrier-free campus. Total enrollment: 2,346 (all undergraduates); 2% part-time, 80% women. Total faculty: 167. Library holdings: 12,050 bound volumes, 149 periodical subscriptions, 501 records/tapes.

Undergraduate Courses offered for part-time students during daytime, summer. Complete part-time degree programs offered during daytime, summer. Adult/continuing education programs available. Career services available to part-time students: individual and group career counseling, individual job placement, employer recruitment on campus. Part-time tuition: $650 per course.

Fashion Institute of Design and Merchandising, San Francisco Campus
San Francisco 94102

Proprietary institution; metropolitan setting. Awards A. Barrier-free campus. Total enrollment: 573 (all undergraduates); 2% part-time, 80% women. Total faculty: 45. Library holdings: 6,000 bound volumes, 149 periodical subscriptions, 450 records/tapes.

Undergraduate Courses offered for part-time students during daytime, summer. Complete part-time degree programs offered during daytime, summer. Adult/continuing education programs available. Career services available to part-time students: individual and group career counseling, individual job placement, employer recruitment on campus. Part-time tuition: $650 per course.

Feather River College
Quincy 95971

Public institution; rural setting. Awards A. Barrier-free campus. Total enrollment: 865 (all undergraduates); 73% part-time, 62% women, 57% over 25. Total faculty: 56. Library holdings: 13,731 bound volumes, 13 titles on microform, 44 periodical subscriptions, 312 records/tapes.

Undergraduate Courses offered for part-time students during daytime, evenings. Complete part-time degree programs offered during daytime, evenings. Adult/continuing education programs available. Career services available to part-time students: individual career counseling, individual job placement. Part-time tuition: $5 per unit for state residents, $73 per unit for nonresidents. State residents taking 6 or more units are charged the full-time rate for tuition.

Foothill College
Los Altos Hills 94022

Public institution; city setting. Awards A. Total enrollment: 14,026 (all undergraduates); 70% part-time, 62% women, 46% over 25. Total faculty: 376. Library holdings: 75,000 bound volumes, 200 periodical subscriptions.

Undergraduate Courses offered for part-time students during daytime, evenings, weekends, summer. Complete part-time degree programs offered during daytime, evenings, weekends, summer. Adult/continuing education programs available. Career services available to part-time students: individual and group career counseling, individual job placement, employer recruitment on campus. Part-time tuition: $3.50 per unit for state residents, $55 per unit for nonresidents. State residents taking 6 or more units are charged the full-time rate for tuition.

Fresno City College
Fresno 93741

Public institution; city setting. Awards A. Barrier-free campus. Total enrollment: 14,013 (all undergraduates); 62% part-time, 54% women, 48% over 25. Total faculty: 378. Library holdings: 52,000 bound volumes, 267 titles on microform, 575 periodical subscriptions, 3,200 records/tapes.

Undergraduate Courses offered for part-time students during daytime, evenings, summer. Complete part-time degree programs offered during daytime, evenings, summer. Career services available to part-time students: individual and group career counseling, individual job placement, employer recruitment on campus. Part-time tuition: $5 per unit for state residents, $73 per unit for nonresidents. State residents taking 6 or more units are charged the full-time rate for tuition.

California / **Colleges Offering Part-Time Degree Programs**

Fresno Pacific College
Fresno 93702

Independent-religious instutition; city setting. Awards A, B, M. Total enrollment: 890. Undergraduate enrollment: 456; 7% part-time, 53% women. Total faculty: 63. Library holdings: 89,000 bound volumes, 650 periodical subscriptions, 2,300 records/tapes.

Graduate Part-time study available in Graduate Program in Education. Degree can be earned exclusively through evening/weekend study in Graduate Program in Education. Basic part-time expenses: $67 per credit tuition plus $990 (one-time fee). Institutional financial aid available to part-time graduate students in Graduate Program in Education.

Fullerton College
Fullerton 92634

Public institution; city setting. Awards A. Total enrollment: 18,950 (all undergraduates); 31% part-time, 65% women, 37% over 25. Total faculty: 600. Library holdings: 90,000 bound volumes, 800 titles on microform, 500 periodical subscriptions, 3,700 records/tapes.

Undergraduate Courses offered for part-time students during daytime, evenings, weekends, summer. Complete part-time degree programs offered during daytime, evenings, weekends, summer. Career services available to part-time students: individual career counseling, individual job placement, employer recruitment on campus. Part-time tuition: $5 per unit for state residents, $76 per unit for nonresidents. State residents taking 6 or more units are charged the full-time rate for tuition.

Gavilan College
Gilroy 95020

Public institution; rural setting. Awards A. Barrier-free campus. Total enrollment: 3,044 (all undergraduates); 60% part-time, 58% women, 42% over 25. Total faculty: 164.

Undergraduate Courses offered for part-time students during daytime, evenings, summer. Complete part-time degree programs offered during daytime, evenings, summer. Adult/continuing education programs available. Career services available to part-time students: individual and group career counseling, individual job placement, employer recruitment on campus. Part-time tuition: $5 per unit for state residents, $83 per unit for nonresidents. State residents taking 6 or more units are charged the full-time rate for tuition.

Glendale Community College
Glendale 91208

Public institution; city setting. Awards A. Total enrollment: 10,797 (all undergraduates); 68% part-time, 54% women, 41% over 25. Total faculty: 405. Library holdings: 55,044 bound volumes, 128 titles on microform, 524 periodical subscriptions, 1,408 records/tapes.

Undergraduate Courses offered for part-time students during daytime, evenings, summer. Complete part-time degree programs offered during daytime, evenings, summer. Adult/continuing education programs available. Career services available to part-time students: individual and group career counseling, individual job placement, employer recruitment on campus. Part-time tuition: $5 per unit for state residents, $90 per unit for nonresidents. State residents taking 6 or more units are charged the full-time rate for tuition.

Golden Gate Baptist Theological Seminary
Mill Valley 94941

Independent-religious institution (graduate only). Total enrollment: 710 (coed; 54% part-time). Total faculty: 40. Library holdings: 102,523 bound volumes, 2,694 microforms.

Graduate Part-time study available in Graduate and Professional Programs. Basic part-time expenses: $275 per semester (minimum) tuition.

Golden Gate University
San Francisco 94105

Independent institution; metropolitan setting. Awards A, B, M, D. Barrier-free campus. Total enrollment: 11,083. Undergraduate enrollment: 2,470; 80% part-time, 40% women. Total faculty: 768. Library holdings: 300,000 bound volumes, 3,000 periodical subscriptions.

Undergraduate Courses offered for part-time students during daytime, evenings, weekends, summer. Complete part-time degree programs offered during daytime, evenings, summer. Adult/continuing education programs available. Career services available to part-time students: individual and group career counseling, individual job placement, employer recruitment on campus. Part-time tuition: $100 per unit.

Graduate Part-time study available in Graduate College, School of Accounting, School of Law. Degree can be earned exclusively through evening/weekend study in School of Law. Basic part-time expenses: $155 per unit tuition plus $25 per semester (minimum) fees. Institutional financial aid available to part-time graduate students in Graduate College, School of Law.

Golden West College
Huntington Beach 92647

Public institution; city setting. Awards A. Barrier-free campus. Total enrollment: 19,100 (all undergraduates); 60% part-time, 52% women. Total faculty: 246. Library holdings: 94,700 bound volumes, 530 periodical subscriptions, 16,000 records/tapes.

Undergraduate Courses offered for part-time students during daytime, evenings, summer. Complete part-time degree programs offered during daytime, evenings, summer. External degree and adult/continuing education programs available. Career services available to part-time students: individual and group career counseling, individual job placement, employer recruitment on campus. Part-time tuition: $5 per unit for state residents, $73 per unit for nonresidents. State residents taking 6 or more units are charged the full-time rate for tuition.

Graduate Theological Union
Berkeley 94709

Independent-religious institution (graduate only). Total enrollment: 401 (coed; 9% part-time). Library holdings: 349,888 bound volumes, 123,380 microforms.

Graduate Part-time study available in Graduate Programs. Basic part-time expenses: $675 per year (minimum) tuition. Institutional financial aid available to part-time graduate students in Graduate Programs.

Colleges Offering Part-Time Degree Programs / *California*

Grantham College of Engineering
Los Angeles 90035

Proprietary institution. Awards A, B (courses conducted through independent study). Total enrollment: 931 (all undergraduates); 100% part-time, 1% women. Total faculty: 5.

Undergraduate Part-time degree programs offered. External degree programs available. Tuition per degree program: $6400 for bachelor's, $4800 for associate.

Grossmont College
El Cajon 92020

Public institution; city setting. Awards A. Total enrollment: 17,000 (all undergraduates); 70% part-time, 57% women. Total faculty: 474. Library holdings: 95,500 bound volumes, 298 titles on microform, 676 periodical subscriptions, 14,600 records/tapes.

Undergraduate Courses offered for part-time students during daytime, evenings, summer. Complete part-time degree programs offered during daytime, evenings, summer. Adult/continuing education programs available. Career services available to part-time students: individual and group career counseling, individual job placement, employer recruitment on campus. Part-time tuition: $5 per unit for state residents, $72 per unit for nonresidents. State residents taking 6 or more units are charged the full-time rate for tuition.

Holy Names College
Oakland 94619

Independent-religious instutition; city setting. Awards B, M. Barrier-free campus. Total enrollment: 632. Undergraduate enrollment: 468; 30% part-time, 74% women. Total faculty: 101. Library holdings: 100,000 bound volumes, 18,000 titles on microform, 533 periodical subscriptions, 5,000 records/tapes.

Undergraduate Courses offered for part-time students during daytime, evenings, weekends, summer. Complete part-time degree programs offered during daytime, evenings, weekends, summer. Adult/continuing education programs available. Career services available to part-time students: individual and group career counseling, individual job placement, employer recruitment on campus. Part-time tuition: $195 per credit hour.

Graduate Part-time study available in Graduate Division. Degree can be earned exclusively through evening/weekend study in Graduate Division. Basic part-time expenses: $195 per unit tuition plus $15 per semester fees. Institutional financial aid available to part-time graduate students in Graduate Division.

Humboldt State University
Arcata 95521

Public institution; rural setting. Awards B, M. Total enrollment: 7,359. Undergraduate enrollment: 6,430; 28% part-time, 47% women, 32% over 25. Total faculty: 488. Library holdings: 300,000 bound volumes, 100,000 titles on microform, 2,100 periodical subscriptions, 8,000 records/tapes.

Undergraduate Courses offered for part-time students during daytime, evenings, summer. Complete part-time degree programs offered during daytime, evenings. Adult/continuing education programs available. Career services available to part-time students: individual and group career counseling, individual job placement, employer recruitment on campus. Part-time tuition: $150 per quarter hour for state residents. Nonresident part-time tuition and fees per quarter (1 to 5 quarter hours) range from $228 to $540.

Graduate Part-time study available in Graduate Studies. Basic part-time expenses: $0 tuition plus $160 per quarter fees for state residents, $78 per unit tuition plus $160 per quarter fees for nonresidents.

Humphreys College
Stockton 95207

Independent institution; city setting. Awards A. Barrier-free campus. Total enrollment: 325 (all undergraduates); 20% part-time, 66% women. Total faculty: 48. Library holdings: 15,000 bound volumes, 60 periodical subscriptions, 100 records/tapes.

Undergraduate Courses offered for part-time students during daytime, evenings, summer. Complete part-time degree programs offered during daytime, evenings, summer. Career services available to part-time students: individual career counseling, individual job placement. Part-time tuition ranges from $57 per unit (for students taking 1 to 7 units) to $627 per quarter (for students taking 8 to 11 units).

Imperial Valley College
Imperial 92251

Public institution; rural setting. Awards A. Barrier-free campus. Total enrollment: 5,200 (all undergraduates); 45% part-time, 50% women. Total faculty: 323. Library holdings: 30,000 bound volumes.

Undergraduate Courses offered for part-time students during daytime, evenings, summer. Complete part-time degree programs offered during daytime, evenings, summer. External degree and adult/continuing education programs available. Career services available to part-time students: individual and group career counseling, individual job placement, employer recruitment on campus. Part-time tuition: $5 per unit for state residents, $78 per unit for nonresidents. State residents taking 6 or more units are charged the full-time rate for tuition.

Indian Valley Colleges
Novato 94947

Public institution; small-town setting. Awards A. Barrier-free campus. Total enrollment: 3,403 (all undergraduates); 80% part-time, 66% women. Total faculty: 145. Library holdings: 35,000 bound volumes, 316 periodical subscriptions, 3,000 records/tapes.

Undergraduate Courses offered for part-time students during daytime, evenings, summer. Complete part-time degree programs offered during daytime, evenings, summer. Adult/continuing education programs available. Career services available to part-time students: individual and group career counseling, individual job placement, employer recruitment on campus. Part-time tuition: $5 per unit for state residents, $92 per unit for nonresidents. State residents taking 6 or more units are charged the full-time rate for tuition.

Jesuit School of Theology at Berkeley
Berkeley 94709

Independent-religious institution (graduate only). Total enrollment: 195 (coed; 30% part-time). Total faculty: 28.

Graduate Part-time study available in Graduate and Professional Programs. Basic part-time expenses: $145 per credit tuition.

California / **Colleges Offering Part-Time Degree Programs**

John F Kennedy University
Orinda 94563

Independent institution; city setting. Awards B, M, D. Barrier-free campus. Total enrollment: 1,853. Undergraduate enrollment: 225; 82% part-time, 71% women, 98% over 25. Total faculty: 262. Library holdings: 36,000 bound volumes, 14 titles on microform, 350 periodical subscriptions, 356 records/tapes.

Undergraduate Courses offered for part-time students during daytime, evenings, weekends, summer. Complete part-time degree programs offered during evenings. Career services available to part-time students: individual and group career counseling. Part-time tuition: $80 per quarter hour.

Graduate Part-time study available in Graduate School of Consciousness Studies, Graduate School of Professional Psychology, School of Liberal and Professional Arts, School of Law, School of Management. Degree can be earned exclusively through evening/weekend study in Graduate School of Consciousness Studies, Graduate School of Professional Psychology, School of Liberal and Professional Arts, School of Law, School of Management. Basic part-time expenses: $108 per unit (minimum) tuition plus $13 per quarter (minimum) fees. Institutional financial aid available to part-time graduate students in Graduate School of Consciousness Studies, Graduate School of Professional Psychology, School of Liberal and Professional Arts, School of Law, School of Management.

King's River Community College
Reedley 93654

Public institution; rural setting. Awards A. Total enrollment: 3,146 (all undergraduates); 53% part-time, 53% women, 50% over 25. Total faculty: 122. Library holdings: 30,000 bound volumes, 205 periodical subscriptions, 2,155 records/tapes.

Undergraduate Courses offered for part-time students during daytime, evenings, summer. Complete part-time degree programs offered during daytime, evenings. Adult/continuing education programs available. Career services available to part-time students: individual and group career counseling. Part-time tuition: $5 per unit for state residents, $78 per unit for nonresidents. State residents taking 6 or more units are charged the full-time rate for tuition.

Lake Tahoe Community College
South Lake Tahoe 95702

Public institution; small-town setting. Awards A. Total enrollment: 1,163 (all undergraduates); 86% part-time, 62% women, 65% over 25. Total faculty: 82. Library holdings: 25,308 bound volumes, 61 titles on microform, 201 periodical subscriptions, 1,274 records/tapes.

Undergraduate Courses offered for part-time students during daytime, evenings, summer. Complete part-time degree programs offered during daytime. Adult/continuing education programs available. Career services available to part-time students: individual and group career counseling. Part-time tuition: $3 per unit for state residents. State residents taking 6 or more units are charged the full-time rate for tuition. Nonresident part-time tuition per quarter (1 to 11 units) ranges from $24.50 to $814.

Laney College
Oakland 94607

Public institution; city setting. Awards A. Barrier-free campus. Total enrollment: 11,687 (all undergraduates); 77% part-time, 50% women, 64% over 25. Total faculty: 329.

Undergraduate Courses offered for part-time students during daytime, evenings, weekends, summer. Complete part-time degree programs offered during daytime, evenings. Adult/continuing education programs available. Career services available to part-time students: individual and group career counseling, individual job placement, employer recruitment on campus. Part-time tuition: $5 per unit for state residents, $72 per unit for nonresidents. State residents taking 6 or more units are charged the full-time rate for tuition.

Lassen College
Susanville 96130

Public institution; rural setting. Awards A. Barrier-free campus. Total enrollment: 2,605 (all undergraduates); 70% part-time, 56% women. Total faculty: 200. Library holdings: 15,000 bound volumes, 100 periodical subscriptions, 150 records/tapes.

Undergraduate Courses offered for part-time students during daytime, evenings, summer. Complete part-time degree programs offered during daytime, evenings, summer. Adult/continuing education programs available. Career services available to part-time students: individual and group career counseling. Part-time tuition: $5 per unit for state residents, $74 per unit for nonresidents. State residents taking 6 or more units are charged the full-time rate for tuition.

LIFE Bible College
Los Angeles 90026

Independent-religious instutition; metropolitan setting. Awards A, B. Barrier-free campus. Total enrollment: 437 (all undergraduates); 37% part-time, 36% women, 50% over 25. Total faculty: 22. Library holdings: 22,750 bound volumes, 92 periodical subscriptions, 664 records/tapes.

Undergraduate Courses offered for part-time students during daytime, evenings, summer. Complete part-time degree programs offered during daytime, evenings. Part-time tuition: $55 per quarter hour.

Life Chiropractic College West
San Lorenzo 94580

Independent institution (graduate only). Total enrollment: 400 (coed; 6% part-time). Total faculty: 60. Library holdings: 7,000 bound volumes.

Graduate Part-time study available in Professional Program. Basic part-time expenses: $64 per hour tuition. Institutional financial aid available to part-time graduate students in Professional Program.

Loma Linda University
Loma Linda 92350

Independent-religious institution (undergraduate and graduate). Total enrollment: 4,853. Graduate enrollment: 2,032 (coed; 33% part-time). Library holdings: 408,288 bound volumes, 138,337 microforms.

Graduate Part-time study available in Graduate School, School of Education, School of Health. Degree can be earned exclusively through evening/weekend study in Graduate School. Basic part-time expenses: $166 per unit tuition. Institutional financial aid available to part-time graduate students in Graduate School, School of Education.

Colleges Offering Part-Time Degree Programs / *California*

Loma Linda University
Riverside 92515

Independent-religious instutition; city setting. Awards A, B, M, D. Barrier-free campus. Total enrollment: 4,853. Undergraduate enrollment: 2,801; 18% part-time, 60% women. Total faculty: 1,794. Library holdings: 408,288 bound volumes, 138,337 titles on microform, 9,448 periodical subscriptions, 10,000 records/tapes.

Undergraduate Courses offered for part-time students during daytime, evenings, summer. Complete part-time degree programs offered during daytime. Adult/continuing education programs available. Career services available to part-time students: individual and group career counseling, individual job placement, employer recruitment on campus. Part-time tuition: $162 per unit.

Long Beach City College
Long Beach 90808

Public institution; city setting. Awards A. Barrier-free campus. Total enrollment: 23,525 (all undergraduates); 75% part-time, 54% women, 62% over 25. Total faculty: 1,320. Library holdings: 250,000 bound volumes.

Undergraduate Courses offered for part-time students during daytime, evenings, weekends, summer. Complete part-time degree programs offered during daytime, evenings, summer. Adult/continuing education programs available. Career services available to part-time students: individual and group career counseling, individual job placement, employer recruitment on campus. Part-time tuition: $5 per unit for state residents, $78 per unit for nonresidents. State residents taking 6 or more units are charged the full-time rate for tuition.

Los Angeles Baptist College
Newhall 91322

Independent-religious instutition; small-town setting. Awards A, B. Total enrollment: 308 (all undergraduates); 8% part-time, 54% women, 5% over 25. Total faculty: 46. Library holdings: 40,000 bound volumes.

Undergraduate Courses offered for part-time students during daytime. Complete part-time degree programs offered during daytime. Career services available to part-time students: individual career counseling, individual job placement. Part-time tuition: $150 per unit.

Los Angeles City College
Los Angeles 90029

Public institution; metropolitan setting. Awards A. Barrier-free campus. Total enrollment: 17,560 (all undergraduates); 50% part-time, 55% women. Total faculty: 750. Library holdings: 156,000 bound volumes, 220 periodical subscriptions.

Undergraduate Courses offered for part-time students during daytime, evenings, summer. Complete part-time degree programs offered during daytime. Adult/continuing education programs available. Career services available to part-time students: individual and group career counseling, individual job placement, employer recruitment on campus. Part-time tuition: $5 per unit for state residents, $95 per unit for nonresidents.

Los Angeles Harbor College
Wilmington 90744

Public institution; metropolitan setting. Awards A. Barrier-free campus. Total enrollment: 12,500 (all undergraduates); 68% part-time, 52% women. Total faculty: 436. Library holdings: 60,000 bound volumes, 500 periodical subscriptions.

Undergraduate Courses offered for part-time students during daytime, evenings, weekends, summer. Complete part-time degree programs offered during daytime, evenings, weekends, summer. External degree and adult/continuing education programs available. Career services available to part-time students: individual and group career counseling, individual job placement, employer recruitment on campus. Part-time tuition: $5 per unit for state residents, $97 per unit for nonresidents. State residents taking 6 or more units are charged the full-time rate for tuition.

Los Angeles Mission College
San Fernando 91340

Public institution; small-town setting. Awards A. Total enrollment: 4,376 (all undergraduates); 90% part-time, 68% women, 12% over 25. Total faculty: 127. Library holdings: 33,000 bound volumes, 62 titles on microform, 450 periodical subscriptions, 1,850 records/tapes.

Undergraduate Courses offered for part-time students during daytime, evenings, summer. Complete part-time degree programs offered during daytime, evenings, summer. External degree and adult/continuing education programs available. Career services available to part-time students: individual and group career counseling, individual job placement, employer recruitment on campus. Part-time tuition: $5 per unit for state residents, $100 per unit for nonresidents. State residents taking 6 or more units are charged the full-time rate for tuition.

Los Angeles Pierce College
Woodland Hills 91371

Public institution; metropolitan setting. Awards A. Barrier-free campus. Total enrollment: 21,260 (all undergraduates); 72% part-time, 51% women, 67% over 25. Total faculty: 583. Library holdings: 100,977 bound volumes, 327 periodical subscriptions, 5,223 records/tapes.

Undergraduate Courses offered for part-time students during daytime, evenings, summer. Complete part-time degree programs offered during daytime, evenings, summer. Adult/continuing education programs available. Career services available to part-time students: individual and group career counseling, individual job placement, employer recruitment on campus. Part-time tuition: $5 per unit for state residents, $95 per unit for nonresidents. State residents taking 6 or more units are charged the full-time rate for tuition.

Los Angeles Southwest College
Los Angeles 90047

Public institution; metropolitan setting. Awards A. Total enrollment: 7,165 (all undergraduates); 33% part-time, 67% women, 75% over 25. Total faculty: 203. Library holdings: 63,191 bound volumes, 120 titles on microform, 397 periodical subscriptions.

Undergraduate Courses offered for part-time students during daytime, evenings. Complete part-time degree programs offered during daytime, evenings. Adult/continuing education programs available. Career services available to part-time students: individual and group career counseling, employer recruitment on campus. Part-time tuition: $5 per unit for state residents, $100 per unit for nonresidents. State residents taking 6 or more units are charged the full-time rate for tuition.

California / **Colleges Offering Part-Time Degree Programs**

Los Angeles Trade-Technical College
Los Angeles 90015

Public institution; metropolitan setting. Awards A. Barrier-free campus. Total enrollment: 18,000 (all undergraduates); 71% part-time, 45% over 25. Total faculty: 558. Library holdings: 97,000 bound volumes, 700 periodical subscriptions, 12,000 records/tapes.

Undergraduate Courses offered for part-time students during daytime, evenings, weekends, summer. Complete part-time degree programs offered during daytime, evenings, weekends, summer. Adult/continuing education programs available. Career services available to part-time students: individual and group career counseling, individual job placement. Part-time tuition: $5 per unit for state residents, $100 per unit for nonresidents. State residents taking 6 or more units are charged the full-time rate for tuition.

Los Angeles Valley College
Van Nuys 91401

Public institution; metropolitan setting. Awards A. Barrier-free campus. Total enrollment: 26,610 (all undergraduates); 75% part-time, 56% women, 50% over 25. Total faculty: 618. Library holdings: 115,000 bound volumes, 8,000 titles on microform, 768 periodical subscriptions, 300 records/tapes.

Undergraduate Courses offered for part-time students during daytime, evenings, summer. Complete part-time degree programs offered during daytime, evenings, summer. Adult/continuing education programs available. Career services available to part-time students: individual and group career counseling, individual job placement, employer recruitment on campus. Part-time tuition: $5 per unit for state residents, $100 per unit for nonresidents. State residents taking 6 or more units are charged the full-time rate for tuition.

Louise Salinger Academy of Fashion
San Francisco 94105

Independent institution; metropolitan setting. Awards A, B. Barrier-free campus. Undergraduate enrollment profile: 35% part-time, 90% women, 15% over 25. Total faculty: 7.

Undergraduate Courses offered for part-time students during daytime, evenings, summer. Complete part-time degree programs offered during daytime, evenings, summer. Career services available to part-time students: individual career counseling, individual job placement. Part-time tuition: $165 per unit.

Loyola Marymount University
Los Angeles 90045

Independent-religious instutition; metropolitan setting. Awards B, M, D. Total enrollment: 6,448. Undergraduate enrollment: 3,924; 8% part-time, 52% women, 7% over 25. Total faculty: 348. Library holdings: 257,968 bound volumes, 27,841 titles on microform, 1,862 periodical subscriptions, 6,145 records/tapes.

Undergraduate Courses offered for part-time students during daytime. Complete part-time degree programs offered during daytime. Adult/continuing education programs available. Career services available to part-time students: individual and group career counseling, individual job placement, employer recruitment on campus. Part-time tuition: $202 per unit.

Graduate Part-time study available in Graduate Division, Loyola Law School. Degree can be earned exclusively through evening/weekend study in Graduate Division, Loyola Law School. Basic part-time expenses: $155 per unit tuition plus $4 per semester fees. Institutional financial aid available to part-time graduate students in Graduate Division, Loyola Law School.

Marymount Palos Verdes College
Rancho Palos Verdes 90274

Independent-religious instutition; small-town setting. Awards A. Total enrollment: 632 (all undergraduates); 3% part-time, 56% women. Total faculty: 59. Library holdings: 35,000 bound volumes, 175 periodical subscriptions, 3,735 records/tapes.

Undergraduate Courses offered for part-time students during daytime, evenings, weekends, summer. Complete part-time degree programs offered during daytime, weekends, summer. Part-time tuition: $195 per unit.

Mendocino College
Ukiah 95482

Public institution; rural setting. Awards A. Barrier-free campus. Total enrollment: 3,410 (all undergraduates); 88% part-time, 66% women, 73% over 25. Total faculty: 160. Library holdings: 15,723 bound volumes, 275 periodical subscriptions, 216 records/tapes.

Undergraduate Courses offered for part-time students during daytime, evenings, weekends, summer. Complete part-time degree programs offered during daytime, evenings, weekends. Adult/continuing education programs available. Career services available to part-time students: individual and group career counseling, individual job placement, employer recruitment on campus. Part-time tuition: $5 per unit for state residents, $85 per unit for nonresidents. State residents taking 6 or more units are charged the full-time rate for tuition.

Menlo College
Atherton 94025

Independent institution; small-town setting. Awards A, B. Barrier-free campus. Total enrollment: 629 (all undergraduates); 1% part-time, 33% women. Total faculty: 68. Library holdings: 48,000 bound volumes, 300 periodical subscriptions.

Undergraduate Courses offered for part-time students during daytime. Complete part-time degree programs offered during daytime. Career services available to part-time students: individual and group career counseling, individual job placement, employer recruitment on campus. Part-time tuition: $285 per credit hour.

Merced College
Merced 95340

Public institution; small-town setting. Awards A. Barrier-free campus. Total enrollment: 6,838 (all undergraduates); 63% part-time, 53% women, 54% over 25. Total faculty: 380. Library holdings: 35,000 bound volumes, 400 periodical subscriptions, 500 records/tapes.

Undergraduate Courses offered for part-time students during daytime, evenings, summer. Complete part-time degree programs offered during daytime, evenings, summer. Adult/continuing education programs available. Career services available to part-time students: individual and group career counseling, individual job placement, employer recruitment on campus. Part-time tuition: $5 per unit for state residents, $78 per unit for nonresidents. State residents taking 6 or more units are charged the full-time rate for tuition.

Colleges Offering Part-Time Degree Programs / California

Merritt College
Oakland 94619

Public institution; city setting. Awards A. Barrier-free campus. Total enrollment: 7,712 (all undergraduates); 70% part-time, 55% women, 49% over 25. Total faculty: 325. Library holdings: 150,000 bound volumes.

Undergraduate Courses offered for part-time students during daytime, evenings, weekends, summer. Complete part-time degree programs offered during daytime, evenings, weekends, summer. Adult/continuing education programs available. Career services available to part-time students: individual and group career counseling, individual job placement, employer recruitment on campus. Part-time tuition: $5 per unit for state residents, $78 per unit for nonresidents. State residents taking 6 or more units are charged the full-time rate for tuition.

Mills College
Oakland 94613

Independent institution; city setting. Awards B, M. Total enrollment: 900. Undergraduate enrollment: 715; 6% part-time, 100% women, 19% over 25. Total faculty: 147. Library holdings: 201,748 bound volumes, 595 periodical subscriptions.

Undergraduate Courses offered for part-time students during daytime. Complete part-time degree programs offered during daytime. Adult/continuing education programs available. Career services available to part-time students: individual and group career counseling, individual job placement, employer recruitment on campus. Part-time tuition: $900 per course.

Graduate Part-time study available in Graduate Studies. Basic part-time expenses: $900 per course tuition plus $40 per semester fees. Institutional financial aid available to part-time graduate students in Graduate Studies.

MiraCosta College
Oceanside 92056

Public institution; city setting. Awards A. Barrier-free campus. Total enrollment: 8,035 (all undergraduates); 85% part-time, 59% women, 57% over 25. Total faculty: 320. Library holdings: 30,000 bound volumes, 357 periodical subscriptions, 2,850 records/tapes.

Undergraduate Courses offered for part-time students during daytime, evenings, weekends, summer. Complete part-time degree programs offered during daytime, evenings. Adult/continuing education programs available. Career services available to part-time students: individual and group career counseling, individual job placement, employer recruitment on campus. Part-time tuition: $5 per unit for state residents, $77 per unit for nonresidents. State residents taking 6 or more units are charged the full-time rate for tuition.

Mission College
Santa Clara 95054

Public institution; city setting. Awards A. Barrier-free campus. Total enrollment: 8,334 (all undergraduates); 84% part-time, 52% women, 54% over 25. Total faculty: 375. Library holdings: 33,900 bound volumes, 90 titles on microform, 445 periodical subscriptions, 5,500 records/tapes.

Undergraduate Courses offered for part-time students during daytime, evenings, weekends, summer. Complete part-time degree programs offered during daytime, evenings, weekends, summer. Adult/continuing education programs available. Career services available to part-time students: individual and group career counseling, individual job placement. Part-time tuition: $5 per unit for state residents, $75 per unit for nonresidents. State residents taking 6 or more units are charged the full-time rate for tuition.

Modesto Junior College
Modesto 95350

Public institution; city setting. Awards A. Total enrollment: 8,487 (all undergraduates); 69% part-time, 53% women, 48% over 25. Total faculty: 375. Library holdings: 65,000 bound volumes, 40 periodical subscriptions, 6,000 records/tapes.

Undergraduate Courses offered for part-time students during daytime, evenings, weekends, summer. Complete part-time degree programs offered during daytime, evenings, weekends, summer. Adult/continuing education programs available. Career services available to part-time students: individual and group career counseling, individual job placement. Part-time tuition: $5 per unit for state residents, $86 per unit for nonresidents. State residents taking 6 or more units are charged the full-time rate for tuition.

Monterey Institute of International Studies
Monterey 93940

Independent institution; small-town setting. Awards B, M. Total enrollment: 382. Undergraduate enrollment: 77; 9% part-time, 70% women. Total faculty: 65. Library holdings: 49,280 bound volumes, 2,461 titles on microform, 271 periodical subscriptions, 7,000 records/tapes.

Undergraduate Courses offered for part-time students during daytime, summer. Complete part-time degree programs offered during daytime, summer. Career services available to part-time students: individual and group career counseling, individual job placement, employer recruitment on campus. Part-time tuition: $240 per unit.

Graduate Part-time study available in Division of American Language and Culture, Division of International Policy Studies, Division of Language Studies and Humanities. Basic part-time expenses: $240 per unit tuition. Institutional financial aid available to part-time graduate students in Division of American Language and Culture, Division of International Policy Studies, Division of Language Studies and Humanities.

Monterey Peninsula College
Monterey 93940

Public institution; small-town setting. Awards A. Barrier-free campus. Total enrollment: 7,199 (all undergraduates); 72% part-time, 57% women. Total faculty: 225. Library holdings: 70,000 bound volumes, 220 periodical subscriptions, 1,721 records/tapes.

Undergraduate Courses offered for part-time students during daytime, evenings, weekends, summer. Complete part-time degree programs offered during daytime, evenings, weekends, summer. Adult/continuing education programs available. Career services available to part-time students: individual and group career counseling, individual job placement. Part-time tuition: $5 per unit for state residents, $80 per unit for nonresidents. State residents taking 6 or more units are charged the full-time rate for tuition.

Moorpark College
Moorpark 93021

Public institution; small-town setting. Awards A. Barrier-free campus. Total enrollment: 9,264 (all undergraduates); 67% part-

California / **Colleges Offering Part-Time Degree Programs**

time, 53% women, 38% over 25. Total faculty: 290. Library holdings: 50,000 bound volumes, 100 periodical subscriptions.

Undergraduate Courses offered for part-time students during daytime, evenings, summer. Complete part-time degree programs offered during daytime, evenings, summer. Adult/continuing education programs available. Career services available to part-time students: individual and group career counseling, individual job placement, employer recruitment on campus. Part-time tuition: $5 per unit for state residents, $97 per unit for nonresidents. State residents taking 6 or more units are charged the full-time rate for tuition.

Mount St Mary's College
Los Angeles 90049

Independent-religious instutition; metropolitan setting. Awards A, B, M. Total enrollment: 1,252. Undergraduate enrollment: 1,104; 15% part-time, 95% women, 15% over 25. Total faculty: 142. Library holdings: 131,440 bound volumes.

Undergraduate Courses offered for part-time students during daytime, evenings, summer. Complete part-time degree programs offered during daytime, evenings, summer. Adult/continuing education programs available. Career services available to part-time students: individual and group career counseling, individual job placement. Part-time tuition: $182 per unit.

Graduate Part-time study available in Graduate Division. Basic part-time expenses: $155 per credit tuition. Institutional financial aid available to part-time graduate students in Graduate Division.

Mt San Antonio College
Walnut 91789

Public institution; small-town setting. Awards A. Barrier-free campus. Total enrollment: 22,934 (all undergraduates); 69% part-time, 53% women, 45% over 25. Total faculty: 681. Library holdings: 93,668 bound volumes, 522 periodical subscriptions, 12,000 records/tapes.

Undergraduate Courses offered for part-time students during daytime, evenings, summer. Complete part-time degree programs offered during daytime, evenings, summer. Adult/continuing education programs available. Career services available to part-time students: individual career counseling, individual job placement, employer recruitment on campus. Part-time tuition: $5 per unit for state residents, $90 per unit for nonresidents. State residents taking 6 or more units are charged the full-time rate for tuition.

Mt San Jacinto College
San Jacinto 92383

Public institution; rural setting. Awards A. Barrier-free campus. Total enrollment: 2,914 (all undergraduates); 80% part-time, 56% women, 58% over 25. Total faculty: 156. Library holdings: 34,000 bound volumes, 230 periodical subscriptions.

Undergraduate Courses offered for part-time students during daytime, evenings, summer. Complete part-time degree programs offered during daytime, evenings. Career services available to part-time students: individual and group career counseling, individual job placement, employer recruitment on campus. Part-time tuition: $5 per unit for state residents, $84 per unit for nonresidents. State residents taking 6 or more units are charged the full-time rate for tuition.

Napa Valley College
Napa 94558

Public institution; city setting. Awards A. Barrier-free campus. Total enrollment: 6,371 (all undergraduates); 21% part-time, 38% women. Total faculty: 294.

Undergraduate Courses offered for part-time students during daytime, evenings, weekends, summer. Complete part-time degree programs offered during daytime, evenings, weekends, summer. Part-time tuition: $5 per unit for state residents, $78 per unit for nonresidents. State residents taking 6 or more units are charged the full-time rate for tuition.

National University
San Diego 92108

Independent institution; metropolitan setting. Awards A, B, M, D. Barrier-free campus. Total enrollment: 7,855. Undergraduate enrollment: 5,374; 41% part-time, 35% women, 76% over 25. Total faculty: 612. Library holdings: 45,000 bound volumes, 10,000 titles on microform, 1,000 periodical subscriptions, 500 records/tapes.

Undergraduate Courses offered for part-time students during daytime, evenings, summer. Complete part-time degree programs offered during daytime, evenings, summer. Adult/continuing education programs available. Career services available to part-time students: individual and group career counseling, individual job placement, employer recruitment on campus. Part-time tuition: $79 per quarter hour.

Graduate Part-time study available in Graduate Studies. Degree can be earned exclusively through evening/weekend study in Graduate Studies. Basic part-time expenses: $395 per course tuition.

Naval Postgraduate School
Monterey 93943

Public institution (graduate only). Total enrollment: 1,518 (primarily men). Total faculty: 225.

Graduate Part-time study available in Graduate Programs. Basic part-time expenses: $0 tuition.

New College of California
San Francisco 94110

Independent institution; metropolitan setting. Awards A, B, M. Total enrollment: 617. Undergraduate enrollment: 447; 34% part-time, 60% women, 75% over 25. Total faculty: 27. Library holdings: 12,000 bound volumes, 1 title on microform, 100 periodical subscriptions, 30 records/tapes.

Undergraduate Courses offered for part-time students during daytime, evenings, weekends, summer. Complete part-time degree programs offered during daytime, evenings, weekends, summer. Career services available to part-time students: individual and group career counseling. Part-time tuition: $120 per credit.

Graduate Part-time study available in Graduate Humanities Division. Degree can be earned exclusively through evening/weekend study in Graduate Humanities Division. Basic part-time expenses: $135 per credit tuition plus $25 per year fees. Institutional financial aid available to part-time graduate students in Graduate Humanities Division.

Colleges Offering Part-Time Degree Programs / *California*

Northrop University
Inglewood 90306

Independent institution; metropolitan setting. Awards A, B, M, D. Barrier-free campus. Total enrollment: 1,522. Undergraduate enrollment: 1,202; 15% part-time, 8% women, 35% over 25. Total faculty: 43. Library holdings: 90,802 bound volumes, 289 periodical subscriptions, 250 records/tapes.

Undergraduate Courses offered for part-time students during daytime, evenings. Complete part-time degree programs offered during daytime, evenings. Career services available to part-time students: individual and group career counseling, individual job placement, employer recruitment on campus. Part-time tuition: $135 per quarter hour.

Occidental College
Los Angeles 90041

Independent institution; metropolitan setting. Awards B, M. Total enrollment: 1,586. Undergraduate enrollment: 1,556; 4% part-time, 50% women, 1% over 25. Total faculty: 134. Library holdings: 400,000 bound volumes, 1,736 periodical subscriptions, 3,100 records/tapes.

Graduate Part-time study available in Graduate Programs. Basic part-time expenses: $951 per course tuition plus $30 per quarter fees. Institutional financial aid available to part-time graduate students in Graduate Programs.

Ohlone College
Fremont 94539

Public institution; city setting. Awards A. Barrier-free campus. Total enrollment: 7,592 (all undergraduates); 74% part-time, 57% women, 43% over 25. Total faculty: 300. Library holdings: 50,000 bound volumes, 525 periodical subscriptions, 15,000 records/tapes.

Undergraduate Courses offered for part-time students during daytime, evenings, summer. Complete part-time degree programs offered during daytime, evenings, summer. Adult/continuing education programs available. Career services available to part-time students: individual and group career counseling, individual job placement, employer recruitment on campus. Part-time tuition: $5 per unit for state residents, $77 per unit for nonresidents. State residents taking 6 or more units are charged the full-time rate for tuition.

Orange Coast College
Costa Mesa 92626

Public institution; city setting. Awards A. Barrier-free campus. Total enrollment: 22,691 (all undergraduates); 69% part-time, 50% women. Total faculty: 877. Library holdings: 95,000 bound volumes, 650 periodical subscriptions, 2,000 records/tapes.

Undergraduate Courses offered for part-time students during daytime, evenings, weekends, summer. Complete part-time degree programs offered during daytime, evenings, weekends, summer. Adult/continuing education programs available. Career services available to part-time students: individual and group career counseling, individual job placement, employer recruitment on campus. Part-time tuition: $5 per unit for state residents, $78 per unit for nonresidents. State residents taking 6 or more units are charged the full-time rate for tuition.

Otis Art Institute of Parsons School of Design
Los Angeles 90057

Independent institution; metropolitan setting. Awards A, B, M. Barrier-free campus. Total enrollment: 710. Undergraduate enrollment: 683; 1% part-time, 62% women. Total faculty: 138. Library holdings: 30,000 bound volumes, 220 periodical subscriptions.

Undergraduate Courses offered for part-time students during evenings, weekends. Complete part-time degree programs offered during evenings, weekends. Adult/continuing education programs available. Career services available to part-time students: individual career counseling, individual job placement. Part-time tuition: $196 per credit.

Oxnard College
Oxnard 93033

Public institution; city setting. Awards A. Barrier-free campus. Total enrollment: 4,998 (all undergraduates); 80% part-time, 54% women, 64% over 25. Total faculty: 255. Library holdings: 24,000 bound volumes, 24 titles on microform, 171 periodical subscriptions, 550 records/tapes.

Undergraduate Courses offered for part-time students during daytime, evenings, weekends, summer. Complete part-time degree programs offered during daytime, evenings, weekends, summer. Adult/continuing education programs available. Career services available to part-time students: individual and group career counseling, individual job placement, employer recruitment on campus. Part-time tuition: $5 per unit for state residents, $97 per unit for nonresidents. State residents taking 6 or more units are charged the full-time rate for tuition.

Pacific Christian College
Fullerton 92631

Independent-religious instutition; city setting. Awards A, B, M. Barrier-free campus. Total enrollment: 483. Undergraduate enrollment: 430; 31% part-time, 47% women, 5% over 25. Total faculty: 42. Library holdings: 43,000 bound volumes, 240 periodical subscriptions, 200 records/tapes.

Undergraduate Courses offered for part-time students during daytime, evenings, summer. Complete part-time degree programs offered during daytime, evenings, summer. Career services available to part-time students: individual and group career counseling, individual job placement, employer recruitment on campus. Part-time tuition: $110 per unit.

Graduate Part-time study available in Graduate School of Church Dynamics. Degree can be earned exclusively through evening/weekend study in Graduate School of Church Dynamics. Basic part-time expenses: $90 per credit tuition. Institutional financial aid available to part-time graduate students in Graduate School of Church Dynamics.

Pacific Coast Junior College
San Diego 92111

Proprietary institution; metropolitan setting. Awards A. Barrier-free campus. Total enrollment: 500 (all undergraduates); 3% part-time, 95% women, 40% over 25. Total faculty: 17. Library holdings: 2,200 bound volumes, 20 periodical subscriptions, 50 records/tapes.

Undergraduate Courses offered for part-time students during daytime, evenings. Complete part-time degree programs offered during daytime, evenings. Career services available to part-time students: individual and group career counseling, individual job

California / **Colleges Offering Part-Time Degree Programs**

placement, employer recruitment on campus. Part-time tuition: $65 per quarter hour.

Pacific Graduate School of Psychology
Menlo Park 94025

Independent institution (graduate only). Total enrollment: 178 (coed; 79% part-time). Total faculty: 25. Library holdings: 5,300 bound volumes.

Graduate Part-time study available in Graduate Programs. Basic part-time expenses: $180 per credit tuition. Institutional financial aid available to part-time graduate students in Graduate Programs.

Pacific Lutheran Theological Seminary
Berkeley 94708

Independent-religious institution (graduate only). Total enrollment: 219 (coed; 19% part-time). Total faculty: 15.

Graduate Part-time study available in Graduate and Professional Programs. Basic part-time expenses: $83 per credit tuition.

Pacific Oaks College
Pasadena 91103

Independent institution (undergraduate and graduate). Total enrollment: 253. Graduate enrollment: 212 (primarily women).

Graduate Part-time study available in Graduate School. Basic part-time expenses: $180 per unit tuition.

Pacific School of Religion
Berkeley 94709

Independent institution (graduate only). Total enrollment: 209 (coed; 20% part-time). Total faculty: 23.

Graduate Part-time study available in Graduate and Professional Programs. Basic part-time expenses: $192.50 per unit tuition. Institutional financial aid available to part-time graduate students in Graduate and Professional Programs.

Pacific Union College
Angwin 94508

Independent-religious instutition; rural setting. Awards A, B, M. Total enrollment: 1,443. Undergraduate enrollment: 1,353; 14% part-time, 53% women, 11% over 25. Total faculty: 160. Library holdings: 198,000 bound volumes, 900 periodical subscriptions.

Undergraduate Courses offered for part-time students during daytime, evenings, summer. Complete part-time degree programs offered during daytime. Career services available to part-time students: individual and group career counseling, individual job placement, employer recruitment on campus. Part-time tuition: $168 per quarter hour.

Graduate Part-time study available in Graduate Division. Basic part-time expenses: $168 per hour tuition. Institutional financial aid available to part-time graduate students in Graduate Division.

Palmer College of Chiropractic–West
Sunnyvale 94087

Independent institution (graduate only). Total enrollment: 656 (coed; 11% part-time). Total faculty: 44. Library holdings: 4,483 bound volumes.

Graduate Part-time study available in Professional Program. Basic part-time expenses: $378 per quarter (minimum) tuition. Institutional financial aid available to part-time graduate students in Professional Program.

Palomar College
San Marcos 92069

Public institution; small-town setting. Awards A. Barrier-free campus. Total enrollment: 17,071 (all undergraduates); 67% part-time, 54% women, 52% over 25. Total faculty: 651. Library holdings: 120,000 bound volumes, 878 periodical subscriptions.

Undergraduate Courses offered for part-time students during daytime, evenings, summer. Complete part-time degree programs offered during daytime, evenings, summer. Adult/continuing education programs available. Career services available to part-time students: individual and group career counseling, individual job placement. Part-time tuition: $5 per unit for state residents, $77 per unit for nonresidents. State residents taking 6 or more units are charged the full-time rate for tuition.

Palo Verde College
Blythe 92225

Public institution; rural setting. Awards A. Barrier-free campus. Total enrollment: 630 (all undergraduates); 80% part-time, 65% women, 55% over 25. Total faculty: 43. Library holdings: 17,500 bound volumes, 50 periodical subscriptions, 1,000 records/tapes.

Undergraduate Courses offered for part-time students during daytime, evenings. Complete part-time degree programs offered during daytime, evenings. Adult/continuing education programs available. Career services available to part-time students: individual career counseling, individual job placement. Part-time tuition: $5 per unit for state residents, $77 per unit for nonresidents. State residents taking 6 or more units are charged the full-time rate for tuition.

Pasadena City College
Pasadena 91106

Public institution; city setting. Awards A. Barrier-free campus. Total enrollment: 18,426 (all undergraduates); 65% part-time, 54% women, 39% over 25. Total faculty: 684. Library holdings: 100,000 bound volumes, 500 periodical subscriptions.

Undergraduate Courses offered for part-time students during daytime, evenings, summer. Complete part-time degree programs offered during daytime, evenings, summer. Adult/continuing education programs available. Career services available to part-time students: individual and group career counseling, individual job placement, employer recruitment on campus. Part-time tuition: $5 per unit for state residents, $90 per unit for nonresidents. State residents taking 6 or more units are charged the full-time rate for tuition.

Patten College
Oakland 94601

Independent institution; city setting. Awards A, B. Barrier-free campus. Total enrollment: 150 (all undergraduates); 40% part-time, 54% women, 60% over 25. Total faculty: 23. Library hold-

Colleges Offering Part-Time Degree Programs / *California*

Patten College (continued)

ings: 18,000 bound volumes, 200 periodical subscriptions, 111 records/tapes.

Undergraduate Courses offered for part-time students during daytime, evenings. Complete part-time degree programs offered during daytime, evenings. Adult/continuing education programs available. Career services available to part-time students: individual career counseling, individual job placement. Part-time tuition: $100 per unit.

Pepperdine University
Malibu 90265

Independent-religious instutition; small-town setting. Awards B, M, D. Barrier-free campus. Total enrollment: 2,622. Undergraduate enrollment: 2,516; 9% part-time, 52% women, 6% over 25. Total faculty: 245. Library holdings: 279,877 bound volumes, 94,560 titles on microform, 2,972 periodical subscriptions, 7,436 records/tapes.

Undergraduate Courses offered for part-time students during daytime, summer. Complete part-time degree programs offered during daytime, summer. Career services available to part-time students: individual and group career counseling, employer recruitment on campus. Part-time tuition: $263 per semester hour.

Graduate Part-time study available in Seaver College. Basic part-time expenses: $263 per credit tuition plus $7.50 per trimester fees. Institutional financial aid available to part-time graduate students in Seaver College.

Pepperdine University, Pepperdine Plaza
Los Angeles 90034

Independent-religious instutition; metropolitan setting. Awards B, M, D. Barrier-free campus. Total enrollment: 3,411. Undergraduate enrollment: 509; 99% part-time, 50% women, 81% over 25. Total faculty: 177. Library holdings: 103,693 bound volumes, 413 periodical subscriptions, 353 records/tapes.

Undergraduate Courses offered for part-time students during evenings, weekends. Complete part-time degree programs offered during evenings, weekends. Adult/continuing education programs available. Career services available to part-time students: individual career counseling. Part-time tuition: $263 per unit.

Graduate Part-time study available in Graduate School of Education and Psychology, School of Business and Management. Degree can be earned exclusively through evening/weekend study in School of Business and Management. Basic part-time expenses: $199 per unit (minimum) tuition. Institutional financial aid available to part-time graduate students in Graduate School of Education and Psychology, School of Business and Management.

Pitzer College
Claremont 91711

Independent institution; small-town setting. Awards B. Total enrollment: 740 (all undergraduates); 10% part-time, 51% women, 10% over 25. Total faculty: 78. Library holdings: 1.5 million bound volumes, 700,050 titles on microform, 7,000 periodical subscriptions, 2,400 records/tapes.

Undergraduate Courses offered for part-time students during daytime, evenings. Complete part-time degree programs offered during daytime. Adult/continuing education programs available. Career services available to part-time students: individual and group career counseling, employer recruitment on campus. Part-time tuition: $1075 per course.

Point Loma Nazarene College
San Diego 92106

Independent-religious instutition; metropolitan setting. Awards B, M. Total enrollment: 1,873. Undergraduate enrollment: 1,667; 9% part-time, 56% women. Total faculty: 136. Library holdings: 176,806 bound volumes, 869 periodical subscriptions.

Undergraduate Courses offered for part-time students during daytime, summer. Complete part-time degree programs offered during daytime, summer. Career services available to part-time students: individual and group career counseling, individual job placement, employer recruitment on campus. Part-time tuition: $89 per quarter hour.

Graduate Part-time study available in Graduate Programs. Basic part-time expenses: $98 per unit tuition plus $15 per quarter fees.

Porterville College
Porterville 93257

Public institution; rural setting. Awards A. Barrier-free campus. Total enrollment: 2,204 (all undergraduates); 65% part-time, 55% women. Total faculty: 174. Library holdings: 20,298 bound volumes, 240 periodical subscriptions, 700 records/tapes.

Undergraduate Courses offered for part-time students during daytime, evenings, summer. Complete part-time degree programs offered during daytime, evenings, summer. Adult/continuing education programs available. Career services available to part-time students: individual and group career counseling, individual job placement. Part-time tuition: $5 per unit for state residents, $73 per unit for nonresidents. State residents taking 6 or more units are charged the full-time rate for tuition.

Rio Hondo Community College
Whittier 90608

Public institution; city setting. Awards A. Barrier-free campus. Total enrollment: 12,547 (all undergraduates); 76% part-time, 42% women, 40% over 25. Total faculty: 347.

Undergraduate Courses offered for part-time students during daytime, evenings, weekends, summer. Complete part-time degree programs offered during daytime, evenings, weekends, summer. Adult/continuing education programs available. Career services available to part-time students: individual and group career counseling, individual job placement, employer recruitment on campus. Part-time tuition: $5 per unit for state residents, $85 per unit for nonresidents. State residents taking 6 or more units are charged the full-time rate for tuition.

Riverside City College
Riverside 92506

Public institution; city setting. Awards A. Barrier-free campus. Total enrollment: 14,201 (all undergraduates); 71% part-time, 56% women, 51% over 25. Total faculty: 483. Library holdings: 76,867 bound volumes, 4,745 titles on microform, 509 periodical subscriptions, 1,411 records/tapes.

Undergraduate Courses offered for part-time students during daytime, evenings, summer. Complete part-time degree programs offered during daytime, evenings, summer. Adult/continuing education programs available. Career services available to part-time students: individual and group career counseling, individual job placement, employer recruitment on campus. Part-time tuition: $5 per unit for state residents, $84 per unit for nonresidents. State residents taking 6 or more units are charged the full-time rate for tuition.

Sacramento City College
Sacramento 95822

Public institution; metropolitan setting. Awards A. Barrier-free campus. Total enrollment: 14,977 (all undergraduates); 67% part-time, 53% women, 45% over 25. Total faculty: 450. Library holdings: 80,000 bound volumes, 400 periodical subscriptions, 1,000 records/tapes.

Undergraduate Courses offered for part-time students during daytime, evenings, summer. Complete part-time degree programs offered during daytime, evenings, summer. Career services available to part-time students: individual and group career counseling, individual job placement, employer recruitment on campus. Part-time tuition: $4.55 per unit for state residents, $79.55 per unit for nonresidents. State residents taking 6 or more units are charged the full-time rate for tuition.

Saddleback Community College
Mission Viejo 92692

Public institution; small-town setting. Awards A. Barrier-free campus. Total enrollment: 23,382 (all undergraduates); 80% part-time, 60% women, 50% over 25. Total faculty: 725. Library holdings: 92,000 bound volumes, 200 periodical subscriptions, 9,800 records/tapes.

Undergraduate Courses offered for part-time students during daytime, evenings, weekends, summer. Complete part-time degree programs offered during daytime, evenings, weekends, summer. Adult/continuing education programs available. Career services available to part-time students: individual and group career counseling, individual job placement. Part-time tuition: $5 per unit for state residents, $83 per unit for nonresidents. State residents taking 6 or more units are charged the full-time rate for tuition.

Saint Mary's College of California
Moraga 94575

Independent-religious instutition; small-town setting. Awards B, M. Barrier-free campus. Total enrollment: 2,675. Undergraduate enrollment: 2,172; 5% part-time, 51% women, 1% over 25. Total faculty: 174. Library holdings: 136,000 bound volumes, 620 periodical subscriptions, 3,100 records/tapes.

Undergraduate Courses offered for part-time students during daytime, evenings, summer. Complete part-time degree programs offered during daytime, evenings, summer. External degree and adult/continuing education programs available. Career services available to part-time students: individual and group career counseling, individual job placement, employer recruitment on campus. Part-time tuition: $740 per course.

San Diego City College
San Diego 92101

Public institution; metropolitan setting. Awards A. Barrier-free campus. Total enrollment: 18,000 (all undergraduates); 74% part-time, 56% women, 52% over 25. Total faculty: 745. Library holdings: 80,000 bound volumes, 600 periodical subscriptions, 1,500 records/tapes.

Undergraduate Courses offered for part-time students during daytime, evenings, weekends, summer. Complete part-time degree programs offered during daytime, evenings, weekends, summer. Career services available to part-time students: individual and group career counseling, individual job placement, employer recruitment on campus. Part-time tuition: $5 per unit for state residents, $78 per unit for nonresidents. State residents taking 6 or more units are charged the full-time rate for tuition.

San Diego Mesa College
San Diego 92111

Public institution; metropolitan setting. Awards A. Barrier-free campus. Total enrollment: 21,000 (all undergraduates); 75% part-time, 51% women. Total faculty: 890. Library holdings: 83,000 bound volumes, 1,314 periodical subscriptions, 712 records/tapes.

Undergraduate Courses offered for part-time students during daytime, evenings, weekends, summer. Complete part-time degree programs offered during daytime, evenings, weekends, summer. External degree and adult/continuing education programs available. Career services available to part-time students: individual and group career counseling, individual job placement. Part-time tuition: $5 per unit for state residents, $78 per unit for nonresidents. State residents taking 6 or more units are charged the full-time rate for tuition.

San Diego Miramar College
San Diego 92126

Public institution; metropolitan setting. Awards A. Total enrollment: 3,681 (all undergraduates); 66% part-time, 38% women, 60% over 25. Total faculty: 303. Library holdings: 4,000 bound volumes.

Undergraduate Courses offered for part-time students during daytime, evenings, weekends, summer. Complete part-time degree programs offered during daytime, evenings, weekends, summer. Adult/continuing education programs available. Career services available to part-time students: individual and group career counseling, individual job placement, employer recruitment on campus. Part-time tuition: $5 per unit for state residents, $73 per unit for nonresidents. State residents taking 6 or more units are charged the full-time rate for tuition.

San Diego State University
San Diego 92182

Public institution; metropolitan setting. Awards B, M, D. Barrier-free campus. Total enrollment: 32,194. Undergraduate enrollment: 26,040; 26% part-time, 50% women. Total faculty: 1,935. Library holdings: 727,730 bound volumes, 8,500 periodical subscriptions, 5,037 records/tapes.

Undergraduate Courses offered for part-time students during daytime, evenings, summer. Complete part-time degree programs offered during daytime, evenings, summer. External degree and adult/continuing education programs available. Career services available to part-time students: individual and group career counseling, individual job placement, employer recruitment on campus. Part-time tuition: $0 for state residents, $117 per unit for nonresidents.

Graduate Part-time study available in Graduate Division and Research. Degree can be earned exclusively through evening/weekend study in Graduate Division and Research. Basic part-time expenses: $0 tuition plus $228.50 per semester fees for state residents, $117 per unit tuition plus $228.50 per semester fees for nonresidents. Institutional financial aid available to part-time graduate students in Graduate Division and Research.

San Francisco Art Institute
San Francisco 94133

Independent institution; metropolitan setting. Awards B, M. Total enrollment: 641. Undergraduate enrollment: 488; 23% part-time, 53% women, 50% over 25. Total faculty: 68. Library holdings: 22,000 bound volumes, 250 periodical subscriptions, 350 records/tapes.

Colleges Offering Part-Time Degree Programs / California

San Francisco Art Institute (continued)

Undergraduate Courses offered for part-time students during daytime, evenings, summer. Complete part-time degree programs offered during daytime, evenings, summer. Career services available to part-time students: individual and group career counseling, individual job placement. Part-time tuition: $830 per course.

San Francisco Conservatory of Music
San Francisco 94122

Independent institution; metropolitan setting. Awards B, M. Barrier-free campus. Total enrollment: 209. Undergraduate enrollment: 159; 20% part-time, 50% women, 29% over 25. Total faculty: 59. Library holdings: 17,000 bound volumes, 56 periodical subscriptions, 6,000 records/tapes.

Undergraduate Courses offered for part-time students during daytime. Complete part-time degree programs offered during daytime. Career services available to part-time students: individual career counseling, individual job placement. Part-time tuition: $255 per semester hour.

Graduate Part-time study available in Graduate Division. Basic part-time expenses: $255 per credit tuition plus $35 per semester fees. Institutional financial aid available to part-time graduate students in Graduate Division.

San Francisco State University
San Francisco 94132

Public institution; metropolitan setting. Awards B, M. Barrier-free campus. Total enrollment: 23,966. Undergraduate enrollment: 18,677; 33% part-time, 56% women. Total faculty: 1,882. Library holdings: 600,000 bound volumes, 540,000 titles on microform, 4,000 periodical subscriptions.

Undergraduate Courses offered for part-time students during daytime, evenings, weekends, summer. Complete part-time degree programs offered during daytime, evenings, summer. Adult/continuing education programs available. Career services available to part-time students: individual and group career counseling, employer recruitment on campus. Part-time tuition and fees per semester (1 to 11 semester hours) range from $210 to $345 for state residents, $318 to $1533 for nonresidents.

Graduate Part-time study available in Graduate Studies and Research. Basic part-time expenses: $0 tuition plus $312 per semester fees for state residents, $117 per unit tuition plus $312 per semester fees for nonresidents.

San Francisco Theological Seminary
San Anselmo 94960

Independent-religious institution (graduate only). Total enrollment: 1,088 (coed; 79% part-time). Total faculty: 217. Library holdings: 400,000 bound volumes.

Graduate Part-time study available in Graduate and Professional Programs. Basic part-time expenses: $137.50 per credit tuition. Institutional financial aid available to part-time graduate students in Graduate and Professional Programs.

San Joaquin Delta College
Stockton 95207

Public institution; city setting. Awards A. Barrier-free campus. Total enrollment: 17,772 (all undergraduates); 68% part-time, 53% women, 49% over 25. Total faculty: 534. Library holdings: 71,427 bound volumes, 734 periodical subscriptions, 2,660 records/tapes.

Undergraduate Courses offered for part-time students during daytime, evenings, summer. Complete part-time degree programs offered during daytime, evenings, summer. Adult/continuing education programs available. Career services available to part-time students: individual and group career counseling, individual job placement, employer recruitment on campus. Part-time tuition: $5 per unit for state residents, $80 per unit for nonresidents. State residents taking 6 or more units are charged the full-time rate for tuition.

San Jose Bible College
San Jose 95108

Independent-religious institution; metropolitan setting. Awards B. Barrier-free campus. Total enrollment: 167 (all undergraduates); 36% part-time, 44% women, 33% over 25. Total faculty: 26. Library holdings: 32,000 bound volumes, 620 titles on microform, 139 periodical subscriptions, 1,150 records/tapes.

Undergraduate Courses offered for part-time students during daytime, evenings. Complete part-time degree programs offered during daytime. Career services available to part-time students: individual career counseling, individual job placement, employer recruitment on campus. Part-time tuition: $70 per quarter hour.

San Jose City College
San Jose 95128

Public institution; metropolitan setting. Awards A. Barrier-free campus. Total enrollment: 13,253 (all undergraduates); 70% part-time, 52% women. Total faculty: 541. Library holdings: 72,000 bound volumes, 500 periodical subscriptions, 3,000 records/tapes.

Undergraduate Courses offered for part-time students during daytime, evenings, weekends, summer. Complete part-time degree programs offered during daytime, evenings, weekends, summer. Adult/continuing education programs available. Career services available to part-time students: individual and group career counseling, individual job placement, employer recruitment on campus. Part-time tuition: $5 per unit for state residents, $83 per unit for nonresidents. State residents taking 6 or more units are charged the full-time rate for tuition.

San Jose State University
San Jose 95192

Public institution; metropolitan setting. Awards B, M. Barrier-free campus. Total enrollment: 25,081. Undergraduate enrollment: 20,711; 32% part-time, 49% women, 40% over 25. Total faculty: 1,674. Library holdings: 700,000 bound volumes, 5,700 periodical subscriptions, 25,000 records/tapes.

Undergraduate Courses offered for part-time students during daytime, evenings, summer. Complete part-time degree programs offered during daytime, evenings, summer. Adult/continuing education programs available. Career services available to part-time students: individual and group career counseling, individual job placement, employer recruitment on campus. Part-time tuition and fees per semester (1 to 11 semester hours) range from $327 to $507 for state residents, $459 to $1629 for nonresidents.

Santa Ana College
Santa Ana 92706

Public institution; city setting. Awards A. Barrier-free campus. Total enrollment: 22,587 (all undergraduates); 82% part-time, 51% women, 55% over 25. Total faculty: 1,056. Library holdings:

80,000 bound volumes, 19 titles on microform, 700 periodical subscriptions, 2,500 records/tapes.

Undergraduate Courses offered for part-time students during daytime, evenings, weekends, summer. Complete part-time degree programs offered during daytime, evenings, weekends, summer. External degree and adult/continuing education programs available. Career services available to part-time students: individual and group career counseling, individual job placement, employer recruitment on campus. Part-time tuition: $5 per unit for state residents, $75 per unit for nonresidents. State residents taking 6 or more units are charged the full-time rate for tuition.

Santa Barbara City College
Santa Barbara 93109

Public institution; city setting. Awards A. Barrier-free campus. Total enrollment: 10,714 (all undergraduates); 70% part-time, 53% women, 43% over 25. Total faculty: 444. Library holdings: 80,355 bound volumes, 535 periodical subscriptions, 4,118 records/tapes.

Undergraduate Courses offered for part-time students during daytime, evenings, summer. Complete part-time degree programs offered during daytime, evenings, summer. Adult/continuing education programs available. Career services available to part-time students: individual and group career counseling, individual job placement, employer recruitment on campus. Part-time tuition: $5 per unit for state residents, $78 per unit for nonresidents. State residents taking 6 or more units are charged the full-time rate for tuition.

Santa Monica College
Santa Monica 90405

Public institution; city setting. Awards A. Barrier-free campus. Total enrollment: 22,650 (all undergraduates); 77% part-time, 57% women. Total faculty: 743. Library holdings: 103,392 bound volumes, 18,915 titles on microform, 500 periodical subscriptions.

Undergraduate Courses offered for part-time students during daytime, evenings, summer. Complete part-time degree programs offered during daytime, evenings, summer. Adult/continuing education programs available. Career services available to part-time students: individual career counseling. Part-time tuition: $5 per unit for state residents, $85 per unit for nonresidents. State residents taking 6 or more units are charged the full-time rate for tuition.

Santa Rosa Junior College
Santa Rosa 95401

Public institution; city setting. Awards A. Barrier-free campus. Total enrollment: 20,053 (all undergraduates); 67% part-time, 56% women, 56% over 25. Total faculty: 334. Library holdings: 83,000 bound volumes, 33,361 titles on microform, 650 periodical subscriptions, 1,300 records/tapes.

Undergraduate Courses offered for part-time students during daytime, evenings, weekends, summer. Complete part-time degree programs offered during daytime, evenings, weekends, summer. Adult/continuing education programs available. Career services available to part-time students: individual and group career counseling, individual job placement, employer recruitment on campus. Part-time tuition: $5 per unit for state residents, $77 per unit for nonresidents. State residents taking 6 or more units are charged the full-time rate for tuition.

School of Theology at Claremont
Claremont 91711

Independent-religious institution (graduate only). Total enrollment: 369 (coed; 61% part-time). Total faculty: 48. Library holdings: 118,191 bound volumes.

Graduate Part-time study available in Graduate and Professional Programs. Basic part-time expenses: $155 per unit (minimum) tuition plus $55 per semester fees. Institutional financial aid available to part-time graduate students in Graduate and Professional Programs.

Scripps College
Claremont 91711

Independent institution; small-town setting. Awards B. Total enrollment: 625 (all undergraduates); 1% part-time, 100% women, 1% over 25. Total faculty: 77. Library holdings: 1.1 million bound volumes, 775,000 titles on microform, 6,543 periodical subscriptions, 16,176 records/tapes.

Undergraduate Courses offered for part-time students during daytime. Complete part-time degree programs offered during daytime. Career services available to part-time students: individual and group career counseling, individual job placement, employer recruitment on campus. Part-time tuition: $1100 per course.

Sierra College
Rocklin 95677

Public institution; rural setting. Awards A. Barrier-free campus. Total enrollment: 9,726 (all undergraduates); 68% part-time, 56% women, 50% over 25. Total faculty: 315. Library holdings: 61,056 bound volumes, 2,150 titles on microform, 275 periodical subscriptions, 7,692 records/tapes.

Undergraduate Courses offered for part-time students during daytime, evenings, summer. Complete part-time degree programs offered during daytime, evenings. Career services available to part-time students: individual and group career counseling, individual job placement, employer recruitment on campus. Part-time tuition: $5 per unit for state residents, $78 per unit for nonresidents. State residents taking 6 or more units are charged the full-time rate for tuition.

Simpson College
San Francisco 94134

Independent-religious instutition; metropolitan setting. Awards B, M. Total enrollment: 306. Undergraduate enrollment: 277; 6% part-time, 48% women. Total faculty: 30. Library holdings: 50,416 bound volumes, 86 titles on microform, 388 periodical subscriptions, 925 records/tapes.

Undergraduate Courses offered for part-time students during daytime, evenings, summer. Complete part-time degree programs offered during daytime, evenings, summer. External degree programs available. Career services available to part-time students: individual and group career counseling, individual job placement, employer recruitment on campus. Part-time tuition: $150 per credit.

Skyline College
San Bruno 94066

Public institution; small-town setting. Awards A. Barrier-free campus. Total enrollment: 7,227 (all undergraduates); 79% part-time, 60% women. Total faculty: 269. Library holdings: 45,000

Colleges Offering Part-Time Degree Programs / *California*

Skyline College (continued)
bound volumes, 4,400 titles on microform, 300 periodical subscriptions, 4,200 records/tapes.

Undergraduate Courses offered for part-time students during daytime, evenings, weekends, summer. Complete part-time degree programs offered during daytime, evenings. Adult/continuing education programs available. Career services available to part-time students: individual and group career counseling, individual job placement, employer recruitment on campus. Part-time tuition: $5 per unit for state residents, $82 per unit for nonresidents. State residents taking 6 or more units are charged the full-time rate for tuition.

Solano Community College
Suisun City 94585

Public institution; small-town setting. Awards A. Barrier-free campus. Total enrollment: 9,299 (all undergraduates); 74% part-time, 50% women. Total faculty: 317. Library holdings: 32,000 bound volumes.

Undergraduate Courses offered for part-time students during daytime, evenings, summer. Complete part-time degree programs offered during daytime, evenings, summer. Adult/continuing education programs available. Career services available to part-time students: individual and group career counseling, individual job placement, employer recruitment on campus. Part-time tuition: $5 per unit for state residents, $75 per unit for nonresidents. State residents taking 6 or more units are charged the full-time rate for tuition.

Sonoma State University
Rohnert Park 94928

Public institution; rural setting. Awards B, M. Barrier-free campus. Total enrollment: 5,380. Undergraduate enrollment: 3,977; 26% part-time, 57% women, 40% over 25. Total faculty: 373. Library holdings: 350,000 bound volumes, 725,000 titles on microform, 2,745 periodical subscriptions, 25,000 records/tapes.

Undergraduate Courses offered for part-time students during daytime, evenings, summer. Complete part-time degree programs offered during daytime, evenings, summer. Adult/continuing education programs available. Career services available to part-time students: individual and group career counseling, individual job placement, employer recruitment on campus. Part-time tuition and fees per semester (1 to 11 units) range from $220 to $355 for state residents, $733 to $1813 for nonresidents.

Graduate Part-time study available in School of Humanities, School of Natural Sciences, School of Social Sciences. Degree can be earned exclusively through evening/weekend study in School of Humanities, School of Social Sciences. Basic part-time expenses: $0 tuition plus $242 per semester fees for state residents, $117 per unit tuition plus $242 per semester fees for nonresidents.

Southern California College
Costa Mesa 92626

Independent-religious instutition; city setting. Awards B, M. Barrier-free campus. Total enrollment: 858. Undergraduate enrollment: 820; 18% part-time, 44% women. Total faculty: 75. Library holdings: 80,000 bound volumes, 458 periodical subscriptions.

Undergraduate Courses offered for part-time students during daytime, evenings, weekends, summer. Complete part-time degree programs offered during daytime, evenings. Adult/continuing education programs available. Career services available to part-time students: individual and group career counseling. Part-time tuition: $142 per credit.

Southwestern College
Chula Vista 92010

Public institution; city setting. Awards A. Barrier-free campus. Total enrollment: 11,687 (all undergraduates); 66% part-time, 50% women, 47% over 25. Total faculty: 393. Library holdings: 66,918 bound volumes, 81 titles on microform, 653 periodical subscriptions, 4,254 records/tapes.

Undergraduate Courses offered for part-time students during daytime, evenings, summer. Complete part-time degree programs offered during daytime, evenings, summer. External degree and adult/continuing education programs available. Career services available to part-time students: individual career counseling, individual job placement, employer recruitment on campus. Part-time tuition: $5 per unit for state residents, $73 per unit for nonresidents. State residents taking 6 or more units are charged the full-time rate for tuition.

Southwestern University School of Law
Los Angeles 90005

Independent institution (graduate only). Total enrollment: 1,307 (coed; 35% part-time). Total faculty: 92. Library holdings: 158,560 bound volumes, 79,704 microforms.

Graduate Part-time study available in Professional Program. Degree can be earned exclusively through evening/weekend study in Professional Program. Basic part-time expenses: $235 per unit tuition. Institutional financial aid available to part-time graduate students in Professional Program.

Sysorex Institute
Cupertino 95014

Proprietary institution; small-town setting. Awards A. Barrier-free campus. Total enrollment: 20 (all undergraduates); 0% part-time, 20% women, 60% over 25. Total faculty: 12. Library holdings: 1,500 bound volumes, 80 periodical subscriptions, 1,000 records/tapes.

Undergraduate Courses offered for part-time students during daytime, evenings, summer. Complete part-time degree programs offered during daytime, evenings, summer. Career services available to part-time students: individual and group career counseling, individual job placement, employer recruitment on campus. Part-time tuition: $70 per credit.

Taft College
Taft 93268

Public institution; small-town setting. Awards A. Total enrollment: 1,393 (all undergraduates); 75% part-time, 50% women, 35% over 25. Total faculty: 80. Library holdings: 28,000 bound volumes, 150 records/tapes.

Undergraduate Courses offered for part-time students during daytime, evenings, weekends, summer. Complete part-time degree programs offered during daytime, evenings, weekends, summer. Adult/continuing education programs available. Career services available to part-time students: individual career counseling, individual job placement, employer recruitment on campus. Part-time tuition: $5 per unit for state residents, $78 per unit for nonresidents. State residents taking 6 or more units are charged the full-time rate for tuition.

California / **Colleges Offering Part-Time Degree Programs**

United States International University
San Diego 92131

Independent institution; metropolitan setting. Awards A, B, M, D. Total enrollment: 3,275. Undergraduate enrollment: 1,541; 14% part-time, 30% women, 50% over 25. Total faculty: 334. Library holdings: 424,217 bound volumes, 1,238 periodical subscriptions.

Undergraduate Courses offered for part-time students during daytime, evenings. Complete part-time degree programs offered during daytime, evenings. Career services available to part-time students: individual career counseling, individual job placement, employer recruitment on campus. Part-time tuition: $130 per unit.

Graduate Part-time study available in School of Business and Management. Basic part-time expenses: $130 per unit tuition. Institutional financial aid available to part-time graduate students in School of Business and Management.

University of California, Davis
Davis 95616

Public institution; small-town setting. Awards B, M, D. Total enrollment: 18,971. Undergraduate enrollment: 13,830; 0% part-time, 54% women, 6% over 25. Total faculty: 1,366. Library holdings: 1.8 million bound volumes, 2.1 million titles on microform, 46,000 periodical subscriptions, 14,600 records/tapes.

Undergraduate Courses offered for part-time students during daytime, summer. Complete part-time degree programs offered during daytime, summer. Adult/continuing education programs available. Part-time tuition: $925 per year for state residents, $2707 per year for nonresidents.

University of California, Irvine
Irvine 92717

Public institution; city setting. Awards B, M, D. Barrier-free campus. Total enrollment: 11,909. Undergraduate enrollment: 9,436; 8% part-time, 51% women. Total faculty: 584. Library holdings: 1.4 million bound volumes, 1 million titles on microform, 10,000 periodical subscriptions, 1,100 records/tapes.

Undergraduate Courses offered for part-time students during daytime, evenings, summer. Complete part-time degree programs offered during daytime. Adult/continuing education programs available. Career services available to part-time students: individual and group career counseling, individual job placement, employer recruitment on campus. Part-time tuition: $895 per year for state residents, $2678 per year for nonresidents.

Graduate Part-time study available in Division of Graduate Studies and Research. Basic part-time expenses: $0 tuition plus $331 per quarter fees for state residents, $594 per quarter tuition plus $331 per quarter fees for nonresidents.

University of California, Riverside
Riverside 92521

Public institution; city setting. Awards B, M, D. Barrier-free campus. Total enrollment: 4,706. Undergraduate enrollment: 3,357; 5% part-time, 48% women. Total faculty: 369. Library holdings: 1.1 million bound volumes, 938,552 titles on microform, 14,200 periodical subscriptions, 21,511 records/tapes.

Undergraduate Courses offered for part-time students during daytime. Complete part-time degree programs offered during daytime. Adult/continuing education programs available. Career services available to part-time students: individual and group career counseling, individual job placement, employer recruitment on campus. Part-time tuition: $955 per year for state residents, $2737 per year for nonresidents.

Graduate Part-time study available in Graduate Division. Degree can be earned exclusively through evening/weekend study in Graduate Division. Basic part-time expenses: $0 tuition plus $318 per quarter fees for state residents, $594 per quarter tuition plus $318 per quarter fees for nonresidents. Institutional financial aid available to part-time graduate students in Graduate Division.

University of California, San Diego
La Jolla 92093

Public institution; metropolitan setting. Awards B, M, D. Total enrollment: 13,670. Undergraduate enrollment: 11,122; 0% part-time, 44% women, 7% over 25. Total faculty: 880. Library holdings: 1.4 million bound volumes, 600,000 titles on microform, 25,000 periodical subscriptions.

Graduate Part-time study available in Graduate Studies. Basic part-time expenses: $0 tuition plus $325 per quarter fees for state residents, $594 per quarter tuition plus $325 per quarter fees for nonresidents.

University of California, San Francisco
San Francisco 94143

Public institution (undergraduate and graduate). Total enrollment: 2,478. Graduate enrollment: 2,391 (coed). Library holdings: 479,000 bound volumes, 621,000 microforms.

Graduate Part-time study available in Graduate Division. Basic part-time expenses: $0 tuition plus $349 per quarter fees for state residents, $1188 per quarter tuition plus $349 per quarter fees for nonresidents. Institutional financial aid available to part-time graduate students in Graduate Division.

University of California, Santa Barbara
Santa Barbara 93106

Public institution; city setting. Awards B, M, D. Barrier-free campus. Total enrollment: 15,489. Undergraduate enrollment: 13,973; 4% part-time, 51% women. Total faculty: 1,112. Library holdings: 1.5 million bound volumes, 1.6 million titles on microform, 18,832 periodical subscriptions, 23,177 records/tapes.

Graduate Part-time study available in Graduate Division. Basic part-time expenses: $0 tuition plus $310 per quarter fees for state residents, $594 per quarter tuition plus $310 per quarter fees for nonresidents. Institutional financial aid available to part-time graduate students in Graduate Division.

University of California, Santa Cruz
Santa Cruz 95064

Public institution; small-town setting. Awards B, M, D. Total enrollment: 6,893. Undergraduate enrollment: 6,351; 8% part-time, 50% women, 18% over 25. Total faculty: 640. Library holdings: 710,000 bound volumes, 200,000 titles on microform, 11,000 periodical subscriptions, 6,500 records/tapes.

Undergraduate Courses offered for part-time students during daytime, evenings, summer. Complete part-time degree programs offered during daytime, evenings, summer. Adult/continuing education programs available. Career services available to part-time students: individual and group career counseling, individual job placement, employer recruitment on campus. Part-time tuition: $1029 per year for state residents, $3507 per year for nonresidents.

Colleges Offering Part-Time Degree Programs / *California*

University of Judaism
Los Angeles 90077

Independent-religious instutition; metropolitan setting. Awards A, B, M, D. Barrier-free campus. Total enrollment: 220. Undergraduate enrollment: 108; 80% part-time, 60% women. Total faculty: 50. Library holdings: 170,000 bound volumes, 500 periodical subscriptions.

Undergraduate Courses offered for part-time students during daytime, evenings, summer. Complete part-time degree programs offered during daytime, evenings, summer. Adult/continuing education programs available. Career services available to part-time students: individual career counseling. Part-time tuition: $150 per unit.

Graduate Part-time study available in David Lieber School of Graduate Studies. Basic part-time expenses: $120 per unit tuition plus $20 per semester fees. Institutional financial aid available to part-time graduate students in David Lieber School of Graduate Studies.

University of La Verne
La Verne 91750

Independent institution; small-town setting. Awards A, B, M, D. Barrier-free campus. Total enrollment: 2,476. Undergraduate enrollment: 1,210; 20% part-time, 52% women. Total faculty: 188. Library holdings: 175,000 bound volumes, 650 periodical subscriptions.

Undergraduate Courses offered for part-time students during daytime, evenings, weekends, summer. Complete part-time degree programs offered during daytime, evenings, weekends, summer. External degree and adult/continuing education programs available. Career services available to part-time students: individual and group career counseling, individual job placement, employer recruitment on campus. Part-time tuition: $175 per semester hour.

Graduate Part-time study available in College of Graduate and Professional Studies, College of Law. Degree can be earned exclusively through evening/weekend study in College of Graduate and Professional Studies. Basic part-time expenses: $175 per semester hour tuition plus $15 per semester fees. Institutional financial aid available to part-time graduate students in College of Graduate and Professional Studies, College of Law.

University of Redlands
Redlands 92374

Independent institution; small-town setting. Awards B, M. Barrier-free campus. Total enrollment: 1,236. Undergraduate enrollment: 1,141; 3% part-time, 56% women, 1% over 25. Total faculty: 184. Library holdings: 300,000 bound volumes, 39,000 titles on microform, 715 periodical subscriptions, 6,500 records/tapes.

Undergraduate Courses offered for part-time students during daytime. Complete part-time degree programs offered during daytime. External degree and adult/continuing education programs available. Career services available to part-time students: individual and group career counseling, individual job placement, employer recruitment on campus. Part-time tuition: $244 per unit.

Graduate Part-time study available in Graduate Studies, Alfred North Whitehead Center. Basic part-time expenses: $260 per unit tuition plus $100 per year fees.

University of San Diego
San Diego 92110

Independent-religious instutition; metropolitan setting. Awards B, M, D. Barrier-free campus. Total enrollment: 5,077. Undergraduate enrollment: 3,274; 8% part-time, 52% women, 5% over 25. Total faculty: 314. Library holdings: 424,000 bound volumes, 10,000 titles on microform, 1,140 periodical subscriptions, 675 records/tapes.

Undergraduate Courses offered for part-time students during daytime, evenings, summer. Complete part-time degree programs offered during daytime, evenings. Adult/continuing education programs available. Career services available to part-time students: individual and group career counseling, individual job placement, employer recruitment on campus. Part-time tuition: $210 per unit.

Graduate Part-time study available in School of Graduate and Continuing Education, School of Law. Basic part-time expenses: $215 per credit tuition plus $25 per year fees. Institutional financial aid available to part-time graduate students in School of Law.

University of San Francisco
San Francisco 94117

Independent-religious instutition; metropolitan setting. Awards B, M, D. Barrier-free campus. Total enrollment: 5,339. Undergraduate enrollment: 2,648; 11% part-time, 51% women. Total faculty: 418. Library holdings: 600,000 bound volumes, 30 titles on microform, 2,400 periodical subscriptions.

Undergraduate Courses offered for part-time students during daytime, evenings, weekends, summer. Complete part-time degree programs offered during daytime, evenings, weekends, summer. External degree and adult/continuing education programs available. Career services available to part-time students: individual and group career counseling, individual job placement, employer recruitment on campus. Part-time tuition: $215 per unit.

University of Santa Clara
Santa Clara 95053

Independent-religious instutition; city setting. Awards B, M, D. Total enrollment: 7,420. Undergraduate enrollment: 3,610; 2% part-time, 49% women, 2% over 25. Total faculty: 444. Library holdings: 406,000 bound volumes, 360,951 titles on microform, 7,000 periodical subscriptions.

Graduate Part-time study available in Division of Counseling Psychology, Leavey School of Business and Administration, School of Engineering, School of Law. Degree can be earned exclusively through evening/weekend study in Division of Counseling Psychology, Leavey School of Business and Administration, School of Engineering, School of Law. Basic part-time expenses: $160 per quarter hour tuition plus $5 per quarter fees. Institutional financial aid available to part-time graduate students in Division of Counseling Psychology, Leavey School of Business and Administration, School of Engineering, School of Law.

University of Southern California
Los Angeles 90089

Independent institution; metropolitan setting. Awards B, M, D. Total enrollment: 29,411. Undergraduate enrollment: 15,888; 16% part-time, 41% women, 8% over 25. Total faculty: 2,441. Library holdings: 2.2 million bound volumes, 32,870 periodical subscriptions.

California / Colleges Offering Part-Time Degree Programs

Undergraduate Courses offered for part-time students during daytime, evenings, summer. Complete part-time degree programs offered during daytime, evenings, summer. Adult/continuing education programs available. Career services available to part-time students: individual and group career counseling, individual job placement, employer recruitment on campus. Part-time tuition: $292 per unit.

University of the Pacific
Stockton 95211

Independent institution; city setting. Awards B, M, D. Total enrollment: 5,877. Undergraduate enrollment: 3,481; 4% part-time, 52% women, 8% over 25. Total faculty: 341. Library holdings: 362,000 bound volumes, 335,000 titles on microform, 3,100 periodical subscriptions, 4,000 records/tapes.

Undergraduate Courses offered for part-time students during daytime, evenings, summer. Complete part-time degree programs offered during daytime. Adult/continuing education programs available. Career services available to part-time students: individual and group career counseling, individual job placement, employer recruitment on campus. Part-time tuition and fees per semester (1/2 to 11 units) range from $290 to $4139.

University of West Los Angeles
Los Angeles 90066

Independent institution; metropolitan setting. Awards B, D. Total enrollment: 454. Undergraduate enrollment: 246; 81% part-time, 80% women, 79% over 25. Total faculty: 22. Library holdings: 31,000 bound volumes, 237 periodical subscriptions, 100 records/tapes.

Undergraduate Courses offered for part-time students during daytime, evenings, summer. Complete part-time degree programs offered during daytime, evenings, summer. Adult/continuing education programs available. Career services available to part-time students: individual and group career counseling, individual job placement, employer recruitment on campus. Part-time tuition: $92 per unit.

Graduate Part-time study available in School of Law. Degree can be earned exclusively through evening/weekend study in School of Law. Basic part-time expenses: $159 per unit tuition plus $43.50 per semester fees. Institutional financial aid available to part-time graduate students in School of Law.

Victor Valley College
Victorville 92392

Public institution; rural setting. Awards A. Barrier-free campus. Total enrollment: 5,200 (all undergraduates); 66% part-time, 52% women, 60% over 25. Total faculty: 135. Library holdings: 3,582 bound volumes, 165 titles on microform, 692 periodical subscriptions, 2,000 records/tapes.

Undergraduate Courses offered for part-time students during daytime, evenings, summer. Complete part-time degree programs offered during daytime, evenings. Career services available to part-time students: individual and group career counseling, individual job placement, employer recruitment on campus. Part-time tuition: $5 per unit for state residents, $73 per unit for nonresidents. State residents taking 6 or more units are charged the full-time rate for tuition.

West Coast Christian College
Fresno 93710

Independent-religious instutition; city setting. Awards A, B. Barrier-free campus. Total enrollment: 252 (all undergraduates); 20% part-time, 34% women, 30% over 25. Total faculty: 21. Library holdings: 28,641 bound volumes, 2,514 titles on microform, 282 periodical subscriptions, 714 records/tapes.

Undergraduate Courses offered for part-time students during daytime. Complete part-time degree programs offered during daytime. Career services available to part-time students: individual career counseling, individual job placement. Part-time tuition: $85 per semester hour.

West Coast University
Los Angeles 90020

Independent institution; metropolitan setting. Awards A, B, M. Barrier-free campus. Total enrollment: 1,400. Undergraduate enrollment: 880; 36% part-time, 20% women, 50% over 25. Total faculty: 250. Library holdings: 11,180 bound volumes, 195 periodical subscriptions.

Undergraduate Courses offered for part-time students during daytime, evenings. Complete part-time degree programs offered during daytime, evenings. Adult/continuing education programs available. Part-time tuition: $169 per unit.

Graduate Part-time study available in College of Business and Management, College of Engineering, College of Letters and Science. Basic part-time expenses: $169 per credit tuition.

Western State University College of Law of Orange County
Fullerton 92631

Proprietary institution; city setting. Awards B, D. Barrier-free campus. Total enrollment: 1,423. Undergraduate enrollment: 394; 73% part-time, 41% women. Total faculty: 56. Library holdings: 40,000 bound volumes, 20,000 titles on microform, 400 periodical subscriptions.

Undergraduate Courses offered for part-time students during daytime, evenings, weekends, summer. Complete part-time degree programs offered during daytime, evenings, weekends, summer. Career services available to part-time students: individual and group career counseling, individual job placement, employer recruitment on campus. Part-time tuition: $185 per unit.

Graduate Part-time study available in Professional Program. Basic part-time expenses: $185 per credit tuition plus $100 per semester fees. Institutional financial aid available to part-time graduate students in Professional Program.

Western State University College of Law of San Diego
San Diego 92110

Proprietary institution; metropolitan setting. Awards B, D. Barrier-free campus. Total enrollment: 719. Undergraduate enrollment: 153; 79% part-time, 42% women, 91% over 25. Total faculty: 51.

Undergraduate Courses offered for part-time students during daytime, evenings, weekends, summer. Complete part-time degree programs offered during daytime, evenings, weekends, summer. Career services available to part-time students: individual and group career counseling, individual job placement, employer recruitment on campus. Part-time tuition: $185 per unit.

Graduate Part-time study available in Professional Program. Basic part-time expenses: $185 per credit tuition plus $100 per semester fees. Institutional financial aid available to part-time graduate students in Professional Program.

Colleges Offering Part-Time Degree Programs / California

West Hills College
Coalinga 93210

Public institution; small-town setting. Awards A. Barrier-free campus. Total enrollment: 2,400 (all undergraduates); 24% part-time, 52% women. Total faculty: 185. Library holdings: 48,264 bound volumes, 500 periodical subscriptions, 1,843 records/tapes.

Undergraduate Courses offered for part-time students during daytime, evenings, summer. Complete part-time degree programs offered during daytime, evenings, summer. Adult/continuing education programs available. Career services available to part-time students: individual and group career counseling, individual job placement, employer recruitment on campus. Part-time tuition: $5 per unit for state residents, $77 per unit for nonresidents. State residents taking 6 or more units are charged the full-time rate for tuition.

West Los Angeles College
Culver City 90230

Public institution; city setting. Awards A. Barrier-free campus. Total enrollment: 9,000 (all undergraduates); 80% part-time, 61% women, 61% over 25. Total faculty: 375. Library holdings: 50,000 bound volumes, 300 periodical subscriptions, 1,200 records/tapes.

Undergraduate Courses offered for part-time students during daytime, evenings, weekends, summer. Complete part-time degree programs offered during daytime, evenings. Adult/continuing education programs available. Career services available to part-time students: individual and group career counseling, individual job placement, employer recruitment on campus. Part-time tuition: $5 per unit for state residents, $95 per unit for nonresidents. State residents taking 6 or more units are charged the full-time rate for tuition.

West Valley College
Saratoga 95070

Public institution; small-town setting. Awards A. Barrier-free campus. Total enrollment: 14,194 (all undergraduates); 71% part-time, 54% women. Total faculty: 500. Library holdings: 60,000 bound volumes, 300 titles on microform, 1,065 periodical subscriptions, 3,500 records/tapes.

Undergraduate Courses offered for part-time students during daytime, evenings. Complete part-time degree programs offered during daytime, evenings. Adult/continuing education programs available. Career services available to part-time students: individual and group career counseling, individual job placement, employer recruitment on campus. Part-time tuition: $5 per unit for state residents, $75 per unit for nonresidents. State residents taking 6 or more units are charged the full-time rate for tuition.

Whittier College
Whittier 90608

Independent institution; city setting. Awards B, M. Barrier-free campus. Total enrollment: 1,750. Undergraduate enrollment: 1,200; 3% part-time, 51% women, 1% over 25. Total faculty: 105. Library holdings: 180,000 bound volumes, 150 titles on microform, 400 periodical subscriptions, 10,000 records/tapes.

Graduate Part-time study available in Graduate Programs. Basic part-time expenses: $240 per credit tuition.

Woodbury University
Los Angeles 90017

Independent institution; metropolitan setting. Awards A, B, M. Barrier-free campus. Total enrollment: 1,003. Undergraduate enrollment: 848; 10% part-time, 45% women. Total faculty: 85. Library holdings: 55,000 bound volumes, 21,500 titles on microform, 500 periodical subscriptions, 450 records/tapes.

Undergraduate Courses offered for part-time students during daytime, evenings, summer. Complete part-time degree programs offered during daytime, evenings, summer. Adult/continuing education programs available. Career services available to part-time students: individual and group career counseling, individual job placement, employer recruitment on campus. Part-time tuition: $115 per quarter hour.

Graduate Part-time study available in Division of Graduate Studies. Degree can be earned exclusively through evening/weekend study in Division of Graduate Studies. Basic part-time expenses: $429 per course tuition. Institutional financial aid available to part-time graduate students in Division of Graduate Studies.

Yeshiva University of Los Angeles
Los Angeles 90035

Independent-religious instutition; metropolitan setting. Awards B. Barrier-free campus. Total enrollment: 75 (all undergraduates); 30% part-time, 0% women, 5% over 25. Total faculty: 10.

Undergraduate Courses offered for part-time students during daytime, evenings. Complete part-time degree programs offered during daytime. Adult/continuing education programs available. Career services available to part-time students: individual and group career counseling, individual job placement, employer recruitment on campus. Part-time tuition: $1100 per year.

Yuba College
Marysville 95901

Public institution; rural setting. Awards A. Barrier-free campus. Total enrollment: 8,496 (all undergraduates); 66% part-time, 60% women, 51% over 25. Total faculty: 267. Library holdings: 61,000 bound volumes, 530 periodical subscriptions.

Undergraduate Courses offered for part-time students during daytime, evenings, summer. Complete part-time degree programs offered during daytime, evenings, summer. Adult/continuing education programs available. Career services available to part-time students: individual and group career counseling, individual job placement, employer recruitment on campus. Part-time tuition: $6 per unit for state residents, $71 per unit for nonresidents. State residents taking 6 or more units are charged the full-time rate for tuition.

COLORADO

Adams State College
Alamosa 81102

Public institution; small-town setting. Awards A, B, M. Barrier-free campus. Total enrollment: 2,087. Undergraduate enrollment: 1,684; 14% part-time, 54% women, 24% over 25. Total faculty: 91. Library holdings: 158,000 bound volumes, 1,500 periodical subscriptions.

Undergraduate Courses offered for part-time students during daytime, evenings, summer. Complete part-time degree programs offered during daytime, evenings, summer. Adult/continuing education programs available. Career services available

Colorado / **Colleges Offering Part-Time Degree Programs**

to part-time students: individual and group career counseling, individual job placement, employer recruitment on campus. Part-time tuition: $28 per credit for state residents, $94 per credit for nonresidents.

Graduate Part-time study available in Division of Graduate Studies. Basic part-time expenses: $28 per credit tuition plus $6 per credit fees for state residents, $84 per credit tuition plus $6 per credit fees for nonresidents.

Aims Community College
Greeley 80632

Public institution; city setting. Awards A. Barrier-free campus. Total enrollment: 6,100 (all undergraduates); 70% part-time, 56% women, 60% over 25. Total faculty: 260. Library holdings: 35,000 bound volumes, 325 titles on microform, 100 periodical subscriptions, 2,000 records/tapes.

Undergraduate Courses offered for part-time students during daytime, evenings, summer. Complete part-time degree programs offered during daytime, evenings, summer. External degree and adult/continuing education programs available. Career services available to part-time students: individual and group career counseling, individual job placement, employer recruitment on campus. Part-time tuition: $12 per quarter hour for area residents, $22 per quarter hour for state residents, $65 per quarter hour for nonresidents.

Arapahoe Community College
Littleton 80120

Public institution; small-town setting. Awards A. Barrier-free campus. Total enrollment: 6,200 (all undergraduates); 65% part-time, 60% women, 53% over 25. Total faculty: 354. Library holdings: 41,151 bound volumes, 9,031 titles on microform, 410 periodical subscriptions.

Undergraduate Courses offered for part-time students during daytime, evenings, summer. Complete part-time degree programs offered during daytime, evenings, summer. Adult/continuing education programs available. Career services available to part-time students: individual career counseling, individual job placement, employer recruitment on campus. Part-time tuition: $38.05 per credit hour for state residents, $119.05 per credit hour for nonresidents.

Blair Junior College
Colorado Springs 80915

Proprietary institution; city setting. Awards A. Barrier-free campus. Total enrollment: 717 (all undergraduates); 2% part-time, 68% women, 72% over 25. Total faculty: 43. Library holdings: 4,000 bound volumes, 47 periodical subscriptions, 300 records/tapes.

Undergraduate Courses offered for part-time students during daytime, evenings. Complete part-time degree programs offered during daytime, evenings. Career services available to part-time students: individual and group career counseling, individual job placement, employer recruitment on campus. Part-time tuition: $64 per credit.

Colorado Mountain College, Alpine Campus
Steamboat Springs 80477

Public institution; rural setting. Awards A. Total enrollment: 138 (all undergraduates); 30% part-time, 30% women, 15% over 25. Total faculty: 112. Library holdings: 1,814 bound volumes, 116 periodical subscriptions.

Undergraduate Courses offered for part-time students during daytime, evenings, weekends, summer. Complete part-time degree programs offered during daytime, evenings. Adult/continuing education programs available. Career services available to part-time students: individual career counseling. Part-time tuition: $14 per credit for area residents, $32 per credit for state residents, $112 per credit for nonresidents.

Colorado Mountain College, Spring Valley Campus
Glenwood Springs 81601

Public institution; rural setting. Awards A. Total enrollment: 741 (all undergraduates); 26% part-time, 52% women, 5% over 25. Total faculty: 58. Library holdings: 32,315 bound volumes, 30,000 titles on microform, 6 periodical subscriptions, 3,000 records/tapes.

Undergraduate Courses offered for part-time students during daytime, evenings, summer. Complete part-time degree programs offered during daytime, evenings, summer. Adult/continuing education programs available. Career services available to part-time students: individual and group career counseling, individual job placement. Part-time tuition: $14 per credit for area residents, $32 per credit for state residents, $112 per credit for nonresidents.

Colorado Mountain College, Timberline Campus
Leadville 80461

Public institution; rural setting. Awards A. Total enrollment: 612 (all undergraduates); 64% part-time, 56% women, 15% over 25. Total faculty: 55. Library holdings: 19,000 bound volumes, 208 periodical subscriptions, 941 records/tapes.

Undergraduate Courses offered for part-time students during daytime, evenings, weekends. Complete part-time degree programs offered during daytime, evenings. Adult/continuing education programs available. Career services available to part-time students: individual career counseling, individual job placement. Part-time tuition: $14 per credit for area residents, $32 per credit for state residents, $112 per credit for nonresidents.

Colorado Northwestern Community College
Rangely 81648

Public institution; small-town setting. Awards A. Total enrollment: 309 (all undergraduates); 10% part-time, 32% women. Total faculty: 62. Library holdings: 13,640 bound volumes.

Undergraduate Courses offered for part-time students during daytime, evenings. Complete part-time degree programs offered during daytime. Adult/continuing education programs available. Career services available to part-time students: individual and group career counseling, individual job placement, employer recruitment on campus. Part-time tuition: $20 per semester hour for state residents, $63 per semester hour for nonresidents.

Colorado School of Mines
Golden 80401

Public institution; small-town setting. Awards B, M, D. Total enrollment: 2,931. Undergraduate enrollment: 2,323; 2% part-time, 20% women, 1% over 25. Total faculty: 210. Library holdings: 250,000 bound volumes, 2,150 periodical subscriptions, 1,200 records/tapes.

Colleges Offering Part-Time Degree Programs / Colorado

Colorado School of Mines (continued)

Graduate Part-time study available in Graduate School. Basic part-time expenses: $81 per semester hour tuition for state residents, $221 per semester hour tuition for nonresidents.

Colorado State University
Fort Collins 80523

Public institution; city setting. Awards B, M, D. Total enrollment: 18,295. Undergraduate enrollment: 15,251; 8% part-time, 50% women, 9% over 25. Total faculty: 1,158. Library holdings: 1.2 million bound volumes, 16,900 periodical subscriptions, 8,300 records/tapes.

Undergraduate Courses offered for part-time students during daytime, evenings, weekends, summer. Complete part-time degree programs offered during daytime. Adult/continuing education programs available. Career services available to part-time students: individual and group career counseling, individual job placement, employer recruitment on campus. Part-time tuition: $48 per credit for state residents, $184 per credit for nonresidents.

Graduate Part-time study available in College of Engineering, College of Veterinary Medicine and Biomedical Sciences. Basic part-time expenses: $56 per credit tuition plus $13 per semester (minimum) fees for state residents, $192 per credit tuition plus $13 per semester (minimum) fees for nonresidents.

Colorado Technical College
Colorado Springs 80907

Proprietary institution; city setting. Awards A, B. Total enrollment: 634 (all undergraduates); 48% part-time, 17% women, 43% over 25. Total faculty: 65. Library holdings: 4,100 bound volumes, 80 periodical subscriptions.

Undergraduate Courses offered for part-time students during daytime, evenings, summer. Complete part-time degree programs offered during daytime, evenings, summer. Career services available to part-time students: individual and group career counseling, individual job placement, employer recruitment on campus. Part-time tuition: $80 per quarter hour.

Denver Auraria Community College
Denver 80204

Public institution; metropolitan setting. Awards A. Barrier-free campus. Total enrollment: 3,687 (all undergraduates); 62% part-time, 52% women, 60% over 25. Total faculty: 293.

Undergraduate Courses offered for part-time students during daytime, evenings, weekends, summer. Complete part-time degree programs offered during daytime, evenings, weekends, summer. Adult/continuing education programs available. Career services available to part-time students: individual and group career counseling, individual job placement, employer recruitment on campus. Part-time tuition: $29.25 per credit hour for state residents, $112.50 per credit hour for nonresidents.

Denver Conservative Baptist Seminary
Denver 80210

Independent-religious institution (graduate only). Total enrollment: 525 (coed; 63% part-time). Total faculty: 47.

Graduate Part-time study available in Graduate and Professional Programs. Degree can be earned exclusively through evening/weekend study in Graduate and Professional Programs. Basic part-time expenses: $80 per quarter hour tuition plus $6 per quarter hour fees.

Denver Institute of Technology
Denver 80221

Proprietary institution; metropolitan setting. Awards A. Barrier-free campus. Total enrollment: 843 (all undergraduates); 2% part-time, 15% women, 40% over 25. Total faculty: 43. Library holdings: 2,500 bound volumes, 74 periodical subscriptions.

Undergraduate Courses offered for part-time students during daytime. Complete part-time degree programs offered during daytime. Part-time tuition: $4.25 per contact hour.

Fort Lewis College
Durango 81301

Public institution; small-town setting. Awards A, B. Total enrollment: 3,685 (all undergraduates); 6% part-time, 43% women. Total faculty: 158. Library holdings: 150,000 bound volumes, 48,000 titles on microform, 850 periodical subscriptions, 3,600 records/tapes.

Undergraduate Courses offered for part-time students during daytime, evenings. Complete part-time degree programs offered during daytime, evenings. Adult/continuing education programs available. Career services available to part-time students: individual and group career counseling, individual job placement, employer recruitment on campus. Part-time tuition: $46 per credit hour for state residents, $194 per credit hour for nonresidents.

Front Range Community College
Westminster 80030

Public institution; small-town setting. Awards A. Barrier-free campus. Total enrollment: 5,500 (all undergraduates); 67% part-time, 56% women. Total faculty: 337. Library holdings: 34,425 bound volumes, 12 periodical subscriptions, 3,018 records/tapes.

Undergraduate Courses offered for part-time students during daytime, evenings, weekends, summer. Complete part-time degree programs offered during daytime, evenings, weekends, summer. Adult/continuing education programs available. Career services available to part-time students: individual career counseling, individual job placement. Part-time tuition: $32.20 per credit hour for state residents, $115.45 per credit hour for nonresidents.

Iliff School of Theology
Denver 80210

Independent-religious institution (graduate only). Total enrollment: 332 (coed; 40% part-time). Total faculty: 63.

Graduate Part-time study available in Graduate and Professional Programs. Basic part-time expenses: $137.50 per quarter hour (minimum) tuition plus $10 per quarter fees. Institutional financial aid available to part-time graduate students in Graduate and Professional Programs.

Intermountain Bible College
Grand Junction 81501

Independent-religious instutition; small-town setting. Awards A, B. Total enrollment: 58 (all undergraduates); 28% part-time, 50% women, 34% over 25. Total faculty: 11. Library holdings: 14,525 bound volumes, 56 periodical subscriptions.

Colorado / **Colleges Offering Part-Time Degree Programs**

Undergraduate Courses offered for part-time students during daytime. Complete part-time degree programs offered during daytime. Adult/continuing education programs available. Career services available to part-time students: individual career counseling. Part-time tuition: $47.50 per semester hour.

Lamar Community College
Lamar 81052

Public institution; rural setting. Awards A. Total enrollment: 621 (all undergraduates); 40% part-time, 62% women, 40% over 25. Total faculty: 45. Library holdings: 30,000 bound volumes, 260 periodical subscriptions.

Undergraduate Courses offered for part-time students during daytime, evenings, weekends. Complete part-time degree programs offered during daytime, evenings, weekends. Adult/continuing education programs available. Part-time tuition: $29.25 per semester hour for state residents, $89.25 per semester hour for nonresidents.

Loretto Heights College
Denver 80236

Independent institution; metropolitan setting. Awards B. Total enrollment: 800 (all undergraduates); 14% part-time, 81% women. Total faculty: 97. Library holdings: 109,400 bound volumes, 4,822 titles on microform, 690 periodical subscriptions.

Undergraduate Courses offered for part-time students during daytime, evenings, weekends, summer. Complete part-time degree programs offered during daytime, weekends. External degree and adult/continuing education programs available. Career services available to part-time students: individual and group career counseling, individual job placement. Part-time tuition: $191 per credit hour.

Mesa College
Grand Junction 81502

Public institution; small-town setting. Awards A, B. Barrier-free campus. Total enrollment: 4,621 (all undergraduates); 44% part-time, 56% women. Total faculty: 155. Library holdings: 85,000 bound volumes, 751 periodical subscriptions, 2,000 records/tapes.

Undergraduate Courses offered for part-time students during daytime, evenings, summer. Complete part-time degree programs offered during daytime, evenings, summer. Adult/continuing education programs available. Career services available to part-time students: individual and group career counseling, individual job placement, employer recruitment on campus. Part-time tuition: $49 per credit hour for state residents, $126 per credit hour for nonresidents.

Metropolitan State College
Denver 80204

Public institution; metropolitan setting. Awards B. Barrier-free campus. Total enrollment: 16,408 (all undergraduates); 54% part-time, 50% women. Total faculty: 705. Library holdings: 700,000 bound volumes, 27,580 titles on microform, 2,801 periodical subscriptions, 5,124 records/tapes.

Undergraduate Courses offered for part-time students during daytime, evenings, summer. Complete part-time degree programs offered during daytime, evenings, summer. External degree and adult/continuing education programs available. Career services available to part-time students: individual and group career counseling, individual job placement, employer recruitment on campus. Part-time tuition: $40 per semester hour for state residents, $167 per semester hour for nonresidents.

Morgan Community College
Fort Morgan 80701

Public institution; rural setting. Awards A. Barrier-free campus. Total enrollment: 643 (all undergraduates); 32% part-time, 38% women. Total faculty: 72. Library holdings: 154 bound volumes, 16 periodical subscriptions, 291 records/tapes.

Undergraduate Courses offered for part-time students during daytime, evenings, summer. Complete part-time degree programs offered during daytime, evenings. Adult/continuing education programs available. Career services available to part-time students: individual and group career counseling, individual job placement. Part-time tuition: $19.50 per credit hour for state residents, $59.50 per credit hour for nonresidents.

Naropa Institute
Boulder 80302

Independent institution; city setting. Awards B, M. Barrier-free campus. Total enrollment: 198. Undergraduate enrollment: 98; 42% part-time, 50% women, 60% over 25. Total faculty: 117. Library holdings: 10,600 bound volumes, 33 periodical subscriptions, 8,290 records/tapes.

Undergraduate Courses offered for part-time students during daytime, evenings, weekends, summer. Complete part-time degree programs offered during daytime. Adult/continuing education programs available. Career services available to part-time students: individual career counseling. Part-time tuition: $80 per quarter hour.

Graduate Part-time study available in Graduate Programs. Basic part-time expenses: $80 per quarter hour tuition plus $5 per quarter (minimum) fees. Institutional financial aid available to part-time graduate students in Graduate Programs.

Nazarene Bible College
Colorado Springs 80935

Independent-religious instutition; city setting. Awards A. Barrier-free campus. Total enrollment: 447 (all undergraduates); 30% part-time, 40% women. Total faculty: 16.

Undergraduate Courses offered for part-time students during daytime, evenings. Complete part-time degree programs offered during daytime, evenings. Part-time tuition: $32.50 per credit hour.

Otero Junior College
La Junta 81050

Public institution; rural setting. Awards A. Total enrollment: 850 (all undergraduates); 45% part-time, 58% women, 32% over 25. Total faculty: 52. Library holdings: 30,000 bound volumes, 350 periodical subscriptions.

Undergraduate Courses offered for part-time students during daytime, evenings. Complete part-time degree programs offered during daytime, evenings. Adult/continuing education programs available. Career services available to part-time students: individual career counseling, individual job placement, employer recruitment on campus. Part-time tuition: $22.50 per quarter hour for state residents, $62.50 per quarter hour for nonresidents.

Colleges Offering Part-Time Degree Programs / Colorado

Parks College
Denver 80221

Proprietary institution; metropolitan setting. Awards A. Barrier-free campus. Total enrollment: 618 (all undergraduates); 32% part-time, 85% women, 11% over 25. Total faculty: 45. Library holdings: 2,000 bound volumes, 100 periodical subscriptions, 50 records/tapes.

Undergraduate Courses offered for part-time students during daytime, evenings, weekends. Complete part-time degree programs offered during daytime, evenings. Career services available to part-time students: individual and group career counseling, individual job placement, employer recruitment on campus. Part-time tuition: $75 per quarter hour.

Pikes Peak Community College
Colorado Springs 80906

Public institution; city setting. Awards A. Barrier-free campus. Total enrollment: 6,025 (all undergraduates); 52% part-time, 46% women, 80% over 25. Total faculty: 200. Library holdings: 43,473 bound volumes, 12,676 titles on microform, 540 periodical subscriptions, 2,948 records/tapes.

Undergraduate Courses offered for part-time students during daytime, evenings, weekends, summer. Complete part-time degree programs offered during daytime, evenings, weekends, summer. Adult/continuing education programs available. Career services available to part-time students: individual and group career counseling, individual job placement, employer recruitment on campus. Part-time tuition: $19.50 per credit hour for state residents, $79.25 per credit hour for nonresidents.

Pueblo Community College
Pueblo 81004

Public institution; city setting. Awards A. Total enrollment: 1,299 (all undergraduates); 20% part-time, 46% women, 62% over 25. Total faculty: 156. Library holdings: 7,000 bound volumes.

Undergraduate Courses offered for part-time students during daytime, evenings. Complete part-time degree programs offered during daytime, evenings. Adult/continuing education programs available. Career services available to part-time students: individual career counseling, individual job placement, employer recruitment on campus. Part-time tuition: $31.75 per semester hour for state residents, $149.50 per semester hour for nonresidents.

Red Rocks Community College
Golden 80401

Public institution; small-town setting. Awards A. Barrier-free campus. Total enrollment: 5,141 (all undergraduates); 73% part-time, 52% women. Total faculty: 244. Library holdings: 38,596 bound volumes, 140 titles on microform, 486 periodical subscriptions, 1,218 records/tapes.

Undergraduate Courses offered for part-time students during daytime, evenings, summer. Complete part-time degree programs offered during daytime, evenings, summer. Adult/continuing education programs available. Career services available to part-time students: individual and group career counseling, individual job placement. Part-time tuition: $31.15 per credit for state residents, $114.40 per credit for nonresidents.

Regis College
Denver 80221

Independent-religious instutition; metropolitan setting. Awards B, M. Total enrollment: 1,220. Undergraduate enrollment: 1,100; 10% part-time, 45% women, 2% over 25. Total faculty: 95. Library holdings: 75,000 bound volumes, 600 periodical subscriptions, 1,500 records/tapes.

Undergraduate Courses offered for part-time students during daytime, evenings. Complete part-time degree programs offered during daytime, evenings. External degree and adult/continuing education programs available. Part-time tuition: $185 per semester hour.

Graduate Part-time study available in Graduate Programs. Degree can be earned exclusively through evening/weekend study in Graduate Programs. Basic part-time expenses: $146 per credit (minimum) tuition.

Rockmont College
Denver 80226

Independent-religious instutition; metropolitan setting. Awards A, B. Total enrollment: 280 (all undergraduates); 19% part-time, 49% women, 15% over 25. Total faculty: 45. Library holdings: 34,622 bound volumes, 258 periodical subscriptions, 420 records/tapes.

Undergraduate Courses offered for part-time students during daytime, evenings, summer. Complete part-time degree programs offered during daytime, evenings, summer. Adult/continuing education programs available. Career services available to part-time students: individual career counseling, individual job placement. Part-time tuition: $155 per semester hour.

Rocky Mountain School of Art
Denver 80218

Proprietary institution; metropolitan setting. Awards A. Total enrollment: 178 (all undergraduates). Total faculty: 28. Library holdings: 700 bound volumes, 15 periodical subscriptions.

Undergraduate Courses offered for part-time students during daytime. Complete part-time degree programs offered during daytime. Career services available to part-time students: individual and group career counseling, individual job placement, employer recruitment on campus. Part-time tuition per quarter (27.5 to 220 hours) ranges from $176 to $975.

Trinidad State Junior College
Trinidad 81082

Public institution; rural setting. Awards A. Total enrollment: 1,784 (all undergraduates); 60% part-time, 31% women. Total faculty: 115. Library holdings: 65,630 bound volumes, 325 periodical subscriptions, 2,035 records/tapes.

Undergraduate Courses offered for part-time students during daytime, evenings, weekends, summer. Complete part-time degree programs offered during daytime, evenings, weekends, summer. Adult/continuing education programs available. Career services available to part-time students: individual and group career counseling, individual job placement, employer recruitment on campus. Part-time tuition: $19.50 per semester hour for state residents, $59.40 per semester hour for nonresidents.

Colorado / Colleges Offering Part-Time Degree Programs

University of Colorado at Boulder
Boulder 80309

Public institution; city setting. Awards B, M, D. Barrier-free campus. Total enrollment: 22,180. Undergraduate enrollment: 17,985; 8% part-time, 46% women, 8% over 25. Total faculty: 1,158. Library holdings: 1.9 million bound volumes, 2.1 million titles on microform, 11,255 periodical subscriptions, 50,000 records/tapes.

Undergraduate Courses offered for part-time students during daytime, evenings, summer. Complete part-time degree programs offered during daytime, summer. Adult/continuing education programs available. Career services available to part-time students: individual and group career counseling, individual job placement, employer recruitment on campus. Part-time tuition and fees per semester (1 to 10 semester hours) range from $217 to $597 for state residents, $847 to $2553 for nonresidents.

Graduate Part-time study available in Graduate School. Basic part-time expenses: $220 per semester (minimum) tuition plus $123 per semester fees for state residents, $847 per semester (minimum) tuition plus $123 per semester fees for nonresidents.

University of Colorado at Colorado Springs
Colorado Springs 80933

Public institution; city setting. Awards B, M. Total enrollment: 5,560. Undergraduate enrollment: 4,047; 44% part-time, 52% women, 57% over 25. Total faculty: 335. Library holdings: 201,740 bound volumes, 2,688 titles on microform, 1,500 periodical subscriptions, 1,433 records/tapes.

Undergraduate Courses offered for part-time students during daytime, evenings, summer. Complete part-time degree programs offered during daytime, evenings, summer. Adult/continuing education programs available. Career services available to part-time students: individual and group career counseling, individual job placement, employer recruitment on campus. Part-time tuition: $39 per semester hour for state residents, $122 per semester hour for nonresidents.

University of Colorado at Denver
Denver 80202

Public institution; metropolitan setting. Awards B, M, D. Barrier-free campus. Total enrollment: 11,365. Undergraduate enrollment: 6,493; 74% part-time, 49% women, 60% over 25. Total faculty: 349. Library holdings: 340,140 bound volumes, 2,801 periodical subscriptions.

Undergraduate Courses offered for part-time students during daytime, evenings, summer. Complete part-time degree programs offered during daytime, evenings, summer. External degree and adult/continuing education programs available. Career services available to part-time students: individual and group career counseling, individual job placement, employer recruitment on campus. Part-time tuition: $41 per credit for state residents, $170 per credit for nonresidents.

Graduate Part-time study available in Graduate School, College of Design and Planning, Graduate School of Business Administration, Graduate School of Public Affairs. Basic part-time expenses: $50 per credit hour tuition for state residents, $189 per credit hour tuition for nonresidents.

University of Denver
Denver 80208

Independent institution; metropolitan setting. Awards B, M, D. Total enrollment: 8,472. Undergraduate enrollment: 4,904; 5% part-time, 50% women, 7% over 25. Total faculty: 487. Library holdings: 901,311 bound volumes, 578,237 titles on microform, 10,594 periodical subscriptions.

Undergraduate Courses offered for part-time students during daytime, evenings, weekends, summer. Complete part-time degree programs offered during daytime, evenings, weekends, summer. Adult/continuing education programs available. Career services available to part-time students: individual and group career counseling, individual job placement, employer recruitment on campus. Part-time tuition: $194 per quarter hour.

Graduate Part-time study available in Graduate School of Arts and Science, College of Law, Graduate School of Business and Public Management, Graduate School of International Studies, Graduate School of Librarianship and Information Management, Graduate School of Social Work. Degree can be earned exclusively through evening/weekend study in College of Law, Graduate School of Business and Public Management, Graduate School of Librarianship and Information Management. Basic part-time expenses: $194 per quarter hour tuition plus $10 per quarter hour fees. Institutional financial aid available to part-time graduate students in Graduate School of Arts and Science, Graduate School of Business and Public Management, Graduate School of International Studies, Graduate School of Librarianship and Information Management, Graduate School of Social Work.

University of Northern Colorado
Greeley 80639

Public institution; city setting. Awards B, M, D. Barrier-free campus. Total enrollment: 9,784. Undergraduate enrollment: 8,362; 6% part-time, 58% women. Total faculty: 650. Library holdings: 800,000 bound volumes.

Undergraduate Courses offered for part-time students during daytime, evenings, summer. Complete part-time degree programs offered during daytime, evenings, summer. External degree and adult/continuing education programs available. Career services available to part-time students: individual and group career counseling, individual job placement, employer recruitment on campus. Part-time tuition: $140 per hour for nonresidents. State resident part-time tuition per hour ranges from $16 (for students taking 1 to 5 hours) to $39 (for students taking 6 to 9 hours).

Graduate Part-time study available in Graduate School. Degree can be earned exclusively through evening/weekend study in Graduate School. Basic part-time expenses: $18 per credit hour (minimum) tuition plus $8 per credit hour fees for state residents, $157 per credit hour (minimum) tuition plus $8 per credit hour fees for nonresidents. Institutional financial aid available to part-time graduate students in Graduate School.

University of Southern Colorado
Pueblo 81001

Public institution; city setting. Awards A, B, M. Barrier-free campus. Total enrollment: 4,982. Undergraduate enrollment: 4,706; 14% part-time, 45% women, 31% over 25. Total faculty: 269. Library holdings: 163,075 bound volumes, 178 titles on microform, 1,246 periodical subscriptions, 4,932 records/tapes.

Undergraduate Courses offered for part-time students during daytime, evenings, summer. Complete part-time degree programs offered during daytime, evenings, summer. Adult/continuing education programs available. Part-time tuition: $49 per semester hour for state residents, $158 per semester hour for nonresidents.

Graduate Part-time study available in School of Applied Science and Engineering Technology, School of Business, School of Education. Degree can be earned exclusively through even-

Colleges Offering Part-Time Degree Programs / Colorado

University of Southern Colorado (continued)

ing/weekend study in School of Applied Science and Engineering Technology, School of Business.Basic part-time expenses: $49 per credit hour tuition plus $8.50 per credit hour fees for state residents, $158 per credit hour tuition plus $8.50 per credit hour fees for nonresidents.

Western Bible College
Morrison 80465

Independent-religious instutition; rural setting. Awards A, B. Total enrollment: 203 (all undergraduates); 20% part-time, 41% women. Total faculty: 20. Library holdings: 35,000 bound volumes, 100 periodical subscriptions, 300 records/tapes.

Undergraduate Courses offered for part-time students during daytime. Complete part-time degree programs offered during daytime. Adult/continuing education programs available. Career services available to part-time students: individual career counseling, employer recruitment on campus. Part-time tuition: $95 per credit hour.

Western State College of Colorado
Gunnison 81230

Public institution; rural setting. Awards B, M. Total enrollment: 2,850. Undergraduate enrollment: 2,648; 6% part-time, 41% women, 5% over 25. Total faculty: 134. Library holdings: 135,000 bound volumes, 3,000 titles on microform, 960 periodical subscriptions, 3,700 records/tapes.

Undergraduate Courses offered for part-time students during daytime, evenings, summer. Complete part-time degree programs offered during daytime, summer. Adult/continuing education programs available. Career services available to part-time students: individual and group career counseling, individual job placement, employer recruitment on campus. Part-time tuition: $27 per semester hour for state residents, $116 per semester hour for nonresidents.

Graduate Part-time study available in Graduate Division.Basic part-time expenses: $27 per credit tuition plus $6.50 per semester (minimum) fees for state residents, $121 per credit tuition plus $6.50 per semester (minimum) fees for nonresidents.

CONNECTICUT

Albertus Magnus College
New Haven 06511

Independent-religious instutition; city setting. Awards A, B. Total enrollment: 571 (all undergraduates); 32% part-time, 98% women. Total faculty: 58. Library holdings: 88,000 bound volumes, 741 periodical subscriptions, 4,400 records/tapes.

Undergraduate Courses offered for part-time students during daytime, weekends. Complete part-time degree programs offered during daytime, weekends. Adult/continuing education programs available. Career services available to part-time students: individual career counseling, individual job placement, employer recruitment on campus. Part-time tuition: $179 per semester hour.

Asnuntuck Community College
Enfield 06082

Public institution; small-town setting. Awards A. Barrier-free campus. Total enrollment: 1,710 (all undergraduates); 87% part-time, 70% women, 87% over 25. Total faculty: 37. Library holdings: 27,000 bound volumes, 180 periodical subscriptions, 1,700 records/tapes.

Undergraduate Courses offered for part-time students during daytime, evenings, summer. Complete part-time degree programs offered during daytime, evenings, summer. Adult/continuing education programs available. Career services available to part-time students: individual career counseling, individual job placement. Part-time tuition: $18.50 per credit for state residents, $37.50 per credit for nonresidents.

Briarwood College
Southington 06489

Proprietary institution; small-town setting. Awards A. Barrier-free campus. Total enrollment: 374 (all undergraduates); 3% part-time, 98% women, 5% over 25. Total faculty: 35. Library holdings: 7,169 bound volumes, 91 periodical subscriptions.

Undergraduate Courses offered for part-time students during daytime, evenings, summer. Complete part-time degree programs offered during daytime. External degree and adult/continuing education programs available. Career services available to part-time students: individual career counseling, individual job placement, employer recruitment on campus. Part-time tuition: $65 per credit hour.

Bridgeport Engineering Institute
Bridgeport 06606

Independent institution; city setting. Awards A, B (part-time evening programs only). Barrier-free campus. Total enrollment: 900 (all undergraduates); 100% part-time, 15% women, 50% over 25. Total faculty: 80. Library holdings: 100,000 bound volumes, 1,000 periodical subscriptions.

Undergraduate Courses offered for part-time students during evenings. Complete part-time degree programs offered during evenings. Part-time tuition: $285 per course.

Central Connecticut State University
New Britain 06050

Public institution; city setting. Awards B, M. Total enrollment: 13,209. Undergraduate enrollment: 10,894; 38% part-time, 48% women, 31% over 25. Total faculty: 638. Library holdings: 370,747 bound volumes, 80,234 titles on microform, 1,620 periodical subscriptions, 6,827 records/tapes.

Undergraduate Courses offered for part-time students during daytime, evenings, summer. Complete part-time degree programs offered during daytime, evenings, summer. Adult/continuing education programs available. Career services available to part-time students: individual and group career counseling, employer recruitment on campus. Part-time tuition: $60 per credit hour for state residents, $60 per credit hour for nonresidents.

Graduate Part-time study available in School of Graduate Studies. Degree can be earned exclusively through evening/weekend study in School of Graduate Studies.Basic part-time expenses: $75 per semester hour tuition plus $20 per semester fees. Institutional financial aid available to part-time graduate students in School of Graduate Studies.

Charter Oak College
Hartford 06106

Public institution; metropolitan setting. Awards A, B (external degree programs only). Total enrollment: 1,200 (all undergraduates); 100% part-time, 35% women, 95% over 25. Total faculty: 55.

Undergraduate Part-time degree programs offered. External degree programs available. One-time enrollment fee: $150 for state residents, $190 for nonresidents for associate program; $300-$350 for state residents, $340-$390 for nonresidents for bachelor's program. Students pay an additional $100 fee for each year after the first year until completion of degree.

Connecticut College
New London 06320

Independent institution; small-town setting. Awards B, M. Total enrollment: 1,806. Undergraduate enrollment: 1,734; 6% part-time, 58% women. Total faculty: 230. Library holdings: 380,000 bound volumes, 2,000 periodical subscriptions, 10,000 records/tapes.

Undergraduate Courses offered for part-time students during daytime, evenings, summer. Complete part-time degree programs offered during daytime. Adult/continuing education programs available. Career services available to part-time students: individual and group career counseling, individual job placement, employer recruitment on campus. Part-time tuition: $117 per credit.

Graduate Part-time study available in Graduate School. Basic part-time expenses: $525 per course tuition. Institutional financial aid available to part-time graduate students in Graduate School.

Eastern Connecticut State University
Willimantic 06226

Public institution; small-town setting. Awards A, B, M. Total enrollment: 3,754. Undergraduate enrollment: 3,475; 38% part-time, 51% women, 18% over 25. Total faculty: 212. Library holdings: 145,000 bound volumes, 600 periodical subscriptions.

Undergraduate Courses offered for part-time students during daytime, evenings, weekends, summer. Complete part-time degree programs offered during daytime, evenings, weekends, summer. Adult/continuing education programs available. Career services available to part-time students: individual and group career counseling, individual job placement, employer recruitment on campus. Part-time tuition: $60 per credit hour for state residents, $60 per credit hour for nonresidents.

Graduate Part-time study available in School of Professional Studies. Degree can be earned exclusively through evening/weekend study in School of Professional Studies. Basic part-time expenses: $70 per credit tuition plus $5 per semester fees. Institutional financial aid available to part-time graduate students in School of Professional Studies.

Fairfield University
Fairfield 06430

Independent-religious instutition; city setting. Awards B, M. Barrier-free campus. Total enrollment: 5,242. Undergraduate enrollment: 2,887; 0% part-time, 50% women, 1% over 25. Total faculty: 323. Library holdings: 178,672 bound volumes, 65,419 titles on microform, 1,433 periodical subscriptions, 2,175 records/tapes.

Undergraduate Courses offered for part-time students during daytime, evenings, summer. Complete part-time degree programs offered during daytime, evenings, summer. Adult/continuing education programs available. Career services available to part-time students: individual and group career counseling, individual job placement, employer recruitment on campus. Part-time tuition: $125 per credit.

Graduate Part-time study available in School of Graduate and Continuing Education, Graduate School of Corporate and Political Communication. Degree can be earned exclusively through evening/weekend study in School of Graduate and Continuing Education, Graduate School of Corporate and Political Communication. Basic part-time expenses: $125 per credit tuition. Institutional financial aid available to part-time graduate students in School of Graduate and Continuing Education.

Greater Hartford Community College
Hartford 06105

Public institution; metropolitan setting. Awards A. Total enrollment: 3,700 (all undergraduates); 65% part-time, 70% women, 50% over 25. Total faculty: 72. Library holdings: 37,356 bound volumes, 382 periodical subscriptions, 2,330 records/tapes.

Undergraduate Courses offered for part-time students during daytime, evenings, weekends, summer. Complete part-time degree programs offered during daytime, evenings, weekends, summer. Adult/continuing education programs available. Career services available to part-time students: individual and group career counseling, individual job placement, employer recruitment on campus. Part-time tuition: $18.50 per credit hour for state residents, $62.50 per credit hour for nonresidents.

Greater New Haven State Technical College
North Haven 06473

Public institution; small-town setting. Awards A. Barrier-free campus. Total enrollment: 1,464 (all undergraduates); 60% part-time, 30% women. Total faculty: 78.

Undergraduate Courses offered for part-time students during evenings, weekends, summer. Complete part-time degree programs offered during evenings. Career services available to part-time students: individual and group career counseling, individual job placement, employer recruitment on campus. Part-time tuition per credit hour ranges from $14 for daytime courses to $31 for evening courses.

Hartford College for Women
Hartford 06105

Independent institution; metropolitan setting. Awards A. Barrier-free campus. Total enrollment: 230 (all undergraduates); 20% part-time, 100% women, 20% over 25. Total faculty: 34. Library holdings: 58,110 bound volumes, 123 periodical subscriptions, 600 records/tapes.

Undergraduate Courses offered for part-time students during daytime, evenings, summer. Complete part-time degree programs offered during daytime. Adult/continuing education programs available. Career services available to part-time students: individual and group career counseling, individual job placement. Part-time tuition: $140 per credit.

Hartford Graduate Center
Hartford 06120

Independent institution (graduate only). Total enrollment: 2,167 (coed; 98% part-time). Total faculty: 71. Library holdings: 25,000 bound volumes.

Graduate Part-time study available in School of Engineering and Science, School of Management. Degree can be earned exclusively through evening/weekend study in School of Engineering and Science, School of Management. Basic part-time expenses: $197.50 per credit tuition for state residents, for nonresidents.

Colleges Offering Part-Time Degree Programs / *Connecticut*

Hartford Seminary
Hartford 06105

Independent institution (graduate only). Total enrollment: 112 (coed; 93% part-time). Total faculty: 17.

Graduate Part-time study available in Graduate Programs. Basic part-time expenses: $120 per credit tuition. Institutional financial aid available to part-time graduate students in Graduate Programs.

Hartford State Technical College
Hartford 06106

Public institution; metropolitan setting. Awards A. Total enrollment: 1,871 (all undergraduates); 56% part-time, 14% women, 5% over 25. Total faculty: 51.

Undergraduate Courses offered for part-time students during evenings, summer. Complete part-time degree programs offered during evenings. Adult/continuing education programs available. Career services available to part-time students: individual and group career counseling, individual job placement, employer recruitment on campus. Part-time tuition: $16 per credit for state residents, $52 per credit for nonresidents.

Holy Apostles College
Cromwell 06416

Independent-religious instutition; small-town setting. Awards A, B, M. Total enrollment: 166. Undergraduate enrollment: 48; 25% part-time, 23% women, 95% over 25. Total faculty: 30. Library holdings: 50,000 bound volumes, 150 periodical subscriptions.

Undergraduate Courses offered for part-time students during daytime, evenings. Complete part-time degree programs offered during daytime, evenings. External degree and adult/continuing education programs available. Part-time tuition: $85 per credit hour.

Housatonic Community College
Bridgeport 06608

Public institution; city setting. Awards A. Barrier-free campus. Total enrollment: 2,693 (all undergraduates); 66% part-time, 56% women. Total faculty: 112. Library holdings: 29,212 bound volumes, 277 periodical subscriptions, 10,488 records/tapes.

Undergraduate Courses offered for part-time students during daytime, evenings, summer. Complete part-time degree programs offered during daytime, evenings, summer. Adult/continuing education programs available. Career services available to part-time students: individual and group career counseling, employer recruitment on campus. Part-time tuition: $77.50 per course for state residents, $209.50 per course for nonresidents.

Manchester Community College
Manchester 06040

Public institution; city setting. Awards A. Barrier-free campus. Total enrollment: 5,000 (all undergraduates); 60% part-time, 66% women. Total faculty: 200.

Undergraduate Courses offered for part-time students during daytime, evenings, weekends, summer. Complete part-time degree programs offered during daytime, evenings, weekends, summer. Part-time tuition and fees per semester (1 to 11 credit hours) range from $40.50 to $67.50 for state residents, $84.50 to $111.50 for nonresidents.

Mattatuck Community College
Waterbury 06708

Public institution; city setting. Awards A. Barrier-free campus. Total enrollment: 3,249 (all undergraduates); 42% part-time, 72% women, 42% over 25. Total faculty: 148. Library holdings: 29,267 bound volumes, 170 periodical subscriptions, 488 records/tapes.

Undergraduate Courses offered for part-time students during daytime, evenings, summer. Complete part-time degree programs offered during daytime, evenings, summer. External degree and adult/continuing education programs available. Career services available to part-time students: individual and group career counseling, individual job placement, employer recruitment on campus. Part-time tuition: $18.50 per credit hour for state residents, $62.50 per credit hour for nonresidents.

Middlesex Community College
Middletown 06457

Public institution; small-town setting. Awards A. Total enrollment: 3,200 (all undergraduates); 60% part-time, 60% women. Total faculty: 75. Library holdings: 45,000 bound volumes, 180 periodical subscriptions, 1,900 records/tapes.

Undergraduate Courses offered for part-time students during daytime, evenings. Complete part-time degree programs offered during daytime, evenings. External degree and adult/continuing education programs available. Career services available to part-time students: individual and group career counseling, individual job placement, employer recruitment on campus. Part-time tuition: $18.50 per credit hour for state residents, $62.50 per credit hour for nonresidents.

Mitchell College
New London 06320

Independent institution; small-town setting. Awards A. Total enrollment: 920 (all undergraduates); 41% part-time, 45% women. Total faculty: 38. Library holdings: 50,000 bound volumes, 150 periodical subscriptions, 300 records/tapes.

Undergraduate Courses offered for part-time students during daytime, evenings, weekends, summer. Complete part-time degree programs offered during daytime, evenings, summer. Adult/continuing education programs available. Career services available to part-time students: individual and group career counseling, individual job placement. Part-time tuition: $65 per credit hour.

Mohegan Community College
Norwich 06360

Public institution; small-town setting. Awards A. Barrier-free campus. Total enrollment: 2,023 (all undergraduates); 75% part-time, 61% women, 70% over 25. Total faculty: 86.

Undergraduate Courses offered for part-time students during daytime, evenings, weekends, summer. Complete part-time degree programs offered during daytime, evenings, weekends, summer. External degree and adult/continuing education programs available. Career services available to part-time students: individual and group career counseling, employer recruitment on campus. Part-time tuition: $18.50 per credit for state residents, $62.50 per credit for nonresidents.

Connecticut / **Colleges Offering Part-Time Degree Programs**

Northwestern Connecticut Community College
Winsted 06098

Public institution; small-town setting. Awards A. Barrier-free campus. Total enrollment: 2,258 (all undergraduates); 75% part-time, 70% women, 75% over 25. Total faculty: 85. Library holdings: 45,580 bound volumes, 1,665 titles on microform, 270 periodical subscriptions, 1,668 records/tapes.

Undergraduate Courses offered for part-time students during daytime, evenings, weekends, summer. Complete part-time degree programs offered during daytime, evenings. External degree and adult/continuing education programs available. Career services available to part-time students: individual and group career counseling, individual job placement. Part-time tuition: $18.50 per credit hour for state residents, $62.50 per credit hour for nonresidents.

Norwalk Community College
Norwalk 06854

Public institution; city setting. Awards A. Barrier-free campus. Total enrollment: 3,383 (all undergraduates); 74% part-time, 64% women, 51% over 25. Total faculty: 105. Library holdings: 50,000 bound volumes, 28,000 titles on microform, 200 periodical subscriptions, 1,300 records/tapes.

Undergraduate Courses offered for part-time students during daytime, evenings, weekends, summer. Complete part-time degree programs offered during daytime, evenings, weekends, summer. Adult/continuing education programs available. Career services available to part-time students: individual and group career counseling. Part-time tuition: $18.50 per credit hour for state residents, $62.50 per credit hour for nonresidents.

Norwalk State Technical College
Norwalk 06854

Public institution; city setting. Awards A. Barrier-free campus. Total enrollment: 835 (all undergraduates); 10% part-time, 12% women, 10% over 25. Total faculty: 100.

Undergraduate Courses offered for part-time students during daytime, evenings, weekends, summer. Complete part-time degree programs offered during daytime, evenings, summer. Adult/continuing education programs available. Part-time tuition: $16 per credit hour for state residents, $52 per credit hour for nonresidents.

Paier College of Art, Inc
Hamden 06511

Proprietary institution; city setting. Awards A, B. Total enrollment: 341 (all undergraduates); 30% part-time, 65% women, 40% over 25. Total faculty: 53. Library holdings: 5,500 bound volumes, 65 periodical subscriptions.

Undergraduate Courses offered for part-time students during daytime, evenings, summer. Complete part-time degree programs offered during daytime. Career services available to part-time students: individual career counseling, individual job placement, employer recruitment on campus. Part-time tuition: $182 per semester hour.

Post College
Waterbury 06708

Independent institution; city setting. Awards A, B. Total enrollment: 1,438 (all undergraduates); 57% part-time, 64% women, 51% over 25. Total faculty: 58. Library holdings: 35,000 bound volumes, 2,000 titles on microform, 335 periodical subscriptions, 550 records/tapes.

Undergraduate Courses offered for part-time students during daytime, evenings, summer. Complete part-time degree programs offered during daytime, evenings. Adult/continuing education programs available. Career services available to part-time students: individual and group career counseling, individual job placement, employer recruitment on campus. Part-time tuition: $150 per credit.

Quinebaug Valley Community College
Danielson 06239

Public institution; rural setting. Awards A. Total enrollment: 1,124 (all undergraduates); 80% part-time, 57% women. Total faculty: 46. Library holdings: 15,000 bound volumes, 165 periodical subscriptions, 600 records/tapes.

Undergraduate Courses offered for part-time students during daytime, evenings. Complete part-time degree programs offered during daytime, evenings. Adult/continuing education programs available. Career services available to part-time students: individual career counseling. Part-time tuition: $18.50 per credit for state residents, $62.50 per credit for nonresidents.

Quinnipiac College
Hamden 06518

Independent institution; city setting. Awards A, B, M. Barrier-free campus. Total enrollment: 2,745. Undergraduate enrollment: 2,460; 30% part-time, 68% women, 27% over 25. Total faculty: 347. Library holdings: 132,405 bound volumes, 17,397 titles on microform, 8,707 periodical subscriptions, 1,679 records/tapes.

Undergraduate Courses offered for part-time students during daytime, evenings, summer. Complete part-time degree programs offered during daytime, evenings. External degree and adult/continuing education programs available. Career services available to part-time students: individual career counseling, individual job placement, employer recruitment on campus. Part-time tuition per credit ranges from $110 for evening courses to $195 for daytime courses.

Graduate Part-time study available in School of Allied Health and Natural Sciences, School of Business. Basic part-time expenses: $140 per credit tuition.

Sacred Heart University
Bridgeport 06606

Independent-religious instutition; city setting. Awards A, B, M. Barrier-free campus. Total enrollment: 4,660. Undergraduate enrollment: 4,066; 61% part-time, 67% women. Total faculty: 333. Library holdings: 120,000 bound volumes, 950 periodical subscriptions.

Undergraduate Courses offered for part-time students during daytime, evenings, weekends, summer. Complete part-time degree programs offered during daytime, evenings, weekends, summer. External degree and adult/continuing education programs available. Career services available to part-time students: individual and group career counseling, individual job placement, employer recruitment on campus. Part-time tuition: $124 per credit.

Graduate Part-time study available in Graduate Programs. Degree can be earned exclusively through evening/weekend study in Graduate Programs. Basic part-time expenses: $127 per credit hour (minimum) tuition plus $10 per semester fees.

Colleges Offering Part-Time Degree Programs / *Connecticut*

Saint Joseph College
West Hartford 06117

Independent-religious instutition; city setting. Awards B, M. Total enrollment: 1,289. Undergraduate enrollment: 785; 27% part-time, 100% women, 18% over 25. Total faculty: 96. Library holdings: 96,500 bound volumes, 5,205 titles on microform, 541 periodical subscriptions, 1,519 records/tapes.

Undergraduate Courses offered for part-time students during daytime, evenings, summer. Complete part-time degree programs offered during daytime, evenings. Adult/continuing education programs available. Career services available to part-time students: individual and group career counseling, individual job placement, employer recruitment on campus. Part-time tuition: $145 per credit.

Graduate Part-time study available in Graduate Division. Basic part-time expenses: $145 per credit hour tuition plus $37.50 per semester fees.

South Central Community College
New Haven 06511

Public institution; city setting. Awards A. Barrier-free campus. Total enrollment: 2,340 (all undergraduates); 69% part-time, 68% women, 63% over 25. Total faculty: 97. Library holdings: 22,957 bound volumes, 140 periodical subscriptions, 3,000 records/tapes.

Undergraduate Courses offered for part-time students during daytime, evenings, summer. Complete part-time degree programs offered during daytime, evenings. External degree and adult/continuing education programs available. Career services available to part-time students: individual and group career counseling, individual job placement, employer recruitment on campus. Part-time tuition and fees per semester (1 to 11 credits) range from $40.50 to $252.50 for state residents, $84.50 to $736.50 for nonresidents.

Southern Connecticut State University
New Haven 06515

Public institution; city setting. Awards B, M. Barrier-free campus. Total enrollment: 10,000. Undergraduate enrollment: 6,500; 5% part-time, 62% women. Total faculty: 657. Library holdings: 372,000 bound volumes, 1,281 periodical subscriptions, 1,700 records/tapes.

Undergraduate Courses offered for part-time students during daytime, evenings, summer. Complete part-time degree programs offered during daytime, evenings, summer. Adult/continuing education programs available. Career services available to part-time students: individual and group career counseling, individual job placement. Part-time tuition: $68 per semester hour for state residents, $68 per semester hour for nonresidents.

Graduate Part-time study available in Graduate Studies and Continuing Education. Degree can be earned exclusively through evening/weekend study in Graduate Studies and Continuing Education. Basic part-time expenses: $76 per credit tuition plus $5 per semester fees.

Thames Valley State Technical College
Norwich 06360

Public institution; small-town setting. Awards A. Barrier-free campus. Total enrollment: 840 (all undergraduates); 12% part-time, 30% women, 3% over 25. Total faculty: 45. Library holdings: 7,650 bound volumes, 110 titles on microform, 114 periodical subscriptions, 150 records/tapes.

Undergraduate Courses offered for part-time students during daytime, evenings, weekends, summer. Complete part-time degree programs offered during daytime, evenings, summer. Adult/continuing education programs available. Career services available to part-time students: individual and group career counseling, individual job placement, employer recruitment on campus. Part-time tuition: $16 per credit for state residents, $52 per credit for nonresidents.

Trinity College
Hartford 06106

Independent institution; metropolitan setting. Awards B, M. Barrier-free campus. Total enrollment: 1,982. Undergraduate enrollment: 1,797; 4% part-time, 47% women, 6% over 25. Total faculty: 154. Library holdings: 650,000 bound volumes, 1,620 periodical subscriptions, 13,000 records/tapes.

Undergraduate Courses offered for part-time students during daytime, evenings, summer. Complete part-time degree programs offered during daytime. External degree and adult/continuing education programs available. Career services available to part-time students: individual and group career counseling, employer recruitment on campus. Part-time tuition: $865 per course.

Graduate Part-time study available in Graduate Programs. Degree can be earned exclusively through evening/weekend study in Graduate Programs. Basic part-time expenses: $120 per semester hour tuition plus $15 per semester fees. Institutional financial aid available to part-time graduate students in Graduate Programs.

Tunxis Community College
Farmington 06032

Public institution; small-town setting. Awards A. Barrier-free campus. Total enrollment: 1,570 (all undergraduates); 49% part-time, 67% women, 29% over 25. Total faculty: 100. Library holdings: 20,000 bound volumes, 200 periodical subscriptions, 300 records/tapes.

Undergraduate Courses offered for part-time students during daytime, evenings, weekends, summer. Complete part-time degree programs offered during daytime, evenings. Adult/continuing education programs available. Career services available to part-time students: individual career counseling, individual job placement, employer recruitment on campus. Part-time tuition: $18.50 per semester hour for state residents, $42 per semester hour for nonresidents.

University of Bridgeport
Bridgeport 06601

Independent institution; city setting. Awards A, B, M, D. Total enrollment: 6,413. Undergraduate enrollment: 4,201; 28% part-time, 47% women. Total faculty: 523. Library holdings: 300,000 bound volumes, 418,000 titles on microform, 1,650 periodical subscriptions, 3,000 records/tapes.

Undergraduate Courses offered for part-time students during daytime, evenings, weekends, summer. Complete part-time degree programs offered during daytime, evenings, weekends. Adult/continuing education programs available. Career services available to part-time students: individual and group career counseling, individual job placement, employer recruitment on campus. Part-time tuition: $157 per credit.

Graduate Part-time study available in College of Arts and Humanities, College of Business and Public Management, College of Health Sciences, College of Science and Engineering (in Connecticut Technology Institute), School of Law. Degree can be earned exclusively through evening/weekend study in College of Arts and Humanities, College of Business and Public Management, College of Health Sciences, College of Science and

Engineering (in Connecticut Technology Institute), School of Law.Basic part-time expenses: $167 per credit tuition plus $20 per semester fees. Institutional financial aid available to part-time graduate students in College of Arts and Humanities, College of Business and Public Management, College of Health Sciences, College of Science and Engineering (in Connecticut Technology Institute), School of Law.

University of Connecticut
Storrs 06268

Public institution; rural setting. Awards B, M, D. Total enrollment: 16,184. Undergraduate enrollment: 12,484; 5% part-time, 52% women, 2% over 25. Total faculty: 1,257. Library holdings: 1.4 million bound volumes, 1.3 million titles on microform, 7,000 periodical subscriptions.

Graduate Part-time study available in Graduate School, School of Law.Basic part-time expenses: $157 per semester (minimum) tuition plus $233 per semester (minimum) fees for state residents, $439 per semester (minimum) tuition plus $233 per semester (minimum) fees for nonresidents.

University of Connecticut at Waterbury
Waterbury 06710

Public institution; city setting. Awards B (nontraditional upper-level program; also offers first 2 years of most baccalaureate programs available at the main campus in Storrs). Total enrollment: 550 (all undergraduates). Total faculty: 52.

Undergraduate Part-time degree programs offered. Courses offered for part-time students during daytime, evenings, weekends, summer. Adult/continuing education programs available. Career services available to part-time students: individual and group career counseling. Part-time tuition and fees per semester (3 to 11 credits) range from $229 to $562 for state residents, $441 to $1343 for nonresidents.

University of Connecticut Health Center
Farmington 06032

Public institution (graduate only). Total enrollment: 646 (coed; 6% part-time). Total faculty: 574.

Graduate Part-time study available in Graduate Programs, School of Dental Medicine.Basic part-time expenses: $390 per semester (minimum) tuition for state residents, $672 per semester (minimum) tuition for nonresidents.

University of Hartford
West Hartford 06117

Independent institution; city setting. Awards A, B, M, D. Barrier-free campus. Total enrollment: 8,062. Undergraduate enrollment: 6,031; 35% part-time, 44% women. Total faculty: 620. Library holdings: 300,000 bound volumes, 50,000 titles on microform, 2,300 periodical subscriptions, 50,000 records/tapes.

Undergraduate Courses offered for part-time students during daytime, evenings, summer. Complete part-time degree programs offered during daytime, evenings, summer. Adult/continuing education programs available. Career services available to part-time students: individual and group career counseling, individual job placement, employer recruitment on campus. Part-time tuition: $165 per credit.

Graduate Part-time study available in Barney School of Business and Public Administration, College of Arts and Sciences, College of Education and Allied Services, Hartford Art School, Hartt School of Music. Degree can be earned exclusively through evening/weekend study in Barney School of Business and Public Administration, Hartford Art School.Basic part-time expenses: $170 per credit tuition plus $25 per semester fees.

University of New Haven
West Haven 06516

Independent institution; city setting. Awards A, B, M. Total enrollment: 7,201. Undergraduate enrollment: 4,728; 57% part-time, 32% women. Total faculty: 478. Library holdings: 145,527 bound volumes, 7,687 titles on microform, 808 periodical subscriptions, 8,956 records/tapes.

Undergraduate Courses offered for part-time students during daytime, evenings, weekends, summer. Complete part-time degree programs offered during daytime, evenings, weekends, summer. Adult/continuing education programs available. Career services available to part-time students: individual and group career counseling, individual job placement, employer recruitment on campus. Part-time tuition: $183 per credit hour.

Graduate Part-time study available in Graduate School.Basic part-time expenses: $165 per credit hour tuition plus $8 per trimester fees. Institutional financial aid available to part-time graduate students in Graduate School.

Waterbury State Technical College
Waterbury 06708

Public institution; city setting. Awards A. Barrier-free campus. Total enrollment: 1,902 (all undergraduates); 62% part-time, 23% women. Total faculty: 97. Library holdings: 13,000 bound volumes.

Undergraduate Courses offered for part-time students during daytime, evenings. Complete part-time degree programs offered during daytime, evenings. Career services available to part-time students: individual and group career counseling, individual job placement, employer recruitment on campus. Part-time tuition: $16 per credit for state residents, $52 per credit for nonresidents. Part-time tuition for evening classes: $31 per credit (for all students).

Wesleyan University
Middletown 06457

Independent institution; small-town setting. Awards B, M, D. Total enrollment: 2,625. Undergraduate enrollment: 2,525; 1% part-time, 48% women, 2% over 25. Total faculty: 269. Library holdings: 1 million bound volumes, 2,700 periodical subscriptions.

Graduate Part-time study available in Graduate Programs, Liberal Studies Program. Degree can be earned exclusively through evening/weekend study in Liberal Studies Program. Basic part-time expenses: $1156 per course tuition. Institutional financial aid available to part-time graduate students in Liberal Studies Program.

Western Connecticut State University
Danbury 06810

Public institution; city setting. Awards A, B, M. Total enrollment: 5,908. Undergraduate enrollment: 4,974; 34% part-time, 59% women, 31% over 25. Total faculty: 220. Library holdings: 128,100 bound volumes, 529 periodical subscriptions, 2,672 records/tapes.

Undergraduate Courses offered for part-time students during daytime, evenings, summer. Complete part-time degree programs offered during daytime, evenings. Adult/continuing education programs available. Career services available to part-time students: individual and group career counseling,

Colleges Offering Part-Time Degree Programs / Connecticut

Western Connecticut State University (continued)
individual job placement, employer recruitment on campus. Part-time tuition: $71 per semester hour for state residents, $71 per semester hour for nonresidents.

Graduate Part-time study available in Division of Graduate Studies. Basic part-time expenses: $86 per credit hour tuition. Institutional financial aid available to part-time graduate students in Division of Graduate Studies.

Yale University
New Haven 06520

Independent institution; city setting. Awards B, M, D. Barrier-free campus. Total enrollment: 10,448. Undergraduate enrollment: 5,106; 0% part-time, 44% women, 1% over 25. Total faculty: 1,741. Library holdings: 7.9 million bound volumes, 1.7 million titles on microform, 52,212 periodical subscriptions, 132,346 records/tapes.

Undergraduate Courses offered for part-time students during daytime, summer. Complete part-time degree programs offered during daytime. Part-time tuition: $880 per course.

Graduate Part-time study available in Graduate School of Arts and Sciences, Divinity School, School of Architecture, School of Nursing. Basic part-time expenses: $1175 per course tuition plus $190 per year fees.

DELAWARE

Delaware State College
Dover 19901

Public institution (undergraduate and graduate). Total enrollment: 2,113. Graduate enrollment: 72 (coed; 94% part-time). Library holdings: 141,469 bound volumes.

Graduate Part-time study available in Graduate Programs. Degree can be earned exclusively through evening/weekend study in Graduate Programs. Basic part-time expenses: $50 per credit hour (minimum) tuition for state residents, $60 per credit hour (minimum) tuition for nonresidents.

Delaware Technical and Community College, Terry Campus
Dover 19901

Public institution; small-town setting. Awards A. Barrier-free campus. Total enrollment: 1,325 (all undergraduates); 59% part-time, 54% women, 45% over 25. Total faculty: 52. Library holdings: 18,339 bound volumes, 2,571 titles on microform, 264 periodical subscriptions, 2,964 records/tapes.

Undergraduate Courses offered for part-time students during daytime, evenings, summer. Complete part-time degree programs offered during daytime, evenings, summer. Adult/continuing education programs available. Career services available to part-time students: individual and group career counseling, individual job placement, employer recruitment on campus. Part-time tuition: $17 per credit hour for state residents, $42.50 per credit hour for nonresidents.

Goldey Beacom College
Wilmington 19808

Independent institution; city setting. Awards A, B. Barrier-free campus. Total enrollment: 1,993 (all undergraduates); 51% part-time, 70% women. Total faculty: 92. Library holdings: 13,000 bound volumes, 11,500 titles on microform, 300 periodical subscriptions.

Undergraduate Courses offered for part-time students during daytime, evenings, weekends, summer. Complete part-time degree programs offered during daytime, evenings, summer. Adult/continuing education programs available. Career services available to part-time students: individual and group career counseling, individual job placement, employer recruitment on campus. Part-time tuition: $105 per credit.

University of Delaware
Newark 19716

Public institution; small-town setting. Awards A, B, M, D. Total enrollment: 15,260. Undergraduate enrollment: 13,241; 1% part-time, 57% women, 5% over 25. Total faculty: 920. Library holdings: 1.8 million bound volumes, 1 million titles on microform, 14,500 periodical subscriptions, 4,000 records/tapes.

Undergraduate Courses offered for part-time students during daytime, evenings, summer. Complete part-time degree programs offered during daytime, evenings, summer. Adult/continuing education programs available. Career services available to part-time students: individual and group career counseling, employer recruitment on campus. Part-time tuition: $71 per credit hour for state residents, $179 per credit hour for nonresidents.

Graduate Part-time study available in College of Agricultural Sciences, College of Arts and Science, College of Business and Economics, College of Education, College of Engineering, College of Human Resources, College of Marine Studies, College of Nursing, College of Urban Affairs and Public Policy, Division of Physical Education, Athletics and Recreation. Basic part-time expenses: $95 per credit hour tuition for state residents, $239 per credit hour tuition for nonresidents.

Wesley College
Dover 19901

Independent-religious institution; small-town setting. Awards A, B. Barrier-free campus. Total enrollment: 1,229 (all undergraduates); 15% part-time, 50% women, 15% over 25. Total faculty: 77. Library holdings: 45,000 bound volumes, 357 periodical subscriptions, 1,671 records/tapes.

Undergraduate Courses offered for part-time students during daytime, evenings, summer. Complete part-time degree programs offered during daytime, evenings, summer. External degree and adult/continuing education programs available. Career services available to part-time students: individual career counseling. Part-time tuition and fees per semester (1 to 11 semester hours) range from $110 to $1565.

Widener University, Delaware Campus
Wilmington 19803

Independent institution; small-town setting. Awards A, B. Total enrollment: 1,180 (all undergraduates); 7% part-time, 60% women. Total faculty: 55. Library holdings: 46,000 bound volumes, 290 titles on microform, 260 periodical subscriptions, 500 records/tapes.

Undergraduate Courses offered for part-time students during daytime, evenings, weekends, summer. Complete part-time degree programs offered during daytime, evenings. Career services available to part-time students: individual and group career counseling, individual job placement, employer recruitment on campus. Part-time tuition per credit ranges from $142 to $155 according to program.

District of Columbia / **Colleges Offering Part-Time Degree Programs**

Wilmington College
New Castle 19720

Independent institution; city setting. Awards A, B, M. Barrier-free campus. Total enrollment: 1,038. Undergraduate enrollment: 890; 70% part-time, 52% women, 65% over 25. Total faculty: 79. Library holdings: 56,500 bound volumes, 1,500 titles on microform, 275 periodical subscriptions, 1,500 records/tapes.

Undergraduate Courses offered for part-time students during daytime, evenings, weekends, summer. Complete part-time degree programs offered during evenings. External degree and adult/continuing education programs available. Career services available to part-time students: individual and group career counseling, individual job placement, employer recruitment on campus. Part-time tuition: $325 per course.

Graduate Part-time study available in Graduate Program in Business.

DISTRICT OF COLUMBIA

American University
Washington 20016

Independent-religious instutition; metropolitan setting. Awards A, B, M, D. Barrier-free campus. Total enrollment: 11,322. Undergraduate enrollment: 4,904; 18% part-time, 56% women, 15% over 25. Total faculty: 1,057. Library holdings: 548,190 bound volumes, 479,259 titles on microform, 4,674 periodical subscriptions, 10,052 records/tapes.

Undergraduate Courses offered for part-time students during daytime, evenings, summer. Complete part-time degree programs offered during evenings, summer. Adult/continuing education programs available. Career services available to part-time students: individual and group career counseling, individual job placement, employer recruitment on campus. Part-time tuition: $254 per semester hour.

Graduate Part-time study available in College of Arts and Sciences, Center for Financial Management, College of Public and International Affairs, Kogod College of Business Administration, Washington College of Law. Degree can be earned exclusively through evening/weekend study in College of Arts and Sciences, Center for Financial Management, College of Public and International Affairs, Kogod College of Business Administration, Washington College of Law.Basic part-time expenses: $267 per semester hour tuition plus $10 per semester fees. Institutional financial aid available to part-time graduate students in Washington College of Law.

Benjamin Franklin University
Washington 20036

Independent institution (undergraduate and graduate). Total enrollment: 325. Graduate enrollment: 25 (coed). Library holdings: 12,000 bound volumes.

Graduate Part-time study available in Graduate Program in Financial Management.Basic part-time expenses: $125 per credit hour tuition plus $25 per semester fees.

Catholic University of America
Washington 20064

Independent-religious instutition; metropolitan setting. Awards B, M, D. Total enrollment: 7,258. Undergraduate enrollment: 2,884; 9% part-time, 52% women. Total faculty: 616. Library holdings: 1 million bound volumes, 26,707 titles on microform, 7,921 periodical subscriptions, 843 records/tapes.

Undergraduate Courses offered for part-time students during daytime, evenings, summer. Complete part-time degree programs offered during daytime, evenings, summer. External degree and adult/continuing education programs available. Career services available to part-time students: individual and group career counseling, employer recruitment on campus. Part-time tuition: $240 per credit.

Graduate Part-time study available in Columbus School of Law, National Catholic School of Social Service, School of Arts and Sciences, School of Education, School of Engineering and Architecture, School of Library and Information Science, School of Music, School of Nursing, School of Philosophy, School of Religious Studies.Basic part-time expenses: $255 per credit hour tuition.

Dominican House of Studies
Washington 20017

Independent-religious institution (graduate only). Total enrollment: 42 (primarily men). Total faculty: 13. Library holdings: 53,826 bound volumes.

Graduate Part-time study available in Graduate and Professional Programs.Basic part-time expenses: $100 per credit tuition plus $80 per semester fees. Institutional financial aid available to part-time graduate students in Graduate and Professional Programs.

Gallaudet College
Washington 20002

Independent institution; metropolitan setting. Awards A, B, M, D (all undergraduate programs except deaf interpreter training open to hearing impaired only). Total enrollment: 1,680. Undergraduate enrollment: 1,200; 6% part-time, 57% women. Total faculty: 280. Library holdings: 168,000 bound volumes, 55,000 titles on microform.

Undergraduate Courses offered for part-time students during daytime. Complete part-time degree programs offered during daytime. Adult/continuing education programs available. Career services available to part-time students: individual and group career counseling, employer recruitment on campus. Part-time tuition: $84.20 per credit hour.

Georgetown University
Washington 20057

Independent-religious instutition; metropolitan setting. Awards B, M, D. Barrier-free campus. Total enrollment: 11,237. Undergraduate enrollment: 5,378; 3% part-time, 51% women. Total faculty: 1,475. Library holdings: 1.5 million bound volumes, 12,500 periodical subscriptions.

Graduate Part-time study available in Graduate School, Law Center.Basic part-time expenses: $284 per credit tuition.

George Washington University
Washington 20052

Independent institution; metropolitan setting. Awards A, B, M, D. Barrier-free campus. Total enrollment: 14,482. Undergraduate enrollment: 5,801; 16% part-time, 49% women, 17% over 25. Total faculty: 1,769. Library holdings: 1.3 million bound volumes, 14,800 periodical subscriptions, 1,300 records/tapes.

Undergraduate Courses offered for part-time students during daytime, evenings, summer. Complete part-time degree programs offered during daytime. Adult/continuing education programs available. Career services available to part-time students:

George Washington University (continued)

individual and group career counseling, individual job placement, employer recruitment on campus. Part-time tuition: $251 per semester hour.

Graduate Part-time study available in Graduate School of Arts and Sciences, National Law Center, School of Education and Human Development, School of Engineering and Applied Science, School of Government and Business Administration, School of Public and International Affairs. Degree can be earned exclusively through evening/weekend study in Graduate School of Arts and Sciences, National Law Center, School of Education and Human Development, School of Engineering and Applied Science, School of Public and International Affairs.Basic part-time expenses: $251 per semester hour tuition plus $7.25 per semester hour fees.

Howard University
Washington 20059

Independent institution; metropolitan setting. Awards B, M, D. Barrier-free campus. Total enrollment: 11,594. Undergraduate enrollment: 8,291; 8% part-time, 56% women. Total faculty: 1,959. Library holdings: 1.3 million bound volumes, 1.4 million titles on microform, 25,078 periodical subscriptions.

Undergraduate Courses offered for part-time students during daytime, evenings, summer. Complete part-time degree programs offered during daytime. Adult/continuing education programs available. Career services available to part-time students: individual and group career counseling, individual job placement, employer recruitment on campus. Part-time tuition: $117 per credit hour.

Graduate Part-time study available in College of Fine Arts, College of Nursing, Graduate School of Arts and Sciences, School of Architecture and Planning, School of Business and Public Administration, School of Communications, School of Divinity, School of Education, School of Engineering, School of Human Ecology, School of Law, School of Social Work. Degree can be earned exclusively through evening/weekend study in School of Business and Public Administration, School of Communications, School of Human Ecology.Basic part-time expenses: $161 per credit tuition plus $190 per semester fees.

Mount Vernon College
Washington 20007

Independent institution; metropolitan setting. Awards A, B. Total enrollment: 489 (all undergraduates); 4% part-time, 100% women, 17% over 25. Total faculty: 48. Library holdings: 30,000 bound volumes, 290 periodical subscriptions, 2,709 records/tapes.

Undergraduate Courses offered for part-time students during daytime, evenings, summer. Complete part-time degree programs offered during daytime, evenings, summer. Adult/continuing education programs available. Part-time tuition: $250 per credit hour.

Southeastern University
Washington 20024

Independent institution; metropolitan setting. Awards A, B, M. Total enrollment: 1,206. Undergraduate enrollment: 838; 80% part-time, 55% women. Total faculty: 150. Library holdings: 11,000 bound volumes, 1,000 periodical subscriptions, 300 records/tapes.

Undergraduate Courses offered for part-time students during daytime, evenings, weekends, summer. Complete part-time degree programs offered during daytime, evenings, weekends, summer. Adult/continuing education programs available. Career services available to part-time students: individual and group career counseling, individual job placement, employer recruitment on campus. Part-time tuition: $125 per credit.

Graduate Part-time study available in Graduate School.Basic part-time expenses: $150 per credit hour tuition plus $35 per trimester fees. Institutional financial aid available to part-time graduate students in Graduate School.

Strayer College
Washington 20005

Proprietary institution; metropolitan setting. Awards A, B. Barrier-free campus. Total enrollment: 1,723 (all undergraduates); 33% part-time, 67% women. Total faculty: 75. Library holdings: 18,500 bound volumes, 320 titles on microform, 133 periodical subscriptions, 15 records/tapes.

Undergraduate Courses offered for part-time students during daytime, evenings, weekends, summer. Complete part-time degree programs offered during daytime, evenings, weekends, summer. External degree and adult/continuing education programs available. Career services available to part-time students: individual and group career counseling, individual job placement, employer recruitment on campus. Part-time tuition: $78 per quarter hour.

Trinity College
Washington 20017

Independent-religious instutition; metropolitan setting. Awards B, M. Total enrollment: 670. Undergraduate enrollment: 550; 11% part-time, 100% women, 9% over 25. Total faculty: 86. Library holdings: 160,000 bound volumes, 605 periodical subscriptions.

Undergraduate Courses offered for part-time students during daytime, evenings, weekends, summer. Complete part-time degree programs offered during daytime, evenings, weekends, summer. Adult/continuing education programs available. Career services available to part-time students: individual and group career counseling, individual job placement, employer recruitment on campus. Part-time tuition: $200 per credit hour.

Graduate Part-time study available in Graduate Programs in Education. Degree can be earned exclusively through evening/weekend study in Graduate Programs in Education.Basic part-time expenses: $195 per hour tuition.

University of the District of Columbia
Washington 20008

Public institution; metropolitan setting. Awards A, B, M. Total enrollment: 13,576. Undergraduate enrollment: 12,472; 72% part-time, 56% women. Total faculty: 905. Library holdings: 389,000 bound volumes, 2,210 periodical subscriptions, 13,331 records/tapes.

Undergraduate Courses offered for part-time students during daytime, evenings, summer. Complete part-time degree programs offered during daytime, evenings, summer. External degree and adult/continuing education programs available. Career services available to part-time students: individual and group career counseling, employer recruitment on campus. Part-time tuition: $19.25 per semester hour for district residents, $96.25 per semester hour for nonresidents.

Graduate Part-time study available in Graduate Studies.Basic part-time expenses: $182 per semester (minimum) tuition plus $17 per semester fees for district residents, $385 per semester (minimum) tuition plus $17 per semester fees for nonresidents.

Wesley Theological Seminary
Washington 20016

Independent-religious institution (graduate only). Total enrollment: 424 (coed; 39% part-time). Total faculty: 36. Library holdings: 106,000 bound volumes.

Graduate Part-time study available in Graduate and Professional Programs. Basic part-time expenses: $135 per semester hour tuition plus $15 per semester fees.

FLORIDA

Baptist Bible Institute
Graceville 32440

Independent-religious instutition; small-town setting. Awards B. Barrier-free campus. Total enrollment: 411 (all undergraduates); 12% part-time, 22% women, 73% over 25. Total faculty: 22. Library holdings: 46,372 bound volumes, 1,879 titles on microform, 330 periodical subscriptions, 3,657 records/tapes.

Undergraduate Courses offered for part-time students during daytime, summer. Complete part-time degree programs offered during daytime. Adult/continuing education programs available. Career services available to part-time students: individual career counseling, individual job placement. Part-time tuition: $30 per semester hour.

Barry University
Miami Shores 33161

Independent-religious instutition; metropolitan setting. Awards B, M, D. Total enrollment: 3,218. Undergraduate enrollment: 2,426; 62% part-time, 60% women, 50% over 25. Total faculty: 205. Library holdings: 120,000 bound volumes, 7,000 titles on microform, 1,200 periodical subscriptions, 7,615 records/tapes.

Undergraduate Courses offered for part-time students during daytime, evenings, weekends, summer. Complete part-time degree programs offered during daytime, evenings. External degree and adult/continuing education programs available. Career services available to part-time students: individual and group career counseling, individual job placement, employer recruitment on campus. Part-time tuition: $165 per credit.

Graduate Part-time study available in Division of Biological and Biomedical Sciences, School of Arts and Sciences, School of Business, School of Computer Science, School of Education, School of Social Work. Degree can be earned exclusively through evening/weekend study in Division of Biological and Biomedical Sciences, School of Arts and Sciences, School of Business, School of Computer Science, School of Education, School of Social Work. Basic part-time expenses: $175 per credit tuition plus $22 per semester (minimum) fees.

Bethune-Cookman College
Daytona Beach 32015

Independent-religious instutition; city setting. Awards B. Total enrollment: 1,724 (all undergraduates); 3% part-time, 58% women, 11% over 25. Total faculty: 122. Library holdings: 112,315 bound volumes, 895 titles on microform, 536 periodical subscriptions, 1,530 records/tapes.

Undergraduate Courses offered for part-time students during daytime, evenings, summer. Complete part-time degree programs offered during daytime, evenings. Adult/continuing education programs available. Career services available to part-time students: individual and group career counseling, individual job placement, employer recruitment on campus. Part-time tuition: $123 per credit hour.

Brevard Community College
Cocoa 32922

Public institution; small-town setting. Awards A. Total enrollment: 11,109 (all undergraduates); 62% part-time, 54% women, 60% over 25. Total faculty: 818. Library holdings: 85,000 bound volumes, 650 periodical subscriptions, 16,000 records/tapes.

Undergraduate Courses offered for part-time students during daytime, evenings, summer. Complete part-time degree programs offered during daytime, evenings, summer. External degree and adult/continuing education programs available. Career services available to part-time students: individual and group career counseling, individual job placement, employer recruitment on campus. Part-time tuition: $19 per credit hour for state residents, $38 per credit hour for nonresidents.

Broward Community College
Fort Lauderdale 33301

Public institution; city setting. Awards A. Barrier-free campus. Total enrollment: 29,074 (all undergraduates); 68% part-time, 60% women, 50% over 25. Total faculty: 705. Library holdings: 200,000 bound volumes, 600 periodical subscriptions.

Undergraduate Courses offered for part-time students during daytime, evenings, weekends, summer. Complete part-time degree programs offered during daytime, evenings, summer. Adult/continuing education programs available. Career services available to part-time students: individual and group career counseling, individual job placement, employer recruitment on campus. Part-time tuition: $20.30 per credit hour for state residents, $43.50 per credit hour for nonresidents.

Central Florida Bible College
Orlando 32806

Independent-religious instutition; metropolitan setting. Awards A, B. Total enrollment: 130 (all undergraduates); 22% part-time, 42% women, 16% over 25. Total faculty: 12. Library holdings: 20,000 bound volumes, 493 titles on microform, 90 periodical subscriptions, 580 records/tapes.

Undergraduate Courses offered for part-time students during daytime, evenings. Complete part-time degree programs offered during daytime, evenings. Adult/continuing education programs available. Career services available to part-time students: individual career counseling. Part-time tuition: $40 per quarter hour.

Central Florida Community College
Ocala 32670

Public institution; small-town setting. Awards A. Total enrollment: 2,929 (all undergraduates); 36% part-time, 55% women. Total faculty: 110. Library holdings: 48,263 bound volumes, 344 periodical subscriptions, 4,456 records/tapes.

Undergraduate Courses offered for part-time students during daytime, evenings, summer. Complete part-time degree programs offered during daytime, evenings, summer. Adult/continuing education programs available. Career services available to part-time students: individual and group career counseling, individual job placement, employer recruitment on campus. Part-time tuition: $19 per credit hour for state residents, $41 per credit hour for nonresidents.

Colleges Offering Part-Time Degree Programs / *Florida*

Chipola Junior College
Marianna 32446

Public institution; rural setting. Awards A. Barrier-free campus. Total enrollment: 1,408 (all undergraduates); 20% part-time, 25% women. Total faculty: 71. Library holdings: 47,558 bound volumes, 155 periodical subscriptions, 2,169 records/tapes.

Undergraduate Courses offered for part-time students during daytime, evenings, summer. Complete part-time degree programs offered during daytime, evenings, summer. Adult/continuing education programs available. Career services available to part-time students: individual and group career counseling, individual job placement. Part-time tuition: $18 per semester hour for state residents, $39 per semester hour for nonresidents.

Clearwater Christian College
Clearwater 33519

Independent-religious instutition; city setting. Awards A, B. Barrier-free campus. Total enrollment: 217 (all undergraduates); 20% part-time, 52% women, 8% over 25. Total faculty: 26. Library holdings: 35,800 bound volumes, 35 titles on microform, 125 periodical subscriptions, 200 records/tapes.

Undergraduate Courses offered for part-time students during daytime, evenings, summer. Complete part-time degree programs offered during daytime, evenings, summer. Adult/continuing education programs available. Career services available to part-time students: individual and group career counseling, individual job placement, employer recruitment on campus. Part-time tuition: $67.50 per credit hour.

College of Boca Raton
Boca Raton 33431

Independent institution; city setting. Awards A, B. Barrier-free campus. Total enrollment: 700 (all undergraduates); 5% part-time, 55% women, 3% over 25. Total faculty: 57. Library holdings: 30,000 bound volumes, 201 periodical subscriptions, 2,000 records/tapes.

Undergraduate Courses offered for part-time students during daytime, evenings, summer. Complete part-time degree programs offered during daytime. Adult/continuing education programs available. Career services available to part-time students: individual and group career counseling, individual job placement, employer recruitment on campus. Part-time tuition: $100 per credit hour.

Daytona Beach Community College
Daytona Beach 32015

Public institution; city setting. Awards A. Total enrollment: 8,260 (all undergraduates); 57% part-time, 60% women. Total faculty: 549. Library holdings: 63,848 bound volumes, 6,335 titles on microform, 470 periodical subscriptions, 2,014 records/tapes.

Undergraduate Courses offered for part-time students during daytime, evenings, weekends, summer. Complete part-time degree programs offered during daytime, evenings, weekends, summer. Adult/continuing education programs available. Career services available to part-time students: individual and group career counseling, individual job placement, employer recruitment on campus. Part-time tuition: $19.95 per semester hour for state residents, $43.05 per semester hour for nonresidents.

Eckerd College
St Petersburg 33733

Independent-religious instutition; metropolitan setting. Awards B. Barrier-free campus. Total enrollment: 1,058 (all undergraduates); 3% part-time, 51% women, 1% over 25. Total faculty: 91. Library holdings: 125,000 bound volumes, 20,000 titles on microform, 1,300 periodical subscriptions, 38,000 records/tapes.

Undergraduate Courses offered for part-time students during daytime, evenings, weekends, summer. Complete part-time degree programs offered during daytime, evenings, weekends, summer. External degree and adult/continuing education programs available. Career services available to part-time students: individual and group career counseling, individual job placement, employer recruitment on campus. Part-time tuition: $715 per credit.

Edison Community College
Fort Myers 33907

Public institution; small-town setting. Awards A. Barrier-free campus. Total enrollment: 5,947 (all undergraduates); 70% part-time, 63% women. Total faculty: 218. Library holdings: 96,000 bound volumes, 785 periodical subscriptions, 6,311 records/tapes.

Undergraduate Courses offered for part-time students during daytime, evenings, weekends, summer. Complete part-time degree programs offered during daytime, evenings, summer. Adult/continuing education programs available. Career services available to part-time students: individual and group career counseling, individual job placement, employer recruitment on campus. Part-time tuition: $20 per credit for state residents, $42 per credit for nonresidents.

Edward Waters College
Jacksonville 32209

Independent-religious instutition; metropolitan setting. Awards B. Total enrollment: 877 (all undergraduates); 10% part-time, 62% women. Total faculty: 43. Library holdings: 120,000 bound volumes, 7,300 periodical subscriptions, 175 records/tapes.

Undergraduate Courses offered for part-time students during daytime, evenings, weekends, summer. Complete part-time degree programs offered during daytime, evenings, weekends, summer. Adult/continuing education programs available. Part-time tuition: $100 per semester hour.

Embry-Riddle Aeronautical University
Daytona Beach 32014

Independent institution; city setting. Awards A, B, M. Total enrollment: 4,994. Undergraduate enrollment: 4,911; 6% part-time, 7% women. Total faculty: 270. Library holdings: 32,000 bound volumes, 28,500 titles on microform, 1,134 periodical subscriptions, 1,000 records/tapes.

Undergraduate Courses offered for part-time students during daytime, evenings, summer. Complete part-time degree programs offered during daytime, evenings, summer. External degree and adult/continuing education programs available. Career services available to part-time students: individual career counseling, individual job placement, employer recruitment on campus. Part-time tuition: $115 per credit hour.

Graduate Part-time study available in Center for Graduate Studies. Degree can be earned exclusively through evening/weekend study in Center for Graduate Studies. Basic part-time expenses: $140 per credit hour tuition. Institutional financial aid available to part-time graduate students in Center for Graduate Studies.

Florida / **Colleges Offering Part-Time Degree Programs**

Embry-Riddle Aeronautical University, International Campus
Bunnell 32010

Independent institution. Awards A, B, M. Total enrollment: 4,404. Undergraduate enrollment: 3,718; 80% part-time, 6% women. Total faculty: 1,104.

Undergraduate Courses offered for part-time students during daytime, evenings, weekends, summer. Complete part-time degree programs offered during daytime, evenings, weekends, summer. External degree programs available. Career services available to part-time students: individual and group career counseling, individual job placement, employer recruitment on campus. Part-time tuition: $70 per credit hour.

Graduate Part-time study available in Graduate Resident Centers. Degree can be earned exclusively through evening/weekend study in Graduate Resident Centers. Basic part-time expenses: $140 per credit hour tuition. Institutional financial aid available to part-time graduate students in Graduate Resident Centers.

Florida Agricultural and Mechanical University
Tallahassee 32307

Public institution; city setting. Awards A, B, M. Total enrollment: 5,175. Undergraduate enrollment: 5,014; 2% part-time, 54% women, 8% over 25. Total faculty: 327. Library holdings: 376,165 bound volumes, 37,322 titles on microform, 2,255 periodical subscriptions, 62,610 records/tapes.

Undergraduate Courses offered for part-time students during daytime, evenings, weekends, summer. Complete part-time degree programs offered during daytime, evenings, weekends, summer. Adult/continuing education programs available. Career services available to part-time students: individual and group career counseling, individual job placement, employer recruitment on campus. Part-time tuition per semester hour ranges from $25 to $28 for state residents, $66 to $91 for nonresidents, according to class level.

Graduate Part-time study available in Graduate Studies. Basic part-time expenses: $46.35 per credit hour tuition for state residents, $136.35 per credit hour tuition for nonresidents.

Florida Atlantic University
Boca Raton 33431

Public institution; city setting. Awards B, M, D (students accepted for freshman admission beginning in fall, 1984). Barrier-free campus. Total enrollment: 7,287. Undergraduate enrollment: 6,086; 52% part-time, 51% women. Total faculty: 508. Library holdings: 410,000 bound volumes, 640,000 titles on microform, 5,000 periodical subscriptions, 14,000 records/tapes.

Undergraduate Courses offered for part-time students during daytime, evenings, summer. Complete part-time degree programs offered during daytime, evenings, summer. Adult/continuing education programs available. Career services available to part-time students: individual and group career counseling, individual job placement, employer recruitment on campus. Part-time tuition per semester hour ranges from $28.84 to $32.77 for state residents, $79.84 to $111.77 for nonresidents, according to class level.

Graduate Part-time study available in College of Business and Public Administration, College of Education, College of Engineering, College of Humanities, College of Science, College of Social Science. Basic part-time expenses: $47.42 per credit tuition for state residents, $137.42 per credit tuition for nonresidents. Institutional financial aid available to part-time graduate students in College of Business and Public Administration.

Florida Institute of Technology
Melbourne 32901

Independent institution; small-town setting. Awards A, B, M, D. Barrier-free campus. Total enrollment: 7,018. Undergraduate enrollment: 3,938; 12% part-time, 30% women, 10% over 25. Total faculty: 392. Library holdings: 133,000 bound volumes, 24,245 titles on microform, 1,000 periodical subscriptions, 260 records/tapes.

Undergraduate Courses offered for part-time students during daytime, evenings, summer. Complete part-time degree programs offered during daytime, evenings, summer. Adult/continuing education programs available. Career services available to part-time students: individual career counseling, individual job placement, employer recruitment on campus. Part-time tuition: $99 per credit.

Graduate Part-time study available in Graduate School. Degree can be earned exclusively through evening/weekend study in Graduate School. Basic part-time expenses: $126 per credit tuition.

Florida Institute of Technology, School of Applied Technology
Jensen Beach 33457

Independent institution; small-town setting. Awards A, B, M. Total enrollment: 971. Undergraduate enrollment: 900; 14% part-time, 23% women, 15% over 25. Total faculty: 80. Library holdings: 20,000 bound volumes, 200 periodical subscriptions.

Undergraduate Courses offered for part-time students during daytime, evenings, summer. Complete part-time degree programs offered during daytime. Adult/continuing education programs available. Career services available to part-time students: individual job placement, employer recruitment on campus. Part-time tuition: $82 per quarter hour.

Florida International University
Miami 33199

Public institution; metropolitan setting. Awards B, M, D. Barrier-free campus. Total enrollment: 10,732. Undergraduate enrollment: 9,541; 53% part-time, 52% women, 41% over 25. Total faculty: 704. Library holdings: 588,242 bound volumes, 1.5 million titles on microform, 4,848 periodical subscriptions, 10,745 records/tapes.

Undergraduate Courses offered for part-time students during daytime, evenings, weekends, summer. Complete part-time degree programs offered during daytime, evenings, summer. Adult/continuing education programs available. Career services available to part-time students: individual career counseling, individual job placement, employer recruitment on campus. Part-time tuition: $29 per semester hour for state residents, $91 per semester hour for nonresidents.

Graduate Part-time study available in College of Arts and Sciences, College of Business Administration, College of Engineering and Applied Sciences, School of Education, School of Hospitality Management, School of Public Affairs and Services. Degree can be earned exclusively through evening/weekend study in College of Arts and Sciences, College of Business Administration, College of Engineering and Applied Sciences, School of Education, School of Hospitality Management, School of Public Affairs and Services. Basic part-time expenses: $45.63 per semester hour tuition plus $17 per semester fees for state residents, $135.63 per semester hour tuition plus $17 per semester fees for nonresidents.

Colleges Offering Part-Time Degree Programs / *Florida*

Florida Keys Community College
Key West 33040

Public institution; small-town setting. Awards A. Barrier-free campus. Total enrollment: 1,568 (all undergraduates); 75% part-time, 58% women, 81% over 25. Total faculty: 76. Library holdings: 23,000 bound volumes, 11,025 titles on microform, 200 periodical subscriptions, 300 records/tapes.

Undergraduate Courses offered for part-time students during daytime, evenings, weekends, summer. Complete part-time degree programs offered during daytime, evenings, summer. Adult/continuing education programs available. Career services available to part-time students: individual and group career counseling, individual job placement, employer recruitment on campus. Part-time tuition: $19 per credit for state residents, $41 per credit for nonresidents.

Florida Memorial College
Miami 33054

Independent-religious instutition; metropolitan setting. Awards B. Barrier-free campus. Total enrollment: 1,750 (all undergraduates); 19% part-time, 52% women. Total faculty: 94. Library holdings: 74,393 bound volumes, 405 periodical subscriptions.

Undergraduate Courses offered for part-time students during daytime, evenings, weekends, summer. Complete part-time degree programs offered during daytime, evenings, weekends, summer. External degree programs available. Career services available to part-time students: individual and group career counseling, individual job placement, employer recruitment on campus. Part-time tuition: $96 per credit.

Florida Southern College
Lakeland 33802

Independent-religious instutition; small-town setting. Awards B, M. Total enrollment: 1,960. Undergraduate enrollment: 1,859; 6% part-time, 52% women. Total faculty: 135. Library holdings: 180,000 bound volumes, 120,000 titles on microform, 800 periodical subscriptions.

Undergraduate Courses offered for part-time students during daytime, evenings. Complete part-time degree programs offered during daytime, evenings. Adult/continuing education programs available. Career services available to part-time students: individual and group career counseling, individual job placement, employer recruitment on campus. Part-time tuition: $110 per semester hour.

Fort Lauderdale College
Fort Lauderdale 33301

Proprietary institution; city setting. Awards A, B. Barrier-free campus. Total enrollment: 720 (all undergraduates); 6% part-time, 19% women. Total faculty: 40. Library holdings: 13,692 bound volumes, 48 periodical subscriptions, 176 records/tapes.

Undergraduate Courses offered for part-time students during daytime, evenings, summer. Complete part-time degree programs offered during daytime, evenings, summer. Adult/continuing education programs available. Career services available to part-time students: individual career counseling, individual job placement, employer recruitment on campus. Part-time tuition: $59 per quarter hour.

Gulf Coast Community College
Panama City 32401

Public institution; small-town setting. Awards A. Barrier-free campus. Total enrollment: 4,000 (all undergraduates); 55% part-time, 52% women, 40% over 25. Total faculty: 140. Library holdings: 80,000 bound volumes, 50,000 titles on microform, 600 periodical subscriptions, 5,000 records/tapes.

Undergraduate Courses offered for part-time students during daytime, evenings, summer. Complete part-time degree programs offered during daytime, evenings, summer. Adult/continuing education programs available. Career services available to part-time students: individual career counseling, individual job placement, employer recruitment on campus. Part-time tuition: $18 per credit hour for state residents, $36 per credit hour for nonresidents.

Hillsborough Community College
Tampa 33622

Public institution; metropolitan setting. Awards A. Barrier-free campus. Total enrollment: 13,159 (all undergraduates); 69% part-time, 59% women, 48% over 25. Total faculty: 735. Library holdings: 75,796 bound volumes, 648 titles on microform, 648 periodical subscriptions, 21,085 records/tapes.

Undergraduate Courses offered for part-time students during daytime, evenings, weekends, summer. Complete part-time degree programs offered during daytime, evenings, weekends, summer. Adult/continuing education programs available. Career services available to part-time students: individual and group career counseling, individual job placement, employer recruitment on campus. Part-time tuition: $20 per credit hour for state residents, $44 per credit hour for nonresidents.

Indian River Community College
Fort Pierce 33450

Public institution; small-town setting. Awards A. Total enrollment: 6,200 (all undergraduates); 60% part-time, 60% women, 15% over 25. Total faculty: 200.

Undergraduate Courses offered for part-time students during daytime, evenings, summer. Complete part-time degree programs offered during daytime, evenings, summer. Adult/continuing education programs available. Career services available to part-time students: individual and group career counseling, individual job placement, employer recruitment on campus. Part-time tuition: $19 per semester hour for state residents, $38 per semester hour for nonresidents.

Jacksonville University
Jacksonville 32211

Independent institution; metropolitan setting. Awards B, M. Total enrollment: 2,270. Undergraduate enrollment: 2,050; 11% part-time, 44% women. Total faculty: 181. Library holdings: 275,170 bound volumes, 12,290 titles on microform, 664 periodical subscriptions, 7,073 records/tapes.

Undergraduate Courses offered for part-time students during daytime, evenings, summer. Complete part-time degree programs offered during daytime, evenings, summer. Adult/continuing education programs available. Career services available to part-time students: individual career counseling, individual job placement, employer recruitment on campus. Part-time tuition: $150 per credit hour.

Graduate Part-time study available in College of Business Administration, Division of Education. Basic part-time expenses: $150 per credit hour tuition plus $90 per semester fees.

Florida / **Colleges Offering Part-Time Degree Programs**

Jones College
Jacksonville 32211

Independent institution; metropolitan setting. Awards A, B. Total enrollment: 1,719 (all undergraduates); 5% part-time, 60% women, 65% over 25. Total faculty: 61. Library holdings: 17,000 bound volumes, 107 periodical subscriptions, 4,500 records/tapes.

Undergraduate Courses offered for part-time students during daytime, evenings, summer. Complete part-time degree programs offered during daytime, evenings. Adult/continuing education programs available. Career services available to part-time students: individual career counseling, employer recruitment on campus. Part-time tuition: $46 per credit.

Lake City Community College
Lake City 32055

Public institution; rural setting. Awards A. Total enrollment: 2,035 (all undergraduates); 40% part-time, 50% women, 37% over 25. Total faculty: 232. Library holdings: 23,453 bound volumes, 275 periodical subscriptions, 1,184 records/tapes.

Undergraduate Courses offered for part-time students during daytime, evenings, summer. Complete part-time degree programs offered during daytime, evenings, summer. Adult/continuing education programs available. Career services available to part-time students: individual career counseling, employer recruitment on campus. Part-time tuition: $18 per semester hour for state residents, $37 per semester hour for nonresidents.

Lake-Sumter Community College
Leesburg 32788

Public institution; small-town setting. Awards A. Barrier-free campus. Total enrollment: 1,835 (all undergraduates); 65% part-time, 64% women. Total faculty: 114. Library holdings: 57,000 bound volumes, 225 titles on microform, 350 periodical subscriptions, 3,750 records/tapes.

Undergraduate Courses offered for part-time students during daytime, evenings, summer. Complete part-time degree programs offered during daytime, evenings, summer. Adult/continuing education programs available. Career services available to part-time students: individual and group career counseling, individual job placement, employer recruitment on campus. Part-time tuition: $19 per semester hour for state residents, $38 per semester hour for nonresidents.

Manatee Junior College
Bradenton 33507

Public institution; small-town setting. Awards A. Barrier-free campus. Total enrollment: 6,728 (all undergraduates); 62% part-time, 59% women. Total faculty: 245. Library holdings: 59,384 bound volumes, 425 periodical subscriptions, 5,736 records/tapes.

Undergraduate Courses offered for part-time students during daytime, evenings, summer. Complete part-time degree programs offered during daytime, evenings, summer. Career services available to part-time students: individual and group career counseling, individual job placement, employer recruitment on campus. Part-time tuition: $19.50 per credit hour for state residents, $41.50 per credit hour for nonresidents.

Miami Christian College
Miami 33167

Independent institution; metropolitan setting. Awards A, B. Total enrollment: 322 (all undergraduates); 18% part-time, 47% women. Total faculty: 18. Library holdings: 31,493 bound volumes, 109 titles on microform, 159 periodical subscriptions, 428 records/tapes.

Undergraduate Courses offered for part-time students during daytime, evenings, summer. Complete part-time degree programs offered during daytime, evenings. Adult/continuing education programs available. Career services available to part-time students: individual career counseling, employer recruitment on campus. Part-time tuition: $125 per semester hour.

Miami-Dade Community College
Miami 33176

Public institution; metropolitan setting. Awards A. Barrier-free campus. Total enrollment: 41,980 (all undergraduates); 64% part-time, 57% women, 32% over 25. Total faculty: 1,956. Library holdings: 331,092 bound volumes, 416,972 titles on microform, 2,861 periodical subscriptions, 16,032 records/tapes.

Undergraduate Courses offered for part-time students during daytime, evenings, weekends, summer. Complete part-time degree programs offered during daytime, evenings, weekends, summer. Adult/continuing education programs available. Career services available to part-time students: individual and group career counseling, individual job placement, employer recruitment on campus. Part-time tuition: $20 per credit hour for state residents, $43 per credit hour for nonresidents.

Morris Junior College of Business
Melbourne 32935

Proprietary institution; small-town setting. Awards A. Barrier-free campus. Total enrollment: 193 (all undergraduates); 17% part-time, 69% women, 45% over 25. Total faculty: 19. Library holdings: 1,549 bound volumes.

Undergraduate Courses offered for part-time students during daytime, evenings. Complete part-time degree programs offered during daytime, evenings. Career services available to part-time students: individual career counseling, individual job placement. Part-time tuition: $44 per quarter hour.

North Florida Junior College
Madison 32340

Public institution; small-town setting. Awards A. Total enrollment: 844 (all undergraduates); 64% part-time, 65% women. Total faculty: 37. Library holdings: 35,000 bound volumes, 20 periodical subscriptions, 7,000 records/tapes.

Undergraduate Courses offered for part-time students during daytime, evenings, weekends, summer. Complete part-time degree programs offered during daytime, evenings, weekends, summer. Adult/continuing education programs available. Career services available to part-time students: individual career counseling, individual job placement, employer recruitment on campus. Part-time tuition: $16 per credit for state residents, $32 per credit for nonresidents.

Nova University
Fort Lauderdale 33314

Independent institution; city setting. Awards B, M, D. Barrier-free campus. Total enrollment: 6,159. Undergraduate enroll-

Colleges Offering Part-Time Degree Programs / Florida

Nova University (continued)
ment: 1,198; 33% part-time, 55% women, 60% over 25. Total faculty: 403. Library holdings: 112,000 bound volumes, 25,060 titles on microform, 2,673 periodical subscriptions, 1,000 records/tapes.

Undergraduate Courses offered for part-time students during daytime, evenings, weekends, summer. Complete part-time degree programs offered during daytime, evenings, weekends, summer. External degree and adult/continuing education programs available. Career services available to part-time students: individual career counseling, individual job placement, employer recruitment on campus. Part-time tuition: $360 per course.

Graduate Part-time study available in Behavioral Sciences Center, Center for Higher Education, Center for School Leadership Development, Center for Science and Engineering, Center for the Advancement of Education, Center for the Study of Administration, Oceanographic Center. Degree can be earned exclusively through evening/weekend study in Behavioral Sciences Center, Center for Higher Education, Center for School Leadership Development, Center for Science and Engineering, Center for the Advancement of Education, Center for the Study of Administration, Oceanographic Center. Basic part-time expenses: $75 per year fees. Institutional financial aid available to part-time graduate students in Behavioral Sciences Center, Center for the Study of Administration.

Okaloosa-Walton Junior College
Niceville 32578

Public institution; small-town setting. Awards A. Barrier-free campus. Total enrollment: 3,825 (all undergraduates); 61% part-time, 50% women. Total faculty: 170. Library holdings: 68,000 bound volumes, 500 periodical subscriptions, 3,400 records/tapes.

Undergraduate Courses offered for part-time students during daytime, evenings, weekends, summer. Complete part-time degree programs offered during daytime, evenings, summer. Adult/continuing education programs available. Career services available to part-time students: individual and group career counseling, individual job placement. Part-time tuition: $18 per credit hour for state residents, $38 per credit hour for nonresidents.

Orlando College
Orlando 32810

Independent institution; metropolitan setting. Awards A, B. Barrier-free campus. Total enrollment: 906 (all undergraduates); 45% part-time, 50% women, 75% over 25. Total faculty: 38. Library holdings: 8,000 bound volumes, 51 periodical subscriptions, 97 records/tapes.

Undergraduate Courses offered for part-time students during daytime, evenings, weekends, summer. Complete part-time degree programs offered during daytime, evenings, summer. Adult/continuing education programs available. Career services available to part-time students: individual and group career counseling, individual job placement, employer recruitment on campus. Part-time tuition: $60 per quarter hour.

Palm Beach Atlantic College
West Palm Beach 33401

Independent-religious instutition; city setting. Awards B. Total enrollment: 711 (all undergraduates); 13% part-time, 53% women. Total faculty: 62. Library holdings: 53,648 bound volumes, 1,841 titles on microform, 331 periodical subscriptions.

Undergraduate Courses offered for part-time students during daytime, evenings, summer. Complete part-time degree programs offered during daytime, evenings. Adult/continuing education programs available. Part-time tuition: $115 per credit hour.

Palm Beach Junior College
Lake Worth 33461

Public institution; small-town setting. Awards A. Barrier-free campus. Total enrollment: 11,600 (all undergraduates); 67% part-time, 59% women. Total faculty: 467. Library holdings: 96,756 bound volumes, 680 periodical subscriptions, 4,349 records/tapes.

Undergraduate Courses offered for part-time students during daytime, evenings, summer. Complete part-time degree programs offered during daytime, evenings, summer. Adult/continuing education programs available. Career services available to part-time students: individual career counseling, employer recruitment on campus. Part-time tuition: $19.95 per semester hour for state residents, $39.90 per semester hour for nonresidents.

Pasco-Hernando Community College
Dade City 33525

Public institution; small-town setting. Awards A. Barrier-free campus. Total enrollment: 3,027 (all undergraduates); 66% part-time, 57% women. Total faculty: 247. Library holdings: 32,500 bound volumes, 20 periodical subscriptions, 900 records/tapes.

Undergraduate Courses offered for part-time students during daytime, evenings, summer. Complete part-time degree programs offered during daytime, evenings, summer. Adult/continuing education programs available. Career services available to part-time students: individual career counseling. Part-time tuition: $19 per semester hour for state residents, $41 per semester hour for nonresidents.

Pensacola Junior College
Pensacola 32504

Public institution; city setting. Awards A. Barrier-free campus. Total enrollment: 8,363 (all undergraduates); 67% part-time, 54% women. Total faculty: 600. Library holdings: 121,000 bound volumes, 1,200 periodical subscriptions, 7,500 records/tapes.

Undergraduate Courses offered for part-time students during daytime, evenings, summer. Complete part-time degree programs offered during daytime, evenings, summer. Adult/continuing education programs available. Career services available to part-time students: individual and group career counseling, individual job placement, employer recruitment on campus. Part-time tuition: $22 per hour for state residents, $44 per hour for nonresidents.

Polk Community College
Winter Haven 33880

Public institution; city setting. Awards A. Barrier-free campus. Total enrollment: 5,200 (all undergraduates); 65% part-time, 60% women, 50% over 25. Total faculty: 250. Library holdings: 77,263 bound volumes, 310 periodical subscriptions, 1,150 records/tapes.

Undergraduate Courses offered for part-time students during daytime, evenings, summer. Complete part-time degree programs offered during daytime, evenings, summer. Adult/continuing education programs available. Career services available to part-time students: individual career counseling, individual

Florida / **Colleges Offering Part-Time Degree Programs**

job placement, employer recruitment on campus. Part-time tuition: $20 per credit hour for state residents, $42 per credit hour for nonresidents.

Prospect Hall College
Hollywood 33020

Proprietary institution; city setting. Awards A. Barrier-free campus. Total enrollment: 387 (all undergraduates); 9% part-time, 50% women. Total faculty: 15.

Undergraduate Courses offered for part-time students during daytime, evenings. Complete part-time degree programs offered during daytime, evenings. Adult/continuing education programs available. Career services available to part-time students: individual and group career counseling, individual job placement, employer recruitment on campus. Part-time tuition: $325 per course.

Rollins College
Winter Park 32789

Independent institution; small-town setting. Awards B, M. Barrier-free campus. Total enrollment: 2,241. Undergraduate enrollment: 1,625; 0% part-time, 60% women. Total faculty: 134. Library holdings: 203,330 bound volumes, 1,000 periodical subscriptions.

Graduate Part-time study available in Graduate Programs in Education and Human Development, Roy E. Crummer Graduate School of Business. Degree can be earned exclusively through evening/weekend study in Graduate Programs in Education and Human Development. Basic part-time expenses: $250 per course tuition.

St Johns River Community College
Palatka 32077

Public institution; small-town setting. Awards A. Barrier-free campus. Total enrollment: 1,660 (all undergraduates); 64% part-time, 62% women, 49% over 25. Total faculty: 96. Library holdings: 46,000 bound volumes, 206 periodical subscriptions, 2,200 records/tapes.

Undergraduate Courses offered for part-time students during daytime, evenings, summer. Complete part-time degree programs offered during daytime, evenings. Adult/continuing education programs available. Career services available to part-time students: individual and group career counseling, individual job placement. Part-time tuition: $18 per credit for state residents, $38 per credit for nonresidents.

Saint Leo College
Saint Leo 33574

Independent-religious instutition; rural setting. Awards A, B. Total enrollment: 1,108 (all undergraduates); 3% part-time, 47% women. Total faculty: 91. Library holdings: 74,000 bound volumes, 15,600 titles on microform, 600 periodical subscriptions.

Undergraduate Courses offered for part-time students during daytime, evenings, weekends, summer. Complete part-time degree programs offered during daytime, evenings, weekends, summer. Adult/continuing education programs available. Career services available to part-time students: individual and group career counseling, individual job placement, employer recruitment on campus. Part-time tuition per semester (1 to 11 credit hours) ranges from $150 to $1950.

St Petersburg Junior College
St Petersburg 33733

Public institution; metropolitan setting. Awards A. Barrier-free campus. Total enrollment: 16,358 (all undergraduates); 54% part-time, 57% women, 60% over 25. Total faculty: 447. Library holdings: 189,549 bound volumes, 861 periodical subscriptions, 12,842 records/tapes.

Undergraduate Courses offered for part-time students during daytime, evenings, summer. Complete part-time degree programs offered during daytime, evenings, summer. Adult/continuing education programs available. Career services available to part-time students: individual and group career counseling. Part-time tuition: $21 per credit hour for state residents, $43 per credit hour for nonresidents.

St Thomas of Villanova University
Miami 33054

Independent-religious instutition; metropolitan setting. Awards A, B, M, D. Total enrollment: 3,401. Undergraduate enrollment: 2,896; 40% part-time, 51% women. Total faculty: 250. Library holdings: 108,000 bound volumes, 50 titles on microform, 650 periodical subscriptions, 2,000 records/tapes.

Undergraduate Courses offered for part-time students during daytime, evenings, weekends, summer. Complete part-time degree programs offered during daytime, evenings, weekends, summer. External degree and adult/continuing education programs available. Career services available to part-time students: individual and group career counseling, individual job placement, employer recruitment on campus. Part-time tuition: $140 per credit.

Santa Fe Community College
Gainesville 32601

Public institution; city setting. Awards A. Barrier-free campus. Total enrollment: 7,499 (all undergraduates); 36% part-time, 56% women. Total faculty: 404. Library holdings: 61,269 bound volumes, 2,450 titles on microform, 442 periodical subscriptions, 1,855 records/tapes.

Undergraduate Courses offered for part-time students during daytime, evenings, summer. Complete part-time degree programs offered during daytime, evenings, summer. Adult/continuing education programs available. Career services available to part-time students: individual and group career counseling, individual job placement, employer recruitment on campus. Part-time tuition: $20 per semester hour for state residents, $40 per semester hour for nonresidents.

Seminole Community College
Sanford 32771

Public institution; small-town setting. Awards A. Barrier-free campus. Total enrollment: 5,152 (all undergraduates); 64% part-time, 55% women, 42% over 25. Total faculty: 345. Library holdings: 70,694 bound volumes, 382 titles on microform, 870 periodical subscriptions, 6,998 records/tapes.

Undergraduate Courses offered for part-time students during daytime, evenings, summer. Complete part-time degree programs offered during daytime, evenings, summer. Adult/continuing education programs available. Career services available to part-time students: individual and group career counseling, individual job placement. Part-time tuition: $19 per credit hour for state residents, $40 per credit hour for nonresidents.

Colleges Offering Part-Time Degree Programs / *Florida*

Spurgeon Baptist Bible College
Mulberry 33860

Independent-religious instutition; rural setting. Awards B. Barrier-free campus. Total enrollment: 52 (all undergraduates); 10% part-time, 27% women. Total faculty: 12.

Undergraduate Courses offered for part-time students during daytime, evenings. Complete part-time degree programs offered during daytime. Adult/continuing education programs available. Part-time tuition: $42 per quarter hour.

Stetson University
DeLand 32720

Independent-religious instutition; small-town setting. Awards B, M. Total enrollment: 2,900. Undergraduate enrollment: 1,950; 5% part-time, 45% women, 2% over 25. Total faculty: 138. Library holdings: 228,811 bound volumes, 3,600 titles on microform, 950 periodical subscriptions, 926 records/tapes.

Undergraduate Courses offered for part-time students during daytime, evenings, summer. Complete part-time degree programs offered during daytime, evenings, summer. Adult/continuing education programs available. Career services available to part-time students: individual career counseling, individual job placement, employer recruitment on campus. Part-time tuition: $165 per hour.

Graduate Part-time study available in College of Liberal Arts, School of Business Administration.Basic part-time expenses: $110 per credit hour tuition. Institutional financial aid available to part-time graduate students in College of Liberal Arts, School of Business Administration.

Tallahassee Community College
Tallahassee 32304

Public institution; city setting. Awards A. Barrier-free campus. Total enrollment: 5,061 (all undergraduates); 57% part-time, 56% women, 33% over 25. Total faculty: 196. Library holdings: 68,952 bound volumes, 662 titles on microform, 627 periodical subscriptions, 5,781 records/tapes.

Undergraduate Courses offered for part-time students during daytime, evenings. Complete part-time degree programs offered during daytime, evenings. Adult/continuing education programs available. Career services available to part-time students: individual and group career counseling. Part-time tuition: $18 per semester hour for state residents, $18 per semester hour for nonresidents.

Tampa College
Tampa 33614

Independent institution; metropolitan setting. Awards A, B. Barrier-free campus. Total enrollment: 1,413 (all undergraduates); 5% part-time, 52% women. Total faculty: 65. Library holdings: 10,500 bound volumes, 75 periodical subscriptions, 500 records/tapes.

Undergraduate Courses offered for part-time students during daytime, evenings, weekends, summer. Complete part-time degree programs offered during daytime, evenings, weekends, summer. Adult/continuing education programs available. Career services available to part-time students: individual career counseling, individual job placement, employer recruitment on campus. Part-time tuition: $55 per credit.

University of Central Florida
Orlando 32816

Public institution; metropolitan setting. Awards A, B, M, D. Barrier-free campus. Total enrollment: 15,648. Undergraduate enrollment: 12,308; 35% part-time, 50% women, 27% over 25. Total faculty: 658. Library holdings: 387,451 bound volumes, 19,323 titles on microform, 3,500 periodical subscriptions, 6,716 records/tapes.

Undergraduate Courses offered for part-time students during daytime, evenings, summer. Complete part-time degree programs offered during daytime, evenings, summer. Adult/continuing education programs available. Career services available to part-time students: individual and group career counseling, individual job placement, employer recruitment on campus. Part-time tuition: $30.89 per semester hour for state residents, $109.89 per semester hour for nonresidents.

Graduate Part-time study available in College of Arts and Sciences, College of Business Administration, College of Education, College of Engineering, College of Health. Degree can be earned exclusively through evening/weekend study in College of Arts and Sciences, College of Business Administration, College of Education, College of Engineering, College of Health.Basic part-time expenses: $45.54 per credit tuition for state residents, $135.54 per credit tuition for nonresidents. Institutional financial aid available to part-time graduate students in College of Arts and Sciences, College of Business Administration, College of Education, College of Engineering, College of Health.

University of Florida
Gainesville 32611

Public institution; city setting. Awards B, M, D. Total enrollment: 34,694. Undergraduate enrollment: 26,656; 11% part-time, 44% women. Total faculty: 2,744. Library holdings: 2.3 million bound volumes, 1.6 million titles on microform, 33,000 periodical subscriptions, 3,650 records/tapes.

Undergraduate Courses offered for part-time students during daytime, evenings, summer. Complete part-time degree programs offered during daytime, summer. Adult/continuing education programs available. Career services available to part-time students: individual and group career counseling, individual job placement, employer recruitment on campus. Part-time tuition: $25 per semester hour for state residents, $66 per semester hour for nonresidents.

Graduate Part-time study available in Graduate School, College of Law, College of Medicine.Basic part-time expenses: $46.30 per credit hour tuition for state residents, $136.30 per credit hour tuition for nonresidents. Institutional financial aid available to part-time graduate students in Graduate School.

University of Miami
Coral Gables 33124

Independent institution; city setting. Awards B, M, D. Barrier-free campus. Total enrollment: 18,145. Undergraduate enrollment: 8,631; 18% part-time, 46% women. Total faculty: 1,515. Library holdings: 1.5 million bound volumes, 1.6 million titles on microform, 17,000 periodical subscriptions.

Undergraduate Courses offered for part-time students during daytime, evenings, summer. Complete part-time degree programs offered during daytime, evenings, summer. Adult/continuing education programs available. Career services available to part-time students: individual and group career counseling, individual job placement, employer recruitment on campus. Part-time tuition: $237 per credit.

Florida / **Colleges Offering Part-Time Degree Programs**

University of North Florida
Jacksonville 32216

Public institution; metropolitan setting. Awards B, M (students accepted for freshman admission beginning in fall 1984). Barrier-free campus. Total enrollment: 5,651. Undergraduate enrollment: 4,336; 74% part-time, 57% women. Total faculty: 200. Library holdings: 300,000 bound volumes, 50,000 titles on microform, 2,900 periodical subscriptions, 6,500 records/tapes.

Undergraduate Courses offered for part-time students during daytime, evenings, summer. Complete part-time degree programs offered during daytime, evenings. Adult/continuing education programs available. Career services available to part-time students: individual career counseling, individual job placement, employer recruitment on campus. Part-time tuition per semester hour ranges from $29.47 to $33.40 for state residents, $80.47 to $112.40 for nonresidents, according to course level.

Graduate Part-time study available in College of Arts and Sciences, College of Business Administration, College of Education, Interdisciplinary Program. Basic part-time expenses: $48.-05 per credit hour tuition for state residents, $138.05 per credit hour tuition for nonresidents. Institutional financial aid available to part-time graduate students in College of Arts and Sciences, College of Business Administration, College of Education, Interdisciplinary Program.

University of Sarasota
Sarasota 33577

Independent institution; city setting. Awards B, M, D (Part-time degree programs only). Total enrollment: 388. Undergraduate enrollment: 20; 100% part-time, 8% women. Total faculty: 24. Library holdings: 40,000 bound volumes, 400,000 titles on microform, 125 periodical subscriptions, 200 records/tapes.

Undergraduate Courses offered for part-time students during evenings, weekends, summer. Complete part-time degree programs offered during evenings, weekends, summer. External degree and adult/continuing education programs available. Career services available to part-time students: individual career counseling. Part-time tuition: $95 per credit.

University of South Florida
Tampa 33620

Public institution; metropolitan setting. Awards A, B, M, D. Total enrollment: 27,301. Undergraduate enrollment: 19,447; 34% part-time, 51% women. Total faculty: 1,192. Library holdings: 851,477 bound volumes, 2,704 titles on microform, 4,423 periodical subscriptions, 29,744 records/tapes.

Undergraduate Courses offered for part-time students during daytime, evenings, weekends, summer. Complete part-time degree programs offered during daytime, evenings, summer. External degree and adult/continuing education programs available. Career services available to part-time students: individual and group career counseling, individual job placement, employer recruitment on campus. Part-time tuition: $28.61 per semester hour for state residents, $79.61 per semester hour for nonresidents.

University of Tampa
Tampa 33606

Independent institution; metropolitan setting. Awards A, B, M. Barrier-free campus. Total enrollment: 2,069. Undergraduate enrollment: 1,916; 15% part-time, 49% women. Total faculty: 161. Library holdings: 186,313 bound volumes, 52,235 titles on microform, 1,712 periodical subscriptions, 3,669 records/tapes.

Undergraduate Courses offered for part-time students during daytime, evenings, summer. Complete part-time degree programs offered during daytime, evenings, summer. Adult/continuing education programs available. Career services available to part-time students: individual and group career counseling, individual job placement, employer recruitment on campus. Part-time tuition: $131 per semester hour.

Graduate Part-time study available in Division of Economics and Business. Basic part-time expenses: $143 per credit tuition.

University of West Florida
Pensacola 32514

Public institution; city setting. Awards B, M. Barrier-free campus. Total enrollment: 6,092. Undergraduate enrollment: 4,817; 47% part-time, 52% women. Total faculty: 342. Library holdings: 386,704 bound volumes, 596,479 titles on microform, 3,551 periodical subscriptions, 3,228 records/tapes.

Undergraduate Courses offered for part-time students during daytime, evenings, summer. Complete part-time degree programs offered during daytime, evenings, summer. External degree and adult/continuing education programs available. Career services available to part-time students: individual and group career counseling, individual job placement, employer recruitment on campus. Part-time tuition: $33.15 per semester hour for state residents, $103 per semester hour for nonresidents.

Graduate Part-time study available in College of Arts and Sciences, College of Business, College of Education. Degree can be earned exclusively through evening/weekend study in College of Arts and Sciences, College of Business, College of Education. Basic part-time expenses: $39.60 per credit tuition for state residents, $112 per credit tuition for nonresidents. Institutional financial aid available to part-time graduate students in College of Arts and Sciences, College of Business, College of Education.

Valencia Community College
Orlando 32802

Public institution; metropolitan setting. Awards A. Barrier-free campus. Total enrollment: 11,123 (all undergraduates); 64% part-time, 56% women. Total faculty: 663. Library holdings: 60,424 bound volumes, 1,051 periodical subscriptions, 3,217 records/tapes.

Undergraduate Courses offered for part-time students during daytime, evenings, weekends, summer. Complete part-time degree programs offered during daytime, evenings, weekends, summer. Adult/continuing education programs available. Career services available to part-time students: individual and group career counseling, individual job placement, employer recruitment on campus. Part-time tuition: $21.25 per semester hour for state residents, $44 per semester hour for nonresidents.

Warner Southern College
Lake Wales 33853

Independent-religious instutition; rural setting. Awards A, B. Total enrollment: 295 (all undergraduates); 9% part-time, 60% women, 17% over 25. Total faculty: 43. Library holdings: 61,068 bound volumes, 3,848 titles on microform, 378 periodical subscriptions, 3,646 records/tapes.

Undergraduate Courses offered for part-time students during daytime, evenings. Complete part-time degree programs offered during daytime, evenings. Adult/continuing education programs available. Career services available to part-time students: individual career counseling, individual job placement. Part-time tuition per semester hour ranges from $75 (for stu-

Warner Southern College (continued)

dents taking 1 to 7 semester hours) to $150 (for students taking 8 to 11 semester hours).

Webber College
Babson Park 33827

Independent institution; rural setting. Awards A, B, M. Total enrollment: 375. Undergraduate enrollment: 355; 24% part-time, 55% women, 30% over 25. Total faculty: 21. Library holdings: 27,000 bound volumes, 30 periodical subscriptions, 775 records/tapes.

Undergraduate Courses offered for part-time students during daytime, evenings, summer. Complete part-time degree programs offered during daytime, evenings, summer. Adult/continuing education programs available. Career services available to part-time students: individual and group career counseling, individual job placement. Part-time tuition: $70 per credit hour.

GEORGIA

Abraham Baldwin Agricultural College
Tifton 31793

Public institution; rural setting. Awards A. Total enrollment: 2,182 (all undergraduates); 7% part-time, 43% women. Total faculty: 140. Library holdings: 60,000 bound volumes, 400 periodical subscriptions.

Undergraduate Courses offered for part-time students during daytime. Complete part-time degree programs offered during daytime. Adult/continuing education programs available. Career services available to part-time students: individual career counseling, individual job placement. Part-time tuition: $16 per quarter hour for state residents, $21 per quarter hour for nonresidents.

Agnes Scott College
Decatur 30030

Independent institution; small-town setting. Awards B. Total enrollment: 543 (all undergraduates); 5% part-time, 100% women, 9% over 25. Total faculty: 81. Library holdings: 172,000 bound volumes, 200 titles on microform, 750 periodical subscriptions, 3,657 records/tapes.

Undergraduate Courses offered for part-time students during daytime. Complete part-time degree programs offered during daytime. Adult/continuing education programs available. Career services available to part-time students: individual and group career counseling, individual job placement, employer recruitment on campus. Part-time tuition: $165 per quarter hour.

Albany State College
Albany 31705

Public institution; city setting. Awards A, B, M. Total enrollment: 1,865. Undergraduate enrollment: 1,727; 23% part-time, 59% women. Total faculty: 127. Library holdings: 127,847 bound volumes, 330,328 titles on microform, 892 periodical subscriptions, 500 records/tapes.

Undergraduate Courses offered for part-time students during daytime, evenings, weekends, summer. Complete part-time degree programs offered during daytime, evenings, weekends, summer. Adult/continuing education programs available. Career services available to part-time students: individual and group career counseling, employer recruitment on campus. Part-time tuition: $24 per quarter hour for state residents, $71 per quarter hour for nonresidents.

Andrew College
Cuthbert 31740

Independent-religious instutition; rural setting. Awards A. Total enrollment: 327 (all undergraduates); 10% part-time, 50% women, 20% over 25. Total faculty: 18. Library holdings: 35,000 bound volumes, 50 periodical subscriptions, 700 records/tapes.

Undergraduate Courses offered for part-time students during daytime, evenings, summer. Complete part-time degree programs offered during daytime, evenings, summer. Adult/continuing education programs available. Part-time tuition: $40 per quarter hour.

Armstrong State College
Savannah 31406

Public institution; city setting. Awards A, B, M. Barrier-free campus. Total enrollment: 2,988 (all undergraduates); 33% part-time, 55% women. Total faculty: 160. Library holdings: 132,000 bound volumes, 800 periodical subscriptions.

Undergraduate Courses offered for part-time students during daytime, evenings, summer. Complete part-time degree programs offered during daytime, evenings, summer. Adult/continuing education programs available. Career services available to part-time students: individual and group career counseling, individual job placement, employer recruitment on campus. Part-time tuition: $46 per quarter hour for state residents, $90 per quarter hour for nonresidents.

Graduate Part-time study available in School of Education, School of Health Professions. Degree can be earned exclusively through evening/weekend study in School of Education, School of Health Professions. Basic part-time expenses: $171 per quarter (minimum) tuition for state residents, $406 per quarter (minimum) tuition for nonresidents. Institutional financial aid available to part-time graduate students in School of Education, School of Health Professions.

Atlanta Christian College
East Point 30344

Independent-religious instutition; city setting. Awards A, B. Barrier-free campus. Total enrollment: 164 (all undergraduates); 20% part-time, 40% women, 35% over 25. Total faculty: 16. Library holdings: 42,000 bound volumes, 15,000 titles on microform, 160 periodical subscriptions.

Undergraduate Courses offered for part-time students during daytime. Complete part-time degree programs offered during daytime. Adult/continuing education programs available. Career services available to part-time students: individual career counseling. Part-time tuition: $75 per semester hour.

Atlanta College of Art
Atlanta 30309

Independent institution; metropolitan setting. Awards B. Barrier-free campus. Total enrollment: 240 (all undergraduates); 6% part-time, 48% women, 28% over 25. Total faculty: 33. Library holdings: 16,000 bound volumes, 210 periodical subscriptions, 150 records/tapes.

Undergraduate Courses offered for part-time students during daytime, evenings, weekends, summer. Complete part-time degree programs offered during daytime, evenings, weekends, summer. Adult/continuing education programs available. Ca-

Georgia / **Colleges Offering Part-Time Degree Programs**

reer services available to part-time students: individual career counseling, individual job placement, employer recruitment on campus. Part-time tuition: $165 per credit.

Atlanta Junior College
Atlanta 30310

Public institution; metropolitan setting. Awards A. Total enrollment: 1,685 (all undergraduates); 39% part-time, 57% women, 40% over 25. Total faculty: 91. Library holdings: 20,000 bound volumes, 85 titles on microform, 320 periodical subscriptions, 1,200 records/tapes.

Undergraduate Courses offered for part-time students during daytime, evenings, summer. Complete part-time degree programs offered during daytime, evenings, summer. Adult/continuing education programs available. Career services available to part-time students: individual and group career counseling, individual job placement, employer recruitment on campus. Part-time tuition and fees per quarter (1 to 12 quarter hours) range from $28 to $225 for state residents, $65 to $656 for nonresidents.

Atlanta University
Atlanta 30314

Independent institution (graduate only). Total enrollment: 1,069 (coed; 46% part-time). Total faculty: 142.

Graduate Part-time study available in School of Arts and Sciences, School of Business Administration, School of Education, School of Library and Information Studies, School of Social Work. Degree can be earned exclusively through evening/weekend study in School of Education. Basic part-time expenses: $150 per semester hour tuition plus $28.50 per semester fees. Institutional financial aid available to part-time graduate students in School of Arts and Sciences, School of Business Administration, School of Education, School of Library and Information Studies, School of Social Work.

Augusta College
Augusta 30910

Public institution; city setting. Awards A, B, M. Total enrollment: 4,252. Undergraduate enrollment: 3,894; 38% part-time, 55% women, 40% over 25. Total faculty: 189. Library holdings: 325,000 bound volumes, 590,253 titles on microform, 2,465 periodical subscriptions, 6,500 records/tapes.

Undergraduate Courses offered for part-time students during daytime, evenings, summer. Complete part-time degree programs offered during daytime, evenings. Adult/continuing education programs available. Career services available to part-time students: individual and group career counseling, individual job placement, employer recruitment on campus. Part-time tuition: $24 per quarter hour for state residents, $71 per quarter hour for nonresidents.

Graduate Part-time study available in Graduate Studies. Basic part-time expenses: $24 per quarter hour tuition plus $40 per quarter fees for state residents, $71 per quarter hour tuition plus $40 per quarter fees for nonresidents. Institutional financial aid available to part-time graduate students in Graduate Studies.

Bainbridge Junior College
Bainbridge 31717

Public institution; small-town setting. Awards A. Barrier-free campus. Total enrollment: 621 (all undergraduates); 56% part-time, 61% women, 37% over 25. Total faculty: 45. Library holdings: 22,412 bound volumes, 75 periodical subscriptions, 1,719 records/tapes.

Undergraduate Courses offered for part-time students during daytime, evenings, weekends, summer. Complete part-time degree programs offered during daytime, evenings, summer. Adult/continuing education programs available. Career services available to part-time students: individual career counseling, individual job placement. Part-time tuition: $18 per quarter hour for state residents, $37 per quarter hour for nonresidents.

Berry College
Mount Berry 30149

Independent institution; small-town setting. Awards A, B, M. Barrier-free campus. Total enrollment: 1,403. Undergraduate enrollment: 1,207; 5% part-time, 60% women. Total faculty: 115. Library holdings: 12,100 bound volumes, 226,000 titles on microform, 1,170 periodical subscriptions.

Undergraduate Courses offered for part-time students during daytime, evenings. Complete part-time degree programs offered during daytime, evenings. Adult/continuing education programs available. Career services available to part-time students: individual and group career counseling, individual job placement, employer recruitment on campus. Part-time tuition: $91 per credit.

Graduate Part-time study available in Graduate Programs. Basic part-time expenses: $91 per hour tuition. Institutional financial aid available to part-time graduate students in Graduate Programs.

Brenau College
Gainesville 30501

Independent institution; small-town setting. Awards B, M. Total enrollment: 1,786. Undergraduate enrollment: 1,509; 17% part-time, 70% women. Total faculty: 149. Library holdings: 54,000 bound volumes, 200 titles on microform, 360 periodical subscriptions, 800 records/tapes.

Undergraduate Courses offered for part-time students during daytime, evenings, weekends, summer. Complete part-time degree programs offered during daytime, evenings, summer. Adult/continuing education programs available. Part-time tuition: $77 per quarter hour. Part-time tuition for Professional College: $50 per quarter hour.

Graduate Part-time study available in Professional College. Degree can be earned exclusively through evening/weekend study in Professional College. Basic part-time expenses: $35 per quarter hour tuition.

Brewton-Parker College
Mt Vernon 30445

Independent-religious instutition; rural setting. Awards A, B. Total enrollment: 1,207 (all undergraduates); 25% part-time, 35% women, 3% over 25. Total faculty: 32. Library holdings: 26,478 bound volumes, 145 periodical subscriptions, 1,585 records/tapes.

Undergraduate Courses offered for part-time students during daytime, evenings, weekends, summer. Complete part-time degree programs offered during daytime, evenings, weekends, summer. Adult/continuing education programs available. Career services available to part-time students: individual and group career counseling, individual job placement. Part-time tuition: $46 per quarter hour.

Colleges Offering Part-Time Degree Programs / *Georgia*

Brunswick Junior College
Brunswick 31520

Public institution; small-town setting. Awards A. Barrier-free campus. Total enrollment: 1,310 (all undergraduates); 30% part-time, 50% women, 40% over 25. Total faculty: 64. Library holdings: 48,000 bound volumes.

Undergraduate Courses offered for part-time students during daytime, evenings. Complete part-time degree programs offered during daytime, evenings. Adult/continuing education programs available. Career services available to part-time students: individual career counseling, individual job placement, employer recruitment on campus. Part-time tuition: $18 per quarter hour for state residents, $55 per quarter hour for nonresidents.

Clark College
Atlanta 30314

Independent-religious instutition; metropolitan setting. Awards B. Total enrollment: 1,936 (all undergraduates); 4% part-time, 64% women. Total faculty: 157. Library holdings: 553,197 bound volumes, 70,000 titles on microform, 1,505 periodical subscriptions.

Undergraduate Courses offered for part-time students during daytime. Complete part-time degree programs offered during daytime. Career services available to part-time students: individual and group career counseling, individual job placement, employer recruitment on campus. Part-time tuition: $120.85 per credit.

Clayton Junior College
Morrow 30260

Public institution; small-town setting. Awards A. Barrier-free campus. Total enrollment: 3,603 (all undergraduates); 49% part-time, 59% women, 28% over 25. Total faculty: 148. Library holdings: 53,299 bound volumes, 518 periodical subscriptions, 3,968 records/tapes.

Undergraduate Courses offered for part-time students during daytime, evenings, summer. Complete part-time degree programs offered during daytime, evenings, summer. Adult/continuing education programs available. Career services available to part-time students: individual and group career counseling, individual job placement, employer recruitment on campus. Part-time tuition: $18 per quarter hour for state residents, $55 per quarter hour for nonresidents.

Columbus College
Columbus 31993

Public institution; city setting. Awards A, B, M. Barrier-free campus. Total enrollment: 4,283. Undergraduate enrollment: 3,876; 40% part-time, 56% women, 25% over 25. Total faculty: 215. Library holdings: 190,000 bound volumes, 221,320 titles on microform, 1,358 periodical subscriptions, 2,630 records/tapes.

Undergraduate Courses offered for part-time students during daytime, evenings, summer. Complete part-time degree programs offered during daytime, evenings, summer. Adult/continuing education programs available. Career services available to part-time students: individual and group career counseling, individual job placement, employer recruitment on campus. Part-time tuition: $24 per quarter hour for state residents, $71 per quarter hour for nonresidents.

Graduate Part-time study available in Graduate Studies. Degree can be earned exclusively through evening/weekend study in Graduate Studies. Basic part-time expenses: $24 per credit tuition plus $42 per quarter fees for state residents, $71 per credit tuition plus $42 per quarter fees for nonresidents. Institutional financial aid available to part-time graduate students in Graduate Studies.

Covenant College
Lookout Mountain 37350

Independent-religious instutition; small-town setting. Awards A, B. Total enrollment: 518 (all undergraduates); 9% part-time, 51% women, 2% over 25. Total faculty: 45. Library holdings: 57,000 bound volumes, 24,000 titles on microform, 546 periodical subscriptions, 6,200 records/tapes.

Undergraduate Courses offered for part-time students during daytime, evenings. Complete part-time degree programs offered during daytime, evenings. External degree programs available. Career services available to part-time students: individual and group career counseling, individual job placement. Part-time tuition: $185 per unit.

Crandall Junior College
Macon 31201

Proprietary institution; city setting. Awards A. Barrier-free campus. Total enrollment: 350 (all undergraduates); 5% part-time, 60% women. Total faculty: 25. Library holdings: 1,100 bound volumes, 29 periodical subscriptions, 200 records/tapes.

Undergraduate Courses offered for part-time students during daytime, evenings, summer. Complete part-time degree programs offered during daytime, evenings, summer. Career services available to part-time students: individual career counseling, individual job placement, employer recruitment on campus. Part-time tuition: $50 per quarter hour.

Dalton Junior College
Dalton 30720

Public institution; small-town setting. Awards A. Total enrollment: 1,755 (all undergraduates); 30% part-time, 50% women, 18% over 25. Total faculty: 70. Library holdings: 60,000 bound volumes, 690 periodical subscriptions, 300 records/tapes.

Undergraduate Courses offered for part-time students during daytime, evenings, summer. Complete part-time degree programs offered during daytime, evenings, summer. Adult/continuing education programs available. Career services available to part-time students: individual and group career counseling, individual job placement, employer recruitment on campus. Part-time tuition: $18 per credit hour for state residents, $54 per credit hour for nonresidents.

DeKalb Community College
Clarkston 30021

Public institution; small-town setting. Awards A. Barrier-free campus. Total enrollment: 20,000 (all undergraduates); 40% part-time, 60% women. Total faculty: 819.

Undergraduate Courses offered for part-time students during daytime, evenings, weekends, summer. Complete part-time degree programs offered during daytime, evenings, weekends, summer. Adult/continuing education programs available. Career services available to part-time students: individual and group career counseling, individual job placement, employer recruitment on campus. Part-time tuition: $17 per quarter hour for area residents, $25 per quarter hour for state residents, $55 per quarter hour for nonresidents.

Georgia / **Colleges Offering Part-Time Degree Programs**

DeVry Institute of Technology
Atlanta 30341

Proprietary institution; metropolitan setting. Awards A, B. Barrier-free campus. Total enrollment: 2,759 (all undergraduates); 9% part-time, 19% women. Total faculty: 82.

Undergraduate Courses offered for part-time students during daytime. Complete part-time degree programs offered during daytime. Adult/continuing education programs available. Career services available to part-time students: individual and group career counseling, individual job placement, employer recruitment on campus. Part-time tuition: $1990 per year (minimum).

Draughon's Junior College
Savannah 31406

Proprietary institution; city setting. Awards A. Barrier-free campus. Total enrollment: 702 (all undergraduates); 26% part-time, 77% women. Total faculty: 48. Library holdings: 4,750 bound volumes, 4 titles on microform, 57 periodical subscriptions, 50 records/tapes.

Undergraduate Courses offered for part-time students during daytime, evenings, summer. Complete part-time degree programs offered during daytime, evenings, summer. Career services available to part-time students: individual career counseling, individual job placement. Part-time tuition per quarter (1 to 11 quarter credits) ranges from $275 to $570 according to course load and program.

Emanuel County Junior College
Swainsboro 30401

Public institution; small-town setting. Awards A. Barrier-free campus. Total enrollment: 414 (all undergraduates); 28% part-time, 58% women. Total faculty: 25. Library holdings: 31,572 bound volumes, 4,366 titles on microform, 482 periodical subscriptions, 964 records/tapes.

Undergraduate Courses offered for part-time students during daytime, evenings, summer. Complete part-time degree programs offered during daytime, evenings. Adult/continuing education programs available. Career services available to part-time students: individual and group career counseling. Part-time tuition: $18 per quarter hour for state residents, $55 per quarter hour for nonresidents.

Emmanuel College School of Christian Ministries
Franklin Springs 30639

Independent-religious instutition; rural setting. Awards B. Total enrollment: 31 (all undergraduates); 0% part-time, 25% women, 25% over 25. Total faculty: 6. Library holdings: 31,000 bound volumes, 62 titles on microform, 225 periodical subscriptions, 1,453 records/tapes.

Undergraduate Courses offered for part-time students during daytime. Complete part-time degree programs offered during daytime. Career services available to part-time students: individual career counseling. Part-time tuition: $60 per credit hour.

Emory University
Atlanta 30322

Independent-religious instutition; metropolitan setting. Awards B, M, D. Barrier-free campus. Total enrollment: 8,052. Undergraduate enrollment: 3,553; 1% part-time, 49% women. Total faculty: 1,309. Library holdings: 1.7 million bound volumes, 966,000 titles on microform, 15,000 periodical subscriptions, 2,491 records/tapes.

Graduate Part-time study available in Candler School of Theology, Division of Allied Health Professions, Graduate School of Arts and Sciences, Nell Hodgson Woodruff School of Nursing, School of Law. Basic part-time expenses: $315 per semester hour tuition plus $3 per semester hour fees. Institutional financial aid available to part-time graduate students in Candler School of Theology, Division of Allied Health Professions, Graduate School of Arts and Sciences.

Floyd Junior College
Rome 30163

Public institution; rural setting. Awards A. Total enrollment: 1,673 (all undergraduates); 49% part-time, 66% women. Total faculty: 63.

Undergraduate Courses offered for part-time students during daytime, evenings, summer. Complete part-time degree programs offered during daytime, evenings, summer. Part-time tuition and fees per quarter (1 to 11 credit hours) range from $28 to $208 for state residents, $65 to $615 for nonresidents.

Fort Valley State College
Fort Valley 31030

Public institution; small-town setting. Awards A, B, M. Barrier-free campus. Total enrollment: 1,870. Undergraduate enrollment: 1,722; 5% part-time, 51% women. Total faculty: 142. Library holdings: 166,910 bound volumes, 1,644 periodical subscriptions.

Undergraduate Courses offered for part-time students during daytime, evenings, summer. Complete part-time degree programs offered during daytime, evenings. Adult/continuing education programs available. Career services available to part-time students: individual and group career counseling, individual job placement, employer recruitment on campus. Part-time tuition: $24 per quarter hour for state residents, $47 per quarter hour for nonresidents.

Graduate Part-time study available in Graduate Division. Basic part-time expenses: $24 per quarter hour tuition for state residents, $71 per quarter hour tuition for nonresidents. Institutional financial aid available to part-time graduate students in Graduate Division.

Gainesville Junior College
Gainesville 30503

Public institution; small-town setting. Awards A. Barrier-free campus. Total enrollment: 1,769 (all undergraduates); 30% part-time, 50% women. Total faculty: 65.

Undergraduate Courses offered for part-time students during daytime, evenings, summer. Complete part-time degree programs offered during daytime, evenings, summer. Adult/continuing education programs available. Career services available to part-time students: individual and group career counseling. Part-time tuition: $18 per quarter hour for state residents, $56 per quarter hour for nonresidents.

Georgia College
Milledgeville 31061

Public institution; small-town setting. Awards A, B, M. Barrier-free campus. Total enrollment: 3,554. Undergraduate enrollment: 2,898; 33% part-time, 56% women. Total faculty: 179.

Colleges Offering Part-Time Degree Programs / Georgia

Georgia College (continued)
Library holdings: 140,409 bound volumes, 1,346 periodical subscriptions, 13,199 records/tapes.

Undergraduate Courses offered for part-time students during daytime, evenings, summer. Complete part-time degree programs offered during daytime, evenings, summer. Adult/continuing education programs available. Career services available to part-time students: individual career counseling, individual job placement, employer recruitment on campus. Part-time tuition: $25 per quarter hour for state residents, $47 per quarter hour for nonresidents.

Graduate Part-time study available in Graduate School. Basic part-time expenses: $72 per quarter (minimum) tuition for state residents, $213 per quarter (minimum) tuition for nonresidents. Institutional financial aid available to part-time graduate students in Graduate School.

Georgia Institute of Technology
Atlanta 30332

Public institution; metropolitan setting. Awards B, M, D. Total enrollment: 10,918. Undergraduate enrollment: 8,775; 6% part-time, 22% women. Total faculty: 603. Library holdings: 1.6 million bound volumes, 1.7 million titles on microform, 6,000 periodical subscriptions.

Undergraduate Courses offered for part-time students during daytime. Complete part-time degree programs offered during daytime. Adult/continuing education programs available. Career services available to part-time students: individual and group career counseling, individual job placement, employer recruitment on campus. Part-time tuition and fees per quarter (1 to 11 quarter hours) range from $28 to $398 for state residents, $68 to $838 for nonresidents.

Graduate Part-time study available in Graduate Studies and Research. Basic part-time expenses: $32 per credit tuition plus $6 per quarter (minimum) fees for state residents, $110 per credit tuition plus $6 per quarter (minimum) fees for nonresidents. Institutional financial aid available to part-time graduate students in Graduate Studies and Research.

Georgia Southern College
Statesboro 30460

Public institution; small-town setting. Awards A, B, M. Total enrollment: 7,018. Undergraduate enrollment: 6,033; 8% part-time, 55% women. Total faculty: 400. Library holdings: 323,517 bound volumes, 584,653 titles on microform, 3,650 periodical subscriptions, 19,008 records/tapes.

Undergraduate Courses offered for part-time students during daytime, evenings, summer. Complete part-time degree programs offered during daytime, evenings, summer. Adult/continuing education programs available. Career services available to part-time students: individual and group career counseling, individual job placement, employer recruitment on campus. Part-time tuition: $24 per quarter hour for state residents, $71 per quarter hour for nonresidents.

Graduate Part-time study available in Graduate School. Degree can be earned exclusively through evening/weekend study in Graduate School. Basic part-time expenses: $24 per quarter hour tuition for state residents, $71 per quarter hour tuition for nonresidents. Institutional financial aid available to part-time graduate students in Graduate School.

Georgia Southwestern College
Americus 31709

Public institution; small-town setting. Awards A, B, M. Total enrollment: 2,344. Undergraduate enrollment: 2,078; 13% part-time, 55% women, 19% over 25. Total faculty: 116. Library holdings: 132,094 bound volumes, 420 periodical subscriptions, 1,234 records/tapes.

Undergraduate Courses offered for part-time students during daytime, evenings, summer. Complete part-time degree programs offered during daytime, evenings, summer. Adult/continuing education programs available. Career services available to part-time students: individual and group career counseling, individual job placement, employer recruitment on campus. Part-time tuition: $24 per quarter hour for state residents, $71 per quarter hour for nonresidents.

Graduate Part-time study available in Graduate Studies. Basic part-time expenses: $24 per quarter hour tuition plus $65 per quarter (minimum) fees for state residents, $71 per quarter hour tuition plus $65 per quarter (minimum) fees for nonresidents. Institutional financial aid available to part-time graduate students in Graduate Studies.

Georgia State University
Atlanta 30303

Public institution; metropolitan setting. Awards A, B, M, D. Barrier-free campus. Total enrollment: 21,512. Undergraduate enrollment: 14,623; 56% part-time, 55% women. Total faculty: 924. Library holdings: 721,480 bound volumes, 1.2 million titles on microform, 4,721 periodical subscriptions, 1,188 records/tapes.

Undergraduate Courses offered for part-time students during daytime, evenings, summer. Complete part-time degree programs offered during daytime, evenings, summer. Adult/continuing education programs available. Career services available to part-time students: individual and group career counseling, individual job placement, employer recruitment on campus. Part-time tuition: $25 per quarter hour for state residents, $85 per quarter hour for nonresidents.

Graduate Part-time study available in College of Arts and Sciences, College of Business Administration, College of Education, College of Health Sciences, College of Law, College of Public and Urban Affairs. Basic part-time expenses: $25 per credit hour tuition plus $20 per quarter fees for state residents, $85 per credit hour tuition plus $20 per quarter fees for nonresidents.

Gordon Junior College
Barnesville 30204

Public institution; small-town setting. Awards A. Barrier-free campus. Total enrollment: 1,510 (all undergraduates); 35% part-time, 61% women, 25% over 25. Total faculty: 81. Library holdings: 60,000 bound volumes, 320 periodical subscriptions, 2,100 records/tapes.

Undergraduate Courses offered for part-time students during daytime, evenings, summer. Complete part-time degree programs offered during daytime, evenings, summer. External degree and adult/continuing education programs available. Career services available to part-time students: individual career counseling. Part-time tuition: $18 per quarter hour for state residents, $37 per quarter hour for nonresidents.

Georgia / **Colleges Offering Part-Time Degree Programs**

Kennesaw College
Marietta 30061

Public institution; small-town setting. Awards A, B. Total enrollment: 5,383 (all undergraduates); 50% part-time, 51% women. Total faculty: 196. Library holdings: 97,500 bound volumes, 13,250 titles on microform, 1,000 periodical subscriptions, 1,400 records/tapes.

Undergraduate Courses offered for part-time students during daytime, evenings, summer. Complete part-time degree programs offered during daytime, evenings, summer. Adult/continuing education programs available. Career services available to part-time students: individual and group career counseling, individual job placement. Part-time tuition: $24 per quarter hour for state residents, $71 per quarter hour for nonresidents.

LaGrange College
LaGrange 30240

Independent-religious instutition; small-town setting. Awards A, B, M. Total enrollment: 987. Undergraduate enrollment: 934; 31% part-time, 60% women. Total faculty: 62. Library holdings: 70,000 bound volumes, 1,800 titles on microform, 370 periodical subscriptions.

Undergraduate Courses offered for part-time students during daytime, evenings, summer. Complete part-time degree programs offered during daytime, evenings, summer. Adult/continuing education programs available. Career services available to part-time students: individual and group career counseling, individual job placement, employer recruitment on campus. Part-time tuition: $61 per quarter hour.

Meadows Junior College
Columbus 31906

Proprietary institution; city setting. Awards A. Barrier-free campus. Total enrollment: 358 (all undergraduates); 2% part-time, 54% women. Total faculty: 28. Library holdings: 4,200 bound volumes, 40 periodical subscriptions.

Undergraduate Courses offered for part-time students during daytime, evenings, weekends, summer. Complete part-time degree programs offered during daytime, evenings, weekends, summer. Career services available to part-time students: individual career counseling, individual job placement, employer recruitment on campus. Part-time tuition: $200 per course.

Mercer University
Macon 31207

Independent-religious instutition; city setting. Awards B, M, D. Barrier-free campus. Total enrollment: 2,886. Undergraduate enrollment: 2,109; 11% part-time, 51% women, 13% over 25. Total faculty: 218. Library holdings: 308,098 bound volumes, 3,581 titles on microform, 2,705 periodical subscriptions, 6,000 records/tapes.

Undergraduate Courses offered for part-time students during daytime, evenings, weekends, summer. Complete part-time degree programs offered during daytime, evenings, summer. External degree and adult/continuing education programs available. Part-time tuition: $597 per course. Part-time tuition for residents of Bibb County and the six adjacent counties, graduates of Macon Junior College, and anyone 30 or older is $476 per course.

Graduate Part-time study available in College of Liberal Arts, School of Business and Economics. Degree can be earned exclusively through evening/weekend study in College of Liberal Arts, School of Business and Economics.Basic part-time expenses: $215 per course (minimum) tuition.

Mercer University in Atlanta
Atlanta 30341

Independent-religious instutition; metropolitan setting. Awards B, M. Total enrollment: 1,868. Undergraduate enrollment: 1,-420; 40% part-time, 52% women, 37% over 25. Total faculty: 101. Library holdings: 63,316 bound volumes, 19,000 titles on microform, 629 periodical subscriptions, 1,688 records/tapes.

Undergraduate Courses offered for part-time students during daytime, evenings, summer. Complete part-time degree programs offered during daytime, evenings, summer. Adult/continuing education programs available. Career services available to part-time students: individual and group career counseling, individual job placement, employer recruitment on campus. Part-time tuition: $80 per quarter hour.

Graduate Part-time study available in College of Arts and Sciences, School of Business and Economics. Degree can be earned exclusively through evening/weekend study in College of Arts and Sciences, School of Business and Economics.Basic part-time expenses: $100 per credit tuition.

Middle Georgia College
Cochran 31014

Public institution; small-town setting. Awards A. Total enrollment: 1,429 (all undergraduates); 20% part-time, 49% women, 16% over 25. Total faculty: 105. Library holdings: 78,775 bound volumes, 672 periodical subscriptions, 5,017 records/tapes.

Undergraduate Courses offered for part-time students during daytime, evenings, summer. Complete part-time degree programs offered during daytime, evenings, summer. Adult/continuing education programs available. Career services available to part-time students: individual and group career counseling. Part-time tuition: $18 per quarter hour for state residents, $55 per quarter hour for nonresidents.

Morris Brown College
Atlanta 30314

Independent-religious instutition; metropolitan setting. Awards B. Total enrollment: 1,268 (all undergraduates); 4% part-time, 66% women, 5% over 25. Total faculty: 84. Library holdings: 104,276 bound volumes.

Undergraduate Courses offered for part-time students during daytime. Complete part-time degree programs offered during daytime. Adult/continuing education programs available. Career services available to part-time students: individual and group career counseling, individual job placement, employer recruitment on campus. Part-time tuition: $129 per semester hour.

North Georgia College
Dahlonega 30597

Public institution; small-town setting. Awards A, B, M. Total enrollment: 1,990. Undergraduate enrollment: 1,770; 15% part-time, 57% women. Total faculty: 140. Library holdings: 120,186 bound volumes, 206,294 titles on microform, 994 periodical subscriptions, 1,741 records/tapes.

Undergraduate Courses offered for part-time students during daytime, evenings, summer. Complete part-time degree programs offered during daytime, evenings, summer. Adult/continuing education programs available. Career services available to part-time students: individual career counseling, individual job placement, employer recruitment on campus. Part-time tuition: $24 per quarter hour for state residents, $47 per quarter hour for nonresidents.

Colleges Offering Part-Time Degree Programs / Georgia

North Georgia College (continued)

Graduate Part-time study available in Graduate Studies. Degree can be earned exclusively through evening/weekend study in Graduate Studies. Basic part-time expenses: $120 per course tuition for state residents, $355 per course tuition for nonresidents.

Oglethorpe University
Atlanta 30319

Independent institution; metropolitan setting. Awards B, M. Total enrollment: 1,030. Undergraduate enrollment: 944; 20% part-time, 51% women. Total faculty: 55. Library holdings: 68,-000 bound volumes, 319 periodical subscriptions, 350 records/tapes.

Undergraduate Courses offered for part-time students during daytime, evenings, weekends, summer. Complete part-time degree programs offered during daytime, evenings, summer. Adult/continuing education programs available. Career services available to part-time students: individual and group career counseling, individual job placement, employer recruitment on campus. Part-time tuition: $290 per semester hour.

Graduate Part-time study available in Graduate Division. Basic part-time expenses: $45 per credit tuition.

Reinhardt College
Waleska 30183

Independent-religious instutition; rural setting. Awards A. Barrier-free campus. Total enrollment: 539 (all undergraduates); 15% part-time, 60% women. Total faculty: 31.

Undergraduate Courses offered for part-time students during daytime, evenings, summer. Complete part-time degree programs offered during daytime, evenings. Part-time tuition: $52.-50 per quarter hour for state residents, $52.50 per quarter hour for nonresidents.

Savannah College of Art and Design
Savannah 31401

Independent institution; city setting. Awards B. Barrier-free campus. Total enrollment: 770 (all undergraduates); 26% part-time, 64% women, 11% over 25. Total faculty: 48. Library holdings: 22,000 bound volumes, 200 periodical subscriptions.

Undergraduate Courses offered for part-time students during daytime, evenings, weekends, summer. Complete part-time degree programs offered during daytime, evenings, weekends, summer. Career services available to part-time students: individual and group career counseling, individual job placement. Part-time tuition: $86 per credit hour.

Savannah State College
Savannah 31404

Public institution (undergraduate and graduate). Total enrollment: 2,125. Graduate enrollment: 130 (coed; 80% part-time). Library holdings: 125,000 bound volumes, 256,000 microforms.

Graduate Part-time study available in School of Business. Degree can be earned exclusively through evening/weekend study in School of Business. Basic part-time expenses: $72 per quarter (minimum) tuition for state residents, $213 per quarter (minimum) tuition for nonresidents.

Shorter College
Rome 30161

Independent-religious instutition; small-town setting. Awards B. Total enrollment: 781 (all undergraduates); 4% part-time, 55% women, 8% over 25. Total faculty: 55. Library holdings: 80,000 bound volumes, 1,000 periodical subscriptions, 4,679 records/tapes.

Undergraduate Courses offered for part-time students during daytime, evenings, summer. Complete part-time degree programs offered during daytime, evenings, summer. Career services available to part-time students: individual career counseling, individual job placement, employer recruitment on campus. Part-time tuition: $100 per semester hour.

Southern Technical Institute
Marietta 30060

Public institution; small-town setting. Awards A, B. Total enrollment: 3,499 (all undergraduates); 35% part-time, 15% women. Total faculty: 175. Library holdings: 75,000 bound volumes, 1,300 periodical subscriptions, 20,000 records/tapes.

Undergraduate Courses offered for part-time students during daytime, evenings. Complete part-time degree programs offered during daytime, evenings. Adult/continuing education programs available. Career services available to part-time students: individual and group career counseling, individual job placement, employer recruitment on campus. Part-time tuition: $24 per quarter hour for state residents, $71 per quarter hour for nonresidents.

South Georgia College
Douglas 31533

Public institution; rural setting. Awards A. Total enrollment: 1,172 (all undergraduates); 30% part-time, 55% women. Total faculty: 65. Library holdings: 75,846 bound volumes, 135 titles on microform, 492 periodical subscriptions, 3,063 records/tapes.

Undergraduate Courses offered for part-time students during daytime, evenings, summer. Complete part-time degree programs offered during daytime, evenings, summer. Adult/continuing education programs available. Career services available to part-time students: individual and group career counseling, employer recruitment on campus. Part-time tuition: $18 per quarter hour for state residents, $37 per quarter hour for nonresidents.

Thomas County Community College
Thomasville 31792

Independent institution; small-town setting. Awards A. Total enrollment: 429 (all undergraduates); 17% part-time, 64% women, 35% over 25. Total faculty: 27. Library holdings: 20,000 bound volumes, 25 titles on microform, 201 periodical subscriptions, 300 records/tapes.

Undergraduate Courses offered for part-time students during daytime, evenings, weekends, summer. Complete part-time degree programs offered during daytime, evenings. Adult/continuing education programs available. Career services available to part-time students: individual career counseling. Part-time tuition: $39 per quarter hour for state residents, $39 per quarter hour for nonresidents.

Georgia / **Colleges Offering Part-Time Degree Programs**

Tift College
Forsyth 31029

Independent-religious instutition; small-town setting. Awards B. Total enrollment: 331 (all undergraduates); 4% part-time, 100% women, 1% over 25. Total faculty: 43. Library holdings: 59,000 bound volumes.

Undergraduate Courses offered for part-time students during daytime, evenings. Complete part-time degree programs offered during daytime, evenings. Adult/continuing education programs available. Career services available to part-time students: individual and group career counseling, individual job placement, employer recruitment on campus. Part-time tuition: $56 per quarter hour.

Toccoa Falls College
Toccoa Falls 30598

Independent-religious instutition; rural setting. Awards A, B. Total enrollment: 613 (all undergraduates); 15% part-time, 50% women, 16% over 25. Total faculty: 46. Library holdings: 58,861 bound volumes, 883 titles on microform, 510 periodical subscriptions, 1,450 records/tapes.

Undergraduate Courses offered for part-time students during daytime, evenings, summer. Complete part-time degree programs offered during daytime. Career services available to part-time students: individual and group career counseling, individual job placement. Part-time tuition: $117 per hour.

Truett-McConnell College
Cleveland 30528

Independent-religious instutition; rural setting. Awards A. Barrier-free campus. Total enrollment: 331 (all undergraduates); 4% part-time, 57% women. Total faculty: 26. Library holdings: 27,500 bound volumes, 21 periodical subscriptions, 1,702 records/tapes.

Undergraduate Courses offered for part-time students during daytime, evenings, summer. Complete part-time degree programs offered during daytime, evenings, summer. External degree programs available. Part-time tuition: $50 per quarter hour.

University of Georgia
Athens 30602

Public institution; small-town setting. Awards A, B, M, D. Total enrollment: 25,042. Undergraduate enrollment: 19,360; 11% part-time, 45% women, 5% over 25. Total faculty: 1,902. Library holdings: 2.2 million bound volumes, 2.4 million titles on microform, 55,319 periodical subscriptions, 385,993 records/tapes.

Undergraduate Courses offered for part-time students during daytime, evenings, summer. Complete part-time degree programs offered during daytime, summer. Adult/continuing education programs available. Career services available to part-time students: individual and group career counseling, individual job placement, employer recruitment on campus. Part-time tuition: $32 per quarter hour for state residents, $95 per quarter hour for nonresidents.

Graduate Part-time study available in Graduate School. Basic part-time expenses: $32 per credit hour tuition for state residents, $95 per credit hour tuition for nonresidents. Institutional financial aid available to part-time graduate students in Graduate School.

Valdosta State College
Valdosta 31698

Public institution; city setting. Awards A, B, M. Barrier-free campus. Total enrollment: 5,835. Undergraduate enrollment: 4,937; 28% part-time, 56% women. Total faculty: 245. Library holdings: 230,000 bound volumes, 500,000 titles on microform, 1,700 periodical subscriptions, 3,500 records/tapes.

Undergraduate Courses offered for part-time students during daytime, evenings. Complete part-time degree programs offered during daytime, evenings. Adult/continuing education programs available. Career services available to part-time students: individual career counseling, individual job placement, employer recruitment on campus. Part-time tuition and fees per quarter (1 to 11 quarter hours) range from $24 to $332 for state residents, $71 to $849 for nonresidents.

Graduate Part-time study available in Division of Graduate Studies. Degree can be earned exclusively through evening/weekend study in Division of Graduate Studies. Basic part-time expenses: $120 per quarter (minimum) tuition for state residents, $355 per quarter (minimum) tuition for nonresidents. Institutional financial aid available to part-time graduate students in Division of Graduate Studies.

Waycross Junior College
Waycross 31501

Public institution; small-town setting. Awards A. Barrier-free campus. Total enrollment: 555 (all undergraduates); 43% part-time, 67% women, 35% over 25. Total faculty: 24. Library holdings: 27,000 bound volumes, 300 periodical subscriptions.

Undergraduate Courses offered for part-time students during daytime, evenings, summer. Complete part-time degree programs offered during daytime, evenings, summer. Adult/continuing education programs available. Career services available to part-time students: individual and group career counseling, individual job placement. Part-time tuition: $18 per quarter hour for state residents, $55 per quarter hour for nonresidents.

Wesleyan College
Macon 31297

Independent-religious instutition; city setting. Awards B. Total enrollment: 431 (all undergraduates); 28% part-time, 100% women. Total faculty: 57. Library holdings: 117,000 bound volumes, 3,202 titles on microform, 575 periodical subscriptions, 4,811 records/tapes.

Undergraduate Courses offered for part-time students during daytime, evenings, summer. Complete part-time degree programs offered during daytime, evenings, summer. External degree and adult/continuing education programs available. Career services available to part-time students: individual and group career counseling, individual job placement, employer recruitment on campus. Part-time tuition: $100 per semester hour for area residents, $100 per semester hour for nonresidents.

West Georgia College
Carrollton 30118

Public institution; small-town setting. Awards A, B, M. Total enrollment: 6,352. Undergraduate enrollment: 5,240; 17% part-time, 60% women. Total faculty: 305. Library holdings: 250,700 bound volumes, 642,832 titles on microform, 1,500 periodical subscriptions, 457 records/tapes.

Undergraduate Courses offered for part-time students during daytime, evenings, summer. Complete part-time degree programs offered during daytime, evenings, summer. Adult/con-

Colleges Offering Part-Time Degree Programs / Georgia

West Georgia College (continued)
tinuing education programs available. Part-time tuition and fees per quarter (1 to 11 credits) range from $24 to $339 for residents, $331 to $876 for nonresidents.
Graduate Part-time study available in Graduate School. Degree can be earned exclusively through evening/weekend study in Graduate School.Basic part-time expenses: $24 per quarter hour tuition for state residents, $71 per quarter hour tuition for nonresidents. Institutional financial aid available to part-time graduate students in Graduate School.

Young Harris College
Young Harris 30582
Independent-religious instutition; rural setting. Awards A. Total enrollment: 526 (all undergraduates); 2% part-time, 49% women, 2% over 25. Total faculty: 32. Library holdings: 40,000 bound volumes, 230 titles on microform, 280 periodical subscriptions, 720 records/tapes.
Undergraduate Courses offered for part-time students during daytime, summer. Complete part-time degree programs offered during daytime. Career services available to part-time students: individual and group career counseling. Part-time tuition: $50 per quarter hour.

GUAM

Guam Community College
Guam Main Facility 96921
Public institution; small-town setting. Awards A. Barrier-free campus. Total enrollment: 612 (all undergraduates); 88% part-time, 45% women. Total faculty: 184. Library holdings: 14,361 bound volumes, 116 titles on microform, 152 periodical subscriptions, 60 records/tapes.
Undergraduate Courses offered for part-time students during daytime, evenings, weekends, summer. Complete part-time degree programs offered during daytime, evenings, weekends, summer. Adult/continuing education programs available. Career services available to part-time students: individual and group career counseling, individual job placement, employer recruitment on campus. Part-time tuition: $5 per semester hour.

University of Guam
Mangilao 96913
Public institution; rural setting. Awards A, B, M. Total enrollment: 2,774. Undergraduate enrollment: 2,386; 29% part-time. Total faculty: 198. Library holdings: 250,000 bound volumes.
Undergraduate Courses offered for part-time students during daytime, evenings, summer. Complete part-time degree programs offered during daytime, evenings, summer. External degree and adult/continuing education programs available. Career services available to part-time students: individual and group career counseling, employer recruitment on campus. Part-time tuition: $19 per credit for territory residents, $43 per credit for nonresidents.
Graduate Part-time study available in Graduate School. Degree can be earned exclusively through evening/weekend study in Graduate School.Basic part-time expenses: $35 per credit hour tuition plus $58 per semester fees for territory residents, $51 per credit hour tuition plus $58 per semester fees for nonresidents. Institutional financial aid available to part-time graduate students in Graduate School.

HAWAII

Brigham Young University–Hawaii Campus
Laie, Oahu 96762
Independent-religious instutition; small-town setting. Awards A, B. Barrier-free campus. Total enrollment: 1,820 (all undergraduates); 5% part-time, 56% women, 22% over 25. Total faculty: 116. Library holdings: 122,000 bound volumes, 18,700 titles on microform, 940 periodical subscriptions, 4,458 records/tapes.
Undergraduate Courses offered for part-time students during daytime, evenings, summer. Complete part-time degree programs offered during daytime, evenings, summer. Adult/continuing education programs available. Career services available to part-time students: individual and group career counseling, individual job placement, employer recruitment on campus. Part-time tuition: $72 per credit hour. Part-time tuition for non–church members: $108 per credit hour.

Chaminade University of Honolulu
Honolulu 96816
Independent-religious instutition; metropolitan setting. Awards A, B, M. Barrier-free campus. Total enrollment: 2,421. Undergraduate enrollment: 2,286; 18% part-time, 46% women. Total faculty: 65. Library holdings: 55,000 bound volumes, 40 titles on microform, 500 periodical subscriptions, 2,144 records/tapes.
Undergraduate Courses offered for part-time students during daytime, evenings, weekends, summer. Complete part-time degree programs offered during daytime, evenings, weekends, summer. Adult/continuing education programs available. Career services available to part-time students: individual and group career counseling, individual job placement, employer recruitment on campus. Part-time tuition: $125 per credit hour.
Graduate Part-time study available in Graduate Program in Business Administration.Basic part-time expenses: $130 per credit tuition.

Hawaii Loa College
Kaneohe 96744
Independent-religious instutition; small-town setting. Awards A, B. Barrier-free campus. Total enrollment: 400 (all undergraduates); 20% part-time, 50% women, 15% over 25. Total faculty: 36. Library holdings: 470,000 bound volumes, 260 periodical subscriptions, 800 records/tapes.
Undergraduate Courses offered for part-time students during daytime, evenings, summer. Complete part-time degree programs offered during daytime. Adult/continuing education programs available. Career services available to part-time students: individual and group career counseling. Part-time tuition per credit hour ranges from $140 for 1 to 6 credit hours to $185 for 7 to 11 credit hours.

Hawaii Pacific College
Honolulu 96813
Independent institution; metropolitan setting. Awards A, B. Total enrollment: 3,108 (all undergraduates); 40% part-time, 30% women. Total faculty: 170. Library holdings: 21,000 bound volumes, 450 periodical subscriptions.
Undergraduate Courses offered for part-time students during daytime, evenings, weekends, summer. Complete part-time degree programs offered during daytime, evenings. Adult/continuing education programs available. Career services available to part-time students: individual and group career counseling,

individual job placement, employer recruitment on campus. Part-time tuition: $80 per credit.

University of Hawaii at Hilo
Hilo 96720

Public institution; small-town setting. Awards A, B. Total enrollment: 3,557 (all undergraduates); 26% part-time, 53% women. Total faculty: 242. Library holdings: 160,000 bound volumes, 75,000 titles on microform, 2,000 periodical subscriptions, 5,000 records/tapes.

Undergraduate Courses offered for part-time students during daytime, evenings, summer. Complete part-time degree programs offered during daytime, evenings, summer. Adult/continuing education programs available. Career services available to part-time students: individual and group career counseling, individual job placement, employer recruitment on campus. Part-time tuition per credit hour ranges from $10 to $32 for state residents, $71 to $120 for nonresidents, according to program.

University of Hawaii at Manoa
Honolulu 96822

Public institution; metropolitan setting. Awards A, B, M, D. Total enrollment: 21,112. Undergraduate enrollment: 15,503; 19% part-time, 53% women, 16% over 25. Total faculty: 1,615. Library holdings: 1.9 million bound volumes, 77,069 titles on microform, 28,619 periodical subscriptions, 5,000 records/tapes.

Undergraduate Courses offered for part-time students during daytime, evenings, summer. Complete part-time degree programs offered during daytime, evenings, summer. Adult/continuing education programs available. Career services available to part-time students: individual job placement, employer recruitment on campus. Part-time tuition: $36 per credit for state residents, $128 per credit for nonresidents.

University of Hawaii–Honolulu Community College
Honolulu 96817

Public institution; metropolitan setting. Awards A. Barrier-free campus. Total enrollment: 5,127 (all undergraduates); 53% part-time, 34% women, 17% over 25. Total faculty: 248. Library holdings: 46,326 bound volumes, 101 titles on microform, 277 periodical subscriptions, 573 records/tapes.

Undergraduate Courses offered for part-time students during daytime, evenings. Complete part-time degree programs offered during daytime, evenings. Career services available to part-time students: individual and group career counseling, individual job placement. Part-time tuition: $10 per semester hour for state residents, $71 per semester hour for nonresidents.

University of Hawaii–Leeward Community College
Pearl City 96782

Public institution; small-town setting. Awards A. Barrier-free campus. Total enrollment: 6,022 (all undergraduates); 52% part-time, 51% women, 37% over 25. Total faculty: 239. Library holdings: 58,430 bound volumes, 306 titles on microform, 328 periodical subscriptions, 5,170 records/tapes.

Undergraduate Courses offered for part-time students during daytime, evenings, weekends, summer. Complete part-time degree programs offered during daytime, evenings, weekends, summer. Adult/continuing education programs available. Career services available to part-time students: individual and group career counseling, individual job placement, employer recruitment on campus. Part-time tuition: $10 per credit for state residents, $71 per credit for nonresidents.

University of Hawaii–Maui Community College
Kahului 96732

Public institution; city setting. Awards A. Barrier-free campus. Total enrollment: 2,287 (all undergraduates); 63% part-time, 62% women. Total faculty: 107. Library holdings: 33,341 bound volumes, 205 titles on microform, 315 periodical subscriptions, 215 records/tapes.

Undergraduate Courses offered for part-time students during daytime, evenings, weekends, summer. Complete part-time degree programs offered during daytime, evenings, weekends, summer. Adult/continuing education programs available. Career services available to part-time students: individual and group career counseling, individual job placement, employer recruitment on campus. Part-time tuition: $10 per credit for state residents, $70 per credit for nonresidents.

University of Hawaii–West Oahu College
Pearl City 96782

Public institution; small-town setting. Awards B. Barrier-free campus. Total enrollment: 433 (all undergraduates); 57% part-time, 46% women, 80% over 25. Total faculty: 21. Library holdings: 17,173 bound volumes, 30 titles on microform, 95 periodical subscriptions, 18 records/tapes.

Undergraduate Courses offered for part-time students during daytime, evenings, weekends, summer. Complete part-time degree programs offered during daytime, evenings, weekends. Career services available to part-time students: individual career counseling. Part-time tuition: $27 per credit for state residents, $92 per credit for nonresidents.

University of Hawaii–Windward Community College
Kaneohe 96744

Public institution; small-town setting. Awards A. Barrier-free campus. Total enrollment: 1,456 (all undergraduates); 61% part-time, 60% women, 40% over 25. Total faculty: 68. Library holdings: 27,534 bound volumes, 160 titles on microform, 301 periodical subscriptions, 1,704 records/tapes.

Undergraduate Courses offered for part-time students during daytime, evenings. Complete part-time degree programs offered during daytime, evenings. Adult/continuing education programs available. Career services available to part-time students: individual and group career counseling, individual job placement, employer recruitment on campus. Part-time tuition: $10 per credit for state residents, $71 per credit for nonresidents.

IDAHO

Boise Bible College
Boise 83714

Independent-religious instutition; city setting. Awards A, B. Total enrollment: 87 (all undergraduates); 60% part-time, 42% women, 33% over 25. Total faculty: 14. Library holdings: 17,375 bound volumes, 924 titles on microform, 105 periodical subscriptions, 426 records/tapes.

Colleges Offering Part-Time Degree Programs / Idaho

Boise Bible College (continued)

Undergraduate Courses offered for part-time students during daytime, evenings. Complete part-time degree programs offered during daytime. Career services available to part-time students: individual career counseling, individual job placement, employer recruitment on campus. Part-time tuition: $70 per hour.

Boise State University
Boise 83725

Public institution; city setting. Awards A, B, M. Total enrollment: 11,236. Undergraduate enrollment: 9,604; 31% part-time, 51% women, 43% over 25. Total faculty: 453. Library holdings: 279,557 bound volumes, 1,932 periodical subscriptions, 9,838 records/tapes.

Undergraduate Courses offered for part-time students during daytime, evenings, summer. Complete part-time degree programs offered during daytime, evenings. Adult/continuing education programs available. Career services available to part-time students: individual and group career counseling, individual job placement, employer recruitment on campus. Part-time tuition: $49.50 per semester hour for state residents, $49.50 per semester hour for nonresidents.

Graduate Part-time study available in Graduate School. Basic part-time expenses: $0 tuition plus $72 per credit fees.

College of Idaho
Caldwell 83605

Independent-religious instutition; small-town setting. Awards B, M. Total enrollment: 885. Undergraduate enrollment: 631; 16% part-time, 50% women. Total faculty: 104. Library holdings: 115,000 bound volumes, 550 periodical subscriptions, 700 records/tapes.

Undergraduate Courses offered for part-time students during daytime, evenings. Complete part-time degree programs offered during daytime, evenings. Adult/continuing education programs available. Career services available to part-time students: individual and group career counseling, individual job placement, employer recruitment on campus. Part-time tuition: $152 per credit.

Graduate Part-time study available in Graduate Studies. Basic part-time expenses: $81 per unit tuition.

College of Southern Idaho
Twin Falls 83301

Public institution; small-town setting. Awards A. Barrier-free campus. Total enrollment: 2,658 (all undergraduates); 55% part-time, 52% women, 34% over 25. Total faculty: 107. Library holdings: 100,000 bound volumes.

Undergraduate Courses offered for part-time students during daytime, evenings, summer. Complete part-time degree programs offered during daytime, evenings, summer. Adult/continuing education programs available. Career services available to part-time students: individual and group career counseling, individual job placement, employer recruitment on campus. Part-time tuition: $37.50 per credit for state residents, $75 per credit for nonresidents.

Idaho State University
Pocatello 83209

Public institution; small-town setting. Awards A, B, M, D. Total enrollment: 6,041. Undergraduate enrollment: 4,815; 30% part-time, 49% women, 59% over 25. Total faculty: 505. Library holdings: 320,000 bound volumes, 290,000 titles on microform, 3,145 periodical subscriptions.

Undergraduate Courses offered for part-time students during daytime, evenings, summer. Complete part-time degree programs offered during daytime, evenings, summer. Adult/continuing education programs available. Career services available to part-time students: individual and group career counseling, individual job placement, employer recruitment on campus. Part-time tuition: $47.50 per credit for state residents, $47.50 per credit for nonresidents.

Graduate Part-time study available in Graduate School. Basic part-time expenses: $0 tuition plus $63.50 per credit hour fees. Institutional financial aid available to part-time graduate students in Graduate School.

Lewis-Clark State College
Lewiston 83501

Public institution; small-town setting. Awards A, B. Total enrollment: 2,165 (all undergraduates); 37% part-time, 57% women. Total faculty: 120.

Undergraduate Courses offered for part-time students during daytime, evenings, weekends, summer. Complete part-time degree programs offered during daytime, evenings, weekends, summer. External degree and adult/continuing education programs available. Career services available to part-time students: individual and group career counseling, individual job placement, employer recruitment on campus. Part-time tuition: $47.50 per credit hour for state residents, $47.50 per credit hour for nonresidents.

North Idaho College
Coeur d'Alene 83814

Public institution; small-town setting. Awards A. Barrier-free campus. Total enrollment: 2,546 (all undergraduates); 38% part-time, 57% women, 49% over 25. Total faculty: 152. Library holdings: 35,198 bound volumes, 2,724 titles on microform, 475 periodical subscriptions, 3,452 records/tapes.

Undergraduate Courses offered for part-time students during daytime, evenings, weekends, summer. Complete part-time degree programs offered during daytime, evenings, summer. External degree and adult/continuing education programs available. Career services available to part-time students: individual and group career counseling, employer recruitment on campus. Part-time tuition: $30 per credit for state residents, $71 per credit for nonresidents.

Northwest Nazarene College
Nampa 83651

Independent-religious instutition; small-town setting. Awards A, B, M. Total enrollment: 1,111. Undergraduate enrollment: 1,072; 6% part-time, 53% women. Total faculty: 85. Library holdings: 115,769 bound volumes, 21,253 titles on microform, 502 periodical subscriptions, 1,806 records/tapes.

Undergraduate Courses offered for part-time students during daytime, evenings, summer. Complete part-time degree programs offered during daytime, summer. Career services available to part-time students: individual and group career counseling, individual job placement, employer recruitment on campus. Part-time tuition: $110 per credit.

Illinois / Colleges Offering Part-Time Degree Programs

Ricks College
Rexburg 83440

Independent-religious instutition; small-town setting. Awards A. Barrier-free campus. Total enrollment: 6,456 (all undergraduates); 21% part-time, 60% women, 3% over 25. Total faculty: 314. Library holdings: 120,374 bound volumes, 120,005 titles on microform, 670 periodical subscriptions, 9,100 records/tapes.

Undergraduate Courses offered for part-time students during daytime, evenings, summer. Complete part-time degree programs offered during daytime, evenings, summer. Adult/continuing education programs available. Career services available to part-time students: individual and group career counseling, individual job placement, employer recruitment on campus. Part-time tuition: $57 per credit hour.

University of Idaho
Moscow 83843

Public institution; small-town setting. Awards B, M, D. Total enrollment: 9,237. Undergraduate enrollment: 7,556; 17% part-time, 38% women, 27% over 25. Total faculty: 576. Library holdings: 625,833 bound volumes, 347,253 titles on microform, 5,426 periodical subscriptions.

Undergraduate Courses offered for part-time students during daytime, summer. Complete part-time degree programs offered during daytime, summer. Adult/continuing education programs available. Career services available to part-time students: individual and group career counseling, individual job placement, employer recruitment on campus. Part-time tuition: $50 per credit for state residents, $50 per credit for nonresidents.

ILLINOIS

Alfred Adler Institute
Chicago 60601

Independent institution (graduate only). Total enrollment: 101 (primarily women; 100% part-time). Total faculty: 27.

Graduate Part-time study available in Graduate Programs in Psychology. Degree can be earned exclusively through evening/weekend study in Graduate Programs in Psychology.Basic part-time expenses: $250 per course tuition plus $6 per quarter fees.

American Academy of Art
Chicago 60604

Proprietary institution; metropolitan setting. Awards A. Total enrollment: 887 (all undergraduates); 50% part-time, 50% women, 6% over 25. Total faculty: 26.

Undergraduate Courses offered for part-time students during evenings, weekends, summer. Complete part-time degree programs offered during evenings, weekends, summer. Career services available to part-time students: individual and group career counseling, individual job placement, employer recruitment on campus. Part-time tuition: $123 per semester hour.

American Conservatory of Music
Chicago 60603

Independent institution; metropolitan setting. Awards A, B, M, D. Barrier-free campus. Total enrollment: 291. Undergraduate enrollment: 243; 47% part-time, 47% women. Total faculty: 131. Library holdings: 8,135 bound volumes, 30 periodical subscriptions, 1,639 records/tapes.

Undergraduate Courses offered for part-time students during daytime, evenings, weekends, summer. Complete part-time degree programs offered during daytime, evenings, weekends, summer. Adult/continuing education programs available. Part-time tuition: $102 per credit.

Graduate Part-time study available in Graduate Studies.Basic part-time expenses: $120 per credit hour (minimum) tuition plus $25 per semester fees.

Augustana College
Rock Island 61201

Independent-religious instutition; city setting. Awards B. Barrier-free campus. Total enrollment: 2,352 (all undergraduates); 6% part-time, 50% women, 4% over 25. Total faculty: 144. Library holdings: 228,783 bound volumes, 29,058 titles on microform, 1,440 periodical subscriptions, 1,665 records/tapes.

Undergraduate Courses offered for part-time students during daytime. Complete part-time degree programs offered during daytime. Career services available to part-time students: individual career counseling, employer recruitment on campus. Part-time tuition: $156 per quarter hour.

Aurora College
Aurora 60506

Independent-religious instutition; city setting. Awards B, M. Total enrollment: 1,490. Undergraduate enrollment: 1,357; 40% part-time, 45% women, 9% over 25. Total faculty: 88. Library holdings: 110,000 bound volumes, 169 titles on microform, 574 periodical subscriptions, 2,459 records/tapes.

Undergraduate Courses offered for part-time students during daytime, evenings, weekends, summer. Complete part-time degree programs offered during daytime, evenings, weekends. Adult/continuing education programs available. Career services available to part-time students: individual and group career counseling, individual job placement, employer recruitment on campus. Part-time tuition: $465 per unit.

Graduate Part-time study available in Center for Graduate Study. Degree can be earned exclusively through evening/weekend study in Center for Graduate Study.Basic part-time expenses: $155 per credit tuition.

Barat College
Lake Forest 60045

Independent-religious instutition; small-town setting. Awards B. Total enrollment: 732 (all undergraduates); 51% part-time, 87% women, 53% over 25. Total faculty: 72. Library holdings: 85,000 bound volumes, 624 periodical subscriptions, 1,000 records/tapes.

Undergraduate Courses offered for part-time students during daytime, evenings, weekends, summer. Complete part-time degree programs offered during daytime, evenings, summer. Adult/continuing education programs available. Career services available to part-time students: individual and group career counseling, individual job placement, employer recruitment on campus. Part-time tuition: $175 per semester hour.

Belleville Area College
Belleville 62221

Public institution; small-town setting. Awards A. Barrier-free campus. Total enrollment: 12,765 (all undergraduates); 74% part-time, 55% women, 55% over 25. Total faculty: 483. Library

Colleges Offering Part-Time Degree Programs / Illinois

Belleville Area College (continued)
holdings: 2,100 bound volumes, 445 periodical subscriptions, 2,119 records/tapes.
Undergraduate Courses offered for part-time students during daytime, evenings, weekends, summer. Complete part-time degree programs offered during daytime, evenings, summer. Adult/continuing education programs available. Career services available to part-time students: individual and group career counseling, individual job placement. Part-time tuition: $23 per credit hour for area residents, $46 per credit hour for state residents, $69 per credit hour for nonresidents.

Bethany Theological Seminary
Oak Brook 60521

Independent-religious institution (graduate only). Total enrollment: 121 (coed; 32% part-time). Total faculty: 20. Library holdings: 130,000 bound volumes, 10,000 microforms.
Graduate Part-time study available in Graduate and Professional Programs. Basic part-time expenses: $67 per hour tuition. Institutional financial aid available to part-time graduate students in Graduate and Professional Programs.

Blackburn College
Carlinville 62626

Independent-religious instutition; small-town setting. Awards B. Total enrollment: 540 (all undergraduates); 9% part-time, 56% women, 5% over 25. Total faculty: 50. Library holdings: 69,487 bound volumes, 400 periodical subscriptions, 3,534 records/tapes.
Undergraduate Courses offered for part-time students during daytime. Complete part-time degree programs offered during daytime. Career services available to part-time students: individual and group career counseling, individual job placement, employer recruitment on campus. Part-time tuition: $170 per semester hour.

Black Hawk College–East Campus
Kewanee 61443

Public institution; rural setting. Awards A. Barrier-free campus. Total enrollment: 1,250 (all undergraduates); 45% part-time, 52% women, 47% over 25. Total faculty: 101. Library holdings: 14,000 bound volumes, 65 periodical subscriptions, 300 records/tapes.
Undergraduate Courses offered for part-time students during daytime, evenings, summer. Complete part-time degree programs offered during daytime, evenings, summer. Adult/continuing education programs available. Career services available to part-time students: individual and group career counseling, individual job placement. Part-time tuition: $29.50 per semester hour for area residents, $57.50 per semester hour for state residents, $79 per semester hour for nonresidents.

Bradley University
Peoria 61625

Independent institution; city setting. Awards B, M. Total enrollment: 5,604. Undergraduate enrollment: 5,040; 6% part-time, 44% women, 7% over 25. Total faculty: 377. Library holdings: 335,000 bound volumes, 315,000 titles on microform, 1,500 periodical subscriptions, 5,000 records/tapes.
Undergraduate Courses offered for part-time students during daytime, evenings, summer. Complete part-time degree programs offered during daytime, evenings, summer. Adult/continuing education programs available. Career services available to part-time students: individual and group career counseling, individual job placement, employer recruitment on campus. Part-time tuition: $157 per credit.
Graduate Part-time study available in Graduate School. Basic part-time expenses: $157 per credit hour (minimum) tuition. Institutional financial aid available to part-time graduate students in Graduate School.

Carl Sandburg College
Galesburg 61401

Public institution; small-town setting. Awards A. Barrier-free campus. Total enrollment: 3,890 (all undergraduates); 68% part-time, 63% women, 60% over 25. Total faculty: 117. Library holdings: 34,000 bound volumes, 75 periodical subscriptions, 2,500 records/tapes.
Undergraduate Courses offered for part-time students during daytime, evenings, weekends, summer. Complete part-time degree programs offered during daytime, evenings, weekends, summer. Adult/continuing education programs available. Career services available to part-time students: individual and group career counseling, individual job placement, employer recruitment on campus. Part-time tuition: $13.75 per quarter hour for area residents, $39.64 per quarter hour for state residents, $54.89 per quarter hour for nonresidents.

Catholic Theological Union at Chicago
Chicago 60615

Independent-religious institution (graduate only). Total enrollment: 312 (coed; 9% part-time). Total faculty: 47. Library holdings: 87,000 bound volumes, 25 microforms.
Graduate Part-time study available in Graduate and Professional Programs. Basic part-time expenses: $105 per credit tuition plus $5 per quarter fees. Institutional financial aid available to part-time graduate students in Graduate and Professional Programs.

Chicago City-Wide College
Chicago 60601

See City Colleges of Chicago, Chicago City-Wide College

Chicago College of Commerce
Chicago 60603

Proprietary institution; metropolitan setting. Awards A. Barrier-free campus. Total enrollment: 457 (all undergraduates); 50% part-time, 95% women, 54% over 25. Total faculty: 25. Library holdings: 1,000 bound volumes, 20 periodical subscriptions, 700 records/tapes.
Undergraduate Courses offered for part-time students during evenings, weekends, summer. Complete part-time degree programs offered during evenings, weekends. Career services available to part-time students: individual career counseling, individual job placement. Part-time tuition: $900 per year.

Chicago School of Professional Psychology
Chicago 60605

Independent institution (graduate only). Total enrollment: 111 (coed; 55% part-time). Total faculty: 24. Library holdings: 7,200 bound volumes, 1,500 microforms.

Illinois / **Colleges Offering Part-Time Degree Programs**

Graduate Part-time study available in Graduate Program. Degree can be earned exclusively through evening/weekend study in Graduate Program.Basic part-time expenses: $260 per semester hour tuition plus $10 per semester fees. Institutional financial aid available to part-time graduate students in Graduate Program.

Chicago State University
Chicago 60628

Public institution; metropolitan setting. Awards B, M. Barrier-free campus. Total enrollment: 7,510. Undergraduate enrollment: 5,875; 36% part-time, 65% women, 42% over 25. Total faculty: 430. Library holdings: 260,000 bound volumes, 350,000 titles on microform, 2,000 periodical subscriptions, 20,000 records/tapes.

Undergraduate Courses offered for part-time students during daytime, evenings, summer. Complete part-time degree programs offered during daytime, evenings, summer. External degree and adult/continuing education programs available. Career services available to part-time students: individual and group career counseling, individual job placement, employer recruitment on campus. Part-time tuition: $38.25 per credit hour for state residents, $114.75 per credit hour for nonresidents.

Graduate Part-time study available in Graduate Division.Basic part-time expenses: $41.75 per hour tuition plus $38 per trimester fees for state residents, $131.25 per hour tuition plus $38 per trimester fees for nonresidents.

Chicago Theological Seminary
Chicago 60637

Independent-religious institution (graduate only). Total enrollment: 133 (coed; 48% part-time). Total faculty: 14.

Graduate Part-time study available in Graduate and Professional Programs.Basic part-time expenses: $356 per course (minimum) tuition plus $10 per quarter fees.

Christ Seminary–Seminex
Chicago 60615

Independent institution (graduate only). Total enrollment: 91 (primarily men; 100% part-time).

Graduate Part-time study available in Graduate Program (offered jointly with Lutheran School of Theology at Chicago).Basic part-time expenses: $1000 per year tuition. Institutional financial aid available to part-time graduate students in Graduate Program (offered jointly with Lutheran School of Theology at Chicago).

City Colleges of Chicago, Chicago City-Wide College
Chicago 60601

Public institution; metropolitan setting. Awards A. Barrier-free campus. Total enrollment: 12,841 (all undergraduates); 96% part-time, 60% women, 85% over 25. Total faculty: 308.

Undergraduate Courses offered for part-time students during daytime, evenings, weekends, summer. Complete part-time degree programs offered during daytime, evenings, summer. External degree and adult/continuing education programs available. Career services available to part-time students: individual and group career counseling, individual job placement, employer recruitment on campus. Part-time tuition: $23 per credit hour for area residents, $40.41 per credit hour for state residents, $52.46 per credit hour for nonresidents.

City Colleges of Chicago, Harry S Truman College
Chicago 60640

Public institution; metropolitan setting. Awards A. Barrier-free campus. Total enrollment: 11,037 (all undergraduates); 84% part-time, 63% women, 74% over 25. Total faculty: 379. Library holdings: 59,750 bound volumes, 395 titles on microform, 250 periodical subscriptions, 21,900 records/tapes.

Undergraduate Courses offered for part-time students during daytime, evenings, weekends, summer. Complete part-time degree programs offered during daytime, evenings, summer. Adult/continuing education programs available. Career services available to part-time students: individual and group career counseling, individual job placement, employer recruitment on campus. Part-time tuition: $23 per credit hour for area residents, $40.41 per credit hour for state residents, $52.46 per credit hour for nonresidents.

City Colleges of Chicago, Kennedy-King College
Chicago 60621

Public institution; metropolitan setting. Awards A. Barrier-free campus. Total enrollment: 8,289 (all undergraduates); 74% part-time, 65% women, 66% over 25. Total faculty: 334. Library holdings: 41,906 bound volumes, 164 titles on microform, 264 periodical subscriptions, 29,422 records/tapes.

Undergraduate Courses offered for part-time students during daytime, evenings, weekends, summer. Complete part-time degree programs offered during daytime, evenings, summer. Adult/continuing education programs available. Career services available to part-time students: individual and group career counseling, individual job placement, employer recruitment on campus. Part-time tuition: $23 per credit hour for area residents, $40.41 per credit hour for state residents, $52.46 per credit hour for nonresidents.

City Colleges of Chicago, Loop College
Chicago 60601

Public institution; metropolitan setting. Awards A. Barrier-free campus. Total enrollment: 9,055 (all undergraduates); 76% part-time, 65% women, 50% over 25. Total faculty: 285. Library holdings: 51,493 bound volumes, 5,569 titles on microform, 309 periodical subscriptions, 37,617 records/tapes.

Undergraduate Courses offered for part-time students during daytime, evenings, weekends, summer. Complete part-time degree programs offered during daytime, evenings, summer. Adult/continuing education programs available. Career services available to part-time students: individual and group career counseling, individual job placement, employer recruitment on campus. Part-time tuition: $23 per credit hour for area residents, $40.41 per credit hour for state residents, $52.46 per credit hour for nonresidents.

City Colleges of Chicago, Malcolm X College
Chicago 60612

Public institution; metropolitan setting. Awards A. Barrier-free campus. Total enrollment: 6,520 (all undergraduates); 69% part-time, 73% women, 64% over 25. Total faculty: 310. Library

Colleges Offering Part-Time Degree Programs / *Illinois*

City Colleges of Chicago, Malcolm X College (continued)
holdings: 39,200 bound volumes, 1,683 titles on microform, 314 periodical subscriptions, 11,260 records/tapes.
Undergraduate Courses offered for part-time students during daytime, evenings, weekends, summer. Complete part-time degree programs offered during daytime, evenings, summer. Adult/continuing education programs available. Career services available to part-time students: individual and group career counseling, individual job placement, employer recruitment on campus. Part-time tuition: $23 per credit hour for area residents, $40.41 per credit hour for state residents, $52.46 per credit hour for nonresidents.

City Colleges of Chicago, Olive-Harvey College
Chicago 60628
Public institution; metropolitan setting. Awards A. Barrier-free campus. Total enrollment: 7,771 (all undergraduates); 78% part-time, 70% women, 66% over 25. Total faculty: 236. Library holdings: 51,893 bound volumes, 4,724 titles on microform, 312 periodical subscriptions, 1,712 records/tapes.
Undergraduate Courses offered for part-time students during daytime, evenings, weekends, summer. Complete part-time degree programs offered during daytime, evenings, summer. Adult/continuing education programs available. Career services available to part-time students: individual and group career counseling, individual job placement, employer recruitment on campus. Part-time tuition: $23 per credit hour for area residents, $40.41 per credit hour for state residents, $52.46 per credit hour for nonresidents.

City Colleges of Chicago, Richard J Daley College
Chicago 60652
Public institution; metropolitan setting. Awards A. Barrier-free campus. Total enrollment: 10,718 (all undergraduates); 87% part-time, 66% women, 57% over 25. Total faculty: 309. Library holdings: 42,645 bound volumes, 87 titles on microform, 394 periodical subscriptions, 36,534 records/tapes.
Undergraduate Courses offered for part-time students during daytime, evenings, weekends, summer. Complete part-time degree programs offered during daytime, evenings, summer. Adult/continuing education programs available. Career services available to part-time students: individual and group career counseling, individual job placement, employer recruitment on campus. Part-time tuition: $23 per credit hour for area residents, $40.41 per credit hour for state residents, $52.46 per credit hour for nonresidents.

City Colleges of Chicago, Wilbur Wright College
Chicago 60634
Public institution; metropolitan setting. Awards A. Barrier-free campus. Total enrollment: 9,382 (all undergraduates); 82% part-time, 62% women, 48% over 25. Total faculty: 338. Library holdings: 67,389 bound volumes, 12,256 titles on microform, 550 periodical subscriptions, 15,165 records/tapes.
Undergraduate Courses offered for part-time students during daytime, evenings, weekends, summer. Complete part-time degree programs offered during daytime, evenings, summer. Adult/continuing education programs available. Career services available to part-time students: individual and group career counseling, individual job placement, employer recruitment on campus. Part-time tuition: $23 per credit hour for area residents, $40.41 per credit hour for state residents, $52.46 per credit hour for nonresidents.

College of Automation
Chicago 60606
Proprietary institution; metropolitan setting. Awards A. Barrier-free campus. Total enrollment: 242 (all undergraduates); 0% part-time, 51% women, 58% over 25. Total faculty: 21. Library holdings: 100 bound volumes, 35 periodical subscriptions.
Undergraduate Courses offered for part-time students during daytime, evenings, summer. Complete part-time degree programs offered during daytime, evenings. Career services available to part-time students: individual and group career counseling, individual job placement, employer recruitment on campus. Part-time tuition: $151 per credit hour.

College of DuPage
Glen Ellyn 60137
Public institution; city setting. Awards A. Barrier-free campus. Total enrollment: 23,303 (all undergraduates); 74% part-time, 56% women, 55% over 25. Total faculty: 1,220. Library holdings: 107,500 bound volumes, 34,185 titles on microform, 739 periodical subscriptions, 19,767 records/tapes.
Undergraduate Courses offered for part-time students during daytime, evenings, weekends, summer. Complete part-time degree programs offered during daytime, evenings, weekends, summer. External degree and adult/continuing education programs available. Career services available to part-time students: individual and group career counseling, individual job placement, employer recruitment on campus. Part-time tuition: $17 per quarter hour for area residents, $37 per quarter hour for state residents, $55 per quarter hour for nonresidents.

College of Lake County
Grayslake 60030
Public institution; rural setting. Awards A. Total enrollment: 12,187 (all undergraduates); 82% part-time, 56% women. Total faculty: 657. Library holdings: 87,193 bound volumes, 398 periodical subscriptions, 2,485 records/tapes.
Undergraduate Courses offered for part-time students during daytime, evenings, weekends, summer. Complete part-time degree programs offered during daytime, evenings, weekends, summer. External degree and adult/continuing education programs available. Career services available to part-time students: individual career counseling, individual job placement, employer recruitment on campus. Part-time tuition: $23.15 per credit hour for area residents, $64.10 per credit hour for state residents, $87.04 per credit hour for nonresidents.

College of St Francis
Joliet 60435
Independent-religious instutition; city setting. Awards B, M. Barrier-free campus. Total enrollment: 1,062. Undergraduate enrollment: 1,021; 20% part-time, 60% women, 12% over 25. Total faculty: 87. Library holdings: 130,000 bound volumes, 480 periodical subscriptions, 5,400 records/tapes.
Undergraduate Courses offered for part-time students during daytime, evenings, summer. Complete part-time degree programs offered during daytime, evenings. External degree and adult/continuing education programs available. Career services available to part-time students: individual and group career

Illinois / **Colleges Offering Part-Time Degree Programs**

counseling, individual job placement, employer recruitment on campus. Part-time tuition: $128 per credit.

Graduate Part-time study available in Graduate Program in Health Services Administration. Degree can be earned exclusively through evening/weekend study in Graduate Program in Health Services Administration. Basic part-time expenses: $130 per semester hour tuition. Institutional financial aid available to part-time graduate students in Graduate Program in Health Services Administration.

Columbia College
Chicago 60605

Independent institution; metropolitan setting. Awards B, M. Barrier-free campus. Total enrollment: 4,754. Undergraduate enrollment: 4,583; 30% part-time, 47% women, 17% over 25. Total faculty: 473.

Undergraduate Courses offered for part-time students during daytime, evenings, weekends, summer. Complete part-time degree programs offered during daytime, evenings, weekends, summer. Career services available to part-time students: individual and group career counseling, individual job placement, employer recruitment on campus. Part-time tuition: $130 per semester hour.

Graduate Part-time study available in Graduate Division. Degree can be earned exclusively through evening/weekend study in Graduate Division. Basic part-time expenses: $158 per credit tuition plus $15 per semester fees.

Concordia College
River Forest 60305

Independent-religious instutition; small-town setting. Awards B, M. Total enrollment: 1,322. Undergraduate enrollment: 1,150; 1% part-time, 65% women. Total faculty: 114. Library holdings: 135,000 bound volumes, 212,000 titles on microform, 800 periodical subscriptions, 3,750 records/tapes.

Graduate Part-time study available in Graduate Studies. Degree can be earned exclusively through evening/weekend study in Graduate Studies. Basic part-time expenses: $90 per credit tuition. Institutional financial aid available to part-time graduate students in Graduate Studies.

Daley College
Chicago 60652

See City Colleges of Chicago, Richard J Daley College

Danville Area Community College
Danville 61832

Public institution; small-town setting. Awards A. Barrier-free campus. Total enrollment: 3,866 (all undergraduates); 60% part-time, 54% women. Total faculty: 219. Library holdings: 30,000 bound volumes, 200 periodical subscriptions, 3,000 records/tapes.

Undergraduate Courses offered for part-time students during daytime, evenings, summer. Complete part-time degree programs offered during daytime, evenings, summer. Adult/continuing education programs available. Career services available to part-time students: individual and group career counseling, individual job placement, employer recruitment on campus. Part-time tuition: $22 per credit for area residents, $60.61 per credit for state residents, $81.56 per credit for nonresidents.

De Lourdes College
Des Plaines 60016

Independent-religious instutition; city setting. Awards B. Barrier-free campus. Total enrollment: 204 (all undergraduates); 83% part-time, 100% women, 95% over 25. Total faculty: 25. Library holdings: 20,400 bound volumes, 145 periodical subscriptions, 3,847 records/tapes.

Undergraduate Courses offered for part-time students during daytime, evenings, summer. Complete part-time degree programs offered during daytime. Part-time tuition: $50 per semester hour.

DePaul University
Chicago 60604

Independent-religious instutition; metropolitan setting. Awards B, M, D. Barrier-free campus. Total enrollment: 12,447. Undergraduate enrollment: 7,694; 46% part-time, 46% women, 40% over 25. Total faculty: 925. Library holdings: 371,076 bound volumes, 15,371 titles on microform, 4,905 periodical subscriptions, 7,110 records/tapes.

Undergraduate Courses offered for part-time students during daytime, evenings, weekends, summer. Complete part-time degree programs offered during daytime, evenings, weekends, summer. Adult/continuing education programs available. Career services available to part-time students: individual and group career counseling, individual job placement, employer recruitment on campus. Part-time tuition: $102 per quarter hour.

Graduate Part-time study available in College of Law, College of Liberal Arts and Sciences, Graduate School of Business, School of Education, School of Music. Basic part-time expenses: $132 per quarter hour tuition plus $10 per quarter fees. Institutional financial aid available to part-time graduate students in College of Law, College of Liberal Arts and Sciences, Graduate School of Business, School of Education, School of Music.

DeVry Institute of Technology
Chicago 60618

Proprietary institution; metropolitan setting. Awards A, B. Barrier-free campus. Total enrollment: 4,838 (all undergraduates); 21% part-time, 16% women. Total faculty: 177.

Undergraduate Courses offered for part-time students during daytime, evenings. Complete part-time degree programs offered during daytime. Adult/continuing education programs available. Career services available to part-time students: individual and group career counseling, individual job placement, employer recruitment on campus. Part-time tuition: $1990 per year.

DeVry Institute of Technology
Lombard 60148

Proprietary institution; small-town setting. Awards A, B. Barrier-free campus. Total enrollment: 2,865 (all undergraduates); 13% part-time, 19% women. Total faculty: 119.

Undergraduate Courses offered for part-time students during daytime. Complete part-time degree programs offered during daytime. Adult/continuing education programs available. Career services available to part-time students: individual and group career counseling, individual job placement, employer recruitment on campus. Part-time tuition: $1990 per year.

Colleges Offering Part-Time Degree Programs / *Illinois*

Eastern Illinois University
Charleston 61920

Public institution; small-town setting. Awards B, M. Total enrollment: 10,028. Undergraduate enrollment: 9,214; 9% part-time, 54% women, 7% over 25. Total faculty: 549. Library holdings: 498,367 bound volumes, 1.2 million titles on microform, 2,880 periodical subscriptions, 35,602 records/tapes.

Undergraduate Courses offered for part-time students during daytime, evenings, summer. Complete part-time degree programs offered during daytime, summer. External degree and adult/continuing education programs available. Career services available to part-time students: individual and group career counseling, individual job placement, employer recruitment on campus. Part-time tuition: $38.25 per credit hour for state residents, $114.75 per credit hour for nonresidents.

Graduate Part-time study available in Graduate School. Basic part-time expenses: $43.75 per semester hour tuition plus $11.65 per semester hour fees for state residents, $131.25 per semester hour tuition plus $11.65 per semester hour fees for nonresidents. Institutional financial aid available to part-time graduate students in Graduate School.

East-West University
Chicago 60605

Independent institution; metropolitan setting. Awards A, B. Barrier-free campus. Total enrollment: 515 (all undergraduates); 3% part-time, 51% women. Total faculty: 29. Library holdings: 16,300 bound volumes.

Undergraduate Courses offered for part-time students during daytime, evenings, summer. Complete part-time degree programs offered during daytime. Career services available to part-time students: individual and group career counseling. Part-time tuition: $110 per quarter hour.

Elgin Community College
Elgin 60120

Public institution; city setting. Awards A. Barrier-free campus. Total enrollment: 6,610 (all undergraduates); 81% part-time, 55% women, 51% over 25. Total faculty: 364. Library holdings: 42,000 bound volumes, 60 titles on microform, 160 periodical subscriptions, 2,600 records/tapes.

Undergraduate Courses offered for part-time students during daytime, evenings, summer. Complete part-time degree programs offered during daytime, evenings, summer. Adult/continuing education programs available. Career services available to part-time students: individual and group career counseling, individual job placement, employer recruitment on campus. Part-time tuition: $25.50 per credit hour for area residents, $66.70 per credit hour for state residents, $89.73 per credit hour for nonresidents.

Elmhurst College
Elmhurst 60126

Independent-religious instutition; city setting. Awards B. Total enrollment: 3,605 (all undergraduates); 47% part-time, 58% women, 35% over 25. Total faculty: 184. Library holdings: 160,000 bound volumes, 830 periodical subscriptions.

Undergraduate Courses offered for part-time students during daytime, evenings, weekends, summer. Complete part-time degree programs offered during daytime, evenings. External degree and adult/continuing education programs available. Part-time tuition: $540 per course.

Eureka College
Eureka 61530

Independent-religious instutition; small-town setting. Awards B. Total enrollment: 503 (all undergraduates); 3% part-time, 48% women, 6% over 25. Total faculty: 52. Library holdings: 75,000 bound volumes.

Undergraduate Courses offered for part-time students during daytime. Complete part-time degree programs offered during daytime. Adult/continuing education programs available. Career services available to part-time students: individual career counseling, individual job placement, employer recruitment on campus. Part-time tuition: $110 per semester hour.

Felician College
Chicago 60659

Independent-religious instutition; metropolitan setting. Awards A. Total enrollment: 403 (all undergraduates); 60% part-time, 82% women, 12% over 25. Total faculty: 30. Library holdings: 60,000 bound volumes, 225 periodical subscriptions, 1,244 records/tapes.

Undergraduate Courses offered for part-time students during daytime, evenings, summer. Complete part-time degree programs offered during daytime, evenings, summer. Adult/continuing education programs available. Career services available to part-time students: individual career counseling. Part-time tuition: $65 per credit.

Forest Institute of Professional Psychology
Des Plaines 60016

Independent institution (graduate only). Total enrollment: 123 (coed; 37% part-time). Total faculty: 35. Library holdings: 8,500 bound volumes, 6,000 microforms.

Graduate Part-time study available in Graduate Programs. Degree can be earned exclusively through evening/weekend study in Graduate Programs. Basic part-time expenses: $150 per credit tuition plus $10 per trimester fees. Institutional financial aid available to part-time graduate students in Graduate Programs.

Garrett-Evangelical Theological Seminary
Evanston 60201

Independent-religious instutition (graduate only). Total enrollment: 340 (coed; 24% part-time). Total faculty: 35. Library holdings: 253,500 bound volumes.

Graduate Part-time study available in Graduate and Professional Programs. Basic part-time expenses: $425 per quarter (minimum) tuition for state residents, for nonresidents. Institutional financial aid available to part-time graduate students in Graduate and Professional Programs.

Gem City College
Quincy 62306

Proprietary institution; small-town setting. Awards A. Barrier-free campus. Total enrollment: 525 (all undergraduates); 5% part-time, 60% women, 10% over 25. Total faculty: 30. Library holdings: 2,700 bound volumes, 40 periodical subscriptions, 15 records/tapes.

Undergraduate Courses offered for part-time students during daytime, evenings, summer. Complete part-time degree pro-

grams offered during daytime. Adult/continuing education programs available. Career services available to part-time students: individual career counseling, individual job placement. Part-time tuition: $55 per quarter hour.

George Williams College
Downers Grove 60515

Independent institution; small-town setting. Awards B, M. Total enrollment: 1,036. Undergraduate enrollment: 551; 22% part-time, 68% women, 30% over 25. Total faculty: 103. Library holdings: 93,000 bound volumes, 600 periodical subscriptions.

Undergraduate Courses offered for part-time students during daytime, evenings, weekends, summer. Complete part-time degree programs offered during daytime, evenings, summer. Adult/continuing education programs available. Career services available to part-time students: individual and group career counseling, individual job placement, employer recruitment on campus. Part-time tuition: $139 per quarter hour.

Graduate Part-time study available in Division of Counseling Psychology, Division of Leisure and Environmental Resources Administration, Division of Natural and Health Sciences, Division of Physical Education, Graduate Division of Social Work Education, School of Management and Organizational Behavior. Degree can be earned exclusively through evening/weekend study in Division of Counseling Psychology, Division of Leisure and Environmental Resources Administration, Division of Natural and Health Sciences, Division of Physical Education, Graduate Division of Social Work Education, School of Management and Organizational Behavior. Basic part-time expenses: $156 per credit tuition plus $2 per credit fees. Institutional financial aid available to part-time graduate students in Division of Counseling Psychology, Division of Leisure and Environmental Resources Administration, Division of Natural and Health Sciences, Division of Physical Education, Graduate Division of Social Work Education, School of Management and Organizational Behavior.

Governors State University
University Park 60466

Public institution; small-town setting. Awards B, M. Barrier-free campus. Total enrollment: 4,546. Undergraduate enrollment: 1,906; 70% part-time, 57% women, 74% over 25. Total faculty: 320. Library holdings: 213,226 bound volumes, 357,794 titles on microform, 2,347 periodical subscriptions, 27,000 records/tapes.

Undergraduate Courses offered for part-time students during daytime, evenings, weekends, summer. Complete part-time degree programs offered during daytime, evenings, weekends, summer. Adult/continuing education programs available. Career services available to part-time students: individual and group career counseling, individual job placement, employer recruitment on campus. Part-time tuition: $42.25 per credit hour for state residents, $126.75 per credit hour for nonresidents.

Graduate Part-time study available in College of Arts and Sciences, College of Business and Public Administration, College of Education, College of Health Professions. Degree can be earned exclusively through evening/weekend study in College of Arts and Sciences, College of Business and Public Administration, College of Education, College of Health Professions. Basic part-time expenses: $45.75 per hour tuition plus $20 per trimester fees for state residents, $137.25 per hour tuition plus $20 per trimester fees for nonresidents. Institutional financial aid available to part-time graduate students in College of Arts and Sciences, College of Business and Public Administration, College of Education, College of Health Professions.

Greenville College
Greenville 62246

Independent-religious instutition; small-town setting. Awards B. Total enrollment: 688 (all undergraduates); 22% part-time, 54% women. Total faculty: 74. Library holdings: 100,000 bound volumes, 450 periodical subscriptions, 2,384 records/tapes.

Undergraduate Courses offered for part-time students during daytime, evenings. Complete part-time degree programs offered during daytime, evenings. Career services available to part-time students: individual and group career counseling, individual job placement, employer recruitment on campus. Part-time tuition: $142 per credit hour.

Highland Community College
Freeport 61032

Public institution; rural setting. Awards A. Barrier-free campus. Total enrollment: 2,534 (all undergraduates); 62% part-time, 59% women, 58% over 25. Total faculty: 103. Library holdings: 33,000 bound volumes, 45 periodical subscriptions, 300 records/tapes.

Undergraduate Courses offered for part-time students during daytime, evenings, summer. Complete part-time degree programs offered during daytime, evenings. Adult/continuing education programs available. Career services available to part-time students: individual and group career counseling, individual job placement, employer recruitment on campus. Part-time tuition: $19 per credit hour for area residents, $54.42 per credit hour for state residents, $76.50 per credit hour for nonresidents.

Illinois Benedictine College
Lisle 60532

Independent-religious instutition; small-town setting. Awards B, M. Total enrollment: 2,345. Undergraduate enrollment: 1,929; 55% part-time, 50% women. Total faculty: 119. Library holdings: 171,000 bound volumes, 5,000 titles on microform, 941 periodical subscriptions, 7,392 records/tapes.

Undergraduate Courses offered for part-time students during daytime, evenings, summer. Complete part-time degree programs offered during daytime, evenings. Adult/continuing education programs available. Career services available to part-time students: individual and group career counseling, individual job placement, employer recruitment on campus. Part-time tuition: $165 per credit hour.

Graduate Part-time study available in Graduate Program in Business Administration. Degree can be earned exclusively through evening/weekend study in Graduate Program in Business Administration. Basic part-time expenses: $500 per course tuition. Institutional financial aid available to part-time graduate students in Graduate Program in Business Administration.

Illinois Central College
East Peoria 61635

Public institution; city setting. Awards A. Barrier-free campus. Total enrollment: 14,469 (all undergraduates); 75% part-time, 58% women. Total faculty: 639. Library holdings: 69,000 bound volumes.

Undergraduate Courses offered for part-time students during daytime, evenings, weekends, summer. Complete part-time degree programs offered during daytime, evenings, weekends, summer. Adult/continuing education programs available. Career services available to part-time students: individual and group career counseling, individual job placement, employer recruitment on campus. Part-time tuition: $20 per semester

Colleges Offering Part-Time Degree Programs / Illinois

Illinois Central College (continued)
hour for area residents, $70 per semester hour for state residents, $95 per semester hour for nonresidents.

Illinois Eastern Community Colleges, Frontier Community College
Fairfield 62837

Public institution; rural setting. Awards A. Barrier-free campus. Total enrollment: 3,529 (all undergraduates); 93% part-time, 70% women. Total faculty: 514. Library holdings: 4,500 bound volumes, 50 titles on microform, 76 periodical subscriptions, 350 records/tapes.

Undergraduate Courses offered for part-time students during daytime, evenings, weekends, summer. Complete part-time degree programs offered during daytime, evenings, weekends, summer. External degree and adult/continuing education programs available. Career services available to part-time students: individual and group career counseling, individual job placement. Part-time tuition: $8 per quarter hour for area residents, $31.76 per quarter hour for state residents, $46.04 per quarter hour for nonresidents.

Illinois Eastern Community Colleges, Lincoln Trail College
Robinson 62454

Public institution; rural setting. Awards A. Barrier-free campus. Total enrollment: 1,285 (all undergraduates); 63% part-time, 59% women, 2% over 25. Total faculty: 116. Library holdings: 21,000 bound volumes, 33 periodical subscriptions, 500 records/tapes.

Undergraduate Courses offered for part-time students during daytime, evenings, weekends, summer. Complete part-time degree programs offered during daytime, evenings, weekends, summer. External degree and adult/continuing education programs available. Career services available to part-time students: individual and group career counseling, individual job placement, employer recruitment on campus. Part-time tuition: $8 per quarter hour for area residents, $31.76 per quarter hour for state residents, $46.04 per quarter hour for nonresidents.

Illinois Eastern Community Colleges, Olney Central College
Olney 62450

Public institution; rural setting. Awards A. Barrier-free campus. Total enrollment: 2,077 (all undergraduates); 60% part-time, 59% women. Total faculty: 130. Library holdings: 27,370 bound volumes, 105 titles on microform, 290 periodical subscriptions, 2,000 records/tapes.

Undergraduate Courses offered for part-time students during daytime, evenings, weekends, summer. Complete part-time degree programs offered during daytime, evenings, weekends, summer. External degree and adult/continuing education programs available. Career services available to part-time students: individual and group career counseling, individual job placement, employer recruitment on campus. Part-time tuition: $8 per quarter hour for area residents, $31.76 per quarter hour for state residents, $46.04 per quarter hour for nonresidents.

Illinois Eastern Community Colleges, Wabash Valley College
Mount Carmel 62863

Public institution; rural setting. Awards A. Total enrollment: 2,709 (all undergraduates); 62% part-time, 38% women. Total faculty: 142. Library holdings: 25,784 bound volumes, 223 titles on microform, 200 periodical subscriptions, 3,116 records/tapes.

Undergraduate Courses offered for part-time students during daytime, evenings, weekends, summer. Complete part-time degree programs offered during daytime, evenings, weekends, summer. External degree and adult/continuing education programs available. Career services available to part-time students: individual and group career counseling, individual job placement, employer recruitment on campus. Part-time tuition: $8 per quarter hour for area residents, $31.76 per quarter hour for state residents, $46.04 per quarter hour for nonresidents.

Illinois Institute of Technology
Chicago 60616

Independent institution; metropolitan setting. Awards B, M, D. Total enrollment: 4,784. Undergraduate enrollment: 3,087; 27% part-time, 18% women, 22% over 25. Total faculty: 520. Library holdings: 955,319 bound volumes, 527,001 titles on microform, 13,255 periodical subscriptions.

Undergraduate Courses offered for part-time students during daytime, evenings. Complete part-time degree programs offered during daytime, evenings. Adult/continuing education programs available. Career services available to part-time students: individual and group career counseling, individual job placement, employer recruitment on campus. Part-time tuition: $230 per semester hour.

Graduate Part-time study available in School of Advanced Studies, Chicago-Kent College of Law. Basic part-time expenses: $230 per credit hour tuition.

Illinois School of Professional Psychology
Chicago 60604

Independent institution (graduate only). Total enrollment: 298 (coed; 58% part-time). Total faculty: 36. Library holdings: 3,800 bound volumes.

Graduate Part-time study available in Graduate Programs. Basic part-time expenses: $165 per credit hour tuition plus $40 per year fees. Institutional financial aid available to part-time graduate students in Graduate Programs.

Illinois State University
Normal 61761

Public institution; city setting. Awards B, M, D. Total enrollment: 19,817. Undergraduate enrollment: 17,715; 8% part-time, 54% women, 62% over 25. Total faculty: 1,080. Library holdings: 954,787 bound volumes, 5,467 periodical subscriptions, 20,125 records/tapes.

Undergraduate Courses offered for part-time students during daytime, evenings, summer. Complete part-time degree programs offered during daytime, evenings, summer. Adult/continuing education programs available. Career services available to part-time students: individual and group career counseling, individual job placement, employer recruitment on campus. Part-time tuition: $36 per credit hour for state residents, $108 per credit hour for nonresidents.

Graduate Part-time study available in Graduate School. Basic part-time expenses: $42.50 per semester hour tuition plus $50.75

per semester fees for state residents, $127.50 per semester hour tuition plus $50.75 per semester fees for nonresidents. Institutional financial aid available to part-time graduate students in Graduate School.

Illinois Technical College
Chicago 60605

Proprietary institution; metropolitan setting. Awards A. Total enrollment: 477 (all undergraduates); 22% part-time, 11% women, 47% over 25. Total faculty: 25. Library holdings: 340,000 bound volumes, 500,000 titles on microform, 1,000 periodical subscriptions.

Undergraduate Courses offered for part-time students during evenings. Complete part-time degree programs offered during evenings. Adult/continuing education programs available. Career services available to part-time students: individual and group career counseling, individual job placement, employer recruitment on campus. Part-time tuition: $103 per credit hour.

Illinois Valley Community College
Oglesby 61348

Public institution; rural setting. Awards A. Barrier-free campus. Total enrollment: 4,300 (all undergraduates); 64% part-time, 56% women. Total faculty: 184. Library holdings: 49,822 bound volumes, 572 periodical subscriptions, 2,004 records/tapes.

Undergraduate Courses offered for part-time students during daytime, evenings, summer. Complete part-time degree programs offered during daytime, evenings, summer. Adult/continuing education programs available. Career services available to part-time students: individual and group career counseling, individual job placement, employer recruitment on campus. Part-time tuition: $14 per semester hour for area residents, $50 per semester hour for state residents, $70 per semester hour for nonresidents.

International Academy of Merchandising and Design
Chicago 60654

Proprietary institution; metropolitan setting. Awards A. Barrier-free campus. Total enrollment: 585 (all undergraduates); 34% part-time, 90% women, 25% over 25. Total faculty: 56. Library holdings: 250 bound volumes, 25 periodical subscriptions.

Undergraduate Courses offered for part-time students during daytime, evenings, summer. Complete part-time degree programs offered during daytime. Adult/continuing education programs available. Career services available to part-time students: individual career counseling. Part-time tuition: $97 per quarter hour.

John A Logan College
Carterville 62918

Public institution; rural setting. Awards A. Total enrollment: 2,421 (all undergraduates); 44% part-time, 56% women, 25% over 25. Total faculty: 67. Library holdings: 26,000 bound volumes, 10 periodical subscriptions, 2,900 records/tapes.

Undergraduate Courses offered for part-time students during daytime, evenings, summer. Complete part-time degree programs offered during daytime, evenings, summer. Adult/continuing education programs available. Career services available to part-time students: individual career counseling, individual job placement. Part-time tuition: $18 per semester hour for area residents, $53.95 per semester hour for state residents, $78.44 per semester hour for nonresidents.

John Marshall Law School
Chicago 60604

Independent institution (graduate only). Total enrollment: 1,609 (coed; 40% part-time). Total faculty: 141. Library holdings: 125,164 bound volumes, 73,450 microforms.

Graduate Part-time study available in Graduate School, Professional Program. Degree can be earned exclusively through evening/weekend study in Graduate School, Professional Program. Basic part-time expenses: $200 per semester hour tuition plus $25 per semester fees.

John Wood Community College
Quincy 62301

Public institution; small-town setting. Awards A. Barrier-free campus. Total enrollment: 4,562 (all undergraduates); 67% part-time, 59% women. Total faculty: 102. Library holdings: 369,700 bound volumes, 1,002 periodical subscriptions, 69,000 records/tapes.

Undergraduate Courses offered for part-time students during daytime, evenings, weekends, summer. Complete part-time degree programs offered during daytime, evenings, weekends, summer. External degree and adult/continuing education programs available. Career services available to part-time students: individual and group career counseling, individual job placement, employer recruitment on campus. Part-time tuition: $20 per credit hour for area residents, $51.60 per credit hour for state residents, $80 per credit hour for nonresidents.

Joliet Junior College
Joliet 60436

Public institution; city setting. Awards A. Barrier-free campus. Total enrollment: 11,078 (all undergraduates); 73% part-time, 53% women. Total faculty: 600. Library holdings: 53,416 bound volumes, 1,180 titles on microform, 516 periodical subscriptions, 6,575 records/tapes.

Undergraduate Courses offered for part-time students during daytime, evenings, weekends, summer. Complete part-time degree programs offered during daytime, evenings. Adult/continuing education programs available. Career services available to part-time students: individual and group career counseling, individual job placement, employer recruitment on campus. Part-time tuition: $20 per credit hour for area residents, $50.28 per credit hour for state residents, $75.89 per credit hour for nonresidents.

Judson College
Elgin 60120

Independent-religious instutition; city setting. Awards B. Barrier-free campus. Total enrollment: 431 (all undergraduates); 6% part-time, 51% women. Total faculty: 50. Library holdings: 40,000 bound volumes, 26,000 titles on microform, 400 periodical subscriptions, 2,000 records/tapes.

Undergraduate Courses offered for part-time students during daytime, evenings. Complete part-time degree programs offered during daytime. Career services available to part-time students: individual and group career counseling, individual job placement, employer recruitment on campus. Part-time tuition: $165 per credit hour.

Colleges Offering Part-Time Degree Programs / Illinois

Kankakee Community College
Kankakee 60901

Public institution; small-town setting. Awards A. Total enrollment: 3,300 (all undergraduates); 67% part-time, 54% women, 25% over 25. Total faculty: 109. Library holdings: 28,000 bound volumes, 310 periodical subscriptions, 700 records/tapes.

Undergraduate Courses offered for part-time students during daytime, evenings, summer. Complete part-time degree programs offered during daytime, evenings, summer. Adult/continuing education programs available. Career services available to part-time students: individual and group career counseling, individual job placement, employer recruitment on campus. Part-time tuition: $18 per credit hour for area residents, $45 per credit hour for state residents, $73 per credit hour for nonresidents.

Kaskaskia College
Centralia 62801

Public institution; rural setting. Awards A. Barrier-free campus. Total enrollment: 3,185 (all undergraduates); 65% part-time, 62% women, 60% over 25. Total faculty: 95. Library holdings: 30,000 bound volumes, 200 periodical subscriptions, 5,000 records/tapes.

Undergraduate Courses offered for part-time students during daytime, evenings, summer. Complete part-time degree programs offered during daytime, evenings, summer. External degree and adult/continuing education programs available. Career services available to part-time students: individual and group career counseling, individual job placement, employer recruitment on campus. Part-time tuition: $19.25 per semester hour for area residents, $52.75 per semester hour for state residents, $78.75 per semester hour for nonresidents.

Kendall College
Evanston 60201

Independent-religious instutition; city setting. Awards A, B. Total enrollment: 327 (all undergraduates); 14% part-time, 65% women, 6% over 25. Total faculty: 34. Library holdings: 26,000 bound volumes, 1,100 titles on microform, 200 periodical subscriptions.

Undergraduate Courses offered for part-time students during daytime. Complete part-time degree programs offered during daytime. Career services available to part-time students: individual career counseling. Part-time tuition: $210 per credit hour.

Kennedy-King College
Chicago 60621

See City Colleges of Chicago, Kennedy-King College

Kishwaukee College
Malta 60150

Public institution; rural setting. Awards A. Total enrollment: 3,391 (all undergraduates); 66% part-time, 57% women, 42% over 25. Total faculty: 209. Library holdings: 30,000 bound volumes, 70 titles on microform, 240 periodical subscriptions, 400 records/tapes.

Undergraduate Courses offered for part-time students during daytime, evenings, summer. Complete part-time degree programs offered during daytime, evenings, summer. External degree and adult/continuing education programs available. Career services available to part-time students: individual and group career counseling, individual job placement, employer recruitment on campus. Part-time tuition: $20 per semester hour for area residents, $50 per semester hour for state residents, $72 per semester hour for nonresidents.

Knox College
Galesburg 61401

Independent institution; small-town setting. Awards B. Total enrollment: 919 (all undergraduates); 3% part-time, 46% women, 2% over 25. Total faculty: 86. Library holdings: 210,000 bound volumes, 650 periodical subscriptions.

Undergraduate Courses offered for part-time students during daytime. Complete part-time degree programs offered during daytime. Adult/continuing education programs available. Career services available to part-time students: individual and group career counseling, individual job placement, employer recruitment on campus. Part-time tuition: $745 per course.

Lake Forest College
Lake Forest 60045

Independent institution; small-town setting. Awards B, M. Total enrollment: 1,030. Undergraduate enrollment: 953; 1% part-time, 48% women. Total faculty: 93. Library holdings: 250,000 bound volumes, 2,000 records/tapes.

Undergraduate Courses offered for part-time students during daytime, evenings, summer. Complete part-time degree programs offered during daytime, evenings, summer. Adult/continuing education programs available. Career services available to part-time students: individual and group career counseling, individual job placement, employer recruitment on campus. Part-time tuition: $1022 per course.

Graduate Part-time study available in Graduate Program.

Lake Forest School of Management
Lake Forest 60045

Independent institution (graduate only). Total enrollment: 445 (coed; 100% part-time). Total faculty: 42.

Graduate Part-time study available in Graduate Programs. Degree can be earned exclusively through evening/weekend study in Graduate Programs. Basic part-time expenses: $630 per course tuition.

Lake Land College
Mattoon 61938

Public institution; rural setting. Awards A. Barrier-free campus. Total enrollment: 3,766 (all undergraduates); 50% part-time, 49% women. Total faculty: 285. Library holdings: 35,000 bound volumes, 450 periodical subscriptions, 5,000 records/tapes.

Undergraduate Courses offered for part-time students during daytime, evenings, weekends, summer. Complete part-time degree programs offered during daytime, evenings, weekends, summer. Adult/continuing education programs available. Career services available to part-time students: individual and group career counseling, individual job placement, employer recruitment on campus. Part-time tuition: $24.25 per semester hour for area residents, $42 per semester hour for state residents, $87 per semester hour for nonresidents.

Illinois / Colleges Offering Part-Time Degree Programs

Lewis and Clark Community College
Godfrey 62035

Public institution; small-town setting. Awards A. Total enrollment: 5,322 (all undergraduates); 64% part-time, 61% women, 50% over 25. Total faculty: 300. Library holdings: 33,800 bound volumes, 12,811 titles on microform, 732 periodical subscriptions, 4,395 records/tapes.

Undergraduate Courses offered for part-time students during daytime, evenings, weekends, summer. Complete part-time degree programs offered during daytime, evenings, summer. Adult/continuing education programs available. Career services available to part-time students: individual and group career counseling, individual job placement, employer recruitment on campus. Part-time tuition: $20.75 per semester hour for area residents, $52.84 per semester hour for state residents, $76.65 per semester hour for nonresidents.

Lewis University
Romeoville 60441

Independent-religious instutition; small-town setting. Awards A, B, M. Total enrollment: 2,811. Undergraduate enrollment: 2,239; 34% part-time, 46% women, 26% over 25. Total faculty: 140. Library holdings: 125,000 bound volumes, 65,000 titles on microform, 650 periodical subscriptions, 1,600 records/tapes.

Undergraduate Courses offered for part-time students during daytime, evenings, weekends, summer. Complete part-time degree programs offered during daytime, evenings, weekends, summer. Adult/continuing education programs available. Career services available to part-time students: individual and group career counseling, individual job placement, employer recruitment on campus. Part-time tuition: $153 per credit hour.

Graduate Part-time study available in College of Arts and Sciences, College of Business, College of Nursing. Degree can be earned exclusively through evening/weekend study in College of Arts and Sciences, College of Business, College of Nursing.Basic part-time expenses: $164 per credit tuition plus $30 per semester fees. Institutional financial aid available to part-time graduate students in College of Arts and Sciences, College of Business.

Lincoln Christian College
Lincoln 62656

Independent-religious instutition; small-town setting. Awards B. Barrier-free campus. Total enrollment: 347 (all undergraduates); 15% part-time, 50% women, 10% over 25. Total faculty: 38. Library holdings: 74,000 bound volumes, 5,000 titles on microform, 450 periodical subscriptions, 11,000 records/tapes.

Undergraduate Courses offered for part-time students during daytime. Complete part-time degree programs offered during daytime. Career services available to part-time students: individual career counseling, individual job placement, employer recruitment on campus. Part-time tuition: $90 per semester hour.

Lincoln Christian Seminary
Lincoln 62656

Independent-religious institution (graduate only). Total enrollment: 155 (coed; 52% part-time). Total faculty: 16.

Graduate Part-time study available in Graduate and Professional Programs.Basic part-time expenses: $65 per credit tuition plus $50 per semester fees. Institutional financial aid available to part-time graduate students in Graduate and Professional Programs.

Lincoln College
Lincoln 62656

Independent institution; small-town setting. Awards A. Total enrollment: 414 (all undergraduates); 10% part-time, 39% women, 2% over 25. Total faculty: 43. Library holdings: 35,000 bound volumes, 303 titles on microform, 352 periodical subscriptions, 1,600 records/tapes.

Undergraduate Courses offered for part-time students during daytime, evenings, summer. Complete part-time degree programs offered during daytime, evenings, summer. Adult/continuing education programs available. Career services available to part-time students: individual and group career counseling, individual job placement, employer recruitment on campus. Part-time tuition: $190 per credit hour.

Lincoln Land Community College
Springfield 62708

Public institution; city setting. Awards A. Barrier-free campus. Total enrollment: 7,089 (all undergraduates); 69% part-time, 54% women, 48% over 25. Total faculty: 391. Library holdings: 67,980 bound volumes, 4,313 titles on microform, 580 periodical subscriptions, 7,611 records/tapes.

Undergraduate Courses offered for part-time students during daytime, evenings, weekends, summer. Complete part-time degree programs offered during daytime, evenings, weekends, summer. External degree and adult/continuing education programs available. Career services available to part-time students: individual and group career counseling, individual job placement, employer recruitment on campus. Part-time tuition: $23 per credit hour for area residents, $71.16 per credit hour for state residents, $92.25 per credit hour for nonresidents.

Loop College
Chicago 60601

See City Colleges of Chicago, Loop College

Loyola University of Chicago
Chicago 60611

Independent-religious instutition; metropolitan setting. Awards B, M, D. Barrier-free campus. Total enrollment: 13,215. Undergraduate enrollment: 8,035; 20% part-time, 55% women. Total faculty: 1,322. Library holdings: 840,000 bound volumes, 5,813 periodical subscriptions, 25,705 records/tapes.

Undergraduate Courses offered for part-time students during daytime, evenings. Complete part-time degree programs offered during daytime, evenings. Adult/continuing education programs available. Career services available to part-time students: individual career counseling, individual job placement, employer recruitment on campus. Part-time tuition: $130 per semester hour.

Graduate Part-time study available in Graduate School, Graduate School of Business, School of Education, School of Law, School of Social Work.Basic part-time expenses: $170 per credit hour tuition. Institutional financial aid available to part-time graduate students in Graduate School, Graduate School of Business, School of Education, School of Law, School of Social Work.

Colleges Offering Part-Time Degree Programs / *Illinois*

Lutheran School of Theology at Chicago
Chicago 60615

Independent-religious institution (graduate only). Total enrollment: 366 (coed; 24% part-time). Total faculty: 32. Library holdings: 334,388 bound volumes, 101,279 microforms.

Graduate Part-time study available in Graduate and Professional Programs. Basic part-time expenses: $160 per course (minimum) tuition plus $5 per quarter (minimum) fees. Institutional financial aid available to part-time graduate students in Graduate and Professional Programs.

MacCormac Junior College
Chicago 60604

Independent institution; metropolitan setting. Awards A. Total enrollment: 760 (all undergraduates); 5% part-time, 70% women, 20% over 25. Total faculty: 50. Library holdings: 10,100 bound volumes, 140 periodical subscriptions, 3,000 records/tapes.

Undergraduate Courses offered for part-time students during daytime, evenings. Complete part-time degree programs offered during daytime, evenings. Adult/continuing education programs available. Career services available to part-time students: individual career counseling, individual job placement, employer recruitment on campus. Part-time tuition: $96 per quarter hour.

MacMurray College
Jacksonville 62650

Independent-religious instutition; small-town setting. Awards A, B. Total enrollment: 626 (all undergraduates); 10% part-time, 65% women, 10% over 25. Total faculty: 71. Library holdings: 145,000 bound volumes, 90 titles on microform, 765 periodical subscriptions, 956 records/tapes.

Undergraduate Courses offered for part-time students during daytime, evenings, summer. Complete part-time degree programs offered during daytime, evenings, summer. Career services available to part-time students: individual and group career counseling, individual job placement, employer recruitment on campus. Part-time tuition: $145 per credit hour.

Malcolm X College
Chicago 60612

See City Colleges of Chicago, Malcolm X College

Mallinckrodt College
Wilmette 60091

Independent-religious instutition; small-town setting. Awards A, B. Barrier-free campus. Total enrollment: 266 (all undergraduates); 71% part-time, 89% women, 63% over 25. Total faculty: 42. Library holdings: 40,000 bound volumes, 125 periodical subscriptions.

Undergraduate Courses offered for part-time students during daytime, evenings, summer. Complete part-time degree programs offered during daytime, evenings. Adult/continuing education programs available. Career services available to part-time students: individual and group career counseling, individual job placement. Part-time tuition: $80 per semester hour.

McCormick Theological Seminary
Chicago 60637

Independent-religious institution (graduate only). Total enrollment: 605 (coed; 73% part-time). Total faculty: 55. Library holdings: 365,000 bound volumes, 104,000 microforms.

Graduate Part-time study available in Graduate and Professional Programs. Basic part-time expenses: $290 per course tuition.

McKendree College
Lebanon 62254

Independent-religious instutition; small-town setting. Awards B. Total enrollment: 1,000 (all undergraduates); 20% part-time, 50% women. Total faculty: 83. Library holdings: 55,637 bound volumes, 400 periodical subscriptions, 825 records/tapes.

Undergraduate Courses offered for part-time students during daytime, evenings, summer. Complete part-time degree programs offered during daytime, evenings, summer. External degree and adult/continuing education programs available. Career services available to part-time students: individual and group career counseling, individual job placement, employer recruitment on campus. Part-time tuition: $128 per credit.

Meadville/Lombard Theological School
Chicago 60637

Independent-religious institution (graduate only). Total enrollment: 34 (coed; 14% part-time). Total faculty: 11. Library holdings: 93,000 bound volumes.

Graduate Part-time study available in Graduate and Professional Programs. Basic part-time expenses: $888 per quarter (minimum) tuition plus $139 per quarter fees. Institutional financial aid available to part-time graduate students in Graduate and Professional Programs.

Metropolitan Business College
Chicago 60659

Proprietary institution; metropolitan setting. Awards A (24-month program). Barrier-free campus. Total enrollment: 174 (all undergraduates); 3% part-time, 40% women. Total faculty: 8. Library holdings: 4,900 bound volumes, 7 periodical subscriptions.

Undergraduate Courses offered for part-time students during daytime, summer. Complete part-time degree programs offered during daytime, summer. Career services available to part-time students: individual and group career counseling, individual job placement, employer recruitment on campus. Part-time tuition: $2280 per year.

Midstate College
Peoria 61602

Proprietary institution; city setting. Awards A. Barrier-free campus. Total enrollment: 422 (all undergraduates); 10% part-time, 75% women, 31% over 25. Total faculty: 27. Library holdings: 9,800 bound volumes, 96 periodical subscriptions, 1,600 records/tapes.

Undergraduate Courses offered for part-time students during daytime, evenings, summer. Complete part-time degree programs offered during daytime, evenings, summer. Career services available to part-time students: individual career counseling, individual job placement, employer recruitment on campus. Part-time tuition: $60 per quarter hour.

Midwest College of Engineering
Lombard 60148

Independent institution; small-town setting. Awards B, M. Total enrollment: 260. Undergraduate enrollment: 222; 84% part-time, 6% women, 85% over 25. Total faculty: 43. Library holdings: 9,767 bound volumes, 125 periodical subscriptions.

Undergraduate Courses offered for part-time students during daytime, evenings, summer. Complete part-time degree programs offered during evenings. Career services available to part-time students: individual career counseling. Part-time tuition: $110 per quarter hour.

Graduate Part-time study available in Graduate Division. Degree can be earned exclusively through evening/weekend study in Graduate Division. Basic part-time expenses: $125 per quarter hour tuition.

Millikin University
Decatur 62522

Independent-religious instutition; city setting. Awards B. Total enrollment: 1,529 (all undergraduates); 8% part-time, 51% women, 6% over 25. Total faculty: 126. Library holdings: 158,000 bound volumes, 8,000 titles on microform, 887 periodical subscriptions, 4,149 records/tapes.

Undergraduate Courses offered for part-time students during daytime, evenings, summer. Complete part-time degree programs offered during daytime, evenings, summer. Adult/continuing education programs available. Career services available to part-time students: individual and group career counseling, individual job placement. Part-time tuition: $153 per credit.

Monmouth College
Monmouth 61462

Independent-religious instutition; small-town setting. Awards B. Total enrollment: 692 (all undergraduates); 1% part-time, 50% women, 2% over 25. Total faculty: 72. Library holdings: 180,000 bound volumes, 800 periodical subscriptions, 1,300 records/tapes.

Undergraduate Courses offered for part-time students during daytime. Complete part-time degree programs offered during daytime. Career services available to part-time students: individual and group career counseling, individual job placement, employer recruitment on campus. Part-time tuition: $650 per course.

Moraine Valley Community College
Palos Hills 60465

Public institution; small-town setting. Awards A. Barrier-free campus. Total enrollment: 13,890 (all undergraduates); 68% part-time, 55% women, 43% over 25. Total faculty: 447. Library holdings: 66,378 bound volumes, 17,000 titles on microform, 600 periodical subscriptions, 30,000 records/tapes.

Undergraduate Courses offered for part-time students during daytime, evenings, weekends, summer. Complete part-time degree programs offered during daytime, evenings, weekends, summer. Adult/continuing education programs available. Career services available to part-time students: individual and group career counseling, individual job placement, employer recruitment on campus. Part-time tuition: $24.05 per semester hour for area residents, $51.55 per semester hour for state residents, $66.55 per semester hour for nonresidents.

Morrison Institute of Techology
Morrison 61270

Independent institution; small-town setting. Awards A. Barrier-free campus. Total enrollment: 270 (all undergraduates); 0% part-time, 11% women, 2% over 25. Total faculty: 10. Library holdings: 10,000 bound volumes, 25 periodical subscriptions.

Undergraduate Courses offered for part-time students during daytime. Complete part-time degree programs offered during daytime. Career services available to part-time students: group career counseling, individual job placement, employer recruitment on campus. Part-time tuition: $96 per credit hour.

Morton College
Cicero 60650

Public institution; metropolitan setting. Awards A. Barrier-free campus. Total enrollment: 4,345 (all undergraduates); 75% part-time, 57% women. Total faculty: 200. Library holdings: 44,651 bound volumes, 354 titles on microform, 306 periodical subscriptions, 1,484 records/tapes.

Undergraduate Courses offered for part-time students during daytime, evenings, weekends, summer. Complete part-time degree programs offered during daytime, evenings, summer. Adult/continuing education programs available. Career services available to part-time students: individual and group career counseling, individual job placement, employer recruitment on campus. Part-time tuition: $18 per semester hour for area residents, $74.57 per semester hour for state residents, $99.25 per semester hour for nonresidents.

Mundelein College
Chicago 60660

Independent-religious instutition; metropolitan setting. Awards B, M. Barrier-free campus. Total enrollment: 1,282. Undergraduate enrollment: 1,209; 52% part-time, 98% women, 49% over 25. Total faculty: 137. Library holdings: 126,500 bound volumes, 613 periodical subscriptions.

Undergraduate Courses offered for part-time students during daytime, weekends, summer. Complete part-time degree programs offered during daytime, weekends, summer. Adult/continuing education programs available. Career services available to part-time students: individual and group career counseling, individual job placement, employer recruitment on campus. Part-time tuition: $504 per course.

Graduate Part-time study available in Graduate Studies. Degree can be earned exclusively through evening/weekend study in Graduate Studies. Basic part-time expenses: $168 per credit tuition plus $10 per trimester fees.

National College of Education
Evanston 60201

Independent institution; city setting. Awards B, M. Total enrollment: 1,050. Undergraduate enrollment: 650; 1% part-time, 80% women, 30% over 25. Total faculty: 118. Library holdings: 100,000 bound volumes, 600 periodical subscriptions, 1,500 records/tapes.

Undergraduate Courses offered for part-time students during daytime, evenings, summer. Complete part-time degree programs offered during daytime, evenings, summer. External degree and adult/continuing education programs available. Career services available to part-time students: individual and group career counseling, individual job placement, employer recruitment on campus. Part-time tuition: $100 per quarter hour.

Colleges Offering Part-Time Degree Programs / *Illinois*

North Central College
Naperville 60566

Independent-religious instutition; small-town setting. Awards B. Total enrollment: 1,628 (all undergraduates); 15% part-time, 43% women. Total faculty: 116. Library holdings: 100,941 bound volumes, 123 titles on microform, 489 periodical subscriptions, 1,261 records/tapes.

Undergraduate Courses offered for part-time students during daytime, evenings, weekends, summer. Complete part-time degree programs offered during daytime, evenings, weekends, summer. Adult/continuing education programs available. Career services available to part-time students: individual career counseling, individual job placement, employer recruitment on campus. Part-time tuition: $716 per course.

Northeastern Illinois University
Chicago 60625

Public institution; metropolitan setting. Awards B, M. Total enrollment: 10,404. Undergraduate enrollment: 8,299; 42% part-time, 54% women, 34% over 25. Total faculty: 455. Library holdings: 475,315 bound volumes, 571,907 titles on microform, 2,553 periodical subscriptions, 26,688 records/tapes.

Undergraduate Courses offered for part-time students during daytime, evenings, summer. Complete part-time degree programs offered during daytime, evenings. External degree and adult/continuing education programs available. Career services available to part-time students: individual and group career counseling, individual job placement, employer recruitment on campus. Part-time tuition: $40.25 per credit hour for state residents, $120.75 per credit hour for nonresidents.

Graduate Part-time study available in Graduate College. Degree can be earned exclusively through evening/weekend study in Graduate College. Basic part-time expenses: $41.25 per hour tuition plus $31 per trimester fees for state residents, $123.75 per hour tuition plus $31 per trimester fees for nonresidents. Institutional financial aid available to part-time graduate students in Graduate College.

Northern Baptist Theological Seminary
Lombard 60148

Independent-religious institution (graduate only). Total enrollment: 240 (coed; 62% part-time). Total faculty: 23.

Graduate Part-time study available in Graduate and Professional Programs. Basic part-time expenses: $85 per credit hour (minimum) tuition plus $55 per year fees. Institutional financial aid available to part-time graduate students in Graduate and Professional Programs.

Northern Illinois University
De Kalb 60115

Public institution; small-town setting. Awards B, M, D. Total enrollment: 24,524. Undergraduate enrollment: 17,976; 10% part-time, 55% women, 8% over 25. Total faculty: 1,207. Library holdings: 1.9 million bound volumes, 3,145 titles on microform, 17,000 periodical subscriptions, 18,200 records/tapes.

Undergraduate Courses offered for part-time students during daytime, evenings, weekends. Complete part-time degree programs offered during daytime, evenings, weekends. Adult/continuing education programs available. Career services available to part-time students: individual and group career counseling, individual job placement, employer recruitment on campus. Part-time tuition: $40 per credit hour for state residents, $120 per credit hour for nonresidents.

Graduate Part-time study available in Graduate School, College of Law. Basic part-time expenses: $42.50 per semester hour tuition plus $15.94 per semester hour fees for state residents, $127.50 per semester hour tuition plus $15.94 per semester hour fees for nonresidents.

North Park College
Chicago 60625

Independent-religious instutition; metropolitan setting. Awards B. Total enrollment: 1,137 (all undergraduates); 5% part-time, 56% women, 4% over 25. Total faculty: 106. Library holdings: 117,000 bound volumes, 21 titles on microform, 606 periodical subscriptions, 3,500 records/tapes.

Undergraduate Courses offered for part-time students during daytime, evenings, summer. Complete part-time degree programs offered during daytime, evenings. Adult/continuing education programs available. Part-time tuition: $124 per quarter hour.

North Park Theological Seminary
Chicago 60625

Independent-religious institution (graduate only). Total enrollment: 137 (coed). Total faculty: 17.

Graduate Part-time study available in Graduate and Professional Programs. Basic part-time expenses: $90 per hour tuition plus $20 per quarter fees. Institutional financial aid available to part-time graduate students in Graduate and Professional Programs.

Northwestern Business College
Chicago 60641

Proprietary institution; metropolitan setting. Awards A. Barrier-free campus. Total enrollment: 312 (all undergraduates); 26% part-time, 80% women, 33% over 25. Total faculty: 18.

Undergraduate Courses offered for part-time students during daytime, evenings, summer. Complete part-time degree programs offered during daytime, evenings. Career services available to part-time students: individual career counseling, individual job placement. Part-time tuition: $60 per credit hour.

Northwestern University
Evanston 60201

Independent institution; city setting. Awards B, M, D. Total enrollment: 15,890. Undergraduate enrollment: 7,222; 1% part-time, 48% women, 1% over 25. Total faculty: 1,783. Library holdings: 3.0 million bound volumes, 1.3 million titles on microform, 33,000 periodical subscriptions, 51,821 records/tapes.

Undergraduate Courses offered for part-time students during daytime, evenings, weekends, summer. Complete part-time degree programs offered during daytime, evenings, weekends, summer. Adult/continuing education programs available. Career services available to part-time students: individual and group career counseling, individual job placement, employer recruitment on campus. Part-time tuition: $1060 per course.

Graduate Part-time study available in Graduate School, J. L. Kellogg Graduate School of Management, School of Music, Technological Institute. Basic part-time expenses: $1145 per course tuition.

Illinois / Colleges Offering Part-Time Degree Programs

Oakton Community College
Des Plaines 60016

Public institution; city setting. Awards A. Barrier-free campus. Total enrollment: 8,639 (all undergraduates); 71% part-time, 54% women, 41% over 25. Total faculty: 392. Library holdings: 53,000 bound volumes, 525 periodical subscriptions, 4,500 records/tapes.

Undergraduate Courses offered for part-time students during daytime, evenings, weekends, summer. Complete part-time degree programs offered during daytime, evenings, weekends, summer. External degree and adult/continuing education programs available. Career services available to part-time students: individual career counseling, individual job placement, employer recruitment on campus. Part-time tuition: $17 per semester hour for area residents, $76.40 per semester hour for state residents, $98.05 per semester hour for nonresidents.

Olive-Harvey College
Chicago 60628

See City Colleges of Chicago, Olive-Harvey College

Olivet Nazarene College
Kankakee 60901

Independent-religious instutition; small-town setting. Awards A, B, M. Barrier-free campus. Total enrollment: 1,773. Undergraduate enrollment: 1,718; 12% part-time, 55% women, 9% over 25. Total faculty: 110. Library holdings: 138,000 bound volumes, 36,000 titles on microform, 900 periodical subscriptions, 3,000 records/tapes.

Undergraduate Courses offered for part-time students during daytime, evenings, summer. Complete part-time degree programs offered during daytime. Adult/continuing education programs available. Career services available to part-time students: individual and group career counseling, individual job placement, employer recruitment on campus. Part-time tuition: $154 per semester hour.

Graduate Part-time study available in Division of Graduate Studies. Basic part-time expenses: $154 per hour tuition plus $10 per semester fees. Institutional financial aid available to part-time graduate students in Division of Graduate Studies.

Parks College of Saint Louis University
Cahokia 62206

Independent-religious instutition; small-town setting. Awards A, B. Barrier-free campus. Total enrollment: 1,072 (all undergraduates); 4% part-time, 8% women, 4% over 25. Total faculty: 57. Library holdings: 34,373 bound volumes, 253 periodical subscriptions.

Undergraduate Courses offered for part-time students during daytime. Complete part-time degree programs offered during daytime. Part-time tuition: $160 per credit hour.

Prairie State College
Chicago Heights 60411

Public institution; small-town setting. Awards A. Barrier-free campus. Total enrollment: 6,100 (all undergraduates); 60% part-time, 53% women, 48% over 25. Total faculty: 410. Library holdings: 65,000 bound volumes, 2,363 titles on microform, 289 periodical subscriptions, 28,019 records/tapes.

Undergraduate Courses offered for part-time students during daytime, evenings, summer. Complete part-time degree programs offered during daytime, evenings. Adult/continuing education programs available. Career services available to part-time students: individual and group career counseling, individual job placement, employer recruitment on campus. Part-time tuition: $27 per credit hour for area residents, $67 per credit hour for state residents, $94 per credit hour for nonresidents.

Quincy College
Quincy 62301

Independent-religious instutition; small-town setting. Awards A, B, M. Total enrollment: 1,759 (all undergraduates); 43% part-time, 54% women, 15% over 25. Total faculty: 104. Library holdings: 200,000 bound volumes, 88,168 titles on microform, 860 periodical subscriptions, 2,129 records/tapes.

Undergraduate Courses offered for part-time students during daytime, evenings. Complete part-time degree programs offered during daytime. Adult/continuing education programs available. Career services available to part-time students: individual and group career counseling, individual job placement, employer recruitment on campus. Part-time tuition: $135 per semester hour.

Rend Lake College
Ina 62846

Public institution; rural setting. Awards A. Total enrollment: 3,114 (all undergraduates); 69% part-time, 45% women, 55% over 25. Total faculty: 180.

Undergraduate Courses offered for part-time students during daytime, evenings, summer. Complete part-time degree programs offered during daytime, evenings, summer. Adult/continuing education programs available. Career services available to part-time students: individual career counseling, individual job placement. Part-time tuition: $18 per credit hour for area residents, $78 per credit hour for state residents, $124 per credit hour for nonresidents.

Richland Community College
Decatur 62526

Public institution; city setting. Awards A. Barrier-free campus. Total enrollment: 3,331 (all undergraduates); 75% part-time, 55% women. Total faculty: 162. Library holdings: 21,375 bound volumes, 108 titles on microform, 275 periodical subscriptions, 1,800 records/tapes.

Undergraduate Courses offered for part-time students during daytime, evenings, summer. Complete part-time degree programs offered during daytime, evenings, summer. Adult/continuing education programs available. Career services available to part-time students: individual career counseling, individual job placement, employer recruitment on campus. Part-time tuition: $23.05 per semester hour for state residents, $82.50 per semester hour for nonresidents.

Rockford College
Rockford 61101

Independent institution; city setting. Awards B, M. Barrier-free campus. Total enrollment: 1,452. Undergraduate enrollment: 1,212; 41% part-time, 60% women, 10% over 25. Total faculty: 136. Library holdings: 130,000 bound volumes, 60 titles on microform, 720 periodical subscriptions, 8,272 records/tapes.

Undergraduate Courses offered for part-time students during daytime, evenings, weekends. Complete part-time degree programs offered during daytime, evenings, weekends. Adult/continuing education programs available. Career services available

Rockford College (continued)

to part-time students: individual and group career counseling, individual job placement, employer recruitment on campus. Part-time tuition: $160 per credit.

Graduate Part-time study available in Graduate Studies. Basic part-time expenses: $160 per credit tuition plus $15 per semester fees.

Rock Valley College
Rockford 61101

Public institution; city setting. Awards A. Barrier-free campus. Total enrollment: 9,590 (all undergraduates); 77% part-time, 52% women, 49% over 25. Total faculty: 555. Library holdings: 60,000 bound volumes, 183 periodical subscriptions, 4,493 records/tapes.

Undergraduate Courses offered for part-time students during daytime, evenings, weekends, summer. Complete part-time degree programs offered during daytime, evenings, weekends, summer. Adult/continuing education programs available. Career services available to part-time students: individual and group career counseling, individual job placement, employer recruitment on campus. Part-time tuition: $26 per credit hour for area residents, $54 per credit hour for state residents, $76 per credit hour for nonresidents.

Roosevelt University
Chicago 60605

Independent institution; metropolitan setting. Awards B, M. Barrier-free campus. Total enrollment: 6,374. Undergraduate enrollment: 4,382; 61% part-time, 54% women, 65% over 25. Total faculty: 476. Library holdings: 400,000 bound volumes, 24,360 titles on microform, 1,500 periodical subscriptions, 10,000 records/tapes.

Undergraduate Courses offered for part-time students during daytime, evenings, weekends, summer. Complete part-time degree programs offered during daytime, evenings, weekends, summer. External degree and adult/continuing education programs available. Career services available to part-time students: individual and group career counseling, individual job placement, employer recruitment on campus. Part-time tuition: $154.50 per semester hour.

Graduate Part-time study available in Graduate Division. Degree can be earned exclusively through evening/weekend study in Graduate Division. Basic part-time expenses: $177.50 per credit tuition. Institutional financial aid available to part-time graduate students in Graduate Division.

Rosary College
River Forest 60305

Independent-religious instutition; small-town setting. Awards B, M. Total enrollment: 1,734. Undergraduate enrollment: 1,027; 27% part-time, 72% women. Total faculty: 136. Library holdings: 268,018 bound volumes, 10,184 titles on microform, 1,072 periodical subscriptions, 4,545 records/tapes.

Undergraduate Courses offered for part-time students during daytime, evenings, weekends, summer. Complete part-time degree programs offered during daytime, evenings, weekends, summer. Adult/continuing education programs available. Career services available to part-time students: individual and group career counseling, individual job placement, employer recruitment on campus. Part-time tuition: $174 per semester hour.

Graduate Part-time study available in Graduate School of Business, Graduate School of Fine Arts (Florence, Italy), Graduate School of Library and Information Science. Basic part-time expenses: $460 per course tuition. Institutional financial aid available to part-time graduate students in Graduate School of Business.

Rush University
Chicago 60612

Independent institution (undergraduate and graduate). Total enrollment: 1,192. Graduate enrollment: 799 (coed; 16% part-time). Library holdings: 92,158 bound volumes, 900 microforms.

Graduate Part-time study available in Graduate College, College of Nursing. Basic part-time expenses: $170 per quarter hour tuition. Institutional financial aid available to part-time graduate students in Graduate College, College of Nursing.

Saint Augustine Community College
Chicago 60640

Independent-religious instutition; metropolitan setting. Awards A. Total enrollment: 1,006 (all undergraduates); 1% part-time, 53% women, 60% over 25. Total faculty: 71. Library holdings: 4,000 bound volumes, 120 periodical subscriptions, 125 records/tapes.

Undergraduate Courses offered for part-time students during daytime, evenings, summer. Complete part-time degree programs offered during daytime, evenings. Part-time tuition: $98 per semester hour.

Saint Xavier College
Chicago 60655

Independent-religious instutition; metropolitan setting. Awards B, M. Barrier-free campus. Total enrollment: 2,367. Undergraduate enrollment: 2,268; 28% part-time, 71% women, 40% over 25. Total faculty: 160. Library holdings: 60,000 bound volumes, 500 periodical subscriptions, 1,000 records/tapes.

Undergraduate Courses offered for part-time students during daytime, evenings, weekends, summer. Complete part-time degree programs offered during daytime, evenings, weekends, summer. Adult/continuing education programs available. Career services available to part-time students: individual career counseling, employer recruitment on campus. Part-time tuition: $161 per semester hour.

Graduate Part-time study available in Graduate Studies. Degree can be earned exclusively through evening/weekend study in Graduate Studies. Basic part-time expenses: $173 per credit hour tuition plus $10 per semester fees. Institutional financial aid available to part-time graduate students in Graduate Studies.

Sangamon State University
Springfield 62708

Public institution; city setting. Awards B, M. Barrier-free campus. Total enrollment: 3,197. Undergraduate enrollment: 1,700; 59% part-time, 50% women, 80% over 25. Total faculty: 222. Library holdings: 279,024 bound volumes, 614,133 titles on microform, 3,112 periodical subscriptions, 25,614 records/tapes.

Undergraduate Courses offered for part-time students during daytime, evenings, weekends, summer. Complete part-time degree programs offered during daytime, evenings, summer. Adult/continuing education programs available. Career services available to part-time students: individual and group career counseling, individual job placement, employer recruitment on campus. Part-time tuition: $40 per semester

Illinois / **Colleges Offering Part-Time Degree Programs**

hour for state residents, $120 per semester hour for nonresidents.

Graduate Part-time study available in Graduate Programs. Basic part-time expenses: $41 per semester hour tuition for state residents, $123 per semester hour tuition for nonresidents.

Sauk Valley College
Dixon 61021

Public institution; rural setting. Awards A. Barrier-free campus. Total enrollment: 3,500 (all undergraduates); 65% part-time, 58% women, 32% over 25. Total faculty: 180. Library holdings: 50,000 bound volumes, 500 periodical subscriptions, 2,000 records/tapes.

Undergraduate Courses offered for part-time students during daytime, evenings, summer. Complete part-time degree programs offered during daytime, evenings, summer. Adult/continuing education programs available. Career services available to part-time students: individual and group career counseling, individual job placement, employer recruitment on campus. Part-time tuition: $27 per credit hour for area residents, $56 per credit hour for state residents, $72 per credit hour for nonresidents.

School of the Art Institute of Chicago
Chicago 60603

Independent institution; metropolitan setting. Awards B, M. Barrier-free campus. Total enrollment: 1,541. Undergraduate enrollment: 923; 38% part-time, 62% women. Total faculty: 168. Library holdings: 18,500 bound volumes, 200 periodical subscriptions, 2,000 records/tapes.

Undergraduate Courses offered for part-time students during daytime, evenings, weekends, summer. Complete part-time degree programs offered during daytime, evenings, weekends, summer. Adult/continuing education programs available. Career services available to part-time students: individual and group career counseling, individual job placement, employer recruitment on campus. Part-time tuition: $205 per semester hour.

Graduate Part-time study available in Graduate Programs. Basic part-time expenses: $205 per credit hour tuition. Institutional financial aid available to part-time graduate students in Graduate Programs.

Seabury-Western Theological Seminary
Evanston 60201

Independent-religious institution (graduate only). Total enrollment: 75 (coed; 9% part-time). Total faculty: 12. Library holdings: 77,090 bound volumes, 240 microforms.

Graduate Part-time study available in Graduate and Professional Programs. Basic part-time expenses: $358 per course tuition. Institutional financial aid available to part-time graduate students in Graduate and Professional Programs.

Shawnee College
Ullin 62992

Public institution; rural setting. Awards A. Barrier-free campus. Total enrollment: 2,550 (all undergraduates); 50% part-time, 55% women, 40% over 25. Total faculty: 219. Library holdings: 37,000 bound volumes, 245 periodical subscriptions.

Undergraduate Courses offered for part-time students during daytime, evenings, summer. Complete part-time degree programs offered during daytime, evenings, summer. Adult/continuing education programs available. Career services available to part-time students: individual and group career counseling, individual job placement, employer recruitment on campus. Part-time tuition: $14 per semester hour for area residents, $47 per semester hour for state residents, $73 per semester hour for nonresidents.

Sherwood Conservatory of Music
Chicago 60605

Independent institution; metropolitan setting. Awards B, M. Total enrollment: 47. Undergraduate enrollment: 40; 38% part-time, 48% women, 45% over 25. Total faculty: 36. Library holdings: 11,000 bound volumes, 1,600 records/tapes.

Undergraduate Courses offered for part-time students during daytime, evenings, summer. Complete part-time degree programs offered during daytime, evenings, summer. Career services available to part-time students: individual career counseling. Part-time tuition: $85 per semester hour.

Graduate Part-time study available in Graduate Program in Music. Basic part-time expenses: $105 per credit hour tuition plus $15 per year fees.

Shimer College
Waukegan 60085

Independent institution; city setting. Awards B. Total enrollment: 100 (all undergraduates); 0% part-time, 40% women, 25% over 25. Total faculty: 15. Library holdings: 200,000 bound volumes, 55 periodical subscriptions, 7,000 records/tapes.

Undergraduate Courses offered for part-time students during daytime, evenings, weekends, summer. Complete part-time degree programs offered during daytime, evenings, weekends, summer. Adult/continuing education programs available. Career services available to part-time students: group career counseling, individual job placement.

Southeastern Illinois College
Harrisburg 62946

Public institution; rural setting. Awards A. Barrier-free campus. Total enrollment: 2,796 (all undergraduates); 60% part-time, 50% women. Total faculty: 183. Library holdings: 25,000 bound volumes, 58 periodical subscriptions, 948 records/tapes.

Undergraduate Courses offered for part-time students during daytime, evenings, summer. Complete part-time degree programs offered during daytime, evenings, summer. Adult/continuing education programs available. Career services available to part-time students: individual and group career counseling, individual job placement, employer recruitment on campus. Part-time tuition: $17 per semester hour for area residents, $50 per semester hour for state residents, $90 per semester hour for nonresidents.

Southern Illinois University at Carbondale
Carbondale 62901

Public institution; rural setting. Awards A, B, M, D. Barrier-free campus. Total enrollment: 23,383. Undergraduate enrollment: 19,246; 8% part-time, 36% women, 20% over 25. Total faculty: 1,478. Library holdings: 1.5 million bound volumes, 1.6 million titles on microform, 16,800 periodical subscriptions.

Undergraduate Courses offered for part-time students during daytime, evenings, summer. Complete part-time degree pro-

Colleges Offering Part-Time Degree Programs / Illinois

Southern Illinois University at Carbondale (continued)
grams offered during daytime, evenings, summer. External degree and adult/continuing education programs available. Career services available to part-time students: individual and group career counseling, individual job placement, employer recruitment on campus. Part-time tuition: $39.75 per semester hour for state residents, $119.25 per semester hour for nonresidents.

Graduate Part-time study available in Graduate School. Basic part-time expenses: $236 per semester (minimum) tuition for state residents, $474 per semester (minimum) tuition for nonresidents. Institutional financial aid available to part-time graduate students in Graduate School.

Southern Illinois University at Edwardsville
Edwardsville 62026

Public institution; rural setting. Awards B, M, D. Barrier-free campus. Total enrollment: 10,360. Undergraduate enrollment: 8,282; 37% part-time, 52% women. Total faculty: 650. Library holdings: 715,000 bound volumes, 5,000 periodical subscriptions, 15,000 records/tapes.

Undergraduate Courses offered for part-time students during daytime, evenings, weekends, summer. Complete part-time degree programs offered during daytime, evenings, weekends, summer. Adult/continuing education programs available. Career services available to part-time students: individual and group career counseling, individual job placement, employer recruitment on campus. Part-time tuition: $26.05 per credit hour for state residents, $78.15 per credit hour for nonresidents.

Graduate Part-time study available in Graduate School. Basic part-time expenses: $29 per credit tuition plus $13 per credit fees for state residents, $84 per credit tuition plus $13 per credit fees for nonresidents. Institutional financial aid available to part-time graduate students in Graduate School.

Spertus College of Judaica
Chicago 60605

Independent institution; metropolitan setting. Awards B, M. Barrier-free campus. Total enrollment: 300. Undergraduate enrollment: 230; 85% part-time, 52% women, 75% over 25. Total faculty: 23. Library holdings: 70,000 bound volumes, 625 periodical subscriptions, 100 records/tapes.

Undergraduate Courses offered for part-time students during daytime, evenings, summer. Complete part-time degree programs offered during daytime, evenings. Adult/continuing education programs available. Career services available to part-time students: individual career counseling, individual job placement. Part-time tuition: $220 per course.

Graduate Part-time study available in Norman and Evelyn Edidin Graduate Institute of Advanced Judaica. Degree can be earned exclusively through evening/weekend study in Norman and Evelyn Edidin Graduate Institute of Advanced Judaica. Basic part-time expenses: $300 per course tuition plus $40 per year fees. Institutional financial aid available to part-time graduate students in Norman and Evelyn Edidin Graduate Institute of Advanced Judaica.

Spoon River College
Canton 61520

Public institution; rural setting. Awards A. Barrier-free campus. Total enrollment: 2,362 (all undergraduates); 63% part-time, 60% women, 50% over 25. Total faculty: 135. Library holdings: 29,000 bound volumes, 2,622 titles on microform, 406 periodical subscriptions, 1,800 records/tapes.

Undergraduate Courses offered for part-time students during daytime, evenings, summer. Complete part-time degree programs offered during daytime. Adult/continuing education programs available. Career services available to part-time students: individual career counseling, individual job placement. Part-time tuition: $27 per semester hour for area residents, $81.74 per semester hour for state residents, $104.30 per semester hour for nonresidents.

Springfield College in Illinois
Springfield 62702

Independent-religious instustition; city setting. Awards A. Total enrollment: 532 (all undergraduates); 52% part-time, 72% women, 2% over 25. Total faculty: 50. Library holdings: 31,370 bound volumes, 4 titles on microform, 181 periodical subscriptions, 1,550 records/tapes.

Undergraduate Courses offered for part-time students during daytime, evenings, weekends, summer. Complete part-time degree programs offered during daytime, evenings. Adult/continuing education programs available. Career services available to part-time students: individual career counseling. Part-time tuition: $127 per semester hour.

Thornton Community College
South Holland 60473

Public institution; small-town setting. Awards A. Barrier-free campus. Total enrollment: 8,500 (all undergraduates); 70% part-time, 60% women, 50% over 25. Total faculty: 313.

Undergraduate Courses offered for part-time students during daytime, evenings, weekends, summer. Complete part-time degree programs offered during daytime, evenings, weekends, summer. Adult/continuing education programs available. Career services available to part-time students: individual and group career counseling, individual job placement, employer recruitment on campus. Part-time tuition: $24 per semester hour for area residents, $51 per semester hour for state residents, $76 per semester hour for nonresidents.

Trinity Christian College
Palos Heights 60463

Independent institution; small-town setting. Awards B. Total enrollment: 460 (all undergraduates); 12% part-time, 55% women. Total faculty: 58. Library holdings: 50,000 bound volumes, 20,000 titles on microform, 300 periodical subscriptions, 285 records/tapes.

Undergraduate Courses offered for part-time students during daytime, evenings. Complete part-time degree programs offered during daytime, evenings. Career services available to part-time students: individual and group career counseling, individual job placement, employer recruitment on campus. Part-time tuition: $165 per credit.

Trinity College
Deerfield 60015

Independent-religious institution; small-town setting. Awards B. Total enrollment: 487 (all undergraduates); 10% part-time, 54% women. Total faculty: 56. Library holdings: 60,000 bound volumes, 20,000 titles on microform, 500 periodical subscriptions, 846 records/tapes.

Undergraduate Courses offered for part-time students during daytime. Complete part-time degree programs offered during

Illinois / Colleges Offering Part-Time Degree Programs

daytime. Adult/continuing education programs available. Part-time tuition per semester ranges from $175 (for students taking 1 to 6 hours) to $225 (for students taking 7 to 11 hours).

Trinity Evangelical Divinity School
Deerfield 60015

Independent-religious institution (graduate only). Total enrollment: 935 (primarily men; 38% part-time). Total faculty: 53.

Graduate Part-time study available in Graduate and Professional Programs. Basic part-time expenses: $129.50 per credit tuition. Institutional financial aid available to part-time graduate students in Graduate and Professional Programs.

Triton College
River Grove 60171

Public institution; small-town setting. Awards A. Barrier-free campus. Total enrollment: 14,258 (all undergraduates); 60% part-time, 50% women, 34% over 25. Total faculty: 722. Library holdings: 70,000 bound volumes, 524 periodical subscriptions, 2,100 records/tapes.

Undergraduate Courses offered for part-time students during daytime, evenings, weekends, summer. Complete part-time degree programs offered during daytime, evenings, weekends, summer. Adult/continuing education programs available. Career services available to part-time students: individual and group career counseling, individual job placement, employer recruitment on campus. Part-time tuition: $22 per credit for area residents, $61 per credit for state residents, $82 per credit for nonresidents.

Truman College
Chicago 60640

See City Colleges of Chicago, Harry S Truman College

University of Chicago
Chicago 60637

Independent institution; metropolitan setting. Awards B, M, D. Total enrollment: 7,833. Undergraduate enrollment: 2,993; 5% part-time, 38% women, 3% over 25. Total faculty: 1,130. Library holdings: 4.6 million bound volumes, 40,000 periodical subscriptions.

Graduate Part-time study available in Graduate School of Business. Basic part-time expenses: $1300 per quarter (minimum) tuition plus $134 per quarter fees.

University of Illinois at Chicago, Health Sciences Center
Chicago 60612

Public institution (undergraduate and graduate). Total enrollment: 4,634. Graduate enrollment: 2,601 (coed; 14% part-time).

Graduate Part-time study available in Graduate College. Basic part-time expenses: $335 per quarter (minimum) tuition for state residents, $737 per quarter (minimum) tuition for nonresidents.

University of Illinois at Chicago, University Center
Chicago 60680

Public institution; metropolitan setting. Awards B, M, D. Barrier-free campus. Total enrollment: 24,651. Undergraduate enrollment: 17,307; 19% part-time, 44% women. Total faculty: 1,209. Library holdings: 1.2 million bound volumes, 792,077 titles on microform, 14,926 periodical subscriptions, 6,525 records/tapes.

Undergraduate Courses offered for part-time students during daytime, evenings, summer. Complete part-time degree programs offered during daytime, evenings, summer. Adult/continuing education programs available. Career services available to part-time students: individual and group career counseling, employer recruitment on campus. Part-time tuition and fees per quarter (1 to 11 quarter hours) range from $271 to $506 for state residents, $561 to $1174 for nonresidents, according to course load and class level.

Graduate Part-time study available in Graduate College. Basic part-time expenses: $201 per quarter (minimum) tuition plus $68 per quarter (minimum) fees for state residents, $603 per quarter (minimum) tuition plus $68 per quarter (minimum) fees for nonresidents. Institutional financial aid available to part-time graduate students in Graduate College.

VanderCook College of Music
Chicago 60616

Independent institution; metropolitan setting. Awards B, M. Total enrollment: 141. Undergraduate enrollment: 95; 10% part-time, 27% women. Total faculty: 26. Library holdings: 18,285 bound volumes, 1,841 titles on microform, 98 periodical subscriptions, 1,680 records/tapes.

Undergraduate Courses offered for part-time students during daytime, weekends, summer. Complete part-time degree programs offered during daytime, weekends, summer. Career services available to part-time students: individual and group career counseling, individual job placement. Part-time tuition: $135 per semester hour.

Waubonsee Community College
Sugar Grove 60554

Public institution; rural setting. Awards A. Barrier-free campus. Total enrollment: 6,165 (all undergraduates); 81% part-time, 58% women. Total faculty: 306. Library holdings: 48,375 bound volumes, 350 periodical subscriptions, 1,387 records/tapes.

Undergraduate Courses offered for part-time students during daytime, evenings. Complete part-time degree programs offered during daytime, evenings. Adult/continuing education programs available. Career services available to part-time students: individual and group career counseling, individual job placement, employer recruitment on campus. Part-time tuition: $20.50 per semester hour for area residents, $64.10 per semester hour for state residents, $85.80 per semester hour for nonresidents.

Western Illinois University
Macomb 61455

Public institution; small-town setting. Awards B, M. Barrier-free campus. Total enrollment: 12,411. Undergraduate enrollment: 10,399; 11% part-time, 47% women, 1% over 25. Total faculty: 693. Library holdings: 515,695 bound volumes, 30,000 titles on microform, 3,600 periodical subscriptions, 4,100 records/tapes.

Colleges Offering Part-Time Degree Programs / Illinois

Western Illinois University (continued)

Undergraduate Courses offered for part-time students during daytime, evenings, summer. Complete part-time degree programs offered during daytime, evenings, summer. External degree and adult/continuing education programs available. Career services available to part-time students: individual and group career counseling, individual job placement, employer recruitment on campus. Part-time tuition per semester hour ranges from $35.75 to $38.75 for state residents, $120.75 to $126.75 for nonresidents, according to class level.

Graduate Part-time study available in School of Graduate Studies. Degree can be earned exclusively through evening/weekend study in School of Graduate Studies. Basic part-time expenses: $43.75 per semester hour tuition plus $37 per semester fees for state residents, $131.75 per semester hour tuition plus $37 per semester fees for nonresidents.

Wheaton College
Wheaton 60187

Independent-religious instutition; small-town setting. Awards B, M. Total enrollment: 2,378. Undergraduate enrollment: 2,094; 1% part-time, 50% women. Total faculty: 150. Library holdings: 200,000 bound volumes, 200 periodical subscriptions, 200 records/tapes.

Graduate Part-time study available in Graduate School. Basic part-time expenses: $179 per semester hour tuition plus $20 per year fees.

William Rainey Harper College
Palatine 60067

Public institution; small-town setting. Awards A. Barrier-free campus. Total enrollment: 21,465 (all undergraduates); 77% part-time, 57% women. Total faculty: 814. Library holdings: 124,545 bound volumes, 268 titles on microform, 663 periodical subscriptions, 9,450 records/tapes.

Undergraduate Courses offered for part-time students during daytime, evenings, weekends, summer. Complete part-time degree programs offered during daytime, evenings, summer. Adult/continuing education programs available. Career services available to part-time students: individual and group career counseling, individual job placement, employer recruitment on campus. Part-time tuition: $27 per semester hour for area residents, $62.94 per semester hour for state residents, $84.70 per semester hour for nonresidents.

Wright College
Chicago 60634

See City Colleges of Chicago, Wilbur Wright College

INDIANA

Ancilla College
Donaldson 46513

Independent-religious instutition; rural setting. Awards A. Barrier-free campus. Total enrollment: 439 (all undergraduates); 60% part-time, 70% women, 40% over 25. Total faculty: 30. Library holdings: 27,800 bound volumes, 22 periodical subscriptions, 3,400 records/tapes.

Undergraduate Courses offered for part-time students during daytime, evenings, summer. Complete part-time degree programs offered during daytime, evenings, summer. Adult/continuing education programs available. Career services available to part-time students: individual and group career counseling, employer recruitment on campus. Part-time tuition: $40 per semester hour.

Anderson College
Anderson 46012

Independent-religious instutition; city setting. Awards A, B, M. Total enrollment: 2,070. Undergraduate enrollment: 1,881; 0% part-time, 55% women. Total faculty: 163. Library holdings: 160,000 bound volumes, 950 periodical subscriptions, 6,700 records/tapes.

Graduate Part-time study available in School of Theology. Basic part-time expenses: $85 per credit tuition plus $10 per semester fees. Institutional financial aid available to part-time graduate students in School of Theology.

Ball State University
Muncie 47306

Public institution; city setting. Awards A, B, M, D. Barrier-free campus. Total enrollment: 18,359. Undergraduate enrollment: 16,356; 11% part-time, 56% women, 19% over 25. Total faculty: 1,220. Library holdings: 1.2 million bound volumes, 157,183 titles on microform, 4,100 periodical subscriptions, 324,320 records/tapes.

Undergraduate Courses offered for part-time students during daytime, evenings, summer. Complete part-time degree programs offered during daytime, evenings, summer. External degree and adult/continuing education programs available. Career services available to part-time students: individual and group career counseling, individual job placement, employer recruitment on campus. Part-time tuition per quarter (1 to 11 credits) ranges from $195 to $370 for state residents, $450 to $825 for nonresidents.

Graduate Part-time study available in Graduate School. Degree can be earned exclusively through evening/weekend study in Graduate School. Basic part-time expenses: $211 per quarter (minimum) tuition for state residents, $466 per quarter (minimum) tuition for nonresidents. Institutional financial aid available to part-time graduate students in Graduate School.

Bethel College
Mishawaka 46545

Independent-religious instutition; city setting. Awards A, B, M. Total enrollment: 547. Undergraduate enrollment: 535; 36% part-time, 61% women. Total faculty: 47. Library holdings: 55,100 bound volumes, 375 periodical subscriptions, 1,500 records/tapes.

Undergraduate Courses offered for part-time students during daytime, evenings. Complete part-time degree programs offered during daytime, evenings. Career services available to part-time students: individual career counseling, individual job placement, employer recruitment on campus. Part-time tuition: $128 per semester hour.

Graduate Part-time study available in Division of Graduate Studies. Basic part-time expenses: $128 per semester hour tuition. Institutional financial aid available to part-time graduate students in Division of Graduate Studies.

Butler University
Indianapolis 46208

Independent institution; metropolitan setting. Awards A, B, M. Total enrollment: 4,058. Undergraduate enrollment: 2,638; 24%

Indiana / **Colleges Offering Part-Time Degree Programs**

part-time, 57% women. Total faculty: 340. Library holdings: 316,133 bound volumes, 6,500 titles on microform, 1,250 periodical subscriptions, 11,000 records/tapes.

Undergraduate Courses offered for part-time students during daytime, evenings, summer. Complete part-time degree programs offered during daytime, evenings, summer. Adult/continuing education programs available. Career services available to part-time students: individual and group career counseling, individual job placement, employer recruitment on campus. Part-time tuition per semester hour ranges from $80 for evening courses to $235 for daytime courses.

Graduate Part-time study available in College of Business Administration, College of Education, College of Liberal Arts and Sciences, College of Pharmacy, Jordan College of Fine Arts. Degree can be earned exclusively through evening/weekend study in College of Business Administration, College of Education, College of Liberal Arts and Sciences, College of Pharmacy, Jordan College of Fine Arts. Basic part-time expenses: $80 per credit (minimum) tuition.

Calumet College
Whiting 46394

Independent-religious instiution; small-town setting. Awards A, B. Barrier-free campus. Total enrollment: 1,297 (all undergraduates); 67% part-time, 61% women, 42% over 25. Total faculty: 83. Library holdings: 106,000 bound volumes, 2,700 titles on microform, 800 periodical subscriptions, 2,600 records/tapes.

Undergraduate Courses offered for part-time students during daytime, evenings, weekends, summer. Complete part-time degree programs offered during daytime, evenings, weekends, summer. External degree and adult/continuing education programs available. Career services available to part-time students: individual and group career counseling, individual job placement, employer recruitment on campus. Part-time tuition: $90 per credit hour.

Clark College
Indianapolis 46202

Proprietary institution; metropolitan setting. Awards A. Barrier-free campus. Total enrollment: 419 (all undergraduates); 8% part-time, 50% women, 20% over 25. Total faculty: 36.

Undergraduate Courses offered for part-time students during daytime, evenings, summer. Complete part-time degree programs offered during daytime, evenings. Career services available to part-time students: individual and group career counseling, individual job placement, employer recruitment on campus. Part-time tuition: $62 per credit hour.

Concordia Theological Seminary
Fort Wayne 46825

Independent-religious institution (graduate only). Total enrollment: 539 (primarily men; 7% part-time). Total faculty: 37. Library holdings: 101,000 bound volumes, 2,800 microforms.

Graduate Part-time study available in Graduate and Professional Programs. Basic part-time expenses: $90 per quarter hour tuition. Institutional financial aid available to part-time graduate students in Graduate and Professional Programs.

DePauw University
Greencastle 46135

Independent-religious instuition; small-town setting. Awards B, M. Total enrollment: 2,381. Undergraduate enrollment: 2,-312; 1% part-time, 50% women. Total faculty: 208. Library holdings: 441,000 bound volumes, 1,277 periodical subscriptions, 3,043 records/tapes.

Undergraduate Courses offered for part-time students during daytime, evenings, summer. Complete part-time degree programs offered during daytime, evenings, summer. Adult/continuing education programs available. Part-time tuition: $870 per course.

Graduate Part-time study available in Graduate Studies. Degree can be earned exclusively through evening/weekend study in Graduate Studies. Basic part-time expenses: $215 per course tuition.

Earlham College
Richmond 47374

Independent-religious instiution; small-town setting. Awards B, M. Total enrollment: 1,058 (all undergraduates); 2% part-time, 54% women. Total faculty: 97. Library holdings: 300,000 bound volumes, 7,000 titles on microform, 1,300 periodical subscriptions, 1,900 records/tapes.

Graduate Part-time study available in Earlham School of Religion. Basic part-time expenses: $350 per trimester (minimum) tuition. Institutional financial aid available to part-time graduate students in Earlham School of Religion.

Fort Wayne Bible College
Fort Wayne 46807

Independent-religious instiution; city setting. Awards A, B. Total enrollment: 433 (all undergraduates); 20% part-time, 43% women, 28% over 25. Total faculty: 70. Library holdings: 53,000 bound volumes, 663 titles on microform, 471 periodical subscriptions, 3,115 records/tapes.

Undergraduate Courses offered for part-time students during daytime, evenings. Complete part-time degree programs offered during daytime, evenings. Adult/continuing education programs available. Career services available to part-time students: individual career counseling, individual job placement, employer recruitment on campus. Part-time tuition: $120 per credit hour.

Goshen College
Goshen 46526

Independent-religious instiution; small-town setting. Awards B. Total enrollment: 1,088 (all undergraduates); 9% part-time, 57% women, 21% over 25. Total faculty: 99. Library holdings: 113,000 bound volumes, 30 titles on microform, 725 periodical subscriptions, 5,000 records/tapes.

Undergraduate Courses offered for part-time students during daytime, evenings, summer. Complete part-time degree programs offered during daytime. Adult/continuing education programs available. Career services available to part-time students: individual and group career counseling, individual job placement, employer recruitment on campus. Part-time tuition: $200 per credit hour.

Grace College
Winona Lake 46590

Independent-religious instiution; small-town setting. Awards A, B. Total enrollment: 915 (all undergraduates); 12% part-time, 55% women, 2% over 25. Total faculty: 48. Library holdings: 103,000 bound volumes, 1,200 periodical subscriptions, 2,750 records/tapes.

Colleges Offering Part-Time Degree Programs / Indiana

Grace College (continued)

Undergraduate Courses offered for part-time students during daytime, evenings. Complete part-time degree programs offered during daytime. Career services available to part-time students: individual and group career counseling, individual job placement, employer recruitment on campus. Part-time tuition: $122 per semester hour.

Grace Theological Seminary
Winona Lake 46590

Independent-religious institution (graduate only). Total enrollment: 451 (primarily men; 53% part-time). Total faculty: 31.
Graduate Part-time study available in Graduate and Professional Programs. Basic part-time expenses: $100 per semester hour tuition plus $41 per semester fees. Institutional financial aid available to part-time graduate students in Graduate and Professional Programs.

Holy Cross Junior College
Notre Dame 46556

Independent-religious instutition; city setting. Awards A. Barrier-free campus. Total enrollment: 383 (all undergraduates); 16% part-time, 37% women, 1% over 25. Total faculty: 26. Library holdings: 12,000 bound volumes, 150 periodical subscriptions.
Undergraduate Courses offered for part-time students during daytime. Complete part-time degree programs offered during daytime. Career services available to part-time students: individual career counseling. Part-time tuition: $70 per credit.

Huntington College
Huntington 46750

Independent-religious instutition; small-town setting. Awards A, B, M. Total enrollment: 462. Undergraduate enrollment: 423; 15% part-time, 48% women. Total faculty: 47. Library holdings: 72,715 bound volumes, 13,216 titles on microform, 567 periodical subscriptions, 1,495 records/tapes.
Undergraduate Courses offered for part-time students during daytime, evenings, summer. Complete part-time degree programs offered during daytime, evenings, summer. Adult/continuing education programs available. Career services available to part-time students: individual and group career counseling, individual job placement, employer recruitment on campus. Part-time tuition: $146 per semester hour.
Graduate Part-time study available in Graduate School. Basic part-time expenses: $340 per course tuition plus $6 per course fees. Institutional financial aid available to part-time graduate students in Graduate School.

Indiana Central University
Indianapolis 46227

Independent-religious instutition; metropolitan setting. Awards A, B, M. Barrier-free campus. Total enrollment: 3,323. Undergraduate enrollment: 2,940; 63% part-time, 70% women. Total faculty: 212. Library holdings: 125,488 bound volumes, 268 titles on microform, 721 periodical subscriptions, 1,188 records/tapes.
Undergraduate Courses offered for part-time students during daytime, evenings, summer. Complete part-time degree programs offered during daytime, evenings, summer. Adult/continuing education programs available. Career services available to part-time students: individual and group career counseling, individual job placement, employer recruitment on campus. Part-time tuition: $206 per semester hour.

Graduate Part-time study available in Graduate School. Basic part-time expenses: $73 per credit hour tuition plus $5 per semester fees.

Indiana Institute of Technology
Fort Wayne 46803

Independent institution; city setting. Awards A, B. Total enrollment: 850 (all undergraduates); 8% part-time, 15% women. Total faculty: 44. Library holdings: 56,000 bound volumes, 1,500 periodical subscriptions, 5,000 records/tapes.
Undergraduate Courses offered for part-time students during daytime, evenings, summer. Complete part-time degree programs offered during daytime, evenings, summer. External degree programs available. Career services available to part-time students: individual career counseling, individual job placement, employer recruitment on campus. Part-time tuition: $138 per credit hour.

Indiana State University
Terre Haute 47809

Public institution; city setting. Awards A, B, M, D. Barrier-free campus. Total enrollment: 11,587. Undergraduate enrollment: 9,945; 15% part-time, 49% women, 13% over 25. Total faculty: 713. Library holdings: 936,294 bound volumes, 528,699 titles on microform, 4,862 periodical subscriptions, 48,049 records/tapes.
Undergraduate Courses offered for part-time students during daytime, evenings, weekends, summer. Complete part-time degree programs offered during daytime, evenings, weekends, summer. Adult/continuing education programs available. Career services available to part-time students: individual and group career counseling, individual job placement, employer recruitment on campus. Part-time tuition: $49.50 per credit hour for state residents, $115 per credit hour for nonresidents.
Graduate Part-time study available in School of Graduate Studies. Basic part-time expenses: $57 per semester hour tuition for state residents, $125 per semester hour tuition for nonresidents. Institutional financial aid available to part-time graduate students in School of Graduate Studies.

Indiana State University Evansville
Evansville 47712

Public institution; city setting. Awards A, B. Barrier-free campus. Total enrollment: 3,806 (all undergraduates); 42% part-time, 56% women, 25% over 25. Total faculty: 174. Library holdings: 152,662 bound volumes, 57,924 titles on microform, 625 periodical subscriptions, 3,748 records/tapes.
Undergraduate Courses offered for part-time students during daytime, evenings, weekends, summer. Complete part-time degree programs offered during daytime, evenings, weekends, summer. Adult/continuing education programs available. Career services available to part-time students: individual and group career counseling, individual job placement, employer recruitment on campus. Part-time tuition: $41 per semester hour for state residents, $100 per semester hour for nonresidents.

Indiana University at Kokomo
Kokomo 46901

Public institution; small-town setting. Awards A, B, M. Barrier-free campus. Total enrollment: 2,735. Undergraduate enrollment: 2,496; 73% part-time, 61% women, 75% over 25. Total faculty: 180. Library holdings: 100,000 bound volumes, 31,800

Indiana / **Colleges Offering Part-Time Degree Programs**

titles on microform, 886 periodical subscriptions, 770 records/tapes.

Undergraduate Courses offered for part-time students during daytime, evenings, summer. Complete part-time degree programs offered during daytime, evenings, summer. External degree and adult/continuing education programs available. Career services available to part-time students: individual and group career counseling, individual job placement, employer recruitment on campus. Part-time tuition: $42.50 per semester hour for state residents, $104.25 per semester hour for nonresidents.

Indiana University at South Bend
South Bend 46634

Public institution; city setting. Awards A, B, M. Barrier-free campus. Total enrollment: 5,610. Undergraduate enrollment: 4,319; 64% part-time, 57% women. Total faculty: 297. Library holdings: 207,000 bound volumes.

Undergraduate Courses offered for part-time students during daytime, evenings, weekends, summer. Complete part-time degree programs offered during daytime, evenings, weekends, summer. Adult/continuing education programs available. Career services available to part-time students: individual career counseling, employer recruitment on campus. Part-time tuition: $42.50 per credit hour for state residents, $104.25 per credit hour for nonresidents.

Graduate Part-time study available in Division of Business and Economics, Division of Education, Division of Public and Environmental Affairs. Basic part-time expenses: $56 per credit tuition for state residents, $124 per credit tuition for nonresidents.

Indiana University Bloomington
Bloomington 47405

Public institution; small-town setting. Awards A, B, M, D. Barrier-free campus. Total enrollment: 33,109. Undergraduate enrollment: 24,357; 3% part-time, 51% women, 6% over 25. Total faculty: 1,561. Library holdings: 4.4 million bound volumes.

Undergraduate Courses offered for part-time students during daytime, evenings, summer. Complete part-time degree programs offered during daytime, evenings, summer. External degree and adult/continuing education programs available. Career services available to part-time students: individual and group career counseling, individual job placement, employer recruitment on campus. Part-time tuition: $50.50 per credit hour for state residents, $142.50 per credit hour for nonresidents.

Graduate Part-time study available in Graduate School, School of Health, Physical Education and Recreation, School of Library and Information Science. Basic part-time expenses: $65.75 per credit tuition for state residents, $180.25 per credit tuition for nonresidents. Institutional financial aid available to part-time graduate students in Graduate School, School of Library and Information Science.

Indiana University East
Richmond 47374

Public institution; small-town setting. Awards A. Barrier-free campus. Total enrollment: 1,399 (all undergraduates); 72% part-time, 60% women. Total faculty: 105. Library holdings: 34,497 bound volumes, 271 titles on microform, 356 periodical subscriptions, 1,250 records/tapes.

Undergraduate Courses offered for part-time students during daytime, evenings, summer. Complete part-time degree programs offered during daytime, evenings, summer. External degree and adult/continuing education programs available. Career services available to part-time students: individual and group career counseling. Part-time tuition: $42.50 per credit for state residents, $104.25 per credit for nonresidents.

Indiana University Northwest
Gary 46408

Public institution; city setting. Awards A, B, M. Total enrollment: 5,116. Undergraduate enrollment: 4,549; 57% part-time, 60% women, 30% over 25. Total faculty: 265. Library holdings: 159,613 bound volumes, 1,413 periodical subscriptions, 95 records/tapes.

Undergraduate Courses offered for part-time students during daytime, evenings, weekends, summer. Complete part-time degree programs offered during daytime, evenings. External degree and adult/continuing education programs available. Career services available to part-time students: individual and group career counseling, individual job placement, employer recruitment on campus. Part-time tuition: $42.50 per credit for state residents, $104.25 per credit for nonresidents.

Graduate Part-time study available in Division of Business and Economics, Division of Education, Division of Public and Environmental Affairs. Degree can be earned exclusively through evening/weekend study in Division of Business and Economics, Division of Education, Division of Public and Environmental Affairs. Basic part-time expenses: $56 per credit tuition plus $6 per semester fees for state residents, $124 per credit tuition plus $6 per semester fees for nonresidents.

Indiana University–Purdue University at Fort Wayne
Fort Wayne 46805

Public institution; city setting. Awards A, B, M. Barrier-free campus. Total enrollment: 10,476. Undergraduate enrollment: 9,571; 55% part-time, 54% women. Total faculty: 583. Library holdings: 225,000 bound volumes, 1,651 periodical subscriptions, 2,700 records/tapes.

Undergraduate Courses offered for part-time students during daytime, evenings, weekends, summer. Complete part-time degree programs offered during daytime, evenings. External degree and adult/continuing education programs available. Career services available to part-time students: individual and group career counseling, individual job placement. Part-time tuition: $42.45 per semester hour for state residents, $105.50 per semester hour for nonresidents.

Graduate Part-time study available in Division of Arts and Letters, School of Engineering, Technology and Nursing, School of Science and Humanities. Basic part-time expenses: $55.65 per credit hour tuition for state residents, $125 per credit hour tuition for nonresidents.

Indiana University–Purdue University at Indianapolis
Indianapolis 46202

Public institution; metropolitan setting. Awards A, B, M, D. Barrier-free campus. Total enrollment: 23,514. Undergraduate enrollment: 16,952; 55% part-time, 50% women, 49% over 25. Total faculty: 1,922. Library holdings: 652,743 bound volumes, 436,255 titles on microform, 10,429 periodical subscriptions.

Undergraduate Courses offered for part-time students during daytime, evenings, weekends, summer. Complete part-time degree programs offered during daytime, evenings, weekends, summer. External degree and adult/continuing education programs available. Career services available to part-time students: individual and group career counseling, individual job

Colleges Offering Part-Time Degree Programs / *Indiana*

Indiana University–Purdue University at Indianapolis (continued)
placement, employer recruitment on campus. Part-time tuition: $46.50 per semester hour for state residents, $123.50 per semester hour for nonresidents.

Graduate Part-time study available in School of Business, School of Education, School of Engineering and Technology, School of Law, School of Nursing, School of Public and Environmental Affairs, School of Science, School of Social Work. Basic part-time expenses: $65.75 per credit tuition for state residents, $180.25 per credit tuition for nonresidents. Institutional financial aid available to part-time graduate students in School of Business, School of Education, School of Engineering and Technology, School of Law, School of Nursing, School of Public and Environmental Affairs, School of Science, School of Social Work.

Indiana University Southeast
New Albany 47150

Public institution; small-town setting. Awards A, B, M. Total enrollment: 4,671. Undergraduate enrollment: 4,189; 58% part-time, 58% women, 53% over 25. Total faculty: 250. Library holdings: 150,000 bound volumes, 967 periodical subscriptions, 4,000 records/tapes.

Undergraduate Courses offered for part-time students during daytime, evenings, weekends, summer. Complete part-time degree programs offered during daytime, evenings, weekends, summer. External degree and adult/continuing education programs available. Career services available to part-time students: individual and group career counseling, individual job placement, employer recruitment on campus. Part-time tuition: $42.50 per credit hour for state residents, $104.25 per credit hour for nonresidents.

Graduate Part-time study available in Division of Education. Degree can be earned exclusively through evening/weekend study in Division of Education. Basic part-time expenses: $56 per credit tuition for state residents, $124 per credit tuition for nonresidents. Institutional financial aid available to part-time graduate students in Division of Education.

Indiana Vocational Technical College–Central Indiana
Indianapolis 46202

Public institution; metropolitan setting. Awards A. Total enrollment: 5,001 (all undergraduates); 45% part-time, 45% women. Total faculty: 236.

Undergraduate Courses offered for part-time students during daytime, evenings, summer. Complete part-time degree programs offered during daytime, evenings, summer. Adult/continuing education programs available. Career services available to part-time students: individual career counseling, individual job placement, employer recruitment on campus. Part-time tuition: $25 per credit for state residents, $42.50 per credit for nonresidents.

Indiana Vocational Technical College–Columbus
Columbus 47203

Public institution; small-town setting. Awards A. Barrier-free campus. Total enrollment: 1,845 (all undergraduates); 50% part-time, 50% women, 55% over 25. Total faculty: 108.

Undergraduate Courses offered for part-time students during daytime, evenings, summer. Complete part-time degree programs offered during daytime, evenings, summer. Adult/continuing education programs available. Career services available to part-time students: individual and group career counseling, individual job placement, employer recruitment on campus. Part-time tuition: $22.75 per credit for state residents, $42.50 per credit for nonresidents.

Indiana Vocational Technical College–Eastcentral
Muncie 47302

Public institution; city setting. Awards A. Barrier-free campus. Total enrollment: 2,266 (all undergraduates); 44% part-time, 38% women, 68% over 25. Total faculty: 116.

Undergraduate Courses offered for part-time students during daytime, evenings, summer. Complete part-time degree programs offered during daytime, evenings, summer. Adult/continuing education programs available. Career services available to part-time students: individual and group career counseling, individual job placement, employer recruitment on campus. Part-time tuition: $22.75 per credit for state residents, $40.50 per credit for nonresidents.

Indiana Vocational Technical College–Kokomo
Kokomo 46901

Public institution; small-town setting. Awards A. Barrier-free campus. Total enrollment: 1,587 (all undergraduates); 52% part-time, 44% women, 70% over 25. Total faculty: 111.

Undergraduate Courses offered for part-time students during daytime, evenings. Complete part-time degree programs offered during daytime, evenings. Adult/continuing education programs available. Career services available to part-time students: individual career counseling, individual job placement. Part-time tuition: $23.10 per credit for state residents, $42.50 per credit for nonresidents.

Indiana Vocational Technical College–Northcentral
South Bend 46619

Public institution; city setting. Awards A. Barrier-free campus. Total enrollment: 2,279 (all undergraduates); 69% part-time, 42% women, 60% over 25. Total faculty: 118. Library holdings: 8,000 bound volumes, 140 periodical subscriptions, 1,000 records/tapes.

Undergraduate Courses offered for part-time students during daytime, evenings, weekends, summer. Complete part-time degree programs offered during daytime, evenings, summer. Adult/continuing education programs available. Career services available to part-time students: individual career counseling, individual job placement. Part-time tuition: $22.75 per credit for state residents, $42.50 per credit for nonresidents.

Indiana Vocational Technical College–Northeast
Fort Wayne 46805

Public institution; city setting. Awards A. Barrier-free campus. Total enrollment: 3,375 (all undergraduates); 70% part-time, 46% women. Total faculty: 141. Library holdings: 8,000 bound volumes, 15 titles on microform, 130 periodical subscriptions, 150 records/tapes.

Undergraduate Courses offered for part-time students during daytime, evenings, summer. Complete part-time degree programs offered during daytime, evenings, summer. Adult/con-

tinuing education programs available. Career services available to part-time students: individual career counseling, individual job placement. Part-time tuition: $22.75 per credit for state residents, $42.50 per credit for nonresidents.

Indiana Vocational Technical College–Northwest
Gary 46409

Public institution; city setting. Awards A. Barrier-free campus. Total enrollment: 3,176 (all undergraduates); 51% part-time, 50% women, 21% over 25. Total faculty: 125. Library holdings: 100 bound volumes, 63 periodical subscriptions, 3,000 records/tapes.

Undergraduate Courses offered for part-time students during daytime, evenings, summer. Complete part-time degree programs offered during daytime, evenings, summer. Adult/continuing education programs available. Career services available to part-time students: individual career counseling, individual job placement. Part-time tuition: $22.75 per credit for state residents, $42.50 per credit for nonresidents.

Indiana Vocational Technical College–Southcentral
Sellersburg 47172

Public institution; small-town setting. Awards A. Total enrollment: 1,484 (all undergraduates); 42% part-time, 41% women, 30% over 25. Total faculty: 113. Library holdings: 4,025 bound volumes, 80 periodical subscriptions.

Undergraduate Courses offered for part-time students during daytime, evenings, summer. Complete part-time degree programs offered during daytime, evenings. Adult/continuing education programs available. Career services available to part-time students: individual and group career counseling, individual job placement. Part-time tuition: $22.75 per credit for state residents, $42.50 per credit for nonresidents.

Indiana Vocational Technical College–Southeast
Madison 47250

Public institution; small-town setting. Awards A. Barrier-free campus. Total enrollment: 718 (all undergraduates); 65% part-time, 57% women, 75% over 25. Total faculty: 74. Library holdings: 1,700 bound volumes, 75 periodical subscriptions, 372 records/tapes.

Undergraduate Courses offered for part-time students during daytime, evenings. Complete part-time degree programs offered during daytime, evenings. Career services available to part-time students: individual and group career counseling, individual job placement, employer recruitment on campus. Part-time tuition: $22.75 per credit for state residents, $42.50 per credit for nonresidents.

Indiana Vocational Technical College–Southwest
Evansville 47710

Public institution; city setting. Awards A. Barrier-free campus. Total enrollment: 1,830 (all undergraduates); 58% part-time, 41% women. Total faculty: 85.

Undergraduate Courses offered for part-time students during daytime, evenings, summer. Complete part-time degree programs offered during daytime, evenings. Career services available to part-time students: individual career counseling, individual job placement, employer recruitment on campus. Part-time tuition: $22.95 per credit hour for state residents, $42.70 per credit hour for nonresidents.

Indiana Vocational Technical College–Wabash Valley
Terre Haute 47802

Public institution; city setting. Awards A. Barrier-free campus. Total enrollment: 1,510 (all undergraduates); 44% part-time, 42% women. Total faculty: 80.

Undergraduate Courses offered for part-time students during daytime, evenings. Complete part-time degree programs offered during daytime, evenings. Adult/continuing education programs available. Career services available to part-time students: individual and group career counseling, individual job placement, employer recruitment on campus. Part-time tuition: $22.75 per credit for state residents, $42.50 per credit for nonresidents.

Indiana Vocational Technical College–Whitewater
Richmond 47374

Public institution; small-town setting. Awards A. Barrier-free campus. Total enrollment: 1,085 (all undergraduates); 57% part-time, 35% women. Total faculty: 75. Library holdings: 6,000 bound volumes.

Undergraduate Courses offered for part-time students during daytime, evenings, weekends, summer. Complete part-time degree programs offered during daytime, evenings, weekends, summer. Adult/continuing education programs available. Career services available to part-time students: individual career counseling, individual job placement. Part-time tuition: $22.75 per credit for state residents, $42.50 per credit for nonresidents.

LaPorte Business College
LaPorte 46350

Proprietary institution; rural setting. Awards A. Barrier-free campus. Total enrollment: 200 (all undergraduates); 20% part-time, 85% women. Total faculty: 14. Library holdings: 1,200 bound volumes, 30 periodical subscriptions, 40 records/tapes.

Undergraduate Courses offered for part-time students during daytime, evenings. Complete part-time degree programs offered during daytime, evenings. Adult/continuing education programs available. Career services available to part-time students: individual and group career counseling, individual job placement. Part-time tuition: $52.50 per credit hour.

Lockyear College, Evansville Campus
Evansville 47706

Proprietary institution; city setting. Awards A. Total enrollment: 585 (all undergraduates); 33% part-time, 60% women, 50% over 25. Total faculty: 18. Library holdings: 7,000 bound volumes, 30 periodical subscriptions, 250 records/tapes.

Undergraduate Courses offered for part-time students during daytime, evenings, summer. Complete part-time degree programs offered during daytime, evenings, summer. Adult/continuing education programs available. Career services available to part-time students: individual career counseling, individual job placement. Part-time tuition: $60 per credit.

Colleges Offering Part-Time Degree Programs / *Indiana*

Lockyear College, Indianapolis Campus
Indianapolis 46202

Proprietary institution; metropolitan setting. Awards A. Barrier-free campus. Total enrollment: 1,300 (all undergraduates); 3% part-time, 60% women, 50% over 25. Total faculty: 15.

Undergraduate Courses offered for part-time students during daytime, evenings, summer. Complete part-time degree programs offered during daytime, evenings, summer. Adult/continuing education programs available. Career services available to part-time students: individual and group career counseling, individual job placement. Part-time tuition: $60 per credit.

Manchester College
North Manchester 46962

Independent-religious instutition; small-town setting. Awards A, B, M. Total enrollment: 1,036. Undergraduate enrollment: 1,024; 6% part-time, 55% women, 5% over 25. Total faculty: 92. Library holdings: 156,000 bound volumes, 750 periodical subscriptions, 4,000 records/tapes.

Undergraduate Courses offered for part-time students during daytime, evenings, summer. Complete part-time degree programs offered during daytime. Career services available to part-time students: individual and group career counseling, individual job placement, employer recruitment on campus. Part-time tuition: $180 per semester hour.

Marian College
Indianapolis 46222

Independent-religious instutition; metropolitan setting. Awards A, B. Barrier-free campus. Total enrollment: 948 (all undergraduates); 25% part-time, 72% women, 4% over 25. Total faculty: 91. Library holdings: 106,000 bound volumes, 535 periodical subscriptions, 1,842 records/tapes.

Undergraduate Courses offered for part-time students during daytime, evenings, summer. Complete part-time degree programs offered during daytime. Adult/continuing education programs available. Career services available to part-time students: individual career counseling, individual job placement, employer recruitment on campus. Part-time tuition: $160 per credit hour.

Marion College
Marion 46952

Independent-religious instutition; small-town setting. Awards A, B, M. Total enrollment: 1,159. Undergraduate enrollment: 1,117; 25% part-time, 57% women. Total faculty: 94. Library holdings: 100,000 bound volumes, 450 periodical subscriptions.

Undergraduate Courses offered for part-time students during daytime, evenings. Complete part-time degree programs offered during daytime, evenings. Adult/continuing education programs available. Career services available to part-time students: individual and group career counseling, individual job placement, employer recruitment on campus. Part-time tuition and fees per semester (1 to 11 semester hours) range from $72 to $2052.

Graduate Part-time study available in Graduate Programs. Degree can be earned exclusively through evening/weekend study in Graduate Programs. Basic part-time expenses: $180 per semester (minimum) tuition plus $12 per credit hour fees. Institutional financial aid available to part-time graduate students in Graduate Programs.

Martin Center College
Indianapolis 46205

Independent institution; metropolitan setting. Awards B. Total enrollment: 142 (all undergraduates); 20% part-time, 65% women, 95% over 25. Total faculty: 65. Library holdings: 750 bound volumes, 130 records/tapes.

Undergraduate Courses offered for part-time students during daytime, evenings, weekends, summer. Complete part-time degree programs offered during daytime, evenings, weekends, summer. Adult/continuing education programs available. Career services available to part-time students: individual and group career counseling, individual job placement. Part-time tuition: $250 per course.

Michiana College of Commerce
South Bend 46614

Proprietary institution; city setting. Awards A. Barrier-free campus. Total enrollment: 235 (all undergraduates); 28% part-time, 78% women, 53% over 25. Total faculty: 12. Library holdings: 3,000 bound volumes, 20 periodical subscriptions, 100 records/tapes.

Undergraduate Courses offered for part-time students during daytime, evenings, weekends, summer. Complete part-time degree programs offered during daytime, evenings. Adult/continuing education programs available. Career services available to part-time students: individual career counseling, individual job placement. Part-time tuition: $40 per credit hour.

Oakland City College
Oakland City 47660

Independent-religious instutition; small-town setting. Awards A, B, M. Barrier-free campus. Total enrollment: 645. Undergraduate enrollment: 635; 12% part-time, 46% women. Total faculty: 50. Library holdings: 67,000 bound volumes, 407 titles on microform, 315 periodical subscriptions, 6,427 records/tapes.

Undergraduate Courses offered for part-time students during daytime, evenings, weekends, summer. Complete part-time degree programs offered during daytime, evenings, weekends, summer. Career services available to part-time students: individual and group career counseling, individual job placement, employer recruitment on campus. Part-time tuition: $87 per quarter hour.

Graduate Part-time study available in Graduate School of Theology. Basic part-time expenses: $50 per quarter hour tuition plus $48.33 per quarter fees. Institutional financial aid available to part-time graduate students in Graduate School of Theology.

Purdue University
West Lafayette 47907

Public institution; small-town setting. Awards A, B, M, D. Total enrollment: 31,856. Undergraduate enrollment: 26,675; 4% part-time, 40% women. Total faculty: 3,100. Library holdings: 1.6 million bound volumes.

Undergraduate Courses offered for part-time students during daytime, evenings, summer. Complete part-time degree programs offered during daytime, evenings, summer. Adult/continuing education programs available. Career services available to part-time students: individual and group career counseling, individual job placement, employer recruitment on campus. Part-time tuition: $56 per semester hour for state residents, $150 per semester hour for nonresidents.

Graduate Part-time study available in Graduate School. Basic part-time expenses: $56 per credit hour tuition for state residents, $150 per credit hour tuition for nonresidents. Institution-

Indiana / **Colleges Offering Part-Time Degree Programs**

al financial aid available to part-time graduate students in Graduate School.

Purdue University Calumet
Hammond 46323

Public institution; city setting. Awards A, B, M. Barrier-free campus. Total enrollment: 7,830. Undergraduate enrollment: 7,142; 60% part-time, 44% women. Total faculty: 389. Library holdings: 125,000 bound volumes, 1,200 periodical subscriptions, 900 records/tapes.

Undergraduate Courses offered for part-time students during daytime, evenings, weekends, summer. Complete part-time degree programs offered during daytime, evenings, weekends, summer. Adult/continuing education programs available. Career services available to part-time students: individual and group career counseling, individual job placement, employer recruitment on campus. Part-time tuition: $42.25 per hour for state residents, $106.75 per hour for nonresidents.

Graduate Part-time study available in Graduate School. Basic part-time expenses: $55.40 per credit hour tuition plus $26 per semester fees for state residents, $126 per credit hour tuition plus $26 per semester fees for nonresidents. Institutional financial aid available to part-time graduate students in Graduate School.

Purdue University North Central
Westville 46391

Public institution; rural setting. Awards A, B (also offers some graduate courses). Total enrollment: 2,560. Undergraduate enrollment: 2,457; 66% part-time, 58% women, 39% over 25. Total faculty: 146. Library holdings: 51,500 bound volumes, 1,650 titles on microform, 371 periodical subscriptions, 525 records/tapes.

Undergraduate Courses offered for part-time students during daytime, evenings, weekends, summer. Complete part-time degree programs offered during daytime, evenings, summer. Adult/continuing education programs available. Career services available to part-time students: individual and group career counseling, individual job placement, employer recruitment on campus. Part-time tuition: $42.25 per credit hour for state residents, $106.75 per credit hour for nonresidents.

Rose-Hulman Institute of Technology
Terre Haute 47803

Independent institution; city setting. Awards B, M. Total enrollment: 1,329. Undergraduate enrollment: 1,300; 0% part-time, 0% women. Total faculty: 96. Library holdings: 52,000 bound volumes, 392 periodical subscriptions, 1,450 records/tapes.

Graduate Part-time study available in Graduate Studies. Basic part-time expenses: $180 per credit tuition.

Saint Francis College
Fort Wayne 46808

Independent-religious instutition; city setting. Awards A, B, M. Total enrollment: 1,267. Undergraduate enrollment: 942; 55% part-time, 76% women, 35% over 25. Total faculty: 90. Library holdings: 71,210 bound volumes, 50,000 titles on microform, 565 periodical subscriptions.

Undergraduate Courses offered for part-time students during daytime, evenings, summer. Complete part-time degree programs offered during daytime, evenings. Adult/continuing education programs available. Career services available to part-time students: individual and group career counseling, individual job placement, employer recruitment on campus. Part-time tuition: $110 per semester hour.

Graduate Part-time study available in Graduate School. Degree can be earned exclusively through evening/weekend study in Graduate School. Basic part-time expenses: $120 per semester hour tuition plus $20 per year fees. Institutional financial aid available to part-time graduate students in Graduate School.

Saint Joseph's College
Rensselaer 47978

Independent-religious instutition; small-town setting. Awards A, B, M. Total enrollment: 991. Undergraduate enrollment: 919; 2% part-time, 41% women. Total faculty: 67. Library holdings: 165,000 bound volumes, 1,740 periodical subscriptions, 32,000 records/tapes.

Undergraduate Courses offered for part-time students during daytime, summer. Complete part-time degree programs offered during daytime, summer. Career services available to part-time students: individual and group career counseling, individual job placement, employer recruitment on campus. Part-time tuition: $167 per credit.

Graduate Part-time study available in Rensselaer Program of Church Music and Liturgy. Basic part-time expenses: $73 per credit tuition plus $30 per summer fees.

Saint Mary-of-the-Woods College
Saint Mary-of-the-Woods 47876

Independent-religious instutition; city setting. Awards A, B. Total enrollment: 650 (all undergraduates); 40% part-time, 100% women. Total faculty: 73. Library holdings: 132,000 bound volumes, 404 periodical subscriptions, 900 records/tapes.

Undergraduate Courses offered for part-time students during daytime. Complete part-time degree programs offered during daytime. External degree and adult/continuing education programs available. Career services available to part-time students: individual and group career counseling, individual job placement, employer recruitment on campus. Part-time tuition: $175 per credit hour.

Saint Meinrad School of Theology
St Meinrad 47577

Independent-religious instutition (graduate only). Total enrollment: 198 (primarily men; 22% part-time). Total faculty: 21. Library holdings: 112,000 bound volumes, 500 microforms.

Graduate Part-time study available in Graduate and Professional Programs. Basic part-time expenses: $110 per credit hour tuition.

Taylor University
Upland 46989

Independent-religious instutition; rural setting. Awards A, B. Total enrollment: 1,559 (all undergraduates); 5% part-time, 55% women. Total faculty: 105. Library holdings: 129,000 bound volumes, 5,000 titles on microform, 800 periodical subscriptions.

Undergraduate Courses offered for part-time students during daytime, summer. Complete part-time degree programs offered during daytime, summer. Career services available to part-time students: individual and group career counseling, individual job placement, employer recruitment on campus. Part-time tuition per semester (1 to 11 credit hours) ranges from $152 to $2035.

Colleges Offering Part-Time Degree Programs / Indiana

Tri-State University
Angola 46703

Independent institution; small-town setting. Awards A, B. Total enrollment: 1,049 (all undergraduates); 9% part-time, 21% women. Total faculty: 77. Library holdings: 116,000 bound volumes, 171 periodical subscriptions, 150 records/tapes.

Undergraduate Courses offered for part-time students during daytime, summer. Complete part-time degree programs offered during daytime, summer. Adult/continuing education programs available. Career services available to part-time students: individual career counseling. Part-time tuition: $98 per credit hour.

University of Evansville
Evansville 47702

Independent-religious instutition; city setting. Awards A, B, M. Total enrollment: 4,626. Undergraduate enrollment: 4,055; 31% part-time, 53% women. Total faculty: 280. Library holdings: 180,000 bound volumes, 110,000 titles on microform, 1,300 periodical subscriptions, 4,500 records/tapes.

Undergraduate Courses offered for part-time students during daytime, evenings, weekends, summer. Complete part-time degree programs offered during daytime, evenings, summer. External degree and adult/continuing education programs available. Career services available to part-time students: individual and group career counseling, individual job placement, employer recruitment on campus. Part-time tuition: $150 per quarter hour.

Graduate Part-time study available in School of Graduate Studies. Degree can be earned exclusively through evening/weekend study in School of Graduate Studies. Basic part-time expenses: $100 per credit tuition.

University of Notre Dame
Notre Dame 46556

Independent-religious instutition; city setting. Awards B, M, D. Total enrollment: 9,400. Undergraduate enrollment: 7,400; 0% part-time, 30% women, 1% over 25. Total faculty: 798. Library holdings: 1.4 million bound volumes, 680,000 titles on microform, 12,000 periodical subscriptions, 7,000 records/tapes.

Graduate Part-time study available in Graduate School. Basic part-time expenses: $385 per credit tuition.

Valparaiso University
Valparaiso 46383

Independent-religious instutition; small-town setting. Awards A, B, M, D. Total enrollment: 3,783. Undergraduate enrollment: 3,300; 3% part-time, 53% women, 15% over 25. Total faculty: 356. Library holdings: 334,000 bound volumes, 115,000 titles on microform, 1,317 periodical subscriptions, 13,662 records/tapes.

Undergraduate Courses offered for part-time students during daytime, evenings, weekends, summer. Complete part-time degree programs offered during daytime, evenings, summer. Adult/continuing education programs available. Career services available to part-time students: individual and group career counseling, individual job placement, employer recruitment on campus. Part-time tuition: $215 per credit hour.

Graduate Part-time study available in Graduate Division. Basic part-time expenses: $90 per semester hour tuition.

Vincennes University
Vincennes 47591

Public institution; small-town setting. Awards A. Total enrollment: 4,896 (all undergraduates); 25% part-time, 49% women, 5% over 25. Total faculty: 182. Library holdings: 40,000 bound volumes, 475 periodical subscriptions, 1,500 records/tapes.

Undergraduate Courses offered for part-time students during daytime, evenings, summer. Complete part-time degree programs offered during daytime, evenings, summer. Adult/continuing education programs available. Career services available to part-time students: individual and group career counseling. Part-time tuition: $39 per credit for state residents, $107 per credit for nonresidents.

IOWA

American Institute of Business
Des Moines 50321

Independent institution; city setting. Awards A. Total enrollment: 1,164 (all undergraduates); 20% part-time, 80% women, 12% over 25. Total faculty: 57. Library holdings: 4,000 bound volumes, 95 periodical subscriptions, 3,842 records/tapes.

Undergraduate Courses offered for part-time students during daytime, evenings, weekends, summer. Complete part-time degree programs offered during daytime, evenings, weekends, summer. Adult/continuing education programs available. Career services available to part-time students: individual career counseling, individual job placement, employer recruitment on campus. Part-time tuition: $78 per quarter hour.

Briar Cliff College
Sioux City 51104

Independent-religious instutition; city setting. Awards A, B. Barrier-free campus. Total enrollment: 1,307 (all undergraduates); 34% part-time, 64% women, 22% over 25. Total faculty: 75. Library holdings: 86,000 bound volumes, 25,000 titles on microform, 450 periodical subscriptions, 3,000 records/tapes.

Undergraduate Courses offered for part-time students during daytime, evenings, weekends, summer. Complete part-time degree programs offered during daytime, evenings, weekends, summer. Adult/continuing education programs available. Career services available to part-time students: individual career counseling, individual job placement, employer recruitment on campus. Part-time tuition: $137.50 per credit hour.

Buena Vista College
Storm Lake 50588

Independent-religious instutition; small-town setting. Awards B. Total enrollment: 904 (all undergraduates); 5% part-time, 48% women, 10% over 25. Total faculty: 70. Library holdings: 80,000 bound volumes, 468 periodical subscriptions, 3,200 records/tapes.

Undergraduate Courses offered for part-time students during daytime, evenings, summer. Complete part-time degree programs offered during daytime, evenings. Adult/continuing education programs available. Career services available to part-time students: individual and group career counseling, individual job placement, employer recruitment on campus. Part-time tuition: $182 per semester hour.

Iowa / Colleges Offering Part-Time Degree Programs

Central University of Iowa
Pella 50219

Independent-religious instutition; small-town setting. Awards B. Total enrollment: 1,535 (all undergraduates); 6% part-time, 54% women. Total faculty: 93. Library holdings: 124,000 bound volumes, 500 titles on microform, 800 periodical subscriptions, 2,624 records/tapes.

Undergraduate Courses offered for part-time students during daytime, evenings, summer. Complete part-time degree programs offered during daytime, evenings, summer. External degree and adult/continuing education programs available. Part-time tuition: $550 per course.

Clarke College
Dubuque 52001

Independent-religious instutition; city setting. Awards B, M. Total enrollment: 906. Undergraduate enrollment: 863; 30% part-time, 71% women, 22% over 25. Total faculty: 79. Library holdings: 120,000 bound volumes, 550 periodical subscriptions, 650 records/tapes.

Undergraduate Courses offered for part-time students during daytime, evenings, summer. Complete part-time degree programs offered during daytime, evenings. Adult/continuing education programs available. Career services available to part-time students: individual and group career counseling, individual job placement, employer recruitment on campus. Part-time tuition: $140 per credit.

Graduate Part-time study available in Graduate Division. Basic part-time expenses: $155 per credit tuition. Institutional financial aid available to part-time graduate students in Graduate Division.

Clinton Community College
Clinton 52732

Public institution; small-town setting. Awards A. Barrier-free campus. Total enrollment: 1,103 (all undergraduates); 44% part-time, 52% women, 30% over 25. Total faculty: 58. Library holdings: 20,000 bound volumes, 150 periodical subscriptions, 1,000 records/tapes.

Undergraduate Courses offered for part-time students during daytime, evenings, summer. Complete part-time degree programs offered during daytime, evenings. Adult/continuing education programs available. Career services available to part-time students: individual and group career counseling, individual job placement, employer recruitment on campus. Part-time tuition: $36 per semester hour for state residents, $54 per semester hour for nonresidents.

Coe College
Cedar Rapids 52402

Independent-religious instutition; city setting. Awards B. Total enrollment: 1,371 (all undergraduates); 21% part-time, 50% women, 20% over 25. Total faculty: 101. Library holdings: 180,000 bound volumes, 560 periodical subscriptions, 6,413 records/tapes.

Undergraduate Courses offered for part-time students during daytime, evenings, summer. Complete part-time degree programs offered during daytime, evenings, summer. Adult/continuing education programs available. Career services available to part-time students: individual and group career counseling, individual job placement, employer recruitment on campus. Part-time tuition: $395 per course.

Cornell College
Mount Vernon 52314

Independent-religious instutition; small-town setting. Awards B. Total enrollment: 961 (all undergraduates); 4% part-time, 45% women, 4% over 25. Total faculty: 95. Library holdings: 185,000 bound volumes, 600 periodical subscriptions, 5,000 records/tapes.

Undergraduate Courses offered for part-time students during daytime, weekends. Complete part-time degree programs offered during daytime. Adult/continuing education programs available. Career services available to part-time students: individual and group career counseling, individual job placement, employer recruitment on campus. Part-time tuition: $875 per course.

Des Moines Area Community College
Ankeny 50021

Public institution; small-town setting. Awards A. Barrier-free campus. Total enrollment: 7,895 (all undergraduates); 53% part-time, 58% women, 32% over 25. Total faculty: 377. Library holdings: 49,000 bound volumes, 600 periodical subscriptions, 1,225 records/tapes.

Undergraduate Courses offered for part-time students during daytime, evenings. Complete part-time degree programs offered during daytime, evenings. Adult/continuing education programs available. Career services available to part-time students: individual and group career counseling, individual job placement, employer recruitment on campus. Part-time tuition: $28 per semester hour for state residents, $56 per semester hour for nonresidents.

Drake University
Des Moines 50311

Independent institution; city setting. Awards B, M, D. Total enrollment: 6,008. Undergraduate enrollment: 4,283; 20% part-time, 51% women. Total faculty: 343. Library holdings: 400,000 bound volumes, 2,000 periodical subscriptions, 6,000 records/tapes.

Undergraduate Courses offered for part-time students during daytime, evenings, weekends, summer. Complete part-time degree programs offered during daytime, evenings, weekends, summer. Adult/continuing education programs available. Career services available to part-time students: individual and group career counseling, individual job placement, employer recruitment on campus. Part-time tuition: $207 per hour.

Graduate Part-time study available in School of Graduate Studies. Basic part-time expenses: $140 per hour (minimum) tuition. Institutional financial aid available to part-time graduate students in School of Graduate Studies.

Ellsworth Community College
Iowa Falls 50126

Public institution; small-town setting. Awards A. Total enrollment: 901 (all undergraduates); 19% part-time, 45% women, 4% over 25. Total faculty: 53. Library holdings: 24,250 bound volumes, 2,300 records/tapes.

Undergraduate Courses offered for part-time students during daytime, evenings, summer. Complete part-time degree programs offered during daytime, evenings, summer. Adult/continuing education programs available. Career services available to part-time students: individual career counseling, individual job placement. Part-time tuition: $30 per credit for state residents, $60 per credit for nonresidents.

Colleges Offering Part-Time Degree Programs / *Iowa*

Faith Baptist Bible College
Ankeny 50021

Independent-religious instutition; small-town setting. Awards A, B, M. Total enrollment: 407. Undergraduate enrollment: 398; 8% part-time, 52% women, 1% over 25. Total faculty: 24. Library holdings: 42,896 bound volumes, 333 periodical subscriptions, 1,365 records/tapes.

Undergraduate Courses offered for part-time students during daytime, evenings, summer. Complete part-time degree programs offered during daytime. Adult/continuing education programs available. Part-time tuition: $110 per semester hour.

Graduate Part-time study available in Graduate Program. Basic part-time expenses: $115 per credit tuition plus $15 per semester (minimum) fees. Institutional financial aid available to part-time graduate students in Graduate Program.

Graceland College
Lamoni 50140

Independent institution; small-town setting. Awards B. Total enrollment: 1,059 (all undergraduates); 11% part-time, 54% women, 1% over 25. Total faculty: 100. Library holdings: 91,114 bound volumes, 1,409 titles on microform, 423 periodical subscriptions, 2,306 records/tapes.

Undergraduate Courses offered for part-time students during daytime, summer. Complete part-time degree programs offered during daytime, summer. Adult/continuing education programs available. Career services available to part-time students: individual and group career counseling, individual job placement, employer recruitment on campus. Part-time tuition: $150 per semester hour.

Grand View College
Des Moines 50316

Independent-religious instutition; city setting. Awards A, B. Barrier-free campus. Total enrollment: 1,307 (all undergraduates); 28% part-time, 58% women, 28% over 25. Total faculty: 99. Library holdings: 80,000 bound volumes, 1,200 titles on microform, 500 periodical subscriptions, 3,400 records/tapes.

Undergraduate Courses offered for part-time students during daytime, evenings, summer. Complete part-time degree programs offered during daytime, evenings, summer. Career services available to part-time students: individual career counseling, individual job placement, employer recruitment on campus. Part-time tuition: $175 per semester hour.

Hawkeye Institute of Technology
Waterloo 50704

Public institution; city setting. Awards A. Barrier-free campus. Total enrollment: 2,080 (all undergraduates); 4% part-time, 47% women, 27% over 25. Total faculty: 137. Library holdings: 13,990 bound volumes, 408 titles on microform, 424 periodical subscriptions, 96 records/tapes.

Undergraduate Courses offered for part-time students during daytime. Complete part-time degree programs offered during daytime. Adult/continuing education programs available. Career services available to part-time students: individual and group career counseling, individual job placement. Part-time tuition: $22 per quarter hour for state residents, $44 per quarter hour for nonresidents.

Indian Hills Community College
Ottumwa 52501

Public institution; small-town setting. Awards A. Total enrollment: 2,399 (all undergraduates); 26% part-time, 53% women, 44% over 25. Total faculty: 68. Library holdings: 17,000 bound volumes.

Undergraduate Courses offered for part-time students during daytime, evenings, summer. Complete part-time degree programs offered during daytime, evenings, summer. Adult/continuing education programs available. Career services available to part-time students: individual career counseling, employer recruitment on campus. Part-time tuition: $30 per credit for state residents, $45 per credit for nonresidents.

Iowa Central Community College
Fort Dodge 50501

Public institution; rural setting. Awards A. Barrier-free campus. Total enrollment: 2,825 (all undergraduates); 26% part-time, 47% women. Total faculty: 103. Library holdings: 61,000 bound volumes, 30 periodical subscriptions, 900 records/tapes.

Undergraduate Courses offered for part-time students during daytime, evenings, summer. Complete part-time degree programs offered during daytime, evenings, summer. Adult/continuing education programs available. Career services available to part-time students: individual and group career counseling, individual job placement, employer recruitment on campus. Part-time tuition: $33.70 per semester hour for state residents, $48.70 per semester hour for nonresidents.

Iowa Lakes Community College, North Attendance Center
Estherville 51334

Public institution; small-town setting. Awards A. Barrier-free campus. Total enrollment: 828 (all undergraduates); 16% part-time, 46% women, 12% over 25. Total faculty: 42. Library holdings: 25,861 bound volumes, 232 titles on microform, 178 periodical subscriptions, 2,832 records/tapes.

Undergraduate Courses offered for part-time students during daytime, evenings, weekends, summer. Complete part-time degree programs offered during daytime, evenings, weekends, summer. Adult/continuing education programs available. Career services available to part-time students: individual and group career counseling, individual job placement. Part-time tuition: $23.50 per quarter hour for state residents, $35.25 per quarter hour for nonresidents.

Iowa Lakes Community College, South Attendance Center
Emmetsburg 50536

Public institution; small-town setting. Awards A. Barrier-free campus. Total enrollment: 700 (all undergraduates); 22% part-time, 46% women, 16% over 25. Total faculty: 53. Library holdings: 12,380 bound volumes, 260 titles on microform, 172 periodical subscriptions, 3,002 records/tapes.

Undergraduate Courses offered for part-time students during daytime, evenings, weekends, summer. Complete part-time degree programs offered during daytime, evenings, weekends, summer. Adult/continuing education programs available. Career services available to part-time students: individual and group career counseling, individual job placement. Part-time tuition: $23.50 per quarter hour for state residents, $35.25 per quarter hour for nonresidents.

Iowa / Colleges Offering Part-Time Degree Programs

Iowa State University
Ames 50011

Public institution; small-town setting. Awards B, M, D. Barrier-free campus. Total enrollment: 26,020. Undergraduate enrollment: 22,209; 7% part-time, 38% women, 10% over 25. Total faculty: 2,098. Library holdings: 1.5 million bound volumes, 1.5 million titles on microform, 19,100 periodical subscriptions, 30,000 records/tapes.

Undergraduate Courses offered for part-time students during daytime, evenings, summer. Complete part-time degree programs offered during daytime, summer. External degree and adult/continuing education programs available. Career services available to part-time students: individual and group career counseling, individual job placement, employer recruitment on campus. Part-time tuition: $52 per credit hour for state residents, $144 per credit hour for nonresidents.

Graduate Part-time study available in Graduate College. Basic part-time expenses: $246 per semester (minimum) tuition. Institutional financial aid available to part-time graduate students in Graduate College.

Iowa Wesleyan College
Mount Pleasant 52641

Independent-religious instutition; small-town setting. Awards A, B. Total enrollment: 721 (all undergraduates); 15% part-time, 62% women, 9% over 25. Total faculty: 55. Library holdings: 98,427 bound volumes, 708 periodical subscriptions, 2,372 records/tapes.

Undergraduate Courses offered for part-time students during daytime, evenings, summer. Complete part-time degree programs offered during daytime, evenings, summer. Adult/continuing education programs available. Career services available to part-time students: individual and group career counseling, individual job placement, employer recruitment on campus. Part-time tuition: $115 per credit hour.

Iowa Western Community College
Council Bluffs 51502

Public institution; city setting. Awards A. Barrier-free campus. Total enrollment: 2,987 (all undergraduates); 39% part-time, 48% women, 10% over 25. Total faculty: 178. Library holdings: 57,587 bound volumes, 392 periodical subscriptions, 1,803 records/tapes.

Undergraduate Courses offered for part-time students during daytime, evenings, weekends, summer. Complete part-time degree programs offered during daytime, evenings, weekends, summer. Adult/continuing education programs available. Career services available to part-time students: individual and group career counseling, individual job placement, employer recruitment on campus. Part-time tuition: $27 per quarter hour for state residents, $40.50 per quarter hour for nonresidents.

Kirkwood Community College
Cedar Rapids 52406

Public institution; city setting. Awards A. Total enrollment: 6,337 (all undergraduates); 41% part-time, 55% women. Total faculty: 461. Library holdings: 48,446 bound volumes, 305 periodical subscriptions, 1,804 records/tapes.

Undergraduate Courses offered for part-time students during daytime, evenings, weekends, summer. Complete part-time degree programs offered during daytime, evenings, weekends, summer. Adult/continuing education programs available. Career services available to part-time students: individual and group career counseling, individual job placement, employer recruitment on campus. Part-time tuition: $20.50 per quarter hour for state residents, $41 per quarter hour for nonresidents.

Loras College
Dubuque 52001

Independent-religious instutition; city setting. Awards A, B, M. Total enrollment: 2,003. Undergraduate enrollment: 1,907; 5% part-time, 44% women. Total faculty: 125. Library holdings: 240,000 bound volumes.

Undergraduate Courses offered for part-time students during daytime, evenings, summer. Complete part-time degree programs offered during daytime, evenings, summer. External degree and adult/continuing education programs available. Career services available to part-time students: individual and group career counseling, individual job placement, employer recruitment on campus. Part-time tuition: $155 per semester hour.

Graduate Part-time study available in Graduate Division. Basic part-time expenses: $160 per hour tuition.

Marshalltown Community College
Marshalltown 50158

Public institution; small-town setting. Awards A. Total enrollment: 1,163 (all undergraduates); 45% part-time, 50% women. Total faculty: 96. Library holdings: 30,000 bound volumes, 330 periodical subscriptions, 2,000 records/tapes.

Undergraduate Courses offered for part-time students during daytime, evenings, summer. Complete part-time degree programs offered during daytime, evenings, summer. Adult/continuing education programs available. Career services available to part-time students: individual and group career counseling, individual job placement, employer recruitment on campus. Part-time tuition: $37.50 per credit hour for state residents, $75 per credit hour for nonresidents.

Marycrest College
Davenport 52804

Independent-religious instutition; city setting. Awards A, B, M. Total enrollment: 1,200. Undergraduate enrollment: 1,084; 57% part-time, 65% women, 56% over 25. Total faculty: 90. Library holdings: 100,001 bound volumes, 11,182 titles on microform, 514 periodical subscriptions, 3,450 records/tapes.

Undergraduate Courses offered for part-time students during daytime, evenings, weekends, summer. Complete part-time degree programs offered during daytime, evenings, weekends, summer. Adult/continuing education programs available. Career services available to part-time students: individual and group career counseling, individual job placement, employer recruitment on campus. Part-time tuition: $165 per credit hour.

Morningside College
Sioux City 51106

Independent-religious instutition; city setting. Awards A, B, M. Total enrollment: 1,246. Undergraduate enrollment: 1,223; 23% part-time, 53% women. Total faculty: 94. Library holdings: 135,000 bound volumes, 60 periodical subscriptions, 5,700 records/tapes.

Undergraduate Courses offered for part-time students during daytime, evenings, summer. Complete part-time degree programs offered during daytime, evenings, summer. Adult/continuing education programs available. Career services available to part-time students: individual career counseling. Part-time tuition: $180 per semester hour.

Colleges Offering Part-Time Degree Programs / *Iowa*

Morningside College (continued)

Graduate Part-time study available in Graduate Division. Basic part-time expenses: $115 per credit tuition.

Mount Mercy College
Cedar Rapids 52402

Independent-religious instutition; city setting. Awards B. Barrier-free campus. Total enrollment: 1,262 (all undergraduates); 32% part-time, 70% women, 15% over 25. Total faculty: 81. Library holdings: 69,000 bound volumes, 429 periodical subscriptions, 866 records/tapes.

Undergraduate Courses offered for part-time students during daytime, evenings, weekends, summer. Complete part-time degree programs offered during daytime, evenings, weekends, summer. Adult/continuing education programs available. Career services available to part-time students: individual and group career counseling, individual job placement, employer recruitment on campus. Part-time tuition: $128 per credit hour.

Mount Saint Clare College
Clinton 52732

Independent-religious instutition; small-town setting. Awards A, B. Barrier-free campus. Total enrollment: 371 (all undergraduates); 21% part-time, 63% women, 18% over 25. Total faculty: 36. Library holdings: 25,000 bound volumes, 350 periodical subscriptions.

Undergraduate Courses offered for part-time students during daytime, evenings, summer. Complete part-time degree programs offered during daytime, evenings, summer. Adult/continuing education programs available. Career services available to part-time students: individual and group career counseling, individual job placement, employer recruitment on campus. Part-time tuition: $120 per semester hour.

Muscatine Community College
Muscatine 52761

Public institution; small-town setting. Awards A. Barrier-free campus. Total enrollment: 1,050 (all undergraduates); 34% part-time, 45% women. Total faculty: 45. Library holdings: 16,559 bound volumes, 210 periodical subscriptions, 963 records/tapes.

Undergraduate Courses offered for part-time students during daytime, evenings, summer. Complete part-time degree programs offered during daytime, evenings, summer. Adult/continuing education programs available. Career services available to part-time students: individual career counseling. Part-time tuition: $32 per credit hour for state residents, $48 per credit hour for nonresidents.

Northeast Iowa Technical Institute–North Center
Calmar 52132

Public institution; small-town setting. Awards A. Barrier-free campus. Total enrollment: 552 (all undergraduates); 13% part-time, 54% women, 27% over 25. Total faculty: 74. Library holdings: 14,195 bound volumes, 312 periodical subscriptions.

Undergraduate Courses offered for part-time students during daytime, evenings, weekends, summer. Complete part-time degree programs offered during daytime. Adult/continuing education programs available. Career services available to part-time students: individual and group career counseling, individual job placement, employer recruitment on campus. Part-time tuition: $22 per credit for state residents, $44 per credit for nonresidents.

North Iowa Area Community College
Mason City 50401

Public institution; rural setting. Awards A. Barrier-free campus. Total enrollment: 2,289 (all undergraduates); 25% part-time, 49% women, 28% over 25. Total faculty: 166. Library holdings: 31,125 bound volumes, 432 periodical subscriptions.

Undergraduate Courses offered for part-time students during daytime, evenings, summer. Complete part-time degree programs offered during daytime, evenings, summer. External degree and adult/continuing education programs available. Career services available to part-time students: individual and group career counseling, individual job placement, employer recruitment on campus. Part-time tuition: $32 per semester hour for state residents, $48 per semester hour for nonresidents.

Open Bible College
Des Moines 50321

Independent-religious instutition; city setting. Awards A, B. Total enrollment: 99 (all undergraduates); 11% part-time, 35% women, 29% over 25. Total faculty: 13. Library holdings: 19,000 bound volumes, 400 titles on microform, 70 periodical subscriptions, 500 records/tapes.

Undergraduate Courses offered for part-time students during daytime. Complete part-time degree programs offered during daytime. Career services available to part-time students: individual and group career counseling. Part-time tuition: $95 per semester hour.

Palmer College of Chiropractic
Davenport 52803

Independent institution (graduate only). Total enrollment: 1,976 (coed; 2% part-time). Total faculty: 114.

Graduate Part-time study available in Professional Program. Basic part-time expenses: $288 per course tuition plus $105 per quarter fees.

St Ambrose College
Davenport 52803

Independent-religious instutition; city setting. Awards B, M. Total enrollment: 2,161. Undergraduate enrollment: 1,840; 56% part-time, 48% women. Total faculty: 144. Library holdings: 125,000 bound volumes, 105 titles on microform, 750 periodical subscriptions, 2,877 records/tapes.

Undergraduate Courses offered for part-time students during daytime, evenings, weekends, summer. Complete part-time degree programs offered during daytime, evenings, weekends. Adult/continuing education programs available. Career services available to part-time students: individual and group career counseling, employer recruitment on campus. Part-time tuition: $168 per credit hour.

Graduate Part-time study available in Graduate School of Business Administration. Degree can be earned exclusively through evening/weekend study in Graduate School of Business Administration. Basic part-time expenses: $168 per hour tuition plus $3 per hour fees. Institutional financial aid available to part-time graduate students in Graduate School of Business Administration.

Iowa / Colleges Offering Part-Time Degree Programs

Scott Community College
Bettendorf 52722

Public institution; city setting. Awards A. Barrier-free campus. Total enrollment: 2,617 (all undergraduates); 54% part-time, 54% women. Total faculty: 121. Library holdings: 21,510 bound volumes, 4 titles on microform, 18 periodical subscriptions, 628 records/tapes.

Undergraduate Courses offered for part-time students during daytime, evenings, weekends, summer. Complete part-time degree programs offered during daytime, evenings, weekends, summer. Adult/continuing education programs available. Career services available to part-time students: individual and group career counseling, individual job placement. Part-time tuition: $40.25 per semester hour for state residents, $58.25 per semester hour for nonresidents.

Simpson College
Indianola 50125

Independent-religious instutition; small-town setting. Awards B. Barrier-free campus. Total enrollment: 1,122 (all undergraduates); 32% part-time, 50% women. Total faculty: 67. Library holdings: 120,000 bound volumes, 3,119 titles on microform, 550 periodical subscriptions, 2,774 records/tapes.

Undergraduate Courses offered for part-time students during daytime, evenings, weekends, summer. Complete part-time degree programs offered during daytime, evenings, summer. Adult/continuing education programs available. Career services available to part-time students: individual career counseling, individual job placement, employer recruitment on campus. Part-time tuition: $98 per credit hour.

Sioux Empire College
Hawarden 51023

Independent institution; rural setting. Awards A. Total enrollment: 220 (all undergraduates); 10% part-time, 50% women, 40% over 25. Total faculty: 33. Library holdings: 10,000 bound volumes, 35 periodical subscriptions, 2,000 records/tapes.

Undergraduate Courses offered for part-time students during daytime, evenings, weekends, summer. Complete part-time degree programs offered during daytime, evenings, weekends, summer. Adult/continuing education programs available. Career services available to part-time students: individual career counseling. Part-time tuition: $125 per credit.

Southeastern Community College, North Campus
West Burlington 52655

Public institution; small-town setting. Awards A. Barrier-free campus. Total enrollment: 1,700 (all undergraduates); 29% part-time, 56% women, 36% over 25. Total faculty: 135. Library holdings: 40,000 bound volumes, 295 periodical subscriptions, 1,024 records/tapes.

Undergraduate Courses offered for part-time students during daytime, evenings, summer. Complete part-time degree programs offered during daytime, evenings, summer. Adult/continuing education programs available. Career services available to part-time students: individual career counseling, individual job placement, employer recruitment on campus. Part-time tuition: $29 per credit hour for state residents, $43.50 per credit hour for nonresidents.

Southeastern Community College, South Campus
Keokuk 52632

Public institution; small-town setting. Awards A. Barrier-free campus. Total enrollment: 470 (all undergraduates); 34% part-time, 62% women. Total faculty: 26. Library holdings: 40,000 bound volumes, 295 periodical subscriptions, 1,024 records/tapes.

Undergraduate Courses offered for part-time students during daytime, evenings, summer. Complete part-time degree programs offered during daytime, evenings, summer. Adult/continuing education programs available. Career services available to part-time students: individual and group career counseling, individual job placement, employer recruitment on campus. Part-time tuition: $29 per semester hour for state residents, $43.50 per semester hour for nonresidents.

Southwestern Community College
Creston 50801

Public institution; rural setting. Awards A. Barrier-free campus. Total enrollment: 654 (all undergraduates); 9% part-time, 43% women, 38% over 25. Total faculty: 47.

Undergraduate Courses offered for part-time students during daytime, evenings. Complete part-time degree programs offered during daytime, evenings. Adult/continuing education programs available. Career services available to part-time students: individual and group career counseling, individual job placement, employer recruitment on campus. Part-time tuition: $30 per hour for state residents, $45 per hour for nonresidents.

University of Dubuque
Dubuque 52001

Independent-religious instutition; city setting. Awards A, B, M, D. Total enrollment: 1,229. Undergraduate enrollment: 1,099; 34% part-time, 46% women. Total faculty: 77. Library holdings: 86,000 bound volumes, 20,000 titles on microform, 450 periodical subscriptions, 3,000 records/tapes.

Undergraduate Courses offered for part-time students during daytime, evenings, weekends, summer. Complete part-time degree programs offered during daytime, evenings, summer. Adult/continuing education programs available. Career services available to part-time students: individual and group career counseling, individual job placement, employer recruitment on campus. Part-time tuition: $155 per credit.

Graduate Part-time study available in Theological Seminary. Basic part-time expenses: $140 per credit tuition.

University of Iowa
Iowa City 52242

Public institution; small-town setting. Awards B, M, D. Barrier-free campus. Total enrollment: 29,599. Undergraduate enrollment: 21,377; 16% part-time, 51% women, 11% over 25. Total faculty: 1,954. Library holdings: 2.5 million bound volumes, 30,000 periodical subscriptions, 10,235 records/tapes.

Undergraduate Courses offered for part-time students during daytime, evenings, weekends, summer. Complete part-time degree programs offered during daytime, summer. External degree and adult/continuing education programs available. Career services available to part-time students: individual and group career counseling, individual job placement, employer recruitment on campus. Part-time tuition and fees per semester (1 to 11 semester hours) range from $104 to $572 for state residents, $104 to $1584 for nonresidents.

Colleges Offering Part-Time Degree Programs / *Iowa*

University of Iowa (continued)

Graduate Part-time study available in Graduate College. Basic part-time expenses: $164 per semester (minimum) tuition. Institutional financial aid available to part-time graduate students in Graduate College.

University of Northern Iowa
Cedar Falls 50613

Public institution; small-town setting. Awards B, M, D. Barrier-free campus. Total enrollment: 13,900. Undergraduate enrollment: 11,200; 14% part-time, 56% women. Total faculty: 683. Library holdings: 583,752 bound volumes, 2,644 periodical subscriptions, 8,110 records/tapes.

Undergraduate Courses offered for part-time students during daytime, evenings, summer. Complete part-time degree programs offered during daytime, evenings, summer. External degree and adult/continuing education programs available. Career services available to part-time students: individual and group career counseling, individual job placement, employer recruitment on campus. Part-time tuition: $50 per semester hour for state residents, $113 per semester hour for nonresidents.

Graduate Part-time study available in Graduate College. Basic part-time expenses: $74 per credit tuition for state residents, $74 per credit (minimum) tuition for nonresidents. Institutional financial aid available to part-time graduate students in Graduate College.

Upper Iowa University
Fayette 52142

Independent institution; small-town setting. Awards B. Barrier-free campus. Total enrollment: 400 (all undergraduates); 5% part-time, 45% women, 10% over 25. Total faculty: 50. Library holdings: 100,000 bound volumes, 100 periodical subscriptions.

Undergraduate Courses offered for part-time students during daytime, evenings, summer. Complete part-time degree programs offered during daytime, evenings, summer. External degree and adult/continuing education programs available. Career services available to part-time students: individual and group career counseling, individual job placement, employer recruitment on campus. Part-time tuition: $190 per semester hour.

Vennard College
University Park 52595

Independent-religious instutition; small-town setting. Awards A, B. Total enrollment: 214 (all undergraduates); 19% part-time, 42% women. Total faculty: 19. Library holdings: 60,000 bound volumes, 150 periodical subscriptions, 650 records/tapes.

Undergraduate Courses offered for part-time students during daytime, evenings, summer. Complete part-time degree programs offered during daytime, evenings, summer. Part-time tuition: $95 per semester hour.

Wartburg College
Waverly 50677

Independent-religious instutition; small-town setting. Awards B. Total enrollment: 1,141 (all undergraduates); 3% part-time, 53% women, 3% over 25. Total faculty: 86. Library holdings: 180,000 bound volumes, 900 periodical subscriptions, 1,000 records/tapes.

Undergraduate Courses offered for part-time students during daytime, evenings, weekends, summer. Complete part-time degree programs offered during daytime, evenings, summer. Adult/continuing education programs available. Career services available to part-time students: individual and group career counseling, individual job placement, employer recruitment on campus. Part-time tuition: $450 per course.

Wartburg Theological Seminary
Dubuque 52001

Independent-religious institution (graduate only). Total enrollment: 229 (coed; 13% part-time). Total faculty: 16. Library holdings: 150,177 bound volumes, 3,500 microforms.

Graduate Part-time study available in Graduate and Professional Programs. Basic part-time expenses: $80 per credit tuition.

Western Iowa Tech Community College
Sioux City 51102

Public institution; city setting. Awards A. Total enrollment: 1,409 (all undergraduates); 1% part-time, 41% women, 28% over 25. Total faculty: 790. Library holdings: 545 periodical subscriptions.

Undergraduate Courses offered for part-time students during daytime, evenings. Complete part-time degree programs offered during daytime, evenings. External degree and adult/continuing education programs available. Career services available to part-time students: individual and group career counseling. Part-time tuition: $19 per quarter hour for state residents, $38 per quarter hour for nonresidents.

Westmar College
Le Mars 51031

Independent-religious instutition; small-town setting. Awards B. Total enrollment: 506 (all undergraduates); 14% part-time, 41% women, 18% over 25. Total faculty: 44. Library holdings: 88,000 bound volumes, 3,113 titles on microform, 401 periodical subscriptions, 7,825 records/tapes.

Undergraduate Courses offered for part-time students during daytime, evenings, summer. Complete part-time degree programs offered during daytime, evenings. Adult/continuing education programs available. Career services available to part-time students: individual career counseling, individual job placement, employer recruitment on campus. Part-time tuition: $130 per semester hour.

William Penn College
Oskaloosa 52577

Independent-religious instutition; small-town setting. Awards B. Total enrollment: 459 (all undergraduates); 3% part-time, 38% women, 2% over 25. Total faculty: 36. Library holdings: 85,000 bound volumes.

Undergraduate Courses offered for part-time students during daytime, evenings, summer. Complete part-time degree programs offered during daytime, summer. External degree and adult/continuing education programs available. Career services available to part-time students: individual and group career counseling, individual job placement. Part-time tuition: $240 per credit hour.

KANSAS

Allen County Community College
Iola 66749

Public institution; small-town setting. Awards A. Total enrollment: 1,941 (all undergraduates); 68% part-time, 65% women. Total faculty: 92. Library holdings: 40,000 bound volumes, 30 periodical subscriptions, 1,000 records/tapes.

Undergraduate Courses offered for part-time students during daytime, evenings, summer. Complete part-time degree programs offered during daytime, evenings, summer. External degree and adult/continuing education programs available. Career services available to part-time students: individual and group career counseling. Part-time tuition: $12 per credit hour for state residents, $58 per credit hour for nonresidents.

Baker University
Baldwin City 66006

Independent-religious instutition; rural setting. Awards B, M. Total enrollment: 826. Undergraduate enrollment: 743; 2% part-time, 53% women, 2% over 25. Total faculty: 55. Library holdings: 66,000 bound volumes, 3,000 titles on microform, 330 periodical subscriptions, 657 records/tapes.

Undergraduate Courses offered for part-time students during daytime, summer. Complete part-time degree programs offered during daytime, summer. Career services available to part-time students: individual career counseling, individual job placement, employer recruitment on campus. Part-time tuition: $135 per credit hour.

Graduate Part-time study available in Graduate Program. Basic part-time expenses: $100 per credit tuition.

Barton County Community College
Great Bend 67530

Public institution; rural setting. Awards A. Total enrollment: 2,640 (all undergraduates); 70% part-time, 48% women. Total faculty: 121. Library holdings: 37,500 bound volumes, 400 periodical subscriptions, 450 records/tapes.

Undergraduate Courses offered for part-time students during daytime, evenings, summer. Complete part-time degree programs offered during daytime, evenings, summer. External degree and adult/continuing education programs available. Career services available to part-time students: individual career counseling, individual job placement, employer recruitment on campus. Part-time tuition: $18.50 per credit hour for state residents, $61.25 per credit hour for nonresidents.

Benedictine College
Atchison 66002

Independent-religious instutition; small-town setting. Awards A, B. Total enrollment: 965 (all undergraduates); 8% part-time, 50% women, 5% over 25. Total faculty: 94. Library holdings: 294,000 bound volumes, 1,000 periodical subscriptions, 24,000 records/tapes.

Undergraduate Courses offered for part-time students during daytime, evenings, summer. Complete part-time degree programs offered during daytime, evenings, summer. Adult/continuing education programs available. Career services available to part-time students: individual and group career counseling, individual job placement, employer recruitment on campus. Part-time tuition: $167 per credit hour.

Bethel College
North Newton 67117

Independent-religious instutition; small-town setting. Awards A, B. Total enrollment: 671 (all undergraduates); 15% part-time, 52% women. Total faculty: 60. Library holdings: 73,000 bound volumes, 2,300 titles on microform, 350 periodical subscriptions, 190 records/tapes.

Undergraduate Courses offered for part-time students during daytime, evenings, weekends, summer. Complete part-time degree programs offered during daytime. Adult/continuing education programs available. Career services available to part-time students: individual and group career counseling, individual job placement, employer recruitment on campus. Part-time tuition per credit hour ranges from $73 (for 1 to 5 credit hours) to $146 (for 6 to 11 credit hours).

Butler County Community College
El Dorado 67042

Public institution; small-town setting. Awards A. Barrier-free campus. Total enrollment: 3,279 (all undergraduates); 60% part-time, 48% women, 57% over 25. Total faculty: 200. Library holdings: 35,000 bound volumes, 13,000 titles on microform, 220 periodical subscriptions, 500 records/tapes.

Undergraduate Courses offered for part-time students during daytime, evenings, summer. Complete part-time degree programs offered during daytime, evenings, summer. Adult/continuing education programs available. Career services available to part-time students: individual career counseling, individual job placement, employer recruitment on campus. Part-time tuition: $20 per credit hour for state residents, $64.50 per credit hour for nonresidents.

Central Baptist Theological Seminary
Kansas City 66102

Independent-religious institution (graduate only). Total enrollment: 139 (coed; 41% part-time). Total faculty: 19. Library holdings: 69,561 bound volumes.

Graduate Part-time study available in Graduate and Professional Programs. Basic part-time expenses: $63 per semester hour (minimum) tuition.

Central College
McPherson 67460

Independent-religious instutition; small-town setting. Awards A. Total enrollment: 323 (all undergraduates); 2% part-time, 52% women, 1% over 25. Total faculty: 26. Library holdings: 25,000 bound volumes.

Undergraduate Courses offered for part-time students during daytime. Complete part-time degree programs offered during daytime. Adult/continuing education programs available. Career services available to part-time students: individual and group career counseling, individual job placement, employer recruitment on campus. Part-time tuition: $113 per credit hour.

Cloud County Community College
Concordia 66901

Public institution; small-town setting. Awards A. Barrier-free campus. Total enrollment: 2,329 (all undergraduates); 74% part-time, 69% women, 54% over 25. Total faculty: 243. Library holdings: 21,000 bound volumes, 591 titles on microform, 215 periodical subscriptions, 2,400 records/tapes.

Colleges Offering Part-Time Degree Programs / *Kansas*

Cloud County Community College (continued)

Undergraduate Courses offered for part-time students during daytime, evenings. Complete part-time degree programs offered during daytime, evenings. Adult/continuing education programs available. Career services available to part-time students: individual career counseling, individual job placement, employer recruitment on campus. Part-time tuition: $29 per credit hour for state residents, $72 per credit hour for nonresidents.

Coffeyville Community College
Coffeyville 67337

Public institution; small-town setting. Awards A. Barrier-free campus. Total enrollment: 1,580 (all undergraduates); 40% part-time, 54% women. Total faculty: 50. Library holdings: 25,611 bound volumes, 238 periodical subscriptions, 1,526 records/tapes.

Undergraduate Courses offered for part-time students during daytime, evenings, weekends, summer. Complete part-time degree programs offered during daytime, evenings, weekends, summer. Adult/continuing education programs available. Career services available to part-time students: individual career counseling. Part-time tuition: $12 per credit hour for state residents, $53.20 per credit hour for nonresidents.

Colby Community College
Colby 67701

Public institution; small-town setting. Awards A. Barrier-free campus. Total enrollment: 898 (all undergraduates); 12% part-time, 60% women. Total faculty: 109. Library holdings: 32,000 bound volumes, 46 periodical subscriptions, 1,000 records/tapes.

Undergraduate Courses offered for part-time students during daytime, evenings, summer. Complete part-time degree programs offered during daytime, evenings, summer. External degree and adult/continuing education programs available. Career services available to part-time students: individual and group career counseling. Part-time tuition: $20 per credit for state residents, $60 per credit for nonresidents.

Dodge City Community College
Dodge City 67801

Public institution; small-town setting. Awards A. Barrier-free campus. Total enrollment: 1,451 (all undergraduates); 49% part-time, 53% women, 10% over 25. Total faculty: 73. Library holdings: 28,000 bound volumes.

Undergraduate Courses offered for part-time students during daytime, evenings, summer. Complete part-time degree programs offered during daytime, evenings, summer. External degree and adult/continuing education programs available. Career services available to part-time students: individual career counseling, individual job placement, employer recruitment on campus. Part-time tuition: $12 per credit hour for state residents, $58 per credit hour for nonresidents.

Emporia State University
Emporia 66801

Public institution; small-town setting. Awards A, B, M. Barrier-free campus. Total enrollment: 5,358. Undergraduate enrollment: 4,056; 14% part-time, 54% women, 17% over 25. Total faculty: 284. Library holdings: 422,433 bound volumes, 167,818 titles on microform, 1,992 periodical subscriptions, 2,482 records/tapes.

Undergraduate Courses offered for part-time students during daytime, evenings, summer. Complete part-time degree programs offered during daytime, evenings, summer. Adult/continuing education programs available. Career services available to part-time students: individual and group career counseling, individual job placement, employer recruitment on campus. Part-time tuition: $33.40 per credit hour for state residents, $67.41 per credit hour for nonresidents.

Graduate Part-time study available in School of Graduate and Professional Studies. Basic part-time expenses: $35.90 per hour tuition for state residents, $72.65 per hour tuition for nonresidents.

Fort Hays State University
Hays 67601

Public institution; small-town setting. Awards A, B, M. Total enrollment: 5,476. Undergraduate enrollment: 3,946; 33% part-time, 57% women, 33% over 25. Total faculty: 264. Library holdings: 546,000 bound volumes, 373,500 titles on microform, 1,300 periodical subscriptions, 1,000 records/tapes.

Undergraduate Courses offered for part-time students during daytime, evenings, weekends, summer. Complete part-time degree programs offered during daytime, summer. Adult/continuing education programs available. Career services available to part-time students: individual and group career counseling, individual job placement, employer recruitment on campus. Part-time tuition: $34 per semester hour for state residents, $68 per semester hour for nonresidents.

Graduate Part-time study available in Graduate School. Basic part-time expenses: $36.50 per credit hour tuition for state residents, $73.25 per credit hour tuition for nonresidents. Institutional financial aid available to part-time graduate students in Graduate School.

Fort Scott Community College
Fort Scott 66701

Public institution; small-town setting. Awards A. Total enrollment: 1,285 (all undergraduates); 40% part-time, 52% women, 15% over 25. Total faculty: 72.

Undergraduate Courses offered for part-time students during daytime, evenings. Complete part-time degree programs offered during daytime, evenings. Adult/continuing education programs available. Career services available to part-time students: individual and group career counseling, individual job placement, employer recruitment on campus. Part-time tuition: $12 per credit hour for state residents, $57.75 per credit hour for nonresidents.

Friends Bible College
Haviland 67059

Independent-religious instutition; rural setting. Awards B. Total enrollment: 143 (all undergraduates); 23% part-time, 50% women, 10% over 25. Total faculty: 18. Library holdings: 23,592 bound volumes, 400 titles on microform, 210 periodical subscriptions, 662 records/tapes.

Undergraduate Courses offered for part-time students during daytime, evenings. Complete part-time degree programs offered during daytime. Career services available to part-time students: individual career counseling, individual job placement, employer recruitment on campus. Part-time tuition: $124 per credit hour.

Kansas / **Colleges Offering Part-Time Degree Programs**

Friends University
Wichita 67213

Independent-religious instutition; city setting. Awards A, B. Total enrollment: 761 (all undergraduates); 20% part-time, 50% women. Total faculty: 58. Library holdings: 88,196 bound volumes, 1,364 titles on microform, 521 periodical subscriptions, 4,400 records/tapes.

Undergraduate Courses offered for part-time students during daytime, evenings. Complete part-time degree programs offered during daytime, evenings. Career services available to part-time students: individual and group career counseling, individual job placement, employer recruitment on campus. Part-time tuition: $131 per semester hour.

Haskell Indian Junior College
Lawrence 66044

Public institution; city setting. Awards A. Total enrollment: 925 (all undergraduates); 5% part-time, 52% women, 1% over 25. Total faculty: 65. Library holdings: 27,000 bound volumes, 6,000 titles on microform, 525 periodical subscriptions.

Undergraduate Courses offered for part-time students during daytime. Complete part-time degree programs offered during daytime. Career services available to part-time students: individual and group career counseling, individual job placement, employer recruitment on campus. Part-time tuition: $0.

Hesston College
Hesston 67062

Independent-religious instutition; small-town setting. Awards A. Total enrollment: 557 (all undergraduates); 12% part-time, 53% women, 12% over 25. Total faculty: 60. Library holdings: 32,000 bound volumes, 260 periodical subscriptions, 736 records/tapes.

Undergraduate Courses offered for part-time students during daytime. Complete part-time degree programs offered during daytime. Career services available to part-time students: individual career counseling, individual job placement. Part-time tuition: $150 per credit hour.

Highland Community College
Highland 66035

Public institution; rural setting. Awards A. Total enrollment: 1,266 (all undergraduates); 61% part-time, 51% women, 28% over 25. Total faculty: 59. Library holdings: 28,000 bound volumes, 42 periodical subscriptions, 768 records/tapes.

Undergraduate Courses offered for part-time students during daytime, evenings, weekends, summer. Complete part-time degree programs offered during daytime, evenings, weekends, summer. Adult/continuing education programs available. Career services available to part-time students: individual and group career counseling. Part-time tuition: $18 per credit hour for state residents, $58 per credit hour for nonresidents.

Hutchinson Community College
Hutchinson 67501

Public institution; small-town setting. Awards A. Barrier-free campus. Total enrollment: 3,805 (all undergraduates); 66% part-time, 52% women, 58% over 25. Total faculty: 233. Library holdings: 49,000 bound volumes, 363 titles on microform, 267 periodical subscriptions, 2,952 records/tapes.

Undergraduate Courses offered for part-time students during daytime, evenings, summer. Complete part-time degree programs offered during daytime, evenings, summer. Adult/continuing education programs available. Career services available to part-time students: individual and group career counseling, individual job placement, employer recruitment on campus. Part-time tuition: $15 per credit hour for state residents, $57.75 per credit hour for nonresidents.

Independence Community College
Independence 67301

Public institution; small-town setting. Awards A. Total enrollment: 957 (all undergraduates); 70% part-time, 58% women, 60% over 25. Total faculty: 67. Library holdings: 29,574 bound volumes, 77 titles on microform, 151 periodical subscriptions, 1,083 records/tapes.

Undergraduate Courses offered for part-time students during daytime, evenings, summer. Complete part-time degree programs offered during daytime, evenings, summer. Adult/continuing education programs available. Career services available to part-time students: individual and group career counseling, individual job placement, employer recruitment on campus. Part-time tuition: $12 per semester hour for state residents, $57.75 per semester hour for nonresidents.

Johnson County Community College
Overland Park 66210

Public institution; city setting. Awards A. Barrier-free campus. Total enrollment: 8,106 (all undergraduates); 71% part-time, 59% women, 50% over 25. Total faculty: 343. Library holdings: 48,000 bound volumes, 270,000 titles on microform, 500 periodical subscriptions, 2,330 records/tapes.

Undergraduate Courses offered for part-time students during daytime, evenings, weekends, summer. Complete part-time degree programs offered during daytime, evenings, summer. Adult/continuing education programs available. Career services available to part-time students: individual and group career counseling, individual job placement, employer recruitment on campus. Part-time tuition: $20.50 per credit hour for state residents, $62.50 per credit hour for nonresidents.

Kansas City Kansas Community College
Kansas City 66112

Public institution; metropolitan setting. Awards A. Barrier-free campus. Total enrollment: 3,300 (all undergraduates); 52% part-time, 52% women, 57% over 25. Total faculty: 222. Library holdings: 57,000 bound volumes, 280 periodical subscriptions, 919 records/tapes.

Undergraduate Courses offered for part-time students during daytime, evenings, summer. Complete part-time degree programs offered during daytime, evenings, summer. Adult/continuing education programs available. Career services available to part-time students: individual career counseling, individual job placement, employer recruitment on campus. Part-time tuition: $17 per credit hour for state residents, $56 per credit hour for nonresidents.

Kansas Newman College
Wichita 67213

Independent-religious instutition; city setting. Awards A, B. Total enrollment: 901 (all undergraduates); 33% part-time, 60% women, 50% over 25. Total faculty: 72. Library holdings: 72,000 bound volumes, 435 periodical subscriptions, 915 records/tapes.

Undergraduate Courses offered for part-time students during daytime, evenings, weekends, summer. Complete part-time de-

Colleges Offering Part-Time Degree Programs / Kansas

Kansas Newman College (continued)

gree programs offered during daytime, evenings, summer. Adult/continuing education programs available. Career services available to part-time students: individual and group career counseling, individual job placement, employer recruitment on campus. Part-time tuition: $124 per semester hour.

Kansas State University
Manhattan 66506

Public institution; small-town setting. Awards A, B, M, D. Total enrollment: 18,470. Undergraduate enrollment: 14,584; 5% part-time, 45% women, 17% over 25. Total faculty: 1,544. Library holdings: 1.5 million bound volumes, 12,000 periodical subscriptions.

Undergraduate Courses offered for part-time students during daytime, evenings, summer. Complete part-time degree programs offered during daytime. External degree and adult/continuing education programs available. Career services available to part-time students: individual and group career counseling, individual job placement, employer recruitment on campus. Part-time tuition and fees per semester (1 to 6 semester hours) range from $112.50 to $247.50 for state residents, $116.50 to $512.50 for nonresidents.

Graduate Part-time study available in Graduate School, College of Veterinary Medicine. Basic part-time expenses: $33 per credit hour tuition plus $89.50 per semester fees for state residents, $94 per credit hour tuition plus $89.50 per semester fees for nonresidents. Institutional financial aid available to part-time graduate students in Graduate School, College of Veterinary Medicine.

Kansas Technical Institute
Salina 67401

Public institution; small-town setting. Awards A. Barrier-free campus. Total enrollment: 710 (all undergraduates); 11% part-time, 25% women, 43% over 25. Total faculty: 42. Library holdings: 19,296 bound volumes, 1 title on microform, 155 periodical subscriptions, 188 records/tapes.

Undergraduate Courses offered for part-time students during daytime. Complete part-time degree programs offered during daytime. Adult/continuing education programs available. Part-time tuition: $20 per semester hour for state residents, $54 per semester hour for nonresidents.

Kansas Wesleyan
Salina 67401

Independent-religious instutition; small-town setting. Awards A, B. Barrier-free campus. Total enrollment: 571 (all undergraduates); 33% part-time, 48% women, 16% over 25. Total faculty: 43. Library holdings: 72,000 bound volumes, 40 periodical subscriptions.

Undergraduate Courses offered for part-time students during daytime, evenings, summer. Complete part-time degree programs offered during daytime, evenings, summer. External degree and adult/continuing education programs available. Career services available to part-time students: individual and group career counseling, individual job placement, employer recruitment on campus. Part-time tuition: $75 per semester hour.

Manhattan Christian College
Manhattan 66502

Independent-religious instutition; small-town setting. Awards A, B. Total enrollment: 228 (all undergraduates); 40% part-time, 44% women, 25% over 25. Total faculty: 21. Library holdings: 24,000 bound volumes, 4,000 titles on microform, 50 periodical subscriptions, 1,000 records/tapes.

Undergraduate Courses offered for part-time students during daytime, evenings, summer. Complete part-time degree programs offered during daytime. Career services available to part-time students: individual and group career counseling, employer recruitment on campus. Part-time tuition: $50 per credit hour.

Marymount College of Kansas
Salina 67401

Independent-religious instutition; small-town setting. Awards A, B. Total enrollment: 709 (all undergraduates); 29% part-time, 61% women. Total faculty: 66. Library holdings: 75,122 bound volumes, 550 periodical subscriptions, 2,711 records/tapes.

Undergraduate Courses offered for part-time students during daytime, evenings, summer. Complete part-time degree programs offered during daytime, evenings, summer. Adult/continuing education programs available. Career services available to part-time students: individual and group career counseling, individual job placement. Part-time tuition ranges from $72 per credit hour (for students taking 1 to 5 credit hours) to $75 per credit hour (for students taking 6 to 11 credit hours).

McPherson College
McPherson 67460

Independent-religious instutition; small-town setting. Awards A, B. Total enrollment: 494 (all undergraduates); 15% part-time, 49% women, 10% over 25. Total faculty: 48. Library holdings: 96,550 bound volumes, 3,892 titles on microform, 471 periodical subscriptions, 1,981 records/tapes.

Undergraduate Courses offered for part-time students during daytime, evenings. Complete part-time degree programs offered during daytime, evenings. Adult/continuing education programs available. Career services available to part-time students: individual career counseling, employer recruitment on campus. Part-time tuition: $135 per credit hour.

Mid-America Nazarene College
Olathe 66061

Independent-religious instutition; small-town setting. Awards A, B. Total enrollment: 1,219 (all undergraduates); 11% part-time, 49% women, 25% over 25. Total faculty: 70. Library holdings: 65,000 bound volumes, 20,000 titles on microform, 400 periodical subscriptions, 1,500 records/tapes.

Undergraduate Courses offered for part-time students during daytime, evenings, summer. Complete part-time degree programs offered during daytime, evenings, summer. Career services available to part-time students: individual and group career counseling, individual job placement, employer recruitment on campus. Part-time tuition: $329 per course.

Neosho County Community College
Chanute 66720

Public institution; small-town setting. Awards A. Barrier-free campus. Total enrollment: 1,043 (all undergraduates); 60% part-

time, 63% women, 56% over 25. Total faculty: 83. Library holdings: 25,000 bound volumes, 200 periodical subscriptions.

Undergraduate Courses offered for part-time students during daytime, evenings, summer. Complete part-time degree programs offered during daytime, evenings, summer. External degree and adult/continuing education programs available. Career services available to part-time students: individual and group career counseling, individual job placement, employer recruitment on campus. Part-time tuition: $12 per credit hour for state residents, $58 per credit hour for nonresidents.

Ottawa University
Ottawa 66067

Independent-religious instutition; small-town setting. Awards B. Total enrollment: 455 (all undergraduates); 6% part-time, 43% women, 5% over 25. Total faculty: 49. Library holdings: 90,000 bound volumes, 4,000 titles on microform, 400 periodical subscriptions, 800 records/tapes.

Undergraduate Courses offered for part-time students during daytime, summer. Complete part-time degree programs offered during daytime, summer. Career services available to part-time students: individual and group career counseling, individual job placement, employer recruitment on campus. Part-time tuition: $125 per credit hour.

Pittsburg State University
Pittsburg 66762

Public institution; small-town setting. Awards A, B, M. Total enrollment: 4,959. Undergraduate enrollment: 3,867; 30% part-time, 51% women. Total faculty: 267. Library holdings: 262,000 bound volumes, 40,000 titles on microform, 1,600 periodical subscriptions, 700 records/tapes.

Undergraduate Courses offered for part-time students during daytime, evenings, summer. Complete part-time degree programs offered during daytime, evenings, summer. Adult/continuing education programs available. Career services available to part-time students: individual and group career counseling, individual job placement, employer recruitment on campus. Part-time tuition: $23.75 per semester hour for state residents, $57.75 per semester hour for nonresidents.

Graduate Part-time study available in Graduate Division. Degree can be earned exclusively through evening/weekend study in Graduate Division. Basic part-time expenses: $26.25 per credit hour tuition for state residents, $63 per credit hour tuition for nonresidents.

Pratt Community College
Pratt 67124

Public institution; rural setting. Awards A. Barrier-free campus. Total enrollment: 480 (all undergraduates); 7% part-time, 45% women, 4% over 25. Total faculty: 32. Library holdings: 25,000 bound volumes.

Undergraduate Courses offered for part-time students during daytime, evenings, summer. Complete part-time degree programs offered during daytime, evenings, summer. Adult/continuing education programs available. Career services available to part-time students: individual career counseling, individual job placement. Part-time tuition: $18 per credit hour for state residents, $60 per credit hour for nonresidents.

St John's College
Winfield 67156

Independent-religious instutition; small-town setting. Awards A, B. Total enrollment: 288 (all undergraduates); 6% part-time, 57% women, 15% over 25. Total faculty: 32. Library holdings: 58,000 bound volumes, 260 periodical subscriptions, 500 records/tapes.

Undergraduate Courses offered for part-time students during daytime, evenings. Complete part-time degree programs offered during daytime. Career services available to part-time students: individual career counseling, employer recruitment on campus. Part-time tuition: $125 per hour.

Saint Mary College
Leavenworth 66048

Independent-religious instutition; small-town setting. Awards A, B. Barrier-free campus. Total enrollment: 1,008 (all undergraduates); 65% part-time, 63% women, 59% over 25. Total faculty: 80. Library holdings: 114,000 bound volumes, 20,229 titles on microform, 477 periodical subscriptions, 5,500 records/tapes.

Undergraduate Courses offered for part-time students during daytime, evenings, weekends, summer. Complete part-time degree programs offered during daytime, evenings, weekends. Adult/continuing education programs available. Career services available to part-time students: individual and group career counseling, employer recruitment on campus. Part-time tuition: $126 per credit.

Saint Mary of the Plains College
Dodge City 67801

Independent-religious instutition; rural setting. Awards B. Total enrollment: 675 (all undergraduates); 10% part-time, 56% women, 2% over 25. Total faculty: 46. Library holdings: 57,472 bound volumes, 373 periodical subscriptions, 931 records/tapes.

Undergraduate Courses offered for part-time students during daytime, evenings. Complete part-time degree programs offered during daytime, evenings. External degree and adult/continuing education programs available. Career services available to part-time students: individual and group career counseling, individual job placement, employer recruitment on campus. Part-time tuition: $65 per credit hour.

Seward County Community College
Liberal 67901

Public institution; rural setting. Awards A. Barrier-free campus. Total enrollment: 1,527 (all undergraduates); 72% part-time, 64% women, 50% over 25. Total faculty: 63. Library holdings: 25,910 bound volumes, 494 titles on microform, 223 periodical subscriptions.

Undergraduate Courses offered for part-time students during daytime, evenings, summer. Complete part-time degree programs offered during daytime, evenings, summer. External degree and adult/continuing education programs available. Career services available to part-time students: individual and group career counseling, individual job placement. Part-time tuition: $16 per credit hour for state residents, $57.50 per credit hour for nonresidents.

Colleges Offering Part-Time Degree Programs / Kansas

Southwestern College
Winfield 67156

Independent-religious instutition; small-town setting. Awards B. Total enrollment: 668 (all undergraduates); 13% part-time, 45% women. Total faculty: 44. Library holdings: 110,000 bound volumes, 500 periodical subscriptions, 200 records/tapes.

Undergraduate Courses offered for part-time students during daytime, evenings, summer. Complete part-time degree programs offered during daytime, summer. Adult/continuing education programs available. Career services available to part-time students: individual and group career counseling, individual job placement, employer recruitment on campus. Part-time tuition: $154 per semester hour.

Tabor College
Hillsboro 67063

Independent-religious instutition; small-town setting. Awards A, B. Total enrollment: 408 (all undergraduates); 9% part-time, 45% women, 6% over 25. Total faculty: 43. Library holdings: 69,500 bound volumes, 1 million titles on microform, 500 periodical subscriptions, 1,500 records/tapes.

Undergraduate Courses offered for part-time students during daytime, evenings, summer. Complete part-time degree programs offered during daytime, evenings, summer. Adult/continuing education programs available. Career services available to part-time students: individual career counseling, individual job placement, employer recruitment on campus. Part-time tuition: $72 per hour.

University of Kansas
Lawrence 66045

Public institution; city setting. Awards B, M, D. Total enrollment: 24,219. Undergraduate enrollment: 17,488; 12% part-time, 47% women. Total faculty: 1,313. Library holdings: 2 million bound volumes, 1 million titles on microform, 22,000 periodical subscriptions, 37,000 records/tapes.

Undergraduate Courses offered for part-time students during daytime. Complete part-time degree programs offered during daytime. Adult/continuing education programs available. Career services available to part-time students: individual and group career counseling, individual job placement, employer recruitment on campus. Part-time tuition: $48 per credit hour for state residents, $104 per credit hour for nonresidents.

University of Kansas College of Health Sciences and Hospital
Kansas City 66103

Public institution; metropolitan setting. Awards B, M, D. Barrier-free campus. Total enrollment: 2,560. Undergraduate enrollment: 516; 9% part-time, 82% women. Total faculty: 682. Library holdings: 134,730 bound volumes, 6,521 titles on microform, 2,049 periodical subscriptions.

Graduate Part-time study available in Graduate School. Basic part-time expenses: $127.10 per semester (minimum) tuition for state residents, $310 per semester (minimum) tuition for nonresidents. Institutional financial aid available to part-time graduate students in Graduate School.

Washburn University of Topeka
Topeka 66621

Public institution; city setting. Awards A, B, M, D. Barrier-free campus. Total enrollment: 6,987. Undergraduate enrollment: 6,083; 51% part-time, 52% women, 42% over 25. Total faculty: 260. Library holdings: 232,000 bound volumes, 250,045 titles on microform, 1,688 periodical subscriptions.

Undergraduate Courses offered for part-time students during daytime, evenings, weekends, summer. Complete part-time degree programs offered during daytime, evenings, weekends, summer. Adult/continuing education programs available. Career services available to part-time students: individual and group career counseling, individual job placement, employer recruitment on campus. Part-time tuition: $53 per credit hour for state residents, $78 per credit hour for nonresidents.

Graduate Part-time study available in College of Arts and Sciences, School of Business. Degree can be earned exclusively through evening/weekend study in College of Arts and Sciences. Basic part-time expenses: $53 per credit tuition for state residents, $78 per credit tuition for nonresidents. Institutional financial aid available to part-time graduate students in College of Arts and Sciences, School of Business.

Wichita State University
Wichita 67208

Public institution; city setting. Awards A, B, M, D. Total enrollment: 20,252. Undergraduate enrollment: 16,647; 51% part-time, 49% women, 45% over 25. Total faculty: 703. Library holdings: 716,364 bound volumes, 430,251 titles on microform, 3,349 periodical subscriptions, 3,320 records/tapes.

Undergraduate Courses offered for part-time students during daytime, evenings, weekends, summer. Complete part-time degree programs offered during daytime, evenings, weekends, summer. Adult/continuing education programs available. Career services available to part-time students: individual and group career counseling, individual job placement, employer recruitment on campus. Part-time tuition: $38.20 per credit hour for state residents, $94 per credit hour for nonresidents.

Graduate Part-time study available in Graduate School. Basic part-time expenses: $32.65 per credit tuition plus $8.20 per credit fees for state residents, $86 per credit tuition plus $8.20 per credit fees for nonresidents. Institutional financial aid available to part-time graduate students in Graduate School.

KENTUCKY

Alice Lloyd College
Pippa Passes 41844

Independent institution; rural setting. Awards A, B. Total enrollment: 548 (all undergraduates); 6% part-time, 52% women. Total faculty: 22. Library holdings: 65,000 bound volumes, 400 periodical subscriptions, 7,000 records/tapes.

Undergraduate Courses offered for part-time students during daytime, evenings, summer. Complete part-time degree programs offered during daytime, evenings, summer. Career services available to part-time students: individual and group career counseling, individual job placement, employer recruitment on campus. Part-time tuition: $100 per credit hour.

Asbury Theological Seminary
Wilmore 40390

Independent institution (graduate only). Total enrollment: 792 (coed; 16% part-time). Total faculty: 52.

Graduate Part-time study available in Graduate and Professional Programs. Basic part-time expenses: $120 per credit hour tuition. Institutional financial aid available to part-time graduate students in Graduate and Professional Programs.

Kentucky / **Colleges Offering Part-Time Degree Programs**

Ashland Community College
Ashland 41101
See University of Kentucky, Ashland Community College

Bellarmine College
Louisville 40205
Independent-religious instutition; metropolitan setting. Awards A, B, M. Total enrollment: 2,870. Undergraduate enrollment: 2,484; 43% part-time, 53% women, 20% over 25. Total faculty: 112. Library holdings: 93,820 bound volumes, 555 periodical subscriptions, 4,377 records/tapes.

Undergraduate Courses offered for part-time students during daytime, evenings, weekends, summer. Complete part-time degree programs offered during daytime, evenings, summer. Adult/continuing education programs available. Career services available to part-time students: individual and group career counseling, individual job placement, employer recruitment on campus. Part-time tuition: $125 per credit.

Graduate Part-time study available in Graduate Programs. Degree can be earned exclusively through evening/weekend study in Graduate Programs. Basic part-time expenses: $140 per credit hour tuition. Institutional financial aid available to part-time graduate students in Graduate Programs.

Bowling Green Junior College of Business
Bowling Green 42101
Proprietary institution; small-town setting. Awards A. Total enrollment: 601 (all undergraduates); 1% part-time, 69% women, 12% over 25. Total faculty: 24. Library holdings: 3,287 bound volumes, 41 periodical subscriptions, 23 records/tapes.

Undergraduate Courses offered for part-time students during daytime, evenings, summer. Complete part-time degree programs offered during daytime, evenings, summer. Adult/continuing education programs available. Career services available to part-time students: individual career counseling, individual job placement, employer recruitment on campus. Part-time tuition: $57 per quarter hour.

Brescia College
Owensboro 42301
Independent-religious instutition; city setting. Awards A, B. Total enrollment: 930 (all undergraduates); 38% part-time, 59% women, 23% over 25. Total faculty: 78. Library holdings: 90,000 bound volumes, 500 periodical subscriptions, 500 records/tapes.

Undergraduate Courses offered for part-time students during daytime, evenings, summer. Complete part-time degree programs offered during daytime, evenings, summer. Adult/continuing education programs available. Career services available to part-time students: individual and group career counseling, individual job placement. Part-time tuition: $103 per credit hour.

Campbellsville College
Campbellsville 42718
Independent-religious instutition; small-town setting. Awards A, B. Total enrollment: 731 (all undergraduates); 16% part-time, 56% women. Total faculty: 56. Library holdings: 86,761 bound volumes, 670 periodical subscriptions, 1,816 records/tapes.

Undergraduate Courses offered for part-time students during daytime, evenings. Complete part-time degree programs offered during daytime, evenings. Career services available to part-time students: individual career counseling. Part-time tuition: $120 per credit.

Cumberland College
Williamsburg 40769
Independent-religious instutition; small-town setting. Awards A, B, M. Total enrollment: 1,956. Undergraduate enrollment: 1,898; 18% part-time, 58% women. Total faculty: 118. Library holdings: 152,351 bound volumes, 350,000 titles on microform, 1,100 periodical subscriptions, 20,000 records/tapes.

Undergraduate Courses offered for part-time students during daytime, evenings, summer. Complete part-time degree programs offered during daytime, evenings, summer. Adult/continuing education programs available. Career services available to part-time students: individual and group career counseling, individual job placement, employer recruitment on campus. Part-time tuition: $100 per credit hour.

Graduate Part-time study available in Graduate Program in Education. Basic part-time expenses: $98 per credit hour tuition.

Draughon's Junior College of Business
Paducah 42001
Proprietary institution; small-town setting. Awards A. Total enrollment: 520 (all undergraduates); 5% part-time, 65% women, 40% over 25. Total faculty: 30.

Undergraduate Courses offered for part-time students during daytime, evenings, summer. Complete part-time degree programs offered during daytime, evenings, summer. Adult/continuing education programs available. Career services available to part-time students: individual and group career counseling, individual job placement, employer recruitment on campus. Part-time tuition: $53 per quarter hour.

Eastern Kentucky University
Richmond 40475
Public institution; small-town setting. Awards A, B, M. Barrier-free campus. Total enrollment: 12,661. Undergraduate enrollment: 11,358; 16% part-time, 56% women, 17% over 25. Total faculty: 739. Library holdings: 717,728 bound volumes, 799,513 titles on microform, 4,089 periodical subscriptions, 4,437 records/tapes.

Undergraduate Courses offered for part-time students during daytime, evenings, summer. Complete part-time degree programs offered during daytime, evenings, summer. External degree and adult/continuing education programs available. Career services available to part-time students: individual and group career counseling, individual job placement, employer recruitment on campus. Part-time tuition: $38 per credit for state residents, $107 per credit for nonresidents.

Graduate Part-time study available in Graduate School. Basic part-time expenses: $55 per credit tuition for state residents, $156 per credit tuition for nonresidents. Institutional financial aid available to part-time graduate students in Graduate School.

Elizabethtown Community College
Elizabethtown 42701
See University of Kentucky, Elizabethtown Community College

Colleges Offering Part-Time Degree Programs / Kentucky

Georgetown College
Georgetown 40324
Independent-religious instutition; small-town setting. Awards B, M. Total enrollment: 1,302. Undergraduate enrollment: 987; 7% part-time, 49% women, 5% over 25. Total faculty: 85. Library holdings: 100,000 bound volumes, 16,000 titles on microform, 470 periodical subscriptions, 3,500 records/tapes.
Undergraduate Courses offered for part-time students during daytime, summer. Complete part-time degree programs offered during daytime, summer. Part-time tuition: $100 per semester hour.

Hazard Community College
Hazard 41701
See University of Kentucky, Hazard Community College

Henderson Community College
Henderson 42420
See University of Kentucky, Henderson Community College

Hopkinsville Community College
Hopkinsville 42240
See University of Kentucky, Hopkinsville Community College

Jefferson Community College
Louisville 40201
See University of Kentucky, Jefferson Community College

Kentucky Junior College of Business
Lexington 40576
Proprietary institution; city setting. Awards A. Barrier-free campus. Total enrollment: 425 (all undergraduates); 20% part-time, 65% women. Total faculty: 56.
Undergraduate Courses offered for part-time students during daytime, evenings. Complete part-time degree programs offered during daytime, evenings. Career services available to part-time students: individual and group career counseling, individual job placement. Part-time tuition: $60 per quarter hour.

Kentucky State University
Frankfort 40601
Public institution; small-town setting. Awards A, B, M. Total enrollment: 2,431. Undergraduate enrollment: 2,345; 49% part-time, 54% women, 48% over 25. Total faculty: 144. Library holdings: 48,773 bound volumes, 38,889 titles on microform, 869 periodical subscriptions, 9,582 records/tapes.
Undergraduate Courses offered for part-time students during daytime, evenings, weekends, summer. Complete part-time degree programs offered during daytime, evenings, weekends, summer. Adult/continuing education programs available. Career services available to part-time students: individual and group career counseling, individual job placement, employer recruitment on campus. Part-time tuition: $35 per semester hour for state residents, $104 per semester hour for nonresidents.
Graduate Part-time study available in School of Public Affairs. Degree can be earned exclusively through evening/weekend study in School of Public Affairs. Basic part-time expenses: $51 per credit tuition for state residents, $152 per credit tuition for nonresidents.

Kentucky Wesleyan College
Owensboro 42301
Independent-religious instutition; city setting. Awards A, B. Total enrollment: 942 (all undergraduates); 29% part-time, 61% women, 30% over 25. Total faculty: 85. Library holdings: 130,000 bound volumes, 657 titles on microform, 402 periodical subscriptions, 13,217 records/tapes.
Undergraduate Courses offered for part-time students during daytime, evenings, summer. Complete part-time degree programs offered during daytime. Adult/continuing education programs available. Career services available to part-time students: individual and group career counseling, individual job placement, employer recruitment on campus. Part-time tuition: $115 per credit hour.

Lees Junior College
Jackson 41339
Independent-religious instutition; rural setting. Awards A. Total enrollment: 310 (all undergraduates); 15% part-time, 53% women. Total faculty: 27. Library holdings: 28,000 bound volumes, 30 titles on microform, 246 periodical subscriptions, 1,607 records/tapes.
Undergraduate Courses offered for part-time students during daytime, evenings. Complete part-time degree programs offered during daytime. Adult/continuing education programs available. Part-time tuition: $80 per credit hour.

Lexington Community College
Lexington 40506
See University of Kentucky, Lexington Community College

Lexington Theological Seminary
Lexington 40508
Independent-religious institution (graduate only). Total enrollment: 135 (coed; 29% part-time). Total faculty: 17. Library holdings: 100,000 bound volumes.
Graduate Part-time study available in Graduate and Professional Programs. Basic part-time expenses: $90 per credit tuition plus $5 per semester fees. Institutional financial aid available to part-time graduate students in Graduate and Professional Programs.

Lindsey Wilson College
Columbia 42728
Independent-religious instutition; small-town setting. Awards A. Total enrollment: 465 (all undergraduates); 41% part-time, 53% women, 28% over 25. Total faculty: 25. Library holdings: 21,753 bound volumes, 360 titles on microform, 170 periodical subscriptions, 1,089 records/tapes.
Undergraduate Courses offered for part-time students during daytime, evenings. Complete part-time degree programs offered during daytime, evenings. Adult/continuing education programs available. Career services available to part-time students: individual career counseling. Part-time tuition: $120 per semester hour.

Kentucky / Colleges Offering Part-Time Degree Programs

Louisville Presbyterian Theological Seminary
Louisville 40205

Independent-religious institution (graduate only). Total enrollment: 260 (coed; 45% part-time). Total faculty: 44. Library holdings: 91,427 bound volumes, 75 microforms.

Graduate Part-time study available in Graduate and Professional Programs.Basic part-time expenses: $100 per credit tuition plus $35 per semester fees. Institutional financial aid available to part-time graduate students in Graduate and Professional Programs.

Louisville Technical Institute
Louisville 40218

Proprietary institution; metropolitan setting. Awards A. Barrier-free campus. Total enrollment: 374 (all undergraduates); 4% part-time, 11% women, 40% over 25. Total faculty: 29.

Undergraduate Courses offered for part-time students during daytime, evenings, weekends, summer. Complete part-time degree programs offered during daytime, evenings. External degree and adult/continuing education programs available. Career services available to part-time students: individual and group career counseling, individual job placement, employer recruitment on campus. Part-time tuition: $80 per credit hour.

Madisonville Community College
Madisonville 42431

See University of Kentucky, Madisonville Community College

Maysville Community College
Maysville 41056

See University of Kentucky, Maysville Community College

Midway College
Midway 40347

Independent-religious instutition; small-town setting. Awards A. Total enrollment: 413 (all undergraduates); 22% part-time, 100% women, 35% over 25. Total faculty: 62. Library holdings: 28,750 bound volumes, 2,637 titles on microform, 210 periodical subscriptions, 4,771 records/tapes.

Undergraduate Courses offered for part-time students during daytime, evenings, summer. Complete part-time degree programs offered during daytime, evenings. Adult/continuing education programs available. Career services available to part-time students: individual career counseling, individual job placement. Part-time tuition: $100 per credit.

Morehead State University
Morehead 40351

Public institution; small-town setting. Awards A, B, M. Barrier-free campus. Total enrollment: 6,505. Undergraduate enrollment: 4,901; 12% part-time, 54% women, 16% over 25. Total faculty: 319. Library holdings: 537,980 bound volumes, 73,249 titles on microform, 2,090 periodical subscriptions, 16,467 records/tapes.

Undergraduate Courses offered for part-time students during daytime, evenings, weekends, summer. Complete part-time degree programs offered during daytime. Adult/continuing education programs available. Career services available to part-time students: individual and group career counseling, individual job placement, employer recruitment on campus. Part-time tuition: $38 per credit hour for state residents, $107 per credit hour for nonresidents.

Graduate Part-time study available in Graduate Programs. Degree can be earned exclusively through evening/weekend study in Graduate Programs.Basic part-time expenses: $55 per credit tuition for state residents, $156 per credit tuition for nonresidents. Institutional financial aid available to part-time graduate students in Graduate Programs.

Murray State University
Murray 42071

Public institution; small-town setting. Awards A, B, M. Barrier-free campus. Total enrollment: 7,600. Undergraduate enrollment: 6,250; 12% part-time, 56% women. Total faculty: 381. Library holdings: 380,000 bound volumes, 2,147 periodical subscriptions, 3,000 records/tapes.

Undergraduate Courses offered for part-time students during daytime, evenings, summer. Complete part-time degree programs offered during daytime, evenings, summer. Adult/continuing education programs available. Career services available to part-time students: individual and group career counseling, individual job placement, employer recruitment on campus. Part-time tuition: $37 per credit hour for state residents, $107 per credit hour for nonresidents.

Graduate Part-time study available in College of Business and Public Affairs, College of Creative Expression, College of Environmental Sciences, College of Human Development and Learning, College of Humanistic Studies, College of Industry and Technology.Basic part-time expenses: $54 per hour tuition for state residents, $156 per hour tuition for nonresidents.

Northern Kentucky University
Highland Heights 41076

Public institution; small-town setting. Awards A, B, M. Barrier-free campus. Total enrollment: 9,377. Undergraduate enrollment: 8,481; 44% part-time, 54% women. Total faculty: 487. Library holdings: 220,665 bound volumes, 624,000 titles on microform, 1,651 periodical subscriptions, 4,607 records/tapes.

Undergraduate Courses offered for part-time students during daytime, evenings, summer. Complete part-time degree programs offered during daytime, evenings, summer. Adult/continuing education programs available. Career services available to part-time students: individual and group career counseling, individual job placement, employer recruitment on campus. Part-time tuition: $37 per semester hour for state residents, $106 per semester hour for nonresidents.

Graduate Part-time study available in Graduate Studies, Salmon P. Chase College of Law. Degree can be earned exclusively through evening/weekend study in Graduate Studies, Salmon P. Chase College of Law.Basic part-time expenses: $53 per semester hour tuition for state residents, $155 per semester hour tuition for nonresidents. Institutional financial aid available to part-time graduate students in Graduate Studies, Salmon P. Chase College of Law.

Owensboro Junior College of Business
Owensboro 42301

Proprietary institution; city setting. Awards A. Barrier-free campus. Total enrollment: 283 (all undergraduates); 6% part-time, 71% women, 35% over 25. Total faculty: 22.

Undergraduate Courses offered for part-time students during daytime, evenings. Complete part-time degree programs offered during daytime, evenings. Career services available to part-time students: individual and group career counseling, individual job

Colleges Offering Part-Time Degree Programs / Kentucky

Owensboro Junior College of Business (continued)
placement, employer recruitment on campus. Part-time tuition: $55 per quarter hour.

Paducah Community College
Paducah 42001
See University of Kentucky, Paducah Community College

Pikeville College
Pikeville 41501
Independent-religious instutition; small-town setting. Awards A, B. Total enrollment: 500 (all undergraduates); 24% part-time, 60% women, 30% over 25. Total faculty: 63. Library holdings: 80,000 bound volumes, 14,500 titles on microform, 470 periodical subscriptions.

Undergraduate Courses offered for part-time students during daytime, evenings, summer. Complete part-time degree programs offered during daytime, evenings, summer. Adult/continuing education programs available. Career services available to part-time students: individual career counseling. Part-time tuition: $110 per semester hour.

Prestonsburg Community College
Prestonsburg 41653
See University of Kentucky, Prestonsburg Community College

St Catharine College
St Catharine 40061
Independent-religious instutition; rural setting. Awards A. Total enrollment: 206 (all undergraduates); 29% part-time, 56% women, 29% over 25. Total faculty: 25. Library holdings: 1,200 bound volumes, 65 titles on microform, 50 periodical subscriptions, 750 records/tapes.

Undergraduate Courses offered for part-time students during daytime, evenings, summer. Complete part-time degree programs offered during daytime, evenings, summer. Adult/continuing education programs available. Career services available to part-time students: individual career counseling. Part-time tuition and fees per semester hour range from $65 (for students taking 1 to 7 semester hours) to $80 (for students taking 8 to 11 semester hours).

Somerset Community College
Somerset 42501
See University of Kentucky, Somerset Community College

Southeast Community College
Cumberland 40823
See University of Kentucky, Southeast Community College

Southern Ohio College, Northern Kentucky Campus
Florence 41042
Proprietary institution; city setting. Awards A. Barrier-free campus. Total enrollment: 425 (all undergraduates); 9% part-time, 48% women, 42% over 25. Total faculty: 35.

Undergraduate Courses offered for part-time students during daytime, evenings, summer. Complete part-time degree programs offered during daytime, evenings. Adult/continuing education programs available. Career services available to part-time students: group career counseling, individual job placement, employer recruitment on campus. Part-time tuition: $62 per credit hour.

Spalding University
Louisville 40203
Independent-religious instutition; metropolitan setting. Awards A, B, M, D. Total enrollment: 1,115. Undergraduate enrollment: 861; 50% part-time, 86% women, 60% over 25. Total faculty: 101. Library holdings: 104,044 bound volumes, 1,667 titles on microform, 632 periodical subscriptions.

Undergraduate Courses offered for part-time students during daytime, weekends. Complete part-time degree programs offered during daytime, weekends. Adult/continuing education programs available. Career services available to part-time students: individual and group career counseling, individual job placement, employer recruitment on campus. Part-time tuition: $115 per semester hour.

Graduate Part-time study available in Graduate Division. Degree can be earned exclusively through evening/weekend study in Graduate Division. Basic part-time expenses: $125 per credit tuition plus $3 per credit fees. Institutional financial aid available to part-time graduate students in Graduate Division.

Sullivan Junior College of Business
Louisville 40232
Proprietary institution; metropolitan setting. Awards A. Barrier-free campus. Total enrollment: 1,664 (all undergraduates); 20% part-time, 70% women, 25% over 25. Total faculty: 67. Library holdings: 7,600 bound volumes, 1,050 titles on microform, 120 periodical subscriptions, 1,100 records/tapes.

Undergraduate Courses offered for part-time students during daytime, evenings, summer. Complete part-time degree programs offered during daytime, evenings, summer. Adult/continuing education programs available. Career services available to part-time students: individual and group career counseling, individual job placement, employer recruitment on campus. Part-time tuition: $62 per credit.

Thomas More College
Crestview Hills 41017
Independent-religious instutition; small-town setting. Awards A, B. Barrier-free campus. Total enrollment: 1,335 (all undergraduates); 42% part-time, 56% women, 33% over 25. Total faculty: 117. Library holdings: 99,000 bound volumes, 654 periodical subscriptions, 1,599 records/tapes.

Undergraduate Courses offered for part-time students during daytime, evenings, weekends, summer. Complete part-time degree programs offered during daytime, evenings, weekends, summer. External degree and adult/continuing education programs available. Career services available to part-time students: individual and group career counseling, individual job placement, employer recruitment on campus. Part-time tuition and fees per credit are $120 for 1 to 6 credits, $140 for 7 to 11 credits.

Kentucky / **Colleges Offering Part-Time Degree Programs**

Transylvania University
Lexington 40508

Independent-religious instutition; city setting. Awards B. Total enrollment: 701 (all undergraduates); 15% part-time, 51% women. Total faculty: 72. Library holdings: 114,000 bound volumes, 945 titles on microform, 442 periodical subscriptions, 260 records/tapes.

Undergraduate Courses offered for part-time students during daytime, evenings. Complete part-time degree programs offered during daytime. Adult/continuing education programs available. Career services available to part-time students: individual and group career counseling, individual job placement, employer recruitment on campus. Part-time tuition: $500 per course.

Union College
Barbourville 40906

Independent-religious instutition; small-town setting. Awards A, B, M. Total enrollment: 794. Undergraduate enrollment: 519; 35% part-time, 54% women, 20% over 25. Total faculty: 72. Library holdings: 75,563 bound volumes, 11,912 titles on microform, 599 periodical subscriptions, 450 records/tapes.

Undergraduate Courses offered for part-time students during daytime, evenings, weekends, summer. Complete part-time degree programs offered during daytime. Adult/continuing education programs available. Career services available to part-time students: individual and group career counseling, individual job placement, employer recruitment on campus. Part-time tuition: $80 per semester hour.

University of Kentucky
Lexington 40536

Public institution; city setting. Awards B, M, D. Total enrollment: 21,616. Undergraduate enrollment: 16,016; 13% part-time, 47% women, 20% over 25. Total faculty: 1,842. Library holdings: 1.8 million bound volumes, 1.9 million titles on microform, 33,000 periodical subscriptions, 10,000 records/tapes.

Undergraduate Courses offered for part-time students during daytime, evenings, summer. Complete part-time degree programs offered during daytime, evenings, summer. Adult/continuing education programs available. Career services available to part-time students: individual and group career counseling, individual job placement, employer recruitment on campus. Part-time tuition: $45 per semester hour for state residents, $132 per semester hour for nonresidents.

Graduate Part-time study available in Graduate School. Basic part-time expenses: $66 per credit hour tuition for state residents, $193 per credit hour tuition for nonresidents.

University of Kentucky, Ashland Community College
Ashland 41101

Public institution; small-town setting. Awards A. Barrier-free campus. Total enrollment: 2,031 (all undergraduates); 47% part-time, 62% women, 30% over 25. Total faculty: 85. Library holdings: 27,000 bound volumes, 8 titles on microform, 310 periodical subscriptions, 7,000 records/tapes.

Undergraduate Courses offered for part-time students during daytime, evenings, summer. Complete part-time degree programs offered during daytime, evenings, summer. Adult/continuing education programs available. Career services available to part-time students: individual career counseling. Part-time tuition: $20 per semester hour for state residents, $59 per semester hour for nonresidents.

University of Kentucky, Elizabethtown Community College
Elizabethtown 42701

Public institution; small-town setting. Awards A. Barrier-free campus. Total enrollment: 2,259 (all undergraduates); 48% part-time, 65% women, 40% over 25. Total faculty: 89. Library holdings: 26,000 bound volumes, 140 titles on microform, 160 periodical subscriptions, 2,200 records/tapes.

Undergraduate Courses offered for part-time students during daytime, evenings, summer. Complete part-time degree programs offered during daytime, evenings, summer. External degree and adult/continuing education programs available. Career services available to part-time students: individual and group career counseling, individual job placement, employer recruitment on campus. Part-time tuition: $18 per credit hour for state residents, $52 per credit hour for nonresidents.

University of Kentucky, Hazard Community College
Hazard 41701

Public institution; rural setting. Awards A. Barrier-free campus. Total enrollment: 514 (all undergraduates); 38% part-time, 64% women, 29% over 25. Total faculty: 25. Library holdings: 30,000 bound volumes, 140 periodical subscriptions, 855 records/tapes.

Undergraduate Courses offered for part-time students during daytime, evenings, summer. Complete part-time degree programs offered during daytime, evenings, summer. Adult/continuing education programs available. Career services available to part-time students: individual and group career counseling, individual job placement, employer recruitment on campus. Part-time tuition: $20 per credit for state residents, $59 per credit for nonresidents.

University of Kentucky, Henderson Community College
Henderson 42420

Public institution; small-town setting. Awards A. Barrier-free campus. Total enrollment: 1,105 (all undergraduates); 50% part-time, 65% women. Total faculty: 49. Library holdings: 19,000 bound volumes, 300 periodical subscriptions, 1,000 records/tapes.

Undergraduate Courses offered for part-time students during daytime. Complete part-time degree programs offered during daytime. Adult/continuing education programs available. Career services available to part-time students: individual and group career counseling, individual job placement. Part-time tuition: $20 per semester hour for state residents, $59 per semester hour for nonresidents.

University of Kentucky, Hopkinsville Community College
Hopkinsville 42240

Public institution; small-town setting. Awards A. Barrier-free campus. Total enrollment: 1,284 (all undergraduates); 54% part-time, 72% women, 78% over 25. Total faculty: 64. Library holdings: 15,000 bound volumes, 5,000 titles on microform, 40 periodical subscriptions, 2,000 records/tapes.

Undergraduate Courses offered for part-time students during daytime, evenings, summer. Complete part-time degree programs offered during daytime, evenings. Adult/continuing education programs available. Career services available to part-time students: individual and group career counseling,

Colleges Offering Part-Time Degree Programs / Kentucky

University of Kentucky, Hopkinsville Community College (continued)

individual job placement, employer recruitment on campus. Part-time tuition: $20 per credit for state residents, $59 per credit for nonresidents.

University of Kentucky, Jefferson Community College
Louisville 40201

Public institution; metropolitan setting. Awards A. Barrier-free campus. Total enrollment: 7,079 (all undergraduates); 60% part-time, 63% women, 54% over 25. Total faculty: 282. Library holdings: 47,889 bound volumes, 1,576 titles on microform, 495 periodical subscriptions, 1,113 records/tapes.

Undergraduate Courses offered for part-time students during daytime, evenings, summer. Complete part-time degree programs offered during daytime, evenings, summer. Adult/continuing education programs available. Career services available to part-time students: individual and group career counseling. Part-time tuition: $18 per semester hour for state residents, $59 per semester hour for nonresidents.

University of Kentucky, Lexington Community College
Lexington 40506

Public institution; city setting. Awards A. Barrier-free campus. Total enrollment: 2,532 (all undergraduates); 53% part-time, 59% women, 25% over 25. Total faculty: 172. Library holdings: 6,500 bound volumes, 40 titles on microform, 200 periodical subscriptions, 600 records/tapes.

Undergraduate Courses offered for part-time students during daytime, evenings, summer. Complete part-time degree programs offered during daytime, evenings, summer. Adult/continuing education programs available. Career services available to part-time students: individual career counseling, individual job placement, employer recruitment on campus. Part-time tuition: $45 per semester hour for state residents, $132 per semester hour for nonresidents.

University of Kentucky, Madisonville Community College
Madisonville 42431

Public institution; small-town setting. Awards A. Barrier-free campus. Total enrollment: 1,410 (all undergraduates); 65% part-time, 68% women. Total faculty: 56. Library holdings: 24,000 bound volumes.

Undergraduate Courses offered for part-time students during daytime, evenings, summer. Complete part-time degree programs offered during daytime, evenings, summer. Adult/continuing education programs available. Career services available to part-time students: individual and group career counseling, individual job placement, employer recruitment on campus. Part-time tuition: $20 per credit hour for state residents, $59 per credit hour for nonresidents.

University of Kentucky, Maysville Community College
Maysville 41056

Public institution; rural setting. Awards A. Barrier-free campus. Total enrollment: 653 (all undergraduates); 42% part-time, 66% women. Total faculty: 35. Library holdings: 23,500 bound volumes, 4,000 titles on microform, 167 periodical subscriptions, 500 records/tapes.

Undergraduate Courses offered for part-time students during daytime, evenings, summer. Complete part-time degree programs offered during daytime, evenings, summer. Adult/continuing education programs available. Career services available to part-time students: individual and group career counseling, employer recruitment on campus. Part-time tuition: $19.50 per semester hour for state residents, $59 per semester hour for nonresidents.

University of Kentucky, Paducah Community College
Paducah 42001

Public institution; small-town setting. Awards A. Barrier-free campus. Total enrollment: 1,885 (all undergraduates); 49% part-time, 66% women, 37% over 25. Total faculty: 73. Library holdings: 32,780 bound volumes, 3,600 titles on microform, 155 periodical subscriptions, 7,720 records/tapes.

Undergraduate Courses offered for part-time students during daytime, evenings, summer. Complete part-time degree programs offered during daytime, evenings, summer. Adult/continuing education programs available. Career services available to part-time students: individual and group career counseling, individual job placement, employer recruitment on campus. Part-time tuition: $20 per credit hour for state residents, $59 per credit hour for nonresidents.

University of Kentucky, Prestonsburg Community College
Prestonsburg 41653

Public institution; rural setting. Awards A. Total enrollment: 919 (all undergraduates); 30% part-time, 61% women. Total faculty: 43. Library holdings: 31,980 bound volumes, 175 periodical subscriptions, 1,636 records/tapes.

Undergraduate Courses offered for part-time students during daytime. Complete part-time degree programs offered during daytime. Adult/continuing education programs available. Career services available to part-time students: individual and group career counseling, individual job placement, employer recruitment on campus. Part-time tuition: $20 per credit hour for state residents, $59 per credit hour for nonresidents.

University of Kentucky, Somerset Community College
Somerset 42501

Public institution; small-town setting. Awards A. Barrier-free campus. Total enrollment: 1,132 (all undergraduates); 20% part-time, 50% women, 45% over 25. Total faculty: 75. Library holdings: 35,461 bound volumes, 117 titles on microform, 294 periodical subscriptions, 3,339 records/tapes.

Undergraduate Courses offered for part-time students during daytime, evenings, summer. Complete part-time degree programs offered during daytime, evenings, summer. Adult/continuing education programs available. Career services available to part-time students: individual and group career counseling, individual job placement, employer recruitment on campus. Part-time tuition: $20 per credit hour for state residents, $59 per credit hour for nonresidents.

University of Kentucky, Southeast Community College
Cumberland 40823

Public institution; small-town setting. Awards A. Barrier-free campus. Total enrollment: 816 (all undergraduates); 72% part-time, 72% women. Total faculty: 48. Library holdings: 25,000 bound volumes, 201 periodical subscriptions, 926 records/tapes.

Undergraduate Courses offered for part-time students during daytime, evenings, summer. Complete part-time degree programs offered during daytime, evenings, summer. Adult/continuing education programs available. Career services available to part-time students: individual and group career counseling. Part-time tuition: $20 per credit hour for state residents, $59 per credit hour for nonresidents.

University of Louisville
Louisville 40292

Public institution; metropolitan setting. Awards A, B, M, D. Total enrollment: 19,750. Undergraduate enrollment: 14,984; 42% part-time, 48% women. Total faculty: 1,426. Library holdings: 956,384 bound volumes, 820,287 titles on microform, 8,750 periodical subscriptions.

Undergraduate Courses offered for part-time students during daytime, evenings, weekends, summer. Complete part-time degree programs offered during daytime, evenings, summer. Adult/continuing education programs available. Career services available to part-time students: individual and group career counseling, individual job placement, employer recruitment on campus. Part-time tuition and fees per semester (1 to 11 credit hours) range from $54 to $526 for state residents, $140 to $1478 for nonresidents.

Graduate Part-time study available in Graduate School, School of Law, Speed Scientific School. Basic part-time expenses: $210 per semester (minimum) tuition for state residents, $591 per semester (minimum) tuition for nonresidents.

Watterson College
Louisville 40218

Proprietary institution; metropolitan setting. Awards A. Barrier-free campus. Total enrollment: 945 (all undergraduates); 7% part-time, 60% women. Total faculty: 90. Library holdings: 5,547 bound volumes, 45 periodical subscriptions, 140 records/tapes.

Undergraduate Courses offered for part-time students during daytime, evenings, summer. Complete part-time degree programs offered during daytime, evenings, summer. Career services available to part-time students: individual and group career counseling, individual job placement, employer recruitment on campus. Part-time tuition: $62 per credit.

Western Kentucky University
Bowling Green 42101

Public institution; small-town setting. Awards A, B, M. Barrier-free campus. Total enrollment: 12,666. Undergraduate enrollment: 10,544; 17% part-time, 52% women. Total faculty: 631. Library holdings: 912,000 bound volumes, 422,200 titles on microform, 6,400 periodical subscriptions, 9,500 records/tapes.

Undergraduate Courses offered for part-time students during daytime, evenings, summer. Complete part-time degree programs offered during daytime, evenings, summer. Adult/continuing education programs available. Career services available to part-time students: individual and group career counseling, individual job placement, employer recruitment on campus.

Part-time tuition: $37 per semester hour for state residents, $106 per semester hour for nonresidents.

Graduate Part-time study available in Graduate College. Basic part-time expenses: $53 per credit tuition for state residents, $155 per credit tuition for nonresidents.

LOUISIANA

Bossier Parish Community College
Bossier City 71111

Public institution; city setting. Awards A. Total enrollment: 1,661 (all undergraduates); 82% part-time, 69% women. Total faculty: 65. Library holdings: 22,075 bound volumes, 104 periodical subscriptions.

Undergraduate Courses offered for part-time students during daytime, evenings, weekends, summer. Complete part-time degree programs offered during daytime, evenings. Adult/continuing education programs available. Career services available to part-time students: individual career counseling. Part-time tuition per semester (1 to 11 semester hours) ranges from $62 to $140.

Centenary College of Louisiana
Shreveport 71134

Independent-religious instutition; city setting. Awards A, B, M. Barrier-free campus. Total enrollment: 1,387. Undergraduate enrollment: 895; 18% part-time, 47% women. Total faculty: 108. Library holdings: 143,147 bound volumes, 856 periodical subscriptions, 975 records/tapes.

Undergraduate Courses offered for part-time students during daytime, evenings, summer. Complete part-time degree programs offered during daytime, evenings, summer. Adult/continuing education programs available. Career services available to part-time students: individual and group career counseling, individual job placement, employer recruitment on campus. Part-time tuition: $140 per semester hour.

Delgado Community College
New Orleans 70119

Public institution; metropolitan setting. Awards A. Barrier-free campus. Total enrollment: 8,733 (all undergraduates); 61% part-time, 44% women, 30% over 25. Total faculty: 550. Library holdings: 38,000 bound volumes, 132 titles on microform, 244 periodical subscriptions, 1,993 records/tapes.

Undergraduate Courses offered for part-time students during daytime, evenings, summer. Complete part-time degree programs offered during daytime, evenings, summer. External degree and adult/continuing education programs available. Career services available to part-time students: individual and group career counseling, individual job placement, employer recruitment on campus. Part-time tuition per semester (1 to 11 semester hours) ranges from $90 to $245 for state residents, $90 to $557 for nonresidents.

Dillard University
New Orleans 70122

Independent-religious instutition; metropolitan setting. Awards B. Total enrollment: 1,142 (all undergraduates); 1% part-time, 71% women. Total faculty: 92. Library holdings: 126,960 bound volumes, 2,411 titles on microform, 631 periodical subscriptions, 1,409 records/tapes.

Colleges Offering Part-Time Degree Programs / Louisiana

Dillard University (continued)

Undergraduate Courses offered for part-time students during daytime. Complete part-time degree programs offered during daytime. Career services available to part-time students: individual and group career counseling, individual job placement, employer recruitment on campus. Part-time tuition: $82.50 per credit hour.

Grambling State University
Grambling 71245

Public institution; small-town setting. Awards A, B, M. Total enrollment: 4,593. Undergraduate enrollment: 4,043; 8% part-time, 52% women. Total faculty: 200. Library holdings: 177,962 bound volumes, 1,217 periodical subscriptions.

Undergraduate Courses offered for part-time students during daytime, evenings, summer. Complete part-time degree programs offered during daytime, evenings, summer. Adult/continuing education programs available. Career services available to part-time students: individual and group career counseling, individual job placement, employer recruitment on campus. Part-time tuition per semester (1 to 11 semester hours) ranges from $219 to $419 for state residents, $219 to $731 for nonresidents.

Graduate Part-time study available in Division of Graduate Studies. Basic part-time expenses: $128 per semester (minimum) tuition.

Louisiana College
Pineville 71359

Independent-religious instutition; small-town setting. Awards A, B. Barrier-free campus. Total enrollment: 1,302 (all undergraduates); 35% part-time, 52% women. Total faculty: 93. Library holdings: 110,000 bound volumes, 62 titles on microform, 551 periodical subscriptions, 1,650 records/tapes.

Undergraduate Courses offered for part-time students during daytime, evenings, summer. Complete part-time degree programs offered during daytime, evenings. External degree and adult/continuing education programs available. Career services available to part-time students: individual career counseling, individual job placement, employer recruitment on campus. Part-time tuition: $66 per credit hour.

Louisiana State University and Agricultural and Mechanical College
Baton Rouge 70803

Public institution; city setting. Awards B, M, D. Total enrollment: 29,863. Undergraduate enrollment: 24,704; 15% part-time, 47% women, 11% over 25. Total faculty: 1,485. Library holdings: 2 million bound volumes, 1.5 million titles on microform, 22,172 periodical subscriptions, 9,575 records/tapes.

Undergraduate Courses offered for part-time students during daytime, evenings. Complete part-time degree programs offered during daytime, evenings. Adult/continuing education programs available. Career services available to part-time students: individual career counseling. Part-time tuition per semester (1 to 11 semester hours) ranges from $135 to $367 for state residents, $195 to $975 for nonresidents.

Graduate Part-time study available in Graduate School, Center for Wetland Resources, School of Veterinary Medicine. Degree can be earned exclusively through evening/weekend study in Graduate School. Basic part-time expenses: $135 per semester (minimum) tuition for state residents, $195 per semester (minimum) tuition for nonresidents.

Louisiana State University at Alexandria
Alexandria 71302

Public institution; rural setting. Awards A. Total enrollment: 2,021 (all undergraduates); 41% part-time, 61% women. Total faculty: 97. Library holdings: 121,619 bound volumes, 127 titles on microform, 824 periodical subscriptions, 772 records/tapes.

Undergraduate Courses offered for part-time students during daytime, evenings, summer. Complete part-time degree programs offered during daytime, evenings, summer. Adult/continuing education programs available. Career services available to part-time students: individual and group career counseling, employer recruitment on campus. Part-time tuition per semester (1 to 11 semester hours) ranges from $80 to $208 for state residents, $255 to $652 for nonresidents.

Louisiana State University at Eunice
Eunice 70535

Public institution; small-town setting. Awards A. Barrier-free campus. Total enrollment: 1,557 (all undergraduates); 63% part-time, 61% women, 32% over 25. Total faculty: 80. Library holdings: 89,652 bound volumes, 113 titles on microform, 750 periodical subscriptions, 2,436 records/tapes.

Undergraduate Courses offered for part-time students during daytime, evenings, summer. Complete part-time degree programs offered during daytime, evenings, summer. Adult/continuing education programs available. Career services available to part-time students: individual and group career counseling. Part-time tuition per semester (1 to 11 credit hours) ranges from $80 to $370 for state residents, $225 to $615 for nonresidents.

Louisiana State University in Shreveport
Shreveport 71115

Public institution; city setting. Awards B, M. Barrier-free campus. Total enrollment: 4,625. Undergraduate enrollment: 4,049; 48% part-time, 55% women, 42% over 25. Total faculty: 196. Library holdings: 168,304 bound volumes, 72,675 titles on microform, 2,135 periodical subscriptions, 388 records/tapes.

Undergraduate Courses offered for part-time students during daytime, evenings, summer. Complete part-time degree programs offered during daytime, evenings, summer. Adult/continuing education programs available. Career services available to part-time students: individual and group career counseling, individual job placement, employer recruitment on campus. Part-time tuition per semester (1 to 11 credit hours) ranges from $120 to $345 for state residents, $310 to $885 for nonresidents.

Graduate Part-time study available in College of Business Administration, College of Education, College of Liberal Arts. Basic part-time expenses: $120 per semester (minimum) tuition for state residents, $240 per semester (minimum) tuition for nonresidents. Institutional financial aid available to part-time graduate students in College of Education.

Louisiana Tech University
Ruston 71272

Public institution; small-town setting. Awards A, B, M, D. Total enrollment: 11,172. Undergraduate enrollment: 9,688; 14% part-time, 43% women, 24% over 25. Total faculty: 466. Library holdings: 289,712 bound volumes, 648,470 titles on microform, 2,017 periodical subscriptions, 2,411 records/tapes.

Undergraduate Courses offered for part-time students during daytime. Complete part-time degree programs offered during daytime. Adult/continuing education programs available. Career services available to part-time students: individual and group career counseling, individual job placement, employer

Louisiana / Colleges Offering Part-Time Degree Programs

recruitment on campus. Part-time tuition: $38 per semester hour for state residents, $66 per semester hour for nonresidents.

Graduate Part-time study available in Graduate School. Basic part-time expenses: $113.50 per quarter (minimum) tuition.

Loyola University, New Orleans
New Orleans 70118

Independent-religious instutition; metropolitan setting. Awards A, B, M. Total enrollment: 4,588. Undergraduate enrollment: 3,545; 23% part-time, 56% women. Total faculty: 309. Library holdings: 305,000 bound volumes, 51,500 titles on microform, 1,600 periodical subscriptions.

Undergraduate Courses offered for part-time students during daytime, evenings, weekends, summer. Complete part-time degree programs offered during daytime, evenings, weekends, summer. Adult/continuing education programs available. Career services available to part-time students: individual and group career counseling, individual job placement, employer recruitment on campus. Part-time tuition: $145 per credit hour.

McNeese State University
Lake Charles 70609

Public institution; city setting. Awards A, B, M. Barrier-free campus. Total enrollment: 8,026. Undergraduate enrollment: 6,491; 20% part-time, 54% women, 21% over 25. Total faculty: 331. Library holdings: 202,870 bound volumes, 52 titles on microform, 1,369 periodical subscriptions, 2,876 records/tapes.

Undergraduate Courses offered for part-time students during daytime, evenings, summer. Complete part-time degree programs offered during daytime, evenings, summer. Adult/continuing education programs available. Career services available to part-time students: individual job placement, employer recruitment on campus. Part-time tuition per semester (1 to 11 credit hours) ranges from $123.50 to $371.50 for state residents, $123.50 to $683.50 for nonresidents.

Graduate Part-time study available in Graduate School. Basic part-time expenses: $85 per semester (minimum) tuition plus $38.50 per semester (minimum) fees. Institutional financial aid available to part-time graduate students in Graduate School.

Newcomb College
New Orleans 70118

See Tulane University, Newcomb College

New Orleans Baptist Theological Seminary
New Orleans 70126

Independent-religious instutition; metropolitan setting. Awards A, M, D. Total enrollment: 1,529. Undergraduate enrollment: 379; 40% part-time, 35% women, 100% over 25. Total faculty: 50. Library holdings: 150,000 bound volumes.

Undergraduate Courses offered for part-time students during daytime, evenings, summer. Complete part-time degree programs offered during daytime, evenings. Adult/continuing education programs available. Career services available to part-time students: individual career counseling. Part-time tuition: $68.75 per course.

Nicholls State University
Thibodaux 70310

Public institution; small-town setting. Awards A, B, M. Barrier-free campus. Total enrollment: 7,445. Undergraduate enrollment: 6,572; 20% part-time, 55% women. Total faculty: 257. Library holdings: 218,298 bound volumes, 360,236 titles on microform, 1,567 periodical subscriptions, 6,958 records/tapes.

Undergraduate Courses offered for part-time students during daytime, evenings, summer. Complete part-time degree programs offered during daytime, evenings, summer. Adult/continuing education programs available. Career services available to part-time students: individual and group career counseling, individual job placement, employer recruitment on campus. Part-time tuition per semester (1 to 11 semester hours) ranges from $100.50 to $346.05 for state residents, $100.50 to $635.40 for nonresidents.

Graduate Part-time study available in Graduate School. Degree can be earned exclusively through evening/weekend study in Graduate School. Basic part-time expenses: $98 per semester (minimum) tuition. Institutional financial aid available to part-time graduate students in Graduate School.

Northeast Louisiana University
Monroe 71209

Public institution; city setting. Awards A, B, M, D. Total enrollment: 11,586. Undergraduate enrollment: 9,963; 17% part-time, 55% women. Total faculty: 478. Library holdings: 433,143 bound volumes, 290,917 titles on microform, 3,617 periodical subscriptions.

Undergraduate Courses offered for part-time students during daytime, evenings, summer. Complete part-time degree programs offered during daytime, evenings, summer. Adult/continuing education programs available. Career services available to part-time students: individual and group career counseling, individual job placement, employer recruitment on campus. Part-time tuition per semester (1 to 11 semester hours) ranges from $100 to $305 for state residents, $100 to $617 for nonresidents.

Graduate Part-time study available in Graduate School. Basic part-time expenses: $100 per semester (minimum) fees. Institutional financial aid available to part-time graduate students in Graduate School.

Northwestern State University of Louisiana
Natchitoches 71497

Public institution; small-town setting. Awards A, B, M, D. Barrier-free campus. Total enrollment: 6,272. Undergraduate enrollment: 4,824; 33% part-time, 55% women, 5% over 25. Total faculty: 225.

Undergraduate Courses offered for part-time students during daytime. Complete part-time degree programs offered during daytime. Adult/continuing education programs available. Career services available to part-time students: individual and group career counseling, individual job placement, employer recruitment on campus. Part-time tuition per semester (1 to 11 credits) ranges from $170 to $230 for state residents, $495 to $555 for nonresidents.

Graduate Part-time study available in Graduate Studies and Research. Basic part-time expenses: $160 per semester (minimum) fees. Institutional financial aid available to part-time graduate students in Graduate Studies and Research.

Colleges Offering Part-Time Degree Programs / Louisiana

Notre Dame Seminary
New Orleans 70118

Independent-religious institution (graduate only). Total enrollment: 106 (primarily men; 18% part-time). Total faculty: 20. Library holdings: 80,000 bound volumes.

Graduate Part-time study available in Graduate School of Theology. Basic part-time expenses: $95 per credit hour tuition plus $25 per semester fees.

Our Lady of Holy Cross College
New Orleans 70114

Independent-religious instutition; metropolitan setting. Awards A, B. Total enrollment: 621 (all undergraduates); 71% part-time, 70% women. Total faculty: 59.

Undergraduate Courses offered for part-time students during daytime, evenings, weekends, summer. Complete part-time degree programs offered during daytime, evenings, weekends, summer. Adult/continuing education programs available. Part-time tuition: $110 per semester hour.

Phillips College of New Orleans
New Orleans 70121

Proprietary institution; metropolitan setting. Awards A. Total enrollment: 902 (all undergraduates); 2% part-time, 48% women. Total faculty: 51.

Undergraduate Courses offered for part-time students during daytime, evenings, summer. Complete part-time degree programs offered during daytime, evenings, summer. Part-time tuition: $85 per quarter hour.

Southeastern Louisiana University
Hammond 70402

Public institution; small-town setting. Awards A, B, M. Total enrollment: 9,019. Undergraduate enrollment: 7,745; 12% part-time, 56% women. Total faculty: 294. Library holdings: 250,000 bound volumes, 1,600 periodical subscriptions, 3,330 records/tapes.

Undergraduate Courses offered for part-time students during daytime. Complete part-time degree programs offered during daytime. Adult/continuing education programs available. Career services available to part-time students: individual and group career counseling, individual job placement, employer recruitment on campus. Part-time tuition per semester (1 to 11 semester hours) ranges from $137 to $404 for state residents, $250 to $716 for nonresidents.

Southern University and Agricultural and Mechanical College
Baton Rouge 70813

Public institution; city setting. Awards A, B, M. Barrier-free campus. Total enrollment: 9,500. Undergraduate enrollment: 8,700; 9% part-time, 53% women. Total faculty: 486.

Undergraduate Courses offered for part-time students during daytime, weekends. Complete part-time degree programs offered during daytime, weekends. Adult/continuing education programs available. Part-time tuition per semester (1 to 11 credits) ranges from $90 to $278 for state residents, $405 to $593 for nonresidents.

Southern University, Shreveport–Bossier City Campus
Shreveport 71107

Public institution; city setting. Awards A. Total enrollment: 722 (all undergraduates); 30% part-time, 66% women. Total faculty: 42. Library holdings: 32,329 bound volumes, 6,639 titles on microform, 355 periodical subscriptions, 775 records/tapes.

Undergraduate Courses offered for part-time students during daytime, evenings, summer. Complete part-time degree programs offered during daytime, evenings, summer. Career services available to part-time students: individual and group career counseling, individual job placement, employer recruitment on campus. Part-time tuition: $84 per course for state residents, $84 per course for nonresidents.

Tulane University
New Orleans 70118

Independent institution; metropolitan setting. Awards A, B, M, D. Total enrollment: 10,700. Undergraduate enrollment: 6,630; 2% part-time, 41% women. Total faculty: 879. Library holdings: 1.4 million bound volumes, 10,958 periodical subscriptions, 9,603 records/tapes.

Graduate Part-time study available in Graduate School, Graduate School of Business Administration, School of Engineering, School of Public Health and Tropical Medicine. Degree can be earned exclusively through evening/weekend study in Graduate School of Business Administration. Basic part-time expenses: $422 per credit hour tuition plus $22.50 per credit hour fees. Institutional financial aid available to part-time graduate students in School of Public Health and Tropical Medicine.

Tulane University, Newcomb College
New Orleans 70118

Independent institution; metropolitan setting. Awards B. Barrier-free campus. Total enrollment: 1,594 (all undergraduates); 6% part-time, 100% women, 4% over 25. Total faculty: 163. Library holdings: 1.4 million bound volumes, 12,518 titles on microform, 1.3 million periodical subscriptions, 10,000 records/tapes.

Undergraduate Courses offered for part-time students during daytime, summer. Complete part-time degree programs offered during daytime. Adult/continuing education programs available. Career services available to part-time students: individual and group career counseling, individual job placement, employer recruitment on campus. Part-time tuition: $305 per credit hour.

University of New Orleans
New Orleans 70148

Public institution; metropolitan setting. Awards A, B, M, D. Total enrollment: 16,317. Undergraduate enrollment: 13,802; 39% part-time, 52% women, 36% over 25. Total faculty: 671. Library holdings: 578,255 bound volumes, 443,211 titles on microform, 7,553 periodical subscriptions, 19,198 records/tapes.

Undergraduate Courses offered for part-time students during daytime, evenings, summer. Complete part-time degree programs offered during daytime, evenings, summer. Adult/continuing education programs available. Career services available to part-time students: individual career counseling, individual job placement, employer recruitment on campus. Part-time tuition and fees per semester (1 to 11 credit hours) range from $194 to $416 for state residents, $443 to $992 for nonresidents.

University of Southwestern Louisiana
Lafayette 70504

Public institution; city setting. Awards A, B, M, D. Total enrollment: 16,266. Undergraduate enrollment: 14,394; 20% part-time, 50% women, 28% over 25. Total faculty: 621. Library holdings: 525,856 bound volumes, 11,799 titles on microform, 6,136 periodical subscriptions, 4,409 records/tapes.

Undergraduate Courses offered for part-time students during daytime, evenings, summer. Complete part-time degree programs offered during daytime, evenings, summer. Adult/continuing education programs available. Career services available to part-time students: individual job placement, employer recruitment on campus. Part-time tuition and fees per semester (1 to 11 semester hours) range from $111 to $324 for state residents, $111 to $636 for nonresidents.

Graduate Part-time study available in Graduate School. Basic part-time expenses: $137.25 per semester (minimum) tuition. Institutional financial aid available to part-time graduate students in Graduate School.

Xavier University of Louisiana
New Orleans 70125

Independent-religious instutition; metropolitan setting. Awards B, M. Total enrollment: 2,243. Undergraduate enrollment: 2,035; 7% part-time, 57% women. Total faculty: 180. Library holdings: 98,194 bound volumes, 660 periodical subscriptions, 7,000 records/tapes.

Graduate Part-time study available in Graduate School. Basic part-time expenses: $120 per semester hour tuition. Institutional financial aid available to part-time graduate students in Graduate School.

MAINE

Andover College
Portland 04103

Proprietary institution; city setting. Awards A. Barrier-free campus. Total enrollment: 575 (all undergraduates); 20% part-time, 60% women. Total faculty: 25. Library holdings: 6,000 bound volumes, 45 periodical subscriptions, 20 records/tapes.

Undergraduate Courses offered for part-time students during daytime, evenings, summer. Complete part-time degree programs offered during daytime, evenings. Adult/continuing education programs available. Career services available to part-time students: individual and group career counseling, individual job placement, employer recruitment on campus. Part-time tuition: $250 per course.

Bangor Theological Seminary
Bangor 04401

Independent-religious institution (graduate only). Total enrollment: 57 (coed; 19% part-time). Total faculty: 25. Library holdings: 73,960 bound volumes, 430 microforms.

Graduate Part-time study available in Professional Program. Basic part-time expenses: $350 per course tuition plus $35 per year fees. Institutional financial aid available to part-time graduate students in Professional Program.

Beal College
Bangor 04401

Proprietary institution; small-town setting. Awards A. Total enrollment: 299 (all undergraduates); 28% part-time, 60% women. Total faculty: 31. Library holdings: 4,509 bound volumes, 72 periodical subscriptions, 50 records/tapes.

Undergraduate Courses offered for part-time students during daytime, evenings, summer. Complete part-time degree programs offered during daytime, evenings, summer. Adult/continuing education programs available. Career services available to part-time students: individual and group career counseling, individual job placement, employer recruitment on campus. Part-time tuition: $95 per credit hour.

Casco Bay College
Portland 04101

Proprietary institution; city setting. Awards A. Barrier-free campus. Total enrollment: 287 (all undergraduates); 2% part-time, 78% women. Total faculty: 21. Library holdings: 3,500 bound volumes.

Undergraduate Courses offered for part-time students during daytime, evenings. Complete part-time degree programs offered during daytime, evenings. Adult/continuing education programs available. Career services available to part-time students: individual and group career counseling, individual job placement, employer recruitment on campus. Part-time tuition: $90 per credit hour.

College of the Atlantic
Bar Harbor 04609

Independent institution; small-town setting. Awards B. Barrier-free campus. Total enrollment: 150 (all undergraduates); 6% part-time, 54% women, 5% over 25. Total faculty: 21. Library holdings: 16,575 bound volumes, 240 periodical subscriptions.

Undergraduate Courses offered for part-time students during daytime, evenings. Complete part-time degree programs offered during daytime, evenings. Career services available to part-time students: individual and group career counseling, individual job placement. Part-time tuition per trimester ranges from $813 to $1755.

Eastern Maine Vocational-Technical Institute
Bangor 04401

Public institution; small-town setting. Awards A. Total enrollment: 566 (all undergraduates); 10% part-time, 31% women, 10% over 25. Total faculty: 52. Library holdings: 8,500 bound volumes, 120 periodical subscriptions, 250 records/tapes.

Undergraduate Courses offered for part-time students during daytime, evenings, summer. Complete part-time degree programs offered during daytime, evenings, summer. Adult/continuing education programs available. Career services available to part-time students: individual career counseling, individual job placement, employer recruitment on campus. Part-time tuition: $25 per credit hour for state residents, $25 per credit hour for nonresidents.

Husson College
Bangor 04401

Independent institution; small-town setting. Awards A, B, M. Barrier-free campus. Total enrollment: 1,475. Undergraduate enrollment: 1,372; 45% part-time, 63% women. Total faculty:

Colleges Offering Part-Time Degree Programs / Maine

Husson College (continued)

100. Library holdings: 33,000 bound volumes, 300 periodical subscriptions.

Undergraduate Courses offered for part-time students during daytime, evenings, weekends, summer. Complete part-time degree programs offered during daytime, evenings, weekends, summer. Adult/continuing education programs available. Career services available to part-time students: individual and group career counseling, individual job placement, employer recruitment on campus. Part-time tuition: $175 per semester hour.

Kennebec Valley Vocational-Technical Institute
Fairfield 04937

Public institution; small-town setting. Awards A. Total enrollment: 120 (all undergraduates); 2% part-time, 59% women, 40% over 25. Total faculty: 32. Library holdings: 5,000 bound volumes, 25 periodical subscriptions, 50 records/tapes.

Undergraduate Courses offered for part-time students during daytime, evenings, weekends, summer. Complete part-time degree programs offered during daytime, evenings, weekends, summer. Adult/continuing education programs available. Career services available to part-time students: individual career counseling. Part-time tuition: $25 per credit hour for state residents, $50 per credit hour for nonresidents.

Mid-State College
Auburn 04210

Proprietary institution; small-town setting. Awards A. Barrier-free campus. Total enrollment: 200 (all undergraduates); 5% part-time, 75% women. Total faculty: 20. Library holdings: 4,253 bound volumes, 20 periodical subscriptions, 64 records/tapes.

Undergraduate Courses offered for part-time students during daytime, evenings, summer. Complete part-time degree programs offered during daytime, evenings, summer. Adult/continuing education programs available. Career services available to part-time students: individual and group career counseling, individual job placement, employer recruitment on campus. Part-time tuition: $190 per course.

Northern Maine Vocational-Technical Institute
Presque Isle 04769

Public institution; small-town setting. Awards A. Barrier-free campus. Total enrollment: 577 (all undergraduates); 2% part-time, 45% women. Total faculty: 43. Library holdings: 11,100 bound volumes, 135 periodical subscriptions.

Undergraduate Courses offered for part-time students during daytime, evenings, summer. Complete part-time degree programs offered during daytime, evenings, summer. Adult/continuing education programs available. Career services available to part-time students: individual career counseling. Part-time tuition: $20 per semester hour for state residents, $40 per semester hour for nonresidents.

Portland School of Art
Portland 04101

Independent institution; city setting. Awards B. Total enrollment: 253 (all undergraduates); 8% part-time, 66% women. Total faculty: 29. Library holdings: 15,000 bound volumes, 65 periodical subscriptions.

Undergraduate Courses offered for part-time students during daytime. Complete part-time degree programs offered during daytime. Adult/continuing education programs available. Part-time tuition: $250 per credit hour.

Southern Maine Vocational-Technical Institute
South Portland 04106

Public institution; city setting. Awards A. Total enrollment: 1,330 (all undergraduates); 1% part-time, 25% women, 50% over 25. Total faculty: 144. Library holdings: 9,000 bound volumes, 190 periodical subscriptions.

Undergraduate Courses offered for part-time students during evenings. Complete part-time degree programs offered during evenings. External degree and adult/continuing education programs available. Part-time tuition: $25 per credit hour for state residents, $50 per credit hour for nonresidents.

Thomas College
Waterville 04901

Independent institution; small-town setting. Awards A, B, M. Total enrollment: 1,018. Undergraduate enrollment: 918; 59% part-time, 54% women, 30% over 25. Total faculty: 45. Library holdings: 18,000 bound volumes, 195 periodical subscriptions.

Undergraduate Courses offered for part-time students during daytime, evenings, weekends, summer. Complete part-time degree programs offered during daytime, evenings, weekends, summer. Adult/continuing education programs available. Career services available to part-time students: individual and group career counseling, individual job placement, employer recruitment on campus. Part-time tuition per course ranges from $165 for evening courses to $535 for daytime courses.

Graduate Part-time study available in Graduate School. Degree can be earned exclusively through evening/weekend study in Graduate School. Basic part-time expenses: $95 per credit hour tuition plus $5 per trimester fees. Institutional financial aid available to part-time graduate students in Graduate School.

Unity College
Unity 04988

Independent institution; rural setting. Awards A, B. Total enrollment: 330 (all undergraduates); 3% part-time, 30% women, 4% over 25. Total faculty: 28. Library holdings: 40,000 bound volumes, 350 periodical subscriptions, 400 records/tapes.

Undergraduate Courses offered for part-time students during daytime. Complete part-time degree programs offered during daytime. Career services available to part-time students: individual and group career counseling, individual job placement, employer recruitment on campus. Part-time tuition: $166 per semester hour.

University of Maine at Augusta
Augusta 04330

Public institution; small-town setting. Awards A, B. Total enrollment: 3,420 (all undergraduates); 79% part-time, 63% women. Total faculty: 238. Library holdings: 37,000 bound volumes, 300 periodical subscriptions, 12,000 records/tapes.

Undergraduate Courses offered for part-time students during daytime, evenings, summer. Complete part-time degree programs offered during daytime, evenings, summer. Adult/con-

tinuing education programs available. Career services available to part-time students: individual and group career counseling. Part-time tuition: $47.10 per credit for state residents, $121 per credit for nonresidents.

University of Maine at Farmington
Farmington 04938

Public institution; small-town setting. Awards A, B. Total enrollment: 2,053 (all undergraduates); 27% part-time, 72% women, 15% over 25. Total faculty: 107. Library holdings: 100,000 bound volumes, 750 periodical subscriptions, 1,209 records/tapes.

Undergraduate Courses offered for part-time students during daytime, evenings, summer. Complete part-time degree programs offered during daytime, evenings, summer. Adult/continuing education programs available. Career services available to part-time students: individual and group career counseling, individual job placement, employer recruitment on campus. Part-time tuition: $47 per credit hour for state residents, $139 per credit hour for nonresidents.

University of Maine at Fort Kent
Fort Kent 04743

Public institution; rural setting. Awards A, B. Barrier-free campus. Total enrollment: 678 (all undergraduates); 51% part-time, 49% women. Total faculty: 22. Library holdings: 43,000 bound volumes, 3,700 titles on microform, 177 periodical subscriptions, 1,408 records/tapes.

Undergraduate Courses offered for part-time students during daytime, evenings, weekends, summer. Complete part-time degree programs offered during daytime, evenings. Career services available to part-time students: individual career counseling, individual job placement. Part-time tuition: $47.10 per credit hour for state residents, $121 per credit hour for nonresidents.

University of Maine at Machias
Machias 04654

Public institution; small-town setting. Awards A, B. Total enrollment: 806 (all undergraduates); 26% part-time, 50% women. Total faculty: 42. Library holdings: 65,000 bound volumes, 310 periodical subscriptions, 1,500 records/tapes.

Undergraduate Courses offered for part-time students during daytime, evenings, summer. Complete part-time degree programs offered during daytime, evenings. Adult/continuing education programs available. Career services available to part-time students: individual and group career counseling, individual job placement, employer recruitment on campus. Part-time tuition: $47.10 per credit for state residents, $121 per credit for nonresidents.

University of Maine at Orono
Orono 04469

Public institution; small-town setting. Awards A, B, M, D. Total enrollment: 11,507. Undergraduate enrollment: 10,445; 21% part-time, 47% women, 24% over 25. Total faculty: 642. Library holdings: 588,000 bound volumes, 378,000 titles on microform, 4,200 periodical subscriptions, 6,200 records/tapes.

Undergraduate Courses offered for part-time students during daytime, evenings, weekends, summer. Complete part-time degree programs offered during daytime, evenings, weekends, summer. Adult/continuing education programs available. Career services available to part-time students: individual and group career counseling, individual job placement, employer recruitment on campus. Part-time tuition: $50.30 per credit hour for state residents, $152 per credit hour for nonresidents.

Graduate Part-time study available in Graduate School. Degree can be earned exclusively through evening/weekend study in Graduate School. Basic part-time expenses: $57.90 per credit tuition plus $20.50 per semester fees for state residents, $174.80 per credit tuition plus $20.50 per semester fees for nonresidents.

University of Maine at Presque Isle
Presque Isle 04769

Public institution; small-town setting. Awards A, B. Total enrollment: 1,187 (all undergraduates); 33% part-time, 53% women, 47% over 25. Total faculty: 86. Library holdings: 80,000 bound volumes.

Undergraduate Courses offered for part-time students during daytime, evenings, summer. Complete part-time degree programs offered during daytime, evenings, summer. External degree and adult/continuing education programs available. Career services available to part-time students: individual and group career counseling, individual job placement, employer recruitment on campus. Part-time tuition: $47.10 per credit hour for state residents, $121 per credit hour for nonresidents.

University of New England
Biddeford 04005

Independent institution; small-town setting. Awards B, D. Total enrollment: 750. Undergraduate enrollment: 470; 20% part-time, 64% women, 5% over 25. Total faculty: 49. Library holdings: 70,000 bound volumes, 495 periodical subscriptions, 500 records/tapes.

Undergraduate Courses offered for part-time students during daytime, evenings, summer. Complete part-time degree programs offered during daytime, evenings, summer. Adult/continuing education programs available. Career services available to part-time students: individual and group career counseling, individual job placement. Part-time tuition: $180 per credit.

University of Southern Maine
Portland 04103

Public institution; small-town setting. Awards A, B, M. Barrier-free campus. Total enrollment: 8,700. Undergraduate enrollment: 7,900; 50% part-time, 58% women. Total faculty: 607. Library holdings: 330,000 bound volumes, 1,568 periodical subscriptions, 500 records/tapes.

Undergraduate Courses offered for part-time students during daytime, evenings, summer. Complete part-time degree programs offered during daytime, evenings, summer. Adult/continuing education programs available. Career services available to part-time students: individual and group career counseling, individual job placement, employer recruitment on campus. Part-time tuition: $50.30 per credit for state residents, $152 per credit for nonresidents.

Graduate Part-time study available in College of Arts and Sciences, College of Education, School of Business, Economics and Management, School of Law, School of Nursing. Basic part-time expenses: $57.90 per credit tuition for state residents, $174.80 per credit tuition for nonresidents. Institutional financial aid available to part-time graduate students in College of Arts and Sciences, College of Education, School of Business, Economics and Management, School of Law, School of Nursing.

Colleges Offering Part-Time Degree Programs / Maine

Westbrook College
Portland 04103

Independent institution; city setting. Awards A, B. Total enrollment: 511 (all undergraduates); 3% part-time, 89% women. Total faculty: 100. Library holdings: 26,602 bound volumes, 267 periodical subscriptions, 146 records/tapes.

Undergraduate Courses offered for part-time students during daytime, evenings, weekends, summer. Complete part-time degree programs offered during daytime, evenings, weekends, summer. External degree and adult/continuing education programs available. Career services available to part-time students: individual career counseling, individual job placement, employer recruitment on campus. Part-time tuition per credit hour ranges from $79 for evening courses to $210 for daytime courses.

MARYLAND

Allegany Community College
Cumberland 21502

Public institution; small-town setting. Awards A. Barrier-free campus. Total enrollment: 2,321 (all undergraduates); 42% part-time, 64% women, 40% over 25. Total faculty: 137. Library holdings: 43,841 bound volumes, 9,159 titles on microform, 427 periodical subscriptions, 1,973 records/tapes.

Undergraduate Courses offered for part-time students during daytime, evenings, summer. Complete part-time degree programs offered during daytime, evenings, summer. Adult/continuing education programs available. Career services available to part-time students: individual and group career counseling, individual job placement, employer recruitment on campus. Part-time tuition: $31 per credit for area residents, $51 per credit for state residents, $91 per credit for nonresidents.

Anne Arundel Community College
Arnold 21012

Public institution; small-town setting. Awards A. Total enrollment: 9,027 (all undergraduates); 71% part-time, 59% women, 49% over 25. Total faculty: 532. Library holdings: 90,982 bound volumes, 15 titles on microform, 520 periodical subscriptions, 1,455 records/tapes.

Undergraduate Courses offered for part-time students during daytime, evenings, weekends, summer. Complete part-time degree programs offered during daytime, evenings, summer. Adult/continuing education programs available. Career services available to part-time students: individual and group career counseling, individual job placement, employer recruitment on campus. Part-time tuition: $28 per semester hour for area residents, $56 per semester hour for state residents, $112 per semester hour for nonresidents.

Baltimore Hebrew College
Baltimore 21215

Independent-religious instutition; metropolitan setting. Awards B, M, D. Total enrollment: 637. Undergraduate enrollment: 547; 32% part-time, 73% women. Total faculty: 17. Library holdings: 30,275 bound volumes, 240 periodical subscriptions.

Undergraduate Courses offered for part-time students during daytime. Complete part-time degree programs offered during daytime. Adult/continuing education programs available. Career services available to part-time students: individual career counseling, individual job placement. Part-time tuition: $65 per credit.

Bowie State College
Bowie 20715

Public institution; small-town setting. Awards B, M. Barrier-free campus. Total enrollment: 2,366. Undergraduate enrollment: 1,800; 23% part-time, 57% women, 28% over 25. Total faculty: 138. Library holdings: 176,000 bound volumes, 283,017 titles on microform, 1,001 periodical subscriptions.

Undergraduate Courses offered for part-time students during daytime, evenings, weekends, summer. Complete part-time degree programs offered during daytime, evenings, weekends, summer. Adult/continuing education programs available. Career services available to part-time students: individual and group career counseling, individual job placement, employer recruitment on campus. Part-time tuition: $42 per credit hour for state residents, $42 per credit hour for nonresidents.

Graduate Part-time study available in Graduate Programs. Degree can be earned exclusively through evening/weekend study in Graduate Programs. Basic part-time expenses: $68 per credit hour tuition plus $32 per semester (minimum) fees. Institutional financial aid available to part-time graduate students in Graduate Programs.

Capital Bible Seminary
Lanham 20706

Independent-religious institution (graduate only). Total enrollment: 136 (primarily men). Total faculty: 8.

Graduate Part-time study available in Graduate and Professional Programs. Basic part-time expenses: $91 per credit tuition plus $45 per year fees.

Capitol Institute of Technology
Laurel 20708

Independent institution; small-town setting. Awards A, B. Barrier-free campus. Total enrollment: 1,076 (all undergraduates); 48% part-time, 9% women, 40% over 25. Total faculty: 57. Library holdings: 10,700 bound volumes, 120 periodical subscriptions, 110 records/tapes.

Undergraduate Courses offered for part-time students during daytime, evenings, weekends, summer. Complete part-time degree programs offered during daytime, evenings, weekends, summer. Career services available to part-time students: individual and group career counseling, individual job placement, employer recruitment on campus. Part-time tuition: $112 per quarter hour.

Catonsville Community College
Catonsville 21228

Public institution; city setting. Awards A. Barrier-free campus. Total enrollment: 10,269 (all undergraduates); 78% part-time, 53% women, 49% over 25. Total faculty: 506. Library holdings: 110,000 bound volumes, 35,000 titles on microform, 1,000 periodical subscriptions, 20,000 records/tapes.

Undergraduate Courses offered for part-time students during daytime, evenings, weekends, summer. Complete part-time degree programs offered during daytime, evenings. Adult/continuing education programs available. Career services available to part-time students: individual and group career counseling, individual job placement, employer recruitment on campus. Part-time tuition: $26 per credit for area residents, $48 per credit for state residents, $97 per credit for nonresidents.

Maryland / Colleges Offering Part-Time Degree Programs

Cecil Community College
North East 21901

Public institution; rural setting. Awards A. Barrier-free campus. Total enrollment: 1,524 (all undergraduates); 79% part-time, 62% women, 82% over 25. Total faculty: 92. Library holdings: 20,311 bound volumes, 200 periodical subscriptions, 576 records/tapes.

Undergraduate Courses offered for part-time students during daytime, evenings, weekends, summer. Complete part-time degree programs offered during daytime, evenings, summer. Adult/continuing education programs available. Career services available to part-time students: individual and group career counseling, individual job placement. Part-time tuition: $21 per credit for area residents, $42 per credit for state residents, $84 per credit for nonresidents.

Charles County Community College
La Plata 20646

Public institution; rural setting. Awards A. Barrier-free campus. Total enrollment: 4,172 (all undergraduates); 80% part-time, 65% women. Total faculty: 218. Library holdings: 37,000 bound volumes, 3,000 titles on microform, 235 periodical subscriptions, 6,000 records/tapes.

Undergraduate Courses offered for part-time students during daytime, evenings, weekends, summer. Complete part-time degree programs offered during daytime, evenings, summer. Adult/continuing education programs available. Career services available to part-time students: individual and group career counseling, individual job placement. Part-time tuition: $28 per credit for area residents, $56 per credit for state residents, $84 per credit for nonresidents.

Chesapeake College
Wye Mills 21679

Public institution; rural setting. Awards A. Total enrollment: 1,906 (all undergraduates); 73% part-time, 70% women, 35% over 25. Total faculty: 126. Library holdings: 28,500 bound volumes, 135 periodical subscriptions, 2,200 records/tapes.

Undergraduate Courses offered for part-time students during daytime, evenings, summer. Complete part-time degree programs offered during daytime, evenings, summer. Adult/continuing education programs available. Career services available to part-time students: individual and group career counseling, individual job placement. Part-time tuition: $23 per credit hour for area residents, $46 per credit hour for state residents, $82 per credit hour for nonresidents.

College of Notre Dame of Maryland
Baltimore 21210

Independent-religious instutition; metropolitan setting. Awards B. Barrier-free campus. Total enrollment: 570 (all undergraduates); 10% part-time, 100% women, 1% over 25. Total faculty: 79. Library holdings: 206,574 bound volumes, 1,565 periodical subscriptions.

Undergraduate Courses offered for part-time students during daytime, weekends. Complete part-time degree programs offered during daytime, weekends. Adult/continuing education programs available. Career services available to part-time students: individual career counseling, individual job placement, employer recruitment on campus. Part-time tuition: $90 per credit.

Graduate Part-time study available in Graduate Studies. Degree can be earned exclusively through evening/weekend study in Graduate Studies. Basic part-time expenses: $125 per credit tuition plus $15 per semester fees.

Columbia Union College
Takoma Park 20912

Independent-religious instutition; small-town setting. Awards A, B. Total enrollment: 874 (all undergraduates); 34% part-time, 56% women. Total faculty: 86. Library holdings: 106,856 bound volumes, 490 periodical subscriptions, 6,642 records/tapes.

Undergraduate Courses offered for part-time students during daytime, evenings, summer. Complete part-time degree programs offered during daytime. External degree programs available. Career services available to part-time students: individual career counseling, individual job placement, employer recruitment on campus. Part-time tuition: $180 per semester hour.

Coppin State College
Baltimore 21216

Public institution; metropolitan setting. Awards B, M. Barrier-free campus. Total enrollment: 2,650. Undergraduate enrollment: 2,350; 23% part-time, 72% women, 20% over 25. Total faculty: 146. Library holdings: 117,645 bound volumes, 96,858 titles on microform, 692 periodical subscriptions, 4,166 records/tapes.

Undergraduate Courses offered for part-time students during daytime, evenings, weekends, summer. Complete part-time degree programs offered during daytime, evenings. Adult/continuing education programs available. Career services available to part-time students: individual and group career counseling, individual job placement, employer recruitment on campus. Part-time tuition: $42 per semester hour for state residents, $42 per semester hour for nonresidents.

Graduate Part-time study available in Division of Graduate Studies. Degree can be earned exclusively through evening/weekend study in Division of Graduate Studies. Basic part-time expenses: $57 per credit tuition plus $34 per semester fees. Institutional financial aid available to part-time graduate students in Division of Graduate Studies.

Dundalk Community College
Baltimore 21222

Public institution; metropolitan setting. Awards A. Barrier-free campus. Total enrollment: 3,270 (all undergraduates); 73% part-time, 53% women. Total faculty: 184. Library holdings: 29,065 bound volumes, 225 periodical subscriptions, 2,185 records/tapes.

Undergraduate Courses offered for part-time students during daytime, evenings, weekends, summer. Complete part-time degree programs offered during daytime, evenings, weekends, summer. Adult/continuing education programs available. Career services available to part-time students: individual and group career counseling, individual job placement, employer recruitment on campus. Part-time tuition: $26 per credit for area residents, $48 per credit for state residents, $97 per credit for nonresidents.

Essex Community College
Baltimore 21237

Public institution; metropolitan setting. Awards A. Total enrollment: 10,203 (all undergraduates); 73% part-time, 60% women, 69% over 25. Total faculty: 448. Library holdings: 100,000 bound volumes, 700 periodical subscriptions, 350 records/tapes.

Colleges Offering Part-Time Degree Programs / Maryland

Essex Community College (continued)

Undergraduate Courses offered for part-time students during daytime, evenings, weekends, summer. Complete part-time degree programs offered during daytime, evenings, weekends, summer. Adult/continuing education programs available. Career services available to part-time students: individual and group career counseling, individual job placement, employer recruitment on campus. Part-time tuition: $26 per credit for area residents, $48 per credit for state residents, $97 per credit for nonresidents.

Frederick Community College
Frederick 21701

Public institution; small-town setting. Awards A. Barrier-free campus. Total enrollment: 3,400 (all undergraduates); 67% part-time, 57% women, 60% over 25. Total faculty: 183. Library holdings: 37,000 bound volumes, 300 periodical subscriptions, 5,000 records/tapes.

Undergraduate Courses offered for part-time students during daytime, evenings, weekends, summer. Complete part-time degree programs offered during daytime, evenings, summer. Adult/continuing education programs available. Career services available to part-time students: individual and group career counseling, individual job placement, employer recruitment on campus. Part-time tuition: $25 per credit hour for area residents, $50 per credit hour for state residents, $100 per credit hour for nonresidents.

Frostburg State College
Frostburg 21532

Public institution; small-town setting. Awards B, M. Total enrollment: 3,400. Undergraduate enrollment: 2,900; 7% part-time, 53% women. Total faculty: 185. Library holdings: 339,500 bound volumes, 875 periodical subscriptions, 41,535 records/tapes.

Undergraduate Courses offered for part-time students during daytime, evenings, summer. Complete part-time degree programs offered during daytime, evenings, summer. Adult/continuing education programs available. Career services available to part-time students: individual and group career counseling. Part-time tuition: $46 per credit hour for state residents, $46 per credit hour for nonresidents.

Graduate Part-time study available in Graduate School. Degree can be earned exclusively through evening/weekend study in Graduate School. Basic part-time expenses: $68 per credit tuition plus $34.50 per semester (minimum) fees.

Garrett Community College
McHenry 21541

Public institution; rural setting. Awards A. Total enrollment: 650 (all undergraduates); 50% part-time, 42% women. Total faculty: 60. Library holdings: 25,000 bound volumes.

Undergraduate Courses offered for part-time students during daytime. Complete part-time degree programs offered during daytime. Career services available to part-time students: individual and group career counseling, individual job placement, employer recruitment on campus. Part-time tuition: $24 per credit hour for area residents, $42 per credit hour for state residents, $98 per credit hour for nonresidents.

Goucher College
Towson 21204

Independent institution; city setting. Awards B, M. Total enrollment: 1,041. Undergraduate enrollment: 893; 11% part-time, 100% women, 8% over 25. Total faculty: 256. Library holdings: 233,000 bound volumes, 6,662 titles on microform, 944 periodical subscriptions, 5,171 records/tapes.

Undergraduate Courses offered for part-time students during daytime. Complete part-time degree programs offered during daytime. Adult/continuing education programs available. Career services available to part-time students: individual and group career counseling, employer recruitment on campus. Part-time tuition: $275 per unit.

Graduate Part-time study available in Graduate Programs in Expressive Arts Therapy. Basic part-time expenses: $215 per credit tuition.

Hagerstown Business College
Hagerstown 21741

Proprietary institution; small-town setting. Awards A. Total enrollment: 264 (all undergraduates); 1% part-time, 97% women, 5% over 25. Total faculty: 24. Library holdings: 3,000 bound volumes, 50 periodical subscriptions, 245 records/tapes.

Undergraduate Courses offered for part-time students during daytime, evenings. Complete part-time degree programs offered during daytime. Adult/continuing education programs available. Career services available to part-time students: individual and group career counseling, individual job placement, employer recruitment on campus. Part-time tuition: $67 per credit hour.

Hagerstown Junior College
Hagerstown 21740

Public institution; small-town setting. Awards A. Barrier-free campus. Total enrollment: 2,637 (all undergraduates); 65% part-time, 55% women. Total faculty: 152. Library holdings: 48,000 bound volumes, 275 periodical subscriptions, 900 records/tapes.

Undergraduate Courses offered for part-time students during daytime, evenings, summer. Complete part-time degree programs offered during daytime, evenings, summer. Adult/continuing education programs available. Career services available to part-time students: individual and group career counseling, individual job placement, employer recruitment on campus. Part-time tuition: $23 per credit hour for area residents, $47 per credit hour for state residents, $72 per credit hour for nonresidents.

Harford Community College
Bel Air 21014

Public institution; small-town setting. Awards A. Total enrollment: 4,792 (all undergraduates); 72% part-time, 61% women, 49% over 25. Total faculty: 301. Library holdings: 44,842 bound volumes, 7,337 titles on microform, 530 periodical subscriptions, 6,356 records/tapes.

Undergraduate Courses offered for part-time students during daytime, evenings, weekends, summer. Complete part-time degree programs offered during daytime, evenings, weekends, summer. Adult/continuing education programs available. Career services available to part-time students: individual and group career counseling, individual job placement. Part-time tuition: $24 per credit hour for area residents, $55 per credit hour for state residents, $95 per credit hour for nonresidents.

Maryland / **Colleges Offering Part-Time Degree Programs**

Hood College
Frederick 21701

Independent-religious instutition; small-town setting. Awards B, M. Total enrollment: 1,750. Undergraduate enrollment: 1,-100; 24% part-time, 87% women, 20% over 25. Total faculty: 128. Library holdings: 140,000 bound volumes, 123,300 titles on microform, 982 periodical subscriptions, 100 records/tapes.

Undergraduate Courses offered for part-time students during daytime, evenings, summer. Complete part-time degree programs offered during daytime, evenings, summer. Adult/continuing education programs available. Career services available to part-time students: individual and group career counseling, individual job placement, employer recruitment on campus. Part-time tuition: $195 per credit.

Graduate Part-time study available in Graduate School. Basic part-time expenses: $105 per credit tuition. Institutional financial aid available to part-time graduate students in Graduate School.

Howard Community College
Columbia 21044

Public institution; city setting. Awards A. Barrier-free campus. Total enrollment: 3,429 (all undergraduates); 76% part-time, 66% women. Total faculty: 221. Library holdings: 27,018 bound volumes.

Undergraduate Courses offered for part-time students during daytime, evenings, weekends, summer. Complete part-time degree programs offered during daytime, evenings, weekends, summer. Adult/continuing education programs available. Career services available to part-time students: individual career counseling, individual job placement. Part-time tuition: $30 per credit hour for area residents, $60 per credit hour for state residents, $120 per credit hour for nonresidents.

Johns Hopkins University
Baltimore 21218

Independent institution; metropolitan setting. Awards B, M, D. Total enrollment: 3,155. Undergraduate enrollment: 2,280; 0% part-time, 32% women, 0% over 25. Total faculty: 332. Library holdings: 1.9 million bound volumes, 1.1 million titles on microform, 12,214 periodical subscriptions, 6,100 records/tapes.

Graduate Part-time study available in School of Continuing Studies, G. W. C. Whiting School of Engineering, School of Advanced International Studies, School of Hygiene and Public Health. Degree can be earned exclusively through evening/weekend study in G. W. C. Whiting School of Engineering. Basic part-time expenses: $8600 per year tuition plus $260 (one-time fee). Institutional financial aid available to part-time graduate students in School of Continuing Studies, G. W. C. Whiting School of Engineering, School of Advanced International Studies, School of Hygiene and Public Health.

Loyola College
Baltimore 21210

Independent-religious instutition; metropolitan setting. Awards B, M. Barrier-free campus. Total enrollment: 6,168. Undergraduate enrollment: 3,423; 24% part-time, 49% women, 15% over 25. Total faculty: 296. Library holdings: 210,000 bound volumes, 276,646 titles on microform, 1,565 periodical subscriptions, 11,600 records/tapes.

Undergraduate Courses offered for part-time students during daytime, evenings, summer. Complete part-time degree programs offered during daytime, evenings, summer. Adult/continuing education programs available. Career services available to part-time students: individual and group career counseling, individual job placement, employer recruitment on campus. Part-time tuition: $618.75 per course.

Graduate Part-time study available in Graduate Programs. Basic part-time expenses: $95 per credit (minimum) tuition plus $25 per semester fees.

Maryland College of Art and Design
Silver Spring 20902

Independent institution; city setting. Awards A. Barrier-free campus. Total enrollment: 63 (all undergraduates); 21% part-time, 46% women, 24% over 25. Total faculty: 15. Library holdings: 8,400 bound volumes, 33 periodical subscriptions, 127 records/tapes.

Undergraduate Courses offered for part-time students during daytime, evenings, summer. Complete part-time degree programs offered during daytime. Adult/continuing education programs available. Career services available to part-time students: individual career counseling. Part-time tuition: $95 per credit.

Maryland Institute, College of Art
Baltimore 21217

Independent institution; metropolitan setting. Awards B, M. Total enrollment: 884. Undergraduate enrollment: 736; 13% part-time, 55% women. Total faculty: 90. Library holdings: 37,-000 bound volumes, 175 periodical subscriptions.

Undergraduate Courses offered for part-time students during daytime, evenings, summer. Complete part-time degree programs offered during daytime, evenings, summer. Adult/continuing education programs available. Career services available to part-time students: individual and group career counseling, individual job placement, employer recruitment on campus. Part-time tuition: $250 per credit.

Graduate Part-time study available in Graduate Studies. Degree can be earned exclusively through evening/weekend study in Graduate Studies. Basic part-time expenses: $260 per credit tuition.

Montgomery College–Germantown Campus
Germantown 20874

Public institution; small-town setting. Awards A. Barrier-free campus. Total enrollment: 2,592 (all undergraduates); 82% part-time, 60% women, 54% over 25. Total faculty: 93. Library holdings: 46,154 bound volumes, 20,000 titles on microform, 522 periodical subscriptions, 2,600 records/tapes.

Undergraduate Courses offered for part-time students during daytime, evenings, weekends, summer. Complete part-time degree programs offered during daytime. Adult/continuing education programs available. Career services available to part-time students: individual career counseling, individual job placement. Part-time tuition: $36.30 per credit for area residents, $69.30 per credit for state residents, $94.60 per credit for nonresidents.

Montgomery College–Rockville Campus
Rockville 20850

Public institution; city setting. Awards A. Barrier-free campus. Total enrollment: 12,947 (all undergraduates); 66% part-time, 52% women, 34% over 25. Total faculty: 576. Library holdings: 108,148 bound volumes, 3,898 titles on microform, 858 periodical subscriptions, 6,353 records/tapes.

Colleges Offering Part-Time Degree Programs / Maryland

Montgomery College–Rockville Campus (continued)

Undergraduate Courses offered for part-time students during daytime, evenings, weekends, summer. Complete part-time degree programs offered during daytime. Adult/continuing education programs available. Career services available to part-time students: individual career counseling, individual job placement, employer recruitment on campus. Part-time tuition: $36.30 per credit for area residents, $69.30 per credit for state residents, $94.60 per credit for nonresidents.

Montgomery College–Takoma Park Campus
Takoma Park 20912

Public institution; small-town setting. Awards A. Barrier-free campus. Total enrollment: 4,775 (all undergraduates); 74% part-time, 63% women, 46% over 25. Total faculty: 195. Library holdings: 51,561 bound volumes, 297 titles on microform, 404 periodical subscriptions, 4,260 records/tapes.

Undergraduate Courses offered for part-time students during daytime, evenings, weekends, summer. Complete part-time degree programs offered during daytime. Adult/continuing education programs available. Career services available to part-time students: individual career counseling, individual job placement. Part-time tuition: $36.30 per credit for area residents, $69.30 per credit for state residents, $94.60 per credit for nonresidents.

Morgan State University
Baltimore 21239

Public institution; metropolitan setting. Awards B, M, D. Total enrollment: 4,555. Undergraduate enrollment: 4,050; 20% part-time, 55% women. Total faculty: 356. Library holdings: 279,823 bound volumes, 1,265 periodical subscriptions, 8,020 records/tapes.

Undergraduate Courses offered for part-time students during daytime, evenings, summer. Complete part-time degree programs offered during daytime, evenings, summer. Adult/continuing education programs available. Career services available to part-time students: individual and group career counseling, individual job placement, employer recruitment on campus. Part-time tuition: $50 per semester hour for state residents, $55 per semester hour for nonresidents.

Graduate Part-time study available in School of Graduate Studies. Basic part-time expenses: $55 per credit tuition plus $35 per semester fees for state residents, $65 per credit tuition plus $35 per semester fees for nonresidents.

Mount Saint Mary's College
Emmitsburg 21727

Independent-religious instutition; rural setting. Awards B, M. Total enrollment: 1,625. Undergraduate enrollment: 1,419; 8% part-time, 45% women. Total faculty: 103. Library holdings: 135,000 bound volumes, 6,000 titles on microform, 675 periodical subscriptions, 1,200 records/tapes.

Undergraduate Courses offered for part-time students during daytime, evenings, summer. Complete part-time degree programs offered during daytime, evenings, summer. Adult/continuing education programs available. Career services available to part-time students: individual and group career counseling, individual job placement, employer recruitment on campus. Part-time tuition: $165 per credit.

Graduate Part-time study available in Graduate School. Degree can be earned exclusively through evening/weekend study in Graduate School. Basic part-time expenses: $115 per credit tuition.

Prince George's Community College
Largo 20772

Public institution; small-town setting. Awards A. Barrier-free campus. Total enrollment: 15,354 (all undergraduates); 72% part-time, 60% women, 42% over 25. Total faculty: 645. Library holdings: 68,675 bound volumes, 7,000 records/tapes.

Undergraduate Courses offered for part-time students during daytime, evenings, weekends, summer. Complete part-time degree programs offered during daytime, evenings, weekends, summer. Adult/continuing education programs available. Career services available to part-time students: individual and group career counseling, individual job placement, employer recruitment on campus. Part-time tuition: $32 per credit hour for area residents, $75 per credit hour for state residents, $125 per credit hour for nonresidents.

St John's College
Annapolis 21404

Independent institution; small-town setting. Awards B, M. Total enrollment: 449. Undergraduate enrollment: 392; 0% part-time, 45% women, 5% over 25. Total faculty: 50. Library holdings: 75,000 bound volumes, 60 periodical subscriptions, 460 records/tapes.

Graduate Part-time study available in Graduate Institute in Liberal Education. Basic part-time expenses: $480 per course tuition. Institutional financial aid available to part-time graduate students in Graduate Institute in Liberal Education.

St Mary's College of Maryland
St Mary's City 20686

Public institution; rural setting. Awards B. Total enrollment: 1,330 (all undergraduates); 14% part-time, 55% women, 10% over 25. Total faculty: 107. Library holdings: 100,615 bound volumes, 17,500 titles on microform, 702 periodical subscriptions, 2,403 records/tapes.

Undergraduate Courses offered for part-time students during daytime, evenings, summer. Complete part-time degree programs offered during daytime, evenings, summer. Adult/continuing education programs available. Career services available to part-time students: individual and group career counseling, individual job placement, employer recruitment on campus. Part-time tuition: $51 per credit for state residents, $51 per credit for nonresidents.

Salisbury State College
Salisbury 21801

Public institution; small-town setting. Awards B, M. Barrier-free campus. Total enrollment: 4,506. Undergraduate enrollment: 3,660; 22% part-time, 50% women. Total faculty: 243. Library holdings: 250,000 bound volumes, 1,800 periodical subscriptions, 8,500 records/tapes.

Undergraduate Courses offered for part-time students during daytime, evenings, summer. Complete part-time degree programs offered during daytime, evenings, summer. Adult/continuing education programs available. Career services available to part-time students: individual and group career counseling, individual job placement, employer recruitment on campus. Part-time tuition: $44 per semester hour for state residents, $58 per semester hour for nonresidents.

Graduate Part-time study available in Graduate Division. Basic part-time expenses: $70 per credit hour tuition plus $16 per semester fees for state residents, $74 per credit hour tuition plus $16 per semester fees for nonresidents. Institutional financial aid available to part-time graduate students in Graduate Division.

Sojourner-Douglass College
Baltimore 21205

Independent institution; metropolitan setting. Awards B. Barrier-free campus. Total enrollment: 447 (all undergraduates); 3% part-time, 80% women. Total faculty: 53. Library holdings: 10,000 bound volumes, 25 periodical subscriptions.

Undergraduate Courses offered for part-time students during daytime, evenings, weekends, summer. Complete part-time degree programs offered during daytime, evenings, weekends, summer. External degree and adult/continuing education programs available. Career services available to part-time students: individual career counseling. Part-time tuition: $110 per credit.

Towson State University
Towson 21204

Public institution; city setting. Awards B, M. Barrier-free campus. Total enrollment: 15,155. Undergraduate enrollment: 13,975; 33% part-time, 57% women, 24% over 25. Total faculty: 883. Library holdings: 386,535 bound volumes, 380,229 titles on microform, 2,337 periodical subscriptions, 14,515 records/tapes.

Undergraduate Courses offered for part-time students during daytime, evenings, weekends, summer. Complete part-time degree programs offered during daytime, evenings, weekends, summer. Adult/continuing education programs available. Career services available to part-time students: individual and group career counseling, individual job placement, employer recruitment on campus. Part-time tuition: $45 per credit for state residents, $45 per credit for nonresidents.

Graduate Part-time study available in Graduate School. Basic part-time expenses: $65 per credit tuition plus $43 per semester fees. Institutional financial aid available to part-time graduate students in Graduate School.

University of Baltimore
Baltimore 21201

Public institution; metropolitan setting. Awards B, M. Barrier-free campus. Total enrollment: 5,128. Undergraduate enrollment: 2,651; 62% part-time, 46% women. Total faculty: 266. Library holdings: 320,501 bound volumes, 52,945 titles on microform, 1,275 periodical subscriptions.

Undergraduate Courses offered for part-time students during daytime, evenings, weekends, summer. Complete part-time degree programs offered during daytime, evenings, weekends, summer. Career services available to part-time students: individual and group career counseling, individual job placement, employer recruitment on campus. Part-time tuition: $51.50 per semester hour for state residents, $51.50 per semester hour for nonresidents.

Graduate Part-time study available in Graduate School, School of Law. Basic part-time expenses: $72.50 per credit hour tuition plus $35.50 per semester (minimum) fees. Institutional financial aid available to part-time graduate students in Graduate School, School of Law.

University of Maryland at Baltimore
Baltimore 21201

Public institution; metropolitan setting. Awards B, M, D. Total enrollment: 4,682. Undergraduate enrollment: 1,135; 8% part-time, 81% women. Total faculty: 1,283. Library holdings: 501,706 bound volumes, 7,803 periodical subscriptions, 1,822 records/tapes.

Undergraduate Courses offered for part-time students during daytime, evenings. Complete part-time degree programs offered during daytime, evenings. Adult/continuing education programs available. Career services available to part-time students: individual career counseling. Part-time tuition: $64 per credit hour for state residents, $64 per credit hour for nonresidents.

Graduate Part-time study available in Graduate School, Dental School, School of Law, School of Medicine, School of Pharmacy, School of Social Work and Community Planning. Basic part-time expenses: $82 per credit tuition plus $95.50 per semester fees for state residents, $145 per credit tuition plus $95.50 per semester fees for nonresidents.

University of Maryland at College Park
College Park 20742

Public institution; small-town setting. Awards B, M, D. Total enrollment: 37,413. Undergraduate enrollment: 29,510; 16% part-time, 46% women, 11% over 25. Total faculty: 2,346. Library holdings: 1.6 million bound volumes, 1.7 million titles on microform, 19,441 periodical subscriptions, 26,000 records/tapes.

Undergraduate Courses offered for part-time students during daytime, evenings, summer. Complete part-time degree programs offered during daytime, evenings, summer. Adult/continuing education programs available. Career services available to part-time students: individual and group career counseling, individual job placement, employer recruitment on campus. Part-time tuition: $68 per semester hour for state residents, $68 per semester hour for nonresidents.

Graduate Part-time study available in Graduate School. Basic part-time expenses: $82 per credit tuition plus $88 per semester fees for state residents, $145 per credit tuition plus $88 per semester fees for nonresidents.

University of Maryland Baltimore County
Catonsville 21228

Public institution; city setting. Awards B, M, D. Barrier-free campus. Total enrollment: 7,966. Undergraduate enrollment: 7,443; 24% part-time, 52% women, 20% over 25. Total faculty: 478. Library holdings: 389,000 bound volumes, 1,705 titles on microform, 3,205 periodical subscriptions, 68,152 records/tapes.

Undergraduate Courses offered for part-time students during daytime, evenings, summer. Complete part-time degree programs offered during daytime, evenings, summer. Adult/continuing education programs available. Career services available to part-time students: individual and group career counseling, individual job placement, employer recruitment on campus. Part-time tuition and fees per semester (1 to 9 credit hours) range from $68 to $612 for state residents, $83 to $627 for nonresidents.

Graduate Part-time study available in Graduate School. Basic part-time expenses: $82 per credit tuition plus $37 per semester (minimum) fees for state residents, $145 per credit tuition plus $37 per semester (minimum) fees for nonresidents. Institutional financial aid available to part-time graduate students in Graduate School.

Colleges Offering Part-Time Degree Programs / *Maryland*

University of Maryland Eastern Shore
Princess Anne 21853

Public institution; rural setting. Awards B, M, D. Total enrollment: 1,223. Undergraduate enrollment: 1,160; 17% part-time, 54% women, 20% over 25. Total faculty: 94. Library holdings: 106,050 bound volumes, 840 periodical subscriptions, 1,564 records/tapes.

Undergraduate Courses offered for part-time students during daytime, evenings, weekends, summer. Complete part-time degree programs offered during daytime. Adult/continuing education programs available. Career services available to part-time students: individual and group career counseling, individual job placement, employer recruitment on campus. Part-time tuition: $65 per credit for state residents, $65 per credit for nonresidents.

Graduate Part-time study available in Graduate Programs. Basic part-time expenses: $82 per credit tuition plus $24 per semester fees for state residents, $145 per credit tuition plus $24 per semester fees for nonresidents. Institutional financial aid available to part-time graduate students in Graduate Programs.

University of Maryland, University College
College Park 20742

Public institution; small-town setting. Awards B, M. Barrier-free campus. Total enrollment: 11,567. Undergraduate enrollment: 10,800; 93% part-time, 51% women, 69% over 25. Total faculty: 675. Library holdings: 1.5 million bound volumes, 1.5 million titles on microform, 16,481 periodical subscriptions, 48,724 records/tapes.

Undergraduate Courses offered for part-time students during daytime, evenings, weekends, summer. Complete part-time degree programs offered during daytime, evenings, weekends, summer. External degree and adult/continuing education programs available. Career services available to part-time students: individual and group career counseling. Part-time tuition: $71 per credit.

Villa Julie College
Stevenson 21153

Independent institution; rural setting. Awards A, B. Barrier-free campus. Total enrollment: 1,031 (all undergraduates); 38% part-time, 93% women. Total faculty: 120. Library holdings: 26,131 bound volumes, 68 titles on microform, 260 periodical subscriptions, 1,280 records/tapes.

Undergraduate Courses offered for part-time students during daytime, evenings, summer. Complete part-time degree programs offered during daytime, evenings, summer. Career services available to part-time students: individual and group career counseling, individual job placement, employer recruitment on campus. Part-time tuition: $80 per credit.

Washington Bible College
Lanham 20706

Independent-religious instutition; small-town setting. Awards B. Barrier-free campus. Total enrollment: 438 (all undergraduates); 44% part-time, 35% women, 52% over 25. Total faculty: 42. Library holdings: 37,000 bound volumes, 702 titles on microform, 250 periodical subscriptions, 1,722 records/tapes.

Undergraduate Courses offered for part-time students during daytime, evenings, weekends, summer. Complete part-time degree programs offered during daytime, evenings, weekends, summer. Adult/continuing education programs available. Career services available to part-time students: individual and group career counseling, individual job placement, employer recruitment on campus. Part-time tuition: $89 per credit hour.

Washington College
Chestertown 21620

Independent institution; small-town setting. Awards B, M. Total enrollment: 797. Undergraduate enrollment: 684; 2% part-time, 50% women. Total faculty: 73. Library holdings: 140,000 bound volumes, 600 periodical subscriptions.

Undergraduate Courses offered for part-time students during daytime, evenings. Complete part-time degree programs offered during daytime, evenings. Adult/continuing education programs available. Career services available to part-time students: individual and group career counseling, individual job placement, employer recruitment on campus. Part-time tuition: $770 per course.

Washington Theological Union
Silver Spring 20903

Independent-religious institution (graduate only). Total enrollment: 314 (coed; 54% part-time). Total faculty: 59. Library holdings: 130,000 bound volumes, 36 microforms.

Graduate Part-time study available in Graduate and Professional Programs. Basic part-time expenses: $209 per credit tuition. Institutional financial aid available to part-time graduate students in Graduate and Professional Programs.

Western Maryland College
Westminster 21157

Independent institution; small-town setting. Awards B, M. Total enrollment: 1,765. Undergraduate enrollment: 1,284; 6% part-time, 55% women, 1% over 25. Total faculty: 133. Library holdings: 130,000 bound volumes, 180,000 titles on microform, 1,000 periodical subscriptions, 600 records/tapes.

Undergraduate Courses offered for part-time students during daytime, summer. Complete part-time degree programs offered during daytime. Career services available to part-time students: individual and group career counseling, individual job placement, employer recruitment on campus. Part-time tuition: $206 per semester hour.

Graduate Part-time study available in Graduate Studies. Basic part-time expenses: $100 per credit tuition.

Wor-Wic Tech Community College
Salisbury 21801

Public institution; small-town setting. Awards A. Total enrollment: 896 (all undergraduates); 74% part-time, 75% women, 64% over 25. Total faculty: 75.

Undergraduate Courses offered for part-time students during daytime, evenings, weekends, summer. Complete part-time degree programs offered during daytime, evenings. Adult/continuing education programs available. Career services available to part-time students: individual and group career counseling, individual job placement, employer recruitment on campus. Part-time tuition: $21 per credit for area residents, $49 per credit for state residents, $99 per credit for nonresidents.

MASSACHUSETTS

American Institute of Banking
Boston 02114

Independent institution; metropolitan setting. Awards A. Total enrollment: 306 (all undergraduates); 100% part-time, 65% women, 80% over 25. Total faculty: 110.

Undergraduate Courses offered for part-time students during evenings, weekends, summer. Complete part-time degree programs offered during evenings. Adult/continuing education programs available. Career services available to part-time students: individual career counseling. Part-time tuition per course: $115 ($200 for computer courses) for students employed by AIB member institutions, $175 ($200 for computer courses) for students employed by nonmember banks, $230 ($400 for computer courses) for students not employed by banks.

American International College
Springfield 01109

Independent institution; city setting. Awards B, M, D. Total enrollment: 2,280. Undergraduate enrollment: 1,325; 7% part-time, 44% women, 2% over 25. Total faculty: 123. Library holdings: 106,324 bound volumes, 12,759 titles on microform, 519 periodical subscriptions, 3,423 records/tapes.

Undergraduate Courses offered for part-time students during daytime, evenings, summer. Complete part-time degree programs offered during daytime, evenings, summer. External degree and adult/continuing education programs available. Career services available to part-time students: individual and group career counseling, individual job placement, employer recruitment on campus. Part-time tuition: $148 per credit.

Graduate Part-time study available in College of Continuing and Graduate Studies. Basic part-time expenses: $154 per credit tuition.

Anna Maria College for Men and Women
Paxton 01612

Independent-religious instutition; small-town setting. Awards A, B, M. Total enrollment: 1,500. Undergraduate enrollment: 585; 12% part-time, 78% women, 6% over 25. Total faculty: 78. Library holdings: 50,000 bound volumes, 280 periodical subscriptions.

Undergraduate Courses offered for part-time students during daytime, evenings, summer. Complete part-time degree programs offered during daytime, evenings, summer. Adult/continuing education programs available. Part-time tuition: $195 per course.

Graduate Part-time study available in Graduate Division. Degree can be earned exclusively through evening/weekend study in Graduate Division. Basic part-time expenses: $195 per course tuition plus $20 per semester fees.

Assumption College
Worcester 01609

Independent-religious instutition; city setting. Awards B, M. Total enrollment: 2,000. Undergraduate enrollment: 1,600; 5% part-time, 50% women, 0% over 25. Total faculty: 148. Library holdings: 152,919 bound volumes, 3,080 titles on microform, 863 periodical subscriptions.

Undergraduate Courses offered for part-time students during daytime, evenings, summer. Complete part-time degree programs offered during daytime, evenings, summer. Adult/continuing education programs available. Career services available to part-time students: individual and group career counseling, individual job placement, employer recruitment on campus. Part-time tuition: $704 per course.

Graduate Part-time study available in Graduate School. Basic part-time expenses: $115 per credit (minimum) tuition.

Babson College
Babson Park 02157

Independent institution; small-town setting. Awards B, M. Total enrollment: 3,137. Undergraduate enrollment: 1,403; 0% part-time, 34% women. Total faculty: 129. Library holdings: 89,997 bound volumes, 127,522 titles on microform, 984 periodical subscriptions.

Graduate Part-time study available in Graduate Program in Business Administration. Degree can be earned exclusively through evening/weekend study in Graduate Program in Business Administration. Basic part-time expenses: $249 per credit tuition.

Bay Path Junior College
Longmeadow 01106

Independent institution; city setting. Awards A. Total enrollment: 660 (all undergraduates); 3% part-time, 100% women, 1% over 25. Total faculty: 35. Library holdings: 30,000 bound volumes, 170 periodical subscriptions, 2,000 records/tapes.

Undergraduate Courses offered for part-time students during daytime. Complete part-time degree programs offered during daytime. Adult/continuing education programs available. Career services available to part-time students: individual and group career counseling, individual job placement, employer recruitment on campus. Part-time tuition: $143 per credit.

Bay State Junior College
Boston 02116

Independent institution; metropolitan setting. Awards A. Total enrollment: 525 (all undergraduates); 11% part-time, 91% women, 6% over 25. Total faculty: 27. Library holdings: 2,500 bound volumes, 50 periodical subscriptions.

Undergraduate Courses offered for part-time students during evenings. Complete part-time degree programs offered during evenings. Adult/continuing education programs available. Career services available to part-time students: individual and group career counseling, individual job placement, employer recruitment on campus. Part-time tuition: $410 per course.

Becker Junior College–Leicester Campus
Leicester 01524

Independent institution; small-town setting. Awards A. Total enrollment: 532 (all undergraduates); 3% part-time, 65% women, 4% over 25. Total faculty: 48. Library holdings: 25,500 bound volumes, 185 periodical subscriptions, 952 records/tapes.

Undergraduate Courses offered for part-time students during daytime, evenings. Complete part-time degree programs offered during daytime, evenings. Adult/continuing education programs available. Career services available to part-time students: individual and group career counseling, individual job placement, employer recruitment on campus. Part-time tuition: $111 per credit.

Colleges Offering Part-Time Degree Programs / *Massachusetts*

Becker Junior College–Worcester Campus
Worcester 01609

Independent institution; city setting. Awards A. Total enrollment: 720 (all undergraduates); 2% part-time, 97% women. Total faculty: 42. Library holdings: 29,000 bound volumes, 185 periodical subscriptions, 1,300 records/tapes.

Undergraduate Courses offered for part-time students during daytime, evenings, summer. Complete part-time degree programs offered during daytime, evenings, summer. Adult/continuing education programs available. Career services available to part-time students: individual and group career counseling, individual job placement, employer recruitment on campus. Part-time tuition: $117 per credit.

Bentley College
Waltham 02254

Independent institution; city setting. Awards A, B, M. Total enrollment: 8,104. Undergraduate enrollment: 3,920; 3% part-time, 50% women. Total faculty: 296. Library holdings: 114,000 bound volumes, 900 periodical subscriptions, 785 records/tapes.

Undergraduate Courses offered for part-time students during daytime, evenings, summer. Complete part-time degree programs offered during daytime, evenings. Adult/continuing education programs available. Career services available to part-time students: individual and group career counseling, individual job placement, employer recruitment on campus. Part-time tuition: $610 per course.

Graduate Part-time study available in Graduate School. Basic part-time expenses: $220 per credit tuition. Institutional financial aid available to part-time graduate students in Graduate School.

Berkshire Christian College
Lenox 01240

Independent-religious instustion; small-town setting. Awards A, B. Barrier-free campus. Total enrollment: 143 (all undergraduates); 10% part-time, 52% women, 10% over 25. Total faculty: 21. Library holdings: 40,600 bound volumes, 19 titles on microform, 415 periodical subscriptions, 1,510 records/tapes.

Undergraduate Courses offered for part-time students during daytime, summer. Complete part-time degree programs offered during daytime. Adult/continuing education programs available. Career services available to part-time students: individual and group career counseling, individual job placement, employer recruitment on campus. Part-time tuition: $155 per credit hour.

Berkshire Community College
Pittsfield 01201

Public institution; city setting. Awards A. Total enrollment: 2,028 (all undergraduates); 34% part-time, 54% women, 30% over 25. Total faculty: 107. Library holdings: 45,423 bound volumes, 87 titles on microform, 331 periodical subscriptions, 2,421 records/tapes.

Undergraduate Courses offered for part-time students during daytime, evenings, summer. Complete part-time degree programs offered during daytime, evenings, summer. Adult/continuing education programs available. Career services available to part-time students: individual and group career counseling, individual job placement, employer recruitment on campus. Part-time tuition and fees per semester (1 to 11 credits) range from $57 to $371 for state residents, $122 to $1086 for nonresidents.

Boston Architectural Center
Boston 02115

Independent institution; metropolitan setting. Awards B. Barrier-free campus. Total enrollment: 653 (all undergraduates); 21% women. Total faculty: 142. Library holdings: 17,875 bound volumes, 120 periodical subscriptions.

Undergraduate Courses offered for part-time students during evenings, summer. Complete part-time degree programs offered during evenings, summer. Adult/continuing education programs available. Part-time tuition: $180 per credit.

Boston College
Chestnut Hill 02167

Independent-religious instutition; city setting. Awards B, M, D. Total enrollment: 14,059. Undergraduate enrollment: 10,504; 18% part-time, 58% women. Total faculty: 857. Library holdings: 921,418 bound volumes, 6,141 periodical subscriptions, 27,000 records/tapes.

Undergraduate Courses offered for part-time students during daytime, evenings, weekends, summer. Complete part-time degree programs offered during daytime, evenings, summer. Adult/continuing education programs available. Career services available to part-time students: individual and group career counseling, individual job placement, employer recruitment on campus. Part-time tuition: $143 per credit.

Graduate Part-time study available in Graduate School of Arts and Sciences, Graduate School of Management, Graduate School of Social Work. Degree can be earned exclusively through evening/weekend study in Graduate School of Management. Basic part-time expenses: $238 per credit tuition. Institutional financial aid available to part-time graduate students in Graduate School of Arts and Sciences, Graduate School of Social Work.

Boston Conservatory
Boston 02215

Independent institution; metropolitan setting. Awards B, M. Total enrollment: 392. Undergraduate enrollment: 325; 5% part-time, 67% women. Total faculty: 95. Library holdings: 23,772 bound volumes, 1 title on microform, 76 periodical subscriptions, 5,297 records/tapes.

Undergraduate Courses offered for part-time students during daytime, summer. Complete part-time degree programs offered during daytime. Adult/continuing education programs available. Career services available to part-time students: individual career counseling. Part-time tuition: $205 per credit.

Graduate Part-time study available in Graduate Program. Basic part-time expenses: $205 per credit hour tuition plus $15 per semester fees.

Boston University
Boston 02215

Independent institution; metropolitan setting. Awards A, B, M, D. Total enrollment: 27,724. Undergraduate enrollment: 12,770; 2% part-time, 51% women. Total faculty: 2,600. Library holdings: 1.5 million bound volumes, 2.0 million titles on microform, 25,400 periodical subscriptions, 20,000 records/tapes.

Undergraduate Courses offered for part-time students during daytime, evenings, summer. Complete part-time degree programs offered during daytime, evenings, summer. Adult/continuing education programs available. Career services available to part-time students: individual and group career counseling, individual job placement, employer recruitment on campus. Part-time tuition: $280 per credit.

Massachusetts / **Colleges Offering Part-Time Degree Programs**

Graduate Part-time study available in Graduate School, College of Engineering, Metropolitan College, Sargent College of Allied Health Professions, School of Education, School of Law, School of Management, School of Medicine, School of Nursing, School of Public Communication, School of Social Work, School of Theology, University Professors' Program. Degree can be earned exclusively through evening/weekend study in Metropolitan College, School of Education, School of Management, School of Public Communication. Basic part-time expenses: $280 per credit tuition plus $30 per semester fees. Institutional financial aid available to part-time graduate students in Graduate School, College of Engineering, Metropolitan College, Sargent College of Allied Health Professions, School of Education, School of Law, School of Management, School of Medicine, School of Nursing, School of Public Communication, School of Social Work, School of Theology, University Professors' Program.

Bradford College
Bradford 01830

Independent institution; small-town setting. Awards A, B. Total enrollment: 380 (all undergraduates); 15% part-time, 52% women, 5% over 25. Total faculty: 44. Library holdings: 55,000 bound volumes, 200 periodical subscriptions, 650 records/tapes.

Undergraduate Courses offered for part-time students during daytime, evenings. Complete part-time degree programs offered during daytime. Adult/continuing education programs available. Career services available to part-time students: individual and group career counseling, individual job placement. Part-time tuition: $90 per credit.

Brandeis University
Waltham 02254

Independent institution; city setting. Awards B, M, D. Total enrollment: 3,245. Undergraduate enrollment: 2,678; 1% part-time, 50% women, 1% over 25. Total faculty: 448. Library holdings: 804,000 bound volumes, 213,000 titles on microform, 3,900 periodical subscriptions, 12,723 records/tapes.

Undergraduate Courses offered for part-time students during daytime, summer. Complete part-time degree programs offered during daytime, summer. Adult/continuing education programs available. Career services available to part-time students: individual and group career counseling, employer recruitment on campus. Part-time tuition: $1169 per course.

Bridgewater State College
Bridgewater 02324

Public institution; small-town setting. Awards B, M. Total enrollment: 4,990. Undergraduate enrollment: 4,950; 4% part-time, 58% women, 12% over 25. Total faculty: 302. Library holdings: 211,004 bound volumes, 88,800 titles on microform, 1,536 periodical subscriptions, 7,021 records/tapes.

Undergraduate Courses offered for part-time students during daytime, evenings, weekends, summer. Complete part-time degree programs offered during daytime, evenings. Adult/continuing education programs available. Career services available to part-time students: individual and group career counseling, individual job placement, employer recruitment on campus. Part-time tuition: $39 per semester hour for state residents, $124 per semester hour for nonresidents.

Graduate Part-time study available in Graduate School. Basic part-time expenses: $55 per semester hour tuition plus $35 per semester fees for state residents, $65 per semester hour tuition plus $35 per semester fees for nonresidents. Institutional financial aid available to part-time graduate students in Graduate School.

Bristol Community College
Fall River 02720

Public institution; city setting. Awards A. Barrier-free campus. Total enrollment: 2,669 (all undergraduates); 24% part-time, 63% women. Total faculty: 127.

Undergraduate Courses offered for part-time students during daytime. Complete part-time degree programs offered during daytime. Adult/continuing education programs available. Career services available to part-time students: individual and group career counseling, individual job placement. Part-time tuition: $26.50 per credit for state residents, $87.50 per credit for nonresidents.

Bunker Hill Community College
Boston 02129

Public institution; metropolitan setting. Awards A. Barrier-free campus. Total enrollment: 3,423 (all undergraduates); 27% part-time, 54% women, 26% over 25. Total faculty: 153. Library holdings: 34,110 bound volumes, 467 titles on microform, 275 periodical subscriptions, 4,680 records/tapes.

Undergraduate Courses offered for part-time students during daytime, evenings, weekends, summer. Complete part-time degree programs offered during daytime, evenings, weekends, summer. External degree and adult/continuing education programs available. Career services available to part-time students: individual and group career counseling, individual job placement, employer recruitment on campus. Part-time tuition: $28 per credit hour for state residents, $95 per credit hour for nonresidents.

Cape Cod Community College
West Barnstable 02668

Public institution; rural setting. Awards A. Total enrollment: 1,893 (all undergraduates); 22% part-time, 60% women, 33% over 25. Total faculty: 141. Library holdings: 55,000 bound volumes, 350 titles on microform, 412 periodical subscriptions, 1,525 records/tapes.

Undergraduate Courses offered for part-time students during daytime, evenings, summer. Complete part-time degree programs offered during daytime, evenings, summer. Adult/continuing education programs available. Career services available to part-time students: individual and group career counseling, individual job placement, employer recruitment on campus. Part-time tuition: $30 per credit hour for state residents, $95 per credit hour for nonresidents.

Central New England College
Worcester 01610

Independent institution; city setting. Awards A, B. Barrier-free campus. Total enrollment: 2,146 (all undergraduates); 80% part-time, 20% women. Total faculty: 129. Library holdings: 35,000 bound volumes, 60 titles on microform, 225 periodical subscriptions, 1,000 records/tapes.

Undergraduate Courses offered for part-time students during daytime, evenings, weekends, summer. Complete part-time degree programs offered during daytime, evenings, weekends, summer. Adult/continuing education programs available. Career services available to part-time students: individual career counseling, individual job placement. Part-time tuition: $90 per credit. Part-time tuition at Westboro Campus: $100 per credit.

Colleges Offering Part-Time Degree Programs / *Massachusetts*

Chamberlayne Junior College
Boston 02116

Independent institution; metropolitan setting. Awards A. Total enrollment: 853 (all undergraduates); 23% part-time, 59% women, 10% over 25. Total faculty: 55. Library holdings: 25,000 bound volumes, 42 periodical subscriptions.

Undergraduate Courses offered for part-time students during daytime, summer. Complete part-time degree programs offered during daytime. Career services available to part-time students: individual and group career counseling, individual job placement, employer recruitment on campus. Part-time tuition: $131 per credit hour.

Clark University
Worcester 01610

Independent institution; city setting. Awards B, M, D. Total enrollment: 2,700. Undergraduate enrollment: 2,050; 2% part-time, 52% women. Total faculty: 175. Library holdings: 480,000 bound volumes, 2,300 periodical subscriptions.

Undergraduate Courses offered for part-time students during daytime, evenings, summer. Complete part-time degree programs offered during daytime, evenings, summer. Adult/continuing education programs available. Career services available to part-time students: individual and group career counseling, individual job placement, employer recruitment on campus. Part-time tuition: $1000 per course.

Graduate Part-time study available in Graduate School, College of Professional and Continuing Education. Degree can be earned exclusively through evening/weekend study in College of Professional and Continuing Education. Basic part-time expenses: $1050 per course tuition. Institutional financial aid available to part-time graduate students in Graduate School, College of Professional and Continuing Education.

Curry College
Milton 02186

Independent institution; small-town setting. Awards B, M. Total enrollment: 1,189. Undergraduate enrollment: 1,167; 6% part-time, 50% women. Total faculty: 112. Library holdings: 110,000 bound volumes, 450 titles on microform, 1,000 periodical subscriptions.

Undergraduate Courses offered for part-time students during daytime, evenings, summer. Complete part-time degree programs offered during daytime, evenings. Adult/continuing education programs available. Career services available to part-time students: individual and group career counseling, individual job placement, employer recruitment on campus. Part-time tuition: $228 per credit hour.

Graduate Part-time study available in Graduate Program in Education. Degree can be earned exclusively through evening/weekend study in Graduate Program in Education. Basic part-time expenses: $100 per credit tuition. Institutional financial aid available to part-time graduate students in Graduate Program in Education.

Dean Junior College
Franklin 02038

Independent institution; small-town setting. Awards A. Total enrollment: 1,013 (all undergraduates); 0% part-time, 60% women, 1% over 25. Total faculty: 82. Library holdings: 49,937 bound volumes, 180 titles on microform, 280 periodical subscriptions, 3,100 records/tapes.

Undergraduate Courses offered for part-time students during daytime, evenings, summer. Complete part-time degree programs offered during daytime, evenings, summer. Career services available to part-time students: individual and group career counseling, individual job placement. Part-time tuition: $55 per credit.

Eastern Nazarene College
Quincy 02170

Independent-religious instutition; city setting. Awards A, B, M. Total enrollment: 888. Undergraduate enrollment: 779; 7% part-time, 58% women, 14% over 25. Total faculty: 66. Library holdings: 93,000 bound volumes, 600 periodical subscriptions.

Undergraduate Courses offered for part-time students during daytime, evenings, summer. Complete part-time degree programs offered during daytime, summer. Adult/continuing education programs available. Career services available to part-time students: individual and group career counseling, individual job placement, employer recruitment on campus. Part-time tuition: $150 per hour.

Graduate Part-time study available in Division of Graduate Studies. Basic part-time expenses: $165 per credit tuition plus $15 per semester fees.

Elms College
Chicopee 01013

Independent-religious instutition; city setting. Awards B. Barrier-free campus. Total enrollment: 741 (all undergraduates); 29% part-time, 100% women, 33% over 25. Total faculty: 75. Library holdings: 79,362 bound volumes, 416 periodical subscriptions, 14,876 records/tapes.

Undergraduate Courses offered for part-time students during daytime, evenings, summer. Complete part-time degree programs offered during daytime, evenings, summer. Adult/continuing education programs available. Career services available to part-time students: individual and group career counseling, individual job placement, employer recruitment on campus. Part-time tuition: $100 per credit.

Emerson College
Boston 02116

Independent institution; metropolitan setting. Awards B, M. Total enrollment: 2,251. Undergraduate enrollment: 1,650; 5% part-time, 57% women, 3% over 25. Total faculty: 167. Library holdings: 85,000 bound volumes, 11,000 titles on microform, 500 periodical subscriptions, 4,000 records/tapes.

Undergraduate Courses offered for part-time students during daytime, evenings, weekends, summer. Complete part-time degree programs offered during daytime, evenings. Adult/continuing education programs available. Career services available to part-time students: individual and group career counseling, individual job placement, employer recruitment on campus. Part-time tuition: $145 per credit.

Graduate Part-time study available in Graduate Studies. Degree can be earned exclusively through evening/weekend study in Graduate Studies. Basic part-time expenses: $220 per credit tuition plus $10 per semester fees. Institutional financial aid available to part-time graduate students in Graduate Studies.

Emmanuel College
Boston 02115

Independent-religious instutition; metropolitan setting. Awards B, M. Total enrollment: 1,259. Undergraduate enrollment: 1,200; 3% part-time, 100% women. Total faculty: 95. Library holdings: 123,040 bound volumes, 973 titles on microform, 550 periodical subscriptions, 3,300 records/tapes.

Undergraduate Courses offered for part-time students during daytime, evenings, summer. Complete part-time degree programs offered during daytime, evenings, summer. Adult/continuing education programs available. Career services available to part-time students: individual and group career counseling, individual job placement, employer recruitment on campus. Part-time tuition: $712.50 per course.

Graduate Part-time study available in Center for Educational and Pastoral Ministry.Basic part-time expenses: $178 per credit tuition. Institutional financial aid available to part-time graduate students in Center for Educational and Pastoral Ministry.

Endicott College
Beverly 01915

Independent institution; small-town setting. Awards A. Total enrollment: 800 (all undergraduates); 2% part-time, 100% women. Total faculty: 75. Library holdings: 48,591 bound volumes, 92 periodical subscriptions, 1,922 records/tapes.

Undergraduate Courses offered for part-time students during daytime. Complete part-time degree programs offered during daytime. Adult/continuing education programs available. Career services available to part-time students: individual and group career counseling, individual job placement, employer recruitment on campus. Part-time tuition: $140 per credit.

Episcopal Divinity School
Cambridge 02138

Independent-religious institution (graduate only). Total enrollment: 127 (coed; 27% part-time). Total faculty: 22. Library holdings: 250,000 bound volumes.

Graduate Part-time study available in Graduate and Professional Programs.Basic part-time expenses: $775 per course tuition. Institutional financial aid available to part-time graduate students in Graduate and Professional Programs.

Fisher Junior College
Boston 02116

Independent institution; metropolitan setting. Awards A. Total enrollment: 680 (all undergraduates); 1% part-time, 100% women, 1% over 25. Total faculty: 45. Library holdings: 26,000 bound volumes, 118 periodical subscriptions.

Undergraduate Courses offered for part-time students during daytime, evenings, weekends, summer. Complete part-time degree programs offered during daytime, evenings, weekends, summer. Adult/continuing education programs available. Career services available to part-time students: individual and group career counseling. Part-time tuition per course ranges from $225 to $260.

Fitchburg State College
Fitchburg 01420

Public institution; small-town setting. Awards B, M. Total enrollment: 6,574. Undergraduate enrollment: 5,519; 3% part-time, 62% women. Total faculty: 512. Library holdings: 170,000 bound volumes, 248,149 titles on microform, 2,286 periodical subscriptions, 11,300 records/tapes.

Undergraduate Courses offered for part-time students during daytime, evenings, summer. Complete part-time degree programs offered during daytime, evenings, summer. Adult/continuing education programs available. Career services available to part-time students: individual and group career counseling, individual job placement, employer recruitment on campus. Part-time tuition: $39 per semester hour for state residents, $124 per semester hour for nonresidents.

Graduate Part-time study available in Division of Graduate and Continuing Education. Degree can be earned exclusively through evening/weekend study in Division of Graduate and Continuing Education.Basic part-time expenses: $40 per credit tuition plus $20 per semester fees for state residents, $50 per credit tuition plus $20 per semester fees for nonresidents. Institutional financial aid available to part-time graduate students in Division of Graduate and Continuing Education.

Framingham State College
Framingham 01701

Public institution; city setting. Awards B, M. Barrier-free campus. Total enrollment: 3,732. Undergraduate enrollment: 3,232; 6% part-time, 65% women, 12% over 25. Total faculty: 214. Library holdings: 140,744 bound volumes, 256,216 titles on microform, 1,100 periodical subscriptions.

Undergraduate Courses offered for part-time students during daytime, evenings, summer. Complete part-time degree programs offered during daytime, evenings, summer. External degree and adult/continuing education programs available. Career services available to part-time students: individual and group career counseling, individual job placement, employer recruitment on campus. Part-time tuition: $142 per course for state residents, $466 per course for nonresidents.

Graduate Part-time study available in Division of Graduate and Continuing Education.Basic part-time expenses: $172 per course tuition plus $56.50 per semester (minimum) fees for state residents, $514 per course tuition plus $56.50 per semester (minimum) fees for nonresidents.

Franklin Institute of Boston
Boston 02116

Independent institution; metropolitan setting. Awards A. Total enrollment: 500 (all undergraduates); 1% part-time, 5% women. Total faculty: 50. Library holdings: 13,000 bound volumes, 60 periodical subscriptions.

Undergraduate Courses offered for part-time students during daytime, evenings. Complete part-time degree programs offered during daytime, evenings. Adult/continuing education programs available. Career services available to part-time students: individual career counseling, individual job placement, employer recruitment on campus. Part-time tuition: $200 per credit.

Gordon College
Wenham 01984

Independent-religious instutition; small-town setting. Awards B. Total enrollment: 1,095 (all undergraduates); 4% part-time, 56% women. Total faculty: 71. Library holdings: 220,000 bound volumes, 12,000 periodical subscriptions.

Undergraduate Courses offered for part-time students during daytime. Complete part-time degree programs offered during daytime. Career services available to part-time students: individual and group career counseling, individual job placement, employer recruitment on campus. Part-time tuition per quarter ranges from $545 (1 to 4 credits) to $1090 (5 to 10 credits).

Colleges Offering Part-Time Degree Programs / *Massachusetts*

Gordon-Conwell Theological Seminary
South Hamilton 01982

Independent institution (graduate only). Total enrollment: 859 (coed; 36% part-time). Total faculty: 49.

Graduate Part-time study available in Graduate and Professional Programs.Basic part-time expenses: $445 per course tuition plus $45 per year (minimum) fees. Institutional financial aid available to part-time graduate students in Graduate and Professional Programs.

Greenfield Community College
Greenfield 01301

Public institution; small-town setting. Awards A. Barrier-free campus. Total enrollment: 1,625 (all undergraduates); 39% part-time, 59% women, 44% over 25. Total faculty: 92. Library holdings: 39,363 bound volumes, 360 periodical subscriptions, 2,471 records/tapes.

Undergraduate Courses offered for part-time students during daytime, evenings, summer. Complete part-time degree programs offered during daytime, evenings, summer. Adult/continuing education programs available. Career services available to part-time students: individual and group career counseling, individual job placement. Part-time tuition: $30 per credit hour for state residents, $95 per credit hour for nonresidents.

Harvard University
Cambridge 02138

Independent institution (undergraduate and graduate). Total enrollment: 16,037. Graduate enrollment: 9,531 (coed; 5% part-time). Library holdings: 10,567,000 bound volumes, 2,643,772 microforms.

Graduate Part-time study available in Divinity School, Graduate School of Design, Graduate School of Education, John F. Kennedy School of Government, School of Public Health, University Extension. Degree can be earned exclusively through evening/weekend study in University Extension. Basic part-time expenses: $1340 per course tuition. Institutional financial aid available to part-time graduate students in Divinity School, Graduate School of Design, Graduate School of Education, School of Public Health.

Hebrew College
Brookline 02146

Independent institution; city setting. Awards A, B, M. Total enrollment: 187. Undergraduate enrollment: 147; 80% part-time, 74% women, 40% over 25. Total faculty: 7. Library holdings: 80,000 bound volumes, 1,000 periodical subscriptions.

Undergraduate Courses offered for part-time students during daytime, evenings, weekends, summer. Complete part-time degree programs offered during daytime, evenings, weekends, summer. Adult/continuing education programs available. Career services available to part-time students: individual career counseling. Part-time tuition: $90 per credit.

Graduate Part-time study available in Graduate Division. Degree can be earned exclusively through evening/weekend study in Graduate Division.Basic part-time expenses: $90 per credit tuition plus $10 per year fees. Institutional financial aid available to part-time graduate students in Graduate Division.

Hellenic College
Brookline 02146

Independent-religious instutition; city setting. Awards B. Total enrollment: 156 (all undergraduates); 1% part-time, 51% women. Total faculty: 37. Library holdings: 85,000 bound volumes, 430 periodical subscriptions.

Undergraduate Courses offered for part-time students during daytime, evenings, summer. Complete part-time degree programs offered during daytime, summer. Adult/continuing education programs available. Part-time tuition: $150 per credit hour.

Holy Cross Greek Orthodox School of Theology
Brookline 02146

Independent-religious institution (graduate only). Total enrollment: 90 (coed; 5% part-time). Total faculty: 18.

Graduate Part-time study available in Graduate and Professional Programs.Basic part-time expenses: $150 per credit tuition plus $125 per year fees. Institutional financial aid available to part-time graduate students in Graduate and Professional Programs.

Holyoke Community College
Holyoke 01040

Public institution; city setting. Awards A. Barrier-free campus. Total enrollment: 3,218 (all undergraduates); 24% part-time, 58% women, 31% over 25. Total faculty: 179. Library holdings: 55,042 bound volumes, 30,663 titles on microform, 232 periodical subscriptions, 3,088 records/tapes.

Undergraduate Courses offered for part-time students during daytime, evenings, summer. Complete part-time degree programs offered during daytime, evenings, summer. Adult/continuing education programs available. Career services available to part-time students: individual and group career counseling, individual job placement, employer recruitment on campus. Part-time tuition: $30 per credit for state residents, $95 per credit for nonresidents.

Labouré College
Boston 02124

Independent-religious instutition; metropolitan setting. Awards A. Total enrollment: 742 (all undergraduates); 52% part-time, 90% women, 54% over 25. Total faculty: 57. Library holdings: 8,600 bound volumes, 150 periodical subscriptions, 800 records/tapes.

Undergraduate Courses offered for part-time students during daytime, evenings, weekends, summer. Complete part-time degree programs offered during daytime, evenings. Adult/continuing education programs available. Career services available to part-time students: individual and group career counseling, employer recruitment on campus. Part-time tuition: $130 per credit.

Lasell Junior College
Newton 02166

Independent institution; city setting. Awards A. Total enrollment: 650 (all undergraduates); 1% part-time, 100% women, 3% over 25. Total faculty: 77. Library holdings: 60,000 bound volumes, 500 periodical subscriptions, 100 records/tapes.

Massachusetts / **Colleges Offering Part-Time Degree Programs**

Undergraduate Courses offered for part-time students during daytime. Complete part-time degree programs offered during daytime. Adult/continuing education programs available. Part-time tuition: $180 per semester hour.

Lesley College
Cambridge 02238

Independent institution; city setting. Awards B, M. Total enrollment: 1,916. Undergraduate enrollment: 500; 1% part-time, 100% women, 1% over 25. Total faculty: 334. Library holdings: 83,000 bound volumes, 300 periodical subscriptions, 2,000 records/tapes.

Undergraduate Courses offered for part-time students during daytime, evenings, weekends, summer. Complete part-time degree programs offered during daytime, evenings, weekends, summer. Adult/continuing education programs available. Part-time tuition: $195 per credit.

Graduate Part-time study available in Graduate School. Basic part-time expenses: $195 per credit tuition plus $30 per semester fees. Institutional financial aid available to part-time graduate students in Graduate School.

Marian Court Junior College of Business
Swampscott 01907

Independent-religious instutition; small-town setting. Awards A. Barrier-free campus. Total enrollment: 222 (all undergraduates); 2% part-time, 100% women, 10% over 25. Total faculty: 21. Library holdings: 3,550 bound volumes, 10 titles on microform, 76 periodical subscriptions, 400 records/tapes.

Undergraduate Courses offered for part-time students during daytime, evenings, summer. Complete part-time degree programs offered during daytime, evenings. Adult/continuing education programs available. Career services available to part-time students: individual and group career counseling, individual job placement, employer recruitment on campus. Part-time tuition: $113 per credit.

Massachusetts Bay Community College
Wellesley Hills 02181

Public institution; small-town setting. Awards A. Barrier-free campus. Total enrollment: 4,360 (all undergraduates); 60% part-time, 60% women. Total faculty: 231. Library holdings: 40,890 bound volumes, 305 periodical subscriptions.

Undergraduate Courses offered for part-time students during daytime, evenings, weekends, summer. Complete part-time degree programs offered during daytime, evenings, weekends, summer. Adult/continuing education programs available. Career services available to part-time students: individual and group career counseling, individual job placement, employer recruitment on campus. Part-time tuition: $30 per credit for state residents, $95 per credit for nonresidents.

Massachusetts College of Pharmacy and Allied Health Sciences
Boston 02115

Independent institution; metropolitan setting. Awards A, B, M, D. Total enrollment: 987. Undergraduate enrollment: 932; 7% part-time, 45% women, 21% over 25. Total faculty: 82. Library holdings: 55,000 bound volumes, 675 periodical subscriptions, 2,710 records/tapes.

Graduate Part-time study available in Graduate and Professional Programs. Basic part-time expenses: $145 per quarter hour tuition.

Massasoit Community College
Brockton 02402

Public institution; city setting. Awards A. Barrier-free campus. Total enrollment: 3,103 (all undergraduates); 51% part-time, 53% women. Total faculty: 138. Library holdings: 66,000 bound volumes.

Undergraduate Courses offered for part-time students during daytime, evenings, summer. Complete part-time degree programs offered during daytime, evenings, summer. Adult/continuing education programs available. Career services available to part-time students: individual and group career counseling, individual job placement, employer recruitment on campus. Part-time tuition: $28 per credit hour for state residents, $95 per credit hour for nonresidents.

Merrimack College
North Andover 01845

Independent-religious instutition; small-town setting. Awards A, B. Total enrollment: 2,159 (all undergraduates); 1% part-time, 46% women. Total faculty: 144. Library holdings: 93,000 bound volumes, 797 periodical subscriptions, 3,340 records/tapes.

Undergraduate Courses offered for part-time students during daytime, evenings, summer. Complete part-time degree programs offered during daytime, evenings, summer. Adult/continuing education programs available. Career services available to part-time students: individual career counseling, individual job placement, employer recruitment on campus. Part-time tuition: $190 per credit.

MGH Institute of Health Professions
Boston 02114

Independent institution (graduate only). Total enrollment: 121 (primarily women; 36% part-time). Total faculty: 46. Library holdings: 54,714 bound volumes.

Graduate Part-time study available in Graduate Programs. Basic part-time expenses: $245 per credit hour tuition. Institutional financial aid available to part-time graduate students in Graduate Programs.

Middlesex Community College
Bedford 01730

Public institution; small-town setting. Awards A. Total enrollment: 1,440 (all undergraduates); 12% part-time, 58% women, 8% over 25. Total faculty: 100. Library holdings: 35,000 bound volumes.

Undergraduate Courses offered for part-time students during daytime, evenings, summer. Complete part-time degree programs offered during daytime, evenings, summer. Adult/continuing education programs available. Part-time tuition: $30 per credit hour for state residents, $95 per credit hour for nonresidents.

Mount Holyoke College
South Hadley 01075

Independent institution; small-town setting. Awards B, M. Total enrollment: 1,920. Undergraduate enrollment: 1,905; 1% part-

Colleges Offering Part-Time Degree Programs / *Massachusetts*

Mount Holyoke College (continued)

time, 100% women, 5% over 25. Total faculty: 230. Library holdings: 485,000 bound volumes, 325 titles on microform, 1,700 periodical subscriptions, 3,448 records/tapes.

Graduate Part-time study available in Graduate Programs. Basic part-time expenses: $295 per credit tuition plus $80 per year fees.

Mount Ida College
Newton Centre 02159

Independent institution; city setting. Awards A, B. Total enrollment: 835 (all undergraduates); 2% part-time, 90% women, 5% over 25. Total faculty: 92. Library holdings: 48,000 bound volumes, 56 titles on microform, 230 periodical subscriptions, 1,500 records/tapes.

Undergraduate Courses offered for part-time students during daytime, evenings. Complete part-time degree programs offered during daytime, evenings. Adult/continuing education programs available. Career services available to part-time students: individual and group career counseling, individual job placement, employer recruitment on campus. Part-time tuition: $140 per credit hour.

Mount Wachusett Community College
Gardner 01440

Public institution; small-town setting. Awards A. Barrier-free campus. Total enrollment: 1,848 (all undergraduates); 29% part-time, 60% women, 30% over 25. Total faculty: 92. Library holdings: 59,000 bound volumes, 275 periodical subscriptions, 1,000 records/tapes.

Undergraduate Courses offered for part-time students during daytime, evenings, summer. Complete part-time degree programs offered during daytime, evenings. Adult/continuing education programs available. Career services available to part-time students: individual career counseling. Part-time tuition: $30 per credit for state residents, $95 per credit for nonresidents.

Newbury Junior College
Boston 02115

Independent institution; metropolitan setting. Awards A. Total enrollment: 1,325 (all undergraduates); 5% part-time, 65% women. Total faculty: 72. Library holdings: 11,000 bound volumes, 28 titles on microform, 132 periodical subscriptions.

Undergraduate Courses offered for part-time students during daytime, evenings, weekends, summer. Complete part-time degree programs offered during daytime, evenings, weekends, summer. Adult/continuing education programs available. Career services available to part-time students: individual and group career counseling, individual job placement, employer recruitment on campus. Part-time tuition per credit ranges from $60 for evening programs to $150 for daytime programs.

New England Conservatory of Music
Boston 02115

Independent institution; metropolitan setting. Awards B, M. Total enrollment: 683. Undergraduate enrollment: 413; 9% part-time, 40% women. Total faculty: 168. Library holdings: 50,000 bound volumes, 165 periodical subscriptions, 15,000 records/tapes.

Undergraduate Courses offered for part-time students during daytime, summer. Complete part-time degree programs offered during daytime. Adult/continuing education programs available. Career services available to part-time students: individual career counseling, individual job placement, employer recruitment on campus. Part-time tuition: $200 per credit hour.

Graduate Part-time study available in Graduate Program in Music. Basic part-time expenses: $400 per credit tuition. Institutional financial aid available to part-time graduate students in Graduate Program in Music.

New England Institute of Applied Arts and Sciences
Boston 02215

Independent institution; metropolitan setting. Awards A. Barrier-free campus. Total enrollment: 132 (all undergraduates); 20% part-time, 23% women. Total faculty: 14. Library holdings: 6,000 bound volumes, 75 periodical subscriptions, 150 records/tapes.

Undergraduate Courses offered for part-time students during daytime, evenings. Complete part-time degree programs offered during daytime, evenings. Adult/continuing education programs available. Career services available to part-time students: individual job placement. Part-time tuition: $145 per credit.

Nichols College
Dudley 01570

Independent institution; small-town setting. Awards B, M. Total enrollment: 990. Undergraduate enrollment: 726; 2% part-time, 35% women, 3% over 25. Total faculty: 39. Library holdings: 65,000 bound volumes, 2,500 titles on microform, 465 periodical subscriptions, 1,000 records/tapes.

Undergraduate Courses offered for part-time students during daytime, evenings, summer. Complete part-time degree programs offered during daytime, evenings, summer. Adult/continuing education programs available. Career services available to part-time students: individual and group career counseling, individual job placement, employer recruitment on campus. Part-time tuition per credit hour is $157.50 for daytime courses, $65 for evening courses.

North Adams State College
North Adams 01247

Public institution; small-town setting. Awards B, M. Total enrollment: 2,500. Undergraduate enrollment: 2,250; 6% part-time, 56% women, 10% over 25. Total faculty: 190. Library holdings: 130,000 bound volumes, 477 titles on microform, 766 periodical subscriptions.

Undergraduate Courses offered for part-time students during daytime, evenings, summer. Complete part-time degree programs offered during daytime, evenings, summer. External degree and adult/continuing education programs available. Career services available to part-time students: individual and group career counseling, employer recruitment on campus. Part-time tuition: $39 per credit for state residents, $124 per credit for nonresidents.

Northeastern University
Boston 02115

Independent institution; metropolitan setting. Awards A, B, M, D. Total enrollment: 36,559. Undergraduate enrollment: 31,450; 44% part-time, 43% women. Total faculty: 2,420. Library holdings: 508,106 bound volumes, 559,658 titles on microform, 3,850 periodical subscriptions, 9,578 records/tapes.

Massachusetts / **Colleges Offering Part-Time Degree Programs**

Undergraduate Courses offered for part-time students during daytime, evenings, weekends, summer. Complete part-time degree programs offered during daytime, evenings, weekends, summer. Adult/continuing education programs available. Career services available to part-time students: individual and group career counseling, individual job placement, employer recruitment on campus. Part-time tuition: $72 per credit.

Graduate Part-time study available in Graduate School of Arts and Sciences, Graduate School of Boston-Bouvé College of Human Development Professions, Graduate School of Business Administration, Graduate School of Criminal Justice, Graduate School of Engineering, Graduate School of Pharmacy and Allied Health Professions. Basic part-time expenses: $165 per credit tuition. Institutional financial aid available to part-time graduate students in Graduate School of Arts and Sciences, Graduate School of Boston-Bouvé College of Human Development Professions, Graduate School of Business Administration, Graduate School of Criminal Justice, Graduate School of Engineering, Graduate School of Pharmacy and Allied Health Professions.

Northern Essex Community College
Haverhill 01830

Public institution; small-town setting. Awards A. Barrier-free campus. Total enrollment: 3,597 (all undergraduates); 26% part-time, 56% women. Total faculty: 349. Library holdings: 52,500 bound volumes, 330 titles on microform, 452 periodical subscriptions, 2,100 records/tapes.

Undergraduate Courses offered for part-time students during daytime, evenings, summer. Complete part-time degree programs offered during daytime, evenings, summer. Adult/continuing education programs available. Career services available to part-time students: individual and group career counseling, individual job placement, employer recruitment on campus. Part-time tuition: $28 per credit for state residents, $95 per credit for nonresidents. Part-time tuition for nonresidents who are eligible for the New England Regional Student Program: $35 per credit.

North Shore Community College
Beverly 01915

Public institution; small-town setting. Awards A. Total enrollment: 2,737 (all undergraduates); 7% part-time, 60% women. Total faculty: 120. Library holdings: 52,000 bound volumes.

Undergraduate Courses offered for part-time students during daytime, evenings, weekends, summer. Complete part-time degree programs offered during daytime, evenings, weekends, summer. External degree and adult/continuing education programs available. Career services available to part-time students: individual and group career counseling. Part-time tuition: $30 per semester hour for state residents, $95 per semester hour for nonresidents.

Pine Manor College
Chestnut Hill 02167

Independent institution; city setting. Awards A, B. Total enrollment: 589 (all undergraduates); 9% part-time, 100% women, 8% over 25. Total faculty: 67. Library holdings: 45,000 bound volumes, 2,430 titles on microform, 268 periodical subscriptions, 1,672 records/tapes.

Undergraduate Courses offered for part-time students during daytime, evenings, summer. Complete part-time degree programs offered during daytime, evenings. Adult/continuing education programs available. Career services available to part-time students: individual and group career counseling. Part-time tuition: $900 per course.

Quincy Junior College
Quincy 02169

Public institution; city setting. Awards A. Total enrollment: 1,110 (all undergraduates); 18% part-time, 69% women. Total faculty: 173. Library holdings: 20,000 bound volumes, 250 periodical subscriptions, 500 records/tapes.

Undergraduate Courses offered for part-time students during daytime, evenings, weekends, summer. Complete part-time degree programs offered during daytime, evenings, weekends, summer. Adult/continuing education programs available. Career services available to part-time students: individual and group career counseling, individual job placement, employer recruitment on campus. Part-time tuition per course ranges from $145 to $215 according to program.

Quinsigamond Community College
Worcester 01606

Public institution; city setting. Awards A. Barrier-free campus. Total enrollment: 2,266 (all undergraduates); 39% part-time, 60% women. Total faculty: 174. Library holdings: 58,519 bound volumes, 110 titles on microform, 350 periodical subscriptions, 6,252 records/tapes.

Undergraduate Courses offered for part-time students during daytime, evenings, summer. Complete part-time degree programs offered during daytime, evenings, summer. Adult/continuing education programs available. Career services available to part-time students: individual and group career counseling, individual job placement, employer recruitment on campus. Part-time tuition: $30 per credit for state residents, $95 per credit for nonresidents. Part-time tuition for evening classes: $38 per credit (for all students).

Regis College
Weston 02193

Independent-religious instutition; small-town setting. Awards B, M. Barrier-free campus. Total enrollment: 1,250. Undergraduate enrollment: 1,132; 20% part-time, 100% women. Total faculty: 91. Library holdings: 124,000 bound volumes, 800 periodical subscriptions.

Undergraduate Courses offered for part-time students during daytime, evenings, summer. Complete part-time degree programs offered during daytime, evenings, summer. Adult/continuing education programs available. Career services available to part-time students: individual and group career counseling, individual job placement, employer recruitment on campus. Part-time tuition: $695 per course.

Graduate Part-time study available in Graduate Division. Basic part-time expenses: $135 per credit tuition plus $20 per year fees. Institutional financial aid available to part-time graduate students in Graduate Division.

Roxbury Community College
Boston 02115

Public institution; metropolitan setting. Awards A. Total enrollment: 1,200 (all undergraduates); 7% part-time, 65% women, 75% over 25. Total faculty: 41. Library holdings: 12,800 bound volumes.

Undergraduate Courses offered for part-time students during daytime, evenings, summer. Complete part-time degree programs offered during daytime, evenings. Adult/continuing education programs available. Career services available to part-time students: individual and group career counseling, employer recruitment on campus. Part-time tuition: $30 per credit for state residents, $95 per credit for nonresidents.

Colleges Offering Part-Time Degree Programs / *Massachusetts*

Salem State College
Salem 01970

Public institution; small-town setting. Awards B, M. Barrier-free campus. Total enrollment: 8,551. Undergraduate enrollment: 5,516; 6% part-time, 60% women. Total faculty: 297. Library holdings: 200,000 bound volumes, 1,168 periodical subscriptions, 63,746 records/tapes.

Undergraduate Courses offered for part-time students during daytime, evenings, summer. Complete part-time degree programs offered during daytime, evenings. Adult/continuing education programs available. Career services available to part-time students: individual and group career counseling, individual job placement, employer recruitment on campus. Part-time tuition: $38 per semester hour for state residents, $45 per semester hour for nonresidents.

School of the Museum of Fine Arts
Boston 02115

Independent institution; metropolitan setting. Awards B, M. Barrier-free campus. Total enrollment: 602. Undergraduate enrollment: 569; 14% part-time, 70% women. Total faculty: 65. Library holdings: 9,000 bound volumes, 80 periodical subscriptions, 50,000 records/tapes.

Undergraduate Courses offered for part-time students during daytime. Complete part-time degree programs offered during daytime. Adult/continuing education programs available. Career services available to part-time students: individual and group career counseling, individual job placement. Part-time tuition: $385 per credit.

Graduate Part-time study available in Graduate Program. Basic part-time expenses: $9280 (one-time fee).

Simmons College
Boston 02115

Independent institution; metropolitan setting. Awards B, M, D. Total enrollment: 2,188. Undergraduate enrollment: 1,723; 11% part-time, 100% women. Total faculty: 277. Library holdings: 189,000 bound volumes, 1,467 periodical subscriptions, 1,674 records/tapes.

Undergraduate Courses offered for part-time students during daytime, summer. Complete part-time degree programs offered during daytime, summer. Adult/continuing education programs available. Career services available to part-time students: individual and group career counseling, individual job placement, employer recruitment on campus. Part-time tuition: $232 per semester hour.

Graduate Part-time study available in Graduate School, Graduate School of Library and Information Science, Graduate School of Management, School of Social Work. Degree can be earned exclusively through evening/weekend study in Graduate School, Graduate School of Library and Information Science, Graduate School of Management. Basic part-time expenses: $240 per credit tuition. Institutional financial aid available to part-time graduate students in Graduate School, Graduate School of Library and Information Science, Graduate School of Management, School of Social Work.

Smith College
Northampton 01063

Independent institution; small-town setting. Awards B, M, D. Total enrollment: 2,684. Undergraduate enrollment: 2,550; 1% part-time, 100% women, 6% over 25. Total faculty: 284. Library holdings: 900,633 bound volumes, 40,000 records/tapes.

Undergraduate Courses offered for part-time students during daytime. Complete part-time degree programs offered during daytime. Adult/continuing education programs available. Career services available to part-time students: individual and group career counseling, individual job placement, employer recruitment on campus. Part-time tuition: $1146 per course.

Graduate Part-time study available in Graduate Studies. Basic part-time expenses: $288 per credit tuition.

Southeastern Massachusetts University
North Dartmouth 02747

Public institution; small-town setting. Awards B, M. Barrier-free campus. Total enrollment: 5,531. Undergraduate enrollment: 5,502; 5% part-time, 50% women. Total faculty: 365. Library holdings: 250,000 bound volumes, 105,000 titles on microform, 1,700 periodical subscriptions, 4,500 records/tapes.

Undergraduate Courses offered for part-time students during daytime, evenings, summer. Complete part-time degree programs offered during daytime, evenings, summer. Adult/continuing education programs available. Career services available to part-time students: individual and group career counseling, individual job placement, employer recruitment on campus. Part-time tuition: $45.50 per semester hour for state residents, $148 per semester hour for nonresidents.

Graduate Part-time study available in Graduate School. Degree can be earned exclusively through evening/weekend study in Graduate School. Basic part-time expenses: $49.66 per credit tuition plus $17.50 per credit fees for state residents, $145.50 per credit tuition plus $17.50 per credit fees for nonresidents.

Springfield College
Springfield 01109

Independent institution; city setting. Awards B, M, D. Total enrollment: 2,378. Undergraduate enrollment: 2,013; 2% part-time, 54% women. Total faculty: 175. Library holdings: 115,000 bound volumes.

Undergraduate Courses offered for part-time students during daytime, evenings, weekends, summer. Complete part-time degree programs offered during daytime, evenings, summer. Adult/continuing education programs available. Career services available to part-time students: individual and group career counseling. Part-time tuition: $155 per credit.

Graduate Part-time study available in Division of Graduate Studies. Degree can be earned exclusively through evening/weekend study in Division of Graduate Studies. Basic part-time expenses: $155 per credit tuition.

Springfield Technical Community College
Springfield 01105

Public institution; city setting. Awards A. Barrier-free campus. Total enrollment: 3,647 (all undergraduates); 17% part-time, 51% women, 31% over 25. Total faculty: 189. Library holdings: 43,000 bound volumes, 280 periodical subscriptions, 7,600 records/tapes.

Undergraduate Courses offered for part-time students during daytime, evenings, weekends, summer. Complete part-time degree programs offered during daytime, evenings, weekends, summer. Adult/continuing education programs available. Career services available to part-time students: individual and group career counseling, individual job placement, employer recruitment on campus. Part-time tuition: $28 per credit for state residents, $95 per credit for nonresidents.

Massachusetts / **Colleges Offering Part-Time Degree Programs**

Stonehill College
North Easton 02357

Independent-religious instutition; small-town setting. Awards B. Barrier-free campus. Total enrollment: 1,741 (all undergraduates); 1% part-time, 54% women, 0% over 25. Total faculty: 132. Library holdings: 118,000 bound volumes, 975 periodical subscriptions, 1,395 records/tapes.

Undergraduate Courses offered for part-time students during daytime, evenings, summer. Complete part-time degree programs offered during daytime, evenings, summer. Adult/continuing education programs available. Career services available to part-time students: individual and group career counseling, individual job placement, employer recruitment on campus. Part-time tuition: $185 per credit.

Suffolk University
Boston 02114

Independent institution; metropolitan setting. Awards A, B, M, D. Total enrollment: 6,294. Undergraduate enrollment: 2,813; 31% part-time, 49% women. Total faculty: 251. Library holdings: 271,400 bound volumes, 368,895 titles on microform, 1,980 periodical subscriptions, 1,006 records/tapes.

Undergraduate Courses offered for part-time students during daytime, evenings, summer. Complete part-time degree programs offered during daytime, evenings, summer. Adult/continuing education programs available. Career services available to part-time students: individual and group career counseling, individual job placement, employer recruitment on campus. Part-time tuition: $384 per course.

Graduate Part-time study available in College of Liberal Arts and Sciences, Law School, School of Management. Degree can be earned exclusively through evening/weekend study in College of Liberal Arts and Sciences, Law School, School of Management.Basic part-time expenses: $170 per credit hour tuition plus $5 per semester fees. Institutional financial aid available to part-time graduate students in College of Liberal Arts and Sciences, Law School, School of Management.

Swain School of Design
New Bedford 02740

Independent institution; city setting. Awards B. Total enrollment: 173 (all undergraduates); 7% part-time, 54% women, 11% over 25. Total faculty: 17. Library holdings: 18,000 bound volumes, 40 periodical subscriptions.

Undergraduate Courses offered for part-time students during daytime, evenings. Complete part-time degree programs offered during daytime, evenings. Career services available to part-time students: individual career counseling, individual job placement. Part-time tuition: $190 per credit.

Tufts University
Medford 02155

Independent institution; city setting. Awards B, M, D. Barrier-free campus. Total enrollment: 7,074. Undergraduate enrollment: 4,425; 0% part-time, 50% women. Total faculty: 445. Library holdings: 638,914 bound volumes, 571,896 titles on microform, 4,357 periodical subscriptions, 31,365 records/tapes.

Graduate Part-time study available in Graduate School of Arts and Sciences, School of Nutrition, School of Veterinary Medicine. Basic part-time expenses: $1160 per course tuition plus $46.50 per semester fees. Institutional financial aid available to part-time graduate students in Graduate School of Arts and Sciences.

University of Lowell
Lowell 01854

Public institution; city setting. Awards A, B, M, D. Total enrollment: 15,977. Undergraduate enrollment: 8,463; 4% part-time, 36% women, 1% over 25. Total faculty: 772. Library holdings: 300,000 bound volumes, 25,000 periodical subscriptions, 9,000 records/tapes.

Undergraduate Courses offered for part-time students during daytime, evenings, summer. Complete part-time degree programs offered during daytime, evenings, summer. Adult/continuing education programs available. Career services available to part-time students: individual and group career counseling, individual job placement, employer recruitment on campus. Part-time tuition: $45 per credit for state residents, $135.50 per credit for nonresidents.

Graduate Part-time study available in Graduate School. Degree can be earned exclusively through evening/weekend study in Graduate School.Basic part-time expenses: $50 per credit tuition plus $50 per semester (minimum) fees for state residents, $145.50 per credit tuition plus $50 per semester (minimum) fees for nonresidents. Institutional financial aid available to part-time graduate students in Graduate School.

University of Massachusetts at Amherst
Amherst 01003

Public institution; small-town setting. Awards A, B, M, D. Total enrollment: 24,500. Undergraduate enrollment: 19,375; 1% part-time, 48% women. Total faculty: 1,465. Library holdings: 1.7 million bound volumes, 13,054 periodical subscriptions, 5,842 records/tapes.

Undergraduate Courses offered for part-time students during daytime, evenings, summer. Complete part-time degree programs offered during daytime, evenings, summer. External degree and adult/continuing education programs available. Career services available to part-time students: individual career counseling, employer recruitment on campus. Part-time tuition: $54 per credit for state residents, $168 per credit for nonresidents.

Graduate Part-time study available in Graduate School. Degree can be earned exclusively through evening/weekend study in Graduate School.Basic part-time expenses: $64 per credit tuition plus $54.50 per semester (minimum) fees for state residents, $176 per credit tuition plus $54.50 per semester (minimum) fees for nonresidents. Institutional financial aid available to part-time graduate students in Graduate School.

University of Massachusetts at Boston
Boston 02125

Public institution; metropolitan setting. Awards B, M, D. Barrier-free campus. Total enrollment: 11,370. Undergraduate enrollment: 10,560; 19% part-time, 54% women, 36% over 25. Total faculty: 594. Library holdings: 325,000 bound volumes, 3,000 periodical subscriptions, 1,162 records/tapes.

Undergraduate Courses offered for part-time students during daytime, evenings, summer. Complete part-time degree programs offered during daytime, evenings. External degree and adult/continuing education programs available. Career services available to part-time students: individual and group career counseling, individual job placement, employer recruitment on campus. Part-time tuition: $54 per credit for state residents, $168 per credit for nonresidents.

Graduate Part-time study available in Graduate Studies.Basic part-time expenses: $64 per credit tuition plus $53.50 per semester (minimum) fees for state residents, $176 per credit tuition plus $53.50 per semester (minimum) fees for nonresidents. Insti-

Colleges Offering Part-Time Degree Programs / Massachusetts

University of Massachusetts at Boston (continued)
tutional financial aid available to part-time graduate students in Graduate Studies.

Wang Institute of Graduate Studies
Tyngsboro 01879

Independent institution (graduate only). Total enrollment: 40 (coed; 72% part-time). Total faculty: 7. Library holdings: 3,700 bound volumes, 2,000 microforms.

Graduate Part-time study available in School of Information Technology.Basic part-time expenses: $300 per credit tuition plus $30 per semester fees.

Wellesley College
Wellesley 02181

Independent institution; small-town setting. Awards B. Barrier-free campus. Total enrollment: 2,170 (all undergraduates); 7% part-time, 100% women, 1% over 25. Total faculty: 311. Library holdings: 600,000 bound volumes, 17,147 titles on microform, 2,780 periodical subscriptions, 12,858 records/tapes.

Undergraduate Courses offered for part-time students during daytime. Complete part-time degree programs offered during daytime. Adult/continuing education programs available. Career services available to part-time students: individual and group career counseling, individual job placement. Part-time tuition: $1158 per course.

Wentworth Institute of Technology
Boston 02115

Independent institution; metropolitan setting. Awards A, B. Total enrollment: 3,300 (all undergraduates); 2% part-time, 7% women. Total faculty: 170. Library holdings: 55,000 bound volumes, 90 titles on microform, 410 periodical subscriptions.

Undergraduate Courses offered for part-time students during daytime, evenings, weekends. Complete part-time degree programs offered during daytime, evenings, weekends. Adult/continuing education programs available. Career services available to part-time students: individual job placement. Part-time tuition: $184 per credit.

Western New England College
Springfield 01119

Independent institution; city setting. Awards A, B, M, D. Total enrollment: 4,716. Undergraduate enrollment: 3,084; 26% part-time, 35% women, 1% over 25. Total faculty: 268. Library holdings: 99,189 bound volumes, 15,000 titles on microform, 1,039 periodical subscriptions, 840 records/tapes.

Undergraduate Courses offered for part-time students during daytime, evenings, summer. Complete part-time degree programs offered during daytime, evenings. Adult/continuing education programs available. Career services available to part-time students: individual and group career counseling, individual job placement, employer recruitment on campus. Part-time tuition: $155 per semester hour.

Graduate Part-time study available in School of Business, School of Law. Degree can be earned exclusively through evening/weekend study in School of Business, School of Law.Basic part-time expenses: $155 per credit hour tuition plus $15 per credit hour fees. Institutional financial aid available to part-time graduate students in School of Business, School of Law.

Westfield State College
Westfield 01085

Public institution; small-town setting. Awards B, M. Total enrollment: 3,200. Undergraduate enrollment: 3,000; 4% part-time, 63% women. Total faculty: 195. Library holdings: 131,000 bound volumes, 860 periodical subscriptions.

Undergraduate Courses offered for part-time students during daytime, evenings, weekends, summer. Complete part-time degree programs offered during daytime, evenings, weekends, summer. Adult/continuing education programs available. Career services available to part-time students: individual and group career counseling, individual job placement, employer recruitment on campus. Part-time tuition: $55 per credit hour for state residents, $76 per credit hour for nonresidents.

Graduate Part-time study available in Division of Graduate Studies.

Weston School of Theology
Cambridge 02138

Independent-religious institution (graduate only). Total enrollment: 188 (coed; 9% part-time). Total faculty: 29. Library holdings: 220,000 bound volumes.

Graduate Part-time study available in Graduate and Professional Programs.Basic part-time expenses: $166 per credit hour tuition plus $20 per semester fees. Institutional financial aid available to part-time graduate students in Graduate and Professional Programs.

Wheaton College
Norton 02766

Independent institution; small-town setting. Awards B. Total enrollment: 1,204 (all undergraduates); 1% part-time, 100% women, 1% over 25. Total faculty: 130. Library holdings: 220,000 bound volumes, 17,000 titles on microform, 1,200 periodical subscriptions, 7,300 records/tapes.

Undergraduate Courses offered for part-time students during daytime. Complete part-time degree programs offered during daytime. Adult/continuing education programs available. Career services available to part-time students: individual and group career counseling, employer recruitment on campus. Part-time tuition: $1144 per course.

Wheelock College
Boston 02215

Independent institution; metropolitan setting. Awards B, M. Total enrollment: 630. Undergraduate enrollment: 473; 1% part-time, 99% women, 6% over 25. Total faculty: 135. Library holdings: 64,345 bound volumes, 3,375 titles on microform, 575 periodical subscriptions, 2,048 records/tapes.

Undergraduate Courses offered for part-time students during daytime. Complete part-time degree programs offered during daytime. Adult/continuing education programs available. Career services available to part-time students: individual and group career counseling, individual job placement, employer recruitment on campus. Part-time tuition: $204 per credit.

Graduate Part-time study available in Graduate School. Degree can be earned exclusively through evening/weekend study in Graduate School.Basic part-time expenses: $175 per credit tuition.

Michigan / **Colleges Offering Part-Time Degree Programs**

Worcester Polytechnic Institute
Worcester 01609

Independent institution; city setting. Awards B, M, D. Total enrollment: 3,895. Undergraduate enrollment: 2,533; 2% part-time, 18% women. Total faculty: 322. Library holdings: 190,000 bound volumes, 650,000 titles on microform, 1,200 periodical subscriptions, 3,800 records/tapes.

Undergraduate Courses offered for part-time students during daytime, evenings. Complete part-time degree programs offered during daytime, evenings. Adult/continuing education programs available. Part-time tuition: $600 per course.

Graduate Part-time study available in Graduate Studies. Degree can be earned exclusively through evening/weekend study in Graduate Studies.Basic part-time expenses: $220 per semester hour tuition.

Worcester State College
Worcester 01602

Public institution; city setting. Awards B, M. Total enrollment: 4,700. Undergraduate enrollment: 3,528; 11% part-time, 60% women, 30% over 25. Total faculty: 171. Library holdings: 161,000 bound volumes, 980 titles on microform, 883 periodical subscriptions, 15,188 records/tapes.

Undergraduate Courses offered for part-time students during daytime, evenings, summer. Complete part-time degree programs offered during daytime, evenings, summer. Adult/continuing education programs available. Career services available to part-time students: individual and group career counseling, individual job placement, employer recruitment on campus. Part-time tuition: $45 per credit for state residents, $116.50 per credit for nonresidents.

MICHIGAN

Adrian College
Adrian 49221

Independent-religious instutition; small-town setting. Awards A, B. Barrier-free campus. Total enrollment: 1,192 (all undergraduates); 8% part-time, 48% women, 5% over 25. Total faculty: 102. Library holdings: 120,000 bound volumes, 3,500 periodical subscriptions, 1,500 records/tapes.

Undergraduate Courses offered for part-time students during daytime, evenings, weekends, summer. Complete part-time degree programs offered during daytime. Adult/continuing education programs available. Career services available to part-time students: individual and group career counseling. Part-time tuition: $130 per credit hour.

Alpena Community College
Alpena 49707

Public institution; small-town setting. Awards A. Total enrollment: 2,093 (all undergraduates); 57% part-time, 50% women, 50% over 25. Total faculty: 122. Library holdings: 29,000 bound volumes.

Undergraduate Courses offered for part-time students during daytime, evenings, summer. Complete part-time degree programs offered during daytime, evenings. Adult/continuing education programs available. Career services available to part-time students: individual and group career counseling, individual job placement, employer recruitment on campus. Part-time tuition: $22 per contact hour for area residents, $32 per contact hour for state residents, $56 per contact hour for nonresidents.

Andrews University
Berrien Springs 49104

Independent-religious instutition; small-town setting. Awards A, B, M, D. Barrier-free campus. Total enrollment: 2,878. Undergraduate enrollment: 1,929; 15% part-time, 52% women, 21% over 25. Total faculty: 240. Library holdings: 448,671 bound volumes, 263,930 titles on microform, 3,297 periodical subscriptions, 26,676 records/tapes.

Undergraduate Courses offered for part-time students during daytime, evenings. Complete part-time degree programs offered during daytime, evenings. Adult/continuing education programs available. Career services available to part-time students: individual career counseling, individual job placement, employer recruitment on campus. Part-time tuition: $146 per quarter hour.

Graduate Part-time study available in School of Graduate Studies, School of Business, School of Education.Basic part-time expenses: $121 per quarter hour tuition.

Aquinas College
Grand Rapids 49506

Independent-religious instutition; city setting. Awards A, B, M. Barrier-free campus. Total enrollment: 2,805. Undergraduate enrollment: 2,400; 50% part-time, 54% women, 54% over 25. Total faculty: 122. Library holdings: 110,000 bound volumes, 15,000 titles on microform, 700 periodical subscriptions, 3,000 records/tapes.

Undergraduate Courses offered for part-time students during daytime, evenings, weekends, summer. Complete part-time degree programs offered during daytime, evenings, weekends, summer. External degree and adult/continuing education programs available. Career services available to part-time students: individual and group career counseling, individual job placement, employer recruitment on campus. Part-time tuition: $112 per credit.

Graduate Part-time study available in Graduate Program in Management. Degree can be earned exclusively through evening/weekend study in Graduate Program in Management.Basic part-time expenses: $135 per credit tuition.

Baker Junior College of Business
Flint 48507

Independent institution; city setting. Awards A. Barrier-free campus. Total enrollment: 1,949 (all undergraduates); 22% part-time, 77% women, 20% over 25. Total faculty: 76. Library holdings: 7,000 bound volumes, 55 titles on microform, 200 periodical subscriptions, 100 records/tapes.

Undergraduate Courses offered for part-time students during daytime, evenings, summer. Complete part-time degree programs offered during daytime, evenings, summer. Career services available to part-time students: individual career counseling, individual job placement. Part-time tuition: $50 per quarter hour.

Bay de Noc Community College
Escanaba 49829

Public institution; rural setting. Awards A. Barrier-free campus. Total enrollment: 1,777 (all undergraduates); 37% part-time, 52% women. Total faculty: 94. Library holdings: 30,000 bound volumes, 200 periodical subscriptions, 1,000 records/tapes.

Undergraduate Courses offered for part-time students during daytime, evenings, weekends, summer. Complete part-time degree programs offered during daytime, evenings, weekends,

Colleges Offering Part-Time Degree Programs / Michigan

Bay de Noc Community College (continued)

summer. Adult/continuing education programs available. Career services available to part-time students: individual and group career counseling, individual job placement, employer recruitment on campus. Part-time tuition: $25 per credit hour for area residents, $34 per credit hour for state residents, $49 per credit hour for nonresidents.

Calvin College
Grand Rapids 49506

Independent-religious instutition; city setting. Awards B, M. Barrier-free campus. Total enrollment: 3,942. Undergraduate enrollment: 3,864; 9% part-time, 52% women, 3% over 25. Total faculty: 255. Library holdings: 435,000 bound volumes, 2,242 periodical subscriptions, 12,000 records/tapes.

Undergraduate Courses offered for part-time students during daytime, evenings, summer. Complete part-time degree programs offered during daytime, evenings, summer. Career services available to part-time students: individual and group career counseling, individual job placement, employer recruitment on campus. Part-time tuition: $620 per course.

Graduate Part-time study available in Graduate Programs. Basic part-time expenses: $620 per course tuition. Institutional financial aid available to part-time graduate students in Graduate Programs.

Center for Creative Studies–College of Art and Design
Detroit 48202

Independent institution; metropolitan setting. Awards B. Barrier-free campus. Total enrollment: 904 (all undergraduates); 35% part-time, 50% women. Total faculty: 152. Library holdings: 15,000 bound volumes, 70 periodical subscriptions.

Undergraduate Courses offered for part-time students during daytime. Complete part-time degree programs offered during daytime. Career services available to part-time students: individual and group career counseling, individual job placement. Part-time tuition: $180 per semester hour.

Central Michigan University
Mount Pleasant 48859

Public institution; small-town setting. Awards B, M, D. Barrier-free campus. Total enrollment: 16,315. Undergraduate enrollment: 14,785; 7% part-time, 55% women, 6% over 25. Total faculty: 740. Library holdings: 684,000 bound volumes, 603,000 titles on microform, 4,800 periodical subscriptions, 17,000 records/tapes.

Undergraduate Courses offered for part-time students during daytime, evenings, summer. Complete part-time degree programs offered during daytime, evenings, summer. External degree and adult/continuing education programs available. Career services available to part-time students: individual and group career counseling, individual job placement, employer recruitment on campus. Part-time tuition: $47 per credit for state residents, $120 per credit for nonresidents.

Graduate Part-time study available in School of Graduate Studies. Basic part-time expenses: $63.50 per credit tuition plus $12.50 per semester (minimum) fees for state residents, $138 per credit tuition plus $12.50 per semester (minimum) fees for nonresidents.

Charles Stewart Mott Community College
Flint 48503

Public institution; city setting. Awards A. Barrier-free campus. Total enrollment: 11,432 (all undergraduates); 73% part-time, 60% women, 43% over 25. Total faculty: 404. Library holdings: 85,570 bound volumes, 4,128 titles on microform, 450 periodical subscriptions, 3,416 records/tapes.

Undergraduate Courses offered for part-time students during daytime, evenings, summer. Complete part-time degree programs offered during daytime, evenings, summer. Adult/continuing education programs available. Career services available to part-time students: individual and group career counseling, individual job placement, employer recruitment on campus. Part-time tuition: $32 per credit hour for area residents, $44.50 per credit hour for state residents, $60 per credit hour for nonresidents.

Cleary College
Ypsilanti 48197

Independent institution; small-town setting. Awards A, B. Barrier-free campus. Total enrollment: 1,089 (all undergraduates); 64% part-time, 79% women. Total faculty: 62. Library holdings: 12,700 bound volumes, 300 periodical subscriptions, 150 records/tapes.

Undergraduate Courses offered for part-time students during daytime, evenings, weekends, summer. Complete part-time degree programs offered during daytime, evenings, weekends, summer. Adult/continuing education programs available. Career services available to part-time students: individual career counseling, individual job placement. Part-time tuition: $65 per credit hour.

Concordia College
Ann Arbor 48105

Independent-religious instutition; city setting. Awards A, B. Barrier-free campus. Total enrollment: 525 (all undergraduates); 6% part-time, 53% women, 4% over 25. Total faculty: 63. Library holdings: 94,432 bound volumes, 1,642 titles on microform, 1,700 periodical subscriptions, 2,000 records/tapes.

Undergraduate Courses offered for part-time students during daytime, evenings, summer. Complete part-time degree programs offered during daytime, evenings, summer. Adult/continuing education programs available. Career services available to part-time students: individual and group career counseling. Part-time tuition: $125 per semester hour.

Davenport College of Business
Grand Rapids 49503

Independent institution; city setting. Awards A. Barrier-free campus. Total enrollment: 4,511 (all undergraduates); 40% part-time, 53% women. Total faculty: 123. Library holdings: 18,000 bound volumes, 120 titles on microform, 180 periodical subscriptions.

Undergraduate Courses offered for part-time students during daytime, evenings, weekends, summer. Complete part-time degree programs offered during daytime, evenings, weekends, summer. Adult/continuing education programs available. Career services available to part-time students: individual career counseling, individual job placement. Part-time tuition: $93 per credit hour.

Michigan / **Colleges Offering Part-Time Degree Programs**

Delta College
University Center 48710

Public institution; rural setting. Awards A. Total enrollment: 10,426 (all undergraduates); 46% part-time, 63% women, 15% over 25. Total faculty: 603. Library holdings: 87,000 bound volumes, 500 periodical subscriptions.

Undergraduate Courses offered for part-time students during daytime, evenings, weekends, summer. Complete part-time degree programs offered during daytime, evenings, weekends, summer. Career services available to part-time students: individual and group career counseling, individual job placement, employer recruitment on campus. Part-time tuition: $31 per semester hour for area residents, $55 per semester hour for state residents, $74 per semester hour for nonresidents.

Detroit College of Business
Dearborn 48126

Independent institution; city setting. Awards A, B. Barrier-free campus. Total enrollment: 2,658 (all undergraduates); 42% part-time, 71% women. Total faculty: 102. Library holdings: 21,000 bound volumes, 15 titles on microform, 250 periodical subscriptions, 402 records/tapes.

Undergraduate Courses offered for part-time students during daytime, evenings. Complete part-time degree programs offered during daytime, evenings. Career services available to part-time students: individual and group career counseling, individual job placement, employer recruitment on campus. Part-time tuition: $67 per quarter hour.

Detroit College of Business–Flint
Flint 48504

Independent institution; city setting. Awards A, B. Total enrollment: 525 (all undergraduates); 23% part-time, 67% women, 38% over 25. Total faculty: 53. Library holdings: 20,000 bound volumes, 250 periodical subscriptions.

Undergraduate Courses offered for part-time students during daytime, evenings, weekends, summer. Complete part-time degree programs offered during daytime, evenings. Adult/continuing education programs available. Career services available to part-time students: individual and group career counseling, individual job placement, employer recruitment on campus. Part-time tuition: $67 per quarter hour.

Detroit College of Business, Grand Rapids Campus
Grand Rapids 49503

Independent institution; city setting. Awards B. Barrier-free campus. Total enrollment: 192 (all undergraduates); 50% part-time, 33% women. Total faculty: 30.

Undergraduate Courses offered for part-time students during daytime, evenings, summer. Complete part-time degree programs offered during daytime, evenings, summer. External degree programs available. Part-time tuition: $93 per credit hour.

Detroit College of Business, Madison Heights Campus
Madison Heights 48071

Independent institution; small-town setting. Awards A. Barrier-free campus. Total enrollment: 452 (all undergraduates); 45% part-time, 66% women, 40% over 25. Total faculty: 36.

Undergraduate Courses offered for part-time students during daytime, evenings, weekends, summer. Complete part-time degree programs offered during daytime, evenings, weekends. Career services available to part-time students: individual career counseling, individual job placement. Part-time tuition: $67 per quarter hour. Part-time tuition per quarter hour is $70 for data processing, word processing programs.

Detroit College of Law
Detroit 48201

Independent institution (graduate only). Total enrollment: 841 (coed; 49% part-time). Total faculty: 52. Library holdings: 71,000 bound volumes, 76,000 microforms.

Graduate Part-time study available in Professional Program. Degree can be earned exclusively through evening/weekend study in Professional Program. Basic part-time expenses: $3600 per year tuition. Institutional financial aid available to part-time graduate students in Professional Program.

Eastern Michigan University
Ypsilanti 48197

Public institution; small-town setting. Awards B, M. Barrier-free campus. Total enrollment: 19,809. Undergraduate enrollment: 14,637; 31% part-time, 54% women, 22% over 25. Total faculty: 843. Library holdings: 664,677 bound volumes, 104,586 titles on microform, 4,181 periodical subscriptions, 22,383 records/tapes.

Undergraduate Courses offered for part-time students during daytime, evenings, summer. Complete part-time degree programs offered during daytime, evenings, summer. Adult/continuing education programs available. Career services available to part-time students: individual and group career counseling, individual job placement, employer recruitment on campus. Part-time tuition: $45.75 per credit hour for state residents, $112 per credit hour for nonresidents.

Graduate Part-time study available in Graduate School. Degree can be earned exclusively through evening/weekend study in Graduate School. Basic part-time expenses: $63 per credit hour tuition plus $23.75 per semester (minimum) fees for state residents, $147 per credit hour tuition plus $23.75 per semester (minimum) fees for nonresidents.

Ferris State College
Big Rapids 49307

Public institution; small-town setting. Awards A, B, M, D. Barrier-free campus. Total enrollment: 10,767. Undergraduate enrollment: 10,647; 7% part-time, 40% women, 11% over 25. Total faculty: 650. Library holdings: 210,000 bound volumes, 1,380 periodical subscriptions, 26,577 records/tapes.

Undergraduate Courses offered for part-time students during daytime, evenings. Complete part-time degree programs offered during daytime, evenings. External degree and adult/continuing education programs available. Career services available to part-time students: individual and group career counseling, individual job placement, employer recruitment on campus. Part-time tuition: $46.50 per quarter hour for state residents, $91 per quarter hour for nonresidents.

Glen Oaks Community College
Centreville 49032

Public institution; rural setting. Awards A. Total enrollment: 1,525 (all undergraduates); 62% part-time, 54% women, 50%

Colleges Offering Part-Time Degree Programs / Michigan

Glen Oaks Community College (continued)
over 25. Total faculty: 93. Library holdings: 33,104 bound volumes, 240 periodical subscriptions, 1,057 records/tapes.

Undergraduate Courses offered for part-time students during daytime, evenings, summer. Complete part-time degree programs offered during daytime. Adult/continuing education programs available. Career services available to part-time students: individual career counseling, individual job placement, employer recruitment on campus. Part-time tuition: $26 per credit hour for state residents, $40 per credit hour for nonresidents.

Gogebic Community College
Ironwood 49938

Public institution; small-town setting. Awards A. Barrier-free campus. Total enrollment: 1,517 (all undergraduates); 20% part-time, 35% women, 35% over 25. Total faculty: 85. Library holdings: 45,000 bound volumes, 3,500 periodical subscriptions, 2,000 records/tapes.

Undergraduate Courses offered for part-time students during daytime, evenings, summer. Complete part-time degree programs offered during daytime, evenings, summer. External degree and adult/continuing education programs available. Career services available to part-time students: individual and group career counseling, individual job placement, employer recruitment on campus. Part-time tuition: $22 per credit hour for area residents, $34 per credit hour for state residents, $48 per credit hour for nonresidents.

Grace Bible College
Grand Rapids 49509

Independent-religious instutition; city setting. Awards A, B. Barrier-free campus. Total enrollment: 139 (all undergraduates); 6% part-time, 50% women, 19% over 25. Total faculty: 21. Library holdings: 30,000 bound volumes, 112 periodical subscriptions, 100 records/tapes.

Undergraduate Courses offered for part-time students during daytime. Complete part-time degree programs offered during daytime. Career services available to part-time students: individual and group career counseling. Part-time tuition: $76 per semester hour.

Grand Rapids Baptist College and Seminary
Grand Rapids 49505

Independent-religious instutition; city setting. Awards A, B, M. Barrier-free campus. Total enrollment: 1,028. Undergraduate enrollment: 761; 12% part-time, 54% women, 20% over 25. Total faculty: 66. Library holdings: 75,000 bound volumes, 620 periodical subscriptions, 2,100 records/tapes.

Undergraduate Courses offered for part-time students during daytime, summer. Complete part-time degree programs offered during daytime, summer. External degree programs available. Career services available to part-time students: individual and group career counseling, individual job placement, employer recruitment on campus. Part-time tuition: $123 per credit hour.

Graduate Part-time study available in Graduate and Professional Programs. Basic part-time expenses: $85 per credit (minimum) tuition plus $95 per semester fees.

Grand Rapids Junior College
Grand Rapids 49503

Public institution; city setting. Awards A. Barrier-free campus. Total enrollment: 9,600 (all undergraduates); 35% part-time, 51% women, 30% over 25. Total faculty: 465. Library holdings: 55,000 bound volumes.

Undergraduate Courses offered for part-time students during daytime, evenings, weekends, summer. Complete part-time degree programs offered during daytime, evenings, weekends, summer. Adult/continuing education programs available. Career services available to part-time students: individual and group career counseling, individual job placement, employer recruitment on campus. Part-time tuition: $31 per credit for area residents, $50 per credit for state residents, $70 per credit for nonresidents.

Grand Valley State College
Allendale 49401

Public institution; rural setting. Awards B, M. Total enrollment: 5,158. Undergraduate enrollment: 4,664; 41% part-time, 53% women. Total faculty: 229. Library holdings: 332,000 bound volumes, 13,000 titles on microform, 1,800 periodical subscriptions.

Undergraduate Courses offered for part-time students during daytime, evenings, weekends, summer. Complete part-time degree programs offered during daytime, evenings, summer. Adult/continuing education programs available. Career services available to part-time students: individual and group career counseling, individual job placement, employer recruitment on campus. Part-time tuition: $63 per credit hour for state residents, $147 per credit hour for nonresidents.

Graduate Part-time study available in F. E. Seidman School of Business and Economics, Graduate School of Education, Graduate School of Health Sciences, Graduate School of Public Administration, Graduate School of Social Work, Kirkhof Graduate School of Nursing. Degree can be earned exclusively through evening/weekend study in Kirkhof Graduate School of Nursing. Basic part-time expenses: $73 per credit tuition for state residents, $161 per credit tuition for nonresidents.

Great Lakes Bible College
Lansing 48901

Independent-religious instutition; city setting. Awards A, B. Barrier-free campus. Total enrollment: 155 (all undergraduates); 8% part-time, 42% women, 13% over 25. Total faculty: 15. Library holdings: 21,946 bound volumes, 1,785 titles on microform, 187 periodical subscriptions, 1,019 records/tapes.

Undergraduate Courses offered for part-time students during daytime, evenings, summer. Complete part-time degree programs offered during daytime, evenings, summer. Career services available to part-time students: individual career counseling. Part-time tuition: $56 per quarter hour.

Henry Ford Community College
Dearborn 48128

Public institution; city setting. Awards A. Barrier-free campus. Total enrollment: 16,138 (all undergraduates); 40% part-time, 48% women, 40% over 25. Total faculty: 896. Library holdings: 14,255 bound volumes, 909 periodical subscriptions, 4,650 records/tapes.

Undergraduate Courses offered for part-time students during daytime, evenings, weekends, summer. Complete part-time degree programs offered during daytime, evenings, weekends, summer. Adult/continuing education programs available. Ca-

reer services available to part-time students: individual and group career counseling, individual job placement, employer recruitment on campus. Part-time tuition: $30 per credit hour for state residents, $42 per credit hour for nonresidents.

Highland Park Community College
Highland Park 48203

Public institution; small-town setting. Awards A. Total enrollment: 2,785 (all undergraduates); 40% part-time, 60% women, 50% over 25. Total faculty: 112. Library holdings: 18,000 bound volumes, 150 periodical subscriptions, 2,187 records/tapes.

Undergraduate Courses offered for part-time students during daytime, evenings, summer. Complete part-time degree programs offered during daytime, evenings, summer. Adult/continuing education programs available. Career services available to part-time students: individual and group career counseling, individual job placement, employer recruitment on campus. Part-time tuition: $25 per semester hour for area residents, $35 per semester hour for state residents, $45 per semester hour for nonresidents.

Hope College
Holland 49423

Independent-religious instutition; small-town setting. Awards B. Barrier-free campus. Total enrollment: 2,530 (all undergraduates); 13% part-time, 51% women. Total faculty: 213. Library holdings: 195,000 bound volumes, 5,970 titles on microform, 1,300 periodical subscriptions, 2,200 records/tapes.

Undergraduate Courses offered for part-time students during daytime, evenings, summer. Complete part-time degree programs offered during daytime, evenings, summer. Adult/continuing education programs available. Career services available to part-time students: group career counseling. Part-time tuition per credit hour is $95 for 1 to 4 credit hours, $130 for 5 to 7 credit hours, $180 for 8 to 11 credit hours.

Jackson Community College
Jackson 49201

Public institution; city setting. Awards A. Barrier-free campus. Total enrollment: 8,000 (all undergraduates); 80% part-time, 51% women, 55% over 25. Total faculty: 300. Library holdings: 40,000 bound volumes, 311 periodical subscriptions, 2,623 records/tapes.

Undergraduate Courses offered for part-time students during daytime, evenings, weekends, summer. Complete part-time degree programs offered during daytime, evenings, weekends, summer. External degree and adult/continuing education programs available. Career services available to part-time students: individual and group career counseling, individual job placement, employer recruitment on campus. Part-time tuition: $29 per credit hour for area residents, $37 per credit hour for state residents, $45 per credit hour for nonresidents.

Jordan College
Cedar Springs 49319

Independent-religious instutition; small-town setting. Awards A, B. Total enrollment: 1,050 (all undergraduates); 14% part-time, 58% women, 70% over 25. Total faculty: 100.

Undergraduate Courses offered for part-time students during daytime, evenings, summer. Complete part-time degree programs offered during daytime, evenings, summer. External degree and adult/continuing education programs available. Career services available to part-time students: individual career counseling, individual job placement. Part-time tuition: $100 per semester hour.

Kalamazoo Valley Community College
Kalamazoo 49009

Public institution; city setting. Awards A. Barrier-free campus. Total enrollment: 9,087 (all undergraduates); 75% part-time, 56% women. Total faculty: 245. Library holdings: 58,659 bound volumes, 491 titles on microform, 465 periodical subscriptions, 3,620 records/tapes.

Undergraduate Courses offered for part-time students during daytime, evenings, weekends, summer. Complete part-time degree programs offered during daytime, evenings. Career services available to part-time students: individual career counseling, individual job placement. Part-time tuition: $21 per credit hour for area residents, $42 per credit hour for state residents, $63 per credit hour for nonresidents.

Kellogg Community College
Battle Creek 49016

Public institution; city setting. Awards A. Barrier-free campus. Total enrollment: 4,941 (all undergraduates); 67% part-time, 61% women. Total faculty: 200. Library holdings: 70,000 bound volumes.

Undergraduate Courses offered for part-time students during daytime, evenings, weekends, summer. Complete part-time degree programs offered during daytime, evenings, weekends, summer. Adult/continuing education programs available. Career services available to part-time students: individual and group career counseling, individual job placement, employer recruitment on campus. Part-time tuition: $24.50 per credit hour for area residents, $40 per credit hour for state residents, $62.50 per credit hour for nonresidents.

Kendall School of Design
Grand Rapids 49503

Independent institution; city setting. Awards A, B. Total enrollment: 654 (all undergraduates); 20% part-time, 55% women, 20% over 25. Total faculty: 57. Library holdings: 8,500 bound volumes, 122 titles on microform, 90 periodical subscriptions, 506 records/tapes.

Undergraduate Courses offered for part-time students during daytime, evenings, summer. Complete part-time degree programs offered during daytime, evenings, summer. Adult/continuing education programs available. Career services available to part-time students: individual career counseling, individual job placement, employer recruitment on campus. Part-time tuition: $133 per credit.

Kirtland Community College
Roscommon 48653

Public institution; rural setting. Awards A. Barrier-free campus. Total enrollment: 1,335 (all undergraduates); 55% part-time, 56% women, 43% over 25. Total faculty: 69. Library holdings: 30,000 bound volumes, 50 periodical subscriptions, 300 records/tapes.

Undergraduate Courses offered for part-time students during daytime, evenings, weekends, summer. Complete part-time degree programs offered during daytime, evenings, weekends, summer. Adult/continuing education programs available. Career services available to part-time students: individual and group career counseling, individual job placement, employer recruitment on campus. Part-time tuition: $20 per credit hour

Colleges Offering Part-Time Degree Programs / Michigan

Kirtland Community College (continued)
for area residents, $26 per credit hour for state residents, $32 per credit hour for nonresidents.

Lake Michigan College
Benton Harbor 49022

Public institution; small-town setting. Awards A. Barrier-free campus. Total enrollment: 3,324 (all undergraduates); 70% part-time, 58% women. Total faculty: 250. Library holdings: 90,000 bound volumes, 10,000 titles on microform, 350 periodical subscriptions, 3,000 records/tapes.

Undergraduate Courses offered for part-time students during daytime, evenings, summer. Complete part-time degree programs offered during daytime, evenings, summer. Adult/continuing education programs available. Career services available to part-time students: individual career counseling, individual job placement, employer recruitment on campus. Part-time tuition: $23 per credit hour for area residents, $31 per credit hour for state residents, $39 per credit hour for nonresidents.

Lake Superior State College
Sault Sainte Marie 49783

Public institution; small-town setting. Awards A, B, M. Total enrollment: 2,820. Undergraduate enrollment: 2,741; 26% part-time, 45% women. Total faculty: 136. Library holdings: 120,000 bound volumes, 710 periodical subscriptions, 517 records/tapes.

Graduate Part-time study available in Graduate Program in Business Administration. Basic part-time expenses: $90 per credit tuition.

Lansing Community College
Lansing 48901

Public institution; city setting. Awards A. Barrier-free campus. Total enrollment: 20,407 (all undergraduates); 73% part-time, 56% women. Total faculty: 1,000. Library holdings: 90,000 bound volumes, 700 periodical subscriptions, 4,000 records/tapes.

Undergraduate Courses offered for part-time students during daytime, evenings, weekends, summer. Complete part-time degree programs offered during daytime, evenings, weekends, summer. External degree and adult/continuing education programs available. Career services available to part-time students: individual and group career counseling, individual job placement, employer recruitment on campus. Part-time tuition: $16 per quarter hour for area residents, $23 per quarter hour for state residents, $33.50 per quarter hour for nonresidents.

Lawrence Institute of Technology
Southfield 48075

Independent institution; city setting. Awards A, B. Barrier-free campus. Total enrollment: 6,230 (all undergraduates); 39% part-time, 20% women. Total faculty: 323. Library holdings: 65,000 bound volumes, 500 titles on microform, 400 periodical subscriptions, 308 records/tapes.

Undergraduate Courses offered for part-time students during daytime, evenings, weekends, summer. Complete part-time degree programs offered during daytime, evenings. Career services available to part-time students: individual and group career counseling, individual job placement, employer recruitment on campus. Part-time tuition: $64 per quarter hour.

Lewis College of Business
Detroit 48235

Independent institution; metropolitan setting. Awards A. Total enrollment: 656 (all undergraduates); 19% part-time, 76% women. Total faculty: 32. Library holdings: 2,500 bound volumes, 50 periodical subscriptions, 81 records/tapes.

Undergraduate Courses offered for part-time students during daytime, evenings. Complete part-time degree programs offered during daytime, evenings. Career services available to part-time students: individual and group career counseling, individual job placement, employer recruitment on campus. Part-time tuition: $150 per credit hour.

Macomb Community College
Warren 48093

Public institution; city setting. Awards A. Barrier-free campus. Total enrollment: 31,152 (all undergraduates); 79% part-time, 48% women, 50% over 25. Total faculty: 775. Library holdings: 125,779 bound volumes, 145 titles on microform, 1,088 periodical subscriptions, 6,150 records/tapes.

Undergraduate Courses offered for part-time students during daytime, evenings, weekends, summer. Complete part-time degree programs offered during daytime, evenings, weekends, summer. Adult/continuing education programs available. Career services available to part-time students: individual and group career counseling, individual job placement, employer recruitment on campus. Part-time tuition: $29.50 per semester hour for area residents, $48 per semester hour for state residents, $58 per semester hour for nonresidents.

Madonna College
Livonia 48150

Independent-religious instutition; city setting. Awards A, B, M. Barrier-free campus. Total enrollment: 3,924. Undergraduate enrollment: 3,752; 58% part-time, 75% women, 54% over 25. Total faculty: 198. Library holdings: 103,720 bound volumes, 27,797 titles on microform, 725 periodical subscriptions, 3,129 records/tapes.

Undergraduate Courses offered for part-time students during daytime, evenings, weekends, summer. Complete part-time degree programs offered during daytime, evenings, summer. Adult/continuing education programs available. Career services available to part-time students: individual and group career counseling, individual job placement, employer recruitment on campus. Part-time tuition: $75 per semester hour.

Graduate Part-time study available in Graduate Program in Administration. Degree can be earned exclusively through evening/weekend study in Graduate Program in Administration. Basic part-time expenses: $110 per semester hour tuition plus $10 per semester fees.

Marygrove College
Detroit 48221

Independent-religious instutition; metropolitan setting. Awards A, B, M. Total enrollment: 1,135. Undergraduate enrollment: 968; 26% part-time, 78% women, 48% over 25. Total faculty: 56. Library holdings: 174,000 bound volumes, 800 periodical subscriptions, 5,000 records/tapes.

Undergraduate Courses offered for part-time students during daytime, evenings. Complete part-time degree programs offered during daytime, evenings. External degree and adult/continuing education programs available. Career services available to part-time students: individual and group career counseling, in-

Michigan / **Colleges Offering Part-Time Degree Programs**

dividual job placement, employer recruitment on campus. Part-time tuition: $136 per credit.

Mercy College of Detroit
Detroit 48219

Independent-religious instutition; metropolitan setting. Awards A, B, M. Total enrollment: 2,257. Undergraduate enrollment: 2,198; 43% part-time, 85% women, 48% over 25. Total faculty: 202. Library holdings: 112,000 bound volumes, 500 periodical subscriptions.

Undergraduate Courses offered for part-time students during daytime, evenings, weekends, summer. Complete part-time degree programs offered during daytime, evenings, weekends, summer. Adult/continuing education programs available. Career services available to part-time students: individual and group career counseling, individual job placement, employer recruitment on campus. Part-time tuition: $126 per credit.

Graduate Part-time study available in Graduate Studies. Degree can be earned exclusively through evening/weekend study in Graduate Studies. Basic part-time expenses: $136 per credit hour tuition plus $20 per semester fees. Institutional financial aid available to part-time graduate students in Graduate Studies.

Michigan Christian College
Rochester 48063

Independent-religious instutition; small-town setting. Awards A, B. Barrier-free campus. Total enrollment: 373 (all undergraduates); 8% part-time, 56% women, 3% over 25. Total faculty: 35. Library holdings: 26,993 bound volumes, 13,247 titles on microform, 240 periodical subscriptions, 355 records/tapes.

Undergraduate Courses offered for part-time students during daytime, evenings, summer. Complete part-time degree programs offered during daytime. Adult/continuing education programs available. Career services available to part-time students: individual and group career counseling. Part-time tuition: $84 per credit hour.

Michigan State University
East Lansing 48824

Public institution; small-town setting. Awards B, M, D. Total enrollment: 41,765. Undergraduate enrollment: 33,784; 8% part-time, 50% women, 17% over 25. Total faculty: 2,551. Library holdings: 2.9 million bound volumes, 1.9 million titles on microform, 19,980 periodical subscriptions, 17,700 records/tapes.

Undergraduate Courses offered for part-time students during daytime, evenings. Complete part-time degree programs offered during daytime, evenings. Adult/continuing education programs available. Career services available to part-time students: individual and group career counseling, individual job placement, employer recruitment on campus. Part-time tuition per quarter hour ranges from $41 to $46 for state residents, $99 to $103 for nonresidents, according to course level.

Graduate Part-time study available in Graduate School, College of Human Medicine, College of Osteopathic Medicine, College of Veterinary Medicine. Basic part-time expenses: $60 per credit tuition plus $13 per quarter fees for state residents, $113.50 per credit tuition plus $13 per quarter fees for nonresidents. Institutional financial aid available to part-time graduate students in Graduate School, College of Human Medicine, College of Osteopathic Medicine, College of Veterinary Medicine.

Michigan Technological University
Houghton 49931

Public institution; small-town setting. Awards A, B, M, D. Total enrollment: 7,414. Undergraduate enrollment: 7,084; 5% part-time, 24% women. Total faculty: 382. Library holdings: 570,415 bound volumes, 107,249 titles on microform, 9,766 periodical subscriptions, 1,802 records/tapes.

Undergraduate Courses offered for part-time students during daytime. Complete part-time degree programs offered during daytime. Career services available to part-time students: individual and group career counseling, individual job placement, employer recruitment on campus. Part-time tuition: $47 per credit hour for state residents, $106 per credit hour for nonresidents.

Graduate Part-time study available in Graduate School. Basic part-time expenses: $147 per quarter (minimum) tuition for state residents, $318 per quarter (minimum) tuition for nonresidents.

Mid Michigan Community College
Harrison 48625

Public institution; rural setting. Awards A. Barrier-free campus. Total enrollment: 2,048 (all undergraduates); 58% part-time, 59% women. Total faculty: 81. Library holdings: 20,397 bound volumes, 11,302 titles on microform, 255 periodical subscriptions.

Undergraduate Courses offered for part-time students during daytime, evenings, summer. Complete part-time degree programs offered during daytime, evenings, summer. Adult/continuing education programs available. Career services available to part-time students: individual and group career counseling, individual job placement, employer recruitment on campus. Part-time tuition: $24 per credit hour for area residents, $34 per credit hour for state residents, $44 per credit hour for nonresidents.

Monroe County Community College
Monroe 48161

Public institution; small-town setting. Awards A. Barrier-free campus. Total enrollment: 2,937 (all undergraduates); 68% part-time, 60% women, 50% over 25. Total faculty: 98. Library holdings: 46,000 bound volumes, 460 titles on microform, 300 periodical subscriptions, 4,500 records/tapes.

Undergraduate Courses offered for part-time students during daytime, evenings, weekends, summer. Complete part-time degree programs offered during daytime, evenings, summer. Adult/continuing education programs available. Career services available to part-time students: individual and group career counseling, individual job placement, employer recruitment on campus. Part-time tuition: $19 per semester hour for area residents, $28 per semester hour for nonresidents.

Montcalm Community College
Sidney 48885

Public institution; rural setting. Awards A. Barrier-free campus. Total enrollment: 1,363 (all undergraduates); 65% part-time, 48% women. Total faculty: 63. Library holdings: 22,000 bound volumes, 120 periodical subscriptions, 950 records/tapes.

Undergraduate Courses offered for part-time students during daytime, evenings, summer. Complete part-time degree programs offered during daytime, evenings, summer. Adult/continuing education programs available. Career services available to part-time students: individual and group career counseling,

Colleges Offering Part-Time Degree Programs / Michigan

Montcalm Community College (continued)

individual job placement. Part-time tuition: $25 per credit hour for area residents, $37.50 per credit hour for nonresidents.

Muskegon Business College
Muskegon 49442

Independent institution; small-town setting. Awards A. Barrier-free campus. Total enrollment: 1,430 (all undergraduates); 10% part-time, 60% women, 38% over 25. Total faculty: 50. Library holdings: 10,000 bound volumes, 100 periodical subscriptions.

Undergraduate Courses offered for part-time students during daytime, evenings, summer. Complete part-time degree programs offered during daytime, evenings, summer. Adult/continuing education programs available. Career services available to part-time students: individual career counseling, individual job placement. Part-time tuition: $48 per credit hour.

Muskegon Community College
Muskegon 49442

Public institution; small-town setting. Awards A. Barrier-free campus. Total enrollment: 5,000 (all undergraduates); 63% part-time, 42% women. Total faculty: 195. Library holdings: 48,597 bound volumes, 366 titles on microform, 450 periodical subscriptions, 10,200 records/tapes.

Undergraduate Courses offered for part-time students during daytime, evenings, weekends, summer. Complete part-time degree programs offered during daytime, evenings, weekends, summer. Adult/continuing education programs available. Career services available to part-time students: individual career counseling, individual job placement, employer recruitment on campus. Part-time tuition: $26 per credit hour for area residents, $36 per credit hour for state residents, $49 per credit hour for nonresidents.

Nazareth College
Nazareth 49074

Independent-religious instutition; city setting. Awards B. Barrier-free campus. Total enrollment: 671 (all undergraduates); 49% part-time, 78% women. Total faculty: 69. Library holdings: 88,879 bound volumes, 6,284 titles on microform, 450 periodical subscriptions, 3,170 records/tapes.

Undergraduate Courses offered for part-time students during daytime, evenings, weekends, summer. Complete part-time degree programs offered during daytime, evenings, weekends. Adult/continuing education programs available. Career services available to part-time students: individual and group career counseling, individual job placement, employer recruitment on campus. Part-time tuition: $140 per semester hour.

North Central Michigan College
Petoskey 49770

Public institution; small-town setting. Awards A. Total enrollment: 1,822 (all undergraduates); 70% part-time, 64% women, 52% over 25. Total faculty: 87. Library holdings: 22,000 bound volumes, 140 periodical subscriptions.

Undergraduate Courses offered for part-time students during daytime, evenings, summer. Complete part-time degree programs offered during daytime, evenings. Career services available to part-time students: individual and group career counseling. Part-time tuition: $26 per semester hour for area residents, $32 per semester hour for nonresidents.

Northern Michigan University
Marquette 49855

Public institution; small-town setting. Awards A, B, M. Total enrollment: 8,283. Undergraduate enrollment: 7,494; 21% part-time, 48% women. Total faculty: 360. Library holdings: 382,805 bound volumes, 528,000 titles on microform, 2,265 periodical subscriptions, 2,405 records/tapes.

Undergraduate Courses offered for part-time students during daytime, evenings, summer. Complete part-time degree programs offered during daytime. Adult/continuing education programs available. Career services available to part-time students: individual and group career counseling, individual job placement, employer recruitment on campus. Part-time tuition: $46 per credit hour for state residents, $106 per credit hour for nonresidents.

Graduate Part-time study available in School of Graduate Studies. Basic part-time expenses: $60.50 per hour tuition for state residents, $106 per hour tuition for nonresidents. Institutional financial aid available to part-time graduate students in School of Graduate Studies.

Northwestern Michigan College
Traverse City 49684

Public institution; small-town setting. Awards A. Barrier-free campus. Total enrollment: 3,432 (all undergraduates); 40% part-time, 51% women. Total faculty: 123. Library holdings: 40,000 bound volumes, 400 periodical subscriptions, 900 records/tapes.

Undergraduate Courses offered for part-time students during daytime, evenings, weekends, summer. Complete part-time degree programs offered during daytime, evenings, weekends, summer. External degree and adult/continuing education programs available. Career services available to part-time students: individual and group career counseling, individual job placement, employer recruitment on campus. Part-time tuition: $20 per quarter hour for area residents, $33 per quarter hour for state residents, $37 per quarter hour for nonresidents.

Northwood Institute
Midland 48640

Independent institution; small-town setting. Awards A, B. Total enrollment: 1,850 (all undergraduates); 3% part-time, 39% women, 5% over 25. Total faculty: 67. Library holdings: 30,000 bound volumes, 220 periodical subscriptions, 500 records/tapes.

Undergraduate Courses offered for part-time students during daytime, weekends, summer. Complete part-time degree programs offered during daytime, weekends, summer. External degree and adult/continuing education programs available. Career services available to part-time students: individual and group career counseling, individual job placement, employer recruitment on campus. Part-time tuition: $100 per credit hour.

Oakland Community College
Bloomfield Hills 48013

Public institution; city setting. Awards A. Total enrollment: 27,267 (all undergraduates); 79% part-time, 58% women, 44% over 25. Total faculty: 642.

Undergraduate Courses offered for part-time students during daytime, evenings, summer. Complete part-time degree programs offered during daytime, evenings, summer. Adult/continuing education programs available. Career services available to part-time students: individual and group career counseling, individual job placement, employer recruitment on campus. Part-time tuition: $24 per semester hour for area residents, $37

Michigan / **Colleges Offering Part-Time Degree Programs**

per semester hour for state residents, $51 per semester hour for nonresidents.

Oakland University
Rochester 48063

Public institution; small-town setting. Awards B, M, D. Barrier-free campus. Total enrollment: 12,084. Undergraduate enrollment: 10,109; 35% part-time, 60% women, 18% over 25. Total faculty: 527. Library holdings: 300,000 bound volumes, 1,723 periodical subscriptions, 8,852 records/tapes.

Undergraduate Courses offered for part-time students during daytime, evenings. Complete part-time degree programs offered during daytime, evenings. Adult/continuing education programs available. Career services available to part-time students: individual and group career counseling, individual job placement, employer recruitment on campus. Part-time tuition and fees per credit hour range from $45.50 to $52 for state residents, $122 to $132 for nonresidents, according to course level.

Graduate Part-time study available in Graduate School. Degree can be earned exclusively through evening/weekend study in Graduate School. Basic part-time expenses: $82 per credit hour tuition plus $38 per semester fees for state residents, $164 per credit hour tuition plus $38 per semester fees for nonresidents.

Olivet College
Olivet 49076

Independent-religious instutition; rural setting. Awards B. Total enrollment: 616 (all undergraduates); 5% part-time, 40% women, 1% over 25. Total faculty: 58. Library holdings: 81,904 bound volumes, 604 titles on microform, 700 periodical subscriptions, 1,230 records/tapes.

Undergraduate Courses offered for part-time students during daytime, evenings, summer. Complete part-time degree programs offered during daytime, evenings, summer. Career services available to part-time students: individual and group career counseling, individual job placement, employer recruitment on campus. Part-time tuition: $165 per semester hour.

Sacred Heart Seminary College
Detroit 48206

Independent-religious instutition; metropolitan setting. Awards A, B. Barrier-free campus. Total enrollment: 210 (all undergraduates); 75% part-time, 15% women. Total faculty: 23. Library holdings: 50,000 bound volumes, 700 titles on microform, 200 periodical subscriptions, 1,400 records/tapes.

Undergraduate Courses offered for part-time students during daytime, evenings, summer. Complete part-time degree programs offered during daytime, evenings, summer. Career services available to part-time students: individual and group career counseling. Part-time tuition: $50 per credit.

Saginaw Valley State College
University Center 48710

Public institution; city setting. Awards B, M. Barrier-free campus. Total enrollment: 4,650. Undergraduate enrollment: 4,151; 46% part-time, 53% women, 48% over 25. Total faculty: 259. Library holdings: 100,075 bound volumes, 452 titles on microform, 691 periodical subscriptions, 3,300 records/tapes.

Undergraduate Courses offered for part-time students during daytime, evenings, summer. Complete part-time degree programs offered during daytime, evenings. Adult/continuing education programs available. Career services available to part-time students: individual career counseling, individual job placement, employer recruitment on campus. Part-time tuition: $52 per semester hour for state residents, $104 per semester hour for nonresidents.

Graduate Part-time study available in School of Business and Management, School of Education. Degree can be earned exclusively through evening/weekend study in School of Business and Management, School of Education. Basic part-time expenses: $69 per credit tuition plus $3 per credit fees for state residents, $138 per credit tuition plus $3 per credit fees for nonresidents.

St John's Provincial Seminary
Plymouth 48170

Independent-religious institution (graduate only). Total enrollment: 117 (coed; 35% part-time). Total faculty: 30. Library holdings: 55,891 bound volumes, 2,312 microforms.

Graduate Part-time study available in Graduate and Professional Programs. Basic part-time expenses: $70 per credit tuition. Institutional financial aid available to part-time graduate students in Graduate and Professional Programs.

Saint Mary's College
Orchard Lake 48033

Independent-religious instutition; small-town setting. Awards A, B. Total enrollment: 256 (all undergraduates); 45% part-time, 50% women, 20% over 25. Total faculty: 40. Library holdings: 46,000 bound volumes, 450 periodical subscriptions, 1,500 records/tapes.

Undergraduate Courses offered for part-time students during daytime, evenings. Complete part-time degree programs offered during daytime, evenings. Adult/continuing education programs available. Career services available to part-time students: individual and group career counseling, individual job placement. Part-time tuition: $75 per credit hour.

Schoolcraft College
Livonia 48152

Public institution; city setting. Awards A. Total enrollment: 8,686 (all undergraduates); 75% part-time, 51% women, 20% over 25. Total faculty: 350.

Undergraduate Courses offered for part-time students during daytime, evenings, summer. Complete part-time degree programs offered during daytime, evenings, summer. Adult/continuing education programs available. Career services available to part-time students: individual and group career counseling, individual job placement, employer recruitment on campus. Part-time tuition: $29.25 per credit hour for area residents, $40 per credit hour for state residents, $59.50 per credit hour for nonresidents.

Siena Heights College
Adrian 49221

Independent-religious instutition; small-town setting. Awards A, B, M. Total enrollment: 1,483. Undergraduate enrollment: 1,414; 49% part-time, 59% women. Total faculty: 113. Library holdings: 91,486 bound volumes, 22,311 titles on microform, 545 periodical subscriptions, 4,206 records/tapes.

Undergraduate Courses offered for part-time students during daytime, evenings, weekends, summer. Complete part-time degree programs offered during daytime, evenings, weekends, summer. External degree and adult/continuing education pro-

161

Colleges Offering Part-Time Degree Programs / *Michigan*

Siena Heights College (continued)

grams available. Career services available to part-time students: individual and group career counseling, individual job placement, employer recruitment on campus. Part-time tuition: $136 per semester hour.

Graduate Part-time study available in Graduate Studies. Degree can be earned exclusively through evening/weekend study in Graduate Studies. Basic part-time expenses: $141 per semester hour tuition.

Southwestern Michigan College
Dowagiac 49047

Public institution; rural setting. Awards A. Barrier-free campus. Total enrollment: 3,000 (all undergraduates); 44% part-time, 56% women, 35% over 25. Total faculty: 170. Library holdings: 26,000 bound volumes, 375 periodical subscriptions, 1,500 records/tapes.

Undergraduate Courses offered for part-time students during daytime, evenings, weekends, summer. Complete part-time degree programs offered during daytime, evenings, weekends, summer. Adult/continuing education programs available. Career services available to part-time students: individual and group career counseling, individual job placement, employer recruitment on campus. Part-time tuition: $26 per credit for area residents, $32 per credit for state residents, $37 per credit for nonresidents.

Spring Arbor College
Spring Arbor 49283

Independent-religious instutition; rural setting. Awards A, B. Total enrollment: 633 (all undergraduates); 15% part-time, 55% women. Total faculty: 60. Library holdings: 75,673 bound volumes, 202 titles on microform, 348 periodical subscriptions, 3,106 records/tapes.

Undergraduate Courses offered for part-time students during daytime, evenings, summer. Complete part-time degree programs offered during daytime, evenings. External degree and adult/continuing education programs available. Career services available to part-time students: individual and group career counseling, individual job placement, employer recruitment on campus. Part-time tuition: $100 per credit.

Suomi College
Hancock 49930

Independent-religious instutition; small-town setting. Awards A. Total enrollment: 598 (all undergraduates); 1% part-time, 62% women, 5% over 25. Total faculty: 43. Library holdings: 22,348 bound volumes, 171 periodical subscriptions, 12,272 records/tapes.

Undergraduate Courses offered for part-time students during daytime, evenings. Complete part-time degree programs offered during daytime, evenings. Adult/continuing education programs available. Career services available to part-time students: individual and group career counseling, individual job placement, employer recruitment on campus. Part-time tuition: $250 per credit.

Thomas M Cooley Law School
Lansing 48933

Independent institution (graduate only). Total enrollment: 1,159 (coed). Total faculty: 93. Library holdings: 79,633 bound volumes, 57,081 microforms.

Graduate Part-time study available in Professional Program. Degree can be earned exclusively through evening/weekend study in Professional Program. Basic part-time expenses: $157 per credit tuition plus $5 per trimester fees. Institutional financial aid available to part-time graduate students in Professional Program.

University of Detroit
Detroit 48221

Independent-religious instutition; metropolitan setting. Awards B, M, D. Total enrollment: 6,310. Undergraduate enrollment: 3,814; 39% part-time, 46% women, 33% over 25. Total faculty: 430. Library holdings: 470,000 bound volumes, 135,000 titles on microform, 1,600 periodical subscriptions, 34,000 records/tapes.

Undergraduate Courses offered for part-time students during daytime, evenings, summer. Complete part-time degree programs offered during daytime, evenings, summer. Adult/continuing education programs available. Career services available to part-time students: individual and group career counseling, individual job placement, employer recruitment on campus. Part-time tuition: $104 per credit hour.

Graduate Part-time study available in College of Business and Administration, College of Engineering and Science, College of Liberal Arts, School of Education and Human Services, School of Law. Degree can be earned exclusively through evening/weekend study in College of Business and Administration. Basic part-time expenses: $184 per credit tuition plus $30 per semester fees.

University of Michigan
Ann Arbor 48109

Public institution; city setting. Awards B, M, D. Barrier-free campus. Total enrollment: 34,289. Undergraduate enrollment: 21,970; 8% part-time, 46% women. Total faculty: 2,768. Library holdings: 5.8 million bound volumes, 52,460 periodical subscriptions, 32,586 records/tapes.

Undergraduate Courses offered for part-time students during daytime, summer. Complete part-time degree programs offered during daytime, summer. Adult/continuing education programs available. Career services available to part-time students: individual and group career counseling, individual job placement, employer recruitment on campus. Part-time tuition and fees per semester (1 to 11 credits) range from $167 to $1146 for state residents, $356 to $3347 for nonresidents, according to course load and class level.

Graduate Part-time study available in Horace H. Rackham School of Graduate Studies, College of Architecture and Urban Planning, College of Pharmacy, Graduate School of Business Administration, Medical School, School of Dentistry, School of Natural Resources, School of Public Health, School of Social Work. Degree can be earned exclusively through evening/weekend study in Graduate School of Business Administration. Basic part-time expenses: $580 per trimester (minimum) tuition plus $12.63 per trimester fees for state residents, $1231 per trimester (minimum) tuition plus $12.63 per trimester fees for nonresidents. Institutional financial aid available to part-time graduate students in Horace H. Rackham School of Graduate Studies, College of Architecture and Urban Planning, College of Pharmacy, Graduate School of Business Administration, Medical School, School of Dentistry, School of Natural Resources, School of Public Health, School of Social Work.

Michigan / Colleges Offering Part-Time Degree Programs

University of Michigan–Dearborn
Dearborn 48128

Public institution; city setting. Awards B, M. Barrier-free campus. Total enrollment: 5,649. Undergraduate enrollment: 5,125; 40% part-time, 48% women, 30% over 25. Total faculty: 300. Library holdings: 225,000 bound volumes, 1,600 periodical subscriptions, 1,200 records/tapes.

Undergraduate Courses offered for part-time students during daytime, evenings. Complete part-time degree programs offered during daytime, evenings. Career services available to part-time students: individual and group career counseling, individual job placement, employer recruitment on campus. Part-time tuition: $70 per credit hour for state residents, $210 per credit hour for nonresidents.

Graduate Part-time study available in Division of Education, School of Engineering, School of Management, Division of Interdisciplinary Studies. Degree can be earned exclusively through evening/weekend study in Division of Education. Basic part-time expenses: $105 per credit hour tuition plus $50 per semester fees for state residents, $340 per credit hour tuition plus $140 per semester fees for nonresidents. Institutional financial aid available to part-time graduate students in School of Engineering.

University of Michigan–Flint
Flint 48502

Public institution; city setting. Awards B, M. Barrier-free campus. Total enrollment: 5,707. Undergraduate enrollment: 5,410; 51% part-time, 54% women, 41% over 25. Total faculty: 233. Library holdings: 135,921 bound volumes, 245,646 titles on microform, 1,000 periodical subscriptions, 2,414 records/tapes.

Undergraduate Courses offered for part-time students during daytime, evenings, weekends, summer. Complete part-time degree programs offered during daytime, evenings, summer. Adult/continuing education programs available. Career services available to part-time students: individual and group career counseling, individual job placement, employer recruitment on campus. Part-time tuition: $63 per credit hour for state residents, $200 per credit hour for nonresidents.

Walsh College of Accountancy and Business Administration
Troy 48007

Independent institution; city setting. Awards B, M. Barrier-free campus. Total enrollment: 2,072. Undergraduate enrollment: 1,575; 61% part-time, 51% women. Total faculty: 76. Library holdings: 12,000 bound volumes, 600 periodical subscriptions.

Undergraduate Courses offered for part-time students during daytime, evenings, weekends, summer. Complete part-time degree programs offered during daytime, evenings. Adult/continuing education programs available. Career services available to part-time students: individual and group career counseling, individual job placement, employer recruitment on campus. Part-time tuition: $77 per credit hour.

Graduate Part-time study available in Graduate Programs. Basic part-time expenses: $105 per semester hour tuition plus $25 per semester fees. Institutional financial aid available to part-time graduate students in Graduate Programs.

Washtenaw Community College
Ann Arbor 48106

Public institution; city setting. Awards A. Barrier-free campus. Total enrollment: 8,733 (all undergraduates); 69% part-time, 49% women. Total faculty: 574. Library holdings: 52,000 bound volumes, 536 periodical subscriptions, 1,804 records/tapes.

Undergraduate Courses offered for part-time students during daytime, evenings, weekends, summer. Complete part-time degree programs offered during daytime, evenings, weekends, summer. External degree and adult/continuing education programs available. Career services available to part-time students: individual and group career counseling, individual job placement, employer recruitment on campus. Part-time tuition: $29 per credit hour for area residents, $46 per credit hour for state residents, $60 per credit hour for nonresidents.

Wayne County Community College
Detroit 48226

Public institution; metropolitan setting. Awards A. Barrier-free campus. Total enrollment: 17,549 (all undergraduates); 65% part-time, 67% women. Total faculty: 850.

Undergraduate Courses offered for part-time students during daytime, evenings, weekends. Complete part-time degree programs offered during daytime, evenings, weekends. Career services available to part-time students: individual and group career counseling, individual job placement, employer recruitment on campus. Part-time tuition: $26 per semester hour for area residents, $37 per semester hour for state residents, $48 per semester hour for nonresidents.

Wayne State University
Detroit 48202

Public institution; metropolitan setting. Awards B, M, D. Barrier-free campus. Total enrollment: 29,639. Undergraduate enrollment: 20,422; 36% part-time, 36% women. Total faculty: 2,148. Library holdings: 1.9 million bound volumes, 1.3 million titles on microform, 14,448 periodical subscriptions.

Undergraduate Courses offered for part-time students during daytime, evenings, weekends, summer. Complete part-time degree programs offered during daytime, evenings, weekends, summer. External degree and adult/continuing education programs available. Career services available to part-time students: individual and group career counseling, individual job placement, employer recruitment on campus. Part-time tuition: $56 per credit hour for state residents, $126 per credit hour for nonresidents.

Graduate Part-time study available in Graduate School, College of Pharmacy and Allied Health Professions, Law School, School of Medicine. Degree can be earned exclusively through evening/weekend study in Graduate School. Basic part-time expenses: $82 per credit tuition plus $40 per semester fees for state residents, $178 per credit tuition plus $40 per semester fees for nonresidents. Institutional financial aid available to part-time graduate students in Law School.

Western Michigan University
Kalamazoo 49008

Public institution; city setting. Awards B, M, D. Total enrollment: 18,542. Undergraduate enrollment: 15,331; 18% part-time, 47% women, 26% over 25. Total faculty: 1,171. Library holdings: 1.2 million bound volumes, 576,844 titles on microform, 11,000 periodical subscriptions, 10,029 records/tapes.

Undergraduate Courses offered for part-time students during daytime, evenings, summer. Complete part-time degree programs offered during daytime. Adult/continuing education programs available. Career services available to part-time students: individual and group career counseling, individual job placement, employer recruitment on campus. Part-time tuition:

Colleges Offering Part-Time Degree Programs / *Michigan*

Western Michigan University (continued)
$46.25 per credit hour for state residents, $111.75 per credit hour for nonresidents.
Graduate Part-time study available in Graduate College. Basic part-time expenses: $61.50 per credit hour tuition for state residents, $149.75 per credit hour tuition for nonresidents. Institutional financial aid available to part-time graduate students in Graduate College.

West Shore Community College
Scottville 49454
Public institution; rural setting. Awards A. Barrier-free campus. Total enrollment: 1,152 (all undergraduates); 47% part-time, 54% women. Total faculty: 67. Library holdings: 12,089 bound volumes, 1,106 titles on microform, 176 periodical subscriptions, 1,300 records/tapes.
Undergraduate Courses offered for part-time students during daytime, evenings, summer. Complete part-time degree programs offered during daytime, evenings, summer. Adult/continuing education programs available. Career services available to part-time students: individual and group career counseling, individual job placement, employer recruitment on campus. Part-time tuition: $25 per credit for area residents, $38 per credit for state residents, $50 per credit for nonresidents.

William Tyndale College
Farmington Hills 48018
Independent-religious instutition; small-town setting. Awards B. Barrier-free campus. Total enrollment: 321 (all undergraduates); 56% part-time, 39% women, 51% over 25. Total faculty: 31. Library holdings: 48,548 bound volumes, 5 titles on microform, 169 periodical subscriptions, 1,950 records/tapes.
Undergraduate Courses offered for part-time students during daytime, evenings, summer. Complete part-time degree programs offered during daytime. Adult/continuing education programs available. Career services available to part-time students: individual career counseling. Part-time tuition: $85 per credit.

MINNESOTA

Anoka-Ramsey Community College
Coon Rapids 55433
Public institution; city setting. Awards A. Barrier-free campus. Total enrollment: 3,880 (all undergraduates); 57% part-time, 60% women. Total faculty: 137. Library holdings: 29,089 bound volumes, 229 periodical subscriptions, 3,052 records/tapes.
Undergraduate Courses offered for part-time students during daytime, evenings, summer. Complete part-time degree programs offered during daytime, evenings, summer. Adult/continuing education programs available. Career services available to part-time students: individual and group career counseling, individual job placement, employer recruitment on campus. Part-time tuition: $24.50 per credit for state residents, $49 per credit for nonresidents.

Augsburg College
Minneapolis 55454
Independent-religious instutition; metropolitan setting. Awards B. Total enrollment: 1,250 (all undergraduates); 4% part-time, 53% women. Total faculty: 183. Library holdings: 145,345 bound volumes, 12,581 titles on microform, 12,586 periodical subscriptions, 1,000 records/tapes.
Undergraduate Courses offered for part-time students during daytime, evenings, weekends, summer. Complete part-time degree programs offered during daytime, weekends. Adult/continuing education programs available. Career services available to part-time students: individual and group career counseling, individual job placement, employer recruitment on campus. Part-time tuition: $775 per course.

Austin Community College
Austin 55912
Public institution; small-town setting. Awards A. Barrier-free campus. Total enrollment: 1,001 (all undergraduates); 37% part-time, 59% women, 38% over 25. Total faculty: 69. Library holdings: 20,000 bound volumes, 268 periodical subscriptions, 2,900 records/tapes.
Undergraduate Courses offered for part-time students during daytime, evenings, summer. Complete part-time degree programs offered during daytime, evenings, summer. Adult/continuing education programs available. Career services available to part-time students: individual and group career counseling, individual job placement. Part-time tuition: $24.50 per quarter hour for state residents, $49 per quarter hour for nonresidents.

Bemidji State University
Bemidji 56601
Public institution; rural setting. Awards A, B, M. Total enrollment: 4,153. Undergraduate enrollment: 3,989; 14% part-time, 48% women, 21% over 25. Total faculty: 229. Library holdings: 265,012 bound volumes, 482,181 titles on microform, 22,247 periodical subscriptions, 3,018 records/tapes.
Undergraduate Courses offered for part-time students during daytime, evenings, summer. Complete part-time degree programs offered during daytime, evenings, summer. External degree and adult/continuing education programs available. Career services available to part-time students: individual and group career counseling, individual job placement, employer recruitment on campus. Part-time tuition: $26.85 per quarter hour for state residents, $53.70 per quarter hour for nonresidents.
Graduate Part-time study available in Graduate Studies. Basic part-time expenses: $34.40 per credit tuition plus $5.05 per credit fees for state residents, $68.80 per credit tuition plus $5.05 per credit fees for nonresidents.

Bethany Lutheran College
Mankato 56001
Independent-religious instutition; small-town setting. Awards A. Total enrollment: 236 (all undergraduates); 0% part-time, 52% women, 3% over 25. Total faculty: 29. Library holdings: 20,000 bound volumes, 235 periodical subscriptions, 1,200 records/tapes.
Undergraduate Courses offered for part-time students during daytime. Complete part-time degree programs offered during daytime. Career services available to part-time students: individual and group career counseling. Part-time tuition: $135 per credit hour.

Bethel College
St Paul 55112
Independent-religious instutition; metropolitan setting. Awards A, B. Total enrollment: 1,931 (all undergraduates); 5%

Minnesota / **Colleges Offering Part-Time Degree Programs**

part-time, 60% women, 1% over 25. Total faculty: 194. Library holdings: 120,000 bound volumes, 640 periodical subscriptions, 3,700 records/tapes.
Undergraduate Courses offered for part-time students during daytime, evenings, weekends, summer. Complete part-time degree programs offered during daytime. Career services available to part-time students: individual and group career counseling, individual job placement, employer recruitment on campus. Part-time tuition: $775 per course.

Bethel Theological Seminary
St Paul 55112
Independent-religious institution (graduate only). Total enrollment: 481 (coed; 42% part-time). Total faculty: 41. Library holdings: 115,000 bound volumes, 2,250 microforms.
Graduate Part-time study available in Graduate and Professional Programs. Basic part-time expenses: $230 per course tuition. Institutional financial aid available to part-time graduate students in Graduate and Professional Programs.

Brainerd Community College
Brainerd 56401
Public institution; small-town setting. Awards A. Total enrollment: 565 (all undergraduates); 30% part-time, 54% women, 30% over 25. Total faculty: 43. Library holdings: 16,052 bound volumes, 4,350 titles on microform, 286 periodical subscriptions, 1,416 records/tapes.
Undergraduate Courses offered for part-time students during daytime, evenings. Complete part-time degree programs offered during daytime, evenings. Career services available to part-time students: individual career counseling. Part-time tuition: $24.50 per quarter hour for state residents, $49 per quarter hour for nonresidents.

College of Saint Benedict
Saint Joseph 56374
Independent-religious instutition; rural setting. Awards A, B. Total enrollment: 1,747 (all undergraduates); 1% part-time, 100% women, 1% over 25. Total faculty: 136. Library holdings: 115,876 bound volumes, 497 titles on microform, 710 periodical subscriptions, 3,632 records/tapes.
Undergraduate Courses offered for part-time students during daytime, evenings. Complete part-time degree programs offered during daytime, evenings. Adult/continuing education programs available. Career services available to part-time students: individual and group career counseling, individual job placement, employer recruitment on campus. Part-time tuition: $190 per credit hour.

College of St Catherine
St Paul 55105
Independent-religious instutition; metropolitan setting. Awards B, M. Total enrollment: 2,291. Undergraduate enrollment: 2,262; 34% part-time, 100% women, 26% over 25. Total faculty: 178. Library holdings: 220,000 bound volumes, 4,503 titles on microform, 1,036 periodical subscriptions, 7,600 records/tapes.
Undergraduate Courses offered for part-time students during daytime, evenings, weekends, summer. Complete part-time degree programs offered during daytime, evenings, weekends, summer. Adult/continuing education programs available. Career services available to part-time students: individual and group career counseling, individual job placement, employer recruitment on campus. Part-time tuition: $670 per course.

College of St Scholastica
Duluth 55811
Independent-religious instutition; city setting. Awards B, M. Total enrollment: 1,307. Undergraduate enrollment: 1,283; 17% part-time, 76% women, 20% over 25. Total faculty: 120. Library holdings: 87,000 bound volumes, 580 periodical subscriptions.
Undergraduate Courses offered for part-time students during daytime, evenings, summer. Complete part-time degree programs offered during daytime. External degree and adult/continuing education programs available. Career services available to part-time students: individual and group career counseling, individual job placement. Part-time tuition: $104 per credit.
Graduate Part-time study available in Graduate Studies. Degree can be earned exclusively through evening/weekend study in Graduate Studies. Basic part-time expenses: $109 per credit tuition plus $50 per quarter fees. Institutional financial aid available to part-time graduate students in Graduate Studies.

College of Saint Teresa
Winona 55987
Independent-religious instutition; small-town setting. Awards B. Total enrollment: 550 (all undergraduates); 5% part-time, 97% women, 10% over 25. Total faculty: 80. Library holdings: 137,008 bound volumes, 524 periodical subscriptions, 14,673 records/tapes.
Undergraduate Courses offered for part-time students during daytime, summer. Complete part-time degree programs offered during daytime, summer. Adult/continuing education programs available. Career services available to part-time students: individual and group career counseling, individual job placement, employer recruitment on campus. Part-time tuition: $110 per credit.

College of St Thomas
St Paul 55105
Independent-religious instutition; metropolitan setting. Awards B, M. Total enrollment: 5,959. Undergraduate enrollment: 4,026; 16% part-time, 42% women. Total faculty: 350. Library holdings: 200,000 bound volumes.
Undergraduate Courses offered for part-time students during daytime, evenings, weekends, summer. Complete part-time degree programs offered during daytime, evenings, weekends, summer. Adult/continuing education programs available. Career services available to part-time students: individual career counseling, individual job placement, employer recruitment on campus. Part-time tuition: $670 per course.
Graduate Part-time study available in Graduate Studies. Basic part-time expenses: $140 per credit (minimum) tuition. Institutional financial aid available to part-time graduate students in Graduate Studies.

Concordia College
St Paul 55104
Independent-religious instutition; metropolitan setting. Awards A, B. Total enrollment: 779 (all undergraduates); 8% part-time, 52% women, 15% over 25. Total faculty: 73. Library holdings: 92,000 bound volumes, 425 periodical subscriptions, 4,000 records/tapes.
Undergraduate Courses offered for part-time students during daytime, evenings, summer. Complete part-time degree programs offered during daytime, evenings, summer. Adult/continuing education programs available. Career services available to part-time students: individual and group career counseling,

Colleges Offering Part-Time Degree Programs / Minnesota

Concordia College (continued)

individual job placement. Part-time tuition: $118 per quarter hour.

Fergus Falls Community College
Fergus Falls 56537

Public institution; small-town setting. Awards A. Barrier-free campus. Total enrollment: 680 (all undergraduates); 11% part-time, 54% women, 14% over 25. Total faculty: 44. Library holdings: 25,000 bound volumes, 32 titles on microform, 375 periodical subscriptions, 3,800 records/tapes.

Undergraduate Courses offered for part-time students during daytime, evenings. Complete part-time degree programs offered during daytime. Career services available to part-time students: individual and group career counseling, individual job placement, employer recruitment on campus. Part-time tuition: $24.50 per credit for state residents, $45 per credit for nonresidents.

Golden Valley Lutheran College
Minneapolis 55422

Independent institution; metropolitan setting. Awards A. Total enrollment: 479 (all undergraduates); 4% part-time, 50% women, 6% over 25. Total faculty: 43. Library holdings: 30,000 bound volumes, 247 periodical subscriptions, 500 records/tapes.

Undergraduate Courses offered for part-time students during daytime, evenings. Complete part-time degree programs offered during daytime. Adult/continuing education programs available. Career services available to part-time students: individual and group career counseling. Part-time tuition: $147 per credit.

Hamline University
St Paul 55104

Independent-religious instutition; metropolitan setting. Awards B, M. Total enrollment: 1,866. Undergraduate enrollment: 1,232; 4% part-time, 50% women. Total faculty: 127. Library holdings: 155,000 bound volumes, 50,000 titles on microform, 700 periodical subscriptions.

Undergraduate Courses offered for part-time students during daytime. Complete part-time degree programs offered during daytime. Adult/continuing education programs available. Career services available to part-time students: individual and group career counseling, individual job placement, employer recruitment on campus. Part-time tuition: $800 per course.

Graduate Part-time study available in College of Liberal Arts, School of Law. Degree can be earned exclusively through evening/weekend study in College of Liberal Arts.Basic part-time expenses: $445 per course tuition. Institutional financial aid available to part-time graduate students in College of Liberal Arts.

Hibbing Community College
Hibbing 55746

Public institution; small-town setting. Awards A. Barrier-free campus. Total enrollment: 842 (all undergraduates); 38% part-time, 55% women. Total faculty: 51. Library holdings: 19,536 bound volumes, 190 periodical subscriptions, 250 records/tapes.

Undergraduate Courses offered for part-time students during daytime, evenings, summer. Complete part-time degree programs offered during daytime, evenings. Adult/continuing education programs available. Career services available to part-time students: individual career counseling, individual job placement, employer recruitment on campus. Part-time tuition: $24.50 per quarter hour for state residents, $49 per quarter hour for nonresidents.

Inver Hills Community College
Inver Grove Heights 55075

Public institution; city setting. Awards A. Barrier-free campus. Total enrollment: 3,668 (all undergraduates); 64% part-time, 55% women, 25% over 25. Total faculty: 186. Library holdings: 30,000 bound volumes, 320 periodical subscriptions, 2,500 records/tapes.

Undergraduate Courses offered for part-time students during daytime, evenings, weekends, summer. Complete part-time degree programs offered during daytime, evenings, summer. External degree and adult/continuing education programs available. Career services available to part-time students: individual and group career counseling, individual job placement, employer recruitment on campus. Part-time tuition: $24.50 per credit for state residents, $49 per credit for nonresidents.

Itasca Community College
Grand Rapids 55744

Public institution; rural setting. Awards A. Total enrollment: 1,009 (all undergraduates); 40% part-time, 62% women, 20% over 25. Total faculty: 110. Library holdings: 765 bound volumes, 40 titles on microform, 106 periodical subscriptions, 943 records/tapes.

Undergraduate Courses offered for part-time students during daytime, evenings, weekends, summer. Complete part-time degree programs offered during daytime, evenings, weekends, summer. Adult/continuing education programs available. Career services available to part-time students: individual and group career counseling, individual job placement, employer recruitment on campus. Part-time tuition: $24.50 per credit for state residents, $49 per credit for nonresidents.

Luther Northwestern Theological Seminary
St Paul 55108

Independent-religious institution (graduate only). Total enrollment: 841 (coed; 19% part-time). Total faculty: 59.

Graduate Part-time study available in Graduate and Professional Programs.Basic part-time expenses: $57.50 per credit tuition. Institutional financial aid available to part-time graduate students in Graduate and Professional Programs.

Macalester College
St Paul 55105

Independent-religious instutition; metropolitan setting. Awards B. Total enrollment: 1,682 (all undergraduates); 2% part-time, 51% women. Total faculty: 149. Library holdings: 292,500 bound volumes, 24,900 titles on microform, 969 periodical subscriptions, 7,400 records/tapes.

Undergraduate Courses offered for part-time students during daytime, summer. Complete part-time degree programs offered during daytime, summer. Adult/continuing education programs available. Career services available to part-time students: individual and group career counseling. Part-time tuition: $850 per course.

Mankato State University
Mankato 56001

Public institution; small-town setting. Awards A, B, M. Barrier-free campus. Total enrollment: 12,700. Undergraduate enrollment: 11,200; 13% part-time, 52% women, 38% over 25. Total faculty: 586. Library holdings: 538,378 bound volumes, 510,272 titles on microform, 2,323 periodical subscriptions, 14,117 records/tapes.

Undergraduate Courses offered for part-time students during daytime, evenings. Complete part-time degree programs offered during daytime, evenings. External degree and adult/continuing education programs available. Career services available to part-time students: individual and group career counseling, individual job placement, employer recruitment on campus. Part-time tuition: $30.90 per quarter hour for state residents, $57.75 per quarter hour for nonresidents.

Graduate Part-time study available in College of Graduate Studies. Basic part-time expenses: $34.40 per quarter hour tuition for state residents, $68.80 per quarter hour tuition for nonresidents. Institutional financial aid available to part-time graduate students in College of Graduate Studies.

Mesabi Community College
Virginia 55792

Public institution; small-town setting. Awards A. Barrier-free campus. Total enrollment: 1,078 (all undergraduates); 47% part-time, 50% women, 25% over 25. Total faculty: 35. Library holdings: 27,500 bound volumes, 12 titles on microform, 145 periodical subscriptions, 10,000 records/tapes.

Undergraduate Courses offered for part-time students during daytime, evenings, weekends, summer. Complete part-time degree programs offered during daytime, evenings. Adult/continuing education programs available. Career services available to part-time students: individual and group career counseling, individual job placement. Part-time tuition: $24.50 per quarter hour for state residents, $49 per quarter hour for nonresidents.

Metropolitan State University
St Paul 55101

Public institution; metropolitan setting. Awards B, M. Total enrollment: 3,529 (all undergraduates); 87% part-time, 59% women. Total faculty: 480.

Undergraduate Courses offered for part-time students during daytime, evenings, weekends, summer. Complete part-time degree programs offered during daytime, evenings, weekends, summer. Adult/continuing education programs available. Career services available to part-time students: individual and group career counseling. Part-time tuition: $101 per course for state residents, $202 per course for nonresidents.

Graduate Part-time study available in Graduate Program in Management and Administration. Degree can be earned exclusively through evening/weekend study in Graduate Program in Management and Administration. Basic part-time expenses: $137.50 per course tuition plus $3 per quarter fees for state residents, $275 per course tuition plus $3 per quarter fees for nonresidents. Institutional financial aid available to part-time graduate students in Graduate Program in Management and Administration.

Minneapolis College of Art and Design
Minneapolis 55404

Independent institution; metropolitan setting. Awards B. Total enrollment: 509 (all undergraduates); 10% part-time, 57% women. Total faculty: 60. Library holdings: 50,000 bound volumes, 175 periodical subscriptions, 720 records/tapes.

Undergraduate Courses offered for part-time students during daytime, evenings, summer. Complete part-time degree programs offered during daytime, evenings, summer. Adult/continuing education programs available. Career services available to part-time students: individual and group career counseling, individual job placement. Part-time tuition: $230 per credit.

Minneapolis Community College
Minneapolis 55403

Public institution; metropolitan setting. Awards A. Total enrollment: 2,919 (all undergraduates); 54% part-time, 57% women, 48% over 25. Total faculty: 161. Library holdings: 23,200 bound volumes, 135 titles on microform, 190 periodical subscriptions, 3,000 records/tapes.

Undergraduate Courses offered for part-time students during daytime, evenings, weekends, summer. Complete part-time degree programs offered during daytime, evenings, weekends, summer. Adult/continuing education programs available. Career services available to part-time students: individual and group career counseling, individual job placement, employer recruitment on campus. Part-time tuition: $24.50 per credit for state residents, $49 per credit for nonresidents.

Moorhead State University
Moorhead 56560

Public institution; city setting. Awards A, B, M. Barrier-free campus. Total enrollment: 7,334. Undergraduate enrollment: 7,053; 22% part-time, 58% women. Total faculty: 343. Library holdings: 300,000 bound volumes, 1,250 periodical subscriptions.

Undergraduate Courses offered for part-time students during daytime, evenings, weekends, summer. Complete part-time degree programs offered during evenings. External degree and adult/continuing education programs available. Career services available to part-time students: individual and group career counseling, individual job placement, employer recruitment on campus. Part-time tuition: $30.35 per credit for state residents, $57.20 per credit for nonresidents.

Graduate Part-time study available in Graduate Studies. Basic part-time expenses: $34.40 per credit tuition plus $4 per credit fees for state residents, $68.80 per credit tuition plus $4 per credit fees for nonresidents.

National Education Center–Brown Institute Campus
Minneapolis 55406

Proprietary institution; metropolitan setting. Awards A. Barrier-free campus. Total enrollment: 1,500 (all undergraduates); 16% part-time, 28% women. Total faculty: 69. Library holdings: 500 bound volumes.

Undergraduate Courses offered for part-time students during daytime, evenings. Complete part-time degree programs offered during daytime, evenings. Career services available to part-time students: individual career counseling, individual job placement, employer recruitment on campus. Part-time tuition: $1720 per year.

Normandale Community College
Bloomington 55431

Public institution; city setting. Awards A. Barrier-free campus. Total enrollment: 6,600 (all undergraduates); 48% part-time,

Colleges Offering Part-Time Degree Programs / Minnesota

Normandale Community College (continued)

55% women. Total faculty: 220. Library holdings: 40,000 bound volumes, 250 periodical subscriptions, 1,200 records/tapes.

Undergraduate Courses offered for part-time students during daytime, evenings, weekends, summer. Complete part-time degree programs offered during daytime, evenings, weekends, summer. Adult/continuing education programs available. Career services available to part-time students: individual and group career counseling, individual job placement, employer recruitment on campus. Part-time tuition: $24.50 per credit for state residents, $49 per credit for nonresidents.

North Central Bible College
Minneapolis 55404

Independent-religious instutition; metropolitan setting. Awards A, B. Total enrollment: 1,082 (all undergraduates); 19% part-time, 46% women. Total faculty: 51. Library holdings: 35,000 bound volumes, 1,000 titles on microform, 120 periodical subscriptions.

Undergraduate Courses offered for part-time students during daytime, evenings, summer. Complete part-time degree programs offered during daytime. Career services available to part-time students: individual and group career counseling, individual job placement, employer recruitment on campus. Part-time tuition: $103 per credit hour.

North Hennepin Community College
Minneapolis 55445

Public institution; metropolitan setting. Awards A. Barrier-free campus. Total enrollment: 4,950 (all undergraduates); 55% part-time, 58% women. Total faculty: 175. Library holdings: 32,000 bound volumes, 300 periodical subscriptions, 2,000 records/tapes.

Undergraduate Courses offered for part-time students during daytime, evenings, weekends, summer. Complete part-time degree programs offered during daytime, evenings. Adult/continuing education programs available. Career services available to part-time students: individual and group career counseling, individual job placement, employer recruitment on campus. Part-time tuition: $24.50 per quarter hour for state residents, $49 per quarter hour for nonresidents.

Northland Community College
Thief River Falls 56701

Public institution; rural setting. Awards A. Barrier-free campus. Total enrollment: 730 (all undergraduates); 56% part-time, 55% women, 36% over 25. Total faculty: 33.

Undergraduate Courses offered for part-time students during daytime, evenings. Complete part-time degree programs offered during daytime, evenings. Adult/continuing education programs available. Career services available to part-time students: individual and group career counseling. Part-time tuition: $24.50 per credit for state residents, $49 per credit for nonresidents.

Northwestern College
Roseville 55113

Independent-religious instutition; metropolitan setting. Awards A, B. Total enrollment: 949 (all undergraduates); 5% part-time, 48% women. Total faculty: 73. Library holdings: 65,375 bound volumes, 510 titles on microform, 500 periodical subscriptions, 2,849 records/tapes.

Undergraduate Courses offered for part-time students during daytime. Complete part-time degree programs offered during daytime. Adult/continuing education programs available. Career services available to part-time students: individual and group career counseling, individual job placement, employer recruitment on campus. Part-time tuition: $125 per credit.

Rochester Community College
Rochester 55904

Public institution; city setting. Awards A. Barrier-free campus. Total enrollment: 3,289 (all undergraduates); 37% part-time, 61% women, 31% over 25. Total faculty: 160. Library holdings: 45,000 bound volumes, 430 periodical subscriptions.

Undergraduate Courses offered for part-time students during daytime, evenings, summer. Complete part-time degree programs offered during daytime, evenings, summer. Adult/continuing education programs available. Career services available to part-time students: individual and group career counseling, individual job placement, employer recruitment on campus. Part-time tuition: $24.50 per quarter hour for state residents, $49 per quarter hour for nonresidents.

St Cloud State University
St Cloud 56301

Public institution; city setting. Awards A, B, M. Total enrollment: 9,846. Undergraduate enrollment: 9,665; 11% part-time, 51% women, 13% over 25. Total faculty: 587. Library holdings: 492,946 bound volumes, 945,051 titles on microform, 3,464 periodical subscriptions, 13,178 records/tapes.

Undergraduate Courses offered for part-time students during daytime, evenings, weekends, summer. Complete part-time degree programs offered during daytime, evenings, summer. Adult/continuing education programs available. Career services available to part-time students: individual and group career counseling. Part-time tuition: $26.85 per credit for state residents, $53.70 per credit for nonresidents.

Graduate Part-time study available in School of Graduate and Continuing Studies. Basic part-time expenses: $34.40 per credit tuition plus $3.80 per credit fees for state residents, $38.80 per credit tuition plus $3.80 per credit fees for nonresidents.

Saint John's University
Collegeville 56321

Independent-religious instutition; rural setting. Awards B, M. Barrier-free campus. Total enrollment: 2,019. Undergraduate enrollment: 1,884; 5% part-time, 0% women, 1% over 25. Total faculty: 158. Library holdings: 304,214 bound volumes, 18,768 titles on microform, 1,273 periodical subscriptions, 5,308 records/tapes.

Graduate Part-time study available in School of Theology. Basic part-time expenses: $250 per credit tuition plus $55 per year fees.

Saint Mary's College
Winona 55987

Independent-religious instutition; small-town setting. Awards B, M. Total enrollment: 1,425. Undergraduate enrollment: 1,187; 1% part-time, 46% women. Total faculty: 102. Library holdings: 160,000 bound volumes, 600 periodical subscriptions, 3,803 records/tapes.

Undergraduate Courses offered for part-time students during daytime. Complete part-time degree programs offered during daytime. External degree and adult/continuing education programs available. Career services available to part-time students: individual and group career counseling, individual job placement, employer recruitment on campus. Part-time tuition: $170 per credit.

Graduate Part-time study available in Graduate Programs. Basic part-time expenses: $170 per credit tuition. Institutional financial aid available to part-time graduate students in Graduate Programs.

St Mary's Junior College
Minneapolis 55454

Independent-religious instutition; metropolitan setting. Awards A. Barrier-free campus. Total enrollment: 890 (all undergraduates); 35% part-time, 90% women, 40% over 25. Total faculty: 90.

Undergraduate Courses offered for part-time students during daytime, evenings, weekends. Complete part-time degree programs offered during daytime, evenings, weekends. Adult/continuing education programs available. Career services available to part-time students: individual and group career counseling. Part-time tuition: $92 per quarter hour.

Saint Paul Seminary
St Paul 55105

Independent-religious institution (graduate only). Total enrollment: 87 (primarily men; 5% part-time). Total faculty: 30.

Graduate Part-time study available in Graduate and Professional Programs. Basic part-time expenses: $148 per credit hour tuition.

Southwest State University
Marshall 56258

Public institution; small-town setting. Awards A, B. Barrier-free campus. Total enrollment: 1,922 (all undergraduates); 19% part-time, 46% women, 25% over 25. Total faculty: 108. Library holdings: 144,000 bound volumes, 24,000 titles on microform, 1,200 periodical subscriptions, 9,500 records/tapes.

Undergraduate Courses offered for part-time students during daytime, evenings, weekends, summer. Complete part-time degree programs offered during daytime, evenings. External degree and adult/continuing education programs available. Career services available to part-time students: individual and group career counseling, individual job placement, employer recruitment on campus. Part-time tuition: $26.85 per quarter hour for state residents, $53.70 per quarter hour for nonresidents.

University of Minnesota, Duluth
Duluth 55812

Public institution; city setting. Awards A, B, M. Barrier-free campus. Total enrollment: 7,525. Undergraduate enrollment: 7,206; 12% part-time, 46% women, 10% over 25. Total faculty: 426. Library holdings: 292,594 bound volumes, 55,891 titles on microform, 2,484 periodical subscriptions, 4,500 records/tapes.

Undergraduate Courses offered for part-time students during daytime, evenings, summer. Complete part-time degree programs offered during daytime, evenings. Adult/continuing education programs available. Career services available to part-time students: individual and group career counseling, individual job placement, employer recruitment on campus. Part-time tuition: $34 per credit for state residents, $86 per credit for nonresidents. Wisconsin residents pay tuition at the rate they would pay if attending a comparable state-supported institution in Wisconsin.

University of Minnesota, Morris
Morris 56267

Public institution; rural setting. Awards B. Total enrollment: 1,603 (all undergraduates); 5% part-time, 49% women. Total faculty: 132. Library holdings: 122,000 bound volumes, 12,714 titles on microform, 741 periodical subscriptions, 1,182 records/tapes.

Undergraduate Courses offered for part-time students during daytime, evenings, summer. Complete part-time degree programs offered during daytime, evenings, summer. External degree and adult/continuing education programs available. Career services available to part-time students: individual career counseling. Part-time tuition: $36.87 per credit for state residents, $101.39 per credit for nonresidents. Wisconsin residents pay tuition at the rate they would pay if attending a comparable state-supported institution in Wisconsin.

University of Minnesota Technical College, Crookston
Crookston 56716

Public institution; rural setting. Awards A. Total enrollment: 1,149 (all undergraduates); 17% part-time, 50% women. Total faculty: 75. Library holdings: 21,000 bound volumes, 60 titles on microform, 640 periodical subscriptions, 1,200 records/tapes.

Undergraduate Courses offered for part-time students during daytime, evenings, summer. Complete part-time degree programs offered during daytime, evenings, summer. External degree and adult/continuing education programs available. Career services available to part-time students: individual and group career counseling, individual job placement, employer recruitment on campus. Part-time tuition: $36.85 per credit for state residents, $102 per credit for nonresidents. Wisconsin residents pay tuition at the rate they would pay if attending a comparable state-supported institution in Wisconsin.

University of Minnesota Technical College, Waseca
Waseca 56093

Public institution; small-town setting. Awards A. Barrier-free campus. Total enrollment: 780 (all undergraduates); 24% part-time, 51% women, 20% over 25. Total faculty: 76. Library holdings: 30,000 bound volumes, 200 titles on microform, 600 periodical subscriptions, 670 records/tapes.

Undergraduate Courses offered for part-time students during daytime, evenings, summer. Complete part-time degree programs offered during daytime, evenings, summer. Career services available to part-time students: individual and group career counseling, individual job placement, employer recruitment on campus. Part-time tuition: $36 per credit for state residents, $101 per credit for nonresidents. Wisconsin, North Dakota, and South Dakota residents pay tuition at the rate they would pay if attending comparable state-supported institutions in their home states.

University of Minnesota, Twin Cities Campus
Minneapolis 55455

Public institution; metropolitan setting. Awards A, B, M, D. Total enrollment: 46,445. Undergraduate enrollment: 34,596;

Colleges Offering Part-Time Degree Programs / Minnesota

University of Minnesota, Twin Cities Campus (continued)

25% part-time, 45% women, 18% over 25. Total faculty: 5,800. Library holdings: 4 million bound volumes, 1.7 million titles on microform, 42,930 periodical subscriptions, 253,599 records/tapes.

Undergraduate Courses offered for part-time students during daytime, evenings, weekends, summer. Complete part-time degree programs offered during daytime, evenings, weekends, summer. External degree and adult/continuing education programs available. Career services available to part-time students: individual and group career counseling, individual job placement, employer recruitment on campus. Part-time tuition: $36.87 per credit for state residents, $101.39 per credit for nonresidents. Wisconsin residents pay tuition at the rate they would pay if attending a comparable state-supported institution in Wisconsin.

Vermillion Community College
Ely 55731

Public institution; rural setting. Awards A. Barrier-free campus. Total enrollment: 520 (all undergraduates); 20% over 25. Total faculty: 39.

Undergraduate Courses offered for part-time students during daytime, evenings, weekends, summer. Complete part-time degree programs offered during daytime, evenings, weekends, summer. Adult/continuing education programs available. Part-time tuition: $24.50 per quarter hour for state residents, $49 per quarter hour for nonresidents.

William Mitchell College of Law
St Paul 55105

Independent institution (graduate only). Total enrollment: 1,100 (coed; 70% part-time). Total faculty: 194. Library holdings: 84,755 bound volumes, 66,468 microforms.

Graduate Part-time study available in Professional Program. Basic part-time expenses: $3950 per year tuition plus $20 per year fees. Institutional financial aid available to part-time graduate students in Professional Program.

Willmar Community College
Willmar 56201

Public institution; small-town setting. Awards A. Barrier-free campus. Total enrollment: 761 (all undergraduates); 18% part-time, 51% women. Total faculty: 58. Library holdings: 19,000 bound volumes, 32 periodical subscriptions, 1,361 records/tapes.

Undergraduate Courses offered for part-time students during daytime, evenings, summer. Complete part-time degree programs offered during daytime, evenings, summer. Adult/continuing education programs available. Career services available to part-time students: individual career counseling, individual job placement, employer recruitment on campus. Part-time tuition: $24.50 per credit for state residents, $49 per credit for nonresidents.

Winona State University
Winona 55987

Public institution; small-town setting. Awards A, B, M. Barrier-free campus. Total enrollment: 5,300. Undergraduate enrollment: 4,900; 10% part-time, 60% women. Total faculty: 270. Library holdings: 200,000 bound volumes, 600,000 titles on microform.

Undergraduate Courses offered for part-time students during daytime, evenings, weekends, summer. Complete part-time degree programs offered during daytime, evenings, weekends, summer. External degree and adult/continuing education programs available. Career services available to part-time students: individual and group career counseling, individual job placement, employer recruitment on campus. Part-time tuition: $27 per quarter hour for state residents, $54 per quarter hour for nonresidents.

Graduate Part-time study available in Graduate Studies. Basic part-time expenses: $34 per credit tuition plus $6.30 per credit fees for state residents, $68 per credit tuition plus $6.30 per credit fees for nonresidents. Institutional financial aid available to part-time graduate students in Graduate Studies.

Worthington Community College
Worthington 56187

Public institution; small-town setting. Awards A. Barrier-free campus. Total enrollment: 750 (all undergraduates); 47% part-time, 53% women, 40% over 25. Total faculty: 48. Library holdings: 31,000 bound volumes, 150 titles on microform, 200 periodical subscriptions, 650 records/tapes.

Undergraduate Courses offered for part-time students during daytime, evenings. Complete part-time degree programs offered during daytime, evenings. Adult/continuing education programs available. Career services available to part-time students: individual and group career counseling, individual job placement. Part-time tuition: $24.50 per quarter hour for state residents, $49 per quarter hour for nonresidents.

MISSISSIPPI

Alcorn State University
Lorman 39096

Public institution (undergraduate and graduate). Total enrollment: 2,555. Graduate enrollment: 235 (coed; 92% part-time).

Graduate Part-time study available in Division of Graduate Studies. Basic part-time expenses: $163.50 per semester (minimum) tuition for state residents, $701.50 per semester (minimum) tuition for nonresidents. Institutional financial aid available to part-time graduate students in Division of Graduate Studies.

Belhaven College
Jackson 39202

Independent-religious instutition; city setting. Awards B. Barrier-free campus. Total enrollment: 875 (all undergraduates); 42% part-time, 55% women. Total faculty: 82. Library holdings: 65,000 bound volumes, 353 periodical subscriptions.

Undergraduate Courses offered for part-time students during daytime, evenings, summer. Complete part-time degree programs offered during daytime, evenings, summer. External degree and adult/continuing education programs available. Career services available to part-time students: individual career counseling, individual job placement, employer recruitment on campus. Part-time tuition: $105 per credit.

Blue Mountain College
Blue Mountain 38610

Independent-religious instutition; small-town setting. Awards B. Total enrollment: 347 (all undergraduates); 16% part-time, 74% women. Total faculty: 32. Library holdings: 46,000 bound

Mississippi / **Colleges Offering Part-Time Degree Programs**

volumes, 11 titles on microform, 218 periodical subscriptions, 1,695 records/tapes.

Undergraduate Courses offered for part-time students during daytime, evenings, weekends, summer. Complete part-time degree programs offered during daytime, evenings, weekends, summer. Career services available to part-time students: individual career counseling. Part-time tuition: $70 per semester hour.

Clarke College
Newton 39345

Independent-religious instutition; small-town setting. Awards A. Total enrollment: 230 (all undergraduates); 8% part-time, 48% women, 25% over 25. Total faculty: 26. Library holdings: 17,644 bound volumes, 52 titles on microform, 146 periodical subscriptions, 390 records/tapes.

Undergraduate Courses offered for part-time students during daytime, evenings, summer. Complete part-time degree programs offered during daytime, evenings, summer. Adult/continuing education programs available. Part-time tuition: $65 per semester hour.

Copiah-Lincoln Junior College
Wesson 39191

Public institution; rural setting. Awards A. Total enrollment: 1,241 (all undergraduates); 28% part-time, 51% women. Total faculty: 94. Library holdings: 32,000 bound volumes, 40 titles on microform, 225 periodical subscriptions.

Undergraduate Courses offered for part-time students during daytime, evenings. Complete part-time degree programs offered during daytime, evenings. Adult/continuing education programs available. Career services available to part-time students: individual career counseling. Part-time tuition: $30 per semester hour for state residents, $60 per semester hour for nonresidents.

Copiah-Lincoln Junior College–Natchez Campus
Natchez 39120

Public institution; small-town setting. Awards A. Barrier-free campus. Total enrollment: 524 (all undergraduates); 73% part-time, 67% women. Total faculty: 45. Library holdings: 12,382 bound volumes, 65 titles on microform, 30 periodical subscriptions, 819 records/tapes.

Undergraduate Courses offered for part-time students during daytime, evenings, summer. Complete part-time degree programs offered during daytime, evenings, summer. Adult/continuing education programs available. Career services available to part-time students: individual career counseling. Part-time tuition: $30 per credit hour for state residents, $60 per credit hour for nonresidents.

Delta State University
Cleveland 38733

Public institution; small-town setting. Awards B, M, D. Barrier-free campus. Total enrollment: 3,713. Undergraduate enrollment: 3,126; 29% part-time, 56% women. Total faculty: 167. Library holdings: 250,000 bound volumes, 1,700 periodical subscriptions, 10,000 records/tapes.

Undergraduate Courses offered for part-time students during daytime, evenings, weekends, summer. Complete part-time degree programs offered during daytime, evenings, weekends, summer. Adult/continuing education programs available. Career services available to part-time students: individual and group career counseling, individual job placement, employer recruitment on campus. Part-time tuition: $36 per semester hour for state residents, $89 per semester hour for nonresidents.

Graduate Part-time study available in School of Graduate Studies. Degree can be earned exclusively through evening/weekend study in School of Graduate Studies. Basic part-time expenses: $48 per semester hour tuition plus $10 per semester fees for state residents, $106 per semester hour tuition plus $10 per semester fees for nonresidents.

East Central Junior College
Decatur 39327

Public institution; rural setting. Awards A. Total enrollment: 850 (all undergraduates); 1% part-time, 45% women. Total faculty: 59.

Undergraduate Courses offered for part-time students during daytime, evenings. Complete part-time degree programs offered during daytime, evenings. Adult/continuing education programs available. Career services available to part-time students: individual and group career counseling, employer recruitment on campus. Part-time tuition: $24 per semester hour for state residents, $24 per semester hour for nonresidents.

East Mississippi Junior College
Scooba 39358

Public institution; rural setting. Awards A. Total enrollment: 400 (all undergraduates); 1% part-time, 42% women, 8% over 25. Total faculty: 35.

Undergraduate Courses offered for part-time students during daytime. Complete part-time degree programs offered during daytime. Adult/continuing education programs available. Part-time tuition: $32 per credit hour for area residents, $32 per credit hour for state residents, $32 per credit hour for nonresidents.

Itawamba Junior College
Fulton 38843

Public institution; small-town setting. Awards A. Barrier-free campus. Total enrollment: 2,500 (all undergraduates); 25% part-time, 53% women, 8% over 25. Total faculty: 151. Library holdings: 34,000 bound volumes.

Undergraduate Courses offered for part-time students during daytime, evenings. Complete part-time degree programs offered during daytime, evenings. Adult/continuing education programs available. Career services available to part-time students: individual and group career counseling, individual job placement. Part-time tuition: $26 per semester hour for area residents, $26 per semester hour for state residents, $26 per semester hour for nonresidents.

Jackson State University
Jackson 39217

Public institution; city setting. Awards B, M, D. Barrier-free campus. Total enrollment: 6,503. Undergraduate enrollment: 5,279; 11% part-time, 54% women. Total faculty: 344. Library holdings: 369,990 bound volumes, 101,192 titles on microform, 2,088 periodical subscriptions, 2,751 records/tapes.

Undergraduate Courses offered for part-time students during daytime, evenings, weekends, summer. Complete part-time degree programs offered during daytime, evenings, weekends, summer. Adult/continuing education programs available. Ca-

Jackson State University (continued)

reer services available to part-time students: individual and group career counseling, individual job placement, employer recruitment on campus. Part-time tuition: $45 per credit hour for state residents, $89.50 per credit hour for nonresidents.

Graduate Part-time study available in Graduate School. Degree can be earned exclusively through evening/weekend study in Graduate School. Basic part-time expenses: $62 per credit hour tuition for state residents, $62 per credit hour tuition plus $62 per credit hour fees for nonresidents.

Jones County Junior College
Ellisville 39437

Public institution; small-town setting. Awards A. Total enrollment: 2,239 (all undergraduates); 10% part-time, 50% women. Total faculty: 119. Library holdings: 53,341 bound volumes, 3,280 titles on microform, 512 periodical subscriptions, 4,204 records/tapes.

Undergraduate Courses offered for part-time students during daytime, evenings. Complete part-time degree programs offered during daytime, evenings. Part-time tuition: $28 per credit hour for area residents, $32 per credit hour for state residents, $32 per credit hour for nonresidents.

Mary Holmes College
West Point 39773

Independent-religious instutition; rural setting. Awards A. Total enrollment: 578 (all undergraduates); 13% part-time, 56% women. Total faculty: 28. Library holdings: 24,521 bound volumes, 1,170 titles on microform, 128 periodical subscriptions.

Undergraduate Courses offered for part-time students during daytime, evenings. Complete part-time degree programs offered during daytime, evenings. Career services available to part-time students: individual career counseling. Part-time tuition: $70 per credit hour.

Meridian Junior College
Meridian 39305

Public institution; small-town setting. Awards A. Total enrollment: 2,800 (all undergraduates); 50% part-time, 50% women, 30% over 25. Total faculty: 151.

Undergraduate Courses offered for part-time students during daytime, evenings, summer. Complete part-time degree programs offered during daytime, evenings, summer. Adult/continuing education programs available. Career services available to part-time students: individual and group career counseling, individual job placement, employer recruitment on campus. Part-time tuition: $22 per semester hour for state residents, $35 per semester hour for nonresidents.

Millsaps College
Jackson 39210

Independent-religious instutition; city setting. Awards B, M. Total enrollment: 1,246. Undergraduate enrollment: 1,173; 25% part-time, 48% women. Total faculty: 95. Library holdings: 205,000 bound volumes, 200 titles on microform, 710 periodical subscriptions, 5,000 records/tapes.

Undergraduate Courses offered for part-time students during daytime, evenings, summer. Complete part-time degree programs offered during daytime, evenings, summer. Adult/continuing education programs available. Career services available to part-time students: individual and group career counseling, individual job placement, employer recruitment on campus. Part-time tuition per semester (1 to 11 semester hours) ranges from $165 to $2215.

Graduate Part-time study available in School of Management. Degree can be earned exclusively through evening/weekend study in School of Management. Basic part-time expenses: $175 per credit tuition plus $3.50 per credit fees. Institutional financial aid available to part-time graduate students in School of Management.

Mississippi College
Clinton 39058

Independent-religious instutition; small-town setting. Awards B, M. Barrier-free campus. Total enrollment: 2,592. Undergraduate enrollment: 1,692; 10% part-time, 48% women, 20% over 25. Total faculty: 155. Library holdings: 200,000 bound volumes, 816 periodical subscriptions, 4,805 records/tapes.

Undergraduate Courses offered for part-time students during daytime, evenings, summer. Complete part-time degree programs offered during daytime, evenings, summer. Adult/continuing education programs available. Career services available to part-time students: individual and group career counseling, individual job placement, employer recruitment on campus. Part-time tuition: $93 per credit hour.

Graduate Part-time study available in Graduate School. Degree can be earned exclusively through evening/weekend study in Graduate School. Basic part-time expenses: $100 per semester hour tuition plus $15 per semester fees. Institutional financial aid available to part-time graduate students in Graduate School.

Mississippi Gulf Coast Junior College, Jackson County Campus
Gautier 39553

Public institution; small-town setting. Awards A. Barrier-free campus. Total enrollment: 1,875 (all undergraduates); 43% women, 45% over 25. Total faculty: 122. Library holdings: 26,000 bound volumes.

Undergraduate Courses offered for part-time students during daytime, evenings, summer. Complete part-time degree programs offered during daytime, summer. Adult/continuing education programs available. Career services available to part-time students: individual and group career counseling, individual job placement, employer recruitment on campus. Part-time tuition: $30 per semester hour for area residents, $47 per semester hour for state residents, $47 per semester hour for nonresidents.

Mississippi Gulf Coast Junior College, Jefferson Davis Campus
Gulfport 39501

Public institution; small-town setting. Awards A. Barrier-free campus. Total enrollment: 3,000 (all undergraduates); 20% part-time, 53% women, 30% over 25. Total faculty: 165. Library holdings: 10,000 bound volumes, 120 periodical subscriptions, 250 records/tapes.

Undergraduate Courses offered for part-time students during daytime, evenings, summer. Complete part-time degree programs offered during daytime, evenings, summer. Adult/continuing education programs available. Career services available to part-time students: individual and group career counseling, individual job placement, employer recruitment on campus. Part-time tuition: $30 per semester hour for area residents, $47 per semester hour for state residents, $47 per semester hour for nonresidents.

Mississippi Gulf Coast Junior College, Perkinston Campus
Perkinston 39573

Public institution; rural setting. Awards A. Barrier-free campus. Total enrollment: 802 (all undergraduates); 1% part-time, 48% women. Total faculty: 55. Library holdings: 21,000 bound volumes, 48 titles on microform.

Undergraduate Courses offered for part-time students during daytime. Complete part-time degree programs offered during daytime. Adult/continuing education programs available. Part-time tuition and fees per semester (1 to 12 semester hours) are $30 for district residents and range from $41 to $75 for state residents, $80 to $230 for nonresidents.

Mississippi State University
Mississippi State 39762

Public institution; small-town setting. Awards B, M, D. Barrier-free campus. Total enrollment: 12,325. Undergraduate enrollment: 10,400; 13% part-time, 39% women, 8% over 25. Total faculty: 864. Library holdings: 992,034 bound volumes, 7,258 periodical subscriptions.

Undergraduate Courses offered for part-time students during daytime, evenings, summer. Complete part-time degree programs offered during daytime, evenings, summer. Adult/continuing education programs available. Career services available to part-time students: individual and group career counseling, individual job placement, employer recruitment on campus. Part-time tuition: $61 per semester hour for state residents, $115 per semester hour for nonresidents.

Graduate Part-time study available in College of Agriculture and Home Economics, College of Arts and Science, College of Business and Industry, College of Education, College of Engineering, School of Accountancy, School of Forest Resources. Basic part-time expenses: $0 tuition plus $67 per credit fees for state residents, $60 per credit tuition plus $121 per credit fees for nonresidents. Institutional financial aid available to part-time graduate students in College of Agriculture and Home Economics, College of Arts and Science, College of Business and Industry, College of Education, College of Engineering, School of Accountancy, School of Forest Resources.

Mississippi University for Women
Columbus 39701

Public institution; small-town setting. Awards A, B, M. Barrier-free campus. Total enrollment: 2,278. Undergraduate enrollment: 2,190; 20% part-time, 84% women, 35% over 25. Total faculty: 144. Library holdings: 266,526 bound volumes, 332,600 titles on microform, 2,055 periodical subscriptions.

Undergraduate Courses offered for part-time students during daytime, evenings, weekends, summer. Complete part-time degree programs offered during daytime, evenings, weekends, summer. Adult/continuing education programs available. Career services available to part-time students: individual and group career counseling, individual job placement, employer recruitment on campus. Part-time tuition: $38.50 per semester hour for state residents, $38.50 per semester hour for nonresidents. Part-time students from out-of-state who live on campus pay an additional $538 fee per semester.

Graduate Part-time study available in Graduate School. Degree can be earned exclusively through evening/weekend study in Graduate School. Basic part-time expenses: $51.50 per credit tuition.

Mississippi Valley State University
Itta Bena 38941

Public institution; small-town setting. Awards A, B, M. Barrier-free campus. Total enrollment: 2,575. Undergraduate enrollment: 2,487; 8% part-time, 52% women. Total faculty: 179. Library holdings: 106,289 bound volumes, 692 periodical subscriptions, 1,268 records/tapes.

Undergraduate Courses offered for part-time students during daytime, evenings, summer. Complete part-time degree programs offered during daytime, evenings, summer. Adult/continuing education programs available. Career services available to part-time students: individual and group career counseling, individual job placement, employer recruitment on campus. Part-time tuition: $34 per semester hour for state residents, $34 per semester hour for nonresidents.

Graduate Part-time study available in Division of Graduate Studies. Degree can be earned exclusively through evening/weekend study in Division of Graduate Studies. Basic part-time expenses: $33 per credit hour tuition for state residents, $66 per credit tuition for nonresidents.

Northeast Mississippi Junior College
Booneville 38829

Public institution; small-town setting. Awards A. Barrier-free campus. Total enrollment: 2,300 (all undergraduates); 9% part-time, 52% women, 23% over 25. Total faculty: 145. Library holdings: 29,879 bound volumes, 378 periodical subscriptions, 941 records/tapes.

Undergraduate Courses offered for part-time students during daytime, evenings, summer. Complete part-time degree programs offered during daytime, evenings, summer. Adult/continuing education programs available. Career services available to part-time students: individual and group career counseling, individual job placement, employer recruitment on campus. Part-time tuition: $25 per semester hour for area residents, $25 per semester hour for state residents, $25 per semester hour for nonresidents.

Pearl River Junior College
Poplarville 39470

Public institution; rural setting. Awards A. Barrier-free campus. Total enrollment: 1,747 (all undergraduates); 10% part-time, 54% women. Total faculty: 107. Library holdings: 39,000 bound volumes, 340 periodical subscriptions, 300 records/tapes.

Undergraduate Courses offered for part-time students during daytime, evenings, summer. Complete part-time degree programs offered during daytime, evenings, summer. Adult/continuing education programs available. Part-time tuition: $25 per semester hour for area residents, $30.42 per semester hour for state residents, $47.92 per semester hour for nonresidents.

Prentiss Normal and Industrial Institute
Prentiss 39474

Independent institution; small-town setting. Awards A. Barrier-free campus. Total enrollment: 153 (all undergraduates); 20% part-time, 69% women, 1% over 25. Total faculty: 15.

Undergraduate Courses offered for part-time students during daytime, evenings. Complete part-time degree programs offered during daytime, evenings. Adult/continuing education programs available. Career services available to part-time students: individual and group career counseling, employer recruitment on campus. Part-time tuition: $62.50 per credit hour.

Colleges Offering Part-Time Degree Programs / *Mississippi*

Rust College
Holly Springs 38635

Independent-religious instutition; rural setting. Awards A, B. Total enrollment: 851 (all undergraduates); 5% part-time, 90% women. Total faculty: 40. Library holdings: 5,951 bound volumes, 325 periodical subscriptions, 735 records/tapes.

Undergraduate Courses offered for part-time students during daytime, evenings. Complete part-time degree programs offered during daytime, evenings. Adult/continuing education programs available. Career services available to part-time students: employer recruitment on campus. Part-time tuition: $80 per credit.

Southeastern Baptist College
Laurel 39440

Independent-religious instutition; small-town setting. Awards A, B. Total enrollment: 83 (all undergraduates); 43% part-time, 37% women, 24% over 25. Total faculty: 14. Library holdings: 15,459 bound volumes, 900 titles on microform, 227 periodical subscriptions, 260 records/tapes.

Undergraduate Courses offered for part-time students during daytime, evenings, summer. Complete part-time degree programs offered during daytime. Adult/continuing education programs available. Career services available to part-time students: individual career counseling. Part-time tuition: $50 per hour.

Southwest Mississippi Junior College
Summit 39666

Public institution; rural setting. Awards A. Barrier-free campus. Total enrollment: 1,435 (all undergraduates); 22% part-time, 56% women. Total faculty: 53. Library holdings: 33,000 bound volumes, 375 titles on microform, 150 periodical subscriptions, 575 records/tapes.

Undergraduate Courses offered for part-time students during evenings, summer. Complete part-time degree programs offered during evenings, summer. Adult/continuing education programs available. Career services available to part-time students: individual and group career counseling, individual job placement, employer recruitment on campus. Part-time tuition: $25 per semester hour for state residents, $25 per semester hour for nonresidents.

Tougaloo College
Tougaloo 39174

Independent institution; city setting. Awards A, B. Total enrollment: 653 (all undergraduates); 5% part-time, 66% women, 10% over 25. Total faculty: 86. Library holdings: 91,251 bound volumes, 4,799 titles on microform, 450 periodical subscriptions, 3,074 records/tapes.

Undergraduate Courses offered for part-time students during daytime, evenings. Complete part-time degree programs offered during daytime, evenings. Adult/continuing education programs available. Career services available to part-time students: individual career counseling, individual job placement, employer recruitment on campus. Part-time tuition: $99 per hour.

University of Mississippi
University 38677

Public institution; small-town setting. Awards B, M, D. Total enrollment: 9,236. Undergraduate enrollment: 7,578; 13% part-time, 47% women. Total faculty: 574. Library holdings: 750,000 bound volumes, 4,696 periodical subscriptions, 400 records/tapes.

Undergraduate Courses offered for part-time students during daytime. Complete part-time degree programs offered during daytime. External degree and adult/continuing education programs available. Career services available to part-time students: individual and group career counseling, individual job placement, employer recruitment on campus. Part-time tuition: $42 per semester hour for state residents, $42 per semester hour for nonresidents.

University of Southern Mississippi
Hattiesburg 39406

Public institution; small-town setting. Awards B, M, D. Barrier-free campus. Total enrollment: 11,333. Undergraduate enrollment: 9,665; 12% part-time, 54% women, 26% over 25. Total faculty: 655. Library holdings: 548,660 bound volumes, 754,303 titles on microform, 4,652 periodical subscriptions, 15,428 records/tapes.

Undergraduate Courses offered for part-time students during daytime, evenings, weekends, summer. Complete part-time degree programs offered during daytime, evenings, summer. Adult/continuing education programs available. Career services available to part-time students: individual and group career counseling, individual job placement, employer recruitment on campus. Part-time tuition: $54 per semester hour for state residents, $99 per semester hour for nonresidents.

Graduate Part-time study available in Graduate School. Basic part-time expenses: $70 per semester hour tuition for state residents, $129 per semester hour tuition for nonresidents.

William Carey College
Hattiesburg 39401

Independent-religious instutition; small-town setting. Awards B, M. Total enrollment: 1,728. Undergraduate enrollment: 1,440; 48% part-time, 60% women, 44% over 25. Total faculty: 110. Library holdings: 110,000 bound volumes, 22,600 titles on microform, 2,175 records/tapes.

Undergraduate Courses offered for part-time students during daytime, evenings, weekends, summer. Complete part-time degree programs offered during daytime, evenings, weekends, summer. Adult/continuing education programs available. Career services available to part-time students: individual career counseling. Part-time tuition: $79 per semester hour.

Graduate Part-time study available in Graduate Division. Degree can be earned exclusively through evening/weekend study in Graduate Division. Basic part-time expenses: $79 per semester hour tuition.

Wood Junior College
Mathiston 39752

Independent-religious instutition; rural setting. Awards A. Total enrollment: 441 (all undergraduates); 38% part-time, 61% women, 25% over 25. Total faculty: 31. Library holdings: 26,000 bound volumes, 31 periodical subscriptions, 1,200 records/tapes.

Undergraduate Courses offered for part-time students during daytime, evenings, summer. Complete part-time degree programs offered during daytime, evenings, summer. Career services available to part-time students: individual career counseling. Part-time tuition: $47 per semester hour.

MISSOURI

Aquinas Institute
St Louis 63108

Independent-religious institution (graduate only). Total enrollment: 92 (coed; 29% part-time). Total faculty: 16. Library holdings: 35,000 bound volumes.

Graduate Part-time study available in Graduate and Professional Programs. Basic part-time expenses: $195 per semester hour tuition plus $15 per semester fees. Institutional financial aid available to part-time graduate students in Graduate and Professional Programs.

Assemblies of God Graduate School
Springfield 65802

Independent-religious institution (graduate only). Total enrollment: 274 (coed; 42% part-time). Total faculty: 25.

Graduate Part-time study available in Graduate and Professional Programs. Basic part-time expenses: $95 per credit hour tuition plus $5 per credit hour fees. Institutional financial aid available to part-time graduate students in Graduate and Professional Programs.

Avila College
Kansas City 64145

Independent-religious instsitution; metropolitan setting. Awards A, B, M. Total enrollment: 1,765. Undergraduate enrollment: 1,556; 56% part-time, 73% women. Total faculty: 214. Library holdings: 71,552 bound volumes, 1,156 titles on microform, 441 periodical subscriptions, 3,631 records/tapes.

Undergraduate Courses offered for part-time students during daytime, evenings, weekends, summer. Complete part-time degree programs offered during daytime, evenings, weekends. Adult/continuing education programs available. Career services available to part-time students: individual and group career counseling, individual job placement, employer recruitment on campus. Part-time tuition per credit hour ranges from $75 for evening courses to $130 for daytime courses.

Graduate Part-time study available in Graduate Programs. Degree can be earned exclusively through evening/weekend study in Graduate Programs. Basic part-time expenses: $125 per credit tuition.

Baptist Bible College
Springfield 65802

Independent-religious instsitution; city setting. Awards A, B. Total enrollment: 1,368 (all undergraduates); 5% part-time, 44% women. Total faculty: 39. Library holdings: 31,000 bound volumes, 1,120 titles on microform, 65 periodical subscriptions, 1,240 records/tapes.

Undergraduate Courses offered for part-time students during daytime, summer. Complete part-time degree programs offered during daytime, summer. Part-time tuition: $25 per hour.

Calvary Bible College
Kansas City 64147

Independent-religious instsitution; metropolitan setting. Awards A, B, M. Barrier-free campus. Total enrollment: 501. Undergraduate enrollment: 468; 22% part-time, 42% women, 15% over 25. Total faculty: 39. Library holdings: 45,000 bound volumes, 180 periodical subscriptions.

Undergraduate Courses offered for part-time students during daytime, evenings. Complete part-time degree programs offered during daytime. Adult/continuing education programs available. Career services available to part-time students: individual career counseling, individual job placement. Part-time tuition: $72.50 per semester hour.

Graduate Part-time study available in Graduate Division. Basic part-time expenses: $77.50 per semester hour tuition plus $240 per semester fees. Institutional financial aid available to part-time graduate students in Graduate Division.

Cardinal Newman College
St Louis 63121

Independent-religious instsitution; metropolitan setting. Awards B. Total enrollment: 110 (all undergraduates); 2% part-time, 40% women, 5% over 25. Total faculty: 28. Library holdings: 22,790 bound volumes, 410 titles on microform, 385 periodical subscriptions, 400 records/tapes.

Undergraduate Courses offered for part-time students during daytime, summer. Complete part-time degree programs offered during daytime. Career services available to part-time students: individual and group career counseling, individual job placement, employer recruitment on campus. Part-time tuition: $120 per credit.

Central Bible College
Springfield 65803

Independent-religious instsitution; city setting. Awards A, B. Total enrollment: 909 (all undergraduates); 1% part-time, 38% women. Total faculty: 51. Library holdings: 105,548 bound volumes, 11,800 titles on microform, 601 periodical subscriptions, 2,709 records/tapes.

Undergraduate Courses offered for part-time students during daytime, evenings, summer. Complete part-time degree programs offered during daytime, evenings, summer. Adult/continuing education programs available. Part-time tuition: $57.50 per semester hour.

Central Christian College of the Bible
Moberly 65270

Independent-religious instsitution; small-town setting. Awards A, B. Barrier-free campus. Total enrollment: 111 (all undergraduates); 21% part-time, 46% women, 11% over 25. Total faculty: 13. Library holdings: 23,432 bound volumes, 79 titles on microform, 113 periodical subscriptions, 114 records/tapes.

Undergraduate Courses offered for part-time students during daytime. Complete part-time degree programs offered during daytime. Career services available to part-time students: individual career counseling, individual job placement. Part-time tuition: $42 per credit.

Central Methodist College
Fayette 65248

Independent-religious instsitution; rural setting. Awards A, B. Total enrollment: 623 (all undergraduates); 6% part-time, 49% women, 5% over 25. Total faculty: 62. Library holdings: 100,000 bound volumes, 400 periodical subscriptions, 3,000 records/tapes.

Undergraduate Courses offered for part-time students during daytime. Complete part-time degree programs offered during daytime. Career services available to part-time students: em-

Colleges Offering Part-Time Degree Programs / Missouri

Central Methodist College (continued)

ployer recruitment on campus. Part-time tuition: $190 per credit hour.

Central Missouri State University
Warrensburg 64093

Public institution; small-town setting. Awards A, B, M. Total enrollment: 9,601. Undergraduate enrollment: 8,350; 6% part-time, 48% women, 18% over 25. Total faculty: 452. Library holdings: 590,000 bound volumes, 555,000 titles on microform, 2,720 periodical subscriptions, 15,262 records/tapes.

Undergraduate Courses offered for part-time students during daytime, evenings, weekends, summer. Complete part-time degree programs offered during daytime, evenings, weekends, summer. External degree and adult/continuing education programs available. Career services available to part-time students: individual and group career counseling, individual job placement, employer recruitment on campus. Part-time tuition: $55 per credit hour for state residents, $55 per credit hour for nonresidents.

Graduate Part-time study available in School of Graduate Studies and Research. Basic part-time expenses: $58 per semester hour tuition. Institutional financial aid available to part-time graduate students in School of Graduate Studies and Research.

Clayton University
St Louis 63105

Independent institution. Awards A, B, M, D (external degree programs only). Total enrollment: 185. Undergraduate enrollment: 46; 30% part-time, 35% women, 100% over 25. Total faculty: 500.

Undergraduate Courses offered for part-time students during daytime, evenings, weekends, summer. Complete part-time degree programs offered during daytime, evenings, weekends, summer. External degree and adult/continuing education programs available. Tuition per degree program: $1500 for associate, $3600 for bachelor's.

Graduate Part-time study available in Behavioral Science Division, Business Division, Education Division, Engineering Division, Human Services Division, Nutritional Science Division, Interdisciplinary Division. Degree can be earned exclusively through evening/weekend study in Behavioral Science Division, Business Division, Education Division, Engineering Division, Human Services Division, Nutritional Science Division, Interdisciplinary Division. Basic part-time expenses: $3600 (one-time fee).

Cleveland Chiropractic College
Kansas City 64131

Independent institution (graduate only). Total enrollment: 428 (coed; 6% part-time).

Graduate Part-time study available in Professional Program. Basic part-time expenses: $85 per hour tuition. Institutional financial aid available to part-time graduate students in Professional Program.

Columbia College
Columbia 65216

Independent institution; city setting. Awards A, B. Total enrollment: 681 (all undergraduates); 17% part-time, 56% women, 10% over 25. Total faculty: 60. Library holdings: 60,000 bound volumes, 19,336 titles on microform, 430 periodical subscriptions, 2,126 records/tapes.

Undergraduate Courses offered for part-time students during daytime, evenings, weekends, summer. Complete part-time degree programs offered during daytime, evenings, summer. External degree and adult/continuing education programs available. Career services available to part-time students: individual and group career counseling, individual job placement, employer recruitment on campus. Part-time tuition: $80 per semester hour.

Covenant Theological Seminary
St Louis 63141

Independent-religious institution (graduate only). Total enrollment: 150 (primarily men; 34% part-time). Total faculty: 16.

Graduate Part-time study available in Graduate and Professional Programs. Basic part-time expenses: $100 per credit (minimum) tuition plus $5 per semester fees.

Crowder College
Neosho 64850

Public institution; rural setting. Awards A. Total enrollment: 1,252 (all undergraduates); 45% part-time, 45% women. Total faculty: 70. Library holdings: 29,364 bound volumes, 34 titles on microform, 274 periodical subscriptions, 2,430 records/tapes.

Undergraduate Courses offered for part-time students during daytime, evenings, summer. Complete part-time degree programs offered during daytime, evenings, summer. Adult/continuing education programs available. Career services available to part-time students: individual and group career counseling, individual job placement. Part-time tuition: $20 per semester hour for area residents, $27 per semester hour for state residents, $60 per semester hour for nonresidents.

Culver-Stockton College
Canton 63435

Independent institution; small-town setting. Awards A, B. Total enrollment: 719 (all undergraduates); 17% part-time, 51% women. Total faculty: 50. Library holdings: 110,656 bound volumes, 325 periodical subscriptions, 1,102 records/tapes.

Undergraduate Courses offered for part-time students during daytime, summer. Complete part-time degree programs offered during daytime, summer. Career services available to part-time students: individual and group career counseling, individual job placement, employer recruitment on campus. Part-time tuition: $175 per hour.

Drury College
Springfield 65802

Independent institution; city setting. Awards B, M. Total enrollment: 1,212. Undergraduate enrollment: 954; 11% part-time, 58% women, 3% over 25. Total faculty: 104. Library holdings: 158,000 bound volumes, 518 periodical subscriptions, 100 records/tapes.

Undergraduate Courses offered for part-time students during daytime, evenings, weekends, summer. Complete part-time degree programs offered during daytime, evenings, weekends, summer. Adult/continuing education programs available. Career services available to part-time students: individual career counseling, individual job placement, employer recruitment on campus. Part-time tuition: $137 per semester hour.

Missouri / Colleges Offering Part-Time Degree Programs

Graduate Part-time study available in Breech School of Business Administration and Economics, Graduate Program in Education. Basic part-time expenses: $66 per hour tuition.

East Central College
Union 63084

Public institution; rural setting. Awards A. Barrier-free campus. Total enrollment: 2,189 (all undergraduates); 58% part-time, 56% women, 42% over 25. Total faculty: 120. Library holdings: 20,000 bound volumes, 245 periodical subscriptions.

Undergraduate Courses offered for part-time students during daytime, evenings, weekends, summer. Complete part-time degree programs offered during daytime, evenings, summer. Adult/continuing education programs available. Career services available to part-time students: individual career counseling, individual job placement, employer recruitment on campus. Part-time tuition: $18 per credit for area residents, $28 per credit for state residents, $40 per credit for nonresidents.

Eden Theological Seminary
St Louis 63119

Independent-religious institution (graduate only). Total enrollment: 204 (coed; 52% part-time). Total faculty: 26.

Graduate Part-time study available in Graduate and Professional Programs. Basic part-time expenses: $105 per credit hour tuition.

Fontbonne College
St Louis 63105

Independent-religious instutition; metropolitan setting. Awards A, B, M. Total enrollment: 940. Undergraduate enrollment: 877; 32% part-time, 75% women, 30% over 25. Total faculty: 129. Library holdings: 85,600 bound volumes, 510 periodical subscriptions, 6,238 records/tapes.

Undergraduate Courses offered for part-time students during daytime, evenings, weekends. Complete part-time degree programs offered during daytime, evenings, weekends. Adult/continuing education programs available. Career services available to part-time students: individual and group career counseling, individual job placement, employer recruitment on campus. Part-time tuition per credit ranges from $125 for evening courses to $160 for daytime courses.

Graduate Part-time study available in Graduate Programs. Basic part-time expenses: $160 per credit tuition.

Hannibal-LaGrange College
Hannibal 63401

Independent-religious instutition; small-town setting. Awards A, B. Total enrollment: 532 (all undergraduates); 13% part-time, 55% women, 37% over 25. Total faculty: 49. Library holdings: 25,000 bound volumes, 265 periodical subscriptions, 1,520 records/tapes.

Undergraduate Courses offered for part-time students during daytime, evenings. Complete part-time degree programs offered during daytime, evenings. External degree and adult/continuing education programs available. Career services available to part-time students: individual career counseling, individual job placement. Part-time tuition: $90 per semester hour.

Harris-Stowe State College
St Louis 63103

Public institution; metropolitan setting. Awards B. Total enrollment: 1,287 (all undergraduates); 32% part-time, 74% women. Total faculty: 66. Library holdings: 50,000 bound volumes.

Undergraduate Courses offered for part-time students during daytime, evenings, summer. Complete part-time degree programs offered during daytime, evenings, summer. Career services available to part-time students: employer recruitment on campus. Part-time tuition: $30 per credit hour for state residents, $57.30 per credit hour for nonresidents.

Jefferson College
Hillsboro 63050

Public institution; rural setting. Awards A. Barrier-free campus. Total enrollment: 2,796 (all undergraduates); 55% part-time, 51% women, 60% over 25. Total faculty: 123. Library holdings: 50,000 bound volumes, 150 periodical subscriptions, 8,900 records/tapes.

Undergraduate Courses offered for part-time students during daytime, evenings, weekends, summer. Complete part-time degree programs offered during daytime, evenings, summer. Adult/continuing education programs available. Career services available to part-time students: individual and group career counseling. Part-time tuition: $14 per semester hour for area residents, $21 per semester hour for state residents, $28 per semester hour for nonresidents.

Kansas City Art Institute
Kansas City 64111

Independent institution; metropolitan setting. Awards B. Total enrollment: 448 (all undergraduates); 8% part-time, 49% women, 22% over 25. Total faculty: 48. Library holdings: 32,000 bound volumes, 115 periodical subscriptions.

Undergraduate Courses offered for part-time students during daytime. Complete part-time degree programs offered during daytime. Adult/continuing education programs available. Career services available to part-time students: individual and group career counseling, individual job placement, employer recruitment on campus. Part-time tuition: $260 per semester hour.

Lincoln University
Jefferson City 65102

Public institution; small-town setting. Awards A, B, M. Total enrollment: 2,895. Undergraduate enrollment: 2,519; 41% part-time, 51% women, 24% over 25. Total faculty: 169. Library holdings: 150,000 bound volumes.

Undergraduate Courses offered for part-time students during daytime, evenings, weekends, summer. Complete part-time degree programs offered during daytime, evenings, weekends, summer. Adult/continuing education programs available. Career services available to part-time students: individual and group career counseling, individual job placement, employer recruitment on campus. Part-time tuition: $35 per credit hour for state residents, $70 per credit hour for nonresidents.

Graduate Part-time study available in School of Graduate and Continuing Education. Degree can be earned exclusively through evening/weekend study in School of Graduate and Continuing Education. Basic part-time expenses: $46 per semester hour fees for state residents, $92 per semester hour fees for nonresidents.

Colleges Offering Part-Time Degree Programs / Missouri

Lindenwood College
St Charles 63301

Independent institution; small-town setting. Awards A, B, M. Total enrollment: 1,865. Undergraduate enrollment: 1,325; 34% part-time, 60% women. Total faculty: 108. Library holdings: 120,000 bound volumes, 25,437 titles on microform, 625 periodical subscriptions, 2,500 records/tapes.

Undergraduate Courses offered for part-time students during daytime, evenings, weekends, summer. Complete part-time degree programs offered during daytime, evenings, weekends, summer. External degree and adult/continuing education programs available. Career services available to part-time students: individual and group career counseling, individual job placement, employer recruitment on campus. Part-time tuition per credit hour ranges from $110 for evening courses to $150 for external degree programs.

Graduate Part-time study available in Graduate Programs. Degree can be earned exclusively through evening/weekend study in Graduate Programs. Basic part-time expenses: $150 per semester hour (minimum) tuition.

Longview Community College
Lee's Summit 64063

Public institution; small-town setting. Awards A. Barrier-free campus. Total enrollment: 5,513 (all undergraduates); 70% part-time, 53% women, 52% over 25. Total faculty: 178. Library holdings: 25,000 bound volumes, 125 periodical subscriptions, 1,500 records/tapes.

Undergraduate Courses offered for part-time students during daytime, evenings, weekends, summer. Complete part-time degree programs offered during daytime, evenings, weekends, summer. Adult/continuing education programs available. Career services available to part-time students: individual and group career counseling, individual job placement, employer recruitment on campus. Part-time tuition: $22 per credit hour for area residents, $30 per credit hour for state residents, $50 per credit hour for nonresidents.

Maple Woods Community College
Kansas City 64156

Public institution; metropolitan setting. Awards A. Barrier-free campus. Total enrollment: 2,647 (all undergraduates); 72% part-time, 58% women, 42% over 25. Total faculty: 122. Library holdings: 19,000 bound volumes, 175 periodical subscriptions.

Undergraduate Courses offered for part-time students during daytime, evenings, weekends, summer. Complete part-time degree programs offered during daytime, evenings, weekends, summer. Adult/continuing education programs available. Career services available to part-time students: individual and group career counseling, individual job placement, employer recruitment on campus. Part-time tuition: $22 per credit hour for area residents, $30 per credit hour for state residents, $50 per credit hour for nonresidents.

Maryville College–Saint Louis
St Louis 63141

Independent institution; metropolitan setting. Awards A, B, M. Total enrollment: 2,050. Undergraduate enrollment: 1,916; 51% part-time, 71% women. Total faculty: 140. Library holdings: 90,000 bound volumes, 550 periodical subscriptions.

Undergraduate Courses offered for part-time students during daytime, evenings, weekends, summer. Complete part-time degree programs offered during daytime, evenings, weekends, summer. Adult/continuing education programs available. Career services available to part-time students: individual career counseling, individual job placement, employer recruitment on campus. Part-time tuition: $160 per credit hour.

Graduate Part-time study available in Division of Education, Division of Management. Degree can be earned exclusively through evening/weekend study in Division of Education, Division of Management. Basic part-time expenses: $160 per credit tuition.

Mineral Area College
Flat River 63601

Public institution; rural setting. Awards A. Barrier-free campus. Total enrollment: 1,685 (all undergraduates); 50% part-time, 63% women, 42% over 25. Total faculty: 70. Library holdings: 25,753 bound volumes, 166 titles on microform, 197 periodical subscriptions, 581 records/tapes.

Undergraduate Courses offered for part-time students during daytime, evenings, weekends, summer. Complete part-time degree programs offered during daytime, evenings. Adult/continuing education programs available. Career services available to part-time students: individual and group career counseling, individual job placement, employer recruitment on campus. Part-time tuition: $16 per credit hour for area residents, $26 per credit hour for state residents, $39 per credit hour for nonresidents.

Missouri Southern State College
Joplin 64801

Public institution; small-town setting. Awards A, B. Total enrollment: 4,305 (all undergraduates); 30% part-time, 52% women, 49% over 25. Total faculty: 206. Library holdings: 140,000 bound volumes, 1,300 periodical subscriptions, 4,252 records/tapes.

Undergraduate Courses offered for part-time students during daytime, evenings, summer. Complete part-time degree programs offered during daytime, evenings, summer. Adult/continuing education programs available. Career services available to part-time students: individual and group career counseling, individual job placement, employer recruitment on campus. Part-time tuition: $32 per credit for state residents, $64 per credit for nonresidents.

Missouri Valley College
Marshall 65340

Independent-religious instutition; small-town setting. Awards A, B. Total enrollment: 410 (all undergraduates); 10% part-time, 37% women, 5% over 25. Total faculty: 37. Library holdings: 100,000 bound volumes, 500 periodical subscriptions.

Undergraduate Courses offered for part-time students during daytime, evenings. Complete part-time degree programs offered during daytime, evenings. Adult/continuing education programs available. Career services available to part-time students: individual and group career counseling, individual job placement, employer recruitment on campus. Part-time tuition: $125 per credit hour.

Missouri Western State College
St Joseph 64507

Public institution; city setting. Awards A, B. Barrier-free campus. Total enrollment: 4,233 (all undergraduates); 30% part-time, 54% women, 30% over 25. Total faculty: 199. Library holdings: 129,913 bound volumes, 1,200 periodical subscriptions, 6,000 records/tapes.

Missouri / **Colleges Offering Part-Time Degree Programs**

Undergraduate Courses offered for part-time students during daytime, evenings, summer. Complete part-time degree programs offered during daytime, evenings, summer. Adult/continuing education programs available. Career services available to part-time students: individual and group career counseling, individual job placement, employer recruitment on campus. Part-time tuition: $55 per credit hour for state residents, $101 per credit hour for nonresidents.

Moberly Area Junior College
Moberly 65270

Public institution; rural setting. Awards A. Total enrollment: 1,200 (all undergraduates); 48% part-time, 48% women, 12% over 25. Total faculty: 68. Library holdings: 15,000 bound volumes, 175 titles on microform, 150 periodical subscriptions, 2,500 records/tapes.

Undergraduate Courses offered for part-time students during daytime, evenings, summer. Complete part-time degree programs offered during daytime, evenings, summer. Adult/continuing education programs available. Career services available to part-time students: individual career counseling, individual job placement, employer recruitment on campus. Part-time tuition: $15 per credit hour for area residents, $30 per credit hour for state residents, $60 per credit hour for nonresidents.

Nazarene Theological Seminary
Kansas City 64131

Independent-religious institution (graduate only). Total enrollment: 459 (coed). Total faculty: 28.

Graduate Part-time study available in Graduate and Professional Programs. Basic part-time expenses: $46 per credit tuition plus $26.50 per semester (minimum) fees.

Northeast Missouri State University
Kirksville 63501

Public institution; small-town setting. Awards B, M. Barrier-free campus. Total enrollment: 6,990. Undergraduate enrollment: 6,338; 14% part-time, 56% women, 15% over 25. Total faculty: 351. Library holdings: 255,327 bound volumes, 781,857 titles on microform, 1,554 periodical subscriptions, 125,833 records/tapes.

Undergraduate Courses offered for part-time students during daytime, evenings, weekends, summer. Complete part-time degree programs offered during daytime, evenings, summer. Adult/continuing education programs available. Career services available to part-time students: individual and group career counseling, individual job placement, employer recruitment on campus. Part-time tuition: $20 per credit for state residents, $40 per credit for nonresidents.

Graduate Part-time study available in Graduate School. Basic part-time expenses: $30 per credit tuition for state residents, $60 per credit tuition for nonresidents.

Northwest Missouri State University
Maryville 64468

Public institution; small-town setting. Awards B, M. Barrier-free campus. Total enrollment: 5,243. Undergraduate enrollment: 4,528; 8% part-time, 51% women, 9% over 25. Total faculty: 255. Library holdings: 235,000 bound volumes, 130,000 titles on microform, 1,648 periodical subscriptions.

Graduate Part-time study available in Graduate School. Basic part-time expenses: $37 per semester hour fees for state residents, $70 per semester hour fees for nonresidents.

Park College
Parkville 64152

Independent-religious instutition; small-town setting. Awards A, B, M. Total enrollment: 488. Undergraduate enrollment: 463; 15% part-time, 46% women, 35% over 25. Total faculty: 40. Library holdings: 98,000 bound volumes, 10,000 periodical subscriptions, 1,000 records/tapes.

Undergraduate Courses offered for part-time students during daytime, evenings, weekends, summer. Complete part-time degree programs offered during daytime, evenings, weekends, summer. External degree and adult/continuing education programs available. Career services available to part-time students: individual and group career counseling, individual job placement, employer recruitment on campus. Part-time tuition: $70 per semester hour.

Graduate Part-time study available in Graduate School of Public Affairs, Graduate School of Religion. Degree can be earned exclusively through evening/weekend study in Graduate School of Public Affairs, Graduate School of Religion. Basic part-time expenses: $120 per semester hour tuition. Institutional financial aid available to part-time graduate students in Graduate School of Public Affairs, Graduate School of Religion.

Penn Valley Community College
Kansas City 64111

Public institution; metropolitan setting. Awards A. Barrier-free campus. Total enrollment: 6,074 (all undergraduates); 70% part-time, 59% women, 35% over 25. Total faculty: 208. Library holdings: 61,802 bound volumes, 15 titles on microform, 240 periodical subscriptions, 2,658 records/tapes.

Undergraduate Courses offered for part-time students during daytime, evenings, weekends, summer. Complete part-time degree programs offered during daytime, evenings, weekends, summer. Adult/continuing education programs available. Career services available to part-time students: individual and group career counseling, individual job placement, employer recruitment on campus. Part-time tuition: $22 per semester hour for area residents, $30 per semester hour for state residents, $50 per semester hour for nonresidents.

Pioneer Community College
Kansas City 64111

Public institution; metropolitan setting. Awards A. Barrier-free campus. Total enrollment: 280 (all undergraduates); 84% part-time, 65% women, 30% over 25. Total faculty: 13. Library holdings: 2,800 bound volumes, 92 periodical subscriptions, 360 records/tapes.

Undergraduate Courses offered for part-time students during daytime, evenings, weekends, summer. Complete part-time degree programs offered during daytime, evenings, weekends, summer. Adult/continuing education programs available. Career services available to part-time students: individual and group career counseling, individual job placement. Part-time tuition: $22 per semester hour for area residents, $27 per semester hour for state residents, $50 per semester hour for nonresidents.

Colleges Offering Part-Time Degree Programs / Missouri

Rockhurst College
Kansas City 64110

Independent-religious instutition; metropolitan setting. Awards B, M. Barrier-free campus. Total enrollment: 3,325. Undergraduate enrollment: 1,556; 12% part-time, 57% women, 7% over 25. Total faculty: 180. Library holdings: 85,000 bound volumes, 289 titles on microform, 647 periodical subscriptions, 1,740 records/tapes.

Undergraduate Courses offered for part-time students during daytime, evenings, weekends, summer. Complete part-time degree programs offered during daytime, evenings. Adult/continuing education programs available. Part-time tuition: $160 per credit hour.

Graduate Part-time study available in Graduate Program in Business Administration.Basic part-time expenses: $150 per credit fees.

Rutledge College
Springfield 65806

Proprietary institution; city setting. Awards A. Barrier-free campus. Total enrollment: 325 (all undergraduates); 20% part-time, 52% women. Total faculty: 19. Library holdings: 3,000 bound volumes, 26 periodical subscriptions, 150 records/tapes.

Undergraduate Courses offered for part-time students during daytime, evenings, summer. Complete part-time degree programs offered during daytime, evenings, summer. Career services available to part-time students: individual and group career counseling, individual job placement. Part-time tuition: $53 per credit hour.

St Louis Community College at Florissant Valley
St Louis 63135

Public institution; metropolitan setting. Awards A. Barrier-free campus. Total enrollment: 12,069 (all undergraduates); 40% part-time, 51% women. Total faculty: 241. Library holdings: 25,000 bound volumes, 100 periodical subscriptions, 1,000 records/tapes.

Undergraduate Courses offered for part-time students during daytime, evenings, weekends, summer. Complete part-time degree programs offered during daytime, evenings, weekends, summer. Adult/continuing education programs available. Career services available to part-time students: individual and group career counseling, individual job placement, employer recruitment on campus. Part-time tuition: $24 per credit hour for area residents, $36 per credit hour for state residents, $47 per credit hour for nonresidents.

St Louis Community College at Forest Park
St Louis 63110

Public institution; metropolitan setting. Awards A. Barrier-free campus. Total enrollment: 8,801 (all undergraduates); 72% part-time, 58% women, 51% over 25. Total faculty: 371. Library holdings: 51,378 bound volumes, 319 titles on microform, 481 periodical subscriptions, 7,757 records/tapes.

Undergraduate Courses offered for part-time students during daytime, evenings, weekends, summer. Complete part-time degree programs offered during daytime, evenings, weekends, summer. Adult/continuing education programs available. Career services available to part-time students: individual and group career counseling, individual job placement. Part-time tuition: $24 per credit hour for area residents, $36 per credit hour for state residents, $47 per credit hour for nonresidents.

St Louis Community College at Meramec
Kirkwood 63122

Public institution; metropolitan setting. Awards A. Barrier-free campus. Total enrollment: 13,568 (all undergraduates); 68% part-time, 57% women, 41% over 25. Total faculty: 422. Library holdings: 72,928 bound volumes, 99 titles on microform, 500 periodical subscriptions, 4,349 records/tapes.

Undergraduate Courses offered for part-time students during daytime, evenings, weekends, summer. Complete part-time degree programs offered during daytime, evenings, weekends, summer. External degree and adult/continuing education programs available. Career services available to part-time students: individual and group career counseling, individual job placement, employer recruitment on campus. Part-time tuition: $24 per semester hour for area residents, $36 per semester hour for state residents, $47 per semester hour for nonresidents.

Saint Louis University
St Louis 63103

Independent-religious instutition; metropolitan setting. Awards A, B, M, D. Total enrollment: 10,059. Undergraduate enrollment: 6,501; 29% part-time, 50% women. Total faculty: 2,236. Library holdings: 1.2 million bound volumes, 7,270 periodical subscriptions, 2,588 records/tapes.

Undergraduate Courses offered for part-time students during daytime, evenings, summer. Complete part-time degree programs offered during daytime, evenings, summer. Adult/continuing education programs available. Career services available to part-time students: individual and group career counseling, individual job placement, employer recruitment on campus. Part-time tuition: $200 per credit.

Graduate Part-time study available in Graduate School, School of Business and Administration, School of Social Service.Basic part-time expenses: $200 per credit hour tuition. Institutional financial aid available to part-time graduate students in Graduate School, School of Business and Administration, School of Social Service.

Saint Mary's College of O'Fallon
O'Fallon 63366

Independent-religious instutition; small-town setting. Awards A. Barrier-free campus. Total enrollment: 687 (all undergraduates); 81% part-time, 82% women, 56% over 25. Total faculty: 51. Library holdings: 45,000 bound volumes, 120 periodical subscriptions, 5,800 records/tapes.

Undergraduate Courses offered for part-time students during daytime, evenings, summer. Complete part-time degree programs offered during daytime, evenings, summer. Career services available to part-time students: individual and group career counseling. Part-time tuition: $90 per credit.

Saint Paul's College
Concordia 64020

Independent-religious instutition; small-town setting. Awards A. Total enrollment: 151 (all undergraduates); 47% part-time, 51% women, 4% over 25. Total faculty: 25. Library holdings: 33,000 bound volumes, 180 periodical subscriptions, 1,500 records/tapes.

Undergraduate Courses offered for part-time students during daytime, evenings. Complete part-time degree programs offered

Missouri / **Colleges Offering Part-Time Degree Programs**

during daytime. Career services available to part-time students: individual and group career counseling. Part-time tuition: $130 per semester hour.

School of the Ozarks
Point Lookout 65726

Independent institution; small-town setting. Awards A, B. Total enrollment: 1,260 (all undergraduates); 10% part-time, 50% women, 10% over 25. Total faculty: 93. Library holdings: 92,000 bound volumes, 40 titles on microform, 600 periodical subscriptions, 3,250 records/tapes.

Undergraduate Courses offered for part-time students during daytime, evenings, summer. Complete part-time degree programs offered during daytime, evenings, summer. Career services available to part-time students: individual and group career counseling, individual job placement, employer recruitment on campus. Part-time tuition: $65 per semester hour.

Southeast Missouri State University
Cape Girardeau 63701

Public institution; small-town setting. Awards A, B, M. Total enrollment: 9,018. Undergraduate enrollment: 8,394; 12% part-time, 54% women, 21% over 25. Total faculty: 464. Library holdings: 294,000 bound volumes, 267,000 titles on microform, 2,464 periodical subscriptions, 12,900 records/tapes.

Undergraduate Courses offered for part-time students during daytime, evenings, weekends, summer. Complete part-time degree programs offered during daytime, summer. Adult/continuing education programs available. Career services available to part-time students: individual and group career counseling, individual job placement, employer recruitment on campus. Part-time tuition: $50 per credit hour for state residents, $98 per credit hour for nonresidents.

Graduate Part-time study available in Graduate School. Degree can be earned exclusively through evening/weekend study in Graduate School. Basic part-time expenses: $52 per credit fees for state residents, $100 per credit fees for nonresidents.

Southwest Baptist University
Bolivar 65613

Independent-religious instutition; small-town setting. Awards A, B. Total enrollment: 1,752 (all undergraduates); 8% part-time, 55% women, 2% over 25. Total faculty: 99. Library holdings: 73,363 bound volumes, 522 periodical subscriptions, 1,089 records/tapes.

Undergraduate Courses offered for part-time students during daytime, evenings, summer. Complete part-time degree programs offered during daytime. Adult/continuing education programs available. Career services available to part-time students: individual and group career counseling, individual job placement, employer recruitment on campus. Part-time tuition: $144 per semester hour.

Southwest Missouri State University
Springfield 65804

Public institution; city setting. Awards A, B, M. Barrier-free campus. Total enrollment: 15,156. Undergraduate enrollment: 14,169; 26% part-time, 53% women, 6% over 25. Total faculty: 685. Library holdings: 397,025 bound volumes, 568,289 titles on microform, 4,157 periodical subscriptions, 6,199 records/tapes.

Undergraduate Courses offered for part-time students during daytime, evenings, summer. Complete part-time degree programs offered during daytime, evenings. Adult/continuing education programs available. Career services available to part-time students: individual career counseling. Part-time tuition: $42 per credit hour for state residents, $42 per credit hour for nonresidents.

Graduate Part-time study available in Graduate School. Basic part-time expenses: $43 per hour tuition for state residents, $43 per hour (minimum) tuition for nonresidents. Institutional financial aid available to part-time graduate students in Graduate School.

State Fair Community College
Sedalia 65301

Public institution; small-town setting. Awards A. Barrier-free campus. Total enrollment: 1,528 (all undergraduates); 49% part-time, 58% women, 50% over 25. Total faculty: 113. Library holdings: 30,000 bound volumes, 100 periodical subscriptions, 1,500 records/tapes.

Undergraduate Courses offered for part-time students during daytime, evenings, weekends, summer. Complete part-time degree programs offered during daytime, evenings, summer. Adult/continuing education programs available. Career services available to part-time students: individual and group career counseling, individual job placement, employer recruitment on campus. Part-time tuition: $15 per semester hour for area residents, $22.50 per semester hour for state residents, $44.50 per semester hour for nonresidents.

Stephens College
Columbia 65215

Independent institution; city setting. Awards A, B. Total enrollment: 1,141 (all undergraduates); 6% part-time, 100% women. Total faculty: 120. Library holdings: 127,000 bound volumes, 525 periodical subscriptions.

Undergraduate Courses offered for part-time students during daytime. Complete part-time degree programs offered during daytime. External degree and adult/continuing education programs available. Part-time tuition: $470 per course.

Tarkio College
Tarkio 64491

Independent-religious instutition; rural setting. Awards A, B. Total enrollment: 537 (all undergraduates); 15% part-time, 40% women, 10% over 25. Total faculty: 35. Library holdings: 70,000 bound volumes, 2,100 titles on microform, 265 periodical subscriptions, 1,400 records/tapes.

Undergraduate Courses offered for part-time students during daytime, evenings, weekends, summer. Complete part-time degree programs offered during daytime, evenings. External degree and adult/continuing education programs available. Part-time tuition: $100 per credit hour.

Three Rivers Community College
Poplar Bluff 63901

Public institution; rural setting. Awards A. Total enrollment: 1,537 (all undergraduates); 40% part-time, 48% women, 40% over 25. Total faculty: 62. Library holdings: 27,000 bound volumes, 150 titles on microform, 385 periodical subscriptions, 500 records/tapes.

Undergraduate Courses offered for part-time students during daytime, evenings, summer. Complete part-time degree programs offered during daytime, evenings, summer. Adult/continuing education programs available. Career services available

Colleges Offering Part-Time Degree Programs / Missouri

Three Rivers Community College (continued)

to part-time students: individual career counseling, individual job placement. Part-time tuition: $18 per credit for area residents, $26 per credit for state residents, $44 per credit for nonresidents.

Trenton Junior College
Trenton 64683

Public institution; rural setting. Awards A. Total enrollment: 626 (all undergraduates); 54% part-time, 72% women, 54% over 25. Total faculty: 51. Library holdings: 13,500 bound volumes, 1,094 titles on microform, 139 periodical subscriptions, 813 records/tapes.

Undergraduate Courses offered for part-time students during daytime, evenings, summer. Complete part-time degree programs offered during daytime, evenings. Adult/continuing education programs available. Career services available to part-time students: individual career counseling, individual job placement. Part-time tuition: $18 per credit for area residents, $28 per credit for state residents, $45 per credit for nonresidents.

University of Missouri–Columbia
Columbia 65211

Public institution; city setting. Awards B, M, D. Barrier-free campus. Total enrollment: 24,059. Undergraduate enrollment: 18,339; 6% part-time, 49% women, 7% over 25. Total faculty: 1,598. Library holdings: 2 million bound volumes, 2 million titles on microform, 20,000 periodical subscriptions.

Undergraduate Courses offered for part-time students during daytime, evenings, summer. Complete part-time degree programs offered during daytime, evenings, summer. Adult/continuing education programs available. Career services available to part-time students: individual and group career counseling, individual job placement, employer recruitment on campus. Part-time tuition: $46 per credit hour for state residents, $138 per credit hour for nonresidents.

Graduate Part-time study available in Graduate School. Basic part-time expenses: $61.80 per credit hour tuition plus $2.80 per credit hour fees for state residents, $159.20 per credit hour tuition plus $2.80 per credit hour fees for nonresidents. Institutional financial aid available to part-time graduate students in Graduate School.

University of Missouri–Kansas City
Kansas City 64110

Public institution; metropolitan setting. Awards B, M, D. Total enrollment: 11,496. Undergraduate enrollment: 6,873; 41% part-time, 52% women, 38% over 25. Total faculty: 1,033. Library holdings: 709,201 bound volumes, 1.2 million titles on microform, 10,413 periodical subscriptions, 20,217 records/tapes.

Undergraduate Courses offered for part-time students during daytime, evenings, weekends, summer. Complete part-time degree programs offered during daytime, evenings, weekends, summer. External degree and adult/continuing education programs available. Career services available to part-time students: individual and group career counseling, individual job placement, employer recruitment on campus. Part-time tuition: $50.50 per credit hour for state residents, $142.40 per credit hour for nonresidents.

Graduate Part-time study available in School of Graduate Studies, School of Dentistry, School of Pharmacy. Basic part-time expenses: $59 per credit tuition plus $4.50 per credit fees for state residents, $59 per credit (minimum) tuition plus $4.50 per credit fees for nonresidents.

University of Missouri–Rolla
Rolla 65401

Public institution; small-town setting. Awards B, M, D. Total enrollment: 7,566. Undergraduate enrollment: 6,315; 9% part-time, 21% women, 8% over 25. Total faculty: 349. Library holdings: 330,000 bound volumes, 2,200 periodical subscriptions, 1,800 records/tapes.

Undergraduate Courses offered for part-time students during daytime, evenings, summer. Complete part-time degree programs offered during daytime, evenings, summer. Adult/continuing education programs available. Career services available to part-time students: individual and group career counseling, individual job placement, employer recruitment on campus. Part-time tuition: $46 per credit hour for state residents, $131 per credit hour for nonresidents.

Graduate Part-time study available in Graduate School. Basic part-time expenses: $0 tuition plus $80 per credit fees for state residents, $101 per credit tuition plus $80 per credit fees for nonresidents. Institutional financial aid available to part-time graduate students in Graduate School.

University of Missouri–St Louis
St Louis 63121

Public institution; metropolitan setting. Awards B, M, D. Barrier-free campus. Total enrollment: 11,558. Undergraduate enrollment: 9,890; 44% part-time, 48% women. Total faculty: 449. Library holdings: 346,964 bound volumes, 2,931 periodical subscriptions.

Undergraduate Courses offered for part-time students during daytime, evenings, summer. Complete part-time degree programs offered during daytime, evenings, summer. Adult/continuing education programs available. Career services available to part-time students: individual and group career counseling, individual job placement, employer recruitment on campus. Part-time tuition: $46 per semester hour for state residents, $138 per semester hour for nonresidents.

Graduate Part-time study available in Graduate School. Basic part-time expenses: $59 per credit hour tuition plus $3.55 per credit hour fees for state residents, $160 per credit hour tuition plus $3.55 per credit hour fees for nonresidents. Institutional financial aid available to part-time graduate students in Graduate School.

Washington University
St Louis 63130

Independent institution; metropolitan setting. Awards B, M, D. Total enrollment: 10,769. Undergraduate enrollment: 4,547; 13% part-time, 41% women. Total faculty: 2,515. Library holdings: 1.9 million bound volumes, 15,558 periodical subscriptions, 24,744 records/tapes.

Undergraduate Courses offered for part-time students during daytime, evenings, summer. Complete part-time degree programs offered during daytime, evenings, summer. Adult/continuing education programs available. Part-time tuition: $100 per credit hour.

Graduate Part-time study available in Graduate School of Arts and Science, George Warren Brown School of Social Work, School of Business and Public Administration, School of Engineering and Applied Science, School of Fine Arts. Basic part-time expenses: $360 per credit tuition. Institutional financial aid available to part-time graduate students in Graduate

School of Arts and Science, George Warren Brown School of Social Work, School of Business and Public Administration.

Webster University
St Louis 63119

Independent institution; metropolitan setting. Awards B, M. Total enrollment: 5,218. Undergraduate enrollment: 1,739; 33% part-time, 67% women. Total faculty: 621. Library holdings: 162,000 bound volumes, 800 periodical subscriptions, 1,800 records/tapes.

Undergraduate Courses offered for part-time students during daytime, evenings, summer. Complete part-time degree programs offered during daytime, evenings, summer. Adult/continuing education programs available. Part-time tuition: $143 per credit hour.

William Jewell College
Liberty 64068

Independent-religious instutition; small-town setting. Awards B. Total enrollment: 1,399 (all undergraduates); 1% part-time, 50% women, 9% over 25. Total faculty: 120. Library holdings: 150,000 bound volumes, 21,000 titles on microform, 625 periodical subscriptions, 11,000 records/tapes.

Undergraduate Courses offered for part-time students during daytime, evenings. Complete part-time degree programs offered during daytime, evenings. Adult/continuing education programs available. Career services available to part-time students: individual and group career counseling, individual job placement, employer recruitment on campus. Part-time tuition: $175 per semester hour.

William Woods College
Fulton 65251

Independent-religious instutition; small-town setting. Awards B. Total enrollment: 796 (all undergraduates); 0% part-time, 100% women, 2% over 25. Total faculty: 69. Library holdings: 160,000 bound volumes, 680 periodical subscriptions.

Undergraduate Courses offered for part-time students during daytime. Complete part-time degree programs offered during daytime. Career services available to part-time students: individual and group career counseling, individual job placement, employer recruitment on campus. Part-time tuition: $180 per credit hour.

MONTANA

Blackfeet Community College
Browning 59417

Independent institution; small-town setting. Awards A. Barrier-free campus. Total enrollment: 247 (all undergraduates); 33% part-time, 65% women, 60% over 25. Total faculty: 31. Library holdings: 10,000 bound volumes, 175 periodical subscriptions.

Undergraduate Courses offered for part-time students during daytime, evenings, weekends. Complete part-time degree programs offered during daytime, evenings. Adult/continuing education programs available. Career services available to part-time students: individual and group career counseling, individual job placement. Part-time tuition: $15 per credit.

Carroll College of Montana
Helena 59625

Independent-religious instutition; small-town setting. Awards A, B. Total enrollment: 1,533 (all undergraduates); 27% part-time, 59% women, 10% over 25. Total faculty: 117. Library holdings: 94,000 bound volumes, 470 periodical subscriptions, 2,000 records/tapes.

Undergraduate Courses offered for part-time students during daytime, evenings, weekends, summer. Complete part-time degree programs offered during daytime, evenings, summer. Adult/continuing education programs available. Career services available to part-time students: individual and group career counseling, individual job placement, employer recruitment on campus. Part-time tuition: $107 per semester hour.

College of Great Falls
Great Falls 59405

Independent-religious instutition; city setting. Awards A, B, M. Total enrollment: 1,192. Undergraduate enrollment: 1,166; 60% part-time, 50% women, 46% over 25. Total faculty: 87. Library holdings: 64,079 bound volumes, 32,232 titles on microform, 450 periodical subscriptions, 2,500 records/tapes.

Undergraduate Courses offered for part-time students during daytime, evenings, summer. Complete part-time degree programs offered during daytime, evenings. Adult/continuing education programs available. Career services available to part-time students: individual and group career counseling, individual job placement, employer recruitment on campus. Part-time tuition: $110 per credit.

Graduate Part-time study available in Graduate Program. Degree can be earned exclusively through evening/weekend study in Graduate Program. Basic part-time expenses: $100 per credit tuition plus $5 per semester fees.

Dawson Community College
Glendive 59330

Public institution; rural setting. Awards A. Barrier-free campus. Total enrollment: 690 (all undergraduates); 61% part-time, 60% women, 55% over 25. Total faculty: 32. Library holdings: 18,500 bound volumes, 200 periodical subscriptions, 500 records/tapes.

Undergraduate Courses offered for part-time students during daytime, evenings, summer. Complete part-time degree programs offered during daytime, evenings, summer. Adult/continuing education programs available. Career services available to part-time students: individual and group career counseling. Part-time tuition: $14 per quarter hour for area residents, $18 per quarter hour for state residents, $28 per quarter hour for nonresidents.

Eastern Montana College
Billings 59101

Public institution; city setting. Awards A, B, M. Barrier-free campus. Total enrollment: 4,424. Undergraduate enrollment: 3,779; 32% part-time, 61% women, 36% over 25. Total faculty: 218. Library holdings: 100,000 bound volumes.

Undergraduate Courses offered for part-time students during daytime, evenings, summer. Complete part-time degree programs offered during daytime, evenings, summer. Adult/continuing education programs available. Career services available to part-time students: individual and group career counseling, individual job placement, employer recruitment on campus. Part-time tuition and fees per quarter (1 to 11 credits) range

Colleges Offering Part-Time Degree Programs / *Montana*

Eastern Montana College (continued)

from $48.50 to $258 for residents, $85.50 to $665 for nonresidents.

Graduate Part-time study available in School of Education. Institutional financial aid available to part-time graduate students in School of Education.

Flathead Valley Community College
Kalispell 59901

Public institution; small-town setting. Awards A. Total enrollment: 1,771 (all undergraduates); 69% part-time, 60% women, 65% over 25. Total faculty: 127. Library holdings: 11,000 bound volumes, 123 periodical subscriptions, 150 records/tapes.

Undergraduate Courses offered for part-time students during daytime, evenings, weekends, summer. Complete part-time degree programs offered during daytime, evenings. Adult/continuing education programs available. Career services available to part-time students: individual and group career counseling. Part-time tuition: $10.50 per quarter hour for area residents, $13.50 per quarter hour for state residents, $24.50 per quarter hour for nonresidents.

Miles Community College
Miles City 59301

Public institution; small-town setting. Awards A. Barrier-free campus. Total enrollment: 798 (all undergraduates); 66% part-time, 64% women, 35% over 25. Total faculty: 54. Library holdings: 13,523 bound volumes, 117 titles on microform, 159 periodical subscriptions, 7,813 records/tapes.

Undergraduate Courses offered for part-time students during daytime, evenings, summer. Complete part-time degree programs offered during daytime, evenings, summer. Adult/continuing education programs available. Career services available to part-time students: individual and group career counseling, individual job placement, employer recruitment on campus. Part-time tuition: $11 per credit for area residents, $18 per credit for state residents, $28 per credit for nonresidents.

Montana College of Mineral Science and Technology
Butte 59701

Public institution; small-town setting. Awards A, B, M. Total enrollment: 2,334. Undergraduate enrollment: 2,044; 23% part-time, 35% women. Total faculty: 134. Library holdings: 77,000 bound volumes, 5,000 titles on microform, 725 periodical subscriptions, 700 records/tapes.

Undergraduate Courses offered for part-time students during daytime, evenings. Complete part-time degree programs offered during daytime, evenings. Adult/continuing education programs available. Career services available to part-time students: individual and group career counseling. Part-time tuition per semester (1 to 11 semester hours) ranges from $49 to $368 for state residents, $120 to $1144 for nonresidents.

Graduate Part-time study available in Graduate School. Basic part-time expenses: $102.75 per semester (minimum) tuition for state residents, $314.25 per semester (minimum) tuition for nonresidents. Institutional financial aid available to part-time graduate students in Graduate School.

Montana State University
Bozeman 59717

Public institution; small-town setting. Awards B, M, D. Total enrollment: 11,447. Undergraduate enrollment: 10,051; 10% part-time, 43% women. Total faculty: 681. Library holdings: 505,000 bound volumes, 10,000 periodical subscriptions, 4,000 records/tapes.

Undergraduate Courses offered for part-time students during daytime, evenings, summer. Complete part-time degree programs offered during daytime. Adult/continuing education programs available. Career services available to part-time students: individual and group career counseling, individual job placement, employer recruitment on campus. Part-time tuition and fees per quarter (1 to 11 credits) range from $35 to $275 for state residents, $82 to $792 for nonresidents.

Graduate Part-time study available in College of Graduate Studies. Basic part-time expenses: $73.80 per quarter (minimum) fees for state residents, $214.80 per quarter (minimum) fees for nonresidents.

Northern Montana College
Havre 59501

Public institution; small-town setting. Awards A, B, M. Barrier-free campus. Total enrollment: 1,859. Undergraduate enrollment: 1,658; 14% part-time, 43% women. Total faculty: 122. Library holdings: 85,000 bound volumes, 200 periodical subscriptions.

Undergraduate Courses offered for part-time students during daytime, evenings, weekends, summer. Complete part-time degree programs offered during daytime, evenings. Adult/continuing education programs available. Career services available to part-time students: individual and group career counseling, individual job placement, employer recruitment on campus. Part-time tuition: $35 per quarter hour for state residents, $76 per quarter hour for nonresidents.

Graduate Part-time study available in Graduate Studies. Degree can be earned exclusively through evening/weekend study in Graduate Studies. Basic part-time expenses: $72 per quarter (minimum) fees for state residents, $184 per quarter (minimum) fees for nonresidents. Institutional financial aid available to part-time graduate students in Graduate Studies.

Rocky Mountain College
Billings 59102

Independent-religious instutition; city setting. Awards B. Total enrollment: 487 (all undergraduates); 2% part-time, 60% women. Total faculty: 45. Library holdings: 65,000 bound volumes, 300 titles on microform, 325 periodical subscriptions, 1,450 records/tapes.

Undergraduate Courses offered for part-time students during daytime, summer. Complete part-time degree programs offered during daytime, summer. Adult/continuing education programs available. Career services available to part-time students: individual career counseling, individual job placement, employer recruitment on campus. Part-time tuition: $145 per semester hour.

Salish Kootenai Community College
Pablo 59855

Independent institution; rural setting. Awards A. Barrier-free campus. Total enrollment: 507 (all undergraduates); 87% part-time, 55% women, 50% over 25. Total faculty: 53. Library holdings: 10,000 bound volumes, 200 periodical subscriptions.

Undergraduate Courses offered for part-time students during daytime, evenings. Complete part-time degree programs offered during daytime, evenings. Career services available to part-time students: individual and group career counseling. Part-time tuition for reservation residents: $20 per credit hour. Nonresident part-time tuiton: $58 per credit hour.

University of Montana
Missoula 59812

Public institution; city setting. Awards A, B, M, D. Total enrollment: 9,350. Undergraduate enrollment: 7,496; 15% part-time, 47% women, 36% over 25. Total faculty: 487. Library holdings: 700,000 bound volumes, 19,200 titles on microform, 4,500 periodical subscriptions, 7,135 records/tapes.

Undergraduate Courses offered for part-time students during daytime, evenings. Complete part-time degree programs offered during daytime, evenings. Adult/continuing education programs available. Career services available to part-time students: individual and group career counseling, individual job placement, employer recruitment on campus. Part-time tuition and fees per quarter (1 to 11 credits) range from $92 to $229 for state residents, $135 to $772 for nonresidents.

Graduate Part-time study available in Graduate School. Basic part-time expenses: $75.50 per quarter (minimum) tuition for state residents, $216.50 per quarter (minimum) tuition for nonresidents. Institutional financial aid available to part-time graduate students in Graduate School.

Western Montana College
Dillon 59725

Public institution; small-town setting. Awards A, B, M. Total enrollment: 960. Undergraduate enrollment: 767; 17% part-time, 45% women. Total faculty: 52. Library holdings: 60,000 bound volumes, 19,500 titles on microform, 390 periodical subscriptions, 500 records/tapes.

Undergraduate Courses offered for part-time students during daytime, evenings, weekends, summer. Complete part-time degree programs offered during daytime, summer. Adult/continuing education programs available. Career services available to part-time students: individual and group career counseling, individual job placement, employer recruitment on campus. Part-time tuition and fees per semester (1 to 7 credits) range from $57 to $187 for state residents, $106 to $534 for nonresidents.

Graduate Part-time study available in Graduate Studies. Degree can be earned exclusively through evening/weekend study in Graduate Studies.

NEBRASKA

Bellevue College
Bellevue 68005

Independent institution; small-town setting. Awards B. Barrier-free campus. Total enrollment: 2,697 (all undergraduates); 60% part-time, 50% women, 60% over 25. Total faculty: 102. Library holdings: 65,000 bound volumes, 300 periodical subscriptions, 1,500 records/tapes.

Undergraduate Courses offered for part-time students during daytime, evenings, summer. Complete part-time degree programs offered during daytime, evenings. Adult/continuing education programs available. Career services available to part-time students: individual and group career counseling, individual job placement, employer recruitment on campus. Part-time tuition: $48 per credit hour.

Bishop Clarkson College of Nursing
Omaha 68131

Independent institution; metropolitan setting. Awards B. Barrier-free campus. Total enrollment: 500 (all undergraduates); 25% part-time, 90% women, 60% over 25. Total faculty: 39. Library holdings: 7,000 bound volumes, 50 titles on microform, 130 periodical subscriptions, 250 records/tapes.

Undergraduate Courses offered for part-time students during daytime, evenings, summer. Complete part-time degree programs offered during daytime, evenings, summer. Career services available to part-time students: individual career counseling. Part-time tuition: $97 per credit.

Central Community College–Grand Island Campus
Grand Island 68802

Public institution; small-town setting. Awards A. Barrier-free campus. Total enrollment: 1,500 (all undergraduates); 86% part-time, 38% women, 65% over 25. Total faculty: 588. Library holdings: 9,107 bound volumes, 333 titles on microform, 56 periodical subscriptions, 1,446 records/tapes.

Undergraduate Courses offered for part-time students during daytime, evenings, summer. Complete part-time degree programs offered during daytime, evenings, summer. External degree and adult/continuing education programs available. Career services available to part-time students: individual and group career counseling, individual job placement, employer recruitment on campus. Part-time tuition: $24 per semester hour for state residents, $36 per semester hour for nonresidents.

Central Community College–Hastings Campus
Hastings 68901

Public institution; small-town setting. Awards A. Barrier-free campus. Total enrollment: 1,975 (all undergraduates); 70% part-time, 49% women, 40% over 25. Total faculty: 86. Library holdings: 17,678 bound volumes, 437 titles on microform, 305 periodical subscriptions, 8,573 records/tapes.

Undergraduate Courses offered for part-time students during daytime, evenings, weekends, summer. Complete part-time degree programs offered during daytime, evenings, weekends, summer. Adult/continuing education programs available. Career services available to part-time students: individual and group career counseling, individual job placement, employer recruitment on campus. Part-time tuition: $24 per semester hour for state residents, $36 per semester hour for nonresidents.

Central Community College–Platte Campus
Columbus 68601

Public institution; rural setting. Awards A. Barrier-free campus. Total enrollment: 985 (all undergraduates); 58% part-time, 59% women, 39% over 25. Total faculty: 55. Library holdings: 31,300 bound volumes, 600 titles on microform, 225 periodical subscriptions, 2,900 records/tapes.

Undergraduate Courses offered for part-time students during daytime, evenings, weekends, summer. Complete part-time degree programs offered during daytime, evenings, weekends, summer. Adult/continuing education programs available. Career services available to part-time students: individual and group career counseling, individual job placement, employer recruitment on campus. Part-time tuition: $24 per semester hour for state residents, $36 per semester hour for nonresidents.

Colleges Offering Part-Time Degree Programs / Nebraska

Chadron State College
Chadron 69337

Public institution; small-town setting. Awards A, B, M. Total enrollment: 1,977. Undergraduate enrollment: 1,558; 27% part-time, 57% women. Total faculty: 104. Library holdings: 187,000 bound volumes, 73,000 titles on microform, 900 periodical subscriptions, 12,000 records/tapes.

Undergraduate Courses offered for part-time students during daytime, evenings, weekends, summer. Complete part-time degree programs offered during daytime. External degree and adult/continuing education programs available. Career services available to part-time students: individual and group career counseling, individual job placement, employer recruitment on campus. Part-time tuition: $27.50 per semester hour for state residents, $46 per semester hour for nonresidents.

Graduate Part-time study available in School of Graduate Studies. Basic part-time expenses: $27.50 per credit tuition plus $6 per semester (minimum) fees for state residents, $46 per credit tuition plus $6 per semester (minimum) fees for nonresidents. Institutional financial aid available to part-time graduate students in School of Graduate Studies.

College of Saint Mary
Omaha 68124

Independent-religious instutition; metropolitan setting. Awards A, B. Total enrollment: 1,207 (all undergraduates); 59% part-time, 84% women, 67% over 25. Total faculty: 114. Library holdings: 41,392 bound volumes, 47 titles on microform, 277 periodical subscriptions, 2,481 records/tapes.

Undergraduate Courses offered for part-time students during daytime, evenings, weekends, summer. Complete part-time degree programs offered during daytime, evenings, weekends. Adult/continuing education programs available. Career services available to part-time students: individual and group career counseling, individual job placement, employer recruitment on campus. Part-time tuition: $143 per credit hour.

Concordia Teachers College
Seward 68434

Independent-religious instutition; small-town setting. Awards B, M. Total enrollment: 959. Undergraduate enrollment: 950; 7% part-time, 52% women, 1% over 25. Total faculty: 101. Library holdings: 135,000 bound volumes, 18,000 titles on microform, 650 periodical subscriptions, 9,000 records/tapes.

Undergraduate Courses offered for part-time students during daytime, evenings, summer. Complete part-time degree programs offered during daytime, evenings, summer. Adult/continuing education programs available. Career services available to part-time students: individual career counseling, individual job placement. Part-time tuition: $117 per credit.

Graduate Part-time study available in Graduate Program in Education. Basic part-time expenses: $117 per credit tuition. Institutional financial aid available to part-time graduate students in Graduate Program in Education.

Creighton University
Omaha 68178

Independent-religious instutition; metropolitan setting. Awards A, B, M, D. Total enrollment: 5,864. Undergraduate enrollment: 4,285; 10% part-time, 47% women, 19% over 25. Total faculty: 986. Library holdings: 443,167 bound volumes, 65,555 titles on microform, 2,893 periodical subscriptions, 6,789 records/tapes.

Undergraduate Courses offered for part-time students during daytime, evenings, weekends, summer. Complete part-time degree programs offered during daytime, evenings, weekends. Adult/continuing education programs available. Career services available to part-time students: individual and group career counseling, individual job placement, employer recruitment on campus. Part-time tuition: $150 per credit.

Graduate Part-time study available in Graduate School, School of Law. Basic part-time expenses: $162 per credit tuition. Institutional financial aid available to part-time graduate students in Graduate School, School of Law.

Dana College
Blair 68008

Independent-religious instutition; small-town setting. Awards B. Total enrollment: 495 (all undergraduates); 5% part-time, 48% women. Total faculty: 58. Library holdings: 126,000 bound volumes, 534 periodical subscriptions.

Undergraduate Courses offered for part-time students during daytime, summer. Complete part-time degree programs offered during daytime, summer. Career services available to part-time students: individual and group career counseling, individual job placement, employer recruitment on campus. Part-time tuition: $160 per credit.

Grace College of the Bible
Omaha 68108

Independent-religious instutition; metropolitan setting. Awards A, B. Total enrollment: 285 (all undergraduates); 17% part-time, 46% women, 7% over 25. Total faculty: 29. Library holdings: 54,000 bound volumes, 270 periodical subscriptions, 1,531 records/tapes.

Undergraduate Courses offered for part-time students during daytime, evenings, summer. Complete part-time degree programs offered during daytime. Adult/continuing education programs available. Career services available to part-time students: individual and group career counseling, individual job placement. Part-time tuition: $88 per semester hour.

Hastings College
Hastings 68901

Independent-religious instutition; small-town setting. Awards B. Total enrollment: 792 (all undergraduates); 8% part-time, 54% women, 6% over 25. Total faculty: 71. Library holdings: 100,697 bound volumes, 800 titles on microform, 516 periodical subscriptions, 1,800 records/tapes.

Undergraduate Courses offered for part-time students during daytime, summer. Complete part-time degree programs offered during daytime, summer. Career services available to part-time students: individual and group career counseling, individual job placement, employer recruitment on campus. Part-time tuition: $190 per semester hour.

Kearney State College
Kearney 68849

Public institution; small-town setting. Awards B, M. Total enrollment: 7,939. Undergraduate enrollment: 6,032; 32% part-time, 59% women. Total faculty: 330. Library holdings: 168,094 bound volumes, 318,789 titles on microform, 1,917 periodical subscriptions.

Undergraduate Courses offered for part-time students during daytime, evenings, weekends, summer. Complete part-time degree programs offered during daytime, evenings, weekends, summer. Adult/continuing education programs available. Career services available to part-time students: individual and

Nebraska / **Colleges Offering Part-Time Degree Programs**

group career counseling, individual job placement, employer recruitment on campus. Part-time tuition: $27.50 per semester hour for state residents, $46 per semester hour for nonresidents.

Graduate Part-time study available in School of Graduate Study. Basic part-time expenses: $27.50 per credit tuition plus $31 per semester fees for state residents, $46 per credit tuition plus $31 per semester fees for nonresidents.

Lincoln School of Commerce
Lincoln 68501

Proprietary institution; city setting. Awards A. Total enrollment: 496 (all undergraduates); 11% part-time, 98% women. Total faculty: 21. Library holdings: 1,283 bound volumes, 25 periodical subscriptions.

Undergraduate Courses offered for part-time students during daytime, evenings, summer. Complete part-time degree programs offered during daytime, evenings. Career services available to part-time students: individual and group career counseling, individual job placement, employer recruitment on campus. Part-time tuition: $45 per credit hour.

McCook Community College
McCook 69001

Public institution; small-town setting. Awards A. Total enrollment: 700 (all undergraduates); 61% part-time, 75% women. Total faculty: 55. Library holdings: 22,000 bound volumes, 245 periodical subscriptions, 2,000 records/tapes.

Undergraduate Courses offered for part-time students during daytime, evenings, summer. Complete part-time degree programs offered during daytime, evenings, summer. Adult/continuing education programs available. Career services available to part-time students: individual career counseling. Part-time tuition: $17 per credit hour for state residents, $21.50 per credit hour for nonresidents.

Metropolitan Technical Community College
Omaha 68103

Public institution; metropolitan setting. Awards A. Total enrollment: 5,745 (all undergraduates); 75% part-time, 53% women, 62% over 25. Total faculty: 345. Library holdings: 39,621 bound volumes, 143 titles on microform, 504 periodical subscriptions, 2,819 records/tapes.

Undergraduate Courses offered for part-time students during daytime, evenings, summer. Complete part-time degree programs offered during daytime, evenings. Adult/continuing education programs available. Career services available to part-time students: individual and group career counseling, individual job placement. Part-time tuition: $16.50 per quarter hour for state residents, $33 per quarter hour for nonresidents.

Midland Lutheran College
Fremont 68025

Independent-religious instutition; small-town setting. Awards A, B. Barrier-free campus. Total enrollment: 855 (all undergraduates); 10% part-time, 53% women, 5% over 25. Total faculty: 90. Library holdings: 105,000 bound volumes, 800 periodical subscriptions, 3,700 records/tapes.

Undergraduate Courses offered for part-time students during daytime, evenings, summer. Complete part-time degree programs offered during daytime, evenings, summer. Adult/continuing education programs available. Career services available to part-time students: individual career counseling, individual job placement, employer recruitment on campus. Part-time tuition: $160 per credit hour.

Mid-Plains Community College
North Platte 69101

Public institution; small-town setting. Awards A. Barrier-free campus. Total enrollment: 1,800 (all undergraduates); 62% part-time, 50% women. Total faculty: 74. Library holdings: 22,000 bound volumes, 200 periodical subscriptions, 500 records/tapes.

Undergraduate Courses offered for part-time students during daytime, evenings, summer. Complete part-time degree programs offered during daytime, evenings, summer. External degree and adult/continuing education programs available. Career services available to part-time students: individual and group career counseling, individual job placement, employer recruitment on campus. Part-time tuition: $17 per credit hour for state residents, $21.50 per credit hour for nonresidents.

Nebraska Christian College
Norfolk 68701

Independent-religious instutition; small-town setting. Awards A, B. Barrier-free campus. Total enrollment: 151 (all undergraduates); 20% part-time, 49% women. Total faculty: 16.

Undergraduate Courses offered for part-time students during daytime. Complete part-time degree programs offered during daytime. Career services available to part-time students: individual career counseling. Part-time tuition: $58 per semester hour.

Nebraska Indian Community College
Winnebago 68071

Public institution; rural setting. Awards A. Total enrollment: 216 (all undergraduates); 55% part-time, 63% women, 80% over 25. Total faculty: 68. Library holdings: 14,000 bound volumes, 95 titles on microform, 91 periodical subscriptions, 275 records/tapes.

Undergraduate Courses offered for part-time students during daytime, evenings, weekends, summer. Complete part-time degree programs offered during daytime, evenings. Adult/continuing education programs available. Career services available to part-time students: individual career counseling. Part-time tuition: $19.50 per credit.

Nebraska Wesleyan University
Lincoln 68504

Independent-religious instutition; city setting. Awards A, B. Total enrollment: 1,246 (all undergraduates); 17% part-time, 54% women, 15% over 25. Total faculty: 104. Library holdings: 180,931 bound volumes, 600 periodical subscriptions, 1,060 records/tapes.

Undergraduate Courses offered for part-time students during daytime, evenings, summer. Complete part-time degree programs offered during daytime, evenings. Adult/continuing education programs available. Career services available to part-time students: individual and group career counseling, individual job placement, employer recruitment on campus. Part-time tuition: $190 per hour.

Colleges Offering Part-Time Degree Programs / Nebraska

Nebraska Western College
Scottsbluff 69361

Public institution; small-town setting. Awards A. Barrier-free campus. Total enrollment: 1,542 (all undergraduates); 65% part-time, 62% women, 54% over 25. Total faculty: 72. Library holdings: 21,200 bound volumes, 3 titles on microform, 225 periodical subscriptions, 2,000 records/tapes.

Undergraduate Courses offered for part-time students during daytime, evenings, summer. Complete part-time degree programs offered during daytime, evenings, summer. Adult/continuing education programs available. Career services available to part-time students: individual and group career counseling, individual job placement. Part-time tuition: $21.30 per credit for state residents, $29 per credit for nonresidents.

Northeast Technical Community College
Norfolk 68701

Public institution; small-town setting. Awards A. Barrier-free campus. Total enrollment: 1,666 (all undergraduates); 35% part-time, 40% women. Total faculty: 117. Library holdings: 25,000 bound volumes, 12 titles on microform, 452 periodical subscriptions, 430 records/tapes.

Undergraduate Courses offered for part-time students during daytime, evenings, summer. Complete part-time degree programs offered during daytime, evenings, summer. Adult/continuing education programs available. Career services available to part-time students: individual career counseling, individual job placement. Part-time tuition: $17.50 per semester hour for state residents, $28 per semester hour for nonresidents.

Peru State College
Peru 68421

Public institution; rural setting. Awards A, B. Barrier-free campus. Total enrollment: 1,306 (all undergraduates); 20% part-time, 55% women. Total faculty: 65. Library holdings: 95,000 bound volumes, 285 periodical subscriptions, 2,000 records/tapes.

Undergraduate Courses offered for part-time students during daytime, evenings, summer. Complete part-time degree programs offered during daytime, evenings, summer. External degree and adult/continuing education programs available. Career services available to part-time students: individual and group career counseling, individual job placement, employer recruitment on campus. Part-time tuition: $27.50 per semester hour for state residents, $46 per semester hour for nonresidents.

Platte Valley Bible College
Scottsbluff 69361

Independent-religious instutition; small-town setting. Awards A, B. Total enrollment: 51 (all undergraduates); 20% part-time, 46% women. Total faculty: 7. Library holdings: 12,000 bound volumes, 10 periodical subscriptions.

Undergraduate Courses offered for part-time students during daytime, evenings. Complete part-time degree programs offered during daytime. Part-time tuition: $30 per credit.

Southeast Community College, Beatrice Campus
Beatrice 68310

Public institution; small-town setting. Awards A. Barrier-free campus. Total enrollment: 191 (all undergraduates); 5% part-time, 55% women, 26% over 25. Total faculty: 20. Library holdings: 2,071 bound volumes, 128 periodical subscriptions.

Undergraduate Courses offered for part-time students during daytime. Complete part-time degree programs offered during daytime. Adult/continuing education programs available. Career services available to part-time students: group career counseling, individual job placement, employer recruitment on campus. Part-time tuition: $17.25 per credit hour for state residents, $24.75 per credit hour for nonresidents.

Southeast Community College, Fairbury Campus
Fairbury 68352

Public institution; small-town setting. Awards A. Total enrollment: 323 (all undergraduates); 23% part-time, 47% women, 30% over 25. Total faculty: 30.

Undergraduate Courses offered for part-time students during daytime, evenings, summer. Complete part-time degree programs offered during daytime, evenings, summer. Adult/continuing education programs available. Career services available to part-time students: individual and group career counseling, individual job placement, employer recruitment on campus. Part-time tuition: $24.75 per credit for state residents, $39.75 per credit for nonresidents.

Southeast Community College, Lincoln Campus
Lincoln 68520

Public institution; city setting. Awards A. Barrier-free campus. Total enrollment: 3,692 (all undergraduates); 66% part-time, 51% women, 46% over 25. Total faculty: 571. Library holdings: 14,500 bound volumes, 300 periodical subscriptions, 4,000 records/tapes.

Undergraduate Courses offered for part-time students during daytime, evenings, weekends, summer. Complete part-time degree programs offered during daytime, evenings, weekends, summer. Adult/continuing education programs available. Career services available to part-time students: individual and group career counseling, individual job placement, employer recruitment on campus. Part-time tuition: $16.50 per credit for state residents, $26.25 per credit for nonresidents.

Union College
Lincoln 68506

Independent-religious instutition; city setting. Awards A, B. Total enrollment: 1,040 (all undergraduates); 15% part-time, 53% women. Total faculty: 86. Library holdings: 109,966 bound volumes, 723 periodical subscriptions.

Undergraduate Courses offered for part-time students during daytime, evenings, summer. Complete part-time degree programs offered during daytime, summer. Career services available to part-time students: individual and group career counseling, individual job placement, employer recruitment on campus. Part-time tuition: $250 per semester hour.

University of Nebraska at Omaha
Omaha 68182

Public institution; metropolitan setting. Awards A, B, M. Barrier-free campus. Total enrollment: 14,531. Undergraduate enrollment: 12,387; 41% part-time, 43% women, 40% over 25. Total faculty: 491. Library holdings: 489,872 bound volumes,

443,545 titles on microform, 5,875 periodical subscriptions, 3,670 records/tapes.
Undergraduate Courses offered for part-time students during daytime, evenings, weekends, summer. Complete part-time degree programs offered during daytime, evenings, weekends, summer. Adult/continuing education programs available. Career services available to part-time students: individual and group career counseling, individual job placement, employer recruitment on campus. Part-time tuition: $38 per semester hour for state residents, $103 per semester hour for nonresidents.
Graduate Part-time study available in Graduate Studies and Research. Basic part-time expenses: $47 per credit tuition plus $56.10 per semester fees for state residents, $112 per credit tuition plus $56.10 per semester fees for nonresidents. Institutional financial aid available to part-time graduate students in Graduate Studies and Research.

University of Nebraska–Lincoln
Lincoln 68588

Public institution; city setting. Awards B, M, D. Total enrollment: 24,336. Undergraduate enrollment: 20,471; 8% part-time, 42% women. Total faculty: 1,077. Library holdings: 1.4 million bound volumes, 18,477 periodical subscriptions.
Undergraduate Courses offered for part-time students during daytime, evenings, summer. Complete part-time degree programs offered during daytime, evenings, summer. Adult/continuing education programs available. Career services available to part-time students: individual and group career counseling, individual job placement, employer recruitment on campus. Part-time tuition: $38 per credit hour for state residents, $103 per credit hour for nonresidents.
Graduate Part-time study available in Graduate College. Basic part-time expenses: $47 per credit hour tuition plus $34.44 per semester (minimum) fees for state residents, $112 per credit hour tuition plus $34.44 per semester (minimum) fees for nonresidents. Institutional financial aid available to part-time graduate students in Graduate College.

University of Nebraska Medical Center
Omaha 68105

Public institution; metropolitan setting. Awards A, B, M, D. Total enrollment: 2,265. Undergraduate enrollment: 951; 43% part-time, 90% women. Total faculty: 602. Library holdings: 190,858 bound volumes, 965 titles on microform, 3,162 periodical subscriptions.
Undergraduate Courses offered for part-time students during daytime. Complete part-time degree programs offered during daytime. Adult/continuing education programs available. Part-time tuition per semester hour ranges from $34 to $38 for state residents, $93.50 to $103 for nonresidents, according to program.
Graduate Part-time study available in Graduate College. Basic part-time expenses: $47 per credit tuition plus $20 per semester fees for state residents, $112 per credit tuition plus $20 per semester fees for nonresidents. Institutional financial aid available to part-time graduate students in Graduate College.

Wayne State College
Wayne 68787

Public institution; small-town setting. Awards B, M. Barrier-free campus. Total enrollment: 2,405. Undergraduate enrollment: 2,065; 26% part-time, 59% women, 18% over 25. Total faculty: 126. Library holdings: 160,000 bound volumes, 4,200 titles on microform, 967 periodical subscriptions, 350,000 records/tapes.
Undergraduate Courses offered for part-time students during daytime, evenings, weekends, summer. Complete part-time degree programs offered during daytime. Adult/continuing education programs available. Career services available to part-time students: individual and group career counseling, individual job placement, employer recruitment on campus. Part-time tuition: $27.50 per credit hour for state residents, $46 per credit hour for nonresidents.
Graduate Part-time study available in Graduate School. Basic part-time expenses: $27.50 per credit hour tuition plus $3.50 per credit hour fees for state residents, $46 per credit hour tuition plus $3.50 per credit hour fees for nonresidents.

Western Nebraska Technical College
Sidney 69162

Public institution; rural setting. Awards A. Barrier-free campus. Total enrollment: 632 (all undergraduates); 59% part-time, 37% women, 68% over 25. Total faculty: 31.
Undergraduate Courses offered for part-time students during daytime, evenings. Complete part-time degree programs offered during daytime. Career services available to part-time students: individual career counseling, individual job placement, employer recruitment on campus. Part-time tuition: $19.30 per semester hour for state residents, $27 per semester hour for nonresidents.

York College
York 68467

Independent-religious instutition; small-town setting. Awards A. Total enrollment: 491 (all undergraduates); 11% part-time, 51% women, 15% over 25. Total faculty: 34. Library holdings: 26,416 bound volumes, 8,588 titles on microform, 250 periodical subscriptions, 1,166 records/tapes.
Undergraduate Courses offered for part-time students during daytime, evenings. Complete part-time degree programs offered during daytime. Career services available to part-time students: individual career counseling. Part-time tuition and fees per semester (1 to 11 credit hours) range from $40 to $715.

NEVADA

Clark County Community College
North Las Vegas 89030

Public institution; city setting. Awards A. Barrier-free campus. Total enrollment: 10,075 (all undergraduates); 84% part-time, 48% women, 33% over 25. Total faculty: 451. Library holdings: 27,000 bound volumes, 300 periodical subscriptions, 2,500 records/tapes.
Undergraduate Courses offered for part-time students during daytime, evenings, summer. Complete part-time degree programs offered during daytime, evenings, summer. Adult/continuing education programs available. Career services available to part-time students: individual and group career counseling, individual job placement, employer recruitment on campus. Part-time tuition: $20.50 per credit hour for state residents. Nonresident part-time tuition and fees per semester (1 to 11 credit hours) range from $20.50 to $1325.50.

Northern Nevada Community College
Elko 89801

Public institution; rural setting. Awards A. Barrier-free campus. Total enrollment: 1,746 (all undergraduates); 83%

Colleges Offering Part-Time Degree Programs / Nevada

Northern Nevada Community College (continued)
part-time, 55% women, 60% over 25. Total faculty: 125. Library holdings: 550 bound volumes, 110 titles on microform, 300 periodical subscriptions, 4,605 records/tapes.

Undergraduate Courses offered for part-time students during daytime, evenings, weekends, summer. Complete part-time degree programs offered during daytime, evenings, weekends, summer. Adult/continuing education programs available. Career services available to part-time students: individual and group career counseling, individual job placement, employer recruitment on campus. Part-time tuition: $20 per semester hour for state residents, $20 per semester hour (minimum) for nonresidents.

Old College
Reno 89503

Independent institution; city setting. Awards B, D. Barrier-free campus. Total enrollment: 180. Undergraduate enrollment: 85; 58% part-time, 30% women. Total faculty: 45. Library holdings: 10,000 bound volumes, 60 periodical subscriptions.

Undergraduate Courses offered for part-time students during daytime, evenings, weekends, summer. Complete part-time degree programs offered during daytime, evenings. External degree and adult/continuing education programs available. Career services available to part-time students: individual and group career counseling. Part-time tuition: $90 per credit.

Graduate Part-time study available in School of Law. Degree can be earned exclusively through evening/weekend study in School of Law. Basic part-time expenses: $1850 per semester tuition. Institutional financial aid available to part-time graduate students in School of Law.

Reno Business College
Reno 89503

Proprietary institution; city setting. Awards A, B. Barrier-free campus. Total enrollment: 190 (all undergraduates); 30% part-time, 62% women, 75% over 25. Total faculty: 27. Library holdings: 5,100 bound volumes, 20 periodical subscriptions, 350 records/tapes.

Undergraduate Courses offered for part-time students during daytime, evenings, weekends, summer. Complete part-time degree programs offered during daytime, evenings, weekends, summer. Adult/continuing education programs available. Career services available to part-time students: individual career counseling, individual job placement. Part-time tuition: $48 per credit.

Sierra Nevada College
Incline Village 89450

Independent institution; small-town setting. Awards A, B, M. Total enrollment: 220. Undergraduate enrollment: 170; 32% part-time, 46% women, 25% over 25. Total faculty: 39. Library holdings: 16,071 bound volumes, 130 periodical subscriptions, 387 records/tapes.

Undergraduate Courses offered for part-time students during daytime, evenings, summer. Complete part-time degree programs offered during daytime, evenings, summer. External degree and adult/continuing education programs available. Career services available to part-time students: individual career counseling. Part-time tuition: $100 per semester hour.

Truckee Meadows Community College
Reno 89512

Public institution; city setting. Awards A. Barrier-free campus. Total enrollment: 8,387 (all undergraduates); 90% part-time, 59% women, 60% over 25. Total faculty: 373. Library holdings: 19,091 bound volumes, 12,960 titles on microform, 310 periodical subscriptions, 12,960 records/tapes.

Undergraduate Courses offered for part-time students during daytime, evenings, weekends, summer. Complete part-time degree programs offered during daytime, evenings, weekends, summer. Adult/continuing education programs available. Career services available to part-time students: individual and group career counseling, individual job placement, employer recruitment on campus. Part-time tuition: $22 per credit for state residents. Nonresident part-time tuition and fees per semester (1 to 11 credits) range from $22 to $1342.

University of Nevada, Las Vegas
Las Vegas 89154

Public institution; city setting. Awards A, B, M, D. Barrier-free campus. Total enrollment: 9,112. Undergraduate enrollment: 8,361; 33% part-time, 49% women, 61% over 25. Total faculty: 451. Library holdings: 439,071 bound volumes, 500,000 titles on microform, 5,300 periodical subscriptions, 21,000 records/tapes.

Undergraduate Courses offered for part-time students during daytime, evenings, summer. Complete part-time degree programs offered during daytime. Adult/continuing education programs available. Career services available to part-time students: individual and group career counseling, individual job placement, employer recruitment on campus. Part-time tuition: $36 per credit hour for state residents, $36 per credit hour for nonresidents.

Graduate Part-time study available in Graduate College. Degree can be earned exclusively through evening/weekend study in Graduate College. Basic part-time expenses: $41 per credit tuition.

University of Nevada Reno
Reno 89557

Public institution; city setting. Awards A, B, M, D. Total enrollment: 8,937. Undergraduate enrollment: 7,173; 26% part-time, 49% women, 34% over 25. Total faculty: 376. Library holdings: 729,023 bound volumes, 363,768 titles on microform, 147 periodical subscriptions, 62,311 records/tapes.

Undergraduate Courses offered for part-time students during daytime, evenings, summer. Complete part-time degree programs offered during daytime, evenings, summer. Adult/continuing education programs available. Career services available to part-time students: individual and group career counseling, individual job placement, employer recruitment on campus. Part-time tuition: $36 per credit for state residents, $36 per credit for nonresidents.

Western Nevada Community College
Carson City 89701

Public institution; small-town setting. Awards A. Barrier-free campus. Total enrollment: 3,006 (all undergraduates); 80% part-time, 65% women, 60% over 25. Total faculty: 126. Library holdings: 14,900 bound volumes, 58 periodical subscriptions, 942 records/tapes.

Undergraduate Courses offered for part-time students during daytime, evenings. Complete part-time degree programs offered during daytime, evenings. Career services available to part-time students: individual career counseling, individual job place-

New Hampshire / **Colleges Offering Part-Time Degree Programs**

ment. Part-time tuition: $20 per credit for state residents, $20 per credit for nonresidents.

NEW HAMPSHIRE

Castle Junior College
Windham 03087

Independent-religious instutition; rural setting. Awards A. Barrier-free campus. Total enrollment: 143 (all undergraduates); 4% part-time, 100% women, 10% over 25. Total faculty: 14. Library holdings: 4,400 bound volumes, 57 periodical subscriptions, 578 records/tapes.

Undergraduate Courses offered for part-time students during daytime. Complete part-time degree programs offered during daytime. Adult/continuing education programs available. Career services available to part-time students: individual job placement, employer recruitment on campus. Part-time tuition: $210 per course.

Colby-Sawyer College
New London 03257

Independent institution; small-town setting. Awards A, B. Total enrollment: 550 (all undergraduates); 5% part-time, 100% women, 10% over 25. Total faculty: 64. Library holdings: 80,000 bound volumes, 25,000 titles on microform, 425 periodical subscriptions, 1,800 records/tapes.

Undergraduate Courses offered for part-time students during daytime, evenings. Complete part-time degree programs offered during daytime. Adult/continuing education programs available. Career services available to part-time students: individual and group career counseling, individual job placement, employer recruitment on campus. Part-time tuition: $240 per credit.

Daniel Webster College
Nashua 03063

Independent institution; city setting. Awards A, B. Total enrollment: 419 (all undergraduates); 4% part-time, 20% women. Total faculty: 30. Library holdings: 17,500 bound volumes, 160 periodical subscriptions.

Undergraduate Courses offered for part-time students during daytime, evenings. Complete part-time degree programs offered during daytime, evenings. Adult/continuing education programs available. Career services available to part-time students: individual and group career counseling, individual job placement, employer recruitment on campus. Part-time tuition: $235 per credit.

Franklin Pierce College
Rindge 03461

Independent institution; rural setting. Awards B. Total enrollment: 991 (all undergraduates); 2% part-time, 42% women. Total faculty: 145. Library holdings: 60,000 bound volumes, 350 periodical subscriptions.

Undergraduate Courses offered for part-time students during daytime, evenings. Complete part-time degree programs offered during daytime, evenings. External degree and adult/continuing education programs available. Career services available to part-time students: individual career counseling. Part-time tuition: $710 per course.

Hawthorne College
Antrim 03440

Independent institution; rural setting. Awards A, B. Total enrollment: 621 (all undergraduates); 3% part-time, 24% women. Total faculty: 50. Library holdings: 65,000 bound volumes, 426 periodical subscriptions, 700 records/tapes.

Undergraduate Courses offered for part-time students during daytime, evenings, weekends. Complete part-time degree programs offered during daytime, evenings, weekends. External degree and adult/continuing education programs available. Career services available to part-time students: individual career counseling, individual job placement. Part-time tuition: $175 per credit.

Hesser College
Manchester 03101

Proprietary institution; city setting. Awards A. Barrier-free campus. Total enrollment: 1,868 (all undergraduates); 30% part-time, 65% women, 40% over 25. Total faculty: 113. Library holdings: 4,917 bound volumes, 51 periodical subscriptions.

Undergraduate Courses offered for part-time students during daytime, evenings, weekends, summer. Complete part-time degree programs offered during daytime, evenings. Adult/continuing education programs available. Career services available to part-time students: individual and group career counseling. Part-time tuition: $130 per credit.

Keene State College
Keene 03431

Public institution; small-town setting. Awards A, B, M. Barrier-free campus. Total enrollment: 2,967. Undergraduate enrollment: 2,899; 9% part-time, 59% women, 17% over 25. Total faculty: 194. Library holdings: 160,000 bound volumes, 35,400 titles on microform, 1,000 periodical subscriptions, 1,200 records/tapes.

Undergraduate Courses offered for part-time students during daytime, evenings, summer. Complete part-time degree programs offered during daytime, evenings, summer. External degree and adult/continuing education programs available. Career services available to part-time students: individual and group career counseling, individual job placement, employer recruitment on campus. Part-time tuition: $70 per credit for state residents, $180 per credit for nonresidents.

Graduate Part-time study available in Graduate Studies. Degree can be earned exclusively through evening/weekend study in Graduate Studies. Basic part-time expenses: $85 per credit hour tuition for state residents, $185 per credit hour tuition for nonresidents. Institutional financial aid available to part-time graduate students in Graduate Studies.

Merrimack Valley College of the University System of New Hampshire
Manchester 03102

Public institution; city setting. Awards A. Barrier-free campus. Total enrollment: 441 (all undergraduates); 10% part-time, 55% women. Total faculty: 73. Library holdings: 15,000 bound volumes, 200 periodical subscriptions, 900 records/tapes.

Undergraduate Courses offered for part-time students during daytime, evenings, summer. Complete part-time degree programs offered during daytime, evenings, summer. Adult/continuing education programs available. Career services available to part-time students: individual and group career counseling. Part-time tuition: $55 per credit for state residents, $150 per credit for nonresidents.

Colleges Offering Part-Time Degree Programs / New Hampshire

New England College
Henniker 03242

Independent institution; rural setting. Awards B, M. Barrier-free campus. Total enrollment: 1,180. Undergraduate enrollment: 1,140; 0% part-time, 60% women. Total faculty: 109. Library holdings: 80,000 bound volumes, 500 periodical subscriptions.

Undergraduate Courses offered for part-time students during daytime. Complete part-time degree programs offered during daytime. External degree and adult/continuing education programs available. Part-time tuition: $220 per credit.

Graduate Part-time study available in School of Graduate and Continuing Studies. Basic part-time expenses: $240 per course tuition plus $10 per semester fees.

New Hampshire College
Manchester 03104

Independent institution; city setting. Awards A, B, M. Total enrollment: 2,763. Undergraduate enrollment: 1,677; 1% part-time, 48% women. Total faculty: 74. Library holdings: 63,000 bound volumes, 33,000 titles on microform, 900 periodical subscriptions, 1,500 records/tapes.

Undergraduate Courses offered for part-time students during daytime, evenings, weekends, summer. Complete part-time degree programs offered during daytime, evenings, weekends, summer. External degree and adult/continuing education programs available. Part-time tuition: $210 per credit hour.

Graduate Part-time study available in Graduate School of Business. Basic part-time expenses: $440 per course tuition.

New Hampshire Technical Institute
Concord 03301

Public institution; small-town setting. Awards A. Barrier-free campus. Total enrollment: 925 (all undergraduates); 7% part-time, 52% women, 35% over 25. Total faculty: 81. Library holdings: 24,000 bound volumes, 32 periodical subscriptions, 75 records/tapes.

Undergraduate Courses offered for part-time students during evenings. Complete part-time degree programs offered during evenings. Adult/continuing education programs available. Career services available to part-time students: individual career counseling, individual job placement, employer recruitment on campus. Part-time tuition: $55 per semester hour for state residents, $55 per semester hour for nonresidents.

New Hampshire Vocational-Technical College
Berlin 03570

Public institution; rural setting. Awards A. Barrier-free campus. Total enrollment: 351 (all undergraduates); 10% part-time, 40% women, 18% over 25. Total faculty: 33. Library holdings: 5,500 bound volumes, 50 periodical subscriptions.

Undergraduate Courses offered for part-time students during daytime, evenings, summer. Complete part-time degree programs offered during daytime, evenings, summer. Adult/continuing education programs available. Career services available to part-time students: individual career counseling. Part-time tuition: $52.25 per credit for state residents, $152 per credit for nonresidents. Part-time tuition for nonresidents who are eligible for the New England Regional Student Program: $70 per credit.

New Hampshire Vocational-Technical College
Laconia 03246

Public institution; small-town setting. Awards A. Barrier-free campus. Total enrollment: 243 (all undergraduates); 10% part-time, 35% women, 11% over 25. Total faculty: 22. Library holdings: 7,943 bound volumes, 17 titles on microform, 72 periodical subscriptions, 248 records/tapes.

Undergraduate Courses offered for part-time students during daytime, evenings. Complete part-time degree programs offered during daytime, evenings. Adult/continuing education programs available. Career services available to part-time students: individual and group career counseling, individual job placement, employer recruitment on campus. Part-time tuition: $52.25 per credit for state residents, $152 per credit for nonresidents. Part-time tuition for nonresidents who are eligible for the New England Regional Student Program: $70 per credit.

New Hampshire Vocational-Technical College
Manchester 03102

Public institution; city setting. Awards A. Barrier-free campus. Total enrollment: 425 (all undergraduates); 3% part-time, 20% women. Total faculty: 31. Library holdings: 10,000 bound volumes, 200 records/tapes.

Undergraduate Courses offered for part-time students during daytime, evenings, summer. Complete part-time degree programs offered during daytime, evenings. External degree and adult/continuing education programs available. Part-time tuition: $52.25 per credit for state residents, $152 per credit for nonresidents. Part-time tuition for nonresidents who are eligible for the New England Regional Student Program: $70 per credit.

New Hampshire Vocational-Technical College
Nashua 03063

Public institution; city setting. Awards A. Barrier-free campus. Total enrollment: 324 (all undergraduates); 5% part-time, 33% women, 10% over 25. Total faculty: 75.

Undergraduate Courses offered for part-time students during daytime, evenings, summer. Complete part-time degree programs offered during daytime, evenings, summer. Adult/continuing education programs available. Career services available to part-time students: individual and group career counseling, individual job placement, employer recruitment on campus. Part-time tuition: $56.25 per credit for state residents, $152 per credit for nonresidents. Part-time tuition for nonresidents who are eligible for the New England Regional Student Program: $70 per credit.

New Hampshire Vocational-Technical College
Stratham 03885

Public institution; small-town setting. Awards A. Barrier-free campus. Total enrollment: 268 (all undergraduates); 5% part-time, 25% women, 22% over 25. Total faculty: 23. Library holdings: 8,900 bound volumes, 7,850 titles on microform, 90 periodical subscriptions.

Undergraduate Courses offered for part-time students during daytime, evenings, summer. Complete part-time degree programs offered during evenings, summer. Adult/continuing education programs available. Career services available to part-time students: individual career counseling, individual job placement. Part-time tuition: $56.25 per credit for state residents, $152 per credit for nonresidents. Part-time tuition for nonresidents who are eligible for the New England Regional Student Program: $70 per credit.

Notre Dame College
Manchester 03104

Independent-religious instutition; city setting. Awards A, B, M. Total enrollment: 741. Undergraduate enrollment: 576; 30% part-time, 87% women. Total faculty: 70. Library holdings: 44,000 bound volumes, 3,052 titles on microform, 278 periodical subscriptions, 2,900 records/tapes.

Undergraduate Courses offered for part-time students during daytime, evenings, summer. Complete part-time degree programs offered during daytime, evenings, summer. Adult/continuing education programs available. Career services available to part-time students: individual and group career counseling, individual job placement. Part-time tuition: $225 per course.

Graduate Part-time study available in Graduate Division. Basic part-time expenses: $95 per credit tuition plus $15 per semester fees. Institutional financial aid available to part-time graduate students in Graduate Division.

Plymouth State College of the University System of New Hampshire
Plymouth 03264

Public institution; small-town setting. Awards A, B, M. Total enrollment: 3,400. Undergraduate enrollment: 3,000; 10% part-time, 50% women. Total faculty: 189. Library holdings: 280,000 bound volumes, 380,000 titles on microform, 1,090 periodical subscriptions, 9,000 records/tapes.

Undergraduate Courses offered for part-time students during daytime, evenings, summer. Complete part-time degree programs offered during daytime, evenings, summer. External degree and adult/continuing education programs available. Career services available to part-time students: individual career counseling, individual job placement, employer recruitment on campus. Part-time tuition: $70 per credit hour for state residents, $165 per credit hour for nonresidents.

Graduate Part-time study available in Graduate Studies. Degree can be earned exclusively through evening/weekend study in Graduate Studies. Basic part-time expenses: $80 per credit tuition plus $10 per semester fees for state residents, $165 per credit tuition plus $15 per semester fees for nonresidents.

Rivier College
Nashua 03060

Independent-religious instutition; city setting. Awards A, B, M. Total enrollment: 2,285. Undergraduate enrollment: 1,504; 52% part-time, 88% women. Total faculty: 170. Library holdings: 104,000 bound volumes, 700 periodical subscriptions, 3,350 records/tapes.

Undergraduate Courses offered for part-time students during daytime, evenings, summer. Complete part-time degree programs offered during daytime, evenings, summer. Adult/continuing education programs available. Career services available to part-time students: individual and group career counseling, individual job placement, employer recruitment on campus. Part-time tuition: $140 per credit.

Graduate Part-time study available in Graduate School. Basic part-time expenses: $130 per credit tuition plus $10 per semester fees. Institutional financial aid available to part-time graduate students in Graduate School.

School for Lifelong Learning of the University System of New Hampshire
Durham 03824

Public institution. Awards A, B. Total enrollment: 1,250 (all undergraduates); 99% part-time, 50% women, 99% over 25. Total faculty: 301.

Undergraduate Courses offered for part-time students during daytime, evenings, weekends, summer. Complete part-time degree programs offered during daytime, evenings, weekends, summer. External degree and adult/continuing education programs available. Career services available to part-time students: individual and group career counseling. Part-time tuition: $55 per semester hour.

University of New Hampshire
Durham 03824

Public institution; small-town setting. Awards A, B, M, D. Total enrollment: 10,300. Undergraduate enrollment: 9,600; 9% part-time, 54% women. Total faculty: 639. Library holdings: 830,000 bound volumes, 24,000 titles on microform, 8,301 periodical subscriptions, 6,923 records/tapes.

Undergraduate Courses offered for part-time students during daytime, evenings, summer. Complete part-time degree programs offered during daytime, evenings. External degree and adult/continuing education programs available. Career services available to part-time students: individual and group career counseling, individual job placement, employer recruitment on campus. Part-time tuition: $55 per credit for state residents, $65 per credit for nonresidents.

Graduate Part-time study available in Graduate School. Basic part-time expenses: $85 per credit hour tuition for state residents, $235 per credit hour tuition for nonresidents. Institutional financial aid available to part-time graduate students in Graduate School.

White Pines College
Chester 03036

Independent institution; small-town setting. Awards A. Total enrollment: 72 (all undergraduates); 22% part-time, 65% women. Total faculty: 13. Library holdings: 24,000 bound volumes, 127 periodical subscriptions, 600 records/tapes.

Undergraduate Courses offered for part-time students during daytime, evenings. Complete part-time degree programs offered during daytime, evenings. Adult/continuing education programs available. Career services available to part-time students: individual and group career counseling. Part-time tuition: $130 per credit.

NEW JERSEY

Atlantic Community College
Mays Landing 08330

Public institution; small-town setting. Awards A. Barrier-free campus. Total enrollment: 4,100 (all undergraduates); 60% part-time, 55% women, 40% over 25. Total faculty: 190. Library holdings: 85,000 bound volumes, 300 periodical subscriptions.

Undergraduate Courses offered for part-time students during daytime, evenings, weekends, summer. Complete part-time de-

Colleges Offering Part-Time Degree Programs / New Jersey

Atlantic Community College (continued)
gree programs offered during daytime, evenings, weekends, summer. Adult/continuing education programs available. Career services available to part-time students: individual and group career counseling, individual job placement, employer recruitment on campus. Part-time tuition: $34.25 per credit for area residents, $99.25 per credit for state residents, $133.50 per credit for nonresidents.

Bergen Community College
Paramus 07652

Public institution; small-town setting. Awards A. Barrier-free campus. Total enrollment: 12,000 (all undergraduates); 62% part-time, 59% women, 41% over 25. Total faculty: 517. Library holdings: 77,000 bound volumes, 500 periodical subscriptions, 5,000 records/tapes.

Undergraduate Courses offered for part-time students during daytime, evenings, weekends, summer. Complete part-time degree programs offered during daytime, evenings, weekends, summer. Adult/continuing education programs available. Career services available to part-time students: individual and group career counseling, individual job placement, employer recruitment on campus. Part-time tuition: $33.35 per credit for area residents, $62.35 per credit for state residents, $91.35 per credit for nonresidents.

Berkeley School
Little Falls 07424

Proprietary institution; small-town setting. Awards A. Total enrollment: 819 (all undergraduates); 24% part-time, 99% women, 5% over 25. Total faculty: 33. Library holdings: 26,000 bound volumes, 126 periodical subscriptions, 1,080 records/tapes.

Undergraduate Courses offered for part-time students during daytime, evenings. Complete part-time degree programs offered during daytime, evenings. Adult/continuing education programs available. Career services available to part-time students: individual and group career counseling, individual job placement. Part-time tuition: $68 per credit.

Bloomfield College
Bloomfield 07003

Independent-religious instutition; small-town setting. Awards B. Total enrollment: 1,730 (all undergraduates); 47% part-time, 63% women, 54% over 25. Total faculty: 134. Library holdings: 97,366 bound volumes, 3,000 titles on microform, 393 periodical subscriptions, 2,897 records/tapes.

Undergraduate Courses offered for part-time students during daytime, evenings, weekends, summer. Complete part-time degree programs offered during daytime, evenings. Adult/continuing education programs available. Career services available to part-time students: individual and group career counseling, individual job placement, employer recruitment on campus. Part-time tuition: $490 per course.

Brookdale Community College
Lincroft 07738

Public institution; small-town setting. Awards A. Barrier-free campus. Total enrollment: 12,021 (all undergraduates); 72% part-time, 60% women. Total faculty: 438. Library holdings: 64,780 bound volumes, 734 periodical subscriptions, 43,739 records/tapes.

Undergraduate Courses offered for part-time students during daytime, evenings, weekends, summer. Complete part-time degree programs offered during daytime, evenings, weekends, summer. Adult/continuing education programs available. Career services available to part-time students: individual and group career counseling, individual job placement, employer recruitment on campus. Part-time tuition: $33.35 per credit for area residents, $62.35 per credit for state residents, $91.35 per credit for nonresidents.

Burlington County College
Pemberton 08068

Public institution; small-town setting. Awards A. Barrier-free campus. Total enrollment: 6,704 (all undergraduates); 72% part-time, 57% women, 51% over 25. Total faculty: 245. Library holdings: 80,000 bound volumes, 553 periodical subscriptions, 3,800 records/tapes.

Undergraduate Courses offered for part-time students during daytime, evenings, weekends, summer. Complete part-time degree programs offered during daytime, evenings, weekends, summer. Adult/continuing education programs available. Career services available to part-time students: individual and group career counseling, individual job placement, employer recruitment on campus. Part-time tuition: $33.50 per credit hour for area residents, $104.50 per credit hour for nonresidents.

Caldwell College
Caldwell 07006

Independent-religious instutition; small-town setting. Awards B. Total enrollment: 718 (all undergraduates); 50% part-time, 100% women. Total faculty: 71. Library holdings: 104,500 bound volumes, 1,457 titles on microform, 425 periodical subscriptions, 7,000 records/tapes.

Undergraduate Courses offered for part-time students during daytime, evenings, summer. Complete part-time degree programs offered during daytime, evenings, summer. External degree and adult/continuing education programs available. Career services available to part-time students: individual and group career counseling, individual job placement, employer recruitment on campus. Part-time tuition: $140 per credit.

Camden College of Arts and Sciences
Camden 08102

See Rutgers University, Camden College of Arts and Sciences

Camden County College
Blackwood 08012

Public institution; small-town setting. Awards A. Total enrollment: 8,815 (all undergraduates); 65% part-time, 61% women, 47% over 25. Total faculty: 375. Library holdings: 69,981 bound volumes, 668 periodical subscriptions, 3,359 records/tapes.

Undergraduate Courses offered for part-time students during daytime, evenings. Complete part-time degree programs offered during daytime, evenings. External degree and adult/continuing education programs available. Career services available to part-time students: individual and group career counseling, individual job placement. Part-time tuition: $21 per credit for area residents, $23 per credit for nonresidents.

New Jersey / **Colleges Offering Part-Time Degree Programs**

Centenary College
Hackettstown 07840

Independent institution; small-town setting. Awards A, B. Total enrollment: 694 (all undergraduates); 5% part-time, 100% women, 3% over 25. Total faculty: 67. Library holdings: 48,000 bound volumes, 12,400 titles on microform, 375 periodical subscriptions, 2,600 records/tapes.

Undergraduate Courses offered for part-time students during daytime, evenings, weekends, summer. Complete part-time degree programs offered during daytime, evenings. External degree and adult/continuing education programs available. Career services available to part-time students: individual and group career counseling, employer recruitment on campus. Part-time tuition: $98 per credit.

College of Saint Elizabeth
Convent Station 07961

Independent-religious instutition; small-town setting. Awards B. Total enrollment: 671 (all undergraduates); 25% part-time, 98% women, 29% over 25. Total faculty: 93. Library holdings: 151,000 bound volumes, 1,200 periodical subscriptions, 4,000 records/tapes.

Undergraduate Courses offered for part-time students during daytime, evenings, weekends, summer. Complete part-time degree programs offered during daytime, weekends. Adult/continuing education programs available. Career services available to part-time students: individual and group career counseling, individual job placement, employer recruitment on campus. Part-time tuition: $156 per semester hour.

County College of Morris
Randolph 07869

Public institution; rural setting. Awards A. Barrier-free campus. Total enrollment: 11,287 (all undergraduates); 61% part-time, 54% women, 43% over 25. Total faculty: 509. Library holdings: 86,491 bound volumes, 9,127 titles on microform, 709 periodical subscriptions, 6,866 records/tapes.

Undergraduate Courses offered for part-time students during daytime, evenings, weekends, summer. Complete part-time degree programs offered during daytime, evenings, weekends, summer. Adult/continuing education programs available. Career services available to part-time students: individual and group career counseling, individual job placement, employer recruitment on campus. Part-time tuition: $29 per credit for state residents, $86 per credit for nonresidents.

Cumberland County College
Vineland 08360

Public institution; small-town setting. Awards A. Barrier-free campus. Total enrollment: 2,377 (all undergraduates); 60% part-time, 67% women, 48% over 25. Total faculty: 94. Library holdings: 51,000 bound volumes, 213 periodical subscriptions, 2,804 records/tapes.

Undergraduate Courses offered for part-time students during daytime, evenings, weekends, summer. Complete part-time degree programs offered during daytime, evenings. Adult/continuing education programs available. Career services available to part-time students: individual and group career counseling, individual job placement, employer recruitment on campus. Part-time tuition: $29 per credit for area residents, $58 per credit for state residents, $116 per credit for nonresidents.

Douglass College
New Brunswick 08903

See Rutgers University, Douglass College

Drew University
Madison 07940

Independent institution; small-town setting. Awards B, M, D. Total enrollment: 2,397. Undergraduate enrollment: 1,486; 7% part-time, 59% women. Total faculty: 187. Library holdings: 450,000 bound volumes, 55,000 titles on microform, 1,500 periodical subscriptions, 2,000 records/tapes.

Undergraduate Courses offered for part-time students during daytime, summer. Complete part-time degree programs offered during daytime, summer. Adult/continuing education programs available. Career services available to part-time students: individual and group career counseling, employer recruitment on campus. Part-time tuition: $291 per credit.

Graduate Part-time study available in Graduate School, Theological School. Degree can be earned exclusively through evening/weekend study in Graduate School. Basic part-time expenses: $1366 per course tuition plus $2.50 per semester (minimum) fees. Institutional financial aid available to part-time graduate students in Graduate School, Theological School.

Essex County College
Newark 07102

Public institution; city setting. Awards A. Barrier-free campus. Total enrollment: 6,749 (all undergraduates); 37% part-time, 60% women, 44% over 25. Total faculty: 352. Library holdings: 56,894 bound volumes, 288,845 titles on microform, 627 periodical subscriptions, 11,504 records/tapes.

Undergraduate Courses offered for part-time students during daytime, evenings, weekends, summer. Complete part-time degree programs offered during daytime, evenings. Adult/continuing education programs available. Career services available to part-time students: individual and group career counseling, individual job placement, employer recruitment on campus. Part-time tuition: $29 per credit hour for area residents, $58 per credit hour for state residents, $87 per credit hour for nonresidents.

Fairleigh Dickinson University, Edward Williams College
Hackensack 07601

Independent institution; city setting. Awards A. Total enrollment: 1,159 (all undergraduates); 32% part-time, 44% women, 26% over 25. Total faculty: 54.

Undergraduate Courses offered for part-time students during daytime, weekends. Complete part-time degree programs offered during daytime, weekends. Career services available to part-time students: individual and group career counseling, individual job placement. Part-time tuition: $170 per semester hour.

Fairleigh Dickinson University, Florham-Madison Campus
Madison 07940

Independent institution; small-town setting. Awards A, B, M. Total enrollment: 4,603. Undergraduate enrollment: 2,798; 38%

Colleges Offering Part-Time Degree Programs / New Jersey

Fairleigh Dickinson University, Florham-Madison Campus (continued)

part-time, 39% women, 16% over 25. Total faculty: 239. Library holdings: 146,000 bound volumes, 1,700 periodical subscriptions.

Undergraduate Courses offered for part-time students during daytime, evenings, summer. Complete part-time degree programs offered during daytime, evenings, summer. Adult/continuing education programs available. Career services available to part-time students: individual career counseling, individual job placement, employer recruitment on campus. Part-time tuition: $170 per credit hour.

Graduate Part-time study available in Leonard Dreyfuss College, Maxwell Becton College of Arts and Sciences, Samuel J. Silberman College of Business Administration. Basic part-time expenses: $202 per credit tuition. Institutional financial aid available to part-time graduate students in Maxwell Becton College of Arts and Sciences, Samuel J. Silberman College of Business Administration.

Fairleigh Dickinson University, Rutherford Campus
Rutherford 07070

Independent institution; small-town setting. Awards B, M. Total enrollment: 3,576. Undergraduate enrollment: 1,929; 38% part-time, 57% women, 26% over 25. Total faculty: 246. Library holdings: 161,000 bound volumes, 2,100 periodical subscriptions.

Undergraduate Courses offered for part-time students during daytime, evenings, summer. Complete part-time degree programs offered during daytime, evenings, summer. Adult/continuing education programs available. Career services available to part-time students: individual career counseling, individual job placement, employer recruitment on campus. Part-time tuition: $170 per credit hour.

Graduate Part-time study available in Maxwell Becton College of Arts and Sciences, Samuel J. Silberman College of Business Administration. Basic part-time expenses: $202 per credit tuition. Institutional financial aid available to part-time graduate students in Maxwell Becton College of Arts and Sciences, Samuel J. Silberman College of Business Administration.

Fairleigh Dickinson University, Teaneck-Hackensack Campus
Teaneck 07666

Independent institution; city setting. Awards A, B, M, D. Total enrollment: 7,347. Undergraduate enrollment: 4,660; 41% part-time, 41% women, 28% over 25. Total faculty: 688. Library holdings: 243,000 bound volumes, 3,500 periodical subscriptions.

Undergraduate Courses offered for part-time students during daytime, evenings, summer. Complete part-time degree programs offered during daytime, evenings, summer. Adult/continuing education programs available. Career services available to part-time students: individual career counseling, individual job placement, employer recruitment on campus. Part-time tuition: $170 per credit hour.

Graduate Part-time study available in College of Science and Engineering, Maxwell Becton College of Liberal Arts, Peter Sammartino College of Education, Samuel J. Silberman College of Business Administration, School of Dentistry. Basic part-time expenses: $202 per credit tuition. Institutional financial aid available to part-time graduate students in School of Dentistry.

Felician College
Lodi 07644

Independent-religious instutition; small-town setting. Awards A, B. Barrier-free campus. Total enrollment: 678 (all undergraduates); 63% part-time, 96% women, 50% over 25. Total faculty: 78. Library holdings: 86,050 bound volumes, 4,000 titles on microform, 524 periodical subscriptions, 1,548 records/tapes.

Undergraduate Courses offered for part-time students during daytime, evenings, summer. Complete part-time degree programs offered during daytime, evenings. Adult/continuing education programs available. Career services available to part-time students: individual and group career counseling. Part-time tuition: $105 per semester hour.

Georgian Court College
Lakewood 08701

Independent-religious instutition; small-town setting. Awards B, M. Total enrollment: 1,498. Undergraduate enrollment: 1,137; 38% part-time, 99% women, 42% over 25. Total faculty: 124. Library holdings: 78,450 bound volumes, 702 periodical subscriptions, 5,800 records/tapes.

Undergraduate Courses offered for part-time students during daytime, evenings, summer. Complete part-time degree programs offered during daytime, evenings, summer. Career services available to part-time students: individual and group career counseling, individual job placement, employer recruitment on campus. Part-time tuition: $105 per credit.

Graduate Part-time study available in Graduate School of Education. Basic part-time expenses: $110 per credit tuition plus $10 per semester fees.

Glassboro State College
Glassboro 08028

Public institution; small-town setting. Awards B, M. Barrier-free campus. Total enrollment: 9,500. Undergraduate enrollment: 9,200; 23% part-time, 57% women. Total faculty: 534. Library holdings: 380,000 bound volumes, 2,000 periodical subscriptions.

Undergraduate Courses offered for part-time students during daytime, evenings, summer. Complete part-time degree programs offered during daytime, evenings, summer. Adult/continuing education programs available. Career services available to part-time students: individual and group career counseling, individual job placement, employer recruitment on campus. Part-time tuition: $42.80 per credit for state residents, $62 per credit for nonresidents.

Graduate Part-time study available in Graduate Studies. Basic part-time expenses: $64 per credit tuition plus $7.10 per credit fees for state residents, $84 per credit tuition plus $7.10 per credit fees for nonresidents. Institutional financial aid available to part-time graduate students in Graduate Studies.

Gloucester County College
Sewell 08080

Public institution; rural setting. Awards A. Total enrollment: 3,847 (all undergraduates); 63% part-time, 51% women, 45% over 25. Total faculty: 143. Library holdings: 55,000 bound volumes, 406 titles on microform, 557 periodical subscriptions, 2,986 records/tapes.

Undergraduate Courses offered for part-time students during daytime, evenings, weekends, summer. Complete part-time degree programs offered during daytime, evenings, weekends. Adult/continuing education programs available. Career services available to part-time students: individual and group

New Jersey / Colleges Offering Part-Time Degree Programs

career counseling, individual job placement. Part-time tuition: $22 per credit hour for area residents, $23 per credit hour for state residents, $104 per credit hour for nonresidents.

Hudson County Community College
Jersey City 07306

Public institution; city setting. Awards A. Total enrollment: 3,451 (all undergraduates); 39% part-time, 58% women, 55% over 25. Total faculty: 187.

Undergraduate Courses offered for part-time students during daytime, evenings, summer. Complete part-time degree programs offered during daytime, evenings. Career services available to part-time students: individual and group career counseling, individual job placement. Part-time tuition: $21 per credit for state residents, $42 per credit for nonresidents.

Jersey City State College
Jersey City 07305

Public institution; city setting. Awards B, M. Barrier-free campus. Total enrollment: 7,464. Undergraduate enrollment: 6,796; 46% part-time, 53% women. Total faculty: 469. Library holdings: 315,000 bound volumes, 1,577 periodical subscriptions.

Undergraduate Courses offered for part-time students during daytime, evenings, weekends, summer. Complete part-time degree programs offered during daytime, evenings, summer. Adult/continuing education programs available. Career services available to part-time students: individual and group career counseling, individual job placement, employer recruitment on campus. Part-time tuition: $41.50 per credit for state residents, $61.50 per credit for nonresidents.

Graduate Part-time study available in Graduate Studies. Degree can be earned exclusively through evening/weekend study in Graduate Studies. Basic part-time expenses: $68 per credit tuition plus $8.50 per credit fees for state residents, $88 per credit tuition plus $8.50 per credit fees for nonresidents.

Kean College of New Jersey
Union 07083

Public institution; city setting. Awards B, M. Barrier-free campus. Total enrollment: 10,561. Undergraduate enrollment: 9,326; 47% part-time, 60% women, 35% over 25. Total faculty: 587. Library holdings: 265,340 bound volumes, 92,467 titles on microform, 1,150 periodical subscriptions, 4,570 records/tapes.

Undergraduate Courses offered for part-time students during daytime, evenings, weekends, summer. Complete part-time degree programs offered during daytime, evenings, weekends, summer. External degree and adult/continuing education programs available. Career services available to part-time students: individual and group career counseling, individual job placement, employer recruitment on campus. Part-time tuition: $39.25 per semester hour for state residents, $59.25 per semester hour for nonresidents.

Graduate Part-time study available in School of Education, School of Humanities, Social Sciences, and Administrative Sciences. Basic part-time expenses: $64 per credit tuition plus $7 per credit fees for state residents, $84 per credit tuition plus $7 per credit fees for nonresidents.

Mercer County Community College
Trenton 08690

Public institution; small-town setting. Awards A. Barrier-free campus. Total enrollment: 6,531 (all undergraduates); 68% part-time, 56% women, 47% over 25. Total faculty: 322. Library holdings: 6,699 bound volumes, 11,616 titles on microform, 923 periodical subscriptions, 3,195 records/tapes.

Undergraduate Courses offered for part-time students during daytime, evenings, weekends, summer. Complete part-time degree programs offered during daytime, evenings, weekends, summer. External degree and adult/continuing education programs available. Career services available to part-time students: individual and group career counseling, individual job placement, employer recruitment on campus. Part-time tuition: $25 per credit for area residents, $47 per credit for state residents, $68 per credit for nonresidents.

Middlesex County College
Edison 08818

Public institution; city setting. Awards A. Barrier-free campus. Total enrollment: 12,020 (all undergraduates); 60% part-time, 60% women, 57% over 25. Total faculty: 620. Library holdings: 75,000 bound volumes.

Undergraduate Courses offered for part-time students during daytime, evenings, weekends, summer. Complete part-time degree programs offered during daytime, evenings, weekends, summer. Adult/continuing education programs available. Career services available to part-time students: individual and group career counseling, individual job placement, employer recruitment on campus. Part-time tuition: $31 per credit for area residents, $62 per credit for state residents, $124 per credit for nonresidents.

Monmouth College
West Long Branch 07764

Independent institution; small-town setting. Awards A, B, M. Barrier-free campus. Total enrollment: 4,135. Undergraduate enrollment: 3,100; 42% part-time, 52% women, 34% over 25. Total faculty: 279. Library holdings: 215,000 bound volumes, 1,800 periodical subscriptions.

Undergraduate Courses offered for part-time students during daytime, evenings, weekends, summer. Complete part-time degree programs offered during daytime, evenings, weekends, summer. Adult/continuing education programs available. Career services available to part-time students: individual and group career counseling, individual job placement, employer recruitment on campus. Part-time tuition: $170 per credit.

Graduate Part-time study available in Graduate Programs. Degree can be earned exclusively through evening/weekend study in Graduate Programs. Basic part-time expenses: $180 per credit tuition plus $55 per semester fees. Institutional financial aid available to part-time graduate students in Graduate Programs.

Montclair State College
Upper Montclair 07043

Public institution; small-town setting. Awards B, M. Total enrollment: 14,949. Undergraduate enrollment: 11,643; 34% part-time, 63% women, 24% over 25. Total faculty: 720. Library holdings: 363,120 bound volumes, 736,960 titles on microform, 2,174 periodical subscriptions, 38,050 records/tapes.

Undergraduate Courses offered for part-time students during evenings, weekends, summer. Complete part-time degree programs offered during evenings, weekends, summer. Adult/continuing education programs available. Career services available to part-time students: individual and group career counseling. Part-time tuition: $34 per semester hour for state residents, $54 per semester hour for nonresidents.

Graduate Part-time study available in Division of Graduate Studies. Basic part-time expenses: $64 per credit tuition plus

Colleges Offering Part-Time Degree Programs / New Jersey

Montclair State College (continued)
$7.75 per credit fees for state residents, $84 per credit tuition plus $7.75 per credit fees for nonresidents. Institutional financial aid available to part-time graduate students in Division of Graduate Studies.

Newark College of Arts and Sciences
Newark 07102
See Rutgers University, Newark College of Arts and Sciences

New Brunswick Theological Seminary
New Brunswick 08901
Independent-religious institution (graduate only). Total enrollment: 90 (coed; 56% part-time). Total faculty: 24.
Graduate Part-time study available in Graduate and Professional Programs. Degree can be earned exclusively through evening/weekend study in Graduate and Professional Programs. Basic part-time expenses: $100 per credit (minimum) tuition plus $50 per year fees.

New Jersey Institute of Technology
Newark 07102
Public institution; city setting. Awards B, M, D. Barrier-free campus. Total enrollment: 7,285. Undergraduate enrollment: 5,663; 38% part-time, 12% women, 24% over 25. Total faculty: 433. Library holdings: 130,000 bound volumes, 4,600 titles on microform, 1,400 periodical subscriptions, 650 records/tapes.
Undergraduate Courses offered for part-time students during daytime, evenings, summer. Complete part-time degree programs offered during daytime, evenings, summer. Adult/continuing education programs available. Career services available to part-time students: individual career counseling, individual job placement, employer recruitment on campus. Part-time tuition: $74.83 per credit for state residents, $149.67 per credit for nonresidents.
Graduate Part-time study available in Graduate Division. Degree can be earned exclusively through evening/weekend study in Graduate Division. Basic part-time expenses: $108 per credit tuition plus $78 per course fees for state residents, $158 per credit tuition plus $78 per course fees for nonresidents.

Northeastern Bible College
Essex Fells 07021
Independent-religious instutition; small-town setting. Awards A, B. Total enrollment: 265 (all undergraduates); 35% part-time, 40% women. Total faculty: 24. Library holdings: 41,000 bound volumes, 325 periodical subscriptions, 1,843 records/tapes.
Undergraduate Courses offered for part-time students during daytime, evenings, summer. Complete part-time degree programs offered during daytime, evenings, summer. Adult/continuing education programs available. Career services available to part-time students: individual and group career counseling, individual job placement, employer recruitment on campus. Part-time tuition: $135 per credit hour.

Ocean County College
Toms River 08753
Public institution; small-town setting. Awards A. Barrier-free campus. Total enrollment: 4,415 (all undergraduates); 31% part-time, 55% women, 7% over 25. Total faculty: 225. Library holdings: 73,000 bound volumes, 215 titles on microform, 430 periodical subscriptions, 4,850 records/tapes.
Undergraduate Courses offered for part-time students during daytime, evenings, weekends, summer. Complete part-time degree programs offered during daytime, evenings, weekends, summer. Adult/continuing education programs available. Career services available to part-time students: individual and group career counseling, individual job placement, employer recruitment on campus. Part-time tuition: $31 per semester hour for area residents, $36 per semester hour for state residents, $124 per semester hour for nonresidents.

Passaic County Community College
Paterson 07509
Public institution; city setting. Awards A. Barrier-free campus. Total enrollment: 2,745 (all undergraduates); 49% part-time, 62% women, 54% over 25. Total faculty: 169. Library holdings: 28,581 bound volumes, 5 titles on microform, 257 periodical subscriptions, 646 records/tapes.
Undergraduate Courses offered for part-time students during daytime, evenings, weekends, summer. Complete part-time degree programs offered during daytime, evenings. Career services available to part-time students: individual career counseling, individual job placement, employer recruitment on campus. Part-time tuition: $29 per credit for state residents, $56 per credit for nonresidents.

Princeton Theological Seminary
Princeton 08542
Independent-religious institution (graduate only). Total enrollment: 873 (coed; 27% part-time). Total faculty: 42.
Graduate Part-time study available in Graduate and Professional Programs. Basic part-time expenses: $440 per course tuition plus $27.50 per semester fees. Institutional financial aid available to part-time graduate students in Graduate and Professional Programs.

Ramapo College of New Jersey
Mahwah 07430
Public institution; small-town setting. Awards B. Barrier-free campus. Total enrollment: 4,303 (all undergraduates); 40% part-time, 51% women, 25% over 25. Total faculty: 210. Library holdings: 150,000 bound volumes, 1,700 periodical subscriptions, 800 records/tapes.
Undergraduate Courses offered for part-time students during daytime, evenings, weekends, summer. Complete part-time degree programs offered during daytime, evenings, weekends. Adult/continuing education programs available. Career services available to part-time students: individual and group career counseling, individual job placement, employer recruitment on campus. Part-time tuition: $44.20 per credit for state residents, $64.20 per credit for nonresidents.

Rider College
Lawrenceville 08648
Independent institution; small-town setting. Awards A, B, M. Barrier-free campus. Total enrollment: 5,349. Undergraduate enrollment: 4,438; 26% part-time, 52% women, 11% over 25. Total faculty: 285. Library holdings: 313,400 bound volumes, 24,800 titles on microform, 1,787 periodical subscriptions.
Undergraduate Courses offered for part-time students during daytime, evenings, summer. Complete part-time degree programs offered during daytime, evenings, summer. Adult/con-

tinuing education programs available. Career services available to part-time students: individual and group career counseling, individual job placement, employer recruitment on campus. Part-time tuition per semester hour ranges from $104 for evening courses to $165 for daytime courses.

Graduate Part-time study available in School of Business Administration, School of Education, School of Liberal Arts and Science. Degree can be earned exclusively through evening/weekend study in School of Business Administration, School of Education, School of Liberal Arts and Science. Basic part-time expenses: $150 per credit tuition. Institutional financial aid available to part-time graduate students in School of Education.

Rutgers University, Camden College of Arts and Sciences
Camden 08102

Public institution; city setting. Awards B. Total enrollment: 2,672 (all undergraduates); 18% part-time, 49% women, 22% over 25. Total faculty: 161. Library holdings: 429,027 bound volumes, 180,529 titles on microform, 3,184 periodical subscriptions, 1,509 records/tapes.

Undergraduate Courses offered for part-time students during daytime, evenings, weekends, summer. Complete part-time degree programs offered during daytime, weekends, summer. Career services available to part-time students: individual and group career counseling, employer recruitment on campus. Part-time tuition: $51 per credit for state residents, $102 per credit for nonresidents.

Rutgers University, College of Nursing
Newark 07102

Public institution; city setting. Awards B. Total enrollment: 495 (all undergraduates); 18% part-time, 93% women, 34% over 25. Total faculty: 52. Library holdings: 777,396 bound volumes, 278,227 titles on microform, 6,133 periodical subscriptions, 5,461 records/tapes.

Undergraduate Courses offered for part-time students during daytime, evenings. Complete part-time degree programs offered during daytime. Career services available to part-time students: individual and group career counseling, employer recruitment on campus. Part-time tuition: $51 per credit for state residents, $102 per credit for nonresidents.

Rutgers University, Douglass College
New Brunswick 08903

Public institution; small-town setting. Awards B. Total enrollment: 3,428 (all undergraduates); 6% part-time, 100% women, 5% over 25. Library holdings: 3.6 million bound volumes, 221,787 titles on microform, 13,492 periodical subscriptions, 35,476 records/tapes.

Undergraduate Courses offered for part-time students during daytime, evenings. Complete part-time degree programs offered during daytime. Career services available to part-time students: individual and group career counseling, employer recruitment on campus. Part-time tuition: $51 per credit for state residents, $102 per credit for nonresidents.

Rutgers University, Newark
Newark 07102

Public institution (undergraduate and graduate). Total enrollment: 9,929. Graduate enrollment: 3,443 (coed; 68% part-time).

Graduate Part-time study available in Graduate School, School of Criminal Justice, School of Law. Degree can be earned exclusively through evening/weekend study in Graduate School, School of Criminal Justice, School of Law. Basic part-time expenses: $91 per credit tuition plus $29.10 per semester fees for state residents, $131 per credit tuition plus $29.10 per semester fees for nonresidents. Institutional financial aid available to part-time graduate students in Graduate School, School of Criminal Justice, School of Law.

Rutgers University, Newark College of Arts and Sciences
Newark 07102

Public institution; city setting. Awards B. Total enrollment: 3,485 (all undergraduates); 14% part-time, 44% women, 16% over 25. Total faculty: 221. Library holdings: 777,396 bound volumes, 278,227 titles on microform, 6,133 periodical subscriptions, 5,461 records/tapes.

Undergraduate Courses offered for part-time students during daytime. Complete part-time degree programs offered during daytime. Adult/continuing education programs available. Career services available to part-time students: individual and group career counseling, employer recruitment on campus. Part-time tuition: $51 per credit for state residents, $102 per credit for nonresidents.

Rutgers University, New Brunswick
New Brunswick 08903

Public institution (undergraduate and graduate). Total enrollment: 33,008. Graduate enrollment: 7,854 (coed; 71% part-time). Library holdings: 2,000,000 bound volumes, 1,805,000 microforms.

Graduate Part-time study available in Graduate School, Graduate School of Education, Graduate School of Social Work, Mason Gross School of the Arts, School of Communication Information and Library Studies. Basic part-time expenses: $91 per credit tuition plus $36.25 per semester fees for state residents, $131 per credit tuition plus $36.25 per semester fees for nonresidents. Institutional financial aid available to part-time graduate students in Graduate School.

Rutgers University, University College–Camden
Camden 08102

Public institution; city setting. Awards B (offers primarily part-time evening degree programs). Total enrollment: 1,193 (all undergraduates); 92% part-time, 49% women, 76% over 25. Total faculty: 16. Library holdings: 429,027 bound volumes, 180,529 titles on microform, 3,184 periodical subscriptions, 1,509 records/tapes.

Undergraduate Courses offered for part-time students during daytime, evenings, weekends, summer. Complete part-time degree programs offered during evenings. Adult/continuing education programs available. Career services available to part-time students: individual and group career counseling, employer recruitment on campus. Part-time tuition: $51 per credit for state residents, $102 per credit for nonresidents.

Colleges Offering Part-Time Degree Programs / New Jersey

Rutgers University, University College–Newark
Newark 07102

Public institution; city setting. Awards B (offers primarily part-time evening degree programs). Total enrollment: 1,784 (all undergraduates); 75% part-time, 56% women, 68% over 25. Total faculty: 40. Library holdings: 777,396 bound volumes, 278,227 titles on microform, 6,133 periodical subscriptions, 5,461 records/tapes.

Undergraduate Courses offered for part-time students during evenings, summer. Complete part-time degree programs offered during evenings, summer. Adult/continuing education programs available. Career services available to part-time students: individual and group career counseling, employer recruitment on campus. Part-time tuition: $51 per credit for state residents, $102 per credit for nonresidents.

Rutgers University, University College–New Brunswick
New Brunswick 08903

Public institution; small-town setting. Awards B (offers primarily part-time evening degree programs). Total enrollment: 3,411 (all undergraduates); 81% part-time, 55% women, 60% over 25. Library holdings: 3.6 million bound volumes, 221,787 titles on microform, 13,492 periodical subscriptions, 35,476 records/tapes.

Undergraduate Courses offered for part-time students during daytime, evenings, summer. Complete part-time degree programs offered during daytime, evenings, summer. Adult/continuing education programs available. Career services available to part-time students: individual and group career counseling, individual job placement, employer recruitment on campus. Part-time tuition: $51 per credit for state residents, $102 per credit for nonresidents.

Saint Peter's College
Jersey City 07306

Independent-religious instutition; city setting. Awards A, B, M. Barrier-free campus. Total enrollment: 2,730. Undergraduate enrollment: 2,613; 25% part-time, 48% women. Total faculty: 315. Library holdings: 240,000 bound volumes, 1,200 periodical subscriptions, 700 records/tapes.

Undergraduate Courses offered for part-time students during daytime, evenings, weekends, summer. Complete part-time degree programs offered during daytime, evenings, weekends, summer. Adult/continuing education programs available. Career services available to part-time students: individual and group career counseling, individual job placement, employer recruitment on campus. Part-time tuition: $139 per credit.

Graduate Part-time study available in Graduate Program in Education. Degree can be earned exclusively through evening/weekend study in Graduate Program in Education. Basic part-time expenses: $149 per credit tuition. Institutional financial aid available to part-time graduate students in Graduate Program in Education.

Salem Community College
Carneys Point 08069

Public institution; rural setting. Awards A. Total enrollment: 1,339 (all undergraduates); 47% part-time, 62% women, 40% over 25. Total faculty: 73. Library holdings: 21,500 bound volumes, 265 periodical subscriptions, 400 records/tapes.

Undergraduate Courses offered for part-time students during daytime, evenings, weekends, summer. Complete part-time degree programs offered during daytime, evenings, weekends, summer. Adult/continuing education programs available. Career services available to part-time students: individual and group career counseling, individual job placement, employer recruitment on campus. Part-time tuition: $31 per credit for area residents, $41 per credit for state residents, $50 per credit for nonresidents.

Seton Hall University
South Orange 07079

Independent-religious institution; small-town setting. Awards B, M, D. Barrier-free campus. Total enrollment: 8,241. Undergraduate enrollment: 6,026; 12% part-time, 50% women. Total faculty: 537. Library holdings: 315,000 bound volumes, 1,700 periodical subscriptions, 2,500 records/tapes.

Undergraduate Courses offered for part-time students during daytime, evenings, summer. Complete part-time degree programs offered during daytime, evenings, summer. Adult/continuing education programs available. Career services available to part-time students: individual and group career counseling, individual job placement, employer recruitment on campus. Part-time tuition: $172 per semester hour.

Graduate Part-time study available in College of Arts and Sciences, College of Nursing, School of Education, School of Law, W. Paul Stillman School of Business. Basic part-time expenses: $189 per credit tuition plus $50 per semester fees. Institutional financial aid available to part-time graduate students in School of Law.

Somerset County College
Somerville 08876

Public institution; small-town setting. Awards A. Barrier-free campus. Total enrollment: 4,870 (all undergraduates); 65% part-time, 60% women. Total faculty: 195.

Undergraduate Courses offered for part-time students during daytime, evenings, weekends, summer. Complete part-time degree programs offered during daytime, evenings, summer. Adult/continuing education programs available. Career services available to part-time students: individual and group career counseling, individual job placement, employer recruitment on campus. Part-time tuition: $29 per credit for area residents, $58 per credit for state residents, $116 per credit for nonresidents.

Stevens Institute of Technology
Hoboken 07030

Independent institution; small-town setting. Awards B, M, D. Barrier-free campus. Total enrollment: 3,062. Undergraduate enrollment: 1,641; 0% part-time, 18% women. Total faculty: 240. Library holdings: 150,000 bound volumes, 20 titles on microform, 1,000 periodical subscriptions.

Graduate Part-time study available in Graduate Division. Degree can be earned exclusively through evening/weekend study in Graduate Division. Basic part-time expenses: $285 per credit tuition.

Stockton State College
Pomona 08240

Public institution; rural setting. Awards B. Barrier-free campus. Total enrollment: 4,923 (all undergraduates); 21% part-time, 46% women, 20% over 25. Total faculty: 215. Library holdings:

New Mexico / **Colleges Offering Part-Time Degree Programs**

115,000 bound volumes, 1,900 periodical subscriptions, 2,200 records/tapes.

Undergraduate Courses offered for part-time students during daytime, evenings, summer. Complete part-time degree programs offered during daytime, evenings, summer. Adult/continuing education programs available. Career services available to part-time students: individual and group career counseling, employer recruitment on campus. Part-time tuition: $43.50 per credit hour for state residents, $63.50 per credit hour for nonresidents.

Thomas A Edison State College
Trenton 08625

Public institution. Awards A, B (external degree programs only). Total enrollment: 4,112 (all undergraduates); 100% part-time.

Undergraduate Part-time degree programs offered. External degree and adult/continuing education programs available. Career services available to part-time students: individual and group career counseling. Tuition: $105 for state residents, $160 for nonresidents in the first year; $80 for state residents, $120 for nonresidents in each subsequent year. Mandatory fees: $3 per credit for state residents, $5 per credit for nonresidents.

Trenton State College
Trenton 08625

Public institution; small-town setting. Awards B, M. Barrier-free campus. Total enrollment: 10,000. Undergraduate enrollment: 7,100; 15% part-time, 60% women, 26% over 25. Total faculty: 500. Library holdings: 450,000 bound volumes, 225,000 titles on microform, 1,700 periodical subscriptions, 12,075 records/tapes.

Undergraduate Courses offered for part-time students during daytime, evenings, summer. Complete part-time degree programs offered during daytime, evenings, summer. Adult/continuing education programs available. Career services available to part-time students: individual and group career counseling, individual job placement, employer recruitment on campus. Part-time tuition: $32 per semester hour for state residents, $52 per semester hour for nonresidents.

Graduate Part-time study available in Graduate Division. Degree can be earned exclusively through evening/weekend study in Graduate Division. Basic part-time expenses: $64 per credit tuition plus $8 per credit fees for state residents, $84 per credit tuition plus $8 per credit fees for nonresidents. Institutional financial aid available to part-time graduate students in Graduate Division.

Upsala College
East Orange 07019

Independent-religious instutition; city setting. Awards B, M. Total enrollment: 1,198. Undergraduate enrollment: 1,158; 42% part-time, 40% women, 2% over 25. Total faculty: 140. Library holdings: 150,190 bound volumes, 1,072 titles on microform, 900 periodical subscriptions, 5,598 records/tapes.

Undergraduate Courses offered for part-time students during daytime, evenings, weekends, summer. Complete part-time degree programs offered during daytime, evenings, weekends, summer. Adult/continuing education programs available. Career services available to part-time students: individual and group career counseling, individual job placement, employer recruitment on campus. Part-time tuition: $595 per course.

Graduate Part-time study available in Graduate Programs. Degree can be earned exclusively through evening/weekend study in Graduate Programs. Basic part-time expenses: $595 per course tuition. Institutional financial aid available to part-time graduate students in Graduate Programs.

Westminster Choir College
Princeton 08540

Independent institution; small-town setting. Awards B, M. Total enrollment: 385. Undergraduate enrollment: 309; 2% part-time, 56% women, 1% over 25. Total faculty: 69. Library holdings: 42,000 bound volumes, 110 periodical subscriptions, 5,000 records/tapes.

Undergraduate Courses offered for part-time students during daytime, summer. Complete part-time degree programs offered during daytime, summer. Adult/continuing education programs available. Career services available to part-time students: individual and group career counseling, individual job placement, employer recruitment on campus. Part-time tuition: $220 per semester hour.

Graduate Part-time study available in Graduate Division. Basic part-time expenses: $310 per credit tuition.

William Paterson College of New Jersey
Wayne 07470

Public institution; small-town setting. Awards B, M. Total enrollment: 12,491. Undergraduate enrollment: 10,265; 38% part-time, 53% women. Total faculty: 601. Library holdings: 285,000 bound volumes, 3,000 periodical subscriptions, 8,000 records/tapes.

Undergraduate Courses offered for part-time students during daytime, evenings, weekends, summer. Complete part-time degree programs offered during daytime, evenings, weekends, summer. Adult/continuing education programs available. Career services available to part-time students: individual and group career counseling, individual job placement, employer recruitment on campus. Part-time tuition: $39.40 per credit for state residents, $59.40 per credit for nonresidents.

NEW MEXICO

College of Santa Fe
Santa Fe 87501

Independent-religious instutition; city setting. Awards A, B. Total enrollment: 857 (all undergraduates); 33% part-time, 59% women. Total faculty: 90. Library holdings: 87,000 bound volumes, 300 periodical subscriptions, 1,000 records/tapes.

Undergraduate Courses offered for part-time students during daytime, evenings, weekends, summer. Complete part-time degree programs offered during daytime, evenings, weekends, summer. External degree and adult/continuing education programs available. Career services available to part-time students: individual and group career counseling, individual job placement, employer recruitment on campus. Part-time tuition: $120 per semester hour.

College of the Southwest
Hobbs 88240

Independent institution; small-town setting. Awards B. Barrier-free campus. Total enrollment: 231 (all undergraduates); 46% part-time, 70% women, 70% over 25. Total faculty: 42. Library holdings: 38,000 bound volumes, 404 periodical subscriptions, 335 records/tapes.

Undergraduate Courses offered for part-time students during daytime, evenings, weekends, summer. Complete part-time de-

Colleges Offering Part-Time Degree Programs / New Mexico

College of the Southwest (continued)

gree programs offered during daytime, evenings, summer. Career services available to part-time students: individual career counseling, employer recruitment on campus. Part-time tuition: $45 per semester hour.

Eastern New Mexico University
Portales 88130

Public institution; small-town setting. Awards A, B, M. Barrier-free campus. Total enrollment: 3,748. Undergraduate enrollment: 3,227; 13% part-time, 50% women. Total faculty: 200. Library holdings: 368,000 bound volumes, 67,230 titles on microform, 1,328 periodical subscriptions, 31,081 records/tapes.

Undergraduate Courses offered for part-time students during daytime, evenings, summer. Complete part-time degree programs offered during daytime, evenings, summer. External degree and adult/continuing education programs available. Career services available to part-time students: individual career counseling, individual job placement, employer recruitment on campus. Part-time tuition: $30.95 per credit for state residents, $95.75 per credit for nonresidents.

Graduate Part-time study available in Graduate Studies. Basic part-time expenses: $30.95 per credit tuition for state residents, $95.75 per credit tuition for nonresidents. Institutional financial aid available to part-time graduate students in Graduate Studies.

Eastern New Mexico University–Roswell
Roswell 88201

Public institution; small-town setting. Awards A. Total enrollment: 1,428 (all undergraduates); 38% part-time, 43% women. Total faculty: 70. Library holdings: 24,000 bound volumes, 7,000 titles on microform, 100 periodical subscriptions.

Undergraduate Courses offered for part-time students during daytime, evenings, weekends. Complete part-time degree programs offered during daytime, evenings. Career services available to part-time students: individual and group career counseling, individual job placement, employer recruitment on campus. Part-time tuition: $17.17 per semester hour for state residents, $44.17 per semester hour for nonresidents.

Institute of American Indian Arts
Santa Fe 87501

Public institution; city setting. Awards A. Total enrollment: 180 (all undergraduates); 4% part-time, 44% women, 20% over 25. Total faculty: 23. Library holdings: 15,000 bound volumes, 70 periodical subscriptions, 400 records/tapes.

Undergraduate Courses offered for part-time students during daytime, summer. Complete part-time degree programs offered during daytime, summer. Adult/continuing education programs available. Career services available to part-time students: individual and group career counseling, individual job placement, employer recruitment on campus.

New Mexico Highlands University
Las Vegas 87701

Public institution; small-town setting. Awards A, B, M. Barrier-free campus. Total enrollment: 2,326. Undergraduate enrollment: 1,647; 24% part-time, 64% women. Total faculty: 126. Library holdings: 300,000 bound volumes, 1,200 periodical subscriptions, 1,000 records/tapes.

Undergraduate Courses offered for part-time students during daytime, evenings, weekends, summer. Complete part-time degree programs offered during daytime, evenings, weekends, summer. Adult/continuing education programs available. Career services available to part-time students: individual and group career counseling, individual job placement, employer recruitment on campus. Part-time tuition: $23.15 per semester hour for state residents, $87.95 per semester hour for nonresidents.

Graduate Part-time study available in Graduate Division. Basic part-time expenses: $23.15 per hour tuition for state residents, $83.95 per hour tuition for nonresidents. Institutional financial aid available to part-time graduate students in Graduate Division.

New Mexico Institute of Mining and Technology
Socorro 87801

Public institution; small-town setting. Awards A, B, M, D. Total enrollment: 1,345. Undergraduate enrollment: 1,136; 13% part-time, 28% women, 30% over 25. Total faculty: 94. Library holdings: 115,123 bound volumes, 11,091 titles on microform, 872 periodical subscriptions, 749 records/tapes.

Graduate Part-time study available in Graduate Studies. Basic part-time expenses: $19.30 per credit hour tuition plus $39 per semester (minimum) fees for state residents, $101.30 per credit hour tuition plus $39 per semester (minimum) fees for nonresidents.

New Mexico Junior College
Hobbs 88240

Public institution; small-town setting. Awards A. Barrier-free campus. Total enrollment: 2,570 (all undergraduates); 63% part-time, 41% over 25. Total faculty: 96. Library holdings: 58,000 bound volumes, 46,000 titles on microform, 20 periodical subscriptions, 18,000 records/tapes.

Undergraduate Courses offered for part-time students during daytime, evenings, weekends, summer. Complete part-time degree programs offered during daytime, evenings, weekends, summer. Adult/continuing education programs available. Career services available to part-time students: individual and group career counseling, individual job placement, employer recruitment on campus. Part-time tuition: $6 per semester hour for area residents, $12 per semester hour for state residents, $18 per semester hour for nonresidents.

New Mexico State University
Las Cruces 88003

Public institution; city setting. Awards A, B, M, D. Barrier-free campus. Total enrollment: 12,926. Undergraduate enrollment: 11,257; 19% part-time, 46% women. Total faculty: 712. Library holdings: 700,000 bound volumes, 530,000 titles on microform, 275,000 periodical subscriptions, 369 records/tapes.

Undergraduate Courses offered for part-time students during daytime, evenings, summer. Complete part-time degree programs offered during daytime, evenings, summer. Adult/continuing education programs available. Career services available to part-time students: individual and group career counseling, individual job placement, employer recruitment on campus. Part-time tuition: $36.25 per semester hour for state residents, $118.25 per semester hour for nonresidents.

Graduate Part-time study available in Graduate School. Basic part-time expenses: $36.25 per credit hour tuition for state residents, $36.25 per credit hour (minimum) tuition for nonresi-

New Mexico / **Colleges Offering Part-Time Degree Programs**

dents. Institutional financial aid available to part-time graduate students in Graduate School.

New Mexico State University–Carlsbad
Carlsbad 88220

Public institution; small-town setting. Awards A. Barrier-free campus. Total enrollment: 850 (all undergraduates); 60% part-time, 62% women, 50% over 25. Total faculty: 55. Library holdings: 25,000 bound volumes, 108 periodical subscriptions, 1,245 records/tapes.

Undergraduate Courses offered for part-time students during daytime, evenings. Complete part-time degree programs offered during daytime, evenings. Adult/continuing education programs available. Career services available to part-time students: individual career counseling. Part-time tuition: $14 per credit hour for state residents, $41 per credit hour for nonresidents.

Northern New Mexico Community College
El Rito 87530

Public institution; rural setting. Awards A. Total enrollment: 1,219 (all undergraduates); 47% part-time, 58% women, 50% over 25. Total faculty: 100. Library holdings: 13,000 bound volumes, 50 titles on microform, 100 periodical subscriptions, 200 records/tapes.

Undergraduate Courses offered for part-time students during daytime, evenings, weekends, summer. Complete part-time degree programs offered during daytime, evenings. Adult/continuing education programs available. Career services available to part-time students: individual and group career counseling, individual job placement, employer recruitment on campus. Part-time tuition: $13 per credit hour for state residents, $40 per credit hour for nonresidents.

St John's College
Santa Fe 87501

Independent institution; city setting. Awards B, M. Total enrollment: 354. Undergraduate enrollment: 301; 1% part-time, 40% women. Total faculty: 44. Library holdings: 53,100 bound volumes, 200 periodical subscriptions, 7,500 records/tapes.

Graduate Part-time study available in Graduate Institute in Liberal Education. Degree can be earned exclusively through evening/weekend study in Graduate Institute in Liberal Education. Basic part-time expenses: $420 per course tuition.

San Juan College
Farmington 87401

Public institution; small-town setting. Awards A. Barrier-free campus. Total enrollment: 2,390 (all undergraduates); 67% part-time, 52% women, 49% over 25. Total faculty: 144. Library holdings: 28,440 bound volumes, 23 titles on microform, 213 periodical subscriptions, 2,454 records/tapes.

Undergraduate Courses offered for part-time students during daytime, evenings, weekends, summer. Complete part-time degree programs offered during daytime, evenings, summer. Adult/continuing education programs available. Career services available to part-time students: individual and group career counseling, individual job placement, employer recruitment on campus. Part-time tuition: $15 per credit for state residents, $42 per credit for nonresidents.

University of Albuquerque
Albuquerque 87140

Independent-religious instutition; city setting. Awards A, B. Total enrollment: 1,800 (all undergraduates); 43% part-time, 52% women, 50% over 25. Total faculty: 148. Library holdings: 78,000 bound volumes, 520 periodical subscriptions.

Undergraduate Courses offered for part-time students during daytime, evenings, weekends, summer. Complete part-time degree programs offered during daytime, evenings, weekends, summer. Adult/continuing education programs available. Career services available to part-time students: individual and group career counseling, individual job placement, employer recruitment on campus. Part-time tuition: $130 per semester hour.

University of New Mexico
Albuquerque 87131

Public institution; city setting. Awards A, B, M, D. Total enrollment: 23,897. Undergraduate enrollment: 19,597; 39% part-time, 52% women, 37% over 25. Total faculty: 1,067. Library holdings: 1.1 million bound volumes, 72,024 titles on microform, 9,317 periodical subscriptions, 23,700 records/tapes.

Undergraduate Courses offered for part-time students during daytime, evenings. Complete part-time degree programs offered during daytime. Adult/continuing education programs available. Career services available to part-time students: individual and group career counseling, individual job placement, employer recruitment on campus. Part-time tuition: $34 per semester hour for state residents. Nonresident part-time tuition per semester hour ranges from $34 for 1 to 6 semester hours to $116 for 7 to 11 semester hours.

University of New Mexico Gallup Branch
Gallup 87301

Public institution; small-town setting. Awards A. Barrier-free campus. Total enrollment: 1,454 (all undergraduates); 70% part-time, 62% women, 50% over 25. Total faculty: 80. Library holdings: 23,000 bound volumes, 100 periodical subscriptions.

Undergraduate Courses offered for part-time students during daytime, evenings. Complete part-time degree programs offered during daytime, evenings. Adult/continuing education programs available. Career services available to part-time students: individual and group career counseling, individual job placement, employer recruitment on campus. Part-time tuition: $14.50 per credit for state residents, $41.50 per credit for nonresidents.

University of New Mexico–Los Alamos
Los Alamos 87544

Public institution; small-town setting. Awards A. Barrier-free campus. Total enrollment: 800 (all undergraduates); 80% part-time, 64% women, 70% over 25. Total faculty: 103. Library holdings: 2,000 bound volumes, 3,000 titles on microform, 50 periodical subscriptions, 20 records/tapes.

Undergraduate Courses offered for part-time students during daytime, evenings, weekends, summer. Complete part-time degree programs offered during daytime, evenings, summer. Adult/continuing education programs available. Career services available to part-time students: individual and group career counseling, individual job placement, employer recruitment on campus. Part-time tuition: $13 per semester hour for state residents, $40 per semester hour for nonresidents.

Colleges Offering Part-Time Degree Programs / New Mexico

Western New Mexico University
Silver City 88061

Public institution; small-town setting. Awards A, B, M. Total enrollment: 1,805. Undergraduate enrollment: 1,561; 35% part-time, 34% women. Total faculty: 75. Library holdings: 117,000 bound volumes, 751 periodical subscriptions, 850 records/tapes.

Undergraduate Courses offered for part-time students during daytime, summer. Complete part-time degree programs offered during daytime, summer. Career services available to part-time students: individual career counseling. Part-time tuition: $23 per credit hour for state residents, $88 per credit hour for nonresidents.

Graduate Part-time study available in Graduate Division. Basic part-time expenses: $15 per hour tuition plus $8 per hour fees for state residents, $15 per hour (minimum) tuition plus $8 per hour (minimum) fees for nonresidents. Institutional financial aid available to part-time graduate students in Graduate Division.

NEW YORK

Academy of Aeronautics
Flushing 11371

Independent institution; metropolitan setting. Awards A, B (B awarded by New York Institute of Technology). Total enrollment: 1,450 (all undergraduates); 22% part-time, 1% women. Total faculty: 68. Library holdings: 50,525 bound volumes, 75 periodical subscriptions, 135 records/tapes.

Undergraduate Courses offered for part-time students during daytime, evenings, summer. Complete part-time degree programs offered during daytime, evenings, summer. Career services available to part-time students: individual career counseling, individual job placement, employer recruitment on campus. Part-time tuition: $108 per credit.

Adelphi University
Garden City 11530

Independent institution; small-town setting. Awards B, M, D. Total enrollment: 11,087. Undergraduate enrollment: 6,455; 19% part-time, 67% women. Total faculty: 857. Library holdings: 393,410 bound volumes, 413,745 titles on microform, 3,044 periodical subscriptions.

Undergraduate Courses offered for part-time students during daytime, evenings, weekends, summer. Complete part-time degree programs offered during daytime. External degree and adult/continuing education programs available. Career services available to part-time students: individual and group career counseling, individual job placement, employer recruitment on campus. Part-time tuition: $181 per credit.

Graduate Part-time study available in School of Arts and Sciences, School of Business Administration. Basic part-time expenses: $195 per credit tuition plus $78 per semester (minimum) fees.

Adirondack Community College
Glens Falls 12801

Public institution; small-town setting. Awards A. Barrier-free campus. Total enrollment: 3,134 (all undergraduates); 48% part-time, 62% women, 47% over 25. Total faculty: 167. Library holdings: 46,000 bound volumes, 400 periodical subscriptions, 1,500 records/tapes.

Undergraduate Courses offered for part-time students during daytime, evenings, summer. Complete part-time degree programs offered during daytime, evenings, summer. Adult/continuing education programs available. Career services available to part-time students: individual and group career counseling, individual job placement, employer recruitment on campus. Part-time tuition: $32 per semester hour for state residents, $64 per semester hour for nonresidents.

Albany Business College
Albany 12210

Proprietary institution; city setting. Awards A. Total enrollment: 484 (all undergraduates); 7% part-time, 70% women, 25% over 25. Total faculty: 43. Library holdings: 2,000 bound volumes, 50 periodical subscriptions.

Undergraduate Courses offered for part-time students during daytime, evenings, weekends, summer. Complete part-time degree programs offered during daytime, evenings, weekends. Part-time tuition: $95 per credit hour.

Albany Medical College of Union University
Albany 12208

Independent institution (graduate only). Total enrollment: 576 (coed). Total faculty: 412.

Graduate Part-time study available in Graduate Studies Program. Basic part-time expenses: $220 per credit tuition. Institutional financial aid available to part-time graduate students in Graduate Studies Program.

Alfred University
Alfred 14802

Independent institution; rural setting. Awards B, M, D. Total enrollment: 2,448. Undergraduate enrollment: 2,141; 5% part-time, 50% women. Total faculty: 176. Library holdings: 200,000 bound volumes, 2,000 periodical subscriptions.

Undergraduate Courses offered for part-time students during daytime. Complete part-time degree programs offered during daytime. Career services available to part-time students: individual and group career counseling, individual job placement, employer recruitment on campus. Part-time tuition: $140 per credit. Part-time tuition for state-supported programs: $140 per credit for state residents, $140 per credit for nonresidents.

Graduate Part-time study available in School of Engineering. Degree can be earned exclusively through evening/weekend study in School of Engineering. Basic part-time expenses: $140 per credit hour tuition. Institutional financial aid available to part-time graduate students in School of Engineering.

Bank Street College of Education
New York 10025

Independent institution (graduate only). Total enrollment: 596 (primarily women; 69% part-time). Total faculty: 78.

Graduate Part-time study available in Graduate School. Basic part-time expenses: $200 per credit tuition plus $60 per semester fees. Institutional financial aid available to part-time graduate students in Graduate School.

Bard College
Annandale-on-Hudson 12504

Independent institution; rural setting. Awards B, M. Total enrollment: 745. Undergraduate enrollment: 696; 4% part-time,

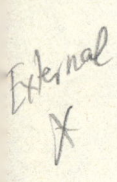

New York / **Colleges Offering Part-Time Degree Programs**

53% women. Total faculty: 90. Library holdings: 160,000 bound volumes, 3,500 titles on microform, 600 periodical subscriptions, 2,500 records/tapes.

Undergraduate Courses offered for part-time students during daytime, summer. Complete part-time degree programs offered during daytime. External degree and adult/continuing education programs available. Career services available to part-time students: individual and group career counseling, individual job placement, employer recruitment on campus. Part-time tuition: $312.50 per credit.

Baruch College
New York 10010

See City University of New York, Bernard M Baruch College

Berkeley School
Hicksville 11801

Proprietary institution; small-town setting. Awards A. Barrier-free campus. Total enrollment: 300 (all undergraduates); 0% part-time, 86% women, 10% over 25. Total faculty: 14. Library holdings: 4,000 bound volumes, 100 periodical subscriptions, 35 records/tapes.

Undergraduate Courses offered for part-time students during daytime, evenings. Complete part-time degree programs offered during daytime, evenings. Adult/continuing education programs available. Career services available to part-time students: individual and group career counseling, individual job placement, employer recruitment on campus. Part-time tuition: $68 per credit hour.

Bramson ORT Technical Institute
New York 10010

Independent institution; metropolitan setting. Awards A. Barrier-free campus. Total enrollment: 289 (all undergraduates); 32% part-time, 45% women. Total faculty: 18. Library holdings: 6,500 bound volumes, 95 periodical subscriptions, 1,000 records/tapes.

Undergraduate Courses offered for part-time students during daytime, evenings, weekends. Complete part-time degree programs offered during daytime, evenings. Career services available to part-time students: individual career counseling, individual job placement. Part-time tuition: $110 per credit.

Briarcliffe Secretarial School
Hicksville 11801

Proprietary institution; small-town setting. Awards A. Total enrollment: 450 (all undergraduates); 40% part-time, 100% women. Total faculty: 48.

Undergraduate Courses offered for part-time students during evenings, weekends, summer. Complete part-time degree programs offered during evenings, weekends. Adult/continuing education programs available. Career services available to part-time students: individual and group career counseling. Part-time tuition: $60 per credit.

Bronx Community College
Bronx 10468

See City University of New York, Bronx Community College

Brooklyn College
Brooklyn 11210

See City University of New York, Brooklyn College

Brooklyn Law School
Brooklyn 11201

Independent institution (graduate only). Total enrollment: 1,186 (coed; 31% part-time). Total faculty: 89.

Graduate Part-time study available in Professional Program. Basic part-time expenses: $5475 per year tuition plus $35 per semester fees for state residents, $7300 per year tuition plus $35 per semester fees for nonresidents. Institutional financial aid available to part-time graduate students in Professional Program.

Broome Community College
Binghamton 13902

Public institution; city setting. Awards A. Barrier-free campus. Total enrollment: 6,841 (all undergraduates); 44% part-time, 49% women, 30% over 25. Total faculty: 563. Library holdings: 60,000 bound volumes, 550 periodical subscriptions, 650 records/tapes.

Undergraduate Courses offered for part-time students during daytime, evenings, summer. Complete part-time degree programs offered during daytime, evenings, summer. Adult/continuing education programs available. Career services available to part-time students: individual and group career counseling, individual job placement. Part-time tuition: $36 per credit hour for state residents, $72 per credit hour for nonresidents.

Bryant and Stratton Business Institute
Buffalo 14202

Proprietary institution; metropolitan setting. Awards A. Total enrollment: 2,275 (all undergraduates); 5% part-time, 65% women, 39% over 25. Total faculty: 182. Library holdings: 2,670 bound volumes, 129 periodical subscriptions, 563 records/tapes.

Undergraduate Courses offered for part-time students during daytime, evenings, weekends, summer. Complete part-time degree programs offered during daytime, evenings, weekends, summer. Adult/continuing education programs available. Career services available to part-time students: individual and group career counseling, individual job placement, employer recruitment on campus. Part-time tuition: $226 per course.

Bryant and Stratton Business Institute
Rochester 14604

Proprietary institution; metropolitan setting. Awards A. Barrier-free campus. Total enrollment: 850 (all undergraduates); 7% part-time, 90% women, 20% over 25. Total faculty: 24. Library holdings: 1,500 bound volumes, 35 periodical subscriptions.

Undergraduate Courses offered for part-time students during daytime, evenings. Complete part-time degree programs offered during daytime, evenings. Adult/continuing education programs available. Career services available to part-time students: group career counseling, individual job placement, employer recruitment on campus. Part-time tuition: $226 per course.

Colleges Offering Part-Time Degree Programs / New York

Bryant and Stratton Business Institute, Eastern Hills Campus
Clarence 14031

Proprietary institution; small-town setting. Awards A. Barrier-free campus. Total enrollment: 989 (all undergraduates); 3% part-time, 75% women, 15% over 25. Total faculty: 38. Library holdings: 200 bound volumes, 78 periodical subscriptions, 245 records/tapes.

Undergraduate Courses offered for part-time students during daytime, evenings, weekends, summer. Complete part-time degree programs offered during daytime, evenings, weekends, summer. Adult/continuing education programs available. Career services available to part-time students: individual and group career counseling, individual job placement, employer recruitment on campus. Part-time tuition: $226 per course.

Bryant and Stratton Powelson Business Institute
Syracuse 13202

Proprietary institution; metropolitan setting. Awards A. Barrier-free campus. Total enrollment: 1,036 (all undergraduates); 10% part-time, 75% women. Total faculty: 28. Library holdings: 1,694 bound volumes, 95 periodical subscriptions, 75 records/tapes.

Undergraduate Courses offered for part-time students during daytime, evenings, weekends, summer. Complete part-time degree programs offered during daytime, evenings. Adult/continuing education programs available. Career services available to part-time students: individual career counseling, individual job placement, employer recruitment on campus. Part-time tuition: $226 per course.

Canisius College
Buffalo 14208

Independent institution; metropolitan setting. Awards B, M. Total enrollment: 4,567. Undergraduate enrollment: 2,495; 33% part-time, 43% women. Total faculty: 271. Library holdings: 248,000 bound volumes, 1,250 periodical subscriptions, 2,400 records/tapes.

Undergraduate Courses offered for part-time students during daytime, evenings, weekends, summer. Complete part-time degree programs offered during daytime, evenings, weekends, summer. Adult/continuing education programs available. Career services available to part-time students: individual and group career counseling, individual job placement, employer recruitment on campus. Part-time tuition: $125 per credit.

Graduate Part-time study available in Graduate Division. Basic part-time expenses: $135 per credit hour tuition plus $4 per credit hour fees. Institutional financial aid available to part-time graduate students in Graduate Division.

Cayuga County Community College
Auburn 13021

Public institution; small-town setting. Awards A. Barrier-free campus. Total enrollment: 3,412 (all undergraduates); 47% part-time, 52% women, 30% over 25. Total faculty: 144. Library holdings: 62,757 bound volumes, 716 periodical subscriptions, 1,473 records/tapes.

Undergraduate Courses offered for part-time students during daytime, evenings, summer. Complete part-time degree programs offered during daytime, evenings, summer. Adult/continuing education programs available. Career services available to part-time students: individual and group career counseling, individual job placement, employer recruitment on campus. Part-time tuition: $38 per credit for state residents, $76 per credit for nonresidents.

Cazenovia College
Cazenovia 13035

Independent institution; rural setting. Awards A. Barrier-free campus. Total enrollment: 711 (all undergraduates); 1% part-time, 95% women, 1% over 25. Total faculty: 72. Library holdings: 35,958 bound volumes, 205 periodical subscriptions, 4,400 records/tapes.

Undergraduate Courses offered for part-time students during daytime. Complete part-time degree programs offered during daytime. Adult/continuing education programs available. Career services available to part-time students: individual and group career counseling, individual job placement, employer recruitment on campus. Part-time tuition: $125 per credit.

Central City Business Institute
Syracuse 13203

Proprietary institution; metropolitan setting. Awards A. Total enrollment: 737 (all undergraduates); 1% part-time, 95% women. Total faculty: 57. Library holdings: 900 bound volumes, 50 periodical subscriptions.

Undergraduate Courses offered for part-time students during evenings, summer. Complete part-time degree programs offered during evenings. Adult/continuing education programs available. Career services available to part-time students: individual and group career counseling, individual job placement, employer recruitment on campus. Part-time tuition: $40 per credit hour.

Christ the King Seminary
East Aurora 14052

Independent-religious institution (graduate only). Total enrollment: 130 (coed; 30% part-time). Total faculty: 25. Library holdings: 100,000 bound volumes, 55 microforms.

Graduate Part-time study available in Graduate and Professional Programs. Degree can be earned exclusively through evening/weekend study in Graduate and Professional Programs. Basic part-time expenses: $100 per credit tuition plus $30 per year fees.

City College
New York 10031

See City University of New York, City College

City University of New York, Bernard M Baruch College
New York 10010

Public institution; metropolitan setting. Awards B, M. Barrier-free campus. Total enrollment: 15,368. Undergraduate enrollment: 12,637; 36% part-time, 57% women. Total faculty: 800. Library holdings: 265,000 bound volumes, 180,000 titles on microform, 1,500 periodical subscriptions.

Undergraduate Courses offered for part-time students during daytime, evenings, summer. Complete part-time degree programs offered during daytime, evenings, summer. Adult/continuing education programs available. Career services available to part-time students: individual and group career counseling,

individual job placement, employer recruitment on campus. Part-time tuition: $47 per credit for state residents, $96 per credit for nonresidents.

Graduate Part-time study available in School of Business and Public Administration.Basic part-time expenses: $82 per credit tuition plus $13.50 per semester (minimum) fees for state residents, $136 per credit tuition plus $13.50 per semester (minimum) fees for nonresidents. Institutional financial aid available to part-time graduate students in School of Business and Public Administration.

City University of New York, Borough of Manhattan Community College
New York 10007

Public institution; metropolitan setting. Awards A. Barrier-free campus. Total enrollment: 11,500 (all undergraduates); 43% part-time, 66% women, 41% over 25. Total faculty: 623. Library holdings: 51,232 bound volumes, 1,400 titles on microform, 525 periodical subscriptions, 500 records/tapes.

Undergraduate Courses offered for part-time students during daytime, evenings, weekends, summer. Complete part-time degree programs offered during daytime, evenings, weekends, summer. Adult/continuing education programs available. Career services available to part-time students: individual and group career counseling, individual job placement, employer recruitment on campus. Part-time tuition: $40 per credit for state residents, $76 per credit for nonresidents.

City University of New York, Bronx Community College
Bronx 10453

Public institution; metropolitan setting. Awards A. Total enrollment: 7,200 (all undergraduates); 27% part-time, 61% women. Total faculty: 426. Library holdings: 75,000 bound volumes, 800 periodical subscriptions.

Undergraduate Courses offered for part-time students during daytime, evenings, weekends, summer. Complete part-time degree programs offered during daytime, evenings, weekends, summer. Adult/continuing education programs available. Career services available to part-time students: individual career counseling. Part-time tuition: $40 per credit for state residents, $76 per credit for nonresidents.

City University of New York, Brooklyn College
Brooklyn 11210

Public institution; metropolitan setting. Awards B, M. Barrier-free campus. Total enrollment: 12,271. Undergraduate enrollment: 10,757; 22% part-time, 52% women. Total faculty: 1,045. Library holdings: 866,395 bound volumes, 818,071 titles on microform, 3,420 periodical subscriptions, 14,373 records/tapes.

Undergraduate Courses offered for part-time students during daytime, evenings, weekends, summer. Complete part-time degree programs offered during daytime, evenings, weekends, summer. Adult/continuing education programs available. Career services available to part-time students: individual and group career counseling, individual job placement, employer recruitment on campus. Part-time tuition: $47 per credit for state residents, $96 per credit for nonresidents.

Graduate Part-time study available in Graduate Division.Basic part-time expenses: $82 per credit tuition plus $28 per semester fees for state residents, $136 per credit tuition plus $28 per semester fees for nonresidents. Institutional financial aid available to part-time graduate students in Graduate Division.

City University of New York, City College
New York 10031

Public institution; metropolitan setting. Awards B, M. Barrier-free campus. Total enrollment: 13,129. Undergraduate enrollment: 10,797; 9% part-time, 42% women. Total faculty: 1,013. Library holdings: 1.0 million bound volumes, 465,000 titles on microform, 3,468 periodical subscriptions, 15,500 records/tapes.

Undergraduate Courses offered for part-time students during daytime, evenings, summer. Complete part-time degree programs offered during daytime, evenings, summer. Adult/continuing education programs available. Career services available to part-time students: individual and group career counseling, individual job placement. Part-time tuition: $47 per credit for state residents, $96 per credit for nonresidents.

Graduate Part-time study available in School of Architecture, School of Education, School of Engineering, School of Liberal Arts and Sciences. Degree can be earned exclusively through evening/weekend study in School of Education, School of Engineering.Basic part-time expenses: $82 per credit tuition plus $15.35 per semester fees for state residents, $136 per credit tuition plus $15.35 per semester fees for nonresidents. Institutional financial aid available to part-time graduate students in School of Architecture, School of Education, School of Engineering, School of Liberal Arts and Sciences.

City University of New York, College of Staten Island
Staten Island 10301

Public institution; metropolitan setting. Awards A, B, M. Barrier-free campus. Total enrollment: 11,100. Undergraduate enrollment: 10,500; 50% part-time, 54% women. Total faculty: 379. Library holdings: 170,000 bound volumes, 321,000 titles on microform, 1,100 periodical subscriptions, 6,200 records/tapes.

Undergraduate Courses offered for part-time students during daytime, evenings, weekends, summer. Complete part-time degree programs offered during daytime, evenings, weekends, summer. External degree and adult/continuing education programs available. Career services available to part-time students: individual and group career counseling, individual job placement, employer recruitment on campus. Part-time tuition: $47 per semester hour for state residents, $96 per semester hour for nonresidents.

Graduate Part-time study available in Graduate Programs. Degree can be earned exclusively through evening/weekend study in Graduate Programs.Basic part-time expenses: $82 per credit tuition plus $18 per semester fees for state residents, $136 per credit tuition plus $18 per semester fees for nonresidents. Institutional financial aid available to part-time graduate students in Graduate Programs.

City University of New York, Fiorello H LaGuardia Community College
Long Island City 11101

Public institution; metropolitan setting. Awards A. Total enrollment: 6,800 (all undergraduates); 10% part-time, 68% women. Total faculty: 368. Library holdings: 41,440 bound volumes, 629 periodical subscriptions, 1,000 records/tapes.

Undergraduate Courses offered for part-time students during daytime, evenings. Complete part-time degree programs offered during daytime, evenings. Adult/continuing education programs available. Career services available to part-time students: individual and group career counseling, individual job placement. Part-time tuition: $47 per credit for state residents, $96 per credit for nonresidents.

Colleges Offering Part-Time Degree Programs / New York

City University of New York, Herbert H Lehman College
Bronx 10468

Public institution; metropolitan setting. Awards B, M. Barrier-free campus. Total enrollment: 10,500. Undergraduate enrollment: 10,000; 38% part-time, 57% women. Total faculty: 820. Library holdings: 350,834 bound volumes, 261,920 titles on microform, 2,000 periodical subscriptions.

Undergraduate Courses offered for part-time students during daytime, evenings, summer. Complete part-time degree programs offered during daytime, evenings, summer. Adult/continuing education programs available. Career services available to part-time students: individual career counseling, employer recruitment on campus. Part-time tuition: $47 per credit for state residents, $96 per credit for nonresidents.

Graduate Part-time study available in Division of Humanities, Division of Natural and Social Sciences, Division of Professional Studies. Degree can be earned exclusively through evening/weekend study in Division of Humanities, Division of Natural and Social Sciences, Division of Professional Studies. Basic part-time expenses: $82 per credit tuition plus $10.50 per semester fees for state residents, $136 per credit tuition plus $10.50 per semester fees for nonresidents. Institutional financial aid available to part-time graduate students in Division of Humanities, Division of Natural and Social Sciences, Division of Professional Studies.

City University of New York, Hunter College
New York 10021

Public institution; metropolitan setting. Awards B, M. Total enrollment: 17,784. Undergraduate enrollment: 14,433; 41% part-time, 75% women. Total faculty: 1,122. Library holdings: 512,710 bound volumes, 4,000 periodical subscriptions, 3,500 records/tapes.

Undergraduate Courses offered for part-time students during daytime, evenings, summer. Complete part-time degree programs offered during daytime, evenings, summer. Career services available to part-time students: individual career counseling, individual job placement. Part-time tuition: $47 per credit for state residents, $96 per credit for nonresidents.

Graduate Part-time study available in Graduate School. Basic part-time expenses: $82 per credit tuition plus $7.85 per semester fees for state residents, $136 per credit tuition plus $7.85 per semester fees for nonresidents. Institutional financial aid available to part-time graduate students in Graduate School.

City University of New York, John Jay College of Criminal Justice
New York 10019

Public institution; metropolitan setting. Awards A, B, M, D. Total enrollment: 6,369. Undergraduate enrollment: 5,864; 35% part-time, 45% women, 34% over 25. Total faculty: 406. Library holdings: 170,000 bound volumes, 14,000 titles on microform, 1,125 periodical subscriptions, 1,150 records/tapes.

Undergraduate Courses offered for part-time students during daytime, evenings, summer. Complete part-time degree programs offered during daytime, evenings. Adult/continuing education programs available. Career services available to part-time students: individual and group career counseling, individual job placement, employer recruitment on campus. Part-time tuition: $47 per credit for state residents, $96 per credit for nonresidents.

Graduate Part-time study available in Graduate Studies. Degree can be earned exclusively through evening/weekend study in Graduate Studies. Basic part-time expenses: $82 per credit tuition plus $17.50 per semester fees for state residents, $136 per credit tuition plus $17.50 per semester fees for nonresidents.

City University of New York, Kingsborough Community College
Brooklyn 11235

Public institution; metropolitan setting. Awards A. Barrier-free campus. Total enrollment: 9,916 (all undergraduates); 39% part-time, 66% women, 17% over 25. Total faculty: 545. Library holdings: 103,084 bound volumes, 8,280 titles on microform, 421 periodical subscriptions, 3,700 records/tapes.

Undergraduate Courses offered for part-time students during daytime, evenings, summer. Complete part-time degree programs offered during daytime, evenings. Adult/continuing education programs available. Career services available to part-time students: individual and group career counseling, individual job placement, employer recruitment on campus. Part-time tuition: $47 per credit for state residents, $96 per credit for nonresidents.

City University of New York, Medgar Evers College
Brooklyn 11225

Public institution; metropolitan setting. Awards A, B. Total enrollment: 2,536 (all undergraduates); 40% part-time, 73% women. Total faculty: 323. Library holdings: 77,568 bound volumes, 18,000 titles on microform, 515 periodical subscriptions, 659 records/tapes.

Undergraduate Courses offered for part-time students during daytime, evenings, weekends. Complete part-time degree programs offered during daytime, evenings. Adult/continuing education programs available. Career services available to part-time students: individual and group career counseling, employer recruitment on campus. Part-time tuition: $40 per credit for state residents, $76 per credit for nonresidents.

City University of New York, New York City Technical College
Brooklyn 11201

Public institution; metropolitan setting. Awards A, B. Barrier-free campus. Total enrollment: 12,077 (all undergraduates); 35% part-time, 49% women, 43% over 25. Total faculty: 1,030. Library holdings: 135,271 bound volumes, 12,586 titles on microform, 548 periodical subscriptions, 1,939 records/tapes.

Undergraduate Courses offered for part-time students during daytime, evenings, weekends, summer. Complete part-time degree programs offered during daytime, evenings. Adult/continuing education programs available. Career services available to part-time students: individual and group career counseling, individual job placement, employer recruitment on campus. Part-time tuition: $47 per credit for state residents, $96 per credit for nonresidents.

City University of New York, Queensborough Community College
Bayside 11364

Public institution; metropolitan setting. Awards A. Barrier-free campus. Total enrollment: 13,401 (all undergraduates); 50% part-time, 55% women, 32% over 25. Total faculty: 697. Library holdings: 128,204 bound volumes, 820 periodical subscriptions, 3,876 records/tapes.

New York / Colleges Offering Part-Time Degree Programs

Undergraduate Courses offered for part-time students during daytime, evenings, weekends, summer. Complete part-time degree programs offered during daytime, evenings, weekends, summer. External degree and adult/continuing education programs available. Career services available to part-time students: individual and group career counseling, individual job placement, employer recruitment on campus. Part-time tuition: $47 per credit for state residents, $96 per credit for nonresidents.

City University of New York, Queens College
Flushing 11367

Public institution; metropolitan setting. Awards B, M. Total enrollment: 17,179. Undergraduate enrollment: 14,231; 31% part-time, 57% women, 3% over 25. Total faculty: 1,435. Library holdings: 600,000 bound volumes, 3,000 periodical subscriptions, 2,000 records/tapes.

Undergraduate Courses offered for part-time students during daytime, evenings, weekends, summer. Complete part-time degree programs offered during daytime, evenings, weekends, summer. External degree and adult/continuing education programs available. Career services available to part-time students: individual and group career counseling, employer recruitment on campus. Part-time tuition: $47 per credit for state residents, $96 per credit for nonresidents.

Graduate Part-time study available in Division of Graduate Studies and Research. Degree can be earned exclusively through evening/weekend study in Division of Graduate Studies and Research. Basic part-time expenses: $82 per credit tuition plus $55.25 per semester fees for state residents, $136 per credit tuition plus $55.25 per semester fees for nonresidents. Institutional financial aid available to part-time graduate students in Division of Graduate Studies and Research.

City University of New York, York College
Jamaica 11451

Public institution; metropolitan setting. Awards B. Total enrollment: 4,200 (all undergraduates); 30% part-time, 65% women. Total faculty: 200. Library holdings: 153,500 bound volumes, 4,009 records/tapes.

Undergraduate Courses offered for part-time students during daytime, evenings, summer. Complete part-time degree programs offered during daytime, evenings, summer. Adult/continuing education programs available. Career services available to part-time students: individual and group career counseling, individual job placement, employer recruitment on campus. Part-time tuition: $47 per credit for state residents, $96 per credit for nonresidents.

Clarkson University
Potsdam 13676

Independent institution; small-town setting. Awards B, M, D. Total enrollment: 4,080. Undergraduate enrollment: 3,680; 2% part-time, 23% women. Total faculty: 231. Library holdings: 131,418 bound volumes, 150,000 titles on microform, 1,360 periodical subscriptions, 1,211 records/tapes.

Graduate Part-time study available in Graduate School. Basic part-time expenses: $243 per credit tuition plus $50 per semester fees.

Clinton Community College
Plattsburgh 12901

Public institution; small-town setting. Awards A. Total enrollment: 1,655 (all undergraduates); 50% part-time, 50% women, 50% over 25. Total faculty: 82. Library holdings: 43,000 bound volumes, 360 periodical subscriptions, 2,950 records/tapes.

Undergraduate Courses offered for part-time students during daytime, evenings, summer. Complete part-time degree programs offered during daytime, evenings, summer. Adult/continuing education programs available. Career services available to part-time students: individual and group career counseling, individual job placement, employer recruitment on campus. Part-time tuition: $35 per credit for state residents, $70 per credit for nonresidents.

Cochran School of Nursing
Yonkers 10701

Independent institution; city setting. Awards A. Barrier-free campus. Total enrollment: 89 (all undergraduates); 2% part-time, 99% women. Total faculty: 16. Library holdings: 1,000 bound volumes, 50 periodical subscriptions.

Undergraduate Courses offered for part-time students during daytime. Complete part-time degree programs offered during daytime. Career services available to part-time students: individual career counseling. Part-time tuition: $97 per credit.

Colgate University
Hamilton 13346

Independent institution; small-town setting. Awards B, M. Total enrollment: 2,594. Undergraduate enrollment: 2,589; 1% part-time, 45% women, 0% over 25. Total faculty: 208. Library holdings: 370,000 bound volumes, 2,001 periodical subscriptions.

Graduate Part-time study available in Graduate Programs. Basic part-time expenses: $1009 per course tuition plus $40 per semester fees. Institutional financial aid available to part-time graduate students in Graduate Programs.

College of Insurance
New York 10007

Independent institution; metropolitan setting. Awards A, B, M. Barrier-free campus. Total enrollment: 602. Undergraduate enrollment: 491; 43% part-time, 40% women. Total faculty: 255. Library holdings: 86,951 bound volumes, 430 periodical subscriptions.

Undergraduate Courses offered for part-time students during daytime, evenings. Complete part-time degree programs offered during daytime, evenings. Adult/continuing education programs available. Career services available to part-time students: individual career counseling, individual job placement. Part-time tuition: $150 per credit.

Graduate Part-time study available in Graduate Division. Degree can be earned exclusively through evening/weekend study in Graduate Division. Basic part-time expenses: $166 per credit (minimum) tuition plus $50 per semester fees. Institutional financial aid available to part-time graduate students in Graduate Division.

College of Mount Saint Vincent
Riverdale 10471

Independent institution; metropolitan setting. Awards A, B. Barrier-free campus. Total enrollment: 1,108 (all undergraduates); 45% part-time, 90% women. Total faculty: 83. Library

Colleges Offering Part-Time Degree Programs / New York

College of Mount Saint Vincent (continued)
holdings: 126,810 bound volumes, 10,824 titles on microform, 560 periodical subscriptions, 9,237 records/tapes.

Undergraduate Courses offered for part-time students during daytime, evenings, weekends, summer. Complete part-time degree programs offered during daytime, evenings, weekends. Adult/continuing education programs available. Career services available to part-time students: individual and group career counseling, individual job placement. Part-time tuition: $145 per credit.

College of New Rochelle
New Rochelle 10801

Independent institution; city setting. Awards B, M. Total enrollment: 2,041. Undergraduate enrollment: 976; 7% part-time, 100% women, 4% over 25. Total faculty: 135. Library holdings: 170,288 bound volumes, 18,222 titles on microform, 1,050 periodical subscriptions, 3,610 records/tapes.

Undergraduate Courses offered for part-time students during daytime, summer. Complete part-time degree programs offered during daytime. Adult/continuing education programs available. Career services available to part-time students: individual and group career counseling, individual job placement, employer recruitment on campus. Part-time tuition: $175 per credit. Part-time tuition for nursing program: $180 per credit.

Graduate Part-time study available in Graduate School. Basic part-time expenses: $131 per credit tuition. Institutional financial aid available to part-time graduate students in Graduate School.

College of New Rochelle, New Resources Division
New Rochelle 10801

Independent institution; city setting. Awards B. Total enrollment: 3,030 (all undergraduates); 14% part-time, 82% women, 90% over 25. Total faculty: 429. Library holdings: 170,288 bound volumes, 18,222 titles on microform, 1,050 periodical subscriptions, 3,610 records/tapes.

Undergraduate Courses offered for part-time students during daytime, evenings, weekends, summer. Complete part-time degree programs offered during daytime, evenings. External degree and adult/continuing education programs available. Career services available to part-time students: individual and group career counseling, employer recruitment on campus. Part-time tuition: $110 per credit.

College of Saint Rose
Albany 12203

Independent institution; city setting. Awards B, M. Total enrollment: 2,378. Undergraduate enrollment: 1,889; 43% part-time, 75% women, 33% over 25. Total faculty: 187. Library holdings: 142,376 bound volumes, 40,703 titles on microform, 866 periodical subscriptions, 359 records/tapes.

Undergraduate Courses offered for part-time students during daytime, evenings, weekends, summer. Complete part-time degree programs offered during daytime, evenings, summer. Adult/continuing education programs available. Career services available to part-time students: individual career counseling, individual job placement, employer recruitment on campus. Part-time tuition: $160 per credit hour.

Graduate Part-time study available in Graduate School. Degree can be earned exclusively through evening/weekend study in Graduate School. Basic part-time expenses: $134 per credit tuition plus $11 per semester fees. Institutional financial aid available to part-time graduate students in Graduate School.

College of Staten Island
Staten Island 10301

See City University of New York, College of Staten Island

Columbia-Greene Community College
Hudson 12534

Public institution; rural setting. Awards A. Barrier-free campus. Total enrollment: 1,300 (all undergraduates); 53% part-time, 54% women, 43% over 25. Total faculty: 59. Library holdings: 30,000 bound volumes, 650 periodical subscriptions, 888 records/tapes.

Undergraduate Courses offered for part-time students during daytime, evenings, summer. Complete part-time degree programs offered during daytime, evenings, summer. Adult/continuing education programs available. Career services available to part-time students: individual career counseling, individual job placement. Part-time tuition: $49 per credit for state residents, $98 per credit for nonresidents.

Columbia University
New York 10027

Independent institution (undergraduate and graduate). Total enrollment: 18,485. Graduate enrollment: 10,587 (coed; 17% part-time). Library holdings: 5,270,432 bound volumes, 2,771,509 microforms.

Graduate Part-time study available in Graduate School of Arts and Sciences. Basic part-time expenses: $2980 per semester tuition. Institutional financial aid available to part-time graduate students in Graduate School of Arts and Sciences.

Columbia University, School of General Studies
New York 10027

Independent institution; metropolitan setting. Awards B. Total enrollment: 2,096 (all undergraduates); 60% part-time, 45% women, 55% over 25. Total faculty: 420. Library holdings: 5 million bound volumes, 58,000 periodical subscriptions.

Undergraduate Courses offered for part-time students during daytime, evenings, summer. Complete part-time degree programs offered during daytime, evenings. Adult/continuing education programs available. Career services available to part-time students: individual and group career counseling, individual job placement, employer recruitment on campus. Part-time tuition: $288 per credit.

Columbia University, School of Nursing
New York 10032

Independent institution; metropolitan setting. Awards B, M. Total enrollment: 362. Undergraduate enrollment: 172; 12% part-time, 94% women, 31% over 25. Total faculty: 61. Library holdings: 5.3 million bound volumes, 2.8 million titles on microform, 60,570 periodical subscriptions.

Undergraduate Courses offered for part-time students during daytime, summer. Complete part-time degree programs offered during daytime. Adult/continuing education programs available. Career services available to part-time students: individual and group career counseling, employer recruitment on campus. Part-time tuition: $328 per credit.

Community College of the Finger Lakes
Canandaigua 14424

Public institution; small-town setting. Awards A. Barrier-free campus. Total enrollment: 1,676 (all undergraduates); 11% part-time, 65% women. Total faculty: 218. Library holdings: 53,391 bound volumes, 590 periodical subscriptions, 1,835 records/tapes.

Undergraduate Courses offered for part-time students during daytime, evenings, weekends, summer. Complete part-time degree programs offered during daytime, evenings, weekends, summer. Adult/continuing education programs available. Career services available to part-time students: individual and group career counseling, individual job placement, employer recruitment on campus. Part-time tuition: $51 per credit hour for state residents, $102 per credit hour for nonresidents.

Cornell University
Ithaca 14853

Independent institution; small-town setting. Awards B, M, D. Total enrollment: 17,146. Undergraduate enrollment: 12,148; 0% part-time, 46% women. Total faculty: 1,553. Library holdings: 5 million bound volumes, 57,000 periodical subscriptions.

Graduate Part-time study available in Graduate School. Basic part-time expenses: $2400 per semester (minimum) tuition. Institutional financial aid available to part-time graduate students in Graduate School.

Corning Community College
Corning 14830

Public institution; rural setting. Awards A. Barrier-free campus. Total enrollment: 2,100 (all undergraduates); 22% part-time, 50% women, 21% over 25. Total faculty: 131. Library holdings: 66,500 bound volumes, 4,300 titles on microform, 475 periodical subscriptions, 3,592 records/tapes.

Undergraduate Courses offered for part-time students during daytime, evenings, weekends, summer. Complete part-time degree programs offered during daytime, evenings. Adult/continuing education programs available. Career services available to part-time students: individual and group career counseling, individual job placement, employer recruitment on campus. Part-time tuition: $50 per credit hour for state residents, $100 per credit hour for nonresidents.

C W Post Campus of Long Island University
Greenvale 11548

See Long Island University, C W Post Campus

Daemen College
Amherst 14226

Independent institution; city setting. Awards B. Barrier-free campus. Total enrollment: 1,623 (all undergraduates); 18% part-time, 65% women. Total faculty: 123. Library holdings: 110,631 bound volumes, 967 titles on microform, 698 periodical subscriptions, 3,875 records/tapes.

Undergraduate Courses offered for part-time students during daytime, evenings, summer. Complete part-time degree programs offered during daytime, evenings. Adult/continuing education programs available. Career services available to part-time students: individual and group career counseling, individual job placement, employer recruitment on campus. Part-time tuition: $160 per credit.

Dominican College of Blauvelt
Orangeburg 10962

Independent institution; rural setting. Awards A, B. Barrier-free campus. Total enrollment: 1,729 (all undergraduates); 56% part-time, 60% women, 35% over 25. Total faculty: 129. Library holdings: 85,000 bound volumes, 650 periodical subscriptions.

Undergraduate Courses offered for part-time students during daytime, evenings, weekends, summer. Complete part-time degree programs offered during daytime, evenings, weekends, summer. Adult/continuing education programs available. Career services available to part-time students: individual and group career counseling, individual job placement, employer recruitment on campus. Part-time tuition: $105 per credit.

Dowling College
Oakdale 11769

Independent institution; small-town setting. Awards B, M. Barrier-free campus. Total enrollment: 2,260. Undergraduate enrollment: 1,922; 22% part-time, 49% women, 26% over 25. Total faculty: 197. Library holdings: 100,000 bound volumes, 246,653 titles on microform, 736 periodical subscriptions.

Undergraduate Courses offered for part-time students during daytime, evenings, weekends, summer. Complete part-time degree programs offered during daytime, evenings, summer. Adult/continuing education programs available. Career services available to part-time students: individual and group career counseling, individual job placement, employer recruitment on campus. Part-time tuition: $145 per credit hour.

Graduate Part-time study available in Graduate Programs. Degree can be earned exclusively through evening/weekend study in Graduate Programs. Basic part-time expenses: $159 per credit tuition plus $35 per semester (minimum) fees.

Dutchess Community College
Poughkeepsie 12601

Public institution; small-town setting. Awards A. Barrier-free campus. Total enrollment: 5,268 (all undergraduates); 37% part-time, 55% women, 38% over 25. Total faculty: 403. Library holdings: 87,882 bound volumes, 9,135 titles on microform, 593 periodical subscriptions.

Undergraduate Courses offered for part-time students during daytime, evenings, summer. Complete part-time degree programs offered during daytime, evenings, summer. Adult/continuing education programs available. Career services available to part-time students: individual career counseling, individual job placement, employer recruitment on campus. Part-time tuition: $48 per credit for state residents, $96 per credit for nonresidents.

D'Youville College
Buffalo 14201

Independent institution; metropolitan setting. Awards B, M. Total enrollment: 1,270. Undergraduate enrollment: 1,252; 24% part-time, 84% women. Total faculty: 102. Library holdings: 86,840 bound volumes, 13,540 titles on microform, 786 periodical subscriptions.

Colleges Offering Part-Time Degree Programs / New York

D'Youville College (continued)

Undergraduate Courses offered for part-time students during daytime, evenings, summer. Complete part-time degree programs offered during daytime, evenings, summer. Adult/continuing education programs available. Career services available to part-time students: individual and group career counseling, individual job placement, employer recruitment on campus. Part-time tuition: $125 per credit.

Graduate Part-time study available in Graduate Program. Degree can be earned exclusively through evening/weekend study in Graduate Program. Basic part-time expenses: $160 per credit hour tuition plus $25 per year fees. Institutional financial aid available to part-time graduate students in Graduate Program.

Elizabeth Seton College
Yonkers 10701

Independent institution; city setting. Awards A. Barrier-free campus. Total enrollment: 1,536 (all undergraduates); 10% part-time, 75% women. Total faculty: 101. Library holdings: 41,000 bound volumes, 263 periodical subscriptions, 1,117 records/tapes.

Undergraduate Courses offered for part-time students during daytime, evenings, weekends, summer. Complete part-time degree programs offered during daytime, evenings, weekends, summer. External degree and adult/continuing education programs available. Career services available to part-time students: individual and group career counseling, individual job placement, employer recruitment on campus. Part-time tuition: $105.50 per credit.

Elmira College
Elmira 14901

Independent institution; small-town setting. Awards A, B, M. Total enrollment: 2,088. Undergraduate enrollment: 1,740; 42% part-time, 66% women, 9% over 25. Total faculty: 258. Library holdings: 230,920 bound volumes, 17,656 titles on microform, 823 periodical subscriptions, 45,000 records/tapes.

Undergraduate Courses offered for part-time students during daytime, evenings, weekends, summer. Complete part-time degree programs offered during daytime, evenings, weekends, summer. Adult/continuing education programs available. Career services available to part-time students: individual and group career counseling, individual job placement. Part-time tuition: $75 per credit.

Graduate Part-time study available in Graduate Programs. Degree can be earned exclusively through evening/weekend study in Graduate Programs. Basic part-time expenses: $110 per credit tuition. Institutional financial aid available to part-time graduate students in Graduate Programs.

Erie Community College, City Campus
Buffalo 14203

Public institution; metropolitan setting. Awards A. Barrier-free campus. Total enrollment: 1,328 (all undergraduates); 45% part-time, 62% women. Total faculty: 103.

Undergraduate Courses offered for part-time students during daytime, evenings, summer. Complete part-time degree programs offered during daytime, evenings. Adult/continuing education programs available. Career services available to part-time students: individual and group career counseling, individual job placement, employer recruitment on campus. Part-time tuition: $36 per credit hour for area residents, $70 per credit hour for state residents, $104 per credit hour for nonresidents.

Erie Community College, South Campus
Orchard Park 14127

Public institution; small-town setting. Awards A. Barrier-free campus. Total enrollment: 3,786 (all undergraduates); 53% part-time, 45% women. Total faculty: 103. Library holdings: 20,000 bound volumes, 800 titles on microform, 200 periodical subscriptions.

Undergraduate Courses offered for part-time students during daytime, evenings, summer. Complete part-time degree programs offered during daytime, evenings. Adult/continuing education programs available. Career services available to part-time students: individual and group career counseling, individual job placement, employer recruitment on campus. Part-time tuition: $36 per credit hour for area residents, $70 per credit hour for state residents, $104 per credit hour for nonresidents.

Fashion Institute of Technology
New York 10001

Public institution; metropolitan setting. Awards A, B. Barrier-free campus. Total enrollment: 3,930 (all undergraduates); 61% part-time, 80% women, 8% over 25. Total faculty: 650. Library holdings: 81,569 bound volumes, 133 titles on microform, 600 periodical subscriptions, 1,095 records/tapes.

Undergraduate Courses offered for part-time students during daytime, evenings, weekends, summer. Complete part-time degree programs offered during daytime, evenings, weekends, summer. Adult/continuing education programs available. Career services available to part-time students: individual and group career counseling, individual job placement. Part-time tuition: $30 per credit for state residents, $60 per credit for nonresidents.

Five Towns College
Seaford 11783

Proprietary institution; city setting. Awards A. Total enrollment: 404 (all undergraduates); 18% part-time, 35% women, 24% over 25. Total faculty: 32. Library holdings: 11,005 bound volumes, 50 titles on microform, 225 periodical subscriptions, 2,000 records/tapes.

Undergraduate Courses offered for part-time students during daytime, evenings, summer. Complete part-time degree programs offered during daytime. Adult/continuing education programs available. Career services available to part-time students: individual and group career counseling, individual job placement, employer recruitment on campus. Part-time tuition: $145 per credit.

Fordham University
Bronx 10458

Independent-religious institution (undergraduate and graduate). Total enrollment: 13,000. Graduate enrollment: 5,239 (coed; 65% part-time).

Graduate Part-time study available in Graduate School of Arts and Sciences, Graduate School of Education, Graduate School of Religion and Religious Education, Graduate School of Social Service, Graduate School of Business Administration, School of Law. Basic part-time expenses: $190 per credit tuition. Institutional financial aid available to part-time graduate students in Graduate School of Arts and Sciences, Graduate School of Education, Graduate School of Religion and Religious Education, Graduate School of Social Service, Graduate School of Business Administration, School of Law.

New York / Colleges Offering Part-Time Degree Programs

Fordham University at Lincoln Center
New York 10023

Independent-religious instutition; metropolitan setting. Awards B, M, D. Barrier-free campus. Total enrollment: 3,983. Undergraduate enrollment: 2,754; 40% part-time, 66% women. Total faculty: 898. Library holdings: 1.3 million bound volumes, 1 million titles on microform, 4,053 periodical subscriptions.

Undergraduate Courses offered for part-time students during daytime, evenings, summer. Complete part-time degree programs offered during daytime, evenings, summer. Adult/continuing education programs available. Career services available to part-time students: individual and group career counseling, individual job placement, employer recruitment on campus. Part-time tuition: $166 per credit hour.

Fulton-Montgomery Community College
Johnstown 12095

Public institution; rural setting. Awards A. Barrier-free campus. Total enrollment: 1,884 (all undergraduates); 40% part-time, 53% women, 35% over 25. Total faculty: 95. Library holdings: 55,000 bound volumes, 325 periodical subscriptions, 1,050 records/tapes.

Undergraduate Courses offered for part-time students during daytime, evenings, weekends, summer. Complete part-time degree programs offered during daytime, evenings, weekends, summer. Adult/continuing education programs available. Career services available to part-time students: individual career counseling, individual job placement, employer recruitment on campus. Part-time tuition: $35 per credit for state residents, $70 per credit for nonresidents.

Genesee Community College
Batavia 14020

Public institution; small-town setting. Awards A. Barrier-free campus. Total enrollment: 2,550 (all undergraduates); 44% part-time, 59% women, 40% over 25. Total faculty: 155. Library holdings: 60,100 bound volumes, 500 periodical subscriptions, 250 records/tapes.

Undergraduate Courses offered for part-time students during daytime, evenings, summer. Complete part-time degree programs offered during daytime, evenings, summer. Adult/continuing education programs available. Career services available to part-time students: individual and group career counseling, individual job placement, employer recruitment on campus. Part-time tuition: $38 per credit for state residents, $76 per credit for nonresidents.

Hartwick College
Oneonta 13820

Independent institution; small-town setting. Awards B. Total enrollment: 1,440 (all undergraduates); 3% part-time, 57% women, 2% over 25. Total faculty: 118. Library holdings: 172,008 bound volumes, 20,216 titles on microform, 679 periodical subscriptions, 4,200 records/tapes.

Undergraduate Courses offered for part-time students during daytime. Complete part-time degree programs offered during daytime. Career services available to part-time students: individual and group career counseling, individual job placement, employer recruitment on campus. Part-time tuition: $828 per course.

Herkimer County Community College
Herkimer 13350

Public institution; small-town setting. Awards A. Barrier-free campus. Total enrollment: 1,840 (all undergraduates); 24% part-time, 50% women, 10% over 25. Total faculty: 88. Library holdings: 50,000 bound volumes, 500 periodical subscriptions, 1,600 records/tapes.

Undergraduate Courses offered for part-time students during daytime, evenings, summer. Complete part-time degree programs offered during daytime, evenings, summer. Adult/continuing education programs available. Career services available to part-time students: individual and group career counseling, individual job placement, employer recruitment on campus. Part-time tuition: $33 per semester hour for state residents, $66 per semester hour for nonresidents.

Hilbert College
Hamburg 14075

Independent institution; small-town setting. Awards A. Total enrollment: 677 (all undergraduates); 33% part-time, 67% women, 39% over 25. Total faculty: 66. Library holdings: 43,083 bound volumes, 315 periodical subscriptions, 3,681 records/tapes.

Undergraduate Courses offered for part-time students during daytime, evenings, summer. Complete part-time degree programs offered during daytime, evenings, summer. Career services available to part-time students: individual and group career counseling, individual job placement. Part-time tuition: $90 per credit.

Hofstra University
Hempstead 11550

Independent institution; city setting. Awards B, M, D. Barrier-free campus. Total enrollment: 11,535. Undergraduate enrollment: 7,433; 17% part-time, 49% women, 2% over 25. Total faculty: 660. Library holdings: 1 million bound volumes, 3,000 periodical subscriptions.

Undergraduate Courses offered for part-time students during daytime, evenings, summer. Complete part-time degree programs offered during daytime, evenings. Adult/continuing education programs available. Career services available to part-time students: individual and group career counseling, individual job placement. Part-time tuition: $179 per credit.

Graduate Part-time study available in College of Liberal Arts and Sciences, New College, School of Business, School of Education.Basic part-time expenses: $191 per semester hour tuition plus $31 per semester (minimum) fees. Institutional financial aid available to part-time graduate students in College of Liberal Arts and Sciences, New College, School of Business, School of Education.

Hudson Valley Community College
Troy 12180

Public institution; city setting. Awards A. Barrier-free campus. Total enrollment: 8,489 (all undergraduates); 32% part-time, 40% women, 35% over 25. Total faculty: 366. Library holdings: 116,233 bound volumes, 40,256 titles on microform, 686 periodical subscriptions, 3,884 records/tapes.

Undergraduate Courses offered for part-time students during daytime, evenings, summer. Complete part-time degree programs offered during daytime, evenings. External degree and adult/continuing education programs available. Career services available to part-time students: individual and group career counseling, individual job placement, employer recruitment on

Colleges Offering Part-Time Degree Programs / New York

Hudson Valley Community College (continued)
campus. Part-time tuition: $46 per credit for state residents, $102 per credit for nonresidents.

Hunter College
New York 10021
See City University of New York, Hunter College

Institute of Design and Construction
Brooklyn 11201
Independent institution; metropolitan setting. Awards A. Barrier-free campus. Total enrollment: 176 (all undergraduates); 50% part-time, 10% women. Total faculty: 20.
Undergraduate Courses offered for part-time students during daytime, evenings. Complete part-time degree programs offered during daytime, evenings. Career services available to part-time students: individual career counseling, individual job placement. Part-time tuition: $70 per credit.

Iona College
New Rochelle 10801
Independent institution; city setting. Awards B, M. Total enrollment: 6,200. Undergraduate enrollment: 3,618; 10% part-time, 38% women. Total faculty: 353. Library holdings: 200,000 bound volumes, 451 titles on microform, 1,067 periodical subscriptions, 2,622 records/tapes.
Undergraduate Courses offered for part-time students during daytime, evenings, weekends, summer. Complete part-time degree programs offered during daytime, evenings, weekends, summer. Adult/continuing education programs available. Career services available to part-time students: individual and group career counseling, individual job placement, employer recruitment on campus. Part-time tuition: $155 per credit.
Graduate Part-time study available in Graduate Studies.

Ithaca College
Ithaca 14850
Independent institution; small-town setting. Awards B, M. Total enrollment: 5,252. Undergraduate enrollment: 5,095; 3% part-time, 55% women, 3% over 25. Total faculty: 415. Library holdings: 275,000 bound volumes, 100,000 titles on microform, 1,962 periodical subscriptions, 13,100 records/tapes.
Undergraduate Courses offered for part-time students during daytime. Complete part-time degree programs offered during daytime. Adult/continuing education programs available. Career services available to part-time students: individual and group career counseling, individual job placement, employer recruitment on campus. Part-time tuition: $205 per credit hour.
Graduate Part-time study available in Graduate Studies. Basic part-time expenses: $205 per credit tuition.

Jamestown Business College
Jamestown 14701
Proprietary institution; small-town setting. Awards A. Total enrollment: 307 (all undergraduates); 1% part-time, 85% women, 13% over 25. Total faculty: 12.
Undergraduate Courses offered for part-time students during daytime. Complete part-time degree programs offered during daytime. Career services available to part-time students: individual and group career counseling, individual job placement, employer recruitment on campus. Part-time tuition: $112.50 per credit hour.

Jamestown Community College
Jamestown 14701
Public institution; small-town setting. Awards A. Barrier-free campus. Total enrollment: 4,371 (all undergraduates); 54% part-time, 56% women, 50% over 25. Total faculty: 229. Library holdings: 48,549 bound volumes, 14,301 titles on microform, 518 periodical subscriptions, 2,707 records/tapes.
Undergraduate Courses offered for part-time students during daytime, evenings, summer. Complete part-time degree programs offered during daytime, evenings, summer. Adult/continuing education programs available. Career services available to part-time students: individual and group career counseling, individual job placement, employer recruitment on campus. Part-time tuition: $35 per credit for state residents, $70 per credit for nonresidents.

Jefferson Community College
Watertown 13601
Public institution; small-town setting. Awards A. Barrier-free campus. Total enrollment: 1,851 (all undergraduates); 42% part-time, 56% women. Total faculty: 108. Library holdings: 49,468 bound volumes, 50 titles on microform, 216 periodical subscriptions, 1,500 records/tapes.
Undergraduate Courses offered for part-time students during daytime, evenings, summer. Complete part-time degree programs offered during daytime, evenings, summer. Adult/continuing education programs available. Career services available to part-time students: individual career counseling, individual job placement, employer recruitment on campus. Part-time tuition: $39 per credit hour.

Jewish Theological Seminary of America
New York 10027
Independent institution; metropolitan setting. Awards B, M, D. Barrier-free campus. Total enrollment: 485. Undergraduate enrollment: 122; 10% part-time, 45% women. Total faculty: 87. Library holdings: 250,000 bound volumes, 675 periodical subscriptions.
Undergraduate Courses offered for part-time students during daytime. Complete part-time degree programs offered during daytime. Adult/continuing education programs available. Career services available to part-time students: individual job placement. Part-time tuition: $175 per credit.
Graduate Part-time study available in Graduate School. Basic part-time expenses: $145 per credit tuition plus $50 per semester fees. Institutional financial aid available to part-time graduate students in Graduate School.

John Jay College of Criminal Justice
New York 10019
See City University of New York, John Jay College of Criminal Justice

Junior College of Albany
Albany 12208
Independent institution; city setting. Awards A. Total enrollment: 970 (all undergraduates); 8% part-time, 70% women, 5%

over 25. Total faculty: 78. Library holdings: 75,000 bound volumes, 800 periodical subscriptions, 1,500 records/tapes.
Undergraduate Courses offered for part-time students during daytime, evenings, summer. Complete part-time degree programs offered during daytime, evenings, summer. Adult/continuing education programs available. Career services available to part-time students: individual career counseling, employer recruitment on campus. Part-time tuition: $130 per credit.

Katharine Gibbs School
New York 10017
Proprietary institution; metropolitan setting. Awards A. Total enrollment: 200 (all undergraduates); 7% part-time, 98% women. Total faculty: 27.
Undergraduate Courses offered for part-time students during evenings. Complete part-time degree programs offered during evenings. Career services available to part-time students: individual and group career counseling, individual job placement, employer recruitment on campus. Part-time tuition: $150 per credit.

Kingsborough Community College
Brooklyn 11235
See City University of New York, Kingsborough Community College

King's College
Briarcliff Manor 10510
Independent-religious instutition; small-town setting. Awards A, B. Total enrollment: 760 (all undergraduates); 4% part-time, 62% women, 4% over 25. Total faculty: 64. Library holdings: 81,866 bound volumes, 9,615 titles on microform, 569 periodical subscriptions, 961 records/tapes.
Undergraduate Courses offered for part-time students during daytime, summer. Complete part-time degree programs offered during daytime. Adult/continuing education programs available. Career services available to part-time students: individual and group career counseling, individual job placement, employer recruitment on campus. Part-time tuition: $198 per semester hour.

LaGuardia Community College
Long Island City 11101
See City University of New York, Fiorello H LaGuardia Community College

Lehman College
Bronx 10468
See City University of New York, Herbert H Lehman College

Le Moyne College
Syracuse 13214
Independent-religious instutition; metropolitan setting. Awards B. Barrier-free campus. Total enrollment: 1,855 (all undergraduates); 2% part-time, 50% women. Total faculty: 176. Library holdings: 150,000 bound volumes, 1,200 periodical subscriptions, 1,800 records/tapes.
Undergraduate Courses offered for part-time students during daytime, evenings. Complete part-time degree programs offered during daytime, evenings. Adult/continuing education programs available. Career services available to part-time students: individual and group career counseling, individual job placement, employer recruitment on campus. Part-time tuition: $130 per credit hour.

Long Island College Hospital School of Nursing
Brooklyn 11201
Independent institution; metropolitan setting. Awards A. Total enrollment: 158 (all undergraduates); 25% part-time, 85% women. Total faculty: 14. Library holdings: 15,000 bound volumes.
Undergraduate Courses offered for part-time students during daytime, evenings. Complete part-time degree programs offered during daytime, evenings. Career services available to part-time students: employer recruitment on campus. Part-time tuition: $90 per credit.

Long Island University, Brooklyn Campus
Brooklyn 11201
Independent institution; metropolitan setting. Awards A, B, M, D. Total enrollment: 4,974. Undergraduate enrollment: 3,294; 21% part-time, 55% women. Total faculty: 406. Library holdings: 341,000 bound volumes, 1,300 periodical subscriptions.
Undergraduate Courses offered for part-time students during daytime, evenings, weekends, summer. Complete part-time degree programs offered during daytime, evenings, summer. Adult/continuing education programs available. Career services available to part-time students: individual and group career counseling, employer recruitment on campus. Part-time tuition: $180 per credit hour.
Graduate Part-time study available in Arnold and Marie Schwartz College of Pharmacy and Health Sciences, Richard L. Conolly College, School of Business and Public Administration. Degree can be earned exclusively through evening/weekend study in Richard L. Conolly College, School of Business and Public Administration.Basic part-time expenses: $180 per credit tuition plus $37.50 per semester fees. Institutional financial aid available to part-time graduate students in Richard L. Conolly College.

Long Island University, C W Post Campus
Greenvale 11548
Independent institution; small-town setting. Awards A, B, M. Total enrollment: 10,488. Undergraduate enrollment: 7,041; 34% part-time, 54% women, 13% over 25. Total faculty: 705. Library holdings: 960,000 bound volumes, 241,694 titles on microform, 4,636 periodical subscriptions, 18,847 records/tapes.
Undergraduate Courses offered for part-time students during daytime, evenings, weekends, summer. Complete part-time degree programs offered during daytime, evenings, weekends, summer. Adult/continuing education programs available. Career services available to part-time students: individual and group career counseling. Part-time tuition: $171 per credit.
Graduate Part-time study available in College of Arts and Sciences, Palmer School of Library and Information Science, School of Business and Public Administration, School of Communication and Computer Sciences, School of Education, School of Health Sciences, School of Professional Accountancy, School of the Arts. Degree can be earned exclusively through evening/weekend study in School of Health Sciences.Basic part-time expenses: $182 per credit tuition plus $48 per semester (minimum)

Colleges Offering Part-Time Degree Programs / New York

Long Island University, C W Post Campus (continued)
fees. Institutional financial aid available to part-time graduate students in College of Arts and Sciences, Palmer School of Library and Information Science, School of Business and Public Administration, School of Communication and Computer Sciences, School of Education, School of Health Sciences, School of Professional Accountancy, School of the Arts.

Long Island University, Southampton Campus
Southampton 11968

Independent institution; rural setting. Awards B, M. Total enrollment: 1,279. Undergraduate enrollment: 1,210; 10% part-time, 50% women. Total faculty: 107. Library holdings: 130,000 bound volumes, 625 periodical subscriptions, 1,150 records/tapes.

Graduate Part-time study available in Graduate Program in Education. Degree can be earned exclusively through evening/weekend study in Graduate Program in Education. Basic part-time expenses: $182 per credit tuition.

Manhattan College
Riverdale 10471

Independent institution; metropolitan setting. Awards A, B, M. Barrier-free campus. Total enrollment: 4,928. Undergraduate enrollment: 4,101; 9% part-time, 33% women, 2% over 25. Total faculty: 415. Library holdings: 270,415 bound volumes, 1,546 periodical subscriptions.

Undergraduate Courses offered for part-time students during daytime, evenings, weekends, summer. Complete part-time degree programs offered during daytime, evenings, weekends, summer. Adult/continuing education programs available. Career services available to part-time students: individual and group career counseling, individual job placement, employer recruitment on campus. Part-time tuition: $145 per credit hour.

Graduate Part-time study available in Graduate Division. Degree can be earned exclusively through evening/weekend study in Graduate Division. Basic part-time expenses: $155 per credit (minimum) tuition plus $25 per semester fees.

Manhattan Community College
New York 10019

See City University of New York, Borough of Manhattan Community College

Manhattan School of Music
New York 10027

Independent institution; metropolitan setting. Awards B, M, D. Total enrollment: 668. Undergraduate enrollment: 427; 10% part-time, 50% women, 10% over 25. Total faculty: 158. Library holdings: 76,000 bound volumes, 77 periodical subscriptions, 25,000 records/tapes.

Graduate Part-time study available in Graduate Programs in Music. Basic part-time expenses: $240 per credit tuition plus $130 per year fees.

Manhattanville College
Purchase 10577

Independent institution; small-town setting. Awards B, M. Barrier-free campus. Total enrollment: 1,300. Undergraduate enrollment: 950; 7% part-time, 63% women. Total faculty: 170. Library holdings: 250,000 bound volumes, 3,000 titles on microform, 1,100 periodical subscriptions.

Undergraduate Courses offered for part-time students during daytime, evenings, summer. Complete part-time degree programs offered during daytime. Adult/continuing education programs available. Career services available to part-time students: individual and group career counseling, individual job placement, employer recruitment on campus. Part-time tuition: $130 per credit.

Graduate Part-time study available in Graduate Programs. Basic part-time expenses: $138 per credit tuition.

Maria College
Albany 12208

Independent institution; city setting. Awards A. Total enrollment: 1,044 (all undergraduates); 63% part-time, 90% women, 33% over 25. Total faculty: 65. Library holdings: 42,000 bound volumes, 300 titles on microform, 230 periodical subscriptions, 300 records/tapes.

Undergraduate Courses offered for part-time students during daytime, evenings, weekends, summer. Complete part-time degree programs offered during daytime, evenings, weekends. Adult/continuing education programs available. Career services available to part-time students: individual career counseling, individual job placement, employer recruitment on campus. Part-time tuition: $85 per credit hour.

Maria Regina College
Syracuse 13208

Independent-religious instutition; city setting. Awards A. Total enrollment: 632 (all undergraduates); 75% part-time, 100% women. Total faculty: 41. Library holdings: 42,000 bound volumes, 250 periodical subscriptions, 1,600 records/tapes.

Undergraduate Courses offered for part-time students during daytime, evenings, weekends. Complete part-time degree programs offered during daytime, evenings, weekends. Adult/continuing education programs available. Career services available to part-time students: individual and group career counseling, individual job placement, employer recruitment on campus. Part-time tuition: $55 per credit hour.

Marist College
Poughkeepsie 12601

Independent institution; small-town setting. Awards B, M. Barrier-free campus. Total enrollment: 2,631. Undergraduate enrollment: 2,291; 10% part-time, 43% women. Total faculty: 120. Library holdings: 90,000 bound volumes, 500 periodical subscriptions, 2,600 records/tapes.

Undergraduate Courses offered for part-time students during daytime, evenings, summer. Complete part-time degree programs offered during daytime, evenings, summer. Adult/continuing education programs available. Career services available to part-time students: individual and group career counseling, individual job placement, employer recruitment on campus. Part-time tuition: $140 per credit.

Graduate Part-time study available in Graduate Programs. Degree can be earned exclusively through evening/weekend study in Graduate Programs. Basic part-time expenses: $190 per credit tuition. Institutional financial aid available to part-time graduate students in Graduate Programs.

New York / **Colleges Offering Part-Time Degree Programs**

Maryknoll School of Theology
Maryknoll 10545

Independent-religious institution (graduate only). Total enrollment: 148 (coed; 36% part-time). Total faculty: 36. Library holdings: 95,000 bound volumes, 75 microforms.

Graduate Part-time study available in Graduate and Professional Programs. Basic part-time expenses: $100 per credit tuition plus $25 per trimester fees. Institutional financial aid available to part-time graduate students in Graduate and Professional Programs.

Marymount College
Tarrytown 10591

Independent institution; small-town setting. Awards B. Barrier-free campus. Total enrollment: 755 (all undergraduates); 3% part-time, 93% women. Total faculty: 128. Library holdings: 110,000 bound volumes, 750 periodical subscriptions, 900 records/tapes.

Undergraduate Courses offered for part-time students during daytime, weekends, summer. Complete part-time degree programs offered during daytime, weekends, summer. Adult/continuing education programs available. Career services available to part-time students: individual and group career counseling, individual job placement, employer recruitment on campus. Part-time tuition: $194 per semester hour.

Marymount Manhattan College
New York 10021

Independent institution; metropolitan setting. Awards B. Barrier-free campus. Total enrollment: 2,052 (all undergraduates); 64% part-time, 91% women, 55% over 25. Total faculty: 177. Library holdings: 77,210 bound volumes, 15 titles on microform, 689 periodical subscriptions, 9,854 records/tapes.

Undergraduate Courses offered for part-time students during daytime, evenings, weekends, summer. Complete part-time degree programs offered during daytime, evenings, weekends, summer. Adult/continuing education programs available. Career services available to part-time students: individual and group career counseling, individual job placement, employer recruitment on campus. Part-time tuition: $160 per credit hour.

Mater Dei College
Ogdensburg 13669

Independent-religious instutition; rural setting. Awards A. Barrier-free campus. Total enrollment: 444 (all undergraduates); 26% part-time, 69% women, 14% over 25. Total faculty: 47. Library holdings: 47,500 bound volumes, 300 periodical subscriptions.

Undergraduate Courses offered for part-time students during daytime, evenings, summer. Complete part-time degree programs offered during daytime, evenings, summer. Adult/continuing education programs available. Career services available to part-time students: individual and group career counseling, individual job placement. Part-time tuition: $74 per credit hour.

Medaille College
Buffalo 14214

Independent institution; metropolitan setting. Awards A, B. Total enrollment: 755 (all undergraduates); 15% part-time, 55% women, 35% over 25. Total faculty: 68. Library holdings: 85,000 bound volumes, 450 periodical subscriptions.

Undergraduate Courses offered for part-time students during daytime, evenings, summer. Complete part-time degree programs offered during daytime, evenings, summer. Adult/continuing education programs available. Career services available to part-time students: individual and group career counseling, individual job placement, employer recruitment on campus. Part-time tuition: $135 per credit hour.

Medgar Evers College
Brooklyn 11225

See City University of New York, Medgar Evers College

Mercy College
Dobbs Ferry 10522

Independent institution; small-town setting. Awards A, B, M. Barrier-free campus. Total enrollment: 9,206 (all undergraduates); 40% part-time, 49% women. Total faculty: 600. Library holdings: 279,000 bound volumes, 1,000 periodical subscriptions, 7,000 records/tapes.

Undergraduate Courses offered for part-time students during daytime, evenings, weekends, summer. Complete part-time degree programs offered during daytime, evenings, weekends, summer. Adult/continuing education programs available. Career services available to part-time students: individual and group career counseling, individual job placement. Part-time tuition: $112 per credit.

Graduate Part-time study available in Graduate Program in Nursing. Basic part-time expenses: $150 per credit tuition. Institutional financial aid available to part-time graduate students in Graduate Program in Nursing.

Mohawk Valley Community College
Utica 13501

Public institution; city setting. Awards A. Barrier-free campus. Total enrollment: 7,400 (all undergraduates); 42% part-time, 50% women. Total faculty: 427. Library holdings: 65,000 bound volumes, 796 periodical subscriptions, 1,700 records/tapes.

Undergraduate Courses offered for part-time students during daytime, evenings, weekends, summer. Complete part-time degree programs offered during daytime, evenings, weekends, summer. Adult/continuing education programs available. Career services available to part-time students: individual and group career counseling, individual job placement, employer recruitment on campus. Part-time tuition: $38.50 per credit for state residents, $115.50 per credit for nonresidents.

Molloy College
Rockville Centre 11570

Independent-religious instutition; small-town setting. Awards A, B. Barrier-free campus. Total enrollment: 1,690 (all undergraduates); 22% part-time, 90% women. Total faculty: 174. Library holdings: 87,500 bound volumes, 1,255 titles on microform, 845 periodical subscriptions, 5,730 records/tapes.

Undergraduate Courses offered for part-time students during daytime, evenings, weekends, summer. Complete part-time degree programs offered during daytime, evenings, weekends, summer. Adult/continuing education programs available. Career services available to part-time students: individual and group career counseling, individual job placement, employer recruitment on campus. Part-time tuition: $135 per credit.

Colleges Offering Part-Time Degree Programs / New York

Monroe Business Institute
Bronx 10468

Proprietary institution; metropolitan setting. Awards A. Barrier-free campus. Total enrollment: 1,900 (all undergraduates); 10% part-time, 65% women, 50% over 25. Total faculty: 49. Library holdings: 3,783 bound volumes, 45 periodical subscriptions, 10 records/tapes.

Undergraduate Courses offered for part-time students during daytime, evenings. Complete part-time degree programs offered during daytime, evenings. Career services available to part-time students: individual and group career counseling, individual job placement. Part-time tuition: $100 per credit.

Monroe Community College
Rochester 14623

Public institution; metropolitan setting. Awards A. Barrier-free campus. Total enrollment: 11,908 (all undergraduates); 49% part-time, 55% women. Total faculty: 547. Library holdings: 83,928 bound volumes, 865 periodical subscriptions, 1,250 records/tapes.

Undergraduate Courses offered for part-time students during daytime, evenings. Complete part-time degree programs offered during daytime, evenings. Adult/continuing education programs available. Career services available to part-time students: individual and group career counseling, individual job placement, employer recruitment on campus. Part-time tuition: $49 per credit for state residents, $98 per credit for nonresidents.

Mount Saint Alphonsus Seminary
Esopus 12429

Independent-religious institution (graduate only). Total enrollment: 44 (primarily men). Total faculty: 18. Library holdings: 78,000 bound volumes, 8,700 microforms.

Graduate Part-time study available in Graduate and Professional Programs. Basic part-time expenses: $3000 per year tuition.

Mount Saint Mary College
Newburgh 12550

Independent institution; city setting. Awards B, M. Total enrollment: 1,079 (all undergraduates); 25% part-time, 80% women. Total faculty: 86. Library holdings: 89,000 bound volumes, 560 periodical subscriptions, 5,000 records/tapes.

Undergraduate Courses offered for part-time students during daytime, evenings, weekends, summer. Complete part-time degree programs offered during daytime, evenings, weekends, summer. Adult/continuing education programs available. Career services available to part-time students: individual and group career counseling, individual job placement, employer recruitment on campus. Part-time tuition: $137 per credit hour.

Nassau Community College
Garden City 11530

Public institution; small-town setting. Awards A. Barrier-free campus. Total enrollment: 21,961 (all undergraduates); 45% part-time, 55% women. Total faculty: 1,285. Library holdings: 144,667 bound volumes, 448 titles on microform, 851 periodical subscriptions, 7,760 records/tapes.

Undergraduate Courses offered for part-time students during daytime, evenings, weekends, summer. Complete part-time degree programs offered during daytime, evenings, weekends, summer. Adult/continuing education programs available. Career services available to part-time students: individual and group career counseling, individual job placement, employer recruitment on campus. Part-time tuition: $44 per credit for state residents, $88 per credit for nonresidents.

Nazareth College of Rochester
Rochester 14610

Independent institution; metropolitan setting. Awards B, M. Total enrollment: 1,836. Undergraduate enrollment: 1,491; 15% part-time, 81% women, 26% over 25. Total faculty: 151. Library holdings: 200,000 bound volumes, 72,122 titles on microform, 1,250 periodical subscriptions, 4,122 records/tapes.

Undergraduate Courses offered for part-time students during daytime, evenings, weekends, summer. Complete part-time degree programs offered during daytime, evenings, summer. Adult/continuing education programs available. Career services available to part-time students: individual and group career counseling, individual job placement, employer recruitment on campus. Part-time tuition: $148 per credit hour.

Graduate Part-time study available in Graduate Program. Degree can be earned exclusively through evening/weekend study in Graduate Program. Basic part-time expenses: $160 per credit tuition.

New School for Social Research
New York 10011

Independent institution (undergraduate and graduate). Total enrollment: 5,795. Graduate enrollment: 3,040 (coed; 84% part-time).

Graduate Part-time study available in Adult Division, Graduate Faculty of Political and Social Science, Graduate School of Management and Urban Professions. Basic part-time expenses: $245 per credit tuition plus $60 per semester fees. Institutional financial aid available to part-time graduate students in Graduate Faculty of Political and Social Science.

New School for Social Research, Seminar College
New York 10011

Independent institution; metropolitan setting. Awards B. Barrier-free campus. Total enrollment: 150 (all undergraduates); 2% part-time, 53% women, 2% over 25. Total faculty: 25. Library holdings: 3.1 million bound volumes, 24,666 periodical subscriptions.

Undergraduate Courses offered for part-time students during daytime, evenings, weekends, summer. Complete part-time degree programs offered during daytime, evenings, summer. Adult/continuing education programs available. Part-time tuition: $227 per credit.

New School for Social Research, Senior College
New York 10011

Independent institution; metropolitan setting. Awards B. Barrier-free campus. Total enrollment: 150 (all undergraduates); 47% part-time, 65% women, 10% over 25. Total faculty: 2,000.

Undergraduate Courses offered for part-time students during daytime, evenings, weekends, summer. Complete part-time degree programs offered during evenings. Part-time tuition: $227 per credit.

New York City Technical College
Brooklyn 11201

See City University of New York, New York City Technical College

New York Institute of Technology
Old Westbury 11568

Independent institution; small-town setting. Awards A, B, M, D. Barrier-free campus. Total enrollment: 12,621. Undergraduate enrollment: 10,272; 33% part-time, 27% women. Total faculty: 987. Library holdings: 130,064 bound volumes, 202,000 titles on microform, 2,760 periodical subscriptions.

Undergraduate Courses offered for part-time students during daytime, evenings, weekends, summer. Complete part-time degree programs offered during daytime, evenings. External degree and adult/continuing education programs available. Career services available to part-time students: individual and group career counseling, individual job placement, employer recruitment on campus. Part-time tuition: $122 per credit.

Graduate Part-time study available in Graduate Division. Degree can be earned exclusively through evening/weekend study in Graduate Division.Basic part-time expenses: $130 per credit tuition. Institutional financial aid available to part-time graduate students in Graduate Division.

New York Law School
New York 10013

Independent institution (graduate only). Total enrollment: 1,395 (coed; 36% part-time). Total faculty: 103. Library holdings: 270,000 bound volumes, 105,000 microforms.

Graduate Part-time study available in Professional Program. Degree can be earned exclusively through evening/weekend study in Professional Program.Basic part-time expenses: $5400 per year tuition plus $100 per year fees. Institutional financial aid available to part-time graduate students in Professional Program.

New York Medical College
Valhalla 10595

Independent institution (graduate only). Total enrollment: 1,135 (coed). Total faculty: 1,120. Library holdings: 110,000 bound volumes, 4,000 microforms.

Graduate Part-time study available in Graduate School of Basic Medical Sciences, Graduate School of Health Sciences. Degree can be earned exclusively through evening/weekend study in Graduate School of Basic Medical Sciences, Graduate School of Health Sciences.Basic part-time expenses: $180 per credit tuition. Institutional financial aid available to part-time graduate students in Graduate School of Basic Medical Sciences, Graduate School of Health Sciences.

New York School of Interior Design
New York 10022

Independent institution; metropolitan setting. Awards A, B. Total enrollment: 783 (all undergraduates); 66% part-time, 88% women, 31% over 25. Total faculty: 75. Library holdings: 3,201 bound volumes, 73 periodical subscriptions.

Undergraduate Courses offered for part-time students during daytime, evenings, summer. Complete part-time degree programs offered during daytime. Adult/continuing education programs available. Career services available to part-time students: individual career counseling, individual job placement. Part-time tuition: $185 per credit.

New York University
New York 10003

Independent institution; metropolitan setting. Awards A, B, M, D. Barrier-free campus. Total enrollment: 23,000. Undergraduate enrollment: 14,013; 25% part-time, 54% women. Total faculty: 5,422. Library holdings: 3.1 million bound volumes, 36,000 titles on microform, 23,686 periodical subscriptions, 17,000 records/tapes.

Undergraduate Courses offered for part-time students during daytime, evenings, weekends, summer. Complete part-time degree programs offered during daytime, evenings, weekends, summer. Adult/continuing education programs available. Career services available to part-time students: individual and group career counseling, individual job placement, employer recruitment on campus. Part-time tuition: $237 per credit.

Graduate Part-time study available in Graduate School of Arts and Science.Basic part-time expenses: $210 per credit tuition plus $12 per credit fees. Institutional financial aid available to part-time graduate students in Graduate School of Arts and Science.

Niagara County Community College
Sanborn 14132

Public institution; rural setting. Awards A. Barrier-free campus. Total enrollment: 4,657 (all undergraduates); 29% part-time, 53% women. Total faculty: 317. Library holdings: 36,572 bound volumes, 350 periodical subscriptions, 11,912 records/tapes.

Undergraduate Courses offered for part-time students during daytime, evenings, weekends, summer. Complete part-time degree programs offered during daytime, evenings, weekends, summer. External degree and adult/continuing education programs available. Career services available to part-time students: individual and group career counseling. Part-time tuition: $38 per semester hour for state residents, $76 per semester hour for nonresidents.

Niagara University
Niagara University 14109

Independent institution; city setting. Awards A, B, M. Total enrollment: 3,600. Undergraduate enrollment: 2,950; 12% part-time, 55% women, 2% over 25. Total faculty: 240. Library holdings: 225,000 bound volumes, 22,121 titles on microform, 1,426 periodical subscriptions, 908 records/tapes.

Undergraduate Courses offered for part-time students during daytime, evenings, summer. Complete part-time degree programs offered during daytime, evenings, summer. Adult/continuing education programs available. Career services available to part-time students: individual and group career counseling, employer recruitment on campus. Part-time tuition: $132 per credit hour.

Graduate Part-time study available in Graduate Division of Arts and Sciences, Graduate Division of Business Administration, Graduate Division of Education.Basic part-time expenses: $135 per hour tuition plus $10 per semester fees.

North Country Community College
Saranac Lake 12983

Public institution; rural setting. Awards A. Barrier-free campus. Total enrollment: 1,587 (all undergraduates); 50%

Colleges Offering Part-Time Degree Programs / New York

North Country Community College (continued)
part-time, 62% women, 43% over 25. Total faculty: 227. Library holdings: 30,600 bound volumes, 328 periodical subscriptions, 816 records/tapes.

Undergraduate Courses offered for part-time students during daytime, evenings, summer. Complete part-time degree programs offered during daytime, evenings, summer. Adult/continuing education programs available. Career services available to part-time students: individual and group career counseling, individual job placement, employer recruitment on campus. Part-time tuition: $30 per credit for state residents, $60 per credit for nonresidents.

Nyack College
Nyack 10960

Independent-religious instutition; small-town setting. Awards A, B, M. Total enrollment: 870. Undergraduate enrollment: 565; 10% part-time, 57% women. Total faculty: 55. Library holdings: 70,000 bound volumes, 100 periodical subscriptions.

Undergraduate Courses offered for part-time students during daytime, summer. Complete part-time degree programs offered during daytime. Career services available to part-time students: individual career counseling, individual job placement, employer recruitment on campus. Part-time tuition: $178 per credit hour.

Graduate Part-time study available in Alliance Theological Seminary.Basic part-time expenses: $92 per credit tuition plus $28.50 per semester (minimum) fees.

Onondaga Community College
Syracuse 13215

Public institution; metropolitan setting. Awards A. Barrier-free campus. Total enrollment: 7,642 (all undergraduates); 50% part-time, 50% women, 40% over 25. Total faculty: 300. Library holdings: 80,953 bound volumes, 752 periodical subscriptions, 118 records/tapes.

Undergraduate Courses offered for part-time students during daytime, evenings, weekends, summer. Complete part-time degree programs offered during daytime, evenings, weekends, summer. External degree and adult/continuing education programs available. Career services available to part-time students: individual and group career counseling, individual job placement, employer recruitment on campus. Part-time tuition: $45 per credit for state residents, $135 per credit for nonresidents.

Orange County Community College
Middletown 10940

Public institution; small-town setting. Awards A. Total enrollment: 5,415 (all undergraduates); 56% part-time, 60% women, 14% over 25. Total faculty: 260. Library holdings: 78,116 bound volumes, 500 titles on microform, 600 periodical subscriptions, 1,454 records/tapes.

Undergraduate Courses offered for part-time students during daytime, evenings, weekends, summer. Complete part-time degree programs offered during daytime, evenings. External degree and adult/continuing education programs available. Career services available to part-time students: individual and group career counseling, individual job placement, employer recruitment on campus. Part-time tuition: $48 per credit for state residents, $96 per credit for nonresidents.

Pace University
New York 10038

Independent institution; metropolitan setting. Awards A, B, M, D. Barrier-free campus. Total enrollment: 10,498. Undergraduate enrollment: 6,684; 39% part-time, 58% women, 44% over 25. Total faculty: 765. Library holdings: 311,697 bound volumes, 23,150 titles on microform, 1,360 periodical subscriptions.

Undergraduate Courses offered for part-time students during daytime, evenings, weekends, summer. Complete part-time degree programs offered during daytime, evenings. Adult/continuing education programs available. Career services available to part-time students: individual and group career counseling, individual job placement, employer recruitment on campus. Part-time tuition: $150 per credit.

Graduate Part-time study available in Dyson College of Arts and Sciences, Lienhard School of Nursing (Pleasantville/Briarcliffe), Lubin Graduate School of Business, School of Education, School of Law (White Plains).Basic part-time expenses: $195 per credit tuition plus $5 per credit fees. Institutional financial aid available to part-time graduate students in Dyson College of Arts and Sciences, Lienhard School of Nursing (Pleasantville/Briarcliffe), Lubin Graduate School of Business, School of Education, School of Law (White Plains).

Pace University, College of White Plains
White Plains 10603

Independent institution; city setting. Awards A, B, M. Total enrollment: 3,455. Undergraduate enrollment: 1,170; 21% part-time, 63% women, 39% over 25. Total faculty: 125. Library holdings: 75,229 bound volumes, 6,723 titles on microform, 806 periodical subscriptions.

Undergraduate Courses offered for part-time students during daytime, evenings, weekends, summer. Complete part-time degree programs offered during daytime, evenings. Adult/continuing education programs available. Career services available to part-time students: individual and group career counseling, individual job placement, employer recruitment on campus. Part-time tuition: $150 per credit.

Pace University–Pleasantville/Briarcliff
Pleasantville 10570

Independent institution; small-town setting. Awards A, B, M, D. Total enrollment: 4,138. Undergraduate enrollment: 3,746; 22% part-time, 57% women, 27% over 25. Total faculty: 520. Library holdings: 207,178 bound volumes, 11,018 titles on microform, 830 periodical subscriptions.

Undergraduate Courses offered for part-time students during daytime, evenings, weekends, summer. Complete part-time degree programs offered during daytime, evenings, weekends, summer. Adult/continuing education programs available. Career services available to part-time students: individual and group career counseling, individual job placement, employer recruitment on campus. Part-time tuition: $150 per credit.

Polytechnic Institute of New York, Brooklyn Campus
Brooklyn 11201

Independent institution; metropolitan setting. Awards B, M, D. Total enrollment: 3,191. Undergraduate enrollment: 1,882; 14% part-time, 13% women. Total faculty: 384. Library holdings: 273,000 bound volumes, 1,261 periodical subscriptions.

Undergraduate Courses offered for part-time students during daytime, evenings, summer. Complete part-time degree programs offered during daytime, evenings, summer. Career ser-

New York / **Colleges Offering Part-Time Degree Programs**

vices available to part-time students: group career counseling, individual job placement, employer recruitment on campus. Part-time tuition: $245 per credit.

Polytechnic Institute of New York, Farmingdale Campus
Farmingdale 11735

Independent institution; small-town setting. Awards B, M, D. Total enrollment: 1,383. Undergraduate enrollment: 711; 11% part-time, 13% women. Total faculty: 384. Library holdings: 32,000 bound volumes.

Undergraduate Courses offered for part-time students during daytime, evenings, summer. Complete part-time degree programs offered during daytime, evenings, summer. Career services available to part-time students: group career counseling, individual job placement, employer recruitment on campus. Part-time tuition: $245 per credit.

Pratt Institute
Brooklyn 11205

Independent institution; metropolitan setting. Awards A, B, M. Total enrollment: 4,062. Undergraduate enrollment: 3,130; 10% part-time, 38% women. Total faculty: 537. Library holdings: 185,000 bound volumes, 16,000 titles on microform, 680 periodical subscriptions, 3,200 records/tapes.

Undergraduate Courses offered for part-time students during daytime, evenings, summer. Complete part-time degree programs offered during daytime, evenings, summer. Adult/continuing education programs available. Career services available to part-time students: individual and group career counseling, individual job placement, employer recruitment on campus. Part-time tuition: $208 per credit.

Graduate Part-time study available in Graduate School of Library and Information Science, School of Architecture, School of Art and Design, School of Liberal Arts and Sciences. Degree can be earned exclusively through evening/weekend study in Graduate School of Library and Information Science.Basic part-time expenses: $236 per credit tuition. Institutional financial aid available to part-time graduate students in Graduate School of Library and Information Science, School of Architecture, School of Art and Design, School of Liberal Arts and Sciences.

Queensborough Community College
Bayside 11364

See City University of New York, Queensborough Community College

Queens College
Flushing 11367

See City University of New York, Queens College

Rensselaer Polytechnic Institute
Troy 12180

Independent institution; city setting. Awards B, M, D. Total enrollment: 6,667. Undergraduate enrollment: 4,701; 0% part-time, 20% women. Total faculty: 638. Library holdings: 300,000 bound volumes, 60 titles on microform, 3,800 periodical subscriptions, 2,016 records/tapes.

Undergraduate Courses offered for part-time students during daytime, evenings, summer. Complete part-time degree programs offered during daytime. Adult/continuing education programs available. Part-time tuition: $275 per credit hour.

Graduate Part-time study available in Graduate School. Degree can be earned exclusively through evening/weekend study in Graduate School.Basic part-time expenses: $275 per credit tuition.

Roberts Wesleyan College
Rochester 14624

Independent-religious instutition; metropolitan setting. Awards A, B. Total enrollment: 668 (all undergraduates); 6% part-time, 68% women, 6% over 25. Total faculty: 85. Library holdings: 85,000 bound volumes, 4,900 titles on microform, 442 periodical subscriptions, 1,879 records/tapes.

Undergraduate Courses offered for part-time students during daytime, evenings, summer. Complete part-time degree programs offered during daytime, evenings, summer. Adult/continuing education programs available. Career services available to part-time students: individual career counseling, individual job placement, employer recruitment on campus. Part-time tuition: $90 per semester hour.

Rochester Business Institute
Rochester 14604

Proprietary institution; metropolitan setting. Awards A. Barrier-free campus. Total enrollment: 332 (all undergraduates); 10% part-time, 85% women. Total faculty: 16. Library holdings: 4,200 bound volumes, 26 periodical subscriptions.

Undergraduate Courses offered for part-time students during daytime, evenings. Complete part-time degree programs offered during daytime. Adult/continuing education programs available. Part-time tuition: $80 per credit hour.

Rochester Institute of Technology
Rochester 14623

Independent institution; metropolitan setting. Awards A, B, M. Total enrollment: 16,005. Undergraduate enrollment: 14,476; 10% part-time, 42% women. Total faculty: 1,170. Library holdings: 300,000 bound volumes, 8,579 periodical subscriptions.

Undergraduate Courses offered for part-time students during daytime, evenings, summer. Complete part-time degree programs offered during daytime, evenings, summer. External degree and adult/continuing education programs available. Career services available to part-time students: individual career counseling, individual job placement, employer recruitment on campus. Part-time tuition: $177 per quarter hour.

Graduate Part-time study available in Graduate Studies.Basic part-time expenses: $188 per credit hour tuition.

Rockland Community College
Suffern 10901

Public institution; small-town setting. Awards A. Barrier-free campus. Total enrollment: 8,386 (all undergraduates); 54% part-time, 54% women, 40% over 25. Total faculty: 328. Library holdings: 120,000 bound volumes, 30,000 titles on microform, 740 periodical subscriptions, 2,500 records/tapes.

Undergraduate Courses offered for part-time students during daytime, evenings, weekends, summer. Complete part-time degree programs offered during daytime, evenings, weekends, summer. External degree and adult/continuing education programs available. Career services available to part-time students:

Colleges Offering Part-Time Degree Programs / New York

Rockland Community College (continued)

individual and group career counseling, individual job placement, employer recruitment on campus. Part-time tuition and fees per semester (1 to 11 semester hours) range from $51 to $534 for state residents, $97 to $1040 for nonresidents.

Russell Sage College
Troy 12180

Independent institution; city setting. Awards B, M. Total enrollment: 1,430. Undergraduate enrollment: 1,400; 2% part-time, 100% women, 20% over 25. Total faculty: 130. Library holdings: 136,936 bound volumes, 7,639 titles on microform, 1,785 periodical subscriptions, 1,800 records/tapes.

Undergraduate Courses offered for part-time students during daytime, evenings. Complete part-time degree programs offered during daytime, evenings. Adult/continuing education programs available. Career services available to part-time students: individual and group career counseling, individual job placement, employer recruitment on campus. Part-time tuition: $205 per credit.

Graduate Part-time study available in Graduate Studies. Basic part-time expenses: $143 per credit (minimum) tuition.

Saint Bernard's Institute
Rochester 14620

Independent-religious institution (graduate only). Total enrollment: 115 (coed; 97% part-time). Total faculty: 12.

Graduate Part-time study available in Graduate and Professional Programs. Degree can be earned exclusively through evening/weekend study in Graduate and Professional Programs. Institutional financial aid available to part-time graduate students in Graduate and Professional Programs.

St Bonaventure University
St Bonaventure 14778

Independent-religious instutition; rural setting. Awards B, M, D. Total enrollment: 2,740. Undergraduate enrollment: 2,271; 1% part-time, 49% women. Total faculty: 185. Library holdings: 255,000 bound volumes, 1,652 periodical subscriptions, 1,085 records/tapes.

Undergraduate Courses offered for part-time students during daytime, evenings, summer. Complete part-time degree programs offered during daytime, evenings, summer. Adult/continuing education programs available. Career services available to part-time students: individual and group career counseling, individual job placement, employer recruitment on campus. Part-time tuition: $140 per credit hour.

Graduate Part-time study available in Graduate School. Degree can be earned exclusively through evening/weekend study in Graduate School. Basic part-time expenses: $140 per credit tuition. Institutional financial aid available to part-time graduate students in Graduate School.

St Francis College
Brooklyn 11201

Independent-religious instutition; metropolitan setting. Awards A, B. Total enrollment: 2,631 (all undergraduates); 38% part-time, 52% women. Total faculty: 125.

Undergraduate Courses offered for part-time students during daytime, evenings, weekends, summer. Complete part-time degree programs offered during daytime, evenings, weekends, summer. Adult/continuing education programs available. Career services available to part-time students: individual and group career counseling, individual job placement, employer recruitment on campus. Part-time tuition: $126 per credit hour.

St John Fisher College
Rochester 14618

Independent institution; metropolitan setting. Awards B, M. Barrier-free campus. Total enrollment: 1,853. Undergraduate enrollment: 1,783; 14% part-time, 50% women, 13% over 25. Total faculty: 182. Library holdings: 140,000 bound volumes, 10,000 titles on microform, 700 periodical subscriptions, 6,000 records/tapes.

Undergraduate Courses offered for part-time students during daytime, evenings, weekends, summer. Complete part-time degree programs offered during daytime, evenings, summer. Adult/continuing education programs available. Career services available to part-time students: individual and group career counseling, individual job placement, employer recruitment on campus. Part-time tuition: $145 per credit hour.

St John's University
Jamaica 11439

Independent-religious instutition; metropolitan setting. Awards A, B, M, D. Barrier-free campus. Total enrollment: 19,287. Undergraduate enrollment: 14,300; 13% part-time, 49% women. Total faculty: 930. Library holdings: 1.1 million bound volumes, 5,402 periodical subscriptions, 31,203 records/tapes.

Undergraduate Courses offered for part-time students during daytime, evenings, weekends. Complete part-time degree programs offered during daytime, evenings, weekends. Adult/continuing education programs available. Career services available to part-time students: individual career counseling, individual job placement, employer recruitment on campus. Part-time tuition: $133 per credit.

Graduate Part-time study available in College of Business Administration, College of Pharmacy and Allied Health Professions, Graduate School of Arts and Sciences, Institute for Advanced Studies in Catholic Doctrine, School of Education and Human Services, School of Law. Basic part-time expenses: $167 per credit tuition. Institutional financial aid available to part-time graduate students in College of Business Administration, Graduate School of Arts and Sciences, School of Education and Human Services, School of Law.

St Joseph's College
Brooklyn 11205

Independent institution; metropolitan setting. Awards B. Barrier-free campus. Total enrollment: 1,050 (all undergraduates); 54% part-time, 80% women, 35% over 25. Total faculty: 113. Library holdings: 132,000 bound volumes, 2,360 titles on microform, 600 periodical subscriptions.

Undergraduate Courses offered for part-time students during daytime, evenings, weekends, summer. Complete part-time degree programs offered during daytime, evenings, weekends, summer. Adult/continuing education programs available. Career services available to part-time students: individual and group career counseling, individual job placement, employer recruitment on campus. Part-time tuition: $118 per credit.

St Joseph's College, Suffolk Campus
Patchogue 11772

Independent institution; small-town setting. Awards B. Barrier-free campus. Total enrollment: 1,397 (all undergraduates); 44%

part-time, 83% women, 20% over 25. Total faculty: 110. Library holdings: 55,000 bound volumes, 2,400 titles on microform, 360 periodical subscriptions, 2,752 records/tapes.

Undergraduate Courses offered for part-time students during daytime, evenings, weekends, summer. Complete part-time degree programs offered during daytime, evenings. Adult/continuing education programs available. Career services available to part-time students: individual and group career counseling, individual job placement, employer recruitment on campus. Part-time tuition: $118 per credit.

St Lawrence University
Canton 13617

Independent institution; rural setting. Awards B, M. Barrier-free campus. Total enrollment: 2,384. Undergraduate enrollment: 2,318; 1% part-time, 50% women. Total faculty: 180. Library holdings: 312,500 bound volumes, 168,000 titles on microform, 1,990 periodical subscriptions, 1,700 records/tapes.

Graduate Part-time study available in Graduate Programs in Education. Basic part-time expenses: $175 per credit hour tuition plus $10 per semester fees. Institutional financial aid available to part-time graduate students in Graduate Programs in Education.

St Thomas Aquinas College
Sparkill 10976

Independent institution; small-town setting. Awards A, B. Total enrollment: 1,566 (all undergraduates); 35% part-time, 50% women, 15% over 25. Total faculty: 67. Library holdings: 90,000 bound volumes, 21,000 titles on microform, 600 periodical subscriptions, 2,563 records/tapes.

Undergraduate Courses offered for part-time students during daytime, evenings, weekends, summer. Complete part-time degree programs offered during daytime, evenings, summer. Adult/continuing education programs available. Career services available to part-time students: individual and group career counseling, individual job placement, employer recruitment on campus. Part-time tuition: $115 per semester hour.

Sarah Lawrence College
Bronxville 10708

Independent institution; small-town setting. Awards B, M. Total enrollment: 987. Undergraduate enrollment: 828; 6% part-time, 80% women. Total faculty: 132. Library holdings: 288,000 bound volumes, 3,000 titles on microform, 1,135 periodical subscriptions, 12,300 records/tapes.

Undergraduate Courses offered for part-time students during daytime, summer. Complete part-time degree programs offered during daytime, summer. Adult/continuing education programs available. Career services available to part-time students: individual and group career counseling, individual job placement, employer recruitment on campus. Part-time tuition: $333 per credit.

Graduate Part-time study available in Graduate Studies. Basic part-time expenses: $278 per credit tuition plus $12.50 per semester fees. Institutional financial aid available to part-time graduate students in Graduate Studies.

Schenectady County Community College
Schenectady 12305

Public institution; city setting. Awards A. Barrier-free campus. Total enrollment: 1,762 (all undergraduates); 36% part-time, 55% women, 37% over 25. Total faculty: 174. Library holdings: 50,834 bound volumes, 179 titles on microform, 402 periodical subscriptions, 3,280 records/tapes.

Undergraduate Courses offered for part-time students during daytime, evenings, weekends, summer. Complete part-time degree programs offered during daytime, evenings. Adult/continuing education programs available. Career services available to part-time students: individual and group career counseling, individual job placement, employer recruitment on campus. Part-time tuition: $45 per credit hour for state residents, $90 per credit hour for nonresidents.

School of Visual Arts
New York 10010

Proprietary institution; metropolitan setting. Awards B, M. Barrier-free campus. Total enrollment: 2,506. Undergraduate enrollment: 2,475; 8% part-time, 48% women. Total faculty: 603. Library holdings: 40,000 bound volumes, 200 periodical subscriptions, 600 records/tapes.

Undergraduate Courses offered for part-time students during daytime, evenings, weekends, summer. Complete part-time degree programs offered during daytime, evenings. Adult/continuing education programs available. Career services available to part-time students: individual career counseling, individual job placement. Part-time tuition: $95 per credit.

Seminary of the Immaculate Conception
Huntington 11743

Independent-religious institution (graduate only). Total enrollment: 199 (coed; 63% part-time). Total faculty: 33. Library holdings: 47,000 bound volumes.

Graduate Part-time study available in Graduate and Professional Programs. Basic part-time expenses: $100 per credit tuition.

Siena College
Loudonville 12211

Independent-religious instutition; city setting. Awards B. Barrier-free campus. Total enrollment: 2,939 (all undergraduates); 22% part-time, 47% women, 2% over 25. Total faculty: 212. Library holdings: 190,000 bound volumes, 1,262 periodical subscriptions.

Undergraduate Courses offered for part-time students during daytime, evenings, weekends, summer. Complete part-time degree programs offered during daytime, evenings, summer. Adult/continuing education programs available. Career services available to part-time students: individual and group career counseling, individual job placement, employer recruitment on campus. Part-time tuition: $95 per credit.

Skidmore College
Saratoga Springs 12866

Independent institution; small-town setting. Awards B. Total enrollment: 2,142 (all undergraduates); 1% part-time, 65% women, 1% over 25. Total faculty: 228. Library holdings: 300,000 bound volumes, 55,000 titles on microform, 1,395 periodical subscriptions, 6,400 records/tapes.

Undergraduate Courses offered for part-time students during daytime, summer. Complete part-time degree programs offered during daytime, summer. External degree and adult/continuing education programs available. Career services available to part-time students: individual and group career counseling, individu-

Colleges Offering Part-Time Degree Programs / New York

Skidmore College (continued)

al job placement, employer recruitment on campus. Part-time tuition: $985 per unit.

Southampton Campus of Long Island University
Southampton 11968

See Long Island University, Southampton Campus

State University of New York Agricultural and Technical College at Alfred
Alfred 14802

Public institution; rural setting. Awards A. Total enrollment: 4,168 (all undergraduates); 4% part-time, 43% women, 3% over 25. Total faculty: 225. Library holdings: 51,802 bound volumes, 11,135 titles on microform, 760 periodical subscriptions, 430 records/tapes.

Undergraduate Courses offered for part-time students during daytime, weekends, summer. Complete part-time degree programs offered during daytime, weekends. Adult/continuing education programs available. Career services available to part-time students: individual career counseling. Part-time tuition: $45 per credit hour for state residents, $107 per credit hour for nonresidents.

State University of New York Agricultural and Technical College at Canton
Canton 13617

Public institution; small-town setting. Awards A. Total enrollment: 2,508 (all undergraduates); 11% part-time, 46% women, 21% over 25. Total faculty: 122. Library holdings: 38,940 bound volumes, 83 titles on microform, 359 periodical subscriptions, 562 records/tapes.

Undergraduate Courses offered for part-time students during daytime, evenings. Complete part-time degree programs offered during daytime, evenings. Adult/continuing education programs available. Career services available to part-time students: individual and group career counseling, individual job placement, employer recruitment on campus. Part-time tuition: $45 per credit for state residents, $105 per credit for nonresidents.

State University of New York Agricultural and Technical College at Cobleskill
Cobleskill 12043

Public institution; rural setting. Awards A. Total enrollment: 2,642 (all undergraduates); 6% part-time, 54% women, 5% over 25. Total faculty: 142. Library holdings: 77,000 bound volumes, 508 periodical subscriptions, 2,968 records/tapes.

Undergraduate Courses offered for part-time students during daytime, evenings, summer. Complete part-time degree programs offered during daytime, evenings, summer. Adult/continuing education programs available. Career services available to part-time students: individual and group career counseling, individual job placement, employer recruitment on campus. Part-time tuition: $45 per credit for state residents, $105 per credit for nonresidents.

State University of New York Agricultural and Technical College at Delhi
Delhi 13753

Public institution; small-town setting. Awards A. Total enrollment: 2,274 (all undergraduates); 1% part-time, 42% women. Total faculty: 135. Library holdings: 50,000 bound volumes, 500 periodical subscriptions.

Undergraduate Courses offered for part-time students during daytime. Complete part-time degree programs offered during daytime. Adult/continuing education programs available. Career services available to part-time students: individual and group career counseling, individual job placement, employer recruitment on campus. Part-time tuition: $45 per credit hour for state residents, $105 per credit hour for nonresidents.

State University of New York Agricultural and Technical College at Farmingdale
Farmingdale 11735

Public institution; small-town setting. Awards A. Barrier-free campus. Total enrollment: 6,229 (all undergraduates); 13% part-time, 51% women. Total faculty: 404. Library holdings: 104,365 bound volumes, 390 titles on microform, 1,028 periodical subscriptions, 18,092 records/tapes.

Undergraduate Courses offered for part-time students during daytime, evenings, weekends, summer. Complete part-time degree programs offered during daytime, evenings. External degree and adult/continuing education programs available. Career services available to part-time students: individual and group career counseling, individual job placement. Part-time tuition: $45 per credit for state residents, $105 per credit for nonresidents.

State University of New York Agricultural and Technical College at Morrisville
Morrisville 13408

Public institution; rural setting. Awards A. Barrier-free campus. Total enrollment: 3,125 (all undergraduates); 11% part-time, 44% women, 15% over 25. Total faculty: 150. Library holdings: 75,177 bound volumes, 532 periodical subscriptions, 2,012 records/tapes.

Undergraduate Courses offered for part-time students during daytime, evenings, summer. Complete part-time degree programs offered during daytime, evenings. Adult/continuing education programs available. Career services available to part-time students: individual and group career counseling, individual job placement, employer recruitment on campus. Part-time tuition: $45 per credit for state residents, $105 per credit for nonresidents.

State University of New York at Albany
Albany 12222

Public institution; city setting. Awards B, M, D. Barrier-free campus. Total enrollment: 16,000. Undergraduate enrollment: 11,300; 4% part-time, 51% women, 6% over 25. Total faculty: 869. Library holdings: 1 million bound volumes, 7,241 periodical subscriptions, 3,542 records/tapes.

Undergraduate Courses offered for part-time students during daytime, evenings, summer. Complete part-time degree programs offered during daytime, evenings. Adult/continuing education programs available. Career services available to part-time students: individual and group career counseling, individual job placement, employer recruitment on campus. Part-time tuition: $45 per credit for state residents, $107 per credit for nonresidents.

Graduate Part-time study available in College of Humanities and Fine Arts, College of Science and Mathematics, College of Social and Behavioral Sciences, Nelson A. Rockefeller College of Public Affairs and Policy, School of Business, School of Education, School of Library and Information Science. Degree can be earned exclusively through evening/weekend study in College of Humanities and Fine Arts, College of Science and Mathematics, College of Social and Behavioral Sciences, Nelson A. Rockefeller College of Public Affairs and Policy, School of Business, School of Education, School of Library and Information Science. Basic part-time expenses: $90 per credit tuition plus $0.85 per credit fees for state residents, $156 per credit tuition plus $0.85 per credit fees for nonresidents.

State University of New York at Binghamton
Binghamton 13901

Public institution; city setting. Awards B, M, D. Barrier-free campus. Total enrollment: 10,701. Undergraduate enrollment: 8,569; 9% part-time, 54% women, 9% over 25. Total faculty: 708. Library holdings: 1.1 million bound volumes, 598,135 titles on microform, 13,729 periodical subscriptions.

Undergraduate Courses offered for part-time students during daytime, evenings, summer. Complete part-time degree programs offered during daytime, evenings, summer. External degree and adult/continuing education programs available. Career services available to part-time students: individual and group career counseling, individual job placement, employer recruitment on campus. Part-time tuition: $45 per credit hour for state residents, $105 per credit hour for nonresidents.

Graduate Part-time study available in Graduate School. Degree can be earned exclusively through evening/weekend study in Graduate School. Basic part-time expenses: $90 per credit tuition plus $2.35 per credit fees for state residents, $156 per credit tuition plus $2.35 per credit fees for nonresidents. Institutional financial aid available to part-time graduate students in Graduate School.

State University of New York at Buffalo
Buffalo 14260

Public institution; metropolitan setting. Awards B, M, D. Total enrollment: 26,406. Undergraduate enrollment: 18,468; 24% part-time, 43% women. Total faculty: 1,957. Library holdings: 2.2 million bound volumes, 2.5 million titles on microform, 13,419 periodical subscriptions, 20,000 records/tapes.

Undergraduate Courses offered for part-time students during daytime, evenings, weekends, summer. Complete part-time degree programs offered during daytime, evenings, weekends, summer. Adult/continuing education programs available. Career services available to part-time students: individual and group career counseling, employer recruitment on campus. Part-time tuition: $45 per credit hour for state residents, $105 per credit hour for nonresidents.

Graduate Part-time study available in Faculty of Arts and Letters, Faculty of Educational Studies, Faculty of Engineering and Applied Sciences, Faculty of Natural Sciences and Mathematics, Faculty of Social Sciences, Roswell Park Graduate Division, School of Architecture and Environmental Design, School of Dentistry, School of Health Related Professions, School of Information and Library Studies, School of Management, School of Nursing, School of Social Work. Degree can be earned exclusively through evening/weekend study in School of Management. Basic part-time expenses: $90 per credit tuition for state residents, $156 per credit tuition for nonresidents.

State University of New York at Stony Brook
Stony Brook 11794

Public institution; small-town setting. Awards B, M, D. Total enrollment: 14,982. Undergraduate enrollment: 11,027; 6% part-time, 49% women, 13% over 25. Total faculty: 1,345. Library holdings: 1.4 million bound volumes, 1.9 million titles on microform, 16,985 periodical subscriptions.

Undergraduate Courses offered for part-time students during daytime, evenings, summer. Complete part-time degree programs offered during daytime, evenings, summer. Adult/continuing education programs available. Career services available to part-time students: individual and group career counseling, individual job placement, employer recruitment on campus. Part-time tuition: $45 per credit for state residents, $105 per credit for nonresidents.

Graduate Part-time study available in Graduate School, School of Allied Health Professions, School of Basic Health Sciences, School of Social Welfare, Center for Continuing Education. Basic part-time expenses: $90 per credit tuition plus $0.85 per credit fees for state residents, $156 per credit tuition plus $0.85 per credit fees for nonresidents.

State University of New York College at Brockport
Brockport 14420

Public institution; small-town setting. Awards B, M. Total enrollment: 7,234. Undergraduate enrollment: 6,043; 9% part-time, 50% women, 16% over 25. Total faculty: 468. Library holdings: 404,600 bound volumes, 1.1 million titles on microform, 3,434 periodical subscriptions, 500 records/tapes.

Undergraduate Courses offered for part-time students during daytime, evenings, weekends, summer. Complete part-time degree programs offered during daytime, evenings, weekends, summer. External degree and adult/continuing education programs available. Career services available to part-time students: individual and group career counseling, individual job placement, employer recruitment on campus. Part-time tuition: $45 per credit hour for state residents, $105 per credit hour for nonresidents.

Graduate Part-time study available in School of Arts and Performance, School of Letters and Sciences, School of Social Professions. Degree can be earned exclusively through evening/weekend study in School of Arts and Performance, School of Letters and Sciences, School of Social Professions. Basic part-time expenses: $90 per credit tuition plus $4.92 per credit fees for state residents, $156 per credit tuition plus $4.92 per credit fees for nonresidents.

State University of New York College at Buffalo
Buffalo 14222

Public institution; metropolitan setting. Awards B, M. Total enrollment: 11,660. Undergraduate enrollment: 10,238; 18% part-time, 55% women. Total faculty: 573. Library holdings: 390,000 bound volumes, 419,400 titles on microform, 2,300 periodical subscriptions, 7,600 records/tapes.

Undergraduate Courses offered for part-time students during daytime, evenings, weekends, summer. Complete part-time degree programs offered during daytime, evenings. Adult/continuing education programs available. Career services available

Colleges Offering Part-Time Degree Programs / New York

State University of New York College at Buffalo (continued)

to part-time students: individual and group career counseling, individual job placement, employer recruitment on campus. Part-time tuition: $45 per semester hour for state residents, $105 per semester hour for nonresidents.

Graduate Part-time study available in Graduate Studies, Research, and Lifelong Learning. Degree can be earned exclusively through evening/weekend study in Graduate Studies, Research, and Lifelong Learning. Basic part-time expenses: $90 per credit tuition plus $0.85 per credit fees for state residents, $156 per credit tuition plus $0.85 per credit fees for nonresidents. Institutional financial aid available to part-time graduate students in Graduate Studies, Research, and Lifelong Learning.

State University of New York College at Cortland
Cortland 13045

Public institution; small-town setting. Awards B, M. Total enrollment: 6,260. Undergraduate enrollment: 5,495; 4% part-time, 59% women, 5% over 25. Total faculty: 347. Library holdings: 212,942 bound volumes, 1,515 periodical subscriptions, 7,605 records/tapes.

Undergraduate Courses offered for part-time students during daytime, evenings, summer. Complete part-time degree programs offered during daytime. Adult/continuing education programs available. Career services available to part-time students: individual and group career counseling, individual job placement, employer recruitment on campus. Part-time tuition: $45 per credit for state residents, $107 per credit for nonresidents.

Graduate Part-time study available in Graduate Studies. Basic part-time expenses: $90 per credit hour tuition plus $14.55 per semester (minimum) fees for state residents, $156 per credit hour tuition plus $14.55 per semester (minimum) fees for nonresidents. Institutional financial aid available to part-time graduate students in Graduate Studies.

State University of New York College at Fredonia
Fredonia 14063

Public institution; small-town setting. Awards B, M. Total enrollment: 5,161. Undergraduate enrollment: 4,897; 11% part-time, 50% women. Total faculty: 238. Library holdings: 350,000 bound volumes, 730,000 titles on microform, 2,044 periodical subscriptions, 12,600 records/tapes.

Undergraduate Courses offered for part-time students during daytime, evenings, summer. Complete part-time degree programs offered during daytime, evenings, summer. Adult/continuing education programs available. Career services available to part-time students: individual and group career counseling, individual job placement, employer recruitment on campus. Part-time tuition: $45 per semester hour for state residents, $105 per semester hour for nonresidents.

Graduate Part-time study available in Graduate Studies. Basic part-time expenses: $90 per credit tuition plus $4.10 per credit fees for state residents, $156 per credit tuition plus $4.10 per credit fees for nonresidents.

State University of New York College at Geneseo
Geneseo 14454

Public institution; rural setting. Awards B, M. Barrier-free campus. Total enrollment: 5,314. Undergraduate enrollment: 4,961; 3% part-time, 66% women, 3% over 25. Total faculty: 284. Library holdings: 372,614 bound volumes, 565,631 titles on microform, 2,460 periodical subscriptions.

Undergraduate Courses offered for part-time students during daytime, evenings, weekends, summer. Complete part-time degree programs offered during daytime, evenings, weekends. Career services available to part-time students: individual and group career counseling, individual job placement, employer recruitment on campus. Part-time tuition: $45 per semester hour for state residents, $107 per semester hour for nonresidents.

Graduate Part-time study available in Graduate Studies and Research. Degree can be earned exclusively through evening/weekend study in Graduate Studies and Research. Basic part-time expenses: $90 per credit tuition plus $0.85 per credit fees for state residents, $156 per credit tuition plus $0.85 per credit fees for nonresidents.

State University of New York College at New Paltz
New Paltz 12561

Public institution; rural setting. Awards B, M. Total enrollment: 7,515. Undergraduate enrollment: 6,129; 22% part-time, 55% women. Total faculty: 391. Library holdings: 350,000 bound volumes, 560,000 titles on microform, 1,560 periodical subscriptions.

Undergraduate Courses offered for part-time students during daytime, evenings, summer. Complete part-time degree programs offered during daytime, evenings, summer. Adult/continuing education programs available. Career services available to part-time students: individual and group career counseling, individual job placement, employer recruitment on campus. Part-time tuition: $45 per credit for state residents, $105 per credit for nonresidents.

Graduate Part-time study available in Graduate Studies. Degree can be earned exclusively through evening/weekend study in Graduate Studies. Basic part-time expenses: $90 per credit tuition plus $0.85 per credit fees for state residents, $156 per credit tuition plus $0.85 per credit fees for nonresidents.

State University of New York College at Old Westbury
Old Westbury 11568

Public institution; small-town setting. Awards B. Barrier-free campus. Total enrollment: 3,865 (all undergraduates); 29% part-time, 53% women, 54% over 25. Total faculty: 141. Library holdings: 150,000 bound volumes, 200,000 titles on microform, 1,500 periodical subscriptions.

Undergraduate Courses offered for part-time students during daytime, evenings, summer. Complete part-time degree programs offered during daytime, evenings. Career services available to part-time students: individual and group career counseling, individual job placement. Part-time tuition: $45 per credit for state residents, $106.67 per credit for nonresidents.

New York / Colleges Offering Part-Time Degree Programs

State University of New York College at Oneonta
Oneonta 13820

Public institution; small-town setting. Awards B, M. Total enrollment: 5,972. Undergraduate enrollment: 5,611; 4% part-time, 58% women. Total faculty: 383. Library holdings: 383,000 bound volumes, 182,119 titles on microform, 2,110 periodical subscriptions, 9,642 records/tapes.

Undergraduate Courses offered for part-time students during daytime, evenings, summer. Complete part-time degree programs offered during daytime, evenings, summer. Adult/continuing education programs available. Career services available to part-time students: individual and group career counseling, individual job placement, employer recruitment on campus. Part-time tuition: $45 per semester hour for state residents, $105 per semester hour for nonresidents.

Graduate Part-time study available in Graduate Studies. Degree can be earned exclusively through evening/weekend study in Graduate Studies. Basic part-time expenses: $90 per credit tuition plus $0.85 per credit fees for state residents, $156 per credit tuition plus $0.85 per credit fees for nonresidents. Institutional financial aid available to part-time graduate students in Graduate Studies.

State University of New York College at Oswego
Oswego 13126

Public institution; small-town setting. Awards B, M. Total enrollment: 7,832. Undergraduate enrollment: 7,211; 5% part-time, 50% women, 4% over 25. Total faculty: 390. Library holdings: 300,000 bound volumes, 900,000 titles on microform, 2,660 periodical subscriptions, 3,500 records/tapes.

Undergraduate Courses offered for part-time students during daytime, evenings, summer. Complete part-time degree programs offered during daytime, summer. Adult/continuing education programs available. Career services available to part-time students: individual and group career counseling, individual job placement, employer recruitment on campus. Part-time tuition: $45 per semester hour for state residents, $105 per semester hour for nonresidents.

Graduate Part-time study available in Graduate Studies. Basic part-time expenses: $90 per credit tuition plus $0.85 per credit fees for state residents, $156 per credit tuition plus $0.85 per credit fees for nonresidents. Institutional financial aid available to part-time graduate students in Graduate Studies.

State University of New York College at Plattsburgh
Plattsburgh 12901

Public institution; small-town setting. Awards B, M. Barrier-free campus. Total enrollment: 5,917. Undergraduate enrollment: 5,554; 7% part-time, 58% women, 8% over 25. Total faculty: 362. Library holdings: 408,647 bound volumes, 461,524 titles on microform, 1,877 periodical subscriptions, 6,096 records/tapes.

Undergraduate Courses offered for part-time students during daytime, evenings, summer. Complete part-time degree programs offered during daytime. Adult/continuing education programs available. Career services available to part-time students: individual career counseling, employer recruitment on campus. Part-time tuition: $45 per credit for state residents, $107 per credit for nonresidents.

Graduate Part-time study available in Faculty of Arts and Science, Faculty of Professional Studies. Basic part-time expenses: $90 per credit tuition plus $4.35 per credit fees for state residents, $156 per credit tuition plus $4.35 per credit fees for nonresidents. Institutional financial aid available to part-time graduate students in Faculty of Arts and Science, Faculty of Professional Studies.

State University of New York College at Potsdam
Potsdam 13676

Public institution; small-town setting. Awards B, M. Total enrollment: 4,860. Undergraduate enrollment: 4,370; 9% part-time, 52% women, 2% over 25. Total faculty: 290. Library holdings: 321,000 bound volumes, 722 titles on microform, 1,850 periodical subscriptions, 13,200 records/tapes.

Graduate Part-time study available in Crane School of Music, School of Graduate, Professional and Lifelong Learning, School of Liberal Studies. Degree can be earned exclusively through evening/weekend study in Crane School of Music, School of Graduate, Professional and Lifelong Learning, School of Liberal Studies. Basic part-time expenses: $90 per credit tuition plus $0.85 per credit fees for state residents, $156 per credit tuition plus $0.85 per credit fees for nonresidents. Institutional financial aid available to part-time graduate students in Crane School of Music, School of Graduate, Professional and Lifelong Learning, School of Liberal Studies.

State University of New York College at Purchase
Purchase 10577

Public institution; small-town setting. Awards B, M. Barrier-free campus. Total enrollment: 2,188 (all undergraduates); 6% part-time, 59% women. Total faculty: 185. Library holdings: 175,000 bound volumes, 1,200 periodical subscriptions, 1,350 records/tapes.

Undergraduate Courses offered for part-time students during daytime, evenings. Complete part-time degree programs offered during daytime, evenings. Adult/continuing education programs available. Career services available to part-time students: individual and group career counseling, individual job placement, employer recruitment on campus. Part-time tuition: $45 per credit hour for state residents, $89.35 per credit hour for nonresidents.

State University of New York College of Environmental Science and Forestry
Syracuse 13210

Public institution; metropolitan setting. Awards A, B, M, D. Barrier-free campus. Total enrollment: 1,555. Undergraduate enrollment: 1,180; 5% part-time, 25% women. Total faculty: 125. Library holdings: 75,000 bound volumes, 975 periodical subscriptions.

Graduate Part-time study available in Graduate Program in Environmental Science, School of Biology, Chemistry, and Ecology, School of Environmental and Resource Engineering, School of Forestry, School of Landscape Architecture. Basic part-time expenses: $90 per credit tuition plus $16.30 per semester (minimum) fees for state residents, $156 per credit tuition plus $16.30 per semester (minimum) fees for nonresidents. Institutional financial aid available to part-time graduate students in Graduate Program in Environmental Science, School of Biology, Chemistry, and Ecology, School of Environmental and Resource Engineering, School of Forestry, School of Landscape Architecture.

Colleges Offering Part-Time Degree Programs / New York

State University of New York College of Technology at Utica/Rome
Utica 13502

Public institution; city setting. Awards B. Total enrollment: 2,552 (all undergraduates); 38% part-time, 40% women. Total faculty: 138. Library holdings: 110,000 bound volumes, 350,000 titles on microform, 2,100 periodical subscriptions, 6,000 records/tapes.

Undergraduate Courses offered for part-time students during daytime, evenings, weekends, summer. Complete part-time degree programs offered during daytime, evenings. Adult/continuing education programs available. Career services available to part-time students: individual and group career counseling, individual job placement, employer recruitment on campus. Part-time tuition: $45 per semester hour for state residents, $105 per semester hour for nonresidents.

State University of New York Empire State College
Saratoga Springs 12866

Public institution. Awards A, B, M (external degree programs only). Total enrollment: 4,735 (all undergraduates); 79% part-time, 43% women, 75% over 25. Total faculty: 255.

Undergraduate Courses offered for part-time students during daytime, evenings, weekends, summer. Complete part-time degree programs offered during daytime, evenings, weekends, summer. External degree programs available. Part-time tuition: $45 per credit for state residents, $107 per credit for nonresidents.

Graduate Part-time study available in Graduate Programs. Degree can be earned exclusively through evening/weekend study in Graduate Programs. Institutional financial aid available to part-time graduate students in Graduate Programs.

State University of New York Maritime College
Bronx 10465

Public institution; metropolitan setting. Awards B, M. Total enrollment: 1,060. Undergraduate enrollment: 930; 0% part-time, 8% women, 3% over 25. Total faculty: 70. Library holdings: 68,000 bound volumes, 70 titles on microform, 600 periodical subscriptions, 5,000 records/tapes.

Graduate Part-time study available in Graduate Program in Transportation Management. Degree can be earned exclusively through evening/weekend study in Graduate Program in Transportation Management. Basic part-time expenses: $90 per credit tuition for state residents, $133 per credit tuition for nonresidents.

State University of New York Upstate Medical Center
Syracuse 13210

Public institution; metropolitan setting. Awards A, B, M, D. Total enrollment: 898. Undergraduate enrollment: 236; 10% part-time, 72% women, 17% over 25. Total faculty: 233. Library holdings: 112,000 bound volumes, 2,100 periodical subscriptions.

Graduate Part-time study available in College of Graduate Studies. Basic part-time expenses: $90 per credit tuition plus $30.05 per semester (minimum) fees for state residents, $156 per credit tuition plus $30.05 per semester (minimum) fees for nonresidents. Institutional financial aid available to part-time graduate students in College of Graduate Studies.

Stenotype Institute
New York 10019

Proprietary institution; metropolitan setting. Awards A. Barrier-free campus. Total enrollment: 360 (all undergraduates); 30% part-time, 60% women, 30% over 25. Total faculty: 29. Library holdings: 500 bound volumes, 20 periodical subscriptions, 250 records/tapes.

Undergraduate Courses offered for part-time students during daytime. Complete part-time degree programs offered during daytime. Adult/continuing education programs available. Career services available to part-time students: individual and group career counseling, individual job placement, employer recruitment on campus. Part-time tuition: $1300 per course.

Suffolk County Community College–Eastern Campus
Riverhead 11901

Public institution; small-town setting. Awards A. Barrier-free campus. Total enrollment: 2,242 (all undergraduates); 51% part-time, 51% women. Total faculty: 38.

Undergraduate Courses offered for part-time students during daytime, evenings, summer. Complete part-time degree programs offered during daytime, evenings, summer. Adult/continuing education programs available. Career services available to part-time students: individual career counseling, individual job placement, employer recruitment on campus. Part-time tuition: $43 per credit for state residents, $86 per credit for nonresidents.

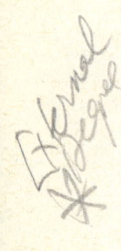

Suffolk County Community College–Selden Campus
Selden 11784

Public institution; small-town setting. Awards A. Barrier-free campus. Total enrollment: 21,000 (all undergraduates); 51% part-time, 51% women. Total faculty: 435. Library holdings: 153,000 bound volumes, 12,800 titles on microform, 1,500 periodical subscriptions, 3,000 records/tapes.

Undergraduate Courses offered for part-time students during daytime, evenings, weekends, summer. Complete part-time degree programs offered during daytime, evenings, weekends, summer. Adult/continuing education programs available. Career services available to part-time students: individual and group career counseling, individual job placement, employer recruitment on campus. Part-time tuition: $43 per credit for state residents, $86 per credit for nonresidents.

Suffolk County Community College–Western Campus
Brentwood 11717

Public institution; city setting. Awards A. Barrier-free campus. Total enrollment: 2,117 (all undergraduates); 51% part-time, 54% women, 46% over 25. Total faculty: 259. Library holdings: 27,000 bound volumes, 200 titles on microform, 360 periodical subscriptions, 7,000 records/tapes.

Undergraduate Courses offered for part-time students during daytime, evenings, summer. Complete part-time degree programs offered during daytime, evenings, summer. Career services available to part-time students: individual and group career counseling, individual job placement, employer recruitment on campus. Part-time tuition: $43 per credit for state residents, $86 per credit for nonresidents.

New York / **Colleges Offering Part-Time Degree Programs**

Sullivan County Community College
Loch Sheldrake 12759

Public institution; rural setting. Awards A. Barrier-free campus. Total enrollment: 1,750 (all undergraduates); 20% part-time, 45% women. Total faculty: 75. Library holdings: 42,000 bound volumes, 510 periodical subscriptions, 2,681 records/tapes.

Undergraduate Courses offered for part-time students during daytime, evenings, summer. Complete part-time degree programs offered during daytime, evenings, summer. Adult/continuing education programs available. Career services available to part-time students: individual and group career counseling, individual job placement. Part-time tuition and fees per semester (1 to 11 credits) range from $58.25 to $593.25 for state residents, $137.25 to $1462.25 for nonresidents.

Syracuse University
Syracuse 13210

Independent institution; metropolitan setting. Awards B, M, D. Total enrollment: 21,288. Undergraduate enrollment: 14,416; 10% part-time, 48% women. Total faculty: 1,233. Library holdings: 2 million bound volumes, 2.1 million titles on microform, 10,000 periodical subscriptions.

Undergraduate Courses offered for part-time students during daytime, evenings, weekends, summer. Complete part-time degree programs offered during daytime, evenings, weekends, summer. Adult/continuing education programs available. Career services available to part-time students: individual and group career counseling, individual job placement, employer recruitment on campus. Part-time tuition: $140 per credit hour.

Graduate Part-time study available in Graduate School. Degree can be earned exclusively through evening/weekend study in Graduate School. Basic part-time expenses: $216 per credit tuition. Institutional financial aid available to part-time graduate students in Graduate School.

Syracuse University, Utica College
Utica 13502

See Utica College of Syracuse University

Teachers College, Columbia University
New York 10027

Independent institution (graduate only). Total enrollment: 3,812 (coed; 72% part-time). Total faculty: 153. Library holdings: 402,722 bound volumes, 262,200 microforms.

Graduate Part-time study available in Division of Educational Institutions and Programs, Division of Health Services, Sciences, and Education, Division of Instruction, Division of Philosophy, the Social Sciences, and Education, Division of Psychology and Education, Interdisciplinary Programs. Degree can be earned exclusively through evening/weekend study in Division of Educational Institutions and Programs, Division of Health Services, Sciences, and Education, Division of Instruction, Division of Philosophy, the Social Sciences, and Education, Division of Psychology and Education. Basic part-time expenses: $265 per credit tuition plus $80 per semester fees. Institutional financial aid available to part-time graduate students in Division of Educational Institutions and Programs, Division of Health Services, Sciences, and Education, Division of Instruction, Division of Philosophy, the Social Sciences, and Education, Division of Psychology and Education, Interdisciplinary Programs.

Technical Career Institutes
New York 10001

Proprietary institution; metropolitan setting. Awards A. Barrier-free campus. Total enrollment: 2,300 (all undergraduates); 30% part-time, 7% women. Total faculty: 90. Library holdings: 5,000 bound volumes, 100 periodical subscriptions.

Undergraduate Courses offered for part-time students during evenings, summer. Complete part-time degree programs offered during evenings. Career services available to part-time students: individual and group career counseling, individual job placement, employer recruitment on campus. Part-time tuition: $63 per quarter hour.

Tompkins Cortland Community College
Dryden 13053

Public institution; rural setting. Awards A. Barrier-free campus. Total enrollment: 3,450 (all undergraduates); 45% part-time, 55% women, 35% over 25. Total faculty: 100.

Undergraduate Courses offered for part-time students during daytime, evenings, weekends, summer. Complete part-time degree programs offered during daytime, evenings, summer. Adult/continuing education programs available. Career services available to part-time students: individual and group career counseling, individual job placement, employer recruitment on campus. Part-time tuition: $40 per credit for state residents, $120 per credit for nonresidents.

Touro College
New York 10036

Independent institution; metropolitan setting. Awards A, B, M, D. Total enrollment: 3,200. Undergraduate enrollment: 2,600; 15% part-time, 60% women, 15% over 25. Total faculty: 253. Library holdings: 120,000 bound volumes, 750 periodical subscriptions.

Undergraduate Courses offered for part-time students during daytime, evenings, summer. Complete part-time degree programs offered during daytime, evenings, summer. Career services available to part-time students: individual and group career counseling. Part-time tuition: $165 per credit.

Graduate Part-time study available in School of Jewish Studies, School of Law. Institutional financial aid available to part-time graduate students in School of Jewish Studies, School of Law.

Trocaire College
Buffalo 14220

Independent institution; metropolitan setting. Awards A. Total enrollment: 980 (all undergraduates); 51% part-time, 92% women, 50% over 25. Total faculty: 97. Library holdings: 41,000 bound volumes, 275 periodical subscriptions, 2,215 records/tapes.

Undergraduate Courses offered for part-time students during daytime, evenings, weekends, summer. Complete part-time degree programs offered during daytime, evenings, weekends. Adult/continuing education programs available. Career services available to part-time students: individual and group career counseling, individual job placement, employer recruitment on campus. Part-time tuition: $82 per credit hour.

Colleges Offering Part-Time Degree Programs / New York

Ulster County Community College
Stone Ridge 12484

Public institution; rural setting. Awards A. Barrier-free campus. Total enrollment: 3,133 (all undergraduates); 49% part-time, 53% women, 40% over 25. Total faculty: 160. Library holdings: 70,000 bound volumes, 62 titles on microform, 452 periodical subscriptions, 2,802 records/tapes.

Undergraduate Courses offered for part-time students during daytime, evenings, weekends, summer. Complete part-time degree programs offered during daytime, evenings, weekends, summer. Adult/continuing education programs available. Career services available to part-time students: individual and group career counseling, individual job placement, employer recruitment on campus. Part-time tuition: $45 per credit for state residents, $135 per credit for nonresidents.

Union College
Schenectady 12308

Independent institution; city setting. Awards B, M, D. Total enrollment: 2,749. Undergraduate enrollment: 2,039; 1% part-time, 40% women, 1% over 25. Total faculty: 205. Library holdings: 422,570 bound volumes, 2,375 periodical subscriptions, 2,333 records/tapes.

Undergraduate Courses offered for part-time students during daytime, evenings, summer. Complete part-time degree programs offered during daytime, evenings, summer. Adult/continuing education programs available. Part-time tuition: $968 per course.

Graduate Part-time study available in Graduate Studies. Degree can be earned exclusively through evening/weekend study in Graduate Studies. Basic part-time expenses: $650 per course tuition. Institutional financial aid available to part-time graduate students in Graduate Studies.

University of Rochester
Rochester 14627

Independent institution; metropolitan setting. Awards B, M, D. Total enrollment: 6,969. Undergraduate enrollment: 4,572; 10% part-time, 42% women. Total faculty: 662. Library holdings: 1.7 million bound volumes, 2.2 million titles on microform, 9,894 periodical subscriptions, 38,276 records/tapes.

Undergraduate Courses offered for part-time students during summer. Complete part-time degree programs offered during summer. Adult/continuing education programs available. Career services available to part-time students: individual and group career counseling, individual job placement, employer recruitment on campus. Part-time tuition per credit hour ranges from $185 to $293 according to program.

Graduate Part-time study available in College of Arts and Science, College of Engineering and Applied Science, Eastman School of Music, Graduate School of Education and Human Development, Graduate School of Management, School of Medicine and Dentistry, School of Nursing. Basic part-time expenses: $258 per hour tuition. Institutional financial aid available to part-time graduate students in College of Arts and Science, College of Engineering and Applied Science, Eastman School of Music, Graduate School of Education and Human Development, Graduate School of Management, School of Medicine and Dentistry, School of Nursing.

University of the State of New York Regents External Degree Program
Albany 12230

Public institution. Awards A, B (external degree programs only). Total enrollment: 18,242 (all undergraduates); 100% part-time, 47% women.

Undergraduate Part-time degree programs offered. External degree programs available. Career services available to part-time students: individual career counseling. Part-time tuition: $175 per year.

Utica College of Syracuse University
Utica 13502

Independent institution; city setting. Awards B. Barrier-free campus. Total enrollment: 1,336 (all undergraduates); 7% part-time, 58% women. Total faculty: 175. Library holdings: 130,055 bound volumes, 1,306 periodical subscriptions.

Undergraduate Courses offered for part-time students during daytime, evenings, summer. Complete part-time degree programs offered during daytime, evenings. Adult/continuing education programs available. Career services available to part-time students: individual and group career counseling, individual job placement, employer recruitment on campus. Part-time tuition: $240 per credit.

Utica School of Commerce
Utica 13501

Proprietary institution; city setting. Awards A. Barrier-free campus. Total enrollment: 385 (all undergraduates); 2% part-time, 70% women, 35% over 25. Total faculty: 15. Library holdings: 2,000 bound volumes, 25 periodical subscriptions, 100 records/tapes.

Undergraduate Courses offered for part-time students during daytime, summer. Complete part-time degree programs offered during daytime, summer. Adult/continuing education programs available. Career services available to part-time students: individual and group career counseling, individual job placement. Part-time tuition: $81 per credit hour.

Vassar College
Poughkeepsie 12601

Independent institution; small-town setting. Awards B, M. Total enrollment: 2,358. Undergraduate enrollment: 2,355; 5% part-time, 60% women. Total faculty: 240. Library holdings: 600,000 bound volumes, 300,000 titles on microform, 3,820 periodical subscriptions, 25,000 records/tapes.

Undergraduate Courses offered for part-time students during daytime. Complete part-time degree programs offered during daytime. Career services available to part-time students: individual and group career counseling, individual job placement, employer recruitment on campus. Part-time tuition: $975 per unit.

Villa Maria College of Buffalo
Buffalo 14225

Independent-religious instutition; metropolitan setting. Awards A. Barrier-free campus. Total enrollment: 660 (all undergraduates); 20% part-time, 66% women, 35% over 25. Total faculty: 63. Library holdings: 54,000 bound volumes, 305 periodical subscriptions, 11,394 records/tapes.

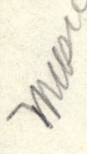

North Carolina / Colleges Offering Part-Time Degree Programs

Undergraduate Courses offered for part-time students during daytime, evenings, weekends, summer. Complete part-time degree programs offered during daytime. Career services available to part-time students: individual and group career counseling, individual job placement. Part-time tuition: $95 per credit.

Wagner College
Staten Island 10301

Independent-religious instutition; metropolitan setting. Awards B, M. Total enrollment: 2,500. Undergraduate enrollment: 1,850; 9% part-time, 55% women, 5% over 25. Total faculty: 216. Library holdings: 226,000 bound volumes, 890 periodical subscriptions, 4,600 records/tapes.

Graduate Part-time study available in Division of Graduate Studies. Degree can be earned exclusively through evening/weekend study in Division of Graduate Studies. Basic part-time expenses: $185 per credit tuition plus $2 per credit fees.

Wells College
Aurora 13026

Independent institution; rural setting. Awards B. Total enrollment: 517 (all undergraduates); 5% part-time, 100% women, 5% over 25. Total faculty: 56. Library holdings: 207,000 bound volumes, 2,800 titles on microform, 631 periodical subscriptions, 858 records/tapes.

Undergraduate Courses offered for part-time students during daytime, evenings. Complete part-time degree programs offered during daytime. Adult/continuing education programs available. Career services available to part-time students: individual and group career counseling, individual job placement, employer recruitment on campus. Part-time tuition: $415 per course.

Westchester Business Institute
White Plains 10602

Proprietary institution; city setting. Awards A. Barrier-free campus. Total enrollment: 570 (all undergraduates); 2% part-time, 70% women, 5% over 25. Total faculty: 29. Library holdings: 6,700 bound volumes, 21 periodical subscriptions.

Undergraduate Courses offered for part-time students during daytime, evenings, summer. Complete part-time degree programs offered during daytime, evenings, summer. Adult/continuing education programs available. Career services available to part-time students: individual and group career counseling, individual job placement, employer recruitment on campus. Part-time tuition: $450 per course.

Westchester Community College
Valhalla 10595

Public institution; small-town setting. Awards A. Barrier-free campus. Total enrollment: 8,357 (all undergraduates); 54% part-time, 49% women, 34% over 25. Total faculty: 419. Library holdings: 87,100 bound volumes.

Undergraduate Courses offered for part-time students during daytime, evenings, weekends, summer. Complete part-time degree programs offered during daytime, evenings. Adult/continuing education programs available. Career services available to part-time students: individual and group career counseling, individual job placement, employer recruitment on campus. Part-time tuition: $47.50 per credit for state residents, $118.75 per credit for nonresidents.

William Smith College
Geneva 14456

Independent institution; small-town setting. Awards B. Total enrollment: 750 (all undergraduates); 1% part-time, 100% women. Total faculty: 143. Library holdings: 230,000 bound volumes, 24,000 titles on microform, 1,300 periodical subscriptions, 10,000 records/tapes.

Undergraduate Courses offered for part-time students during daytime. Complete part-time degree programs offered during daytime. Adult/continuing education programs available. Part-time tuition: $980 per course.

York College
Jamaica 11451

See City University of New York, York College

NORTH CAROLINA

Anson Technical College
Ansonville 28007

Public institution; rural setting. Awards A. Total enrollment: 623 (all undergraduates); 71% part-time, 48% women. Total faculty: 86. Library holdings: 16,863 bound volumes, 154 periodical subscriptions, 183 records/tapes.

Undergraduate Courses offered for part-time students during daytime, evenings, summer. Complete part-time degree programs offered during daytime, evenings, summer. Adult/continuing education programs available. Career services available to part-time students: individual and group career counseling, individual job placement, employer recruitment on campus. Part-time tuition: $4.25 per quarter hour for state residents, $21.25 per quarter hour for nonresidents.

Appalachian State University
Boone 28608

Public institution; small-town setting. Awards B, M. Total enrollment: 10,222. Undergraduate enrollment: 9,056; 6% part-time, 50% women. Total faculty: 584. Library holdings: 543,141 bound volumes, 393,524 titles on microform, 4,878 periodical subscriptions, 29,754 records/tapes.

Undergraduate Courses offered for part-time students during daytime, summer. Complete part-time degree programs offered during daytime, summer. Adult/continuing education programs available. Career services available to part-time students: individual and group career counseling, individual job placement, employer recruitment on campus. Part-time tuition and fees per semester (1 to 11 hours) range from $51 to $334 for state residents, $371 to $1293 for nonresidents.

Graduate Part-time study available in Cratis D. Williams Graduate School. Basic part-time expenses: $103 per semester (minimum) tuition for state residents, $743 per semester (minimum) tuition for nonresidents.

Asheville-Buncombe Technical College
Asheville 28801

Public institution; city setting. Awards A. Barrier-free campus. Total enrollment: 2,619 (all undergraduates); 45% part-time, 53% women. Total faculty: 260. Library holdings: 25,888 bound volumes, 214 titles on microform, 233 periodical subscriptions, 2,419 records/tapes.

Colleges Offering Part-Time Degree Programs / North Carolina

Asheville-Buncombe Technical College (continued)

Undergraduate Courses offered for part-time students during daytime, evenings. Complete part-time degree programs offered during daytime, evenings. Career services available to part-time students: individual career counseling, individual job placement. Part-time tuition: $4.25 per quarter hour for state residents, $21.25 per quarter hour for nonresidents.

Atlantic Christian College
Wilson 27893

Independent-religious instutition; small-town setting. Awards B. Total enrollment: 1,526 (all undergraduates); 16% part-time, 66% women. Total faculty: 110. Library holdings: 115,535 bound volumes, 15,891 titles on microform, 548 periodical subscriptions, 4,264 records/tapes.

Undergraduate Courses offered for part-time students during daytime, evenings, summer. Complete part-time degree programs offered during daytime, evenings, summer. Adult/continuing education programs available. Career services available to part-time students: individual career counseling, individual job placement, employer recruitment on campus. Part-time tuition: $140 per semester hour.

Beaufort County Community College
Washington 27889

Public institution; rural setting. Awards A. Barrier-free campus. Total enrollment: 964 (all undergraduates); 44% part-time, 57% women, 57% over 25. Total faculty: 72. Library holdings: 25,000 bound volumes, 140 periodical subscriptions, 2,759 records/tapes.

Undergraduate Courses offered for part-time students during daytime, evenings, summer. Complete part-time degree programs offered during daytime, evenings, summer. Adult/continuing education programs available. Career services available to part-time students: individual career counseling, individual job placement, employer recruitment on campus. Part-time tuition: $4.25 per quarter hour for state residents, $21.25 per quarter hour for nonresidents.

Bladen Technical College
Dublin 28332

Public institution; rural setting. Awards A. Total enrollment: 430 (all undergraduates); 30% part-time, 52% women, 45% over 25. Total faculty: 35. Library holdings: 15,000 bound volumes, 100 periodical subscriptions.

Undergraduate Courses offered for part-time students during daytime, evenings, summer. Complete part-time degree programs offered during daytime, evenings, summer. Adult/continuing education programs available. Career services available to part-time students: individual career counseling, individual job placement. Part-time tuition: $4.25 per quarter hour for state residents, $21.25 per quarter hour for nonresidents.

Blanton's Junior College
Asheville 28801

Proprietary institution; city setting. Awards A. Barrier-free campus. Total enrollment: 238 (all undergraduates); 28% part-time, 71% women. Total faculty: 11. Library holdings: 5,324 bound volumes, 65 periodical subscriptions.

Undergraduate Courses offered for part-time students during daytime, evenings. Complete part-time degree programs offered during daytime, evenings. Adult/continuing education programs available. Career services available to part-time students: individual career counseling, individual job placement. Part-time tuition: $48 per quarter hour.

Blue Ridge Technical College
Flat Rock 28731

Public institution; small-town setting. Awards A. Barrier-free campus. Total enrollment: 1,041 (all undergraduates); 53% part-time, 50% women, 57% over 25. Total faculty: 76. Library holdings: 15,000 bound volumes, 12 periodical subscriptions, 707 records/tapes.

Undergraduate Courses offered for part-time students during daytime, evenings, summer. Complete part-time degree programs offered during daytime, evenings, summer. Adult/continuing education programs available. Career services available to part-time students: individual and group career counseling, individual job placement, employer recruitment on campus. Part-time tuition: $4.25 per credit hour for state residents, $21.25 per credit hour for nonresidents.

Brunswick Technical College
Supply 28462

Public institution; rural setting. Awards A. Barrier-free campus. Total enrollment: 281 (all undergraduates); 67% part-time, 67% women, 85% over 25. Total faculty: 45. Library holdings: 4,500 bound volumes, 20 titles on microform, 80 periodical subscriptions, 150 records/tapes.

Undergraduate Courses offered for part-time students during daytime, evenings, summer. Complete part-time degree programs offered during daytime, evenings. Adult/continuing education programs available. Career services available to part-time students: individual career counseling, individual job placement. Part-time tuition: $4.25 per credit hour for state residents, $21.25 per credit hour for nonresidents.

Caldwell Community College and Technical Institute
Hudson 28638

Public institution; small-town setting. Awards A. Barrier-free campus. Total enrollment: 2,323 (all undergraduates); 53% part-time, 59% women, 50% over 25. Total faculty: 137. Library holdings: 23,000 bound volumes, 1,900 titles on microform, 50 periodical subscriptions, 1,500 records/tapes.

Undergraduate Courses offered for part-time students during daytime, evenings, summer. Complete part-time degree programs offered during daytime, evenings, summer. Adult/continuing education programs available. Career services available to part-time students: individual and group career counseling, individual job placement, employer recruitment on campus. Part-time tuition: $4.25 per credit hour for state residents, $21.25 per credit hour for nonresidents.

Campbell University
Buies Creek 27506

Independent-religious instutition; rural setting. Awards A, B, M, D. Barrier-free campus. Total enrollment: 3,500. Undergraduate enrollment: 1,973; 10% part-time, 49% women, 12% over 25. Total faculty: 120. Library holdings: 158,500 bound volumes, 100,000 titles on microform, 920 periodical subscriptions, 2,137 records/tapes.

Undergraduate Courses offered for part-time students during daytime, evenings, weekends, summer. Complete part-time degree programs offered during daytime, evenings, weekends,

summer. Adult/continuing education programs available. Career services available to part-time students: individual and group career counseling, individual job placement, employer recruitment on campus. Part-time tuition: $80 per semester hour for state residents, $80 per semester hour for nonresidents.

Cape Fear Technical Institute
Wilmington 28401

Public institution; city setting. Awards A. Barrier-free campus. Total enrollment: 1,900 (all undergraduates); 30% part-time, 37% women. Total faculty: 67. Library holdings: 18,132 bound volumes, 347 periodical subscriptions, 400 records/tapes.

Undergraduate Courses offered for part-time students during daytime, evenings, summer. Complete part-time degree programs offered during daytime, evenings, summer. Adult/continuing education programs available. Career services available to part-time students: individual career counseling, individual job placement, employer recruitment on campus. Part-time tuition: $4.25 per credit hour for state residents, $21.25 per credit hour for nonresidents.

Carteret Technical College
Morehead City 28557

Public institution; small-town setting. Awards A. Total enrollment: 1,089 (all undergraduates); 52% part-time, 54% women. Total faculty: 58. Library holdings: 21,000 bound volumes, 193 titles on microform, 165 periodical subscriptions, 1,500 records/tapes.

Undergraduate Courses offered for part-time students during daytime, evenings. Complete part-time degree programs offered during daytime, evenings. Adult/continuing education programs available. Career services available to part-time students: individual career counseling, individual job placement, employer recruitment on campus. Part-time tuition: $4.25 per quarter hour for state residents, $21.25 per quarter hour for nonresidents.

Catawba College
Salisbury 28144

Independent-religious instutition; small-town setting. Awards B. Total enrollment: 961 (all undergraduates); 11% part-time, 48% women. Total faculty: 64. Library holdings: 150,000 bound volumes, 24,000 titles on microform, 1,050 periodical subscriptions, 2,100 records/tapes.

Undergraduate Courses offered for part-time students during daytime, evenings, summer. Complete part-time degree programs offered during daytime, evenings, summer. Adult/continuing education programs available. Career services available to part-time students: individual and group career counseling, individual job placement, employer recruitment on campus. Part-time tuition: $150 per semester hour.

Catawba Valley Technical College
Hickory 28601

Public institution; small-town setting. Awards A. Barrier-free campus. Total enrollment: 2,550 (all undergraduates); 50% part-time, 48% women, 52% over 25. Total faculty: 146. Library holdings: 25,824 bound volumes, 72 titles on microform, 12 periodical subscriptions, 130 records/tapes.

Undergraduate Courses offered for part-time students during daytime, evenings. Complete part-time degree programs offered during daytime, evenings. Adult/continuing education programs available. Career services available to part-time students: individual career counseling, individual job placement. Part-time tuition: $4.25 per credit hour for state residents, $21.25 per credit hour for nonresidents.

Cecils Junior College of Business
Asheville 28806

Proprietary institution; city setting. Awards A. Barrier-free campus. Total enrollment: 297 (all undergraduates); 15% part-time, 69% women. Total faculty: 13. Library holdings: 7,500 bound volumes, 25 periodical subscriptions.

Undergraduate Courses offered for part-time students during daytime, evenings, summer. Complete part-time degree programs offered during daytime, evenings, summer. Adult/continuing education programs available. Career services available to part-time students: individual and group career counseling, individual job placement. Part-time tuition: $48 per quarter hour.

Central Carolina Technical College
Sanford 27330

Public institution; small-town setting. Awards A. Barrier-free campus. Total enrollment: 2,039 (all undergraduates); 49% part-time, 52% women, 95% over 25. Total faculty: 130. Library holdings: 22,884 bound volumes, 238 periodical subscriptions, 3,791 records/tapes.

Undergraduate Courses offered for part-time students during daytime, evenings, summer. Complete part-time degree programs offered during daytime, evenings. Adult/continuing education programs available. Career services available to part-time students: individual and group career counseling, individual job placement, employer recruitment on campus. Part-time tuition: $4.25 per quarter hour for state residents, $21.25 per quarter hour for nonresidents.

Central Piedmont Community College
Charlotte 28235

Public institution; city setting. Awards A. Total enrollment: 14,363 (all undergraduates); 67% part-time, 60% women. Total faculty: 1,111. Library holdings: 67,192 bound volumes, 229 periodical subscriptions.

Undergraduate Courses offered for part-time students during daytime, evenings, weekends, summer. Complete part-time degree programs offered during daytime, evenings, weekends, summer. Adult/continuing education programs available. Career services available to part-time students: individual and group career counseling, individual job placement, employer recruitment on campus. Part-time tuition: $4.25 per credit hour for state residents, $21.25 per credit hour for nonresidents.

Chowan College
Murfreesboro 27855

Independent-religious instutition; rural setting. Awards A. Total enrollment: 989 (all undergraduates); 1% part-time, 35% women, 0% over 25. Total faculty: 71. Library holdings: 76,000 bound volumes, 387 periodical subscriptions, 1,859 records/tapes.

Undergraduate Courses offered for part-time students during daytime, summer. Complete part-time degree programs offered during daytime, summer. Career services available to part-time students: individual and group career counseling. Part-time tuition: $60 per semester hour.

Colleges Offering Part-Time Degree Programs / North Carolina

Cleveland Technical College
Shelby 28150

Public institution; small-town setting. Awards A. Barrier-free campus. Total enrollment: 1,223 (all undergraduates); 56% part-time, 51% women, 70% over 25. Total faculty: 83. Library holdings: 23,000 bound volumes, 182 periodical subscriptions.

Undergraduate Courses offered for part-time students during daytime, evenings, summer. Complete part-time degree programs offered during daytime, evenings, summer. Adult/continuing education programs available. Career services available to part-time students: individual career counseling, individual job placement, employer recruitment on campus. Part-time tuition: $4.25 per quarter hour for state residents, $21.25 per quarter hour for nonresidents.

Coastal Carolina Community College
Jacksonville 28540

Public institution; small-town setting. Awards A. Barrier-free campus. Total enrollment: 2,705 (all undergraduates); 46% part-time, 49% women, 50% over 25. Total faculty: 122. Library holdings: 33,000 bound volumes, 250 periodical subscriptions, 750 records/tapes.

Undergraduate Courses offered for part-time students during daytime, evenings. Complete part-time degree programs offered during daytime, evenings. Adult/continuing education programs available. Career services available to part-time students: individual career counseling, individual job placement. Part-time tuition: $4.25 per credit hour for state residents, $21.25 per credit hour for nonresidents.

College of the Albemarle
Elizabeth City 27909

Public institution; small-town setting. Awards A. Barrier-free campus. Total enrollment: 1,470 (all undergraduates); 45% part-time, 63% women. Total faculty: 81. Library holdings: 36,065 bound volumes, 1,626 titles on microform, 250 periodical subscriptions, 1,726 records/tapes.

Undergraduate Courses offered for part-time students during daytime, evenings, summer. Complete part-time degree programs offered during daytime, evenings, summer. Adult/continuing education programs available. Career services available to part-time students: individual and group career counseling, individual job placement, employer recruitment on campus. Part-time tuition: $4.25 per quarter hour for state residents, $21.25 per quarter hour for nonresidents.

Craven Community College
New Bern 28560

Public institution; rural setting. Awards A. Barrier-free campus. Total enrollment: 1,816 (all undergraduates); 55% part-time, 52% women, 40% over 25. Total faculty: 137. Library holdings: 18,645 bound volumes, 228 periodical subscriptions, 2,079 records/tapes.

Undergraduate Courses offered for part-time students during daytime, evenings, summer. Complete part-time degree programs offered during daytime, evenings, summer. Adult/continuing education programs available. Career services available to part-time students: individual and group career counseling, individual job placement, employer recruitment on campus. Part-time tuition: $4.25 per quarter hour for state residents, $21.25 per quarter hour for nonresidents.

Davidson County Community College
Lexington 27292

Public institution; rural setting. Awards A. Total enrollment: 2,366 (all undergraduates); 46% part-time, 51% women, 56% over 25. Total faculty: 111. Library holdings: 34,875 bound volumes, 305 periodical subscriptions, 3,242 records/tapes.

Undergraduate Courses offered for part-time students during daytime, evenings, weekends, summer. Complete part-time degree programs offered during daytime, evenings. Adult/continuing education programs available. Career services available to part-time students: individual and group career counseling, individual job placement, employer recruitment on campus. Part-time tuition: $4.25 per quarter hour for state residents, $21.25 per quarter hour for nonresidents.

Duke University
Durham 27706

Independent institution; city setting. Awards B, M, D. Barrier-free campus. Total enrollment: 9,285. Undergraduate enrollment: 5,984; 1% part-time, 47% women. Total faculty: 1,442. Library holdings: 3.3 million bound volumes, 496,840 titles on microform, 29,667 periodical subscriptions, 1,539 records/tapes.

Graduate Part-time study available in Graduate School, Divinity School, School of Forestry and Environmental Studies. Basic part-time expenses: $246 per credit tuition. Institutional financial aid available to part-time graduate students in School of Forestry and Environmental Studies.

Durham Technical Institute
Durham 27703

Public institution; city setting. Awards A. Barrier-free campus. Total enrollment: 3,931 (all undergraduates); 20% part-time, 58% women. Total faculty: 120. Library holdings: 19,084 bound volumes, 250 periodical subscriptions, 1,082 records/tapes.

Undergraduate Courses offered for part-time students during daytime, evenings, weekends, summer. Complete part-time degree programs offered during daytime, evenings, summer. Adult/continuing education programs available. Career services available to part-time students: individual career counseling, individual job placement, employer recruitment on campus. Part-time tuition: $4.25 per credit hour for state residents, $21.25 per credit hour for nonresidents.

East Carolina University
Greenville 27834

Public institution; small-town setting. Awards B, M, D. Total enrollment: 13,358. Undergraduate enrollment: 11,282; 9% part-time, 56% women. Total faculty: 864. Library holdings: 706,742 bound volumes, 704,000 titles on microform, 8,368 periodical subscriptions, 7,500 records/tapes.

Undergraduate Courses offered for part-time students during daytime, evenings, summer. Complete part-time degree programs offered during daytime, evenings, summer. Adult/continuing education programs available. Career services available to part-time students: individual and group career counseling, individual job placement, employer recruitment on campus. Part-time tuition per semester (1 to 11 semester hours) ranges from $51 to $154 for state residents, $340 to $1021 for nonresidents.

Graduate Part-time study available in Graduate School.

North Carolina / **Colleges Offering Part-Time Degree Programs**

East Coast Bible College
Charlotte 28214

Independent-religious instutition; city setting. Awards A, B. Total enrollment: 251 (all undergraduates); 18% part-time, 32% women. Total faculty: 15. Library holdings: 11,000 bound volumes, 400 titles on microform, 110 periodical subscriptions.

Undergraduate Courses offered for part-time students during daytime, evenings. Complete part-time degree programs offered during daytime, evenings. Part-time tuition: $58 per semester hour.

Edgecombe Technical College
Tarboro 27886

Public institution; small-town setting. Awards A. Barrier-free campus. Total enrollment: 1,250 (all undergraduates); 40% part-time, 48% women, 75% over 25. Total faculty: 68. Library holdings: 22,000 bound volumes, 125 periodical subscriptions, 2,000 records/tapes.

Undergraduate Courses offered for part-time students during daytime, evenings, summer. Complete part-time degree programs offered during daytime, evenings, summer. Adult/continuing education programs available. Career services available to part-time students: individual and group career counseling, individual job placement, employer recruitment on campus. Part-time tuition: $4.25 per quarter hour for state residents, $21.25 per quarter hour for nonresidents.

Elon College
Elon College 27244

Independent-religious instutition; small-town setting. Awards A, B, M. Total enrollment: 2,715 (all undergraduates); 12% part-time, 44% women. Total faculty: 149. Library holdings: 152,000 bound volumes, 5,000 titles on microform, 645 periodical subscriptions, 2,437 records/tapes.

Undergraduate Courses offered for part-time students during daytime, evenings, summer. Complete part-time degree programs offered during daytime. Adult/continuing education programs available. Career services available to part-time students: individual and group career counseling, individual job placement, employer recruitment on campus. Part-time tuition: $65 per semester hour.

Fayetteville State University
Fayetteville 28301

Public institution; city setting. Awards A, B, M. Total enrollment: 2,666. Undergraduate enrollment: 2,447; 13% part-time, 54% women, 34% over 25. Total faculty: 183. Library holdings: 143,429 bound volumes, 712 titles on microform, 1,461 periodical subscriptions, 1,909 records/tapes.

Undergraduate Courses offered for part-time students during daytime, evenings, weekends, summer. Complete part-time degree programs offered during daytime, evenings, weekends, summer. Adult/continuing education programs available. Career services available to part-time students: individual and group career counseling, individual job placement, employer recruitment on campus. Part-time tuition and fees per semester (1 to 11 credit hours) range from $128 to $393 for state residents, $409 to $1193 for nonresidents.

Graduate Part-time study available in Graduate School. Degree can be earned exclusively through evening/weekend study in Graduate School. Basic part-time expenses: $94 per semester (minimum) tuition for state residents, $656 per semester (minimum) tuition for nonresidents.

Fayetteville Technical Institute
Fayetteville 28303

Public institution; city setting. Awards A. Total enrollment: 5,711 (all undergraduates); 44% part-time, 53% women, 60% over 25. Total faculty: 218. Library holdings: 37,981 bound volumes, 291 periodical subscriptions, 1,952 records/tapes.

Undergraduate Courses offered for part-time students during daytime, evenings, summer. Complete part-time degree programs offered during daytime, evenings, summer. Adult/continuing education programs available. Career services available to part-time students: individual and group career counseling, employer recruitment on campus. Part-time tuition: $4.25 per quarter hour for state residents, $21.25 per quarter hour for nonresidents.

Forsyth Technical Institute
Winston-Salem 27103

Public institution; city setting. Awards A. Total enrollment: 2,951 (all undergraduates); 48% part-time, 55% women. Total faculty: 193. Library holdings: 32,105 bound volumes, 53 titles on microform, 245 periodical subscriptions, 3,099 records/tapes.

Undergraduate Courses offered for part-time students during daytime, evenings, summer. Complete part-time degree programs offered during daytime, evenings. Adult/continuing education programs available. Career services available to part-time students: individual and group career counseling, individual job placement, employer recruitment on campus. Part-time tuition: $4.25 per credit hour for state residents, $21.25 per credit hour for nonresidents.

Gardner-Webb College
Boiling Springs 28017

Independent-religious instutition; small-town setting. Awards A, B, M. Barrier-free campus. Total enrollment: 1,878. Undergraduate enrollment: 1,773; 9% part-time, 49% women. Total faculty: 152. Library holdings: 250,000 bound volumes, 900 periodical subscriptions, 9,000 records/tapes.

Undergraduate Courses offered for part-time students during daytime, evenings, summer. Complete part-time degree programs offered during daytime, evenings, summer. Adult/continuing education programs available. Career services available to part-time students: individual job placement, employer recruitment on campus. Part-time tuition: $115 per semester hour.

Graduate Part-time study available in Graduate Studies. Degree can be earned exclusively through evening/weekend study in Graduate Studies. Basic part-time expenses: $72 per semester hour tuition.

Gaston College
Dallas 28034

Public institution; small-town setting. Awards A. Barrier-free campus. Total enrollment: 3,318 (all undergraduates); 45% part-time, 10% women. Total faculty: 151. Library holdings: 42,000 bound volumes, 206 periodical subscriptions, 1,281 records/tapes.

Undergraduate Courses offered for part-time students during daytime, evenings, summer. Complete part-time degree programs offered during daytime, evenings, summer. Adult/continuing education programs available. Career services available to part-time students: individual career counseling, individual job placement, employer recruitment on campus. Part-time tuition: $4.25 per credit hour for state residents, $21.25 per credit hour for nonresidents.

Colleges Offering Part-Time Degree Programs / North Carolina

Greensboro College
Greensboro 27401

Independent-religious instutition; city setting. Awards B. Total enrollment: 576 (all undergraduates); 10% part-time, 65% women, 1% over 25. Total faculty: 50. Library holdings: 80,000 bound volumes, 2,000 titles on microform, 375 periodical subscriptions, 1,760 records/tapes.

Undergraduate Courses offered for part-time students during daytime, summer. Complete part-time degree programs offered during daytime, summer. Career services available to part-time students: individual and group career counseling, individual job placement, employer recruitment on campus. Part-time tuition: $110 per semester hour.

Guilford College
Greensboro 27410

Independent-religious instutition; city setting. Awards A, B. Total enrollment: 1,112 (all undergraduates); 1% part-time, 43% women, 2% over 25. Total faculty: 127. Library holdings: 200,000 bound volumes, 1,000 periodical subscriptions, 2,700 records/tapes.

Undergraduate Courses offered for part-time students during daytime, evenings, summer. Complete part-time degree programs offered during daytime, evenings, summer. Adult/continuing education programs available. Career services available to part-time students: individual and group career counseling, individual job placement, employer recruitment on campus. Part-time tuition: $97 per credit.

Guilford Technical Community College
Jamestown 27282

Public institution; city setting. Awards A. Total enrollment: 4,671 (all undergraduates); 54% part-time, 50% women, 50% over 25. Total faculty: 244. Library holdings: 39,516 bound volumes, 172 titles on microform, 491 periodical subscriptions, 7,125 records/tapes.

Undergraduate Courses offered for part-time students during daytime, evenings, weekends, summer. Complete part-time degree programs offered during daytime, evenings. Adult/continuing education programs available. Career services available to part-time students: individual and group career counseling, individual job placement, employer recruitment on campus. Part-time tuition: $4.25 per quarter hour for state residents, $21.25 per quarter hour for nonresidents.

Halifax Community College
Weldon 27890

Public institution; rural setting. Awards A. Barrier-free campus. Total enrollment: 1,117 (all undergraduates); 48% part-time, 70% women. Total faculty: 68. Library holdings: 24,412 bound volumes, 4,920 titles on microform, 177 periodical subscriptions, 1,988 records/tapes.

Undergraduate Courses offered for part-time students during daytime, evenings, summer. Complete part-time degree programs offered during daytime, evenings, summer. Adult/continuing education programs available. Career services available to part-time students: individual and group career counseling, individual job placement, employer recruitment on campus. Part-time tuition: $4.25 per credit hour for state residents, $21.25 per credit hour for nonresidents.

Haywood Technical College
Clyde 28721

Public institution; rural setting. Awards A. Barrier-free campus. Total enrollment: 1,015 (all undergraduates); 34% part-time, 40% women, 40% over 25. Total faculty: 77. Library holdings: 24,050 bound volumes, 105 titles on microform, 205 periodical subscriptions, 185 records/tapes.

Undergraduate Courses offered for part-time students during daytime, evenings. Complete part-time degree programs offered during daytime, evenings. Adult/continuing education programs available. Career services available to part-time students: individual job placement. Part-time tuition: $4.25 per quarter hour for state residents, $21.25 per quarter hour for nonresidents.

High Point College
High Point 27262

Independent-religious instutition; city setting. Awards B. Total enrollment: 1,359 (all undergraduates); 13% part-time, 52% women. Total faculty: 61. Library holdings: 140,000 bound volumes, 1,700 titles on microform.

Undergraduate Courses offered for part-time students during daytime, evenings. Complete part-time degree programs offered during daytime, evenings. Adult/continuing education programs available. Career services available to part-time students: individual career counseling, individual job placement, employer recruitment on campus. Part-time tuition: $110 per semester hour.

Isothermal Community College
Spindale 28160

Public institution; rural setting. Awards A. Barrier-free campus. Total enrollment: 2,650 (all undergraduates); 65% part-time, 57% women. Total faculty: 162. Library holdings: 26,000 bound volumes, 15 periodical subscriptions, 1,170 records/tapes.

Undergraduate Courses offered for part-time students during daytime, evenings, weekends, summer. Complete part-time degree programs offered during daytime, evenings, weekends, summer. External degree and adult/continuing education programs available. Career services available to part-time students: individual career counseling, individual job placement, employer recruitment on campus. Part-time tuition: $4.25 per quarter hour for state residents, $21.25 per quarter hour for nonresidents.

James Sprunt Technical College
Kenansville 28349

Public institution; rural setting. Awards A. Barrier-free campus. Total enrollment: 763 (all undergraduates); 31% part-time, 62% women. Total faculty: 45. Library holdings: 22,500 bound volumes, 190 periodical subscriptions.

Undergraduate Courses offered for part-time students during daytime, evenings, summer. Complete part-time degree programs offered during daytime, evenings. Adult/continuing education programs available. Career services available to part-time students: individual career counseling, individual job placement, employer recruitment on campus. Part-time tuition: $4.25 per quarter hour for state residents, $21.25 per quarter hour for nonresidents.

North Carolina / **Colleges Offering Part-Time Degree Programs**

Johnson C Smith University
Charlotte 28216

Independent-religious instution; city setting. Awards B. Total enrollment: 1,130 (all undergraduates); 3% part-time, 51% women, 2% over 25. Total faculty: 95. Library holdings: 100,000 bound volumes, 8,000 titles on microform, 795 periodical subscriptions.

Undergraduate Courses offered for part-time students during daytime, evenings, summer. Complete part-time degree programs offered during daytime, summer. Adult/continuing education programs available. Career services available to part-time students: individual and group career counseling, individual job placement, employer recruitment on campus. Part-time tuition: $85 per semester hour.

John Wesley College
High Point 27260

Independent-religious instution; city setting. Awards A, B. Barrier-free campus. Total enrollment: 84 (all undergraduates); 40% part-time, 35% women, 68% over 25. Total faculty: 11. Library holdings: 25,000 bound volumes, 101 periodical subscriptions.

Undergraduate Courses offered for part-time students during daytime, evenings. Complete part-time degree programs offered during daytime, evenings. Career services available to part-time students: individual career counseling. Part-time tuition: $70 per semester hour.

Lenoir Community College
Kinston 28502

Public institution; small-town setting. Awards A. Barrier-free campus. Total enrollment: 2,154 (all undergraduates); 46% part-time, 54% women. Total faculty: 105. Library holdings: 44,000 bound volumes, 330 periodical subscriptions.

Undergraduate Courses offered for part-time students during daytime, evenings, summer. Complete part-time degree programs offered during daytime, evenings, summer. Adult/continuing education programs available. Career services available to part-time students: individual and group career counseling, individual job placement, employer recruitment on campus. Part-time tuition: $4.25 per quarter hour for state residents, $21.25 per quarter hour for nonresidents.

Lenoir-Rhyne College
Hickory 28603

Independent-religious instution; small-town setting. Awards B, M. Total enrollment: 1,382. Undergraduate enrollment: 1,350; 14% part-time, 58% women, 3% over 25. Total faculty: 112. Library holdings: 107,380 bound volumes, 68,400 titles on microform, 762 periodical subscriptions.

Undergraduate Courses offered for part-time students during daytime, evenings, summer. Complete part-time degree programs offered during daytime, evenings, summer. Adult/continuing education programs available. Part-time tuition: $70 per credit hour.

Graduate Part-time study available in Graduate Program in Education. Degree can be earned exclusively through evening/weekend study in Graduate Program in Education. Basic part-time expenses: $70 per semester hour tuition.

Livingstone College
Salisbury 28144

Independent-religious instution; small-town setting. Awards B. Total enrollment: 780 (all undergraduates); 5% part-time, 42% women, 6% over 25. Total faculty: 77. Library holdings: 69,075 bound volumes.

Undergraduate Courses offered for part-time students during daytime. Complete part-time degree programs offered during daytime. Career services available to part-time students: individual and group career counseling, individual job placement, employer recruitment on campus. Part-time tuition: $68.75 per hour.

Louisburg College
Louisburg 27549

Independent-religious instution; small-town setting. Awards A. Total enrollment: 730 (all undergraduates); 4% part-time, 43% women, 2% over 25. Total faculty: 45. Library holdings: 50,700 bound volumes, 200 periodical subscriptions, 4,000 records/tapes.

Undergraduate Courses offered for part-time students during daytime, evenings, weekends, summer. Complete part-time degree programs offered during daytime, weekends, summer. Adult/continuing education programs available. Career services available to part-time students: individual career counseling. Part-time tuition: $70 per semester hour.

Mars Hill College
Mars Hill 28754

Independent-religious instution; rural setting. Awards B. Total enrollment: 1,481 (all undergraduates); 15% part-time, 54% women, 14% over 25. Total faculty: 92. Library holdings: 87,227 bound volumes, 4,839 titles on microform, 417 periodical subscriptions, 11,000 records/tapes.

Undergraduate Courses offered for part-time students during daytime, evenings, summer. Complete part-time degree programs offered during daytime, evenings. External degree and adult/continuing education programs available. Career services available to part-time students: individual and group career counseling, individual job placement, employer recruitment on campus. Part-time tuition: $115 per credit hour.

Martin Community College
Williamston 27892

Public institution; rural setting. Awards A. Total enrollment: 778 (all undergraduates); 57% part-time, 59% women, 51% over 25. Total faculty: 47. Library holdings: 19,850 bound volumes, 737 titles on microform, 156 periodical subscriptions, 1,654 records/tapes.

Undergraduate Courses offered for part-time students during daytime, evenings, summer. Complete part-time degree programs offered during daytime, evenings. Adult/continuing education programs available. Career services available to part-time students: individual and group career counseling, individual job placement, employer recruitment on campus. Part-time tuition: $4.25 per credit hour for state residents, $21.25 per credit hour for nonresidents.

Mayland Technical College
Spruce Pine 28777

Public institution; rural setting. Awards A. Barrier-free campus. Total enrollment: 720 (all undergraduates); 50% part-time,

Colleges Offering Part-Time Degree Programs / North Carolina

Mayland Technical College (continued)
53% women. Total faculty: 46. Library holdings: 13,464 bound volumes, 75 periodical subscriptions, 2,270 records/tapes.

Undergraduate Courses offered for part-time students during daytime, evenings, summer. Complete part-time degree programs offered during daytime, evenings, summer. Adult/continuing education programs available. Career services available to part-time students: individual and group career counseling, individual job placement, employer recruitment on campus. Part-time tuition: $4.25 per quarter hour for state residents, $21.25 per quarter hour for nonresidents.

McDowell Technical College
Marion 28752

Public institution; rural setting. Awards A. Barrier-free campus. Total enrollment: 602 (all undergraduates); 44% part-time, 57% women. Total faculty: 45. Library holdings: 15,503 bound volumes, 140 periodical subscriptions, 1,607 records/tapes.

Undergraduate Courses offered for part-time students during daytime, evenings, weekends, summer. Complete part-time degree programs offered during daytime, evenings, weekends, summer. Adult/continuing education programs available. Career services available to part-time students: individual and group career counseling, individual job placement, employer recruitment on campus. Part-time tuition: $4.25 per quarter hour for state residents, $21.25 per quarter hour for nonresidents.

Meredith College
Raleigh 27607

Independent-religious instutition; city setting. Awards B, M. Barrier-free campus. Total enrollment: 1,507. Undergraduate enrollment: 1,486; 11% part-time, 100% women. Total faculty: 129. Library holdings: 100,000 bound volumes, 55,000 titles on microform, 550 periodical subscriptions, 3,500 records/tapes.

Undergraduate Courses offered for part-time students during daytime, evenings, summer. Complete part-time degree programs offered during daytime, summer. Adult/continuing education programs available. Career services available to part-time students: individual and group career counseling, individual job placement, employer recruitment on campus. Part-time tuition: $140 per semester hour.

Methodist College
Fayetteville 28301

Independent-religious instutition; city setting. Awards A, B. Total enrollment: 643 (all undergraduates); 6% part-time, 44% women. Total faculty: 50. Library holdings: 69,823 bound volumes, 95 titles on microform, 433 periodical subscriptions, 2,476 records/tapes.

Undergraduate Courses offered for part-time students during daytime, evenings, weekends, summer. Complete part-time degree programs offered during daytime, evenings, summer. Adult/continuing education programs available. Career services available to part-time students: individual and group career counseling, individual job placement, employer recruitment on campus. Part-time tuition: $110 per semester hour.

Mitchell Community College
Statesville 28677

Public institution; small-town setting. Awards A. Barrier-free campus. Total enrollment: 1,453 (all undergraduates); 52% part-time, 58% women, 58% over 25. Total faculty: 76. Library holdings: 30,000 bound volumes, 6 periodical subscriptions, 1,159 records/tapes.

Undergraduate Courses offered for part-time students during daytime, evenings, summer. Complete part-time degree programs offered during daytime, evenings, summer. Adult/continuing education programs available. Career services available to part-time students: individual and group career counseling, individual job placement, employer recruitment on campus. Part-time tuition: $4.25 per quarter hour for state residents, $21.25 per quarter hour for nonresidents.

Montgomery Technical College
Troy 27371

Public institution; rural setting. Awards A. Barrier-free campus. Total enrollment: 589 (all undergraduates); 48% part-time, 27% women, 54% over 25. Total faculty: 36. Library holdings: 16,000 bound volumes, 150 titles on microform, 200 periodical subscriptions, 300 records/tapes.

Undergraduate Courses offered for part-time students during daytime, evenings, summer. Complete part-time degree programs offered during daytime, evenings, summer. Adult/continuing education programs available. Career services available to part-time students: individual and group career counseling, individual job placement, employer recruitment on campus. Part-time tuition: $4.25 per quarter hour for state residents, $21.25 per quarter hour for nonresidents.

Montreat-Anderson College
Montreat 28757

Independent-religious instutition; rural setting. Awards A. Total enrollment: 382 (all undergraduates); 2% part-time, 49% women, 6% over 25. Total faculty: 29. Library holdings: 48,090 bound volumes, 14 titles on microform, 250 periodical subscriptions, 1,200 records/tapes.

Undergraduate Courses offered for part-time students during daytime. Complete part-time degree programs offered during daytime. Career services available to part-time students: individual and group career counseling. Part-time tuition: $50 per credit hour.

Mount Olive College
Mount Olive 28365

Independent-religious instutition; small-town setting. Awards A. Barrier-free campus. Total enrollment: 345 (all undergraduates); 10% part-time, 51% women, 14% over 25. Total faculty: 30. Library holdings: 35,000 bound volumes, 3,098 titles on microform, 225 periodical subscriptions.

Undergraduate Courses offered for part-time students during daytime, evenings, summer. Complete part-time degree programs offered during daytime, evenings, summer. Adult/continuing education programs available. Career services available to part-time students: individual career counseling. Part-time tuition: $72 per semester hour.

North Carolina / **Colleges Offering Part-Time Degree Programs**

Nash Technical College
Rocky Mount 27804

Public institution; rural setting. Awards A. Barrier-free campus. Total enrollment: 1,554 (all undergraduates); 65% part-time, 57% women, 61% over 25. Total faculty: 90. Library holdings: 19,331 bound volumes, 118 periodical subscriptions.

Undergraduate Courses offered for part-time students during daytime, evenings, summer. Complete part-time degree programs offered during daytime, evenings, summer. Adult/continuing education programs available. Career services available to part-time students: individual career counseling, individual job placement. Part-time tuition: $4.25 per credit for state residents, $21.25 per credit for nonresidents.

North Carolina Agricultural and Technical State University
Greensboro 27411

Public institution; city setting. Awards B, M. Total enrollment: 5,622. Undergraduate enrollment: 5,058; 9% part-time, 42% women, 16% over 25. Total faculty: 376. Library holdings: 309,718 bound volumes, 56,697 titles on microform, 1,536 periodical subscriptions, 16,522 records/tapes.

Undergraduate Courses offered for part-time students during daytime, evenings, summer. Complete part-time degree programs offered during daytime, evenings, summer. Adult/continuing education programs available. Career services available to part-time students: individual and group career counseling, individual job placement, employer recruitment on campus. Part-time tuition and fees per semester (1 to 11 semester hours) range from $103 to $393 for state residents, $423 to $1352 for nonresidents.

Graduate Part-time study available in Graduate School. Degree can be earned exclusively through evening/weekend study in Graduate School. Basic part-time expenses: $103 per semester (minimum) tuition for state residents, $742 per semester (minimum) tuition for nonresidents. Institutional financial aid available to part-time graduate students in Graduate School.

North Carolina Central University
Durham 27707

Public institution; city setting. Awards B, M. Total enrollment: 5,228. Undergraduate enrollment: 4,368; 22% part-time, 62% women, 18% over 25. Total faculty: 379. Library holdings: 341,050 bound volumes, 274 periodical subscriptions.

Undergraduate Courses offered for part-time students during daytime, evenings. Complete part-time degree programs offered during daytime, evenings. Adult/continuing education programs available. Career services available to part-time students: individual career counseling, individual job placement, employer recruitment on campus. Part-time tuition and fees per semester (1 to 11 semester hours) range from $70 to $211 for state residents, $359 to $1078 for nonresidents.

Graduate Part-time study available in Graduate School, School of Business, School of Library Science, School of Law. Degree can be earned exclusively through evening/weekend study in School of Law. Basic part-time expenses: $93 per semester (minimum) tuition plus $42 per semester (minimum) fees for state residents, $382 per semester (minimum) tuition plus $42 per semester (minimum) fees for nonresidents. Institutional financial aid available to part-time graduate students in Graduate School, School of Business, School of Library Science, School of Law.

North Carolina State University at Raleigh
Raleigh 27695

Public institution; city setting. Awards A, B, M, D. Total enrollment: 22,632. Undergraduate enrollment: 17,662; 17% part-time, 32% women. Total faculty: 1,606. Library holdings: 1 million bound volumes, 7,000 periodical subscriptions.

Undergraduate Courses offered for part-time students during daytime, evenings, summer. Complete part-time degree programs offered during daytime, evenings, summer. Adult/continuing education programs available. Career services available to part-time students: individual and group career counseling, individual job placement, employer recruitment on campus. Part-time tuition per semester (1 to 11 semester hours) ranges from $101 to $303 for state residents, $396 to $1189 for nonresidents.

Graduate Part-time study available in Graduate School. Basic part-time expenses: $173 per semester (minimum) tuition for state residents, $828 per semester (minimum) tuition for nonresidents.

North Carolina Wesleyan College
Rocky Mount 27801

Independent-religious instutition; small-town setting. Awards B. Total enrollment: 1,157 (all undergraduates); 30% part-time, 48% women, 25% over 25. Total faculty: 40. Library holdings: 67,549 bound volumes, 700 periodical subscriptions, 300 records/tapes.

Undergraduate Courses offered for part-time students during daytime, evenings, summer. Complete part-time degree programs offered during daytime, evenings, summer. External degree and adult/continuing education programs available. Career services available to part-time students: individual and group career counseling, individual job placement, employer recruitment on campus. Part-time tuition: $70 per semester hour.

Pamlico Technical College
Grantsboro 28529

Public institution; rural setting. Awards A. Barrier-free campus. Total enrollment: 163 (all undergraduates); 47% part-time, 52% women, 80% over 25. Total faculty: 36. Library holdings: 13,000 bound volumes, 54 titles on microform, 138 periodical subscriptions, 2,050 records/tapes.

Undergraduate Courses offered for part-time students during daytime, evenings, summer. Complete part-time degree programs offered during daytime, evenings, summer. Adult/continuing education programs available. Career services available to part-time students: individual and group career counseling, individual job placement. Part-time tuition: $4.25 per credit hour for state residents, $21.25 per credit hour for nonresidents.

Peace College
Raleigh 27604

Independent institution; city setting. Awards A. Barrier-free campus. Total enrollment: 480 (all undergraduates); 6% part-time, 100% women. Total faculty: 33. Library holdings: 36,000 bound volumes.

Undergraduate Courses offered for part-time students during daytime. Complete part-time degree programs offered during daytime. Adult/continuing education programs available. Career services available to part-time students: individual and group career counseling. Part-time tuition: $95 per semester hour.

Colleges Offering Part-Time Degree Programs / North Carolina

Pembroke State University
Pembroke 28372

Public institution; rural setting. Awards B, M. Barrier-free campus. Total enrollment: 2,122. Undergraduate enrollment: 1,924; 16% part-time, 48% women, 15% over 25. Total faculty: 134. Library holdings: 171,247 bound volumes, 27,497 titles on microform, 1,036 periodical subscriptions.

Undergraduate Courses offered for part-time students during daytime, evenings, summer. Complete part-time degree programs offered during daytime, evenings, summer. Adult/continuing education programs available. Career services available to part-time students: individual and group career counseling, individual job placement, employer recruitment on campus. Part-time tuition and fees per semester (1 to 11 semester hours) range from $44 to $271 for state residents, $298 to $1034 for nonresidents.

Graduate Part-time study available in Graduate Studies. Basic part-time expenses: $44 per semester (minimum) tuition for state residents, $298 per semester (minimum) tuition for nonresidents.

Pfeiffer College
Misenheimer 28109

Independent-religious instutition; rural setting. Awards B. Total enrollment: 821 (all undergraduates); 21% part-time, 45% women, 19% over 25. Total faculty: 61. Library holdings: 101,000 bound volumes, 8,593 titles on microform, 434 periodical subscriptions, 2,214 records/tapes.

Undergraduate Courses offered for part-time students during daytime, evenings, summer. Complete part-time degree programs offered during daytime, evenings, summer. Career services available to part-time students: individual and group career counseling, individual job placement, employer recruitment on campus. Part-time tuition: $96 per semester hour.

Piedmont Bible College
Winston-Salem 27101

Independent-religious instutition; city setting. Awards B. Total enrollment: 382 (all undergraduates); 17% part-time, 37% women, 31% over 25. Total faculty: 22. Library holdings: 44,981 bound volumes, 598 titles on microform, 221 periodical subscriptions, 1,622 records/tapes.

Undergraduate Courses offered for part-time students during daytime, evenings, summer. Complete part-time degree programs offered during daytime, evenings, summer. Adult/continuing education programs available. Career services available to part-time students: individual career counseling, individual job placement, employer recruitment on campus. Part-time tuition: $100 per credit hour.

Piedmont Technical College
Roxboro 27573

Public institution; small-town setting. Awards A. Barrier-free campus. Total enrollment: 670 (all undergraduates); 40% part-time, 58% women. Total faculty: 50. Library holdings: 16,841 bound volumes, 233 titles on microform, 290 periodical subscriptions, 13,947 records/tapes.

Undergraduate Courses offered for part-time students during daytime, evenings, summer. Complete part-time degree programs offered during daytime, evenings, summer. Adult/continuing education programs available. Career services available to part-time students: individual and group career counseling, individual job placement, employer recruitment on campus. Part-time tuition: $4.25 per credit hour for state residents, $21.25 per credit hour for nonresidents.

Pitt Community College
Greenville 27835

Public institution; small-town setting. Awards A. Barrier-free campus. Total enrollment: 2,723 (all undergraduates); 48% part-time, 63% women, 40% over 25. Total faculty: 110. Library holdings: 20,000 bound volumes, 400 periodical subscriptions, 300 records/tapes.

Undergraduate Courses offered for part-time students during daytime, evenings. Complete part-time degree programs offered during daytime, evenings. Adult/continuing education programs available. Career services available to part-time students: individual and group career counseling, individual job placement. Part-time tuition: $4.25 per quarter hour for state residents, $21.25 per quarter hour for nonresidents.

Queens College
Charlotte 28274

Independent-religious instutition; city setting. Awards B, M. Total enrollment: 1,175. Undergraduate enrollment: 1,026; 45% part-time, 95% women. Total faculty: 117. Library holdings: 110,000 bound volumes, 700 periodical subscriptions, 50 records/tapes.

Undergraduate Courses offered for part-time students during daytime, evenings, weekends, summer. Complete part-time degree programs offered during daytime, evenings, weekends, summer. Adult/continuing education programs available. Career services available to part-time students: individual and group career counseling, individual job placement, employer recruitment on campus. Part-time tuition: $125 per credit hour.

Graduate Part-time study available in Graduate School. Degree can be earned exclusively through evening/weekend study in Graduate School. Basic part-time expenses: $130 per credit hour tuition plus $7 per semester fees. Institutional financial aid available to part-time graduate students in Graduate School.

Randolph Technical College
Asheboro 27203

Public institution; small-town setting. Awards A. Barrier-free campus. Total enrollment: 1,173 (all undergraduates); 49% part-time, 54% women, 50% over 25. Total faculty: 55. Library holdings: 23,225 bound volumes, 2,600 titles on microform, 250 periodical subscriptions, 3,507 records/tapes.

Undergraduate Courses offered for part-time students during daytime, evenings, summer. Complete part-time degree programs offered during daytime, evenings, summer. Adult/continuing education programs available. Career services available to part-time students: individual and group career counseling, individual job placement, employer recruitment on campus. Part-time tuition: $4.75 per quarter hour for state residents, $21.75 per quarter hour for nonresidents.

Richmond Technical College
Hamlet 28345

Public institution; rural setting. Awards A. Barrier-free campus. Total enrollment: 1,062 (all undergraduates); 20% part-time, 50% women, 50% over 25. Total faculty: 111. Library holdings: 23,013 bound volumes, 131 periodical subscriptions, 203 records/tapes.

Undergraduate Courses offered for part-time students during daytime, evenings, summer. Complete part-time degree programs offered during daytime, evenings. Adult/continuing education programs available. Career services available to part-time students: group career counseling, individual job placement, employer recruitment on campus. Part-time tuition: $4.25 per credit hour for state residents, $21.25 per credit hour for nonresidents.

Roanoke Bible College
Elizabeth City 27909

Independent-religious instutition; small-town setting. Awards A, B. Total enrollment: 177 (all undergraduates); 14% part-time, 50% women, 20% over 25. Total faculty: 16. Library holdings: 25,000 bound volumes, 20 titles on microform, 140 periodical subscriptions, 2,000 records/tapes.

Undergraduate Courses offered for part-time students during daytime. Complete part-time degree programs offered during daytime. Career services available to part-time students: individual career counseling, individual job placement. Part-time tuition: $44 per semester hour.

Roanoke-Chowan Technical College
Ahoskie 27910

Public institution; rural setting. Awards A. Barrier-free campus. Total enrollment: 650 (all undergraduates); 30% part-time, 69% women. Total faculty: 53. Library holdings: 24,500 bound volumes, 221 periodical subscriptions, 5,203 records/tapes.

Undergraduate Courses offered for part-time students during daytime, evenings, summer. Complete part-time degree programs offered during daytime, evenings, summer. Adult/continuing education programs available. Career services available to part-time students: individual and group career counseling, individual job placement, employer recruitment on campus. Part-time tuition: $4.25 per quarter hour for state residents, $21.25 per quarter hour for nonresidents.

Rockingham Community College
Wentworth 27375

Public institution; rural setting. Awards A. Total enrollment: 1,734 (all undergraduates); 47% part-time, 61% women. Total faculty: 138. Library holdings: 32,000 bound volumes, 203 periodical subscriptions, 2,012 records/tapes.

Undergraduate Courses offered for part-time students during daytime, evenings, summer. Complete part-time degree programs offered during daytime, evenings. Adult/continuing education programs available. Career services available to part-time students: individual and group career counseling, individual job placement. Part-time tuition: $4.25 per quarter hour for state residents, $21.25 per quarter hour for nonresidents.

Rowan Technical College
Salisbury 28144

Public institution; small-town setting. Awards A. Barrier-free campus. Total enrollment: 2,100 (all undergraduates); 40% part-time, 50% women. Total faculty: 130.

Undergraduate Courses offered for part-time students during daytime, evenings, summer. Complete part-time degree programs offered during daytime, evenings, summer. Adult/continuing education programs available. Career services available to part-time students: individual career counseling, individual job placement, employer recruitment on campus. Part-time tuition: $4.25 per credit for state residents, $21.25 per credit for nonresidents.

Rutledge College
Fayetteville 28301

Proprietary institution; city setting. Awards A. Barrier-free campus. Total enrollment: 450 (all undergraduates); 5% part-time, 56% women, 40% over 25. Total faculty: 11. Library holdings: 6,100 bound volumes, 38 periodical subscriptions, 100 records/tapes.

Undergraduate Courses offered for part-time students during daytime, evenings, summer. Complete part-time degree programs offered during daytime, evenings, summer. Career services available to part-time students: individual and group career counseling, individual job placement, employer recruitment on campus. Part-time tuition: $53 per credit hour.

Sacred Heart College
Belmont 28012

Independent-religious instutition; small-town setting. Awards A, B. Barrier-free campus. Total enrollment: 405 (all undergraduates); 10% part-time, 61% women, 25% over 25. Total faculty: 60. Library holdings: 57,550 bound volumes, 200 periodical subscriptions.

Undergraduate Courses offered for part-time students during daytime, evenings, summer. Complete part-time degree programs offered during daytime, evenings, summer. Adult/continuing education programs available. Career services available to part-time students: individual career counseling, individual job placement. Part-time tuition: $105 per semester hour.

St Andrews Presbyterian College
Laurinburg 28352

Independent-religious instutition; small-town setting. Awards B. Barrier-free campus. Total enrollment: 724 (all undergraduates); 8% part-time, 50% women. Total faculty: 57. Library holdings: 98,231 bound volumes, 20,117 titles on microform, 471 periodical subscriptions, 3,750 records/tapes.

Undergraduate Courses offered for part-time students during daytime, evenings, summer. Complete part-time degree programs offered during daytime. Adult/continuing education programs available. Career services available to part-time students: individual career counseling, individual job placement, employer recruitment on campus. Part-time tuition: $168 per credit.

Saint Augustine's College
Raleigh 27611

Independent-religious instutition; city setting. Awards B. Total enrollment: 1,641 (all undergraduates); 12% part-time, 54% women, 8% over 25. Total faculty: 84. Library holdings: 99,658 bound volumes, 460 periodical subscriptions, 680 records/tapes.

Undergraduate Courses offered for part-time students during daytime, evenings, summer. Complete part-time degree programs offered during daytime, evenings, summer. Adult/continuing education programs available. Career services available to part-time students: individual career counseling, individual job placement, employer recruitment on campus. Part-time tuition: $54 per semester hour.

Colleges Offering Part-Time Degree Programs / North Carolina

Salem College
Winston-Salem 27108

Independent-religious instutition; city setting. Awards B. Total enrollment: 596 (all undergraduates); 6% part-time, 100% women, 16% over 25. Total faculty: 69. Library holdings: 111,612 bound volumes, 7,212 titles on microform, 424 periodical subscriptions, 5,000 records/tapes.

Undergraduate Courses offered for part-time students during daytime, evenings, summer. Complete part-time degree programs offered during daytime, evenings, summer. External degree and adult/continuing education programs available. Career services available to part-time students: individual and group career counseling, individual job placement, employer recruitment on campus. Part-time tuition: $330 per course.

Sampson Technical College
Clinton 28328

Public institution; rural setting. Awards A. Barrier-free campus. Total enrollment: 876 (all undergraduates); 48% part-time, 61% women. Total faculty: 66. Library holdings: 16,000 bound volumes, 53 periodical subscriptions, 1,361 records/tapes.

Undergraduate Courses offered for part-time students during daytime, evenings. Complete part-time degree programs offered during daytime, evenings. Adult/continuing education programs available. Career services available to part-time students: individual career counseling, individual job placement, employer recruitment on campus. Part-time tuition: $4.25 per quarter hour for state residents, $21.25 per quarter hour for nonresidents.

Sandhills Community College
Carthage 28327

Public institution; rural setting. Awards A. Barrier-free campus. Total enrollment: 1,937 (all undergraduates); 41% part-time, 62% women, 48% over 25. Total faculty: 105. Library holdings: 42,845 bound volumes, 6,017 titles on microform.

Undergraduate Courses offered for part-time students during daytime, evenings, summer. Complete part-time degree programs offered during daytime, evenings, summer. Adult/continuing education programs available. Career services available to part-time students: individual and group career counseling, individual job placement, employer recruitment on campus. Part-time tuition: $4.25 per quarter hour for state residents, $21.25 per quarter hour for nonresidents.

Shaw University
Raleigh 27611

Independent-religious instutition; city setting. Awards B. Total enrollment: 1,922 (all undergraduates); 5% part-time, 44% women. Total faculty: 83. Library holdings: 79,374 bound volumes.

Undergraduate Courses offered for part-time students during daytime, evenings, summer. Complete part-time degree programs offered during daytime, evenings, summer. External degree and adult/continuing education programs available. Career services available to part-time students: individual and group career counseling, individual job placement, employer recruitment on campus. Part-time tuition: $91.67 per credit hour.

Southeastern Community College
Whiteville 28472

Public institution; rural setting. Awards A. Total enrollment: 1,911 (all undergraduates); 47% part-time, 52% women, 45% over 25. Total faculty: 212. Library holdings: 36,920 bound volumes, 386 periodical subscriptions, 4,185 records/tapes.

Undergraduate Courses offered for part-time students during daytime, evenings, summer. Complete part-time degree programs offered during daytime, evenings, summer. External degree and adult/continuing education programs available. Career services available to part-time students: individual and group career counseling, individual job placement, employer recruitment on campus. Part-time tuition: $4.25 per quarter hour for state residents, $21.25 per quarter hour for nonresidents.

Southwestern Technical College
Sylva 28779

Public institution; small-town setting. Awards A. Barrier-free campus. Total enrollment: 1,190 (all undergraduates); 48% part-time, 48% women. Total faculty: 79. Library holdings: 21,063 bound volumes, 210 periodical subscriptions, 810 records/tapes.

Undergraduate Courses offered for part-time students during daytime, evenings, summer. Complete part-time degree programs offered during daytime, evenings, summer. Adult/continuing education programs available. Career services available to part-time students: individual career counseling, individual job placement. Part-time tuition: $4.25 per quarter hour for state residents, $21.25 per quarter hour for nonresidents.

Stanly Technical College
Albemarle 28001

Public institution; small-town setting. Awards A. Barrier-free campus. Total enrollment: 909 (all undergraduates); 62% part-time, 60% women. Total faculty: 57. Library holdings: 22,645 bound volumes, 110 periodical subscriptions, 5,858 records/tapes.

Undergraduate Courses offered for part-time students during daytime, evenings, summer. Complete part-time degree programs offered during daytime, evenings, summer. External degree and adult/continuing education programs available. Career services available to part-time students: individual career counseling, individual job placement, employer recruitment on campus. Part-time tuition: $4.25 per credit for state residents, $21.25 per credit for nonresidents.

Surry Community College
Dobson 27017

Public institution; rural setting. Awards A. Total enrollment: 2,112 (all undergraduates); 35% part-time, 45% women, 60% over 25. Total faculty: 75. Library holdings: 20,000 bound volumes.

Undergraduate Courses offered for part-time students during daytime, evenings, summer. Complete part-time degree programs offered during daytime, evenings, summer. Adult/continuing education programs available. Career services available to part-time students: individual and group career counseling, individual job placement, employer recruitment on campus. Part-time tuition: $4.25 per quarter hour for state residents, $21.50 per quarter hour for nonresidents.

North Carolina / **Colleges Offering Part-Time Degree Programs**

Technical College of Alamance
Haw River 27258

Public institution; rural setting. Awards A. Barrier-free campus. Total enrollment: 1,600 (all undergraduates); 35% part-time, 45% women, 58% over 25. Total faculty: 120. Library holdings: 24,000 bound volumes, 25 periodical subscriptions.

Undergraduate Courses offered for part-time students during daytime, evenings, summer. Complete part-time degree programs offered during daytime, evenings, summer. Adult/continuing education programs available. Career services available to part-time students: individual and group career counseling, individual job placement, employer recruitment on campus. Part-time tuition: $4.25 per quarter hour for state residents, $21.75 per quarter hour for nonresidents.

Tri-County Community College
Murphy 28906

Public institution; rural setting. Awards A. Barrier-free campus. Total enrollment: 721 (all undergraduates); 53% part-time, 62% women, 52% over 25. Total faculty: 35. Library holdings: 16,224 bound volumes, 94 titles on microform, 306 periodical subscriptions, 1,000 records/tapes.

Undergraduate Courses offered for part-time students during daytime, evenings, summer. Complete part-time degree programs offered during daytime, evenings, summer. Adult/continuing education programs available. Career services available to part-time students: individual career counseling, individual job placement, employer recruitment on campus. Part-time tuition: $4.25 per quarter hour for state residents, $21.25 per quarter hour for nonresidents.

University of North Carolina at Asheville
Asheville 28814

Public institution; city setting. Awards B. Barrier-free campus. Total enrollment: 2,648 (all undergraduates); 45% part-time, 54% women, 42% over 25. Total faculty: 168. Library holdings: 126,912 bound volumes, 15,000 titles on microform, 800 periodical subscriptions.

Undergraduate Courses offered for part-time students during daytime, evenings, summer. Complete part-time degree programs offered during daytime, evenings, summer. Adult/continuing education programs available. Career services available to part-time students: individual and group career counseling, individual job placement, employer recruitment on campus. Part-time tuition per semester (1 to 11 credits) ranges from $88 to $263 for state residents, $342 to $1026 for nonresidents.

University of North Carolina at Chapel Hill
Chapel Hill 27514

Public institution; small-town setting. Awards B, M, D. Total enrollment: 21,757. Undergraduate enrollment: 14,558; 7% part-time, 57% women. Total faculty: 1,900. Library holdings: 2.9 million bound volumes, 1.8 million titles on microform, 38,510 periodical subscriptions, 32,001 records/tapes.

Graduate Part-time study available in Graduate School, School of Law, School of Pharmacy. Basic part-time expenses: $120 per semester (minimum) tuition plus $144 per semester fees for state residents, $775 per semester (minimum) tuition plus $144 per semester fees for nonresidents.

University of North Carolina at Charlotte
Charlotte 28223

Public institution; city setting. Awards B, M. Barrier-free campus. Total enrollment: 10,347. Undergraduate enrollment: 9,007; 24% part-time, 46% women, 21% over 25. Total faculty: 646. Library holdings: 346,741 bound volumes, 104,562 titles on microform, 5,028 periodical subscriptions, 31,247 records/tapes.

Undergraduate Courses offered for part-time students during daytime, evenings, summer. Complete part-time degree programs offered during daytime, evenings, summer. Adult/continuing education programs available. Career services available to part-time students: individual and group career counseling, individual job placement, employer recruitment on campus. State resident part-time tuition per semester (1 to 11 semester hours) ranges from $76 to $299. Nonresident part-time tuition per semester (1 to 8 semester hours) ranges from $396 to $1177.

Graduate Part-time study available in Graduate Studies. Basic part-time expenses: $103 per semester (minimum) tuition plus $25 per semester (minimum) fees for state residents, $742 per semester (minimum) tuition plus $25 per semester (minimum) fees for nonresidents.

University of North Carolina at Greensboro
Greensboro 27412

Public institution; city setting. Awards B, M, D. Total enrollment: 9,924. Undergraduate enrollment: 7,326; 17% part-time, 68% women, 18% over 25. Total faculty: 627. Library holdings: 686,185 bound volumes, 1.4 million titles on microform, 6,038 periodical subscriptions, 7,287 records/tapes.

Undergraduate Courses offered for part-time students during daytime, evenings, summer. Complete part-time degree programs offered during daytime, evenings. Adult/continuing education programs available. Career services available to part-time students: individual and group career counseling, individual job placement, employer recruitment on campus. Part-time tuition and fees per semester (1 to 11 semester hours) range from $88 to $316 for state residents, $416 to $1299 for nonresidents.

Graduate Part-time study available in Graduate School. Basic part-time expenses: $120 per semester (minimum) tuition for state residents, $776 per semester (minimum) tuition for nonresidents.

University of North Carolina at Wilmington
Wilmington 28403

Public institution; city setting. Awards A, B, M. Total enrollment: 5,432. Undergraduate enrollment: 5,217; 18% part-time, 53% women, 17% over 25. Total faculty: 315. Library holdings: 223,403 bound volumes, 1,828 titles on microform, 3,511 periodical subscriptions, 5,296 records/tapes.

Undergraduate Courses offered for part-time students during daytime, evenings, summer. Complete part-time degree programs offered during daytime. Adult/continuing education programs available. Career services available to part-time students: individual and group career counseling, individual job placement, employer recruitment on campus. Part-time tuition and fees per semester (1 to 11 credits) range from $84.50 to $314 for state residents, $365.50 to $1158 for nonresidents.

Graduate Part-time study available in Graduate Program in Marine Biology, School of Business, School of Education. Degree can be earned exclusively through evening/weekend study in

Colleges Offering Part-Time Degree Programs / North Carolina

University of North Carolina at Wilmington (continued)

School of Business, School of Education. Basic part-time expenses: $117.50 per semester (minimum) fees for state residents, $626 per semester (minimum) fees for nonresidents.

Vance-Granville Community College
Henderson 27536

Public institution; small-town setting. Awards A. Barrier-free campus. Total enrollment: 1,131 (all undergraduates); 43% part-time, 56% women, 45% over 25. Total faculty: 85. Library holdings: 22,000 bound volumes, 260 periodical subscriptions, 2,000 records/tapes.

Undergraduate Courses offered for part-time students during daytime, evenings. Complete part-time degree programs offered during daytime, evenings. Adult/continuing education programs available. Career services available to part-time students: individual and group career counseling, individual job placement, employer recruitment on campus. Part-time tuition: $4.25 per credit hour for state residents, $21.25 per credit hour for nonresidents.

Wake Forest University
Winston-Salem 27109

Independent-religious instutition; city setting. Awards B, M, D. Barrier-free campus. Total enrollment: 4,818. Undergraduate enrollment: 3,147; 3% part-time, 39% women. Total faculty: 1,128. Library holdings: 849,987 bound volumes, 307,253 titles on microform, 11,634 periodical subscriptions, 1,542 records/tapes.

Undergraduate Courses offered for part-time students during daytime, summer. Complete part-time degree programs offered during daytime. Adult/continuing education programs available. Career services available to part-time students: individual and group career counseling, individual job placement, employer recruitment on campus. Part-time tuition: $170 per credit.

Graduate Part-time study available in Graduate School, Babcock Graduate School of Management. Degree can be earned exclusively through evening/weekend study in Babcock Graduate School of Management. Basic part-time expenses: $180 per hour tuition. Institutional financial aid available to part-time graduate students in Graduate School, Babcock Graduate School of Management.

Wake Technical College
Raleigh 27603

Public institution; city setting. Awards A. Barrier-free campus. Total enrollment: 3,354 (all undergraduates); 19% part-time, 52% women, 48% over 25. Total faculty: 120. Library holdings: 30,000 bound volumes, 851 titles on microform, 271 periodical subscriptions, 400 records/tapes.

Undergraduate Courses offered for part-time students during daytime, evenings, summer. Complete part-time degree programs offered during daytime, evenings, summer. Adult/continuing education programs available. Career services available to part-time students: individual and group career counseling, individual job placement, employer recruitment on campus. Part-time tuition: $4.25 per quarter hour for state residents, $21.50 per quarter hour for nonresidents.

Warren Wilson College
Swannanoa 28778

Independent-religious instutition; rural setting. Awards B, M. Total enrollment: 476. Undergraduate enrollment: 443; 2% part-time, 55% women, 3% over 25. Total faculty: 82. Library holdings: 83,000 bound volumes, 500 periodical subscriptions, 100 records/tapes.

Undergraduate Courses offered for part-time students during daytime. Complete part-time degree programs offered during daytime. Adult/continuing education programs available. Career services available to part-time students: individual and group career counseling, individual job placement, employer recruitment on campus. Part-time tuition per semester (1 to 12 credits) ranges from $90 to $1440.

Wayne Community College
Goldsboro 27530

Public institution; city setting. Awards A. Barrier-free campus. Total enrollment: 2,186 (all undergraduates); 30% part-time, 54% women, 50% over 25. Total faculty: 142. Library holdings: 35,526 bound volumes, 450 titles on microform, 242 periodical subscriptions, 12,590 records/tapes.

Undergraduate Courses offered for part-time students during daytime, evenings. Complete part-time degree programs offered during daytime, evenings. Adult/continuing education programs available. Career services available to part-time students: individual career counseling, individual job placement, employer recruitment on campus. Part-time tuition: $4.25 per credit hour for state residents, $21.25 per credit hour for nonresidents.

Western Carolina University
Cullowhee 28723

Public institution; rural setting. Awards B, M. Total enrollment: 6,027. Undergraduate enrollment: 5,202; 8% part-time, 47% women, 12% over 25. Total faculty: 359. Library holdings: 338,808 bound volumes, 695,643 titles on microform, 2,351 periodical subscriptions, 1,083 records/tapes.

Undergraduate Courses offered for part-time students during daytime, evenings, weekends, summer. Complete part-time degree programs offered during daytime, evenings, weekends. Adult/continuing education programs available. Career services available to part-time students: individual and group career counseling, individual job placement, employer recruitment on campus. Part-time tuition and fees per semester (1 to 11 credit hours) range from $68 to $343 for state residents, $357 to $1209 for nonresidents.

Graduate Part-time study available in Graduate School. Degree can be earned exclusively through evening/weekend study in Graduate School. Basic part-time expenses: $142.15 per semester (minimum) tuition for state residents, $781.15 per semester (minimum) tuition for nonresidents. Institutional financial aid available to part-time graduate students in Graduate School.

Western Piedmont Community College
Morganton 28655

Public institution; small-town setting. Awards A. Barrier-free campus. Total enrollment: 2,100 (all undergraduates); 65% part-time, 64% women. Total faculty: 99. Library holdings: 31,195 bound volumes, 200 periodical subscriptions, 6,480 records/tapes.

Undergraduate Courses offered for part-time students during daytime, evenings, summer. Complete part-time degree programs offered during daytime, evenings, summer. Adult/con-

tinuing education programs available. Career services available to part-time students: individual and group career counseling, individual job placement. Part-time tuition: $4.25 per quarter hour for state residents, $21.25 per quarter hour for nonresidents.

Wilkes Community College
Wilkesboro 28697

Public institution; small-town setting. Awards A. Barrier-free campus. Total enrollment: 2,631 (all undergraduates); 65% part-time, 65% women, 58% over 25. Total faculty: 158. Library holdings: 45,300 bound volumes, 2,843 titles on microform, 54 periodical subscriptions, 9,600 records/tapes.

Undergraduate Courses offered for part-time students during daytime, evenings, weekends, summer. Complete part-time degree programs offered during daytime, evenings, summer. Adult/continuing education programs available. Career services available to part-time students: individual and group career counseling, individual job placement, employer recruitment on campus. Part-time tuition: $4.25 per credit hour for state residents, $21.25 per credit hour for nonresidents.

Wingate College
Wingate 28174

Independent-religious instutition; small-town setting. Awards A, B. Total enrollment: 1,500 (all undergraduates); 5% part-time, 50% women, 3% over 25. Total faculty: 78. Library holdings: 89,100 bound volumes, 125 titles on microform, 350 periodical subscriptions, 2,820 records/tapes.

Undergraduate Courses offered for part-time students during daytime, evenings, summer. Complete part-time degree programs offered during daytime, summer. External degree programs available. Career services available to part-time students: individual and group career counseling, individual job placement, employer recruitment on campus. Part-time tuition: $86 per credit hour.

Winston-Salem State University
Winston-Salem 27110

Public institution; city setting. Awards B. Total enrollment: 2,224 (all undergraduates); 17% part-time, 60% women. Total faculty: 145. Library holdings: 144,238 bound volumes, 1,157 periodical subscriptions, 2,747 records/tapes.

Undergraduate Courses offered for part-time students during daytime, evenings, summer. Complete part-time degree programs offered during daytime, evenings, summer. Adult/continuing education programs available. Career services available to part-time students: individual career counseling, individual job placement, employer recruitment on campus. Part-time tuition and fees per semester (1 to 11 semester hours) range from $76 to $250 for state residents, $330 to $1093 for nonresidents.

NORTH DAKOTA

Bismarck Junior College
Bismarck 58501

Public institution; small-town setting. Awards A. Total enrollment: 2,450 (all undergraduates); 38% part-time, 51% women, 30% over 25. Total faculty: 109. Library holdings: 33,000 bound volumes, 325 periodical subscriptions, 2,400 records/tapes.

Undergraduate Courses offered for part-time students during daytime, evenings, summer. Complete part-time degree programs offered during daytime, evenings, summer. Adult/continuing education programs available. Career services available to part-time students: individual career counseling. Part-time tuition: $28 per credit for area residents, $32 per credit for state residents, $39 per credit for nonresidents.

Dickinson State College
Dickinson 58601

Public institution; small-town setting. Awards A, B. Total enrollment: 1,234 (all undergraduates); 14% part-time, 57% women. Total faculty: 90.

Undergraduate Courses offered for part-time students during daytime. Complete part-time degree programs offered during daytime. Part-time tuition: $20.16 per quarter hour for state residents, $38.16 per quarter hour for nonresidents.

Jamestown College
Jamestown 58401

Independent-religious instutition; small-town setting. Awards B. Total enrollment: 580 (all undergraduates); 16% part-time, 50% women, 13% over 25. Total faculty: 48. Library holdings: 68,000 bound volumes, 15,800 titles on microform, 365 periodical subscriptions.

Undergraduate Courses offered for part-time students during daytime, evenings, summer. Complete part-time degree programs offered during daytime, evenings, summer. Adult/continuing education programs available. Career services available to part-time students: individual and group career counseling, individual job placement, employer recruitment on campus. Part-time tuition: $160 per semester hour.

Mary College
Bismarck 58501

Independent-religious instutition; rural setting. Awards B, M. Barrier-free campus. Total enrollment: 1,122 (all undergraduates); 12% part-time, 73% women. Total faculty: 76. Library holdings: 46,457 bound volumes, 556 titles on microform, 390 periodical subscriptions, 4,475 records/tapes.

Undergraduate Courses offered for part-time students during daytime, evenings, weekends, summer. Complete part-time degree programs offered during daytime, evenings, weekends, summer. External degree and adult/continuing education programs available. Career services available to part-time students: individual and group career counseling, individual job placement, employer recruitment on campus. Part-time tuition: $102 per credit hour.

Mayville State College
Mayville 58257

Public institution; rural setting. Awards A, B. Total enrollment: 759 (all undergraduates); 9% part-time, 50% women, 13% over 25. Total faculty: 59. Library holdings: 79,000 bound volumes, 4,500 titles on microform, 600 periodical subscriptions, 3,490 records/tapes.

Undergraduate Courses offered for part-time students during daytime, summer. Complete part-time degree programs offered during daytime, summer. Adult/continuing education programs available. Career services available to part-time students: individual and group career counseling, individual job placement, employer recruitment on campus. Part-time tuition: $21.41 per quarter hour for state residents, $40.57 per quarter hour for nonresidents.

Colleges Offering Part-Time Degree Programs / North Dakota

Minot State College
Minot 58701

Public institution; small-town setting. Awards A, B, M. Total enrollment: 2,985. Undergraduate enrollment: 2,924; 13% part-time, 60% women, 26% over 25. Total faculty: 138. Library holdings: 91,800 bound volumes, 800 periodical subscriptions, 2,000 records/tapes.

Undergraduate Courses offered for part-time students during daytime, evenings, summer. Complete part-time degree programs offered during daytime, evenings, summer. Adult/continuing education programs available. Career services available to part-time students: individual career counseling, individual job placement, employer recruitment on campus. Part-time tuition: $24.50 per quarter hour for state residents, $44.42 per quarter hour for nonresidents.

Graduate Part-time study available in School of Graduate Studies. Basic part-time expenses: $31 per quarter hour tuition for state residents, $49 per quarter hour tuition for nonresidents. Institutional financial aid available to part-time graduate students in School of Graduate Studies.

North Dakota State School of Science
Wahpeton 58075

Public institution; rural setting. Awards A. Total enrollment: 3,171 (all undergraduates); 2% part-time, 32% women, 11% over 25. Total faculty: 185. Library holdings: 65,840 bound volumes, 560 titles on microform, 1,040 periodical subscriptions, 3,065 records/tapes.

Undergraduate Courses offered for part-time students during daytime, evenings, summer. Complete part-time degree programs offered during daytime. Adult/continuing education programs available. Career services available to part-time students: individual and group career counseling, individual job placement, employer recruitment on campus. Part-time tuition: $21.83 per quarter hour for state residents, $39.75 per quarter hour for nonresidents.

North Dakota State University–Bottineau Branch and Institute of Forestry
Bottineau 58318

Public institution; rural setting. Awards A. Total enrollment: 493 (all undergraduates); 35% part-time, 40% women. Total faculty: 26. Library holdings: 45,000 bound volumes, 260 periodical subscriptions.

Undergraduate Courses offered for part-time students during daytime. Complete part-time degree programs offered during daytime. Adult/continuing education programs available. Career services available to part-time students: individual career counseling, individual job placement. Part-time tuition: $24.95 per credit for state residents, $44.87 per credit for nonresidents.

Northwest Bible College
Minot 58701

Independent-religious instutition; small-town setting. Awards A, B. Total enrollment: 166 (all undergraduates); 30% part-time, 45% women. Total faculty: 12. Library holdings: 33,500 bound volumes, 192 periodical subscriptions, 1,200 records/tapes.

Undergraduate Courses offered for part-time students during daytime. Complete part-time degree programs offered during daytime. Part-time tuition: $71.50 per semester hour.

Tri-College University
Fargo 58105

Independent institution (graduate only). Total enrollment: 279 (coed; 97% part-time). Total faculty: 9. Library holdings: 700,000 bound volumes.

Graduate Part-time study available in Graduate Programs in Education. Basic part-time expenses: $32 per credit hour tuition for state residents, $61 per credit hour tuition for nonresidents. Institutional financial aid available to part-time graduate students in Graduate Programs in Education.

University of North Dakota
Grand Forks 58202

Public institution; rural setting. Awards A, B, M, D. Barrier-free campus. Total enrollment: 11,053. Undergraduate enrollment: 9,003; 5% part-time, 46% women. Total faculty: 650.

Undergraduate Courses offered for part-time students during daytime. Complete part-time degree programs offered during daytime. Career services available to part-time students: individual and group career counseling, individual job placement, employer recruitment on campus. Part-time tuition: $45 per credit hour for state residents, $82.75 per credit hour for nonresidents.

Graduate Part-time study available in Graduate School. Degree can be earned exclusively through evening/weekend study in Graduate School. Basic part-time expenses: $51 per credit tuition for state residents, $95 per credit tuition for nonresidents.

University of North Dakota–Williston Center
Williston 58801

Public institution; small-town setting. Awards A. Total enrollment: 624 (all undergraduates); 9% part-time, 47% women, 30% over 25. Total faculty: 50.

Undergraduate Courses offered for part-time students during daytime, evenings. Complete part-time degree programs offered during daytime, evenings. Adult/continuing education programs available. Part-time tuition: $30 per credit hour for state residents, $60 per credit hour for nonresidents.

Valley City State College
Valley City 58072

Public institution; small-town setting. Awards A, B. Total enrollment: 1,167 (all undergraduates); 21% part-time, 57% women. Total faculty: 66. Library holdings: 74,500 bound volumes, 7,400 titles on microform, 516 periodical subscriptions, 820 records/tapes.

Undergraduate Courses offered for part-time students during daytime, evenings, summer. Complete part-time degree programs offered during daytime, evenings. External degree and adult/continuing education programs available. Career services available to part-time students: individual and group career counseling, individual job placement, employer recruitment on campus. Part-time tuition: $21.42 per quarter hour for state residents, $39.33 per quarter hour for nonresidents.

NORTHERN MARIANA ISLANDS

Northern Marianas College
Saipan 96950

Public institution; rural setting. Awards A. Barrier-free campus. Total enrollment: 173 (all undergraduates); 84% part-time, 65% women, 50% over 25. Total faculty: 20.

Undergraduate Courses offered for part-time students during daytime, evenings, summer. Complete part-time degree programs offered during daytime, evenings. Adult/continuing education programs available. Career services available to part-time students: individual career counseling. Part-time tuition: $30 per credit.

OHIO

Air Force Institute of Technology
Wright-Patterson AFB 45433

Public institution (graduate only). Total enrollment: 991. Graduate enrollment: 882 (primarily men; 16% part-time). Total faculty: 149.

Graduate Part-time study available in School of Engineering, School of Systems and Logistics. Basic part-time expenses: $0 tuition.

Antioch College
Yellow Springs 45387

Independent institution; small-town setting. Awards B, M. Total enrollment: 531 (all undergraduates); 6% part-time, 52% women, 18% over 25. Total faculty: 57. Library holdings: 243,410 bound volumes, 20,000 titles on microform, 1,500 periodical subscriptions, 4,200 records/tapes.

Undergraduate Courses offered for part-time students during daytime, evenings, weekends. Complete part-time degree programs offered during daytime. Adult/continuing education programs available. Career services available to part-time students: individual and group career counseling, individual job placement, employer recruitment on campus. Part-time tuition: $200 per credit.

Antioch International
Yellow Springs 45387

Independent institution (graduate only). Total enrollment: 132. Graduate enrollment: 115 (coed). Total faculty: 22.

Graduate Part-time study available in Graduate Program. Basic part-time expenses: $4335 per year tuition.

Art Academy of Cincinnati
Cincinnati 45202

Independent institution; metropolitan setting. Awards B. Total enrollment: 225 (all undergraduates); 20% part-time, 50% women, 16% over 25. Total faculty: 28. Library holdings: 50,000 bound volumes.

Undergraduate Courses offered for part-time students during daytime, evenings, summer. Complete part-time degree programs offered during daytime. Adult/continuing education programs available. Career services available to part-time students: individual career counseling, employer recruitment on campus. Part-time tuition: $100 per credit hour.

Ashland College
Ashland 44805

Independent-religious instutition; small-town setting. Awards A, B, M. Total enrollment: 3,110. Undergraduate enrollment: 1,896; 9% part-time, 50% women, 1% over 25. Total faculty: 122. Library holdings: 165,309 bound volumes, 120,543 titles on microform, 21,676 periodical subscriptions, 4,697 records/tapes.

Undergraduate Courses offered for part-time students during daytime, evenings, weekends, summer. Complete part-time degree programs offered during daytime, evenings, weekends, summer. External degree and adult/continuing education programs available. Career services available to part-time students: individual and group career counseling, individual job placement, employer recruitment on campus. Part-time tuition: $186 per semester hour.

Graduate Part-time study available in School of Business Administration and Economics, School of Education and Related Professions, Theological Seminary. Degree can be earned exclusively through evening/weekend study in School of Business Administration and Economics. Basic part-time expenses: $132 per credit tuition. Institutional financial aid available to part-time graduate students in Theological Seminary.

Athenaeum of Ohio
Cincinnati 45230

Independent-religious institution (graduate only). Total enrollment: 117 (coed; 9% part-time). Total faculty: 57.

Graduate Part-time study available in Mount Saint Mary's Seminary of the West, Lay Pastoral Ministry Division. Basic part-time expenses: $72 per credit tuition.

Baldwin-Wallace College
Berea 44017

Independent-religious instutition; small-town setting. Awards B, M. Barrier-free campus. Total enrollment: 3,651. Undergraduate enrollment: 2,986; 41% part-time, 50% women. Total faculty: 209. Library holdings: 200,000 bound volumes, 102,865 titles on microform, 1,002 periodical subscriptions, 18,300 records/tapes.

Undergraduate Courses offered for part-time students during daytime, evenings, weekends, summer. Complete part-time degree programs offered during daytime, evenings, weekends, summer. Adult/continuing education programs available. Career services available to part-time students: individual and group career counseling, individual job placement, employer recruitment on campus. Part-time tuition: $127 per credit hour.

Graduate Part-time study available in Graduate Programs. Degree can be earned exclusively through evening/weekend study in Graduate Programs. Basic part-time expenses: $105 per credit hour (minimum) tuition plus $13 per quarter fees.

Belmont Technical College
St Clairsville 43950

Public institution; rural setting. Awards A. Barrier-free campus. Total enrollment: 1,300 (all undergraduates); 58% part-time, 50% women, 15% over 25. Total faculty: 75. Library holdings: 4,500 bound volumes, 130 periodical subscriptions.

Undergraduate Courses offered for part-time students during daytime, evenings, summer. Complete part-time degree programs offered during daytime, evenings, summer. Career services available to part-time students: individual and group career counseling, individual job placement, employer recruitment on campus. Part-time tuition: $21 per credit for state residents, $26 per credit for nonresidents.

Colleges Offering Part-Time Degree Programs / Ohio

Bluffton College
Bluffton 45817

Independent-religious instutition; small-town setting. Awards B. Total enrollment: 610 (all undergraduates); 14% part-time, 48% women, 3% over 25. Total faculty: 59. Library holdings: 94,000 bound volumes, 15,500 titles on microform, 700 periodical subscriptions.

Undergraduate Courses offered for part-time students during daytime. Complete part-time degree programs offered during daytime. Adult/continuing education programs available. Career services available to part-time students: individual and group career counseling, individual job placement, employer recruitment on campus. Part-time tuition: $552 per unit.

Bowling Green State University
Bowling Green 43403

Public institution; small-town setting. Awards A, B, M, D. Total enrollment: 16,866. Undergraduate enrollment: 14,865; 5% part-time, 57% women, 5% over 25. Total faculty: 848. Library holdings: 736,082 bound volumes, 1.2 million titles on microform, 7,301 periodical subscriptions, 60,132 records/tapes.

Undergraduate Courses offered for part-time students during daytime, evenings, summer. Complete part-time degree programs offered during daytime, summer. Adult/continuing education programs available. Career services available to part-time students: individual and group career counseling, individual job placement, employer recruitment on campus. Part-time tuition: $91 per credit hour for state residents, $196 per credit hour for nonresidents.

Graduate Part-time study available in Graduate College. Basic part-time expenses: $118 per credit hour tuition for state residents, $224 per credit hour tuition for nonresidents.

Bowling Green State University–Firelands College
Huron 44839

Public institution; rural setting. Awards A (also offers some graduate courses). Barrier-free campus. Total enrollment: 1,239. Undergraduate enrollment: 1,153; 58% part-time, 59% women. Total faculty: 63. Library holdings: 31,452 bound volumes, 20 titles on microform, 229 periodical subscriptions, 600 records/tapes.

Undergraduate Courses offered for part-time students during daytime, evenings, weekends, summer. Complete part-time degree programs offered during daytime, evenings. Adult/continuing education programs available. Career services available to part-time students: individual and group career counseling, individual job placement. Part-time tuition: $74.50 per credit hour for state residents, $180.50 per credit hour for nonresidents.

Capital University
Columbus 43209

Independent-religious instutition; metropolitan setting. Awards B, M. Total enrollment: 2,537. Undergraduate enrollment: 1,636; 10% part-time, 56% women, 5% over 25. Total faculty: 192. Library holdings: 210,000 bound volumes, 957 periodical subscriptions, 11,044 records/tapes.

Undergraduate Courses offered for part-time students during daytime, evenings, summer. Complete part-time degree programs offered during daytime. External degree programs available. Career services available to part-time students: individual and group career counseling, individual job placement, employer recruitment on campus. Part-time tuition: $190 per semester hour.

Graduate Part-time study available in Graduate School of Administration. Basic part-time expenses: $140 per semester hour tuition.

Case Western Reserve University
Cleveland 44106

Independent institution; metropolitan setting. Awards B, M, D. Total enrollment: 8,698. Undergraduate enrollment: 3,552; 13% part-time, 32% women. Total faculty: 1,535. Library holdings: 1.6 million bound volumes, 370,000 titles on microform, 13,775 periodical subscriptions, 13,995 records/tapes.

Undergraduate Courses offered for part-time students during daytime. Complete part-time degree programs offered during daytime. Adult/continuing education programs available. Career services available to part-time students: individual and group career counseling, individual job placement, employer recruitment on campus. Part-time tuition: $319 per credit.

Graduate Part-time study available in School of Graduate Studies, Frances Payne Bolton School of Nursing, Matthew A. Baxter School of Information and Library Science, School of Applied Social Sciences, Weatherhead School of Management. Degree can be earned exclusively through evening/weekend study in School of Graduate Studies, Weatherhead School of Management. Basic part-time expenses: $319 per credit tuition. Institutional financial aid available to part-time graduate students in Frances Payne Bolton School of Nursing, School of Applied Social Sciences, Weatherhead School of Management.

Cedarville College
Cedarville 45314

Independent-religious instutition; rural setting. Awards B. Total enrollment: 1,793 (all undergraduates); 4% part-time, 53% women, 4% over 25. Total faculty: 121. Library holdings: 85,672 bound volumes, 15,188 titles on microform, 900 periodical subscriptions.

Undergraduate Courses offered for part-time students during daytime, summer. Complete part-time degree programs offered during daytime. Career services available to part-time students: individual and group career counseling, individual job placement, employer recruitment on campus. Part-time tuition: $69 per quarter hour.

Central Ohio Technical College
Newark 43055

Public institution; small-town setting. Awards A. Barrier-free campus. Total enrollment: 1,245 (all undergraduates); 52% part-time, 58% women, 43% over 25. Total faculty: 91. Library holdings: 45,000 bound volumes, 3,994 titles on microform, 407 periodical subscriptions, 2,500 records/tapes.

Undergraduate Courses offered for part-time students during daytime, evenings, summer. Complete part-time degree programs offered during daytime, evenings. Adult/continuing education programs available. Career services available to part-time students: individual and group career counseling, individual job placement, employer recruitment on campus. Part-time tuition: $30.50 per quarter hour for state residents, $43.50 per quarter hour for nonresidents.

Central State University
Wilberforce 45384

Public institution; rural setting. Awards A, B. Total enrollment: 2,310 (all undergraduates); 15% part-time, 49% women. Total faculty: 154. Library holdings: 130,000 bound volumes, 250,000 titles on microform, 500 periodical subscriptions, 400 records/tapes.

Undergraduate Courses offered for part-time students during daytime, evenings, summer. Complete part-time degree programs offered during daytime, evenings, summer. Adult/continuing education programs available. Career services available to part-time students: individual and group career counseling, individual job placement, employer recruitment on campus. Part-time tuition: $32 per quarter hour for state residents, $64 per quarter hour for nonresidents.

Chatfield College
St Martin 45118

Independent institution; rural setting. Awards A. Barrier-free campus. Total enrollment: 140 (all undergraduates); 82% part-time, 69% women, 50% over 25. Total faculty: 25. Library holdings: 18,000 bound volumes, 1,178 records/tapes.

Undergraduate Courses offered for part-time students during daytime, evenings, summer. Complete part-time degree programs offered during daytime, evenings, summer. Adult/continuing education programs available. Career services available to part-time students: individual and group career counseling. Part-time tuition: $70 per credit.

Cincinnati Bible College
Cincinnati 45204

Independent-religious instutition; metropolitan setting. Awards A, B. Total enrollment: 612 (all undergraduates); 17% part-time, 44% women, 10% over 25. Total faculty: 45. Library holdings: 40,268 bound volumes, 265 titles on microform, 285 periodical subscriptions, 4,130 records/tapes.

Undergraduate Courses offered for part-time students during daytime, evenings, summer. Complete part-time degree programs offered during daytime. Career services available to part-time students: individual career counseling, individual job placement. Part-time tuition: $54 per semester hour.

Cincinnati Christian Seminary
Cincinnati 45204

Independent-religious institution (graduate only). Total enrollment: 287 (coed; 75% part-time). Total faculty: 12. Library holdings: 40,268 bound volumes.

Graduate Part-time study available in Graduate School. Basic part-time expenses: $82 per credit tuition.

Cincinnati Metropolitan College
St Bernard 45217

Proprietary institution; small-town setting. Awards A. Total enrollment: 408 (all undergraduates); 5% part-time, 70% women, 85% over 25. Total faculty: 22.

Undergraduate Courses offered for part-time students during daytime, evenings, summer. Complete part-time degree programs offered during daytime, evenings. Adult/continuing education programs available. Career services available to part-time students: individual job placement. Part-time tuition: $295 per quarter hour.

Cincinnati Technical College
Cincinnati 45223

Public institution; metropolitan setting. Awards A. Barrier-free campus. Total enrollment: 3,993 (all undergraduates); 35% part-time, 47% women, 40% over 25. Total faculty: 203. Library holdings: 12,631 bound volumes, 438 periodical subscriptions, 450 records/tapes.

Undergraduate Courses offered for part-time students during daytime, evenings, weekends. Complete part-time degree programs offered during daytime, evenings, weekends. Adult/continuing education programs available. Career services available to part-time students: individual and group career counseling, individual job placement. Part-time tuition: $22 per credit for state residents, $40 per credit for nonresidents.

Clark Technical College
Springfield 45501

Public institution; city setting. Awards A. Barrier-free campus. Total enrollment: 2,689 (all undergraduates); 56% part-time, 63% women. Total faculty: 166. Library holdings: 28,500 bound volumes, 650 titles on microform, 450 periodical subscriptions, 2,413 records/tapes.

Undergraduate Courses offered for part-time students during daytime, evenings, summer. Complete part-time degree programs offered during daytime, evenings. Adult/continuing education programs available. Career services available to part-time students: individual career counseling, individual job placement, employer recruitment on campus. Part-time tuition: $25 per quarter hour for state residents, $50 per quarter hour for nonresidents.

Clermont General and Technical College
Batavia 45103

See University of Cincinnati, Clermont General and Technical College

Cleveland College of Jewish Studies
Beachwood 44122

Independent institution; metropolitan setting. Awards B, M. Barrier-free campus. Total enrollment: 150. Undergraduate enrollment: 125; 90% part-time, 80% women. Total faculty: 25. Library holdings: 15,000 bound volumes, 100 periodical subscriptions, 500 records/tapes.

Undergraduate Courses offered for part-time students during daytime, evenings, summer. Complete part-time degree programs offered during daytime, evenings. Part-time tuition: $45 per credit.

Graduate Part-time study available in Graduate Programs. Basic part-time expenses: $45 per credit tuition.

Cleveland Institute of Art
Cleveland 44106

Independent institution; metropolitan setting. Awards B. Total enrollment: 557 (all undergraduates); 10% part-time, 54% women, 10% over 25. Total faculty: 112. Library holdings: 40,000 bound volumes, 100 titles on microform, 225 periodical subscriptions, 1,000 records/tapes.

Undergraduate Courses offered for part-time students during daytime, summer. Complete part-time degree programs offered during daytime, summer. Adult/continuing education programs available. Part-time tuition: $155 per credit hour.

Colleges Offering Part-Time Degree Programs / Ohio

Cleveland Institute of Electronics
Cleveland 44114

Proprietary institution. Awards A (courses conducted through independent study). Total enrollment: 26,800 (all undergraduates); 100% part-time, 6% women, 60% over 25. Total faculty: 63. Library holdings: 5,000 bound volumes, 38 periodical subscriptions.

Undergraduate Part-time degree programs offered. External degree programs available. Part-time tuition: $1500 per year.

Cleveland State University
Cleveland 44115

Public institution; metropolitan setting. Awards B, M, D. Barrier-free campus. Total enrollment: 18,942. Undergraduate enrollment: 14,195; 41% part-time, 43% women, 28% over 25. Total faculty: 710. Library holdings: 640,000 bound volumes, 360,000 titles on microform, 4,000 periodical subscriptions, 6,000 records/tapes.

Undergraduate Courses offered for part-time students during daytime, evenings. Complete part-time degree programs offered during daytime, evenings. Adult/continuing education programs available. Career services available to part-time students: individual and group career counseling, individual job placement, employer recruitment on campus. Part-time tuition: $47 per quarter hour for state residents, $94 per quarter hour for nonresidents.

Graduate Part-time study available in College of Arts and Sciences, College of Education, College of Urban Affairs, Fenn College of Engineering, James J. Nance College of Business Administration. Basic part-time expenses: $53 per credit tuition for state residents, $106 per credit tuition for nonresidents.

College of Mount St Joseph on the Ohio
Mount St Joseph 45051

Independent-religious instutition; metropolitan setting. Awards A, B, M. Barrier-free campus. Total enrollment: 1,753. Undergraduate enrollment: 1,665; 50% part-time, 96% women, 53% over 25. Total faculty: 116. Library holdings: 105,000 bound volumes, 525 periodical subscriptions.

Undergraduate Courses offered for part-time students during daytime, evenings, weekends, summer. Complete part-time degree programs offered during daytime, evenings, weekends, summer. Adult/continuing education programs available. Career services available to part-time students: individual career counseling, individual job placement, employer recruitment on campus. Part-time tuition: $137 per credit hour.

Graduate Part-time study available in Graduate Program in Education. Degree can be earned exclusively through evening/weekend study in Graduate Program in Education. Basic part-time expenses: $110 per semester hour tuition.

Columbus College of Art and Design
Columbus 43215

Independent institution; metropolitan setting. Awards B. Total enrollment: 941 (all undergraduates); 17% part-time, 52% women. Total faculty: 69. Library holdings: 20,450 bound volumes, 2,300 titles on microform, 142 periodical subscriptions, 380 records/tapes.

Undergraduate Courses offered for part-time students during daytime, evenings, summer. Complete part-time degree programs offered during daytime, evenings, summer. Adult/continuing education programs available. Career services available to part-time students: individual career counseling, individual job placement, employer recruitment on campus. Part-time tuition: $150 per semester hour.

Columbus Technical Institute
Columbus 43216

Public institution; metropolitan setting. Awards A. Barrier-free campus. Total enrollment: 9,550 (all undergraduates); 47% part-time, 50% women. Total faculty: 465. Library holdings: 21,165 bound volumes, 118 titles on microform, 392 periodical subscriptions, 3,946 records/tapes.

Undergraduate Courses offered for part-time students during daytime, evenings, weekends, summer. Complete part-time degree programs offered during daytime, evenings, summer. Adult/continuing education programs available. Career services available to part-time students: individual and group career counseling, individual job placement, employer recruitment on campus. Part-time tuition: $32 per quarter hour for state residents, $72 per quarter hour for nonresidents.

Cuyahoga Community College, Eastern Campus
Warrensville Township 44122

Public institution; small-town setting. Awards A. Barrier-free campus. Total enrollment: 5,929 (all undergraduates); 79% part-time, 68% women, 62% over 25. Total faculty: 215. Library holdings: 35,000 bound volumes, 5,000 titles on microform, 200 periodical subscriptions, 1,060 records/tapes.

Undergraduate Courses offered for part-time students during daytime, evenings, weekends, summer. Complete part-time degree programs offered during daytime, evenings, weekends, summer. Adult/continuing education programs available. Career services available to part-time students: individual and group career counseling, individual job placement, employer recruitment on campus. Part-time tuition: $20 per credit hour for area residents, $27 per credit hour for state residents, $43 per credit hour for nonresidents.

Cuyahoga Community College, Western Campus
Parma 44130

Public institution; city setting. Awards A. Barrier-free campus. Total enrollment: 11,996 (all undergraduates); 75% part-time, 61% women, 50% over 25. Total faculty: 436. Library holdings: 51,269 bound volumes, 371 periodical subscriptions, 3,168 records/tapes.

Undergraduate Courses offered for part-time students during daytime, evenings, weekends, summer. Complete part-time degree programs offered during daytime, evenings, weekends, summer. Adult/continuing education programs available. Career services available to part-time students: individual and group career counseling, individual job placement, employer recruitment on campus. Part-time tuition: $20 per credit hour for area residents, $27 per credit hour for state residents, $43 per credit hour for nonresidents.

Defiance College
Defiance 43512

Independent-religious instutition; small-town setting. Awards A, B. Total enrollment: 917 (all undergraduates); 26% part-time, 40% women, 13% over 25. Total faculty: 75. Library holdings: 90,311 bound volumes, 843 periodical subscriptions, 4,825 records/tapes.

Ohio / Colleges Offering Part-Time Degree Programs

Undergraduate Courses offered for part-time students during daytime, evenings, summer. Complete part-time degree programs offered during daytime, evenings, summer. External degree and adult/continuing education programs available. Career services available to part-time students: individual and group career counseling, individual job placement, employer recruitment on campus. Part-time tuition: $95 per hour.

DeVry Institute of Technology
Columbus 43209

Proprietary institution; metropolitan setting. Awards A, B. Barrier-free campus. Total enrollment: 4,440 (all undergraduates); 6% part-time, 14% women. Total faculty: 238.

Undergraduate Courses offered for part-time students during daytime, evenings. Complete part-time degree programs offered during daytime. Adult/continuing education programs available. Career services available to part-time students: individual and group career counseling, individual job placement, employer recruitment on campus. Part-time tuition: $1990 per year.

Dyke College
Cleveland 44115

Independent institution; metropolitan setting. Awards A, B. Total enrollment: 1,482 (all undergraduates); 32% part-time, 65% women, 35% over 25. Total faculty: 128. Library holdings: 12,000 bound volumes, 800 titles on microform, 130 periodical subscriptions, 1,920 records/tapes.

Undergraduate Courses offered for part-time students during daytime, evenings, weekends, summer. Complete part-time degree programs offered during daytime, evenings, weekends, summer. External degree and adult/continuing education programs available. Career services available to part-time students: individual and group career counseling, individual job placement, employer recruitment on campus. Part-time tuition: $110 per credit.

Edison State Community College
Piqua 45356

Public institution; small-town setting. Awards A. Barrier-free campus. Total enrollment: 2,595 (all undergraduates); 74% part-time, 60% women, 41% over 25. Total faculty: 136. Library holdings: 23,000 bound volumes, 30 titles on microform, 120 periodical subscriptions, 300 records/tapes.

Undergraduate Courses offered for part-time students during daytime, evenings, summer. Complete part-time degree programs offered during daytime, evenings, summer. Adult/continuing education programs available. Career services available to part-time students: individual and group career counseling, individual job placement. Part-time tuition: $21 per credit hour for state residents, $40 per credit hour for nonresidents.

Findlay College
Findlay 45840

Independent-religious instutition; small-town setting. Awards A, B. Total enrollment: 1,157 (all undergraduates); 34% part-time, 58% women. Total faculty: 99. Library holdings: 103,021 bound volumes, 510 titles on microform, 645 periodical subscriptions, 4,560 records/tapes.

Undergraduate Courses offered for part-time students during daytime, evenings, weekends, summer. Complete part-time degree programs offered during daytime, evenings, weekends, summer. Adult/continuing education programs available. Career services available to part-time students: individual and group career counseling, individual job placement, employer recruitment on campus. Part-time tuition: $167 per semester hour.

Franklin University
Columbus 43215

Independent institution; metropolitan setting. Awards A, B. Barrier-free campus. Total enrollment: 4,857 (all undergraduates); 60% part-time, 53% women. Total faculty: 218. Library holdings: 52,869 bound volumes, 11,026 titles on microform, 1,200 periodical subscriptions, 639 records/tapes.

Undergraduate Courses offered for part-time students during daytime, evenings, weekends, summer. Complete part-time degree programs offered during daytime, evenings, weekends, summer. Adult/continuing education programs available. Career services available to part-time students: individual and group career counseling, individual job placement, employer recruitment on campus. Part-time tuition: $85 per credit hour.

God's Bible School and College
Cincinnati 45210

Independent-religious instutition; metropolitan setting. Awards B. Total enrollment: 338 (all undergraduates); 10% part-time, 49% women, 13% over 25. Total faculty: 22. Library holdings: 25,121 bound volumes, 202 titles on microform, 70 periodical subscriptions, 750 records/tapes.

Undergraduate Courses offered for part-time students during daytime. Complete part-time degree programs offered during daytime. Career services available to part-time students: individual job placement. Part-time tuition: $50 per semester hour.

Harding Business College
Marion 43302

Proprietary institution; small-town setting. Awards A. Total enrollment: 200 (all undergraduates); 0% part-time, 72% women, 26% over 25. Total faculty: 15. Library holdings: 1,500 bound volumes, 8 periodical subscriptions.

Undergraduate Courses offered for part-time students during daytime, evenings. Complete part-time degree programs offered during daytime, evenings. Career services available to part-time students: individual career counseling, individual job placement. Part-time tuition: $55 per credit hour.

Hebrew Union College–Jewish Institute of Religion
Cincinnati 45220

Independent-religious institution (graduate only). Total enrollment: 188 (coed; 16% part-time). Total faculty: 30.

Graduate Part-time study available in School of Graduate Studies. Basic part-time expenses: $575 per course tuition.

Heidelberg College
Tiffin 44883

Independent-religious instutition; small-town setting. Awards B. Total enrollment: 843 (all undergraduates); 7% part-time, 44% women. Total faculty: 79. Library holdings: 144,000 bound volumes, 870 titles on microform, 800 periodical subscriptions, 4,854 records/tapes.

Colleges Offering Part-Time Degree Programs / Ohio

Heidelberg College (continued)

Undergraduate Courses offered for part-time students during daytime, evenings, weekends, summer. Complete part-time degree programs offered during daytime, weekends, summer. External degree and adult/continuing education programs available. Career services available to part-time students: individual and group career counseling, individual job placement, employer recruitment on campus. Part-time tuition: $155 per semester hour.

Hiram College
Hiram 44234

Independent-religious instutition; rural setting. Awards B. Total enrollment: 1,209 (all undergraduates); 2% part-time, 45% women, 2% over 25. Total faculty: 80. Library holdings: 157,000 bound volumes, 790 periodical subscriptions, 7,200 records/tapes.

Undergraduate Courses offered for part-time students during daytime, weekends. Complete part-time degree programs offered during daytime, weekends. Adult/continuing education programs available. Career services available to part-time students: individual career counseling, individual job placement, employer recruitment on campus. Part-time tuition: $169 per credit hour.

Hocking Technical College
Nelsonville 45764

Public institution; rural setting. Awards A. Barrier-free campus. Total enrollment: 3,736 (all undergraduates); 30% part-time, 38% women, 45% over 25. Total faculty: 147. Library holdings: 15,000 bound volumes, 260 periodical subscriptions.

Undergraduate Courses offered for part-time students during daytime, evenings, summer. Complete part-time degree programs offered during daytime, evenings, summer. Adult/continuing education programs available. Career services available to part-time students: individual and group career counseling, individual job placement, employer recruitment on campus. Part-time tuition: $30 per quarter hour for state residents, $60 per quarter hour for nonresidents.

Jefferson Technical College
Steubenville 43952

Public institution; small-town setting. Awards A. Barrier-free campus. Total enrollment: 1,822 (all undergraduates); 54% part-time, 50% women, 46% over 25. Total faculty: 108. Library holdings: 19,800 bound volumes, 50 titles on microform, 190 periodical subscriptions, 2,105 records/tapes.

Undergraduate Courses offered for part-time students during daytime, evenings, weekends, summer. Complete part-time degree programs offered during daytime, evenings. Adult/continuing education programs available. Career services available to part-time students: individual and group career counseling, individual job placement, employer recruitment on campus. Part-time tuition: $15 per quarter hour for area residents, $18 per quarter hour for state residents, $30 per quarter hour for nonresidents.

John Carroll University
University Heights 44118

Independent-religious instutition; small-town setting. Awards B, M. Total enrollment: 3,900. Undergraduate enrollment: 3,200; 18% part-time, 47% women. Total faculty: 223. Library holdings: 389,000 bound volumes, 5,000 titles on microform, 500 periodical subscriptions, 2,700 records/tapes.

Undergraduate Courses offered for part-time students during daytime, evenings, summer. Complete part-time degree programs offered during daytime, evenings, summer. Adult/continuing education programs available. Career services available to part-time students: individual career counseling, individual job placement, employer recruitment on campus. Part-time tuition: $149 per credit hour.

Graduate Part-time study available in Graduate School. Basic part-time expenses: $164 per credit tuition.

Kent State University
Kent 44242

Public institution; small-town setting. Awards B, M, D. Total enrollment: 19,687. Undergraduate enrollment: 15,991; 17% part-time, 51% women, 8% over 25. Total faculty: 1,188. Library holdings: 1.5 million bound volumes, 900,000 titles on microform, 8,700 periodical subscriptions.

Undergraduate Courses offered for part-time students during daytime, evenings, weekends, summer. Complete part-time degree programs offered during daytime, evenings. Adult/continuing education programs available. Career services available to part-time students: individual and group career counseling, individual job placement, employer recruitment on campus. Part-time tuition: $98 per semester hour for state residents, $155 per semester hour for nonresidents.

Graduate Part-time study available in Graduate College, Graduate School of Education, Graduate School of Management. Basic part-time expenses: $101.25 per credit tuition for state residents, $161.25 per credit tuition for nonresidents.

Kent State University, Ashtabula Campus
Ashtabula 44004

Public institution; small-town setting. Awards A (also offers upper-level courses applicable toward the bachelor's degree awarded by the main campus in Kent). Barrier-free campus. Total enrollment: 1,030 (all undergraduates); 55% part-time, 60% women, 53% over 25. Total faculty: 59. Library holdings: 46,113 bound volumes, 311 periodical subscriptions, 1,746 records/tapes.

Undergraduate Courses offered for part-time students during daytime, evenings, summer. Complete part-time degree programs offered during daytime, evenings, summer. Adult/continuing education programs available. Career services available to part-time students: individual career counseling, individual job placement. Part-time tuition: $69 per semester hour for state residents, $129 per semester hour for nonresidents.

Kent State University, East Liverpool Campus
East Liverpool 43920

Public institution; small-town setting. Awards A (also offers upper-level courses applicable toward the bachelor's degree awarded by the main campus in Kent). Barrier-free campus. Total enrollment: 685 (all undergraduates); 49% part-time, 70% women. Total faculty: 40. Library holdings: 31,000 bound volumes, 110 periodical subscriptions.

Undergraduate Courses offered for part-time students during daytime, evenings, summer. Complete part-time degree programs offered during daytime, evenings, summer. Adult/continuing education programs available. Career services available to part-time students: individual career counseling, individual

Ohio / Colleges Offering Part-Time Degree Programs

job placement. Part-time tuition: $69 per semester hour for state residents, $129 per semester hour for nonresidents.

Kent State University, Geauga Campus
Burton Township 44021

Public institution; rural setting. Awards A. Barrier-free campus. Total enrollment: 350 (all undergraduates); 60% part-time, 64% women, 58% over 25. Total faculty: 29. Library holdings: 12,000 bound volumes, 150 periodical subscriptions, 100 records/tapes.

Undergraduate Courses offered for part-time students during daytime, evenings, weekends, summer. Complete part-time degree programs offered during daytime, evenings, summer. Adult/continuing education programs available. Career services available to part-time students: individual and group career counseling, individual job placement, employer recruitment on campus. Part-time tuition: $69 per semester hour for state residents, $119 per semester hour for nonresidents.

Kent State University, Salem Campus
Salem 44460

Public institution; rural setting. Awards A. Total enrollment: 621 (all undergraduates); 63% part-time, 53% women, 40% over 25. Total faculty: 39. Library holdings: 23,000 bound volumes, 20 periodical subscriptions, 200 records/tapes.

Undergraduate Courses offered for part-time students during daytime, evenings, summer. Complete part-time degree programs offered during daytime, evenings, summer. Adult/continuing education programs available. Career services available to part-time students: individual and group career counseling, individual job placement, employer recruitment on campus. Part-time tuition: $69 per semester hour for state residents, $119 per semester hour for nonresidents.

Kent State University, Stark Campus
Canton 44720

Public institution; city setting. Awards A (also offers upper-level courses applicable toward the bachelor's degree awarded by the main campus in Kent). Barrier-free campus. Total enrollment: 1,776 (all undergraduates); 60% part-time, 61% women. Total faculty: 98. Library holdings: 69,637 bound volumes, 600 titles on microform, 369 periodical subscriptions, 2,062 records/tapes.

Undergraduate Courses offered for part-time students during daytime, evenings, summer. Complete part-time degree programs offered during daytime, evenings, summer. Adult/continuing education programs available. Career services available to part-time students: individual career counseling. Part-time tuition: $65.50 per semester hour for state residents, $164.95 per semester hour for nonresidents.

Kent State University, Trumbull Campus
Warren 44483

Public institution; city setting. Awards A (also offers upper-level courses applicable toward the bachelor's degree awarded by the main campus in Kent). Barrier-free campus. Total enrollment: 1,626 (all undergraduates); 55% part-time, 63% women, 47% over 25. Total faculty: 85. Library holdings: 20,000 bound volumes, 280 periodical subscriptions.

Undergraduate Courses offered for part-time students during daytime, evenings, weekends, summer. Complete part-time degree programs offered during daytime, evenings, weekends, summer. Adult/continuing education programs available. Career services available to part-time students: individual career counseling, individual job placement, employer recruitment on campus. Part-time tuition: $69 per credit hour for state residents, $129 per credit hour for nonresidents.

Kent State University, Tuscarawas Campus
New Philadelphia 44663

Public institution; small-town setting. Awards A. Barrier-free campus. Total enrollment: 944 (all undergraduates); 52% part-time, 58% women. Total faculty: 51. Library holdings: 37,500 bound volumes, 2,662 titles on microform, 52 periodical subscriptions, 1,706 records/tapes.

Undergraduate Courses offered for part-time students during daytime, evenings, summer. Complete part-time degree programs offered during daytime, evenings, summer. Adult/continuing education programs available. Career services available to part-time students: individual career counseling. Part-time tuition: $69 per semester hour for state residents, $119 per semester hour for nonresidents.

Kettering College of Medical Arts
Kettering 45429

Independent-religious instutition; city setting. Awards A. Barrier-free campus. Total enrollment: 490 (all undergraduates); 12% part-time, 78% women, 40% over 25. Total faculty: 73. Library holdings: 53,513 bound volumes, 1,044 periodical subscriptions, 4,882 records/tapes.

Undergraduate Courses offered for part-time students during daytime. Complete part-time degree programs offered during daytime. Career services available to part-time students: individual career counseling, employer recruitment on campus. Part-time tuition: $72 per credit hour.

Lake Erie College
Painesville 44077

Independent institution; small-town setting. Awards B, M. Total enrollment: 1,171. Undergraduate enrollment: 797; 10% part-time, 80% women. Total faculty: 78. Library holdings: 120,000 bound volumes, 375 titles on microform, 590 periodical subscriptions, 2,000 records/tapes.

Undergraduate Courses offered for part-time students during daytime, evenings, weekends, summer. Complete part-time degree programs offered during daytime, evenings. External degree and adult/continuing education programs available. Career services available to part-time students: individual and group career counseling, individual job placement, employer recruitment on campus. Part-time tuition: $130 per credit hour.

Graduate Part-time study available in Graduate Programs. Basic part-time expenses: $130 per semester hour (minimum) tuition.

Lakeland Community College
Mentor 44060

Public institution; small-town setting. Awards A. Barrier-free campus. Total enrollment: 9,234 (all undergraduates); 75% part-time, 57% women. Total faculty: 390. Library holdings: 66,896 bound volumes, 310 periodical subscriptions, 584 records/tapes.

Undergraduate Courses offered for part-time students during daytime, evenings, weekends, summer. Complete part-time degree programs offered during daytime, evenings, weekends, summer. External degree and adult/continuing education pro-

Colleges Offering Part-Time Degree Programs / Ohio

Lakeland Community College (continued)

grams available. Career services available to part-time students: individual job placement. Part-time tuition: $21 per quarter hour for area residents, $25 per quarter hour for state residents, $52.50 per quarter hour for nonresidents.

Lima Technical College
Lima 45804

Public institution; small-town setting. Awards A. Total enrollment: 2,165 (all undergraduates); 35% part-time, 61% women, 43% over 25. Total faculty: 115. Library holdings: 47,440 bound volumes, 507 periodical subscriptions, 1,951 records/tapes.

Undergraduate Courses offered for part-time students during daytime, evenings, summer. Complete part-time degree programs offered during daytime, evenings. Adult/continuing education programs available. Career services available to part-time students: individual and group career counseling, individual job placement, employer recruitment on campus. Part-time tuition: $28.75 per credit hour for state residents, $58 per credit hour for nonresidents.

Lorain County Community College
Elyria 44035

Public institution; city setting. Awards A. Barrier-free campus. Total enrollment: 7,173 (all undergraduates); 60% part-time, 59% women, 50% over 25. Total faculty: 320. Library holdings: 95,826 bound volumes, 9,086 titles on microform, 642 periodical subscriptions, 4,992 records/tapes.

Undergraduate Courses offered for part-time students during daytime, evenings, weekends, summer. Complete part-time degree programs offered during daytime, evenings, summer. Adult/continuing education programs available. Career services available to part-time students: individual and group career counseling, individual job placement, employer recruitment on campus. Part-time tuition: $22.50 per quarter hour for area residents, $30.50 per quarter hour for state residents, $63.50 per quarter hour for nonresidents.

Lourdes College
Sylvania 43560

Independent-religious instutition; small-town setting. Awards A, B. Barrier-free campus. Total enrollment: 762 (all undergraduates); 68% part-time, 93% women, 38% over 25. Total faculty: 38. Library holdings: 37,399 bound volumes, 1,325 titles on microform, 234 periodical subscriptions, 400 records/tapes.

Undergraduate Courses offered for part-time students during daytime, evenings, weekends, summer. Complete part-time degree programs offered during daytime, evenings, weekends, summer. Adult/continuing education programs available. Career services available to part-time students: individual and group career counseling. Part-time tuition: $73 per semester hour.

Malone College
Canton 44709

Independent-religious instutition; city setting. Awards A, B. Barrier-free campus. Total enrollment: 876 (all undergraduates); 25% part-time, 55% women. Total faculty: 68. Library holdings: 101,000 bound volumes, 38,500 titles on microform, 645 periodical subscriptions, 4,913 records/tapes.

Undergraduate Courses offered for part-time students during daytime, evenings, summer. Complete part-time degree programs offered during daytime, evenings, summer. Adult/continuing education programs available. Career services available to part-time students: individual and group career counseling, individual job placement, employer recruitment on campus. Part-time tuition: $100 per credit hour.

Mansfield Business College
Mansfield 44905

Proprietary institution; city setting. Awards A. Barrier-free campus. Total enrollment: 448 (all undergraduates); 0% part-time, 61% women, 41% over 25. Total faculty: 19. Library holdings: 5,000 bound volumes, 23 periodical subscriptions, 500 records/tapes.

Undergraduate Courses offered for part-time students during daytime, evenings, summer. Complete part-time degree programs offered during daytime, evenings, summer. Adult/continuing education programs available. Career services available to part-time students: individual career counseling, individual job placement, employer recruitment on campus. Part-time tuition: $60 per credit hour.

Marietta College
Marietta 45750

Independent institution; small-town setting. Awards B, M. Total enrollment: 1,250. Undergraduate enrollment: 1,245; 10% part-time, 36% women. Total faculty: 104. Library holdings: 257,530 bound volumes, 2,188 periodical subscriptions.

Undergraduate Courses offered for part-time students during daytime, evenings, summer. Complete part-time degree programs offered during daytime, evenings, summer. Adult/continuing education programs available. Career services available to part-time students: individual career counseling, individual job placement, employer recruitment on campus. Part-time tuition: $215 per credit hour.

Graduate Part-time study available in Graduate Program. Basic part-time expenses: $135 per credit tuition for state residents, for nonresidents.

Marion Technical College
Marion 43302

Public institution; small-town setting. Awards A. Barrier-free campus. Total enrollment: 1,516 (all undergraduates); 54% part-time, 59% women. Total faculty: 80. Library holdings: 30,000 bound volumes.

Undergraduate Courses offered for part-time students during daytime, evenings, summer. Complete part-time degree programs offered during daytime, evenings, summer. Adult/continuing education programs available. Career services available to part-time students: individual and group career counseling, individual job placement, employer recruitment on campus. Part-time tuition: $31 per credit hour for state residents, $74 per credit hour for nonresidents.

Medical College of Ohio
Toledo 43699

Public institution (graduate only). Total enrollment: 730 (coed; 9% part-time). Total faculty: 488.

Graduate Part-time study available in Graduate School. Basic part-time expenses: $56 per credit hour (minimum) tuition for state residents, $71 per credit hour (minimum) tuition for nonresidents.

Ohio / Colleges Offering Part-Time Degree Programs

Methodist Theological School in Ohio
Delaware 43015

Independent-religious institution (graduate only). Total enrollment: 241 (coed; 15% part-time). Total faculty: 25.

Graduate Part-time study available in Graduate and Professional Programs. Basic part-time expenses: $416 per unit tuition.

Miami-Jacobs Junior College of Business
Dayton 45401

Proprietary institution; metropolitan setting. Awards A. Total enrollment: 750 (all undergraduates); 2% part-time, 75% women, 40% over 25. Total faculty: 34. Library holdings: 5,000 bound volumes, 60 periodical subscriptions, 265 records/tapes.

Undergraduate Courses offered for part-time students during daytime, evenings, summer. Complete part-time degree programs offered during daytime, evenings. Career services available to part-time students: individual and group career counseling, individual job placement. Part-time tuition: $55 per credit.

Miami University
Oxford 45056

Public institution; small-town setting. Awards B, M, D. Total enrollment: 14,870. Undergraduate enrollment: 13,423; 4% part-time, 56% women. Total faculty: 770. Library holdings: 1.1 million bound volumes, 5,000 periodical subscriptions.

Undergraduate Courses offered for part-time students during daytime, summer. Complete part-time degree programs offered during daytime. Adult/continuing education programs available. Career services available to part-time students: individual and group career counseling, individual job placement, employer recruitment on campus. Part-time tuition: $99.25 per credit hour for state residents, $188.75 per credit hour for nonresidents.

Graduate Part-time study available in School of Education and Allied Professions. Basic part-time expenses: $0 tuition plus $105.50 per credit hour fees for state residents, $89.50 per credit hour tuition plus $105.50 per credit hour fees for nonresidents.

Miami University–Hamilton Campus
Hamilton 45011

Public institution; city setting. Awards A. Barrier-free campus. Total enrollment: 1,778 (all undergraduates); 65% part-time, 59% women, 25% over 25. Total faculty: 51. Library holdings: 64,090 bound volumes, 280 titles on microform, 377 periodical subscriptions, 455 records/tapes.

Undergraduate Courses offered for part-time students during daytime, evenings, summer. Complete part-time degree programs offered during daytime, evenings, summer. Adult/continuing education programs available. Career services available to part-time students: individual and group career counseling, individual job placement. Part-time tuition: $77.75 per credit hour for state residents, $163.25 per credit hour for nonresidents.

Miami University–Middletown Campus
Middletown 45042

Public institution; city setting. Awards A. Barrier-free campus. Total enrollment: 1,718. Undergraduate enrollment: 1,671; 60% part-time, 61% women, 60% over 25. Total faculty: 143. Library holdings: 75,000 bound volumes, 500 periodical subscriptions, 6,000 records/tapes.

Undergraduate Courses offered for part-time students during daytime, evenings, summer. Complete part-time degree programs offered during daytime, evenings, summer. Adult/continuing education programs available. Career services available to part-time students: individual and group career counseling, individual job placement, employer recruitment on campus. Part-time tuition: $77.75 per semester hour for state residents, $163.25 per semester hour for nonresidents.

Mount Union College
Alliance 44601

Independent-religious instutition; small-town setting. Awards B. Barrier-free campus. Total enrollment: 989 (all undergraduates); 3% part-time, 45% women, 2% over 25. Total faculty: 94. Library holdings: 200,000 bound volumes, 975 periodical subscriptions.

Undergraduate Courses offered for part-time students during daytime, evenings, summer. Complete part-time degree programs offered during daytime, evenings, summer. Adult/continuing education programs available. Part-time tuition: $300 per credit hour.

Mount Vernon Nazarene College
Mt Vernon 43050

Independent-religious instutition; small-town setting. Awards A, B. Total enrollment: 1,052 (all undergraduates); 15% part-time, 51% women. Total faculty: 72. Library holdings: 75,000 bound volumes, 450 periodical subscriptions, 2,200 records/tapes.

Undergraduate Courses offered for part-time students during daytime, evenings, weekends, summer. Complete part-time degree programs offered during daytime, evenings. Adult/continuing education programs available. Career services available to part-time students: individual and group career counseling, individual job placement, employer recruitment on campus. Part-time tuition: $140 per credit hour.

Muskingum College
New Concord 43762

Independent-religious instutition; rural setting. Awards B. Total enrollment: 1,017 (all undergraduates); 5% part-time, 48% women, 1% over 25. Total faculty: 83. Library holdings: 176,000 bound volumes, 52,000 titles on microform, 700 periodical subscriptions, 4,600 records/tapes.

Undergraduate Courses offered for part-time students during daytime, evenings, summer. Complete part-time degree programs offered during daytime, summer. External degree and adult/continuing education programs available. Career services available to part-time students: individual and group career counseling, individual job placement, employer recruitment on campus. Part-time tuition: $215 per credit hour.

North Central Technical College
Mansfield 44906

Public institution; city setting. Awards A. Barrier-free campus. Total enrollment: 2,088 (all undergraduates); 51% part-time, 53% women, 50% over 25. Total faculty: 113. Library holdings: 41,117 bound volumes, 106 titles on microform, 427 periodical subscriptions, 12,200 records/tapes.

Undergraduate Courses offered for part-time students during daytime, evenings, weekends, summer. Complete part-time degree programs offered during daytime, evenings. Adult/continuing education programs available. Career services available

Colleges Offering Part-Time Degree Programs / Ohio

North Central Technical College (continued)
to part-time students: individual and group career counseling, individual job placement, employer recruitment on campus. Part-time tuition per quarter (1 to 11 quarter credits) ranges from $118 to $367 for state residents, $224 to $700 for nonresidents.

Northwestern Business College–Technical Center
Lima 45805

Proprietary institution; small-town setting. Awards A. Barrier-free campus. Total enrollment: 710 (all undergraduates); 1% part-time, 35% women. Total faculty: 70.

Undergraduate Courses offered for part-time students during daytime, evenings. Complete part-time degree programs offered during daytime, evenings. Adult/continuing education programs available. Career services available to part-time students: individual job placement. Part-time tuition ranges from $36 per credit hour to $500 per course, according to program.

Northwest Technical College
Archbold 43502

Public institution; rural setting. Awards A. Barrier-free campus. Total enrollment: 939 (all undergraduates); 58% part-time, 51% women, 60% over 25. Total faculty: 79. Library holdings: 12,000 bound volumes, 160 periodical subscriptions, 1,850 records/tapes.

Undergraduate Courses offered for part-time students during daytime, evenings, weekends, summer. Complete part-time degree programs offered during daytime, evenings. Adult/continuing education programs available. Career services available to part-time students: individual and group career counseling, individual job placement, employer recruitment on campus. Part-time tuition: $26 per quarter hour for state residents, $51 per quarter hour for nonresidents.

Notre Dame College of Ohio
Cleveland 44121

Independent-religious instutition; metropolitan setting. Awards A, B. Total enrollment: 750 (all undergraduates); 35% part-time, 100% women, 50% over 25. Total faculty: 68. Library holdings: 85,000 bound volumes, 485 periodical subscriptions.

Undergraduate Courses offered for part-time students during daytime, evenings, weekends, summer. Complete part-time degree programs offered during daytime, evenings, weekends, summer. Career services available to part-time students: individual and group career counseling, individual job placement, employer recruitment on campus. Part-time tuition: $105 per semester hour.

Oberlin College
Oberlin 44074

Independent institution; small-town setting. Awards B, M. Barrier-free campus. Total enrollment: 2,898. Undergraduate enrollment: 2,887; 2% part-time, 54% women. Total faculty: 226. Library holdings: 870,000 bound volumes, 170,000 titles on microform, 3,300 periodical subscriptions, 2,800 records/tapes.
Graduate Part-time study available in College of Arts and Sciences, Conservatory of Music. Basic part-time expenses: $380 per credit tuition plus $190 per year fees. Institutional financial aid available to part-time graduate students in College of Arts and Sciences, Conservatory of Music.

Ohio Dominican College
Columbus 43219

Independent-religious instutition; metropolitan setting. Awards A, B. Barrier-free campus. Total enrollment: 1,020 (all undergraduates); 37% part-time, 60% women, 37% over 25. Total faculty: 82. Library holdings: 102,833 bound volumes, 167 titles on microform, 537 periodical subscriptions, 2,585 records/tapes.

Undergraduate Courses offered for part-time students during daytime, evenings, weekends, summer. Complete part-time degree programs offered during daytime, weekends. Adult/continuing education programs available. Career services available to part-time students: individual and group career counseling, individual job placement, employer recruitment on campus. Part-time tuition: $147 per credit hour.

Ohio Institute of Photography
Dayton 45439

Proprietary institution; metropolitan setting. Awards A. Barrier-free campus. Total enrollment: 225 (all undergraduates); 25% part-time, 28% women, 20% over 25. Total faculty: 21. Library holdings: 250 bound volumes, 12 periodical subscriptions, 25 records/tapes.

Undergraduate Courses offered for part-time students during daytime, evenings. Complete part-time degree programs offered during daytime, evenings. Career services available to part-time students: individual career counseling, individual job placement. Part-time tuition: $105 per credit.

Ohio State University
Columbus 43210

Public institution; metropolitan setting. Awards B, M, D. Barrier-free campus. Total enrollment: 53,757. Undergraduate enrollment: 41,247; 15% part-time, 45% women, 14% over 25. Total faculty: 3,262. Library holdings: 3.7 million bound volumes, 27,519 periodical subscriptions.

Undergraduate Courses offered for part-time students during daytime, evenings, weekends, summer. Complete part-time degree programs offered during daytime, evenings, summer. Adult/continuing education programs available. Career services available to part-time students: individual and group career counseling, individual job placement, employer recruitment on campus. Part-time tuition and fees per quarter (1 to 11 quarter hours) range from $90 to $501 for state residents, $162 to $1299 for nonresidents.
Graduate Part-time study available in Graduate School, College of Dentistry, College of Medicine, College of Optometry, College of Pharmacy, College of Veterinary Medicine. Basic part-time expenses: $215 per quarter (minimum) tuition for state residents, $518 per quarter (minimum) tuition for nonresidents. Institutional financial aid available to part-time graduate students in Graduate School, College of Dentistry, College of Medicine, College of Optometry, College of Pharmacy, College of Veterinary Medicine.

Ohio State University Agricultural Technical Institute
Wooster 44691

Public institution; small-town setting. Awards A. Barrier-free campus. Total enrollment: 739 (all undergraduates); 7% part-time, 25% women, 11% over 25. Total faculty: 32. Library holdings: 13,720 bound volumes, 521 periodical subscriptions.

Undergraduate Courses offered for part-time students during daytime, summer. Complete part-time degree programs offered during daytime, summer. Adult/continuing education programs available. Career services available to part-time students: individual career counseling, individual job placement, employer recruitment on campus. Part-time tuition and fees per quarter (1 to 11 quarter hours) range from $90 to $501 for state residents, $162 to $1299 for nonresidents.

Ohio State University–Lima Campus
Lima 45804

Public institution; small-town setting. Awards A, B (also offers some graduate courses). Barrier-free campus. Total enrollment: 985. Undergraduate enrollment: 963; 28% part-time, 57% women, 26% over 25. Total faculty: 34. Library holdings: 60,793 bound volumes, 503 periodical subscriptions.

Undergraduate Courses offered for part-time students during daytime, evenings, summer. Complete part-time degree programs offered during daytime, evenings, summer. Adult/continuing education programs available. Career services available to part-time students: individual and group career counseling. Part-time tuition and fees per quarter (1 to 11 quarter hours) range from $90 to $501 for state residents, $162 to $1299 for nonresidents.

Ohio State University–Mansfield Campus
Mansfield 44906

Public institution; city setting. Awards A, B (also offers some graduate courses). Barrier-free campus. Total enrollment: 1,124. Undergraduate enrollment: 1,048; 31% part-time, 59% women, 31% over 25. Total faculty: 36. Library holdings: 45,261 bound volumes, 431 periodical subscriptions.

Undergraduate Courses offered for part-time students during daytime, evenings, summer. Complete part-time degree programs offered during daytime, evenings, summer. Adult/continuing education programs available. Career services available to part-time students: individual and group career counseling. Part-time tuition and fees per quarter (1 to 11 quarter hours) range from $90 to $501 for state residents, $162 to $1299 for nonresidents.

Ohio State University–Marion Campus
Marion 43302

Public institution; small-town setting. Awards A, B (also offers some graduate courses). Barrier-free campus. Total enrollment: 830. Undergraduate enrollment: 765; 35% part-time, 55% women, 33% over 25. Total faculty: 25. Library holdings: 32,256 bound volumes, 237 periodical subscriptions.

Undergraduate Courses offered for part-time students during daytime, evenings, summer. Complete part-time degree programs offered during daytime, evenings, summer. Adult/continuing education programs available. Career services available to part-time students: individual and group career counseling, individual job placement, employer recruitment on campus. Part-time tuition and fees per quarter (1 to 11 quarter hours) range from $90 to $501 for state residents, $162 to $1299 for nonresidents.

Ohio State University–Newark Campus
Newark 43055

Public institution; small-town setting. Awards A, B (also offers some graduate courses). Barrier-free campus. Total enrollment: 924. Undergraduate enrollment: 895; 36% part-time, 50% women, 26% over 25. Total faculty: 27. Library holdings: 42,000 bound volumes, 386 periodical subscriptions.

Undergraduate Courses offered for part-time students during daytime, evenings, summer. Complete part-time degree programs offered during daytime, evenings, summer. Adult/continuing education programs available. Career services available to part-time students: individual career counseling, individual job placement, employer recruitment on campus. Part-time tuition and fees per quarter (1 to 11 quarter hours) range from $90 to $501 for state residents, $162 to $1299 for nonresidents.

Ohio University
Athens 45701

Public institution; small-town setting. Awards A, B, M, D. Total enrollment: 14,646. Undergraduate enrollment: 12,095; 13% part-time, 47% women, 7% over 25. Total faculty: 759. Library holdings: 1.2 million bound volumes, 700,000 titles on microform, 30,000 periodical subscriptions, 300,000 records/tapes.

Undergraduate Courses offered for part-time students during daytime, summer. Complete part-time degree programs offered during daytime. External degree and adult/continuing education programs available. Career services available to part-time students: individual and group career counseling, individual job placement, employer recruitment on campus. Part-time tuition: $63 per quarter hour for state residents, $127 per quarter hour for nonresidents.

Ohio University–Chillicothe
Chillicothe 45601

Public institution; small-town setting. Awards A, B (also offers some graduate courses). Barrier-free campus. Total enrollment: 1,168 (all undergraduates); 58% part-time, 70% women. Total faculty: 73. Library holdings: 59,500 bound volumes, 412 periodical subscriptions.

Undergraduate Courses offered for part-time students during daytime, evenings, weekends, summer. Complete part-time degree programs offered during daytime, evenings, weekends, summer. Adult/continuing education programs available. Career services available to part-time students: individual career counseling, individual job placement. Part-time tuition: $48 per credit for state residents, $106 per credit for nonresidents.

Ohio University–Ironton
Ironton 45638

Public institution; small-town setting. Awards A, B (also offers some graduate courses). Total enrollment: 880. Undergraduate enrollment: 730; 20% part-time, 50% women, 60% over 25. Total faculty: 80. Library holdings: 10,000 bound volumes, 50 titles on microform, 17 periodical subscriptions, 200 records/tapes.

Undergraduate Courses offered for part-time students during evenings, weekends, summer. Complete part-time degree programs offered during evenings. Adult/continuing education programs available. Part-time tuition: $44 per credit hour for state residents, $47 per credit hour for nonresidents.

Ohio University–Lancaster
Lancaster 43130

Public institution; small-town setting. Awards A, B, M. Barrier-free campus. Total enrollment: 1,550. Undergraduate enrollment: 1,450; 64% part-time, 60% women. Total faculty: 106. Library holdings: 52,000 bound volumes, 110,000 titles on microform, 320 periodical subscriptions, 18,300 records/tapes.

Undergraduate Courses offered for part-time students during daytime, evenings, weekends, summer. Complete part-time de-

Colleges Offering Part-Time Degree Programs / Ohio

Ohio University–Lancaster (continued)
gree programs offered during daytime, evenings, weekends, summer. Adult/continuing education programs available. Career services available to part-time students: individual and group career counseling, individual job placement, employer recruitment on campus. Part-time tuition: $48 per quarter hour for state residents, $106 per quarter hour for nonresidents.

Ohio University–Zanesville
Zanesville 43701

Public institution; small-town setting. Awards A, B (also offers some graduate courses). Barrier-free campus. Total enrollment: 904. Undergraduate enrollment: 847; 57% part-time, 69% women. Total faculty: 61. Library holdings: 55,000 bound volumes, 271 periodical subscriptions, 1,541 records/tapes.

Undergraduate Courses offered for part-time students during daytime, evenings, weekends, summer. Complete part-time degree programs offered during daytime, evenings. External degree and adult/continuing education programs available. Career services available to part-time students: individual and group career counseling, individual job placement. Part-time tuition: $48 per quarter hour for state residents, $106 per quarter hour for nonresidents.

Ohio Wesleyan University
Delaware 43015

Independent-religious instutition; small-town setting. Awards B. Total enrollment: 1,546 (all undergraduates); 1% part-time, 53% women, 1% over 25. Total faculty: 161. Library holdings: 400,000 bound volumes, 500 titles on microform, 1,250 periodical subscriptions.

Undergraduate Courses offered for part-time students during daytime. Complete part-time degree programs offered during daytime. Career services available to part-time students: individual and group career counseling, individual job placement, employer recruitment on campus. Part-time tuition: $775 per unit.

Otterbein College
Westerville 43081

Independent-religious instutition; small-town setting. Awards A, B. Total enrollment: 1,594 (all undergraduates); 28% part-time, 61% women. Total faculty: 109. Library holdings: 141,511 bound volumes, 62,875 titles on microform, 915 periodical subscriptions, 6,600 records/tapes.

Undergraduate Courses offered for part-time students during daytime, evenings, summer. Complete part-time degree programs offered during daytime, evenings. Adult/continuing education programs available. Career services available to part-time students: individual and group career counseling, individual job placement, employer recruitment on campus. Part-time tuition: $127 per credit hour.

Owens Technical College
Toledo 43699

Public institution; metropolitan setting. Awards A. Barrier-free campus. Total enrollment: 4,833 (all undergraduates); 51% part-time, 52% women. Total faculty: 335. Library holdings: 33,000 bound volumes, 200 records/tapes.

Undergraduate Courses offered for part-time students during daytime, evenings, weekends, summer. Complete part-time degree programs offered during daytime, evenings, weekends, summer. Adult/continuing education programs available. Career services available to part-time students: individual and group career counseling, individual job placement, employer recruitment on campus. Part-time tuition: $39 per credit hour for state residents, $74 per credit hour for nonresidents.

Raymond Walters General and Technical College
Cincinnati 45236

See University of Cincinnati, Raymond Walters General and Technical College

RETS Tech Center
Centerville 45459

Proprietary institution; city setting. Awards A. Barrier-free campus. Total enrollment: 80 (all undergraduates); 0% part-time, 40% women, 20% over 25. Total faculty: 18. Library holdings: 250 bound volumes, 5 periodical subscriptions, 25 records/tapes.

Undergraduate Courses offered for part-time students during daytime, evenings. Complete part-time degree programs offered during daytime, evenings. Adult/continuing education programs available. Career services available to part-time students: individual and group career counseling, individual job placement, employer recruitment on campus. Part-time tuition: $92 per credit.

Rio Grande College/Community College
Rio Grande 45674

Independent institution; rural setting. Awards A, B. Total enrollment: 1,553 (all undergraduates); 28% part-time, 54% women. Total faculty: 92. Library holdings: 60,000 bound volumes, 500 periodical subscriptions, 1,200 records/tapes.

Undergraduate Courses offered for part-time students during daytime, evenings. Complete part-time degree programs offered during daytime, evenings. Adult/continuing education programs available. Career services available to part-time students: individual and group career counseling, individual job placement, employer recruitment on campus. Part-time tuition: $24 per quarter hour for area residents, $29 per quarter hour for state residents, $96 per quarter hour for nonresidents. Juniors and seniors pay nonresident tuition rate regardless of residence.

Saint Mary Seminary
Cleveland 44108

Independent-religious institution (graduate only). Total enrollment: 96 (primarily men; 16% part-time). Total faculty: 23. Library holdings: 45,559 bound volumes, 912 microforms.

Graduate Part-time study available in Graduate and Professional Programs.Basic part-time expenses: $90 per quarter hour tuition.

Shawnee State Community College
Portsmouth 45662

Public institution; city setting. Awards A. Barrier-free campus. Total enrollment: 1,910 (all undergraduates); 41% part-time, 59% women. Total faculty: 167.

Undergraduate Courses offered for part-time students during daytime, evenings, summer. Complete part-time degree programs offered during daytime, evenings, summer. Career services available to part-time students: individual and group career counseling, individual job placement, employer recruitment on campus. Part-time tuition: $26 per quarter hour for state residents, $28 per quarter hour for nonresidents.

Sinclair Community College
Dayton 45402

Public institution; metropolitan setting. Awards A. Barrier-free campus. Total enrollment: 18,491 (all undergraduates); 74% part-time, 60% women. Total faculty: 881. Library holdings: 93,089 bound volumes, 204 titles on microform, 549 periodical subscriptions, 2,493 records/tapes.

Undergraduate Courses offered for part-time students during daytime, evenings, weekends, summer. Complete part-time degree programs offered during daytime, evenings, weekends, summer. External degree and adult/continuing education programs available. Career services available to part-time students: individual and group career counseling, individual job placement, employer recruitment on campus. Part-time tuition: $22 per quarter hour for area residents, $29 per quarter hour for state residents, $41 per quarter hour for nonresidents.

Southern Ohio College, Cincinnati Campus
Cincinnati 45237

Proprietary institution; metropolitan setting. Awards A. Barrier-free campus. Total enrollment: 1,300 (all undergraduates); 4% part-time, 60% women, 60% over 25. Total faculty: 75.

Undergraduate Courses offered for part-time students during daytime, evenings. Complete part-time degree programs offered during daytime, evenings. Career services available to part-time students: individual and group career counseling, individual job placement, employer recruitment on campus. Part-time tuition: $65 per credit hour.

Southern Ohio College, Fairfield Campus
Fairfield 45014

Proprietary institution; small-town setting. Awards A. Barrier-free campus. Total enrollment: 957 (all undergraduates); 15% part-time, 60% women. Total faculty: 97. Library holdings: 3,600 bound volumes, 35 periodical subscriptions, 150 records/tapes.

Undergraduate Courses offered for part-time students during daytime, evenings, summer. Complete part-time degree programs offered during daytime, evenings, summer. Adult/continuing education programs available. Career services available to part-time students: individual and group career counseling. Part-time tuition: $62 per credit.

Southern Ohio College, Northeast Campus
Akron 44312

Proprietary institution; city setting. Awards A. Barrier-free campus. Total enrollment: 712 (all undergraduates); 5% part-time, 65% women, 45% over 25. Total faculty: 60. Library holdings: 2,150 bound volumes, 34 periodical subscriptions.

Undergraduate Courses offered for part-time students during daytime, evenings, summer. Complete part-time degree programs offered during daytime, evenings. Career services available to part-time students: individual career counseling, individual job placement, employer recruitment on campus. Part-time tuition: $62 per credit hour.

Southern State Community College
Hillsboro 45133

Public institution; rural setting. Awards A. Barrier-free campus. Total enrollment: 1,267 (all undergraduates); 66% part-time, 67% women, 55% over 25. Total faculty: 119. Library holdings: 17,829 bound volumes, 1,834 titles on microform, 389 periodical subscriptions, 1,319 records/tapes.

Undergraduate Courses offered for part-time students during daytime, evenings, summer. Complete part-time degree programs offered during daytime, evenings. Career services available to part-time students: individual career counseling, individual job placement. Part-time tuition: $30 per quarter hour for state residents, $34 per quarter hour for nonresidents.

Southwestern College of Business
Kettering 45429

Proprietary institution; city setting. Awards A. Barrier-free campus. Total enrollment: 325 (all undergraduates); 1% part-time, 80% women. Total faculty: 18.

Undergraduate Courses offered for part-time students during daytime, evenings, summer. Complete part-time degree programs offered during evenings, summer. Part-time tuition: $300 per course.

Stark Technical College
Canton 44720

Public institution; city setting. Awards A. Barrier-free campus. Total enrollment: 3,500 (all undergraduates); 55% part-time, 48% women, 43% over 25. Total faculty: 169. Library holdings: 49,559 bound volumes, 1,300 records/tapes.

Undergraduate Courses offered for part-time students during daytime, evenings, summer. Complete part-time degree programs offered during daytime, evenings. Adult/continuing education programs available. Career services available to part-time students: individual and group career counseling, individual job placement, employer recruitment on campus. Part-time tuition: $26 per quarter hour for state residents, $46 per quarter hour for nonresidents.

Stautzenberger College
Toledo 43623

Proprietary institution; metropolitan setting. Awards A. Barrier-free campus. Total enrollment: 2,100 (all undergraduates); 10% part-time, 63% women, 35% over 25. Total faculty: 165. Library holdings: 18,000 bound volumes, 1,000 titles on microform, 65 periodical subscriptions, 500 records/tapes.

Undergraduate Courses offered for part-time students during daytime, evenings, weekends, summer. Complete part-time degree programs offered during daytime, evenings, weekends, summer. Adult/continuing education programs available. Career services available to part-time students: individual and group career counseling, individual job placement, employer recruitment on campus. Part-time tuition: $51 per credit.

Terra Technical College
Fremont 43420

Public institution; small-town setting. Awards A. Barrier-free campus. Total enrollment: 2,228 (all undergraduates); 60% part-time, 12% women. Total faculty: 110. Library holdings: 15,885 bound volumes, 414 periodical subscriptions, 2,075 records/tapes.

Colleges Offering Part-Time Degree Programs / Ohio

Terra Technical College (continued)

Undergraduate Courses offered for part-time students during daytime, evenings. Complete part-time degree programs offered during daytime, evenings. Adult/continuing education programs available. Career services available to part-time students: individual and group career counseling, individual job placement, employer recruitment on campus. Part-time tuition: $23 per quarter hour for state residents, $52 per quarter hour for nonresidents.

Tiffin University
Tiffin 44883

Independent institution; small-town setting. Awards A, B. Total enrollment: 528 (all undergraduates); 22% part-time, 52% women, 27% over 25. Total faculty: 34. Library holdings: 9,572 bound volumes, 1,496 titles on microform, 66 periodical subscriptions, 228 records/tapes.

Undergraduate Courses offered for part-time students during daytime, evenings, weekends, summer. Complete part-time degree programs offered during daytime, evenings. Adult/continuing education programs available. Career services available to part-time students: individual and group career counseling, individual job placement, employer recruitment on campus. Part-time tuition: $299 per course.

Trinity Lutheran Seminary
Columbus 43209

Independent-religious institution (graduate only). Total enrollment: 348 (coed; 17% part-time). Total faculty: 26. Library holdings: 85,000 bound volumes, 3,000 microforms.

Graduate Part-time study available in Graduate and Professional Programs. Basic part-time expenses: $165 per unit tuition. Institutional financial aid available to part-time graduate students in Graduate and Professional Programs.

United Theological Seminary
Dayton 45406

Independent-religious institution (graduate only). Total enrollment: 342 (coed; 9% part-time). Total faculty: 35.

Graduate Part-time study available in Graduate and Professional Programs. Degree can be earned exclusively through evening/weekend study in Graduate and Professional Programs. Basic part-time expenses: $275 per course tuition plus $12 per quarter fees.

University of Akron
Akron 44325

Public institution; city setting. Awards A, B, M, D. Total enrollment: 27,022. Undergraduate enrollment: 23,301; 40% part-time, 50% women. Total faculty: 1,487. Library holdings: 1 million bound volumes, 687,926 titles on microform, 5,013 periodical subscriptions, 10,391 records/tapes.

Undergraduate Courses offered for part-time students during daytime, evenings, summer. Complete part-time degree programs offered during daytime, evenings, summer. Adult/continuing education programs available. Career services available to part-time students: individual and group career counseling, individual job placement, employer recruitment on campus. Part-time tuition: $63.50 per credit for state residents, $126.50 per credit for nonresidents.

Graduate Part-time study available in Graduate School. Basic part-time expenses: $68 per credit hour tuition plus $6 per credit hour fees for state residents, $121 per credit hour tuition plus $6 per credit hour fees for nonresidents.

University of Cincinnati
Cincinnati 45221

Public institution; metropolitan setting. Awards A, B, M, D. Barrier-free campus. Total enrollment: 31,734. Undergraduate enrollment: 25,637; 40% part-time, 49% women. Total faculty: 2,606. Library holdings: 1.5 million bound volumes, 8,500 periodical subscriptions.

Undergraduate Courses offered for part-time students during daytime, evenings, summer. Complete part-time degree programs offered during evenings. Adult/continuing education programs available. Career services available to part-time students: individual and group career counseling. Part-time tuition: $55 per credit for state residents, $132 per credit for nonresidents.

Graduate Part-time study available in Division of Graduate Studies and Research, College of Medicine. Degree can be earned exclusively through evening/weekend study in Division of Graduate Studies and Research. Basic part-time expenses: $83 per credit tuition for state residents, $164 per credit tuition for nonresidents.

University of Cincinnati, Clermont General and Technical College
Batavia 45103

Public institution; rural setting. Awards A. Total enrollment: 505 (all undergraduates); 69% part-time, 57% women, 51% over 25. Total faculty: 82. Library holdings: 16,015 bound volumes, 550 titles on microform, 185 periodical subscriptions, 194 records/tapes.

Undergraduate Courses offered for part-time students during daytime, evenings, weekends, summer. Complete part-time degree programs offered during daytime, evenings. Adult/continuing education programs available. Career services available to part-time students: individual and group career counseling, individual job placement. Part-time tuition: $53 per quarter hour for state residents, $128 per quarter hour for nonresidents.

University of Cincinnati, Raymond Walters General and Technical College
Cincinnati 45236

Public institution; metropolitan setting. Awards A. Barrier-free campus. Total enrollment: 3,800 (all undergraduates); 50% part-time, 65% women, 40% over 25. Total faculty: 100.

Undergraduate Courses offered for part-time students during daytime, evenings. Complete part-time degree programs offered during daytime, evenings. Adult/continuing education programs available. Career services available to part-time students: individual and group career counseling, individual job placement, employer recruitment on campus. Part-time tuition: $50 per credit for state residents, $120 per credit for nonresidents.

University of Dayton
Dayton 45469

Independent-religious instutition; metropolitan setting. Awards A, B, M, D. Barrier-free campus. Total enrollment: 10,577. Undergraduate enrollment: 7,180; 14% part-time, 45% women, 10% over 25. Total faculty: 685. Library holdings: 625,625 bound volumes, 283,027 titles on microform, 2,348 periodical subscriptions, 1,400 records/tapes.

Undergraduate Courses offered for part-time students during daytime, evenings, summer. Complete part-time degree programs offered during daytime, evenings, summer. Adult/continuing education programs available. Career services available to part-time students: individual and group career counseling, individual job placement, employer recruitment on campus. Part-time tuition: $123 per semester hour.

University of Steubenville
Steubenville 43952

Independent-religious instutition; small-town setting. Awards A, B, M. Total enrollment: 934. Undergraduate enrollment: 850; 23% part-time, 55% women. Total faculty: 66. Library holdings: 170,000 bound volumes, 700 periodical subscriptions, 5,200 records/tapes.

Undergraduate Courses offered for part-time students during daytime, evenings, summer. Complete part-time degree programs offered during daytime, evenings. Adult/continuing education programs available. Career services available to part-time students: individual and group career counseling, individual job placement, employer recruitment on campus. Part-time tuition: $145 per credit hour.

Graduate Part-time study available in School of Business, School of Theology. Degree can be earned exclusively through evening/weekend study in School of Business. Basic part-time expenses: $155 per credit tuition.

University of Toledo
Toledo 43606

Public institution; metropolitan setting. Awards A, B, M, D. Barrier-free campus. Total enrollment: 21,652. Undergraduate enrollment: 18,486; 30% part-time, 50% women. Total faculty: 1,194. Library holdings: 1 million bound volumes, 5,000 periodical subscriptions.

Undergraduate Courses offered for part-time students during daytime, evenings, summer. Complete part-time degree programs offered during daytime, evenings, summer. Adult/continuing education programs available. Career services available to part-time students: individual and group career counseling, individual job placement, employer recruitment on campus. Part-time tuition: $45 per quarter hour for state residents, $98 per quarter hour for nonresidents.

Graduate Part-time study available in Graduate School, College of Law. Degree can be earned exclusively through evening/weekend study in Graduate School, College of Law. Basic part-time expenses: $173.10 per quarter (minimum) fees for state residents, $343 per quarter (minimum) fees for nonresidents. Institutional financial aid available to part-time graduate students in Graduate School.

Urbana College
Urbana 43078

Independent-religious instutition; small-town setting. Awards A, B. Total enrollment: 573 (all undergraduates); 20% part-time, 43% women. Total faculty: 94. Library holdings: 50,000 bound volumes, 9,483 titles on microform, 840 periodical subscriptions, 2,500 records/tapes.

Undergraduate Courses offered for part-time students during daytime, evenings, summer. Complete part-time degree programs offered during daytime, evenings. External degree and adult/continuing education programs available. Career services available to part-time students: individual and group career counseling, individual job placement, employer recruitment on campus. Part-time tuition: $100 per credit hour.

Ursuline College
Pepper Pike 44124

Independent-religious instutition; small-town setting. Awards A, B, M. Total enrollment: 1,318. Undergraduate enrollment: 1,299; 28% part-time, 96% women. Total faculty: 90. Library holdings: 73,000 bound volumes, 325 periodical subscriptions, 225 records/tapes.

Undergraduate Courses offered for part-time students during daytime, evenings, weekends, summer. Complete part-time degree programs offered during daytime, evenings. External degree and adult/continuing education programs available. Career services available to part-time students: individual and group career counseling, individual job placement, employer recruitment on campus. Part-time tuition: $115 per semester hour.

Graduate Part-time study available in Graduate Studies. Basic part-time expenses: $120 per credit hour tuition plus $20 per year fees. Institutional financial aid available to part-time graduate students in Graduate Studies.

Walsh College
Canton 44720

Independent-religious instutition; city setting. Awards A, B, M. Total enrollment: 1,205. Undergraduate enrollment: 1,116; 46% part-time, 60% women, 40% over 25. Total faculty: 108. Library holdings: 90,000 bound volumes, 100 titles on microform, 550 periodical subscriptions, 300 records/tapes.

Undergraduate Courses offered for part-time students during daytime, evenings, weekends, summer. Complete part-time degree programs offered during daytime, evenings, summer. External degree and adult/continuing education programs available. Career services available to part-time students: individual and group career counseling, individual job placement, employer recruitment on campus. Part-time tuition: $110 per credit hour.

Washington Technical College
Marietta 45750

Public institution; small-town setting. Awards A. Barrier-free campus. Total enrollment: 552 (all undergraduates); 47% part-time, 50% women, 50% over 25. Total faculty: 74. Library holdings: 15,000 bound volumes, 68 titles on microform, 200 periodical subscriptions, 300 records/tapes.

Undergraduate Courses offered for part-time students during daytime, evenings, weekends, summer. Complete part-time degree programs offered during daytime, evenings. Adult/continuing education programs available. Career services available to part-time students: individual and group career counseling, individual job placement. Part-time tuition: $22 per quarter hour for state residents, $38 per quarter hour for nonresidents.

Wilmington College of Ohio
Wilmington 45177

Independent-religious instutition; rural setting. Awards B. Total enrollment: 857 (all undergraduates); 4% part-time, 38% women. Total faculty: 59. Library holdings: 108,000 bound volumes, 555 periodical subscriptions, 2,500 records/tapes.

Undergraduate Courses offered for part-time students during daytime, summer. Complete part-time degree programs offered during daytime, summer. Adult/continuing education programs available. Career services available to part-time students: individual and group career counseling, individual job placement, employer recruitment on campus. Part-time tuition: $142 per credit.

Colleges Offering Part-Time Degree Programs / Ohio

Wittenberg University
Springfield 45501

Independent-religious instutition; city setting. Awards B. Total enrollment: 2,142 (all undergraduates); 4% part-time, 53% women. Total faculty: 174. Library holdings: 350,000 bound volumes, 58,248 titles on microform, 1,150 periodical subscriptions, 15,500 records/tapes.

Undergraduate Courses offered for part-time students during daytime, evenings, weekends, summer. Complete part-time degree programs offered during daytime, evenings, summer. Adult/continuing education programs available. Career services available to part-time students: individual and group career counseling, individual job placement, employer recruitment on campus. Part-time tuition: $800 per course.

Wright State University
Dayton 45435

Public institution; metropolitan setting. Awards A, B, M, D. Barrier-free campus. Total enrollment: 15,452. Undergraduate enrollment: 12,103; 40% part-time, 50% women, 44% over 25. Total faculty: 878. Library holdings: 380,650 bound volumes, 565,306 titles on microform, 5,155 periodical subscriptions.

Undergraduate Courses offered for part-time students during daytime, evenings, summer. Complete part-time degree programs offered during daytime, evenings. Adult/continuing education programs available. Career services available to part-time students: individual and group career counseling, individual job placement, employer recruitment on campus. Part-time tuition: $51 per credit hour for state residents, $102 per credit hour for nonresidents.

Graduate Part-time study available in School of Graduate Studies.Basic part-time expenses: $64 per quarter hour tuition for state residents, $115 per quarter hour tuition for nonresidents.

Wright State University, Western Ohio Branch Campus
Celina 45822

Public institution; rural setting. Awards A. Barrier-free campus. Total enrollment: 950 (all undergraduates); 62% part-time, 53% women, 33% over 25. Total faculty: 36. Library holdings: 26,000 bound volumes, 347 periodical subscriptions, 200 records/tapes.

Undergraduate Courses offered for part-time students during daytime, evenings, summer. Complete part-time degree programs offered during daytime, evenings, summer. Adult/continuing education programs available. Career services available to part-time students: individual career counseling, individual job placement. Part-time tuition: $46 per credit hour for state residents, $92 per credit hour for nonresidents.

Xavier University
Cincinnati 45207

Independent-religious instutition; metropolitan setting. Awards A, B, M. Total enrollment: 6,950. Undergraduate enrollment: 3,985; 18% part-time, 52% women. Total faculty: 343. Library holdings: 300,000 bound volumes, 2,000 periodical subscriptions, 2,000 records/tapes.

Undergraduate Courses offered for part-time students during daytime, evenings, weekends, summer. Complete part-time degree programs offered during daytime, evenings, weekends, summer. Adult/continuing education programs available. Career services available to part-time students: individual and group career counseling, individual job placement, employer recruitment on campus. Part-time tuition: $169 per semester hour.

Graduate Part-time study available in Graduate School.Basic part-time expenses: $126 per semester hour tuition. Institutional financial aid available to part-time graduate students in Graduate School.

Youngstown State University
Youngstown 44555

Public institution; city setting. Awards A, B, M. Barrier-free campus. Total enrollment: 15,849. Undergraduate enrollment: 14,684; 35% part-time, 47% women, 32% over 25. Total faculty: 785. Library holdings: 491,114 bound volumes, 632,141 titles on microform, 2,950 periodical subscriptions.

Undergraduate Courses offered for part-time students during daytime, evenings, weekends, summer. Complete part-time degree programs offered during daytime, evenings, weekends, summer. Adult/continuing education programs available. Career services available to part-time students: individual and group career counseling, individual job placement, employer recruitment on campus. Part-time tuition: $32 per quarter hour for state residents, $59 per quarter hour for nonresidents.

Graduate Part-time study available in Graduate School.Basic part-time expenses: $37 per quarter hour tuition plus $6 per quarter hour fees for state residents, $64 per quarter hour tuition plus $6 per quarter hour fees for nonresidents. Institutional financial aid available to part-time graduate students in Graduate School.

OKLAHOMA

Bacone College
Muskogee 74401

Independent-religious instutition; small-town setting. Awards A. Total enrollment: 430 (all undergraduates); 17% part-time, 68% women, 50% over 25. Total faculty: 41. Library holdings: 32,000 bound volumes, 250 periodical subscriptions, 400 records/tapes.

Undergraduate Courses offered for part-time students during daytime, evenings, weekends, summer. Complete part-time degree programs offered during daytime, evenings, summer. Adult/continuing education programs available. Career services available to part-time students: individual career counseling, employer recruitment on campus. Part-time tuition: $55 per semester hour.

Bartlesville Wesleyan College
Bartlesville 74006

Independent-religious instutition; small-town setting. Awards A, B. Total enrollment: 802 (all undergraduates); 52% part-time, 58% women. Total faculty: 59. Library holdings: 55,000 bound volumes, 31,000 titles on microform, 212 periodical subscriptions, 1,156 records/tapes.

Undergraduate Courses offered for part-time students during daytime, evenings, weekends, summer. Complete part-time degree programs offered during daytime, evenings, summer. Adult/continuing education programs available. Career services available to part-time students: individual career counseling, individual job placement, employer recruitment on campus. Part-time tuition: $105 per hour.

Oklahoma / Colleges Offering Part-Time Degree Programs

Bethany Nazarene College
Bethany 73008

Independent-religious instutition; small-town setting. Awards A, B, M. Total enrollment: 1,320. Undergraduate enrollment: 1,222; 19% part-time, 53% women, 16% over 25. Total faculty: 100. Library holdings: 102,000 bound volumes, 42,109 titles on microform, 650 periodical subscriptions, 1,700 records/tapes.

Undergraduate Courses offered for part-time students during daytime. Complete part-time degree programs offered during daytime. Adult/continuing education programs available. Career services available to part-time students: individual and group career counseling, individual job placement, employer recruitment on campus. Part-time tuition: $94 per credit hour.

Graduate Part-time study available in Graduate Studies. Basic part-time expenses: $94 per semester hour tuition plus $6.92 per semester hour fees.

Cameron University
Lawton 73505

Public institution; city setting. Awards A, B. Total enrollment: 5,194 (all undergraduates); 38% part-time, 50% women, 40% over 25. Total faculty: 325. Library holdings: 140,000 bound volumes, 1,435 periodical subscriptions, 1,810 records/tapes.

Undergraduate Courses offered for part-time students during daytime, evenings, summer. Complete part-time degree programs offered during daytime, evenings, summer. Adult/continuing education programs available. Career services available to part-time students: group career counseling, individual job placement, employer recruitment on campus. Part-time tuition: $18.95 per semester hour for state residents, $54.00 per semester hour for nonresidents.

Carl Albert Junior College
Poteau 74953

Public institution; small-town setting. Awards A. Barrier-free campus. Total enrollment: 2,146 (all undergraduates); 40% part-time, 48% women. Total faculty: 66. Library holdings: 14,000 bound volumes, 350 records/tapes.

Undergraduate Courses offered for part-time students during daytime, evenings. Complete part-time degree programs offered during daytime. Career services available to part-time students: individual and group career counseling, individual job placement, employer recruitment on campus. Part-time tuition: $14.35 per credit hour for state residents, $37.15 per credit hour for nonresidents.

Central State University
Edmond 73034

Public institution; small-town setting. Awards B, M. Total enrollment: 12,309. Undergraduate enrollment: 8,845; 37% part-time, 56% women. Total faculty: 430. Library holdings: 551,402 bound volumes, 4,752 periodical subscriptions.

Undergraduate Courses offered for part-time students during daytime, evenings, summer. Complete part-time degree programs offered during daytime, evenings, summer. Adult/continuing education programs available. Career services available to part-time students: individual and group career counseling, individual job placement, employer recruitment on campus. Part-time tuition: $19.22 per credit hour for state residents, $51.92 per credit hour for nonresidents.

Graduate Part-time study available in Graduate School. Basic part-time expenses: $23.22 per credit hour tuition for state residents, $65.07 per credit hour tuition for nonresidents.

Connors State College
Warner 74469

Public institution; rural setting. Awards A. Total enrollment: 1,487 (all undergraduates); 46% part-time, 58% women, 1% over 25. Total faculty: 62. Library holdings: 1,000 bound volumes, 150 titles on microform, 25 periodical subscriptions, 3,686 records/tapes.

Undergraduate Courses offered for part-time students during daytime, evenings, summer. Complete part-time degree programs offered during evenings, summer. Adult/continuing education programs available. Career services available to part-time students: individual career counseling. Part-time tuition: $14.85 per semester hour for state residents, $41.70 per semester hour for nonresidents.

East Central Oklahoma State University
Ada 74820

Public institution; small-town setting. Awards B, M. Barrier-free campus. Total enrollment: 4,268. Undergraduate enrollment: 3,649; 30% part-time, 59% women. Total faculty: 210. Library holdings: 203,301 bound volumes, 293,094 titles on microform, 1,300 periodical subscriptions, 5,131 records/tapes.

Undergraduate Courses offered for part-time students during daytime, evenings. Complete part-time degree programs offered during daytime, evenings. Adult/continuing education programs available. Career services available to part-time students: individual career counseling, individual job placement, employer recruitment on campus. Part-time tuition per semester hour ranges from $18.80 to $20.15 for state residents, $51.50 to $56.25 for nonresidents, according to course level.

Graduate Part-time study available in Graduate School. Degree can be earned exclusively through evening/weekend study in Graduate School. Basic part-time expenses: $20.55 per hour tuition plus $5 per hour fees for state residents, $56.95 per hour tuition plus $5 per hour fees for nonresidents.

Eastern Oklahoma State College
Wilburton 74578

Public institution; rural setting. Awards A. Total enrollment: 2,104 (all undergraduates); 67% part-time, 54% women, 60% over 25. Total faculty: 60. Library holdings: 41,376 bound volumes, 2,003 titles on microform, 248 periodical subscriptions, 2,671 records/tapes.

Undergraduate Courses offered for part-time students during daytime, evenings, weekends, summer. Complete part-time degree programs offered during daytime, evenings, weekends, summer. Adult/continuing education programs available. Career services available to part-time students: individual career counseling, individual job placement, employer recruitment on campus. Part-time tuition: $15.35 per semester hour for state residents, $42.30 per semester hour for nonresidents.

El Reno Junior College
El Reno 73036

Public institution; rural setting. Awards A. Barrier-free campus. Total enrollment: 2,220 (all undergraduates); 78% part-time, 49% women, 66% over 25. Total faculty: 51. Library holdings: 15,532 bound volumes, 2,008 titles on microform, 647 periodical subscriptions, 2,207 records/tapes.

Undergraduate Courses offered for part-time students during daytime, evenings, summer. Complete part-time degree programs offered during daytime, evenings, summer. Adult/continuing education programs available. Career services available to part-time students: individual and group career counseling,

Colleges Offering Part-Time Degree Programs / Oklahoma

El Reno Junior College (continued)
individual job placement, employer recruitment on campus. Part-time tuition: $11.35 per semester hour for state residents, $36.75 per semester hour for nonresidents.

Hillsdale Free Will Baptist College
Moore 73153

Independent-religious instutition; small-town setting. Awards A, B. Total enrollment: 173 (all undergraduates); 19% part-time, 51% women, 16% over 25. Total faculty: 22. Library holdings: 12,123 bound volumes, 46 titles on microform, 140 periodical subscriptions, 114 records/tapes.

Undergraduate Courses offered for part-time students during daytime, evenings, summer. Complete part-time degree programs offered during daytime. Part-time tuition: $47.50 per semester hour.

Langston University
Langston 73050

Public institution; rural setting. Awards B. Barrier-free campus. Total enrollment: 2,229 (all undergraduates); 6% part-time, 47% women. Total faculty: 201. Library holdings: 147,000 bound volumes, 3,175 titles on microform, 300 periodical subscriptions, 600 records/tapes.

Undergraduate Courses offered for part-time students during daytime, evenings, weekends, summer. Complete part-time degree programs offered during daytime, evenings, weekends, summer. Adult/continuing education programs available. Career services available to part-time students: individual and group career counseling, individual job placement, employer recruitment on campus. Part-time tuition: $20.30 per credit hour for state residents, $37.70 per credit hour for nonresidents.

Midwest Christian College
Oklahoma City 73111

Independent-religious instutition; metropolitan setting. Awards A, B. Total enrollment: 82 (all undergraduates); 21% part-time, 42% women. Total faculty: 17. Library holdings: 19,533 bound volumes, 60 titles on microform, 21 periodical subscriptions, 1,500 records/tapes.

Undergraduate Courses offered for part-time students during daytime, evenings, summer. Complete part-time degree programs offered during daytime. Part-time tuition: $40 per credit hour.

Northeastern Oklahoma Agricultural and Mechanical College
Miami 74354

Public institution; small-town setting. Awards A. Barrier-free campus. Total enrollment: 2,865 (all undergraduates); 25% part-time, 45% women, 20% over 25. Total faculty: 110. Library holdings: 51,103 bound volumes, 50 periodical subscriptions, 2,800 records/tapes.

Undergraduate Courses offered for part-time students during daytime, evenings. Complete part-time degree programs offered during daytime, evenings. Adult/continuing education programs available. Career services available to part-time students: individual and group career counseling, individual job placement, employer recruitment on campus. Part-time tuition: $13.85 per credit hour for state residents, $40.80 per credit hour for nonresidents.

Northeastern Oklahoma State University
Tahlequah 74464

Public institution; small-town setting. Awards B, M, D. Barrier-free campus. Total enrollment: 7,444. Undergraduate enrollment: 5,902; 32% part-time, 54% women. Total faculty: 220. Library holdings: 180,567 bound volumes, 2,107 periodical subscriptions, 3,691 records/tapes.

Undergraduate Courses offered for part-time students during daytime, evenings. Complete part-time degree programs offered during daytime, evenings. Adult/continuing education programs available. Career services available to part-time students: individual career counseling, individual job placement, employer recruitment on campus. Part-time tuition per credit hour ranges from $19.30 to $20.60 for state residents, $52 to $56.75 for nonresidents, according to course level.

Graduate Part-time study available in Graduate College. Basic part-time expenses: $23.30 per hour tuition plus $6 per semester fees for state residents, $65.15 per hour tuition plus $6 per semester fees for nonresidents.

Northwestern Oklahoma State University
Alva 73717

Public institution; small-town setting. Awards B, M. Total enrollment: 1,863. Undergraduate enrollment: 1,585; 32% part-time, 52% women. Total faculty: 82. Library holdings: 257,838 bound volumes, 340,000 titles on microform, 1,481 periodical subscriptions, 4,206 records/tapes.

Undergraduate Courses offered for part-time students during daytime, evenings, summer. Complete part-time degree programs offered during daytime. Adult/continuing education programs available. Part-time tuition per credit hour ranges from $18.80 to $20.15 for state residents, $51.50 to $56.25 for nonresidents, according to course level.

Graduate Part-time study available in Division of Education, Psychology, and Health and Physical Education, Division of Social Science. Degree can be earned exclusively through evening/weekend study in Division of Social Science. Basic part-time expenses: $22.80 per credit tuition for state residents, $64.65 per credit tuition for nonresidents.

Oklahoma Baptist University
Shawnee 74801

Independent-religious instutition; small-town setting. Awards A, B. Total enrollment: 1,527 (all undergraduates); 18% part-time, 52% women, 15% over 25. Total faculty: 134. Library holdings: 140,000 bound volumes, 99,000 titles on microform, 693 periodical subscriptions, 6,594 records/tapes.

Undergraduate Courses offered for part-time students during daytime, evenings, summer. Complete part-time degree programs offered during daytime. Adult/continuing education programs available. Career services available to part-time students: individual career counseling, individual job placement, employer recruitment on campus. Part-time tuition: $90 per credit hour.

Oklahoma City University
Oklahoma City 73106

Independent-religious instutition; metropolitan setting. Awards B, M. Barrier-free campus. Total enrollment: 3,264. Undergraduate enrollment: 1,603; 41% part-time, 53% women. Total faculty: 201. Library holdings: 155,800 bound volumes, 700 periodical subscriptions, 4,000 records/tapes.

Undergraduate Courses offered for part-time students during daytime, evenings, weekends, summer. Complete part-time degree programs offered during daytime, evenings, weekends, summer. External degree and adult/continuing education programs available. Career services available to part-time students: individual and group career counseling, individual job placement, employer recruitment on campus. Part-time tuition: $108 per semester hour.

Graduate Part-time study available in Petree College of Arts and Sciences, School of Law, School of Management and Business Sciences, School of Music and Performing Arts, School of Religion and Church Vocations. Degree can be earned exclusively through evening/weekend study in Petree College of Arts and Sciences, School of Law, School of Management and Business Sciences, School of Religion and Church Vocations. Basic part-time expenses: $129 per credit tuition plus $15 per semester fees. Institutional financial aid available to part-time graduate students in Petree College of Arts and Sciences, School of Law, School of Management and Business Sciences, School of Music and Performing Arts, School of Religion and Church Vocations.

Oklahoma Panhandle State University
Goodwell 73939

Public institution; rural setting. Awards B. Total enrollment: 1,354 (all undergraduates); 21% part-time, 47% women, 11% over 25. Total faculty: 62. Library holdings: 84,000 bound volumes, 300 titles on microform, 400 periodical subscriptions, 1,600 records/tapes.

Undergraduate Courses offered for part-time students during daytime, evenings, summer. Complete part-time degree programs offered during daytime, evenings, summer. Adult/continuing education programs available. Career services available to part-time students: individual career counseling, individual job placement. Part-time tuition: $16 per credit hour for state residents, $45.60 per credit hour for nonresidents.

Oklahoma State University
Stillwater 74078

Public institution; small-town setting. Awards A, B, M, D. Total enrollment: 22,823. Undergraduate enrollment: 18,754; 7% part-time, 42% women, 9% over 25. Total faculty: 1,921. Library holdings: 1.3 million bound volumes, 1.2 million titles on microform, 14,200 periodical subscriptions, 1,000 records/tapes.

Undergraduate Courses offered for part-time students during daytime, summer. Complete part-time degree programs offered during daytime, summer. External degree and adult/continuing education programs available. Career services available to part-time students: individual and group career counseling, individual job placement, employer recruitment on campus. Part-time tuition per semester hour ranges from $25.95 to $29.25 for state residents, $76.15 to $87.45 for nonresidents, according to course level.

Graduate Part-time study available in Graduate College. Basic part-time expenses: $29.65 per credit hour tuition plus $4.50 per credit hour fees for state residents, $99.65 per credit hour tuition plus $4.50 per credit hour fees for nonresidents. Institutional financial aid available to part-time graduate students in Graduate College.

Oklahoma State University Technical Institute
Oklahoma City 73107

Public institution; metropolitan setting. Awards A. Barrier-free campus. Total enrollment: 2,880 (all undergraduates); 77% part-time, 44% women, 80% over 25. Total faculty: 149. Library holdings: 12,000 bound volumes, 213 periodical subscriptions.

Undergraduate Courses offered for part-time students during daytime, evenings, weekends, summer. Complete part-time degree programs offered during daytime, evenings, weekends, summer. Adult/continuing education programs available. Career services available to part-time students: individual and group career counseling, individual job placement, employer recruitment on campus. Part-time tuition: $23.55 per semester hour for state residents, $73.75 per semester hour for nonresidents.

Oral Roberts University
Tulsa 74171

Independent-religious instutition; metropolitan setting. Awards B, M, D. Barrier-free campus. Total enrollment: 4,507. Undergraduate enrollment: 3,603; 8% part-time, 52% women, 8% over 25. Total faculty: 563. Library holdings: 578,439 bound volumes, 820,554 titles on microform, 6,313 periodical subscriptions, 12,000 records/tapes.

Graduate Part-time study available in Graduate School of Business, Graduate School of Education. Degree can be earned exclusively through evening/weekend study in Graduate School of Business. Basic part-time expenses: $155 per credit tuition plus $40 per semester fees. Institutional financial aid available to part-time graduate students in Graduate School of Education.

Phillips University
Enid 73702

Independent-religious instutition; city setting. Awards A, B, M, D. Barrier-free campus. Total enrollment: 1,284. Undergraduate enrollment: 947; 26% part-time, 55% women, 12% over 25. Total faculty: 121. Library holdings: 248,541 bound volumes, 1,205 periodical subscriptions, 7,561 records/tapes.

Undergraduate Courses offered for part-time students during daytime, evenings, summer. Complete part-time degree programs offered during daytime, evenings, summer. Adult/continuing education programs available. Career services available to part-time students: individual and group career counseling, individual job placement, employer recruitment on campus. Part-time tuition: $115 per credit hour.

Graduate Part-time study available in Center for Graduate Studies, Graduate Seminary. Basic part-time expenses: $125 per credit tuition plus $15 per semester (minimum) fees.

Rogers State College
Claremore 74017

Public institution; small-town setting. Awards A. Barrier-free campus. Total enrollment: 3,282 (all undergraduates); 48% part-time, 54% women, 30% over 25. Total faculty: 106. Library holdings: 24,000 bound volumes, 60 titles on microform, 200 periodical subscriptions, 500 records/tapes.

Undergraduate Courses offered for part-time students during daytime, evenings, summer. Complete part-time degree programs offered during daytime, evenings. Adult/continuing education programs available. Career services available to part-time students: individual and group career counseling. Part-time tuition: $16.35 per credit hour for state residents, $43.75 per credit hour for nonresidents.

Colleges Offering Part-Time Degree Programs / Oklahoma

Rose State College
Midwest City 73110

Public institution; city setting. Awards A. Barrier-free campus. Total enrollment: 9,250 (all undergraduates); 81% part-time, 54% women, 60% over 25. Total faculty: 272. Library holdings: 65,000 bound volumes, 800 periodical subscriptions, 3,500 records/tapes.

Undergraduate Courses offered for part-time students during daytime, evenings, weekends, summer. Complete part-time degree programs offered during daytime, evenings, weekends, summer. Adult/continuing education programs available. Career services available to part-time students: individual and group career counseling, individual job placement, employer recruitment on campus. Part-time tuition: $12.85 per credit hour for state residents, $39.80 per credit hour for nonresidents.

Seminole Junior College
Seminole 74868

Public institution; small-town setting. Awards A. Barrier-free campus. Total enrollment: 1,437 (all undergraduates); 18% part-time, 52% women. Total faculty: 67. Library holdings: 21,827 bound volumes, 50 periodical subscriptions, 524 records/tapes.

Undergraduate Courses offered for part-time students during daytime, evenings, weekends, summer. Complete part-time degree programs offered during daytime, evenings, weekends, summer. Adult/continuing education programs available. Career services available to part-time students: individual and group career counseling, individual job placement, employer recruitment on campus. Part-time tuition: $15.35 per credit hour for state residents, $42.30 per credit hour for nonresidents.

Southeastern Oklahoma State University
Durant 74701

Public institution; small-town setting. Awards A, B, M. Total enrollment: 4,340. Undergraduate enrollment: 3,731; 26% part-time, 51% women, 36% over 25. Total faculty: 165. Library holdings: 150,000 bound volumes, 11,000 titles on microform, 748 periodical subscriptions.

Undergraduate Courses offered for part-time students during daytime, evenings, summer. Complete part-time degree programs offered during daytime, evenings, summer. Adult/continuing education programs available. Career services available to part-time students: individual and group career counseling, individual job placement. Part-time tuition per credit hour ranges from $19.30 to $20.60 for state residents, $52 to $56.75 for nonresidents, according to course level.

Graduate Part-time study available in Graduate School. Degree can be earned exclusively through evening/weekend study in Graduate School. Basic part-time expenses: $23.30 per hour tuition plus $5 per semester fees for state residents, $65.15 per hour tuition plus $5 per semester fees for nonresidents. Institutional financial aid available to part-time graduate students in Graduate School.

Southwestern College of Christian Ministries
Bethany 73008

Independent-religious instutition; small-town setting. Awards B. Total enrollment: 66 (all undergraduates); 28% part-time, 43% women, 18% over 25. Total faculty: 10. Library holdings: 10,000 bound volumes, 1,500 titles on microform, 100 periodical subscriptions.

Undergraduate Courses offered for part-time students during daytime, evenings, summer. Complete part-time degree programs offered during daytime. Adult/continuing education programs available. Career services available to part-time students: individual career counseling, individual job placement. Part-time tuition: $65 per credit hour.

Southwestern Oklahoma State University
Weatherford 73096

Public institution; small-town setting. Awards A, B, M. Total enrollment: 5,116. Undergraduate enrollment: 4,220; 14% part-time, 51% women, 5% over 25. Total faculty: 213. Library holdings: 445,827 bound volumes, 489,015 titles on microform, 1,865 periodical subscriptions.

Undergraduate Courses offered for part-time students during daytime, evenings, summer. Complete part-time degree programs offered during daytime, evenings, summer. Adult/continuing education programs available. Career services available to part-time students: individual career counseling, individual job placement, employer recruitment on campus. Part-time tuition per semester hour ranges from $18.80 to $20.15 for state residents, $51.50 to $56.25 for nonresidents, according to course level.

Graduate Part-time study available in Graduate School. Degree can be earned exclusively through evening/weekend study in Graduate School. Basic part-time expenses: $22.80 per credit tuition for state residents, $64.65 per credit tuition for nonresidents.

Tulsa Junior College
Tulsa 74135

Public institution; metropolitan setting. Awards A. Barrier-free campus. Total enrollment: 15,153 (all undergraduates); 70% part-time, 61% women. Total faculty: 650. Library holdings: 100,000 bound volumes.

Undergraduate Courses offered for part-time students during daytime, evenings, summer. Complete part-time degree programs offered during daytime, evenings, summer. Adult/continuing education programs available. Career services available to part-time students: individual and group career counseling, individual job placement, employer recruitment on campus. Part-time tuition: $15.35 per hour for state residents, $42.50 per hour for nonresidents.

University of Oklahoma
Norman 73019

Public institution; city setting. Awards B, M, D. Total enrollment: 21,493. Undergraduate enrollment: 16,464; 15% part-time, 42% women, 14% over 25. Total faculty: 920. Library holdings: 1.9 million bound volumes, 1.4 million titles on microform, 16,957 periodical subscriptions.

Undergraduate Courses offered for part-time students during daytime, evenings, weekends, summer. Complete part-time degree programs offered during daytime, evenings, weekends, summer. Adult/continuing education programs available. Career services available to part-time students: individual and group career counseling, individual job placement, employer recruitment on campus. Part-time tuition: $22.60 per credit hour for state residents, $72.80 per credit hour for nonresidents.

Graduate Part-time study available in College of Environmental Design. Basic part-time expenses: $30.60 per hour tuition plus $65 per semester fees for state residents, $100.60 per hour tuition plus $65 per semester fees for nonresidents. Institutional financial aid available to part-time graduate students in College of Environmental Design.

Oregon / **Colleges Offering Part-Time Degree Programs**

University of Oklahoma Health Sciences Center
Oklahoma City 73190

Public institution; metropolitan setting. Awards B, M, D. Barrier-free campus. Total enrollment: 3,236. Undergraduate enrollment: 933; 8% part-time, 45% women. Total faculty: 690. Library holdings: 155,434 bound volumes, 650 titles on microform, 2,304 periodical subscriptions, 3,327 records/tapes.

Graduate Part-time study available in Graduate College. Degree can be earned exclusively through evening/weekend study in Graduate College.Basic part-time expenses: $30.30 per credit hour tuition plus $19 per semester fees for state residents, $100.30 per credit hour tuition plus $19 per semester fees for nonresidents. Institutional financial aid available to part-time graduate students in Graduate College.

University of Tulsa
Tulsa 74104

Independent-religious instutition; metropolitan setting. Awards B, M, D. Barrier-free campus. Total enrollment: 5,769. Undergraduate enrollment: 4,216; 24% part-time, 48% women, 27% over 25. Total faculty: 449. Library holdings: 1.4 million bound volumes, 680,000 titles on microform, 6,198 periodical subscriptions, 3,200 records/tapes.

Undergraduate Courses offered for part-time students during daytime, evenings, summer. Complete part-time degree programs offered during daytime. Adult/continuing education programs available. Career services available to part-time students: individual career counseling, individual job placement, employer recruitment on campus. Part-time tuition: $130 per credit hour.

Graduate Part-time study available in Graduate School, College of Law.Basic part-time expenses: $175 per credit tuition. Institutional financial aid available to part-time graduate students in Graduate School.

Western Oklahoma State College
Altus 73521

Public institution; rural setting. Awards A. Barrier-free campus. Total enrollment: 1,984 (all undergraduates); 40% part-time, 48% women, 53% over 25. Total faculty: 66.

Undergraduate Courses offered for part-time students during daytime, evenings, summer. Complete part-time degree programs offered during daytime, evenings, summer. Adult/continuing education programs available. Career services available to part-time students: individual career counseling. Part-time tuition: $14.35 per semester hour for state residents, $41.30 per semester hour for nonresidents.

OREGON

Blue Mountain Community College
Pendleton 97801

Public institution; rural setting. Awards A. Total enrollment: 2,061 (all undergraduates); 84% part-time, 55% women. Total faculty: 152. Library holdings: 36,737 bound volumes, 433 periodical subscriptions.

Undergraduate Courses offered for part-time students during daytime, evenings. Complete part-time degree programs offered during daytime. Adult/continuing education programs available. Part-time tuition: $15 per hour for area residents, $22 per hour for state residents, $60 per hour for nonresidents.

Central Oregon Community College
Bend 97701

Public institution; rural setting. Awards A. Total enrollment: 2,072 (all undergraduates); 46% part-time, 57% women, 54% over 25. Total faculty: 142. Library holdings: 28,000 bound volumes, 32 titles on microform, 318 periodical subscriptions, 500 records/tapes.

Undergraduate Courses offered for part-time students during daytime, evenings. Complete part-time degree programs offered during daytime, evenings. Adult/continuing education programs available. Career services available to part-time students: individual and group career counseling, individual job placement, employer recruitment on campus. Part-time tuition: $19.50 per credit hour for area residents, $19.50 per credit hour for state residents, $19.50 per credit hour for nonresidents.

Chemeketa Community College
Salem 97309

Public institution; city setting. Awards A. Barrier-free campus. Total enrollment: 11,129 (all undergraduates); 72% part-time, 55% women. Total faculty: 573. Library holdings: 45,000 bound volumes, 1,300 periodical subscriptions.

Undergraduate Courses offered for part-time students during daytime, evenings, weekends. Complete part-time degree programs offered during daytime, evenings. Adult/continuing education programs available. Career services available to part-time students: individual career counseling, individual job placement, employer recruitment on campus. Part-time tuition: $20 per credit hour for area residents, $30 per credit hour for state residents, $75 per credit hour for nonresidents.

Clackamas Community College
Oregon City 97045

Public institution; small-town setting. Awards A. Total enrollment: 4,650 (all undergraduates); 83% part-time, 61% women, 12% over 25. Total faculty: 353. Library holdings: 48,502 bound volumes, 328 titles on microform, 400 periodical subscriptions, 3,017 records/tapes.

Undergraduate Courses offered for part-time students during daytime, evenings, weekends, summer. Complete part-time degree programs offered during daytime, evenings. Adult/continuing education programs available. Career services available to part-time students: individual and group career counseling, individual job placement, employer recruitment on campus. Part-time tuition: $20 per credit hour for state residents, $73 per credit hour for nonresidents.

Clatsop Community College
Astoria 97103

Public institution; small-town setting. Awards A. Total enrollment: 2,553 (all undergraduates); 86% part-time, 55% women. Total faculty: 164. Library holdings: 35,000 bound volumes, 1,200 records/tapes.

Undergraduate Courses offered for part-time students during daytime, evenings, weekends, summer. Complete part-time degree programs offered during daytime, evenings. Adult/continuing education programs available. Career services available to part-time students: individual and group career counseling, individual job placement. Part-time tuition: $16 per credit for state residents, $62 per credit for nonresidents.

Colleges Offering Part-Time Degree Programs / Oregon

Columbia Christian College
Portland 97220

Independent-religious instutition; metropolitan setting. Awards B. Total enrollment: 263 (all undergraduates); 8% part-time, 48% women. Total faculty: 33. Library holdings: 36,000 bound volumes, 26,191 titles on microform, 230 periodical subscriptions, 1,291 records/tapes.

Undergraduate Courses offered for part-time students during daytime, evenings. Complete part-time degree programs offered during daytime. Career services available to part-time students: individual career counseling. Part-time tuition: $76 per credit.

Eastern Oregon State College
La Grande 97850

Public institution; rural setting. Awards A, B, M. Total enrollment: 1,674. Undergraduate enrollment: 1,595; 21% part-time, 51% women, 27% over 25. Total faculty: 126. Library holdings: 94,000 bound volumes, 29,200 titles on microform, 1,150 periodical subscriptions, 3,787 records/tapes.

Undergraduate Courses offered for part-time students during daytime, evenings, weekends, summer. Complete part-time degree programs offered during daytime. External degree and adult/continuing education programs available. Career services available to part-time students: individual and group career counseling, individual job placement, employer recruitment on campus. Part-time tuition: $65 per credit hour.

Graduate Part-time study available in Graduate Studies. Basic part-time expenses: $235 per quarter (minimum) tuition.

Judson Baptist College
The Dalles 97058

Independent-religious instutition; small-town setting. Awards A, B. Barrier-free campus. Total enrollment: 272 (all undergraduates); 9% part-time, 51% women, 4% over 25. Total faculty: 30. Library holdings: 36,000 bound volumes, 55 titles on microform, 190 periodical subscriptions, 700 records/tapes.

Undergraduate Courses offered for part-time students during daytime, evenings, summer. Complete part-time degree programs offered during daytime. Adult/continuing education programs available. Career services available to part-time students: individual and group career counseling, individual job placement. Part-time tuition: $80 per quarter hour.

Lane Community College
Eugene 97405

Public institution; city setting. Awards A. Barrier-free campus. Total enrollment: 7,920 (all undergraduates); 40% part-time, 52% women, 52% over 25. Total faculty: 343. Library holdings: 50,000 bound volumes, 700 periodical subscriptions.

Undergraduate Courses offered for part-time students during daytime. Complete part-time degree programs offered during daytime. Adult/continuing education programs available. Career services available to part-time students: individual and group career counseling, individual job placement, employer recruitment on campus. Part-time tuition: $18 per credit for area residents, $30 per credit for state residents, $75 per credit for nonresidents.

Lewis and Clark College
Portland 97219

Independent-religious instutition; metropolitan setting. Awards B, M. Barrier-free campus. Total enrollment: 3,037. Undergraduate enrollment: 1,640; 2% part-time, 52% women. Total faculty: 165. Library holdings: 197,000 bound volumes, 11,425 titles on microform, 1,074 periodical subscriptions, 3,000 records/tapes.

Undergraduate Courses offered for part-time students during daytime, summer. Complete part-time degree programs offered during daytime, summer. Career services available to part-time students: individual and group career counseling, individual job placement, employer recruitment on campus. Part-time tuition: $991 per credit.

Graduate Part-time study available in Graduate School of Professional Studies, Northwestern School of Law, School of Music. Degree can be earned exclusively through evening/weekend study in Northwestern School of Law. Basic part-time expenses: $296 per course tuition. Institutional financial aid available to part-time graduate students in Northwestern School of Law.

Linfield College
McMinnville 97128

Independent-religious instutition; small-town setting. Awards B, M. Total enrollment: 1,180. Undergraduate enrollment: 1,147; 5% part-time, 51% women, 1% over 25. Total faculty: 112. Library holdings: 110,000 bound volumes, 25,000 titles on microform, 750 periodical subscriptions, 3,472 records/tapes.

Undergraduate Courses offered for part-time students during daytime, evenings, weekends, summer. Complete part-time degree programs offered during daytime, evenings, weekends, summer. External degree and adult/continuing education programs available. Career services available to part-time students: individual and group career counseling, individual job placement, employer recruitment on campus. Part-time tuition: $185 per semester hour.

Graduate Part-time study available in Graduate Studies in Education. Degree can be earned exclusively through evening/weekend study in Graduate Studies in Education. Basic part-time expenses: $110 per semester hour tuition.

Marylhurst College for Lifelong Learning
Marylhurst 97036

Independent institution; small-town setting. Awards B, M. Total enrollment: 892. Undergraduate enrollment: 866; 78% part-time, 70% women, 90% over 25. Total faculty: 147. Library holdings: 114,016 bound volumes, 3,425 titles on microform, 260 periodical subscriptions, 9,400 records/tapes.

Undergraduate Courses offered for part-time students during daytime, evenings, weekends, summer. Complete part-time degree programs offered during daytime, evenings, weekends, summer. Adult/continuing education programs available. Career services available to part-time students: individual and group career counseling. Part-time tuition: $105 per quarter hour.

Mount Angel Seminary
St Benedict 97373

Independent-religious instutition; rural setting. Awards B, M. Total enrollment: 110. Undergraduate enrollment: 46; 0% part-time, 0% women, 11% over 25. Total faculty: 31. Library holdings: 100,000 bound volumes, 640 periodical subscriptions.

Graduate Part-time study available in Graduate and Professional Programs. Basic part-time expenses: $100 per credit hour tuition.

Oregon / **Colleges Offering Part-Time Degree Programs**

Mt Hood Community College
Gresham 97030

Public institution; city setting. Awards A. Barrier-free campus. Total enrollment: 8,984 (all undergraduates); 62% part-time, 55% women, 60% over 25. Total faculty: 566. Library holdings: 61,000 bound volumes, 420 periodical subscriptions, 6,400 records/tapes.

Undergraduate Courses offered for part-time students during daytime, evenings, summer. Complete part-time degree programs offered during daytime, evenings, summer. Adult/continuing education programs available. Career services available to part-time students: individual and group career counseling, individual job placement, employer recruitment on campus. Part-time tuition: $24 per quarter hour for area residents, $34 per quarter hour for state residents, $72 per quarter hour for nonresidents.

Multnomah School of the Bible
Portland 97220

Independent-religious institution; metropolitan setting. Awards A, B, M. Barrier-free campus. Total enrollment: 682. Undergraduate enrollment: 561; 9% part-time, 38% women, 25% over 25. Total faculty: 52. Library holdings: 35,044 bound volumes, 4,162 titles on microform, 422 periodical subscriptions, 1,064 records/tapes.

Graduate Part-time study available in Graduate Division. Basic part-time expenses: $115 per credit tuition.

Oregon Graduate Center
Beaverton 97006

Independent institution (graduate only). Total enrollment: 104 (coed; 30% part-time). Total faculty: 61.

Graduate Part-time study available in Graduate Studies. Basic part-time expenses: $150 per credit tuition plus $25 per quarter fees.

Oregon Institute of Technology
Klamath Falls 97601

Public institution; small-town setting. Awards A, B. Total enrollment: 2,698 (all undergraduates); 20% part-time, 32% women. Total faculty: 193. Library holdings: 63,000 bound volumes, 1,265 periodical subscriptions.

Undergraduate Courses offered for part-time students during daytime, evenings, summer. Complete part-time degree programs offered during daytime, evenings, summer. Adult/continuing education programs available. Career services available to part-time students: individual and group career counseling, individual job placement, employer recruitment on campus. Part-time tuition per quarter (1 to 11 quarter hours) ranges from $57 to $434 for state residents, $57 to $1347 for nonresidents.

Oregon State University
Corvallis 97331

Public institution; small-town setting. Awards B, M, D. Total enrollment: 16,119. Undergraduate enrollment: 13,392; 8% part-time, 41% women. Total faculty: 1,150. Library holdings: 963,642 bound volumes, 1.0 million titles on microform, 17,168 periodical subscriptions.

Graduate Part-time study available in Graduate School, College of Veterinary Medicine. Basic part-time expenses: $198 per quarter (minimum) tuition plus $64 per quarter (minimum) fees for state residents, $336 per quarter (minimum) tuition plus $64 per quarter (minimum) fees for nonresidents.

Pacific Northwest College of Art
Portland 97205

Independent institution; metropolitan setting. Awards B. Barrier-free campus. Total enrollment: 167 (all undergraduates); 4% part-time, 65% women. Total faculty: 33. Library holdings: 15,500 bound volumes, 67 periodical subscriptions.

Undergraduate Courses offered for part-time students during daytime, summer. Complete part-time degree programs offered during daytime. Adult/continuing education programs available. Career services available to part-time students: individual career counseling. Part-time tuition: $155 per semester hour.

Pacific University
Forest Grove 97116

Independent institution; small-town setting. Awards B, M, D. Total enrollment: 1,071. Undergraduate enrollment: 873; 2% part-time, 46% women. Total faculty: 98. Library holdings: 133,000 bound volumes, 21,500 titles on microform, 835 periodical subscriptions, 9,391 records/tapes.

Undergraduate Courses offered for part-time students during daytime, evenings. Complete part-time degree programs offered during daytime, evenings. Adult/continuing education programs available. Career services available to part-time students: individual and group career counseling, employer recruitment on campus. Part-time tuition: $225 per semester hour.

Portland Community College
Portland 97219

Public institution; metropolitan setting. Awards A. Barrier-free campus. Total enrollment: 19,250 (all undergraduates); 63% part-time, 51% women, 67% over 25. Total faculty: 1,647. Library holdings: 79,000 bound volumes, 5,500 titles on microform, 750 periodical subscriptions, 7,700 records/tapes.

Undergraduate Courses offered for part-time students during daytime, evenings, summer. Complete part-time degree programs offered during daytime, evenings. External degree and adult/continuing education programs available. Career services available to part-time students: individual and group career counseling, individual job placement. Part-time tuition: $21 per credit hour for area residents, $43 per credit hour for state residents, $70 per credit hour for nonresidents.

Portland State University
Portland 97207

Public institution; metropolitan setting. Awards B, M, D. Barrier-free campus. Total enrollment: 14,497. Undergraduate enrollment: 10,375; 40% part-time, 49% women, 38% over 25. Total faculty: 709. Library holdings: 669,590 bound volumes, 711,770 titles on microform, 10,474 periodical subscriptions, 19,465 records/tapes.

Undergraduate Courses offered for part-time students during daytime, evenings, weekends, summer. Complete part-time degree programs offered during daytime, evenings, summer. Adult/continuing education programs available. Part-time tuition and fees per quarter (1 to 11 credit hours) range from $64 to $434 for state residents, $64 to $1237 for nonresidents.

Graduate Part-time study available in Graduate Studies. Degree can be earned exclusively through evening/weekend study in Graduate Studies. Basic part-time expenses: $231 per quarter

Colleges Offering Part-Time Degree Programs / Oregon

Portland State University (continued)

(minimum) tuition. Institutional financial aid available to part-time graduate students in Graduate Studies.

Rogue Community College
Grants Pass 97527

Public institution; rural setting. Awards A. Barrier-free campus. Total enrollment: 2,842 (all undergraduates); 77% part-time, 61% women, 75% over 25. Total faculty: 267. Library holdings: 30,000 bound volumes, 169 periodical subscriptions, 482 records/tapes.

Undergraduate Courses offered for part-time students during daytime, evenings, weekends, summer. Complete part-time degree programs offered during daytime, evenings. Adult/continuing education programs available. Career services available to part-time students: individual and group career counseling, individual job placement, employer recruitment on campus. Part-time tuition: $16 per credit for area residents, $28 per credit for state residents, $64 per credit for nonresidents.

Southern Oregon State College
Ashland 97520

Public institution; small-town setting. Awards A, B, M. Total enrollment: 4,535. Undergraduate enrollment: 3,961; 13% part-time, 51% women. Total faculty: 240. Library holdings: 200,000 bound volumes, 365,000 titles on microform, 4,700 periodical subscriptions.

Undergraduate Courses offered for part-time students during daytime, evenings, summer. Complete part-time degree programs offered during daytime, evenings, summer. Adult/continuing education programs available. Career services available to part-time students: individual and group career counseling, individual job placement, employer recruitment on campus. Part-time tuition and fees per quarter (1 to 11 credits) range from $66 to $441 for state residents, $100 to $1123 for nonresidents.

Graduate Part-time study available in Graduate School. Basic part-time expenses: $228 per quarter (minimum) tuition. Institutional financial aid available to part-time graduate students in Graduate School.

Southwestern Oregon Community College
Coos Bay 97420

Public institution; small-town setting. Awards A. Total enrollment: 4,080 (all undergraduates); 79% part-time, 52% women, 60% over 25. Total faculty: 245. Library holdings: 52,164 bound volumes, 2,743 titles on microform, 484 periodical subscriptions, 5,907 records/tapes.

Undergraduate Courses offered for part-time students during daytime, evenings, weekends. Complete part-time degree programs offered during daytime, evenings. Adult/continuing education programs available. Career services available to part-time students: individual and group career counseling. Part-time tuition: $19 per credit for area residents, $38 per credit for state residents, $57 per credit for nonresidents.

Treasure Valley Community College
Ontario 97914

Public institution; small-town setting. Awards A. Barrier-free campus. Total enrollment: 1,993 (all undergraduates); 65% part-time, 58% women, 20% over 25. Total faculty: 75. Library holdings: 28,000 bound volumes, 150 periodical subscriptions, 250 records/tapes.

Undergraduate Courses offered for part-time students during daytime, evenings. Complete part-time degree programs offered during daytime, evenings. Adult/continuing education programs available. Career services available to part-time students: individual and group career counseling. Part-time tuition: $22 per credit for state residents, $44 per credit for nonresidents.

Umpqua Community College
Roseburg 97470

Public institution; rural setting. Awards A. Barrier-free campus. Total enrollment: 1,650 (all undergraduates); 45% part-time, 55% women. Total faculty: 250. Library holdings: 41,000 bound volumes, 20 periodical subscriptions, 800 records/tapes.

Undergraduate Courses offered for part-time students during daytime, evenings, summer. Complete part-time degree programs offered during daytime, evenings, summer. Adult/continuing education programs available. Career services available to part-time students: individual and group career counseling, individual job placement, employer recruitment on campus. Part-time tuition and fees per quarter (1 to 11 credits) range from $38 to $211 for district residents, $91 to $388 for state residents, $231 to $979 for nonresidents.

University of Oregon
Eugene 97403

Public institution; city setting. Awards B, M, D. Total enrollment: 15,478. Undergraduate enrollment: 11,467; 14% part-time, 49% women. Total faculty: 1,287. Library holdings: 1.8 million bound volumes, 960,000 titles on microform, 20,000 periodical subscriptions, 4,000 records/tapes.

Graduate Part-time study available in Graduate School. Basic part-time expenses: $275 per quarter (minimum) tuition for state residents, $413 per quarter (minimum) tuition for nonresidents.

University of Portland
Portland 97203

Independent-religious instutition; metropolitan setting. Awards B, M. Total enrollment: 2,847. Undergraduate enrollment: 2,224; 18% part-time, 47% women, 20% over 25. Total faculty: 176. Library holdings: 200,000 bound volumes, 125,000 titles on microform, 1,300 periodical subscriptions, 3,000 records/tapes.

Undergraduate Courses offered for part-time students during daytime, evenings, summer. Complete part-time degree programs offered during daytime, evenings. Adult/continuing education programs available. Career services available to part-time students: individual and group career counseling, individual job placement, employer recruitment on campus. Part-time tuition: $172 per semester hour.

Graduate Part-time study available in Graduate School. Degree can be earned exclusively through evening/weekend study in Graduate School. Basic part-time expenses: $165 per semester hour tuition. Institutional financial aid available to part-time graduate students in Graduate School.

Warner Pacific College
Portland 97215

Independent-religious instutition; metropolitan setting. Awards A, B, M. Total enrollment: 426. Undergraduate enrollment: 420; 17% part-time, 50% women. Total faculty: 49. Library holdings:

52,000 bound volumes, 250 periodical subscriptions, 1,500 records/tapes.

Undergraduate Courses offered for part-time students during daytime, evenings, summer. Complete part-time degree programs offered during daytime. Adult/continuing education programs available. Career services available to part-time students: group career counseling, employer recruitment on campus. Part-time tuition: $100 per quarter hour.

Graduate Part-time study available in Center for Christian Ministries. Basic part-time expenses: $50 per quarter hour tuition plus $10 per quarter (minimum) fees.

Western Baptist College
Salem 97301

Independent-religious instutition; city setting. Awards A, B. Total enrollment: 290 (all undergraduates); 12% part-time, 50% women, 14% over 25. Total faculty: 29. Library holdings: 29,000 bound volumes, 296 periodical subscriptions, 1,608 records/tapes.

Undergraduate Courses offered for part-time students during daytime. Complete part-time degree programs offered during daytime. Career services available to part-time students: individual career counseling. Part-time tuition: $95 per credit.

Western Conservative Baptist Seminary
Portland 97215

Independent-religious institution (graduate only). Total enrollment: 485 (primarily men; 46% part-time). Total faculty: 38.

Graduate Part-time study available in Graduate and Professional Programs. Basic part-time expenses: $85 per credit tuition. Institutional financial aid available to part-time graduate students in Graduate and Professional Programs.

Western Evangelical Seminary
Portland 97222

Independent-religious institution (graduate only). Total enrollment: 256 (coed; 41% part-time). Total faculty: 17. Library holdings: 42,000 bound volumes, 800 microforms.

Graduate Part-time study available in Graduate and Professional Programs. Basic part-time expenses: $75 per credit tuition plus $12 per quarter fees. Institutional financial aid available to part-time graduate students in Graduate and Professional Programs.

Western Oregon State College
Monmouth 97361

Public institution; small-town setting. Awards B, M. Barrier-free campus. Total enrollment: 2,527. Undergraduate enrollment: 2,051; 23% part-time, 63% women, 25% over 25. Total faculty: 200. Library holdings: 190,000 bound volumes, 400 periodical subscriptions, 9,000 records/tapes.

Undergraduate Courses offered for part-time students during daytime, evenings, summer. Complete part-time degree programs offered during daytime, evenings, summer. Adult/continuing education programs available. Career services available to part-time students: individual job placement, employer recruitment on campus. Part-time tuition per quarter (3 to 11 credit hours) ranges from $113 to $429 for state residents, $113 to $1111 for nonresidents.

Graduate Part-time study available in Graduate Studies. Basic part-time expenses: $215 per quarter (minimum) tuition.

Willamette University
Salem 97301

Independent-religious instutition; city setting. Awards B, M, D. Total enrollment: 1,850. Undergraduate enrollment: 1,260; 1% part-time, 50% women, 3% over 25. Total faculty: 172. Library holdings: 136,000 bound volumes, 5,200 titles on microform, 1,150 periodical subscriptions, 2,600 records/tapes.

Undergraduate Courses offered for part-time students during daytime. Complete part-time degree programs offered during daytime. Adult/continuing education programs available. Career services available to part-time students: individual and group career counseling. Part-time tuition: $198 per semester hour.

Graduate Part-time study available in College of Law, Geo. H. Atkinson Graduate School of Administration. Degree can be earned exclusively through evening/weekend study in Geo. H. Atkinson Graduate School of Administration. Basic part-time expenses: $212 per semester hour tuition plus $10 per semester fees. Institutional financial aid available to part-time graduate students in College of Law, Geo. H. Atkinson Graduate School of Administration.

PENNSYLVANIA

Academy of the New Church
Bryn Athyn 19009

Independent-religious instutition; small-town setting. Awards A, B (also offers graduate-level Bachelor of Theology degree). Total enrollment: 160. Undergraduate enrollment: 151; 9% part-time, 50% women, 15% over 25. Total faculty: 37. Library holdings: 110,000 bound volumes, 356 periodical subscriptions, 3,400 records/tapes.

Undergraduate Courses offered for part-time students during daytime, evenings. Complete part-time degree programs offered during daytime, evenings. Career services available to part-time students: individual and group career counseling. Part-time tuition: $60 per credit.

Albright College
Reading 19603

Independent-religious instutition; city setting. Awards B. Total enrollment: 1,413 (all undergraduates); 4% part-time, 56% women, 0% over 25. Total faculty: 126. Library holdings: 140,000 bound volumes, 7,100 titles on microform, 1,050 periodical subscriptions, 3,610 records/tapes.

Undergraduate Courses offered for part-time students during daytime, evenings, summer. Complete part-time degree programs offered during daytime, evenings, summer. Adult/continuing education programs available. Career services available to part-time students: individual and group career counseling, individual job placement, employer recruitment on campus. Part-time tuition: $220 per credit.

Allegheny College
Meadville 16335

Independent-religious instutition; small-town setting. Awards B, M. Total enrollment: 1,955. Undergraduate enrollment: 1,900; 1% part-time, 49% women, 1% over 25. Total faculty: 161. Library holdings: 330,000 bound volumes, 1,114 periodical subscriptions, 400 records/tapes.

Undergraduate Courses offered for part-time students during daytime, summer. Complete part-time degree programs offered during daytime, summer. Career services available to part-time

Allegheny College (continued)
students: individual and group career counseling, individual job placement, employer recruitment on campus. Part-time tuition: $705 per course.

Graduate Part-time study available in Graduate Programs in Education. Basic part-time expenses: $778 per course tuition.

Allentown Business School
Allentown 18101

Proprietary institution; city setting. Awards A. Barrier-free campus. Total enrollment: 900 (all undergraduates); 15% part-time, 70% women, 20% over 25. Total faculty: 18.

Undergraduate Courses offered for part-time students during daytime, weekends. Complete part-time degree programs offered during daytime, weekends. Adult/continuing education programs available. Career services available to part-time students: individual job placement. Part-time tuition: $230 per course.

Allentown College of St Francis de Sales
Center Valley 18034

Independent-religious instutition; rural setting. Awards B. Total enrollment: 742 (all undergraduates); 5% part-time, 54% women, 1% over 25. Total faculty: 66. Library holdings: 135,000 bound volumes, 700 periodical subscriptions, 500 records/tapes.

Undergraduate Courses offered for part-time students during daytime, evenings, summer. Complete part-time degree programs offered during daytime, evenings. Adult/continuing education programs available. Career services available to part-time students: individual and group career counseling, individual job placement, employer recruitment on campus. Part-time tuition: $155 per credit.

Alliance College
Cambridge Springs 16403

Independent institution; rural setting. Awards A, B. Total enrollment: 270 (all undergraduates); 26% part-time, 36% women, 9% over 25. Total faculty: 35. Library holdings: 80,000 bound volumes, 500 periodical subscriptions.

Undergraduate Courses offered for part-time students during daytime, evenings. Complete part-time degree programs offered during daytime, evenings. Career services available to part-time students: individual and group career counseling. Part-time tuition: $95 per semester hour.

Alvernia College
Reading 19607

Independent-religious instutition; city setting. Awards A, B. Total enrollment: 706 (all undergraduates); 45% part-time, 66% women. Total faculty: 80. Library holdings: 67,500 bound volumes, 1,450 titles on microform, 300 periodical subscriptions, 4,250 records/tapes.

Undergraduate Courses offered for part-time students during daytime, evenings, weekends. Complete part-time degree programs offered during daytime, evenings, weekends. Adult/continuing education programs available. Career services available to part-time students: individual and group career counseling, individual job placement. Part-time tuition: $125 per credit.

American College
Bryn Mawr 19010

Independent institution (graduate only). Total enrollment: 2,100 (primarily men; 100% part-time). Total faculty: 70.

Graduate Part-time study available in Graduate School of Financial Sciences, Richard D. Irwin Graduate School of Management. Degree can be earned exclusively through evening/weekend study in Graduate School of Financial Sciences, Richard D. Irwin Graduate School of Management. Basic part-time expenses: $225 per course tuition. Institutional financial aid available to part-time graduate students in Graduate School of Financial Sciences, Richard D. Irwin Graduate School of Management.

Antonelli Institute of Art and Photography
Plymouth Meeting 19462

Proprietary institution; metropolitan setting. Awards A. Barrier-free campus. Total enrollment: 325 (all undergraduates); 10% part-time, 40% women. Total faculty: 23. Library holdings: 5,000 bound volumes, 1,000 periodical subscriptions.

Undergraduate Courses offered for part-time students during evenings. Complete part-time degree programs offered during evenings. Adult/continuing education programs available. Career services available to part-time students: individual and group career counseling, individual job placement, employer recruitment on campus. Part-time tuition: $140 per credit hour.

Baptist Bible College of Pennsylvania
Clarks Summit 18411

Independent-religious instutition; small-town setting. Awards A, B, M. Total enrollment: 761. Undergraduate enrollment: 701; 26% part-time, 52% women. Total faculty: 49. Library holdings: 74,000 bound volumes, 3,200 titles on microform, 490 periodical subscriptions, 3,200 records/tapes.

Undergraduate Courses offered for part-time students during daytime, evenings, summer. Complete part-time degree programs offered during daytime. Career services available to part-time students: individual and group career counseling, individual job placement, employer recruitment on campus. Part-time tuition: $105 per credit.

Graduate Part-time study available in School of Theology. Basic part-time expenses: $100 per semester hour (minimum) tuition plus $240 per semester fees. Institutional financial aid available to part-time graduate students in School of Theology.

Beaver College
Glenside 19038

Independent-religious instutition; small-town setting. Awards A, B, M. Total enrollment: 2,210. Undergraduate enrollment: 1,351; 47% part-time, 74% women. Total faculty: 160. Library holdings: 107,000 bound volumes, 7,956 titles on microform, 659 periodical subscriptions, 2,000 records/tapes.

Undergraduate Courses offered for part-time students during daytime, evenings, summer. Complete part-time degree programs offered during daytime, evenings. Adult/continuing education programs available. Career services available to part-time students: individual and group career counseling, individual job placement, employer recruitment on campus. Part-time tuition: $181 per credit.

Graduate Part-time study available in Graduate Studies. Basic part-time expenses: $138 per credit tuition.

Pennsylvania / **Colleges Offering Part-Time Degree Programs**

Berean Institute
Philadelphia 19130

Independent institution; metropolitan setting. Awards A. Barrier-free campus. Total enrollment: 335 (all undergraduates); 5% part-time, 90% women, 20% over 25. Total faculty: 18. Library holdings: 2,700 bound volumes, 48 periodical subscriptions, 150 records/tapes.

Undergraduate Courses offered for part-time students during daytime, evenings. Complete part-time degree programs offered during daytime, evenings. Career services available to part-time students: individual and group career counseling, individual job placement, employer recruitment on campus. Part-time tuition: $40 per unit.

Bloomsburg University of Pennsylvania
Bloomsburg 17815

Public institution; small-town setting. Awards A, B, M. Total enrollment: 6,316. Undergraduate enrollment: 5,809; 15% part-time, 59% women, 10% over 25. Total faculty: 340. Library holdings: 300,370 bound volumes, 1.3 million titles on microform, 1,465 periodical subscriptions, 6,752 records/tapes.

Undergraduate Courses offered for part-time students during daytime, evenings, summer. Complete part-time degree programs offered during daytime, evenings, summer. Adult/continuing education programs available. Career services available to part-time students: individual and group career counseling, individual job placement, employer recruitment on campus. Part-time tuition: $66 per semester hour for state residents, $115 per semester hour for nonresidents.

Graduate Part-time study available in School of Graduate and Extended Studies. Basic part-time expenses: $87 per credit hour tuition for state residents, $92 per credit hour tuition for nonresidents. Institutional financial aid available to part-time graduate students in School of Graduate and Extended Studies.

Bryn Mawr College
Bryn Mawr 19010

Independent institution; small-town setting. Awards B, M, D. Barrier-free campus. Total enrollment: 1,590. Undergraduate enrollment: 1,156; 3% part-time, 100% women, 1% over 25. Total faculty: 199. Library holdings: 794,000 bound volumes, 2,300 periodical subscriptions.

Undergraduate Courses offered for part-time students during daytime, summer. Complete part-time degree programs offered during daytime. Adult/continuing education programs available. Career services available to part-time students: individual and group career counseling, individual job placement, employer recruitment on campus. Part-time tuition: $600 per course.

Graduate Part-time study available in Graduate School of Arts and Sciences, Graduate School of Social Work and Social Research. Basic part-time expenses: $1415 per course tuition. Institutional financial aid available to part-time graduate students in Graduate School of Arts and Sciences, Graduate School of Social Work and Social Research.

Bucknell University
Lewisburg 17837

Independent institution; small-town setting. Awards B, M. Total enrollment: 3,338. Undergraduate enrollment: 3,157; 1% part-time, 48% women, 1% over 25. Total faculty: 252. Library holdings: 450,000 bound volumes, 167,000 titles on microform, 5,300 periodical subscriptions, 4,000 records/tapes.

Undergraduate Courses offered for part-time students during daytime. Complete part-time degree programs offered during daytime. Part-time tuition: $1125 per course.

Graduate Part-time study available in Graduate Studies. Basic part-time expenses: $1050 per course tuition plus $60 per semester fees.

Bucks County Community College
Newtown 18940

Public institution; small-town setting. Awards A. Barrier-free campus. Total enrollment: 10,203 (all undergraduates); 64% part-time, 54% women, 45% over 25. Total faculty: 337. Library holdings: 103,000 bound volumes, 760 periodical subscriptions, 10,000 records/tapes.

Undergraduate Courses offered for part-time students during daytime, evenings, weekends, summer. Complete part-time degree programs offered during daytime, evenings, weekends, summer. Adult/continuing education programs available. Career services available to part-time students: individual and group career counseling, individual job placement, employer recruitment on campus. Part-time tuition: $36 per credit for area residents, $72 per credit for state residents, $108 per credit for nonresidents.

Butler County Community College
Butler 16001

Public institution; rural setting. Awards A. Barrier-free campus. Total enrollment: 1,250 (all undergraduates); 40% part-time, 60% women. Total faculty: 65. Library holdings: 40,000 bound volumes, 302 periodical subscriptions, 1,100 records/tapes.

Undergraduate Courses offered for part-time students during daytime, evenings, weekends, summer. Complete part-time degree programs offered during daytime, evenings, weekends, summer. Adult/continuing education programs available. Career services available to part-time students: individual and group career counseling, individual job placement. Part-time tuition: $42 per credit for area residents, $84 per credit for state residents, $126 per credit for nonresidents.

Cabrini College
Radnor 19087

Independent-religious instutition; small-town setting. Awards B, M. Total enrollment: 800. Undergraduate enrollment: 657; 14% part-time, 79% women, 1% over 25. Total faculty: 75. Library holdings: 70,000 bound volumes, 3,000 titles on microform, 370 periodical subscriptions, 650 records/tapes.

Undergraduate Courses offered for part-time students during daytime, evenings, summer. Complete part-time degree programs offered during daytime, evenings, summer. Adult/continuing education programs available. Career services available to part-time students: individual and group career counseling, employer recruitment on campus. Part-time tuition: $130 per credit.

Graduate Part-time study available in Graduate Division. Degree can be earned exclusively through evening/weekend study in Graduate Division. Basic part-time expenses: $135 per credit tuition plus $35 per semester fees. Institutional financial aid available to part-time graduate students in Graduate Division.

Colleges Offering Part-Time Degree Programs / Pennsylvania

California University of Pennsylvania
California 15419

Public institution; small-town setting. Awards A, B, M. Total enrollment: 4,877. Undergraduate enrollment: 4,418; 20% part-time, 45% women, 5% over 25. Total faculty: 305. Library holdings: 231,025 bound volumes, 910,343 titles on microform, 1,200 periodical subscriptions, 25,000 records/tapes.

Undergraduate Courses offered for part-time students during daytime, evenings, summer. Complete part-time degree programs offered during daytime, evenings, summer. Adult/continuing education programs available. Career services available to part-time students: individual and group career counseling, individual job placement, employer recruitment on campus. Part-time tuition: $66 per credit for state residents, $115 per credit for nonresidents.

Carlow College
Pittsburgh 15213

Independent-religious instutition; metropolitan setting. Awards B, M. Total enrollment: 991. Undergraduate enrollment: 979; 24% part-time, 97% women. Total faculty: 117. Library holdings: 110,699 bound volumes, 192 titles on microform, 421 periodical subscriptions, 6,389 records/tapes.

Undergraduate Courses offered for part-time students during daytime, evenings, weekends, summer. Complete part-time degree programs offered during daytime, weekends. Adult/continuing education programs available. Career services available to part-time students: individual and group career counseling, individual job placement, employer recruitment on campus. Part-time tuition: $170 per credit.

Graduate Part-time study available in Graduate Program in Education. Basic part-time expenses: $180 per credit tuition plus $20 per credit fees.

Carnegie-Mellon University
Pittsburgh 15213

Independent institution; metropolitan setting. Awards B, M, D. Total enrollment: 5,818. Undergraduate enrollment: 4,130; 3% part-time, 35% women, 1% over 25. Total faculty: 511. Library holdings: 622,046 bound volumes, 43,514 titles on microform, 2,819 periodical subscriptions, 112,623 records/tapes.

Graduate Part-time study available in Carnegie Institute of Technology, College of Fine Arts, Mellon College of Science, School of Urban and Public Affairs. Basic part-time expenses: $126 per unit tuition. Institutional financial aid available to part-time graduate students in School of Urban and Public Affairs.

Cedar Crest College
Allentown 18104

Independent-religious instutition; city setting. Awards B. Total enrollment: 1,142 (all undergraduates); 35% part-time, 98% women, 20% over 25. Total faculty: 123. Library holdings: 286,165 bound volumes, 18,764 titles on microform, 1,483 periodical subscriptions, 2,927 records/tapes.

Undergraduate Courses offered for part-time students during daytime, evenings, weekends, summer. Complete part-time degree programs offered during daytime, evenings, weekends, summer. Adult/continuing education programs available. Career services available to part-time students: individual and group career counseling, employer recruitment on campus. Part-time tuition: $195 per credit hour.

Central Pennsylvania Business School
Summerdale 17093

Proprietary institution; small-town setting. Awards A. Barrier-free campus. Total enrollment: 752 (all undergraduates); 7% part-time, 86% women, 4% over 25. Total faculty: 47. Library holdings: 7,000 bound volumes, 30 titles on microform, 106 periodical subscriptions, 800 records/tapes.

Undergraduate Courses offered for part-time students during daytime, evenings, summer. Complete part-time degree programs offered during daytime, summer. Adult/continuing education programs available. Career services available to part-time students: individual and group career counseling, individual job placement, employer recruitment on campus. Part-time tuition: $83 per credit.

Chatham College
Pittsburgh 15232

Independent institution; metropolitan setting. Awards B. Barrier-free campus. Total enrollment: 610 (all undergraduates); 20% part-time, 100% women, 25% over 25. Total faculty: 70. Library holdings: 120,000 bound volumes, 566 periodical subscriptions, 1,606 records/tapes.

Undergraduate Courses offered for part-time students during daytime, evenings. Complete part-time degree programs offered during daytime, evenings. Adult/continuing education programs available. Career services available to part-time students: individual and group career counseling, individual job placement, employer recruitment on campus. Part-time tuition: $705 per unit.

Chestnut Hill College
Philadelphia 19118

Independent-religious instutition; metropolitan setting. Awards A, B, M. Total enrollment: 819. Undergraduate enrollment: 770; 24% part-time, 99% women. Total faculty: 100. Library holdings: 118,000 bound volumes, 775 titles on microform, 995 periodical subscriptions, 1,667 records/tapes.

Undergraduate Courses offered for part-time students during daytime, evenings, summer. Complete part-time degree programs offered during daytime, evenings, summer. Adult/continuing education programs available. Career services available to part-time students: individual and group career counseling, individual job placement, employer recruitment on campus. Part-time tuition: $80 per semester hour.

Graduate Part-time study available in Graduate Division. Degree can be earned exclusively through evening/weekend study in Graduate Division. Basic part-time expenses: $105 per credit tuition plus $15 per semester fees.

Cheyney University of Pennsylvania
Cheyney 19319

Public institution; rural setting. Awards B, M. Barrier-free campus. Total enrollment: 1,992. Undergraduate enrollment: 1,867; 10% part-time, 55% women. Total faculty: 163. Library holdings: 132,000 bound volumes, 8,600 titles on microform, 18,000 periodical subscriptions.

Undergraduate Courses offered for part-time students during daytime, evenings. Complete part-time degree programs offered during daytime, evenings. Adult/continuing education programs available. Career services available to part-time students: individual and group career counseling, individual job placement, employer recruitment on campus. Part-time tuition: $62 per credit hour for state residents, $108 per credit hour for nonresidents.

Pennsylvania / **Colleges Offering Part-Time Degree Programs**

Graduate Part-time study available in School of Graduate Studies. Degree can be earned exclusively through evening/weekend study in School of Graduate Studies. Basic part-time expenses: $82 per credit tuition plus $27.50 per semester fees. Institutional financial aid available to part-time graduate students in School of Graduate Studies.

Churchman Business School
Easton 18042

Proprietary institution; small-town setting. Awards A. Total enrollment: 230 (all undergraduates); 7% part-time, 65% women. Total faculty: 10. Library holdings: 5,000 bound volumes, 15 periodical subscriptions.

Undergraduate Courses offered for part-time students during daytime, evenings. Complete part-time degree programs offered during daytime, evenings. Adult/continuing education programs available. Career services available to part-time students: group career counseling, individual job placement, employer recruitment on campus. Part-time tuition: $340 per course.

Clarion University of Pennsylvania
Clarion 16214

Public institution; small-town setting. Awards A, B, M. Barrier-free campus. Total enrollment: 4,841. Undergraduate enrollment: 4,636; 5% part-time, 52% women, 5% over 25. Total faculty: 320. Library holdings: 350,000 bound volumes, 1,446 periodical subscriptions, 2,667 records/tapes.

Undergraduate Courses offered for part-time students during daytime, evenings, summer. Complete part-time degree programs offered during daytime, evenings, summer. Adult/continuing education programs available. Part-time tuition: $62 per credit for state residents, $80 per credit for nonresidents.

Graduate Part-time study available in School of Graduate Studies and Continuing Education. Degree can be earned exclusively through evening/weekend study in School of Graduate Studies and Continuing Education. Basic part-time expenses: $87 per credit tuition plus $7.50 per semester (minimum) fees for state residents, $92 per credit tuition plus $7.50 per semester (minimum) fees for nonresidents. Institutional financial aid available to part-time graduate students in School of Graduate Studies and Continuing Education.

Clarion University of Pennsylvania, Venango Campus
Oil City 16301

Public institution; small-town setting. Awards A, B. Barrier-free campus. Total enrollment: 556 (all undergraduates); 68% part-time, 55% women. Total faculty: 33. Library holdings: 25,000 bound volumes, 74 titles on microform, 200 periodical subscriptions.

Undergraduate Courses offered for part-time students during daytime, evenings, weekends, summer. Complete part-time degree programs offered during daytime, evenings. Adult/continuing education programs available. Career services available to part-time students: individual career counseling. Part-time tuition: $66 per credit hour for state residents, $115 per credit hour for nonresidents.

College Misericordia
Dallas 18612

Independent-religious instutition; small-town setting. Awards A, B, M. Barrier-free campus. Total enrollment: 1,303. Undergraduate enrollment: 1,193; 24% part-time, 72% women. Total faculty: 128. Library holdings: 69,549 bound volumes, 772 periodical subscriptions, 10,303 records/tapes.

Undergraduate Courses offered for part-time students during daytime, evenings, weekends, summer. Complete part-time degree programs offered during daytime, evenings, weekends, summer. Adult/continuing education programs available. Part-time tuition per credit ranges from $100 to $108 according to program.

Community College of Allegheny County–Boyce Campus
Monroeville 15146

Public institution; city setting. Awards A. Barrier-free campus. Total enrollment: 4,810 (all undergraduates); 65% part-time, 50% women, 50% over 25. Total faculty: 80. Library holdings: 55,000 bound volumes, 60 periodical subscriptions, 2,670 records/tapes.

Undergraduate Courses offered for part-time students during daytime, evenings, weekends, summer. Complete part-time degree programs offered during daytime, evenings, weekends, summer. Adult/continuing education programs available. Career services available to part-time students: individual career counseling, individual job placement, employer recruitment on campus. Part-time tuition: $33 per credit for area residents, $66 per credit for state residents, $99 per credit for nonresidents.

Community College of Allegheny County–College Center North
Pittsburgh 15237

Public institution; metropolitan setting. Awards A. Barrier-free campus. Total enrollment: 4,014 (all undergraduates); 84% part-time, 40% women. Total faculty: 196. Library holdings: 17,685 bound volumes, 160 titles on microform, 309 periodical subscriptions, 1,260 records/tapes.

Undergraduate Courses offered for part-time students during daytime, evenings, weekends, summer. Complete part-time degree programs offered during daytime, evenings, weekends, summer. Adult/continuing education programs available. Career services available to part-time students: individual and group career counseling, individual job placement, employer recruitment on campus. Part-time tuition: $33 per credit for area residents, $66 per credit for state residents, $99 per credit for nonresidents.

Community College of Beaver County
Monaca 15061

Public institution; small-town setting. Awards A. Total enrollment: 2,200 (all undergraduates); 49% part-time, 51% women, 56% over 25. Total faculty: 87. Library holdings: 35,000 bound volumes, 300 periodical subscriptions, 1,200 records/tapes.

Undergraduate Courses offered for part-time students during daytime, evenings, summer. Complete part-time degree programs offered during daytime, evenings, summer. Adult/continuing education programs available. Career services available to part-time students: individual career counseling, individual job placement, employer recruitment on campus. Part-time tuition: $35 per credit for area residents, $78 per credit for state residents, $121 per credit for nonresidents.

Colleges Offering Part-Time Degree Programs / *Pennsylvania*

Community College of Philadelphia
Philadelphia 19130

Public institution; metropolitan setting. Awards A. Barrier-free campus. Total enrollment: 10,500 (all undergraduates); 49% part-time, 69% women, 40% over 25. Total faculty: 756. Library holdings: 133,000 bound volumes, 680 periodical subscriptions.

Undergraduate Courses offered for part-time students during daytime, evenings, weekends, summer. Complete part-time degree programs offered during daytime, evenings, weekends, summer. Adult/continuing education programs available. Career services available to part-time students: individual and group career counseling, individual job placement, employer recruitment on campus. Part-time tuition: $38 per semester hour for area residents, $76 per semester hour for state residents, $114 per semester hour for nonresidents.

Dean Institute of Technology
Pittsburgh 15226

Proprietary institution; metropolitan setting. Awards A. Barrier-free campus. Total enrollment: 380 (all undergraduates); 25% part-time, 10% women, 15% over 25. Total faculty: 23.

Undergraduate Courses offered for part-time students during daytime, evenings. Complete part-time degree programs offered during daytime, evenings. Career services available to part-time students: individual and group career counseling, individual job placement, employer recruitment on campus. Part-time tuition: $1890 per year.

Delaware County Community College
Media 19063

Public institution; small-town setting. Awards A. Barrier-free campus. Total enrollment: 7,547 (all undergraduates); 63% part-time, 57% women, 40% over 25. Total faculty: 498. Library holdings: 60,600 bound volumes, 47,000 titles on microform, 510 periodical subscriptions, 4,000 records/tapes.

Undergraduate Courses offered for part-time students during daytime, evenings, weekends, summer. Complete part-time degree programs offered during daytime, evenings, weekends. Adult/continuing education programs available. Career services available to part-time students: individual and group career counseling, individual job placement, employer recruitment on campus. Part-time tuition: $31 per credit for area residents, $66 per credit for state residents, $101 per credit for nonresidents. State residents from cooperating districts pay area-resident tuition.

Delaware Valley College of Science and Agriculture
Doylestown 18901

Independent institution; rural setting. Awards B. Total enrollment: 1,305 (all undergraduates); 3% part-time, 33% women. Total faculty: 91. Library holdings: 60,000 bound volumes, 2,900 titles on microform, 611 periodical subscriptions, 665 records/tapes.

Undergraduate Courses offered for part-time students during daytime, evenings, summer. Complete part-time degree programs offered during daytime, evenings, summer. Adult/continuing education programs available. Career services available to part-time students: individual and group career counseling, individual job placement, employer recruitment on campus. Part-time tuition: $135 per credit.

Dickinson College
Carlisle 17013

Independent-religious instutition; small-town setting. Awards B. Total enrollment: 1,776 (all undergraduates); 0% part-time, 54% women, 0% over 25. Total faculty: 126. Library holdings: 365,000 bound volumes, 122,400 titles on microform, 1,184 periodical subscriptions, 6,400 records/tapes.

Undergraduate Courses offered for part-time students during daytime, summer. Complete part-time degree programs offered during daytime. Adult/continuing education programs available. Part-time tuition: $1300 per course.

Drexel University
Philadelphia 19104

Independent institution; metropolitan setting. Awards B, M, D. Barrier-free campus. Total enrollment: 12,687. Undergraduate enrollment: 7,296; 27% part-time, 35% women. Total faculty: 373. Library holdings: 400,000 bound volumes, 8,000 periodical subscriptions, 2,537 records/tapes.

Undergraduate Courses offered for part-time students during daytime, evenings, summer. Complete part-time degree programs offered during daytime, evenings, summer. Adult/continuing education programs available. Part-time tuition: $168 per credit hour.

Dropsie College for Hebrew and Cognate Learning
Philadelphia 19132

Independent institution (graduate only). Total enrollment: 46 (coed; 10% part-time). Total faculty: 10.

Graduate Part-time study available in Graduate Programs. Basic part-time expenses: $400 per course tuition plus $75 per semester fees.

Duquesne University
Pittsburgh 15282

Independent-religious instutition; metropolitan setting. Awards A, B, M, D. Total enrollment: 6,340. Undergraduate enrollment: 4,287; 11% part-time, 55% women. Total faculty: 492. Library holdings: 445,000 bound volumes, 3,645 periodical subscriptions, 6,550 records/tapes.

Undergraduate Courses offered for part-time students during daytime, evenings, summer. Complete part-time degree programs offered during daytime, evenings, summer. Adult/continuing education programs available. Career services available to part-time students: individual and group career counseling, individual job placement, employer recruitment on campus. Part-time tuition: $170 per credit.

Graduate Part-time study available in Graduate School of Liberal Arts and Sciences, School of Business and Administration, School of Music. Degree can be earned exclusively through evening/weekend study in School of Music. Basic part-time expenses: $180 per credit tuition plus $11 per credit fees. Institutional financial aid available to part-time graduate students in Graduate School of Liberal Arts and Sciences, School of Music.

Eastern Baptist Theological Seminary
Philadelphia 19151

Independent-religious institution (graduate only). Total enrollment: 373 (coed; 65% part-time). Total faculty: 39. Library holdings: 92,869 bound volumes, 532 microforms.

Pennsylvania / **Colleges Offering Part-Time Degree Programs**

Graduate Part-time study available in Graduate and Professional Programs.Basic part-time expenses: $110 per credit tuition.

Eastern College
St Davids 19087

Independent-religious instutition; small-town setting. Awards B, M. Barrier-free campus. Total enrollment: 907. Undergraduate enrollment: 813; 32% part-time, 67% women. Total faculty: 77. Library holdings: 72,928 bound volumes, 14,906 titles on microform, 530 periodical subscriptions, 2,271 records/tapes.

Undergraduate Courses offered for part-time students during daytime, evenings, summer. Complete part-time degree programs offered during daytime, evenings, summer. Adult/continuing education programs available. Career services available to part-time students: individual and group career counseling, employer recruitment on campus. Part-time tuition: $154 per credit.

Graduate Part-time study available in Graduate Program in Business Administration. Degree can be earned exclusively through evening/weekend study in Graduate Program in Business Administration.Basic part-time expenses: $160 per credit tuition plus $20 per semester fees.

East Stroudsburg University of Pennsylvania
East Stroudsburg 18301

Public institution; small-town setting. Awards A, B, M. Total enrollment: 4,065. Undergraduate enrollment: 3,724; 7% part-time, 56% women. Total faculty: 217. Library holdings: 300,032 bound volumes, 641,655 titles on microform, 2,810 periodical subscriptions, 7,327 records/tapes.

Undergraduate Courses offered for part-time students during daytime. Complete part-time degree programs offered during daytime. Adult/continuing education programs available. Career services available to part-time students: individual and group career counseling, individual job placement, employer recruitment on campus. Part-time tuition: $66 per credit for state residents, $115 per credit for nonresidents.

Graduate Part-time study available in Graduate School.Basic part-time expenses: $87 per credit tuition plus $14.75 per semester (minimum) fees for state residents, $92 per credit tuition plus $14.75 per semester (minimum) fees for nonresidents.

Edinboro University of Pennsylvania
Edinboro 16444

Public institution; small-town setting. Awards A, B, M. Barrier-free campus. Total enrollment: 5,913. Undergraduate enrollment: 5,352; 14% part-time, 52% women. Total faculty: 339. Library holdings: 360,077 bound volumes, 1 million titles on microform, 1,639 periodical subscriptions, 22,006 records/tapes.

Undergraduate Courses offered for part-time students during daytime, evenings, weekends, summer. Complete part-time degree programs offered during daytime, evenings, weekends, summer. Adult/continuing education programs available. Career services available to part-time students: individual and group career counseling, individual job placement, employer recruitment on campus. Part-time tuition: $62 per credit for state residents, $108 per credit for nonresidents.

Graduate Part-time study available in Graduate Studies. Degree can be earned exclusively through evening/weekend study in Graduate Studies.Basic part-time expenses: $87 per credit tuition plus $2.50 per semester (minimum) fees for state residents, $92 per credit tuition plus $2.50 per semester (minimum) fees for nonresidents. Institutional financial aid available to part-time graduate students in Graduate Studies.

Elizabethtown College
Elizabethtown 17022

Independent-religious instutition; small-town setting. Awards A, B. Total enrollment: 1,864 (all undergraduates); 18% part-time, 59% women. Total faculty: 135. Library holdings: 170,000 bound volumes, 225 titles on microform, 827 periodical subscriptions, 6,328 records/tapes.

Undergraduate Courses offered for part-time students during daytime, evenings, summer. Complete part-time degree programs offered during daytime, evenings, summer. External degree and adult/continuing education programs available. Career services available to part-time students: individual and group career counseling, individual job placement, employer recruitment on campus. Part-time tuition: $190 per credit.

Evangelical School of Theology
Myerstown 17067

Independent-religious institution (graduate only). Total enrollment: 77 (primarily men; 53% part-time). Total faculty: 17.

Graduate Part-time study available in Graduate and Professional Programs.Basic part-time expenses: $95 per credit tuition. Institutional financial aid available to part-time graduate students in Graduate and Professional Programs.

Franklin and Marshall College
Lancaster 17604

Independent institution; city setting. Awards B. Barrier-free campus. Total enrollment: 2,010 (all undergraduates); 2% part-time, 48% women, 1% over 25. Total faculty: 164. Library holdings: 210,000 bound volumes, 70,000 titles on microform, 1,700 periodical subscriptions.

Undergraduate Courses offered for part-time students during daytime, evenings, summer. Complete part-time degree programs offered during daytime, evenings, summer. Adult/continuing education programs available. Career services available to part-time students: individual and group career counseling, individual job placement, employer recruitment on campus. Part-time tuition: $1360 per course.

Gannon University
Erie 16541

Independent-religious instutition; city setting. Awards A, B, M. Total enrollment: 3,600. Undergraduate enrollment: 2,950; 25% part-time, 45% women, 5% over 25. Total faculty: 251. Library holdings: 187,000 bound volumes, 22,000 titles on microform, 1,150 periodical subscriptions, 750 records/tapes.

Undergraduate Courses offered for part-time students during daytime, evenings, summer. Complete part-time degree programs offered during daytime, evenings, summer. External degree and adult/continuing education programs available. Career services available to part-time students: individual career counseling, individual job placement, employer recruitment on campus. Part-time tuition: $135 per credit.

Graduate Part-time study available in School of Graduate Studies.Basic part-time expenses: $155 per credit tuition. Institutional financial aid available to part-time graduate students in School of Graduate Studies.

Colleges Offering Part-Time Degree Programs / *Pennsylvania*

Geneva College
Beaver Falls 15010

Independent-religious instutition; small-town setting. Awards A, B. Total enrollment: 1,290 (all undergraduates); 11% part-time, 40% women. Total faculty: 101. Library holdings: 120,000 bound volumes, 66,000 titles on microform, 650 periodical subscriptions, 2,500 records/tapes.

Undergraduate Courses offered for part-time students during daytime, evenings. Complete part-time degree programs offered during daytime, evenings. Adult/continuing education programs available. Career services available to part-time students: individual and group career counseling, individual job placement, employer recruitment on campus. Part-time tuition: $136 per credit.

Gettysburg College
Gettysburg 17325

Independent-religious instutition; small-town setting. Awards B. Total enrollment: 1,850 (all undergraduates); 1% part-time, 50% women, 0% over 25. Total faculty: 132. Library holdings: 274,000 bound volumes, 38,000 titles on microform, 1,100 periodical subscriptions, 59,000 records/tapes.

Undergraduate Courses offered for part-time students during daytime. Complete part-time degree programs offered during daytime. Adult/continuing education programs available. Career services available to part-time students: individual and group career counseling, individual job placement, employer recruitment on campus. Part-time tuition: $680 per course.

Gratz College
Philadelphia 19141

Independent-religious instutition; metropolitan setting. Awards B, M. Total enrollment: 303. Undergraduate enrollment: 256; 70% part-time, 67% women, 70% over 25. Total faculty: 19. Library holdings: 40,000 bound volumes, 100 periodical subscriptions, 62,500 records/tapes.

Undergraduate Courses offered for part-time students during daytime, evenings, weekends, summer. Complete part-time degree programs offered during daytime, evenings, weekends, summer. Adult/continuing education programs available. Career services available to part-time students: individual and group career counseling. Part-time tuition: $65 per credit.

Graduate Part-time study available in Graduate Programs. Basic part-time expenses: $75 per credit tuition plus $30 per year fees.

Grove City College
Grove City 16127

Independent-religious instutition; small-town setting. Awards B. Total enrollment: 2,186 (all undergraduates); 2% part-time, 48% women, 1% over 25. Total faculty: 120. Library holdings: 138,500 bound volumes, 62,200 titles on microform, 643 periodical subscriptions, 312 records/tapes.

Undergraduate Courses offered for part-time students during daytime. Complete part-time degree programs offered during daytime. Part-time tuition: $125 per credit.

Gwynedd-Mercy College
Gwynedd Valley 19437

Independent-religious instutition; small-town setting. Awards A, B, M. Barrier-free campus. Total enrollment: 2,191. Undergraduate enrollment: 2,167; 42% part-time, 94% women, 20% over 25. Total faculty: 218. Library holdings: 71,000 bound volumes, 1,300 titles on microform, 600 periodical subscriptions, 900 records/tapes.

Undergraduate Courses offered for part-time students during daytime, evenings, summer. Complete part-time degree programs offered during daytime, evenings, summer. Adult/continuing education programs available. Career services available to part-time students: individual and group career counseling, individual job placement, employer recruitment on campus. Part-time tuition: $135 per credit.

Hahnemann University
Philadelphia 19102

Independent institution; metropolitan setting. Awards A, B, M, D. Barrier-free campus. Total enrollment: 2,036. Undergraduate enrollment: 982; 7% part-time, 70% women, 32% over 25. Total faculty: 350. Library holdings: 68,000 bound volumes, 1,000 periodical subscriptions, 400 records/tapes.

Undergraduate Courses offered for part-time students during daytime, evenings. Complete part-time degree programs offered during daytime, evenings. Adult/continuing education programs available. Career services available to part-time students: individual and group career counseling. Part-time tuition per credit hour ranges from $73 to $133 according to program.

Graduate Part-time study available in Graduate School. Basic part-time expenses: $225 per credit tuition. Institutional financial aid available to part-time graduate students in Graduate School.

Harcum Junior College
Bryn Mawr 19010

Independent institution; small-town setting. Awards A. Total enrollment: 885 (all undergraduates); 10% part-time, 99% women. Total faculty: 71. Library holdings: 35,000 bound volumes, 250 periodical subscriptions.

Undergraduate Courses offered for part-time students during daytime, evenings, summer. Complete part-time degree programs offered during daytime, evenings. Adult/continuing education programs available. Career services available to part-time students: individual career counseling. Part-time tuition: $117 per credit hour. Part-time tuition for evening classes: $84 per credit.

Harrisburg Area Community College
Harrisburg 17110

Public institution; city setting. Awards A. Barrier-free campus. Total enrollment: 6,696 (all undergraduates); 64% part-time, 57% women, 48% over 25. Total faculty: 291. Library holdings: 90,659 bound volumes, 201 titles on microform, 661 periodical subscriptions, 3,195 records/tapes.

Undergraduate Courses offered for part-time students during daytime, evenings, weekends, summer. Complete part-time degree programs offered during daytime, evenings, weekends, summer. Adult/continuing education programs available. Career services available to part-time students: individual and group career counseling, individual job placement, employer recruitment on campus. Part-time tuition: $31.25 per credit hour for area residents, $62.50 per credit hour for state residents, $93.75 per credit hour for nonresidents.

Holy Family College
Philadelphia 19114

Independent-religious instutition; metropolitan setting. Awards B. Barrier-free campus. Total enrollment: 1,506 (all undergraduates); 58% part-time, 85% women. Total faculty: 125. Library holdings: 90,740 bound volumes, 390 periodical subscriptions, 6,431 records/tapes.

Undergraduate Courses offered for part-time students during daytime, evenings, summer. Complete part-time degree programs offered during daytime, evenings, summer. Adult/continuing education programs available. Career services available to part-time students: individual and group career counseling, individual job placement, employer recruitment on campus. Part-time tuition: $90 per credit. Part-time tuition for nursing program: $100 per credit.

Hussian School of Art
Philadelphia 19107

Proprietary institution; metropolitan setting. Awards A (4-year program). Barrier-free campus. Total enrollment: 200 (all undergraduates); 0% part-time, 50% women, 5% over 25. Total faculty: 28. Library holdings: 50,000 bound volumes, 100 periodical subscriptions, 1,000 records/tapes.

Undergraduate Courses offered for part-time students during daytime. Complete part-time degree programs offered during daytime. Career services available to part-time students: individual and group career counseling, individual job placement, employer recruitment on campus. Part-time tuition: $320 per course.

ICS Center for Degree Studies
Scranton 18515

Proprietary institution. Awards A (courses conducted through independent study). Total enrollment: 6,000 (all undergraduates); 10% part-time, 30% women, 80% over 25. Total faculty: 40.

Undergraduate Courses offered for part-time students during daytime. Complete part-time degree programs offered during daytime. External degree programs available. Part-time tuition: $45 per credit.

Immaculata College
Immaculata 19345

Independent-religious instutition; small-town setting. Awards A, B, M. Barrier-free campus. Total enrollment: 1,918. Undergraduate enrollment: 1,809; 50% part-time, 95% women. Total faculty: 112. Library holdings: 140,000 bound volumes, 575 periodical subscriptions, 500 records/tapes.

Undergraduate Courses offered for part-time students during daytime, evenings, summer. Complete part-time degree programs offered during daytime, evenings. Adult/continuing education programs available. Career services available to part-time students: individual and group career counseling, individual job placement, employer recruitment on campus. Part-time tuition: $100 per semester hour.

Graduate Part-time study available in Graduate Program in Bicultural/Bilingual Studies. Degree can be earned exclusively through evening/weekend study in Graduate Program in Bicultural/Bilingual Studies. Basic part-time expenses: $125 per credit tuition plus $20 per semester fees. Institutional financial aid available to part-time graduate students in Graduate Program in Bicultural/Bilingual Studies.

Indiana University of Pennsylvania
Indiana 15705

Public institution; small-town setting. Awards A, B, M, D. Total enrollment: 12,526. Undergraduate enrollment: 11,482; 7% part-time, 57% women, 5% over 25. Total faculty: 700. Library holdings: 515,000 bound volumes, 1.3 million titles on microform, 3,900 periodical subscriptions, 8,000 records/tapes.

Undergraduate Courses offered for part-time students during daytime, evenings, summer. Complete part-time degree programs offered during daytime, evenings, summer. Adult/continuing education programs available. Career services available to part-time students: individual and group career counseling, individual job placement, employer recruitment on campus. Part-time tuition: $62 per semester hour for state residents, $108 per semester hour for nonresidents.

Graduate Part-time study available in Graduate School. Basic part-time expenses: $87 per credit tuition plus $29 per semester fees for state residents, $92 per credit tuition plus $29 per semester fees for nonresidents. Institutional financial aid available to part-time graduate students in Graduate School.

Juniata College
Huntingdon 16652

Independent institution; small-town setting. Awards B. Total enrollment: 1,274 (all undergraduates); 1% part-time, 45% women, 1% over 25. Total faculty: 97. Library holdings: 204,000 bound volumes, 45,000 titles on microform, 812 periodical subscriptions, 4,800 records/tapes.

Undergraduate Courses offered for part-time students during daytime, evenings. Complete part-time degree programs offered during daytime. Adult/continuing education programs available. Part-time tuition: $900 per unit.

Keystone Junior College
La Plume 18440

Independent institution; rural setting. Awards A. Total enrollment: 730 (all undergraduates); 5% part-time, 54% women, 1% over 25. Total faculty: 74. Library holdings: 34,790 bound volumes, 256 periodical subscriptions, 590 records/tapes.

Undergraduate Courses offered for part-time students during daytime, weekends, summer. Complete part-time degree programs offered during daytime, weekends, summer. Adult/continuing education programs available. Career services available to part-time students: individual and group career counseling, individual job placement, employer recruitment on campus. Part-time tuition: $100 per credit.

Keystone Secretarial and Business Administration School
Swarthmore 19081

Proprietary institution; small-town setting. Awards A. Total enrollment: 195 (all undergraduates); 2% part-time, 98% women, 6% over 25. Total faculty: 18. Library holdings: 2,200 bound volumes, 27 periodical subscriptions, 130 records/tapes.

Undergraduate Courses offered for part-time students during daytime, evenings. Complete part-time degree programs offered during daytime. Adult/continuing education programs available. Career services available to part-time students: individual career counseling, individual job placement, employer recruitment on campus. Part-time tuition: $1190 per year.

Colleges Offering Part-Time Degree Programs / *Pennsylvania*

King's College
Wilkes-Barre 18711

Independent-religious instutition; city setting. Awards A, B. Barrier-free campus. Total enrollment: 2,309 (all undergraduates); 7% part-time, 49% women. Total faculty: 151. Library holdings: 160,000 bound volumes, 28,000 titles on microform, 1,100 periodical subscriptions, 4,935 records/tapes.

Undergraduate Courses offered for part-time students during daytime, evenings, summer. Complete part-time degree programs offered during daytime, evenings, summer. Adult/continuing education programs available. Career services available to part-time students: individual career counseling, individual job placement, employer recruitment on campus. Part-time tuition: $113 per credit hour.

Kutztown University of Pennsylvania
Kutztown 19530

Public institution; small-town setting. Awards B, M. Total enrollment: 6,453. Undergraduate enrollment: 6,040; 17% part-time, 58% women, 5% over 25. Total faculty: 303. Library holdings: 320,400 bound volumes, 859,000 titles on microform, 1,976 periodical subscriptions, 1,500 records/tapes.

Undergraduate Courses offered for part-time students during daytime, evenings, weekends, summer. Complete part-time degree programs offered during daytime, evenings, weekends, summer. Adult/continuing education programs available. Career services available to part-time students: individual and group career counseling, individual job placement, employer recruitment on campus. Part-time tuition: $62 per credit for state residents, $108 per credit for nonresidents.

Graduate Part-time study available in College of Graduate Studies.Basic part-time expenses: $87 per credit tuition for state residents, $92 per credit tuition for nonresidents.

Lackawanna Junior College
Scranton 18505

Independent institution; city setting. Awards A. Total enrollment: 1,243 (all undergraduates); 30% part-time, 65% women, 30% over 25. Total faculty: 97. Library holdings: 24,500 bound volumes, 185 periodical subscriptions, 1,450 records/tapes.

Undergraduate Courses offered for part-time students during daytime, evenings, summer. Complete part-time degree programs offered during daytime, evenings, summer. Adult/continuing education programs available. Career services available to part-time students: individual and group career counseling, individual job placement, employer recruitment on campus. Part-time tuition: $91 per credit.

Lafayette College
Easton 18042

Independent-religious instutition; small-town setting. Awards B. Barrier-free campus. Total enrollment: 2,050 (all undergraduates); 15% part-time, 43% women. Total faculty: 205. Library holdings: 376,000 bound volumes, 10,200 titles on microform, 1,700 periodical subscriptions, 6,200 records/tapes.

Undergraduate Courses offered for part-time students during daytime, evenings, summer. Complete part-time degree programs offered during daytime, evenings, summer. Adult/continuing education programs available. Career services available to part-time students: individual and group career counseling, individual job placement, employer recruitment on campus. Part-time tuition: $125 per credit.

Lancaster Bible College
Lancaster 17601

Independent-religious instutition; city setting. Awards A, B. Barrier-free campus. Total enrollment: 363 (all undergraduates); 32% part-time, 40% women. Total faculty: 25. Library holdings: 41,000 bound volumes, 353 periodical subscriptions.

Undergraduate Courses offered for part-time students during daytime, evenings. Complete part-time degree programs offered during daytime, evenings. Adult/continuing education programs available. Career services available to part-time students: individual career counseling, individual job placement. Part-time tuition: $140 per credit hour.

Lancaster Theological Seminary
Lancaster 17603

Independent-religious institution (graduate only). Total enrollment: 253 (coed; 77% part-time). Total faculty: 29.

Graduate Part-time study available in Graduate and Professional Programs.Basic part-time expenses: $110 per credit tuition.

La Roche College
Pittsburgh 15237

Independent-religious instutition; metropolitan setting. Awards B, M. Total enrollment: 1,723. Undergraduate enrollment: 1,588; 52% part-time, 73% women, 35% over 25. Total faculty: 111. Library holdings: 61,000 bound volumes, 2,000 titles on microform, 750 periodical subscriptions, 1,700 records/tapes.

Undergraduate Courses offered for part-time students during daytime, evenings, summer. Complete part-time degree programs offered during daytime, evenings. Adult/continuing education programs available. Career services available to part-time students: individual and group career counseling, individual job placement, employer recruitment on campus. Part-time tuition: $145 per credit.

Graduate Part-time study available in Graduate Studies in Human Resources Management. Degree can be earned exclusively through evening/weekend study in Graduate Studies in Human Resources Management.Basic part-time expenses: $165 per credit tuition.

La Salle University
Philadelphia 19141

Independent-religious instutition; metropolitan setting. Awards B, M. Total enrollment: 6,725. Undergraduate enrollment: 5,624; 38% part-time, 48% women, 7% over 25. Total faculty: 289. Library holdings: 300,000 bound volumes.

Undergraduate Courses offered for part-time students during daytime, evenings, weekends, summer. Complete part-time degree programs offered during daytime, evenings, weekends, summer. Adult/continuing education programs available. Career services available to part-time students: individual and group career counseling, individual job placement, employer recruitment on campus. Part-time tuition: $180 per credit hour.

Graduate Part-time study available in Division of Arts and Sciences, Division of Business Administration. Degree can be earned exclusively through evening/weekend study in Division of Arts and Sciences, Division of Business Administration.Basic part-time expenses: $180 per credit hour tuition plus $25 per semester fees.

Pennsylvania / **Colleges Offering Part-Time Degree Programs**

Lebanon Valley College
Annville 17003

Independent-religious instutition; small-town setting. Awards B. Total enrollment: 946 (all undergraduates); 13% part-time, 53% women. Total faculty: 90. Library holdings: 120,000 bound volumes, 20,000 titles on microform, 599 periodical subscriptions, 4,000 records/tapes.

Undergraduate Courses offered for part-time students during daytime, evenings, weekends, summer. Complete part-time degree programs offered during daytime, evenings, weekends, summer. Adult/continuing education programs available. Career services available to part-time students: individual and group career counseling, individual job placement, employer recruitment on campus. Part-time tuition: $135 per credit.

Lehigh County Community College
Schnecksville 18078

Public institution; rural setting. Awards A. Barrier-free campus. Total enrollment: 3,500 (all undergraduates); 58% part-time, 52% women, 55% over 25. Total faculty: 120. Library holdings: 40,000 bound volumes, 440 periodical subscriptions, 25,335 records/tapes.

Undergraduate Courses offered for part-time students during daytime, evenings, summer. Complete part-time degree programs offered during daytime, evenings, summer. Adult/continuing education programs available. Career services available to part-time students: individual and group career counseling, individual job placement, employer recruitment on campus. Part-time tuition: $35 per credit for area residents, $76 per credit for state residents, $117 per credit for nonresidents.

Lehigh University
Bethlehem 18015

Independent institution; city setting. Awards B, M, D. Total enrollment: 6,042. Undergraduate enrollment: 4,348; 1% part-time, 33% women. Total faculty: 422. Library holdings: 786,000 bound volumes, 507,744 titles on microform, 8,000 periodical subscriptions, 9,712 records/tapes.

Graduate Part-time study available in Graduate School. Basic part-time expenses: $365 per credit tuition.

Lincoln University
Lincoln University 19352

Public institution; rural setting. Awards A, B, M. Total enrollment: 1,250. Undergraduate enrollment: 1,000; 2% part-time, 55% women, 15% over 25. Total faculty: 88. Library holdings: 168,000 bound volumes, 20,020 titles on microform, 600 periodical subscriptions.

Undergraduate Courses offered for part-time students during daytime. Complete part-time degree programs offered during daytime. Adult/continuing education programs available. Career services available to part-time students: individual and group career counseling, individual job placement, employer recruitment on campus. Part-time tuition: $65 per credit hour for state residents, $95 per credit hour for nonresidents.

Lock Haven University of Pennsylvania
Lock Haven 17745

Public institution; small-town setting. Awards B. Barrier-free campus. Total enrollment: 2,661 (all undergraduates); 4% part-time, 51% women, 6% over 25. Total faculty: 173. Library holdings: 304,000 bound volumes, 12,306 titles on microform, 1,238 periodical subscriptions, 2,824 records/tapes.

Undergraduate Courses offered for part-time students during daytime, evenings, summer. Complete part-time degree programs offered during daytime, summer. Adult/continuing education programs available. Part-time tuition: $66 per credit for state residents, $115 per credit for nonresidents.

Luzerne County Community College
Nanticoke 18634

Public institution; small-town setting. Awards A. Barrier-free campus. Total enrollment: 4,183 (all undergraduates); 63% part-time, 62% women, 41% over 25. Total faculty: 213. Library holdings: 54,000 bound volumes, 13,518 titles on microform, 508 periodical subscriptions, 754 records/tapes.

Undergraduate Courses offered for part-time students during daytime, evenings, weekends, summer. Complete part-time degree programs offered during daytime. Adult/continuing education programs available. Career services available to part-time students: individual and group career counseling, individual job placement, employer recruitment on campus. Part-time tuition: $33 per semester hour for area residents, $66 per semester hour for state residents, $99 per semester hour for nonresidents.

Lycoming College
Williamsport 17701

Independent-religious instutition; small-town setting. Awards B. Total enrollment: 1,205 (all undergraduates); 1% part-time, 48% women. Total faculty: 75. Library holdings: 145,000 bound volumes, 900 periodical subscriptions, 1,400 records/tapes.

Undergraduate Courses offered for part-time students during daytime, evenings, summer. Complete part-time degree programs offered during daytime. Part-time tuition: $193.75 per semester hour.

Lyons School of Business
New Castle 16101

Proprietary institution; small-town setting. Awards A. Total enrollment: 212 (all undergraduates); 20% part-time, 61% women, 53% over 25. Total faculty: 17. Library holdings: 4,000 bound volumes, 20 periodical subscriptions.

Undergraduate Courses offered for part-time students during daytime, evenings, summer. Complete part-time degree programs offered during daytime, evenings, summer. Adult/continuing education programs available. Career services available to part-time students: individual career counseling, individual job placement, employer recruitment on campus. Part-time tuition: $58 per credit.

Manor Junior College
Jenkintown 19046

Independent-religious instutition; small-town setting. Awards A. Total enrollment: 422 (all undergraduates); 36% part-time, 95% women. Total faculty: 41. Library holdings: 26,500 bound volumes, 200 periodical subscriptions.

Undergraduate Courses offered for part-time students during daytime, evenings, summer. Complete part-time degree programs offered during daytime, evenings, summer. Adult/continuing education programs available. Career services available to part-time students: individual career counseling, individual job placement. Part-time tuition: $95 per credit hour.

Colleges Offering Part-Time Degree Programs / *Pennsylvania*

Mansfield University of Pennsylvania
Mansfield 16933

Public institution; rural setting. Awards A, B, M. Total enrollment: 2,900. Undergraduate enrollment: 2,713; 15% part-time, 54% women, 8% over 25. Total faculty: 205. Library holdings: 184,018 bound volumes, 2,044 periodical subscriptions, 7,317 records/tapes.

Undergraduate Courses offered for part-time students during daytime, evenings, summer. Complete part-time degree programs offered during daytime, evenings, summer. Adult/continuing education programs available. Career services available to part-time students: individual and group career counseling, individual job placement, employer recruitment on campus. Part-time tuition: $66 per credit for state residents, $115 per credit for nonresidents.

Graduate Part-time study available in Graduate Studies. Degree can be earned exclusively through evening/weekend study in Graduate Studies. Basic part-time expenses: $87 per credit hour tuition plus $23 per semester fees for state residents, $92 per credit hour tuition plus $23 per semester fees for nonresidents.

Marywood College
Scranton 18509

Independent-religious instutition; city setting. Awards B, M. Barrier-free campus. Total enrollment: 3,116. Undergraduate enrollment: 2,115; 29% part-time, 85% women, 17% over 25. Total faculty: 198. Library holdings: 168,760 bound volumes, 24,411 titles on microform, 1,143 periodical subscriptions, 7,565 records/tapes.

Undergraduate Courses offered for part-time students during daytime, evenings, weekends, summer. Complete part-time degree programs offered during daytime, evenings, weekends, summer. External degree and adult/continuing education programs available. Career services available to part-time students: individual and group career counseling, individual job placement, employer recruitment on campus. Part-time tuition: $112 per credit.

Graduate Part-time study available in Graduate School of Arts and Sciences, Graduate School of Social Work. Degree can be earned exclusively through evening/weekend study in Graduate School of Arts and Sciences, Graduate School of Social Work. Basic part-time expenses: $120 per credit tuition plus $20 per semester fees. Institutional financial aid available to part-time graduate students in Graduate School of Arts and Sciences.

Medical College of Pennsylvania
Philadelphia 19129

Independent institution (graduate only). Total enrollment: 542 (coed; 6% part-time). Library holdings: 35,036 bound volumes.

Graduate Part-time study available in Graduate School of Medical Sciences. Basic part-time expenses: $110 per credit (minimum) tuition plus $400 per year fees.

Mercyhurst College
Erie 16546

Independent-religious instutition; city setting. Awards A, B, M. Total enrollment: 1,654. Undergraduate enrollment: 1,612; 30% part-time, 55% women. Total faculty: 103. Library holdings: 70,000 bound volumes, 20,000 titles on microform, 600 periodical subscriptions.

Undergraduate Courses offered for part-time students during daytime, evenings, weekends, summer. Complete part-time degree programs offered during daytime, evenings, weekends, summer. Adult/continuing education programs available. Career services available to part-time students: individual and group career counseling, individual job placement, employer recruitment on campus. Part-time tuition: $165 per credit.

Graduate Part-time study available in Graduate Program. Degree can be earned exclusively through evening/weekend study in Graduate Program. Basic part-time expenses: $501 per course tuition plus $25 per semester fees. Institutional financial aid available to part-time graduate students in Graduate Program.

Messiah College
Grantham 17027

Independent-religious instutition; small-town setting. Awards B. Barrier-free campus. Total enrollment: 1,612 (all undergraduates); 8% part-time, 55% women. Total faculty: 113. Library holdings: 130,000 bound volumes, 1,000 periodical subscriptions, 3,600 records/tapes.

Undergraduate Courses offered for part-time students during daytime, evenings. Complete part-time degree programs offered during daytime, evenings. Adult/continuing education programs available. Career services available to part-time students: individual and group career counseling, individual job placement, employer recruitment on campus. Part-time tuition: $200 per credit.

Millersville University of Pennsylvania
Millersville 17551

Public institution; small-town setting. Awards B, M. Total enrollment: 6,721. Undergraduate enrollment: 6,270; 20% part-time, 57% women. Total faculty: 360. Library holdings: 390,000 bound volumes, 2,600 periodical subscriptions.

Undergraduate Courses offered for part-time students during daytime, evenings, weekends, summer. Complete part-time degree programs offered during daytime, evenings, weekends, summer. Adult/continuing education programs available. Career services available to part-time students: individual and group career counseling, individual job placement, employer recruitment on campus. Part-time tuition: $62 per credit for state residents, $108 per credit for nonresidents.

Graduate Part-time study available in Graduate School. Degree can be earned exclusively through evening/weekend study in Graduate School. Basic part-time expenses: $87 per credit tuition plus $10 per semester fees for state residents, $92 per credit tuition plus $10 per semester fees for nonresidents. Institutional financial aid available to part-time graduate students in Graduate School.

Moore College of Art
Philadelphia 19103

Independent institution; metropolitan setting. Awards B. Barrier-free campus. Total enrollment: 628 (all undergraduates); 15% part-time, 100% women, 1% over 25. Total faculty: 80. Library holdings: 33,000 bound volumes, 4 titles on microform, 340 periodical subscriptions, 1,500 records/tapes.

Undergraduate Courses offered for part-time students during daytime. Complete part-time degree programs offered during daytime. Adult/continuing education programs available. Career services available to part-time students: individual job placement. Part-time tuition: $250 per credit.

Pennsylvania / **Colleges Offering Part-Time Degree Programs**

Moravian College
Bethlehem 18018

Independent institution; city setting. Awards B. Total enrollment: 1,233 (all undergraduates); 4% part-time, 48% women, 2% over 25. Total faculty: 146. Library holdings: 162,000 bound volumes, 1,186 periodical subscriptions.

Undergraduate Courses offered for part-time students during daytime, evenings, summer. Complete part-time degree programs offered during daytime, evenings, summer. Adult/continuing education programs available. Career services available to part-time students: individual and group career counseling, individual job placement, employer recruitment on campus. Part-time tuition: $750 per course.

Moravian Theological Seminary
Bethlehem 18018

Independent-religious institution (graduate only). Total enrollment: 77 (coed; 40% part-time). Total faculty: 18. Library holdings: 170,000 bound volumes, 8,354 microforms.

Graduate Part-time study available in Graduate and Professional Programs. Basic part-time expenses: $145 per credit tuition plus $20 per semester fees.

Mount Aloysius Junior College
Cresson 16630

Independent-religious instutition; rural setting. Awards A. Total enrollment: 525 (all undergraduates); 20% part-time, 79% women, 25% over 25. Total faculty: 61. Library holdings: 35,000 bound volumes, 100 titles on microform, 108 periodical subscriptions, 450 records/tapes.

Undergraduate Courses offered for part-time students during daytime, evenings, summer. Complete part-time degree programs offered during daytime. Adult/continuing education programs available. Career services available to part-time students: individual and group career counseling, individual job placement, employer recruitment on campus. Part-time tuition ranges from $125 to $185 per credit according to program.

Muhlenberg College
Allentown 18104

Independent-religious instutition; city setting. Awards B. Total enrollment: 1,530 (all undergraduates); 3% part-time, 47% women, 0% over 25. Total faculty: 140. Library holdings: 190,000 bound volumes, 16,000 titles on microform, 725 periodical subscriptions.

Undergraduate Courses offered for part-time students during daytime, evenings, summer. Complete part-time degree programs offered during daytime, evenings. Adult/continuing education programs available. Career services available to part-time students: individual and group career counseling, individual job placement, employer recruitment on campus. Part-time tuition: $235 per credit.

National Education Center–Thompson Institute Campus
Harrisburg 17111

Proprietary institution; city setting. Awards A. Barrier-free campus. Total enrollment: 633 (all undergraduates); 18% part-time, 48% women, 25% over 25. Total faculty: 37. Library holdings: 850 bound volumes, 15 periodical subscriptions.

Undergraduate Courses offered for part-time students during daytime, evenings. Complete part-time degree programs offered during daytime. Adult/continuing education programs available. Career services available to part-time students: individual and group career counseling, individual job placement, employer recruitment on campus. Part-time tuition: $300 per course.

Neumann College
Aston 19014

Independent-religious instutition; small-town setting. Awards B, M. Barrier-free campus. Total enrollment: 1,006. Undergraduate enrollment: 965; 46% part-time, 73% women. Total faculty: 84. Library holdings: 73,163 bound volumes, 625 periodical subscriptions, 3,000 records/tapes.

Undergraduate Courses offered for part-time students during daytime, evenings, summer. Complete part-time degree programs offered during daytime, evenings, summer. Adult/continuing education programs available. Career services available to part-time students: individual and group career counseling, individual job placement, employer recruitment on campus. Part-time tuition: $110 per credit.

Graduate Part-time study available in Graduate Program in Pastoral Counseling. Degree can be earned exclusively through evening/weekend study in Graduate Program in Pastoral Counseling. Basic part-time expenses: $150 per credit tuition plus $35 per semester fees.

Northampton County Area Community College
Bethlehem 18017

Public institution; city setting. Awards A. Barrier-free campus. Total enrollment: 4,580 (all undergraduates); 67% part-time, 62% women. Total faculty: 205. Library holdings: 59,210 bound volumes, 490 periodical subscriptions, 3,918 records/tapes.

Undergraduate Courses offered for part-time students during daytime, evenings, summer. Complete part-time degree programs offered during daytime, evenings, summer. External degree and adult/continuing education programs available. Career services available to part-time students: individual and group career counseling, individual job placement, employer recruitment on campus. Part-time tuition: $40 per credit hour for area residents, $83 per credit hour for state residents, $126 per credit hour for nonresidents.

Peirce Junior College
Philadelphia 19102

Independent institution; metropolitan setting. Awards A. Barrier-free campus. Total enrollment: 1,826 (all undergraduates); 42% part-time, 73% women. Total faculty: 97. Library holdings: 35,398 bound volumes, 231 periodical subscriptions, 8,860 records/tapes.

Undergraduate Courses offered for part-time students during daytime, evenings, weekends, summer. Complete part-time degree programs offered during daytime, evenings, weekends, summer. Adult/continuing education programs available. Career services available to part-time students: individual and group career counseling, individual job placement, employer recruitment on campus. Part-time tuition: $130 per credit.

Colleges Offering Part-Time Degree Programs / *Pennsylvania*

Pennsylvania College of Optometry
Philadelphia 19141

Independent institution; metropolitan setting. Awards B, D (B is incidental bachelor's). Barrier-free campus. Total enrollment: 581. Undergraduate enrollment profile: 0% part-time, 25% women. Total faculty: 63. Library holdings: 9,700 bound volumes, 259 periodical subscriptions.

Graduate Part-time study available in Graduate and Professional Programs. Degree can be earned exclusively through evening/weekend study in Graduate and Professional Programs.

Pennsylvania Institute of Technology
Media 19063

Independent institution; small-town setting. Awards A. Total enrollment: 456 (all undergraduates); 29% part-time, 11% women, 32% over 25. Total faculty: 30. Library holdings: 10,000 bound volumes, 145 periodical subscriptions.

Undergraduate Courses offered for part-time students during daytime, evenings. Complete part-time degree programs offered during daytime, evenings. Career services available to part-time students: individual career counseling, individual job placement, employer recruitment on campus. Part-time tuition: $214 per course.

Pennsylvania State University–Behrend College
Erie 16563

Public institution; city setting. Awards A, B, M. Total enrollment: 1,972. Undergraduate enrollment: 1,963; 13% part-time, 36% women, 6% over 25. Total faculty: 111. Library holdings: 59,081 bound volumes, 34,186 titles on microform, 666 periodical subscriptions, 1,627 records/tapes.

Graduate Part-time study available in Graduate Center.Basic part-time expenses: $107 per credit tuition for state residents, $228 per credit tuition for nonresidents. Institutional financial aid available to part-time graduate students in Graduate Center.

Pennsylvania State University–Capitol Campus
Middletown 17057

Public institution; small-town setting. Awards B, M. Total enrollment: 2,452. Undergraduate enrollment: 1,701; 28% part-time, 30% women, 31% over 25. Total faculty: 148. Library holdings: 125,836 bound volumes, 710,249 titles on microform, 1,359 periodical subscriptions.

Undergraduate Courses offered for part-time students during daytime, evenings. Complete part-time degree programs offered during daytime. Adult/continuing education programs available. Career services available to part-time students: individual career counseling, individual job placement, employer recruitment on campus. Part-time tuition: $107 per credit for state residents, $215 per credit for nonresidents.

Graduate Part-time study available in Graduate Center. Degree can be earned exclusively through evening/weekend study in Graduate Center.Basic part-time expenses: $107 per credit tuition for state residents, $228 per credit tuition for nonresidents. Institutional financial aid available to part-time graduate students in Graduate Center.

Pennsylvania State University–King of Prussia Center for Graduate Studies
King of Prussia 19406

Public institution (graduate only). Total enrollment: 224 (coed; 99% part-time). Total faculty: 9. Library holdings: 14,679 bound volumes, 2,077 microforms.

Graduate Part-time study available in Graduate Studies and Continuing Education.Basic part-time expenses: $140 per credit tuition for state residents, $228 per credit tuition for nonresidents. Institutional financial aid available to part-time graduate students in Graduate Studies and Continuing Education.

Pennsylvania State University–Milton S Hershey Medical Center
Hershey 17033

Public institution (graduate only). Total enrollment: 461 (coed; 7% part-time). Total faculty: 592.

Graduate Part-time study available in Graduate Programs. Basic part-time expenses: $114 per credit tuition for state residents, $228 per credit tuition for nonresidents. Institutional financial aid available to part-time graduate students in Graduate Programs.

Pennsylvania State University–University Park Campus
University Park 16802

Public institution; small-town setting. Awards A, B, M, D. Total enrollment: 33,445. Undergraduate enrollment: 28,308; 5% part-time, 44% women, 3% over 25. Total faculty: 1,760. Library holdings: 1.8 million bound volumes, 1.5 million titles on microform, 16,001 periodical subscriptions, 11,890 records/tapes.

Graduate Part-time study available in Graduate School.Basic part-time expenses: $114 per credit tuition for state residents, $228 per credit tuition for nonresidents. Institutional financial aid available to part-time graduate students in Graduate School.

Penn Technical Institute
Pittsburgh 15222

Proprietary institution; metropolitan setting. Awards A. Total enrollment: 528 (all undergraduates); 5% women. Total faculty: 21.

Undergraduate Courses offered for part-time students during evenings. Complete part-time degree programs offered during evenings. Career services available to part-time students: individual job placement, employer recruitment on campus.

Philadelphia College of Art
Philadelphia 19102

Independent institution; metropolitan setting. Awards B, M. Total enrollment: 1,659. Undergraduate enrollment: 1,629; 6% part-time, 55% women, 70% over 25. Total faculty: 234. Library holdings: 36,498 bound volumes, 197 periodical subscriptions, 1,003 records/tapes.

Undergraduate Courses offered for part-time students during daytime, evenings, weekends, summer. Complete part-time degree programs offered during daytime, evenings. Adult/continuing education programs available. Career services available to part-time students: individual and group career counseling, individual job placement, employer recruitment on campus. Part-time tuition: $260 per credit.

Graduate Part-time study available in Graduate Studies. Basic part-time expenses: $295 per credit tuition.

Philadelphia College of Bible
Langhorne 19047

Independent-religious instutition; small-town setting. Awards B. Total enrollment: 577 (all undergraduates); 19% part-time, 45% women, 31% over 25. Total faculty: 40. Library holdings: 46,511 bound volumes, 548 periodical subscriptions, 3,076 records/tapes.

Undergraduate Courses offered for part-time students during daytime, evenings, summer. Complete part-time degree programs offered during daytime, evenings. Adult/continuing education programs available. Career services available to part-time students: individual career counseling. Part-time tuition: $146 per credit.

Philadelphia College of Pharmacy and Science
Philadelphia 19104

Independent institution; metropolitan setting. Awards B, M, D. Barrier-free campus. Total enrollment: 1,119. Undergraduate enrollment: 1,019; 1% part-time, 52% women. Total faculty: 149. Library holdings: 35,000 bound volumes, 800 periodical subscriptions, 1,000 records/tapes.

Graduate Part-time study available in Graduate Studies. Basic part-time expenses: $230 per credit tuition.

Philadelphia College of Textiles and Science
Philadelphia 19144

Independent institution; metropolitan setting. Awards B, M. Total enrollment: 1,851. Undergraduate enrollment: 1,755; 15% part-time, 51% women, 12% over 25. Total faculty: 125. Library holdings: 65,000 bound volumes, 1,200 periodical subscriptions, 700 records/tapes.

Undergraduate Courses offered for part-time students during daytime, evenings, summer. Complete part-time degree programs offered during daytime, evenings, summer. Adult/continuing education programs available. Career services available to part-time students: individual and group career counseling, individual job placement, employer recruitment on campus. Part-time tuition: $180 per credit.

Graduate Part-time study available in Graduate Program in Business Administration. Basic part-time expenses: $180 per credit tuition plus $20 per semester fees.

Philadelphia College of the Performing Arts
Philadelphia 19102

Independent institution; metropolitan setting. Awards B, M. Total enrollment: 397. Undergraduate enrollment: 373; 10% part-time, 51% women. Total faculty: 135. Library holdings: 18,000 bound volumes, 100 periodical subscriptions, 14,000 records/tapes.

Undergraduate Courses offered for part-time students during daytime. Complete part-time degree programs offered during daytime. Adult/continuing education programs available. Career services available to part-time students: individual and group career counseling, individual job placement. Part-time tuition: $250 per credit hour.

Graduate Part-time study available in School of Music. Basic part-time expenses: $7000 per year tuition plus $30 per year fees.

Pinebrook Junior College
Coopersburg 18036

Independent-religious instutition; small-town setting. Awards A. Barrier-free campus. Total enrollment: 125 (all undergraduates); 6% part-time, 52% women. Total faculty: 20. Library holdings: 33,000 bound volumes.

Undergraduate Courses offered for part-time students during daytime, evenings. Complete part-time degree programs offered during daytime, evenings. Adult/continuing education programs available. Career services available to part-time students: individual career counseling. Part-time tuition per semester hour ranges from $96 (for students taking 1 to 7 semester hours) to $120 (for students taking 8 to 11 semester hours).

Pittsburgh Technical Institute
Pittsburgh 15222

Proprietary institution; metropolitan setting. Awards A. Barrier-free campus. Total enrollment: 265 (all undergraduates); 1% part-time, 30% women, 12% over 25. Total faculty: 21. Library holdings: 10,000 bound volumes, 150 periodical subscriptions.

Undergraduate Courses offered for part-time students during evenings. Complete part-time degree programs offered during evenings. Career services available to part-time students: individual and group career counseling, individual job placement, employer recruitment on campus. Part-time tuition: $2160 per year.

Pittsburgh Theological Seminary
Pittsburgh 15206

Independent-religious institution (graduate only). Total enrollment: 412 (coed; 30% part-time). Total faculty: 22.

Graduate Part-time study available in Graduate and Professional Programs. Basic part-time expenses: $90 per credit tuition plus $18 per quarter fees.

Point Park College
Pittsburgh 15222

Independent institution; metropolitan setting. Awards A, B, M. Total enrollment: 2,665. Undergraduate enrollment: 2,561; 59% part-time, 40% women, 35% over 25. Total faculty: 151. Library holdings: 105,107 bound volumes, 24,000 titles on microform, 528 periodical subscriptions, 1,886 records/tapes.

Undergraduate Courses offered for part-time students during daytime, evenings, weekends, summer. Complete part-time degree programs offered during daytime, evenings, weekends, summer. Adult/continuing education programs available. Career services available to part-time students: individual and group career counseling, individual job placement, employer recruitment on campus. Part-time tuition: $128 per credit.

Graduate Part-time study available in Graduate Program in Journalism and Communications. Degree can be earned exclusively through evening/weekend study in Graduate Program in Journalism and Communications. Basic part-time expenses: $140 per credit tuition. Institutional financial aid available to part-time graduate students in Graduate Program in Journalism and Communications.

Colleges Offering Part-Time Degree Programs / *Pennsylvania*

Reading Area Community College
Reading 19603

Public institution; city setting. Awards A. Barrier-free campus. Total enrollment: 1,625 (all undergraduates); 64% part-time, 68% women. Total faculty: 82. Library holdings: 18,500 bound volumes, 35 titles on microform, 245 periodical subscriptions, 1,100 records/tapes.

Undergraduate Courses offered for part-time students during daytime, evenings, summer. Complete part-time degree programs offered during daytime, evenings, summer. External degree and adult/continuing education programs available. Career services available to part-time students: individual and group career counseling, individual job placement, employer recruitment on campus. Part-time tuition: $35 per credit for area residents, $70 per credit for state residents, $105 per credit for nonresidents.

Robert Morris College
Coraopolis 15108

Independent institution; small-town setting. Awards A, B, M. Total enrollment: 5,522. Undergraduate enrollment: 5,069; 39% part-time, 57% women, 40% over 25. Total faculty: 223. Library holdings: 93,005 bound volumes, 25,000 titles on microform, 950 periodical subscriptions, 21,010 records/tapes.

Undergraduate Courses offered for part-time students during daytime, evenings, weekends, summer. Complete part-time degree programs offered during daytime, evenings, summer. Adult/continuing education programs available. Career services available to part-time students: individual career counseling, individual job placement, employer recruitment on campus. Part-time tuition: $96 per credit.

Graduate Part-time study available in Graduate Studies. Degree can be earned exclusively through evening/weekend study in Graduate Studies.Basic part-time expenses: $116 per credit tuition. Institutional financial aid available to part-time graduate students in Graduate Studies.

Rosemont College
Rosemont 19010

Independent-religious instutition; small-town setting. Awards B. Total enrollment: 591 (all undergraduates); 6% part-time, 100% women, 6% over 25. Total faculty: 86. Library holdings: 140,619 bound volumes, 19,968 titles on microform, 650 periodical subscriptions, 250 records/tapes.

Undergraduate Courses offered for part-time students during daytime. Complete part-time degree programs offered during daytime. Adult/continuing education programs available. Career services available to part-time students: individual and group career counseling, employer recruitment on campus. Part-time tuition: $640 per unit.

St Charles Borromeo Seminary
Philadelphia 19151

Independent-religious instutition; metropolitan setting. Awards B, M. Total enrollment: 537. Undergraduate enrollment: 367; 68% part-time, 0% women, 64% over 25. Total faculty: 64. Library holdings: 180,689 bound volumes, 35 titles on microform, 512 periodical subscriptions, 3,393 records/tapes.

Undergraduate Courses offered for part-time students during daytime, evenings, summer. Complete part-time degree programs offered during daytime, evenings, summer. Adult/continuing education programs available. Career services available to part-time students: individual and group career counseling. Part-time tuition: $75 per course.

Graduate Part-time study available in Graduate and Professional Programs.Basic part-time expenses: $50 per credit tuition.

Saint Francis College
Loretto 15940

Independent-religious instutition; rural setting. Awards A, B, M. Total enrollment: 1,600. Undergraduate enrollment: 1,050; 6% part-time, 51% women. Total faculty: 87. Library holdings: 160,700 bound volumes, 100 titles on microform, 902 periodical subscriptions, 2,100 records/tapes.

Undergraduate Courses offered for part-time students during daytime, evenings, summer. Complete part-time degree programs offered during daytime, evenings, summer. Adult/continuing education programs available. Career services available to part-time students: individual and group career counseling, individual job placement, employer recruitment on campus. Part-time tuition: $143 per credit.

Graduate Part-time study available in Continuing Education, Graduate School of Industrial Relations. Degree can be earned exclusively through evening/weekend study in Continuing Education, Graduate School of Industrial Relations.Basic part-time expenses: $153 per credit tuition plus $20 per semester fees. Institutional financial aid available to part-time graduate students in Graduate School of Industrial Relations.

Saint Joseph's University
Philadelphia 19131

Independent-religious instutition; metropolitan setting. Awards A, B, M. Total enrollment: 6,251. Undergraduate enrollment: 2,433; 5% part-time, 46% women. Total faculty: 190. Library holdings: 206,000 bound volumes, 244,000 titles on microform, 1,450 periodical subscriptions, 1,846 records/tapes.

Undergraduate Courses offered for part-time students during evenings, weekends, summer. Complete part-time degree programs offered during evenings, weekends, summer. Adult/continuing education programs available. Career services available to part-time students: individual and group career counseling, individual job placement, employer recruitment on campus. Part-time tuition: $115 per credit hour.

Graduate Part-time study available in Graduate Programs. Basic part-time expenses: $148 per credit tuition. Institutional financial aid available to part-time graduate students in Graduate Programs.

Saint Vincent College
Latrobe 15650

Independent-religious instutition; rural setting. Awards B. Total enrollment: 901 (all undergraduates); 6% part-time, 15% women, 6% over 25. Total faculty: 84. Library holdings: 215,527 bound volumes, 935 periodical subscriptions, 3,972 records/tapes.

Undergraduate Courses offered for part-time students during daytime, evenings, weekends, summer. Complete part-time degree programs offered during daytime, evenings, summer. Adult/continuing education programs available. Career services available to part-time students: individual and group career counseling, individual job placement, employer recruitment on campus. Part-time tuition: $160 per credit.

Pennsylvania / **Colleges Offering Part-Time Degree Programs**

Saint Vincent Seminary
Latrobe 15650

Independent-religious institution (graduate only). Total enrollment: 54 (primarily men; 24% part-time). Total faculty: 20. Library holdings: 218,860 bound volumes, 94,100 microforms.

Graduate Part-time study available in Graduate and Professional Programs.Basic part-time expenses: $140 per credit tuition. Institutional financial aid available to part-time graduate students in Graduate and Professional Programs.

Seton Hill College
Greensburg 15601

Independent-religious instutition; small-town setting. Awards B. Barrier-free campus. Total enrollment: 968 (all undergraduates); 20% part-time, 100% women, 17% over 25. Total faculty: 81. Library holdings: 70,000 bound volumes, 88 titles on microform, 345 periodical subscriptions, 900 records/tapes.

Undergraduate Courses offered for part-time students during daytime, evenings, weekends, summer. Complete part-time degree programs offered during daytime, evenings, weekends, summer. Adult/continuing education programs available. Career services available to part-time students: individual and group career counseling, individual job placement, employer recruitment on campus. Part-time tuition: $144 per credit. 15% discount on part-time tuition for early registration.

Shippensburg University of Pennsylvania
Shippensburg 17257

Public institution; small-town setting. Awards B, M. Total enrollment: 6,033. Undergraduate enrollment: 4,904; 7% part-time, 54% women, 7% over 25. Total faculty: 318. Library holdings: 364,950 bound volumes, 1.1 million titles on microform, 2,384 periodical subscriptions.

Undergraduate Courses offered for part-time students during daytime, evenings, summer. Complete part-time degree programs offered during daytime, evenings, summer. Adult/continuing education programs available. Career services available to part-time students: individual and group career counseling, individual job placement, employer recruitment on campus. Part-time tuition: $66 per credit hour for state residents, $115 per credit hour for nonresidents.

Graduate Part-time study available in School of Graduate Studies.Basic part-time expenses: $87 per credit tuition plus $10 per semester (minimum) fees for state residents, $92 per credit tuition plus $10 per semester (minimum) fees for nonresidents. Institutional financial aid available to part-time graduate students in School of Graduate Studies.

Slippery Rock University of Pennsylvania
Slippery Rock 16057

Public institution; rural setting. Awards B, M. Total enrollment: 5,782. Undergraduate enrollment: 5,061; 9% part-time, 53% women, 4% over 25. Total faculty: 341. Library holdings: 434,247 bound volumes, 636,234 titles on microform, 1,376 periodical subscriptions, 13,843 records/tapes.

Undergraduate Courses offered for part-time students during daytime, evenings, summer. Complete part-time degree programs offered during daytime, evenings, summer. Adult/continuing education programs available. Career services available to part-time students: individual and group career counseling, individual job placement, employer recruitment on campus. Part-time tuition: $62 per credit hour for state residents, $108 per credit hour for nonresidents.

Graduate Part-time study available in Graduate School. Degree can be earned exclusively through evening/weekend study in Graduate School.Basic part-time expenses: $87 per credit tuition plus $19.50 per credit fees for state residents, $92 per credit tuition plus $19.50 per credit fees for nonresidents.

Spring Garden College
Philadelphia 19118

Independent institution; metropolitan setting. Awards A, B. Total enrollment: 1,450 (all undergraduates); 45% part-time, 21% women. Total faculty: 110. Library holdings: 25,000 bound volumes, 472 periodical subscriptions.

Undergraduate Courses offered for part-time students during daytime, evenings, summer. Complete part-time degree programs offered during daytime, evenings. Adult/continuing education programs available. Career services available to part-time students: individual and group career counseling, individual job placement, employer recruitment on campus. Part-time tuition: $130 per credit.

Susquehanna University
Selinsgrove 17870

Independent-religious instutition; small-town setting. Awards A, B. Total enrollment: 1,445 (all undergraduates); 1% part-time, 48% women. Total faculty: 117. Library holdings: 125,000 bound volumes, 25,000 titles on microform, 1,180 periodical subscriptions, 6,000 records/tapes.

Undergraduate Courses offered for part-time students during daytime, evenings, summer. Complete part-time degree programs offered during daytime, evenings, summer. Adult/continuing education programs available. Career services available to part-time students: individual career counseling, individual job placement, employer recruitment on campus. Part-time tuition: $690 per course.

Temple University
Philadelphia 19122

Public institution; metropolitan setting. Awards A, B, M, D. Total enrollment: 24,786. Undergraduate enrollment: 16,249; 19% part-time, 48% women. Total faculty: 2,564. Library holdings: 1.8 million bound volumes, 14,000 periodical subscriptions, 13,669 records/tapes.

Undergraduate Courses offered for part-time students during daytime, evenings, summer. Complete part-time degree programs offered during daytime, evenings. Adult/continuing education programs available. Career services available to part-time students: individual and group career counseling, individual job placement, employer recruitment on campus. Part-time tuition: $100 per credit hour for state residents, $136 per credit hour for nonresidents.

Graduate Part-time study available in Graduate School, School of Dentistry, School of Law, School of Medicine.Basic part-time expenses: $133 per credit hour tuition for state residents, $167 per credit hour tuition for nonresidents.

Temple University, Ambler Campus
Ambler 19002

Public institution; small-town setting. Awards A, B, M, D. Barrier-free campus. Total enrollment: 4,140. Undergraduate enrollment: 3,235; 41% part-time, 48% women. Total faculty: 205.

Colleges Offering Part-Time Degree Programs / *Pennsylvania*

Temple University, Ambler Campus (continued)
Library holdings: 60,000 bound volumes, 576 periodical subscriptions, 3,000 records/tapes.

Undergraduate Courses offered for part-time students during daytime, evenings, summer. Complete part-time degree programs offered during daytime, evenings. Adult/continuing education programs available. Career services available to part-time students: individual and group career counseling, individual job placement, employer recruitment on campus. Part-time tuition: $100 per credit hour for state residents, $136 per credit hour for nonresidents.

Thomas Jefferson University
Philadelphia 19107

Independent institution; metropolitan setting. Awards B, M, D. Barrier-free campus. Total enrollment: 1,434. Undergraduate enrollment: 612; 6% part-time, 88% women. Total faculty: 73. Library holdings: 125,000 bound volumes, 1,715 periodical subscriptions, 300 records/tapes.

Undergraduate Courses offered for part-time students during daytime, evenings, summer. Complete part-time degree programs offered during daytime, evenings, summer. Adult/continuing education programs available. Career services available to part-time students: individual career counseling. Part-time tuition per credit ranges from $110 for lower division courses to $225 for upper division courses.

Graduate Part-time study available in College of Graduate Studies. Basic part-time expenses: $130 per credit tuition.

Triangle Institute of Technology
Greensburg 15601

Proprietary institution; small-town setting. Awards A. Barrier-free campus. Total enrollment: 180 (all undergraduates); 20% part-time, 15% women, 40% over 25. Total faculty: 19. Library holdings: 300 bound volumes, 4 periodical subscriptions.

Undergraduate Courses offered for part-time students during daytime, evenings, summer. Complete part-time degree programs offered during daytime, evenings, summer. Adult/continuing education programs available. Career services available to part-time students: individual and group career counseling, individual job placement, employer recruitment on campus. Part-time tuition per credit ranges from $26 to $31.67 according to program.

United Wesleyan College
Allentown 18103

Independent-religious instutition; city setting. Awards A, B. Total enrollment: 218 (all undergraduates); 17% part-time, 33% women, 40% over 25. Total faculty: 17. Library holdings: 30,000 bound volumes, 400 titles on microform, 40 periodical subscriptions, 100 records/tapes.

Undergraduate Courses offered for part-time students during daytime, evenings, summer. Complete part-time degree programs offered during daytime, evenings, summer. Career services available to part-time students: individual and group career counseling, individual job placement, employer recruitment on campus. Part-time tuition: $155 per semester hour.

University of Pennsylvania
Philadelphia 19104

Independent institution; metropolitan setting. Awards A, B, M, D. Total enrollment: 22,000. Undergraduate enrollment: 9,200; 40% women. Total faculty: 2,500. Library holdings: 3.1 million bound volumes, 1.4 million titles on microform, 44,000 periodical subscriptions, 26,000 records/tapes.

Undergraduate Courses offered for part-time students during daytime, evenings, weekends, summer. Complete part-time degree programs offered during daytime, evenings, weekends, summer. Adult/continuing education programs available. Career services available to part-time students: individual and group career counseling, individual job placement, employer recruitment on campus. Part-time tuition: $370 per course.

Graduate Part-time study available in School of Arts and Sciences, Graduate School of Education, School of Nursing. Degree can be earned exclusively through evening/weekend study in School of Nursing. Basic part-time expenses: $1220 per course tuition plus $55 per course fees.

University of Pittsburgh
Pittsburgh 15260

Public institution; metropolitan setting. Awards B, M, D. Barrier-free campus. Total enrollment: 29,425. Undergraduate enrollment: 19,301; 36% part-time, 47% women. Total faculty: 2,683. Library holdings: 2.5 million bound volumes, 1.7 million titles on microform, 20,091 periodical subscriptions.

Undergraduate Courses offered for part-time students during daytime, evenings, weekends, summer. Complete part-time degree programs offered during daytime, evenings, weekends, summer. External degree and adult/continuing education programs available. Career services available to part-time students: individual and group career counseling, individual job placement, employer recruitment on campus. Part-time tuition: $88 per credit for state residents, $176 per credit for nonresidents.

Graduate Part-time study available in Faculty of Arts and Sciences, Graduate School of Business, Graduate School of Public and International Affairs, Graduate School of Public Health, School of Education, School of Engineering, School of Health Related Professions, School of Law, School of Library and Information Science, School of Nursing, School of Pharmacy, School of Social Work. Degree can be earned exclusively through evening/weekend study in Graduate School of Business, Graduate School of Public and International Affairs, School of Health Related Professions, School of Library and Information Science. Basic part-time expenses: $131 per credit tuition plus $2 per semester fees for state residents, $262 per credit tuition plus $2 per semester fees for nonresidents. Institutional financial aid available to part-time graduate students in Faculty of Arts and Sciences, Graduate School of Public Health, School of Education, School of Engineering, School of Law.

University of Pittsburgh at Bradford
Bradford 16701

Public institution; small-town setting. Awards A, B. Barrier-free campus. Total enrollment: 1,100 (all undergraduates); 30% part-time, 45% women, 33% over 25. Total faculty: 59. Library holdings: 60,000 bound volumes, 1,000 titles on microform, 420 periodical subscriptions, 860 records/tapes.

Undergraduate Courses offered for part-time students during daytime, evenings, summer. Complete part-time degree programs offered during daytime, evenings, summer. Adult/continuing education programs available. Career services available to part-time students: individual and group career counseling, individual job placement, employer recruitment on campus.

Pennsylvania / Colleges Offering Part-Time Degree Programs

Part-time tuition per credit hour ranges from $85 to $110 for state residents, $170 to $220 for nonresidents, according to program.

University of Pittsburgh at Greensburg
Greensburg 15601

Public institution; small-town setting. Awards B. Total enrollment: 1,400 (all undergraduates); 46% part-time, 49% women, 35% over 25. Total faculty: 51. Library holdings: 55,000 bound volumes.

Undergraduate Courses offered for part-time students during daytime, evenings, weekends, summer. Complete part-time degree programs offered during daytime, evenings, summer. External degree and adult/continuing education programs available. Career services available to part-time students: individual career counseling. Part-time tuition: $85 per credit for state residents, $170 per credit for nonresidents.

University of Pittsburgh at Johnstown
Johnstown 15904

Public institution; small-town setting. Awards B. Barrier-free campus. Total enrollment: 3,319 (all undergraduates); 24% part-time, 46% women. Total faculty: 133. Library holdings: 100,000 bound volumes, 500 periodical subscriptions, 4,500 records/tapes.

Undergraduate Courses offered for part-time students during daytime, evenings, summer. Complete part-time degree programs offered during daytime, evenings, summer. Adult/continuing education programs available. Career services available to part-time students: individual and group career counseling, individual job placement, employer recruitment on campus. Part-time tuition: $88 per credit for state residents, $176 per credit for nonresidents.

University of Pittsburgh at Titusville
Titusville 16354

Public institution; small-town setting. Awards A. Total enrollment: 375 (all undergraduates); 24% part-time, 60% women, 22% over 25. Total faculty: 37. Library holdings: 32,000 bound volumes, 190 periodical subscriptions, 155 records/tapes.

Undergraduate Courses offered for part-time students during daytime, evenings, summer. Complete part-time degree programs offered during daytime, evenings, summer. Adult/continuing education programs available. Career services available to part-time students: individual career counseling, individual job placement. Part-time tuition: $82 per credit for state residents, $164 per credit for nonresidents.

University of Scranton
Scranton 18510

Independent-religious instutition; city setting. Awards A, B, M. Barrier-free campus. Total enrollment: 4,801. Undergraduate enrollment: 4,023; 10% part-time, 47% women, 14% over 25. Total faculty: 269. Library holdings: 230,000 bound volumes, 19,400 titles on microform, 1,300 periodical subscriptions, 1,500 records/tapes.

Undergraduate Courses offered for part-time students during daytime, evenings, summer. Complete part-time degree programs offered during daytime, evenings, summer. Adult/continuing education programs available. Career services available to part-time students: individual and group career counseling, individual job placement, employer recruitment on campus. Part-time tuition: $129 per credit hour.

Graduate Part-time study available in Graduate School. Degree can be earned exclusively through evening/weekend study in Graduate School. Basic part-time expenses: $137 per credit tuition plus $15 per semester fees. Institutional financial aid available to part-time graduate students in Graduate School.

Ursinus College
Collegeville 19426

Independent-religious instutition; small-town setting. Awards A, B. Barrier-free campus. Total enrollment: 1,104 (all undergraduates); 5% part-time, 47% women, 4% over 25. Total faculty: 100. Library holdings: 174,000 bound volumes, 114,200 titles on microform, 700 periodical subscriptions, 6,000 records/tapes.

Undergraduate Courses offered for part-time students during daytime, evenings, summer. Complete part-time degree programs offered during daytime, evenings, summer. Adult/continuing education programs available. Career services available to part-time students: individual career counseling, individual job placement, employer recruitment on campus. Part-time tuition: $200 per semester hour.

Villa Maria College
Erie 16505

Independent-religious instutition; city setting. Awards A, B. Total enrollment: 609 (all undergraduates); 18% part-time, 99% women, 25% over 25. Total faculty: 72. Library holdings: 43,100 bound volumes, 310 periodical subscriptions, 1,221 records/tapes.

Undergraduate Courses offered for part-time students during daytime, evenings, summer. Complete part-time degree programs offered during daytime, evenings, summer. Adult/continuing education programs available. Career services available to part-time students: individual career counseling, individual job placement. Part-time tuition: $150 per credit.

Villanova University
Villanova 19085

Independent-religious instutition; small-town setting. Awards A, B, M, D. Total enrollment: 11,190. Undergraduate enrollment: 6,217; 13% part-time, 45% women, 1% over 25. Total faculty: 493. Library holdings: 500,000 bound volumes, 3,200 periodical subscriptions.

Undergraduate Courses offered for part-time students during daytime, evenings, weekends, summer. Complete part-time degree programs offered during daytime, evenings, weekends, summer. Adult/continuing education programs available. Career services available to part-time students: individual career counseling. Part-time tuition: $150 per credit hour.

Graduate Part-time study available in Graduate School, College of Commerce and Finance, School of Law. Degree can be earned exclusively through evening/weekend study in Graduate School, College of Commerce and Finance, School of Law. Basic part-time expenses: $165 per credit tuition plus $28 per semester fees.

Waynesburg College
Waynesburg 15370

Independent-religious instutition; small-town setting. Awards A, B, M. Barrier-free campus. Total enrollment: 780. Undergraduate enrollment: 710; 7% part-time, 45% women. Total faculty: 64. Library holdings: 117,000 bound volumes, 3,450 titles on microform, 700 periodical subscriptions, 1,370 records/tapes.

Colleges Offering Part-Time Degree Programs / *Pennsylvania*

Waynesburg College (continued)

Undergraduate Courses offered for part-time students during daytime, evenings, summer. Complete part-time degree programs offered during daytime, evenings, summer. Adult/continuing education programs available. Career services available to part-time students: individual and group career counseling, individual job placement, employer recruitment on campus. Part-time tuition: $220 per semester hour.

Graduate Part-time study available in Graduate Program in Business Administration. Degree can be earned exclusively through evening/weekend study in Graduate Program in Business Administration. Basic part-time expenses: $160 per credit hour tuition.

West Chester University of Pennsylvania
West Chester 19383

Public institution; small-town setting. Awards A, B, M. Total enrollment: 9,586. Undergraduate enrollment: 8,449; 22% part-time, 57% women, 16% over 25. Total faculty: 529. Library holdings: 427,552 bound volumes, 363,610 titles on microform, 2,450 periodical subscriptions, 15,000 records/tapes.

Undergraduate Courses offered for part-time students during daytime, evenings, summer. Complete part-time degree programs offered during daytime, evenings, summer. Adult/continuing education programs available. Career services available to part-time students: individual and group career counseling, individual job placement, employer recruitment on campus. Part-time tuition: $66 per credit for state residents, $115 per credit for nonresidents.

Westminster College
New Wilmington 16172

Independent-religious instutition; small-town setting. Awards B, M. Total enrollment: 1,542. Undergraduate enrollment: 1,463; 3% part-time, 51% women, 1% over 25. Total faculty: 143. Library holdings: 220,000 bound volumes, 5,000 titles on microform, 1,210 periodical subscriptions, 1,500 records/tapes.

Undergraduate Courses offered for part-time students during daytime, evenings, summer. Complete part-time degree programs offered during daytime, evenings, summer. Adult/continuing education programs available. Career services available to part-time students: individual and group career counseling, individual job placement, employer recruitment on campus. Part-time tuition: $575 per course.

Graduate Part-time study available in Graduate Program in Education. Basic part-time expenses: $575 per course tuition. Institutional financial aid available to part-time graduate students in Graduate Program in Education.

Westminster Theological Seminary
Philadelphia 19118

Independent-religious institution (graduate only). Total enrollment: 423 (primarily men; 41% part-time). Total faculty: 27.

Graduate Part-time study available in Graduate and Professional Programs. Basic part-time expenses: $120 per credit tuition plus $15 per year fees.

Westmoreland County Community College
Youngwood 15697

Public institution; rural setting. Awards A. Barrier-free campus. Total enrollment: 3,242 (all undergraduates); 59% part-time, 61% women. Total faculty: 165. Library holdings: 32,714 bound volumes, 2,382 titles on microform, 632 periodical subscriptions, 1,100 records/tapes.

Undergraduate Courses offered for part-time students during daytime, evenings, weekends, summer. Complete part-time degree programs offered during daytime, evenings, weekends, summer. Adult/continuing education programs available. Career services available to part-time students: individual career counseling, individual job placement. Part-time tuition: $34 per credit for area residents, $73 per credit for state residents, $107 per credit for nonresidents.

Widener University
Chester 19013

Independent institution (undergraduate and graduate). Total enrollment: 7,338. Graduate enrollment: 2,125 (coed; 49% part-time).

Graduate Part-time study available in Delaware Law School, School of Engineering, School of Management, School of Nursing. Basic part-time expenses: $165 per credit tuition plus $15 per semester fees.

Widener University, Pennsylvania Campus
Chester 19013

Independent institution; city setting. Awards A, B, M, D. Barrier-free campus. Total enrollment: 5,425. Undergraduate enrollment: 4,401; 32% part-time, 45% women, 29% over 25. Total faculty: 202. Library holdings: 180,000 bound volumes, 20,000 titles on microform, 1,500 periodical subscriptions, 3,000 records/tapes.

Undergraduate Courses offered for part-time students during daytime, evenings. Complete part-time degree programs offered during daytime, evenings. Adult/continuing education programs available. Career services available to part-time students: individual and group career counseling, individual job placement. Part-time tuition: $198 per credit.

Wilkes College
Wilkes-Barre 18766

Independent institution; city setting. Awards B, M. Total enrollment: 2,808. Undergraduate enrollment: 1,860; 20% part-time, 48% women. Total faculty: 198. Library holdings: 180,000 bound volumes, 400,000 titles on microform, 1,250 periodical subscriptions.

Undergraduate Courses offered for part-time students during daytime, evenings, weekends, summer. Complete part-time degree programs offered during daytime, evenings, weekends, summer. External degree and adult/continuing education programs available. Career services available to part-time students: individual career counseling, individual job placement, employer recruitment on campus. Part-time tuition: $115 per credit.

Graduate Part-time study available in Graduate Division. Degree can be earned exclusively through evening/weekend study in Graduate Division. Basic part-time expenses: $150 per credit tuition.

Williamsport Area Community College
Williamsport 17701

Public institution; small-town setting. Awards A. Barrier-free campus. Total enrollment: 3,955 (all undergraduates); 21% part-

time, 36% women, 25% over 25. Total faculty: 281. Library holdings: 36,000 bound volumes, 475 periodical subscriptions, 4,535 records/tapes.

Undergraduate Courses offered for part-time students during daytime, evenings, weekends, summer. Complete part-time degree programs offered during daytime, evenings. Adult/continuing education programs available. Career services available to part-time students: individual career counseling, individual job placement, employer recruitment on campus. Part-time tuition: $37.75 per credit for area residents, $85.65 per credit for state residents, $126 per credit for nonresidents.

Williamsport School of Commerce
Williamsport 17701

Proprietary institution; small-town setting. Awards A. Total enrollment: 157 (all undergraduates); 3% part-time, 93% women. Total faculty: 5.

Undergraduate Courses offered for part-time students during daytime, summer. Complete part-time degree programs offered during daytime, summer. Career services available to part-time students: individual and group career counseling, individual job placement, employer recruitment on campus. Part-time tuition: $220 per course.

Wilson College
Chambersburg 17201

Independent-religious instutition; small-town setting. Awards A, B. Total enrollment: 313 (all undergraduates); 33% part-time, 100% women. Total faculty: 58. Library holdings: 152,472 bound volumes, 377 periodical subscriptions, 921 records/tapes.

Undergraduate Courses offered for part-time students during daytime, evenings. Complete part-time degree programs offered during daytime, evenings. Adult/continuing education programs available. Career services available to part-time students: individual and group career counseling, individual job placement, employer recruitment on campus. Part-time tuition: $650 per course.

York College of Pennsylvania
York 17405

Independent institution; city setting. Awards A, B, M. Total enrollment: 4,533. Undergraduate enrollment: 4,413; 45% part-time, 60% women, 30% over 25. Total faculty: 230. Library holdings: 100,941 bound volumes, 998 periodical subscriptions, 7,347 records/tapes.

Undergraduate Courses offered for part-time students during daytime, evenings, weekends, summer. Complete part-time degree programs offered during daytime, evenings. Adult/continuing education programs available. Career services available to part-time students: individual and group career counseling, individual job placement, employer recruitment on campus. Part-time tuition: $75 per credit hour.

Graduate Part-time study available in Graduate Program in Business Administration. Degree can be earned exclusively through evening/weekend study in Graduate Program in Business Administration. Basic part-time expenses: $105 per credit tuition plus $15 per semester fees. Institutional financial aid available to part-time graduate students in Graduate Program in Business Administration.

PUERTO RICO

American College of Puerto Rico
Bayamón 00619

Independent institution; city setting. Awards A, B. Barrier-free campus. Total enrollment: 3,789 (all undergraduates); 4% part-time, 70% women. Total faculty: 138. Library holdings: 18,132 bound volumes, 300 periodical subscriptions.

Undergraduate Courses offered for part-time students during daytime, evenings, summer. Complete part-time degree programs offered during daytime, evenings, summer. Adult/continuing education programs available. Career services available to part-time students: individual and group career counseling, individual job placement. Part-time tuition: $50 per credit.

Antillian College
Mayagüez 00708

Independent-religious instutition; city setting. Awards A, B. Total enrollment: 894 (all undergraduates); 14% part-time, 61% women, 24% over 25. Total faculty: 75. Library holdings: 78,328 bound volumes, 1,796 titles on microform, 460 periodical subscriptions, 6,780 records/tapes.

Undergraduate Courses offered for part-time students during daytime, evenings, weekends, summer. Complete part-time degree programs offered during daytime, summer. Career services available to part-time students: individual career counseling, individual job placement, employer recruitment on campus. Part-time tuition: $56 per credit.

Caguas City College
Caguas 00626

Proprietary institution; city setting. Awards A, B. Barrier-free campus. Total enrollment: 909 (all undergraduates). Total faculty: 25. Library holdings: 7,000 bound volumes, 105 periodical subscriptions.

Undergraduate Courses offered for part-time students during daytime, evenings. Complete part-time degree programs offered during daytime, evenings. External degree and adult/continuing education programs available. Part-time tuition: $50 per credit.

Caribbean Center for Advanced Studies
Santurce 00940

Independent institution (graduate only). Total enrollment: 358 (coed; 41% part-time). Total faculty: 19. Library holdings: 8,552 bound volumes, 45 microforms.

Graduate Part-time study available in Graduate Programs in Psychology. Degree can be earned exclusively through evening/weekend study in Graduate Programs in Psychology. Basic part-time expenses: $130 per credit tuition plus $165 per semester fees.

Caribbean University College
Bayamón 00619

Independent institution; city setting. Awards A, B. Total enrollment: 2,706 (all undergraduates); 14% part-time, 65% women, 25% over 25. Total faculty: 116. Library holdings: 12,051 bound volumes, 123 periodical subscriptions, 31 records/tapes.

Undergraduate Courses offered for part-time students during daytime, evenings. Complete part-time degree programs offered during daytime, evenings. Adult/continuing education pro-

Colleges Offering Part-Time Degree Programs / *Puerto Rico*

Caribbean University College (continued)

grams available. Career services available to part-time students: individual career counseling. Part-time tuition: $30 per credit hour.

Catholic University of Puerto Rico
Ponce 00732

Independent-religious instutition; city setting. Awards A, B, M. Barrier-free campus. Total enrollment: 13,816. Undergraduate enrollment: 12,914; 23% part-time, 65% women. Total faculty: 632. Library holdings: 315,395 bound volumes, 65,920 titles on microform, 1,836 periodical subscriptions, 7,950 records/tapes.

Undergraduate Courses offered for part-time students during daytime, evenings. Complete part-time degree programs offered during daytime, evenings. Adult/continuing education programs available. Part-time tuition: $50 per credit.

Graduate Part-time study available in Graduate School in Hispanic Studies, Graduate School of Business Administration, Graduate School of Education, Graduate School of Nursing, School of Law. Degree can be earned exclusively through evening/weekend study in Graduate School in Hispanic Studies, Graduate School of Business Administration, Graduate School of Education, Graduate School of Nursing, School of Law. Basic part-time expenses: $85 per credit hour tuition plus $53 per semester fees. Institutional financial aid available to part-time graduate students in Graduate School in Hispanic Studies, Graduate School of Business Administration, Graduate School of Education, Graduate School of Nursing, School of Law.

Catholic University of Puerto Rico, Mayagüez Center
Mayagüez 00708

Independent-religious instutition; small-town setting. Awards A, B. Total enrollment: 1,007 (all undergraduates); 30% part-time, 65% women, 6% over 25. Total faculty: 82. Library holdings: 15,000 bound volumes, 137 periodical subscriptions, 300 records/tapes.

Undergraduate Courses offered for part-time students during daytime, evenings, summer. Complete part-time degree programs offered during daytime, evenings, summer. Adult/continuing education programs available. Career services available to part-time students: individual and group career counseling. Part-time tuition: $50 per credit.

Centro de Estudios Avanzados de Puerto Rico y el Caribe
San Juan 00904

Independent institution (graduate only). Total enrollment: 230 (coed; 72% part-time). Total faculty: 15. Library holdings: 6,000 bound volumes, 27 microforms.

Graduate Part-time study available in Graduate Program. Degree can be earned exclusively through evening/weekend study in Graduate Program. Basic part-time expenses: $50 per credit tuition plus $35 per semester fees. Institutional financial aid available to part-time graduate students in Graduate Program.

Electronic Data Processing College of Puerto Rico
Hato Rey 00918

Proprietary institution; city setting. Awards A, B. Barrier-free campus. Total enrollment: 2,600 (all undergraduates); 14% part-time, 33% women. Total faculty: 91. Library holdings: 9,160 bound volumes, 112 periodical subscriptions.

Undergraduate Courses offered for part-time students during daytime, evenings. Complete part-time degree programs offered during daytime, evenings. Career services available to part-time students: individual and group career counseling, individual job placement, employer recruitment on campus. Part-time tuition: $45 per credit.

Evangelical Seminary of Puerto Rico
Hato Rey 00918

Independent-religious institution (graduate only). Total enrollment: 159 (coed; 67% part-time). Total faculty: 9.

Graduate Part-time study available in Graduate and Professional Programs. Degree can be earned exclusively through evening/weekend study in Graduate and Professional Programs. Basic part-time expenses: $55 per credit tuition.

Huertas Business College
Caguas 00625

Proprietary institution; city setting. Awards A. Total enrollment: 684 (all undergraduates); 34% part-time, 67% women. Total faculty: 28. Library holdings: 5,524 bound volumes, 1,144 periodical subscriptions, 1,181 records/tapes.

Undergraduate Courses offered for part-time students during evenings. Complete part-time degree programs offered during evenings. Career services available to part-time students: individual and group career counseling, individual job placement. Part-time tuition: $43 per credit.

Instituto Comercial de Puerto Rico Junior College
Hato Rey 00919

Proprietary institution; metropolitan setting. Awards A. Barrier-free campus. Total enrollment: 1,687 (all undergraduates); 18% part-time, 63% women. Total faculty: 85. Library holdings: 5,000 bound volumes, 60 periodical subscriptions, 2,000 records/tapes.

Undergraduate Courses offered for part-time students during daytime, evenings. Complete part-time degree programs offered during daytime, evenings. Career services available to part-time students: individual and group career counseling, individual job placement, employer recruitment on campus. Part-time tuition: $50 per credit.

Instituto Técnico Comercial Junior College
Río Piedras 00926

Proprietary institution; metropolitan setting. Awards A. Barrier-free campus. Total enrollment: 937 (all undergraduates); 16% part-time, 64% women. Total faculty: 46.

Undergraduate Courses offered for part-time students during daytime, evenings. Complete part-time degree programs offered during daytime, evenings. Adult/continuing education programs available. Career services available to part-time students: individual and group career counseling. Part-time tuition: $40 per credit.

Puerto Rico / **Colleges Offering Part-Time Degree Programs**

Inter American University of Puerto Rico, Aguadilla Regional College
Aguadilla 00603

Independent institution; small-town setting. Awards A. Total enrollment: 2,379 (all undergraduates); 14% part-time, 62% women. Total faculty: 118. Library holdings: 19,290 bound volumes, 196 periodical subscriptions, 8,065 records/tapes.

Undergraduate Courses offered for part-time students during daytime, evenings, weekends. Complete part-time degree programs offered during daytime, evenings. Part-time tuition: $55 per semester hour.

Inter American University of Puerto Rico, Barranquitas Regional College
Barranquitas 00615

Independent institution; small-town setting. Awards A. Barrier-free campus. Total enrollment: 1,249 (all undergraduates); 11% part-time, 63% women. Total faculty: 53. Library holdings: 21,994 bound volumes, 208 periodical subscriptions, 4,941 records/tapes.

Undergraduate Courses offered for part-time students during daytime, evenings, weekends, summer. Complete part-time degree programs offered during daytime, evenings, weekends, summer. Career services available to part-time students: individual career counseling, individual job placement. Part-time tuition: $55 per semester hour.

Inter American University of Puerto Rico, Fajardo Regional College
Fajardo 00648

Independent institution; small-town setting. Awards A. Total enrollment: 1,750 (all undergraduates); 20% part-time, 61% women. Total faculty: 76. Library holdings: 22,073 bound volumes, 176 periodical subscriptions, 5,621 records/tapes.

Undergraduate Courses offered for part-time students during daytime, evenings, weekends. Complete part-time degree programs offered during daytime, evenings. Part-time tuition: $55 per semester hour.

Inter American University of Puerto Rico, Guayama Regional College
Guayama 00654

Independent institution; small-town setting. Awards A. Barrier-free campus. Total enrollment: 1,162 (all undergraduates); 12% part-time, 71% women. Total faculty: 70. Library holdings: 20,572 bound volumes, 163 periodical subscriptions, 9,662 records/tapes.

Undergraduate Courses offered for part-time students during daytime, evenings, weekends. Complete part-time degree programs offered during daytime, evenings. Part-time tuition: $55 per semester hour.

Inter American University of Puerto Rico, Metropolitan Campus
Hato Rey 00919

Independent institution; metropolitan setting. Awards A, B, M. Total enrollment: 15,421. Undergraduate enrollment: 11,346; 25% part-time, 53% women. Total faculty: 571.

Undergraduate Courses offered for part-time students during daytime, evenings, weekends, summer. Complete part-time degree programs offered during daytime, evenings, weekends, summer. External degree and adult/continuing education programs available. Career services available to part-time students: individual and group career counseling, individual job placement. Part-time tuition: $55 per credit.

Graduate Part-time study available in Graduate Programs, School of Law. Institutional financial aid available to part-time graduate students in Graduate Programs, School of Law.

Inter American University of Puerto Rico, Ponce Regional College
Ponce 00731

Independent institution; city setting. Awards A. Total enrollment: 1,951 (all undergraduates); 18% part-time, 65% women. Total faculty: 97. Library holdings: 18,833 bound volumes, 244 periodical subscriptions, 5,743 records/tapes.

Undergraduate Courses offered for part-time students during daytime, evenings, weekends. Complete part-time degree programs offered during daytime, evenings. Part-time tuition: $55 per semester hour.

Inter American University of Puerto Rico, San Germán Campus
San Germán 00753

Independent institution (undergraduate and graduate). Total enrollment: 7,430. Graduate enrollment: 383 (coed; 75% part-time). Library holdings: 91,088 bound volumes.

Graduate Part-time study available in Graduate Programs. Degree can be earned exclusively through evening/weekend study in Graduate Programs. Basic part-time expenses: $80 per credit tuition plus $60 per semester fees. Institutional financial aid available to part-time graduate students in Graduate Programs.

Universidad del Turabo
Caguas 00626

Independent institution; city setting. Awards A, B, M. Barrier-free campus. Total enrollment: 6,800 (all undergraduates); 14% part-time, 59% women. Total faculty: 190.

Undergraduate Courses offered for part-time students during daytime, evenings, weekends. Complete part-time degree programs offered during daytime, evenings. Career services available to part-time students: individual and group career counseling. Part-time tuition: $50 per credit.

Universidad Politécnica de Puerto Rico
Hato Rey 00918

Independent institution; metropolitan setting. Awards B. Barrier-free campus. Total enrollment: 893 (all undergraduates); 23% part-time, 9% women, 55% over 25. Total faculty: 55. Library holdings: 9,000 bound volumes, 135 periodical subscriptions, 79 records/tapes.

Undergraduate Courses offered for part-time students during daytime, evenings, summer. Complete part-time degree programs offered during evenings. Career services available to part-time students: individual and group career counseling, individual job placement, employer recruitment on campus. Part-time tuition: $45 per credit.

Colleges Offering Part-Time Degree Programs / Puerto Rico

University of Puerto Rico, Arecibo Technological University College
Arecibo 00613

Public institution; city setting. Awards A, B. Barrier-free campus. Total enrollment: 3,569 (all undergraduates); 10% part-time, 66% women, 22% over 25. Total faculty: 171. Library holdings: 50,000 bound volumes, 380 titles on microform, 450 periodical subscriptions, 2,036 records/tapes.

Undergraduate Courses offered for part-time students during daytime, evenings, weekends, summer. Complete part-time degree programs offered during daytime. Adult/continuing education programs available. Career services available to part-time students: individual and group career counseling, individual job placement, employer recruitment on campus. Part-time tuition per credit ranges from $10 to $15 for commonwealth residents, according to program. Nonresident students who are U.S. citizens pay an amount equal to the rate for nonresidents at a state university in their home state.

University of Puerto Rico, Carolina Regional College
Carolina 00630

Public institution; city setting. Awards A. Barrier-free campus. Total enrollment: 1,337 (all undergraduates); 10% part-time, 60% women, 3% over 25. Total faculty: 79. Library holdings: 17,691 bound volumes, 45 titles on microform, 334 periodical subscriptions, 458 records/tapes.

Undergraduate Courses offered for part-time students during daytime. Complete part-time degree programs offered during daytime. External degree and adult/continuing education programs available. Career services available to part-time students: individual career counseling, individual job placement. Part-time tuition: $15 per credit for commonwealth residents. Nonresident students who are U.S. citizens pay an amount equal to half the rate for nonresidents at a state university in their home state.

University of Puerto Rico, Cayey University College
Cayey 00633

Public institution; small-town setting. Awards B. Total enrollment: 2,565 (all undergraduates); 12% part-time, 52% women. Total faculty: 139. Library holdings: 76,158 bound volumes, 219 periodical subscriptions, 426 records/tapes.

Undergraduate Courses offered for part-time students during evenings, weekends, summer. Complete part-time degree programs offered during evenings, weekends, summer. Career services available to part-time students: individual career counseling, individual job placement, employer recruitment on campus. Part-time tuition: $15 per credit.

University of Puerto Rico, Humacao University College
Humacao 00661

Public institution; small-town setting. Awards A, B. Barrier-free campus. Total enrollment: 3,134 (all undergraduates); 19% part-time, 64% women. Total faculty: 221. Library holdings: 68,643 bound volumes, 1,253 titles on microform, 818 periodical subscriptions.

Undergraduate Courses offered for part-time students during daytime, evenings, weekends, summer. Complete part-time degree programs offered during daytime, evenings, weekends, summer. External degree and adult/continuing education programs available. Career services available to part-time students: individual and group career counseling, employer recruitment on campus. Part-time tuition: $15 per credit hour for commonwealth residents. Nonresident students who are U.S. citizens pay an amount equal to the rate for nonresidents at a state university in their home state.

University of Puerto Rico, Mayagüez
Mayagüez 00708

Public institution; city setting. Awards A, B, M, D. Barrier-free campus. Total enrollment: 8,808. Undergraduate enrollment: 8,553; 13% part-time, 40% women. Total faculty: 553. Library holdings: 213,178 bound volumes, 219,243 titles on microform, 2,630 periodical subscriptions, 5,147 records/tapes.

Graduate Part-time study available in Graduate Studies. Degree can be earned exclusively through evening/weekend study in Graduate Studies. Basic part-time expenses: $45 per credit tuition for commonwealth residents, $1500 per semester tuition for nonresidents.

University of Puerto Rico, Ponce Technological University College
Ponce 00732

Public institution; city setting. Awards A, B. Barrier-free campus. Total enrollment: 1,867 (all undergraduates); 7% part-time, 59% women. Total faculty: 118. Library holdings: 32,338 bound volumes, 28 titles on microform, 251 periodical subscriptions, 1,949 records/tapes.

Undergraduate Courses offered for part-time students during daytime, evenings. Complete part-time degree programs offered during daytime, evenings. Adult/continuing education programs available. Career services available to part-time students: individual and group career counseling, individual job placement, employer recruitment on campus. Part-time tuition: $15 per credit for commonwealth residents. Nonresident students who are U.S. citizens pay an amount equal to the rate for nonresidents at a state university in their home state.

University of Puerto Rico, Río Piedras
Río Piedras 00931

Public institution; city setting. Awards B, M, D. Barrier-free campus. Total enrollment: 18,864. Undergraduate enrollment: 16,325; 27% part-time, 60% women. Total faculty: 1,102. Library holdings: 2.4 million bound volumes, 2,970 periodical subscriptions, 17,941 records/tapes.

Undergraduate Courses offered for part-time students during daytime, evenings, weekends, summer. Complete part-time degree programs offered during daytime, evenings. Adult/continuing education programs available. Career services available to part-time students: individual career counseling, individual job placement, employer recruitment on campus. Part-time tuition: $15 per credit for commonwealth residents. Nonresident students who are U.S. citizens pay an amount equal to the rate for nonresidents at a state university in their home state.

University of the Sacred Heart
Santurce 00914

Independent-religious institution; metropolitan setting. Awards A, B. Barrier-free campus. Total enrollment: 7,985 (all undergraduates); 22% part-time, 61% women, 16% over 25. Total faculty: 330. Library holdings: 85,864 bound volumes, 34,969 titles on microform, 864 periodical subscriptions, 4,842 records/tapes.

Undergraduate Courses offered for part-time students during daytime, evenings. Complete part-time degree programs offered during daytime, evenings. Career services available to part-time students: individual and group career counseling. Part-time tuition: $55 per credit.

RHODE ISLAND

Barrington College
Barrington 02806

Independent-religious instutition; small-town setting. Awards A, B. Barrier-free campus. Total enrollment: 453 (all undergraduates); 17% part-time, 58% women, 12% over 25. Total faculty: 50. Library holdings: 67,512 bound volumes, 44 titles on microform, 214 periodical subscriptions, 1,864 records/tapes.

Undergraduate Courses offered for part-time students during daytime, evenings, summer. Complete part-time degree programs offered during daytime, evenings. Adult/continuing education programs available. Career services available to part-time students: individual and group career counseling, individual job placement, employer recruitment on campus. Part-time tuition: $170 per credit.

Brown University
Providence 02912

Independent institution; city setting. Awards B, M, D. Total enrollment: 6,869. Undergraduate enrollment: 5,402; 1% part-time, 49% women, 1% over 25. Total faculty: 523. Library holdings: 1.8 million bound volumes, 778,000 titles on microform, 14,579 periodical subscriptions, 20,055 records/tapes.

Graduate Part-time study available in Graduate School. Basic part-time expenses: $1242 per course tuition. Institutional financial aid available to part-time graduate students in Graduate School.

Bryant College
Smithfield 02917

Independent institution; small-town setting. Awards B, M. Barrier-free campus. Total enrollment: 6,763. Undergraduate enrollment: 3,128; 1% part-time, 48% women. Total faculty: 164. Library holdings: 103,000 bound volumes, 152 titles on microform, 844 periodical subscriptions, 641 records/tapes.

Undergraduate Courses offered for part-time students during daytime, evenings, weekends, summer. Complete part-time degree programs offered during daytime, evenings, weekends, summer. Adult/continuing education programs available. Career services available to part-time students: individual and group career counseling, employer recruitment on campus. Part-time tuition: $174 per course.

Graduate Part-time study available in Graduate School. Basic part-time expenses: $300 per course tuition.

Community College of Rhode Island, Flanagan Campus
Lincoln 02865

Public institution; city setting. Awards A. Barrier-free campus. Total enrollment: 3,120 (all undergraduates); 40% part-time, 62% women. Total faculty: 179. Library holdings: 25,000 bound volumes, 296 titles on microform, 535 periodical subscriptions, 2,600 records/tapes.

Undergraduate Courses offered for part-time students during daytime, evenings, weekends, summer. Complete part-time degree programs offered during daytime, evenings, weekends, summer. Adult/continuing education programs available. Career services available to part-time students: individual and group career counseling, individual job placement, employer recruitment on campus. Part-time tuition: $30 per credit.

Community College of Rhode Island, Knight Campus
Warwick 02886

Public institution; city setting. Awards A. Barrier-free campus. Total enrollment: 4,483 (all undergraduates); 40% part-time, 62% women. Total faculty: 519. Library holdings: 75,802 bound volumes, 1,397 periodical subscriptions, 8,671 records/tapes.

Undergraduate Courses offered for part-time students during daytime, evenings, weekends, summer. Complete part-time degree programs offered during daytime, evenings, weekends, summer. External degree and adult/continuing education programs available. Career services available to part-time students: individual and group career counseling, individual job placement, employer recruitment on campus. Part-time tuition: $30 per credit.

Johnson & Wales College
Providence 02903

Independent institution; city setting. Awards A, B. Total enrollment: 4,250 (all undergraduates); 1% part-time, 47% women, 1% over 25. Total faculty: 125. Library holdings: 18,500 bound volumes, 60 periodical subscriptions, 150 records/tapes.

Undergraduate Courses offered for part-time students during daytime, evenings, weekends, summer. Complete part-time degree programs offered during daytime, evenings, weekends, summer. Adult/continuing education programs available. Career services available to part-time students: individual career counseling, individual job placement, employer recruitment on campus. Part-time tuition: $162 per credit.

Providence College
Providence 02918

Independent-religious instutition; city setting. Awards A, B, M, D. Total enrollment: 4,735. Undergraduate enrollment: 3,697; 1% part-time, 49% women. Total faculty: 252. Library holdings: 218,493 bound volumes, 23,631 titles on microform, 1,892 periodical subscriptions, 1,088 records/tapes.

Undergraduate Courses offered for part-time students during daytime, evenings, summer. Complete part-time degree programs offered during evenings, summer. Adult/continuing education programs available. Career services available to part-time students: individual and group career counseling, individual job placement, employer recruitment on campus. Part-time tuition per semester hour ranges from $53 for evening courses to $265 for daytime courses.

Graduate Part-time study available in Graduate School. Basic part-time expenses: $70 per credit (minimum) tuition.

Rhode Island College
Providence 02908

Public institution; city setting. Awards B, M. Barrier-free campus. Total enrollment: 9,178. Undergraduate enrollment: 7,676;

Colleges Offering Part-Time Degree Programs / Rhode Island

Rhode Island College (continued)

40% part-time, 63% women. Total faculty: 506. Library holdings: 270,000 bound volumes, 360,000 titles on microform, 2,100 periodical subscriptions, 2,000 records/tapes.

Undergraduate Courses offered for part-time students during daytime, evenings, summer. Complete part-time degree programs offered during daytime, evenings, summer. Adult/continuing education programs available. Career services available to part-time students: individual and group career counseling, individual job placement, employer recruitment on campus. Part-time tuition: $55 per credit for state residents, $135 per credit for nonresidents.

Graduate Part-time study available in Division of Graduate Studies. Basic part-time expenses: $62 per credit tuition plus $12 per semester fees for state residents, $130 per credit tuition plus $12 per semester fees for nonresidents.

Roger Williams College
Bristol 02809

Independent institution; small-town setting. Awards A, B. Barrier-free campus. Total enrollment: 2,500 (all undergraduates); 8% part-time, 45% women, 1% over 25. Total faculty: 120. Library holdings: 900,000 bound volumes, 12,000 titles on microform, 800 periodical subscriptions, 3,700 records/tapes.

Undergraduate Courses offered for part-time students during daytime, evenings, weekends, summer. Complete part-time degree programs offered during daytime, evenings, weekends, summer. External degree and adult/continuing education programs available. Career services available to part-time students: individual and group career counseling, individual job placement, employer recruitment on campus. Part-time tuition per course ranges from $175 for evening courses to $677 for daytime courses.

Salve Regina–The Newport College
Newport 02840

Independent-religious instutition; small-town setting. Awards A, B, M. Total enrollment: 2,120. Undergraduate enrollment: 1,751; 30% part-time, 75% women. Total faculty: 176. Library holdings: 80,000 bound volumes, 510 periodical subscriptions, 796 records/tapes.

Undergraduate Courses offered for part-time students during daytime, evenings, weekends, summer. Complete part-time degree programs offered during daytime, evenings, weekends, summer. Adult/continuing education programs available. Career services available to part-time students: individual and group career counseling, individual job placement, employer recruitment on campus. Part-time tuition per credit hour ranges from $110 for evening courses to $180 for daytime courses.

Graduate Part-time study available in Graduate School. Degree can be earned exclusively through evening/weekend study in Graduate School. Basic part-time expenses: $180 per credit tuition plus $30 per trimester fees. Institutional financial aid available to part-time graduate students in Graduate School.

University of Rhode Island
Kingston 02881

Public institution; small-town setting. Awards A, B, M, D. Total enrollment: 10,239. Undergraduate enrollment: 8,604; 7% part-time, 50% women. Total faculty: 857. Library holdings: 750,000 bound volumes, 650,000 titles on microform.

Undergraduate Courses offered for part-time students during daytime, evenings, weekends, summer. Complete part-time degree programs offered during daytime, evenings, weekends, summer. Adult/continuing education programs available. Career services available to part-time students: individual and group career counseling, individual job placement, employer recruitment on campus. Part-time tuition: $58 per credit for state residents, $203 per credit for nonresidents.

SOUTH CAROLINA

Aiken Technical College
Aiken 29802

Public institution; rural setting. Awards A. Barrier-free campus. Total enrollment: 1,201 (all undergraduates); 69% part-time, 40% women, 46% over 25. Total faculty: 135. Library holdings: 14,402 bound volumes, 54 periodical subscriptions, 6,672 records/tapes.

Undergraduate Courses offered for part-time students during daytime, evenings, summer. Complete part-time degree programs offered during daytime, evenings, summer. Adult/continuing education programs available. Career services available to part-time students: individual career counseling, individual job placement, employer recruitment on campus. Part-time tuition: $14 per credit hour for state residents, $21 per credit hour for nonresidents.

Anderson College
Anderson 29621

Independent-religious instutition; small-town setting. Awards A. Total enrollment: 972 (all undergraduates); 7% part-time, 59% women, 15% over 25. Total faculty: 57. Library holdings: 30,596 bound volumes, 150 periodical subscriptions.

Undergraduate Courses offered for part-time students during daytime, evenings, summer. Complete part-time degree programs offered during daytime, evenings, summer. External degree and adult/continuing education programs available. Part-time tuition: $70 per semester hour.

Baptist College at Charleston
Charleston 29411

Independent-religious instutition; city setting. Awards A, B, M. Barrier-free campus. Total enrollment: 1,966. Undergraduate enrollment: 1,940; 4% part-time, 61% women, 6% over 25. Total faculty: 102. Library holdings: 136,000 bound volumes, 962 periodical subscriptions, 900 records/tapes.

Undergraduate Courses offered for part-time students during daytime, evenings, summer. Complete part-time degree programs offered during daytime, evenings, summer. External degree programs available. Career services available to part-time students: individual and group career counseling, individual job placement, employer recruitment on campus. Part-time tuition: $79 per credit hour.

Beaufort Technical College
Beaufort 29902

Public institution; small-town setting. Awards A. Barrier-free campus. Total enrollment: 1,043 (all undergraduates); 46% part-time, 48% women, 75% over 25. Total faculty: 150. Library holdings: 12,751 bound volumes, 7,538 records/tapes.

Undergraduate Courses offered for part-time students during daytime, evenings, weekends, summer. Complete part-time degree programs offered during daytime, evenings, summer. Adult/continuing education programs available. Career ser-

South Carolina / **Colleges Offering Part-Time Degree Programs**

vices available to part-time students: individual and group career counseling, individual job placement, employer recruitment on campus. Part-time tuition: $15 per credit hour for area residents, $16 per credit hour for state residents, $21 per credit hour for nonresidents.

Benedict College
Columbia 29204

Independent-religious instutition; city setting. Awards B. Total enrollment: 1,457 (all undergraduates); 0% part-time, 63% women, 1% over 25. Total faculty: 97. Library holdings: 131,061 bound volumes, 5,142 titles on microform, 446 periodical subscriptions, 2,579 records/tapes.

Undergraduate Courses offered for part-time students during daytime. Complete part-time degree programs offered during daytime. Career services available to part-time students: individual and group career counseling, individual job placement, employer recruitment on campus. Part-time tuition: $90 per semester hour.

Bob Jones University
Greenville 29614

Independent-religious instutition; city setting. Awards A, B, M, D. Total enrollment: 4,619. Undergraduate enrollment: 4,266; 3% part-time, 52% women. Total faculty: 329. Library holdings: 190,000 bound volumes, 15,000 titles on microform, 730 periodical subscriptions, 6,500 records/tapes.

Undergraduate Courses offered for part-time students during daytime, summer. Complete part-time degree programs offered during daytime, summer. Career services available to part-time students: individual career counseling, individual job placement, employer recruitment on campus. Part-time tuition: $110 per semester hour.

Graduate Part-time study available in School of Education, School of Fine Arts, School of Religion.Basic part-time expenses: $110 per semester hour tuition plus $47.50 per semester (minimum) fees.

Central Wesleyan College
Central 29630

Independent-religious instutition; small-town setting. Awards B. Barrier-free campus. Total enrollment: 404 (all undergraduates); 14% part-time, 55% women. Total faculty: 40. Library holdings: 58,500 bound volumes, 325 titles on microform, 360 periodical subscriptions, 1,500 records/tapes.

Undergraduate Courses offered for part-time students during daytime, evenings, summer. Complete part-time degree programs offered during daytime, evenings, summer. Career services available to part-time students: individual and group career counseling. Part-time tuition: $140 per hour.

Chesterfield-Marlboro Technical College
Cheraw 29520

Public institution; rural setting. Awards A. Barrier-free campus. Total enrollment: 625 (all undergraduates); 32% part-time, 50% women, 66% over 25. Total faculty: 42. Library holdings: 15,441 bound volumes, 520 titles on microform, 108 periodical subscriptions, 514 records/tapes.

Undergraduate Courses offered for part-time students during daytime, evenings, weekends, summer. Complete part-time degree programs offered during daytime. Adult/continuing education programs available. Career services available to part-time students: individual and group career counseling, individual job placement, employer recruitment on campus. Part-time tuition: $14.58 per quarter hour for area residents, $15.42 per quarter hour for state residents, $21.67 per quarter hour for nonresidents.

The Citadel
Charleston 29409

Public institution; city setting. Awards B, M. Barrier-free campus. Total enrollment: 3,123. Undergraduate enrollment: 1,993; 0% part-time, 0% women, 0% over 25. Total faculty: 150. Library holdings: 250,000 bound volumes, 407,000 titles on microform, 1,450 periodical subscriptions.

Undergraduate Courses offered for part-time students during evenings, summer. Complete part-time degree programs offered during evenings, summer. Adult/continuing education programs available. Part-time tuition: $65 per semester hour for state residents, $65 per semester hour for nonresidents.

Graduate Part-time study available in Graduate Studies.Basic part-time expenses: $65 per credit tuition plus $5 per semester fees.

Claflin College
Orangeburg 29115

Independent-religious instutition; small-town setting. Awards B. Total enrollment: 633 (all undergraduates); 1% part-time, 64% women. Total faculty: 65.

Undergraduate Courses offered for part-time students during daytime. Complete part-time degree programs offered during daytime. Part-time tuition: $55 per credit hour.

Clemson University
Clemson 29631

Public institution; small-town setting. Awards B, M, D. Barrier-free campus. Total enrollment: 12,459. Undergraduate enrollment: 10,330; 4% part-time, 40% women. Total faculty: 1,005. Library holdings: 801,023 bound volumes, 102,028 titles on microform, 13,390 periodical subscriptions.

Graduate Part-time study available in Graduate School. Degree can be earned exclusively through evening/weekend study in Graduate School.Basic part-time expenses: $60 per semester hour tuition.

Coker College
Hartsville 29550

Independent institution; small-town setting. Awards B. Total enrollment: 355 (all undergraduates); 14% part-time, 58% women. Total faculty: 45. Library holdings: 60,000 bound volumes, 300 periodical subscriptions, 800 records/tapes.

Undergraduate Courses offered for part-time students during daytime, evenings, summer. Complete part-time degree programs offered during daytime, evenings. Adult/continuing education programs available. Career services available to part-time students: individual and group career counseling, individual job placement, employer recruitment on campus. Part-time tuition: $195 per semester hour.

College of Charleston
Charleston 29424

Public institution; city setting. Awards B, M. Barrier-free campus. Total enrollment: 5,323. Undergraduate enrollment: 5,091; 25% part-time, 63% women, 16% over 25. Total faculty: 326.

Colleges Offering Part-Time Degree Programs / *South Carolina*

College of Charleston (continued)
Library holdings: 215,000 bound volumes, 2,000 periodical subscriptions, 2,300 records/tapes.

Undergraduate Courses offered for part-time students during daytime, evenings, summer. Complete part-time degree programs offered during daytime. Adult/continuing education programs available. Career services available to part-time students: individual and group career counseling, individual job placement, employer recruitment on campus. Part-time tuition: $65 per semester hour for state residents, $65 per semester hour for nonresidents.

Graduate Part-time study available in Graduate Studies. Degree can be earned exclusively through evening/weekend study in Graduate Studies. Basic part-time expenses: $65 per hour tuition.

Columbia Bible College
Columbia 29230

Independent-religious instutition; city setting. Awards A, B, M. Total enrollment: 923. Undergraduate enrollment: 594; 13% part-time, 40% women, 30% over 25. Total faculty: 49. Library holdings: 63,689 bound volumes, 2,116 titles on microform, 625 periodical subscriptions, 10,551 records/tapes.

Graduate Part-time study available in Graduate School of Bible and Missions. Basic part-time expenses: $97 per credit tuition plus $46 per quarter fees. Institutional financial aid available to part-time graduate students in Graduate School of Bible and Missions.

Columbia College
Columbia 29203

Independent-religious instutition; city setting. Awards B, M. Total enrollment: 1,100. Undergraduate enrollment: 1,071; 18% part-time, 100% women. Total faculty: 76. Library holdings: 145,000 bound volumes, 630 titles on microform, 766 periodical subscriptions, 7,703 records/tapes.

Undergraduate Courses offered for part-time students during daytime, evenings. Complete part-time degree programs offered during daytime, evenings. Adult/continuing education programs available. Career services available to part-time students: individual and group career counseling, individual job placement, employer recruitment on campus. Part-time tuition: $140 per credit.

Graduate Part-time study available in Graduate Programs. Basic part-time expenses: $60 per semester hour tuition.

Columbia Junior College of Business
Columbia 29203

Proprietary institution; city setting. Awards A. Barrier-free campus. Total enrollment: 583 (all undergraduates); 7% part-time, 61% women, 15% over 25. Total faculty: 32.

Undergraduate Courses offered for part-time students during daytime, evenings, summer. Complete part-time degree programs offered during daytime, evenings. Career services available to part-time students: individual and group career counseling, individual job placement, employer recruitment on campus. Part-time tuition: $195 per course.

Converse College
Spartanburg 29301

Independent institution; city setting. Awards B, M. Total enrollment: 1,083. Undergraduate enrollment: 692; 1% part-time, 100% women, 11% over 25. Total faculty: 85. Library holdings: 115,000 bound volumes, 520 periodical subscriptions, 7,800 records/tapes.

Undergraduate Courses offered for part-time students during daytime, evenings, summer. Complete part-time degree programs offered during daytime, evenings, summer. Adult/continuing education programs available. Career services available to part-time students: individual and group career counseling, individual job placement, employer recruitment on campus. Part-time tuition: $150 per credit hour.

Graduate Part-time study available in Graduate Programs in Education, School of Music. Basic part-time expenses: $70 per semester hour tuition. Institutional financial aid available to part-time graduate students in Graduate Programs in Education, School of Music.

Denmark Technical College
Denmark 29042

Public institution; rural setting. Awards A. Barrier-free campus. Total enrollment: 783 (all undergraduates); 9% part-time, 51% women, 25% over 25. Total faculty: 44. Library holdings: 16,200 bound volumes, 12,101 titles on microform, 152 periodical subscriptions, 915 records/tapes.

Undergraduate Courses offered for part-time students during daytime, evenings, summer. Complete part-time degree programs offered during daytime, evenings, summer. Adult/continuing education programs available. Career services available to part-time students: individual and group career counseling, individual job placement, employer recruitment on campus. Part-time tuition: $12 per credit.

Erskine College
Due West 29639

Independent-religious instutition; rural setting. Awards B. Barrier-free campus. Total enrollment: 489 (all undergraduates); 5% part-time, 45% women, 1% over 25. Total faculty: 53. Library holdings: 130,000 bound volumes.

Undergraduate Courses offered for part-time students during daytime, summer. Complete part-time degree programs offered during daytime, summer. Career services available to part-time students: individual and group career counseling, individual job placement, employer recruitment on campus. Part-time tuition: $120 per semester hour.

Erskine Theological Seminary
Due West 29639

Independent-religious institution (graduate only). Total enrollment: 122 (coed; 6% part-time). Total faculty: 15.

Graduate Part-time study available in Graduate and Professional Programs. Basic part-time expenses: $75 per semester hour (minimum) tuition.

Florence-Darlington Technical College
Florence 29501

Public institution; rural setting. Awards A. Barrier-free campus. Total enrollment: 2,174 (all undergraduates); 28% part-time, 45% women. Total faculty: 178. Library holdings: 25,966 bound volumes, 1,574 titles on microform, 267 periodical subscriptions, 143 records/tapes.

Undergraduate Courses offered for part-time students during daytime, evenings. Complete part-time degree programs offered during daytime, evenings. Adult/continuing education pro-

South Carolina / Colleges Offering Part-Time Degree Programs

grams available. Part-time tuition: $17 per credit hour for area residents, $21 per credit hour for state residents, $28 per credit hour for nonresidents.

Francis Marion College
Florence 29501

Public institution; rural setting. Awards A, B, M. Barrier-free campus. Total enrollment: 3,131. Undergraduate enrollment: 2,782; 21% part-time, 52% women, 18% over 25. Total faculty: 137. Library holdings: 200,122 bound volumes, 45,782 titles on microform, 1,403 periodical subscriptions, 6,442 records/tapes.

Undergraduate Courses offered for part-time students during daytime, evenings, summer. Complete part-time degree programs offered during daytime, evenings, summer. Adult/continuing education programs available. Career services available to part-time students: individual and group career counseling, individual job placement, employer recruitment on campus. Part-time tuition: $47 per semester hour for state residents, $94 per semester hour for nonresidents.

Graduate Part-time study available in Graduate Programs. Degree can be earned exclusively through evening/weekend study in Graduate Programs. Basic part-time expenses: $53 per semester hour tuition for state residents, $106 per semester hour tuition for nonresidents.

Furman University
Greenville 29613

Independent-religious instutition; city setting. Awards B, M. Barrier-free campus. Total enrollment: 2,625. Undergraduate enrollment: 2,441; 2% part-time, 49% women, 2% over 25. Total faculty: 163. Library holdings: 285,000 bound volumes, 1,600 periodical subscriptions, 1,400 records/tapes.

Undergraduate Courses offered for part-time students during daytime, evenings, summer. Complete part-time degree programs offered during daytime, evenings, summer. Adult/continuing education programs available. Career services available to part-time students: individual and group career counseling, individual job placement, employer recruitment on campus. Part-time tuition: $167 per credit.

Greenville Technical College
Greenville 29606

Public institution; city setting. Awards A. Barrier-free campus. Total enrollment: 9,103 (all undergraduates); 60% part-time, 50% women, 33% over 25. Total faculty: 377. Library holdings: 37,700 bound volumes, 413 periodical subscriptions, 1,500 records/tapes.

Undergraduate Courses offered for part-time students during daytime, evenings, summer. Complete part-time degree programs offered during daytime, evenings, summer. Adult/continuing education programs available. Career services available to part-time students: individual and group career counseling, individual job placement, employer recruitment on campus. Part-time tuition: $15.50 per quarter hour for area residents, $17.25 per quarter hour for state residents, $28.75 per quarter hour for nonresidents.

Lander College
Greenwood 29646

Public institution; small-town setting. Awards B, M. Barrier-free campus. Total enrollment: 2,136. Undergraduate enrollment: 2,075; 15% part-time, 62% women, 12% over 25. Total faculty: 113. Library holdings: 109,338 bound volumes, 34,419 titles on microform, 805 periodical subscriptions.

Undergraduate Courses offered for part-time students during daytime, evenings, summer. Complete part-time degree programs offered during daytime, evenings. Adult/continuing education programs available. Career services available to part-time students: individual and group career counseling, individual job placement, employer recruitment on campus. Part-time tuition: $60 per semester hour for state residents, $60 per semester hour for nonresidents.

Lutheran Theological Southern Seminary
Columbia 29203

Independent-religious institution (graduate only). Total enrollment: 181 (coed; 32% part-time). Total faculty: 21.

Graduate Part-time study available in Graduate and Professional Programs. Basic part-time expenses: $90 per semester hour tuition plus $15 per year fees. Institutional financial aid available to part-time graduate students in Graduate and Professional Programs.

Midlands Technical College
Columbia 29202

Public institution; city setting. Awards A. Barrier-free campus. Total enrollment: 4,967 (all undergraduates); 41% part-time, 48% women, 40% over 25. Total faculty: 457. Library holdings: 59,336 bound volumes, 193 titles on microform, 193 periodical subscriptions, 839 records/tapes.

Undergraduate Courses offered for part-time students during daytime, evenings, summer. Complete part-time degree programs offered during daytime, evenings, summer. Adult/continuing education programs available. Career services available to part-time students: individual and group career counseling, individual job placement, employer recruitment on campus. Part-time tuition: $21 per credit hour for area residents, $27 per credit hour for state residents, $53 per credit hour for nonresidents.

Morris College
Sumter 29150

Independent-religious instutition; small-town setting. Awards B. Total enrollment: 584 (all undergraduates); 4% part-time, 63% women. Total faculty: 44. Library holdings: 119,204 bound volumes, 604 periodical subscriptions, 1,000 records/tapes.

Undergraduate Courses offered for part-time students during daytime, evenings. Complete part-time degree programs offered during daytime, evenings. Career services available to part-time students: individual and group career counseling, individual job placement, employer recruitment on campus. Part-time tuition: $111 per credit hour.

North Greenville College
Tigerville 29688

Independent-religious instutition; rural setting. Awards A. Barrier-free campus. Total enrollment: 485 (all undergraduates); 12% part-time, 38% women, 3% over 25. Total faculty: 34. Library holdings: 34,521 bound volumes, 874 titles on microform, 10 periodical subscriptions, 2,595 records/tapes.

Undergraduate Courses offered for part-time students during daytime, evenings, summer. Complete part-time degree programs offered during daytime, evenings, summer. Adult/con-

Colleges Offering Part-Time Degree Programs / South Carolina

North Greenville College (continued)
tinuing education programs available. Career services available to part-time students: individual and group career counseling, individual job placement, employer recruitment on campus. Part-time tuition: $125 per semester hour.

Orangeburg-Calhoun Technical College
Orangeburg 29115

Public institution; rural setting. Awards A. Barrier-free campus. Total enrollment: 976 (all undergraduates); 30% part-time, 40% women. Total faculty: 177. Library holdings: 13,500 bound volumes, 210 periodical subscriptions, 1,110 records/tapes.

Undergraduate Courses offered for part-time students during daytime, evenings, summer. Complete part-time degree programs offered during daytime, evenings, summer. Adult/continuing education programs available. Career services available to part-time students: individual and group career counseling, individual job placement, employer recruitment on campus. Part-time tuition: $14.60 per credit hour for area residents, $18.75 per credit hour for state residents, $23 per credit hour for nonresidents.

Piedmont Technical College
Greenwood 29648

Public institution; small-town setting. Awards A. Total enrollment: 1,700 (all undergraduates); 5% part-time, 20% women, 35% over 25. Total faculty: 175.

Undergraduate Courses offered for part-time students during daytime, evenings, summer. Complete part-time degree programs offered during daytime, evenings. Adult/continuing education programs available. Career services available to part-time students: individual career counseling, individual job placement, employer recruitment on campus. Part-time tuition: $16 per quarter hour for area residents, $17.50 per quarter hour for state residents, $22 per quarter hour for nonresidents.

Presbyterian College
Clinton 29325

Independent-religious instutition; small-town setting. Awards B. Total enrollment: 895 (all undergraduates); 1% part-time, 42% women. Total faculty: 92. Library holdings: 135,000 bound volumes, 4,500 titles on microform, 700 periodical subscriptions, 2,500 records/tapes.

Undergraduate Courses offered for part-time students during daytime. Complete part-time degree programs offered during daytime. Career services available to part-time students: individual and group career counseling, individual job placement, employer recruitment on campus. Part-time tuition: $175 per credit.

Rutledge College
Columbia 29201

Proprietary institution; city setting. Awards A. Total enrollment: 461 (all undergraduates); 1% part-time, 80% women, 39% over 25. Total faculty: 18. Library holdings: 15,000 bound volumes, 15 periodical subscriptions.

Undergraduate Courses offered for part-time students during daytime, evenings, summer. Complete part-time degree programs offered during daytime, evenings, summer. Career services available to part-time students: individual and group career counseling, individual job placement. Part-time tuition: $49 per quarter hour.

Rutledge College
Greenville 29601

Proprietary institution; city setting. Awards A. Barrier-free campus. Total enrollment: 300 (all undergraduates); 5% part-time, 80% women. Total faculty: 17. Library holdings: 2,500 bound volumes, 80 periodical subscriptions.

Undergraduate Courses offered for part-time students during daytime, evenings, summer. Complete part-time degree programs offered during daytime, evenings, summer. Adult/continuing education programs available. Career services available to part-time students: individual career counseling, individual job placement. Part-time tuition: $53 per quarter hour.

Rutledge College
North Charleston 29406

Proprietary institution; city setting. Awards A. Barrier-free campus. Total enrollment: 600 (all undergraduates); 10% part-time, 65% women, 33% over 25. Total faculty: 18.

Undergraduate Courses offered for part-time students during daytime, evenings. Complete part-time degree programs offered during daytime, evenings. Career services available to part-time students: individual and group career counseling, individual job placement. Part-time tuition: $49 per quarter hour.

Rutledge College
Spartanburg 29303

Proprietary institution; city setting. Awards A. Barrier-free campus. Total enrollment: 458 (all undergraduates); 8% part-time, 84% women. Total faculty: 17. Library holdings: 2,800 bound volumes, 40 periodical subscriptions, 70 records/tapes.

Undergraduate Courses offered for part-time students during daytime, evenings, summer. Complete part-time degree programs offered during daytime, evenings, summer. Adult/continuing education programs available. Career services available to part-time students: individual and group career counseling, individual job placement. Part-time tuition: $53 per quarter hour.

South Carolina State College
Orangeburg 29117

Public institution; small-town setting. Awards B, M. Total enrollment: 4,187. Undergraduate enrollment: 3,709; 15% part-time, 52% women. Total faculty: 250. Library holdings: 228,028 bound volumes, 276,102 titles on microform, 1,096 periodical subscriptions.

Undergraduate Courses offered for part-time students during daytime. Complete part-time degree programs offered during daytime. Adult/continuing education programs available. Career services available to part-time students: individual and group career counseling, individual job placement. Part-time tuition: $45 per semester hour for state residents, $85 per semester hour for nonresidents.

Spartanburg Methodist College
Spartanburg 29301

Independent-religious instutition; city setting. Awards A. Barrier-free campus. Total enrollment: 1,072 (all undergraduates); 10% part-time, 40% women. Total faculty: 76. Library holdings: 27,250 bound volumes, 52 titles on microform, 165 periodical subscriptions, 1,085 records/tapes.

South Carolina / **Colleges Offering Part-Time Degree Programs**

Undergraduate Courses offered for part-time students during daytime, evenings, weekends, summer. Complete part-time degree programs offered during daytime, evenings, weekends, summer. Part-time tuition: $70 per semester hour.

Spartanburg Technical College
Spartanburg 29303

Public institution; city setting. Awards A. Barrier-free campus. Total enrollment: 2,025 (all undergraduates); 30% part-time, 40% women. Total faculty: 180.

Undergraduate Courses offered for part-time students during daytime, evenings. Complete part-time degree programs offered during daytime, evenings. Adult/continuing education programs available. Career services available to part-time students: individual and group career counseling, individual job placement, employer recruitment on campus. Part-time tuition: $12.75 per quarter hour for area residents, $15.75 per quarter hour for state residents, $34.75 per quarter hour for nonresidents.

Sumter Area Technical College
Sumter 29150

Public institution; small-town setting. Awards A. Barrier-free campus. Total enrollment: 1,738 (all undergraduates); 37% part-time, 39% women, 44% over 25. Total faculty: 231. Library holdings: 18,550 bound volumes, 44 periodical subscriptions, 1,529 records/tapes.

Undergraduate Courses offered for part-time students during daytime, evenings, summer. Complete part-time degree programs offered during daytime, evenings, summer. Adult/continuing education programs available. Career services available to part-time students: individual and group career counseling, individual job placement, employer recruitment on campus. Part-time tuition: $15 per quarter hour for area residents, $17 per quarter hour for state residents, $24 per quarter hour for nonresidents.

Tri-County Technical College
Pendleton 29670

Public institution; rural setting. Awards A. Barrier-free campus. Total enrollment: 2,405 (all undergraduates); 38% part-time, 49% women. Total faculty: 150. Library holdings: 37,000 bound volumes.

Undergraduate Courses offered for part-time students during daytime, evenings. Complete part-time degree programs offered during daytime, evenings. Adult/continuing education programs available. Career services available to part-time students: individual and group career counseling, individual job placement, employer recruitment on campus. Part-time tuition: $13 per quarter hour for state residents, $26 per quarter hour for nonresidents.

Trident Technical College
Charleston 29411

Public institution; city setting. Awards A. Barrier-free campus. Total enrollment: 5,189 (all undergraduates); 55% part-time, 54% women. Total faculty: 288.

Undergraduate Courses offered for part-time students during daytime, evenings, weekends, summer. Complete part-time degree programs offered during daytime, evenings. Part-time tuition: $15 per credit hour for area residents, $17 per credit hour for state residents, $30 per credit hour for nonresidents.

University of South Carolina
Columbia 29208

Public institution; city setting. Awards B, M, D. Barrier-free campus. Total enrollment: 24,296. Undergraduate enrollment: 16,123; 18% part-time, 50% women, 16% over 25. Total faculty: 1,253. Library holdings: 2 million bound volumes, 2.2 million titles on microform, 16,200 periodical subscriptions, 5,118 records/tapes.

Undergraduate Courses offered for part-time students during daytime, evenings, weekends, summer. Complete part-time degree programs offered during daytime, evenings, summer. Adult/continuing education programs available. Career services available to part-time students: individual and group career counseling, individual job placement, employer recruitment on campus. Part-time tuition: $58 per semester hour for state residents, $125 per semester hour for nonresidents.

Graduate Part-time study available in Graduate School. Basic part-time expenses: $60 per semester hour tuition.

University of South Carolina at Aiken
Aiken 29801

Public institution; small-town setting. Awards A, B. Barrier-free campus. Total enrollment: 1,932 (all undergraduates); 39% part-time, 53% women, 33% over 25. Total faculty: 150. Library holdings: 76,630 bound volumes, 11,600 titles on microform, 1,125 periodical subscriptions, 430 records/tapes.

Undergraduate Courses offered for part-time students during daytime, evenings, summer. Complete part-time degree programs offered during daytime, evenings, summer. Adult/continuing education programs available. Career services available to part-time students: individual and group career counseling, individual job placement, employer recruitment on campus. Part-time tuition: $42 per semester hour for state residents, $84 per semester hour for nonresidents.

University of South Carolina at Beaufort
Beaufort 29902

Public institution; small-town setting. Awards A. Total enrollment: 500 (all undergraduates); 55% part-time, 45% women, 50% over 25. Total faculty: 40. Library holdings: 30,000 bound volumes, 300 periodical subscriptions.

Undergraduate Courses offered for part-time students during daytime, evenings, summer. Complete part-time degree programs offered during daytime, evenings, summer. Adult/continuing education programs available. Career services available to part-time students: individual and group career counseling, individual job placement. Part-time tuition: $40 per credit hour for state residents, $80 per credit hour for nonresidents.

University of South Carolina at Lancaster
Lancaster 29720

Public institution; small-town setting. Awards A. Barrier-free campus. Total enrollment: 791 (all undergraduates); 45% part-time, 66% women, 39% over 25. Total faculty: 44. Library holdings: 50,000 bound volumes, 500 periodical subscriptions.

Undergraduate Courses offered for part-time students during evenings. Complete part-time degree programs offered during evenings. Adult/continuing education programs available. Career services available to part-time students: individual career counseling. Part-time tuition: $40 per hour for state residents, $80 per hour for nonresidents.

Colleges Offering Part-Time Degree Programs / South Carolina

University of South Carolina at Salkehatchie
Allendale 29810

Public institution; rural setting. Awards A. Barrier-free campus. Total enrollment: 464 (all undergraduates); 40% part-time, 65% women. Total faculty: 36. Library holdings: 28,000 bound volumes, 300 periodical subscriptions, 600 records/tapes.

Undergraduate Courses offered for part-time students during daytime, evenings, summer. Complete part-time degree programs offered during daytime, evenings. Adult/continuing education programs available. Career services available to part-time students: individual career counseling. Part-time tuition: $40 per semester hour for state residents, $80 per semester hour for nonresidents.

University of South Carolina at Spartanburg
Spartanburg 29303

Public institution; city setting. Awards A, B. Barrier-free campus. Total enrollment: 2,728 (all undergraduates); 40% part-time, 60% women, 35% over 25. Total faculty: 189. Library holdings: 125,000 bound volumes, 4,000 titles on microform.

Undergraduate Courses offered for part-time students during daytime, evenings, summer. Complete part-time degree programs offered during daytime, evenings, summer. Adult/continuing education programs available. Career services available to part-time students: individual and group career counseling, individual job placement, employer recruitment on campus. Part-time tuition: $42 per credit hour for state residents, $84 per credit hour for nonresidents.

University of South Carolina at Sumter
Sumter 29150

Public institution; small-town setting. Awards A. Barrier-free campus. Total enrollment: 1,147 (all undergraduates); 48% part-time, 52% women. Total faculty: 44. Library holdings: 40,186 bound volumes, 339 periodical subscriptions, 575 records/tapes.

Undergraduate Courses offered for part-time students during daytime, evenings, summer. Complete part-time degree programs offered during daytime, evenings, summer. Adult/continuing education programs available. Career services available to part-time students: individual and group career counseling, employer recruitment on campus. Part-time tuition: $40 per semester hour for state residents, $80 per semester hour for nonresidents.

University of South Carolina–Coastal Carolina College
Conway 29526

Public institution; rural setting. Awards A, B. Barrier-free campus. Total enrollment: 2,470 (all undergraduates); 30% part-time, 51% women, 27% over 25. Total faculty: 140. Library holdings: 80,000 bound volumes, 850 periodical subscriptions, 4,000 records/tapes.

Undergraduate Courses offered for part-time students during daytime, evenings, summer. Complete part-time degree programs offered during daytime, evenings, summer. Adult/continuing education programs available. Career services available to part-time students: individual and group career counseling, individual job placement, employer recruitment on campus. Part-time tuition: $42 per semester hour for state residents, $84 per semester hour for nonresidents.

Voorhees College
Denmark 29042

Independent-religious instutition; small-town setting. Awards A, B. Total enrollment: 585 (all undergraduates); 2% part-time, 64% women. Total faculty: 56. Library holdings: 90,000 bound volumes, 5,829 periodical subscriptions, 264 records/tapes.

Undergraduate Courses offered for part-time students during daytime, evenings. Complete part-time degree programs offered during daytime, evenings. Adult/continuing education programs available. Career services available to part-time students: individual and group career counseling, individual job placement, employer recruitment on campus. Part-time tuition: $66 per credit hour.

Williamsburg Technical College
Kingstree 29556

Public institution; rural setting. Awards A. Barrier-free campus. Total enrollment: 438 (all undergraduates); 53% part-time, 52% women. Total faculty: 35.

Undergraduate Courses offered for part-time students during daytime, evenings, summer. Complete part-time degree programs offered during daytime, evenings, summer. Adult/continuing education programs available. Career services available to part-time students: individual and group career counseling, individual job placement. Part-time tuition: $11 per credit hour.

Winthrop College
Rock Hill 29733

Public institution; small-town setting. Awards B, M. Barrier-free campus. Total enrollment: 4,999. Undergraduate enrollment: 4,093; 20% part-time, 69% women. Total faculty: 313. Library holdings: 301,500 bound volumes, 632,581 titles on microform, 3,187 periodical subscriptions, 1,160 records/tapes.

Undergraduate Courses offered for part-time students during daytime, evenings, summer. Complete part-time degree programs offered during daytime, evenings. Adult/continuing education programs available. Career services available to part-time students: individual and group career counseling, employer recruitment on campus. Part-time tuition: $49 per credit hour for state residents, $89 per credit hour for nonresidents.

Graduate Part-time study available in College of Arts and Sciences, School of Business Administration, School of Consumer Science and Allied Professions, School of Education, School of Music. Basic part-time expenses: $52 per hour tuition. Institutional financial aid available to part-time graduate students in College of Arts and Sciences, School of Business Administration, School of Consumer Science and Allied Professions, School of Education.

Wofford College
Spartanburg 29301

Independent-religious instutition; city setting. Awards B. Barrier-free campus. Total enrollment: 1,046 (all undergraduates); 7% part-time, 28% women. Total faculty: 75. Library holdings: 200,000 bound volumes, 19,738 titles on microform, 631 periodical subscriptions.

Undergraduate Courses offered for part-time students during daytime, summer. Complete part-time degree programs offered during daytime, summer. Adult/continuing education programs available. Career services available to part-time students: individual and group career counseling, individual job placement, employer recruitment on campus. Part-time tuition: $160 per semester hour.

York Technical College
Rock Hill 29730

Public institution; small-town setting. Awards A. Barrier-free campus. Total enrollment: 2,189 (all undergraduates); 34% part-time, 41% women. Total faculty: 111.

Undergraduate Courses offered for part-time students during daytime, evenings, summer. Complete part-time degree programs offered during daytime, evenings, summer. Adult/continuing education programs available. Career services available to part-time students: individual and group career counseling, individual job placement, employer recruitment on campus. Part-time tuition: $11 per credit for area residents, $13.25 per credit for state residents, $22 per credit for nonresidents.

SOUTH DAKOTA

Augustana College
Sioux Falls 57197

Independent-religious instutition; city setting. Awards A, B, M. Total enrollment: 1,957. Undergraduate enrollment: 1,906; 12% part-time, 59% women, 5% over 25. Total faculty: 163. Library holdings: 235,000 bound volumes, 1,100 periodical subscriptions, 5,067 records/tapes.

Undergraduate Courses offered for part-time students during daytime, evenings, weekends, summer. Complete part-time degree programs offered during daytime, evenings, weekends, summer. Adult/continuing education programs available. Career services available to part-time students: individual and group career counseling, individual job placement, employer recruitment on campus. Part-time tuition: $100 per credit.

Black Hills State College
Spearfish 57783

Public institution; small-town setting. Awards A, B, M (M in summer session only). Total enrollment: 2,218 (all undergraduates); 3% part-time, 54% women, 11% over 25. Total faculty: 104. Library holdings: 200,000 bound volumes, 30,000 titles on microform, 700 periodical subscriptions, 200 records/tapes.

Undergraduate Courses offered for part-time students during daytime, evenings, summer. Complete part-time degree programs offered during daytime, evenings, summer. External degree and adult/continuing education programs available. Career services available to part-time students: individual and group career counseling, individual job placement, employer recruitment on campus. Part-time tuition: $29.50 per semester hour for state residents, $62.50 per semester hour for nonresidents.

Community College of the North Central University Center
Sioux Falls 57105

Independent institution; city setting. Awards A. Barrier-free campus. Total enrollment: 310 (all undergraduates); 70% part-time, 68% women. Total faculty: 63. Library holdings: 78,000 bound volumes, 590 titles on microform, 395 periodical subscriptions, 4,785 records/tapes.

Undergraduate Courses offered for part-time students during daytime, evenings, summer. Complete part-time degree programs offered during daytime, evenings, summer. External degree and adult/continuing education programs available. Career services available to part-time students: individual and group career counseling. Part-time tuition: $58 per quarter hour.

Dakota State College
Madison 57042

Public institution; rural setting. Awards A, B. Total enrollment: 1,246 (all undergraduates); 12% part-time, 58% women. Total faculty: 72. Library holdings: 11,649 bound volumes, 28 titles on microform, 115 periodical subscriptions, 3,727 records/tapes.

Undergraduate Courses offered for part-time students during daytime, evenings, summer. Complete part-time degree programs offered during daytime, summer. External degree programs available. Career services available to part-time students: individual and group career counseling, individual job placement, employer recruitment on campus. Part-time tuition: $29.50 per credit hour for state residents, $62.50 per credit hour for nonresidents.

Dakota Wesleyan University
Mitchell 57301

Independent-religious instutition; small-town setting. Awards A, B. Total enrollment: 495 (all undergraduates); 23% part-time, 65% women. Total faculty: 60. Library holdings: 73,000 bound volumes, 3,500 titles on microform, 352 periodical subscriptions, 5,500 records/tapes.

Undergraduate Courses offered for part-time students during daytime, evenings, weekends, summer. Complete part-time degree programs offered during daytime, evenings, weekends, summer. Adult/continuing education programs available. Career services available to part-time students: individual and group career counseling, individual job placement, employer recruitment on campus. Part-time tuition: $500 per unit.

Freeman Junior College
Freeman 57029

Independent-religious instutition; rural setting. Awards A. Total enrollment: 68 (all undergraduates); 10% part-time, 68% women, 30% over 25. Total faculty: 25. Library holdings: 17,500 bound volumes, 70 periodical subscriptions.

Undergraduate Courses offered for part-time students during daytime, evenings, summer. Complete part-time degree programs offered during daytime. Adult/continuing education programs available. Career services available to part-time students: individual and group career counseling. Part-time tuition: $130 per credit.

Mount Marty College
Yankton 57078

Independent-religious instutition; small-town setting. Awards A, B, M. Barrier-free campus. Total enrollment: 650. Undergraduate enrollment: 645; 22% part-time, 70% women. Total faculty: 58. Library holdings: 77,000 bound volumes, 700 periodical subscriptions, 7,600 records/tapes.

Undergraduate Courses offered for part-time students during daytime, evenings. Complete part-time degree programs offered during daytime, evenings. Adult/continuing education programs available. Career services available to part-time students: individual career counseling, individual job placement, employer recruitment on campus. Part-time tuition: $110 per credit hour.

Graduate Part-time study available in Graduate Program in Anesthesia. Basic part-time expenses: $300 per semester (minimum) tuition plus $85 per semester fees.

Colleges Offering Part-Time Degree Programs / South Dakota

National College
Rapid City 57709

Proprietary institution; city setting. Awards A, B. Barrier-free campus. Total enrollment: 1,033 (all undergraduates); 9% part-time, 57% women. Total faculty: 63. Library holdings: 25,543 bound volumes, 26 titles on microform, 597 periodical subscriptions, 1,050 records/tapes.

Undergraduate Courses offered for part-time students during daytime, evenings, summer. Complete part-time degree programs offered during daytime, evenings. Adult/continuing education programs available. Career services available to part-time students: individual and group career counseling, individual job placement, employer recruitment on campus. Part-time tuition: $113 per credit hour.

North American Baptist Seminary
Sioux Falls 57105

Independent-religious institution (graduate only). Total enrollment: 186 (coed; 44% part-time). Total faculty: 20.

Graduate Part-time study available in Graduate and Professional Programs. Basic part-time expenses: $140 per credit tuition. Institutional financial aid available to part-time graduate students in Graduate and Professional Programs.

Northern State College
Aberdeen 57401

Public institution; small-town setting. Awards A, B, M. Total enrollment: 2,718. Undergraduate enrollment: 2,546; 27% part-time, 58% women, 27% over 25. Total faculty: 110. Library holdings: 126,518 bound volumes, 26,234 titles on microform, 803 periodical subscriptions, 2,700 records/tapes.

Undergraduate Courses offered for part-time students during daytime, evenings, summer. Complete part-time degree programs offered during daytime, evenings, summer. Adult/continuing education programs available. Career services available to part-time students: individual and group career counseling, individual job placement, employer recruitment on campus. Part-time tuition: $29.50 per semester hour for state residents, $62.50 per semester hour for nonresidents.

Graduate Part-time study available in Division of Graduate Studies. Basic part-time expenses: $44 per hour tuition plus $6.25 per hour fees for state residents, $82 per hour tuition plus $6.25 per hour fees for nonresidents. Institutional financial aid available to part-time graduate students in Division of Graduate Studies.

Oglala Lakota College
Kyle 57752

Public institution; rural setting. Awards A, B. Barrier-free campus. Total enrollment: 643 (all undergraduates); 51% part-time, 62% women. Total faculty: 57. Library holdings: 23,000 bound volumes, 110 periodical subscriptions, 200 records/tapes.

Undergraduate Courses offered for part-time students during daytime, evenings, summer. Complete part-time degree programs offered during daytime, evenings, summer. Adult/continuing education programs available. Career services available to part-time students: individual career counseling. Part-time tuition: $20 per credit hour for state residents, $40 per credit hour for nonresidents.

Presentation College
Aberdeen 57401

Independent-religious instutition; small-town setting. Awards A. Barrier-free campus. Total enrollment: 352 (all undergraduates); 35% part-time, 88% women, 45% over 25. Total faculty: 40. Library holdings: 1,223 bound volumes, 12 titles on microform, 190 periodical subscriptions, 1,553 records/tapes.

Undergraduate Courses offered for part-time students during daytime, evenings, summer. Complete part-time degree programs offered during daytime. Adult/continuing education programs available. Career services available to part-time students: individual career counseling. Part-time tuition: $95 per semester hour.

Sioux Falls College
Sioux Falls 57105

Independent-religious instutition; city setting. Awards A, B, M. Total enrollment: 872. Undergraduate enrollment: 868; 32% part-time, 62% women, 20% over 25. Total faculty: 60. Library holdings: 76,500 bound volumes, 500 periodical subscriptions, 4,600 records/tapes.

Undergraduate Courses offered for part-time students during daytime, evenings, weekends, summer. Complete part-time degree programs offered during daytime, evenings. Adult/continuing education programs available. Career services available to part-time students: individual career counseling, individual job placement, employer recruitment on campus. Part-time tuition: $98 per semester hour.

Graduate Part-time study available in Graduate Program in Education. Degree can be earned exclusively through evening/weekend study in Graduate Program in Education. Basic part-time expenses: $105 per hour (minimum) tuition. Institutional financial aid available to part-time graduate students in Graduate Program in Education.

South Dakota School of Mines and Technology
Rapid City 57701

Public institution; city setting. Awards B, M, D. Total enrollment: 2,908. Undergraduate enrollment: 2,686; 23% part-time, 30% women. Total faculty: 137. Library holdings: 180,000 bound volumes, 1,000 periodical subscriptions.

Graduate Part-time study available in Graduate Division. Basic part-time expenses: $46 per credit hour tuition plus $7.17 per credit hour fees for state residents, $89 per credit hour tuition plus $7.17 per credit hour fees for nonresidents. Institutional financial aid available to part-time graduate students in Graduate Division.

South Dakota State University
Brookings 57007

Public institution; rural setting. Awards A, B, M, D. Total enrollment: 7,028. Undergraduate enrollment: 6,393; 9% part-time, 49% women. Total faculty: 401. Library holdings: 300,000 bound volumes, 121,472 titles on microform, 3,000 periodical subscriptions, 1,349 records/tapes.

Undergraduate Courses offered for part-time students during daytime, evenings, weekends, summer. Complete part-time degree programs offered during daytime. Adult/continuing education programs available. Career services available to part-time students: individual and group career counseling, individual job placement, employer recruitment on campus. Part-time tuition: $30.65 per credit for state residents, $69.51 per credit for nonresidents.

Graduate Part-time study available in Graduate School. Basic part-time expenses: $46 per credit tuition plus $12 per credit fees for state residents, $89 per credit tuition plus $12 per credit fees for nonresidents.

University of South Dakota
Vermillion 57069

Public institution; small-town setting. Awards A, B, M, D. Total enrollment: 6,001. Undergraduate enrollment: 4,679; 2% part-time, 51% women. Total faculty: 440. Library holdings: 482,410 bound volumes, 4,609 periodical subscriptions, 12,928 records/tapes.

Undergraduate Courses offered for part-time students during daytime, evenings, summer. Complete part-time degree programs offered during daytime, evenings, summer. External degree and adult/continuing education programs available. Career services available to part-time students: individual career counseling, individual job placement, employer recruitment on campus. Part-time tuition: $30.50 per credit for state residents, $69.50 per credit for nonresidents.

Graduate Part-time study available in Graduate School. Basic part-time expenses: $46 per hour tuition plus $10.05 per hour fees for state residents, $89 per hour tuition plus $10.05 per hour fees for nonresidents. Institutional financial aid available to part-time graduate students in Graduate School.

Yankton College
Yankton 57078

Independent-religious instutition; small-town setting. Awards A, B. Total enrollment: 304 (all undergraduates); 11% part-time, 41% women, 15% over 25. Total faculty: 40. Library holdings: 61,000 bound volumes, 390 periodical subscriptions, 5,200 records/tapes.

Undergraduate Courses offered for part-time students during daytime, evenings, summer. Complete part-time degree programs offered during daytime, evenings, summer. Adult/continuing education programs available. Career services available to part-time students: individual and group career counseling, individual job placement, employer recruitment on campus. Part-time tuition per semester hour ranges from $115 (for students taking 1 to 8 semester hours) to $160 (for students taking 9 to 11 semester hours).

TENNESSEE

American Baptist College of American Baptist Theological Seminary
Nashville 37207

Independent-religious instutition; metropolitan setting. Awards B. Total enrollment: 150 (all undergraduates); 10% part-time, 15% women. Total faculty: 12. Library holdings: 25,232 bound volumes, 167 periodical subscriptions.

Undergraduate Courses offered for part-time students during daytime, evenings, summer. Complete part-time degree programs offered during daytime, evenings, summer. Adult/continuing education programs available. Career services available to part-time students: group career counseling. Part-time tuition: $81 per credit hour.

Aquinas Junior College
Nashville 37205

Independent-religious instutition; metropolitan setting. Awards A. Total enrollment: 148 (all undergraduates); 60% part-time, 40% women. Total faculty: 47. Library holdings: 20,000 bound volumes, 170 periodical subscriptions, 1,300 records/tapes.

Undergraduate Courses offered for part-time students during daytime, evenings, summer. Complete part-time degree programs offered during daytime, evenings, summer. External degree programs available. Career services available to part-time students: individual career counseling. Part-time tuition: $65 per semester hour.

Austin Peay State University
Clarksville 37044

Public institution; city setting. Awards A, B, M. Total enrollment: 5,393. Undergraduate enrollment: 5,122; 28% part-time, 56% women, 29% over 25. Total faculty: 257. Library holdings: 213,330 bound volumes, 962 periodical subscriptions, 4,425 records/tapes.

Undergraduate Courses offered for part-time students during daytime, evenings, summer. Complete part-time degree programs offered during daytime. Adult/continuing education programs available. Career services available to part-time students: individual career counseling, individual job placement, employer recruitment on campus. Part-time tuition: $29 per quarter hour for state residents, $86 per quarter hour for nonresidents.

Belmont College
Nashville 37203

Independent-religious instutition; metropolitan setting. Awards A, B. Total enrollment: 2,041 (all undergraduates); 24% part-time, 50% women, 27% over 25. Total faculty: 181. Library holdings: 87,783 bound volumes, 2,342 titles on microform, 500 periodical subscriptions, 11,587 records/tapes.

Undergraduate Courses offered for part-time students during daytime, evenings, weekends, summer. Complete part-time degree programs offered during daytime, evenings, summer. Adult/continuing education programs available. Career services available to part-time students: individual and group career counseling, individual job placement, employer recruitment on campus. Part-time tuition: $121 per semester hour.

Bethel College
McKenzie 38201

Independent-religious instutition; small-town setting. Awards B. Total enrollment: 515 (all undergraduates); 12% part-time, 51% women. Total faculty: 46. Library holdings: 65,000 bound volumes, 305 periodical subscriptions.

Undergraduate Courses offered for part-time students during daytime, evenings, summer. Complete part-time degree programs offered during daytime, evenings, summer. Adult/continuing education programs available. Career services available to part-time students: individual and group career counseling, individual job placement, employer recruitment on campus. Part-time tuition: $50 per quarter hour.

Colleges Offering Part-Time Degree Programs / *Tennessee*

Bryan College
Dayton 37321

Independent-religious instutition; small-town setting. Awards B. Total enrollment: 585 (all undergraduates); 12% part-time, 60% women, 3% over 25. Total faculty: 49. Library holdings: 65,000 bound volumes, 7,000 titles on microform, 425 periodical subscriptions, 3,000 records/tapes.

Undergraduate Courses offered for part-time students during daytime. Complete part-time degree programs offered during daytime. Career services available to part-time students: individual and group career counseling, individual job placement, employer recruitment on campus. Part-time tuition: $140 per semester hour.

Carson-Newman College
Jefferson City 37760

Independent-religious instutition; small-town setting. Awards B. Total enrollment: 1,763 (all undergraduates); 4% part-time, 50% women, 10% over 25. Total faculty: 113. Library holdings: 147,000 bound volumes, 1,700 periodical subscriptions, 1,410 records/tapes.

Undergraduate Courses offered for part-time students during daytime, evenings, summer. Complete part-time degree programs offered during daytime. External degree and adult/continuing education programs available. Career services available to part-time students: individual and group career counseling, individual job placement, employer recruitment on campus. Part-time tuition: $137 per semester hour.

Chattanooga State Technical Community College
Chattanooga 37406

Public institution; city setting. Awards A. Barrier-free campus. Total enrollment: 5,456 (all undergraduates); 57% part-time, 58% women, 45% over 25. Total faculty: 172. Library holdings: 48,000 bound volumes, 2,020 titles on microform, 500 periodical subscriptions, 4,055 records/tapes.

Undergraduate Courses offered for part-time students during daytime, evenings, weekends, summer. Complete part-time degree programs offered during daytime, evenings, summer. Adult/continuing education programs available. Career services available to part-time students: individual and group career counseling, individual job placement, employer recruitment on campus. Part-time tuition: $15 per quarter hour for state residents, $72 per quarter hour for nonresidents.

Christian Brothers College
Memphis 38104

Independent-religious instutition; metropolitan setting. Awards A, B. Total enrollment: 1,493 (all undergraduates); 15% part-time, 43% women, 15% over 25. Total faculty: 150. Library holdings: 79,577 bound volumes, 128 periodical subscriptions, 1,172 records/tapes.

Undergraduate Courses offered for part-time students during daytime, evenings. Complete part-time degree programs offered during daytime, evenings. Career services available to part-time students: individual and group career counseling, individual job placement, employer recruitment on campus. Part-time tuition: $95 per semester hour.

Church of God School of Theology
Cleveland 37311

Independent-religious institution (graduate only). Total enrollment: 256 (primarily men; 35% part-time). Total faculty: 21. Library holdings: 103,474 bound volumes, 3,834 microforms.

Graduate Part-time study available in Graduate and Professional Programs. Basic part-time expenses: $50 per credit tuition plus $10 per semester fees. Institutional financial aid available to part-time graduate students in Graduate and Professional Programs.

Cleveland State Community College
Cleveland 37320

Public institution; small-town setting. Awards A. Barrier-free campus. Total enrollment: 3,544 (all undergraduates); 63% part-time, 57% women, 49% over 25. Total faculty: 141. Library holdings: 51,700 bound volumes, 432 periodical subscriptions, 8,699 records/tapes.

Undergraduate Courses offered for part-time students during daytime, evenings. Complete part-time degree programs offered during daytime, evenings. Adult/continuing education programs available. Career services available to part-time students: individual and group career counseling, individual job placement, employer recruitment on campus. Part-time tuition: $15 per quarter hour for state residents, $57 per quarter hour for nonresidents.

Columbia State Community College
Columbia 38401

Public institution; small-town setting. Awards A. Barrier-free campus. Total enrollment: 2,533 (all undergraduates); 59% part-time, 59% women. Total faculty: 105. Library holdings: 60,000 bound volumes.

Undergraduate Courses offered for part-time students during daytime, evenings, summer. Complete part-time degree programs offered during daytime, evenings. Adult/continuing education programs available. Career services available to part-time students: individual career counseling, individual job placement, employer recruitment on campus. Part-time tuition: $15 per quarter hour.

Cooper Institute
Knoxville 37927

Proprietary institution; city setting. Awards A. Barrier-free campus. Total enrollment: 153 (all undergraduates); 5% part-time, 55% women, 62% over 25. Total faculty: 10. Library holdings: 4,054 bound volumes, 14 titles on microform, 111 periodical subscriptions, 60 records/tapes.

Undergraduate Courses offered for part-time students during daytime, evenings. Complete part-time degree programs offered during daytime, evenings. Career services available to part-time students: individual career counseling, individual job placement. Part-time tuition: $48 per quarter hour.

Cumberland College of Tennessee
Lebanon 37087

Independent institution; small-town setting. Awards A, B. Total enrollment: 617 (all undergraduates); 40% part-time, 59% women, 30% over 25. Total faculty: 55. Library holdings: 32,000 bound volumes, 130 periodical subscriptions, 450 records/tapes.

Undergraduate Courses offered for part-time students during daytime, evenings, summer. Complete part-time degree pro-

grams offered during daytime, evenings, summer. Adult/continuing education programs available. Career services available to part-time students: individual career counseling. Part-time tuition: $95 per semester hour.

David Lipscomb College
Nashville 37203

Independent-religious instutition; metropolitan setting. Awards A, B, M. Total enrollment: 2,360. Undergraduate enrollment: 2,321; 7% part-time, 52% women, 1% over 25. Total faculty: 149. Library holdings: 145,468 bound volumes, 8,793 titles on microform, 841 periodical subscriptions, 2,100 records/tapes.

Undergraduate Courses offered for part-time students during daytime, summer. Complete part-time degree programs offered during daytime. Career services available to part-time students: individual career counseling, individual job placement, employer recruitment on campus. Part-time tuition: $59 per quarter hour.

Graduate Part-time study available in Graduate Program in Bible Studies. Basic part-time expenses: $65 per quarter hour tuition plus $25 per quarter fees.

Dyersburg State Community College
Dyersburg 38024

Public institution; small-town setting. Awards A. Barrier-free campus. Total enrollment: 1,696 (all undergraduates); 57% part-time, 57% women. Total faculty: 81. Library holdings: 31,893 bound volumes, 315 periodical subscriptions, 375 records/tapes.

Undergraduate Courses offered for part-time students during daytime, evenings, summer. Complete part-time degree programs offered during daytime, evenings, summer. Adult/continuing education programs available. Career services available to part-time students: individual career counseling. Part-time tuition: $15 per quarter hour for state residents, $72 per quarter hour for nonresidents.

East Tennessee State University
Johnson City 37614

Public institution; small-town setting. Awards A, B, M, D. Barrier-free campus. Total enrollment: 9,805. Undergraduate enrollment: 8,325; 22% part-time, 54% women, 38% over 25. Total faculty: 429. Library holdings: 615,899 bound volumes, 503,108 titles on microform, 2,845 periodical subscriptions, 22,013 records/tapes.

Undergraduate Courses offered for part-time students during daytime, evenings, summer. Complete part-time degree programs offered during daytime, evenings, summer. Adult/continuing education programs available. Career services available to part-time students: individual career counseling, individual job placement, employer recruitment on campus. Part-time tuition: $42 per credit hour for state residents, $127 per credit hour for nonresidents.

Graduate Part-time study available in School of Graduate Studies, Quillen-Dishner College of Medicine. Basic part-time expenses: $56 per semester hour tuition for state residents, $142 per semester hour tuition for nonresidents.

Edmondson Junior College
Chattanooga 37411

Proprietary institution; city setting. Awards A. Barrier-free campus. Total enrollment: 525 (all undergraduates); 15% part-time, 90% women, 80% over 25. Total faculty: 36.

Undergraduate Courses offered for part-time students during daytime, evenings. Complete part-time degree programs offered during daytime, evenings. Career services available to part-time students: individual career counseling, individual job placement. Part-time tuition: $60 per credit hour.

Emmanuel School of Religion
Johnson City 37601

Independent-religious institution (graduate only). Total enrollment: 147 (primarily men; 45% part-time). Total faculty: 13. Library holdings: 60,000 bound volumes, 10,000 microforms.

Graduate Part-time study available in Graduate and Professional Programs. Basic part-time expenses: $75 per credit tuition plus $25 per semester fees. Institutional financial aid available to part-time graduate students in Graduate and Professional Programs.

Fisk University
Nashville 37203

Independent-religious instutition; metropolitan setting. Awards B, M. Total enrollment: 694. Undergraduate enrollment: 674; 2% part-time, 68% women. Total faculty: 77. Library holdings: 188,400 bound volumes, 596 periodical subscriptions.

Graduate Part-time study available in Graduate Programs. Basic part-time expenses: $180 per credit hour tuition plus $15 per credit hour fees.

Freed-Hardeman College
Henderson 38340

Independent-religious instutition; small-town setting. Awards B. Barrier-free campus. Total enrollment: 1,146 (all undergraduates); 5% part-time, 53% women. Total faculty: 80. Library holdings: 111,000 bound volumes, 4,600 titles on microform, 628 periodical subscriptions, 4,900 records/tapes.

Undergraduate Courses offered for part-time students during daytime, evenings, summer. Complete part-time degree programs offered during daytime, summer. Adult/continuing education programs available. Career services available to part-time students: individual and group career counseling, individual job placement, employer recruitment on campus. Part-time tuition: $90 per semester hour.

Harding Graduate School of Religion
Memphis 38117

Independent institution (graduate only). Total enrollment: 235 (primarily men; 48% part-time). Total faculty: 15.

Graduate Part-time study available in Graduate Programs. Basic part-time expenses: $103 per semester hour tuition plus $3 per semester fees. Institutional financial aid available to part-time graduate students in Graduate Programs.

Jackson State Community College
Jackson 38301

Public institution; small-town setting. Awards A. Total enrollment: 2,966 (all undergraduates); 57% part-time, 63% women, 40% over 25. Total faculty: 114. Library holdings: 51,822 bound volumes, 1,899 titles on microform, 347 periodical subscriptions, 1,457 records/tapes.

Undergraduate Courses offered for part-time students during daytime, evenings, summer. Complete part-time degree pro-

Colleges Offering Part-Time Degree Programs / *Tennessee*

Jackson State Community College (continued)
grams offered during daytime, evenings, summer. Adult/continuing education programs available. Career services available to part-time students: individual and group career counseling. Part-time tuition: $15 per quarter hour for state residents, $72 per quarter hour for nonresidents.

Johnson Bible College
Knoxville 37920

Independent-religious instutition; rural setting. Awards A, B. Total enrollment: 376 (all undergraduates); 10% part-time, 44% women. Total faculty: 28. Library holdings: 44,000 bound volumes, 12,000 titles on microform, 26 periodical subscriptions, 3,800 records/tapes.

Undergraduate Courses offered for part-time students during daytime. Complete part-time degree programs offered during daytime. Adult/continuing education programs available. Career services available to part-time students: individual job placement, employer recruitment on campus. Part-time tuition: $73.34 per semester hour.

King College
Bristol 37620

Independent-religious instutition; small-town setting. Awards B. Total enrollment: 503 (all undergraduates); 13% part-time, 45% women, 5% over 25. Total faculty: 50. Library holdings: 89,765 bound volumes, 3,100 titles on microform, 450 periodical subscriptions, 600 records/tapes.

Undergraduate Courses offered for part-time students during daytime, evenings, summer. Complete part-time degree programs offered during daytime. Career services available to part-time students: individual career counseling, individual job placement, employer recruitment on campus. Part-time tuition: $100 per semester hour.

Lambuth College
Jackson 38301

Independent-religious instutition; small-town setting. Awards B. Total enrollment: 820 (all undergraduates); 17% part-time, 58% women, 12% over 25. Total faculty: 77. Library holdings: 103,891 bound volumes, 434 periodical subscriptions, 1,510 records/tapes.

Undergraduate Courses offered for part-time students during daytime, evenings. Complete part-time degree programs offered during daytime, evenings. Career services available to part-time students: individual and group career counseling, individual job placement, employer recruitment on campus. Part-time tuition: $59 per credit hour.

LeMoyne-Owen College
Memphis 38126

Independent-religious instutition; metropolitan setting. Awards B. Total enrollment: 950 (all undergraduates); 3% part-time, 64% women, 15% over 25. Total faculty: 77.

Undergraduate Courses offered for part-time students during daytime. Complete part-time degree programs offered during daytime. Adult/continuing education programs available. Part-time tuition: $110 per credit hour.

Lincoln Memorial University
Harrogate 37752

Independent institution; rural setting. Awards A, B, M. Total enrollment: 1,418. Undergraduate enrollment: 1,383; 28% part-time, 65% women. Total faculty: 80. Library holdings: 55,000 bound volumes.

Undergraduate Courses offered for part-time students during daytime, evenings. Complete part-time degree programs offered during daytime, evenings. External degree and adult/continuing education programs available. Career services available to part-time students: individual career counseling. Part-time tuition: $55 per credit hour.

Graduate Part-time study available in Graduate Program in Education. Degree can be earned exclusively through evening/weekend study in Graduate Program in Education. Basic part-time expenses: $60 per quarter hour tuition plus $35 per quarter fees. Institutional financial aid available to part-time graduate students in Graduate Program in Education.

Martin College
Pulaski 38478

Independent-religious instutition; small-town setting. Awards A. Total enrollment: 350 (all undergraduates); 1% part-time, 52% women. Total faculty: 26. Library holdings: 26,000 bound volumes.

Undergraduate Courses offered for part-time students during daytime. Complete part-time degree programs offered during daytime. Adult/continuing education programs available. Career services available to part-time students: individual career counseling, employer recruitment on campus. Part-time tuition per semester hour ranges from $37 (for students 25 or older) to $74 (for students under 25).

Maryville College
Maryville 37801

Independent-religious instutition; small-town setting. Awards B. Total enrollment: 651 (all undergraduates); 10% part-time, 45% women. Total faculty: 55. Library holdings: 118,000 bound volumes, 6,500 titles on microform, 550 periodical subscriptions, 800 records/tapes.

Undergraduate Courses offered for part-time students during daytime, evenings, weekends, summer. Complete part-time degree programs offered during daytime, evenings, weekends, summer. Adult/continuing education programs available. Career services available to part-time students: individual career counseling, individual job placement. Part-time tuition: $160 per semester hour.

Memphis Academy of Arts
Memphis 38112

Independent institution; metropolitan setting. Awards B. Barrier-free campus. Total enrollment: 207 (all undergraduates); 12% part-time, 53% women, 28% over 25. Total faculty: 27. Library holdings: 21,000 bound volumes, 110 periodical subscriptions.

Undergraduate Courses offered for part-time students during daytime, evenings, summer. Complete part-time degree programs offered during daytime, evenings, summer. Adult/continuing education programs available. Career services available to part-time students: individual career counseling, employer recruitment on campus. Part-time tuition: $170 per semester hour.

Tennessee / Colleges Offering Part-Time Degree Programs

Memphis State University
Memphis 38152

Public institution; metropolitan setting. Awards B, M, D. Barrier-free campus. Total enrollment: 22,040. Undergraduate enrollment: 16,954; 30% part-time, 53% women, 25% over 25. Total faculty: 901. Library holdings: 900,000 bound volumes, 594,437 titles on microform, 6,900 periodical subscriptions, 11,775 records/tapes.

Undergraduate Courses offered for part-time students during daytime, evenings, weekends, summer. Complete part-time degree programs offered during daytime, evenings, summer. Adult/continuing education programs available. Career services available to part-time students: individual career counseling, individual job placement, employer recruitment on campus. Part-time tuition: $40 per semester hour for state residents, $125 per semester hour for nonresidents.

Graduate Part-time study available in Graduate School, Cecil C. Humphreys School of Law. Degree can be earned exclusively through evening/weekend study in Cecil C. Humphreys School of Law. Basic part-time expenses: $54 per credit tuition plus $1 per credit (minimum) fees for state residents, $139 per credit tuition plus $1 per credit (minimum) fees for nonresidents.

Memphis Theological Seminary
Memphis 38104

Independent-religious institution (graduate only). Total enrollment: 153 (coed; 30% part-time). Total faculty: 20. Library holdings: 64,516 bound volumes, 746 microforms.

Graduate Part-time study available in Graduate and Professional Programs. Basic part-time expenses: $72 per credit tuition plus $10.50 per semester (minimum) fees.

Mid-America Baptist Theological Seminary
Memphis 38104

Independent-religious institution (graduate only). Total enrollment: 376 (primarily men; 17% part-time). Total faculty: 26.

Graduate Part-time study available in Graduate and Professional Programs. Basic part-time expenses: $100 per semester (minimum) tuition plus $20 per semester fees.

Middle Tennessee State University
Murfreesboro 37132

Public institution; small-town setting. Awards A, B, M, D. Barrier-free campus. Total enrollment: 11,369. Undergraduate enrollment: 9,735; 23% part-time, 50% women, 30% over 25. Total faculty: 478. Library holdings: 453,006 bound volumes, 245,955 titles on microform, 2,836 periodical subscriptions.

Undergraduate Courses offered for part-time students during daytime, evenings, summer. Complete part-time degree programs offered during daytime, evenings. Adult/continuing education programs available. Career services available to part-time students: individual and group career counseling, individual job placement, employer recruitment on campus. Part-time tuition: $39 per hour for state residents, $124 per hour for nonresidents.

Graduate Part-time study available in Graduate School. Basic part-time expenses: $54 per credit tuition for state residents, $140 per credit tuition for nonresidents. Institutional financial aid available to part-time graduate students in Graduate School.

Mid-South Bible College
Memphis 38112

Independent institution; metropolitan setting. Awards B. Barrier-free campus. Total enrollment: 139 (all undergraduates); 38% part-time, 32% women. Total faculty: 21. Library holdings: 22,100 bound volumes, 4 titles on microform, 240 periodical subscriptions, 880 records/tapes.

Undergraduate Courses offered for part-time students during daytime, evenings, summer. Complete part-time degree programs offered during daytime, evenings, summer. Adult/continuing education programs available. Career services available to part-time students: individual and group career counseling. Part-time tuition: $106 per hour.

Milligan College
Milligan College 37682

Independent-religious instutition; rural setting. Awards A, B. Total enrollment: 694 (all undergraduates); 6% part-time, 55% women, 7% over 25. Total faculty: 71. Library holdings: 115,000 bound volumes, 400 periodical subscriptions.

Undergraduate Courses offered for part-time students during daytime, evenings, summer. Complete part-time degree programs offered during daytime, evenings. Career services available to part-time students: individual career counseling, individual job placement, employer recruitment on campus. Part-time tuition: $125 per credit hour.

Motlow State Community College
Tullahoma 37388

Public institution; small-town setting. Awards A. Barrier-free campus. Total enrollment: 2,186 (all undergraduates); 56% part-time, 63% women, 40% over 25. Total faculty: 83. Library holdings: 1,475 bound volumes, 157 titles on microform, 360 periodical subscriptions, 1,348 records/tapes.

Undergraduate Courses offered for part-time students during daytime, evenings, summer. Complete part-time degree programs offered during daytime, evenings, summer. Adult/continuing education programs available. Career services available to part-time students: individual career counseling, individual job placement, employer recruitment on campus. Part-time tuition: $13 per quarter hour for state residents, $64 per quarter hour for nonresidents.

Nashville State Technical Institute
Nashville 37209

Public institution; metropolitan setting. Awards A. Barrier-free campus. Total enrollment: 6,003 (all undergraduates); 71% part-time, 50% women, 49% over 25. Total faculty: 222. Library holdings: 28,695 bound volumes, 13,910 titles on microform, 255 periodical subscriptions, 2,568 records/tapes.

Undergraduate Courses offered for part-time students during daytime, evenings, weekends, summer. Complete part-time degree programs offered during daytime, evenings. Adult/continuing education programs available. Career services available to part-time students: individual and group career counseling, individual job placement, employer recruitment on campus. Part-time tuition: $15 per quarter hour for state residents, $72 per quarter hour for nonresidents.

Colleges Offering Part-Time Degree Programs / Tennessee

O'More College of Design
Franklin 37064

Independent institution; small-town setting. Awards A, B. Total enrollment: 130 (all undergraduates); 27% part-time, 90% women. Total faculty: 14. Library holdings: 1,500 bound volumes.

Undergraduate Courses offered for part-time students during daytime. Complete part-time degree programs offered during daytime. Career services available to part-time students: individual job placement. Part-time tuition: $150 per semester hour.

Roane State Community College
Harriman 37748

Public institution; rural setting. Awards A. Barrier-free campus. Total enrollment: 3,550 (all undergraduates); 54% part-time, 57% women, 33% over 25. Total faculty: 115. Library holdings: 32,000 bound volumes, 470 periodical subscriptions, 1,675 records/tapes.

Undergraduate Courses offered for part-time students during daytime, evenings, summer. Complete part-time degree programs offered during daytime, evenings, summer. Adult/continuing education programs available. Career services available to part-time students: individual career counseling, individual job placement, employer recruitment on campus. Part-time tuition: $15 per quarter hour for state residents, $72 per quarter hour for nonresidents.

Rutledge College
Memphis 38118

Proprietary institution; metropolitan setting. Awards A. Barrier-free campus. Total enrollment: 350 (all undergraduates); 5% part-time, 60% women, 45% over 25. Total faculty: 24. Library holdings: 2,500 bound volumes, 22 periodical subscriptions.

Undergraduate Courses offered for part-time students during daytime, evenings, summer. Complete part-time degree programs offered during daytime, evenings, summer. Career services available to part-time students: individual career counseling, individual job placement, employer recruitment on campus. Part-time tuition: $53 per quarter hour.

Scarritt College
Nashville 37203

Independent-religious institution (graduate only). Total enrollment: 84 (coed; 13% part-time). Total faculty: 14.

Graduate Part-time study available in Graduate Programs. Basic part-time expenses: $150 per credit tuition. Institutional financial aid available to part-time graduate students in Graduate Programs.

Shelby State Community College
Memphis 38104

Public institution; metropolitan setting. Awards A. Barrier-free campus. Total enrollment: 5,289 (all undergraduates); 51% part-time, 70% women, 49% over 25. Total faculty: 249. Library holdings: 51,622 bound volumes, 4,246 titles on microform, 388 periodical subscriptions, 2,507 records/tapes.

Undergraduate Courses offered for part-time students during daytime, evenings, summer. Complete part-time degree programs offered during daytime, evenings, summer. Adult/continuing education programs available. Career services available to part-time students: individual and group career counseling, individual job placement, employer recruitment on campus. Part-time tuition: $15 per quarter hour for state residents, $72 per quarter hour for nonresidents.

Southern College of Optometry
Memphis 38104

Independent institution (undergraduate and graduate). Graduate enrollment: 487 (coed; 1% part-time).

Graduate Part-time study available in Graduate and Professional Programs. Basic part-time expenses: $185 per hour tuition.

Southern College of Seventh-Day Adventists
Collegedale 37315

Independent-religious instutition; small-town setting. Awards A, B. Barrier-free campus. Total enrollment: 1,625 (all undergraduates); 25% part-time, 56% women. Total faculty: 130. Library holdings: 110,000 bound volumes, 890 periodical subscriptions.

Undergraduate Courses offered for part-time students during daytime, summer. Complete part-time degree programs offered during daytime. Adult/continuing education programs available. Part-time tuition: $177 per semester hour.

State Technical Institute at Knoxville
Knoxville 37919

Public institution; city setting. Awards A. Barrier-free campus. Total enrollment: 3,009 (all undergraduates); 63% part-time, 45% women. Total faculty: 170. Library holdings: 8,000 bound volumes, 250 periodical subscriptions, 65 records/tapes.

Undergraduate Courses offered for part-time students during daytime, evenings, summer. Complete part-time degree programs offered during daytime, evenings, summer. Adult/continuing education programs available. Career services available to part-time students: individual and group career counseling, individual job placement, employer recruitment on campus. Part-time tuition: $13 per credit hour for state residents, $64 per credit hour for nonresidents.

State Technical Institute at Memphis
Memphis 38134

Public institution; metropolitan setting. Awards A. Barrier-free campus. Total enrollment: 6,984 (all undergraduates); 60% part-time, 42% women, 50% over 25. Total faculty: 262. Library holdings: 32,700 bound volumes, 4,479 titles on microform, 270 periodical subscriptions, 1,387 records/tapes.

Undergraduate Courses offered for part-time students during daytime, evenings, weekends, summer. Complete part-time degree programs offered during daytime, evenings, weekends, summer. External degree and adult/continuing education programs available. Career services available to part-time students: individual and group career counseling, individual job placement, employer recruitment on campus. Part-time tuition: $15 per quarter hour for state residents, $72 per quarter hour for nonresidents.

Tennessee State University
Nashville 37203

Public institution; metropolitan setting. Awards A, B, M, D. Barrier-free campus. Total enrollment: 8,131. Undergraduate

Tennessee / **Colleges Offering Part-Time Degree Programs**

enrollment: 6,750; 40% part-time, 55% women. Total faculty: 522. Library holdings: 419,730 bound volumes, 759 titles on microform.
Undergraduate Courses offered for part-time students during daytime, evenings, weekends, summer. Complete part-time degree programs offered during daytime, evenings, weekends, summer. External degree and adult/continuing education programs available. Part-time tuition per semester (1 to 12 hours) ranges from $42 to $439 for state residents, $127 to $1423 for nonresidents.
Graduate Part-time study available in Graduate School. Basic part-time expenses: $169 per semester (minimum) tuition for state residents, $424 per semester (minimum) tuition for nonresidents.

Tennessee Technological University
Cookeville 38505

Public institution; small-town setting. Awards A, B, M, D. Total enrollment: 7,848. Undergraduate enrollment: 7,057; 4% part-time, 49% women, 18% over 25. Total faculty: 400. Library holdings: 519,002 bound volumes, 450,000 titles on microform, 3,400 periodical subscriptions, 40,070 records/tapes.
Graduate Part-time study available in Graduate School. Degree can be earned exclusively through evening/weekend study in Graduate School. Basic part-time expenses: $0 tuition plus $37 per quarter hour fees for state residents, $57 per quarter hour tuition plus $37 per quarter hour fees for nonresidents.

Tennessee Temple University
Chattanooga 37404

Independent-religious instutition; city setting. Awards B, M, D. Total enrollment: 2,909. Undergraduate enrollment: 2,631; 18% part-time, 45% women, 25% over 25. Total faculty: 139. Library holdings: 109,292 bound volumes, 5,785 titles on microform, 870 periodical subscriptions, 1,545 records/tapes.
Undergraduate Courses offered for part-time students during daytime, evenings, summer. Complete part-time degree programs offered during daytime, evenings, summer. Adult/continuing education programs available. Career services available to part-time students: individual and group career counseling, individual job placement, employer recruitment on campus. Part-time tuition: $100 per credit hour.

Tennessee Wesleyan College
Athens 37303

Independent-religious instutition; small-town setting. Awards B. Total enrollment: 497 (all undergraduates); 10% part-time, 50% women, 20% over 25. Total faculty: 38.
Undergraduate Courses offered for part-time students during daytime. Complete part-time degree programs offered during daytime. Adult/continuing education programs available. Career services available to part-time students: individual job placement, employer recruitment on campus. Part-time tuition: $75 per quarter hour.

Tomlinson College
Cleveland 37311

Independent-religious instutition; small-town setting. Awards A. Total enrollment: 270 (all undergraduates); 5% part-time, 54% women, 10% over 25. Total faculty: 21. Library holdings: 27,429 bound volumes, 489 periodical subscriptions, 1,546 records/tapes.

Undergraduate Courses offered for part-time students during daytime, evenings. Complete part-time degree programs offered during daytime, evenings. External degree and adult/continuing education programs available. Career services available to part-time students: individual and group career counseling. Part-time tuition: $77.50 per semester hour.

Trevecca Nazarene College
Nashville 37203

Independent-religious instutition; metropolitan setting. Awards A, B, M. Total enrollment: 987 (all undergraduates); 11% part-time, 51% women. Total faculty: 104. Library holdings: 83,520 bound volumes, 17,518 titles on microform, 439 periodical subscriptions, 1,700 records/tapes.
Undergraduate Courses offered for part-time students during daytime, evenings, weekends, summer. Complete part-time degree programs offered during daytime, evenings, weekends, summer. Adult/continuing education programs available. Career services available to part-time students: individual and group career counseling, individual job placement, employer recruitment on campus. Part-time tuition: $87 per quarter hour.

Tri-Cities State Technical Institute
Blountville 37617

Public institution; small-town setting. Awards A. Barrier-free campus. Total enrollment: 1,700 (all undergraduates); 40% part-time, 33% women, 35% over 25. Total faculty: 120. Library holdings: 10,000 bound volumes, 500 periodical subscriptions.
Undergraduate Courses offered for part-time students during daytime, evenings. Complete part-time degree programs offered during daytime, evenings. Career services available to part-time students: individual and group career counseling, individual job placement, employer recruitment on campus. Part-time tuition: $14 per quarter hour for state residents, $65 per quarter hour for nonresidents.

Tusculum College
Greeneville 37743

Independent-religious instutition; small-town setting. Awards B. Total enrollment: 411 (all undergraduates); 10% part-time, 52% women, 11% over 25. Total faculty: 46. Library holdings: 61,000 bound volumes, 8,000 titles on microform, 800 periodical subscriptions, 1,400 records/tapes.
Undergraduate Courses offered for part-time students during daytime, evenings, summer. Complete part-time degree programs offered during daytime, evenings, summer. Adult/continuing education programs available. Career services available to part-time students: individual and group career counseling, individual job placement, employer recruitment on campus. Part-time tuition per semester (1 to 11 credit hours) ranges from $40 to $1410.

Union University
Jackson 38305

Independent-religious instutition; small-town setting. Awards A, B. Barrier-free campus. Total enrollment: 1,431 (all undergraduates); 22% part-time, 63% women. Total faculty: 91. Library holdings: 84,500 bound volumes, 740 periodical subscriptions, 4,061 records/tapes.
Undergraduate Courses offered for part-time students during daytime, evenings. Complete part-time degree programs offered during daytime, evenings. Adult/continuing education programs available. Career services available to part-time students:

Colleges Offering Part-Time Degree Programs / *Tennessee*

Union University (continued)
individual career counseling, individual job placement. Part-time tuition: $110 per semester hour.

University of Tennessee at Chattanooga
Chattanooga 37402

Public institution; city setting. Awards B, M. Total enrollment: 7,834. Undergraduate enrollment: 6,474; 25% part-time, 49% women. Total faculty: 415. Library holdings: 316,485 bound volumes, 592,604 titles on microform, 3,000 periodical subscriptions, 4,253 records/tapes.

Undergraduate Courses offered for part-time students during daytime, evenings, summer. Complete part-time degree programs offered during daytime, evenings, summer. Adult/continuing education programs available. Career services available to part-time students: individual and group career counseling, individual job placement, employer recruitment on campus. Part-time tuition: $43 per semester hour for state residents, $119 per semester hour for nonresidents.

Graduate Part-time study available in Graduate Division. Basic part-time expenses: $72 per semester hour fees for state residents, $174 per semester hour tuition for nonresidents.

University of Tennessee at Martin
Martin 38238

Public institution; small-town setting. Awards A, B, M. Barrier-free campus. Total enrollment: 5,696. Undergraduate enrollment: 5,249; 13% part-time, 50% women. Total faculty: 255. Library holdings: 300,000 bound volumes, 143,496 titles on microform, 1,626 periodical subscriptions, 5,683 records/tapes.

Undergraduate Courses offered for part-time students during daytime, evenings, summer. Complete part-time degree programs offered during daytime, evenings, summer. External degree and adult/continuing education programs available. Career services available to part-time students: individual and group career counseling, individual job placement. Part-time tuition: $27 per credit hour for state residents, $82 per credit hour for nonresidents.

Graduate Part-time study available in Graduate Studies. Basic part-time expenses: $44 per quarter hour tuition for state residents, $117 per quarter hour tuition for nonresidents. Institutional financial aid available to part-time graduate students in Graduate Studies.

University of Tennessee Center for the Health Sciences
Memphis 38163

Public institution; metropolitan setting. Awards B, M, D. Total enrollment: 1,988. Undergraduate enrollment: 620; 1% part-time, 75% women. Total faculty: 686. Library holdings: 124,617 bound volumes, 127 titles on microform, 2,276 periodical subscriptions.

Graduate Part-time study available in Graduate School of Medical Sciences. Basic part-time expenses: $156 per quarter (minimum) tuition plus $50 per quarter fees for state residents, $318 per quarter (minimum) tuition plus $50 per quarter fees for nonresidents.

University of Tennessee, Knoxville
Knoxville 37996

Public institution; city setting. Awards B, M, D. Barrier-free campus. Total enrollment: 27,018. Undergraduate enrollment: 20,555; 17% part-time, 44% women, 17% over 25. Total faculty: 1,334. Library holdings: 1.4 million bound volumes, 1.4 million titles on microform, 21,952 periodical subscriptions, 20,647 records/tapes.

Undergraduate Courses offered for part-time students during daytime, evenings, summer. Complete part-time degree programs offered during daytime. Adult/continuing education programs available. Career services available to part-time students: individual and group career counseling, individual job placement, employer recruitment on campus. Part-time tuition: $36 per quarter hour for state residents. Nonresident part-time tuition and fees per quarter range from $82 to $925.

Graduate Part-time study available in College of Business Administration, College of Communications, College of Education, College of Engineering, College of Home Economics, College of Liberal Arts, College of Nursing, Graduate School of Planning, Graduate School of Social Work. Degree can be earned exclusively through evening/weekend study in College of Business Administration, College of Education, College of Engineering, College of Liberal Arts, Graduate School of Planning, Graduate School of Social Work. Basic part-time expenses: $50 per credit tuition plus $3 per credit fees for state residents, $118 per credit tuition plus $3 per credit fees for nonresidents.

University of Tennessee–Oak Ridge
Oak Ridge 37830

Public institution (graduate only). Total enrollment: 46 (coed; 10% part-time). Total faculty: 81.

Graduate Part-time study available in Graduate School of Biomedical Sciences. Basic part-time expenses: $50 per credit tuition plus $3 per credit fees for state residents, $115 per credit tuition plus $3 per credit fees for nonresidents.

University of Tennessee Space Institute
Tullahoma 37388

Public institution (graduate only). Total enrollment: 354 (primarily men; 76% part-time). Total faculty: 77. Library holdings: 12,245 bound volumes, 130,000 microforms.

Graduate Part-time study available in Graduate Programs. Basic part-time expenses: $50 per credit tuition plus $6 per quarter (minimum) fees for state residents, $115 per credit tuition plus $6 per quarter (minimum) fees for nonresidents. Institutional financial aid available to part-time graduate students in Graduate Programs.

University of the South
Sewanee 37375

Independent-religious instutition; rural setting. Awards B, M, D. Total enrollment: 1,163. Undergraduate enrollment: 1,088; 3% part-time, 42% women. Total faculty: 116. Library holdings: 435,000 bound volumes, 1,850 periodical subscriptions, 2,200 records/tapes.

Graduate Part-time study available in School of Theology.

Vanderbilt University
Nashville 37240

Independent institution; metropolitan setting. Awards B, M, D. Total enrollment: 8,500. Undergraduate enrollment: 5,200; 2% part-time, 51% women, 0% over 25. Total faculty: 1,985. Library holdings: 1.6 million bound volumes, 5,000 periodical subscriptions.

Graduate Part-time study available in Divinity School, George Peabody College for Teachers, Owen Graduate School of Management, School of Engineering. Degree can be earned exclusively through evening/weekend study in George Peabody College for Teachers. Basic part-time expenses: $313 per semester hour tuition plus $17 per semester fees.

Volunteer State Community College
Gallatin 37066

Public institution; small-town setting. Awards A. Barrier-free campus. Total enrollment: 3,774 (all undergraduates); 65% part-time, 63% women, 51% over 25. Total faculty: 178. Library holdings: 35,286 bound volumes, 151 titles on microform, 280 periodical subscriptions, 2,737 records/tapes.

Undergraduate Courses offered for part-time students during daytime, evenings, weekends, summer. Complete part-time degree programs offered during daytime, evenings. Adult/continuing education programs available. Career services available to part-time students: individual and group career counseling, individual job placement, employer recruitment on campus. Part-time tuition: $15 per quarter hour for state residents, $57 per quarter hour for nonresidents.

Walters State Community College
Morristown 37814

Public institution; small-town setting. Awards A. Total enrollment: 3,982 (all undergraduates); 65% part-time, 65% women, 48% over 25. Total faculty: 220. Library holdings: 41,575 bound volumes, 350 titles on microform, 490 periodical subscriptions, 1,194 records/tapes.

Undergraduate Courses offered for part-time students during daytime, evenings, summer. Complete part-time degree programs offered during daytime, evenings, summer. Adult/continuing education programs available. Career services available to part-time students: individual and group career counseling, individual job placement. Part-time tuition: $15 per quarter hour for state residents, $72 per quarter hour for nonresidents.

TEXAS

Abilene Christian University
Abilene 79699

Independent-religious instutition; city setting. Awards A, B, M. Total enrollment: 4,656. Undergraduate enrollment: 4,106; 15% part-time, 50% women, 7% over 25. Total faculty: 251. Library holdings: 252,515 bound volumes, 385,670 titles on microform, 1,814 periodical subscriptions, 29,003 records/tapes.

Undergraduate Courses offered for part-time students during daytime, evenings, summer. Complete part-time degree programs offered during daytime, summer. Adult/continuing education programs available. Career services available to part-time students: individual and group career counseling, individual job placement, employer recruitment on campus. Part-time tuition: $84 per semester hour.

Graduate Part-time study available in Graduate School. Degree can be earned exclusively through evening/weekend study in Graduate School.Basic part-time expenses: $84 per semester hour tuition plus $15 per semester hour fees.

Alvin Community College
Alvin 77511

Public institution; small-town setting. Awards A. Barrier-free campus. Total enrollment: 3,926 (all undergraduates); 62% part-time, 57% women, 51% over 25. Total faculty: 150. Library holdings: 31,000 bound volumes, 250 periodical subscriptions, 2,300 records/tapes.

Undergraduate Courses offered for part-time students during daytime, evenings, weekends, summer. Complete part-time degree programs offered during daytime, evenings, summer. Adult/continuing education programs available. Career services available to part-time students: individual and group career counseling, individual job placement, employer recruitment on campus. Part-time tuition and fees per semester (1 to 11 semester hours) range from $25 to $44 for area residents, $42 to $101 for state residents, $42 to $244 for nonresidents.

Amarillo College
Amarillo 79178

Public institution; city setting. Awards A. Barrier-free campus. Total enrollment: 6,394 (all undergraduates); 72% part-time, 58% women, 54% over 25. Total faculty: 321. Library holdings: 76,405 bound volumes, 12,350 titles on microform, 519 periodical subscriptions, 7,646 records/tapes.

Undergraduate Courses offered for part-time students during daytime, evenings, weekends, summer. Complete part-time degree programs offered during daytime, evenings, summer. Adult/continuing education programs available. Career services available to part-time students: individual and group career counseling, individual job placement, employer recruitment on campus. Part-time tuition per semester (1 to 11 semester hours) ranges from $28.75 to $107.25 for area residents, $34 to $165 for state residents, $61 to $285 for nonresidents.

Amber University
Garland 75041

Independent institution; city setting. Awards B, M. Barrier-free campus. Total enrollment: 1,050. Undergraduate enrollment: 450; 90% part-time, 40% women. Total faculty: 55. Library holdings: 21,000 bound volumes, 120 periodical subscriptions.

Undergraduate Courses offered for part-time students during daytime, evenings, weekends, summer. Complete part-time degree programs offered during daytime, evenings, weekends, summer. Adult/continuing education programs available. Career services available to part-time students: individual career counseling, individual job placement. Part-time tuition: $90 per semester hour.

Graduate Part-time study available in Graduate School.Basic part-time expenses: $90 per hour tuition.

American Technological University
Killeen 76540

Independent institution; small-town setting. Awards B, M. Barrier-free campus. Total enrollment: 526. Undergraduate enrollment: 283; 80% part-time, 34% women, 80% over 25. Total faculty: 27. Library holdings: 71,510 bound volumes, 64,721 titles on microform, 600 periodical subscriptions, 2,855 records/tapes.

Undergraduate Courses offered for part-time students during daytime, evenings, weekends, summer. Complete part-time degree programs offered during daytime, evenings, weekends, summer. Adult/continuing education programs available. Career services available to part-time students: individual and

Colleges Offering Part-Time Degree Programs / Texas

American Technological University (continued)
group career counseling, individual job placement, employer recruitment on campus. Part-time tuition: $76 per credit.

Graduate Part-time study available in Graduate Programs. Basic part-time expenses: $86 per credit tuition plus $27 per semester fees. Institutional financial aid available to part-time graduate students in Graduate Programs.

Angelina College
Lufkin 75902

Public institution; small-town setting. Awards A. Barrier-free campus. Total enrollment: 2,694 (all undergraduates); 60% part-time, 55% women, 62% over 25. Total faculty: 141. Library holdings: 45,000 bound volumes, 1,000 periodical subscriptions, 500 records/tapes.

Undergraduate Courses offered for part-time students during daytime, evenings, summer. Complete part-time degree programs offered during daytime, evenings, summer. Adult/continuing education programs available. Career services available to part-time students: individual and group career counseling, individual job placement, employer recruitment on campus. Part-time tuition and fees per semester (1 to 11 semester hours) range from $29 to $110 for area residents, $30 to $120 for state residents, $28 to $266 for nonresidents.

Angelo State University
San Angelo 76909

Public institution; city setting. Awards A, B, M. Total enrollment: 6,345. Undergraduate enrollment: 5,999; 24% part-time, 51% women, 19% over 25. Total faculty: 227. Library holdings: 330,528 bound volumes, 219,570 titles on microform, 2,330 periodical subscriptions, 2,908 records/tapes.

Undergraduate Courses offered for part-time students during daytime, evenings, summer. Complete part-time degree programs offered during daytime. Adult/continuing education programs available. Career services available to part-time students: individual and group career counseling, individual job placement, employer recruitment on campus. Part-time tuition and fees per semester (1 to 11 semester hours) range from $81 to $206 for state residents, $71 to $596 for nonresidents. Part-time tuition for all nursing students: $37 to 202 per semester.

Graduate Part-time study available in Graduate School. Degree can be earned exclusively through evening/weekend study in Graduate School. Basic part-time expenses: $50 per semester (minimum) tuition plus $63 per semester (minimum) fees for state residents, $40 per semester hour tuition plus $63 per semester (minimum) fees for nonresidents.

Arlington Baptist College
Arlington 76012

Independent-religious instutition; city setting. Awards B. Total enrollment: 381 (all undergraduates); 25% part-time, 45% women, 50% over 25. Total faculty: 24. Library holdings: 23,000 bound volumes, 340 records/tapes.

Undergraduate Courses offered for part-time students during daytime, evenings. Complete part-time degree programs offered during daytime, evenings. Career services available to part-time students: individual and group career counseling, individual job placement, employer recruitment on campus. Part-time tuition: $45 per semester hour.

Austin Community College
Austin 78768

Public institution; city setting. Awards A. Total enrollment: 16,674 (all undergraduates); 77% part-time, 51% women. Total faculty: 802. Library holdings: 51,180 bound volumes, 120 titles on microform, 780 periodical subscriptions, 2,113 records/tapes.

Undergraduate Courses offered for part-time students during daytime, evenings, summer. Complete part-time degree programs offered during daytime, evenings, summer. Adult/continuing education programs available. Career services available to part-time students: individual and group career counseling, individual job placement, employer recruitment on campus. Part-time tuition: $18 per semester hour for state residents, $45 per semester hour for nonresidents.

Baptist Missionary Association Theological Seminary
Jacksonville 75766

Independent-religious institution (graduate only). Total enrollment: 53 (primarily men; 66% part-time). Total faculty: 14.

Graduate Part-time study available in Graduate and Professional Programs. Institutional financial aid available to part-time graduate students in Graduate and Professional Programs.

Baylor University
Waco 76798

Independent-religious instutition; city setting. Awards B, M, D. Barrier-free campus. Total enrollment: 10,818. Undergraduate enrollment: 9,496; 4% part-time, 54% women, 7% over 25. Total faculty: 585. Library holdings: 1.4 million bound volumes, 342,378 titles on microform, 6,016 periodical subscriptions, 344,095 records/tapes.

Undergraduate Courses offered for part-time students during daytime, evenings, summer. Complete part-time degree programs offered during summer. Adult/continuing education programs available. Career services available to part-time students: individual and group career counseling, individual job placement, employer recruitment on campus. Part-time tuition: $107 per semester hour.

Graduate Part-time study available in Graduate School, School of Law. Basic part-time expenses: $107 per credit hour tuition plus $2.50 per semester fees.

Bee County College
Beeville 78102

Public institution; rural setting. Awards A. Barrier-free campus. Total enrollment: 2,226 (all undergraduates); 37% part-time, 54% women. Total faculty: 102. Library holdings: 39,000 bound volumes, 100 periodical subscriptions, 1,500 records/tapes.

Undergraduate Courses offered for part-time students during daytime, evenings, summer. Complete part-time degree programs offered during daytime. Adult/continuing education programs available. Career services available to part-time students: individual and group career counseling, individual job placement, employer recruitment on campus. Part-time tuition: $4 per semester hour for area residents, $9 per semester hour for state residents, $40 per semester hour for nonresidents.

Texas / Colleges Offering Part-Time Degree Programs

Bishop College
Dallas 75241

Independent-religious instutition; metropolitan setting. Awards B. Total enrollment: 1,196 (all undergraduates); 1% part-time, 32% women. Total faculty: 61. Library holdings: 167,500 bound volumes, 38 records/tapes.

Undergraduate Courses offered for part-time students during daytime, evenings, weekends, summer. Complete part-time degree programs offered during daytime, evenings, weekends, summer. Adult/continuing education programs available. Career services available to part-time students: individual and group career counseling, individual job placement, employer recruitment on campus. Part-time tuition: $108 per semester hour.

Blinn College
Brenham 77833

Public institution; small-town setting. Awards A. Barrier-free campus. Total enrollment: 3,380 (all undergraduates); 33% part-time, 41% women, 16% over 25. Total faculty: 123. Library holdings: 80,000 bound volumes, 125 titles on microform, 525 periodical subscriptions, 2,080 records/tapes.

Undergraduate Courses offered for part-time students during daytime. Complete part-time degree programs offered during daytime. Adult/continuing education programs available. Career services available to part-time students: individual and group career counseling, employer recruitment on campus. Part-time tuition: $40 per semester hour for nonresidents. State resident part-time tuition per semester (1 to 11 semester hours) ranges from $25 to $44.

Brazosport College
Lake Jackson 77566

Public institution; small-town setting. Awards A. Barrier-free campus. Total enrollment: 3,607 (all undergraduates); 50% part-time, 43% women, 46% over 25. Total faculty: 190. Library holdings: 42,877 bound volumes, 600 periodical subscriptions.

Undergraduate Courses offered for part-time students during daytime, evenings, summer. Complete part-time degree programs offered during daytime, evenings, summer. Adult/continuing education programs available. Career services available to part-time students: individual and group career counseling, individual job placement, employer recruitment on campus. Part-time tuition: $17 per semester hour for nonresidents. Part-time tuition and fees per semester (1 to 11 semester hours) range from $27.50 to $57.50 for area residents, $27.50 to $72.50 for state residents.

Cedar Valley College
Lancaster 75134

Public institution; small-town setting. Awards A. Barrier-free campus. Total enrollment: 2,276 (all undergraduates); 73% part-time, 59% women. Total faculty: 105.

Undergraduate Courses offered for part-time students during daytime, evenings, weekends. Complete part-time degree programs offered during daytime, evenings, weekends. Part-time tuition and fees per semester (1 to 11 credit hours) range from $33 to $330 for state residents, $60 to $659 for nonresidents.

Central Texas College
Killeen 76541

Public institution; small-town setting. Awards A. Barrier-free campus. Total enrollment: 5,740 (all undergraduates); 46% part-time, 40% women, 20% over 25. Total faculty: 131. Library holdings: 58,395 bound volumes, 64,664 titles on microform, 481 periodical subscriptions, 697 records/tapes.

Undergraduate Courses offered for part-time students during daytime, evenings, weekends, summer. Complete part-time degree programs offered during daytime, evenings, weekends, summer. External degree and adult/continuing education programs available. Career services available to part-time students: individual and group career counseling, individual job placement, employer recruitment on campus. Part-time tuition and fees per semester (1 to 11 semester hours) range from $30 to $101 for state residents, $100 to $295 for nonresidents.

Cisco Junior College
Cisco 76437

Public institution; rural setting. Awards A. Barrier-free campus. Total enrollment: 1,592 (all undergraduates); 40% part-time, 40% women, 45% over 25. Total faculty: 113.

Undergraduate Courses offered for part-time students during daytime, evenings, weekends, summer. Complete part-time degree programs offered during daytime, evenings. Career services available to part-time students: individual career counseling, employer recruitment on campus. Part-time tuition per semester (1 to 11 credit hours) ranges from $51 to $144 for county residents, $53 to $166 for state residents, $71 to $326 for nonresidents.

Clarendon College
Clarendon 79226

Public institution; rural setting. Awards A. Barrier-free campus. Total enrollment: 686 (all undergraduates); 20% part-time, 53% women, 16% over 25. Total faculty: 48. Library holdings: 20,000 bound volumes.

Undergraduate Courses offered for part-time students during daytime, evenings, weekends, summer. Complete part-time degree programs offered during daytime, evenings, weekends, summer. Adult/continuing education programs available. Career services available to part-time students: individual and group career counseling, employer recruitment on campus. Part-time tuition and fees per semester (1 to 11 semester hours) range from $25 to $44 for district residents, $40 to $59 for state residents, $45 to $202 for nonresidents.

College of the Mainland
Texas City 77591

Public institution; small-town setting. Awards A. Total enrollment: 2,630 (all undergraduates); 71% part-time, 56% women, 43% over 25. Total faculty: 182.

Undergraduate Courses offered for part-time students during daytime, evenings, summer. Complete part-time degree programs offered during daytime, evenings, summer. Adult/continuing education programs available. Career services available to part-time students: individual and group career counseling, individual job placement, employer recruitment on campus. Part-time tuition: $17.50 per semester hour for nonresidents. State resident part-time tuition per semester (1 to 11 semester hours) ranges from $28 to $49.50.

Colleges Offering Part-Time Degree Programs / Texas

Concordia Lutheran College
Austin 78705

Independent-religious instutition; city setting. Awards A, B. Total enrollment: 465 (all undergraduates); 6% part-time, 51% women, 1% over 25. Total faculty: 46. Library holdings: 32,527 bound volumes, 145 titles on microform, 467 periodical subscriptions, 2,429 records/tapes.

Undergraduate Courses offered for part-time students during daytime, summer. Complete part-time degree programs offered during daytime, summer. Career services available to part-time students: individual career counseling. Part-time tuition: $115 per semester hour.

Cooke County College
Gainesville 76240

Public institution; rural setting. Awards A. Barrier-free campus. Total enrollment: 1,701 (all undergraduates); 63% part-time, 58% women, 45% over 25. Total faculty: 88. Library holdings: 39,485 bound volumes, 4,220 titles on microform, 353 periodical subscriptions, 1,698 records/tapes.

Undergraduate Courses offered for part-time students during daytime, evenings. Complete part-time degree programs offered during daytime, evenings. Adult/continuing education programs available. Career services available to part-time students: individual and group career counseling. Part-time tuition per semester (1 to 11 semester hours) ranges from $40 to $88 for district residents, $45 to $99 for state residents, $63 to $231 for nonresidents.

Corpus Christi State University
Corpus Christi 78412

Public institution; city setting. Awards B, M. Barrier-free campus. Total enrollment: 3,567. Undergraduate enrollment: 1,885; 52% part-time, 55% women. Total faculty: 154. Library holdings: 220,780 bound volumes, 1,791 periodical subscriptions, 3,967 records/tapes.

Undergraduate Courses offered for part-time students during daytime, evenings, summer. Complete part-time degree programs offered during daytime, evenings, summer. Career services available to part-time students: individual and group career counseling, individual job placement, employer recruitment on campus. Part-time tuition: $5 per semester hour for state residents, $45 per semester hour for nonresidents.

Graduate Part-time study available in Graduate Programs. Degree can be earned exclusively through evening/weekend study in Graduate Programs. Basic part-time expenses: $50 per semester (minimum) tuition plus $11 per semester hour fees for state residents, $40 per semester hour tuition plus $11 per semester hour fees for nonresidents. Institutional financial aid available to part-time graduate students in Graduate Programs.

Dallas Baptist College
Dallas 75211

Independent-religious instutition; metropolitan setting. Awards B, M. Total enrollment: 1,437. Undergraduate enrollment: 1,337; 45% part-time, 45% women. Total faculty: 48.

Undergraduate Courses offered for part-time students during daytime, evenings, summer. Complete part-time degree programs offered during daytime, evenings, summer. External degree and adult/continuing education programs available. Career services available to part-time students: individual job placement, employer recruitment on campus. Part-time tuition: $105 per credit.

Dallas Bible College
Dallas 75228

Independent institution; metropolitan setting. Awards A, B, M. Barrier-free campus. Total enrollment: 228. Undergraduate enrollment: 216; 38% part-time, 34% women, 50% over 25. Total faculty: 29. Library holdings: 32,000 bound volumes, 200 periodical subscriptions.

Undergraduate Courses offered for part-time students during daytime, evenings, summer. Complete part-time degree programs offered during daytime. External degree and adult/continuing education programs available. Career services available to part-time students: individual and group career counseling, individual job placement. Part-time tuition: $80 per semester hour.

Dallas Christian College
Dallas 75234

Independent-religious instutition; metropolitan setting. Awards A, B. Total enrollment: 145 (all undergraduates); 36% part-time, 46% women, 7% over 25. Total faculty: 17. Library holdings: 35,000 bound volumes, 80 periodical subscriptions, 100 records/tapes.

Undergraduate Courses offered for part-time students during daytime. Complete part-time degree programs offered during daytime. Career services available to part-time students: individual career counseling, individual job placement. Part-time tuition: $55 per semester hour.

Del Mar College
Corpus Christi 78404

Public institution; city setting. Awards A. Total enrollment: 8,330 (all undergraduates); 64% part-time, 58% women, 33% over 25. Total faculty: 337. Library holdings: 125,524 bound volumes, 690 periodical subscriptions, 6,419 records/tapes.

Undergraduate Courses offered for part-time students during daytime, evenings, summer. Complete part-time degree programs offered during daytime, evenings, summer. Adult/continuing education programs available. Career services available to part-time students: individual and group career counseling, individual job placement, employer recruitment on campus. Part-time tuition: $9 per semester hour for area residents, $14 per semester hour for state residents, $25 per semester hour for nonresidents.

DeVry Institute of Technology
Irving 75062

Proprietary institution; city setting. Awards A, B. Barrier-free campus. Total enrollment: 2,306 (all undergraduates); 13% part-time, 11% women. Total faculty: 87.

Undergraduate Courses offered for part-time students during daytime, evenings. Complete part-time degree programs offered during daytime. Adult/continuing education programs available. Career services available to part-time students: individual and group career counseling, individual job placement, employer recruitment on campus. Part-time tuition: $1990 per year.

Eastfield College
Mesquite 75150

Public institution; small-town setting. Awards A. Barrier-free campus. Total enrollment: 8,894 (all undergraduates); 55% part-time, 55% women, 51% over 25. Total faculty: 316.

Texas / Colleges Offering Part-Time Degree Programs

Undergraduate Courses offered for part-time students during daytime, evenings, summer. Complete part-time degree programs offered during daytime, evenings, summer. Adult/continuing education programs available. Career services available to part-time students: individual career counseling, individual job placement, employer recruitment on campus. Part-time tuition per semester (1 to 11 credit hours) ranges from $33 to $118 for district residents, $33 to $330 for state residents, $60 to $659 for nonresidents.

East Texas Baptist University
Marshall 75670

Independent-religious instutition; small-town setting. Awards A, B. Total enrollment: 814 (all undergraduates); 18% part-time, 49% women. Total faculty: 56. Library holdings: 100,795 bound volumes, 3,369 titles on microform, 576 periodical subscriptions, 4,881 records/tapes.

Undergraduate Courses offered for part-time students during daytime, evenings, summer. Complete part-time degree programs offered during daytime, evenings, summer. Adult/continuing education programs available. Career services available to part-time students: individual and group career counseling, individual job placement. Part-time tuition: $80 per semester hour.

East Texas State University
Commerce 75428

Public institution; small-town setting. Awards B, M, D. Total enrollment: 7,578. Undergraduate enrollment: 4,620; 22% part-time, 52% women. Total faculty: 363. Library holdings: 939,095 bound volumes, 296,742 titles on microform, 2,622 periodical subscriptions, 1,773 records/tapes.

Undergraduate Courses offered for part-time students during daytime, evenings, weekends, summer. Complete part-time degree programs offered during daytime, evenings, weekends, summer. Adult/continuing education programs available. Career services available to part-time students: individual career counseling, individual job placement, employer recruitment on campus. Part-time tuition: $54.75 per semester hour for nonresidents. State resident part-time tuition per semester (1 to 11 semester hours) ranges from $64.75 to $212.25.

Graduate Part-time study available in Graduate School. Basic part-time expenses: $50 per semester (minimum) tuition plus $14.75 per hour fees for state residents, $40 per hour tuition plus $14.75 per hour fees for nonresidents.

El Centro College
Dallas 75202

Public institution; metropolitan setting. Awards A. Barrier-free campus. Total enrollment: 6,373 (all undergraduates); 77% part-time, 66% women, 64% over 25. Total faculty: 308. Library holdings: 58,000 bound volumes, 330 periodical subscriptions, 4,380 records/tapes.

Undergraduate Courses offered for part-time students during daytime, evenings, weekends, summer. Complete part-time degree programs offered during daytime, evenings, weekends, summer. Adult/continuing education programs available. Career services available to part-time students: individual and group career counseling, individual job placement, employer recruitment on campus. Part-time tuition and fees per semester (1 to 11 credit hours) range from $33 to $118 for district residents, $33 to $330 for state residents, $60 to $659 for nonresidents.

El Paso Community College
El Paso 79998

Public institution; metropolitan setting. Awards A. Barrier-free campus. Total enrollment: 13,500 (all undergraduates); 63% part-time, 54% women, 50% over 25. Total faculty: 695. Library holdings: 53,519 bound volumes, 400 titles on microform, 422 periodical subscriptions, 3,800 records/tapes.

Undergraduate Courses offered for part-time students during daytime, evenings, weekends, summer. Complete part-time degree programs offered during daytime, evenings, weekends, summer. External degree and adult/continuing education programs available. Career services available to part-time students: individual career counseling, individual job placement, employer recruitment on campus. Part-time tuition: $40 per semester hour for nonresidents. State resident part-time tuition per semester (1 to 11 semester hours) ranges from $50 to $114.

Frank Phillips College
Borger 79007

Public institution; small-town setting. Awards A. Barrier-free campus. Total enrollment: 1,010 (all undergraduates); 25% part-time, 55% women. Total faculty: 86. Library holdings: 28,000 bound volumes, 1,975 titles on microform, 196 periodical subscriptions, 1,553 records/tapes.

Undergraduate Courses offered for part-time students during daytime, evenings, weekends, summer. Complete part-time degree programs offered during daytime, evenings, weekends, summer. Adult/continuing education programs available. Career services available to part-time students: individual and group career counseling, individual job placement, employer recruitment on campus. Part-time tuition and fees per semester (1 to 11 credit hours) range from $92 to $131 for district residents, $98 to $177 for state residents, $140 to $252 for nonresidents.

Galveston College
Galveston 77550

Public institution; city setting. Awards A. Total enrollment: 1,830 (all undergraduates); 53% part-time, 67% women, 50% over 25. Total faculty: 121. Library holdings: 36,836 bound volumes, 2,981 titles on microform, 388 periodical subscriptions, 1,500 records/tapes.

Undergraduate Courses offered for part-time students during daytime, evenings, summer. Complete part-time degree programs offered during daytime, evenings, summer. Adult/continuing education programs available. Career services available to part-time students: individual career counseling, individual job placement, employer recruitment on campus. Part-time tuition per semester (1 to 11 credit hours) ranges from $25 to $44 for state residents, $60 to $200 for nonresidents.

Grayson County College
Denison 75020

Public institution; rural setting. Awards A. Barrier-free campus. Total enrollment: 4,790 (all undergraduates); 76% part-time, 61% women, 53% over 25. Total faculty: 201. Library holdings: 48,000 bound volumes, 150 periodical subscriptions, 500 records/tapes.

Undergraduate Courses offered for part-time students during daytime, evenings, weekends, summer. Complete part-time degree programs offered during daytime, evenings, summer. Adult/continuing education programs available. Career services available to part-time students: individual career counseling. Part-time tuition per semester (1 to 11 credits)

Colleges Offering Part-Time Degree Programs / Texas

Grayson County College (continued)
ranges from $28 to $110 for district residents, $30 to $132 for state residents, $30 to $255 for nonresidents.

Gulf-Coast Bible College
Houston 77270

Independent-religious instutition; metropolitan setting. Awards A, B. Total enrollment: 332 (all undergraduates); 28% part-time, 41% women. Total faculty: 21. Library holdings: 50,000 bound volumes, 150 periodical subscriptions, 469 records/tapes.

Undergraduate Courses offered for part-time students during daytime. Complete part-time degree programs offered during daytime. Adult/continuing education programs available. Career services available to part-time students: individual career counseling, individual job placement. Part-time tuition: $92 per credit.

Hardin-Simmons University
Abilene 79698

Independent-religious instutition; city setting. Awards B, M. Total enrollment: 1,927. Undergraduate enrollment: 1,776; 27% part-time, 50% women, 22% over 25. Total faculty: 128. Library holdings: 169,000 bound volumes, 19,000 titles on microform, 966 periodical subscriptions, 7,148 records/tapes.

Undergraduate Courses offered for part-time students during daytime, evenings, weekends, summer. Complete part-time degree programs offered during daytime, evenings, weekends, summer. Adult/continuing education programs available. Career services available to part-time students: individual and group career counseling, individual job placement, employer recruitment on campus. Part-time tuition: $98 per semester hour.

Graduate Part-time study available in Graduate School. Degree can be earned exclusively through evening/weekend study in Graduate School. Basic part-time expenses: $98 per credit tuition plus $1.11 per credit fees.

Henderson County Junior College
Athens 75751

Public institution; small-town setting. Awards A. Total enrollment: 3,690 (all undergraduates); 68% part-time, 46% women, 48% over 25. Total faculty: 154. Library holdings: 23,000 bound volumes, 5,731 titles on microform, 225 periodical subscriptions, 2,000 records/tapes.

Undergraduate Courses offered for part-time students during daytime, evenings, summer. Complete part-time degree programs offered during daytime, evenings. Adult/continuing education programs available. Career services available to part-time students: individual career counseling, individual job placement. Part-time tuition and fees per semester (1 to 11 semester hours) range from $30 to $78 for district residents, $42 to $118 for state residents, $62 to $217 for nonresidents.

Hill Junior College
Hillsboro 76645

Public institution; small-town setting. Awards A. Barrier-free campus. Total enrollment: 1,234 (all undergraduates); 40% part-time, 61% women, 40% over 25. Total faculty: 55. Library holdings: 30,500 bound volumes, 300 periodical subscriptions, 775 records/tapes.

Undergraduate Courses offered for part-time students during daytime, evenings, summer. Complete part-time degree programs offered during daytime, evenings, summer. Adult/continuing education programs available. Career services available to part-time students: individual and group career counseling, individual job placement, employer recruitment on campus. Part-time tuition per semester (1 to 11 semester hours) ranges from $30 to $112.50 for district residents, $44 to $140 for state residents, $76 to $246 for nonresidents.

Houston Baptist University
Houston 77074

Independent-religious instutition; metropolitan setting. Awards A, B, M. Total enrollment: 3,522. Undergraduate enrollment: 3,111; 23% part-time, 58% women, 50% over 25. Total faculty: 158. Library holdings: 111,539 bound volumes, 6,384 titles on microform, 712 periodical subscriptions, 2,166 records/tapes.

Undergraduate Courses offered for part-time students during daytime, evenings, summer. Complete part-time degree programs offered during daytime, evenings, summer. Adult/continuing education programs available. Career services available to part-time students: individual career counseling, individual job placement, employer recruitment on campus. Part-time tuition: $110 per quarter hour.

Graduate Part-time study available in College of Business and Economics. Basic part-time expenses: $400 per course (minimum) tuition.

Houston Community College System
Houston 77270

Public institution; metropolitan setting. Awards A. Total enrollment: 25,298 (all undergraduates); 67% part-time, 61% women, 58% over 25. Total faculty: 1,400.

Undergraduate Courses offered for part-time students during daytime, evenings, weekends, summer. Complete part-time degree programs offered during daytime, evenings, weekends, summer. Adult/continuing education programs available. Career services available to part-time students: individual career counseling, individual job placement, employer recruitment on campus. Part-time tuition and fees per semester (1 to 11 semester hours) range from $69 to $203 for district residents, $73 to $247 for state residents, $88 to $621 for nonresidents.

Howard College at Big Spring
Big Spring 79720

Public institution; small-town setting. Awards A. Total enrollment: 1,170 (all undergraduates); 60% part-time, 52% women, 45% over 25. Total faculty: 80. Library holdings: 32,297 bound volumes, 2,259 titles on microform, 136 periodical subscriptions, 547 records/tapes.

Undergraduate Courses offered for part-time students during daytime, evenings, summer. Complete part-time degree programs offered during daytime, evenings, summer. Adult/continuing education programs available. Career services available to part-time students: individual career counseling, individual job placement, employer recruitment on campus. Part-time tuition: $4 per semester hour for state residents, $20 per semester hour for nonresidents.

Howard Payne University
Brownwood 76801

Independent-religious instutition; small-town setting. Awards B. Total enrollment: 1,067 (all undergraduates); 17% part-time, 49% women, 15% over 25. Total faculty: 83. Library holdings:

109,100 bound volumes, 2,247 titles on microform, 713 periodical subscriptions, 2,457 records/tapes.

Undergraduate Courses offered for part-time students during daytime. Complete part-time degree programs offered during daytime. Adult/continuing education programs available. Career services available to part-time students: individual and group career counseling, individual job placement, employer recruitment on campus. Part-time tuition: $75 per semester hour.

Huston-Tillotson College
Austin 78702

Independent-religious instutition; city setting. Awards B. Total enrollment: 502 (all undergraduates); 11% part-time, 33% women. Total faculty: 45. Library holdings: 64,157 bound volumes, 81 titles on microform, 399 periodical subscriptions, 2,482 records/tapes.

Undergraduate Courses offered for part-time students during daytime, summer. Complete part-time degree programs offered during daytime, summer. Part-time tuition: $78 per credit hour.

Incarnate Word College
San Antonio 78209

Independent-religious instutition; metropolitan setting. Awards B, M. Total enrollment: 1,321. Undergraduate enrollment: 1,125; 37% part-time, 75% women. Total faculty: 115. Library holdings: 149,930 bound volumes, 20,929 titles on microform, 600 periodical subscriptions, 32,944 records/tapes.

Undergraduate Courses offered for part-time students during daytime, evenings, summer. Complete part-time degree programs offered during daytime, evenings. Adult/continuing education programs available. Career services available to part-time students: individual and group career counseling, individual job placement, employer recruitment on campus. Part-time tuition: $131 per semester hour.

Graduate Part-time study available in Division of Humanities and Fine Arts, Division of Natural Sciences, Division of Professional Studies, Division of Social Sciences and Business Administration. Degree can be earned exclusively through evening/weekend study in Division of Professional Studies, Division of Social Sciences and Business Administration. Basic part-time expenses: $141 per semester hour tuition plus $37 per semester fees. Institutional financial aid available to part-time graduate students in Division of Humanities and Fine Arts, Division of Natural Sciences, Division of Professional Studies, Division of Social Sciences and Business Administration.

Jacksonville College
Jacksonville 75766

Independent-religious instutition; small-town setting. Awards A. Barrier-free campus. Total enrollment: 300 (all undergraduates); 20% part-time, 40% women, 2% over 25. Total faculty: 30. Library holdings: 21,500 bound volumes, 160 periodical subscriptions, 1,050 records/tapes.

Undergraduate Courses offered for part-time students during daytime. Complete part-time degree programs offered during daytime. Adult/continuing education programs available. Career services available to part-time students: individual and group career counseling. Part-time tuition: $55 per semester hour.

Jarvis Christian College
Hawkins 75765

Independent-religious instutition; rural setting. Awards A, B. Total enrollment: 590 (all undergraduates); 3% part-time, 49% women. Total faculty: 48.

Undergraduate Courses offered for part-time students during daytime, evenings. Complete part-time degree programs offered during daytime, evenings. Adult/continuing education programs available. Part-time tuition: $100 per semester hour.

Kilgore College
Kilgore 75662

Public institution; small-town setting. Awards A. Total enrollment: 4,543 (all undergraduates); 48% part-time, 56% women, 36% over 25. Total faculty: 185. Library holdings: 70,294 bound volumes, 220 titles on microform, 375 periodical subscriptions, 6,994 records/tapes.

Undergraduate Courses offered for part-time students during daytime, evenings, summer. Complete part-time degree programs offered during daytime, evenings, summer. Adult/continuing education programs available. Career services available to part-time students: individual and group career counseling, individual job placement, employer recruitment on campus. Part-time tuition per semester (1 to 11 semester hours) ranges from $25 to $66 for area residents, $25 to $121 for state residents, $27 to $200 for nonresidents.

Lamar University
Beaumont 77710

Public institution; city setting. Awards A, B, M, D. Barrier-free campus. Total enrollment: 14,638. Undergraduate enrollment: 14,129; 36% part-time, 51% women. Total faculty: 572. Library holdings: 414,738 bound volumes, 3,158 periodical subscriptions.

Undergraduate Courses offered for part-time students during daytime, evenings, summer. Complete part-time degree programs offered during daytime, evenings, summer. Adult/continuing education programs available. Career services available to part-time students: individual career counseling, individual job placement, employer recruitment on campus. Part-time tuition: $4 per semester hour for state residents, $40 per semester hour for nonresidents.

Graduate Part-time study available in College of Graduate Studies. Basic part-time expenses: $50 per semester (minimum) tuition plus $107 per semester (minimum) fees for state residents, $40 per semester hour tuition plus $107 per semester (minimum) fees for nonresidents. Institutional financial aid available to part-time graduate students in College of Graduate Studies.

Laredo State University
Laredo 78040

Public institution; city setting. Awards B, M. Barrier-free campus. Total enrollment: 932. Undergraduate enrollment: 449; 48% part-time, 60% women. Total faculty: 50. Library holdings: 139,800 bound volumes, 250,070 titles on microform, 1,102 periodical subscriptions, 1,782 records/tapes.

Undergraduate Courses offered for part-time students during daytime, evenings, weekends, summer. Complete part-time degree programs offered during daytime, evenings, summer. Career services available to part-time students: individual career counseling, individual job placement, employer recruitment on campus. Part-time tuition: $46 per semester hour for nonresidents. State resident part-time tuition and fees per semester (1 to 11 semester hours) range from $56 to $116.

Colleges Offering Part-Time Degree Programs / Texas

Laredo State University (continued)

Graduate Part-time study available in Division of Graduate Studies. Basic part-time expenses: $50 per semester (minimum) tuition plus $18 per semester (minimum) fees for state residents, $40 per credit tuition plus $18 per semester (minimum) fees for nonresidents. Institutional financial aid available to part-time graduate students in Division of Graduate Studies.

LeTourneau College
Longview 75607

Independent-religious instutition; city setting. Awards A, B. Barrier-free campus. Total enrollment: 1,045 (all undergraduates); 8% part-time, 10% women. Total faculty: 72. Library holdings: 97,000 bound volumes, 35,000 titles on microform, 575 periodical subscriptions, 2,500 records/tapes.

Undergraduate Courses offered for part-time students during daytime. Complete part-time degree programs offered during daytime. Adult/continuing education programs available. Career services available to part-time students: individual and group career counseling, individual job placement, employer recruitment on campus. Part-time tuition: $187 per semester hour.

Lubbock Christian College
Lubbock 79407

Independent-religious instutition; city setting. Awards A, B. Total enrollment: 1,000 (all undergraduates); 15% part-time, 51% women, 5% over 25. Total faculty: 97. Library holdings: 60,000 bound volumes, 600 periodical subscriptions, 450 records/tapes.

Undergraduate Courses offered for part-time students during daytime, evenings, summer. Complete part-time degree programs offered during daytime, evenings, summer. Adult/continuing education programs available. Career services available to part-time students: individual career counseling, individual job placement, employer recruitment on campus. Part-time tuition per semester hour ranges from $55 (for students taking 1 to 6 semester hours) to $99 (for students taking 7 to 11 semester hours).

McLennan Community College
Waco 76708

Public institution; city setting. Awards A. Barrier-free campus. Total enrollment: 4,313 (all undergraduates); 54% part-time, 59% women, 49% over 25. Total faculty: 216. Library holdings: 58,495 bound volumes, 4,439 titles on microform, 469 periodical subscriptions, 7,093 records/tapes.

Undergraduate Courses offered for part-time students during daytime, evenings, weekends, summer. Complete part-time degree programs offered during daytime, evenings, weekends, summer. Adult/continuing education programs available. Career services available to part-time students: individual and group career counseling, individual job placement, employer recruitment on campus. Part-time tuition: $7 per semester hour for area residents, $8 per semester hour for state residents, $30 per semester hour for nonresidents.

McMurry College
Abilene 79697

Independent-religious instutition; city setting. Awards A, B. Total enrollment: 1,602 (all undergraduates); 46% part-time, 48% women, 33% over 25. Total faculty: 121. Library holdings: 126,538 bound volumes, 456 periodical subscriptions.

Undergraduate Courses offered for part-time students during daytime, evenings, weekends, summer. Complete part-time degree programs offered during daytime, evenings, summer. Adult/continuing education programs available. Career services available to part-time students: individual and group career counseling, individual job placement, employer recruitment on campus. Part-time tuition: $92 per semester hour.

Midland College
Midland 79705

Public institution; city setting. Awards A. Barrier-free campus. Total enrollment: 3,350 (all undergraduates); 72% part-time, 54% women, 48% over 25. Total faculty: 174.

Undergraduate Courses offered for part-time students during daytime, evenings, summer. Complete part-time degree programs offered during daytime, evenings, summer. Adult/continuing education programs available. Career services available to part-time students: individual and group career counseling, individual job placement, employer recruitment on campus. Part-time tuition and fees per semester (1 to 11 semester hours) range from $31 to $71 for district residents, $37 to $100 for state residents, $57 to $233 for nonresidents.

Midwestern State University
Wichita Falls 76308

Public institution; city setting. Awards A, B, M. Total enrollment: 5,125. Undergraduate enrollment: 4,436; 48% part-time, 53% women. Total faculty: 215. Library holdings: 375,000 bound volumes, 235,500 titles on microform, 2,000 periodical subscriptions, 6,045 records/tapes.

Undergraduate Courses offered for part-time students during daytime, evenings, summer. Complete part-time degree programs offered during daytime, evenings, summer. Adult/continuing education programs available. Career services available to part-time students: individual and group career counseling, individual job placement, employer recruitment on campus. Part-time tuition per semester (1 to 11 semester hours) ranges from $75.50 to $180.50 for state residents, $65.50 to $570.50 for nonresidents.

Graduate Part-time study available in Graduate Studies. Degree can be earned exclusively through evening/weekend study in Graduate Studies. Basic part-time expenses: $50 per semester (minimum) tuition plus $51.75 per semester (minimum) fees for state residents, $40 per credit tuition plus $51.75 per semester (minimum) fees for nonresidents. Institutional financial aid available to part-time graduate students in Graduate Studies.

Mountain View College
Dallas 75211

Public institution; metropolitan setting. Awards A. Total enrollment: 5,891 (all undergraduates); 69% part-time, 50% women, 50% over 25. Total faculty: 245.

Undergraduate Courses offered for part-time students during daytime, evenings, weekends, summer. Complete part-time degree programs offered during daytime, evenings, summer. Adult/continuing education programs available. Career services available to part-time students: individual and group career counseling, individual job placement, employer recruitment on campus. Part-time tuition and fees per semester (1 to 11 semester hours) range frome $33 to $118 for area residents, $33 to $330 for state residents, $60 to $659 for nonresidents.

Texas / **Colleges Offering Part-Time Degree Programs**

Navarro College
Corsicana 75110

Public institution; small-town setting. Awards A. Barrier-free campus. Total enrollment: 2,359 (all undergraduates); 50% part-time, 64% women. Total faculty: 118. Library holdings: 33,900 bound volumes, 600 titles on microform, 50 periodical subscriptions, 1,006 records/tapes.

Undergraduate Courses offered for part-time students during daytime, evenings, summer. Complete part-time degree programs offered during daytime, evenings, summer. Adult/continuing education programs available. Career services available to part-time students: individual and group career counseling, individual job placement, employer recruitment on campus. Part-time tuition and fees per semester (1 to 11 semester hours) range from $58 to $185 for state residents, $56 to $538 for nonresidents.

North Harris County College
Houston 77073

Public institution; metropolitan setting. Awards A. Barrier-free campus. Total enrollment: 10,222 (all undergraduates); 73% part-time, 56% women, 43% over 25. Total faculty: 424. Library holdings: 39,926 bound volumes, 396 titles on microform, 515 periodical subscriptions, 846 records/tapes.

Undergraduate Courses offered for part-time students during daytime, evenings, weekends, summer. Complete part-time degree programs offered during daytime, evenings, summer. Adult/continuing education programs available. Career services available to part-time students: individual and group career counseling, individual job placement, employer recruitment on campus. Part-time tuition and fees per semester (1 to 11 credit hours) range from $35 to $58 for area residents, $42 to $142 for state residents, $45 to $210 for nonresidents.

North Lake College
Irving 75038

Public institution; city setting. Awards A. Barrier-free campus. Total enrollment: 5,151 (all undergraduates); 65% part-time, 52% women, 55% over 25. Total faculty: 206. Library holdings: 18,281 bound volumes, 1,457 titles on microform, 416 periodical subscriptions, 2,704 records/tapes.

Undergraduate Courses offered for part-time students during daytime, evenings, weekends, summer. Complete part-time degree programs offered during daytime, evenings, summer. Career services available to part-time students: individual and group career counseling, employer recruitment on campus. Part-time tuition per semester (1 to 11 credit hours) ranges from $33 to $118 for county residents, $33 to $330 for state residents, $60 to $659 for nonresidents.

North Texas State University
Denton 76203

Public institution; city setting. Awards B, M, D. Barrier-free campus. Total enrollment: 20,234. Undergraduate enrollment: 14,149; 21% part-time, 51% women. Total faculty: 840. Library holdings: 1.5 million bound volumes, 255,765 titles on microform, 4,429 periodical subscriptions, 73,834 records/tapes.

Undergraduate Courses offered for part-time students during daytime, evenings, weekends, summer. Complete part-time degree programs offered during daytime, evenings, weekends, summer. Adult/continuing education programs available. Career services available to part-time students: individual and group career counseling, individual job placement, employer recruitment on campus. Part-time tuition and fees per semester range from $92 to $212 for state residents, $82 to $602 for nonresidents.

Graduate Part-time study available in Graduate School. Basic part-time expenses: $50 per semester (minimum) tuition plus $66 per semester (minimum) fees for state residents, $40 per credit hour tuition plus $66 per semester (minimum) fees for nonresidents.

Northwood Institute, Texas Campus
Cedar Hill 75104

Independent institution; rural setting. Awards A. Total enrollment: 177 (all undergraduates); 2% part-time, 35% women, 15% over 25. Total faculty: 17. Library holdings: 26,000 bound volumes, 20 titles on microform, 207 periodical subscriptions, 195 records/tapes.

Undergraduate Courses offered for part-time students during daytime, summer. Complete part-time degree programs offered during daytime, summer. External degree and adult/continuing education programs available. Career services available to part-time students: individual and group career counseling, individual job placement, employer recruitment on campus. Part-time tuition: $95 per credit.

Oblate School of Theology
San Antonio 78216

Independent-religious institution (graduate only). Total enrollment: 91 (coed; 49% part-time). Total faculty: 22. Library holdings: 35,300 bound volumes, 640 microforms.

Graduate Part-time study available in Graduate and Professional Programs. Basic part-time expenses: $114 per credit tuition plus $35 per semester (minimum) fees. Institutional financial aid available to part-time graduate students in Graduate and Professional Programs.

Our Lady of the Lake University of San Antonio
San Antonio 78285

Independent-religious instutition; metropolitan setting. Awards B, M. Total enrollment: 1,758. Undergraduate enrollment: 1,257; 50% part-time, 68% women, 34% over 25. Total faculty: 95. Library holdings: 145,339 bound volumes, 25,696 titles on microform, 766 periodical subscriptions, 7,372 records/tapes.

Undergraduate Courses offered for part-time students during daytime, evenings, weekends, summer. Complete part-time degree programs offered during daytime, evenings, weekends, summer. Adult/continuing education programs available. Career services available to part-time students: individual and group career counseling, individual job placement, employer recruitment on campus. Part-time tuition: $122 per credit hour.

Graduate Part-time study available in College of Arts and Sciences, Jersig School-Speech Pathology, School of Business and Public Administration, School of Education and Clinical Studies, Worden School of Social Service. Degree can be earned exclusively through evening/weekend study in School of Business and Public Administration. Basic part-time expenses: $127 per semester hour tuition plus $26 per semester fees. Institutional financial aid available to part-time graduate students in School of Education and Clinical Studies, Worden School of Social Service.

Colleges Offering Part-Time Degree Programs / *Texas*

Pan American University
Edinburg 78539

Public institution; rural setting. Awards A, B, M. Total enrollment: 9,622. Undergraduate enrollment: 8,687; 43% part-time, 58% women. Total faculty: 415. Library holdings: 224,012 bound volumes, 12,673 titles on microform, 2,454 periodical subscriptions, 3,943 records/tapes.

Undergraduate Courses offered for part-time students during daytime, evenings, weekends, summer. Complete part-time degree programs offered during daytime, evenings, summer. Adult/continuing education programs available. Career services available to part-time students: individual and group career counseling, individual job placement, employer recruitment on campus. Part-time tuition: $40 per semester hour for nonresidents. State resident part-time tuition per semester (1 to 11 semester hours) ranges from $54 to $94.

Panola Junior College
Carthage 75633

Public institution; small-town setting. Awards A. Barrier-free campus. Total enrollment: 1,272 (all undergraduates); 45% part-time, 62% women. Total faculty: 47. Library holdings: 26,000 bound volumes, 165 periodical subscriptions, 750 records/tapes.

Undergraduate Courses offered for part-time students during daytime, evenings, summer. Complete part-time degree programs offered during daytime, evenings, summer. Adult/continuing education programs available. Career services available to part-time students: individual and group career counseling, individual job placement. Part-time tuition and fees per semester (1 to 11 semester hours) range from $35 to $79 for district residents, $80 to $240 for state residents, $90 to $245 for nonresidents.

Paris Junior College
Paris 75460

Public institution; rural setting. Awards A. Barrier-free campus. Total enrollment: 2,186 (all undergraduates); 48% part-time, 53% women, 30% over 25. Total faculty: 128. Library holdings: 29,095 bound volumes, 6,517 titles on microform, 396 periodical subscriptions, 3,876 records/tapes.

Undergraduate Courses offered for part-time students during daytime, evenings, summer. Complete part-time degree programs offered during daytime, evenings, summer. External degree and adult/continuing education programs available. Career services available to part-time students: individual and group career counseling, individual job placement, employer recruitment on campus. Part-time tuition per semester ranges from $51 to $132 for area residents, $86 to $172 for state residents, $70 to $495 for nonresidents, according to course load and program.

Paul Quinn College
Waco 76704

Independent-religious instutition; city setting. Awards B. Total enrollment: 467 (all undergraduates); 5% part-time, 53% women. Total faculty: 42. Library holdings: 87,000 bound volumes, 35,000 titles on microform, 167 periodical subscriptions, 1,000 records/tapes.

Undergraduate Courses offered for part-time students during daytime, evenings, summer. Complete part-time degree programs offered during daytime, evenings, summer. External degree programs available. Career services available to part-time students: individual career counseling, individual job placement, employer recruitment on campus. Part-time tuition: $72 per semester hour.

Prairie View A&M University
Prairie View 77445

Public institution; small-town setting. Awards B, M. Total enrollment: 4,495. Undergraduate enrollment: 4,000; 2% part-time, 49% women. Total faculty: 332.

Undergraduate Courses offered for part-time students during daytime, evenings, weekends, summer. Complete part-time degree programs offered during daytime, evenings, weekends, summer. External degree and adult/continuing education programs available. Career services available to part-time students: individual and group career counseling, individual job placement, employer recruitment on campus. Part-time tuition: $4 per credit hour for state residents, $40 per credit hour for nonresidents.

Ranger Junior College
Ranger 76470

Public institution; rural setting. Awards A. Total enrollment: 800 (all undergraduates); 30% part-time, 20% women. Total faculty: 55.

Undergraduate Courses offered for part-time students during daytime, evenings, summer. Complete part-time degree programs offered during daytime, evenings, summer. Adult/continuing education programs available. Career services available to part-time students: individual career counseling. Part-time tuition per semester (1 to 11 semester hours) ranges from $33 to $132 for state residents, $59 to $275 for nonresidents.

Rice University
Houston 77251

Independent institution; metropolitan setting. Awards B, M, D. Barrier-free campus. Total enrollment: 3,719. Undergraduate enrollment: 2,643; 0% part-time, 33% women. Total faculty: 421. Library holdings: 1.2 million bound volumes, 75,000 titles on microform, 9,000 periodical subscriptions, 15,000 records/tapes.

Graduate Part-time study available in Graduate Programs. Basic part-time expenses: $160 per semester hour tuition plus $50 per semester fees.

Richland College
Dallas 75243

Public institution; metropolitan setting. Awards A. Barrier-free campus. Total enrollment: 13,483 (all undergraduates); 73% part-time, 55% women, 53% over 25. Total faculty: 570. Library holdings: 60,000 bound volumes, 2,309 titles on microform, 342 periodical subscriptions, 4,000 records/tapes.

Undergraduate Courses offered for part-time students during daytime, evenings, weekends, summer. Complete part-time degree programs offered during daytime, evenings, weekends, summer. Adult/continuing education programs available. Career services available to part-time students: individual and group career counseling, individual job placement, employer recruitment on campus. Part-time tuition per semester (1 to 11 credits) ranges from $33 to $118 for county residents, $33 to $330 for state residents, $60 to $659 for nonresidents.

Texas / **Colleges Offering Part-Time Degree Programs**

St Edward's University
Austin 78704

Independent-religious instutition; city setting. Awards B, M. Total enrollment: 2,557. Undergraduate enrollment: 2,210; 20% part-time, 48% women, 40% over 25. Total faculty: 141. Library holdings: 150,000 bound volumes, 600 periodical subscriptions.

Undergraduate Courses offered for part-time students during daytime, evenings, summer. Complete part-time degree programs offered during daytime, evenings, summer. External degree and adult/continuing education programs available. Career services available to part-time students: individual and group career counseling, individual job placement, employer recruitment on campus. Part-time tuition: $120 per credit hour.

Graduate Part-time study available in Center for Business and Public Administration, Center for Teaching and Learning. Degree can be earned exclusively through evening/weekend study in Center for Business and Public Administration.Basic part-time expenses: $145 per credit tuition plus $7 per trimester fees.

St Mary's University of San Antonio
San Antonio 78284

Independent-religious instutition; metropolitan setting. Awards B, M, D. Total enrollment: 3,233. Undergraduate enrollment: 2,154; 18% part-time, 48% women, 34% over 25. Total faculty: 187. Library holdings: 348,202 bound volumes, 15,000 titles on microform, 1,115 periodical subscriptions, 12,400 records/tapes.

Undergraduate Courses offered for part-time students during daytime, evenings, summer. Complete part-time degree programs offered during daytime, evenings. Adult/continuing education programs available. Career services available to part-time students: individual and group career counseling, individual job placement, employer recruitment on campus. Part-time tuition: $137 per semester hour.

Graduate Part-time study available in Graduate School. Degree can be earned exclusively through evening/weekend study in Graduate School.Basic part-time expenses: $155 per credit tuition plus $29 per semester fees.

Sam Houston State University
Huntsville 77341

Public institution; small-town setting. Awards B, M, D. Total enrollment: 10,580. Undergraduate enrollment: 8,997; 8% part-time, 51% women, 21% over 25. Total faculty: 372. Library holdings: 600,000 bound volumes, 375,000 titles on microform, 4,500 periodical subscriptions, 12,000 records/tapes.

Undergraduate Courses offered for part-time students during daytime. Complete part-time degree programs offered during daytime. Adult/continuing education programs available. Part-time tuition: $100 per year for state residents, $40 per semester hour for nonresidents.

Graduate Part-time study available in College of Arts and Sciences, College of Business Administration, College of Criminal Justice, College of Education and Applied Science, School of Library Science.Basic part-time expenses: $50 per semester (minimum) tuition plus $65 per semester (minimum) fees for state residents, $40 per hour tuition plus $65 per semester (minimum) fees for nonresidents.

San Antonio College
San Antonio 78284

Public institution; metropolitan setting. Awards A. Barrier-free campus. Total enrollment: 22,147 (all undergraduates); 61% part-time, 55% women, 53% over 25. Total faculty: 964. Library holdings: 263,326 bound volumes, 63,384 titles on microform, 1,921 periodical subscriptions, 9,584 records/tapes.

Undergraduate Courses offered for part-time students during daytime, evenings, summer. Complete part-time degree programs offered during daytime, evenings, summer. Adult/continuing education programs available. Career services available to part-time students: individual and group career counseling, individual job placement, employer recruitment on campus. Part-time tuition and fees per semester (1 to 11 semester hours) range from $50 to $78 for area residents, $70 to $130 for state residents, $70 to $251 for nonresidents.

San Jacinto College–Central Campus
Pasadena 77505

Public institution; city setting. Awards A. Barrier-free campus. Total enrollment: 9,296 (all undergraduates); 65% part-time, 49% women, 42% over 25. Total faculty: 394. Library holdings: 100,000 bound volumes, 400 periodical subscriptions, 2,000 records/tapes.

Undergraduate Courses offered for part-time students during daytime, evenings, weekends, summer. Complete part-time degree programs offered during daytime, evenings, weekends, summer. Adult/continuing education programs available. Career services available to part-time students: individual career counseling, individual job placement, employer recruitment on campus. Part-time tuition: $4 per semester hour for area residents, $14 per semester hour for state residents, $17 per semester hour for nonresidents.

San Jacinto College–North Campus
Houston 77049

Public institution; metropolitan setting. Awards A. Total enrollment: 3,650 (all undergraduates); 69% part-time, 52% women. Total faculty: 165. Library holdings: 36,460 bound volumes, 5,802 titles on microform, 435 periodical subscriptions, 861 records/tapes.

Undergraduate Courses offered for part-time students during daytime, evenings, weekends, summer. Complete part-time degree programs offered during daytime, evenings, weekends, summer. Adult/continuing education programs available. Career services available to part-time students: individual career counseling, individual job placement. Part-time tuition and fees per semester (1 to 11 semester hours) range from $25 to $44 for district residents, $35 to $154 for state residents, $25 to $187 for nonresidents.

San Jacinto College–South Campus
Houston 77089

Public institution; metropolitan setting. Awards A. Barrier-free campus. Total enrollment: 3,513 (all undergraduates); 78% part-time, 58% women, 46% over 25. Total faculty: 133. Library holdings: 30,000 bound volumes, 761 titles on microform, 634 periodical subscriptions, 96 records/tapes.

Undergraduate Courses offered for part-time students during daytime, evenings, weekends, summer. Complete part-time degree programs offered during daytime, evenings, weekends, summer. Adult/continuing education programs available. Career services available to part-time students: individual and group career counseling, individual job placement, employer recruitment on campus. Part-time tuition: $25 per semester hour for area residents, $51 per semester hour for state residents, $120 per semester hour for nonresidents.

Colleges Offering Part-Time Degree Programs / Texas

Schreiner College
Kerrville 78028

Independent-religious instutition; small-town setting. Awards A, B. Total enrollment: 488 (all undergraduates); 22% part-time, 50% women, 20% over 25. Total faculty: 39. Library holdings: 26,000 bound volumes, 247 periodical subscriptions.

Undergraduate Courses offered for part-time students during daytime, evenings, summer. Complete part-time degree programs offered during daytime. Part-time tuition: $120 per credit hour.

Southern Methodist University
Dallas 75275

Independent institution; metropolitan setting. Awards B, M, D. Barrier-free campus. Total enrollment: 9,149. Undergraduate enrollment: 6,086; 10% part-time, 50% women. Total faculty: 622. Library holdings: 1.2 million bound volumes, 214,487 titles on microform, 5,341 periodical subscriptions, 12,892 records/tapes.

Undergraduate Courses offered for part-time students during daytime, summer. Complete part-time degree programs offered during daytime, summer. Adult/continuing education programs available. Career services available to part-time students: individual and group career counseling, individual job placement, employer recruitment on campus. Part-time tuition: $290 per credit hour.

Graduate Part-time study available in Dedman College, Edwin L. Cox School of Business, Meadows School of the Arts, Perkins School of Theology, School of Engineering and Applied Science, School of Law. Basic part-time expenses: $256 per credit tuition plus $34 per semester (minimum) fees. Institutional financial aid available to part-time graduate students in Dedman College, Meadows School of the Arts.

South Plains College
Levelland 79336

Public institution; small-town setting. Awards A. Barrier-free campus. Total enrollment: 3,565 (all undergraduates); 40% part-time, 50% women, 18% over 25. Total faculty: 206.

Undergraduate Courses offered for part-time students during daytime, evenings, summer. Complete part-time degree programs offered during daytime, evenings, summer. Adult/continuing education programs available. Career services available to part-time students: individual career counseling, employer recruitment on campus. Part-time tuition and fees per semester (1 to 11 credits) range from $40 to $66 for area residents, $41 to $77 for state residents, $75 to $222 for nonresidents.

South Texas College of Law
Houston 77002

Independent institution (graduate only). Total enrollment: 1,164 (coed; 49% part-time). Total faculty: 43. Library holdings: 155,000 bound volumes.

Graduate Part-time study available in Professional Program. Degree can be earned exclusively through evening/weekend study in Professional Program. Basic part-time expenses: $1450 per trimester tuition plus $79 per trimester fees. Institutional financial aid available to part-time graduate students in Professional Program.

SouthWest Collegiate Institute for the Deaf
Big Spring 79720

Public institution; small-town setting. Awards A. Barrier-free campus. Total enrollment: 115 (all undergraduates); 0% part-time, 40% women. Total faculty: 23. Library holdings: 33,197 bound volumes, 20 titles on microform, 225 periodical subscriptions, 1,129 records/tapes.

Undergraduate Courses offered for part-time students during daytime, evenings, summer. Complete part-time degree programs offered during daytime. Career services available to part-time students: individual and group career counseling. Part-time tuition per semester (1 to 11 credits) ranges from $131 to $195 for state residents, $398 to $458 for nonresidents.

Southwestern Adventist College
Keene 76059

Independent-religious instutition; small-town setting. Awards A, B. Barrier-free campus. Total enrollment: 708 (all undergraduates); 20% part-time, 53% women, 24% over 25. Total faculty: 62. Library holdings: 81,481 bound volumes, 11,466 titles on microform, 481 periodical subscriptions, 11,012 records/tapes.

Undergraduate Courses offered for part-time students during daytime. Complete part-time degree programs offered during daytime. External degree programs available. Career services available to part-time students: individual career counseling, individual job placement. Part-time tuition: $195 per semester hour.

Southwestern Assemblies of God College
Waxahachie 75165

Independent-religious instutition; small-town setting. Awards A, B. Total enrollment: 325 (all undergraduates); 5% part-time, 46% women, 30% over 25. Total faculty: 33. Library holdings: 84,873 bound volumes, 429 periodical subscriptions, 1,567 records/tapes.

Undergraduate Courses offered for part-time students during daytime, evenings, summer. Complete part-time degree programs offered during daytime. Career services available to part-time students: individual and group career counseling, individual job placement, employer recruitment on campus. Part-time tuition: $60 per semester hour.

Southwestern Baptist Theological Seminary
Fort Worth 76122

Independent-religious institution (graduate only). Total enrollment: 5,036. Graduate enrollment: 4,922 (primarily men; 36% part-time). Total faculty: 170. Library holdings: 576,656 bound volumes, 21,670 microforms.

Graduate Part-time study available in School of Church Music, School of Religious Education, School of Theology. Degree can be earned exclusively through evening/weekend study in School of Church Music, School of Religious Education, School of Theology. Basic part-time expenses: $300 per semester (minimum) tuition plus $30 per semester fees.

Texas / Colleges Offering Part-Time Degree Programs

Southwestern Christian College
Terrell 75160

Independent-religious instutition; small-town setting. Awards A, B. Total enrollment: 306 (all undergraduates); 5% part-time, 55% women, 1% over 25. Total faculty: 26. Library holdings: 1,100 bound volumes, 200 periodical subscriptions.

Undergraduate Courses offered for part-time students during daytime, evenings. Complete part-time degree programs offered during daytime. Career services available to part-time students: group career counseling. Part-time tuition: $89 per hour.

Southwestern Junior College of the Assemblies of God
Waxahachie 75165

Independent-religious instutition; small-town setting. Awards A. Total enrollment: 440 (all undergraduates); 4% part-time, 51% women, 30% over 25. Total faculty: 20. Library holdings: 84,873 bound volumes, 6,629 titles on microform, 496 periodical subscriptions, 1,567 records/tapes.

Undergraduate Courses offered for part-time students during daytime, evenings. Complete part-time degree programs offered during daytime. Career services available to part-time students: individual career counseling, individual job placement, employer recruitment on campus. Part-time tuition: $60 per semester hour.

Southwest Texas Junior College
Uvalde 78801

Public institution; small-town setting. Awards A. Barrier-free campus. Total enrollment: 2,179 (all undergraduates); 55% part-time, 40% women. Total faculty: 135.

Undergraduate Courses offered for part-time students during daytime, evenings. Complete part-time degree programs offered during daytime, evenings. External degree and adult/continuing education programs available. Career services available to part-time students: individual and group career counseling, employer recruitment on campus. Part-time tuition and fees per semester (1 to 11 semester hours) range from $40 to $121 for district residents, $44 to $165 for state residents, $55 to $517 for nonresidents.

Southwest Texas State University
San Marcos 78666

Public institution; small-town setting. Awards A, B, M. Total enrollment: 18,317. Undergraduate enrollment: 16,476; 16% part-time, 56% women, 12% over 25. Total faculty: 843. Library holdings: 647,424 bound volumes, 202,208 titles on microform, 3,923 periodical subscriptions, 3,374 records/tapes.

Undergraduate Courses offered for part-time students during daytime, evenings, summer. Complete part-time degree programs offered during daytime, evenings, summer. Adult/continuing education programs available. Career services available to part-time students: individual and group career counseling, individual job placement, employer recruitment on campus. Part-time tuition and fees per semester (1 to 11 semester hours) range from $86 to $190 for state residents, $76 to $580 for nonresidents.

Graduate Part-time study available in Graduate School. Degree can be earned exclusively through evening/weekend study in Graduate School. Basic part-time expenses: $50 per semester (minimum) tuition plus $71 per semester (minimum) fees for state residents, $40 per semester hour tuition plus $71 per semester (minimum) fees for nonresidents. Institutional financial aid available to part-time graduate students in Graduate School.

Stephen F Austin State University
Nacogdoches 75962

Public institution; small-town setting. Awards B, M, D. Barrier-free campus. Total enrollment: 12,500. Undergraduate enrollment: 10,500; 5% part-time, 54% women. Total faculty: 470. Library holdings: 381,895 bound volumes, 303,818 titles on microform, 3,076 periodical subscriptions, 2,056 records/tapes.

Undergraduate Courses offered for part-time students during daytime, evenings, weekends, summer. Complete part-time degree programs offered during daytime, evenings, weekends, summer. Adult/continuing education programs available. Career services available to part-time students: individual and group career counseling, individual job placement, employer recruitment on campus. Part-time tuition: $100 per year for state residents, $40 per semester hour for nonresidents.

Graduate Part-time study available in Graduate School. Degree can be earned exclusively through evening/weekend study in Graduate School. Basic part-time expenses: $50 per semester (minimum) tuition plus $45.50 per semester (minimum) fees for state residents, $40 per semester hour tuition plus $45.50 per semester (minimum) fees for nonresidents. Institutional financial aid available to part-time graduate students in Graduate School.

Sul Ross State University
Alpine 79832

Public institution; small-town setting. Awards A, B, M. Total enrollment: 2,448. Undergraduate enrollment: 1,827; 21% part-time, 46% women. Total faculty: 150. Library holdings: 216,789 bound volumes, 20,000 titles on microform, 1,411 periodical subscriptions, 2,000 records/tapes.

Graduate Part-time study available in Graduate School. Basic part-time expenses: $50 per semester (minimum) tuition plus $46.50 per semester (minimum) fees for state residents, $40 per semester hour tuition plus $46.50 per semester (minimum) fees for nonresidents.

Tarleton State University
Stephenville 76402

Public institution; small-town setting. Awards A, B, M. Total enrollment: 4,430. Undergraduate enrollment: 3,619; 14% part-time, 50% women. Total faculty: 166.

Undergraduate Courses offered for part-time students during daytime, evenings, summer. Complete part-time degree programs offered during daytime, evenings, summer. Adult/continuing education programs available. Career services available to part-time students: individual career counseling, individual job placement, employer recruitment on campus. Part-time tuition: $4 per semester hour for state residents, $40 per semester hour for nonresidents.

Tarrant County Junior College
Fort Worth 76102

Public institution; metropolitan setting. Awards A. Barrier-free campus. Total enrollment: 27,452 (all undergraduates); 77% part-time, 53% women, 47% over 25. Total faculty: 1,099. Library holdings: 142,250 bound volumes, 1,250 titles on microform, 2,952 periodical subscriptions, 16,200 records/tapes.

Undergraduate Courses offered for part-time students during daytime, evenings, summer. Complete part-time degree pro-

Colleges Offering Part-Time Degree Programs / Texas

Tarrant County Junior College (continued)
grams offered during daytime, evenings, summer. Adult/continuing education programs available. Career services available to part-time students: individual career counseling, individual job placement, employer recruitment on campus. Part-time tuition: $4 per semester hour for area residents, $7 per semester hour for state residents, $40 per semester hour for nonresidents.

Texarkana Community College
Texarkana 75501

Public institution; small-town setting. Awards A. Total enrollment: 3,700 (all undergraduates); 64% part-time, 56% women. Total faculty: 200. Library holdings: 32,500 bound volumes, 228 periodical subscriptions, 3,210 records/tapes.

Undergraduate Courses offered for part-time students during daytime, evenings, summer. Complete part-time degree programs offered during daytime, evenings, summer. Adult/continuing education programs available. Part-time tuition per semester (1 to 11 semester hours) ranges from $38 to $105 for district residents, $47 to $138 for state residents, $71 to $247.50 for nonresidents.

Texas A&I University
Kingsville 78363

Public institution; small-town setting. Awards B, M, D. Barrier-free campus. Total enrollment: 5,560. Undergraduate enrollment: 4,358; 14% part-time, 48% women. Total faculty: 226. Library holdings: 420,279 bound volumes, 203,915 titles on microform, 2,122 periodical subscriptions, 4,837 records/tapes.

Undergraduate Courses offered for part-time students during daytime, evenings, summer. Complete part-time degree programs offered during daytime. Adult/continuing education programs available. Career services available to part-time students: individual career counseling, individual job placement, employer recruitment on campus. Part-time tuition and fees per semester (1 to 12 credits) range from $98 to $212 for state residents, $168 to $642 for nonresidents.

Graduate Part-time study available in College of Graduate Studies.Basic part-time expenses: $50 per semester (minimum) tuition plus $48 per semester (minimum) fees for state residents, $40 per semester hour tuition plus $48 per semester (minimum) fees for nonresidents. Institutional financial aid available to part-time graduate students in College of Graduate Studies.

Texas A&M University
College Station 77843

Public institution; city setting. Awards B, M, D. Total enrollment: 36,846. Undergraduate enrollment: 29,980; 7% part-time, 37% women, 5% over 25. Total faculty: 2,182. Library holdings: 1.4 million bound volumes, 2.0 million titles on microform, 16,886 periodical subscriptions, 256 records/tapes.

Undergraduate Courses offered for part-time students during daytime, evenings, summer. Complete part-time degree programs offered during daytime, summer. Adult/continuing education programs available. Career services available to part-time students: individual and group career counseling, individual job placement, employer recruitment on campus. Part-time tuition and fees per semester (1 to 12 semester hours) range from $90.30 to $203.60 for state residents, $80.30 to $633.60 for nonresidents.

Texas A&M University at Galveston
Galveston 77553

Public institution; city setting. Awards B. Barrier-free campus. Total enrollment: 552 (all undergraduates); 13% part-time, 25% women. Total faculty: 70. Library holdings: 40,000 bound volumes, 30,000 titles on microform, 700 periodical subscriptions, 100 records/tapes.

Undergraduate Courses offered for part-time students during daytime. Complete part-time degree programs offered during daytime. Career services available to part-time students: individual career counseling, individual job placement, employer recruitment on campus. Part-time tuition: $4 per credit hour for state residents, $40 per credit hour for nonresidents.

Texas Christian University
Fort Worth 76129

Independent-religious instutition; metropolitan setting. Awards B, M, D. Total enrollment: 6,878. Undergraduate enrollment: 4,776; 10% part-time, 56% women. Total faculty: 519. Library holdings: 1.2 million bound volumes, 9,000 periodical subscriptions.

Undergraduate Courses offered for part-time students during daytime, evenings. Complete part-time degree programs offered during daytime, evenings. Adult/continuing education programs available. Career services available to part-time students: individual and group career counseling, individual job placement, employer recruitment on campus. Part-time tuition: $150 per semester hour.

Texas Lutheran College
Seguin 78155

Independent-religious instutition; small-town setting. Awards B. Total enrollment: 978 (all undergraduates); 6% part-time, 51% women, 3% over 25. Total faculty: 78. Library holdings: 112,000 bound volumes, 2,000 titles on microform, 622 periodical subscriptions, 8,000 records/tapes.

Undergraduate Courses offered for part-time students during daytime, summer. Complete part-time degree programs offered during daytime, summer. Adult/continuing education programs available. Career services available to part-time students: individual and group career counseling, individual job placement, employer recruitment on campus. Part-time tuition: $112 per credit hour.

Texas Southern University
Houston 77004

Public institution; metropolitan setting. Awards B, M, D. Barrier-free campus. Total enrollment: 9,002. Undergraduate enrollment: 7,028; 28% part-time, 46% women. Total faculty: 600. Library holdings: 250,000 bound volumes, 125 periodical subscriptions, 300 records/tapes.

Undergraduate Courses offered for part-time students during daytime, evenings, weekends, summer. Complete part-time degree programs offered during daytime, evenings, weekends, summer. Adult/continuing education programs available. Career services available to part-time students: individual and group career counseling, employer recruitment on campus. Part-time tuition and fees per semester (1 to 12 semester hours) range from $75.75 to $238 for state residents, $65.75 to $668 for nonresidents.

Graduate Part-time study available in Graduate School. Degree can be earned exclusively through evening/weekend study in Graduate School.Basic part-time expenses: $50 per semester (minimum) tuition plus $55.25 per semester (minimum) fees for state residents, $40 per credit tuition plus $55.25 per semester (minimum) fees for nonresidents.

Texas Southmost College
Brownsville 78520

Public institution; city setting. Awards A. Barrier-free campus. Total enrollment: 4,776 (all undergraduates); 50% part-time, 60% women, 31% over 25. Total faculty: 100. Library holdings: 90,000 bound volumes, 1,903 periodical subscriptions.

Undergraduate Courses offered for part-time students during daytime, evenings, weekends, summer. Complete part-time degree programs offered during daytime, evenings, weekends, summer. Adult/continuing education programs available. Career services available to part-time students: individual career counseling, individual job placement. Part-time tuition per semester (1 to 11 semester hours) ranges from $44.25 to $145.75 for district residents, $46 to $165 for state residents, $53 to $508 for nonresidents.

Texas State Technical Institute–Amarillo Campus
Amarillo 79111

Public institution; city setting. Awards A. Barrier-free campus. Total enrollment: 1,065 (all undergraduates); 10% part-time, 21% women. Total faculty: 115. Library holdings: 14,200 bound volumes, 145 titles on microform, 297 periodical subscriptions, 600 records/tapes.

Undergraduate Courses offered for part-time students during daytime, evenings, summer. Complete part-time degree programs offered during daytime, evenings, summer. Adult/continuing education programs available. Career services available to part-time students: individual career counseling, individual job placement, employer recruitment on campus. Part-time tuition: $5 per quarter hour for state residents, $20 per quarter hour for nonresidents.

Texas State Technical Institute–Harlingen Campus
Harlingen 78550

Public institution; small-town setting. Awards A. Barrier-free campus. Total enrollment: 2,081 (all undergraduates); 1% part-time, 33% women. Total faculty: 128. Library holdings: 14,700 bound volumes, 300 titles on microform, 45 periodical subscriptions, 250 records/tapes.

Undergraduate Courses offered for part-time students during daytime, evenings. Complete part-time degree programs offered during daytime, evenings. Adult/continuing education programs available. Part-time tuition: $5 per quarter hour for state residents, $20 per quarter hour for nonresidents.

Texas State Technical Institute–Sweetwater Campus
Sweetwater 79556

Public institution; rural setting. Awards A. Barrier-free campus. Total enrollment: 638 (all undergraduates); 25% part-time, 28% women, 30% over 25. Total faculty: 55. Library holdings: 13,283 bound volumes, 76 titles on microform, 170 periodical subscriptions, 3,236 records/tapes.

Undergraduate Courses offered for part-time students during daytime, evenings, summer. Complete part-time degree programs offered during daytime, evenings, summer. Adult/continuing education programs available. Career services available to part-time students: individual and group career counseling, individual job placement, employer recruitment on campus. Part-time tuition: $5 per quarter hour for state residents, $20 per quarter hour for nonresidents.

Texas State Technical Institute–Waco Campus
Waco 76705

Public institution; city setting. Awards A. Barrier-free campus. Total enrollment: 5,133 (all undergraduates); 10% part-time, 15% women. Total faculty: 319. Library holdings: 50,264 bound volumes, 59,159 titles on microform, 511 periodical subscriptions, 543 records/tapes.

Undergraduate Courses offered for part-time students during daytime, evenings, summer. Complete part-time degree programs offered during daytime, evenings, summer. Adult/continuing education programs available. Career services available to part-time students: individual and group career counseling, individual job placement, employer recruitment on campus. Part-time tuition: $5 per quarter hour for state residents, $20 per quarter hour for nonresidents.

Texas Tech University
Lubbock 79409

Public institution; city setting. Awards B, M, D. Total enrollment: 23,704. Undergraduate enrollment: 19,755; 12% part-time, 43% women. Total faculty: 1,571. Library holdings: 1.5 million bound volumes, 6,600 periodical subscriptions.

Undergraduate Courses offered for part-time students during daytime, evenings. Complete part-time degree programs offered during daytime, evenings. Adult/continuing education programs available. Career services available to part-time students: individual career counseling. Part-time tuition: $400 per year for state residents. Nonresident part-time tuition and fees per semester (1 to 12 semester hours) range from $190 to $630.

Graduate Part-time study available in Graduate School, School of Law. Basic part-time expenses: $50 per semester (minimum) tuition plus $46.75 per semester (minimum) fees for state residents, $40 per hour tuition plus $46.75 per semester (minimum) fees for nonresidents. Institutional financial aid available to part-time graduate students in Graduate School.

Texas Wesleyan College
Fort Worth 76105

Independent-religious instutition; metropolitan setting. Awards B, M. Barrier-free campus. Total enrollment: 1,629. Undergraduate enrollment: 1,480; 36% part-time, 57% women, 34% over 25. Total faculty: 113. Library holdings: 126,030 bound volumes, 840 periodical subscriptions, 600 records/tapes.

Undergraduate Courses offered for part-time students during daytime, evenings, summer. Complete part-time degree programs offered during daytime, evenings, summer. Career services available to part-time students: individual and group career counseling, individual job placement, employer recruitment on campus. Part-time tuition: $125 per semester hour.

Graduate Part-time study available in Graduate Programs. Basic part-time expenses: $125 per credit hour tuition plus $30 per semester fees. Institutional financial aid available to part-time graduate students in Graduate Programs.

Colleges Offering Part-Time Degree Programs / Texas

Texas Woman's University
Denton 76204

Public institution; city setting. Awards B, M, D. Barrier-free campus. Total enrollment: 8,483. Undergraduate enrollment: 4,251; 27% part-time, 96% women. Total faculty: 648. Library holdings: 693,110 bound volumes, 317,651 titles on microform, 4,371 periodical subscriptions, 6,706 records/tapes.

Undergraduate Courses offered for part-time students during daytime, evenings, weekends, summer. Complete part-time degree programs offered during daytime, evenings, weekends, summer. Adult/continuing education programs available. Career services available to part-time students: individual and group career counseling, individual job placement, employer recruitment on campus. Part-time tuition and fees per semester (1 to 12 semester hours) range from $63.25 to $198 for state residents, $53.25 to $528 for nonresidents.

Trinity University
San Antonio 78284

Independent institution; metropolitan setting. Awards B, M. Total enrollment: 3,027. Undergraduate enrollment: 2,441; 19% part-time, 52% women, 4% over 25. Total faculty: 274. Library holdings: 399,544 bound volumes, 191,494 titles on microform, 2,718 periodical subscriptions, 15,000 records/tapes.

Undergraduate Courses offered for part-time students during daytime. Complete part-time degree programs offered during daytime. Adult/continuing education programs available. Career services available to part-time students: individual and group career counseling, individual job placement, employer recruitment on campus. Part-time tuition: $225 per semester hour.

Graduate Part-time study available in Division of Behavioral Sciences, Division of Business and Administrative Studies, Division of Humanities and Arts, Division of Sciences, Mathematics and Engineering. Basic part-time expenses: $225 per credit hour tuition plus $0.50 per credit hour fees. Institutional financial aid available to part-time graduate students in Division of Behavioral Sciences.

Tyler Junior College
Tyler 75711

Public institution; city setting. Awards A. Total enrollment: 7,771 (all undergraduates); 15% part-time, 58% women, 38% over 25. Total faculty: 320. Library holdings: 68,144 bound volumes, 233 titles on microform, 350 periodical subscriptions, 14,366 records/tapes.

Undergraduate Courses offered for part-time students during daytime, evenings, summer. Complete part-time degree programs offered during daytime, evenings, summer. Adult/continuing education programs available. Career services available to part-time students: individual career counseling, individual job placement, employer recruitment on campus. Part-time tuition: $4 per semester hour for area residents, $7 per semester hour for state residents, $40 per semester hour for nonresidents.

University of Dallas
Irving 75061

Independent-religious instutition; city setting. Awards B, M, D. Total enrollment: 2,600. Undergraduate enrollment: 1,070; 5% part-time, 49% women, 0% over 25. Total faculty: 182. Library holdings: 218,800 bound volumes, 70,034 titles on microform, 1,148 periodical subscriptions, 2,075 records/tapes.

Undergraduate Courses offered for part-time students during daytime, summer. Complete part-time degree programs offered during daytime, summer. Adult/continuing education programs available. Career services available to part-time students: individual career counseling, employer recruitment on campus. Part-time tuition: $156 per credit.

Graduate Part-time study available in Braniff Graduate School. Degree can be earned exclusively through evening/weekend study in Braniff Graduate School. Basic part-time expenses: $168 per hour tuition plus $4 per hour fees. Institutional financial aid available to part-time graduate students in Braniff Graduate School.

University of Houston–Clear Lake
Houston 77058

Public institution; metropolitan setting. Awards B, M. Barrier-free campus. Total enrollment: 6,498. Undergraduate enrollment: 3,583; 61% part-time, 58% women, 69% over 25. Total faculty: 226. Library holdings: 260,000 bound volumes, 380,000 titles on microform, 1,500 periodical subscriptions.

Undergraduate Courses offered for part-time students during daytime, evenings, summer. Complete part-time degree programs offered during daytime, evenings, summer. Career services available to part-time students: individual and group career counseling, individual job placement, employer recruitment on campus. Part-time tuition and fees per semester (1 to 11 semester hours) range from $101 to $228 for state residents, $91 to $618 for nonresidents.

Graduate Part-time study available in School of Business and Public Administration, School of Human Sciences and Humanities, School of Professional Education, School of Sciences and Technologies. Degree can be earned exclusively through evening/weekend study in School of Business and Public Administration, School of Human Sciences and Humanities, School of Professional Education, School of Sciences and Technologies. Basic part-time expenses: $50 per semester (minimum) tuition plus $73 per semester (minimum) fees for state residents, $40 per hour tuition plus $73 per semester (minimum) fees for nonresidents. Institutional financial aid available to part-time graduate students in School of Business and Public Administration, School of Human Sciences and Humanities, School of Professional Education, School of Sciences and Technologies.

University of Houston–Downtown
Houston 77002

Public institution; metropolitan setting. Awards B. Barrier-free campus. Total enrollment: 6,323 (all undergraduates); 53% part-time, 46% women, 55% over 25. Total faculty: 273. Library holdings: 85,000 bound volumes, 600 periodical subscriptions, 3,500 records/tapes.

Undergraduate Courses offered for part-time students during daytime, evenings, weekends, summer. Complete part-time degree programs offered during daytime, evenings, weekends, summer. Adult/continuing education programs available. Career services available to part-time students: individual and group career counseling, individual job placement, employer recruitment on campus. Part-time tuition and fees per semester (1 to 11 hours) range from $112 to $235 for state residents, $102 to $585 for nonresidents.

University of Houston–University Park
Houston 77004

Public institution; metropolitan setting. Awards B, M, D. Barrier-free campus. Total enrollment: 31,500. Undergraduate enrollment: 18,755; 46% part-time, 44% women. Total faculty:

Texas / Colleges Offering Part-Time Degree Programs

2,323. Library holdings: 1.3 million bound volumes, 1.5 million titles on microform, 13,400 periodical subscriptions.

Undergraduate Courses offered for part-time students during daytime, evenings, summer. Complete part-time degree programs offered during daytime, evenings, summer. Adult/continuing education programs available. Career services available to part-time students: individual and group career counseling, individual job placement, employer recruitment on campus. Part-time tuition and fees per semester (1 to 11 semester hours) range from $102 to $200 for state residents, $92 to $590 for nonresidents.

Graduate Part-time study available in Bates College of Law, College of Architecture, College of Business Administration, College of Education, College of Humanities and Fine Arts, College of Optometry, Collen College of Engineering, Graduate School of Social Work. Basic part-time expenses: $50 per semester (minimum) tuition plus $62.50 per semester (minimum) fees for state residents, $40 per credit hour tuition plus $62.50 per semester (minimum) fees for nonresidents. Institutional financial aid available to part-time graduate students in Bates College of Law, College of Business Administration, College of Education, College of Humanities and Fine Arts, College of Optometry, Collen College of Engineering, Graduate School of Social Work.

University of Mary Hardin-Baylor
Belton 76513

Independent-religious instutition; small-town setting. Awards B, M. Total enrollment: 1,270. Undergraduate enrollment: 1,230; 20% part-time, 57% women, 10% over 25. Total faculty: 74. Library holdings: 108,000 bound volumes, 50,000 titles on microform, 41 periodical subscriptions.

Undergraduate Courses offered for part-time students during daytime, evenings, summer. Complete part-time degree programs offered during daytime, evenings, summer. Adult/continuing education programs available. Career services available to part-time students: individual career counseling, individual job placement, employer recruitment on campus. Part-time tuition: $95 per semester hour.

University of St Thomas
Houston 77006

Independent-religious instutition; metropolitan setting. Awards B, M, D. Barrier-free campus. Total enrollment: 2,068. Undergraduate enrollment: 1,600; 35% part-time, 55% women. Total faculty: 167. Library holdings: 100,000 bound volumes, 1,000 titles on microform, 15,000 periodical subscriptions, 12,000 records/tapes.

Undergraduate Courses offered for part-time students during daytime, evenings, weekends, summer. Complete part-time degree programs offered during daytime, evenings, weekends, summer. Adult/continuing education programs available. Career services available to part-time students: individual and group career counseling, individual job placement, employer recruitment on campus. Part-time tuition: $125 per credit hour.

Graduate Part-time study available in Cameron School of Business, Center for Thomistic Studies, School of Education, School of Theology. Basic part-time expenses: $125 per credit tuition plus $125 per semester fees. Institutional financial aid available to part-time graduate students in Cameron School of Business.

University of Texas at Arlington
Arlington 76019

Public institution; city setting. Awards B, M, D. Total enrollment: 23,175. Undergraduate enrollment: 20,098; 40% part-time, 43% women, 42% over 25. Total faculty: 940. Library holdings: 750,000 bound volumes, 3,000 periodical subscriptions.

Undergraduate Courses offered for part-time students during daytime, evenings, summer. Complete part-time degree programs offered during daytime, evenings. Adult/continuing education programs available. Career services available to part-time students: individual and group career counseling, individual job placement, employer recruitment on campus. Part-time tuition and fees per semester (1 to 11 semester hours) range from $72.25 to $214.75 for state residents, $62.25 to $604.75 for nonresidents.

Graduate Part-time study available in Graduate School. Basic part-time expenses: $100.75 per semester (minimum) tuition for state residents, $170.75 per semester (minimum) tuition for nonresidents.

University of Texas at Austin
Austin 78712

Public institution; city setting. Awards B, M, D. Total enrollment: 47,631. Undergraduate enrollment: 36,687; 12% part-time, 47% women, 12% over 25. Total faculty: 2,100. Library holdings: 5 million bound volumes, 2.2 million titles on microform, 60,000 periodical subscriptions, 5,000 records/tapes.

Graduate Part-time study available in Graduate School. Basic part-time expenses: $50 per semester (minimum) tuition plus $76.15 per semester (minimum) fees for state residents, $40 per hour tuition plus $76.15 per semester (minimum) fees for nonresidents. Institutional financial aid available to part-time graduate students in Graduate School.

University of Texas at Dallas
Richardson 75080

Public institution; metropolitan setting. Awards B, M, D. Barrier-free campus. Total enrollment: 7,455. Undergraduate enrollment: 4,179; 65% part-time, 52% women. Total faculty: 382. Library holdings: 421,000 bound volumes, 2,809 periodical subscriptions, 2,000 records/tapes.

Undergraduate Courses offered for part-time students during daytime, evenings, weekends, summer. Complete part-time degree programs offered during daytime, evenings, summer. Adult/continuing education programs available. Career services available to part-time students: individual and group career counseling, individual job placement, employer recruitment on campus. Part-time tuition and fees per semester (1 to 11 semester hours) range from $79 to $154 for state residents, $69 to $543.50 for nonresidents.

Graduate Part-time study available in School of Arts and Humanities, School of General Studies, School of Human Development, School of Management, School of Natural Science and Mathematics, School of Social Sciences. Degree can be earned exclusively through evening/weekend study in School of Arts and Humanities, School of General Studies, School of Human Development, School of Management, School of Natural Science and Mathematics, School of Social Sciences. Basic part-time expenses: $50 per semester (minimum) tuition plus $28.50 per semester (minimum) fees for state residents, $40 per semester hour tuition plus $28.50 per semester (minimum) fees for nonresidents. Institutional financial aid available to part-time graduate students in School of Arts and Humanities, School of General Studies, School of Human Development, School of Management, School of Natural Science and Mathematics, School of Social Sciences.

Colleges Offering Part-Time Degree Programs / Texas

University of Texas at El Paso
El Paso 79968

Public institution; metropolitan setting. Awards B, M, D. Total enrollment: 15,268. Undergraduate enrollment: 13,351; 33% part-time, 49% women, 40% over 25. Total faculty: 595. Library holdings: 797,885 bound volumes, 244,815 titles on microform, 4,300 periodical subscriptions, 3,031 records/tapes.

Undergraduate Courses offered for part-time students during daytime, evenings, summer. Complete part-time degree programs offered during daytime, evenings, summer. Adult/continuing education programs available. Career services available to part-time students: individual career counseling, individual job placement, employer recruitment on campus. Part-time tuition: $100 per year for state residents, $40 per credit for nonresidents.

Graduate Part-time study available in Graduate School. Basic part-time expenses: $50 per semester (minimum) tuition plus $11.25 per hour fees for state residents, $40 per hour tuition plus $11.25 per hour fees for nonresidents. Institutional financial aid available to part-time graduate students in Graduate School.

University of Texas at San Antonio
San Antonio 78285

Public institution; metropolitan setting. Awards B, M. Barrier-free campus. Total enrollment: 11,890. Undergraduate enrollment: 10,359; 52% women. Total faculty: 579. Library holdings: 423,002 bound volumes, 320,756 titles on microform, 3,083 periodical subscriptions, 5,713 records/tapes.

Undergraduate Courses offered for part-time students during daytime, evenings, summer. Complete part-time degree programs offered during daytime, evenings, summer. Adult/continuing education programs available. Career services available to part-time students: individual career counseling, employer recruitment on campus. Part-time tuition and fees per semester (1 to 11 semester hours) range from $78 to $203 for state residents, $68 to $468 for nonresidents.

Graduate Part-time study available in College of Business, College of Fine Arts and Humanities, College of Science and Mathematics, College of Social and Behavioral Sciences. Basic part-time expenses: $50 per semester (minimum) tuition plus $52.50 per semester (minimum) fees for state residents, $40 per hour tuition plus $52.50 per semester (minimum) fees for nonresidents. Institutional financial aid available to part-time graduate students in College of Business, College of Fine Arts and Humanities, College of Science and Mathematics, College of Social and Behavioral Sciences.

University of Texas at Tyler
Tyler 75701

Public institution; city setting. Awards B, M. Barrier-free campus. Total enrollment: 3,142. Undergraduate enrollment: 1,942; 62% part-time, 62% women, 60% over 25. Total faculty: 199. Library holdings: 143,391 bound volumes, 1,196 periodical subscriptions, 3,800 records/tapes.

Undergraduate Courses offered for part-time students during daytime, evenings, summer. Complete part-time degree programs offered during daytime, evenings, summer. Adult/continuing education programs available. Part-time tuition: $53.50 per semester hour for nonresidents. State resident part-time tuition per semester (1 to 11 semester hours) ranges from $64 to $199.

Graduate Part-time study available in Graduate Studies. Basic part-time expenses: $50 per semester (minimum) tuition plus $40.50 per semester (minimum) fees for state residents, $40 per semester hour tuition plus $40.50 per semester (minimum) fees for nonresidents. Institutional financial aid available to part-time graduate students in Graduate Studies.

University of Texas Health Science Center at Houston
Houston 77225

Public institution; metropolitan setting. Awards B, M, D. Total enrollment: 2,679. Undergraduate enrollment: 514; 19% part-time, 16% women. Total faculty: 874. Library holdings: 303,000 bound volumes, 7,500 periodical subscriptions.

Undergraduate Courses offered for part-time students during daytime, evenings, summer. Complete part-time degree programs offered during daytime, summer. Adult/continuing education programs available. Career services available to part-time students: individual and group career counseling. Part-time tuition: $238 per year for state residents, $733 per year for nonresidents.

Graduate Part-time study available in Graduate School of Biomedical Sciences, School of Nursing, School of Public Health. Basic part-time expenses: $33 per quarter tuition plus $5 per hour fees for state residents, $26.67 per hour tuition plus $5 per hour fees for nonresidents.

University of Texas Health Science Center at San Antonio
San Antonio 78284

Public institution; metropolitan setting. Awards B, M. Barrier-free campus. Total enrollment: 624. Undergraduate enrollment: 464; 31% part-time, 86% women, 61% over 25. Total faculty: 64. Library holdings: 100,000 bound volumes, 2,200 periodical subscriptions.

Undergraduate Courses offered for part-time students during daytime, evenings, weekends, summer. Complete part-time degree programs offered during daytime, evenings, weekends. Adult/continuing education programs available. Career services available to part-time students: individual career counseling. Part-time tuition and fees per semester (1 to 11 credits) range from $50.25 to $74.25.

University of Texas Medical Branch at Galveston
Galveston 77550

Public institution; city setting. Awards B, M, D. Total enrollment: 1,766. Undergraduate enrollment: 735; 2% part-time, 65% women. Total faculty: 450.

Undergraduate Courses offered for part-time students during daytime. Complete part-time degree programs offered during daytime. Part-time tuition per semester (1 to 11 semester hours) ranges from $40.25 to $120.25 for state residents, $40.25 to $506.75 for nonresidents, according to course load and program.

Graduate Part-time study available in Graduate School of Biomedical Sciences. Basic part-time expenses: $50 per semester (minimum) tuition plus $5 per semester hour fees for state residents, $40 per semester hour tuition plus $5 per semester hour fees for nonresidents.

University of Texas of the Permian Basin
Odessa 79762

Public institution; city setting. Awards B, M. Barrier-free campus. Total enrollment: 1,983. Undergraduate enrollment: 1,423; 67% part-time, 68% women, 62% over 25. Total faculty: 102.

Library holdings: 360,000 bound volumes, 1,241 periodical subscriptions.

Undergraduate Courses offered for part-time students during daytime, evenings, summer. Complete part-time degree programs offered during daytime, evenings, summer. Career services available to part-time students: individual job placement, employer recruitment on campus. Part-time tuition: $100 per year for state residents, $40 per semester hour for nonresidents.

Graduate Part-time study available in College of Arts and Education, College of Business Administration, College of Science and Engineering. Degree can be earned exclusively through evening/weekend study in College of Arts and Education, College of Business Administration, College of Science and Engineering. Basic part-time expenses: $50 per semester (minimum) tuition plus $9 per credit fees for state residents, $40 per credit tuition plus $9 per credit fees for nonresidents. Institutional financial aid available to part-time graduate students in College of Arts and Education.

Vernon Regional Junior College
Vernon 76384

Public institution; small-town setting. Awards A. Barrier-free campus. Total enrollment: 1,800 (all undergraduates); 45% part-time, 60% women, 43% over 25. Total faculty: 103. Library holdings: 20,000 bound volumes, 150 periodical subscriptions, 303 records/tapes.

Undergraduate Courses offered for part-time students during daytime, evenings, summer. Complete part-time degree programs offered during daytime, evenings, summer. Adult/continuing education programs available. Career services available to part-time students: individual and group career counseling, individual job placement. Part-time tuition and fees per semester (1 to 11 semester hours) range from $38.50 to $53.50 for county residents, $43.50 to $79.50 for state residents, $43.50 to $458.50 for nonresidents.

Victoria College
Victoria 77901

Public institution; city setting. Awards A. Barrier-free campus. Total enrollment: 2,850 (all undergraduates); 60% part-time, 62% women. Total faculty: 120. Library holdings: 150,000 bound volumes, 186,000 titles on microform, 1,500 periodical subscriptions, 11,000 records/tapes.

Undergraduate Courses offered for part-time students during daytime, evenings, summer. Complete part-time degree programs offered during daytime, evenings, summer. Adult/continuing education programs available. Career services available to part-time students: individual and group career counseling, individual job placement, employer recruitment on campus. Part-time tuition and fees per semester (1 to 11 credits) range from $27 to $54 for county residents, $40 to $89 for state residents, $40 to $210 for nonresidents.

Wayland Baptist University
Plainview 79072

Independent-religious instuition; small-town setting. Awards A, B, M. Total enrollment: 1,695. Undergraduate enrollment: 1,540; 50% part-time, 30% women, 50% over 25. Total faculty: 92. Library holdings: 85,383 bound volumes, 515 periodical subscriptions, 2,591 records/tapes.

Undergraduate Courses offered for part-time students during daytime, evenings. Complete part-time degree programs offered during daytime, evenings. External degree and adult/continuing education programs available. Career services available to part-time students: individual and group career counseling, individual job placement, employer recruitment on campus. Part-time tuition: $70 per semester hour.

Weatherford College
Weatherford 76086

Public institution; small-town setting. Awards A. Barrier-free campus. Total enrollment: 1,596 (all undergraduates); 55% part-time, 55% women, 50% over 25. Total faculty: 74. Library holdings: 46,550 bound volumes, 104 periodical subscriptions, 1,124 records/tapes.

Undergraduate Courses offered for part-time students during daytime, evenings, summer. Complete part-time degree programs offered during daytime, evenings, summer. Adult/continuing education programs available. Career services available to part-time students: individual and group career counseling, individual job placement, employer recruitment on campus. Part-time tuition and fees per semester (1 to 11 semester hours) range from $42 to $81 for state residents, $37 to $224 for nonresidents.

Western Texas College
Snyder 79549

Public institution; small-town setting. Awards A. Barrier-free campus. Total enrollment: 1,214 (all undergraduates); 40% part-time, 51% women, 43% over 25. Total faculty: 75. Library holdings: 33,895 bound volumes, 212 periodical subscriptions.

Undergraduate Courses offered for part-time students during daytime, evenings, summer. Complete part-time degree programs offered during daytime, evenings, summer. Adult/continuing education programs available. Career services available to part-time students: individual and group career counseling, individual job placement, employer recruitment on campus. Part-time tuition and fees per semester (1 to 11 semester hours) range from $36 to $87 for state residents, $71 to $242 for nonresidents.

West Texas State University
Canyon 79016

Public institution; small-town setting. Awards B, M. Total enrollment: 6,805. Undergraduate enrollment: 5,496; 20% part-time, 53% women, 29% over 25. Total faculty: 364. Library holdings: 270,075 bound volumes, 26,291 titles on microform, 239 periodical subscriptions.

Undergraduate Courses offered for part-time students during daytime, evenings, summer. Complete part-time degree programs offered during daytime, evenings, summer. Adult/continuing education programs available. Career services available to part-time students: individual career counseling, employer recruitment on campus. Part-time tuition and fees per semester (1 to 11 semester hours) range from $68 to $186 for state residents, $68 to $576 for nonresidents.

Graduate Part-time study available in Graduate School. Basic part-time expenses: $50 per semester (minimum) tuition plus $45.50 per semester (minimum) fees for state residents, $40 per semester hour tuition plus $45.50 per semester (minimum) fees for nonresidents. Institutional financial aid available to part-time graduate students in Graduate School.

Wharton County Junior College
Wharton 77488

Public institution; rural setting. Awards A. Barrier-free campus. Total enrollment: 2,466 (all undergraduates); 25% part-time, 52% women. Total faculty: 139. Library holdings:

Colleges Offering Part-Time Degree Programs / Texas

Wharton County Junior College (continued)

51,478 bound volumes, 536 periodical subscriptions, 1,352 records/tapes.

Undergraduate Courses offered for part-time students during daytime, evenings, summer. Complete part-time degree programs offered during daytime, evenings, summer. Adult/continuing education programs available. Career services available to part-time students: individual career counseling, individual job placement, employer recruitment on campus. Part-time tuition: $7 per semester hour for area residents, $10.25 per semester hour for state residents, $46.25 per semester hour for nonresidents.

Wiley College
Marshall 75670

Independent-religious instutition; small-town setting. Awards A, B. Total enrollment: 557 (all undergraduates); 3% part-time, 56% women, 14% over 25. Total faculty: 48. Library holdings: 77,407 bound volumes, 955 titles on microform, 298 periodical subscriptions, 500 records/tapes.

Undergraduate Courses offered for part-time students during daytime, evenings, summer. Complete part-time degree programs offered during daytime, evenings, summer. Adult/continuing education programs available. Career services available to part-time students: individual and group career counseling, individual job placement, employer recruitment on campus. Part-time tuition: $80 per credit hour.

TRUST TERRITORY OF THE PACIFIC ISLANDS

Micronesian Occupational College
Koror, Palau 96940, Western Caroline Islands

Public institution; small-town setting. Awards A. Total enrollment: 441 (all undergraduates); 7% part-time, 24% women, 5% over 25. Total faculty: 34. Library holdings: 8,265 bound volumes, 96 periodical subscriptions, 480 records/tapes.

Undergraduate Courses offered for part-time students during daytime, evenings, summer. Complete part-time degree programs offered during daytime, evenings, summer. Adult/continuing education programs available. Career services available to part-time students: individual and group career counseling, individual job placement. Part-time tuition per quarter ranges from $1008 (for students taking 6 to 8 credits) to $1440 (for students taking 9 to 11 credits).

UTAH

Brigham Young University
Provo 84602

Independent-religious instutition; city setting. Awards A, B, M, D. Barrier-free campus. Total enrollment: 26,963. Undergraduate enrollment: 24,619; 18% part-time, 44% women, 17% over 25. Total faculty: 1,536.

Undergraduate Courses offered for part-time students during daytime, summer. Complete part-time degree programs offered during daytime, summer. External degree and adult/continuing education programs available. Part-time tuition: $71 per credit. Part-time tuition for non–church members: $107 per credit.

Dixie College
St George 84770

Public institution; rural setting. Awards A. Total enrollment: 1,904 (all undergraduates); 35% part-time, 50% women, 20% over 25. Total faculty: 87. Library holdings: 49,000 bound volumes, 200 periodical subscriptions.

Undergraduate Courses offered for part-time students during daytime. Complete part-time degree programs offered during daytime. Adult/continuing education programs available. Career services available to part-time students: individual and group career counseling, individual job placement, employer recruitment on campus. Part-time tuition per quarter (1 to 9 credit hours) ranges from $27 to $213 for state residents, $65 to $557 for nonresidents.

Latter-Day Saints Business College
Salt Lake City 84111

Independent-religious instutition; metropolitan setting. Awards A. Barrier-free campus. Total enrollment: 968 (all undergraduates); 15% part-time, 65% women, 20% over 25. Total faculty: 38. Library holdings: 3,820 bound volumes, 148 periodical subscriptions, 196 records/tapes.

Undergraduate Courses offered for part-time students during daytime, evenings, summer. Complete part-time degree programs offered during daytime, evenings. Adult/continuing education programs available. Career services available to part-time students: individual and group career counseling, individual job placement, employer recruitment on campus. Part-time tuition: $20 per credit hour for evening programs, $250 per quarter for daytime programs.

Snow College
Ephraim 84627

Public institution; rural setting. Awards A. Barrier-free campus. Total enrollment: 1,306 (all undergraduates); 5% part-time, 49% women, 9% over 25. Total faculty: 60. Library holdings: 80,000 bound volumes, 120 periodical subscriptions, 8,500 records/tapes.

Undergraduate Courses offered for part-time students during daytime, evenings, weekends, summer. Complete part-time degree programs offered during daytime, evenings, weekends, summer. External degree and adult/continuing education programs available. Career services available to part-time students: individual and group career counseling, individual job placement, employer recruitment on campus. Part-time tuition and fees per quarter (1 to 9 quarter hours) range from $39 to $176 for state residents, $114 to $524 for nonresidents.

Southern Utah State College
Cedar City 84720

Public institution; small-town setting. Awards B. Barrier-free campus. Total enrollment: 2,543 (all undergraduates); 19% part-time, 51% women. Total faculty: 114. Library holdings: 144,206 bound volumes, 47,070 titles on microform, 923 periodical subscriptions, 35,718 records/tapes.

Undergraduate Courses offered for part-time students during daytime. Complete part-time degree programs offered during daytime. Adult/continuing education programs available. Career services available to part-time students: individual and group career counseling, individual job placement, employer recruitment on campus. Part-time tuition: $22 per quarter hour for state residents, $69 per quarter hour for nonresidents.

Stevens Henager College
Ogden 84401

Proprietary institution; city setting. Awards A. Total enrollment: 1,002 (all undergraduates); 36% part-time, 66% women, 50% over 25. Total faculty: 43. Library holdings: 6,000 bound volumes, 30 periodical subscriptions, 100 records/tapes.

Undergraduate Courses offered for part-time students during daytime, evenings, summer. Complete part-time degree programs offered during daytime, evenings. Adult/continuing education programs available. Career services available to part-time students: individual and group career counseling, individual job placement. Part-time tuition and fees per quarter (1 to 11 quarter hours) range from $140 to $720.

University of Utah
Salt Lake City 84112

Public institution; metropolitan setting. Awards B, M, D. Barrier-free campus. Total enrollment: 24,911. Undergraduate enrollment: 20,890; 31% part-time, 41% women. Total faculty: 2,734. Library holdings: 2 million bound volumes, 2 million titles on microform, 14,300 periodical subscriptions, 5,000 records/tapes.

Undergraduate Courses offered for part-time students during daytime, evenings, weekends, summer. Complete part-time degree programs offered during daytime. Adult/continuing education programs available. Career services available to part-time students: individual and group career counseling, individual job placement, employer recruitment on campus. Part-time tuition and fees per quarter (1 to 14 credit hours) range from $123 to $370 for state residents, $298 to $1052 for nonresidents.

Graduate Part-time study available in Graduate School, Graduate School of Architecture, Graduate School of Business, Graduate School of Social Work, State College of Mines and Mineral Industries. Degree can be earned exclusively through evening/weekend study in Graduate School of Business. Basic part-time expenses: $161 per quarter (minimum) tuition for state residents, $414 per quarter (minimum) tuition for nonresidents. Institutional financial aid available to part-time graduate students in Graduate School, Graduate School of Social Work, State College of Mines and Mineral Industries.

Utah State University
Logan 84322

Public institution; small-town setting. Awards B, M, D. Total enrollment: 11,849. Undergraduate enrollment: 9,407; 22% part-time, 43% women, 51% over 25. Total faculty: 504. Library holdings: 981,225 bound volumes, 782,204 titles on microform, 6,787 periodical subscriptions, 17,669 records/tapes.

Undergraduate Courses offered for part-time students during daytime, evenings, summer. Complete part-time degree programs offered during daytime, evenings, summer. External degree and adult/continuing education programs available. Career services available to part-time students: individual and group career counseling, individual job placement, employer recruitment on campus. Part-time tuition and fees per quarter (1 to 12 quarter hours) range from $60 to $286 for state residents, $162 to $784 for nonresidents.

Graduate Part-time study available in School of Graduate Studies. Basic part-time expenses: $94 per quarter (minimum) tuition for state residents, $268 per quarter (minimum) tuition for nonresidents. Institutional financial aid available to part-time graduate students in School of Graduate Studies.

Utah Technical College at Provo
Provo 84603

Public institution; city setting. Awards A. Barrier-free campus. Total enrollment: 5,593 (all undergraduates); 34% part-time, 38% women, 44% over 25. Total faculty: 300. Library holdings: 19,050 bound volumes, 416 periodical subscriptions, 200 records/tapes.

Undergraduate Courses offered for part-time students during daytime, evenings, weekends. Complete part-time degree programs offered during daytime, evenings, weekends. Adult/continuing education programs available. Career services available to part-time students: individual career counseling, individual job placement, employer recruitment on campus. Part-time tuition and fees per quarter (1 to 11 credits) range from $64 to $243 for state residents, $134 to $636 for nonresidents.

Utah Technical College at Salt Lake
Salt Lake City 84131

Public institution; metropolitan setting. Awards A. Total enrollment: 8,200 (all undergraduates); 40% part-time, 33% women, 60% over 25. Total faculty: 205. Library holdings: 26,000 bound volumes, 400 periodical subscriptions, 3,800 records/tapes.

Undergraduate Courses offered for part-time students during daytime, evenings, summer. Complete part-time degree programs offered during daytime, evenings, summer. Adult/continuing education programs available. Career services available to part-time students: individual and group career counseling, individual job placement, employer recruitment on campus. Part-time tuition and fees per quarter (1 to 11 credits) range from $45 to $216 for state residents, $115 to $594 for nonresidents.

Weber State College
Ogden 84408

Public institution; city setting. Awards A, B, M. Barrier-free campus. Total enrollment: 10,348. Undergraduate enrollment: 10,249; 20% part-time, 42% women, 46% over 25. Total faculty: 476. Library holdings: 239,894 bound volumes, 2,160 periodical subscriptions, 2,502 records/tapes.

Undergraduate Courses offered for part-time students during daytime, evenings, weekends, summer. Complete part-time degree programs offered during daytime, evenings, summer. Adult/continuing education programs available. Career services available to part-time students: individual and group career counseling, individual job placement, employer recruitment on campus. Part-time tuition: $58 per credit hour for state residents, $186 per credit hour for nonresidents.

Graduate Part-time study available in School of Education. Basic part-time expenses: $79 per quarter (minimum) tuition for state residents, $207 per quarter (minimum) tuition for nonresidents.

Westminster College of Salt Lake City
Salt Lake City 84105

Independent institution; metropolitan setting. Awards B, M. Total enrollment: 1,291. Undergraduate enrollment: 1,195; 54% part-time, 54% women, 45% over 25. Total faculty: 79. Library holdings: 61,000 bound volumes, 150 titles on microform, 320 periodical subscriptions, 2,000 records/tapes.

Undergraduate Courses offered for part-time students during daytime, evenings, weekends, summer. Complete part-time degree programs offered during daytime, evenings. Adult/continuing education programs available. Career services available to part-time students: individual and group career counseling,

Colleges Offering Part-Time Degree Programs / Utah

Westminster College of Salt Lake City (continued)
individual job placement, employer recruitment on campus. Part-time tuition: $135 per semester hour.

Graduate Part-time study available in School of Arts and Sciences, School of Business. Degree can be earned exclusively through evening/weekend study in School of Arts and Sciences. Basic part-time expenses: $145 per credit (minimum) tuition. Institutional financial aid available to part-time graduate students in School of Arts and Sciences, School of Business.

VERMONT

Bennington College
Bennington 05201

Independent institution; rural setting. Awards B, M. Barrier-free campus. Total enrollment: 640. Undergraduate enrollment: 600; 0% part-time, 65% women, 1% over 25. Total faculty: 80. Library holdings: 85,000 bound volumes, 4,794 titles on microform, 625 periodical subscriptions, 807 records/tapes.

Graduate Part-time study available in Graduate Programs. Basic part-time expenses: $11,720 per year tuition plus $50 per year fees.

Burlington College
Burlington 05401

Independent institution; small-town setting. Awards A, B. Barrier-free campus. Total enrollment: 182 (all undergraduates); 32% part-time, 69% women. Total faculty: 51.

Undergraduate Courses offered for part-time students during daytime, evenings, summer. Complete part-time degree programs offered during daytime, evenings, summer. External degree programs available. Career services available to part-time students: individual career counseling. Part-time tuition: $135 per credit.

Castleton State College
Castleton 05735

Public institution; rural setting. Awards A, B, M. Total enrollment: 2,200. Undergraduate enrollment: 1,800; 30% part-time, 55% women, 20% over 25. Total faculty: 113. Library holdings: 100,000 bound volumes, 33,500 titles on microform, 222 periodical subscriptions, 15,000 records/tapes.

Undergraduate Courses offered for part-time students during daytime, evenings, summer. Complete part-time degree programs offered during daytime, evenings, summer. External degree and adult/continuing education programs available. Career services available to part-time students: individual and group career counseling, individual job placement, employer recruitment on campus. Part-time tuition: $66 per credit for state residents, $150 per credit for nonresidents.

Graduate Part-time study available in Graduate School. Degree can be earned exclusively through evening/weekend study in Graduate School. Basic part-time expenses: $70 per credit tuition plus $42 per semester (minimum) fees for state residents, $160 per credit tuition plus $42 per semester (minimum) fees for nonresidents. Institutional financial aid available to part-time graduate students in Graduate School.

Champlain College
Burlington 05402

Independent institution; small-town setting. Awards A. Total enrollment: 1,277 (all undergraduates); 13% part-time, 71% women, 11% over 25. Total faculty: 74. Library holdings: 30,300 bound volumes, 4,163 titles on microform, 252 periodical subscriptions, 1,130 records/tapes.

Undergraduate Courses offered for part-time students during daytime, evenings, summer. Complete part-time degree programs offered during daytime, evenings, summer. Adult/continuing education programs available. Career services available to part-time students: individual and group career counseling, individual job placement, employer recruitment on campus. Part-time tuition: $120 per credit hour.

College of St Joseph the Provider
Rutland 05701

Independent-religious instutition; rural setting. Awards A, B, M. Barrier-free campus. Total enrollment: 386. Undergraduate enrollment: 332; 50% part-time, 74% women, 30% over 25. Total faculty: 44. Library holdings: 21,279 bound volumes, 364 titles on microform, 106 periodical subscriptions, 548 records/tapes.

Undergraduate Courses offered for part-time students during daytime, evenings, summer. Complete part-time degree programs offered during daytime, evenings, summer. Adult/continuing education programs available. Career services available to part-time students: individual and group career counseling, individual job placement, employer recruitment on campus. Part-time tuition: $72 per credit.

Community College of Vermont
Waterbury 05676

Public institution; rural setting. Awards A. Barrier-free campus. Total enrollment: 866 (all undergraduates); 88% part-time, 70% women, 75% over 25. Total faculty: 326.

Undergraduate Courses offered for part-time students during daytime, evenings, weekends, summer. Complete part-time degree programs offered during daytime, evenings, weekends, summer. External degree and adult/continuing education programs available. Career services available to part-time students: individual and group career counseling. Part-time tuition: $40 per credit for state residents, $80 per credit for nonresidents.

Green Mountain College
Poultney 05764

Independent institution; small-town setting. Awards A, B. Total enrollment: 325 (all undergraduates); 4% part-time, 55% women. Total faculty: 45. Library holdings: 64,200 bound volumes, 30,000 titles on microform, 155 periodical subscriptions, 1,420 records/tapes.

Undergraduate Courses offered for part-time students during daytime, evenings. Complete part-time degree programs offered during daytime, evenings. Career services available to part-time students: individual career counseling, individual job placement, employer recruitment on campus. Part-time tuition: $165 per credit.

Johnson State College
Johnson 05656

Public institution; rural setting. Awards A, B, M. Total enrollment: 1,237. Undergraduate enrollment: 952; 17% part-time,

Vermont / Colleges Offering Part-Time Degree Programs

50% women, 4% over 25. Total faculty: 101. Library holdings: 96,000 bound volumes, 6,750 titles on microform, 600 periodical subscriptions, 1,468 records/tapes.

Undergraduate Courses offered for part-time students during daytime, evenings, summer. Complete part-time degree programs offered during daytime, evenings, summer. External degree and adult/continuing education programs available. Career services available to part-time students: individual and group career counseling, individual job placement. Part-time tuition: $66 per credit for state residents, $150 per credit for nonresidents.

Graduate Part-time study available in Graduate Program in Education. Basic part-time expenses: $70 per credit tuition plus $4.17 per credit fees for state residents, $160 per credit tuition plus $4.17 per credit fees for nonresidents.

Lyndon State College
Lyndonville 05851

Public institution; rural setting. Awards A, B, M. Total enrollment: 1,052. Undergraduate enrollment: 1,010; 5% part-time, 47% women. Total faculty: 86. Library holdings: 65,000 bound volumes, 4,000 titles on microform, 4,000 periodical subscriptions, 1,300 records/tapes.

Undergraduate Courses offered for part-time students during daytime, evenings, summer. Complete part-time degree programs offered during daytime. Adult/continuing education programs available. Career services available to part-time students: individual and group career counseling. Part-time tuition: $70 per credit hour for state residents, $160 per credit hour for nonresidents.

Graduate Part-time study available in Graduate Program in Education. Degree can be earned exclusively through evening/weekend study in Graduate Program in Education. Basic part-time expenses: $70 per credit tuition for state residents, $160 per credit tuition for nonresidents.

Marlboro College
Marlboro 05344

Independent institution; rural setting. Awards B. Barrier-free campus. Total enrollment: 190 (all undergraduates); 9% part-time, 50% women, 10% over 25. Total faculty: 35. Library holdings: 49,595 bound volumes, 3,736 titles on microform, 238 periodical subscriptions, 4,000 records/tapes.

Undergraduate Courses offered for part-time students during daytime. Complete part-time degree programs offered during daytime. Career services available to part-time students: individual and group career counseling. Part-time tuition: $270 per credit.

Norwich University, Vermont College
Montpelier 05602

Independent institution; small-town setting. Awards A, B, M. Total enrollment: 880. Undergraduate enrollment: 636; 13% part-time, 77% women, 5% over 25. Total faculty: 56. Library holdings: 32,000 bound volumes, 250 titles on microform, 300 periodical subscriptions, 1,070 records/tapes.

Undergraduate Courses offered for part-time students during daytime, evenings, weekends, summer. Complete part-time degree programs offered during daytime, evenings, weekends, summer. External degree and adult/continuing education programs available. Career services available to part-time students: individual career counseling. Part-time tuition: $150 per credit hour.

Graduate Part-time study available in Division of Alternative Education and Graduate Studies. Degree can be earned exclusively through evening/weekend study in Division of Alternative Education and Graduate Studies. Basic part-time expenses: $5000 per year tuition.

School for International Training
Brattleboro 05301

Independent institution; small-town setting. Awards B, M. Total enrollment: 656. Undergraduate enrollment: 147; 0% part-time, 60% women, 1% over 25. Total faculty: 35. Library holdings: 27,000 bound volumes, 3,300 titles on microform, 230 periodical subscriptions, 5,000 records/tapes.

Graduate Part-time study available in Graduate Programs. Basic part-time expenses: $200 per credit tuition.

Southern Vermont College
Bennington 05201

Independent institution; small-town setting. Awards A, B. Total enrollment: 650 (all undergraduates); 19% part-time, 52% women, 20% over 25. Total faculty: 32. Library holdings: 25,000 bound volumes, 5 titles on microform, 100 periodical subscriptions, 150 records/tapes.

Undergraduate Courses offered for part-time students during daytime, evenings, weekends, summer. Complete part-time degree programs offered during daytime, evenings, weekends, summer. External degree and adult/continuing education programs available. Career services available to part-time students: individual and group career counseling, individual job placement, employer recruitment on campus. Part-time tuition: $118 per credit.

Trinity College
Burlington 05401

Independent-religious instutition; city setting. Awards A, B. Total enrollment: 953 (all undergraduates); 60% part-time, 79% women. Total faculty: 65. Library holdings: 40,211 bound volumes, 42,738 titles on microform, 294 periodical subscriptions, 592 records/tapes.

Undergraduate Courses offered for part-time students during daytime, evenings, weekends, summer. Complete part-time degree programs offered during daytime, evenings, weekends, summer. Adult/continuing education programs available. Career services available to part-time students: individual and group career counseling, employer recruitment on campus. Part-time tuition: $168 per credit.

University of Vermont
Burlington 05405

Public institution; small-town setting. Awards A, B, M, D. Barrier-free campus. Total enrollment: 8,717. Undergraduate enrollment: 7,724; 5% part-time, 57% women, 5% over 25. Total faculty: 857. Library holdings: 770,000 bound volumes, 500,000 titles on microform, 8,500 periodical subscriptions, 8,600 records/tapes.

Undergraduate Courses offered for part-time students during daytime, evenings, summer. Complete part-time degree programs offered during daytime. Adult/continuing education programs available. Career services available to part-time students: individual and group career counseling, individual job placement, employer recruitment on campus. Part-time tuition: $107 per credit for state residents, $282 per credit for nonresidents.

Colleges Offering Part-Time Degree Programs / *Vermont*

University of Vermont (continued)

Graduate Part-time study available in Graduate College, College of Medicine. Basic part-time expenses: $107 per credit tuition for state residents, $282 per credit tuition for nonresidents.

Vermont College
Montpelier 05602

See Norwich University, Vermont College

Vermont Law School
South Royalton 05068

Independent institution (graduate only). Total enrollment: 386 (coed). Total faculty: 42. Library holdings: 100,000 bound volumes, 125,000 microforms.

Graduate Part-time study available in Environmental Law Center. Basic part-time expenses: $6750 per year tuition plus $50 per year fees.

VIRGINIA

Averett College
Danville 24541

Independent-religious instutition; city setting. Awards A, B, M. Total enrollment: 1,000. Undergraduate enrollment: 970; 25% part-time, 66% women, 30% over 25. Total faculty: 54. Library holdings: 76,000 bound volumes, 11,069 titles on microform, 452 periodical subscriptions, 450 records/tapes.

Undergraduate Courses offered for part-time students during daytime, evenings, summer. Complete part-time degree programs offered during daytime, evenings, summer. Adult/continuing education programs available. Career services available to part-time students: individual and group career counseling, individual job placement, employer recruitment on campus. Part-time tuition: $110 per credit hour.

Graduate Part-time study available in Graduate Studies. Basic part-time expenses: $110 per semester hour tuition.

Bluefield College
Bluefield 24605

Independent-religious instutition; small-town setting. Awards A, B. Total enrollment: 382 (all undergraduates); 12% part-time, 50% women, 12% over 25. Total faculty: 32. Library holdings: 40,000 bound volumes, 160 periodical subscriptions, 250 records/tapes.

Undergraduate Courses offered for part-time students during daytime. Complete part-time degree programs offered during daytime. Adult/continuing education programs available. Career services available to part-time students: individual career counseling, individual job placement. Part-time tuition: $75 per semester hour.

Blue Ridge Community College
Weyers Cave 24486

Public institution; rural setting. Awards A. Barrier-free campus. Total enrollment: 2,187 (all undergraduates); 67% part-time, 58% women, 55% over 25. Total faculty: 102. Library holdings: 37,287 bound volumes, 453 periodical subscriptions, 1,450 records/tapes.

Undergraduate Courses offered for part-time students during daytime, evenings, summer. Complete part-time degree programs offered during daytime, evenings, summer. Adult/continuing education programs available. Career services available to part-time students: individual and group career counseling, individual job placement, employer recruitment on campus. Part-time tuition: $15.25 per quarter hour for state residents, $66 per quarter hour for nonresidents.

Bridgewater College
Bridgewater 22812

Independent-religious instutition; small-town setting. Awards B. Total enrollment: 873 (all undergraduates); 4% part-time, 48% women, 1% over 25. Total faculty: 70. Library holdings: 140,000 bound volumes, 500 periodical subscriptions, 8,820 records/tapes.

Undergraduate Courses offered for part-time students during daytime, evenings, summer. Complete part-time degree programs offered during daytime, summer. Adult/continuing education programs available. Career services available to part-time students: individual and group career counseling, employer recruitment on campus. Part-time tuition: $135 per credit.

CBN University
Virginia Beach 23463

Independent institution (graduate only). Total enrollment: 348 (coed; 71% part-time). Total faculty: 38.

Graduate Part-time study available in School of Biblical Studies, School of Business Administration, School of Communication, School of Education, School of Public Policy. Basic part-time expenses: $80 per quarter hour tuition. Institutional financial aid available to part-time graduate students in School of Biblical Studies, School of Business Administration, School of Communication, School of Education, School of Public Policy.

Central Virginia Community College
Lynchburg 24502

Public institution; city setting. Awards A. Barrier-free campus. Total enrollment: 3,839 (all undergraduates); 68% part-time, 50% women, 30% over 25. Total faculty: 142. Library holdings: 38,000 bound volumes, 266 periodical subscriptions, 1,100 records/tapes.

Undergraduate Courses offered for part-time students during daytime, evenings, summer. Complete part-time degree programs offered during daytime, evenings, summer. Adult/continuing education programs available. Career services available to part-time students: individual and group career counseling, individual job placement, employer recruitment on campus. Part-time tuition: $15.25 per credit for state residents, $66 per credit for nonresidents.

Christopher Newport College
Newport News 23606

Public institution; city setting. Awards B. Barrier-free campus. Total enrollment: 4,398 (all undergraduates); 55% part-time, 56% women, 44% over 25. Total faculty: 120. Library holdings: 95,934 bound volumes, 28,008 titles on microform, 704 periodical subscriptions, 1,808 records/tapes.

Undergraduate Courses offered for part-time students during daytime, evenings, weekends, summer. Complete part-time degree programs offered during daytime, evenings, weekends, summer. External degree and adult/continuing education pro-

Virginia / **Colleges Offering Part-Time Degree Programs**

grams available. Career services available to part-time students: individual and group career counseling, individual job placement, employer recruitment on campus. Part-time tuition: $48 per semester hour for state residents, $79 per semester hour for nonresidents.

College of William and Mary
Williamsburg 23185

Public institution; small-town setting. Awards B, M, D. Total enrollment: 6,607. Undergraduate enrollment: 4,731; 1% part-time, 55% women, 1% over 25. Total faculty: 537. Library holdings: 764,372 bound volumes, 539,911 titles on microform, 6,282 periodical subscriptions, 16,842 records/tapes.

Undergraduate Courses offered for part-time students during daytime, summer. Complete part-time degree programs offered during daytime, summer. Career services available to part-time students: individual and group career counseling, individual job placement, employer recruitment on campus. Part-time tuition: $67 per credit for state residents, $181 per credit for nonresidents.

Graduate Part-time study available in Marshall-Wythe School of Law, School of Education. Basic part-time expenses: $67 per credit tuition for state residents, $181 per credit tuition for nonresidents. Institutional financial aid available to part-time graduate students in School of Education.

Dabney S Lancaster Community College
Clifton Forge 24422

Public institution; rural setting. Awards A. Total enrollment: 1,224 (all undergraduates); 63% part-time, 57% women. Total faculty: 79. Library holdings: 33,086 bound volumes, 378 periodical subscriptions, 1,100 records/tapes.

Undergraduate Courses offered for part-time students during daytime, evenings, summer. Complete part-time degree programs offered during daytime, evenings, summer. Adult/continuing education programs available. Career services available to part-time students: individual and group career counseling, individual job placement, employer recruitment on campus. Part-time tuition: $15.50 per quarter hour for state residents, $66.25 per quarter hour for nonresidents.

Danville Community College
Danville 24541

Public institution; city setting. Awards A. Total enrollment: 2,617 (all undergraduates); 40% part-time, 51% women. Total faculty: 112.

Undergraduate Courses offered for part-time students during daytime, evenings. Complete part-time degree programs offered during daytime, evenings. Adult/continuing education programs available. Career services available to part-time students: individual career counseling, individual job placement. Part-time tuition: $15.25 per credit for state residents, $66 per credit for nonresidents.

Eastern Mennonite College
Harrisonburg 22801

Independent-religious instutition; small-town setting. Awards A, B. Barrier-free campus. Total enrollment: 891 (all undergraduates); 5% part-time, 62% women. Total faculty: 84. Library holdings: 108,500 bound volumes, 4,406 titles on microform, 867 periodical subscriptions, 3,044 records/tapes.

Undergraduate Courses offered for part-time students during daytime, evenings, summer. Complete part-time degree programs offered during daytime. Adult/continuing education programs available. Career services available to part-time students: individual career counseling, individual job placement, employer recruitment on campus. Part-time tuition: $198 per semester hour.

Eastern Shore Community College
Melfa 23410

Public institution; rural setting. Awards A. Barrier-free campus. Total enrollment: 307 (all undergraduates); 62% part-time, 63% women. Total faculty: 25. Library holdings: 20,200 bound volumes, 100 titles on microform, 69 periodical subscriptions, 500 records/tapes.

Undergraduate Courses offered for part-time students during daytime, evenings, summer. Complete part-time degree programs offered during daytime, evenings, summer. Adult/continuing education programs available. Career services available to part-time students: individual career counseling, individual job placement, employer recruitment on campus. Part-time tuition: $15.25 per quarter hour for state residents, $66 per quarter hour for nonresidents.

Ferrum College
Ferrum 24088

Independent-religious instutition; rural setting. Awards A, B. Total enrollment: 1,577 (all undergraduates); 9% part-time, 34% women, 1% over 25. Total faculty: 95. Library holdings: 75,000 bound volumes, 410 titles on microform, 732 periodical subscriptions, 1,000 records/tapes.

Undergraduate Courses offered for part-time students during daytime, evenings, summer. Complete part-time degree programs offered during daytime, summer. Adult/continuing education programs available. Career services available to part-time students: individual career counseling. Part-time tuition: $90 per semester hour.

George Mason University
Fairfax 22030

Public institution; small-town setting. Awards B, M, D. Total enrollment: 14,545. Undergraduate enrollment: 10,909; 37% part-time, 55% women. Total faculty: 756. Library holdings: 236,249 bound volumes, 385,000 titles on microform, 3,500 periodical subscriptions, 2,489 records/tapes.

Undergraduate Courses offered for part-time students during daytime, evenings, summer. Complete part-time degree programs offered during daytime, evenings, summer. Adult/continuing education programs available. Career services available to part-time students: individual and group career counseling, individual job placement, employer recruitment on campus. Part-time tuition: $63 per credit hour for state residents, $122 per credit hour for nonresidents.

Graduate Part-time study available in Graduate School, School of Law. Degree can be earned exclusively through evening/weekend study in Graduate School. Basic part-time expenses: $40 per credit hour tuition plus $23 per credit hour fees for state residents, $99 per credit hour tuition plus $23 per credit hour fees for nonresidents. Institutional financial aid available to part-time graduate students in Graduate School.

Germanna Community College
Locust Grove 22508

Public institution; rural setting. Awards A. Barrier-free campus. Total enrollment: 1,907 (all undergraduates); 76%

Colleges Offering Part-Time Degree Programs / Virginia

Germanna Community College (continued)
part-time, 60% women, 50% over 25. Total faculty: 84. Library holdings: 22,412 bound volumes, 998 titles on microform, 160 periodical subscriptions, 1,474 records/tapes.

Undergraduate Courses offered for part-time students during daytime, evenings, weekends, summer. Complete part-time degree programs offered during daytime, evenings. Career services available to part-time students: individual career counseling, individual job placement, employer recruitment on campus. Part-time tuition: $15.25 per credit for state residents, $66 per credit for nonresidents.

Graham Bible College
Meadowview 24361

Independent-religious instutition; rural setting. Awards A, B. Total enrollment: 35 (all undergraduates); 29% part-time, 37% women, 26% over 25. Total faculty: 6. Library holdings: 21,000 bound volumes, 83 periodical subscriptions.

Undergraduate Courses offered for part-time students during daytime, evenings. Complete part-time degree programs offered during daytime, evenings. Career services available to part-time students: individual career counseling. Part-time tuition: $75 per semester hour.

Hampton Institute
Hampton 23668

Independent institution; city setting. Awards B, M. Total enrollment: 4,063. Undergraduate enrollment: 3,714; 8% part-time, 59% women, 1% over 25. Total faculty: 238. Library holdings: 235,000 bound volumes, 35,000 titles on microform, 1,200 periodical subscriptions, 2 million records/tapes.

Undergraduate Courses offered for part-time students during daytime, evenings, summer. Complete part-time degree programs offered during daytime, evenings. External degree and adult/continuing education programs available. Career services available to part-time students: individual and group career counseling, individual job placement, employer recruitment on campus. Part-time tuition: $95 per semester hour.

Graduate Part-time study available in Graduate School. Degree can be earned exclusively through evening/weekend study in Graduate School. Basic part-time expenses: $95 per credit tuition plus $10 per semester fees.

Hollins College
Hollins College 24020

Independent institution; city setting. Awards B, M. Total enrollment: 970. Undergraduate enrollment: 881; 5% part-time, 100% women, 5% over 25. Total faculty: 91. Library holdings: 215,000 bound volumes, 29,400 titles on microform, 1,250 periodical subscriptions, 8,000 records/tapes.

Undergraduate Courses offered for part-time students during daytime. Complete part-time degree programs offered during daytime. Adult/continuing education programs available. Career services available to part-time students: individual and group career counseling, individual job placement, employer recruitment on campus. Part-time tuition: $195 per credit.

Graduate Part-time study available in Graduate Programs. Basic part-time expenses: $225 per course (minimum) tuition.

James Madison University
Harrisonburg 22807

Public institution; small-town setting. Awards B, M. Total enrollment: 9,242. Undergraduate enrollment: 8,182; 3% part-time, 55% women, 4% over 25. Total faculty: 548. Library holdings: 310,000 bound volumes, 508,000 titles on microform, 2,500 periodical subscriptions, 2,000 records/tapes.

Undergraduate Courses offered for part-time students during daytime, evenings, summer. Complete part-time degree programs offered during daytime, evenings, summer. Adult/continuing education programs available. Career services available to part-time students: individual and group career counseling, individual job placement, employer recruitment on campus. Part-time tuition: $63 per credit for state residents, $107 per credit for nonresidents.

Graduate Part-time study available in Graduate School. Degree can be earned exclusively through evening/weekend study in Graduate School. Basic part-time expenses: $70 per credit tuition for state residents, $125 per credit tuition for nonresidents.

John Tyler Community College
Chester 23831

Public institution; small-town setting. Awards A. Barrier-free campus. Total enrollment: 4,332 (all undergraduates); 74% part-time, 59% women, 66% over 25. Total faculty: 196. Library holdings: 30,488 bound volumes, 25,221 titles on microform, 358 periodical subscriptions, 5,705 records/tapes.

Undergraduate Courses offered for part-time students during daytime, evenings, summer. Complete part-time degree programs offered during daytime, evenings, summer. External degree and adult/continuing education programs available. Career services available to part-time students: individual and group career counseling, individual job placement, employer recruitment on campus. Part-time tuition: $15.25 per credit hour for state residents, $66 per credit hour for nonresidents.

J Sargeant Reynolds Community College
Richmond 23241

Public institution; metropolitan setting. Awards A. Barrier-free campus. Total enrollment: 11,300 (all undergraduates); 65% part-time, 65% women. Total faculty: 488. Library holdings: 52,280 bound volumes, 417 titles on microform, 800 periodical subscriptions, 593 records/tapes.

Undergraduate Courses offered for part-time students during daytime, evenings, weekends, summer. Complete part-time degree programs offered during daytime, evenings, weekends, summer. Adult/continuing education programs available. Career services available to part-time students: individual and group career counseling, individual job placement, employer recruitment on campus. Part-time tuition: $15.25 per credit for state residents, $66 per credit for nonresidents.

Liberty Baptist College
Lynchburg 24506

Independent-religious instutition; city setting. Awards A, B, M. Barrier-free campus. Total enrollment: 4,207. Undergraduate enrollment: 3,967; 12% part-time, 49% women. Total faculty: 207. Library holdings: 200,000 bound volumes, 160,000 titles on microform, 550 periodical subscriptions, 2,000 records/tapes.

Undergraduate Courses offered for part-time students during daytime, evenings, summer. Complete part-time degree programs offered during daytime. Career services available to part-time students: individual and group career counseling, individual job placement, employer recruitment on campus. Part-time tuition: $105 per semester hour.

Graduate Part-time study available in Liberty Baptist Theological Seminary, School of Education, School of Religion. Basic part-time expenses: $105 per credit tuition plus $50 per semester fees.

Longwood College
Farmville 23901

Public institution; small-town setting. Awards B, M. Total enrollment: 2,590. Undergraduate enrollment: 2,539; 5% part-time, 70% women, 1% over 25. Total faculty: 158. Library holdings: 179,313 bound volumes, 1,278 periodical subscriptions, 3,307 records/tapes.

Undergraduate Courses offered for part-time students during daytime, evenings, summer. Complete part-time degree programs offered during daytime. Adult/continuing education programs available. Career services available to part-time students: individual and group career counseling, individual job placement, employer recruitment on campus. Part-time tuition: $49 per credit hour for state residents, $100 per credit hour for nonresidents.

Graduate Part-time study available in Graduate Programs. Degree can be earned exclusively through evening/weekend study in Graduate Programs. Basic part-time expenses: $55 per credit tuition for state residents, $100 per credit tuition for nonresidents. Institutional financial aid available to part-time graduate students in Graduate Programs.

Lord Fairfax Community College
Middletown 22645

Public institution; rural setting. Awards A. Barrier-free campus. Total enrollment: 1,872 (all undergraduates); 73% part-time, 62% women. Total faculty: 78. Library holdings: 33,302 bound volumes, 12,000 titles on microform, 300 periodical subscriptions, 2,720 records/tapes.

Undergraduate Courses offered for part-time students during daytime, evenings, weekends, summer. Complete part-time degree programs offered during daytime, evenings. Adult/continuing education programs available. Career services available to part-time students: individual and group career counseling, individual job placement, employer recruitment on campus. Part-time tuition: $15.25 per credit for state residents, $66 per credit for nonresidents.

Lynchburg College
Lynchburg 24501

Independent-religious instutition; city setting. Awards B, M. Total enrollment: 2,207. Undergraduate enrollment: 1,719; 9% part-time, 53% women. Total faculty: 152. Library holdings: 131,034 bound volumes, 51,279 titles on microform, 618 periodical subscriptions, 18,632 records/tapes.

Undergraduate Courses offered for part-time students during daytime, evenings, summer. Complete part-time degree programs offered during daytime, evenings, summer. Adult/continuing education programs available. Career services available to part-time students: individual and group career counseling, individual job placement, employer recruitment on campus. Part-time tuition: $95 per credit hour.

Mary Baldwin College
Staunton 24401

Independent-religious instutition; small-town setting. Awards B. Total enrollment: 660 (all undergraduates); 2% part-time, 100% women. Total faculty: 78. Library holdings: 150,000 bound volumes, 600 periodical subscriptions, 5,000 records/tapes.

Undergraduate Courses offered for part-time students during daytime, evenings. Complete part-time degree programs offered during daytime, evenings. External degree and adult/continuing education programs available. Career services available to part-time students: individual and group career counseling, employer recruitment on campus. Part-time tuition: $206.67 per semester hour.

Marymount College of Virginia
Arlington 22207

Independent-religious instutition; metropolitan setting. Awards A, B, M. Total enrollment: 1,868. Undergraduate enrollment: 1,225; 24% part-time, 96% women, 20% over 25. Total faculty: 173. Library holdings: 60,000 bound volumes, 62,000 titles on microform, 431 periodical subscriptions, 215 records/tapes.

Undergraduate Courses offered for part-time students during daytime, evenings. Complete part-time degree programs offered during daytime, evenings. Career services available to part-time students: individual and group career counseling, individual job placement, employer recruitment on campus. Part-time tuition: $150 per semester hour.

Graduate Part-time study available in Division of Arts and Sciences, Division of Business Administration, Division of Education, Division of Health Services, Division of Human Resource Development. Degree can be earned exclusively through evening/weekend study in Division of Arts and Sciences, Division of Business Administration, Division of Education, Division of Human Resource Development. Basic part-time expenses: $160 per credit tuition.

Mary Washington College
Fredericksburg 22401

Public institution; small-town setting. Awards B, M. Total enrollment: 2,990. Undergraduate enrollment: 2,610; 7% part-time, 75% women, 7% over 25. Total faculty: 169. Library holdings: 280,000 bound volumes, 1,324 periodical subscriptions, 1,590 records/tapes.

Undergraduate Courses offered for part-time students during daytime, evenings, weekends, summer. Complete part-time degree programs offered during daytime, evenings, weekends, summer. Adult/continuing education programs available. Career services available to part-time students: individual and group career counseling, individual job placement, employer recruitment on campus. Part-time tuition: $46 per semester hour for state residents, $97 per semester hour for nonresidents.

Graduate Part-time study available in Graduate Studies. Degree can be earned exclusively through evening/weekend study in Graduate Studies. Basic part-time expenses: $55 per credit tuition for state residents, $103 per credit tuition for nonresidents.

Mountain Empire Community College
Big Stone Gap 24219

Public institution; small-town setting. Awards A. Barrier-free campus. Total enrollment: 2,400 (all undergraduates); 60% part-time, 50% women, 30% over 25. Total faculty: 90. Library holdings: 21,272 bound volumes, 250 titles on microform, 100 periodical subscriptions, 200 records/tapes.

Colleges Offering Part-Time Degree Programs / Virginia

Mountain Empire Community College (continued)

Undergraduate Courses offered for part-time students during daytime, evenings, summer. Complete part-time degree programs offered during daytime, evenings, summer. External degree and adult/continuing education programs available. Career services available to part-time students: individual and group career counseling, individual job placement, employer recruitment on campus. Part-time tuition: $15.25 per quarter hour for state residents, $66 per quarter hour for nonresidents.

National Business College
Lynchburg 24501

Proprietary institution; city setting. Awards A. Total enrollment: 185 (all undergraduates); 7% part-time, 65% women, 50% over 25. Total faculty: 15. Library holdings: 1,500 bound volumes, 10 periodical subscriptions.

Undergraduate Courses offered for part-time students during daytime, evenings, summer. Complete part-time degree programs offered during daytime, evenings, summer. Adult/continuing education programs available. Career services available to part-time students: individual and group career counseling, individual job placement, employer recruitment on campus. Part-time tuition: $60 per quarter hour.

New River Community College
Dublin 24084

Public institution; rural setting. Awards A. Barrier-free campus. Total enrollment: 2,936 (all undergraduates); 68% part-time, 58% women. Total faculty: 168. Library holdings: 23,266 bound volumes, 238 periodical subscriptions, 572 records/tapes.

Undergraduate Courses offered for part-time students during daytime, evenings, summer. Complete part-time degree programs offered during daytime, evenings, summer. Adult/continuing education programs available. Career services available to part-time students: individual and group career counseling, individual job placement, employer recruitment on campus. Part-time tuition: $15.25 per quarter hour for state residents, $66 per quarter hour for nonresidents.

Norfolk State University
Norfolk 23504

Public institution; city setting. Awards A, B, M. Barrier-free campus. Total enrollment: 7,400. Undergraduate enrollment: 6,600; 10% part-time, 58% women. Total faculty: 410. Library holdings: 200,000 bound volumes, 1,000 titles on microform, 2,300 periodical subscriptions.

Undergraduate Courses offered for part-time students during daytime, evenings, summer. Complete part-time degree programs offered during daytime, evenings, summer. Adult/continuing education programs available. Career services available to part-time students: individual and group career counseling, individual job placement, employer recruitment on campus. Part-time tuition: $55 per semester hour for state residents, $96 per semester hour for nonresidents.

Graduate Part-time study available in School of Graduate Studies.Basic part-time expenses: $55 per semester hour tuition plus $18 per semester fees for state residents, $96 per semester hour tuition plus $18 per semester fees for nonresidents.

Northern Virginia Community College
Annandale 22003

Public institution; metropolitan setting. Awards A. Barrier-free campus. Total enrollment: 35,067 (all undergraduates); 74% part-time, 56% women. Total faculty: 1,422. Library holdings: 223,740 bound volumes, 1,887 periodical subscriptions.

Undergraduate Courses offered for part-time students during daytime, evenings, weekends, summer. Complete part-time degree programs offered during daytime, evenings, weekends, summer. Adult/continuing education programs available. Career services available to part-time students: individual and group career counseling, individual job placement. Part-time tuition: $15.25 per credit hour for state residents, $66 per credit hour for nonresidents.

Old Dominion University
Norfolk 23508

Public institution; city setting. Awards B, M, D. Total enrollment: 14,966. Undergraduate enrollment: 11,673; 24% part-time, 50% women. Total faculty: 717. Library holdings: 475,000 bound volumes.

Undergraduate Courses offered for part-time students during daytime, evenings, summer. Complete part-time degree programs offered during daytime, evenings, summer. External degree and adult/continuing education programs available. Career services available to part-time students: individual and group career counseling, individual job placement, employer recruitment on campus. Part-time tuition: $61 per credit hour for state residents, $115 per credit hour for nonresidents.

Graduate Part-time study available in Darden School of Education, School of Arts and Letters, School of Business Administration, School of Engineering, School of Sciences and Health Professions.Basic part-time expenses: $72 per credit tuition for state residents, $157 per credit tuition for nonresidents.

Patrick Henry Community College
Martinsville 24112

Public institution; rural setting. Awards A. Barrier-free campus. Total enrollment: 902 (all undergraduates); 69% part-time, 67% women. Total faculty: 63. Library holdings: 32,000 bound volumes, 325 periodical subscriptions, 809 records/tapes.

Undergraduate Courses offered for part-time students during daytime, evenings, weekends, summer. Complete part-time degree programs offered during daytime, evenings, weekends, summer. Adult/continuing education programs available. Career services available to part-time students: individual and group career counseling, individual job placement. Part-time tuition: $15.25 per credit hour for state residents, $66 per credit hour for nonresidents.

Paul D Camp Community College
Franklin 23851

Public institution; small-town setting. Awards A. Barrier-free campus. Total enrollment: 1,115 (all undergraduates); 61% part-time, 60% women. Total faculty: 65. Library holdings: 22,000 bound volumes, 772 titles on microform, 307 periodical subscriptions, 1,530 records/tapes.

Undergraduate Courses offered for part-time students during daytime, evenings, weekends, summer. Complete part-time degree programs offered during daytime, evenings, weekends, summer. Adult/continuing education programs available. Career services available to part-time students: individual and group career counseling, individual job placement, employer recruitment on campus. Part-time tuition: $13.50 per credit hour for state residents, $58 per credit hour for nonresidents.

Piedmont Virginia Community College
Charlottesville 22901

Public institution; small-town setting. Awards A. Barrier-free campus. Total enrollment: 3,716 (all undergraduates); 76% part-time, 65% women, 60% over 25. Total faculty: 160. Library holdings: 22,000 bound volumes, 199 periodical subscriptions.

Undergraduate Courses offered for part-time students during daytime, evenings, weekends, summer. Complete part-time degree programs offered during daytime, evenings, weekends, summer. Adult/continuing education programs available. Career services available to part-time students: individual and group career counseling, individual job placement, employer recruitment on campus. Part-time tuition: $15.25 per quarter hour for state residents, $66 per quarter hour for nonresidents.

Presbyterian School of Christian Education
Richmond 23227

Independent-religious institution (graduate only). Total enrollment: 136 (coed; 4% part-time). Total faculty: 16.

Graduate Part-time study available in Graduate Programs. Basic part-time expenses: $68.75 per credit tuition.

Protestant Episcopal Theological Seminary in Virginia
Alexandria 22304

Independent-religious institution (graduate only). Total enrollment: 235 (coed; 29% part-time). Total faculty: 36.

Graduate Part-time study available in Graduate and Professional Programs. Basic part-time expenses: $150 per credit tuition.

Radford University
Radford 24142

Public institution; small-town setting. Awards B, M. Total enrollment: 6,285. Undergraduate enrollment: 5,677; 4% part-time, 66% women. Total faculty: 290. Library holdings: 175,000 bound volumes, 2,153 periodical subscriptions, 20,000 records/tapes.

Undergraduate Courses offered for part-time students during daytime, evenings, summer. Complete part-time degree programs offered during daytime, evenings. Adult/continuing education programs available. Career services available to part-time students: individual and group career counseling, individual job placement, employer recruitment on campus. Part-time tuition: $66 per semester hour for state residents, $97 per semester hour for nonresidents.

Graduate Part-time study available in Graduate School. Basic part-time expenses: $70 per credit tuition for state residents, $78 per credit tuition for nonresidents.

Randolph-Macon Woman's College
Lynchburg 24503

Independent-religious instutition; city setting. Awards B. Total enrollment: 750 (all undergraduates); 1% part-time, 100% women, 5% over 25. Total faculty: 83. Library holdings: 141,000 bound volumes, 683 periodical subscriptions.

Undergraduate Courses offered for part-time students during daytime. Complete part-time degree programs offered during daytime. Adult/continuing education programs available. Career services available to part-time students: individual and group career counseling, individual job placement, employer recruitment on campus. Part-time tuition: $400 per semester hour.

Richard Bland College
Petersburg 23805

Public institution; rural setting. Awards A. Barrier-free campus. Total enrollment: 1,026 (all undergraduates); 45% part-time, 70% women, 30% over 25. Total faculty: 60. Library holdings: 52,315 bound volumes, 73 titles on microform, 199 periodical subscriptions, 2,709 records/tapes.

Undergraduate Courses offered for part-time students during daytime, evenings, summer. Complete part-time degree programs offered during daytime, evenings, summer. Career services available to part-time students: individual career counseling, individual job placement. Part-time tuition: $46 per semester hour for state residents, $119 per semester hour for nonresidents.

Roanoke College
Salem 24153

Independent-religious instutition; small-town setting. Awards B. Barrier-free campus. Total enrollment: 1,378 (all undergraduates); 21% part-time, 50% women, 16% over 25. Total faculty: 91. Library holdings: 140,000 bound volumes, 690 periodical subscriptions, 2,600 records/tapes.

Undergraduate Courses offered for part-time students during daytime, evenings, summer. Complete part-time degree programs offered during daytime, evenings, summer. Adult/continuing education programs available. Career services available to part-time students: individual and group career counseling, individual job placement, employer recruitment on campus. Part-time tuition: $280 per unit.

Saint Paul's College
Lawrenceville 23868

Independent-religious instutition; small-town setting. Awards B. Total enrollment: 701 (all undergraduates); 2% part-time, 50% women, 1% over 25. Total faculty: 49. Library holdings: 40,000 bound volumes, 205 periodical subscriptions, 3,000 records/tapes.

Undergraduate Courses offered for part-time students during daytime. Complete part-time degree programs offered during daytime. Career services available to part-time students: individual and group career counseling, individual job placement, employer recruitment on campus. Part-time tuition: $112.10 per credit.

Shenandoah College and Conservatory of Music
Winchester 22601

Independent-religious instutition; small-town setting. Awards A, B, M. Barrier-free campus. Total enrollment: 927. Undergraduate enrollment: 875; 25% part-time, 60% women. Total faculty: 128. Library holdings: 77,600 bound volumes, 400 titles on microform, 500 periodical subscriptions, 7,250 records/tapes.

Undergraduate Courses offered for part-time students during daytime, evenings, summer. Complete part-time degree pro-

Colleges Offering Part-Time Degree Programs / Virginia

Shenandoah College and Conservatory of Music (continued)
grams offered during daytime, evenings, summer. Adult/continuing education programs available. Career services available to part-time students: individual and group career counseling, individual job placement, employer recruitment on campus. Part-time tuition per semester hour ranges from $100 (1 to 6 semester hours) to $165 (7 to 11 semester hours).
Graduate Part-time study available in School of Business Administration, Conservatory of Music. Basic part-time expenses: $160 per credit hour tuition for state residents, for nonresidents.

Southside Virginia Community College
Alberta 23821
Public institution; rural setting. Awards A. Total enrollment: 1,670 (all undergraduates); 69% part-time, 64% women, 55% over 25. Total faculty: 105. Library holdings: 30,000 bound volumes, 300 periodical subscriptions, 3,000 records/tapes.
Undergraduate Courses offered for part-time students during daytime, evenings, summer. Complete part-time degree programs offered during daytime, evenings. Adult/continuing education programs available. Career services available to part-time students: individual and group career counseling, individual job placement, employer recruitment on campus. Part-time tuition: $15.25 per quarter hour for state residents, $66 per quarter hour for nonresidents.

Southwest Virginia Community College
Richlands 24641
Public institution; rural setting. Awards A. Barrier-free campus. Total enrollment: 3,173 (all undergraduates); 60% part-time, 51% women, 35% over 25. Total faculty: 150. Library holdings: 38,888 bound volumes, 30,000 titles on microform, 370 periodical subscriptions, 5,600 records/tapes.
Undergraduate Courses offered for part-time students during daytime, evenings, summer. Complete part-time degree programs offered during daytime, evenings, summer. Adult/continuing education programs available. Career services available to part-time students: individual and group career counseling, individual job placement, employer recruitment on campus. Part-time tuition: $15.25 per quarter hour for state residents, $66 per quarter hour for nonresidents.

Sweet Briar College
Sweet Briar 24595
Independent institution; rural setting. Awards B. Total enrollment: 738 (all undergraduates); 1% part-time, 100% women. Total faculty: 87. Library holdings: 180,157 bound volumes, 4,800 titles on microform, 813 periodical subscriptions, 2,250 records/tapes.
Undergraduate Courses offered for part-time students during daytime, evenings. Complete part-time degree programs offered during daytime. Adult/continuing education programs available. Career services available to part-time students: individual and group career counseling, individual job placement, employer recruitment on campus. Part-time tuition: $826 per course.

Thomas Nelson Community College
Hampton 23670
Public institution; city setting. Awards A. Barrier-free campus. Total enrollment: 6,901 (all undergraduates); 71% part-time, 53% women, 56% over 25. Total faculty: 276. Library holdings: 51,130 bound volumes, 4,042 titles on microform, 550 periodical subscriptions, 3,497 records/tapes.
Undergraduate Courses offered for part-time students during daytime, evenings, weekends, summer. Complete part-time degree programs offered during daytime, evenings, weekends, summer. External degree and adult/continuing education programs available. Career services available to part-time students: individual and group career counseling, individual job placement, employer recruitment on campus. Part-time tuition: $15.25 per credit for state residents, $66 per credit for nonresidents.

Tidewater Community College, Chesapeake Campus
Chesapeake 23320
Public institution; city setting. Awards A. Barrier-free campus. Total enrollment: 2,178 (all undergraduates); 75% part-time, 55% women, 58% over 25. Total faculty: 123. Library holdings: 30,468 bound volumes, 86 titles on microform, 261 periodical subscriptions, 424 records/tapes.
Undergraduate Courses offered for part-time students during daytime, evenings, weekends, summer. Complete part-time degree programs offered during daytime, evenings, summer. External degree and adult/continuing education programs available. Career services available to part-time students: individual and group career counseling, individual job placement, employer recruitment on campus. Part-time tuition: $15.25 per quarter hour for state residents, $66 per quarter hour for nonresidents.

Tidewater Community College, Frederick Campus
Portsmouth 23703
Public institution; city setting. Awards A. Barrier-free campus. Total enrollment: 4,710 (all undergraduates); 72% part-time, 60% women, 58% over 25. Total faculty: 242. Library holdings: 52,832 bound volumes, 154 titles on microform, 310 periodical subscriptions, 500 records/tapes.
Undergraduate Courses offered for part-time students during daytime, evenings, weekends, summer. Complete part-time degree programs offered during daytime, evenings, summer. External degree and adult/continuing education programs available. Career services available to part-time students: individual and group career counseling, individual job placement, employer recruitment on campus. Part-time tuition: $15.25 per quarter hour for state residents, $66 per quarter hour for nonresidents.

Tidewater Community College, Virginia Beach Campus
Virginia Beach 23456
Public institution; city setting. Awards A. Barrier-free campus. Total enrollment: 9,067 (all undergraduates); 73% part-time, 55% women, 54% over 25. Total faculty: 440. Library holdings: 31,246 bound volumes, 278 titles on microform, 497 periodical subscriptions, 370 records/tapes.
Undergraduate Courses offered for part-time students during daytime, evenings, weekends, summer. Complete part-time degree programs offered during daytime, evenings, summer. External degree and adult/continuing education programs available. Career services available to part-time students: individual and group career counseling, individual job placement, employer recruitment on campus. Part-time tuition:

$15.25 per quarter hour for state residents, $66 per quarter hour for nonresidents.

University of Richmond
Richmond 23173

Independent-religious instutition; metropolitan setting. Awards B, M. Total enrollment: 4,300. Undergraduate enrollment: 2,742; 2% part-time, 45% women. Total faculty: 364. Library holdings: 400,000 bound volumes, 13,975 titles on microform, 2,890 periodical subscriptions, 7,152 records/tapes.

Undergraduate Courses offered for part-time students during daytime, evenings, summer. Complete part-time degree programs offered during daytime, evenings, summer. Adult/continuing education programs available. Career services available to part-time students: individual and group career counseling, employer recruitment on campus. Part-time tuition: $335 per semester hour.

Graduate Part-time study available in Graduate School, Richard S. Reynolds Graduate Division of Business. Degree can be earned exclusively through evening/weekend study in Graduate School, Richard S. Reynolds Graduate Division of Business. Basic part-time expenses: $85 per credit hour (minimum) tuition.

Virginia Commonwealth University
Richmond 23284

Public institution; metropolitan setting. Awards B, M, D. Total enrollment: 20,402. Undergraduate enrollment: 15,405; 40% part-time, 61% women, 25% over 25. Total faculty: 1,960. Library holdings: 646,067 bound volumes, 150,533 titles on microform, 8,676 periodical subscriptions, 8,981 records/tapes.

Undergraduate Courses offered for part-time students during daytime, evenings, weekends, summer. Complete part-time degree programs offered during daytime, evenings, summer. Adult/continuing education programs available. Career services available to part-time students: individual and group career counseling, employer recruitment on campus. Part-time tuition: $54 per credit for state residents, $123 per credit for nonresidents.

Graduate Part-time study available in School of Graduate Studies, School of Pharmacy. Basic part-time expenses: $93 per credit hour tuition plus $9 per credit hour fees for state residents, $175 per credit hour tuition plus $9 per credit hour fees for nonresidents. Institutional financial aid available to part-time graduate students in School of Graduate Studies.

Virginia Highlands Community College
Abingdon 24210

Public institution; small-town setting. Awards A. Barrier-free campus. Total enrollment: 1,501 (all undergraduates); 45% part-time, 56% women, 40% over 25. Total faculty: 95. Library holdings: 25,753 bound volumes, 1,117 records/tapes.

Undergraduate Courses offered for part-time students during daytime, evenings. Complete part-time degree programs offered during daytime, evenings. Adult/continuing education programs available. Career services available to part-time students: individual and group career counseling, individual job placement, employer recruitment on campus. Part-time tuition: $15.25 per quarter hour for state residents, $66 per quarter hour for nonresidents.

Virginia Intermont College
Bristol 24201

Independent-religious instutition; city setting. Awards A, B. Total enrollment: 575 (all undergraduates); 6% part-time, 87% women. Total faculty: 56. Library holdings: 58,033 bound volumes, 407 periodical subscriptions.

Undergraduate Courses offered for part-time students during daytime, evenings. Complete part-time degree programs offered during daytime, evenings. Career services available to part-time students: individual career counseling, individual job placement. Part-time tuition per semester (1 to 11 semester hours) ranges from $100 to $1375.

Virginia Polytechnic Institute and State University
Blacksburg 24061

Public institution; small-town setting. Awards B, M, D. Total enrollment: 21,357. Undergraduate enrollment: 17,942; 3% part-time, 41% women, 19% over 25. Total faculty: 1,846. Library holdings: 1.4 million bound volumes, 3.4 million titles on microform, 12,353 periodical subscriptions, 6,564 records/tapes.

Undergraduate Courses offered for part-time students during daytime, summer. Complete part-time degree programs offered during daytime, summer. Adult/continuing education programs available. Career services available to part-time students: individual and group career counseling, individual job placement, employer recruitment on campus. Part-time tuition: $56 per credit hour for state residents, $117 per credit hour for nonresidents.

Graduate Part-time study available in Graduate School. Degree can be earned exclusively through evening/weekend study in Graduate School. Basic part-time expenses: $216 per quarter (minimum) tuition plus $10 per quarter fees for state residents, $237 per quarter (minimum) tuition plus $10 per quarter fees for nonresidents.

Virginia State University
Petersburg 23803

Public institution; small-town setting. Awards B, M. Total enrollment: 3,956. Undergraduate enrollment: 3,553; 9% part-time, 54% women, 27% over 25. Total faculty: 266. Library holdings: 213,103 bound volumes, 374,284 titles on microform, 1,677 periodical subscriptions, 54,117 records/tapes.

Undergraduate Courses offered for part-time students during daytime, evenings, weekends, summer. Complete part-time degree programs offered during daytime, weekends, summer. Adult/continuing education programs available. Career services available to part-time students: individual career counseling, individual job placement, employer recruitment on campus. Part-time tuition: $60 per credit for state residents, $90 per credit for nonresidents.

Graduate Part-time study available in School of Graduate Studies. Basic part-time expenses: $65 per credit hour tuition for state residents, $95 per credit hour tuition for nonresidents. Institutional financial aid available to part-time graduate students in School of Graduate Studies.

Virginia Wesleyan College
Norfolk 23502

Independent-religious instutition; city setting. Awards B. Barrier-free campus. Total enrollment: 926 (all undergraduates); 14% part-time, 58% women, 17% over 25. Total faculty: 72. Library holdings: 70,000 bound volumes, 597 periodical subscriptions, 1,782 records/tapes.

Colleges Offering Part-Time Degree Programs / Virginia

Virginia Wesleyan College (continued)

Undergraduate Courses offered for part-time students during daytime, evenings, summer. Complete part-time degree programs offered during daytime. Adult/continuing education programs available. Career services available to part-time students: individual and group career counseling. Part-time tuition: $198 per semester hour.

Virginia Western Community College
Roanoke 24038

Public institution; city setting. Awards A. Barrier-free campus. Total enrollment: 3,200 (all undergraduates); 52% part-time, 59% women, 65% over 25. Total faculty: 218. Library holdings: 50,000 bound volumes, 550 periodical subscriptions, 2,650 records/tapes.

Undergraduate Courses offered for part-time students during daytime, evenings, weekends, summer. Complete part-time degree programs offered during daytime, evenings, weekends, summer. Adult/continuing education programs available. Career services available to part-time students: individual and group career counseling, individual job placement, employer recruitment on campus. Part-time tuition: $15.25 per quarter hour for state residents, $75 per quarter hour for nonresidents.

VIRGIN ISLANDS

College of the Virgin Islands
Charlotte Amalie, St Thomas 00802

Public institution; small-town setting. Awards A, B, M. Total enrollment: 2,864. Undergraduate enrollment: 2,680; 75% part-time, 72% women. Total faculty: 165. Library holdings: 85,288 bound volumes, 446,380 titles on microform, 1,077 periodical subscriptions, 8,828 records/tapes.

Undergraduate Courses offered for part-time students during daytime, evenings. Complete part-time degree programs offered during daytime, evenings. Adult/continuing education programs available. Career services available to part-time students: individual and group career counseling, individual job placement, employer recruitment on campus. Part-time tuition: $33 per semester hour for territory residents, $33 per semester hour for nonresidents.

Graduate Part-time study available in Graduate Programs. Degree can be earned exclusively through evening/weekend study in Graduate Programs. Basic part-time expenses: $66 per credit tuition plus $10 per semester fees for territory residents, $132 per credit tuition plus $10 per semester fees for nonresidents.

WASHINGTON

Bellevue Community College
Bellevue 98007

Public institution; city setting. Awards A. Barrier-free campus. Total enrollment: 6,323 (all undergraduates); 68% part-time, 65% women, 50% over 25. Total faculty: 386. Library holdings: 40,000 bound volumes, 142 titles on microform, 506 periodical subscriptions, 5,042 records/tapes.

Undergraduate Courses offered for part-time students during daytime, evenings, summer. Complete part-time degree programs offered during daytime, evenings. Adult/continuing education programs available. Career services available to part-time students: individual and group career counseling, individual job placement, employer recruitment on campus. Part-time tuition: $19.35 per quarter hour for state residents, $76.10 per quarter hour for nonresidents.

Big Bend Community College
Moses Lake 98837

Public institution; rural setting. Awards A. Barrier-free campus. Total enrollment: 2,202 (all undergraduates); 78% part-time, 45% women, 29% over 25. Total faculty: 159. Library holdings: 36,953 bound volumes, 325 periodical subscriptions, 2,200 records/tapes.

Undergraduate Courses offered for part-time students during daytime, evenings, summer. Complete part-time degree programs offered during daytime, evenings, summer. Adult/continuing education programs available. Career services available to part-time students: individual job placement. Part-time tuition: $19.35 per quarter hour for state residents, $76.15 per quarter hour for nonresidents.

Centralia College
Centralia 98531

Public institution; small-town setting. Awards A. Barrier-free campus. Total enrollment: 3,248 (all undergraduates); 5% part-time, 56% women, 66% over 25. Total faculty: 270. Library holdings: 31,000 bound volumes, 225 periodical subscriptions, 500 records/tapes.

Undergraduate Courses offered for part-time students during daytime, evenings, summer. Complete part-time degree programs offered during daytime, evenings, summer. External degree and adult/continuing education programs available. Career services available to part-time students: individual and group career counseling, individual job placement, employer recruitment on campus. Part-time tuition: $19.35 per credit for state residents, $76.15 per credit for nonresidents.

Central Washington University
Ellensburg 98926

Public institution; small-town setting. Awards B, M. Total enrollment: 7,121. Undergraduate enrollment: 6,152; 16% part-time, 50% women, 26% over 25. Total faculty: 304. Library holdings: 344,854 bound volumes, 90,150 titles on microform, 2,137 periodical subscriptions, 17,370 records/tapes.

Undergraduate Courses offered for part-time students during daytime, evenings, summer. Complete part-time degree programs offered during daytime, evenings, summer. External degree and adult/continuing education programs available. Career services available to part-time students: individual and group career counseling, individual job placement, employer recruitment on campus. Part-time tuition: $34 per credit for state residents, $116 per credit for nonresidents.

Graduate Part-time study available in Graduate Studies. Basic part-time expenses: $48 per credit tuition plus $10 per quarter fees for state residents, $141 per credit tuition plus $10 per quarter fees for nonresidents.

City University
Bellevue 98008

Independent institution; city setting. Awards A, B, M. Total enrollment: 2,838. Undergraduate enrollment: 1,813; 51% part-time, 49% women, 90% over 25. Total faculty: 220. Library holdings: 5,000 bound volumes, 50 periodical subscriptions.

Undergraduate Courses offered for part-time students during daytime, evenings, weekends, summer. Complete part-time de-

gree programs offered during daytime, evenings, weekends, summer. Part-time tuition: $70 per quarter hour.

Clark College
Vancouver 98663

Public institution; city setting. Awards A. Barrier-free campus. Total enrollment: 8,200 (all undergraduates); 50% part-time, 55% women. Total faculty: 300. Library holdings: 40,000 bound volumes, 500 periodical subscriptions, 500 records/tapes.

Undergraduate Courses offered for part-time students during daytime, evenings, summer. Complete part-time degree programs offered during daytime, evenings, summer. Adult/continuing education programs available. Career services available to part-time students: individual and group career counseling, individual job placement, employer recruitment on campus. Part-time tuition: $19.35 per credit hour for state residents, $76.10 per credit hour for nonresidents.

Columbia Basin College
Pasco 99301

Public institution; small-town setting. Awards A. Barrier-free campus. Total enrollment: 5,000 (all undergraduates); 50% part-time, 52% women, 50% over 25. Total faculty: 310. Library holdings: 51,006 bound volumes, 7,490 titles on microform, 2,603 periodical subscriptions, 12,201 records/tapes.

Undergraduate Courses offered for part-time students during daytime, evenings, summer. Complete part-time degree programs offered during daytime, evenings, summer. Adult/continuing education programs available. Career services available to part-time students: individual career counseling, individual job placement, employer recruitment on campus. Part-time tuition: $19.10 per quarter hour for state residents, $75.75 per quarter hour for nonresidents.

Cornish Institute
Seattle 98102

Independent institution; metropolitan setting. Awards B. Total enrollment: 540 (all undergraduates); 30% part-time, 59% women. Total faculty: 123. Library holdings: 10,000 bound volumes, 100 periodical subscriptions, 2,500 records/tapes.

Undergraduate Courses offered for part-time students during daytime, evenings, summer. Complete part-time degree programs offered during daytime, evenings, summer. Adult/continuing education programs available. Career services available to part-time students: individual career counseling, individual job placement. Part-time tuition: $175 per semester hour.

Eastern Washington University
Cheney 99004

Public institution; small-town setting. Awards B, M. Barrier-free campus. Total enrollment: 8,493. Undergraduate enrollment: 7,046; 8% part-time, 52% women. Total faculty: 390. Library holdings: 333,989 bound volumes, 72,003 titles on microform, 4,634 periodical subscriptions, 15,556 records/tapes.

Undergraduate Courses offered for part-time students during daytime, evenings, weekends, summer. Complete part-time degree programs offered during daytime, evenings, weekends, summer. External degree and adult/continuing education programs available. Career services available to part-time students: individual and group career counseling, individual job placement, employer recruitment on campus. Part-time tuition: $34 per quarter hour for state residents, $116 per quarter hour for nonresidents.

Graduate Part-time study available in Graduate School. Basic part-time expenses: $48 per credit tuition for state residents, $141 per credit tuition for nonresidents.

Edmonds Community College
Lynnwood 98036

Public institution; city setting. Awards A. Barrier-free campus. Total enrollment: 6,199 (all undergraduates); 58% part-time, 53% women. Total faculty: 242. Library holdings: 30,022 bound volumes, 468 periodical subscriptions, 5,000 records/tapes.

Undergraduate Courses offered for part-time students during daytime, evenings, weekends, summer. Complete part-time degree programs offered during daytime, evenings, summer. Adult/continuing education programs available. Career services available to part-time students: individual and group career counseling, individual job placement, employer recruitment on campus. Part-time tuition: $19.35 per credit hour for state residents, $76.15 per credit hour for nonresidents.

Everett Community College
Everett 98201

Public institution; city setting. Awards A. Barrier-free campus. Total enrollment: 5,863 (all undergraduates); 54% part-time, 56% women. Total faculty: 310. Library holdings: 50,918 bound volumes, 3,323 titles on microform, 492 periodical subscriptions, 7,242 records/tapes.

Undergraduate Courses offered for part-time students during daytime, evenings, summer. Complete part-time degree programs offered during daytime, evenings, summer. Adult/continuing education programs available. Career services available to part-time students: individual and group career counseling, individual job placement, employer recruitment on campus. Part-time tuition: $19.35 per credit for state residents, $76.15 per credit for nonresidents.

Evergreen State College
Olympia 98505

Public institution; small-town setting. Awards B, M. Barrier-free campus. Total enrollment: 2,717. Undergraduate enrollment: 2,654; 19% part-time, 52% women, 46% over 25. Total faculty: 165. Library holdings: 165,475 bound volumes, 74,580 titles on microform, 2,663 periodical subscriptions, 8,566 records/tapes.

Undergraduate Courses offered for part-time students during daytime, evenings, weekends, summer. Complete part-time degree programs offered during daytime, evenings, weekends, summer. External degree and adult/continuing education programs available. Career services available to part-time students: individual and group career counseling, individual job placement, employer recruitment on campus. Part-time tuition: $33 per credit hour for state residents, $116 per credit hour for nonresidents.

Graduate Part-time study available in Graduate Programs. Basic part-time expenses: $47 per credit tuition for state residents, $140 per credit tuition for nonresidents.

Fort Steilacoom Community College
Tacoma 98498

Public institution; city setting. Awards A. Barrier-free campus. Total enrollment: 7,998 (all undergraduates); 55% part-time, 45% women, 51% over 25. Total faculty: 284. Library holdings: 39,046 bound volumes, 255 periodical subscriptions, 833 records/tapes.

Colleges Offering Part-Time Degree Programs / *Washington*

Fort Steilacoom Community College (continued)

Undergraduate Courses offered for part-time students during daytime, evenings, summer. Complete part-time degree programs offered during daytime, evenings, summer. Adult/continuing education programs available. Career services available to part-time students: individual and group career counseling, individual job placement, employer recruitment on campus. Part-time tuition: $19.35 per credit for state residents, $76.15 per credit for nonresidents.

Gonzaga University
Spokane 99258

Independent-religious instutition; city setting. Awards B, M, D. Total enrollment: 3,464. Undergraduate enrollment: 2,241; 10% part-time, 54% women, 7% over 25. Total faculty: 287. Library holdings: 303,411 bound volumes, 560 titles on microform, 1,514 periodical subscriptions, 3,027 records/tapes.

Undergraduate Courses offered for part-time students during daytime, evenings, weekends, summer. Complete part-time degree programs offered during daytime. Adult/continuing education programs available. Career services available to part-time students: individual career counseling, individual job placement, employer recruitment on campus. Part-time tuition: $180 per credit.

Graduate Part-time study available in Graduate School. Basic part-time expenses: $170 per credit tuition. Institutional financial aid available to part-time graduate students in Graduate School.

Grays Harbor College
Aberdeen 98520

Public institution; small-town setting. Awards A. Barrier-free campus. Total enrollment: 1,008 (all undergraduates); 60% part-time, 53% women, 30% over 25. Total faculty: 132. Library holdings: 40,500 bound volumes, 64 periodical subscriptions, 2,000 records/tapes.

Undergraduate Courses offered for part-time students during daytime, evenings, summer. Complete part-time degree programs offered during daytime, evenings, summer. Adult/continuing education programs available. Career services available to part-time students: individual career counseling. Part-time tuition: $19.30 per quarter hour for state residents, $76.17 per quarter hour for nonresidents.

Green River Community College
Auburn 98002

Public institution; rural setting. Awards A. Barrier-free campus. Total enrollment: 5,783 (all undergraduates); 45% part-time, 50% women, 45% over 25. Total faculty: 194. Library holdings: 37,000 bound volumes, 2,050 titles on microform, 450 periodical subscriptions, 2,500 records/tapes.

Undergraduate Courses offered for part-time students during daytime, evenings, summer. Complete part-time degree programs offered during daytime, evenings, summer. Adult/continuing education programs available. Career services available to part-time students: individual and group career counseling, individual job placement, employer recruitment on campus. Part-time tuition: $19.36 per quarter hour for state residents, $76.16 per quarter hour for nonresidents.

Griffin College
Seattle 98121

Proprietary institution; metropolitan setting. Awards A, B. Barrier-free campus. Total enrollment: 712 (all undergraduates); 25% part-time, 80% women, 50% over 25. Total faculty: 75. Library holdings: 2,500 bound volumes.

Undergraduate Courses offered for part-time students during daytime, evenings. Complete part-time degree programs offered during daytime, evenings. Career services available to part-time students: individual career counseling, individual job placement. Part-time tuition: $44 per credit.

Heritage College
Toppenish 98948

Independent institution; rural setting. Awards A, B, M. Barrier-free campus. Total enrollment: 332. Undergraduate enrollment: 303; 62% part-time, 48% women. Total faculty: 74. Library holdings: 40,000 bound volumes, 500 records/tapes.

Undergraduate Courses offered for part-time students during daytime, evenings, weekends, summer. Complete part-time degree programs offered during daytime, evenings, weekends, summer. Adult/continuing education programs available. Career services available to part-time students: individual and group career counseling, individual job placement. Part-time tuition: $100 per semester hour.

Graduate Part-time study available in Graduate Program in Education. Basic part-time expenses: $115 per credit tuition.

Highline Community College
Midway 98032

Public institution; small-town setting. Awards A. Total enrollment: 10,460 (all undergraduates); 50% part-time, 60% women. Total faculty: 426.

Undergraduate Courses offered for part-time students during daytime, evenings, summer. Complete part-time degree programs offered during daytime, evenings. Career services available to part-time students: individual and group career counseling, individual job placement, employer recruitment on campus. Part-time tuition: $19.35 per quarter hour for state residents, $76.15 per quarter hour for nonresidents.

Lower Columbia College
Longview 98632

Public institution; small-town setting. Awards A. Barrier-free campus. Total enrollment: 3,800 (all undergraduates); 62% part-time, 57% women, 50% over 25. Total faculty: 150. Library holdings: 25,800 bound volumes, 350 periodical subscriptions, 500 records/tapes.

Undergraduate Courses offered for part-time students during daytime, evenings, summer. Complete part-time degree programs offered during daytime, evenings, summer. Adult/continuing education programs available. Career services available to part-time students: individual and group career counseling, individual job placement. Part-time tuition: $19.30 per quarter hour for state residents, $76.10 per quarter hour for nonresidents.

Lutheran Bible Institute of Seattle
Issaquah 98027

Independent-religious instutition; rural setting. Awards A, B. Barrier-free campus. Total enrollment: 199 (all undergradu-

ates); 12% part-time, 42% women, 19% over 25. Total faculty: 18.
Undergraduate Courses offered for part-time students during daytime, summer. Complete part-time degree programs offered during daytime, summer. Adult/continuing education programs available. Career services available to part-time students: individual career counseling, individual job placement, employer recruitment on campus. Part-time tuition: $60 per quarter hour.

North Seattle Community College
Seattle 98103

Public institution; metropolitan setting. Awards A. Barrier-free campus. Total enrollment: 7,352 (all undergraduates); 59% part-time, 53% women. Total faculty: 272. Library holdings: 33,491 bound volumes, 392 periodical subscriptions, 248 records/tapes.
Undergraduate Courses offered for part-time students during daytime, evenings, summer. Complete part-time degree programs offered during daytime, evenings, summer. Adult/continuing education programs available. Career services available to part-time students: individual and group career counseling, individual job placement, employer recruitment on campus. Part-time tuition: $18.65 per credit for state residents, $75.45 per credit for nonresidents.

Olympic College
Bremerton 98310

Public institution; small-town setting. Awards A. Barrier-free campus. Total enrollment: 6,470 (all undergraduates); 60% part-time, 44% women, 65% over 25. Total faculty: 259. Library holdings: 56,101 bound volumes, 419 periodical subscriptions.
Undergraduate Courses offered for part-time students during daytime, evenings, weekends, summer. Complete part-time degree programs offered during daytime, evenings, weekends, summer. Adult/continuing education programs available. Career services available to part-time students: individual and group career counseling, individual job placement, employer recruitment on campus. Part-time tuition: $19.35 per quarter hour for state residents, $76.15 per quarter hour for nonresidents.

Pacific Lutheran University
Tacoma 98447

Independent-religious instutition; city setting. Awards B, M. Barrier-free campus. Total enrollment: 3,533. Undergraduate enrollment: 2,885; 20% part-time, 55% women. Total faculty: 291. Library holdings: 283,131 bound volumes, 1,546 periodical subscriptions, 2,500 records/tapes.
Undergraduate Courses offered for part-time students during daytime, evenings, summer. Complete part-time degree programs offered during daytime, evenings, summer. Adult/continuing education programs available. Career services available to part-time students: individual and group career counseling, individual job placement, employer recruitment on campus. Part-time tuition: $185 per semester hour.
Graduate Part-time study available in Division of Graduate Studies.Basic part-time expenses: $185 per semester hour tuition.

Peninsula College
Port Angeles 98362

Public institution; small-town setting. Awards A. Barrier-free campus. Total enrollment: 730 (all undergraduates); 35% part-time, 60% women, 59% over 25. Total faculty: 47. Library holdings: 34,883 bound volumes, 1,165 titles on microform, 362 periodical subscriptions, 2,064 records/tapes.
Undergraduate Courses offered for part-time students during daytime, evenings, summer. Complete part-time degree programs offered during daytime, evenings, summer. Adult/continuing education programs available. Career services available to part-time students: individual and group career counseling, individual job placement. Part-time tuition: $18.90 per credit for state residents, $75.70 per credit for nonresidents.

Puget Sound College of the Bible
Edmonds 98020

Independent-religious instutition; small-town setting. Awards B. Total enrollment: 142 (all undergraduates); 15% part-time, 48% women. Total faculty: 14. Library holdings: 25,000 bound volumes, 628 titles on microform, 309 periodical subscriptions, 281 records/tapes.
Undergraduate Courses offered for part-time students during daytime, evenings. Complete part-time degree programs offered during daytime, evenings. Career services available to part-time students: individual career counseling, individual job placement. Part-time tuition: $65 per quarter hour.

Saint Martin's College
Lacey 98503

Independent-religious instutition; small-town setting. Awards A, B, M. Barrier-free campus. Total enrollment: 550. Undergraduate enrollment: 533; 26% part-time, 43% women, 60% over 25. Total faculty: 60. Library holdings: 88,956 bound volumes, 355 periodical subscriptions.
Undergraduate Courses offered for part-time students during daytime, evenings, summer. Complete part-time degree programs offered during daytime, evenings, summer. Adult/continuing education programs available. Career services available to part-time students: individual career counseling, individual job placement, employer recruitment on campus. Part-time tuition: $183 per credit.
Graduate Part-time study available in Graduate Program in Education.Basic part-time expenses: $183 per credit hour tuition. Institutional financial aid available to part-time graduate students in Graduate Program in Education.

Seattle Central Community College
Seattle 98122

Public institution; metropolitan setting. Awards A. Barrier-free campus. Total enrollment: 8,483 (all undergraduates); 42% part-time, 52% women, 61% over 25. Total faculty: 345. Library holdings: 62,481 bound volumes, 189 titles on microform, 536 periodical subscriptions, 2,537 records/tapes.
Undergraduate Courses offered for part-time students during daytime, evenings, summer. Complete part-time degree programs offered during daytime, evenings, summer. External degree and adult/continuing education programs available. Career services available to part-time students: individual and group career counseling, employer recruitment on campus. Part-time tuition: $18.65 per quarter hour for state residents, $75.45 per quarter hour for nonresidents.

Seattle Pacific University
Seattle 98119

Independent-religious instutition; metropolitan setting. Awards B, M. Total enrollment: 2,869. Undergraduate enrollment: 2,-

Colleges Offering Part-Time Degree Programs / Washington

Seattle Pacific University (continued)

377; 12% part-time, 60% women. Total faculty: 199. Library holdings: 120,206 bound volumes, 222,000 titles on microform, 1,040 periodical subscriptions, 3,025 records/tapes.

Undergraduate Courses offered for part-time students during daytime, evenings, weekends, summer. Complete part-time degree programs offered during daytime, evenings, weekends, summer. External degree and adult/continuing education programs available. Career services available to part-time students: individual and group career counseling, individual job placement, employer recruitment on campus. Part-time tuition: $70 per credit.

Graduate Part-time study available in Graduate, Professional, and Continuing Studies. Degree can be earned exclusively through evening/weekend study in Graduate, Professional, and Continuing Studies. Basic part-time expenses: $84 per credit (minimum) tuition.

Seattle University
Seattle 98122

Independent-religious instutition; metropolitan setting. Awards B, M, D. Total enrollment: 4,686. Undergraduate enrollment: 3,564; 25% part-time, 55% women. Total faculty: 306. Library holdings: 200,000 bound volumes, 2,000 periodical subscriptions.

Undergraduate Courses offered for part-time students during daytime, evenings, summer. Complete part-time degree programs offered during daytime, evenings, summer. Adult/continuing education programs available. Career services available to part-time students: individual and group career counseling, individual job placement, employer recruitment on campus. Part-time tuition: $125 per quarter hour.

Shoreline Community College
Seattle 98133

Public institution; metropolitan setting. Awards A. Barrier-free campus. Total enrollment: 5,514 (all undergraduates); 30% part-time, 56% women, 40% over 25. Total faculty: 285. Library holdings: 70,000 bound volumes, 700 periodical subscriptions, 7,000 records/tapes.

Undergraduate Courses offered for part-time students during daytime, evenings, summer. Complete part-time degree programs offered during daytime, evenings, summer. Adult/continuing education programs available. Career services available to part-time students: individual and group career counseling, individual job placement. Part-time tuition and fees per semester (1 to 9 credit hours) range from $38.10 to $171.45 for state residents, $151.70 to $682.65 for nonresidents.

Skagit Valley College
Mount Vernon 98273

Public institution; small-town setting. Awards A. Barrier-free campus. Total enrollment: 1,609 (all undergraduates); 25% part-time, 54% women. Total faculty: 213. Library holdings: 54,171 bound volumes, 112 titles on microform, 394 periodical subscriptions, 6,840 records/tapes.

Undergraduate Courses offered for part-time students during daytime, evenings, summer. Complete part-time degree programs offered during daytime, evenings, summer. Adult/continuing education programs available. Career services available to part-time students: individual and group career counseling, individual job placement. Part-time tuition: $19.35 per credit for state residents, $76.15 per credit for nonresidents.

South Puget Sound Community College
Olympia 98502

Public institution; small-town setting. Awards A. Total enrollment: 3,531 (all undergraduates); 73% part-time, 62% women, 71% over 25. Total faculty: 175. Library holdings: 7,200 bound volumes, 50 periodical subscriptions, 1,100 records/tapes.

Undergraduate Courses offered for part-time students during daytime, evenings, summer. Complete part-time degree programs offered during daytime, evenings, summer. Adult/continuing education programs available. Career services available to part-time students: individual and group career counseling, individual job placement, employer recruitment on campus. Part-time tuition: $19.35 per credit for state residents, $76.15 per credit for nonresidents.

South Seattle Community College
Seattle 98106

Public institution; metropolitan setting. Awards A. Barrier-free campus. Total enrollment: 4,676 (all undergraduates); 60% part-time, 44% women, 60% over 25. Total faculty: 256. Library holdings: 26,640 bound volumes, 75 titles on microform, 312 periodical subscriptions, 2,326 records/tapes.

Undergraduate Courses offered for part-time students during daytime, evenings, weekends, summer. Complete part-time degree programs offered during daytime, evenings, weekends, summer. Adult/continuing education programs available. Career services available to part-time students: individual and group career counseling. Part-time tuition: $18.65 per quarter hour for state residents, $75.45 per quarter hour for nonresidents.

Spokane Community College
Spokane 99207

Public institution; city setting. Awards A. Barrier-free campus. Total enrollment: 5,258 (all undergraduates); 38% part-time, 45% women, 37% over 25. Total faculty: 262. Library holdings: 21,574 bound volumes, 2,952 titles on microform, 536 periodical subscriptions, 675 records/tapes.

Undergraduate Courses offered for part-time students during daytime, evenings, summer. Complete part-time degree programs offered during daytime, evenings, summer. Adult/continuing education programs available. Career services available to part-time students: individual career counseling, individual job placement, employer recruitment on campus. Part-time tuition: $19.10 per credit for state residents, $75.90 per credit for nonresidents.

Spokane Falls Community College
Spokane 99204

Public institution; city setting. Awards A. Barrier-free campus. Total enrollment: 5,379 (all undergraduates); 45% part-time, 53% women, 32% over 25. Total faculty: 193. Library holdings: 44,449 bound volumes, 370 titles on microform, 867 periodical subscriptions, 480 records/tapes.

Undergraduate Courses offered for part-time students during daytime, evenings, weekends. Complete part-time degree programs offered during daytime, evenings, weekends. Adult/continuing education programs available. Career services available to part-time students: individual and group career counseling. Part-time tuition: $19.10 per credit for state residents, $75.90 per credit for nonresidents.

Washington / Colleges Offering Part-Time Degree Programs

Tacoma Community College
Tacoma 98465

Public institution; city setting. Awards A. Barrier-free campus. Total enrollment: 4,100 (all undergraduates); 39% part-time, 56% women. Total faculty: 310. Library holdings: 71,080 bound volumes, 687 periodical subscriptions.

Undergraduate Courses offered for part-time students during daytime, evenings, weekends, summer. Complete part-time degree programs offered during daytime, evenings, weekends, summer. Adult/continuing education programs available. Career services available to part-time students: individual and group career counseling. Part-time tuition: $19.10 per quarter hour for state residents, $75.90 per quarter hour for nonresidents.

University of Puget Sound
Tacoma 98416

Independent-religious instutition; city setting. Awards B, M. Total enrollment: 4,021. Undergraduate enrollment: 2,852; 11% part-time, 56% women, 14% over 25. Total faculty: 183. Library holdings: 300,000 bound volumes, 44,647 titles on microform, 1,259 periodical subscriptions, 3,300 records/tapes.

Undergraduate Courses offered for part-time students during daytime, evenings, summer. Complete part-time degree programs offered during daytime. Adult/continuing education programs available. Career services available to part-time students: individual and group career counseling, individual job placement, employer recruitment on campus. Part-time tuition: $792 per course.

Graduate Part-time study available in Graduate Studies. Basic part-time expenses: $792 per course tuition.

University of Washington
Seattle 98195

Public institution; metropolitan setting. Awards B, M, D. Total enrollment: 34,308. Undergraduate enrollment: 23,529; 17% part-time, 48% women, 19% over 25. Total faculty: 2,600. Library holdings: 4 million bound volumes, 3 million titles on microform, 39,500 periodical subscriptions.

Undergraduate Courses offered for part-time students during daytime, evenings, summer. Complete part-time degree programs offered during daytime, evenings, summer. Adult/continuing education programs available. Career services available to part-time students: individual and group career counseling, individual job placement, employer recruitment on campus. Part-time tuition: $44 per quarter hour for state residents, $120 per quarter hour for nonresidents.

Walla Walla College
College Place 99324

Independent-religious instutition; small-town setting. Awards A, B, M. Barrier-free campus. Total enrollment: 1,660. Undergraduate enrollment: 1,576; 11% part-time, 46% women, 3% over 25. Total faculty: 151. Library holdings: 144,789 bound volumes, 1,012 titles on microform, 1,007 periodical subscriptions, 2,350 records/tapes.

Undergraduate Courses offered for part-time students during daytime, summer. Complete part-time degree programs offered during daytime, summer. Career services available to part-time students: individual career counseling, individual job placement, employer recruitment on campus. Part-time tuition: $145 per credit.

Graduate Part-time study available in Graduate School. Degree can be earned exclusively through evening/weekend study in Graduate School. Basic part-time expenses: $149 per credit tuition plus $22 per quarter fees. Institutional financial aid available to part-time graduate students in Graduate School.

Walla Walla Community College
Walla Walla 99362

Public institution; small-town setting. Awards A. Barrier-free campus. Total enrollment: 5,000 (all undergraduates); 55% part-time, 51% women, 56% over 25. Total faculty: 252. Library holdings: 34,500 bound volumes, 42 titles on microform, 317 periodical subscriptions, 10,504 records/tapes.

Undergraduate Courses offered for part-time students during daytime, evenings, weekends, summer. Complete part-time degree programs offered during daytime, evenings. Adult/continuing education programs available. Career services available to part-time students: individual and group career counseling, individual job placement. Part-time tuition: $19.35 per credit for state residents, $76.15 per credit for nonresidents.

Wenatchee Valley College
Wenatchee 98801

Public institution; rural setting. Awards A. Barrier-free campus. Total enrollment: 2,929 (all undergraduates); 54% part-time, 58% women. Total faculty: 190.

Undergraduate Courses offered for part-time students during daytime, evenings, summer. Complete part-time degree programs offered during daytime, evenings, summer. External degree and adult/continuing education programs available. Career services available to part-time students: individual career counseling, individual job placement. Part-time tuition: $19.35 per credit for state residents, $76.15 per credit for nonresidents.

Western Washington University
Bellingham 98225

Public institution; small-town setting. Awards B, M. Total enrollment: 9,617. Undergraduate enrollment: 8,634; 5% part-time, 51% women, 21% over 25. Total faculty: 504. Library holdings: 418,859 bound volumes, 92,643 titles on microform, 4,464 periodical subscriptions, 9,650 records/tapes.

Undergraduate Courses offered for part-time students during daytime, evenings, summer. Complete part-time degree programs offered during daytime. Adult/continuing education programs available. Career services available to part-time students: individual and group career counseling, individual job placement, employer recruitment on campus. Part-time tuition: $34 per quarter hour for state residents, $116 per quarter hour for nonresidents.

Graduate Part-time study available in School of Education, College of Arts and Sciences, College of Business and Economics, College of Fine and Performing Arts. Degree can be earned exclusively through evening/weekend study in College of Business and Economics. Basic part-time expenses: $48 per credit tuition for state residents, $141 per credit tuition for nonresidents.

Whatcom Community College
Bellingham 98226

Public institution; rural setting. Awards A. Total enrollment: 575 (all undergraduates); 20% part-time, 45% women, 44% over 25. Total faculty: 130. Library holdings: 8,781 bound volumes, 176 periodical subscriptions, 1,543 records/tapes.

Colleges Offering Part-Time Degree Programs / *Washington*

Whatcom Community College (continued)

Undergraduate Courses offered for part-time students during daytime, evenings, summer. Complete part-time degree programs offered during daytime, evenings, summer. External degree and adult/continuing education programs available. Career services available to part-time students: individual and group career counseling. Part-time tuition: $18.65 per credit for state residents, $75.50 per credit for nonresidents.

Whitworth College
Spokane 99251

Independent-religious instutition; city setting. Awards B, M. Barrier-free campus. Total enrollment: 1,884. Undergraduate enrollment: 1,216; 23% part-time, 52% women. Total faculty: 90. Library holdings: 91,762 bound volumes, 46,180 titles on microform, 800 periodical subscriptions, 1,600 records/tapes.

Undergraduate Courses offered for part-time students during daytime, evenings, weekends, summer. Complete part-time degree programs offered during daytime, evenings, weekends, summer. External degree and adult/continuing education programs available. Career services available to part-time students: individual and group career counseling, individual job placement, employer recruitment on campus. Part-time tuition per semester (1 to 3 courses) ranges from $450 to $2700.

Graduate Part-time study available in Graduate Studies in Education. Basic part-time expenses: $350 per course tuition.

Yakima Valley Community College
Yakima 98907

Public institution; small-town setting. Awards A. Total enrollment: 4,773 (all undergraduates); 55% part-time, 61% women, 50% over 25. Total faculty: 312. Library holdings: 40,000 bound volumes, 250 periodical subscriptions, 4,300 records/tapes.

Undergraduate Courses offered for part-time students during daytime, evenings, summer. Complete part-time degree programs offered during daytime, evenings, summer. Adult/continuing education programs available. Career services available to part-time students: individual and group career counseling, individual job placement. Part-time tuition: $19.35 per credit for state residents, $76.15 per credit for nonresidents.

WEST VIRGINIA

Alderson-Broaddus College
Philippi 26416

Independent-religious instutition; rural setting. Awards B. Total enrollment: 817 (all undergraduates); 7% part-time, 62% women. Total faculty: 81. Library holdings: 84,000 bound volumes, 2,647 titles on microform, 397 periodical subscriptions, 4,000 records/tapes.

Undergraduate Courses offered for part-time students during daytime, summer. Complete part-time degree programs offered during daytime, summer. Adult/continuing education programs available. Career services available to part-time students: individual and group career counseling, individual job placement, employer recruitment on campus. Part-time tuition: $156 per credit hour.

Beckley College
Beckley 25801

Independent institution; small-town setting. Awards A. Total enrollment: 1,707 (all undergraduates); 59% part-time, 62% women, 55% over 25. Total faculty: 66. Library holdings: 12,470 bound volumes, 105 periodical subscriptions, 894 records/tapes.

Undergraduate Courses offered for part-time students during daytime, evenings, summer. Complete part-time degree programs offered during daytime, evenings, summer. Career services available to part-time students: individual and group career counseling, individual job placement, employer recruitment on campus. Part-time tuition: $43 per semester hour.

Bethany College
Bethany 26032

Independent-religious instutition; rural setting. Awards B. Total enrollment: 823 (all undergraduates); 1% part-time, 45% women. Total faculty: 79. Library holdings: 145,000 bound volumes, 14,729 titles on microform, 587 periodical subscriptions, 2,308 records/tapes.

Undergraduate Courses offered for part-time students during daytime. Complete part-time degree programs offered during daytime. Adult/continuing education programs available. Career services available to part-time students: individual and group career counseling, employer recruitment on campus. Part-time tuition: $230 per credit hour.

Bluefield State College
Bluefield 24701

Public institution; small-town setting. Awards A, B. Total enrollment: 2,380 (all undergraduates); 50% part-time, 54% women, 65% over 25. Total faculty: 145. Library holdings: 104,398 bound volumes, 232,227 titles on microform, 519 periodical subscriptions, 9,093 records/tapes.

Undergraduate Courses offered for part-time students during daytime, evenings, summer. Complete part-time degree programs offered during daytime, evenings, summer. Adult/continuing education programs available. Career services available to part-time students: individual and group career counseling, individual job placement, employer recruitment on campus. Part-time tuition per semester (1 to 11 semester hours) ranges from $39 to $370.75 for state residents, $98 to $1012.25 for nonresidents.

Concord College
Athens 24712

Public institution; small-town setting. Awards B. Total enrollment: 2,176 (all undergraduates); 23% part-time, 56% women. Total faculty: 123. Library holdings: 145,000 bound volumes, 6,385 titles on microform, 541 periodical subscriptions, 1,627 records/tapes.

Undergraduate Courses offered for part-time students during daytime, evenings, summer. Complete part-time degree programs offered during daytime, evenings, summer. Career services available to part-time students: individual and group career counseling, individual job placement, employer recruitment on campus. Part-time tuition per semester (1 to 11 semester hours) ranges from $23 to $377 for state residents, $82 to $1018 for nonresidents.

West Virginia / **Colleges Offering Part-Time Degree Programs**

Fairmont State College
Fairmont 26554

Public institution; small-town setting. Awards A, B. Total enrollment: 4,844 (all undergraduates); 34% part-time, 55% women, 30% over 25. Total faculty: 312. Library holdings: 156,822 bound volumes, 728 periodical subscriptions, 5,281 records/tapes.

Undergraduate Courses offered for part-time students during daytime, evenings. Complete part-time degree programs offered during daytime. Adult/continuing education programs available. Career services available to part-time students: individual and group career counseling, individual job placement, employer recruitment on campus. Part-time tuition and fees per semester (1 to 11 credit hours) range from $46 to $371 for state residents, $105 to $1019 for nonresidents.

Huntington Junior College of Business
Huntington 25701

Proprietary institution; city setting. Awards A. Total enrollment: 486 (all undergraduates); 2% part-time, 60% women, 40% over 25. Total faculty: 22. Library holdings: 1,900 bound volumes, 35 periodical subscriptions, 100 records/tapes.

Undergraduate Courses offered for part-time students during daytime, evenings. Complete part-time degree programs offered during evenings. Career services available to part-time students: individual career counseling, individual job placement, employer recruitment on campus. Part-time tuition: $240 per course.

Marshall University
Huntington 25701

Public institution; city setting. Awards A, B, M, D. Barrier-free campus. Total enrollment: 11,657. Undergraduate enrollment: 8,600; 39% part-time, 54% women, 47% over 25. Total faculty: 514. Library holdings: 334,780 bound volumes, 2,760 periodical subscriptions, 10,092 records/tapes.

Undergraduate Courses offered for part-time students during daytime, evenings, summer. Complete part-time degree programs offered during daytime, evenings, summer. Adult/continuing education programs available. Career services available to part-time students: individual and group career counseling, individual job placement, employer recruitment on campus. Part-time tuition per semester (1 to 11 semester hours) ranges from $30 to $429.50 for state residents, $97 to $1166.50 for nonresidents.

Graduate Part-time study available in Graduate School. Degree can be earned exclusively through evening/weekend study in Graduate School. Basic part-time expenses: $43 per credit hour fees for state residents, $140 per credit hour fees for nonresidents. Institutional financial aid available to part-time graduate students in Graduate School.

Potomac State College of West Virginia University
Keyser 26726

Public institution; small-town setting. Awards A. Total enrollment: 1,123 (all undergraduates); 37% part-time, 49% women, 4% over 25. Total faculty: 60. Library holdings: 35,066 bound volumes, 147 titles on microform, 140 periodical subscriptions, 2,243 records/tapes.

Undergraduate Courses offered for part-time students during daytime, evenings, summer. Complete part-time degree programs offered during daytime, evenings, summer. Adult/continuing education programs available. Career services available to part-time students: individual and group career counseling, individual job placement, employer recruitment on campus. Part-time tuition per semester (1 to 11 hours) ranges from $27 to $347 for state residents, $85 to $1018 for nonresidents.

Salem College
Salem 26426

Independent institution; rural setting. Awards A, B, M. Total enrollment: 1,289. Undergraduate enrollment: 1,200; 30% part-time, 55% women, 15% over 25. Total faculty: 96. Library holdings: 125,000 bound volumes, 94,000 titles on microform, 270 periodical subscriptions, 2,462 records/tapes.

Undergraduate Courses offered for part-time students during daytime, evenings, summer. Complete part-time degree programs offered during daytime, evenings. External degree and adult/continuing education programs available. Career services available to part-time students: individual and group career counseling, individual job placement, employer recruitment on campus. Part-time tuition: $44 per semester hour.

Graduate Part-time study available in Graduate School. Degree can be earned exclusively through evening/weekend study in Graduate School. Basic part-time expenses: $60 per credit hour tuition plus $5 per semester fees.

Shepherd College
Shepherdstown 25443

Public institution; small-town setting. Awards A, B. Total enrollment: 3,507 (all undergraduates); 40% part-time, 59% women, 42% over 25. Total faculty: 136. Library holdings: 450,000 bound volumes, 14,500 titles on microform, 680 periodical subscriptions, 3,500 records/tapes.

Undergraduate Courses offered for part-time students during daytime, evenings, weekends, summer. Complete part-time degree programs offered during daytime, evenings, summer. External degree and adult/continuing education programs available. Career services available to part-time students: individual and group career counseling, individual job placement, employer recruitment on campus. Part-time tuition per semester hour (1 to 11 semester hours) ranges from $26 to $373 for state residents, $85 to $1015 for nonresidents.

Southern West Virginia Community College
Logan 25601

Public institution; rural setting. Awards A. Barrier-free campus. Total enrollment: 2,059 (all undergraduates); 57% part-time, 50% women, 80% over 25. Total faculty: 127. Library holdings: 28,000 bound volumes, 198 periodical subscriptions, 663 records/tapes.

Undergraduate Courses offered for part-time students during daytime, evenings, summer. Complete part-time degree programs offered during daytime, evenings, summer. Adult/continuing education programs available. Career services available to part-time students: individual career counseling, individual job placement. Part-time tuition: $22 per credit hour for state residents, $77 per credit hour for nonresidents.

University of Charleston
Charleston 25304

Independent institution; city setting. Awards A, B, M. Total enrollment: 2,316. Undergraduate enrollment: 2,301; 67% part-time, 64% women, 25% over 25. Total faculty: 133. Library

Colleges Offering Part-Time Degree Programs / West Virginia

University of Charleston (continued)
holdings: 100,000 bound volumes, 600 titles on microform, 450 periodical subscriptions.

Undergraduate Courses offered for part-time students during daytime, evenings, weekends, summer. Complete part-time degree programs offered during daytime, evenings, summer. External degree and adult/continuing education programs available. Career services available to part-time students: individual and group career counseling. Part-time tuition per credit hour ranges from $80 (for 1 to 6 credit hours) to $160 (for 7 to 11 credit hours).

Graduate Part-time study available in Graduate Center. Degree can be earned exclusively through evening/weekend study in Graduate Center. Basic part-time expenses: $160 per credit tuition. Institutional financial aid available to part-time graduate students in Graduate Center.

West Liberty State College
West Liberty 26074

Public institution; rural setting. Awards A, B. Total enrollment: 2,540 (all undergraduates); 18% part-time, 54% women. Total faculty: 131. Library holdings: 198,000 bound volumes, 1,250 periodical subscriptions, 8,700 records/tapes.

Undergraduate Courses offered for part-time students during daytime, evenings, weekends, summer. Complete part-time degree programs offered during daytime. External degree programs available. Career services available to part-time students: individual and group career counseling, individual job placement, employer recruitment on campus. Part-time tuition per semester (1 to 11 semester hours) ranges from $29 to $374 for state residents, $87 to $1022 for nonresidents.

West Virginia College of Graduate Studies
Institute 25112

Public institution (graduate only). Total enrollment: 3,341 (coed; 93% part-time). Total faculty: 158.

Graduate Part-time study available in Division of Behavioral Studies and Humanities, Division of Business and Management, Division of Education, Division of Engineering and Science. Degree can be earned exclusively through evening/weekend study in Division of Behavioral Studies and Humanities, Division of Business and Management, Division of Education, Division of Engineering and Science. Basic part-time expenses: $37 per credit hour tuition for state residents, $131 per credit hour tuition for nonresidents. Institutional financial aid available to part-time graduate students in Division of Behavioral Studies and Humanities, Division of Business and Management, Division of Education, Division of Engineering and Science.

West Virginia Institute of Technology
Montgomery 25136

Public institution; small-town setting. Awards A, B, M. Total enrollment: 3,439. Undergraduate enrollment: 3,385; 31% part-time, 33% women. Total faculty: 185. Library holdings: 141,966 bound volumes, 315,855 titles on microform, 747 periodical subscriptions.

Undergraduate Courses offered for part-time students during daytime, evenings. Complete part-time degree programs offered during daytime, evenings. Adult/continuing education programs available. Career services available to part-time students: individual and group career counseling, individual job placement, employer recruitment on campus. Part-time tuition and fees per semester (1 to 11 semester hours) range from $27 to $376 for state residents, $84 to $1018 for nonresidents.

Graduate Part-time study available in School of Engineering and Physical Sciences. Basic part-time expenses: $85 per semester (minimum) tuition for state residents, $289 per semester (minimum) tuition for nonresidents.

West Virginia Northern Community College
Wheeling 26003

Public institution; city setting. Awards A. Total enrollment: 3,830 (all undergraduates); 72% part-time, 66% women, 63% over 25. Total faculty: 170. Library holdings: 30,474 bound volumes, 214 periodical subscriptions, 1,095 records/tapes.

Undergraduate Courses offered for part-time students during daytime, evenings. Complete part-time degree programs offered during daytime, evenings. Adult/continuing education programs available. Career services available to part-time students: individual and group career counseling, individual job placement, employer recruitment on campus. Part-time tuition: $22 per credit hour for state residents, $77 per credit hour for nonresidents.

West Virginia State College
Institute 25112

Public institution; small-town setting. Awards A, B. Barrier-free campus. Total enrollment: 4,731 (all undergraduates); 51% part-time, 53% women. Total faculty: 210. Library holdings: 201,112 bound volumes, 27,782 titles on microform, 671 periodical subscriptions, 6,829 records/tapes.

Undergraduate Courses offered for part-time students during daytime, evenings, summer. Complete part-time degree programs offered during daytime, evenings, summer. External degree and adult/continuing education programs available. Career services available to part-time students: individual and group career counseling, individual job placement, employer recruitment on campus. Part-time tuition per semester (1 to 11 credit hours) ranges from $46 to $371 for state residents, $109 to $1034 for nonresidents.

West Virginia University
Morgantown 26506

Public institution; small-town setting. Awards B, M, D. Total enrollment: 20,624. Undergraduate enrollment: 14,951; 7% part-time, 44% women, 7% over 25. Total faculty: 2,367. Library holdings: 1 million bound volumes, 860,185 titles on microform, 9,425 periodical subscriptions, 11,454 records/tapes.

Undergraduate Courses offered for part-time students during daytime. Complete part-time degree programs offered during daytime. Adult/continuing education programs available. Career services available to part-time students: individual and group career counseling, individual job placement, employer recruitment on campus. Part-time tuition: $31 per credit hour for state residents, $114 per credit hour for nonresidents.

Graduate Part-time study available in College of Agriculture and Forestry, College of Arts and Sciences, College of Business and Economics, College of Creative Arts, College of Engineering, College of Human Resources and Education, College of Law, College of Mineral and Energy Resources, Perley Isaac Reed School of Journalism, School of Nursing, School of Physical Education, School of Social Work. Basic part-time expenses: $45 per credit hour tuition plus $45 per semester (minimum) fees for state residents, $164 per credit hour tuition plus $45 per semester (minimum) fees for nonresidents. Institutional financial aid available to part-time graduate students in College of

Agriculture and Forestry, College of Arts and Sciences, College of Business and Economics, College of Creative Arts, College of Engineering, College of Human Resources and Education, College of Mineral and Energy Resources, Perley Isaac Reed School of Journalism, School of Nursing, School of Physical Education, School of Social Work.

West Virginia University, Potomac State College
Keyser 26726

See Potomac State College of West Virginia University

West Virginia Wesleyan College
Buckhannon 26201

Independent-religious instutition; small-town setting. Awards A, B, M. Barrier-free campus. Total enrollment: 1,497. Undergraduate enrollment: 1,484; 4% part-time, 59% women. Total faculty: 114. Library holdings: 145,000 bound volumes, 650 periodical subscriptions.

Undergraduate Courses offered for part-time students during daytime, evenings, summer. Complete part-time degree programs offered during daytime, evenings, summer. External degree and adult/continuing education programs available. Career services available to part-time students: individual and group career counseling, individual job placement, employer recruitment on campus. Part-time tuition: $180 per credit hour.

Wheeling College
Wheeling 26003

Independent-religious instutition; city setting. Awards B, M. Total enrollment: 1,046. Undergraduate enrollment: 934; 32% part-time, 50% women, 9% over 25. Total faculty: 72. Library holdings: 116,325 bound volumes, 28,192 titles on microform, 640 periodical subscriptions, 1,255 records/tapes.

Undergraduate Courses offered for part-time students during daytime, evenings, summer. Complete part-time degree programs offered during daytime, evenings, summer. Adult/continuing education programs available. Career services available to part-time students: individual and group career counseling, individual job placement, employer recruitment on campus. Part-time tuition: $150 per credit hour.

Graduate Part-time study available in Graduate Programs. Degree can be earned exclusively through evening/weekend study in Graduate Programs.Basic part-time expenses: $150 per credit hour tuition.

WISCONSIN

Alverno College
Milwaukee 53215

Independent institution; metropolitan setting. Awards A, B. Barrier-free campus. Total enrollment: 1,330 (all undergraduates); 48% part-time, 100% women, 72% over 25. Total faculty: 138. Library holdings: 86,189 bound volumes, 144,930 titles on microform, 925 periodical subscriptions, 7,094 records/tapes.

Undergraduate Courses offered for part-time students during daytime, evenings, weekends, summer. Complete part-time degree programs offered during daytime, weekends. Adult/continuing education programs available. Career services available to part-time students: individual and group career counseling, individual job placement, employer recruitment on campus. Part-time tuition: $182 per credit.

Beloit College
Beloit 53511

Independent-religious instutition; small-town setting. Awards B, M. Total enrollment: 1,079. Undergraduate enrollment: 1,060; 3% part-time, 48% women, 1% over 25. Total faculty: 97. Library holdings: 250,000 bound volumes, 630 periodical subscriptions, 450 records/tapes.

Undergraduate Courses offered for part-time students during daytime, evenings. Complete part-time degree programs offered during daytime, evenings. Adult/continuing education programs available. Part-time tuition: $920 per unit.

Graduate Part-time study available in Graduate Program in Education.Basic part-time expenses: $920 per unit tuition. Institutional financial aid available to part-time graduate students in Graduate Program in Education.

Blackhawk Technical Institute
Janesville 53547

Public institution; city setting. Awards A. Total enrollment: 2,331 (all undergraduates); 30% part-time, 53% women, 56% over 25. Total faculty: 174. Library holdings: 18,000 bound volumes, 10 periodical subscriptions, 310 records/tapes.

Undergraduate Courses offered for part-time students during daytime, evenings, summer. Complete part-time degree programs offered during daytime, evenings, summer. Adult/continuing education programs available. Career services available to part-time students: individual and group career counseling, individual job placement, employer recruitment on campus. Part-time tuition: $18.40 per credit for area residents, $51.99 per credit for state residents, $89 per credit for nonresidents.

Cardinal Stritch College
Milwaukee 53217

Independent-religious instutition; metropolitan setting. Awards A, B, M. Barrier-free campus. Total enrollment: 1,763. Undergraduate enrollment: 1,000; 26% part-time, 80% women, 43% over 25. Total faculty: 147. Library holdings: 77,623 bound volumes, 431 periodical subscriptions, 5,200 records/tapes.

Undergraduate Courses offered for part-time students during daytime, evenings, summer. Complete part-time degree programs offered during daytime. Adult/continuing education programs available. Career services available to part-time students: individual and group career counseling, individual job placement, employer recruitment on campus. Part-time tuition: $135 per credit hour.

Graduate Part-time study available in Graduate Division.Basic part-time expenses: $135 per credit tuition. Institutional financial aid available to part-time graduate students in Graduate Division.

Carroll College
Waukesha 53186

Independent-religious instutition; city setting. Awards B. Total enrollment: 1,194 (all undergraduates); 3% part-time, 52% women. Total faculty: 107. Library holdings: 155,955 bound volumes, 575 periodical subscriptions, 162 records/tapes.

Undergraduate Courses offered for part-time students during daytime, evenings, summer. Complete part-time degree programs offered during daytime, evenings, summer. Adult/continuing education programs available. Career services available to part-time students: individual and group career counseling, individual job placement, employer recruitment on campus. Part-time tuition: $150 per semester hour.

Colleges Offering Part-Time Degree Programs / *Wisconsin*

Carthage College
Kenosha 53141

Independent-religious instutition; city setting. Awards B, M. Barrier-free campus. Total enrollment: 1,410. Undergraduate enrollment: 1,321; 29% part-time, 50% women. Total faculty: 97. Library holdings: 186,400 bound volumes, 4,069 titles on microform, 657 periodical subscriptions.

Undergraduate Courses offered for part-time students during daytime, evenings, summer. Complete part-time degree programs offered during daytime, evenings, summer. Adult/continuing education programs available. Career services available to part-time students: individual career counseling, individual job placement, employer recruitment on campus. Part-time tuition: $150 per credit hour.

Concordia College Wisconsin
Mequon 53092

Independent-religious instutition; small-town setting. Awards A, B. Barrier-free campus. Total enrollment: 784 (all undergraduates); 22% part-time, 56% women. Total faculty: 59. Library holdings: 53,000 bound volumes, 6,570 titles on microform, 280 periodical subscriptions, 2,399 records/tapes.

Undergraduate Courses offered for part-time students during daytime, evenings, summer. Complete part-time degree programs offered during daytime, evenings, summer. Adult/continuing education programs available. Career services available to part-time students: individual career counseling, individual job placement, employer recruitment on campus. Part-time tuition: $165 per credit hour.

District One Technical Institute
Eau Claire 54701

Public institution; city setting. Awards A. Barrier-free campus. Total enrollment: 3,500 (all undergraduates); 10% part-time, 50% women. Total faculty: 175. Library holdings: 40,000 bound volumes, 997 periodical subscriptions, 2,000 records/tapes.

Undergraduate Courses offered for part-time students during daytime, evenings, summer. Complete part-time degree programs offered during daytime. Adult/continuing education programs available. Career services available to part-time students: individual and group career counseling, individual job placement, employer recruitment on campus. Part-time tuition: $18 per credit for area residents, $52 per credit for state residents, $107 per credit for nonresidents.

Edgewood College
Madison 53711

Independent-religious instutition; city setting. Awards A, B. Barrier-free campus. Total enrollment: 797 (all undergraduates); 49% part-time, 77% women, 58% over 25. Total faculty: 71. Library holdings: 64,855 bound volumes, 24,437 titles on microform, 444 periodical subscriptions, 8,000 records/tapes.

Undergraduate Courses offered for part-time students during daytime, evenings, weekends, summer. Complete part-time degree programs offered during daytime, weekends. Adult/continuing education programs available. Career services available to part-time students: individual and group career counseling, individual job placement, employer recruitment on campus. Part-time tuition: $140 per credit.

Fox Valley Technical Institute
Appleton 54913

Public institution; city setting. Awards A. Barrier-free campus. Total enrollment: 4,760 (all undergraduates); 35% part-time, 53% women. Total faculty: 700.

Undergraduate Courses offered for part-time students during daytime, evenings, summer. Complete part-time degree programs offered during daytime, evenings, summer. Adult/continuing education programs available. Career services available to part-time students: individual and group career counseling, individual job placement, employer recruitment on campus. Part-time tuition: $18.30 per credit for area residents, $48 per credit for state residents, $109 per credit for nonresidents.

Gateway Technical Institute
Kenosha 53141

Public institution; city setting. Awards A. Barrier-free campus. Total enrollment: 4,205 (all undergraduates); 60% part-time, 55% women, 15% over 25. Total faculty: 93. Library holdings: 42,758 bound volumes, 3,665 titles on microform, 386 periodical subscriptions, 10,916 records/tapes.

Undergraduate Courses offered for part-time students during daytime, evenings, summer. Complete part-time degree programs offered during daytime, evenings. Career services available to part-time students: individual career counseling, individual job placement, employer recruitment on campus. Part-time tuition: $18.40 per credit for area residents, $51.90 per credit for state residents, $108 per credit for nonresidents.

Gateway Technical Institute
Racine 53403

Public institution; city setting. Awards A. Barrier-free campus. Total enrollment: 2,260 (all undergraduates); 66% part-time, 52% women. Total faculty: 140. Library holdings: 13,853 bound volumes, 976 titles on microform, 110 periodical subscriptions, 2,059 records/tapes.

Undergraduate Courses offered for part-time students during evenings, weekends. Complete part-time degree programs offered during evenings. Career services available to part-time students: individual and group career counseling, individual job placement. Part-time tuition: $18.40 per credit for area residents, $51.90 per credit for state residents, $108 per credit for nonresidents.

Holy Redeemer College
Waterford 53185

Independent-religious instutition; rural setting. Awards A, B. Barrier-free campus. Total enrollment: 60 (all undergraduates); 0% part-time, 0% women, 25% over 25. Total faculty: 22. Library holdings: 35,326 bound volumes, 282 titles on microform, 273 periodical subscriptions, 566 records/tapes.

Undergraduate Courses offered for part-time students during daytime, evenings. Complete part-time degree programs offered during daytime. Adult/continuing education programs available. Career services available to part-time students: individual career counseling. Part-time tuition: $85 per credit.

Institute of Paper Chemistry
Appleton 54911

Independent institution (graduate only). Total enrollment: 106 (coed). Total faculty: 42. Library holdings: 40,000 bound volumes, 3,500 microforms.

Wisconsin / Colleges Offering Part-Time Degree Programs

Graduate Part-time study available in Graduate Programs. Basic part-time expenses: $90 per quarter hour tuition.

Lakeland College
Sheboygan 53082

Independent-religious instutition; rural setting. Awards B. Total enrollment: 386 (all undergraduates); 48% part-time, 43% women. Total faculty: 38. Library holdings: 55,000 bound volumes, 22,500 titles on microform, 250 periodical subscriptions, 1,600 records/tapes.

Undergraduate Courses offered for part-time students during daytime, evenings, summer. Complete part-time degree programs offered during daytime, evenings, summer. External degree and adult/continuing education programs available. Career services available to part-time students: individual and group career counseling, individual job placement, employer recruitment on campus. Part-time tuition: $500 per course.

Lakeshore Technical Institute
Cleveland 53015

Public institution; rural setting. Awards A. Barrier-free campus. Total enrollment: 3,500 (all undergraduates); 55% part-time, 60% women. Total faculty: 121. Library holdings: 30,000 bound volumes, 500 periodical subscriptions, 3,500 records/tapes.

Undergraduate Courses offered for part-time students during daytime, evenings, weekends, summer. Complete part-time degree programs offered during daytime, evenings, weekends. Adult/continuing education programs available. Career services available to part-time students: individual and group career counseling, individual job placement, employer recruitment on campus. Part-time tuition: $18.40 per credit for state residents, $107.70 per credit for nonresidents.

Lawrence University
Appleton 54912

Independent institution; city setting. Awards B. Total enrollment: 1,066 (all undergraduates); 4% part-time, 51% women, 1% over 25. Total faculty: 112. Library holdings: 248,893 bound volumes, 126,818 titles on microform, 1,103 periodical subscriptions, 3,253 records/tapes.

Undergraduate Courses offered for part-time students during daytime. Complete part-time degree programs offered during daytime. Career services available to part-time students: individual and group career counseling, individual job placement, employer recruitment on campus. Part-time tuition: $928 per course.

Madison Area Technical College
Madison 53703

Public institution; city setting. Awards A. Barrier-free campus. Total enrollment: 6,889 (all undergraduates); 45% part-time, 50% women, 65% over 25. Total faculty: 350.

Undergraduate Courses offered for part-time students during daytime, evenings. Complete part-time degree programs offered during daytime, evenings. Adult/continuing education programs available. Career services available to part-time students: individual and group career counseling, individual job placement, employer recruitment on campus. Part-time tuition: $18.40 per credit for area residents, $51.90 per credit for state residents, $107.70 per credit for nonresidents.

Madison Business College
Madison 53705

Proprietary institution; city setting. Awards A. Barrier-free campus. Total enrollment: 403 (all undergraduates); 15% part-time, 73% women. Total faculty: 16. Library holdings: 8,380 bound volumes, 65 periodical subscriptions, 330 records/tapes.

Undergraduate Courses offered for part-time students during daytime, summer. Complete part-time degree programs offered during daytime, summer. Career services available to part-time students: individual career counseling, individual job placement, employer recruitment on campus. Part-time tuition: $305 per course.

Marquette University
Milwaukee 53233

Independent-religious instutition; metropolitan setting. Awards A, B, M, D. Barrier-free campus. Total enrollment: 11,722. Undergraduate enrollment: 9,121; 13% part-time, 46% women, 7% over 25. Total faculty: 931. Library holdings: 700,000 bound volumes, 10,000 periodical subscriptions.

Undergraduate Courses offered for part-time students during daytime, evenings, summer. Complete part-time degree programs offered during daytime, evenings. Adult/continuing education programs available. Career services available to part-time students: individual and group career counseling, individual job placement, employer recruitment on campus. Part-time tuition: $165 per credit.

Graduate Part-time study available in Graduate School, School of Dentistry. Basic part-time expenses: $165 per credit tuition. Institutional financial aid available to part-time graduate students in Graduate School, School of Dentistry.

Mid-State Technical Institute
Wisconsin Rapids 54494

Public institution; small-town setting. Awards A. Barrier-free campus. Total enrollment: 1,800 (all undergraduates); 43% part-time, 52% women. Total faculty: 89. Library holdings: 19,780 bound volumes, 80 titles on microform, 415 periodical subscriptions, 1,540 records/tapes.

Undergraduate Courses offered for part-time students during daytime, evenings, summer. Complete part-time degree programs offered during daytime, evenings, summer. Adult/continuing education programs available. Career services available to part-time students: individual and group career counseling, individual job placement, employer recruitment on campus. Part-time tuition: $18.40 per credit for area residents, $51.90 per credit for state residents, $107.70 per credit for nonresidents.

Milwaukee Area Technical College
Milwaukee 53203

Public institution; metropolitan setting. Awards A. Total enrollment: 16,991 (all undergraduates); 69% part-time, 56% women, 45% over 25. Total faculty: 1,991. Library holdings: 45,000 bound volumes, 360 periodical subscriptions, 300 records/tapes.

Undergraduate Courses offered for part-time students during daytime, evenings. Complete part-time degree programs offered during daytime, evenings. Adult/continuing education programs available. Career services available to part-time students: individual and group career counseling, individual job placement, employer recruitment on campus. Part-time tuition per credit hour ranges from $18.40 to $28.40 for district residents, $28.40 to $51.90 for state residents, $77.20 to $107.70 for nonresidents, according to program.

Colleges Offering Part-Time Degree Programs / Wisconsin

Milwaukee Institute of Art and Design
Milwaukee 53202

Independent institution; metropolitan setting. Awards B. Total enrollment: 306 (all undergraduates); 10% part-time, 47% women. Total faculty: 35. Library holdings: 14,000 bound volumes, 55 periodical subscriptions.

Undergraduate Courses offered for part-time students during daytime, evenings, summer. Complete part-time degree programs offered during daytime. Adult/continuing education programs available. Career services available to part-time students: individual and group career counseling, individual job placement, employer recruitment on campus. Part-time tuition: $110 per credit.

Milwaukee School of Engineering
Milwaukee 53201

Independent institution; metropolitan setting. Awards A, B, M. Total enrollment: 1,925. Undergraduate enrollment: 1,413; 10% part-time, 4% women. Total faculty: 98. Library holdings: 30,000 bound volumes, 20 titles on microform, 350 periodical subscriptions, 30 records/tapes.

Undergraduate Courses offered for part-time students during daytime, evenings, summer. Complete part-time degree programs offered during daytime, evenings, summer. Adult/continuing education programs available. Career services available to part-time students: individual and group career counseling, individual job placement, employer recruitment on campus. Part-time tuition per quarter hour ranges from $110 for evening classes to $157 for daytime classes.

Graduate Part-time study available in Graduate School. Degree can be earned exclusively through evening/weekend study in Graduate School. Basic part-time expenses: $145 per credit tuition.

Moraine Park Technical Institute
Fond du Lac 54935

Public institution; small-town setting. Awards A. Barrier-free campus. Total enrollment: 3,011 (all undergraduates); 35% part-time, 50% women. Total faculty: 247. Library holdings: 25,000 bound volumes, 25 titles on microform, 353 periodical subscriptions, 4,500 records/tapes.

Undergraduate Courses offered for part-time students during daytime, evenings, weekends, summer. Complete part-time degree programs offered during daytime, evenings, summer. External degree and adult/continuing education programs available. Career services available to part-time students: individual and group career counseling, individual job placement, employer recruitment on campus. Part-time tuition: $18.40 per credit for area residents, $51.90 per credit for state residents, $107.70 per credit for nonresidents.

Mount Mary College
Milwaukee 53222

Independent-religious instutition; metropolitan setting. Awards B, M. Barrier-free campus. Total enrollment: 1,144. Undergraduate enrollment: 1,115; 45% part-time, 100% women, 41% over 25. Total faculty: 119. Library holdings: 103,572 bound volumes, 74 titles on microform, 780 periodical subscriptions, 12,828 records/tapes.

Undergraduate Courses offered for part-time students during daytime, evenings, weekends, summer. Complete part-time degree programs offered during daytime, evenings, summer. Adult/continuing education programs available. Career services available to part-time students: individual and group career counseling, individual job placement, employer recruitment on campus. Part-time tuition per semester (1 to 11 credits) ranges from $125 to $1650.

Mount Senario College
Ladysmith 54848

Independent institution; small-town setting. Awards A, B. Barrier-free campus. Total enrollment: 498 (all undergraduates); 23% part-time, 54% women. Total faculty: 54. Library holdings: 42,000 bound volumes, 300 periodical subscriptions, 11,500 records/tapes.

Undergraduate Courses offered for part-time students during daytime, evenings, weekends, summer. Complete part-time degree programs offered during daytime, evenings, weekends, summer. External degree and adult/continuing education programs available. Career services available to part-time students: individual and group career counseling, individual job placement, employer recruitment on campus. Part-time tuition per credit hour ranges from $75 (for students taking 1 to 6 credit hours) to $120 (for students taking 7 to 11 credit hours).

Nashotah House
Nashotah 53058

Independent-religious institution (graduate only). Total enrollment: 79 (primarily men; 1% part-time). Total faculty: 9. Library holdings: 68,000 bound volumes.

Graduate Part-time study available in Graduate and Professional Programs. Basic part-time expenses: $125 per credit tuition. Institutional financial aid available to part-time graduate students in Graduate and Professional Programs.

Nicolet College and Technical Institute
Rhinelander 54501

Public institution; rural setting. Awards A. Total enrollment: 1,254 (all undergraduates); 62% part-time, 56% women. Total faculty: 92. Library holdings: 35,000 bound volumes, 500 periodical subscriptions, 5,000 records/tapes.

Undergraduate Courses offered for part-time students during daytime, evenings, summer. Complete part-time degree programs offered during daytime, evenings, summer. Adult/continuing education programs available. Career services available to part-time students: individual and group career counseling, individual job placement, employer recruitment on campus. Part-time tuition per credit ranges from $18.40 to $28.40 for area residents, $28.40 to $33.50 for state residents, $77.20 to $107.70 for nonresidents, according to program.

North Central Technical Institute
Wausau 54401

Public institution; small-town setting. Awards A. Barrier-free campus. Total enrollment: 3,983 (all undergraduates); 47% part-time, 50% women, 50% over 25. Total faculty: 139. Library holdings: 38,269 bound volumes, 354 periodical subscriptions, 3,481 records/tapes.

Undergraduate Courses offered for part-time students during daytime. Complete part-time degree programs offered during daytime. Adult/continuing education programs available. Career services available to part-time students: individual and group career counseling, individual job placement, employer recruitment on campus. Part-time tuition: $18.40 per credit for area residents, $51.90 per credit for state residents, $107.70 per credit for nonresidents.

Wisconsin / **Colleges Offering Part-Time Degree Programs**

Northland College
Ashland 54806

Independent-religious instutition; small-town setting. Awards B. Total enrollment: 657 (all undergraduates); 5% part-time, 46% women. Total faculty: 46. Library holdings: 70,300 bound volumes, 400 periodical subscriptions.

Undergraduate Courses offered for part-time students during daytime, evenings, summer. Complete part-time degree programs offered during daytime, evenings, summer. Adult/continuing education programs available. Career services available to part-time students: individual and group career counseling, individual job placement, employer recruitment on campus. Part-time tuition: $100 per credit.

Ripon College
Ripon 54971

Independent institution; small-town setting. Awards B. Total enrollment: 900 (all undergraduates); 1% part-time, 41% women, 1% over 25. Total faculty: 94. Library holdings: 150,000 bound volumes, 14,000 titles on microform, 650 periodical subscriptions.

Undergraduate Courses offered for part-time students during daytime. Complete part-time degree programs offered during daytime. Career services available to part-time students: individual and group career counseling, individual job placement, employer recruitment on campus. Part-time tuition: $255 per credit.

Saint Francis Seminary, School of Pastoral Ministry
Milwaukee 53207

Independent-religious institution (graduate only). Total enrollment: 83 (primarily men; 42% part-time). Total faculty: 16.

Graduate Part-time study available in Graduate and Professional Programs. Basic part-time expenses: $100 per credit tuition.

Silver Lake College
Manitowoc 54220

Independent-religious instutition; small-town setting. Awards A, B. Barrier-free campus. Total enrollment: 438 (all undergraduates); 50% part-time, 60% women, 38% over 25. Total faculty: 67. Library holdings: 60,000 bound volumes, 288 periodical subscriptions, 17,000 records/tapes.

Undergraduate Courses offered for part-time students during daytime, evenings, summer. Complete part-time degree programs offered during daytime, evenings, summer. Adult/continuing education programs available. Career services available to part-time students: individual and group career counseling, individual job placement. Part-time tuition: $85 per credit.

Southwest Wisconsin Vocational-Technical Institute
Fennimore 53809

Public institution; rural setting. Awards A. Total enrollment: 1,450 (all undergraduates). Total faculty: 116. Library holdings: 26,750 bound volumes, 1,200 titles on microform, 220 periodical subscriptions, 2,387 records/tapes.

Undergraduate Courses offered for part-time students during daytime. Complete part-time degree programs offered during daytime. Adult/continuing education programs available. Career services available to part-time students: individual and group career counseling, individual job placement, employer recruitment on campus. Part-time tuition: $18.40 per credit for area residents, $51.90 per credit for state residents, $107.70 per credit for nonresidents.

Stratton College
Milwaukee 53202

Proprietary institution; metropolitan setting. Awards A. Barrier-free campus. Total enrollment: 558 (all undergraduates); 17% part-time, 74% women. Total faculty: 32. Library holdings: 5,000 bound volumes, 60 periodical subscriptions, 200 records/tapes.

Undergraduate Courses offered for part-time students during daytime, evenings, summer. Complete part-time degree programs offered during daytime, evenings, summer. Adult/continuing education programs available. Career services available to part-time students: individual and group career counseling, individual job placement, employer recruitment on campus. Part-time tuition: $75 per credit.

University of Wisconsin Center–Baraboo/Sauk County
Baraboo 53913

Public institution; rural setting. Awards A. Barrier-free campus. Total enrollment: 508 (all undergraduates); 43% part-time, 43% women. Total faculty: 37. Library holdings: 39,200 bound volumes, 2,500 titles on microform, 165 periodical subscriptions.

Undergraduate Courses offered for part-time students during daytime, evenings, summer. Complete part-time degree programs offered during daytime, evenings, summer. Adult/continuing education programs available. Career services available to part-time students: individual and group career counseling, individual job placement. Part-time tuition: $39.70 per credit for state residents, $136.50 per credit for nonresidents. Minnesota residents pay tuition at the rate they would pay if attending a comparable state-supported institution in Minnesota.

University of Wisconsin Center–Barron County
Rice Lake 54868

Public institution; small-town setting. Awards A. Barrier-free campus. Total enrollment: 349 (all undergraduates); 18% part-time, 47% women, 21% over 25. Total faculty: 26. Library holdings: 39,479 bound volumes, 233 periodical subscriptions, 6,600 records/tapes.

Undergraduate Courses offered for part-time students during daytime. Complete part-time degree programs offered during daytime. Adult/continuing education programs available. Career services available to part-time students: individual career counseling. Part-time tuition: $42 per credit for state residents, $142 per credit for nonresidents. Minnesota residents pay tuition at the rate they would pay if attending a comparable state-supported institution in Minnesota.

University of Wisconsin Center–Fox Valley
Menasha 54952

Public institution; city setting. Awards A. Barrier-free campus. Total enrollment: 1,194 (all undergraduates); 51% part-time, 55% women, 36% over 25. Total faculty: 53. Library holdings:

Colleges Offering Part-Time Degree Programs / Wisconsin

University of Wisconsin Center–Fox Valley (continued)
26,000 bound volumes, 20 titles on microform, 225 periodical subscriptions, 1,300 records/tapes.
Undergraduate Courses offered for part-time students during daytime, evenings, summer. Complete part-time degree programs offered during daytime, evenings, summer. Adult/continuing education programs available. Career services available to part-time students: individual and group career counseling. Part-time tuition: $39.35 per credit for state residents, $135.35 per credit for nonresidents. Minnesota residents pay tuition at the rate they would pay if attending a comparable state-supported institution in Minnesota.

University of Wisconsin Center– Manitowoc County
Manitowoc 54220
Public institution; small-town setting. Awards A. Barrier-free campus. Total enrollment: 513 (all undergraduates); 30% part-time, 49% women, 26% over 25. Total faculty: 25. Library holdings: 23,000 bound volumes, 125 periodical subscriptions, 2,000 records/tapes.
Undergraduate Courses offered for part-time students during daytime, evenings, summer. Complete part-time degree programs offered during daytime, evenings, summer. External degree and adult/continuing education programs available. Career services available to part-time students: individual career counseling. Part-time tuition: $39.58 per credit for state residents, $135.50 per credit for nonresidents. Minnesota residents pay tuition at the rate they would pay if attending a comparable state-supported institution in Minnesota.

University of Wisconsin Center– Marathon County
Wausau 54401
Public institution; small-town setting. Awards A. Barrier-free campus. Total enrollment: 1,282 (all undergraduates); 30% part-time, 52% women, 24% over 25. Total faculty: 71. Library holdings: 31,840 bound volumes, 85 titles on microform, 203 periodical subscriptions, 1,485 records/tapes.
Undergraduate Courses offered for part-time students during daytime, evenings, summer. Complete part-time degree programs offered during daytime, evenings, summer. Adult/continuing education programs available. Career services available to part-time students: individual and group career counseling. Part-time tuition: $39.60 per credit for state residents, $135.60 per credit for nonresidents. Minnesota residents pay tuition at the rate they would pay if attending a comparable state-supported institution in Minnesota.

University of Wisconsin Center– Marinette County
Marinette 54143
Public institution; small-town setting. Awards A. Barrier-free campus. Total enrollment: 427 (all undergraduates); 40% part-time, 58% women, 38% over 25. Total faculty: 25. Library holdings: 23,000 bound volumes, 135 periodical subscriptions, 2,000 records/tapes.
Undergraduate Courses offered for part-time students during daytime, evenings, summer. Complete part-time degree programs offered during daytime, evenings, summer. Adult/continuing education programs available. Career services available to part-time students: individual and group career counseling. Part-time tuition: $40.10 per credit for state residents, $136.10 per credit for nonresidents. Minnesota residents pay tuition at the rate they would pay if attending a comparable state-supported institution in Minnesota.

University of Wisconsin Center– Marshfield/Wood County
Marshfield 54449
Public institution; small-town setting. Awards A. Total enrollment: 628 (all undergraduates); 53% part-time, 67% women. Total faculty: 37. Library holdings: 29,000 bound volumes, 40 periodical subscriptions, 3,000 records/tapes.
Undergraduate Courses offered for part-time students during daytime, evenings, summer. Complete part-time degree programs offered during daytime, evenings, summer. Adult/continuing education programs available. Career services available to part-time students: individual and group career counseling. Part-time tuition: $40.15 per credit for state residents, $136.15 per credit for nonresidents.

University of Wisconsin Center–Richland
Richland 53581
Public institution; rural setting. Awards A. Barrier-free campus. Total enrollment: 285 (all undergraduates); 23% part-time, 56% women, 30% over 25. Total faculty: 24. Library holdings: 35,000 bound volumes, 148 periodical subscriptions, 900 records/tapes.
Undergraduate Courses offered for part-time students during daytime, evenings, summer. Complete part-time degree programs offered during daytime, evenings, summer. Adult/continuing education programs available. Career services available to part-time students: individual career counseling, individual job placement. Part-time tuition: $42.50 per credit for state residents, $142.50 per credit for nonresidents. Minnesota residents pay tuition at the rate they would pay if attending a comparable state-supported institution in Minnesota.

University of Wisconsin Center–Rock County
Janesville 53545
Public institution; city setting. Awards A. Total enrollment: 850 (all undergraduates); 50% part-time, 60% women, 50% over 25. Total faculty: 36. Library holdings: 60,000 bound volumes, 200 periodical subscriptions, 2,500 records/tapes.
Undergraduate Courses offered for part-time students during daytime, evenings, summer. Complete part-time degree programs offered during daytime, evenings, summer. External degree and adult/continuing education programs available. Career services available to part-time students: individual and group career counseling. Part-time tuition: $39.55 per credit for state residents, $135.55 per credit for nonresidents. Minnesota residents pay tuition at the rate they would pay if attending a comparable state-supported institution in Minnesota.

University of Wisconsin Center– Sheboygan County
Sheboygan 53081
Public institution; small-town setting. Awards A. Total enrollment: 695 (all undergraduates); 35% part-time, 50% women, 35% over 25. Total faculty: 42. Library holdings: 32,000 bound volumes, 300 periodical subscriptions, 2,000 records/tapes.
Undergraduate Courses offered for part-time students during daytime, evenings, summer. Complete part-time degree programs offered during daytime, evenings, summer. Adult/con-

tinuing education programs available. Career services available to part-time students: individual and group career counseling. Part-time tuition: $39.45 per credit for state residents, $135.45 per credit for nonresidents. Minnesota residents pay tuition at the rate they would pay if attending a comparable state-supported institution in Minnesota.

University of Wisconsin Center–Washington County
West Bend 53095

Public institution; small-town setting. Awards A. Barrier-free campus. Total enrollment: 764 (all undergraduates); 31% part-time, 48% women, 23% over 25. Total faculty: 46. Library holdings: 34,000 bound volumes, 16 titles on microform, 211 periodical subscriptions, 2,100 records/tapes.

Undergraduate Courses offered for part-time students during daytime, evenings, summer. Complete part-time degree programs offered during daytime, evenings, summer. Career services available to part-time students: individual and group career counseling. Part-time tuition: $39.80 per credit for state residents, $135.80 per credit for nonresidents. Minnesota residents pay tuition at the rate they would pay if attending a comparable state-supported institution in Minnesota.

University of Wisconsin Center–Waukesha County
Waukesha 53186

Public institution; city setting. Awards A. Barrier-free campus. Total enrollment: 2,200 (all undergraduates); 51% part-time, 55% women. Total faculty: 90. Library holdings: 39,000 bound volumes, 5,663 titles on microform, 253 periodical subscriptions, 1,855 records/tapes.

Undergraduate Courses offered for part-time students during daytime, evenings, weekends, summer. Complete part-time degree programs offered during daytime, evenings, summer. Adult/continuing education programs available. Career services available to part-time students: individual career counseling. Part-time tuition: $39.45 per credit for state residents, $135.45 per credit for nonresidents. Minnesota residents pay tuition at the rate they would pay if attending a comparable state-supported institution in Minnesota.

University of Wisconsin–Eau Claire
Eau Claire 54701

Public institution; city setting. Awards A, B, M. Total enrollment: 11,072. Undergraduate enrollment: 10,530; 9% part-time, 56% women, 12% over 25. Total faculty: 577. Library holdings: 453,984 bound volumes, 2,319 periodical subscriptions, 5,414 records/tapes.

Undergraduate Courses offered for part-time students during daytime, evenings, summer. Complete part-time degree programs offered during daytime, evenings, summer. Adult/continuing education programs available. Career services available to part-time students: individual and group career counseling, individual job placement, employer recruitment on campus. Part-time tuition: $50.30 per credit for state residents, $153.80 per credit for nonresidents. Minnesota residents pay tuition at the rate they would pay if attending a comparable state-supported institution in Minnesota.

Graduate Part-time study available in School of Graduate Studies. Basic part-time expenses: $73 per credit tuition plus $9.75 per credit fees for state residents, $228.50 per credit tuition plus $9.75 per credit fees for nonresidents. Institutional financial aid available to part-time graduate students in School of Graduate Studies.

University of Wisconsin–Green Bay
Green Bay 54302

Public institution; city setting. Awards A, B, M. Barrier-free campus. Total enrollment: 4,880. Undergraduate enrollment: 4,454; 33% part-time, 56% women, 32% over 25. Total faculty: 243. Library holdings: 270,000 bound volumes, 504,000 titles on microform, 2,600 periodical subscriptions, 30,000 records/tapes.

Undergraduate Courses offered for part-time students during daytime, evenings, summer. Complete part-time degree programs offered during daytime, evenings, summer. External degree and adult/continuing education programs available. Career services available to part-time students: individual and group career counseling, individual job placement, employer recruitment on campus. Part-time tuition: $49.25 per credit for state residents, $153.25 per credit for nonresidents. Minnesota residents pay tuition at the rate they would pay if attending a comparable state-supported institution in Minnesota.

Graduate Part-time study available in Graduate Studies. Basic part-time expenses: $252 per semester (minimum) tuition for state residents, $719 per semester (minimum) tuition for nonresidents.

University of Wisconsin–La Crosse
La Crosse 54601

Public institution; city setting. Awards A, B, M. Total enrollment: 9,849. Undergraduate enrollment: 9,125; 4% part-time, 55% women, 11% over 25. Total faculty: 425. Library holdings: 341,224 bound volumes, 6,600 titles on microform, 2,377 periodical subscriptions, 837 records/tapes.

Undergraduate Courses offered for part-time students during daytime, evenings, weekends, summer. Complete part-time degree programs offered during daytime, evenings, weekends, summer. Adult/continuing education programs available. Career services available to part-time students: individual and group career counseling, individual job placement, employer recruitment on campus. Part-time tuition: $50.45 per credit for state residents, $153.95 per credit for nonresidents. Minnesota residents pay tuition at the rate they would pay if attending a comparable state-supported institution in Minnesota.

Graduate Part-time study available in College of Arts, Letters and Science, College of Business Administration, College of Education and Graduate Studies, College of Health, Physical Education and Recreation. Basic part-time expenses: $75.05 per credit tuition for state residents, $219.55 per credit tuition for nonresidents.

University of Wisconsin–Madison
Madison 53706

Public institution; city setting. Awards B, M, D. Total enrollment: 43,075. Undergraduate enrollment: 29,268; 9% part-time, 46% women, 8% over 25. Total faculty: 2,269. Library holdings: 3.6 million bound volumes.

Undergraduate Courses offered for part-time students during daytime, evenings, summer. Complete part-time degree programs offered during daytime. Career services available to part-time students: individual and group career counseling, individual job placement, employer recruitment on campus. Part-time tuition: $54 per credit hour for state residents, $175.25 per credit hour for nonresidents. Minnesota residents pay tuition at the rate they would pay if attending a comparable state-supported institution in Minnesota.

Graduate Part-time study available in Graduate School. Basic part-time expenses: $112 per credit tuition for state residents, $333 per credit tuition for nonresidents. Institutional financial aid available to part-time graduate students in Graduate School.

Colleges Offering Part-Time Degree Programs / Wisconsin

University of Wisconsin–Milwaukee
Milwaukee 53201

Public institution; metropolitan setting. Awards B, M, D. Total enrollment: 26,468. Undergraduate enrollment: 21,995; 43% part-time, 51% women, 30% over 25. Total faculty: 1,200. Library holdings: 1.3 million bound volumes, 1 million titles on microform, 9,559 periodical subscriptions, 129,746 records/tapes.

Undergraduate Courses offered for part-time students during daytime, evenings, weekends, summer. Complete part-time degree programs offered during daytime, evenings, weekends, summer. Adult/continuing education programs available. Career services available to part-time students: individual and group career counseling, individual job placement, employer recruitment on campus. Part-time tuition per semester (1 to 11 credit hours) ranges from $81 to $621 for state residents, $202 to $1955 for nonresidents. Minnesota residents pay tuition at the rate they would pay if attending a comparable state-supported institution in Minnesota.

Graduate Part-time study available in Graduate School. Basic part-time expenses: $136.95 per credit tuition for state residents, $358 per credit tuition for nonresidents. Institutional financial aid available to part-time graduate students in Graduate School.

University of Wisconsin–Oshkosh
Oshkosh 54901

Public institution; city setting. Awards A, B, M. Barrier-free campus. Total enrollment: 11,200. Undergraduate enrollment: 9,200; 19% part-time, 52% women, 7% over 25. Total faculty: 600. Library holdings: 600,000 bound volumes, 1,800 periodical subscriptions.

Undergraduate Courses offered for part-time students during daytime, evenings, weekends, summer. Complete part-time degree programs offered during daytime, evenings, weekends, summer. Adult/continuing education programs available. Career services available to part-time students: individual and group career counseling, individual job placement, employer recruitment on campus. Part-time tuition: $49.16 per semester hour for state residents, $152.66 per semester hour for nonresidents. Minnesota residents pay tuition at the rate they would pay if attending a comparable state-supported institution in Minnesota.

Graduate Part-time study available in Graduate School. Degree can be earned exclusively through evening/weekend study in Graduate School. Basic part-time expenses: $84.05 per credit fees for state residents, $239.50 per credit fees for nonresidents. Institutional financial aid available to part-time graduate students in Graduate School.

University of Wisconsin–Parkside
Kenosha 53141

Public institution; city setting. Awards B, M. Barrier-free campus. Total enrollment: 5,990. Undergraduate enrollment: 5,602; 49% part-time, 47% women, 40% over 25. Total faculty: 280. Library holdings: 300,000 bound volumes.

Undergraduate Courses offered for part-time students during daytime, evenings, summer. Complete part-time degree programs offered during daytime, evenings, summer. Adult/continuing education programs available. Career services available to part-time students: individual and group career counseling, individual job placement, employer recruitment on campus. Part-time tuition and fees per semester (1 to 11 credits) range from $62 to $525 for state residents, $166 to $1664 for nonresidents. Minnesota residents pay tuition at the rate they would pay if attending a comparable state-supported institution in Minnesota.

Graduate Part-time study available in Division of Business and Administrative Science, Graduate Program in Public Administration. Degree can be earned exclusively through evening/weekend study in Division of Business and Administrative Science. Basic part-time expenses: $260 per semester (minimum) tuition for state residents, $727 per semester (minimum) tuition for nonresidents. Institutional financial aid available to part-time graduate students in Division of Business and Administrative Science, Graduate Program in Public Administration.

University of Wisconsin–Platteville
Platteville 53818

Public institution; small-town setting. Awards A, B, M. Total enrollment: 5,480. Undergraduate enrollment: 5,200; 10% part-time, 40% women, 5% over 25. Total faculty: 244. Library holdings: 180,000 bound volumes, 1,600 periodical subscriptions, 2,400 records/tapes.

Undergraduate Courses offered for part-time students during daytime. Complete part-time degree programs offered during daytime. External degree and adult/continuing education programs available. Career services available to part-time students: individual career counseling, individual job placement, employer recruitment on campus. Part-time tuition: $40.75 per credit for state residents, $144.25 per credit for nonresidents. Minnesota residents pay tuition at the rate they would pay if attending a comparable state-supported institution in Minnesota.

Graduate Part-time study available in Graduate Studies. Basic part-time expenses: $79.20 per credit tuition for state residents, $235 per credit tuition for nonresidents.

University of Wisconsin–River Falls
River Falls 54022

Public institution; small-town setting. Awards A, B, M. Total enrollment: 5,368. Undergraduate enrollment: 4,944; 8% part-time, 49% women, 12% over 25. Total faculty: 279. Library holdings: 184,706 bound volumes, 395,333 titles on microform, 1,455 periodical subscriptions, 8,184 records/tapes.

Undergraduate Courses offered for part-time students during daytime. Complete part-time degree programs offered during daytime. External degree and adult/continuing education programs available. Career services available to part-time students: individual and group career counseling, individual job placement, employer recruitment on campus. Part-time tuition and fees per quarter (1 to 11 quarter hours) range from $46 to $374 for state residents, $115 to $1133 for nonresidents. Minnesota residents pay tuition at the rate they would pay if attending a comparable state-supported institution in Minnesota.

Graduate Part-time study available in Graduate School. Basic part-time expenses: $174.63 per quarter (minimum) fees for state residents, $486 per quarter (minimum) fees for nonresidents. Institutional financial aid available to part-time graduate students in Graduate School.

University of Wisconsin–Stevens Point
Stevens Point 54481

Public institution; small-town setting. Awards A, B, M. Barrier-free campus. Total enrollment: 8,906. Undergraduate enrollment: 8,378; 13% part-time, 51% women, 16% over 25. Total faculty: 455. Library holdings: 285,000 bound volumes, 90,000 titles on microform, 2,000 periodical subscriptions, 5,000 records/tapes.

Undergraduate Courses offered for part-time students during daytime, evenings, weekends, summer. Complete part-time degree programs offered during daytime, evenings, summer. Adult/continuing education programs available. Career services available to part-time students: individual and group career counseling, individual job placement, employer recruitment on campus. Part-time tuition: $56.60 per semester hour for state residents, $156.35 per semester hour for nonresidents. Minnesota residents pay tuition at the rate they would pay if attending a comparable state-supported institution in Minnesota.

Graduate Part-time study available in Graduate School. Basic part-time expenses: $272 per semester (minimum) fees for state residents, $739 per semester (minimum) fees for nonresidents. Institutional financial aid available to part-time graduate students in Graduate School.

University of Wisconsin–Stout
Menomonie 54751

Public institution; small-town setting. Awards B, M. Total enrollment: 7,470. Undergraduate enrollment: 6,933; 5% part-time, 46% women, 14% over 25. Total faculty: 383. Library holdings: 175,000 bound volumes, 460,000 titles on microform, 2,200 periodical subscriptions, 2,000 records/tapes.

Undergraduate Courses offered for part-time students during daytime, evenings, summer. Complete part-time degree programs offered during daytime. External degree and adult/continuing education programs available. Career services available to part-time students: individual and group career counseling, individual job placement, employer recruitment on campus. Part-time tuition: $40.75 per credit for state residents, $144.25 per credit for nonresidents. Minnesota residents pay tuition at the rate they would pay if attending a comparable state-supported institution in Minnesota.

Graduate Part-time study available in Graduate College. Basic part-time expenses: $273 per semester (minimum) tuition for state residents, $740 per semester (minimum) tuition for nonresidents.

University of Wisconsin–Superior
Superior 54880

Public institution; small-town setting. Awards A, B, M. Total enrollment: 2,219. Undergraduate enrollment: 1,820; 17% part-time, 48% women, 27% over 25. Total faculty: 144. Library holdings: 230,000 bound volumes, 6,100 titles on microform, 850 periodical subscriptions, 1,500 records/tapes.

Undergraduate Courses offered for part-time students during daytime, evenings, weekends, summer. Complete part-time degree programs offered during daytime, evenings, weekends, summer. External degree and adult/continuing education programs available. Career services available to part-time students: individual and group career counseling, individual job placement, employer recruitment on campus. Part-time tuition and fees per quarter (1 to 11 credit hours) range from $33 to $329 for state residents, $99 to $1061 for nonresidents. Minnesota residents pay tuition at the rate they would pay if attending a comparable state-supported institution in Minnesota.

Graduate Part-time study available in Graduate Studies. Basic part-time expenses: $175.41 per quarter (minimum) tuition for state residents, $486 per quarter (minimum) tuition for nonresidents.

University of Wisconsin–Whitewater
Whitewater 53190

Public institution; small-town setting. Awards A, B, M. Barrier-free campus. Total enrollment: 10,493. Undergraduate enrollment: 9,171; 10% part-time, 50% women, 21% over 25. Total faculty: 617. Library holdings: 298,000 bound volumes, 575,000 titles on microform, 2,040 periodical subscriptions, 21,500 records/tapes.

Undergraduate Courses offered for part-time students during daytime, evenings, summer. Complete part-time degree programs offered during daytime, evenings, summer. External degree and adult/continuing education programs available. Career services available to part-time students: individual and group career counseling, individual job placement, employer recruitment on campus. Part-time tuition: $49.85 per credit for state residents, $153.35 per credit for nonresidents. Minnesota residents pay tuition at the rate they would pay if attending a comparable state-supported institution in Minnesota.

Graduate Part-time study available in School of Graduate Studies. Basic part-time expenses: $82.64 per credit tuition for state residents, $238.14 per credit tuition for nonresidents. Institutional financial aid available to part-time graduate students in School of Graduate Studies.

Viterbo College
La Crosse 54601

Independent-religious instutition; city setting. Awards B. Barrier-free campus. Total enrollment: 1,173 (all undergraduates); 31% part-time, 80% women, 17% over 25. Total faculty: 120. Library holdings: 68,000 bound volumes, 10 titles on microform, 550 periodical subscriptions, 3,200 records/tapes.

Undergraduate Courses offered for part-time students during daytime, evenings, summer. Complete part-time degree programs offered during daytime, evenings, summer. Adult/continuing education programs available. Career services available to part-time students: individual and group career counseling, individual job placement, employer recruitment on campus. Part-time tuition per semester (1 to 11 credits) ranges from $60 to $1920.

Western Wisconsin Technical Institute
La Crosse 54601

Public institution; city setting. Awards A. Barrier-free campus. Total enrollment: 2,500 (all undergraduates); 25% part-time, 50% women, 25% over 25. Total faculty: 883.

Undergraduate Courses offered for part-time students during daytime, evenings. Complete part-time degree programs offered during daytime, evenings. Adult/continuing education programs available. Career services available to part-time students: individual and group career counseling, individual job placement, employer recruitment on campus. Part-time tuition: $12.25 per credit for area residents, $34.60 per credit for state residents, $71.80 per credit for nonresidents.

Wisconsin Conservatory of Music
Milwaukee 53202

Independent institution; metropolitan setting. Awards A, B, M. Total enrollment: 115. Undergraduate enrollment: 104; 19% part-time, 30% women, 40% over 25. Total faculty: 54. Library holdings: 25,000 bound volumes, 35 periodical subscriptions, 12,000 records/tapes.

Undergraduate Courses offered for part-time students during daytime, summer. Complete part-time degree programs offered during daytime, summer. Adult/continuing education pro-

Wisconsin Conservatory of Music (continued)
grams available. Career services available to part-time students: individual career counseling. Part-time tuition: $220 per credit.

Wisconsin Indianhead Technical Institute, Ashland Campus
Ashland 54806

Public institution; small-town setting. Awards A. Total enrollment: 403 (all undergraduates); 42% part-time, 54% women. Total faculty: 20. Library holdings: 6,788 bound volumes, 85 periodical subscriptions, 260 records/tapes.

Undergraduate Courses offered for part-time students during daytime, evenings, summer. Complete part-time degree programs offered during daytime, evenings, summer. Career services available to part-time students: individual and group career counseling, individual job placement, employer recruitment on campus. Part-time tuition: $18.40 per credit for area residents, $51.90 per credit for state residents, $107.70 per credit for nonresidents.

Wisconsin Indianhead Technical Institute, New Richmond Campus
New Richmond 54017

Public institution; small-town setting. Awards A. Total enrollment: 1,301 (all undergraduates); 71% part-time, 53% women. Total faculty: 34. Library holdings: 6,100 bound volumes, 2,242 titles on microform, 160 periodical subscriptions, 2,015 records/tapes.

Undergraduate Courses offered for part-time students during daytime, evenings, summer. Complete part-time degree programs offered during daytime, evenings, summer. Career services available to part-time students: individual and group career counseling, individual job placement, employer recruitment on campus. Part-time tuition: $18.40 per credit for area residents, $51.90 per credit for state residents, $107.70 per credit for nonresidents.

Wisconsin Indianhead Technical Institute, Rice Lake Campus
Rice Lake 54868

Public institution; small-town setting. Awards A. Total enrollment: 1,317 (all undergraduates); 65% part-time, 42% women. Total faculty: 44. Library holdings: 33,000 bound volumes, 10,000 titles on microform, 147 periodical subscriptions, 9,000 records/tapes.

Undergraduate Courses offered for part-time students during daytime, evenings. Complete part-time degree programs offered during daytime, evenings. Adult/continuing education programs available. Career services available to part-time students: individual and group career counseling, individual job placement, employer recruitment on campus. Part-time tuition: $18.40 per credit for area residents, $51.90 per credit for state residents, $107.70 per credit for nonresidents.

Wisconsin Indianhead Technical Institute, Superior Campus
Superior 54880

Public institution; small-town setting. Awards A. Barrier-free campus. Total enrollment: 1,128 (all undergraduates); 57% part-time, 49% women. Total faculty: 43. Library holdings: 11,217 bound volumes, 165 periodical subscriptions, 552 records/tapes.

Undergraduate Courses offered for part-time students during daytime, evenings, summer. Complete part-time degree programs offered during daytime, evenings, summer. Part-time tuition: $18.40 per credit for area residents, $51.90 per credit for state residents, $107.70 per credit for nonresidents.

Wisconsin Lutheran College
Milwaukee 53226

Independent-religious instutition; metropolitan setting. Awards A. Barrier-free campus. Total enrollment: 107 (all undergraduates); 13% part-time, 61% women. Total faculty: 25. Library holdings: 75,000 bound volumes, 200 periodical subscriptions, 3,000 records/tapes.

Undergraduate Courses offered for part-time students during daytime, evenings. Complete part-time degree programs offered during daytime, evenings. Adult/continuing education programs available. Career services available to part-time students: individual career counseling. Part-time tuition: $115 per credit.

Wisconsin School of Professional Psychology
Milwaukee 53221

Independent institution (graduate only). Total enrollment: 40 (85% part-time). Total faculty: 30.

Graduate Part-time study available in Graduate Program in Clinical Psychology. Degree can be earned exclusively through evening/weekend study in Graduate Program in Clinical Psychology. Basic part-time expenses: $550 per course tuition. Institutional financial aid available to part-time graduate students in Graduate Program in Clinical Psychology.

WYOMING

Casper College
Casper 82601

Public institution; city setting. Awards A. Total enrollment: 1,972 (all undergraduates); 11% part-time, 51% women, 38% over 25. Total faculty: 190. Library holdings: 60,000 bound volumes, 250 periodical subscriptions.

Undergraduate Courses offered for part-time students during daytime, evenings, summer. Complete part-time degree programs offered during daytime, evenings. Adult/continuing education programs available. Career services available to part-time students: individual and group career counseling, employer recruitment on campus. Part-time tuition: $18 per credit hour for state residents, $75 per credit hour for nonresidents.

Central Wyoming College
Riverton 82501

Public institution; rural setting. Awards A. Barrier-free campus. Total enrollment: 1,140 (all undergraduates); 49% part-time, 59% women. Total faculty: 68. Library holdings: 25,000 bound volumes, 300 periodical subscriptions, 2,500 records/tapes.

Undergraduate Courses offered for part-time students during daytime, evenings, summer. Complete part-time degree programs offered during daytime, evenings, summer. Adult/continuing education programs available. Career services available to part-time students: individual and group career counseling, individual job placement. Part-time tuition: $16 per credit.

Wyoming / Colleges Offering Part-Time Degree Programs

Eastern Wyoming College
Torrington 82240

Public institution; rural setting. Awards A. Barrier-free campus. Total enrollment: 1,351 (all undergraduates); 66% part-time, 60% women, 37% over 25. Total faculty: 53. Library holdings: 23,500 bound volumes, 126 titles on microform, 168 periodical subscriptions, 1,800 records/tapes.

Undergraduate Courses offered for part-time students during daytime, evenings. Complete part-time degree programs offered during daytime, evenings. External degree and adult/continuing education programs available. Career services available to part-time students: individual and group career counseling, individual job placement. Part-time tuition: $14 per semester hour for state residents, $14 per semester hour for nonresidents.

Laramie County Community College
Cheyenne 82007

Public institution; city setting. Awards A. Barrier-free campus. Total enrollment: 3,510 (all undergraduates); 70% part-time, 56% women. Total faculty: 162. Library holdings: 20,933 bound volumes.

Undergraduate Courses offered for part-time students during daytime, evenings, summer. Complete part-time degree programs offered during daytime, evenings, summer. Adult/continuing education programs available. Career services available to part-time students: individual and group career counseling, individual job placement, employer recruitment on campus. Part-time tuition: $18.25 per credit hour for state residents, $51.25 per credit hour for nonresidents.

Northwest Community College
Powell 82435

Public institution; rural setting. Awards A. Barrier-free campus. Total enrollment: 1,370 (all undergraduates); 55% part-time, 60% women, 10% over 25. Total faculty: 140. Library holdings: 32,000 bound volumes, 400 records/tapes.

Undergraduate Courses offered for part-time students during daytime, evenings. Complete part-time degree programs offered during daytime, evenings. Adult/continuing education programs available. Career services available to part-time students: individual career counseling. Part-time tuition: $17 per credit for state residents, $42 per credit for nonresidents.

Sheridan College
Sheridan 82801

Public institution; small-town setting. Awards A. Barrier-free campus. Total enrollment: 1,215 (all undergraduates); 53% part-time, 59% women. Total faculty: 133. Library holdings: 34,900 bound volumes, 385 periodical subscriptions, 1,200 records/tapes.

Undergraduate Courses offered for part-time students during daytime, evenings. Complete part-time degree programs offered during daytime, evenings. Adult/continuing education programs available. Career services available to part-time students: individual and group career counseling. Part-time tuition: $22.50 per semester hour for state residents, $22.50 per semester hour for nonresidents.

University of Wyoming
Laramie 82071

Public institution; small-town setting. Awards B, M, D. Barrier-free campus. Total enrollment: 10,270. Undergraduate enrollment: 8,264; 15% part-time, 44% women. Total faculty: 868. Library holdings: 800,000 bound volumes, 350,136 titles on microform, 9,723 periodical subscriptions, 6,114 records/tapes.

Undergraduate Courses offered for part-time students during daytime, summer. Complete part-time degree programs offered during daytime, summer. Adult/continuing education programs available. Career services available to part-time students: individual and group career counseling, individual job placement, employer recruitment on campus. Part-time tuition: $30 per semester hour for state residents, $93 per semester hour for nonresidents.

Graduate Part-time study available in Graduate School. Basic part-time expenses: $96 per semester (minimum) tuition for state residents, $285 per semester (minimum) tuition for nonresidents.

Western Wyoming Community College
Rock Springs 82901

Public institution; small-town setting. Awards A. Barrier-free campus. Total enrollment: 1,661 (all undergraduates); 71% part-time, 65% women, 52% over 25. Total faculty: 81. Library holdings: 20,000 bound volumes, 50 periodical subscriptions, 500 records/tapes.

Undergraduate Courses offered for part-time students during daytime, evenings, weekends, summer. Complete part-time degree programs offered during daytime, evenings, summer. Adult/continuing education programs available. Career services available to part-time students: individual and group career counseling, individual job placement, employer recruitment on campus. Part-time tuition: $18 per semester hour for state residents, $21 per semester hour for nonresidents.

SECTION 2
Directories of Specialized Information

This section lists the colleges in Section 1 that offer particular types of undergraduate programs: part-time evening, part-time weekend, part-time summer, and external degree. A part-time evening program is one that enables a student to earn a degree by attending classes exclusively in the evening. Similarly, part-time weekend and summer programs enable students to earn degrees by attending exclusively during those periods. External degree programs emphasize off-campus, self-directed study. They usually require no more than 25 percent of degree credit to be earned through traditional class attendance and grant credit for documented on-the-job and other training and for experiential learning.

Colleges Offering Part-Time Evening Programs	365
Colleges Offering Part-Time Weekend Programs	379
Colleges Offering Part-Time Summer Programs	382
Colleges Offering External Degree Programs	393

Directories of Specialized Information

Colleges Offering Part-Time Evening Programs

Academy of Aeronautics, NY
Academy of Art College, CA
Academy of the New Church, PA
Adams State College, CO
Adirondack Community College, NY
Aiken Technical College, SC
Aims Community College, CO
Alabama Agricultural and Mechanical University, AL
Alabama Aviation and Technical College, AL
Alabama Christian College, AL
Alabama State University, AL
Alaska Bible College, AK
Alaska Pacific University, AK
Albany Business College, NY
Albany State College, GA
Albright College, PA
Alexander City State Junior College, AL
Alice Lloyd College, KY
Allan Hancock College, CA
Allegany Community College, MD
Allen County Community College, KS
Allentown College of St Francis de Sales, PA
Alliance College, PA
Alpena Community College, MI
Alvernia College, PA
Alvin Community College, TX
Amarillo College, TX
Amber University, TX
American Academy of Art, IL
American Baptist College of American Baptist Theological Seminary, TN
American College of Puerto Rico, PR
American Conservatory of Music, IL
American Indian Bible College, AZ
American Institute of Banking, MA
American Institute of Business, IA
American International College, MA
American River College, CA
American Technological University, TX
American University, DC
Ancilla College, IN
Anderson College, SC
Andover College, ME
Andrew College, GA
Andrews University, MI
Angelina College, TX
Anna Maria College for Men and Women, MA
Anne Arundel Community College, MD
Anoka-Ramsey Community College, MN
Anson Technical College, NC
Antelope Valley College, CA
Antioch University West, CA
Antonelli Institute of Art and Photography, PA
Aquinas College, MI
Aquinas Junior College, TN
Arapahoe Community College, CO
Arizona College of the Bible, AZ
Arizona State University, AZ
Arizona Western College, AZ
Arkansas State University, AR
Arkansas State University–Beebe Branch, AR
Arkansas Tech University, AR
Arlington Baptist College, TX
Armstrong College, CA
Armstrong State College, GA
Asheville-Buncombe Technical College, NC
Ashland College, OH
Asnuntuck Community College, CT
Assumption College, MA
Athens State College, AL
Atlanta College of Art, GA
Atlanta Junior College, GA
Atlantic Christian College, NC
Atlantic Community College, NJ
Auburn University at Montgomery, AL
Augusta College, GA
Augustana College, SD
Aurora College, IL
Austin Community College, MN
Austin Community College, TX
Averett College, VA
Avila College, MO
Bacone College, OK
Bainbridge Junior College, GA
Baker Junior College of Business, MI
Bakersfield College, CA
Baldwin-Wallace College, OH
Ball State University, IN
Baptist College at Charleston, SC
Barat College, IL
Barrington College, RI
Barry University, FL
Barstow College, CA
Bartlesville Wesleyan College, OK
Barton County Community College, KS
Bay de Noc Community College, MI
Bay State Junior College, MA
Bay-Valley Tech, CA
Beal College, ME
Beaufort County Community College, NC
Beaufort Technical College, SC
Beaver College, PA
Becker Junior College–Leicester Campus, MA
Becker Junior College–Worcester Campus, MA
Beckley College, WV
Belhaven College, MS
Bellarmine College, KY
Belleville Area College, IL
Bellevue College, NE
Bellevue Community College, WA
Belmont College, TN
Belmont Technical College, OH
Beloit College, WI
Bemidji State University, MN
Benedictine College, KS
Bentley College, MA
Berean Institute, PA
Bergen Community College, NJ
Berkeley School, NJ
Berkeley School, Hicksville, NY
Berkshire Community College, MA
Berry College, GA
Bethel College, IN
Bethel College, TN
Bethune-Cookman College, FL
Big Bend Community College, WA
Birmingham-Southern College, AL
Bishop Clarkson College of Nursing, NE
Bishop College, TX
Bismarck Junior College, ND
Blackfeet Community College, MT
Black Hawk College–East Campus, IL
Blackhawk Technical Institute, WI
Black Hills State College, SD
Bladen Technical College, NC
Blair Junior College, CO
Blanton's Junior College, NC
Bloomfield College, NJ
Bloomsburg University of Pennsylvania, PA
Bluefield State College, WV
Blue Mountain College, MS
Blue Ridge Community College, VA
Blue Ridge Technical College, NC

Directories of Specialized Information

Part-Time Evening Programs (continued)
Boise State University, ID
Bossier Parish Community College, LA
Boston Architectural Center, MA
Boston College, MA
Boston University, MA
Bowie State College, MD
Bowling Green Junior College of Business, KY
Bowling Green State University–Firelands College, OH
Bradley University, IL
Brainerd Community College, MN
Bramson ORT Technical Institute, NY
Brazosport College, TX
Brenau College, GA
Brescia College, KY
Brevard Community College, FL
Brewer State Junior College, AL
Brewton-Parker College, GA
Briar Cliff College, IA
Briarcliffe Secretarial School, NY
Bridgeport Engineering Institute, CT
Bridgewater State College, MA
Brigham Young University–Hawaii Campus, HI
Brookdale Community College, NJ
Broome Community College, NY
Broward Community College, FL
Brunswick Junior College, GA
Brunswick Technical College, NC
Bryant and Stratton Business Institute, Buffalo, NY
Bryant and Stratton Business Institute, Rochester, NY
Bryant and Stratton Business Institute, Eastern Hills Campus, NY
Bryant and Stratton Powelson Business Institute, NY
Bryant College, RI
Bucks County Community College, PA
Buena Vista College, IA
Bunker Hill Community College, MA
Burlington College, VT
Burlington County College, NJ
Butler County Community College, KS
Butler County Community College, PA
Butler University, IN
Butte College, CA
Cabrillo College, CA
Cabrini College, PA
Caguas City College, PR
Caldwell College, NJ
Caldwell Community College and Technical Institute, NC
California Baptist College, CA
California Lutheran College, CA
California State College, Bakersfield, CA
California State College, San Bernardino, CA
California State College, Stanislaus, CA
California State Polytechnic University, Pomona, CA
California State University, Chico, CA
California State University, Dominguez Hills, CA
California State University, Fresno, CA
California State University, Fullerton, CA
California State University, Hayward, CA
California State University, Long Beach, CA
California State University, Los Angeles, CA
California State University, Northridge, CA
California State University, Sacramento, CA
California University of Pennsylvania, PA
Calumet College, IN
Calvin College, MI
Camden County College, NJ
Cameron University, OK
Campbellsville College, KY
Campbell University, NC
Canisius College, NY
Cape Cod Community College, MA

Cape Fear Technical Institute, NC
Capitol Institute of Technology, MD
Caribbean University College, PR
Carl Sandburg College, IL
Carroll College, WI
Carroll College of Montana, MT
Carteret Technical College, NC
Carthage College, WI
Casco Bay College, ME
Casper College, WY
Castleton State College, VT
Catawba College, NC
Catawba Valley Technical College, NC
Catholic University of America, DC
Catholic University of Puerto Rico, PR
Catholic University of Puerto Rico, Mayagüez Center, PR
Catonsville Community College, MD
Cayuga County Community College, NY
Cecil Community College, MD
Cecils Junior College of Business, NC
Cedar Crest College, PA
Cedar Valley College, TX
Centenary College, NJ
Centenary College of Louisiana, LA
Central Arizona College, AZ
Central Bible College, MO
Central Carolina Technical College, NC
Central City Business Institute, NY
Central Community College–Grand Island Campus, NE
Central Community College–Hastings Campus, NE
Central Community College–Platte Campus, NE
Central Connecticut State University, CT
Central Florida Bible College, FL
Central Florida Community College, FL
Centralia College, WA
Central Michigan University, MI
Central Missouri State University, MO
Central New England College, MA
Central Ohio Technical College, OH
Central Oregon Community College, OR
Central Piedmont Community College, NC
Central State University, OH
Central State University, OK
Central Texas College, TX
Central University of Iowa, IA
Central Virginia Community College, VA
Central Washington University, WA
Central Wesleyan College, SC
Central Wyoming College, WY
Cerritos College, CA
Cerro Coso Community College, CA
Chabot College, CA
Chaffey College, CA
Chaminade University of Honolulu, HI
Champlain College, VT
Chapman College, CA
Charles County Community College, MD
Charles Stewart Mott Community College, MI
Chatfield College, OH
Chatham College, PA
Chattahoochee Valley State Community College, AL
Chattanooga State Technical Community College, TN
Chemeketa Community College, OR
Chesapeake College, MD
Chestnut Hill College, PA
Cheyney University of Pennsylvania, PA
Chicago College of Commerce, IL
Chicago State University, IL
Chipola Junior College, FL
Christian Brothers College, TN
Christopher Newport College, VA
Churchman Business School, PA
Cincinnati Metropolitan College, OH

Directories of Specialized Information

Cincinnati Technical College, OH
Cisco Junior College, TX
The Citadel, SC
Citrus College, CA
City College of San Francisco, CA
City Colleges of Chicago, Chicago City-Wide College, IL
City Colleges of Chicago, Harry S Truman College, IL
City Colleges of Chicago, Kennedy-King College, IL
City Colleges of Chicago, Loop College, IL
City Colleges of Chicago, Malcolm X College, IL
City Colleges of Chicago, Olive-Harvey College, IL
City Colleges of Chicago, Richard J Daley College, IL
City Colleges of Chicago, Wilbur Wright College, IL
City University, WA
City University of New York, Bernard M Baruch College, NY
City University of New York, Borough of Manhattan Community College, NY
City University of New York, Bronx Community College, NY
City University of New York, Brooklyn College, NY
City University of New York, City College, NY
City University of New York, College of Staten Island, NY
City University of New York, Fiorello H LaGuardia Community College, NY
City University of New York, Herbert H Lehman College, NY
City University of New York, Hunter College, NY
City University of New York, John Jay College of Criminal Justice, NY
City University of New York, Kingsborough Community College, NY
City University of New York, Medgar Evers College, NY
City University of New York, New York City Technical College, NY
City University of New York, Queensborough Community College, NY
City University of New York, Queens College, NY
City University of New York, York College, NY
Clackamas Community College, OR
Clarendon College, TX
Clarion University of Pennsylvania, Clarion, PA
Clarion University of Pennsylvania, Venango Campus, PA
Clark College, IN
Clark College, WA
Clark County Community College, NV
Clarke College, IA
Clarke College, MS
Clark Technical College, OH
Clark University, MA
Clatsop Community College, OR
Clayton Junior College, GA
Clayton University, MO
Clearwater Christian College, FL
Cleary College, MI
Cleveland College of Jewish Studies, OH
Cleveland State Community College, TN
Cleveland State University, OH
Cleveland Technical College, NC
Clinton Community College, IA
Clinton Community College, NY
Cloud County Community College, KS
Coastal Carolina Community College, NC
Coastline Community College, CA
Cochise College, AZ
Coe College, IA
Coffeyville Community College, KS
Cogswell College, CA
Cogswell College Silicon Valley, CA
Coker College, SC
Colby Community College, KS
College Misericordia, PA
College of Automation, IL
College of DuPage, IL
College of Ganado, AZ

College of Great Falls, MT
College of Idaho, ID
College of Insurance, NY
College of Lake County, IL
College of Mount St Joseph on the Ohio, OH
College of Mount Saint Vincent, NY
College of New Rochelle, New Resources Division, NY
College of Notre Dame, CA
College of Saint Benedict, MN
College of St Catherine, MN
College of St Francis, IL
College of St Joseph the Provider, VT
College of Saint Mary, NE
College of Saint Rose, NY
College of St Thomas, MN
College of Santa Fe, NM
College of Southern Idaho, ID
College of the Albemarle, NC
College of the Atlantic, ME
College of the Canyons, CA
College of the Center for Early Education, CA
College of the Desert, CA
College of the Mainland, TX
College of the Ozarks, AR
College of the Redwoods, CA
College of the Sequoias, CA
College of the Siskiyous, CA
College of the Southwest, NM
College of the Virgin Islands, VI
Colorado Mountain College, Alpine Campus, CO
Colorado Mountain College, Spring Valley Campus, CO
Colorado Mountain College, Timberline Campus, CO
Colorado Technical College, CO
Columbia Basin College, WA
Columbia College, Columbia, CA
Columbia College, Hollywood, CA
Columbia College, IL
Columbia College, MO
Columbia College, SC
Columbia-Greene Community College, NY
Columbia Junior College of Business, SC
Columbia State Community College, TN
Columbia University, School of General Studies, NY
Columbus College, GA
Columbus College of Art and Design, OH
Columbus Technical Institute, OH
Community College of Allegheny County–Boyce Campus, PA
Community College of Allegheny County–College Center North, PA
Community College of Beaver County, PA
Community College of Philadelphia, PA
Community College of Rhode Island, Flanagan Campus, RI
Community College of Rhode Island, Knight Campus, RI
Community College of the Air Force, AL
Community College of the Finger Lakes, NY
Community College of the North Central University Center, SD
Community College of Vermont, VT
Compton Community College, CA
Concord College, WV
Concordia College, AL
Concordia College, St Paul, MN
Concordia College Wisconsin, WI
Concordia Teachers College, NE
Condie Junior College of Business and Technology, CA
Connors State College, OK
Contra Costa College, CA
Converse College, SC
Cooke County College, TX
Cooper Institute, TN
Copiah-Lincoln Junior College, MS
Copiah-Lincoln Junior College–Natchez Campus, MS
Coppin State College, MD

367

Directories of Specialized Information

Part-Time Evening Programs (continued)

Corning Community College, NY
Cornish Institute, WA
Corpus Christi State University, TX
Cosumnes River College, CA
County College of Morris, NJ
Covenant College, GA
Crafton Hills College, CA
Crandall Junior College, GA
Craven Community College, NC
Creighton University, NE
Crowder College, MO
Cuesta College, CA
Cumberland College, KY
Cumberland College of Tennessee, TN
Cumberland County College, NJ
Curry College, MA
Cuyahoga Community College, Eastern Campus, OH
Cuyahoga Community College, Western Campus, OH
Cuyamaca College, CA
Cypress College, CA
Dabney S Lancaster Community College, VA
Daemen College, NY
Dakota Wesleyan University, SD
Dallas Baptist College, TX
Dalton Junior College, GA
Daniel Webster College, NH
Danville Area Community College, IL
Danville Community College, VA
Davenport College of Business, MI
Davidson County Community College, NC
Dawson Community College, MT
Daytona Beach Community College, FL
Dean Institute of Technology, PA
Dean Junior College, MA
De Anza College, CA
Defiance College, OH
DeKalb Community College, GA
Delaware County Community College, PA
Delaware Technical and Community College, Terry Campus, DE
Delaware Valley College of Science and Agriculture, PA
Delgado Community College, LA
Del Mar College, TX
Delta College, MI
Delta State University, MS
Denmark Technical College, SC
Denver Auraria Community College, CO
DePaul University, IL
DePauw University, IN
Des Moines Area Community College, IA
Detroit College of Business, Dearborn, MI
Detroit College of Business–Flint, MI
Detroit College of Business, Grand Rapids Campus, MI
Detroit College of Business, Madison Heights Campus, MI
Dodge City Community College, KS
Dominican College of Blauvelt, NY
Dowling College, NY
D-Q University, CA
Drake University, IA
Draughon's Junior College, GA
Draughon's Junior College of Business, KY
Drexel University, PA
Drury College, MO
Dundalk Community College, MD
Duquesne University, PA
Durham Technical Institute, NC
Dutchess Community College, NY
Dyersburg State Community College, TN
Dyke College, OH
D'Youville College, NY
East Arkansas Community College, AR

East Carolina University, NC
East Central College, MO
East Central Junior College, MS
East Central Oklahoma State University, OK
East Coast Bible College, NC
Eastern Arizona College, AZ
Eastern College, PA
Eastern Connecticut State University, CT
Eastern Kentucky University, KY
Eastern Maine Vocational-Technical Institute, ME
Eastern Michigan University, MI
Eastern Montana College, MT
Eastern New Mexico University, NM
Eastern New Mexico University–Roswell, NM
Eastern Oklahoma State College, OK
Eastern Shore Community College, VA
Eastern Washington University, WA
Eastern Wyoming College, WY
Eastfield College, TX
East Tennessee State University, TN
East Texas Baptist University, TX
East Texas State University, Commerce, TX
Eckerd College, FL
Ed E Reid State Technical College, AL
Edgecombe Technical College, NC
Edinboro University of Pennsylvania, PA
Edison Community College, FL
Edison State Community College, OH
Edmonds Community College, WA
Edmondson Junior College, TN
Edward Waters College, FL
El Centro College, TX
Electronic Data Processing College of Puerto Rico, PR
Elgin Community College, IL
Elizabeth Seton College, NY
Elizabethtown College, PA
Ellsworth Community College, IA
Elmhurst College, IL
Elmira College, NY
Elms College, MA
El Paso Community College, TX
El Reno Junior College, OK
Emanuel County Junior College, GA
Embry-Riddle Aeronautical University, Daytona Beach, FL
Embry-Riddle Aeronautical University, International Campus, FL
Emerson College, MA
Emmanuel College, MA
Emporia State University, KS
Enterprise State Junior College, AL
Erie Community College, City Campus, NY
Erie Community College, South Campus, NY
Essex Community College, MD
Essex County College, NJ
Everett Community College, WA
Evergreen State College, WA
Evergreen Valley College, CA
Fairfield University, CT
Fairleigh Dickinson University, Florham-Madison Campus, NJ
Fairleigh Dickinson University, Rutherford Campus, NJ
Fairleigh Dickinson University, Teaneck-Hackensack Campus, NJ
Fashion Institute of Technology, NY
Fayetteville State University, NC
Fayetteville Technical Institute, NC
Feather River College, CA
Felician College, IL
Felician College, NJ
Ferris State College, MI
Findlay College, OH
Fisher Junior College, MA
Fitchburg State College, MA

Directories of Specialized Information

Flathead Valley Community College, MT
Florence-Darlington Technical College, SC
Florida Agricultural and Mechanical University, FL
Florida Atlantic University, FL
Florida Institute of Technology, FL
Florida International University, FL
Florida Keys Community College, FL
Florida Memorial College, FL
Florida Southern College, FL
Floyd Junior College, GA
Fontbonne College, MO
Foothill College, CA
Fordham University at Lincoln Center, NY
Forsyth Technical Institute, NC
Fort Lauderdale College, FL
Fort Lewis College, CO
Fort Scott Community College, KS
Fort Steilacoom Community College, WA
Fort Valley State College, GA
Fort Wayne Bible College, IN
Fox Valley Technical Institute, WI
Framingham State College, MA
Francis Marion College, SC
Franklin and Marshall College, PA
Franklin Institute of Boston, MA
Franklin Pierce College, NH
Franklin University, OH
Frank Phillips College, TX
Frederick Community College, MD
Fresno City College, CA
Friends University, KS
Front Range Community College, CO
Frostburg State College, MD
Fullerton College, CA
Fulton-Montgomery Community College, NY
Furman University, SC
Gadsden State Junior College, AL
Gainesville Junior College, GA
Galveston College, TX
Gannon University, PA
Gardner-Webb College, NC
Garland County Community College, AR
Gaston College, NC
Gateway Technical Institute, Kenosha, WI
Gateway Technical Institute, Racine, WI
Gavilan College, CA
Genesee Community College, NY
Geneva College, PA
George Corley Wallace State Community College, Selma, AL
George C Wallace State Community College, Dothan, AL
George Mason University, VA
George Williams College, IL
Georgia College, GA
Georgian Court College, NJ
Georgia Southern College, GA
Georgia Southwestern College, GA
Georgia State University, GA
Germanna Community College, VA
Glassboro State College, NJ
Glendale Community College, AZ
Glendale Community College, CA
Gloucester County College, NJ
Gogebic Community College, MI
Golden Gate University, CA
Golden West College, CA
Goldey Beacom College, DE
Gordon Junior College, GA
Governors State University, IL
Graham Bible College, VA
Grambling State University, LA
Grand Canyon College, AZ
Grand Rapids Junior College, MI
Grand Valley State College, MI

Grand View College, IA
Gratz College, PA
Grays Harbor College, WA
Grayson County College, TX
Greater Hartford Community College, CT
Greater New Haven State Technical College, CT
Great Lakes Bible College, MI
Greenfield Community College, MA
Green Mountain College, VT
Green River Community College, WA
Greenville College, IL
Greenville Technical College, SC
Griffin College, Seattle, WA
Grossmont College, CA
Guam Community College, GU
Guilford College, NC
Guilford Technical Community College, NC
Gulf Coast Community College, FL
Gwynedd-Mercy College, PA
Hagerstown Junior College, MD
Hahnemann University, PA
Halifax Community College, NC
Hampton Institute, VA
Hannibal-LaGrange College, MO
Harcum Junior College, PA
Harding Business College, Marion, OH
Hardin-Simmons University, TX
Harford Community College, MD
Harrisburg Area Community College, PA
Harris-Stowe State College, MO
Hartford State Technical College, CT
Hawaii Pacific College, HI
Hawthorne College, NH
Haywood Technical College, NC
Hebrew College, MA
Henderson County Junior College, TX
Henderson State University, AR
Henry Ford Community College, MI
Heritage College, WA
Herkimer County Community College, NY
Hesser College, NH
Hibbing Community College, MN
Highland Community College, IL
Highland Community College, KS
Highland Park Community College, MI
Highline Community College, WA
High Point College, NC
Hilbert College, NY
Hill Junior College, TX
Hillsborough Community College, FL
Hocking Technical College, OH
Hofstra University, NY
Holy Apostles College, CT
Holy Family College, PA
Holy Names College, CA
Holyoke Community College, MA
Hood College, MD
Hope College, MI
Housatonic Community College, CT
Houston Baptist University, TX
Houston Community College System, TX
Howard College at Big Spring, TX
Howard Community College, MD
Hudson County Community College, NJ
Hudson Valley Community College, NY
Huertas Business College, PR
Humboldt State University, CA
Humphreys College, CA
Huntingdon College, AL
Huntington College, IN
Huntington Junior College of Business, WV
Husson College, ME
Hutchinson Community College, KS

Directories of Specialized Information

Part-Time Evening Programs (continued)

Idaho State University, ID
Illinois Benedictine College, IL
Illinois Central College, IL
Illinois Eastern Community Colleges, Frontier Community College, IL
Illinois Eastern Community Colleges, Lincoln Trail College, IL
Illinois Eastern Community Colleges, Olney Central College, IL
Illinois Eastern Community Colleges, Wabash Valley College, IL
Illinois Institute of Technology, IL
Illinois State University, IL
Illinois Technical College, IL
Illinois Valley Community College, IL
Immaculata College, PA
Imperial Valley College, CA
Incarnate Word College, TX
Independence Community College, KS
Indiana Central University, IN
Indiana Institute of Technology, IN
Indiana State University, Terre Haute, IN
Indiana State University Evansville, IN
Indiana University at Kokomo, IN
Indiana University at South Bend, IN
Indiana University Bloomington, IN
Indiana University East, IN
Indiana University Northwest, IN
Indiana University of Pennsylvania, PA
Indiana University–Purdue University at Fort Wayne, IN
Indiana University–Purdue University at Indianapolis, IN
Indiana University Southeast, IN
Indiana Vocational Technical College–Central Indiana, IN
Indiana Vocational Technical College–Columbus, IN
Indiana Vocational Technical College–Eastcentral, IN
Indiana Vocational Technical College–Kokomo, IN
Indiana Vocational Technical College–Northcentral, IN
Indiana Vocational Technical College–Northeast, IN
Indiana Vocational Technical College–Northwest, IN
Indiana Vocational Technical College–Southcentral, IN
Indiana Vocational Technical College–Southeast, IN
Indiana Vocational Technical College–Southwest, IN
Indiana Vocational Technical College–Wabash Valley, IN
Indiana Vocational Technical College–Whitewater, IN
Indian Hills Community College, IA
Indian River Community College, FL
Indian Valley Colleges, CA
Institute of Design and Construction, NY
Instituto Comercial de Puerto Rico Junior College, PR
Instituto Técnico Comercial Junior College, PR
Inter American University of Puerto Rico, Aguadilla Regional College, PR
Inter American University of Puerto Rico, Barranquitas Regional College, PR
Inter American University of Puerto Rico, Fajardo Regional College, PR
Inter American University of Puerto Rico, Guayama Regional College, PR
Inter American University of Puerto Rico, Metropolitan Campus, PR
Inter American University of Puerto Rico, Ponce Regional College, PR
Inver Hills Community College, MN
Iona College, NY
Iowa Central Community College, IA
Iowa Lakes Community College, North Attendance Center, IA
Iowa Lakes Community College, South Attendance Center, IA
Iowa Wesleyan College, IA
Iowa Western Community College, IA
Isothermal Community College, NC
Itasca Community College, MN
Itawamba Junior College, MS
Jackson Community College, MI
Jackson State Community College, TN
Jackson State University, MS
Jacksonville State University, AL
Jacksonville University, FL
James H Faulkner State Junior College, AL
James Madison University, VA
James Sprunt Technical College, NC
Jamestown College, ND
Jamestown Community College, NY
Jarvis Christian College, TX
Jefferson College, MO
Jefferson Community College, NY
Jefferson Davis State Junior College, AL
Jefferson State Junior College, AL
Jefferson Technical College, OH
Jersey City State College, NJ
John A Logan College, IL
John Carroll University, OH
John C Calhoun State Community College, AL
John F Kennedy University, CA
Johnson & Wales College, RI
Johnson County Community College, KS
Johnson State College, VT
John Tyler Community College, VA
John Wesley College, NC
John Wood Community College, IL
Joliet Junior College, IL
Jones College, FL
Jones County Junior College, MS
Jordan College, MI
J Sargeant Reynolds Community College, VA
Junior College of Albany, NY
Kalamazoo Valley Community College, MI
Kankakee Community College, IL
Kansas City Kansas Community College, KS
Kansas Newman College, KS
Kansas Wesleyan, KS
Kaskaskia College, IL
Katharine Gibbs School, New York, NY
Kean College of New Jersey, NJ
Kearney State College, NE
Keene State College, NH
Kellogg Community College, MI
Kendall School of Design, MI
Kennebec Valley Vocational-Technical Institute, ME
Kennesaw College, GA
Kent State University, OH
Kent State University, Ashtabula Campus, OH
Kent State University, East Liverpool Campus, OH
Kent State University, Geauga Campus, OH
Kent State University, Salem Campus, OH
Kent State University, Stark Campus, OH
Kent State University, Trumbull Campus, OH
Kent State University, Tuscarawas Campus, OH
Kentucky Junior College of Business, KY
Kentucky State University, KY
Kilgore College, TX
King's College, PA
King's River Community College, CA
Kirkwood Community College, IA
Kirtland Community College, MI
Kishwaukee College, IL
Kutztown University of Pennsylvania, PA
Labouré College, MA
Lackawanna Junior College, PA
Lafayette College, PA
LaGrange College, GA
Lake City Community College, FL
Lake Erie College, OH
Lake Forest College, IL

Directories of Specialized Information

Lake Land College, IL
Lakeland College, WI
Lakeland Community College, OH
Lake Michigan College, MI
Lakeshore Technical Institute, WI
Lake-Sumter Community College, FL
Lamar Community College, CO
Lamar University, TX
Lambuth College, TN
Lancaster Bible College, PA
Lander College, SC
Laney College, CA
Langston University, OK
Lansing Community College, MI
LaPorte Business College, IN
Laramie County Community College, WY
Laredo State University, TX
La Roche College, PA
La Salle University, PA
Lassen College, CA
Latter-Day Saints Business College, UT
Lawrence Institute of Technology, MI
Lebanon Valley College, PA
Lehigh County Community College, PA
Le Moyne College, NY
Lenoir Community College, NC
Lenoir-Rhyne College, NC
Lesley College, MA
Lewis and Clark Community College, IL
Lewis-Clark State College, ID
Lewis College of Business, MI
Lewis University, IL
LIFE Bible College, CA
Lima Technical College, OH
Lincoln College, IL
Lincoln Land Community College, IL
Lincoln Memorial University, TN
Lincoln School of Commerce, NE
Lincoln University, MO
Lindenwood College, MO
Lindsey Wilson College, KY
Linfield College, OR
Lockyear College, Evansville Campus, IN
Lockyear College, Indianapolis Campus, IN
Long Beach City College, CA
Long Island College Hospital School of Nursing, NY
Long Island University, Brooklyn Campus, NY
Long Island University, C W Post Campus, NY
Longview Community College, MO
Lorain County Community College, OH
Loras College, IA
Lord Fairfax Community College, VA
Los Angeles Harbor College, CA
Los Angeles Mission College, CA
Los Angeles Pierce College, CA
Los Angeles Southwest College, CA
Los Angeles Trade-Technical College, CA
Los Angeles Valley College, CA
Louise Salinger Academy of Fashion, CA
Louisiana College, LA
Louisiana State University and Agricultural and Mechanical College, LA
Louisiana State University at Alexandria, LA
Louisiana State University at Eunice, LA
Louisiana State University in Shreveport, LA
Louisville Technical Institute, KY
Lourdes College, OH
Lower Columbia College, WA
Loyola College, MD
Loyola University, New Orleans, LA
Loyola University of Chicago, IL
Lubbock Christian College, TX
Lurleen B Wallace State Junior College, AL

Lynchburg College, VA
Lyons School of Business, PA
MacCormac Junior College, IL
MacMurray College, IL
Macomb Community College, MI
Madison Area Technical College, WI
Madonna College, MI
Mallinckrodt College, IL
Malone College, OH
Manatee Junior College, FL
Manchester Community College, CT
Manhattan College, NY
Mankato State University, MN
Manor Junior College, PA
Mansfield Business College, OH
Mansfield University of Pennsylvania, PA
Maple Woods Community College, MO
Maria College, NY
Marian Court Junior College of Business, MA
Maria Regina College, NY
Maricopa Technical Community College, AZ
Marietta College, OH
Marion College, IN
Marion Technical College, OH
Marist College, NY
Marquette University, WI
Marshalltown Community College, IA
Marshall University, WV
Mars Hill College, NC
Martin Center College, IN
Martin Community College, NC
Mary Baldwin College, VA
Mary College, ND
Marycrest College, IA
Marygrove College, MI
Mary Holmes College, MS
Maryland Institute, College of Art, MD
Marylhurst College for Lifelong Learning, OR
Marymount College of Kansas, KS
Marymount College of Virginia, VA
Marymount Manhattan College, NY
Maryville College, TN
Maryville College–Saint Louis, MO
Mary Washington College, VA
Marywood College, PA
Massachusetts Bay Community College, MA
Massasoit Community College, MA
Mater Dei College, NY
Mattatuck Community College, CT
Mayland Technical College, NC
McCook Community College, NE
McDowell Technical College, NC
McKendree College, IL
McLennan Community College, TX
McMurry College, TX
McNeese State University, LA
McPherson College, KS
Meadows Junior College, GA
Medaille College, NY
Memphis Academy of Arts, TN
Memphis State University, TN
Mendocino College, CA
Merced College, CA
Mercer County Community College, NJ
Mercer University, Macon, GA
Mercer University in Atlanta, GA
Mercy College, NY
Mercy College of Detroit, MI
Mercyhurst College, PA
Meridian Junior College, MS
Merrimack College, MA
Merrimack Valley College of the University System of New Hampshire, NH

Directories of Specialized Information

Part-Time Evening Programs (continued)
Merritt College, CA
Mesabi Community College, MN
Mesa College, CO
Messiah College, PA
Methodist College, NC
Metropolitan State College, CO
Metropolitan State University, MN
Metropolitan Technical Community College, NE
Miami Christian College, FL
Miami-Dade Community College, FL
Miami-Jacobs Junior College of Business, OH
Miami University–Hamilton Campus, OH
Miami University–Middletown Campus, OH
Michiana College of Commerce, IN
Michigan State University, MI
Micronesian Occupational College, TT
Mid-America Nazarene College, KS
Middle Georgia College, GA
Middlesex Community College, CT
Middlesex Community College, MA
Middlesex County College, NJ
Middle Tennessee State University, TN
Midland College, TX
Midland Lutheran College, NE
Midlands Technical College, SC
Mid Michigan Community College, MI
Mid-Plains Community College, NE
Mid-South Bible College, TN
Midstate College, IL
Mid-State College, ME
Mid-State Technical Institute, WI
Midway College, KY
Midwest College of Engineering, IL
Midwestern State University, TX
Miles College, AL
Miles Community College, MT
Millersville University of Pennsylvania, PA
Milligan College, TN
Millikin University, IL
Millsaps College, MS
Milwaukee Area Technical College, WI
Milwaukee School of Engineering, WI
Mineral Area College, MO
Minneapolis College of Art and Design, MN
Minneapolis Community College, MN
Minot State College, ND
MiraCosta College, CA
Mission College, CA
Mississippi College, MS
Mississippi County Community College, AR
Mississippi Gulf Coast Junior College, Jefferson Davis Campus, MS
Mississippi State University, MS
Mississippi University for Women, MS
Mississippi Valley State University, MS
Missouri Southern State College, MO
Missouri Valley College, MO
Missouri Western State College, MO
Mitchell College, CT
Mitchell Community College, NC
Moberly Area Junior College, MO
Mobile College, AL
Modesto Junior College, CA
Mohave Community College, AZ
Mohawk Valley Community College, NY
Mohegan Community College, CT
Molloy College, NY
Monmouth College, NJ
Monroe Business Institute, NY
Monroe Community College, NY
Monroe County Community College, MI

Montana College of Mineral Science and Technology, MT
Montcalm Community College, MI
Montclair State College, NJ
Monterey Peninsula College, CA
Montgomery Technical College, NC
Moorhead State University, MN
Moorpark College, CA
Moraine Park Technical Institute, WI
Moraine Valley Community College, IL
Moravian College, PA
Morgan Community College, CO
Morgan State University, MD
Morningside College, IA
Morris College, SC
Morris Junior College of Business, FL
Morton College, IL
Motlow State Community College, TN
Mountain Empire Community College, VA
Mountain View College, TX
Mt Hood Community College, OR
Mount Ida College, MA
Mount Marty College, SD
Mount Mary College, WI
Mount Mercy College, IA
Mount Olive College, NC
Mount Saint Clare College, IA
Mount Saint Mary College, NY
Mount St Mary's College, CA
Mount Saint Mary's College, MD
Mt San Antonio College, CA
Mt San Jacinto College, CA
Mount Senario College, WI
Mount Union College, OH
Mount Vernon College, DC
Mount Vernon Nazarene College, OH
Mount Wachusett Community College, MA
Muhlenberg College, PA
Murray State University, KY
Muscatine Community College, IA
Muskegon Business College, MI
Muskegon Community College, MI
Napa Valley College, CA
Nash Technical College, NC
Nashville State Technical Institute, TN
Nassau Community College, NY
National Business College, Lynchburg, VA
National College, SD
National College of Education, IL
National Education Center–Brown Institute Campus, MN
National University, CA
Navajo Community College, AZ
Navarro College, TX
Nazarene Bible College, CO
Nazareth College, MI
Nazareth College of Rochester, NY
Nebraska Indian Community College, NE
Nebraska Wesleyan University, NE
Nebraska Western College, NE
Neosho County Community College, KS
Neumann College, PA
Newbury Junior College, MA
New College of California, CA
New England Institute of Applied Arts and Sciences, MA
New Hampshire College, NH
New Hampshire Technical Institute, NH
New Hampshire Vocational-Technical College, Berlin, NH
New Hampshire Vocational-Technical College, Laconia, NH
New Hampshire Vocational-Technical College, Manchester, NH
New Hampshire Vocational-Technical College, Nashua, NH
New Hampshire Vocational-Technical College, Stratham, NH
New Jersey Institute of Technology, NJ
New Mexico Highlands University, NM

Directories of Specialized Information

New Mexico Junior College, NM
New Mexico State University, NM
New Mexico State University–Carlsbad, NM
New Orleans Baptist Theological Seminary, LA
New River Community College, VA
New School for Social Research, Seminar College, NY
New School for Social Research, Senior College, NY
New York Institute of Technology, NY
New York University, NY
Niagara County Community College, NY
Niagara University, NY
Nicholls State University, LA
Nichols College, MA
Nicolet College and Technical Institute, WI
Norfolk State University, VA
Normandale Community College, MN
North Adams State College, MA
Northampton County Area Community College, PA
North Arkansas Community College, AR
North Carolina Agricultural and Technical State University, NC
North Carolina Central University, NC
North Carolina State University at Raleigh, NC
North Carolina Wesleyan College, NC
North Central College, IL
North Central Michigan College, MI
North Central Technical College, OH
North Country Community College, NY
Northeast Alabama State Junior College, AL
Northeastern Bible College, NJ
Northeastern Illinois University, IL
Northeastern Oklahoma Agricultural and Mechanical College, OK
Northeastern Oklahoma State University, OK
Northeastern University, MA
Northeast Louisiana University, LA
Northeast Mississippi Junior College, MS
Northeast Missouri State University, MO
Northeast Technical Community College, NE
Northern Arizona University, AZ
Northern Essex Community College, MA
Northern Illinois University, IL
Northern Kentucky University, KY
Northern Maine Vocational-Technical Institute, ME
Northern Marianas College, CM
Northern Montana College, MT
Northern Nevada Community College, NV
Northern New Mexico Community College, NM
Northern State College, SD
Northern Virginia Community College, VA
North Florida Junior College, FL
North Georgia College, GA
North Greenville College, SC
North Harris County College, TX
North Hennepin Community College, MN
North Idaho College, ID
North Iowa Area Community College, IA
North Lake College, TX
Northland College, WI
Northland Community College, MN
Northland Pioneer College, AZ
North Park College, IL
Northrop University, CA
North Seattle Community College, WA
North Shore Community College, MA
North Texas State University, TX
Northwest Community College, WY
Northwestern Business College, IL
Northwestern Business College–Technical Center, OH
Northwestern Connecticut Community College, CT
Northwestern Michigan College, MI
Northwestern University, Evanston, IL
Northwest Technical College, OH

Norwalk Community College, CT
Norwalk State Technical College, CT
Norwich University, Vermont College, VT
Notre Dame College, NH
Notre Dame College of Ohio, OH
Nova University, FL
Oakland City College, IN
Oakland Community College, MI
Oakland University, MI
Oakton Community College, IL
Ocean County College, NJ
Oglala Lakota College, SD
Oglethorpe University, GA
Ohio Institute of Photography, OH
Ohio State University, Columbus, OH
Ohio State University–Lima Campus, OH
Ohio State University–Mansfield Campus, OH
Ohio State University–Marion Campus, OH
Ohio State University–Newark Campus, OH
Ohio University–Chillicothe, OH
Ohio University–Ironton, OH
Ohio University–Lancaster, OH
Ohio University–Zanesville, OH
Ohlone College, CA
Okaloosa-Walton Junior College, FL
Oklahoma City University, OK
Oklahoma Panhandle State University, OK
Oklahoma State University Technical Institute, OK
Old College, NV
Old Dominion University, VA
Olivet College, MI
Olympic College, WA
Onondaga Community College, NY
Opelika State Technical College, AL
Orangeburg-Calhoun Technical College, SC
Orange Coast College, CA
Orange County Community College, NY
Oregon Institute of Technology, OR
Orlando College, FL
Otero Junior College, CO
Otis Art Institute of Parsons School of Design, CA
Otterbein College, OH
Our Lady of Holy Cross College, LA
Our Lady of the Lake University of San Antonio, TX
Owensboro Junior College of Business, KY
Owens Technical College, OH
Oxnard College, CA
Pace University, New York, NY
Pace University, College of White Plains, NY
Pace University–Pleasantville/Briarcliff, NY
Pacific Christian College, CA
Pacific Coast Junior College, CA
Pacific Lutheran University, WA
Pacific University, OR
Palm Beach Atlantic College, FL
Palm Beach Junior College, FL
Palomar College, CA
Palo Verde College, CA
Pamlico Technical College, NC
Pan American University, TX
Panola Junior College, TX
Paris Junior College, TX
Park College, MO
Parks College, CO
Pasadena City College, CA
Pasco-Hernando Community College, FL
Passaic County Community College, NJ
Patrick Henry Community College, VA
Patten College, CA
Paul D Camp Community College, VA
Paul Quinn College, TX
Pearl River Junior College, MS
Peirce Junior College, PA

Directories of Specialized Information

Part-Time Evening Programs (continued)

Pembroke State University, NC
Peninsula College, WA
Pennsylvania Institute of Technology, PA
Penn Technical Institute, PA
Penn Valley Community College, MO
Pensacola Junior College, FL
Pepperdine University, Pepperdine Plaza, CA
Peru State College, NE
Pfeiffer College, NC
Philadelphia College of Art, PA
Philadelphia College of Bible, PA
Philadelphia College of Textiles and Science, PA
Phillips College of New Orleans, LA
Phillips County Community College, AR
Phillips University, OK
Phoenix College, AZ
Piedmont Bible College, NC
Piedmont Technical College, NC
Piedmont Technical College, SC
Piedmont Virginia Community College, VA
Pikes Peak Community College, CO
Pikeville College, KY
Pima Community College, AZ
Pinebrook Junior College, PA
Pine Manor College, MA
Pioneer Community College, MO
Pitt Community College, NC
Pittsburgh Technical Institute, PA
Pittsburg State University, KS
Plymouth State College of the University System of New Hampshire, NH
Point Park College, PA
Polk Community College, FL
Polytechnic Institute of New York, Brooklyn Campus, NY
Polytechnic Institute of New York, Farmingdale Campus, NY
Porterville College, CA
Portland Community College, OR
Portland State University, OR
Post College, CT
Potomac State College of West Virginia University, WV
Prairie State College, IL
Prairie View A&M University, TX
Pratt Community College, KS
Pratt Institute, NY
Prentiss Normal and Industrial Institute, MS
Prince George's Community College, MD
Prospect Hall College, FL
Providence College, RI
Pueblo Community College, CO
Puget Sound College of the Bible, WA
Purdue University, West Lafayette, IN
Purdue University Calumet, IN
Purdue University North Central, IN
Queens College, NC
Quincy Junior College, MA
Quinebaug Valley Community College, CT
Quinnipiac College, CT
Quinsigamond Community College, MA
Radford University, VA
Ramapo College of New Jersey, NJ
Randolph Technical College, NC
Ranger Junior College, TX
Reading Area Community College, PA
Red Rocks Community College, CO
Regis College, CO
Regis College, MA
Reinhardt College, GA
Rend Lake College, IL
Reno Business College, NV
RETS Tech Center, OH
Rhode Island College, RI

Richard Bland College, VA
Richland College, TX
Richland Community College, IL
Richmond Technical College, NC
Ricks College, ID
Rider College, NJ
Rio Grande College/Community College, OH
Rio Hondo Community College, CA
Riverside City College, CA
Rivier College, NH
Roane State Community College, TN
Roanoke-Chowan Technical College, NC
Roanoke College, VA
Robert Morris College, PA
Roberts Wesleyan College, NY
Rochester Community College, MN
Rochester Institute of Technology, NY
Rockford College, IL
Rockhurst College, MO
Rockingham Community College, NC
Rockland Community College, NY
Rockmont College, CO
Rock Valley College, IL
Rogers State College, OK
Roger Williams College, RI
Rogue Community College, OR
Roosevelt University, IL
Rosary College, IL
Rose State College, OK
Rowan Technical College, NC
Roxbury Community College, MA
Russell Sage College, NY
Rust College, MS
Rutgers University, University College–Camden, NJ
Rutgers University, University College–Newark, NJ
Rutgers University, University College–New Brunswick, NJ
Rutledge College, MO
Rutledge College, Fayetteville, NC
Rutledge College, Columbia, SC
Rutledge College, Greenville, SC
Rutledge College, North Charleston, SC
Rutledge College, Spartanburg, SC
Rutledge College, TN
Sacramento City College, CA
Sacred Heart College, NC
Sacred Heart Seminary College, MI
Sacred Heart University, CT
Saddleback Community College, CA
Saginaw Valley State College, MI
St Ambrose College, IA
Saint Augustine Community College, IL
Saint Augustine's College, NC
St Bonaventure University, NY
St Catharine College, KY
St Charles Borromeo Seminary, PA
St Cloud State University, MN
St Edward's University, TX
Saint Francis College, IN
St Francis College, NY
Saint Francis College, PA
St John Fisher College, NY
St Johns River Community College, FL
St John's University, NY
Saint Joseph College, CT
St Joseph's College, Brooklyn, NY
St Joseph's College, Suffolk Campus, NY
Saint Joseph's University, PA
Saint Leo College, FL
St Louis Community College at Florissant Valley, MO
St Louis Community College at Forest Park, MO
St Louis Community College at Meramec, MO
Saint Louis University, MO
Saint Martin's College, WA

374

Directories of Specialized Information

Saint Mary College, KS
Saint Mary of the Plains College, KS
Saint Mary's College, MI
Saint Mary's College of California, CA
St Mary's College of Maryland, MD
Saint Mary's College of O'Fallon, MO
St Mary's Junior College, MN
St Mary's University of San Antonio, TX
St Petersburg Junior College, FL
Saint Peter's College, Jersey City, NJ
St Thomas Aquinas College, NY
St Thomas of Villanova University, FL
Saint Vincent College, PA
Saint Xavier College, IL
Salem College, NC
Salem College, WV
Salem Community College, NJ
Salem State College, MA
Salisbury State College, MD
Salish Kootenai Community College, MT
Salve Regina–The Newport College, RI
Samford University, AL
Sampson Technical College, NC
San Antonio College, TX
Sandhills Community College, NC
San Diego City College, CA
San Diego Mesa College, CA
San Diego Miramar College, CA
San Diego State University, CA
San Francisco Art Institute, CA
San Francisco State University, CA
Sangamon State University, IL
San Jacinto College–Central Campus, TX
San Jacinto College–North Campus, TX
San Jacinto College–South Campus, TX
San Joaquin Delta College, CA
San Jose City College, CA
San Jose State University, CA
San Juan College, NM
Santa Ana College, CA
Santa Barbara City College, CA
Santa Fe Community College, FL
Santa Monica College, CA
Santa Rosa Junior College, CA
Sauk Valley College, IL
Savannah College of Art and Design, GA
Schenectady County Community College, NY
Schoolcraft College, MI
School for Lifelong Learning of the University System of New Hampshire, NH
School of the Art Institute of Chicago, IL
School of the Ozarks, MO
School of Visual Arts, NY
Scott Community College, IA
S D Bishop State Junior College, AL
Seattle Central Community College, WA
Seattle Pacific University, WA
Seattle University, WA
Selma University, AL
Seminole Community College, FL
Seminole Junior College, OK
Seton Hall University, NJ
Seton Hill College, PA
Seward County Community College, KS
Shawnee College, IL
Shawnee State Community College, OH
Shaw University, NC
Shelby State Community College, TN
Sheldon Jackson College, AK
Shenandoah College and Conservatory of Music, VA
Shepherd College, WV
Sheridan College, WY
Sherwood Conservatory of Music, IL

Shimer College, IL
Shippensburg University of Pennsylvania, PA
Shoreline Community College, WA
Shorter College, AR
Shorter College, GA
Siena College, NY
Siena Heights College, MI
Sierra College, CA
Sierra Nevada College, NV
Silver Lake College, WI
Simpson College, CA
Simpson College, IA
Sinclair Community College, OH
Sioux Empire College, IA
Sioux Falls College, SD
Skagit Valley College, WA
Skyline College, CA
Slippery Rock University of Pennsylvania, PA
Snead State Junior College, AL
Snow College, UT
Sojourner-Douglass College, MD
Solano Community College, CA
Somerset County College, NJ
Sonoma State University, CA
South Central Community College, CT
Southeast Community College, Fairbury Campus, NE
Southeast Community College, Lincoln Campus, NE
Southeastern Community College, NC
Southeastern Community College, North Campus, IA
Southeastern Community College, South Campus, IA
Southeastern Illinois College, IL
Southeastern Massachusetts University, MA
Southeastern Oklahoma State University, OK
Southeastern University, DC
Southern Arkansas University, AR
Southern Arkansas University–El Dorado Branch, AR
Southern Arkansas University Tech, AR
Southern Baptist College, AR
Southern California College, CA
Southern Connecticut State University, CT
Southern Illinois University at Carbondale, IL
Southern Illinois University at Edwardsville, IL
Southern Institute, AL
Southern Maine Vocational-Technical Institute, ME
Southern Ohio College, Cincinnati Campus, OH
Southern Ohio College, Fairfield Campus, OH
Southern Ohio College, Northeast Campus, OH
Southern Ohio College, Northern Kentucky Campus, KY
Southern Oregon State College, OR
Southern State Community College, OH
Southern Technical Institute, GA
Southern Union State Junior College, AL
Southern University, Shreveport–Bossier City Campus, LA
Southern Vermont College, VT
Southern West Virginia Community College, WV
South Georgia College, GA
South Mountain Community College, AZ
South Plains College, TX
South Puget Sound Community College, WA
South Seattle Community College, WA
Southside Virginia Community College, VA
Southwestern College, CA
Southwestern College of Business, Kettering, OH
Southwestern Community College, IA
Southwestern Michigan College, MI
Southwestern Oklahoma State University, OK
Southwestern Oregon Community College, OR
Southwestern Technical College, NC
Southwest Mississippi Junior College, MS
Southwest Missouri State University, MO
Southwest State Technical College, AL
Southwest State University, MN
Southwest Texas Junior College, TX

375

Directories of Specialized Information

Part-Time Evening Programs (continued)

Southwest Texas State University, TX
Southwest Virginia Community College, VA
Spartanburg Methodist College, SC
Spartanburg Technical College, SC
Spertus College of Judaica, IL
Spokane Community College, WA
Spokane Falls Community College, WA
Spring Arbor College, MI
Springfield College, MA
Springfield College in Illinois, IL
Springfield Technical Community College, MA
Spring Garden College, PA
Spring Hill College, AL
Stanly Technical College, NC
Stark Technical College, OH
State Fair Community College, MO
State Technical Institute at Knoxville, TN
State Technical Institute at Memphis, TN
State University of New York Agricultural and Technical College at Canton, NY
State University of New York Agricultural and Technical College at Cobleskill, NY
State University of New York Agricultural and Technical College at Farmingdale, NY
State University of New York Agricultural and Technical College at Morrisville, NY
State University of New York at Albany, NY
State University of New York at Binghamton, NY
State University of New York at Buffalo, NY
State University of New York at Stony Brook, NY
State University of New York College at Brockport, NY
State University of New York College at Buffalo, NY
State University of New York College at Fredonia, NY
State University of New York College at Geneseo, NY
State University of New York College at New Paltz, NY
State University of New York College at Old Westbury, NY
State University of New York College at Oneonta, NY
State University of New York College at Purchase, NY
State University of New York College of Technology at Utica/Rome, NY
State University of New York Empire State College, NY
Stautzenberger College, OH
Stephen F Austin State University, TX
Stetson University, FL
Stevens Henager College, UT
Stockton State College, NJ
Stonehill College, MA
Stratton College, WI
Strayer College, DC
Suffolk County Community College–Eastern Campus, NY
Suffolk County Community College–Selden Campus, NY
Suffolk County Community College–Western Campus, NY
Suffolk University, MA
Sullivan County Community College, NY
Sullivan Junior College of Business, KY
Sumter Area Technical College, SC
Suomi College, MI
Surry Community College, NC
Susquehanna University, PA
Swain School of Design, MA
Syracuse University, NY
Sysorex Institute, CA
Tabor College, KS
Tacoma Community College, WA
Taft College, CA
Tallahassee Community College, FL
Tampa College, FL
Tarkio College, MO
Tarleton State University, TX
Tarrant County Junior College, TX
Technical Career Institutes, NY

Technical College of Alamance, NC
Temple University, Philadelphia, PA
Temple University, Ambler Campus, PA
Tennessee State University, TN
Tennessee Temple University, TN
Terra Technical College, OH
Texarkana Community College, TX
Texas Christian University, TX
Texas Southern University, TX
Texas Southmost College, TX
Texas State Technical Institute–Amarillo Campus, TX
Texas State Technical Institute–Harlingen Campus, TX
Texas State Technical Institute–Sweetwater Campus, TX
Texas State Technical Institute–Waco Campus, TX
Texas Tech University, TX
Texas Wesleyan College, TX
Texas Woman's University, TX
Thames Valley State Technical College, CT
Thomas College, ME
Thomas County Community College, GA
Thomas Jefferson University, PA
Thomas More College, KY
Thomas Nelson Community College, VA
Thornton Community College, IL
Three Rivers Community College, MO
Tidewater Community College, Chesapeake Campus, VA
Tidewater Community College, Frederick Campus, VA
Tidewater Community College, Virginia Beach Campus, VA
Tiffin University, OH
Tift College, GA
Tomlinson College, TN
Tompkins Cortland Community College, NY
Tougaloo College, MS
Touro College, NY
Towson State University, MD
Treasure Valley Community College, OR
Trenholm State Technical College, AL
Trenton Junior College, MO
Trenton State College, NJ
Trevecca Nazarene College, TN
Triangle Institute of Technology, Greensburg, PA
Tri-Cities State Technical Institute, TN
Tri-County Community College, NC
Tri-County Technical College, SC
Trident Technical College, SC
Trinidad State Junior College, CO
Trinity Christian College, IL
Trinity College, DC
Trinity College, VT
Triton College, IL
Trocaire College, NY
Troy State University, Troy, AL
Troy State University at Dothan/Fort Rucker, AL
Troy State University in Montgomery, AL
Truckee Meadows Community College, NV
Truett-McConnell College, GA
Tulsa Junior College, OK
Tunxis Community College, CT
Tusculum College, TN
Tyler Junior College, TX
Ulster County Community College, NY
Umpqua Community College, OR
Union College, NY
Union University, TN
United States International University, CA
United Wesleyan College, PA
Universidad del Turabo, PR
Universidad Politécnica de Puerto Rico, PR
University of Akron, OH
University of Alabama, University, AL
University of Alabama in Birmingham, AL
University of Alaska, Anchorage, AK
University of Alaska, Anchorage Community College, AK

Directories of Specialized Information

University of Alaska, Fairbanks, AK
University of Alaska, Islands Community College, AK
University of Alaska, Juneau, AK
University of Alaska, Ketchikan Community College, AK
University of Alaska, Matanuska-Susitna Community College, AK
University of Alaska, Tanana Valley Community College, AK
University of Albuquerque, NM
University of Arizona, AZ
University of Arkansas at Little Rock, AR
University of Arkansas at Monticello, AR
University of Arkansas at Pine Bluff, AR
University of Baltimore, MD
University of Bridgeport, CT
University of California, Santa Cruz, CA
University of Central Florida, FL
University of Charleston, WV
University of Cincinnati, OH
University of Cincinnati, Clermont General and Technical College, OH
University of Cincinnati, Raymond Walters General and Technical College, OH
University of Colorado at Colorado Springs, CO
University of Colorado at Denver, CO
University of Dayton, OH
University of Delaware, DE
University of Denver, CO
University of Detroit, MI
University of Dubuque, IA
University of Evansville, IN
University of Guam, GU
University of Hartford, CT
University of Hawaii at Hilo, HI
University of Hawaii at Manoa, HI
University of Hawaii–Honolulu Community College, HI
University of Hawaii–Leeward Community College, HI
University of Hawaii–Maui Community College, HI
University of Hawaii–West Oahu College, HI
University of Hawaii–Windward Community College, HI
University of Houston–Clear Lake, TX
University of Houston–Downtown, TX
University of Houston–University Park, TX
University of Illinois at Chicago, University Center, IL
University of Judaism, CA
University of Kentucky, KY
University of Kentucky, Ashland Community College, KY
University of Kentucky, Elizabethtown Community College, KY
University of Kentucky, Hazard Community College, KY
University of Kentucky, Hopkinsville Community College, KY
University of Kentucky, Jefferson Community College, KY
University of Kentucky, Lexington Community College, KY
University of Kentucky, Madisonville Community College, KY
University of Kentucky, Maysville Community College, KY
University of Kentucky, Paducah Community College, KY
University of Kentucky, Somerset Community College, KY
University of Kentucky, Southeast Community College, KY
University of La Verne, CA
University of Louisville, KY
University of Lowell, MA
University of Maine at Augusta, ME
University of Maine at Farmington, ME
University of Maine at Fort Kent, ME
University of Maine at Machias, ME
University of Maine at Orono, ME
University of Maine at Presque Isle, ME
University of Mary Hardin-Baylor, TX
University of Maryland at Baltimore, MD
University of Maryland at College Park, MD
University of Maryland Baltimore County, MD
University of Maryland, University College, MD

University of Massachusetts at Amherst, MA
University of Massachusetts at Boston, MA
University of Miami, FL
University of Michigan–Dearborn, MI
University of Michigan–Flint, MI
University of Minnesota, Duluth, MN
University of Minnesota, Morris, MN
University of Minnesota Technical College, Crookston, MN
University of Minnesota Technical College, Waseca, MN
University of Minnesota, Twin Cities Campus, MN
University of Missouri–Columbia, MO
University of Missouri–Kansas City, MO
University of Missouri–Rolla, MO
University of Missouri–St Louis, MO
University of Montana, MT
University of Nebraska at Omaha, NE
University of Nebraska–Lincoln, NE
University of Nevada Reno, NV
University of New England, ME
University of New Hampshire, NH
University of New Haven, CT
University of New Mexico Gallup Branch, NM
University of New Mexico–Los Alamos, NM
University of New Orleans, LA
University of North Alabama, AL
University of North Carolina at Asheville, NC
University of North Carolina at Charlotte, NC
University of North Carolina at Greensboro, NC
University of North Dakota–Williston Center, ND
University of Northern Colorado, CO
University of Northern Iowa, IA
University of North Florida, FL
University of Oklahoma, OK
University of Pennsylvania, PA
University of Pittsburgh, Pittsburgh, PA
University of Pittsburgh at Bradford, PA
University of Pittsburgh at Greensburg, PA
University of Pittsburgh at Johnstown, PA
University of Pittsburgh at Titusville, PA
University of Portland, OR
University of Puerto Rico, Cayey University College, PR
University of Puerto Rico, Humacao University College, PR
University of Puerto Rico, Ponce Technological University College, PR
University of Puerto Rico, Río Piedras, PR
University of Rhode Island, RI
University of Richmond, VA
University of St Thomas, TX
University of San Diego, CA
University of San Francisco, CA
University of Sarasota, FL
University of Scranton, PA
University of South Alabama, AL
University of South Carolina, Columbia, SC
University of South Carolina at Aiken, SC
University of South Carolina at Beaufort, SC
University of South Carolina at Lancaster, SC
University of South Carolina at Salkehatchie, SC
University of South Carolina at Spartanburg, SC
University of South Carolina at Sumter, SC
University of South Carolina–Coastal Carolina College, SC
University of South Dakota, SD
University of Southern California, CA
University of Southern Colorado, CO
University of Southern Maine, ME
University of Southern Mississippi, MS
University of South Florida, FL
University of Southwestern Louisiana, LA
University of Steubenville, OH
University of Tampa, FL
University of Tennessee at Chattanooga, TN
University of Tennessee at Martin, TN
University of Texas at Arlington, TX

Directories of Specialized Information

Part-Time Evening Programs (continued)
University of Texas at Dallas, TX
University of Texas at El Paso, TX
University of Texas at San Antonio, TX
University of Texas at Tyler, TX
University of Texas Health Science Center at San Antonio, TX
University of Texas of the Permian Basin, TX
University of the District of Columbia, DC
University of the Sacred Heart, PR
University of Toledo, OH
University of Washington, WA
University of West Florida, FL
University of West Los Angeles, CA
University of Wisconsin Center–Baraboo/Sauk County, WI
University of Wisconsin Center–Fox Valley, WI
University of Wisconsin Center–Manitowoc County, WI
University of Wisconsin Center–Marathon County, WI
University of Wisconsin Center–Marinette County, WI
University of Wisconsin Center–Marshfield/Wood County, WI
University of Wisconsin Center–Richland, WI
University of Wisconsin Center–Rock County, WI
University of Wisconsin Center–Sheboygan County, WI
University of Wisconsin Center–Washington County, WI
University of Wisconsin Center–Waukesha County, WI
University of Wisconsin–Eau Claire, WI
University of Wisconsin–Green Bay, WI
University of Wisconsin–La Crosse, WI
University of Wisconsin–Milwaukee, WI
University of Wisconsin–Oshkosh, WI
University of Wisconsin–Parkside, WI
University of Wisconsin–Stevens Point, WI
University of Wisconsin–Superior, WI
University of Wisconsin–Whitewater, WI
Upper Iowa University, IA
Upsala College, NJ
Urbana College, OH
Ursinus College, PA
Ursuline College, OH
Utah State University, UT
Utah Technical College at Provo, UT
Utah Technical College at Salt Lake, UT
Utica College of Syracuse University, NY
Valdosta State College, GA
Valencia Community College, FL
Valley City State College, ND
Valparaiso University, IN
Vance-Granville Community College, NC
Vennard College, IA
Vermillion Community College, MN
Vernon Regional Junior College, TX
Victoria College, TX
Victor Valley College, CA
Villa Julie College, MD
Villa Maria College, PA
Villanova University, PA
Vincennes University, IN
Virginia Commonwealth University, VA
Virginia Highlands Community College, VA
Virginia Intermont College, VA
Virginia Western Community College, VA
Viterbo College, WI
Volunteer State Community College, TN
Voorhees College, SC
Wake Technical College, NC
Walker College, AL
Wallace State Community College, AL
Walla Walla Community College, WA
Walsh College, OH
Walsh College of Accountancy and Business Administration, MI
Walters State Community College, TN

Warner Southern College, FL
Wartburg College, IA
Washburn University of Topeka, KS
Washington Bible College, MD
Washington College, MD
Washington Technical College, OH
Washington University, MO
Washtenaw Community College, MI
Waterbury State Technical College, CT
Watterson College, KY
Waubonsee Community College, IL
Waycross Junior College, GA
Wayland Baptist University, TX
Wayne Community College, NC
Wayne County Community College, MI
Waynesburg College, PA
Wayne State University, MI
Weatherford College, TX
Webber College, FL
Weber State College, UT
Webster University, MO
Wenatchee Valley College, WA
Wentworth Institute of Technology, MA
Wesleyan College, GA
Wesley College, DE
Westark Community College, AR
Westbrook College, ME
Westchester Business Institute, NY
Westchester Community College, NY
West Chester University of Pennsylvania, PA
West Coast University, CA
Western Carolina University, NC
Western Connecticut State University, CT
Western Illinois University, IL
Western International University, AZ
Western Iowa Tech Community College, IA
Western Kentucky University, KY
Western Nevada Community College, NV
Western New England College, MA
Western Oklahoma State College, OK
Western Oregon State College, OR
Western Piedmont Community College, NC
Western State University College of Law of Orange County, CA
Western State University College of Law of San Diego, CA
Western Texas College, TX
Western Wisconsin Technical Institute, WI
Western Wyoming Community College, WY
Westfield State College, MA
West Georgia College, GA
West Hills College, CA
West Los Angeles College, CA
Westmar College, IA
Westminster College, PA
Westminster College of Salt Lake City, UT
Westmoreland County Community College, PA
West Shore Community College, MI
West Texas State University, TX
West Valley College, CA
West Virginia Institute of Technology, WV
West Virginia Northern Community College, WV
West Virginia State College, WV
West Virginia Wesleyan College, WV
Wharton County Junior College, TX
Whatcom Community College, WA
Wheeling College, WV
White Pines College, NH
Whitworth College, WA
Wichita State University, KS
Widener University, Delaware Campus, DE
Widener University, Pennsylvania Campus, PA
Wiley College, TX
Wilkes College, PA

378

Directories of Specialized Information

Wilkes Community College, NC
William Carey College, MS
William Jewell College, MO
William Paterson College of New Jersey, NJ
William Rainey Harper College, IL
Williamsburg Technical College, SC
Williamsport Area Community College, PA
Willmar Community College, MN
Wilmington College, DE
Wilson College, PA
Winona State University, MN
Winston-Salem State University, NC
Winthrop College, SC
Wisconsin Indianhead Technical Institute, Ashland Campus, WI
Wisconsin Indianhead Technical Institute, New Richmond Campus, WI
Wisconsin Indianhead Technical Institute, Rice Lake Campus, WI
Wisconsin Indianhead Technical Institute, Superior Campus, WI
Wisconsin Lutheran College, WI
Wittenberg University, OH
Woodbury University, CA
Wood Junior College, MS
Worcester Polytechnic Institute, MA
Worcester State College, MA
Worthington Community College, MN
Wor-Wic Tech Community College, MD
Wright State University, OH
Wright State University, Western Ohio Branch Campus, OH
Xavier University, OH
Yakima Valley Community College, WA
Yankton College, SD
Yavapai College, AZ
York College of Pennsylvania, PA
York Technical College, SC
Youngstown State University, OH
Yuba College, CA

Colleges Offering Part-Time Weekend Programs

Alabama Aviation and Technical College, AL
Alabama State University, AL
Albany Business College, NY
Albany State College, GA
Albertus Magnus College, CT
Allentown Business School, PA
Alvernia College, PA
Alverno College, WI
Amber University, TX
American Academy of Art, IL
American Conservatory of Music, IL
American Institute of Business, IA
American Technological University, TX
Aquinas College, MI
Arkansas State University–Beebe Branch, AR
Ashland College, OH
Athens State College, AL
Atlanta College of Art, GA
Atlantic Community College, NJ
Auburn University at Montgomery, AL
Augsburg College, MN
Augustana College, SD
Aurora College, IL
Avila College, MO
Baldwin-Wallace College, OH
Barstow College, CA
Bay de Noc Community College, MI
Bergen Community College, NJ
Bishop College, TX

Blue Mountain College, MS
Bowie State College, MD
Brewton-Parker College, GA
Briar Cliff College, IA
Briarcliffe Secretarial School, NY
Brookdale Community College, NJ
Bryant and Stratton Business Institute, Buffalo, NY
Bryant and Stratton Business Institute, Eastern Hills Campus, NY
Bryant College, RI
Bucks County Community College, PA
Bunker Hill Community College, MA
Burlington County College, NJ
Butler County Community College, PA
California State University, Chico, CA
California State University, Long Beach, CA
California State University, Sacramento, CA
Calumet College, IN
Campbell University, NC
Canisius College, NY
Capitol Institute of Technology, MD
Carlow College, PA
Carl Sandburg College, IL
Cedar Crest College, PA
Cedar Valley College, TX
Central Community College–Hastings Campus, NE
Central Community College–Platte Campus, NE
Central Missouri State University, MO
Central New England College, MA
Central Piedmont Community College, NC
Central Texas College, TX
Chabot College, CA
Chaminade University of Honolulu, HI
Chattahoochee Valley State Community College, AL
Chicago College of Commerce, IL
Christopher Newport College, VA
Cincinnati Technical College, OH
Citrus College, CA
City University, WA
City University of New York, Borough of Manhattan Community College, NY
City University of New York, Bronx Community College, NY
City University of New York, Brooklyn College, NY
City University of New York, College of Staten Island, NY
City University of New York, Queensborough Community College, NY
City University of New York, Queens College, NY
Clarendon College, TX
Clayton University, MO
Cleary College, MI
Cochise College, AZ
Coffeyville Community College, KS
College Misericordia, PA
College of DuPage, IL
College of Lake County, IL
College of Mount St Joseph on the Ohio, OH
College of Mount Saint Vincent, NY
College of Notre Dame of Maryland, MD
College of St Catherine, MN
College of Saint Elizabeth, NJ
College of Saint Mary, NE
College of St Thomas, MN
College of Santa Fe, NM
College of the Sequoias, CA
College of the Siskiyous, CA
Columbia College, IL
Community College of Allegheny County–Boyce Campus, PA
Community College of Allegheny County–College Center North, PA
Community College of Philadelphia, PA
Community College of Rhode Island, Flanagan Campus, RI
Community College of Rhode Island, Knight Campus, RI
Community College of the Finger Lakes, NY

Directories of Specialized Information

Part-Time Weekend Programs (continued)
Community College of Vermont, VT
Contra Costa College, CA
County College of Morris, NJ
Creighton University, NE
Cuyahoga Community College, Eastern Campus, OH
Cuyahoga Community College, Western Campus, OH
Cypress College, CA
Dakota Wesleyan University, SD
Davenport College of Business, MI
Daytona Beach Community College, FL
DeKalb Community College, GA
Delaware County Community College, PA
Delta College, MI
Delta State University, MS
Denver Auraria Community College, CO
DePaul University, IL
Detroit College of Business, Madison Heights Campus, MI
Dominican College of Blauvelt, NY
Drake University, IA
Drury College, MO
Dundalk Community College, MD
Dyke College, OH
Eastern Connecticut State University, CT
Eastern Oklahoma State College, OK
Eastern Washington University, WA
East Texas State University, Commerce, TX
Eckerd College, FL
Edgewood College, WI
Edinboro University of Pennsylvania, PA
Edward Waters College, FL
El Centro College, TX
Elizabeth Seton College, NY
Elmira College, NY
El Paso Community College, TX
Embry-Riddle Aeronautical University, International Campus, FL
Essex Community College, MD
Evergreen State College, WA
Evergreen Valley College, CA
Fairleigh Dickinson University, Edward Williams College, NJ
Fashion Institute of Technology, NY
Fayetteville State University, NC
Findlay College, OH
Fisher Junior College, MA
Florida Agricultural and Mechanical University, FL
Florida Memorial College, FL
Fontbonne College, MO
Foothill College, CA
Franklin University, OH
Frank Phillips College, TX
Front Range Community College, CO
Fullerton College, CA
Fulton-Montgomery Community College, NY
Gloucester County College, NJ
Governors State University, IL
Grand Rapids Junior College, MI
Gratz College, PA
Greater Hartford Community College, CT
Guam Community College, GU
Hardin-Simmons University, TX
Harford Community College, MD
Harrisburg Area Community College, PA
Hawthorne College, NH
Hebrew College, MA
Heidelberg College, OH
Henry Ford Community College, MI
Heritage College, WA
Highland Community College, KS
Hillsborough Community College, FL
Hiram College, OH
Holy Names College, CA

Houston Community College System, TX
Howard Community College, MD
Husson College, ME
Illinois Central College, IL
Illinois Eastern Community Colleges, Frontier Community College, IL
Illinois Eastern Community Colleges, Lincoln Trail College, IL
Illinois Eastern Community Colleges, Olney Central College, IL
Illinois Eastern Community Colleges, Wabash Valley College, IL
Indiana State University, Terre Haute, IN
Indiana State University Evansville, IN
Indiana University at South Bend, IN
Indiana University–Purdue University at Indianapolis, IN
Indiana University Southeast, IN
Indiana Vocational Technical College–Whitewater, IN
Inter American University of Puerto Rico, Barranquitas Regional College, PR
Inter American University of Puerto Rico, Metropolitan Campus, PR
Iona College, NY
Iowa Lakes Community College, North Attendance Center, IA
Iowa Lakes Community College, South Attendance Center, IA
Iowa Western Community College, IA
Isothermal Community College, NC
Itasca Community College, MN
Jackson Community College, MI
Jackson State University, MS
Johnson & Wales College, RI
John Wood Community College, IL
J Sargeant Reynolds Community College, VA
Kean College of New Jersey, NJ
Kearney State College, NE
Kellogg Community College, MI
Kennebec Valley Vocational-Technical Institute, ME
Kent State University, Trumbull Campus, OH
Kentucky State University, KY
Keystone Junior College, PA
Kirkwood Community College, IA
Kirtland Community College, MI
Kutztown University of Pennsylvania, PA
Lake Land College, IL
Lakeland Community College, OH
Lakeshore Technical Institute, WI
Lamar Community College, CO
Langston University, OK
Lansing Community College, MI
La Salle University, PA
Lebanon Valley College, PA
Lesley College, MA
Lewis-Clark State College, ID
Lewis University, IL
Lincoln Land Community College, IL
Lincoln University, MO
Lindenwood College, MO
Linfield College, OR
Long Island University, C W Post Campus, NY
Longview Community College, MO
Loretto Heights College, CO
Los Angeles Harbor College, CA
Los Angeles Trade-Technical College, CA
Louisburg College, NC
Lourdes College, OH
Loyola University, New Orleans, LA
Macomb Community College, MI
Manchester Community College, CT
Manhattan College, NY
Maple Woods Community College, MO
Maria College, NY
Maria Regina College, NY

Directories of Specialized Information

Martin Center College, IN
Mary College, ND
Marycrest College, IA
Marylhurst College for Lifelong Learning, OR
Marymount College, NY
Marymount Manhattan College, NY
Marymount Palos Verdes College, CA
Maryville College, TN
Maryville College–Saint Louis, MO
Mary Washington College, VA
Marywood College, PA
Massachusetts Bay Community College, MA
McDowell Technical College, NC
McLennan Community College, TX
Meadows Junior College, GA
Mendocino College, CA
Mercer County Community College, NJ
Mercy College, NY
Mercy College of Detroit, MI
Mercyhurst College, PA
Merritt College, CA
Metropolitan State University, MN
Miami-Dade Community College, FL
Middlesex County College, NJ
Millersville University of Pennsylvania, PA
Minneapolis Community College, MN
Mission College, CA
Mississippi University for Women, MS
Modesto Junior College, CA
Mohave Community College, AZ
Mohawk Valley Community College, NY
Mohegan Community College, CT
Molloy College, NY
Monmouth College, NJ
Montclair State College, NJ
Monterey Peninsula College, CA
Moraine Valley Community College, IL
Mount Mercy College, IA
Mount Saint Mary College, NY
Mount Senario College, WI
Mundelein College, IL
Muskegon Community College, MI
Napa Valley College, CA
Nassau Community College, NY
Nazareth College, MI
Newbury Junior College, MA
New College of California, CA
New Hampshire College, NH
New Mexico Highlands University, NM
New Mexico Junior College, NM
New York University, NY
Niagara County Community College, NY
Normandale Community College, MN
North Central College, IL
Northeast Alabama State Junior College, AL
Northeastern University, MA
Northern Illinois University, IL
Northern Nevada Community College, NV
Northern Virginia Community College, VA
North Florida Junior College, FL
North Shore Community College, MA
North Texas State University, TX
Northwestern Michigan College, MI
Northwestern University, Evanston, IL
Northwood Institute, MI
Norwalk Community College, CT
Norwich University, Vermont College, VT
Notre Dame College of Ohio, OH
Nova University, FL
Oakland City College, IN
Oakton Community College, IL
Ocean County College, NJ
Ohio Dominican College, OH

Ohio University–Chillicothe, OH
Ohio University–Lancaster, OH
Oklahoma City University, OK
Oklahoma State University Technical Institute, OK
Olympic College, WA
Onondaga Community College, NY
Orange Coast College, CA
Otis Art Institute of Parsons School of Design, CA
Our Lady of Holy Cross College, LA
Our Lady of the Lake University of San Antonio, TX
Owens Technical College, OH
Oxnard College, CA
Pace University–Pleasantville/Briarcliff, NY
Park College, MO
Patrick Henry Community College, VA
Paul D Camp Community College, VA
Peirce Junior College, PA
Penn Valley Community College, MO
Pepperdine University, Pepperdine Plaza, CA
Piedmont Virginia Community College, VA
Pikes Peak Community College, CO
Pioneer Community College, MO
Point Park College, PA
Prairie View A&M University, TX
Prince George's Community College, MD
Purdue University Calumet, IN
Queens College, NC
Quincy Junior College, MA
Ramapo College of New Jersey, NJ
Reno Business College, NV
Richland College, TX
Rio Hondo Community College, CA
Rockford College, IL
Rockland Community College, NY
Rock Valley College, IL
Roger Williams College, RI
Roosevelt University, IL
Rosary College, IL
Rose State College, OK
Rutgers University, Camden College of Arts and Sciences, NJ
Sacred Heart University, CT
Saddleback Community College, CA
St Ambrose College, IA
St Francis College, NY
St John's University, NY
St Joseph's College, Brooklyn, NY
Saint Joseph's University, PA
Saint Leo College, FL
St Louis Community College at Florissant Valley, MO
St Louis Community College at Forest Park, MO
St Louis Community College at Meramec, MO
Saint Mary College, KS
St Mary's Junior College, MN
Saint Peter's College, Jersey City, NJ
St Thomas of Villanova University, FL
Saint Xavier College, IL
Salem Community College, NJ
Salve Regina–The Newport College, RI
San Diego City College, CA
San Diego Mesa College, CA
San Diego Miramar College, CA
San Jacinto College–Central Campus, TX
San Jacinto College–North Campus, TX
San Jacinto College–South Campus, TX
San Jose City College, CA
Santa Ana College, CA
Santa Rosa Junior College, CA
Savannah College of Art and Design, GA
School for Lifelong Learning of the University System of New Hampshire, NH
School of the Art Institute of Chicago, IL
Scott Community College, IA
Seattle Pacific University, WA

Directories of Specialized Information

Part-Time Weekend Programs (continued)

Seminole Junior College, OK
Seton Hill College, PA
Shimer College, IL
Siena Heights College, MI
Sinclair Community College, OH
Sioux Empire College, IA
Snow College, UT
Sojourner-Douglass College, MD
Southeast Community College, Lincoln Campus, NE
Southeastern University, DC
Southern Illinois University at Edwardsville, IL
Southern University and Agricultural and Mechanical College, LA
Southern Vermont College, VT
South Seattle Community College, WA
Southwestern Michigan College, MI
Spalding University, KY
Spartanburg Methodist College, SC
Spokane Falls Community College, WA
Springfield Technical Community College, MA
State Technical Institute at Memphis, TN
State University of New York Agricultural and Technical College at Alfred, NY
State University of New York at Buffalo, NY
State University of New York College at Brockport, NY
State University of New York College at Geneseo, NY
State University of New York Empire State College, NY
Stautzenberger College, OH
Stephen F Austin State University, TX
Strayer College, DC
Suffolk County Community College–Selden Campus, NY
Syracuse University, NY
Tacoma Community College, WA
Taft College, CA
Tampa College, FL
Tennessee State University, TN
Texas Southern University, TX
Texas Southmost College, TX
Texas Woman's University, TX
Thomas College, ME
Thomas More College, KY
Thomas Nelson Community College, VA
Thornton Community College, IL
Towson State University, MD
Trevecca Nazarene College, TN
Trinidad State Junior College, CO
Trinity College, DC
Trinity College, VT
Triton College, IL
Trocaire College, NY
Troy State University in Montgomery, AL
Truckee Meadows Community College, NV
Ulster County Community College, NY
University of Alabama, University, AL
University of Alabama in Birmingham, AL
University of Alaska, Anchorage, AK
University of Alaska, Ketchikan Community College, AK
University of Albuquerque, NM
University of Arkansas at Pine Bluff, AR
University of Baltimore, MD
University of Bridgeport, CT
University of Denver, CO
University of Hawaii–Leeward Community College, HI
University of Hawaii–Maui Community College, HI
University of Hawaii–West Oahu College, HI
University of Houston–Downtown, TX
University of La Verne, CA
University of Maine at Orono, ME
University of Maryland, University College, MD
University of Minnesota, Twin Cities Campus, MN
University of Missouri–Kansas City, MO

University of Nebraska at Omaha, NE
University of New Haven, CT
University of Oklahoma, OK
University of Pennsylvania, PA
University of Pittsburgh, Pittsburgh, PA
University of Puerto Rico, Cayey University College, PR
University of Puerto Rico, Humacao University College, PR
University of Rhode Island, RI
University of St Thomas, TX
University of San Francisco, CA
University of Sarasota, FL
University of Texas Health Science Center at San Antonio, TX
University of Wisconsin–La Crosse, WI
University of Wisconsin–Milwaukee, WI
University of Wisconsin–Oshkosh, WI
University of Wisconsin–Superior, WI
Upsala College, NJ
Utah Technical College at Provo, UT
Valencia Community College, FL
VanderCook College of Music, IL
Vermillion Community College, MN
Villanova University, PA
Virginia State University, VA
Virginia Western Community College, VA
Washburn University of Topeka, KS
Washington Bible College, MD
Washtenaw Community College, MI
Wayne County Community College, MI
Wayne State University, MI
Wentworth Institute of Technology, MA
Westbrook College, ME
Western Carolina University, NC
Western State University College of Law of Orange County, CA
Western State University College of Law of San Diego, CA
Westfield State College, MA
Westmoreland County Community College, PA
Whitworth College, WA
Wichita State University, KS
Wilkes College, PA
William Carey College, MS
William Paterson College of New Jersey, NJ
Winona State University, MN
Xavier University, OH
Youngstown State University, OH

Colleges Offering Part-Time Summer Programs

Abilene Christian University, TX
Academy of Aeronautics, NY
Academy of Art College, CA
Adams State College, CO
Adirondack Community College, NY
Aiken Technical College, SC
Aims Community College, CO
Alabama Agricultural and Mechanical University, AL
Alabama Aviation and Technical College, AL
Alabama State University, AL
Alaska Pacific University, AK
Albany State College, GA
Albright College, PA
Alderson-Broaddus College, WV
Alexander City State Junior College, AL
Alice Lloyd College, KY
Allan Hancock College, CA
Allegany Community College, MD
Allegheny College, PA
Allen County Community College, KS
Alvin Community College, TX
Amarillo College, TX

Directories of Specialized Information

Amber University, TX
American Academy of Art, IL
American Baptist College of American Baptist Theological Seminary, TN
American College of Puerto Rico, PR
American Conservatory of Music, IL
American Institute of Business, IA
American International College, MA
American River College, CA
American Samoa Community College, AS
American Technological University, TX
American University, DC
Ancilla College, IN
Anderson College, SC
Andrew College, GA
Angelina College, TX
Anna Maria College for Men and Women, MA
Anne Arundel Community College, MD
Anoka-Ramsey Community College, MN
Anson Technical College, NC
Antelope Valley College, CA
Antillian College, PR
Antioch University West, CA
Appalachian State University, NC
Aquinas College, MI
Aquinas Junior College, TN
Arapahoe Community College, CO
Arizona College of the Bible, AZ
Arizona State University, AZ
Arkansas State University–Beebe Branch, AR
Arkansas Tech University, AR
Armstrong College, CA
Armstrong State College, GA
Ashland College, OH
Asnuntuck Community College, CT
Assumption College, MA
Athens State College, AL
Atlanta College of Art, GA
Atlanta Junior College, GA
Atlantic Christian College, NC
Atlantic Community College, NJ
Auburn University, AL
Auburn University at Montgomery, AL
Augustana College, SD
Austin Community College, MN
Austin Community College, TX
Averett College, VA
Bacone College, OK
Bainbridge Junior College, GA
Baker Junior College of Business, MI
Bakersfield College, CA
Baker University, KS
Baldwin-Wallace College, OH
Ball State University, IN
Baptist Bible College, MO
Baptist College at Charleston, SC
Barat College, IL
Barstow College, CA
Bartlesville Wesleyan College, OK
Barton County Community College, KS
Bay de Noc Community College, MI
Baylor University, TX
Beal College, ME
Beaufort County Community College, NC
Beaufort Technical College, SC
Becker Junior College–Worcester Campus, MA
Beckley College, WV
Belhaven College, MS
Bellarmine College, KY
Belleville Area College, IL
Belmont College, TN
Belmont Technical College, OH
Bemidji State University, MN

Benedictine College, KS
Bergen Community College, NJ
Berkshire Community College, MA
Bethel College, TN
Big Bend Community College, WA
Bishop Clarkson College of Nursing, NE
Bishop College, TX
Bismarck Junior College, ND
Black Hawk College–East Campus, IL
Blackhawk Technical Institute, WI
Black Hills State College, SD
Bladen Technical College, NC
Bloomsburg University of Pennsylvania, PA
Bluefield State College, WV
Blue Mountain College, MS
Blue Ridge Community College, VA
Blue Ridge Technical College, NC
Bob Jones University, SC
Boston Architectural Center, MA
Boston College, MA
Boston University, MA
Bowie State College, MD
Bowling Green Junior College of Business, KY
Bowling Green State University, OH
Bradley University, IL
Brandeis University, MA
Brazosport College, TX
Brenau College, GA
Brescia College, KY
Brevard Community College, FL
Brewer State Junior College, AL
Brewton-Parker College, GA
Briar Cliff College, IA
Bridgewater College, VA
Brigham Young University, UT
Brigham Young University–Hawaii Campus, HI
Brookdale Community College, NJ
Broome Community College, NY
Broward Community College, FL
Bryant and Stratton Business Institute, Buffalo, NY
Bryant and Stratton Business Institute, Eastern Hills Campus, NY
Bryant College, RI
Bucks County Community College, PA
Bunker Hill Community College, MA
Burlington College, VT
Burlington County College, NJ
Butler County Community College, KS
Butler County Community College, PA
Butler University, IN
Butte College, CA
Cabrillo College, CA
Cabrini College, PA
Caldwell College, NJ
Caldwell Community College and Technical Institute, NC
California Baptist College, CA
California College of Arts and Crafts, CA
California Lutheran College, CA
California Polytechnic State University, San Luis Obispo, CA
California State College, San Bernardino, CA
California State Polytechnic University, Pomona, CA
California State University, Chico, CA
California State University, Fresno, CA
California State University, Hayward, CA
California State University, Long Beach, CA
California State University, Los Angeles, CA
California State University, Northridge, CA
California State University, Sacramento, CA
California University of Pennsylvania, PA
Calumet College, IN
Calvin College, MI
Cameron University, OK
Campbell University, NC

Directories of Specialized Information

Part-Time Summer Programs (continued)
Canisius College, NY
Cape Cod Community College, MA
Cape Fear Technical Institute, NC
Capitol Institute of Technology, MD
Carl Sandburg College, IL
Carroll College, WI
Carroll College of Montana, MT
Carthage College, WI
Castleton State College, VT
Catawba College, NC
Catholic University of America, DC
Catholic University of Puerto Rico, Mayagüez Center, PR
Cayuga County Community College, NY
Cecil Community College, MD
Cecils Junior College of Business, NC
Cedar Crest College, PA
Centenary College of Louisiana, LA
Central Bible College, MO
Central Community College–Grand Island Campus, NE
Central Community College–Hastings Campus, NE
Central Community College–Platte Campus, NE
Central Connecticut State University, CT
Central Florida Community College, FL
Centralia College, WA
Central Michigan University, MI
Central Missouri State University, MO
Central New England College, MA
Central Pennsylvania Business School, PA
Central Piedmont Community College, NC
Central State University, OH
Central State University, OK
Central Texas College, TX
Central University of Iowa, IA
Central Virginia Community College, VA
Central Washington University, WA
Central Wesleyan College, SC
Central Wyoming College, WY
Cerritos College, CA
Chabot College, CA
Chaffey College, CA
Chaminade University of Honolulu, HI
Champlain College, VT
Chapman College, CA
Charles County Community College, MD
Charles Stewart Mott Community College, MI
Chatfield College, OH
Chattahoochee Valley State Community College, AL
Chattanooga State Technical Community College, TN
Chesapeake College, MD
Chestnut Hill College, PA
Chicago State University, IL
Chipola Junior College, FL
Chowan College, NC
Christopher Newport College, VA
The Citadel, SC
Citrus College, CA
City College of San Francisco, CA
City Colleges of Chicago, Chicago City-Wide College, IL
City Colleges of Chicago, Harry S Truman College, IL
City Colleges of Chicago, Kennedy-King College, IL
City Colleges of Chicago, Loop College, IL
City Colleges of Chicago, Malcolm X College, IL
City Colleges of Chicago, Olive-Harvey College, IL
City Colleges of Chicago, Richard J Daley College, IL
City Colleges of Chicago, Wilbur Wright College, IL
City University, WA
City University of New York, Bernard M Baruch College, NY
City University of New York, Borough of Manhattan Community College, NY
City University of New York, Bronx Community College, NY
City University of New York, Brooklyn College, NY

City University of New York, City College, NY
City University of New York, College of Staten Island, NY
City University of New York, Herbert H Lehman College, NY
City University of New York, Hunter College, NY
City University of New York, Queensborough Community College, NY
City University of New York, Queens College, NY
City University of New York, York College, NY
Clarendon College, TX
Clarion University of Pennsylvania, Clarion, PA
Clark College, WA
Clark County Community College, NV
Clarke College, MS
Clark University, MA
Clayton Junior College, GA
Clayton University, MO
Clearwater Christian College, FL
Cleary College, MI
Cleveland Institute of Art, OH
Cleveland Technical College, NC
Clinton Community College, NY
Coastline Community College, CA
Cochise College, AZ
Coe College, IA
Coffeyville Community College, KS
Cogswell College, CA
Colby Community College, KS
College Misericordia, PA
College of DuPage, IL
College of Ganado, AZ
College of Lake County, IL
College of Mount St Joseph on the Ohio, OH
College of Notre Dame, CA
College of St Catherine, MN
College of St Joseph the Provider, VT
College of Saint Rose, NY
College of Saint Teresa, MN
College of St Thomas, MN
College of Santa Fe, NM
College of Southern Idaho, ID
College of the Albemarle, NC
College of the Canyons, CA
College of the Center for Early Education, CA
College of the Mainland, TX
College of the Ozarks, AR
College of the Redwoods, CA
College of the Sequoias, CA
College of the Siskiyous, CA
College of the Southwest, NM
College of William and Mary, VA
Colorado Mountain College, Spring Valley Campus, CO
Colorado Technical College, CO
Columbia Basin College, WA
Columbia College, Hollywood, CA
Columbia College, IL
Columbia College, MO
Columbia-Greene Community College, NY
Columbus College, GA
Columbus College of Art and Design, OH
Columbus Technical Institute, OH
Community College of Allegheny County–Boyce Campus, PA
Community College of Allegheny County–College Center North, PA
Community College of Beaver County, PA
Community College of Philadelphia, PA
Community College of Rhode Island, Flanagan Campus, RI
Community College of Rhode Island, Knight Campus, RI
Community College of the Finger Lakes, NY
Community College of the North Central University Center, SD
Community College of Vermont, VT
Compton Community College, CA

Directories of Specialized Information

Concord College, WV
Concordia College, MI
Concordia College, St Paul, MN
Concordia College Wisconsin, WI
Concordia Lutheran College, TX
Concordia Teachers College, NE
Condie Junior College of Business and Technology, CA
Connors State College, OK
Contra Costa College, CA
Converse College, SC
Copiah-Lincoln Junior College–Natchez Campus, MS
Cornish Institute, WA
Corpus Christi State University, TX
Cosumnes River College, CA
County College of Morris, NJ
Crafton Hills College, CA
Crandall Junior College, GA
Craven Community College, NC
Crowder College, MO
Crowley's Ridge College, AR
Cuesta College, CA
Culver-Stockton College, MO
Cumberland College, KY
Cumberland College of Tennessee, TN
Cuyahoga Community College, Eastern Campus, OH
Cuyahoga Community College, Western Campus, OH
Cypress College, CA
Dabney S Lancaster Community College, VA
Dakota State College, SD
Dakota Wesleyan University, SD
Dallas Baptist College, TX
Dalton Junior College, GA
Dana College, NE
Danville Area Community College, IL
Davenport College of Business, MI
Dawson Community College, MT
Daytona Beach Community College, FL
Dean Junior College, MA
De Anza College, CA
Defiance College, OH
DeKalb Community College, GA
Delaware Technical and Community College, Terry Campus, DE
Delaware Valley College of Science and Agriculture, PA
Delgado Community College, LA
Del Mar College, TX
Delta College, MI
Delta State University, MS
Denmark Technical College, SC
Denver Auraria Community College, CO
DePaul University, IL
DePauw University, IN
Detroit College of Business, Grand Rapids Campus, MI
Dodge City Community College, KS
Dominican College of Blauvelt, NY
Dowling College, NY
Drake University, IA
Draughon's Junior College, GA
Draughon's Junior College of Business, KY
Drew University, NJ
Drexel University, PA
Drury College, MO
Dundalk Community College, MD
Duquesne University, PA
Durham Technical Institute, NC
Dutchess Community College, NY
Dyersburg State Community College, TN
Dyke College, OH
D'Youville College, NY
East Carolina University, NC
East Central College, MO
Eastern College, PA
Eastern Connecticut State University, CT

Eastern Illinois University, IL
Eastern Kentucky University, KY
Eastern Maine Vocational-Technical Institute, ME
Eastern Michigan University, MI
Eastern Montana College, MT
Eastern Nazarene College, MA
Eastern New Mexico University, NM
Eastern Oklahoma State College, OK
Eastern Shore Community College, VA
Eastern Washington University, WA
Eastfield College, TX
East Tennessee State University, TN
East Texas Baptist University, TX
East Texas State University, Commerce, TX
Eckerd College, FL
Ed E Reid State Technical College, AL
Edgecombe Technical College, NC
Edinboro University of Pennsylvania, PA
Edison Community College, FL
Edison State Community College, OH
Edmonds Community College, WA
Edward Waters College, FL
El Centro College, TX
Elgin Community College, IL
Elizabeth Seton College, NY
Elizabethtown College, PA
Ellsworth Community College, IA
Elmira College, NY
Elms College, MA
El Paso Community College, TX
El Reno Junior College, OK
Embry-Riddle Aeronautical University, Daytona Beach, FL
Embry-Riddle Aeronautical University, International Campus, FL
Emmanuel College, MA
Emporia State University, KS
Enterprise State Junior College, AL
Erskine College, SC
Essex Community College, MD
Everett Community College, WA
Evergreen State College, WA
Evergreen Valley College, CA
Fairfield University, CT
Fairleigh Dickinson University, Florham-Madison Campus, NJ
Fairleigh Dickinson University, Rutherford Campus, NJ
Fairleigh Dickinson University, Teaneck-Hackensack Campus, NJ
Fashion Institute of Design and Merchandising, Los Angeles Campus, CA
Fashion Institute of Design and Merchandising, San Francisco Campus, CA
Fashion Institute of Technology, NY
Fayetteville State University, NC
Fayetteville Technical Institute, NC
Felician College, IL
Ferrum College, VA
Findlay College, OH
Fisher Junior College, MA
Fitchburg State College, MA
Florida Agricultural and Mechanical University, FL
Florida Atlantic University, FL
Florida Institute of Technology, FL
Florida International University, FL
Florida Keys Community College, FL
Florida Memorial College, FL
Floyd Junior College, GA
Foothill College, CA
Fordham University at Lincoln Center, NY
Fort Hays State University, KS
Fort Lauderdale College, FL
Fort Steilacoom Community College, WA
Fox Valley Technical Institute, WI

Directories of Specialized Information

Part-Time Summer Programs (continued)

Framingham State College, MA
Francis Marion College, SC
Franklin and Marshall College, PA
Franklin University, OH
Frank Phillips College, TX
Frederick Community College, MD
Freed-Hardeman College, TN
Fresno City College, CA
Front Range Community College, CO
Frostburg State College, MD
Fullerton College, CA
Fulton-Montgomery Community College, NY
Furman University, SC
Gadsden State Junior College, AL
Gainesville Junior College, GA
Galveston College, TX
Gannon University, PA
Gardner-Webb College, NC
Garland County Community College, AR
Gaston College, NC
Gavilan College, CA
Genesee Community College, NY
George C Wallace State Community College, Dothan, AL
George Mason University, VA
Georgetown College, KY
George Williams College, IL
Georgia College, GA
Georgian Court College, NJ
Georgia Southern College, GA
Georgia Southwestern College, GA
Georgia State University, GA
Glassboro State College, NJ
Glendale Community College, AZ
Glendale Community College, CA
Gogebic Community College, MI
Golden Gate University, CA
Golden West College, CA
Goldey Beacom College, DE
Gordon Junior College, GA
Governors State University, IL
Graceland College, IA
Grambling State University, LA
Grand Canyon College, AZ
Grand Rapids Baptist College and Seminary, MI
Grand Rapids Junior College, MI
Grand Valley State College, MI
Grand View College, IA
Gratz College, PA
Grays Harbor College, WA
Grayson County College, TX
Greater Hartford Community College, CT
Great Lakes Bible College, MI
Greenfield Community College, MA
Green River Community College, WA
Greensboro College, NC
Greenville Technical College, SC
Grossmont College, CA
Guam Community College, GU
Guilford College, NC
Gulf Coast Community College, FL
Gwynedd-Mercy College, PA
Hagerstown Junior College, MD
Halifax Community College, NC
Harding University, AR
Hardin-Simmons University, TX
Harford Community College, MD
Harrisburg Area Community College, PA
Harris-Stowe State College, MO
Hastings College, NE
Hebrew College, MA
Heidelberg College, OH

Hellenic College, MA
Henderson State University, AR
Henry Ford Community College, MI
Heritage College, WA
Herkimer County Community College, NY
Highland Community College, KS
Highland Park Community College, MI
Hilbert College, NY
Hill Junior College, TX
Hillsborough Community College, FL
Hocking Technical College, OH
Holy Family College, PA
Holy Names College, CA
Holyoke Community College, MA
Hood College, MD
Hope College, MI
Housatonic Community College, CT
Houston Baptist University, TX
Houston Community College System, TX
Howard College at Big Spring, TX
Howard Community College, MD
Humphreys College, CA
Huntingdon College, AL
Huntington College, IN
Husson College, ME
Huston-Tillotson College, TX
Hutchinson Community College, KS
Idaho State University, ID
Illinois Central College, IL
Illinois Eastern Community Colleges, Frontier Community College, IL
Illinois Eastern Community Colleges, Lincoln Trail College, IL
Illinois Eastern Community Colleges, Olney Central College, IL
Illinois Eastern Community Colleges, Wabash Valley College, IL
Illinois State University, IL
Illinois Valley Community College, IL
Imperial Valley College, CA
Independence Community College, KS
Indiana Central University, IN
Indiana Institute of Technology, IN
Indiana State University, Terre Haute, IN
Indiana State University Evansville, IN
Indiana University at Kokomo, IN
Indiana University at South Bend, IN
Indiana University Bloomington, IN
Indiana University East, IN
Indiana University of Pennsylvania, PA
Indiana University–Purdue University at Indianapolis, IN
Indiana University Southeast, IN
Indiana Vocational Technical College–Central Indiana, IN
Indiana Vocational Technical College–Columbus, IN
Indiana Vocational Technical College–Eastcentral, IN
Indiana Vocational Technical College–Northcentral, IN
Indiana Vocational Technical College–Northeast, IN
Indiana Vocational Technical College–Northwest, IN
Indiana Vocational Technical College–Whitewater, IN
Indian Hills Community College, IA
Indian River Community College, FL
Indian Valley Colleges, CA
Institute of American Indian Arts, NM
Inter American University of Puerto Rico, Barranquitas Regional College, PR
Inter American University of Puerto Rico, Metropolitan Campus, PR
Inver Hills Community College, MN
Iona College, NY
Iowa Central Community College, IA
Iowa Lakes Community College, North Attendance Center, IA
Iowa Lakes Community College, South Attendance Center, IA

Directories of Specialized Information

Iowa State University, IA
Iowa Wesleyan College, IA
Iowa Western Community College, IA
Isothermal Community College, NC
Itasca Community College, MN
Jackson Community College, MI
Jackson State Community College, TN
Jackson State University, MS
Jacksonville State University, AL
Jacksonville University, FL
James H Faulkner State Junior College, AL
James Madison University, VA
Jamestown College, ND
Jamestown Community College, NY
Jefferson College, MO
Jefferson Community College, NY
Jefferson Davis State Junior College, AL
Jefferson State Junior College, AL
Jersey City State College, NJ
John A Logan College, IL
John Carroll University, OH
John C Calhoun State Community College, AL
Johnson & Wales College, RI
Johnson County Community College, KS
Johnson C Smith University, NC
Johnson State College, VT
John Tyler Community College, VA
John Wood Community College, IL
Jordan College, MI
J Sargeant Reynolds Community College, VA
Junior College of Albany, NY
Kankakee Community College, IL
Kansas City Kansas Community College, KS
Kansas Newman College, KS
Kansas Wesleyan, KS
Kaskaskia College, IL
Kean College of New Jersey, NJ
Kearney State College, NE
Keene State College, NH
Kellogg Community College, MI
Kendall School of Design, MI
Kennebec Valley Vocational-Technical Institute, ME
Kennesaw College, GA
Kent State University, Ashtabula Campus, OH
Kent State University, East Liverpool Campus, OH
Kent State University, Geauga Campus, OH
Kent State University, Salem Campus, OH
Kent State University, Stark Campus, OH
Kent State University, Trumbull Campus, OH
Kent State University, Tuscarawas Campus, OH
Kentucky State University, KY
Keystone Junior College, PA
Kilgore College, TX
King's College, PA
Kirkwood Community College, IA
Kirtland Community College, MI
Kishwaukee College, IL
Kutztown University of Pennsylvania, PA
Lackawanna Junior College, PA
Lafayette College, PA
LaGrange College, GA
Lake City Community College, FL
Lake Forest College, IL
Lake Land College, IL
Lakeland College, WI
Lakeland Community College, OH
Lake Michigan College, MI
Lake-Sumter Community College, FL
Lamar University, TX
Langston University, OK
Lansing Community College, MI
Laramie County Community College, WY
Laredo State University, TX

La Salle University, PA
Lassen College, CA
Lebanon Valley College, PA
Lehigh County Community College, PA
Lenoir Community College, NC
Lenoir-Rhyne College, NC
Lesley College, MA
Lewis and Clark College, OR
Lewis and Clark Community College, IL
Lewis-Clark State College, ID
Lewis University, IL
Lincoln College, IL
Lincoln Land Community College, IL
Lincoln University, MO
Lindenwood College, MO
Linfield College, OR
Livingston University, AL
Lock Haven University of Pennsylvania, PA
Lockyear College, Evansville Campus, IN
Lockyear College, Indianapolis Campus, IN
Long Beach City College, CA
Long Island University, Brooklyn Campus, NY
Long Island University, C W Post Campus, NY
Longview Community College, MO
Lorain County Community College, OH
Loras College, IA
Los Angeles Harbor College, CA
Los Angeles Mission College, CA
Los Angeles Pierce College, CA
Los Angeles Trade-Technical College, CA
Los Angeles Valley College, CA
Louisburg College, NC
Louise Salinger Academy of Fashion, CA
Louisiana State University at Alexandria, LA
Louisiana State University at Eunice, LA
Louisiana State University in Shreveport, LA
Lourdes College, OH
Lower Columbia College, WA
Loyola College, MD
Loyola University, New Orleans, LA
Lubbock Christian College, TX
Lurleen B Wallace State Junior College, AL
Lutheran Bible Institute of Seattle, WA
Lynchburg College, VA
Lyons School of Business, PA
Macalester College, MN
MacMurray College, IL
Macomb Community College, MI
Madison Business College, WI
Madonna College, MI
Malone College, OH
Manatee Junior College, FL
Manchester Community College, CT
Manhattan College, NY
Manor Junior College, PA
Mansfield Business College, OH
Mansfield University of Pennsylvania, PA
Maple Woods Community College, MO
Maricopa Technical Community College, AZ
Marietta College, OH
Marion Technical College, OH
Marist College, NY
Marshalltown Community College, IA
Marshall University, WV
Martin Center College, IN
Mary College, ND
Marycrest College, IA
Maryland Institute, College of Art, MD
Marylhurst College for Lifelong Learning, OR
Marymount College, NY
Marymount College of Kansas, KS
Marymount Manhattan College, NY
Marymount Palos Verdes College, CA

387

Directories of Specialized Information

Part-Time Summer Programs (continued)

Maryville College, TN
Maryville College–Saint Louis, MO
Mary Washington College, VA
Marywood College, PA
Massachusetts Bay Community College, MA
Massasoit Community College, MA
Mater Dei College, NY
Mattatuck Community College, CT
Mayland Technical College, NC
Mayville State College, ND
McCook Community College, NE
McDowell Technical College, NC
McKendree College, IL
McLennan Community College, TX
McMurry College, TX
McNeese State University, LA
Meadows Junior College, GA
Medaille College, NY
Memphis Academy of Arts, TN
Memphis State University, TN
Merced College, CA
Mercer County Community College, NJ
Mercer University, Macon, GA
Mercer University in Atlanta, GA
Mercy College, NY
Mercy College of Detroit, MI
Mercyhurst College, PA
Meredith College, NC
Meridian Junior College, MS
Merrimack College, MA
Merrimack Valley College of the University System of New Hampshire, NH
Merritt College, CA
Mesa College, CO
Methodist College, NC
Metropolitan Business College, IL
Metropolitan State College, CO
Metropolitan State University, MN
Miami-Dade Community College, FL
Miami University–Hamilton Campus, OH
Miami University–Middletown Campus, OH
Micronesian Occupational College, TT
Mid-America Nazarene College, KS
Middle Georgia College, GA
Middlesex Community College, MA
Middlesex County College, NJ
Midland College, TX
Midland Lutheran College, NE
Midlands Technical College, SC
Mid Michigan Community College, MI
Mid-Plains Community College, NE
Mid-South Bible College, TN
Midstate College, IL
Mid-State College, ME
Mid-State Technical Institute, WI
Midwestern State University, TX
Miles College, AL
Miles Community College, MT
Millersville University of Pennsylvania, PA
Millikin University, IL
Millsaps College, MS
Milwaukee School of Engineering, WI
Minneapolis College of Art and Design, MN
Minneapolis Community College, MN
Minot State College, ND
Mission College, CA
Mississippi College, MS
Mississippi County Community College, AR
Mississippi Gulf Coast Junior College, Jackson County Campus, MS
Mississippi Gulf Coast Junior College, Jefferson Davis Campus, MS
Mississippi State University, MS
Mississippi University for Women, MS
Mississippi Valley State University, MS
Missouri Southern State College, MO
Missouri Western State College, MO
Mitchell College, CT
Mitchell Community College, NC
Moberly Area Junior College, MO
Mobile College, AL
Modesto Junior College, CA
Mohave Community College, AZ
Mohawk Valley Community College, NY
Mohegan Community College, CT
Molloy College, NY
Monmouth College, NJ
Monroe County Community College, MI
Montcalm Community College, MI
Montclair State College, NJ
Monterey Institute of International Studies, CA
Monterey Peninsula College, CA
Montgomery Technical College, NC
Moorpark College, CA
Moraine Park Technical Institute, WI
Moraine Valley Community College, IL
Moravian College, PA
Morgan State University, MD
Morningside College, IA
Morton College, IL
Motlow State Community College, TN
Mountain Empire Community College, VA
Mountain View College, TX
Mt Hood Community College, OR
Mount Mary College, WI
Mount Mercy College, IA
Mount Olive College, NC
Mount Saint Clare College, IA
Mount Saint Mary College, NY
Mount St Mary's College, CA
Mount Saint Mary's College, MD
Mt San Antonio College, CA
Mount Senario College, WI
Mount Union College, OH
Mount Vernon College, DC
Mundelein College, IL
Murray State University, KY
Muscatine Community College, IA
Muskegon Business College, MI
Muskegon Community College, MI
Muskingum College, OH
Napa Valley College, CA
Nash Technical College, NC
Nassau Community College, NY
National Business College, Lynchburg, VA
National College of Education, IL
National University, CA
Navajo Community College, AZ
Navarro College, TX
Nazareth College of Rochester, NY
Nebraska Western College, NE
Neosho County Community College, KS
Neumann College, PA
Newbury Junior College, MA
New College of California, CA
New Hampshire College, NH
New Hampshire Vocational-Technical College, Berlin, NH
New Hampshire Vocational-Technical College, Nashua, NH
New Hampshire Vocational-Technical College, Stratham, NH
New Jersey Institute of Technology, NJ
New Mexico Highlands University, NM
New Mexico Junior College, NM
New Mexico State University, NM

Directories of Specialized Information

New River Community College, VA
New School for Social Research, Seminar College, NY
New York University, NY
Niagara County Community College, NY
Niagara University, NY
Nicholls State University, LA
Nichols College, MA
Nicolet College and Technical Institute, WI
Norfolk State University, VA
Normandale Community College, MN
North Adams State College, MA
Northampton County Area Community College, PA
North Arkansas Community College, AR
North Carolina Agricultural and Technical State University, NC
North Carolina State University at Raleigh, NC
North Carolina Wesleyan College, NC
North Central College, IL
North Country Community College, NY
Northeast Alabama State Junior College, AL
Northeastern Bible College, NJ
Northeastern University, MA
Northeast Louisiana University, LA
Northeast Mississippi Junior College, MS
Northeast Missouri State University, MO
Northeast Technical Community College, NE
Northern Arizona University, AZ
Northern Essex Community College, MA
Northern Kentucky University, KY
Northern Maine Vocational-Technical Institute, ME
Northern Nevada Community College, NV
Northern State College, SD
Northern Virginia Community College, VA
North Florida Junior College, FL
North Georgia College, GA
North Greenville College, SC
North Harris County College, TX
North Idaho College, ID
North Iowa Area Community College, IA
North Lake College, TX
Northland College, WI
North Seattle Community College, WA
North Shore Community College, MA
North Texas State University, TX
Northwestern Michigan College, MI
Northwestern University, Evanston, IL
Northwest Nazarene College, ID
Northwood Institute, MI
Northwood Institute, Texas Campus, TX
Norwalk Community College, CT
Norwalk State Technical College, CT
Norwich University, Vermont College, VT
Notre Dame College, NH
Notre Dame College of Ohio, OH
Nova University, FL
Oakland City College, IN
Oakland Community College, MI
Oakton Community College, IL
Ocean County College, NJ
Oglala Lakota College, SD
Oglethorpe University, GA
Ohio State University, Columbus, OH
Ohio State University Agricultural Technical Institute, OH
Ohio State University–Lima Campus, OH
Ohio State University–Mansfield Campus, OH
Ohio State University–Marion Campus, OH
Ohio State University–Newark Campus, OH
Ohio University–Chillicothe, OH
Ohio University–Lancaster, OH
Ohlone College, CA
Okaloosa-Walton Junior College, FL
Oklahoma City University, OK
Oklahoma Panhandle State University, OK

Oklahoma State University, OK
Oklahoma State University Technical Institute, OK
Old Dominion University, VA
Olivet College, MI
Olympic College, WA
Onondaga Community College, NY
Orangeburg-Calhoun Technical College, SC
Orange Coast College, CA
Oregon Institute of Technology, OR
Orlando College, FL
Ottawa University, KS
Our Lady of Holy Cross College, LA
Our Lady of the Lake University of San Antonio, TX
Owens Technical College, OH
Oxnard College, CA
Pace University–Pleasantville/Briarcliff, NY
Pacific Christian College, CA
Pacific Lutheran University, WA
Palm Beach Junior College, FL
Palomar College, CA
Pamlico Technical College, NC
Pan American University, TX
Panola Junior College, TX
Paris Junior College, TX
Park College, MO
Pasadena City College, CA
Pasco-Hernando Community College, FL
Patrick Henry Community College, VA
Paul D Camp Community College, VA
Paul Quinn College, TX
Pearl River Junior College, MS
Peirce Junior College, PA
Pembroke State University, NC
Peninsula College, WA
Penn Valley Community College, MO
Pensacola Junior College, FL
Pepperdine University, Malibu, CA
Peru State College, NE
Pfeiffer College, NC
Philadelphia College of Textiles and Science, PA
Phillips College of New Orleans, LA
Phillips University, OK
Phoenix College, AZ
Piedmont Bible College, NC
Piedmont Technical College, NC
Piedmont Virginia Community College, VA
Pikes Peak Community College, CO
Pikeville College, KY
Pima Community College, AZ
Pioneer Community College, MO
Pittsburg State University, KS
Plymouth State College of the University System of New Hampshire, NH
Point Loma Nazarene College, CA
Point Park College, PA
Polk Community College, FL
Polytechnic Institute of New York, Brooklyn Campus, NY
Polytechnic Institute of New York, Farmingdale Campus, NY
Porterville College, CA
Portland State University, OR
Potomac State College of West Virginia University, WV
Prairie View A&M University, TX
Pratt Community College, KS
Pratt Institute, NY
Prince George's Community College, MD
Providence College, RI
Purdue University, West Lafayette, IN
Purdue University Calumet, IN
Purdue University North Central, IN
Queens College, NC
Quincy Junior College, MA
Quinsigamond Community College, MA
Randolph Technical College, NC

Directories of Specialized Information

Part-Time Summer Programs (continued)

Ranger Junior College, TX
Reading Area Community College, PA
Red Rocks Community College, CO
Regis College, MA
Rend Lake College, IL
Reno Business College, NV
Rhode Island College, RI
Richard Bland College, VA
Richland College, TX
Richland Community College, IL
Ricks College, ID
Rider College, NJ
Rio Hondo Community College, CA
Riverside City College, CA
Rivier College, NH
Roane State Community College, TN
Roanoke-Chowan Technical College, NC
Roanoke College, VA
Robert Morris College, PA
Roberts Wesleyan College, NY
Rochester Community College, MN
Rochester Institute of Technology, NY
Rockland Community College, NY
Rockmont College, CO
Rock Valley College, IL
Rocky Mountain College, MT
Roger Williams College, RI
Roosevelt University, IL
Rosary College, IL
Rose State College, OK
Rowan Technical College, NC
Rutgers University, Camden College of Arts and Sciences, NJ
Rutgers University, University College–Newark, NJ
Rutgers University, University College–New Brunswick, NJ
Rutledge College, MO
Rutledge College, Fayetteville, NC
Rutledge College, Columbia, SC
Rutledge College, Greenville, SC
Rutledge College, Spartanburg, SC
Rutledge College, TN
Sacramento City College, CA
Sacred Heart College, NC
Sacred Heart Seminary College, MI
Sacred Heart University, CT
Saddleback Community College, CA
Saint Augustine's College, NC
St Bonaventure University, NY
St Catharine College, KY
St Charles Borromeo Seminary, PA
St Cloud State University, MN
St Edward's University, TX
St Francis College, NY
Saint Francis College, PA
St John Fisher College, NY
Saint Joseph's College, IN
St Joseph's College, Brooklyn, NY
Saint Joseph's University, PA
Saint Leo College, FL
St Louis Community College at Florissant Valley, MO
St Louis Community College at Forest Park, MO
St Louis Community College at Meramec, MO
Saint Louis University, MO
Saint Martin's College, WA
Saint Mary's College of California, CA
St Mary's College of Maryland, MD
Saint Mary's College of O'Fallon, MO
St Petersburg Junior College, FL
Saint Peter's College, Jersey City, NJ
St Thomas Aquinas College, NY
St Thomas of Villanova University, FL
Saint Vincent College, PA

Saint Xavier College, IL
Salem College, NC
Salem Community College, NJ
Salve Regina–The Newport College, RI
Samford University, AL
San Antonio College, TX
Sandhills Community College, NC
San Diego City College, CA
San Diego Mesa College, CA
San Diego Miramar College, CA
San Diego State University, CA
San Francisco Art Institute, CA
San Francisco State University, CA
Sangamon State University, IL
San Jacinto College–Central Campus, TX
San Jacinto College–North Campus, TX
San Jacinto College–South Campus, TX
San Joaquin Delta College, CA
San Jose City College, CA
San Jose State University, CA
San Juan College, NM
Santa Ana College, CA
Santa Barbara City College, CA
Santa Fe Community College, FL
Santa Monica College, CA
Santa Rosa Junior College, CA
Sarah Lawrence College, NY
Sauk Valley College, IL
Savannah College of Art and Design, GA
Schoolcraft College, MI
School for Lifelong Learning of the University System of New Hampshire, NH
School of the Art Institute of Chicago, IL
School of the Ozarks, MO
Scott Community College, IA
Seattle Central Community College, WA
Seattle Pacific University, WA
Seattle University, WA
Seminole Community College, FL
Seminole Junior College, OK
Seton Hall University, NJ
Seton Hill College, PA
Seward County Community College, KS
Shawnee College, IL
Shawnee State Community College, OH
Shaw University, NC
Shelby State Community College, TN
Shenandoah College and Conservatory of Music, VA
Shepherd College, WV
Sherwood Conservatory of Music, IL
Shimer College, IL
Shippensburg University of Pennsylvania, PA
Shoreline Community College, WA
Shorter College, AR
Shorter College, GA
Siena College, NY
Siena Heights College, MI
Sierra Nevada College, NV
Silver Lake College, WI
Simmons College, MA
Simpson College, CA
Simpson College, IA
Sinclair Community College, OH
Sioux Empire College, IA
Skagit Valley College, WA
Skidmore College, NY
Slippery Rock University of Pennsylvania, PA
Snow College, UT
Sojourner-Douglass College, MD
Solano Community College, CA
Somerset County College, NJ
Sonoma State University, CA
Southeast Community College, Fairbury Campus, NE

Directories of Specialized Information

Southeast Community College, Lincoln Campus, NE
Southeastern Community College, NC
Southeastern Community College, North Campus, IA
Southeastern Community College, South Campus, IA
Southeastern Illinois College, IL
Southeastern Massachusetts University, MA
Southeastern Oklahoma State University, OK
Southeastern University, DC
Southeast Missouri State University, MO
Southern Arkansas University Tech, AR
Southern Connecticut State University, CT
Southern Illinois University at Carbondale, IL
Southern Illinois University at Edwardsville, IL
Southern Methodist University, TX
Southern Ohio College, Fairfield Campus, OH
Southern Oregon State College, OR
Southern Union State Junior College, AL
Southern University, Shreveport–Bossier City Campus, LA
Southern Vermont College, VT
Southern West Virginia Community College, WV
South Georgia College, GA
South Plains College, TX
South Puget Sound Community College, WA
South Seattle Community College, WA
Southwestern College, CA
Southwestern College, KS
Southwestern College of Business, Kettering, OH
Southwestern Michigan College, MI
Southwestern Oklahoma State University, OK
Southwestern Technical College, NC
Southwest Mississippi Junior College, MS
Southwest Texas State University, TX
Southwest Virginia Community College, VA
Spartanburg Methodist College, SC
Spokane Community College, WA
Springfield College, MA
Springfield Technical Community College, MA
Stanly Technical College, NC
State Fair Community College, MO
State Technical Institute at Knoxville, TN
State Technical Institute at Memphis, TN
State University of New York Agricultural and Technical College at Cobleskill, NY
State University of New York at Binghamton, NY
State University of New York at Buffalo, NY
State University of New York at Stony Brook, NY
State University of New York College at Brockport, NY
State University of New York College at Fredonia, NY
State University of New York College at New Paltz, NY
State University of New York College at Oneonta, NY
State University of New York College at Oswego, NY
State University of New York Empire State College, NY
Stautzenberger College, OH
Stephen F Austin State University, TX
Stetson University, FL
Stockton State College, NJ
Stonehill College, MA
Stratton College, WI
Strayer College, DC
Suffolk County Community College–Eastern Campus, NY
Suffolk County Community College–Selden Campus, NY
Suffolk County Community College–Western Campus, NY
Suffolk University, MA
Sullivan County Community College, NY
Sullivan Junior College of Business, KY
Sumter Area Technical College, SC
Surry Community College, NC
Susquehanna University, PA
Syracuse University, NY
Sysorex Institute, CA
Tabor College, KS
Tacoma Community College, WA
Taft College, CA

Tampa College, FL
Tarleton State University, TX
Tarrant County Junior College, TX
Taylor University, IN
Technical College of Alamance, NC
Tennessee State University, TN
Tennessee Temple University, TN
Texarkana Community College, TX
Texas A&M University, College Station, TX
Texas Lutheran College, TX
Texas Southern University, TX
Texas Southmost College, TX
Texas State Technical Institute–Amarillo Campus, TX
Texas State Technical Institute–Sweetwater Campus, TX
Texas State Technical Institute–Waco Campus, TX
Texas Wesleyan College, TX
Texas Woman's University, TX
Thames Valley State Technical College, CT
Thomas College, ME
Thomas Jefferson University, PA
Thomas More College, KY
Thomas Nelson Community College, VA
Thornton Community College, IL
Three Rivers Community College, MO
Tidewater Community College, Chesapeake Campus, VA
Tidewater Community College, Frederick Campus, VA
Tidewater Community College, Virginia Beach Campus, VA
Tompkins Cortland Community College, NY
Touro College, NY
Towson State University, MD
Trenton State College, NJ
Trevecca Nazarene College, TN
Triangle Institute of Technology, Greensburg, PA
Tri-County Community College, NC
Trinidad State Junior College, CO
Trinity College, DC
Trinity College, VT
Tri-State University, IN
Triton College, IL
Troy State University, Troy, AL
Troy State University at Dothan/Fort Rucker, AL
Troy State University in Montgomery, AL
Truckee Meadows Community College, NV
Truett-McConnell College, GA
Tulsa Junior College, OK
Tusculum College, TN
Tyler Junior College, TX
Ulster County Community College, NY
Umpqua Community College, OR
Union College, NE
Union College, NY
United Wesleyan College, PA
University of Akron, OH
University of Alabama, University, AL
University of Alabama in Birmingham, AL
University of Alaska, Anchorage, AK
University of Alaska, Anchorage Community College, AK
University of Alaska, Fairbanks, AK
University of Alaska, Juneau, AK
University of Alaska, Ketchikan Community College, AK
University of Alaska, Matanuska-Susitna Community College, AK
University of Albuquerque, NM
University of Arizona, AZ
University of Arkansas at Little Rock, AR
University of Arkansas at Monticello, AR
University of Baltimore, MD
University of California, Davis, CA
University of California, Santa Cruz, CA
University of Central Arkansas, AR
University of Central Florida, FL
University of Charleston, WV
University of Colorado at Boulder, CO

Directories of Specialized Information

Part-Time Summer Programs (continued)

University of Colorado at Colorado Springs, CO
University of Colorado at Denver, CO
University of Dallas, TX
University of Dayton, OH
University of Delaware, DE
University of Denver, CO
University of Detroit, MI
University of Dubuque, IA
University of Evansville, IN
University of Florida, FL
University of Georgia, GA
University of Guam, GU
University of Hartford, CT
University of Hawaii at Hilo, HI
University of Hawaii at Manoa, HI
University of Hawaii–Leeward Community College, HI
University of Hawaii–Maui Community College, HI
University of Houston–Clear Lake, TX
University of Houston–Downtown, TX
University of Houston–University Park, TX
University of Idaho, ID
University of Illinois at Chicago, University Center, IL
University of Iowa, IA
University of Judaism, CA
University of Kentucky, KY
University of Kentucky, Ashland Community College, KY
University of Kentucky, Elizabethtown Community College, KY
University of Kentucky, Hazard Community College, KY
University of Kentucky, Jefferson Community College, KY
University of Kentucky, Lexington Community College, KY
University of Kentucky, Madisonville Community College, KY
University of Kentucky, Maysville Community College, KY
University of Kentucky, Paducah Community College, KY
University of Kentucky, Somerset Community College, KY
University of Kentucky, Southeast Community College, KY
University of La Verne, CA
University of Louisville, KY
University of Lowell, MA
University of Maine at Augusta, ME
University of Maine at Farmington, ME
University of Maine at Orono, ME
University of Maine at Presque Isle, ME
University of Mary Hardin-Baylor, TX
University of Maryland at College Park, MD
University of Maryland Baltimore County, MD
University of Maryland, University College, MD
University of Massachusetts at Amherst, MA
University of Miami, FL
University of Michigan, Ann Arbor, MI
University of Michigan–Flint, MI
University of Minnesota, Morris, MN
University of Minnesota Technical College, Crookston, MN
University of Minnesota Technical College, Waseca, MN
University of Minnesota, Twin Cities Campus, MN
University of Missouri–Columbia, MO
University of Missouri–Kansas City, MO
University of Missouri–Rolla, MO
University of Missouri–St Louis, MO
University of Montevallo, AL
University of Nebraska at Omaha, NE
University of Nebraska–Lincoln, NE
University of Nevada Reno, NV
University of New England, ME
University of New Haven, CT
University of New Mexico–Los Alamos, NM
University of New Orleans, LA
University of North Carolina at Asheville, NC
University of North Carolina at Charlotte, NC
University of Northern Colorado, CO

University of Northern Iowa, IA
University of Oklahoma, OK
University of Pennsylvania, PA
University of Pittsburgh, Pittsburgh, PA
University of Pittsburgh at Bradford, PA
University of Pittsburgh at Greensburg, PA
University of Pittsburgh at Johnstown, PA
University of Pittsburgh at Titusville, PA
University of Puerto Rico, Cayey University College, PR
University of Puerto Rico, Humacao University College, PR
University of Rhode Island, RI
University of Richmond, VA
University of Rochester, NY
University of St Thomas, TX
University of San Francisco, CA
University of Sarasota, FL
University of Scranton, PA
University of South Alabama, AL
University of South Carolina, Columbia, SC
University of South Carolina at Aiken, SC
University of South Carolina at Beaufort, SC
University of South Carolina at Spartanburg, SC
University of South Carolina at Sumter, SC
University of South Carolina–Coastal Carolina College, SC
University of South Dakota, SD
University of Southern California, CA
University of Southern Colorado, CO
University of Southern Maine, ME
University of Southern Mississippi, MS
University of South Florida, FL
University of Southwestern Louisiana, LA
University of Tampa, FL
University of Tennessee at Chattanooga, TN
University of Tennessee at Martin, TN
University of Texas at Dallas, TX
University of Texas at El Paso, TX
University of Texas at San Antonio, TX
University of Texas at Tyler, TX
University of Texas Health Science Center at Houston, TX
University of Texas of the Permian Basin, TX
University of the District of Columbia, DC
University of Toledo, OH
University of Washington, WA
University of West Florida, FL
University of West Los Angeles, CA
University of Wisconsin Center–Baraboo/Sauk County, WI
University of Wisconsin Center–Fox Valley, WI
University of Wisconsin Center–Manitowoc County, WI
University of Wisconsin Center–Marathon County, WI
University of Wisconsin Center–Marinette County, WI
University of Wisconsin Center–Marshfield/Wood County, WI
University of Wisconsin Center–Richland, WI
University of Wisconsin Center–Rock County, WI
University of Wisconsin Center–Sheboygan County, WI
University of Wisconsin Center–Washington County, WI
University of Wisconsin Center–Waukesha County, WI
University of Wisconsin–Eau Claire, WI
University of Wisconsin–Green Bay, WI
University of Wisconsin–La Crosse, WI
University of Wisconsin–Milwaukee, WI
University of Wisconsin–Oshkosh, WI
University of Wisconsin–Parkside, WI
University of Wisconsin–Stevens Point, WI
University of Wisconsin–Superior, WI
University of Wisconsin–Whitewater, WI
University of Wyoming, WY
Upper Iowa University, IA
Upsala College, NJ
Urbana College, OH
Ursinus College, PA
Utah State University, UT
Utah Technical College at Salt Lake, UT
Utica School of Commerce, NY

Directories of Specialized Information

Valencia Community College, FL
Valparaiso University, IN
VanderCook College of Music, IL
Vennard College, IA
Vermillion Community College, MN
Vernon Regional Junior College, TX
Victoria College, TX
Villa Julie College, MD
Villa Maria College, PA
Villanova University, PA
Vincennes University, IN
Virginia Commonwealth University, VA
Virginia Polytechnic Institute and State University, VA
Virginia State University, VA
Virginia Western Community College, VA
Viterbo College, WI
Wake Technical College, NC
Walker College, AL
Wallace State Community College, AL
Walla Walla College, WA
Walsh College, OH
Walters State Community College, TN
Wartburg College, IA
Washburn University of Topeka, KS
Washington Bible College, MD
Washington University, MO
Washtenaw Community College, MI
Watterson College, KY
Waycross Junior College, GA
Waynesburg College, PA
Wayne State University, MI
Weatherford College, TX
Webber College, FL
Weber State College, UT
Webster University, MO
Wenatchee Valley College, WA
Wesleyan College, GA
Wesley College, DE
Westark Community College, AR
Westbrook College, ME
Westchester Business Institute, NY
West Chester University of Pennsylvania, PA
Western Illinois University, IL
Western International University, AZ
Western Kentucky University, KY
Western Montana College, MT
Western New Mexico University, NM
Western Oklahoma State College, OK
Western Oregon State College, OR
Western Piedmont Community College, NC
Western State College of Colorado, CO
Western State University College of Law of Orange County, CA
Western State University College of Law of San Diego, CA
Western Texas College, TX
Western Wyoming Community College, WY
Westfield State College, MA
West Georgia College, GA
West Hills College, CA
Westminster Choir College, NJ
Westminster College, PA
Westmoreland County Community College, PA
West Shore Community College, MI
West Texas State University, TX
West Virginia State College, WV
West Virginia Wesleyan College, WV
Wharton County Junior College, TX
Whatcom Community College, WA
Wheeling College, WV
Whitworth College, WA
Wichita State University, KS
Wiley College, TX
Wilkes College, PA

Wilkes Community College, NC
William Carey College, MS
William Paterson College of New Jersey, NJ
William Penn College, IA
William Rainey Harper College, IL
Williamsburg Technical College, SC
Williamsport School of Commerce, PA
Willmar Community College, MN
Wilmington College of Ohio, OH
Wingate College, NC
Winona State University, MN
Winston-Salem State University, NC
Wisconsin Conservatory of Music, WI
Wisconsin Indianhead Technical Institute, Ashland Campus, WI
Wisconsin Indianhead Technical Institute, New Richmond Campus, WI
Wisconsin Indianhead Technical Institute, Superior Campus, WI
Wittenberg University, OH
Wofford College, SC
Woodbury University, CA
Wood Junior College, MS
Worcester State College, MA
Wright State University, Western Ohio Branch Campus, OH
Xavier University, OH
Yakima Valley Community College, WA
Yankton College, SD
Yavapai College, AZ
York Technical College, SC
Youngstown State University, OH
Yuba College, CA

Colleges Offering External Degree Programs

Adelphi University, NY
Aims Community College, CO
Allen County Community College, KS
American International College, MA
Anderson College, SC
Antioch University West, CA
Aquinas College, MI
Aquinas Junior College, TN
Ashland College, OH
Athens State College, AL
Ball State University, IN
Baptist College at Charleston, SC
Bard College, NY
Barry University, FL
Barton County Community College, KS
Belhaven College, MS
Bemidji State University, MN
Black Hills State College, SD
Brevard Community College, FL
Briarwood College, CT
Brigham Young University, UT
Bunker Hill Community College, MA
Burlington College, VT
Butte College, CA
Caguas City College, PR
Caldwell College, NJ
California Baptist College, CA
California State College, San Bernardino, CA
California State University, Chico, CA
California State University, Dominguez Hills, CA
California State University, Northridge, CA
California State University, Sacramento, CA
Calumet College, IN
Camden County College, NJ
Capital University, OH
Carson-Newman College, TN
Castleton State College, VT

Directories of Specialized Information

External Degree Programs (continued)

Catholic University of America, DC
Centenary College, NJ
Central Community College–Grand Island Campus, NE
Centralia College, WA
Central Michigan University, MI
Central Missouri State University, MO
Central Texas College, TX
Central University of Iowa, IA
Central Washington University, WA
Chadron State College, NE
Charter Oak College, CT
Chicago State University, IL
Christopher Newport College, VA
City Colleges of Chicago, Chicago City-Wide College, IL
City University of New York, College of Staten Island, NY
City University of New York, Queensborough Community College, NY
City University of New York, Queens College, NY
Clayton University, MO
Cleveland Institute of Electronics, OH
Coastline Community College, CA
Cogswell College, CA
Colby Community College, KS
College of DuPage, IL
College of Lake County, IL
College of New Rochelle, New Resources Division, NY
College of St Francis, IL
College of St Scholastica, MN
College of Santa Fe, NM
College of the Ozarks, AR
Columbia College, MO
Columbia Union College, MD
Community College of Rhode Island, Knight Campus, RI
Community College of the North Central University Center, SD
Community College of Vermont, VT
Covenant College, GA
Crafton Hills College, CA
Dakota State College, SD
Dallas Baptist College, TX
Dallas Bible College, TX
De Anza College, CA
Defiance College, OH
Delgado Community College, LA
Detroit College of Business, Grand Rapids Campus, MI
Dodge City Community College, KS
Dyke College, OH
Eastern Illinois University, IL
Eastern Kentucky University, KY
Eastern New Mexico University, NM
Eastern Oregon State College, OR
Eastern Washington University, WA
Eastern Wyoming College, WY
Eckerd College, FL
Elizabeth Seton College, NY
Elizabethtown College, PA
Elmhurst College, IL
El Paso Community College, TX
Embry-Riddle Aeronautical University, Daytona Beach, FL
Embry-Riddle Aeronautical University, International Campus, FL
Evergreen State College, WA
Ferris State College, MI
Florida Memorial College, FL
Framingham State College, MA
Franklin Pierce College, NH
Gannon University, PA
Gogebic Community College, MI
Golden West College, CA
Gordon Junior College, GA
Grand Rapids Baptist College and Seminary, MI

Grantham College of Engineering, CA
Hampton Institute, VA
Hannibal-LaGrange College, MO
Hawthorne College, NH
Heidelberg College, OH
Holy Apostles College, CT
Hudson Valley Community College, NY
ICS Center for Degree Studies, PA
Illinois Eastern Community Colleges, Frontier Community College, IL
Illinois Eastern Community Colleges, Lincoln Trail College, IL
Illinois Eastern Community Colleges, Olney Central College, IL
Illinois Eastern Community Colleges, Wabash Valley College, IL
Imperial Valley College, CA
Indiana Institute of Technology, IN
Indiana University at Kokomo, IN
Indiana University Bloomington, IN
Indiana University East, IN
Indiana University Northwest, IN
Indiana University–Purdue University at Fort Wayne, IN
Indiana University–Purdue University at Indianapolis, IN
Indiana University Southeast, IN
Inter American University of Puerto Rico, Metropolitan Campus, PR
Inver Hills Community College, MN
Iowa State University, IA
Isothermal Community College, NC
Jackson Community College, MI
James H Faulkner State Junior College, AL
Johnson State College, VT
John Tyler Community College, VA
John Wood Community College, IL
Jordan College, MI
Kansas State University, KS
Kansas Wesleyan, KS
Kaskaskia College, IL
Kean College of New Jersey, NJ
Keene State College, NH
Kishwaukee College, IL
Lake Erie College, OH
Lakeland College, WI
Lakeland Community College, OH
Lansing Community College, MI
Lewis-Clark State College, ID
Lincoln Land Community College, IL
Lincoln Memorial University, TN
Lindenwood College, MO
Linfield College, OR
Loras College, IA
Loretto Heights College, CO
Los Angeles Harbor College, CA
Los Angeles Mission College, CA
Louisiana College, LA
Louisville Technical Institute, KY
Mankato State University, MN
Mars Hill College, NC
Mary Baldwin College, VA
Mary College, ND
Marygrove College, MI
Marywood College, PA
Mattatuck Community College, CT
McKendree College, IL
Mercer County Community College, NJ
Mercer University, Macon, GA
Metropolitan State College, CO
Middlesex Community College, CT
Mid-Plains Community College, NE
Mohegan Community College, CT
Moorhead State University, MN
Moraine Park Technical Institute, WI

Directories of Specialized Information

Mountain Empire Community College, VA
Mount Senario College, WI
Muskingum College, OH
National College of Education, IL
Neosho County Community College, KS
New England College, NH
New Hampshire College, NH
New Hampshire Vocational-Technical College, Manchester, NH
New York Institute of Technology, NY
Niagara County Community College, NY
North Adams State College, MA
Northampton County Area Community College, PA
North Arkansas Community College, AR
North Carolina Wesleyan College, NC
Northeastern Illinois University, IL
Northern Arizona University, AZ
North Idaho College, ID
North Iowa Area Community College, IA
North Shore Community College, MA
Northwestern Connecticut Community College, CT
Northwestern Michigan College, MI
Northwood Institute, MI
Northwood Institute, Texas Campus, TX
Norwich University, Vermont College, VT
Nova University, FL
Oakton Community College, IL
Ohio University, Athens, OH
Ohio University–Zanesville, OH
Oklahoma City University, OK
Oklahoma State University, OK
Old College, NV
Old Dominion University, VA
Onondaga Community College, NY
Orange County Community College, NY
Paris Junior College, TX
Park College, MO
Paul Quinn College, TX
Peru State College, NE
Plymouth State College of the University System of New Hampshire, NH
Portland Community College, OR
Prairie View A&M University, TX
Quinnipiac College, CT
Reading Area Community College, PA
Regis College, CO
Rochester Institute of Technology, NY
Rockland Community College, NY
Roger Williams College, RI
Roosevelt University, IL
Sacred Heart University, CT
St Edward's University, TX
St Louis Community College at Meramec, MO
Saint Mary of the Plains College, KS
Saint Mary-of-the-Woods College, IN
Saint Mary's College, MN
Saint Mary's College of California, CA
St Thomas of Villanova University, FL
Salem College, NC
Salem College, WV
Samford University, AL
San Diego Mesa College, CA
San Diego State University, CA
Santa Ana College, CA
School for Lifelong Learning of the University System of New Hampshire, NH
Seattle Central Community College, WA
Seattle Pacific University, WA
Seward County Community College, KS
Shaw University, NC
Sheldon Jackson College, AK
Shepherd College, WV
Siena Heights College, MI

Sierra Nevada College, NV
Simpson College, CA
Sinclair Community College, OH
Skidmore College, NY
Snow College, UT
Sojourner-Douglass College, MD
South Central Community College, CT
Southeastern Community College, NC
Southern Illinois University at Carbondale, IL
Southern Maine Vocational-Technical Institute, ME
Southern Vermont College, VT
Southwestern Adventist College, TX
Southwestern College, CA
Southwest State University, MN
Southwest Texas Junior College, TX
Spring Arbor College, MI
Spring Hill College, AL
Stanly Technical College, NC
State Technical Institute at Memphis, TN
State University of New York Agricultural and Technical College at Farmingdale, NY
State University of New York at Binghamton, NY
State University of New York College at Brockport, NY
State University of New York Empire State College, NY
Stephens College, MO
Strayer College, DC
Tarkio College, MO
Tennessee State University, TN
Thomas A Edison State College, NJ
Thomas More College, KY
Thomas Nelson Community College, VA
Tidewater Community College, Chesapeake Campus, VA
Tidewater Community College, Frederick Campus, VA
Tidewater Community College, Virginia Beach Campus, VA
Tomlinson College, TN
Trinity College, CT
Truett-McConnell College, GA
University of Alabama, University, AL
University of Alaska, Ketchikan Community College, AK
University of Charleston, WV
University of Colorado at Denver, CO
University of Evansville, IN
University of Guam, GU
University of Iowa, IA
University of Kentucky, Elizabethtown Community College, KY
University of La Verne, CA
University of Maine at Presque Isle, ME
University of Maryland, University College, MD
University of Massachusetts at Amherst, MA
University of Massachusetts at Boston, MA
University of Minnesota, Morris, MN
University of Minnesota Technical College, Crookston, MN
University of Minnesota, Twin Cities Campus, MN
University of Mississippi, MS
University of Missouri–Kansas City, MO
University of New Hampshire, NH
University of Northern Colorado, CO
University of Northern Iowa, IA
University of Pittsburgh, Pittsburgh, PA
University of Pittsburgh at Greensburg, PA
University of Puerto Rico, Carolina Regional College, PR
University of Puerto Rico, Humacao University College, PR
University of Redlands, CA
University of San Francisco, CA
University of Sarasota, FL
University of South Dakota, SD
University of South Florida, FL
University of Tennessee at Martin, TN
University of the District of Columbia, DC
University of the State of New York Regents External Degree Program, NY
University of West Florida, FL

Directories of Specialized Information

External Degree Programs (continued)

University of Wisconsin Center–Manitowoc County, WI
University of Wisconsin Center–Rock County, WI
University of Wisconsin–Green Bay, WI
University of Wisconsin–Platteville, WI
University of Wisconsin–River Falls, WI
University of Wisconsin–Stout, WI
University of Wisconsin–Superior, WI
University of Wisconsin–Whitewater, WI
Upper Iowa University, IA
Urbana College, OH
Ursuline College, OH
Utah State University, UT
Valley City State College, ND
Walsh College, OH
Washtenaw Community College, MI
Wayland Baptist University, TX

Wayne State University, MI
Wenatchee Valley College, WA
Wesleyan College, GA
Wesley College, DE
Westbrook College, ME
Western Illinois University, IL
Western International University, AZ
Western Iowa Tech Community College, IA
West Liberty State College, WV
West Virginia State College, WV
West Virginia Wesleyan College, WV
Whatcom Community College, WA
Whitworth College, WA
Wilkes College, PA
William Penn College, IA
Wilmington College, DE
Wingate College, NC
Winona State University, MN

Index to Colleges

Abilene Christian University, TX	313
Abraham Baldwin Agricultural College, GA	70
Academy of Aeronautics, NY	204
Academy of Art College, CA	18
Academy of the New Church, PA	271
Adams State College, CO*	46
Adelphi University, NY	204
Adirondack Community College, NY	204
Adrian College, MI	153
Agnes Scott College, GA	70
Aiken Technical College, SC	296
Aims Community College, CO	47
Air Force Institute of Technology, OH	247
Alabama Agricultural and Mechanical University, AL	3
Alabama Aviation and Technical College, AL	3
Alabama Christian College, AL	3
Alabama State University, AL	3
Alabama Technical College, AL	3
Alaska Bible College, AK	10
Alaska Pacific University, AK	10
Albany Business College, NY	204
Albany Medical College of Union University, NY	204
Albany State College, GA	70
Albertus Magnus College, CT	52
Albright College, PA	271
Alcorn State University, MS	170
Alderson-Broaddus College, WV	350
Alexander City State Junior College, AL	3
Alfred Adler Institute, IL	81
Alfred University, NY	204
Alice Lloyd College, KY	120
Allan Hancock College, CA	18
Allegany Community College, MD	134
Allegheny College, PA	271
Allen County Community College, KS	115
Allentown Business School, PA	272
Allentown College of St Francis de Sales, PA	272
Alliance College, PA	272
Alpena Community College, MI	153
Alvernia College, PA	272
Alverno College, WI	353
Alvin Community College, TX	313
Amarillo College, TX	313
Amber University, TX	313
American Academy of Art, IL	81
American Baptist College of American Baptist Theological Seminary, TN	305
American Baptist Seminary of the West, CA	19
American College, PA	272
American College of Puerto Rico, PR	291
American Conservatory of Music, IL	81
American Graduate School of International Management, AZ	12
American Indian Bible College, AZ	12
American Institute of Banking, MA	141
American Institute of Business, IA	108
American International College, MA	141
American River College, CA	19
American Samoa Community College, AS	12
American Technological University, TX	313
American University, DC*	59
Ancilla College, IN	100
Anderson College, IN	100
Anderson College, SC	296
Andover College, ME	131
Andrew College, GA	70
Andrews University, MI*	153
Angelina College, TX	314
Angelo State University, TX	314
Anna Maria College for Men and Women, MA	141
Anne Arundel Community College, MD	134
Anoka-Ramsey Community College, MN	164
Anson Technical College, NC	231
Antelope Valley College, CA	19
Antillian College, PR	291
Antioch College, OH	247
Antioch International, OH	247
Antioch University West, CA	19
Antonelli Institute of Art and Photography, PA	272
Appalachian State University, NC*	231
Aquinas College, MI	153
Aquinas Institute, MO	175
Aquinas Junior College, TN	305
Arapahoe Community College, CO	47
Arizona College of the Bible, AZ	12
Arizona State University, AZ*	12
Arizona Western College, AZ	12
Arkansas College, AR	15
Arkansas State University, AR	15
Arkansas State University–Beebe Branch, AR	15
Arkansas Tech University, AR	15
Arlington Baptist College, TX	314
Armstrong College, CA	19
Armstrong State College, GA*	70
Art Academy of Cincinnati, OH	247
Asbury Theological Seminary, KY	120
Asheville-Buncombe Technical College, NC	231
Ashland College, OH	247
Ashland Community College, KY—See University of Kentucky, Ashland Community College	
Asnuntuck Community College, CT	52
Assemblies of God Graduate School, MO	175
Assumption College, MA	141
Athenaeum of Ohio, OH	247
Athens State College, AL	3
Atlanta Christian College, GA	70
Atlanta College of Art, GA	70
Atlanta Junior College, GA	71
Atlanta University, GA	71
Atlantic Christian College, NC	232
Atlantic Community College, NJ	193
Auburn University, AL*	3
Auburn University at Montgomery, AL*	4
Augsburg College, MN	164
Augusta College, GA*	71
Augustana College, IL	81
Augustana College, SD	303
Aurora College, IL	81
Austin Community College, MN	164
Austin Community College, TX	314
Austin Peay State University, TN	305
Averett College, VA	336
Avila College, MO	175
Azusa Pacific University, CA	19
Babson College, MA	141
Bacone College, OK	262
Bainbridge Junior College, GA	71
Baker Junior College of Business, MI	153
Bakersfield College, CA	19
Baker University, KS	115
Baldwin-Wallace College, OH	247
Ball State University, IN*	100
Baltimore Hebrew College, MD	134
Bangor Theological Seminary, ME	131
Bank Street College of Education, NY	204
Baptist Bible College, MO	175
Baptist Bible College of Pennsylvania, PA	272
Baptist Bible Institute, FL	61
Baptist College at Charleston, SC	296
Baptist Missionary Association Theological Seminary, TX	314
Barat College, IL	81
Bard College, NY	204
Barrington College, RI	295
Barry University, FL	61
Barstow College, CA	19

*Member of National University Continuing Education Association

Index to Colleges

Bartlesville Wesleyan College, OK	262
Barton County Community College, KS	115
Baruch College, NY—See City University of New York, Bernard M Baruch College	
Bay de Noc Community College, MI	153
Baylor University, TX*	314
Bay Path Junior College, MA	141
Bay State Junior College, MA	141
Bay-Valley Tech, CA	20
Beal College, ME	131
Beaufort County Community College, NC	232
Beaufort Technical College, SC	296
Beaver College, PA	272
Becker Junior College–Leicester Campus, MA	141
Becker Junior College–Worcester Campus, MA	142
Beckley College, WV	350
Bee County College, TX	314
Belhaven College, MS	170
Bellarmine College, KY	121
Belleville Area College, IL	81
Bellevue College, NE	185
Bellevue Community College, WA	344
Belmont College, TN	305
Belmont Technical College, OH	247
Beloit College, WI	353
Bemidji State University, MN	164
Benedict College, SC	297
Benedictine College, KS	115
Benjamin Franklin University, DC	59
Bennington College, VT	334
Bentley College, MA	142
Berean Institute, PA	273
Bergen Community College, NJ	194
Berkeley School, NJ	194
Berkeley School, Hicksville, NY	205
Berkshire Christian College, MA	142
Berkshire Community College, MA	142
Berry College, GA	71
Bethany College, WV	350
Bethany Lutheran College, MN	164
Bethany Nazarene College, OK	263
Bethany Theological Seminary, IL	82
Bethel College, IN	100
Bethel College, KS	115
Bethel College, MN	164
Bethel College, TN	305
Bethel Theological Seminary, MN	165
Bethune-Cookman College, FL	61
Big Bend Community College, WA	344
Biola University, CA	20
Birmingham-Southern College, AL	4
Bishop Clarkson College of Nursing, NE	185
Bishop College, TX	315
Bismarck Junior College, ND*	245
Blackburn College, IL	82
Blackfeet Community College, MT	183
Black Hawk College–East Campus, IL	82
Blackhawk Technical Institute, WI	353
Black Hills State College, SD	303
Bladen Technical College, NC	232
Blair Junior College, CO	47
Blanton's Junior College, NC	232
Blinn College, TX	315
Bloomfield College, NJ	194
Bloomsburg University of Pennsylvania, PA*	273
Bluefield College, VA	336
Bluefield State College, WV	350
Blue Mountain College, MS	170
Blue Mountain Community College, OR	267
Blue Ridge Community College, VA	336
Blue Ridge Technical College, NC	232
Bluffton College, OH	248
Bob Jones University, SC	297
Boise Bible College, ID	79
Boise State University, ID*	80
Bossier Parish Community College, LA	127
Boston Architectural Center, MA	142
Boston College, MA	142
Boston Conservatory, MA	142
Boston University, MA	142
Bowie State College, MD	134
Bowling Green Junior College of Business, KY	121
Bowling Green State University, OH*	248
Bowling Green State University–Firelands College, OH	248
Bradford College, MA	143
Bradley University, IL*	82
Brainerd Community College, MN	165
Bramson ORT Technical Institute, NY	205
Brandeis University, MA	143
Brazosport College, TX	315
Brenau College, GA	71
Brescia College, KY	121
Brevard Community College, FL	61
Brewer State Junior College, AL	4
Brewton-Parker College, GA	71
Briar Cliff College, IA	108
Briarcliffe Secretarial School, NY	205
Briarwood College, CT	52
Bridgeport Engineering Institute, CT	52
Bridgewater College, VA	336
Bridgewater State College, MA	143
Brigham Young University, UT*	332
Brigham Young University–Hawaii Campus, HI	78
Bristol Community College, MA	143
Bronx Community College, NY—See City University of New York, Bronx Community College	
Brookdale Community College, NJ	194
Brooklyn College, NY—See City University of New York, Brooklyn College	
Brooklyn Law School, NY	205
Broome Community College, NY	205
Broward Community College, FL	61
Brown University, RI	295
Brunswick Junior College, GA	72
Brunswick Technical College, NC	232
Bryan College, TN	306
Bryant and Stratton Business Institute, Buffalo, NY	205
Bryant and Stratton Business Institute, Rochester, NY	205
Bryant and Stratton Business Institute, Eastern Hills Campus, NY	206
Bryant and Stratton Powelson Business Institute, NY	206
Bryant College, RI	295
Bryn Mawr College, PA	273
Bucknell University, PA	273
Bucks County Community College, PA	273
Buena Vista College, IA	108
Bunker Hill Community College, MA	143
Burlington College, VT	334
Burlington County College, NJ	194
Butler County Community College, KS	115
Butler County Community College, PA	273
Butler University, IN	100
Butte College, CA	20
Cabrillo College, CA	20
Cabrini College, PA	273
Caguas City College, PR	291
Caldwell College, NJ	194
Caldwell Community College and Technical Institute, NC	232
California Baptist College, CA	20
California College of Arts and Crafts, CA	20
California Institute of Integral Studies, CA	20
California Institute of the Arts, CA	21
California Lutheran College, CA	21
California Polytechnic State University, San Luis Obispo, CA	21

398

Index to Colleges

College	Page
California School of Professional Psychology, Berkeley, CA	21
California State College, Bakersfield, CA	21
California State College, San Bernardino, CA	21
California State College, Stanislaus, CA	21
California State Polytechnic University, Pomona, CA*	22
California State University, Chico, CA	22
California State University, Dominguez Hills, CA*	22
California State University, Fresno, CA	22
California State University, Fullerton, CA	22
California State University, Hayward, CA*	22
California State University, Long Beach, CA*	23
California State University, Los Angeles, CA*	23
California State University, Northridge, CA*	23
California State University, Sacramento, CA*	23
California University of Pennsylvania, PA	274
Calumet College, IN	101
Calvary Bible College, MO	175
Calvin College, MI	154
Camden College of Arts and Sciences, NJ—See Rutgers University, Camden College of Arts and Sciences	
Camden County College, NJ	194
Cameron University, OK	263
Campbellsville College, KY	121
Campbell University, NC	232
Canisius College, NY	206
Cape Cod Community College, MA	143
Cape Fear Technical Institute, NC	233
Capital Bible Seminary, MD	134
Capital University, OH	248
Capitol Institute of Technology, MD	134
Cardinal Newman College, MO	175
Cardinal Stritch College, WI	353
Caribbean Center for Advanced Studies, PR	291
Caribbean University College, PR	291
Carl Albert Junior College, OK	263
Carlow College, PA	274
Carl Sandburg College, IL	82
Carnegie-Mellon University, PA	274
Carroll College, WI	353
Carroll College of Montana, MT	183
Carson-Newman College, TN	306
Carteret Technical College, NC	233
Carthage College, WI	354
Casco Bay College, ME	131
Case Western Reserve University, OH	248
Casper College, WY	362
Castle Junior College, NH	191
Castleton State College, VT	334
Catawba College, NC	233
Catawba Valley Technical College, NC	233
Catholic Theological Union at Chicago, IL	82
Catholic University of America, DC	59
Catholic University of Puerto Rico, PR	292
Catholic University of Puerto Rico, Mayagüez Center, PR	292
Catonsville Community College, MD	134
Cayuga County Community College, NY	206
Cazenovia College, NY	206
CBN University, VA	336
Cecil Community College, MD	135
Cecils Junior College of Business, NC	233
Cedar Crest College, PA	274
Cedar Valley College, TX	315
Cedarville College, OH	248
Centenary College, NJ	195
Centenary College of Louisiana, LA	127
Center for Creative Studies–College of Art and Design, MI	154
Central Arizona College, AZ	13
Central Baptist College, AR	16
Central Baptist Theological Seminary, KS	115
Central Bible College, MO	175
Central Carolina Technical College, NC	233
Central Christian College of the Bible, MO	175
Central City Business Institute, NY	206
Central College, KS	115
Central Community College–Grand Island Campus, NE	185
Central Community College–Hastings Campus, NE	185
Central Community College–Platte Campus, NE	185
Central Connecticut State University, CT	52
Central Florida Bible College, FL	61
Central Florida Community College, FL	61
Centralia College, WA	344
Central Methodist College, MO	175
Central Michigan University, MI*	154
Central Missouri State University, MO	176
Central New England College, MA	143
Central Ohio Technical College, OH	248
Central Oregon Community College, OR	267
Central Pennsylvania Business School, PA	274
Central Piedmont Community College, NC	233
Central State University, OH	249
Central State University, OK	263
Central Texas College, TX	315
Central University of Iowa, IA	109
Central Virginia Community College, VA	336
Central Washington University, WA*	344
Central Wesleyan College, SC	297
Central Wyoming College, WY	362
Centro de Estudios Avanzados de Puerto Rico y el Caribe, PR	292
Cerritos College, CA	23
Cerro Coso Community College, CA	24
Chabot College, CA	24
Chadron State College, NE	186
Chaffey College, CA	24
Chamberlayne Junior College, MA	144
Chaminade University of Honolulu, HI	78
Champlain College, VT	334
Chapman College, CA	24
Charles County Community College, MD	135
Charles Stewart Mott Community College, MI	154
Charter Oak College, CT	52
Chatfield College, OH	249
Chatham College, PA	274
Chattahoochee Valley State Community College, AL	4
Chattanooga State Technical Community College, TN	306
Chemeketa Community College, OR	267
Chesapeake College, MD	135
Chesterfield-Marlboro Technical College, SC	297
Chestnut Hill College, PA	274
Cheyney University of Pennsylvania, PA	274
Chicago City-Wide College, IL—See City Colleges of Chicago, Chicago City-Wide College	
Chicago College of Commerce, IL	82
Chicago School of Professional Psychology, IL	82
Chicago State University, IL*	83
Chicago Theological Seminary, IL	83
Chipola Junior College, FL	62
Chowan College, NC	233
Christ College Irvine, CA	24
Christian Brothers College, TN	306
Christopher Newport College, VA	336
Christ Seminary–Seminex, IL	83
Christ the King Seminary, NY	206
Church Divinity School of the Pacific, CA	24
Churchman Business School, PA	275
Church of God School of Theology, TN	306
Cincinnati Bible College, OH	249
Cincinnati Christian Seminary, OH	249
Cincinnati Metropolitan College, OH	249
Cincinnati Technical College, OH	249
Cisco Junior College, TX	315
The Citadel, SC	297

*Member of National University Continuing Education Association

Index to Colleges

College	Page
Citrus College, CA	24
City College, NY—See City University of New York, City College	
City College of San Francisco, CA	24
City Colleges of Chicago, Chicago City-Wide College, IL	83
City Colleges of Chicago, Harry S Truman College, IL	83
City Colleges of Chicago, Kennedy-King College, IL	83
City Colleges of Chicago, Loop College, IL	83
City Colleges of Chicago, Malcolm X College, IL	83
City Colleges of Chicago, Olive-Harvey College, IL	84
City Colleges of Chicago, Richard J Daley College, IL	84
City Colleges of Chicago, Wilbur Wright College, IL	84
City University, WA	344
City University of New York, Bernard M Baruch College, NY	206
City University of New York, Borough of Manhattan Community College, NY	207
City University of New York, Bronx Community College, NY	207
City University of New York, Brooklyn College, NY	207
City University of New York, City College, NY	207
City University of New York, College of Staten Island, NY	207
City University of New York, Fiorello H LaGuardia Community College, NY	207
City University of New York, Herbert H Lehman College, NY	208
City University of New York, Hunter College, NY	208
City University of New York, John Jay College of Criminal Justice, NY	208
City University of New York, Kingsborough Community College, NY	208
City University of New York, Medgar Evers College, NY	208
City University of New York, New York City Technical College, NY	208
City University of New York, Queensborough Community College, NY	208
City University of New York, Queens College, NY*	209
City University of New York, York College, NY	209
Clackamas Community College, OR	267
Claflin College, SC	297
Claremont Graduate School, CA	25
Clarendon College, TX	315
Clarion University of Pennsylvania, Clarion, PA*	275
Clarion University of Pennsylvania, Venango Campus, PA*	275
Clark College, GA	72
Clark College, IN	101
Clark College, WA	345
Clark County Community College, NV	189
Clarke College, IA	109
Clarke College, MS	171
Clarkson University, NY	209
Clark Technical College, OH	249
Clark University, MA*	144
Clatsop Community College, OR	267
Clayton Junior College, GA	72
Clayton University, MO	176
Clearwater Christian College, FL	62
Cleary College, MI	154
Clemson University, SC	297
Clermont General and Technical College, OH—See University of Cincinnati, Clermont General and Technical College	
Cleveland Chiropractic College, MO	176
Cleveland College of Jewish Studies, OH	249
Cleveland Institute of Art, OH	249
Cleveland Institute of Electronics, OH	250
Cleveland State Community College, TN	306
Cleveland State University, OH	250
Cleveland Technical College, NC	234
Clinton Community College, IA	109
Clinton Community College, NY	209
Cloud County Community College, KS	115
Coastal Carolina Community College, NC	234
Coastline Community College, CA	25
Cochise College, AZ	13
Cochran School of Nursing, NY	209
Coe College, IA	109
Coffeyville Community College, KS	116
Cogswell College, CA*	25
Cogswell College Silicon Valley, CA	25
Coker College, SC	297
Colby Community College, KS	116
Colby-Sawyer College, NH	191
Colgate University, NY	209
College Misericordia, PA	275
College of Alameda, CA	25
College of Automation, IL	84
College of Boca Raton, FL	62
College of Charleston, SC*	297
College of DuPage, IL	84
College of Ganado, AZ	13
College of Great Falls, MT	183
College of Idaho, ID	80
College of Insurance, NY	209
College of Lake County, IL	84
College of Mount St Joseph on the Ohio, OH	250
College of Mount Saint Vincent, NY	209
College of New Rochelle, NY	210
College of New Rochelle, New Resources Division, NY	210
College of Notre Dame, CA	25
College of Notre Dame of Maryland, MD	135
College of Saint Benedict, MN	165
College of St Catherine, MN*	165
College of Saint Elizabeth, NJ	195
College of St Francis, IL*	84
College of St Joseph the Provider, VT	334
College of Saint Mary, NE*	186
College of Saint Rose, NY	210
College of St Scholastica, MN	165
College of Saint Teresa, MN	165
College of St Thomas, MN*	165
College of Santa Fe, NM	201
College of Southern Idaho, ID	80
College of Staten Island, NY—See City University of New York, College of Staten Island	
College of the Albemarle, NC	234
College of the Atlantic, ME	131
College of the Canyons, CA	25
College of the Center for Early Education, CA	25
College of the Desert, CA	25
College of the Mainland, TX	315
College of the Ozarks, AR	16
College of the Redwoods, CA	26
College of the Sequoias, CA	26
College of the Siskiyous, CA	26
College of the Southwest, NM	201
College of the Virgin Islands, VI	344
College of William and Mary, VA	337
Colorado Mountain College, Alpine Campus, CO	47
Colorado Mountain College, Spring Valley Campus, CO	47
Colorado Mountain College, Timberline Campus, CO	47
Colorado Northwestern Community College, CO	47
Colorado School of Mines, CO	47
Colorado State University, CO*	48
Colorado Technical College, CO	48
Columbia Basin College, WA	345
Columbia Bible College, SC	298
Columbia Christian College, OR	268
Columbia College, Columbia, CA	26
Columbia College, Hollywood, CA	26
Columbia College, IL	85
Columbia College, MO*	176
Columbia College, SC	298

Index to Colleges

College	Page
Columbia-Greene Community College, NY	210
Columbia Junior College of Business, SC	298
Columbia State Community College, TN	306
Columbia Union College, MD	135
Columbia University, NY	210
Columbia University, School of General Studies, NY	210
Columbia University, School of Nursing, NY	210
Columbus College, GA*	72
Columbus College of Art and Design, OH	250
Columbus Technical Institute, OH	250
Community College of Allegheny County–Boyce Campus, PA	275
Community College of Allegheny County–College Center North, PA	275
Community College of Beaver County, PA	275
Community College of Philadelphia, PA	276
Community College of Rhode Island, Flanagan Campus, RI	295
Community College of Rhode Island, Knight Campus, RI	295
Community College of the Air Force, AL*	4
Community College of the Finger Lakes, NY	211
Community College of the North Central University Center, SD	303
Community College of Vermont, VT	334
Compton Community College, CA	26
Concord College, WV	350
Concordia College, AL	4
Concordia College, IL	85
Concordia College, MI	154
Concordia College, St Paul, MN	165
Concordia College Wisconsin, WI	354
Concordia Lutheran College, TX	316
Concordia Teachers College, NE	186
Concordia Theological Seminary, IN	101
Condie Junior College of Business and Technology, CA	26
Connecticut College, CT	53
Connors State College, OK	263
Consortium of the California State University, CA	27
Contra Costa College, CA	27
Converse College, SC	298
Cooke County College, TX	316
Cooper Institute, TN	306
Copiah-Lincoln Junior College, MS	171
Copiah-Lincoln Junior College–Natchez Campus, MS	171
Coppin State College, MD	135
Cornell College, IA	109
Cornell University, NY*	211
Corning Community College, NY	211
Cornish Institute, WA	345
Corpus Christi State University, TX	316
Cosumnes River College, CA	27
County College of Morris, NJ	195
Covenant College, GA	72
Covenant Theological Seminary, MO	176
Crafton Hills College, CA	27
Crandall Junior College, GA	72
Craven Community College, NC	234
Creighton University, NE	186
Crowder College, MO	176
Crowley's Ridge College, AR	16
Cuesta College, CA	27
Culver-Stockton College, MO	176
Cumberland College, KY	121
Cumberland College of Tennessee, TN	306
Cumberland County College, NJ	195
Curry College, MA	144
Cuyahoga Community College, Eastern Campus, OH	250
Cuyahoga Community College, Western Campus, OH	250
Cuyamaca College, CA	27
C W Post Campus of Long Island University, NY—See Long Island University, C W Post Campus	
Cypress College, CA	27
Dabney S Lancaster Community College, VA	337
Daemen College, NY	211
Dakota State College, SD	303
Dakota Wesleyan University, SD	303
Daley College, IL—See City Colleges of Chicago, Richard J Daley College	
Dallas Baptist College, TX	316
Dallas Bible College, TX	316
Dallas Christian College, TX	316
Dalton Junior College, GA	72
Dana College, NE	186
Daniel Webster College, NH	191
Danville Area Community College, IL	85
Danville Community College, VA	337
Davenport College of Business, MI	154
David Lipscomb College, TN	307
Davidson County Community College, NC	234
Dawson Community College, MT	183
Daytona Beach Community College, FL	62
Dean Institute of Technology, PA	276
Dean Junior College, MA	144
De Anza College, CA	27
Defiance College, OH	250
DeKalb Community College, GA	72
Delaware County Community College, PA	276
Delaware State College, DE*	58
Delaware Technical and Community College, Terry Campus, DE	58
Delaware Valley College of Science and Agriculture, PA	276
Delgado Community College, LA	127
Del Mar College, TX	316
De Lourdes College, IL	85
Delta College, MI	155
Delta State University, MS	171
Denmark Technical College, SC	298
Denver Auraria Community College, CO	48
Denver Conservative Baptist Seminary, CO	48
Denver Institute of Technology, CO	48
DePaul University, IL	85
DePauw University, IN	101
Des Moines Area Community College, IA	109
Detroit College of Business, Dearborn, MI	155
Detroit College of Business–Flint, MI	155
Detroit College of Business, Grand Rapids Campus, MI	155
Detroit College of Business, Madison Heights Campus, MI	155
Detroit College of Law, MI	155
DeVry Institute of Technology, GA	73
DeVry Institute of Technology, Chicago, IL	85
DeVry Institute of Technology, Lombard, IL	85
DeVry Institute of Technology, OH	251
DeVry Institute of Technology, TX	316
Dickinson College, PA	276
Dickinson State College, ND	245
Dillard University, LA	127
District One Technical Institute, WI	354
Dixie College, UT	332
Dodge City Community College, KS	116
Dominican College of Blauvelt, NY	211
Dominican College of San Rafael, CA	27
Dominican House of Studies, DC	59
Douglass College, NJ—See Rutgers University, Douglass College	
Dowling College, NY	211
D-Q University, CA	28
Drake University, IA*	109
Draughon's Junior College, GA	73
Draughon's Junior College of Business, KY	121
Drew University, NJ	195
Drexel University, PA	276
Dropsie College for Hebrew and Cognate Learning, PA	276
Drury College, MO	176
Duke University, NC	234
Dundalk Community College, MD	135

*Member of National University Continuing Education Association

401

Index to Colleges

Duquesne University, PA	276
Durham Technical Institute, NC	234
Dutchess Community College, NY	211
Dyersburg State Community College, TN	307
Dyke College, OH	251
D'Youville College, NY	211
Earlham College, IN	101
East Arkansas Community College, AR	16
East Carolina University, NC*	234
East Central College, MO	177
East Central Junior College, MS	171
East Central Oklahoma State University, OK	263
East Coast Bible College, NC	235
Eastern Arizona College, AZ	13
Eastern Baptist Theological Seminary, PA	276
Eastern College, PA	277
Eastern Connecticut State University, CT	53
Eastern Illinois University, IL*	86
Eastern Kentucky University, KY*	121
Eastern Maine Vocational-Technical Institute, ME	131
Eastern Mennonite College, VA	337
Eastern Michigan University, MI*	155
Eastern Montana College, MT	183
Eastern Nazarene College, MA	144
Eastern New Mexico University, NM*	202
Eastern New Mexico University–Roswell, NM	202
Eastern Oklahoma State College, OK	263
Eastern Oregon State College, OR*	268
Eastern Shore Community College, VA	337
Eastern Washington University, WA	345
Eastern Wyoming College, WY	363
Eastfield College, TX	316
East Mississippi Junior College, MS	171
East Stroudsburg University of Pennsylvania, PA*	277
East Tennessee State University, TN*	307
East Texas Baptist University, TX	317
East Texas State University, Commerce, TX	317
East-West University, IL	86
Eckerd College, FL	62
Eden Theological Seminary, MO	177
Ed E Reid State Technical College, AL	4
Edgecombe Technical College, NC	235
Edgewood College, WI	354
Edinboro University of Pennsylvania, PA	277
Edison Community College, FL	62
Edison State Community College, OH	251
Edmonds Community College, WA	345
Edmondson Junior College, TN	307
Edward Waters College, FL	62
El Centro College, TX	317
Electronic Data Processing College of Puerto Rico, PR	292
Elgin Community College, IL	86
Elizabeth Seton College, NY	212
Elizabethtown College, PA	277
Elizabethtown Community College, KY—See University of Kentucky, Elizabethtown Community College	
Ellsworth Community College, IA	109
Elmhurst College, IL*	86
Elmira College, NY	212
Elms College, MA	144
Elon College, NC	235
El Paso Community College, TX	317
El Reno Junior College, OK	263
Emanuel County Junior College, GA	73
Embry-Riddle Aeronautical University, Daytona Beach, FL	62
Embry-Riddle Aeronautical University, International Campus, FL	63
Embry-Riddle Aeronautical University, Prescott Campus, AZ	13
Emerson College, MA	144
Emmanuel College, MA	144
Emmanuel College School of Christian Ministries, GA	73
Emmanuel School of Religion, TN	307
Emory University, GA	73
Emporia State University, KS	116
Endicott College, MA	145
Enterprise State Junior College, AL	5
Episcopal Divinity School, MA	145
Erie Community College, City Campus, NY	212
Erie Community College, South Campus, NY	212
Erskine College, SC	298
Erskine Theological Seminary, SC	298
Essex Community College, MD	135
Essex County College, NJ	195
Eureka College, IL	86
Evangelical School of Theology, PA	277
Evangelical Seminary of Puerto Rico, PR	292
Everett Community College, WA	345
Evergreen State College, WA	345
Evergreen Valley College, CA	28
Fairfield University, CT	53
Fairleigh Dickinson University, Edward Williams College, NJ	195
Fairleigh Dickinson University, Florham-Madison Campus, NJ	195
Fairleigh Dickinson University, Rutherford Campus, NJ	196
Fairleigh Dickinson University, Teaneck-Hackensack Campus, NJ	196
Fairmont State College, WV	351
Faith Baptist Bible College, IA	110
Fashion Institute of Design and Merchandising, Los Angeles Campus, CA	28
Fashion Institute of Design and Merchandising, San Francisco Campus, CA	28
Fashion Institute of Technology, NY	212
Fayetteville State University, NC	235
Fayetteville Technical Institute, NC	235
Feather River College, CA	28
Felician College, IL	86
Felician College, NJ	196
Fergus Falls Community College, MN	166
Ferris State College, MI*	155
Ferrum College, VA	337
Findlay College, OH	251
Fisher Junior College, MA	145
Fisk University, TN	307
Fitchburg State College, MA	145
Five Towns College, NY	212
Flathead Valley Community College, MT	184
Florence-Darlington Technical College, SC	298
Florida Agricultural and Mechanical University, FL*	63
Florida Atlantic University, FL*	63
Florida Institute of Technology, FL	63
Florida Institute of Technology, School of Applied Technology, FL	63
Florida International University, FL*	63
Florida Keys Community College, FL	64
Florida Memorial College, FL	64
Florida Southern College, FL	64
Floyd Junior College, GA	73
Fontbonne College, MO	177
Foothill College, CA	28
Fordham University, NY	212
Fordham University at Lincoln Center, NY	213
Forest Institute of Professional Psychology, IL	86
Forsyth Technical Institute, NC	235
Fort Hays State University, KS	116
Fort Lauderdale College, FL	64
Fort Lewis College, CO	48
Fort Scott Community College, KS	116
Fort Steilacoom Community College, WA	345
Fort Valley State College, GA	73
Fort Wayne Bible College, IN	101
Fox Valley Technical Institute, WI	354
Framingham State College, MA	145

402

Index to Colleges

Francis Marion College, SC	299
Franklin and Marshall College, PA*	277
Franklin Institute of Boston, MA	145
Franklin Pierce College, NH	191
Franklin University, OH	251
Frank Phillips College, TX	317
Frederick Community College, MD	136
Freed-Hardeman College, TN	307
Freeman Junior College, SD	303
Fresno City College, CA	28
Fresno Pacific College, CA	29
Friends Bible College, KS	116
Friends University, KS	117
Front Range Community College, CO	48
Frostburg State College, MD	136
Fullerton College, CA	29
Fulton-Montgomery Community College, NY	213
Furman University, SC	299
Gadsden State Junior College, AL	5
Gainesville Junior College, GA	73
Gallaudet College, DC	59
Galveston College, TX	317
Gannon University, PA	277
Gardner-Webb College, NC	235
Garland County Community College, AR	16
Garrett Community College, MD	136
Garrett-Evangelical Theological Seminary, IL	86
Gaston College, NC	235
Gateway Technical Institute, Kenosha, WI	354
Gateway Technical Institute, Racine, WI	354
Gavilan College, CA	29
Gem City College, IL	86
Genesee Community College, NY	213
Geneva College, PA	278
George Corley Wallace State Community College, Selma, AL	5
George C Wallace State Community College, Dothan, AL	5
George Mason University, VA*	337
Georgetown College, KY	122
Georgetown University, DC	59
George Washington University, DC*	59
George Williams College, IL	87
Georgia College, GA	73
Georgia Institute of Technology, GA*	74
Georgian Court College, NJ	196
Georgia Southern College, GA*	74
Georgia Southwestern College, GA*	74
Georgia State University, GA*	74
Germanna Community College, VA	337
Gettysburg College, PA	278
Glassboro State College, NJ	196
Glendale Community College, AZ	13
Glendale Community College, CA	29
Glen Oaks Community College, MI	155
Gloucester County College, NJ	196
God's Bible School and College, OH	251
Gogebic Community College, MI	156
Golden Gate Baptist Theological Seminary, CA	29
Golden Gate University, CA	29
Golden Valley Lutheran College, MN	166
Golden West College, CA	29
Goldey Beacom College, DE	58
Gonzaga University, WA	346
Gordon College, MA	145
Gordon-Conwell Theological Seminary, MA	146
Gordon Junior College, GA	74
Goshen College, IN	101
Goucher College, MD	136
Governors State University, IL*	87
Grace Bible College, MI	156
Grace College, IN	101
Grace College of the Bible, NE	186
Graceland College, IA	110
Grace Theological Seminary, IN	102
Graduate Theological Union, CA	29
Graham Bible College, VA	338
Grambling State University, LA	128
Grand Canyon College, AZ	13
Grand Rapids Baptist College and Seminary, MI	156
Grand Rapids Junior College, MI	156
Grand Valley State College, MI*	156
Grand View College, IA	110
Grantham College of Engineering, CA	30
Gratz College, PA	278
Grays Harbor College, WA	346
Grayson County College, TX	317
Greater Hartford Community College, CT	53
Greater New Haven State Technical College, CT	53
Great Lakes Bible College, MI	156
Greenfield Community College, MA	146
Green Mountain College, VT	334
Green River Community College, WA	346
Greensboro College, NC	236
Greenville College, IL	87
Greenville Technical College, SC	299
Griffin College, Seattle, WA	346
Grossmont College, CA	30
Grove City College, PA	278
Guam Community College, GU	78
Guilford College, NC	236
Guilford Technical Community College, NC	236
Gulf-Coast Bible College, TX	318
Gulf Coast Community College, FL	64
Gwynedd-Mercy College, PA	278
Hagerstown Business College, MD	136
Hagerstown Junior College, MD	136
Hahnemann University, PA	278
Halifax Community College, NC	236
Hamline University, MN	166
Hampton Institute, VA	338
Hannibal-LaGrange College, MO	177
Harcum Junior College, PA	278
Harding Business College, Marion, OH	251
Harding Graduate School of Religion, TN	307
Harding University, AR	16
Hardin-Simmons University, TX	318
Harford Community College, MD	136
Harrisburg Area Community College, PA	278
Harris-Stowe State College, MO	177
Hartford College for Women, CT	53
Hartford Graduate Center, CT	53
Hartford Seminary, CT	54
Hartford State Technical College, CT	54
Hartwick College, NY	213
Harvard University, MA*	146
Haskell Indian Junior College, KS	117
Hastings College, NE	186
Hawaii Loa College, HI	78
Hawaii Pacific College, HI	78
Hawkeye Institute of Technology, IA	110
Hawthorne College, NH	191
Haywood Technical College, NC	236
Hazard Community College, KY—See University of Kentucky, Hazard Community College	
Hebrew College, MA	146
Hebrew Union College–Jewish Institute of Religion, OH	251
Heidelberg College, OH	251
Hellenic College, MA	146
Henderson Community College, KY—See University of Kentucky, Henderson Community College	
Henderson County Junior College, TX	318
Henderson State University, AR	16
Henry Ford Community College, MI	156
Heritage College, WA	346
Herkimer County Community College, NY	213

*Member of National University Continuing Education Association

Index to Colleges

Hesser College, NH	191
Hesston College, KS	117
Hibbing Community College, MN	166
Highland Community College, IL	87
Highland Community College, KS	117
Highland Park Community College, MI	157
Highline Community College, WA	346
High Point College, NC	236
Hilbert College, NY	213
Hill Junior College, TX	318
Hillsborough Community College, FL	64
Hillsdale Free Will Baptist College, OK	264
Hiram College, OH	252
Hocking Technical College, OH	252
Hofstra University, NY	213
Hollins College, VA	338
Holy Apostles College, CT	54
Holy Cross Greek Orthodox School of Theology, MA	146
Holy Cross Junior College, IN	102
Holy Family College, PA	279
Holy Names College, CA	30
Holyoke Community College, MA	146
Holy Redeemer College, WI	354
Hood College, MD	137
Hope College, MI	157
Hopkinsville Community College, KY—See University of Kentucky, Hopkinsville Community College	
Housatonic Community College, CT	54
Houston Baptist University, TX	318
Houston Community College System, TX	318
Howard College at Big Spring, TX	318
Howard Community College, MD	137
Howard Payne University, TX	318
Howard University, DC	60
Hudson County Community College, NJ	197
Hudson Valley Community College, NY	213
Huertas Business College, PR	292
Humboldt State University, CA*	30
Humphreys College, CA	30
Hunter College, NY—See City University of New York, Hunter College	
Huntingdon College, AL	5
Huntington College, IN	102
Huntington Junior College of Business, WV	351
Hussian School of Art, PA	279
Husson College, ME	131
Huston-Tillotson College, TX	319
Hutchinson Community College, KS	117
ICS Center for Degree Studies, PA	279
Idaho State University, ID*	80
Iliff School of Theology, CO	48
Illinois Benedictine College, IL	87
Illinois Central College, IL	87
Illinois Eastern Community Colleges, Frontier Community College, IL	88
Illinois Eastern Community Colleges, Lincoln Trail College, IL	88
Illinois Eastern Community Colleges, Olney Central College, IL	88
Illinois Eastern Community Colleges, Wabash Valley College, IL	88
Illinois Institute of Technology, IL	88
Illinois School of Professional Psychology, IL	88
Illinois State University, IL*	88
Illinois Technical College, IL	89
Illinois Valley Community College, IL	89
Immaculata College, PA	279
Imperial Valley College, CA	30
Incarnate Word College, TX	319
Independence Community College, KS	117
Indiana Central University, IN	102
Indiana Institute of Technology, IN	102
Indiana State University, Terre Haute, IN*	102
Indiana State University Evansville, IN	102
Indiana University at Kokomo, IN	102
Indiana University at South Bend, IN*	103
Indiana University Bloomington, IN*	103
Indiana University East, IN	103
Indiana University Northwest, IN	103
Indiana University of Pennsylvania, PA*	279
Indiana University–Purdue University at Fort Wayne, IN	103
Indiana University–Purdue University at Indianapolis, IN*	103
Indiana University Southeast, IN	104
Indiana Vocational Technical College–Central Indiana, IN	104
Indiana Vocational Technical College–Columbus, IN	104
Indiana Vocational Technical College–Eastcentral, IN	104
Indiana Vocational Technical College–Kokomo, IN	104
Indiana Vocational Technical College–Northcentral, IN	104
Indiana Vocational Technical College–Northeast, IN	104
Indiana Vocational Technical College–Northwest, IN	105
Indiana Vocational Technical College–Southcentral, IN	105
Indiana Vocational Technical College–Southeast, IN	105
Indiana Vocational Technical College–Southwest, IN	105
Indiana Vocational Technical College–Wabash Valley, IN	105
Indiana Vocational Technical College–Whitewater, IN	105
Indian Hills Community College, IA	110
Indian River Community College, FL	64
Indian Valley Colleges, CA	30
Institute of American Indian Arts, NM	202
Institute of Design and Construction, NY	214
Institute of Paper Chemistry, WI	354
Instituto Comercial de Puerto Rico Junior College, PR	292
Instituto Técnico Comercial Junior College, PR	292
Inter American University of Puerto Rico, Aguadilla Regional College, PR	293
Inter American University of Puerto Rico, Barranquitas Regional College, PR	293
Inter American University of Puerto Rico, Fajardo Regional College, PR	293
Inter American University of Puerto Rico, Guayama Regional College, PR	293
Inter American University of Puerto Rico, Metropolitan Campus, PR	293
Inter American University of Puerto Rico, Ponce Regional College, PR	293
Inter American University of Puerto Rico, San Germán Campus, PR	293
Intermountain Bible College, CO	48
International Academy of Merchandising and Design, IL	89
International Bible College, AL	5
Inver Hills Community College, MN	166
Iona College, NY	214
Iowa Central Community College, IA	110
Iowa Lakes Community College, North Attendance Center, IA	110
Iowa Lakes Community College, South Attendance Center, IA	110
Iowa State University, IA*	111
Iowa Wesleyan College, IA	111
Iowa Western Community College, IA	111
Isothermal Community College, NC	236
Itasca Community College, MN	166
Itawamba Junior College, MS	171
Ithaca College, NY	214
Jackson Community College, MI	157
Jackson State Community College, TN	307
Jackson State University, MS	171
Jacksonville College, TX	319
Jacksonville State University, AL	5
Jacksonville University, FL	64
James H Faulkner State Junior College, AL	5
James Madison University, VA	338

Index to Colleges

James Sprunt Technical College, NC	236
Jamestown Business College, NY	214
Jamestown College, ND	245
Jamestown Community College, NY	214
Jarvis Christian College, TX	319
Jefferson College, MO	177
Jefferson Community College, KY—See University of Kentucky, Jefferson Community College	
Jefferson Community College, NY	214
Jefferson Davis State Junior College, AL	6
Jefferson State Junior College, AL	6
Jefferson Technical College, OH	252
Jersey City State College, NJ	197
Jesuit School of Theology at Berkeley, CA	30
Jewish Theological Seminary of America, NY	214
John A Logan College, IL	89
John Brown University, AR	16
John Carroll University, OH	252
John C Calhoun State Community College, AL	6
John F Kennedy University, CA	31
John Jay College of Criminal Justice, NY—See City University of New York, John Jay College of Criminal Justice	
John Marshall Law School, IL	89
Johns Hopkins University, MD*	137
Johnson & Wales College, RI	295
Johnson Bible College, TN	308
Johnson County Community College, KS	117
Johnson C Smith University, NC	237
Johnson State College, VT	334
John Tyler Community College, VA	338
John Wesley College, NC	237
John Wood Community College, IL	89
Joliet Junior College, IL	89
Jones College, FL	65
Jones County Junior College, MS	172
Jordan College, MI	157
J Sargeant Reynolds Community College, VA	338
Judson Baptist College, OR	268
Judson College, AL	6
Judson College, IL	89
Juniata College, PA	279
Junior College of Albany, NY	214
Kalamazoo Valley Community College, MI	157
Kankakee Community College, IL	90
Kansas City Art Institute, MO	177
Kansas City Kansas Community College, KS	117
Kansas Newman College, KS	117
Kansas State University, KS*	118
Kansas Technical Institute, KS	118
Kansas Wesleyan, KS	118
Kaskaskia College, IL	90
Katharine Gibbs School, New York, NY	215
Kean College of New Jersey, NJ	197
Kearney State College, NE	186
Keene State College, NH	191
Kellogg Community College, MI	157
Kendall College, IL	90
Kendall School of Design, MI	157
Kennebec Valley Vocational-Technical Institute, ME	132
Kennedy-King College, IL—See City Colleges of Chicago, Kennedy-King College	
Kennesaw College, GA*	75
Kent State University, OH*	252
Kent State University, Ashtabula Campus, OH	252
Kent State University, East Liverpool Campus, OH	252
Kent State University, Geauga Campus, OH	253
Kent State University, Salem Campus, OH	253
Kent State University, Stark Campus, OH	253
Kent State University, Trumbull Campus, OH	253
Kent State University, Tuscarawas Campus, OH	253
Kentucky Junior College of Business, KY	122
Kentucky State University, KY	122
Kentucky Wesleyan College, KY	122
Kettering College of Medical Arts, OH	253
Keystone Junior College, PA	279
Keystone Secretarial and Business Administration School, PA	279
Kilgore College, TX	319
King College, TN	308
Kingsborough Community College, NY—See City University of New York, Kingsborough Community College	
King's College, NY	215
King's College, PA	280
King's River Community College, CA	31
Kirkwood Community College, IA	111
Kirtland Community College, MI	157
Kishwaukee College, IL	90
Knox College, IL	90
Kutztown University of Pennsylvania, PA	280
Labouré College, MA	146
Lackawanna Junior College, PA	280
Lafayette College, PA	280
LaGrange College, GA	75
LaGuardia Community College, NY—See City University of New York, Fiorello H LaGuardia Community College	
Lake City Community College, FL	65
Lake Erie College, OH	253
Lake Forest College, IL	90
Lake Forest School of Management, IL	90
Lake Land College, IL	90
Lakeland College, WI	355
Lakeland Community College, OH	253
Lake Michigan College, MI	158
Lakeshore Technical Institute, WI	355
Lake-Sumter Community College, FL	65
Lake Superior State College, MI	158
Lake Tahoe Community College, CA	31
Lamar Community College, CO	49
Lamar University, TX	319
Lambuth College, TN	308
Lancaster Bible College, PA	280
Lancaster Theological Seminary, PA	280
Lander College, SC	299
Lane Community College, OR	268
Laney College, CA	31
Langston University, OK	264
Lansing Community College, MI	158
LaPorte Business College, IN	105
Laramie County Community College, WY	363
Laredo State University, TX	319
La Roche College, PA	280
La Salle University, PA	280
Lasell Junior College, MA*	146
Lassen College, CA	31
Latter-Day Saints Business College, UT	332
Lawrence Institute of Technology, MI	158
Lawrence University, WI	355
Lebanon Valley College, PA	281
Lees Junior College, KY	122
Lehigh County Community College, PA	281
Lehigh University, PA	281
Lehman College, NY—See City University of New York, Herbert H Lehman College	
Le Moyne College, NY	215
LeMoyne-Owen College, TN	308
Lenoir Community College, NC	237
Lenoir-Rhyne College, NC	237
Lesley College, MA	147
LeTourneau College, TX	320
Lewis and Clark College, OR	268
Lewis and Clark Community College, IL	91
Lewis-Clark State College, ID	80
Lewis College of Business, MI	158

Member of National University Continuing Education Association

Index to Colleges

Lewis University, IL	91
Lexington Community College, KY—See University of Kentucky, Lexington Community College	
Lexington Theological Seminary, KY	122
Liberty Baptist College, VA	338
LIFE Bible College, CA	31
Life Chiropractic College West, CA	31
Lima Technical College, OH	254
Lincoln Christian College, IL	91
Lincoln Christian Seminary, IL	91
Lincoln College, IL	91
Lincoln Land Community College, IL	91
Lincoln Memorial University, TN	308
Lincoln School of Commerce, NE	187
Lincoln University, MO	177
Lincoln University, PA	281
Lindenwood College, MO	178
Lindsey Wilson College, KY	122
Linfield College, OR	268
Livingstone College, NC	237
Livingston University, AL	6
Lock Haven University of Pennsylvania, PA	281
Lockyear College, Evansville Campus, IN	105
Lockyear College, Indianapolis Campus, IN	106
Loma Linda University, CA	31
Loma Linda University, CA	32
Long Beach City College, CA	32
Long Island College Hospital School of Nursing, NY	215
Long Island University, Brooklyn Campus, NY	215
Long Island University, C W Post Campus, NY	215
Long Island University, Southampton Campus, NY	216
Longview Community College, MO	178
Longwood College, VA	339
Loop College, IL—See City Colleges of Chicago, Loop College	
Lorain County Community College, OH	254
Loras College, IA	111
Lord Fairfax Community College, VA	339
Loretto Heights College, CO	49
Los Angeles Baptist College, CA	32
Los Angeles City College, CA	32
Los Angeles Harbor College, CA	32
Los Angeles Mission College, CA	32
Los Angeles Pierce College, CA	32
Los Angeles Southwest College, CA	32
Los Angeles Trade-Technical College, CA	33
Los Angeles Valley College, CA	33
Louisburg College, NC	237
Louise Salinger Academy of Fashion, CA	33
Louisiana College, LA	128
Louisiana State University and Agricultural and Mechanical College, LA*	128
Louisiana State University at Alexandria, LA	128
Louisiana State University at Eunice, LA	128
Louisiana State University in Shreveport, LA*	128
Louisiana Tech University, LA	128
Louisville Presbyterian Theological Seminary, KY	123
Louisville Technical Institute, KY	123
Lourdes College, OH	254
Lower Columbia College, WA	346
Loyola College, MD*	137
Loyola Marymount University, CA	33
Loyola University, New Orleans, LA	129
Loyola University of Chicago, IL*	91
Lubbock Christian College, TX	320
Lurleen B Wallace State Junior College, AL	6
Lutheran Bible Institute of Seattle, WA	346
Lutheran School of Theology at Chicago, IL	92
Lutheran Theological Southern Seminary, SC	299
Luther Northwestern Theological Seminary, MN	166
Luzerne County Community College, PA	281
Lycoming College, PA	281
Lynchburg College, VA	339
Lyndon State College, VT	335
Lyons School of Business, PA	281
Macalester College, MN	166
MacCormac Junior College, IL	92
MacMurray College, IL	92
Macomb Community College, MI	158
Madison Area Technical College, WI	355
Madison Business College, WI	355
Madisonville Community College, KY—See University of Kentucky, Madisonville Community College	
Madonna College, MI	158
Malcolm X College, IL—See City Colleges of Chicago, Malcolm X College	
Mallinckrodt College, IL	92
Malone College, OH	254
Manatee Junior College, FL	65
Manchester College, IN	106
Manchester Community College, CT	54
Manhattan Christian College, KS	118
Manhattan College, NY	216
Manhattan Community College, NY—See City University of New York, Borough of Manhattan Community College	
Manhattan School of Music, NY	216
Manhattanville College, NY	216
Mankato State University, MN	167
Manor Junior College, PA	281
Mansfield Business College, OH	254
Mansfield University of Pennsylvania, PA*	282
Maple Woods Community College, MO	178
Maria College, NY	216
Marian College, IN	106
Marian Court Junior College of Business, MA	147
Maria Regina College, NY	216
Maricopa Technical Community College, AZ	13
Marietta College, OH	254
Marion College, IN	106
Marion Technical College, OH	254
Marist College, NY	216
Marlboro College, VT	335
Marquette University, WI	355
Marshalltown Community College, IA	111
Marshall University, WV	351
Mars Hill College, NC	237
Martin Center College, IN	106
Martin College, TN	308
Martin Community College, NC	237
Mary Baldwin College, VA	339
Mary College, ND	245
Marycrest College, IA	111
Marygrove College, MI	158
Mary Holmes College, MS	172
Maryknoll School of Theology, NY	217
Maryland College of Art and Design, MD	137
Maryland Institute, College of Art, MD	137
Marylhurst College for Lifelong Learning, OR	268
Marymount College, NY	217
Marymount College of Kansas, KS	118
Marymount College of Virginia, VA	339
Marymount Manhattan College, NY	217
Marymount Palos Verdes College, CA	33
Maryville College, TN	308
Maryville College–Saint Louis, MO	178
Mary Washington College, VA	339
Marywood College, PA	282
Massachusetts Bay Community College, MA	147
Massachusetts College of Pharmacy and Allied Health Sciences, MA	147
Massasoit Community College, MA	147
Mater Dei College, NY	217
Mattatuck Community College, CT	54
Mayland Technical College, NC	237

Index to Colleges

Maysville Community College, KY—See University of Kentucky, Maysville Community College	
Mayville State College, ND	245
McCook Community College, NE	187
McCormick Theological Seminary, IL	92
McDowell Technical College, NC	238
McKendree College, IL	92
McLennan Community College, TX	320
McMurry College, TX	320
McNeese State University, LA	129
McPherson College, KS	118
Meadows Junior College, GA	75
Meadville/Lombard Theological School, IL	92
Medaille College, NY	217
Medgar Evers College, NY—See City University of New York, Medgar Evers College	
Medical College of Ohio, OH	254
Medical College of Pennsylvania, PA	282
Memphis Academy of Arts, TN	308
Memphis State University, TN*	309
Memphis Theological Seminary, TN	309
Mendocino College, CA	33
Menlo College, CA	33
Merced College, CA	33
Mercer County Community College, NJ	197
Mercer University, Macon, GA	75
Mercer University in Atlanta, GA	75
Mercy College, NY	217
Mercy College of Detroit, MI	159
Mercyhurst College, PA	282
Meredith College, NC	238
Meridian Junior College, MS	172
Merrimack College, MA	147
Merrimack Valley College of the University System of New Hampshire, NH	191
Merritt College, CA	34
Mesabi Community College, MN	167
Mesa College, CO*	49
Messiah College, PA	282
Methodist College, NC	238
Methodist Theological School in Ohio, OH	255
Metropolitan Business College, IL	92
Metropolitan State College, CO	49
Metropolitan State University, MN	167
Metropolitan Technical Community College, NE	187
MGH Institute of Health Professions, MA	147
Miami Christian College, FL	65
Miami-Dade Community College, FL	65
Miami-Jacobs Junior College of Business, OH	255
Miami University, OH*	255
Miami University–Hamilton Campus, OH	255
Miami University–Middletown Campus, OH	255
Michiana College of Commerce, IN	106
Michigan Christian College, MI	159
Michigan State University, MI*	159
Michigan Technological University, MI*	159
Micronesian Occupational College, TT	332
Mid-America Baptist Theological Seminary, TN	309
Mid-America Nazarene College, KS	118
Middle Georgia College, GA	75
Middlesex Community College, CT	54
Middlesex Community College, MA	147
Middlesex County College, NJ	197
Middle Tennessee State University, TN	309
Midland College, TX	320
Midland Lutheran College, NE	187
Midlands Technical College, SC	299
Mid Michigan Community College, MI	159
Mid-Plains Community College, NE	187
Mid-South Bible College, TN	309
Midstate College, IL	92
Mid-State College, ME	132
Mid-State Technical Institute, WI	355
Midway College, KY	123
Midwest Christian College, OK	264
Midwest College of Engineering, IL	93
Midwestern State University, TX	320
Miles College, AL	6
Miles Community College, MT	184
Millersville University of Pennsylvania, PA	282
Milligan College, TN	309
Millikin University, IL	93
Millsaps College, MS	172
Mills College, CA	34
Milwaukee Area Technical College, WI	355
Milwaukee Institute of Art and Design, WI	356
Milwaukee School of Engineering, WI	356
Mineral Area College, MO	178
Minneapolis College of Art and Design, MN	167
Minneapolis Community College, MN	167
Minot State College, ND	246
MiraCosta College, CA	34
Mission College, CA	34
Mississippi College, MS	172
Mississippi County Community College, AR	16
Mississippi Gulf Coast Junior College, Jackson County Campus, MS	172
Mississippi Gulf Coast Junior College, Jefferson Davis Campus, MS	172
Mississippi Gulf Coast Junior College, Perkinston Campus, MS	173
Mississippi State University, MS*	173
Mississippi University for Women, MS	173
Mississippi Valley State University, MS	173
Missouri Southern State College, MO	178
Missouri Valley College, MO	178
Missouri Western State College, MO	178
Mitchell College, CT	54
Mitchell Community College, NC	238
Moberly Area Junior College, MO	179
Mobile College, AL	6
Modesto Junior College, CA	34
Mohave Community College, AZ	13
Mohawk Valley Community College, NY	217
Mohegan Community College, CT	54
Molloy College, NY	217
Monmouth College, IL	93
Monmouth College, NJ	197
Monroe Business Institute, NY	218
Monroe Community College, NY	218
Monroe County Community College, MI	159
Montana College of Mineral Science and Technology, MT	184
Montana State University, MT	184
Montcalm Community College, MI	159
Montclair State College, NJ	197
Monterey Institute of International Studies, CA	34
Monterey Peninsula College, CA	34
Montgomery College–Germantown Campus, MD	137
Montgomery College–Rockville Campus, MD	137
Montgomery College–Takoma Park Campus, MD	138
Montgomery Technical College, NC	238
Montreat-Anderson College, NC	238
Moore College of Art, PA	282
Moorhead State University, MN	167
Moorpark College, CA	34
Moraine Park Technical Institute, WI	356
Moraine Valley Community College, IL	93
Moravian College, PA	283
Moravian Theological Seminary, PA	283
Morehead State University, KY	123
Morgan Community College, CO	49
Morgan State University, MD*	138
Morningside College, IA	111
Morris Brown College, GA	75
Morris College, SC	299

*Member of National University Continuing Education Association

Index to Colleges

Morris Junior College of Business, FL	65
Morrison Institute of Techology, IL	93
Morton College, IL	93
Motlow State Community College, TN	309
Mountain Empire Community College, VA	339
Mountain View College, TX	320
Mount Aloysius Junior College, PA	283
Mount Angel Seminary, OR	268
Mount Holyoke College, MA	147
Mt Hood Community College, OR	269
Mount Ida College, MA	148
Mount Marty College, SD	303
Mount Mary College, WI	356
Mount Mercy College, IA	112
Mount Olive College, NC	238
Mount Saint Alphonsus Seminary, NY	218
Mount Saint Clare College, IA	112
Mount Saint Mary College, NY	218
Mount St Mary's College, CA	35
Mount Saint Mary's College, MD	138
Mt San Antonio College, CA	35
Mt San Jacinto College, CA	35
Mount Senario College, WI	356
Mount Union College, OH	255
Mount Vernon College, DC	60
Mount Vernon Nazarene College, OH	255
Mount Wachusett Community College, MA	148
Muhlenberg College, PA	283
Multnomah School of the Bible, OR	269
Mundelein College, IL	93
Murray State University, KY*	123
Muscatine Community College, IA	112
Muskegon Business College, MI	160
Muskegon Community College, MI	160
Muskingum College, OH	255
Napa Valley College, CA	35
Naropa Institute, CO	49
Nashotah House, WI	356
Nash Technical College, NC	239
Nashville State Technical Institute, TN	309
Nassau Community College, NY	218
National Business College, Lynchburg, VA	340
National College, SD	304
National College of Education, IL	93
National Education Center–Brown Institute Campus, MN	167
National Education Center–Thompson Institute Campus, PA	283
National University, CA*	35
Navajo Community College, AZ	14
Naval Postgraduate School, CA	35
Navarro College, TX	321
Nazarene Bible College, CO	49
Nazarene Theological Seminary, MO	179
Nazareth College, MI	160
Nazareth College of Rochester, NY	218
Nebraska Christian College, NE	187
Nebraska Indian Community College, NE	187
Nebraska Wesleyan University, NE	187
Nebraska Western College, NE	188
Neosho County Community College, KS	118
Neumann College, PA	283
Newark College of Arts and Sciences, NJ—See Rutgers University, Newark College of Arts and Sciences	
New Brunswick Theological Seminary, NJ	198
Newbury Junior College, MA	148
New College of California, CA	35
Newcomb College, LA—See Tulane University, Newcomb College	
New England College, NH	192
New England Conservatory of Music, MA	148
New England Institute of Applied Arts and Sciences, MA	148
New Hampshire College, NH	192
New Hampshire Technical Institute, NH	192
New Hampshire Vocational-Technical College, Berlin, NH	192
New Hampshire Vocational-Technical College, Laconia, NH	192
New Hampshire Vocational-Technical College, Manchester, NH	192
New Hampshire Vocational-Technical College, Nashua, NH	192
New Hampshire Vocational-Technical College, Stratham, NH	192
New Jersey Institute of Technology, NJ	198
New Mexico Highlands University, NM	202
New Mexico Institute of Mining and Technology, NM	202
New Mexico Junior College, NM	202
New Mexico State University, NM*	202
New Mexico State University–Carlsbad, NM	203
New Orleans Baptist Theological Seminary, LA	129
New River Community College, VA	340
New School for Social Research, NY	218
New School for Social Research, Seminar College, NY	218
New School for Social Research, Senior College, NY	218
New York City Technical College, NY—See City University of New York, New York City Technical College	
New York Institute of Technology, NY	219
New York Law School, NY	219
New York Medical College, NY	219
New York School of Interior Design, NY	219
New York University, NY*	219
Niagara County Community College, NY	219
Niagara University, NY	219
Nicholls State University, LA	129
Nichols College, MA	148
Nicolet College and Technical Institute, WI	356
Norfolk State University, VA	340
Normandale Community College, MN	167
North Adams State College, MA	148
North American Baptist Seminary, SD	304
Northampton County Area Community College, PA	283
North Arkansas Community College, AR	17
North Carolina Agricultural and Technical State University, NC	239
North Carolina Central University, NC*	239
North Carolina State University at Raleigh, NC*	239
North Carolina Wesleyan College, NC	239
North Central Bible College, MN	168
North Central College, IL	94
North Central Michigan College, MI	160
North Central Technical College, OH	255
North Central Technical Institute, WI	356
North Country Community College, NY	219
North Dakota State School of Science, ND	246
North Dakota State University–Bottineau Branch and Institute of Forestry, ND	246
Northeast Alabama State Junior College, AL	7
Northeastern Bible College, NJ	198
Northeastern Illinois University, IL	94
Northeastern Oklahoma Agricultural and Mechanical College, OK	264
Northeastern Oklahoma State University, OK	264
Northeastern University, MA	148
Northeast Iowa Technical Institute–North Center, IA	112
Northeast Louisiana University, LA	129
Northeast Mississippi Junior College, MS	173
Northeast Missouri State University, MO	179
Northeast Technical Community College, NE	188
Northern Arizona University, AZ	14
Northern Baptist Theological Seminary, IL	94
Northern Essex Community College, MA	149
Northern Illinois University, IL*	94
Northern Kentucky University, KY*	123

408

Index to Colleges

Northern Maine Vocational-Technical Institute, ME	132
Northern Marianas College, CM	247
Northern Michigan University, MI	160
Northern Montana College, MT	184
Northern Nevada Community College, NV	189
Northern New Mexico Community College, NM	203
Northern State College, SD	304
Northern Virginia Community College, VA	340
North Florida Junior College, FL	65
North Georgia College, GA	75
North Greenville College, SC	299
North Harris County College, TX	321
North Hennepin Community College, MN	168
North Idaho College, ID	80
North Iowa Area Community College, IA	112
North Lake College, TX	321
Northland College, WI	357
Northland Community College, MN	168
Northland Pioneer College, AZ	14
North Park College, IL	94
North Park Theological Seminary, IL	94
Northrop University, CA	36
North Seattle Community College, WA	347
North Shore Community College, MA	149
North Texas State University, TX	321
Northwest Bible College, ND	246
Northwest Community College, WY	363
Northwestern Business College, IL	94
Northwestern Business College–Technical Center, OH	256
Northwestern College, MN	168
Northwestern Connecticut Community College, CT	55
Northwestern Michigan College, MI	160
Northwestern Oklahoma State University, OK	264
Northwestern State University of Louisiana, LA*	129
Northwestern University, Evanston, IL	94
Northwest Missouri State University, MO	179
Northwest Nazarene College, ID	80
Northwest Technical College, OH	256
Northwood Institute, MI	160
Northwood Institute, Texas Campus, TX	321
Norwalk Community College, CT	55
Norwalk State Technical College, CT	55
Norwich University, Vermont College, VT	335
Notre Dame College, NH	193
Notre Dame College of Ohio, OH	256
Notre Dame Seminary, LA	130
Nova University, FL*	65
Nyack College, NY	220
Oakland City College, IN	106
Oakland Community College, MI	160
Oakland University, MI*	161
Oakton Community College, IL	95
Oakwood College, AL	7
Oberlin College, OH	256
Oblate School of Theology, TX	321
Occidental College, CA	36
Ocean County College, NJ	198
Oglala Lakota College, SD	304
Oglethorpe University, GA	76
Ohio Dominican College, OH	256
Ohio Institute of Photography, OH	256
Ohio State University, Columbus, OH*	256
Ohio State University Agricultural Technical Institute, OH	256
Ohio State University–Lima Campus, OH	257
Ohio State University–Mansfield Campus, OH	257
Ohio State University–Marion Campus, OH	257
Ohio State University–Newark Campus, OH	257
Ohio University, Athens, OH*	257
Ohio University–Chillicothe, OH	257
Ohio University–Ironton, OH	257
Ohio University–Lancaster, OH	257
Ohio University–Zanesville, OH	258
Ohio Wesleyan University, OH	258
Ohlone College, CA	36
Okaloosa-Walton Junior College, FL	66
Oklahoma Baptist University, OK	264
Oklahoma City University, OK	264
Oklahoma Panhandle State University, OK	265
Oklahoma State University, OK*	265
Oklahoma State University Technical Institute, OK	265
Old College, NV	190
Old Dominion University, VA*	340
Olive-Harvey College, IL—See City Colleges of Chicago, Olive-Harvey College	
Olivet College, MI	161
Olivet Nazarene College, IL	95
Olympic College, WA	347
O'More College of Design, TN	310
Onondaga Community College, NY	220
Opelika State Technical College, AL	7
Open Bible College, IA	112
Oral Roberts University, OK	265
Orangeburg-Calhoun Technical College, SC	300
Orange Coast College, CA	36
Orange County Community College, NY	220
Oregon Graduate Center, OR	269
Oregon Institute of Technology, OR	269
Oregon State University, OR*	269
Orlando College, FL	66
Otero Junior College, CO	49
Otis Art Institute of Parsons School of Design, CA	36
Ottawa University, KS	119
Otterbein College, OH	258
Our Lady of Holy Cross College, LA	130
Our Lady of the Lake University of San Antonio, TX	321
Owensboro Junior College of Business, KY	123
Owens Technical College, OH	258
Oxnard College, CA	36
Pace University, New York, NY*	220
Pace University, College of White Plains, NY	220
Pace University–Pleasantville/Briarcliff, NY	220
Pacific Christian College, CA	36
Pacific Coast Junior College, CA	36
Pacific Graduate School of Psychology, CA	37
Pacific Lutheran Theological Seminary, CA	37
Pacific Lutheran University, WA	347
Pacific Northwest College of Art, OR	269
Pacific Oaks College, CA	37
Pacific School of Religion, CA	37
Pacific Union College, CA	37
Pacific University, OR	269
Paducah Community College, KY—See University of Kentucky, Paducah Community College	
Paier College of Art, Inc, CT	55
Palm Beach Atlantic College, FL	66
Palm Beach Junior College, FL	66
Palmer College of Chiropractic, IA	112
Palmer College of Chiropractic–West, CA	37
Palomar College, CA	37
Palo Verde College, CA	37
Pamlico Technical College, NC	239
Pan American University, TX	322
Panola Junior College, TX	322
Paris Junior College, TX	322
Park College, MO	179
Parks College, CO	50
Parks College of Saint Louis University, IL	95
Pasadena City College, CA	37
Pasco-Hernando Community College, FL	66
Passaic County Community College, NJ	198
Patrick Henry Community College, VA	340
Patten College, CA	37
Paul D Camp Community College, VA	340
Paul Quinn College, TX	322
Peace College, NC	239

*Member of National University Continuing Education Association

Index to Colleges

Pearl River Junior College, MS	173
Peirce Junior College, PA	283
Pembroke State University, NC	240
Peninsula College, WA	347
Pennsylvania College of Optometry, PA	284
Pennsylvania Institute of Technology, PA	284
Pennsylvania State University–Behrend College, PA*	284
Pennsylvania State University–Capitol Campus, PA*	284
Pennsylvania State University–King of Prussia Center for Graduate Studies, PA*	284
Pennsylvania State University–Milton S Hershey Medical Center, PA	284
Pennsylvania State University–University Park Campus, PA*	284
Penn Technical Institute, PA	284
Penn Valley Community College, MO	179
Pensacola Junior College, FL	66
Pepperdine University, Malibu, CA	38
Pepperdine University, Pepperdine Plaza, CA	38
Peru State College, NE	188
Pfeiffer College, NC	240
Philadelphia College of Art, PA	284
Philadelphia College of Bible, PA	285
Philadelphia College of Pharmacy and Science, PA	285
Philadelphia College of Textiles and Science, PA	285
Philadelphia College of the Performing Arts, PA	285
Phillips College of New Orleans, LA	130
Phillips County Community College, AR	17
Phillips University, OK	265
Phoenix College, AZ	14
Piedmont Bible College, NC	240
Piedmont Technical College, NC	240
Piedmont Technical College, SC	300
Piedmont Virginia Community College, VA	341
Pikes Peak Community College, CO	50
Pikeville College, KY	124
Pima Community College, AZ	14
Pinebrook Junior College, PA	285
Pine Manor College, MA	149
Pioneer Community College, MO	179
Pitt Community College, NC	240
Pittsburgh Technical Institute, PA	285
Pittsburgh Theological Seminary, PA	285
Pittsburg State University, KS*	119
Pitzer College, CA	38
Platte Valley Bible College, NE	188
Plymouth State College of the University System of New Hampshire, NH	193
Point Loma Nazarene College, CA	38
Point Park College, PA	285
Polk Community College, FL	66
Polytechnic Institute of New York, Brooklyn Campus, NY	220
Polytechnic Institute of New York, Farmingdale Campus, NY	221
Porterville College, CA	38
Portland Community College, OR	269
Portland School of Art, ME	132
Portland State University, OR*	269
Post College, CT	55
Potomac State College of West Virginia University, WV	351
Prairie State College, IL	95
Prairie View A&M University, TX	322
Pratt Community College, KS	119
Pratt Institute, NY	221
Prentiss Normal and Industrial Institute, MS	173
Presbyterian College, SC	300
Presbyterian School of Christian Education, VA	341
Presentation College, SD	304
Prestonsburg Community College, KY—See University of Kentucky, Prestonsburg Community College	
Prince George's Community College, MD	138
Princeton Theological Seminary, NJ	198
Prospect Hall College, FL	67
Protestant Episcopal Theological Seminary in Virginia, VA	341
Providence College, RI	295
Pueblo Community College, CO	50
Puget Sound College of the Bible, WA	347
Purdue University, West Lafayette, IN*	106
Purdue University Calumet, IN*	107
Purdue University North Central, IN	107
Queensborough Community College, NY—See City University of New York, Queensborough Community College	
Queens College, NY—See City University of New York, Queens College	
Queens College, NC*	240
Quincy College, IL	95
Quincy Junior College, MA	149
Quinebaug Valley Community College, CT	55
Quinnipiac College, CT	55
Quinsigamond Community College, MA	149
Radford University, VA	341
Ramapo College of New Jersey, NJ	198
Randolph-Macon Woman's College, VA	341
Randolph Technical College, NC	240
Ranger Junior College, TX	322
Raymond Walters General and Technical College, OH—See University of Cincinnati, Raymond Walters General and Technical College	
Reading Area Community College, PA	286
Red Rocks Community College, CO	50
Regis College, CO*	50
Regis College, MA	149
Reinhardt College, GA	76
Rend Lake College, IL	95
Reno Business College, NV	190
Rensselaer Polytechnic Institute, NY	221
RETS Tech Center, OH	258
Rhode Island College, RI*	295
Rice University, TX	322
Richard Bland College, VA	341
Richland College, TX	322
Richland Community College, IL	95
Richmond Technical College, NC	240
Ricks College, ID	81
Rider College, NJ	198
Rio Grande College/Community College, OH	258
Rio Hondo Community College, CA	38
Ripon College, WI	357
Riverside City College, CA	38
Rivier College, NH	193
Roane State Community College, TN	310
Roanoke Bible College, NC	241
Roanoke-Chowan Technical College, NC	241
Roanoke College, VA	341
Robert Morris College, PA	286
Roberts Wesleyan College, NY	221
Rochester Business Institute, NY	221
Rochester Community College, MN	168
Rochester Institute of Technology, NY*	221
Rockford College, IL	95
Rockhurst College, MO	180
Rockingham Community College, NC	241
Rockland Community College, NY	221
Rockmont College, CO	50
Rock Valley College, IL	96
Rocky Mountain College, MT	184
Rocky Mountain School of Art, CO	50
Rogers State College, OK	265
Roger Williams College, RI	296
Rogue Community College, OR	270
Rollins College, FL	67
Roosevelt University, IL*	96
Rosary College, IL	96

Index to Colleges

Rose-Hulman Institute of Technology, IN	107
Rosemont College, PA	286
Rose State College, OK	266
Rowan Technical College, NC	241
Roxbury Community College, MA	149
Rush University, IL	96
Russell Sage College, NY	222
Rust College, MS	174
Rutgers University, Camden College of Arts and Sciences, NJ*	199
Rutgers University, College of Nursing, NJ*	199
Rutgers University, Douglass College, NJ*	199
Rutgers University, Newark, NJ*	199
Rutgers University, Newark College of Arts and Sciences, NJ*	199
Rutgers University, New Brunswick, NJ*	199
Rutgers University, University College–Camden, NJ*	199
Rutgers University, University College–Newark, NJ*	200
Rutgers University, University College–New Brunswick, NJ*	200
Rutledge College, MO	180
Rutledge College, Fayetteville, NC	241
Rutledge College, Columbia, SC	300
Rutledge College, Greenville, SC	300
Rutledge College, North Charleston, SC	300
Rutledge College, Spartanburg, SC	300
Rutledge College, TN	310
Sacramento City College, CA	39
Sacred Heart College, NC	241
Sacred Heart Seminary College, MI	161
Sacred Heart University, CT	55
Saddleback Community College, CA	39
Saginaw Valley State College, MI	161
St Ambrose College, IA	112
St Andrews Presbyterian College, NC	241
Saint Augustine Community College, IL	96
Saint Augustine's College, NC	241
Saint Bernard's Institute, NY	222
St Bonaventure University, NY	222
St Catharine College, KY	124
St Charles Borromeo Seminary, PA	286
St Cloud State University, MN	168
St Edward's University, TX	323
Saint Francis College, IN	107
St Francis College, NY	222
Saint Francis College, PA	286
Saint Francis Seminary, School of Pastoral Ministry, WI	357
St John Fisher College, NY*	222
St John's College, KS	119
St John's College, MD	138
St John's College, NM	203
St John's Provincial Seminary, MI	161
St Johns River Community College, FL	67
Saint John's University, MN	168
St John's University, NY	222
Saint Joseph College, CT	56
Saint Joseph's College, IN	107
St Joseph's College, Brooklyn, NY	222
St Joseph's College, Suffolk Campus, NY	222
Saint Joseph's University, PA	286
St Lawrence University, NY	223
Saint Leo College, FL	67
St Louis Community College at Florissant Valley, MO	180
St Louis Community College at Forest Park, MO	180
St Louis Community College at Meramec, MO	180
Saint Louis University, MO	180
Saint Martin's College, WA	347
Saint Mary College, KS	119
Saint Mary of the Plains College, KS	119
Saint Mary-of-the-Woods College, IN	107
Saint Mary's College, MI	161
Saint Mary's College, MN	168
Saint Mary's College of California, CA	39
St Mary's College of Maryland, MD	138
Saint Mary's College of O'Fallon, MO	180
Saint Mary Seminary, OH	258
St Mary's Junior College, MN	169
St Mary's University of San Antonio, TX	323
Saint Meinrad School of Theology, IN	107
Saint Paul's College, MO	180
Saint Paul's College, VA	341
Saint Paul Seminary, MN	169
St Petersburg Junior College, FL	67
Saint Peter's College, Jersey City, NJ	200
St Thomas Aquinas College, NY	223
St Thomas of Villanova University, FL	67
Saint Vincent College, PA	286
Saint Vincent Seminary, PA	287
Saint Xavier College, IL	96
Salem College, NC	242
Salem College, WV	351
Salem Community College, NJ	200
Salem State College, MA	150
Salisbury State College, MD	138
Salish Kootenai Community College, MT	184
Salve Regina–The Newport College, RI	296
Samford University, AL	7
Sam Houston State University, TX	323
Sampson Technical College, NC	242
San Antonio College, TX	323
Sandhills Community College, NC	242
San Diego City College, CA	39
San Diego Mesa College, CA	39
San Diego Miramar College, CA	39
San Diego State University, CA*	39
San Francisco Art Institute, CA	39
San Francisco Conservatory of Music, CA	40
San Francisco State University, CA*	40
San Francisco Theological Seminary, CA	40
Sangamon State University, IL	96
San Jacinto College–Central Campus, TX	323
San Jacinto College–North Campus, TX	323
San Jacinto College–South Campus, TX	323
San Joaquin Delta College, CA	40
San Jose Bible College, CA	40
San Jose City College, CA	40
San Jose State University, CA*	40
San Juan College, NM	203
Santa Ana College, CA	40
Santa Barbara City College, CA	41
Santa Fe Community College, FL	67
Santa Monica College, CA	41
Santa Rosa Junior College, CA	41
Sarah Lawrence College, NY	223
Sauk Valley College, IL	97
Savannah College of Art and Design, GA	76
Savannah State College, GA*	76
Scarritt College, TN	310
Schenectady County Community College, NY	223
Schoolcraft College, MI	161
School for International Training, VT	335
School for Lifelong Learning of the University System of New Hampshire, NH*	193
School of the Art Institute of Chicago, IL	97
School of the Museum of Fine Arts, MA	150
School of Theology at Claremont, CA	41
School of the Ozarks, MO	181
School of Visual Arts, NY	223
Schreiner College, TX	324
Scott Community College, IA	113
Scripps College, CA	41
S D Bishop State Junior College, AL	7
Seabury-Western Theological Seminary, IL	97
Seattle Central Community College, WA	347
Seattle Pacific University, WA	347

*Member of National University Continuing Education Association

Index to Colleges

Seattle University, WA	348
Selma University, AL	7
Seminary of the Immaculate Conception, NY	223
Seminole Community College, FL	67
Seminole Junior College, OK	266
Seton Hall University, NJ	200
Seton Hill College, PA	287
Seward County Community College, KS	119
Shawnee College, IL	97
Shawnee State Community College, OH	258
Shaw University, NC	242
Shelby State Community College, TN	310
Sheldon Jackson College, AK	11
Shelton State Community College, AL	7
Shenandoah College and Conservatory of Music, VA	341
Shepherd College, WV	351
Sheridan College, WY	363
Sherwood Conservatory of Music, IL	97
Shimer College, IL	97
Shippensburg University of Pennsylvania, PA	287
Shoreline Community College, WA	348
Shorter College, AR	17
Shorter College, GA	76
Siena College, NY	223
Siena Heights College, MI	161
Sierra College, CA	41
Sierra Nevada College, NV	190
Silver Lake College, WI	357
Simmons College, MA	150
Simpson College, CA	41
Simpson College, IA	113
Sinclair Community College, OH	259
Sioux Empire College, IA	113
Sioux Falls College, SD	304
Skagit Valley College, WA	348
Skidmore College, NY	223
Skyline College, CA	41
Slippery Rock University of Pennsylvania, PA	287
Smith College, MA	150
Snead State Junior College, AL	7
Snow College, UT	332
Sojourner-Douglass College, MD	139
Solano Community College, CA	42
Somerset Community College, KY—See University of Kentucky, Somerset Community College	
Somerset County College, NJ	200
Sonoma State University, CA	42
Southampton Campus of Long Island University, NY—See Long Island University, Southampton Campus	
South Carolina State College, SC	300
South Central Community College, CT	56
South Dakota School of Mines and Technology, SD	304
South Dakota State University, SD*	304
Southeast Community College, KY—See University of Kentucky, Southeast Community College	
Southeast Community College, Beatrice Campus, NE	188
Southeast Community College, Fairbury Campus, NE	188
Southeast Community College, Lincoln Campus, NE	188
Southeastern Baptist College, MS	174
Southeastern Bible College, AL	8
Southeastern Community College, NC	242
Southeastern Community College, North Campus, IA	113
Southeastern Community College, South Campus, IA	113
Southeastern Illinois College, IL	97
Southeastern Louisiana University, LA	130
Southeastern Massachusetts University, MA	150
Southeastern Oklahoma State University, OK	266
Southeastern University, DC*	60
Southeast Missouri State University, MO	181
Southern Arkansas University, AR	17
Southern Arkansas University–El Dorado Branch, AR	17
Southern Arkansas University Tech, AR	17
Southern Baptist College, AR	17
Southern California College, CA	42
Southern College of Optometry, TN	310
Southern College of Seventh-Day Adventists, TN	310
Southern Connecticut State University, CT	56
Southern Illinois University at Carbondale, IL*	97
Southern Illinois University at Edwardsville, IL	98
Southern Institute, AL	8
Southern Maine Vocational-Technical Institute, ME	132
Southern Methodist University, TX*	324
Southern Ohio College, Cincinnati Campus, OH	259
Southern Ohio College, Fairfield Campus, OH	259
Southern Ohio College, Northeast Campus, OH	259
Southern Ohio College, Northern Kentucky Campus, KY	124
Southern Oregon State College, OR*	270
Southern State Community College, OH	259
Southern Technical Institute, GA	76
Southern Union State Junior College, AL	8
Southern University and Agricultural and Mechanical College, LA	130
Southern University, Shreveport–Bossier City Campus, LA	130
Southern Utah State College, UT	332
Southern Vermont College, VT	335
Southern West Virginia Community College, WV	351
South Georgia College, GA	76
South Mountain Community College, AZ	14
South Plains College, TX	324
South Puget Sound Community College, WA	348
South Seattle Community College, WA	348
Southside Virginia Community College, VA	342
South Texas College of Law, TX	324
Southwest Baptist University, MO	181
SouthWest Collegiate Institute for the Deaf, TX	324
Southwestern Adventist College, TX	324
Southwestern Assemblies of God College, TX*	324
Southwestern Baptist Theological Seminary, TX	324
Southwestern Christian College, TX	325
Southwestern College, CA	42
Southwestern College, KS	120
Southwestern College of Business, Kettering, OH	259
Southwestern College of Christian Ministries, OK	266
Southwestern Community College, IA	113
Southwestern Junior College of the Assemblies of God, TX	325
Southwestern Michigan College, MI	162
Southwestern Oklahoma State University, OK	266
Southwestern Oregon Community College, OR	270
Southwestern Technical College, NC	242
Southwestern University School of Law, CA	42
Southwest Mississippi Junior College, MS	174
Southwest Missouri State University, MO	181
Southwest State Technical College, AL	8
Southwest State University, MN	169
Southwest Texas Junior College, TX	325
Southwest Texas State University, TX	325
Southwest Virginia Community College, VA	342
Southwest Wisconsin Vocational-Technical Institute, WI	357
Spalding University, KY	124
Spartanburg Methodist College, SC	300
Spartanburg Technical College, SC	301
Spertus College of Judaica, IL	98
Spokane Community College, WA	348
Spokane Falls Community College, WA	348
Spoon River College, IL	98
Spring Arbor College, MI	162
Springfield College, MA	150
Springfield College in Illinois, IL	98
Springfield Technical Community College, MA	150
Spring Garden College, PA	287
Spring Hill College, AL	8
Spurgeon Baptist Bible College, FL	68
Stanly Technical College, NC	242

Index to Colleges

Stark Technical College, OH	259
State Fair Community College, MO	181
State Technical Institute at Knoxville, TN	310
State Technical Institute at Memphis, TN	310
State University of New York Agricultural and Technical College at Alfred, NY	224
State University of New York Agricultural and Technical College at Canton, NY	224
State University of New York Agricultural and Technical College at Cobleskill, NY	224
State University of New York Agricultural and Technical College at Delhi, NY	224
State University of New York Agricultural and Technical College at Farmingdale, NY	224
State University of New York Agricultural and Technical College at Morrisville, NY	224
State University of New York at Albany, NY*	224
State University of New York at Binghamton, NY*	225
State University of New York at Buffalo, NY*	225
State University of New York at Stony Brook, NY	225
State University of New York College at Brockport, NY	225
State University of New York College at Buffalo, NY	225
State University of New York College at Cortland, NY	226
State University of New York College at Fredonia, NY	226
State University of New York College at Geneseo, NY	226
State University of New York College at New Paltz, NY	226
State University of New York College at Old Westbury, NY	226
State University of New York College at Oneonta, NY	227
State University of New York College at Oswego, NY*	227
State University of New York College at Plattsburgh, NY	227
State University of New York College at Potsdam, NY	227
State University of New York College at Purchase, NY	227
State University of New York College of Environmental Science and Forestry, NY	227
State University of New York College of Technology at Utica/Rome, NY	228
State University of New York Empire State College, NY	228
State University of New York Maritime College, NY	228
State University of New York Upstate Medical Center, NY	228
Stautzenberger College, OH	259
Stenotype Institute, NY	228
Stephen F Austin State University, TX	325
Stephens College, MO	181
Stetson University, FL*	68
Stevens Henager College, UT	333
Stevens Institute of Technology, NJ	200
Stockton State College, NJ	200
Stonehill College, MA	151
Stratton College, WI	357
Strayer College, DC	60
Suffolk County Community College–Eastern Campus, NY	228
Suffolk County Community College–Selden Campus, NY	228
Suffolk County Community College–Western Campus, NY	228
Suffolk University, MA	151
Sullivan County Community College, NY	229
Sullivan Junior College of Business, KY	124
Sul Ross State University, TX	325
Sumter Area Technical College, SC	301
Suomi College, MI	162
Surry Community College, NC	242
Susquehanna University, PA	287
Swain School of Design, MA	151
Sweet Briar College, VA	342
Syracuse University, NY*	229
Syracuse University, Utica College, NY—See Utica College of Syracuse University	
Sysorex Institute, CA	42
Tabor College, KS	120
Tacoma Community College, WA	349
Taft College, CA	42
Talladega College, AL	8
Tallahassee Community College, FL	68
Tampa College, FL	68
Tarkio College, MO	181
Tarleton State University, TX	325
Tarrant County Junior College, TX	325
Taylor University, IN	107
Teachers College, Columbia University, NY	229
Technical Career Institutes, NY	229
Technical College of Alamance, NC	243
Temple University, Philadelphia, PA*	287
Temple University, Ambler Campus, PA	287
Tennessee State University, TN*	310
Tennessee Technological University, TN*	311
Tennessee Temple University, TN	311
Tennessee Wesleyan College, TN	311
Terra Technical College, OH	259
Texarkana Community College, TX	326
Texas A&I University, TX	326
Texas A&M University, College Station, TX*	326
Texas A&M University at Galveston, TX	326
Texas Christian University, TX*	326
Texas Lutheran College, TX	326
Texas Southern University, TX	326
Texas Southmost College, TX	327
Texas State Technical Institute–Amarillo Campus, TX	327
Texas State Technical Institute–Harlingen Campus, TX	327
Texas State Technical Institute–Sweetwater Campus, TX	327
Texas State Technical Institute–Waco Campus, TX	327
Texas Tech University, TX*	327
Texas Wesleyan College, TX	327
Texas Woman's University, TX	328
Thames Valley State Technical College, CT	56
Thomas A Edison State College, NJ*	201
Thomas College, ME	132
Thomas County Community College, GA	76
Thomas Jefferson University, PA	288
Thomas M Cooley Law School, MI	162
Thomas More College, KY	124
Thomas Nelson Community College, VA	342
Thornton Community College, IL	98
Three Rivers Community College, MO	181
Tidewater Community College, Chesapeake Campus, VA	342
Tidewater Community College, Frederick Campus, VA	342
Tidewater Community College, Virginia Beach Campus, VA	342
Tiffin University, OH	260
Tift College, GA	77
Toccoa Falls College, GA	77
Tomlinson College, TN	311
Tompkins Cortland Community College, NY	229
Tougaloo College, MS	174
Touro College, NY	229
Towson State University, MD	139
Transylvania University, KY	125
Treasure Valley Community College, OR	270
Trenholm State Technical College, AL	8
Trenton Junior College, MO	182
Trenton State College, NJ	201
Trevecca Nazarene College, TN	311
Triangle Institute of Technology, Greensburg, PA	288
Tri-Cities State Technical Institute, TN	311
Tri-College University, ND	246
Tri-County Community College, NC	243
Tri-County Technical College, SC	301
Trident Technical College, SC	301
Trinidad State Junior College, CO	50
Trinity Christian College, IL	98
Trinity College, CT	56
Trinity College, DC	60

*Member of National University Continuing Education Association

Index to Colleges

Trinity College, IL	98
Trinity College, VT	335
Trinity Evangelical Divinity School, IL	99
Trinity Lutheran Seminary, OH	260
Trinity University, TX*	328
Tri-State University, IN	108
Triton College, IL	99
Trocaire College, NY	229
Troy State University, Troy, AL	8
Troy State University at Dothan/Fort Rucker, AL	9
Troy State University in Montgomery, AL	9
Truckee Meadows Community College, NV	190
Truett-McConnell College, GA	77
Truman College, IL—See City Colleges of Chicago, Harry S Truman College	
Tufts University, MA*	151
Tulane University, LA	130
Tulane University, Newcomb College, LA	130
Tulsa Junior College, OK	266
Tunxis Community College, CT	56
Tusculum College, TN	311
Tuskegee Institute, AL	9
Tyler Junior College, TX	328
Ulster County Community College, NY	230
Umpqua Community College, OR	270
Union College, KY	125
Union College, NE	188
Union College, NY	230
Union University, TN	311
United States International University, CA	43
United States Sports Academy, AL*	9
United Theological Seminary, OH	260
United Wesleyan College, PA	288
Unity College, ME	132
Universidad del Turabo, PR	293
Universidad Politécnica de Puerto Rico, PR	293
University of Akron, OH	260
University of Alabama, University, AL*	9
University of Alabama in Birmingham, AL*	9
University of Alabama in Huntsville, AL	9
University of Alaska, Anchorage, AK*	11
University of Alaska, Anchorage Community College, AK	11
University of Alaska, Fairbanks, AK*	11
University of Alaska, Islands Community College, AK	11
University of Alaska, Juneau, AK	11
University of Alaska, Ketchikan Community College, AK	11
University of Alaska, Matanuska-Susitna Community College, AK	12
University of Alaska, Tanana Valley Community College, AK	12
University of Albuquerque, NM	203
University of Arizona, AZ*	14
University of Arkansas, Fayetteville, AR	17
University of Arkansas at Little Rock, AR*	18
University of Arkansas at Monticello, AR	18
University of Arkansas at Pine Bluff, AR	18
University of Arkansas for Medical Sciences, AR	18
University of Baltimore, MD	139
University of Bridgeport, CT	56
University of California, Davis, CA	43
University of California, Irvine, CA*	43
University of California, Riverside, CA	43
University of California, San Diego, CA*	43
University of California, San Francisco, CA*	43
University of California, Santa Barbara, CA	43
University of California, Santa Cruz, CA	43
University of Central Arkansas, AR	18
University of Central Florida, FL	68
University of Charleston, WV	351
University of Chicago, IL*	99
University of Cincinnati, OH*	260
University of Cincinnati, Clermont General and Technical College, OH	260
University of Cincinnati, Raymond Walters General and Technical College, OH	260
University of Colorado at Boulder, CO*	51
University of Colorado at Colorado Springs, CO	51
University of Colorado at Denver, CO	51
University of Connecticut, Storrs, CT*	57
University of Connecticut at Waterbury, CT	57
University of Connecticut Health Center, CT	57
University of Dallas, TX	328
University of Dayton, OH	260
University of Delaware, DE*	58
University of Denver, CO*	51
University of Detroit, MI	162
University of Dubuque, IA	113
University of Evansville, IN	108
University of Florida, FL*	68
University of Georgia, GA*	77
University of Guam, GU	78
University of Hartford, CT	57
University of Hawaii at Hilo, HI	79
University of Hawaii at Manoa, HI*	79
University of Hawaii–Honolulu Community College, HI	79
University of Hawaii–Leeward Community College, HI	79
University of Hawaii–Maui Community College, HI	79
University of Hawaii–West Oahu College, HI	79
University of Hawaii–Windward Community College, HI	79
University of Houston–Clear Lake, TX	328
University of Houston–Downtown, TX	328
University of Houston–University Park, TX	328
University of Idaho, ID	81
University of Illinois at Chicago, Health Sciences Center, IL*	99
University of Illinois at Chicago, University Center, IL*	99
University of Iowa, IA*	113
University of Judaism, CA	44
University of Kansas, KS*	120
University of Kansas College of Health Sciences and Hospital, KS	120
University of Kentucky, KY*	125
University of Kentucky, Ashland Community College, KY	125
University of Kentucky, Elizabethtown Community College, KY	125
University of Kentucky, Hazard Community College, KY	125
University of Kentucky, Henderson Community College, KY	125
University of Kentucky, Hopkinsville Community College, KY	125
University of Kentucky, Jefferson Community College, KY	126
University of Kentucky, Lexington Community College, KY	126
University of Kentucky, Madisonville Community College, KY	126
University of Kentucky, Maysville Community College, KY	126
University of Kentucky, Paducah Community College, KY	126
University of Kentucky, Prestonsburg Community College, KY	126
University of Kentucky, Somerset Community College, KY	126
University of Kentucky, Southeast Community College, KY	127
University of La Verne, CA	44
University of Louisville, KY*	127
University of Lowell, MA*	151
University of Maine at Augusta, ME	132
University of Maine at Farmington, ME	133
University of Maine at Fort Kent, ME	133

Index to Colleges

College	Page
University of Maine at Machias, ME	133
University of Maine at Orono, ME*	133
University of Maine at Presque Isle, ME	133
University of Mary Hardin-Baylor, TX	329
University of Maryland at Baltimore, MD	139
University of Maryland at College Park, MD*	139
University of Maryland Baltimore County, MD	139
University of Maryland Eastern Shore, MD*	140
University of Maryland, University College, MD	140
University of Massachusetts at Amherst, MA*	151
University of Massachusetts at Boston, MA*	151
University of Miami, FL*	68
University of Michigan, Ann Arbor, MI*	162
University of Michigan–Dearborn, MI	163
University of Michigan–Flint, MI	163
University of Minnesota, Duluth, MN*	169
University of Minnesota, Morris, MN*	169
University of Minnesota Technical College, Crookston, MN	169
University of Minnesota Technical College, Waseca, MN	169
University of Minnesota, Twin Cities Campus, MN*	169
University of Mississippi, MS*	174
University of Missouri–Columbia, MO*	182
University of Missouri–Kansas City, MO*	182
University of Missouri–Rolla, MO*	182
University of Missouri–St Louis, MO*	182
University of Montana, MT	185
University of Montevallo, AL	10
University of Nebraska at Omaha, NE*	188
University of Nebraska–Lincoln, NE*	189
University of Nebraska Medical Center, NE*	189
University of Nevada, Las Vegas, NV*	190
University of Nevada Reno, NV*	190
University of New England, ME	133
University of New Hampshire, NH*	193
University of New Haven, CT	57
University of New Mexico, NM*	203
University of New Mexico Gallup Branch, NM	203
University of New Mexico–Los Alamos, NM	203
University of New Orleans, LA*	130
University of North Alabama, AL	10
University of North Carolina at Asheville, NC	243
University of North Carolina at Chapel Hill, NC*	243
University of North Carolina at Charlotte, NC	243
University of North Carolina at Greensboro, NC*	243
University of North Carolina at Wilmington, NC	243
University of North Dakota, ND*	246
University of North Dakota–Williston Center, ND	246
University of Northern Colorado, CO*	51
University of Northern Iowa, IA*	114
University of North Florida, FL*	69
University of Notre Dame, IN*	108
University of Oklahoma, OK*	266
University of Oklahoma Health Sciences Center, OK	267
University of Oregon, OR*	270
University of Pennsylvania, PA*	288
University of Phoenix, AZ	15
University of Pittsburgh, Pittsburgh, PA*	288
University of Pittsburgh at Bradford, PA	288
University of Pittsburgh at Greensburg, PA	289
University of Pittsburgh at Johnstown, PA	289
University of Pittsburgh at Titusville, PA	289
University of Portland, OR	270
University of Puerto Rico, Arecibo Technological University College, PR	294
University of Puerto Rico, Carolina Regional College, PR	294
University of Puerto Rico, Cayey University College, PR	294
University of Puerto Rico, Humacao University College, PR	294
University of Puerto Rico, Mayagüez, PR*	294
University of Puerto Rico, Ponce Technological University College, PR	294
University of Puerto Rico, Río Piedras, PR*	294
University of Puget Sound, WA	349
University of Redlands, CA	44
University of Rhode Island, RI*	296
University of Richmond, VA	343
University of Rochester, NY	230
University of St Thomas, TX	329
University of San Diego, CA	44
University of San Francisco, CA	44
University of Santa Clara, CA	44
University of Sarasota, FL	69
University of Scranton, PA	289
University of South Alabama, AL*	10
University of South Carolina, Columbia, SC*	301
University of South Carolina at Aiken, SC*	301
University of South Carolina at Beaufort, SC	301
University of South Carolina at Lancaster, SC	301
University of South Carolina at Salkehatchie, SC*	302
University of South Carolina at Spartanburg, SC	302
University of South Carolina at Sumter, SC*	302
University of South Carolina–Coastal Carolina College, SC*	302
University of South Dakota, SD*	305
University of Southern California, CA*	44
University of Southern Colorado, CO	51
University of Southern Maine, ME	133
University of Southern Mississippi, MS*	174
University of South Florida, FL*	69
University of Southwestern Louisiana, LA	131
University of Steubenville, OH	261
University of Tampa, FL	69
University of Tennessee at Chattanooga, TN*	312
University of Tennessee at Martin, TN	312
University of Tennessee Center for the Health Sciences, TN	312
University of Tennessee, Knoxville, TN*	312
University of Tennessee–Oak Ridge, TN	312
University of Tennessee Space Institute, TN	312
University of Texas at Arlington, TX	329
University of Texas at Austin, TX*	329
University of Texas at Dallas, TX	329
University of Texas at El Paso, TX	330
University of Texas at San Antonio, TX	330
University of Texas at Tyler, TX	330
University of Texas Health Science Center at Houston, TX	330
University of Texas Health Science Center at San Antonio, TX	330
University of Texas Medical Branch at Galveston, TX	330
University of Texas of the Permian Basin, TX	330
University of the District of Columbia, DC*	60
University of the Pacific, CA	45
University of the Sacred Heart, PR	294
University of the South, TN	312
University of the State of New York Regents External Degree Program, NY	230
University of Toledo, OH	261
University of Tulsa, OK*	267
University of Utah, UT*	333
University of Vermont, VT*	335
University of Washington, WA*	349
University of West Florida, FL	69
University of West Los Angeles, CA	45
University of Wisconsin Center–Baraboo/Sauk County, WI*	357
University of Wisconsin Center–Barron County, WI*	357
University of Wisconsin Center–Fox Valley, WI*	357
University of Wisconsin Center–Manitowoc County, WI*	358
University of Wisconsin Center–Marathon County, WI*	358
University of Wisconsin Center–Marinette County, WI*	358
University of Wisconsin Center–Marshfield/Wood County, WI*	358
University of Wisconsin Center–Richland, WI*	358

*Member of National University Continuing Education Association

Index to Colleges

College	Page
University of Wisconsin Center–Rock County, WI*	358
University of Wisconsin Center–Sheboygan County, WI*	358
University of Wisconsin Center–Washington County, WI*	359
University of Wisconsin Center–Waukesha County, WI*	359
University of Wisconsin–Eau Claire, WI*	359
University of Wisconsin–Green Bay, WI*	359
University of Wisconsin–La Crosse, WI*	359
University of Wisconsin–Madison, WI*	359
University of Wisconsin–Milwaukee, WI*	360
University of Wisconsin–Oshkosh, WI*	360
University of Wisconsin–Parkside, WI*	360
University of Wisconsin–Platteville, WI*	360
University of Wisconsin–River Falls, WI*	360
University of Wisconsin–Stevens Point, WI*	360
University of Wisconsin–Stout, WI*	361
University of Wisconsin–Superior, WI*	361
University of Wisconsin–Whitewater, WI*	361
University of Wyoming, WY*	363
Upper Iowa University, IA*	114
Upsala College, NJ	201
Urbana College, OH	261
Ursinus College, PA	289
Ursuline College, OH	261
Utah State University, UT*	333
Utah Technical College at Provo, UT	333
Utah Technical College at Salt Lake, UT	333
Utica College of Syracuse University, NY	230
Utica School of Commerce, NY	230
Valdosta State College, GA	77
Valencia Community College, FL	69
Valley City State College, ND	246
Valparaiso University, IN	108
Vance-Granville Community College, NC	244
Vanderbilt University, TN	312
VanderCook College of Music, IL	99
Vassar College, NY	230
Vennard College, IA	114
Vermillion Community College, MN	170
Vermont College, VT—See Norwich University, Vermont College	
Vermont Law School, VT	336
Vernon Regional Junior College, TX	331
Victoria College, TX	331
Victor Valley College, CA	45
Villa Julie College, MD	140
Villa Maria College, PA	289
Villa Maria College of Buffalo, NY	230
Villanova University, PA	289
Vincennes University, IN	108
Virginia Commonwealth University, VA*	343
Virginia Highlands Community College, VA	343
Virginia Intermont College, VA	343
Virginia Polytechnic Institute and State University, VA*	343
Virginia State University, VA	343
Virginia Wesleyan College, VA	343
Virginia Western Community College, VA	344
Viterbo College, WI	361
Volunteer State Community College, TN	313
Voorhees College, SC	302
Wagner College, NY	231
Wake Forest University, NC	244
Wake Technical College, NC	244
Walker College, AL	10
Wallace State Community College, AL	10
Walla Walla College, WA	349
Walla Walla Community College, WA	349
Walsh College, OH	261
Walsh College of Accountancy and Business Administration, MI	163
Walters State Community College, TN	313
Wang Institute of Graduate Studies, MA	152
Warner Pacific College, OR	270
Warner Southern College, FL	69
Warren Wilson College, NC	244
Wartburg College, IA	114
Wartburg Theological Seminary, IA	114
Washburn University of Topeka, KS	120
Washington Bible College, MD	140
Washington College, MD	140
Washington Technical College, OH	261
Washington Theological Union, MD	140
Washington University, MO	182
Washtenaw Community College, MI	163
Waterbury State Technical College, CT	57
Watterson College, KY	127
Waubonsee Community College, IL	99
Waycross Junior College, GA	77
Wayland Baptist University, TX	331
Wayne Community College, NC	244
Wayne County Community College, MI	163
Waynesburg College, PA	289
Wayne State College, NE	189
Wayne State University, MI*	163
Weatherford College, TX	331
Webber College, FL	70
Weber State College, UT*	333
Webster University, MO*	183
Wellesley College, MA	152
Wells College, NY	231
Wenatchee Valley College, WA	349
Wentworth Institute of Technology, MA	152
Wesleyan College, GA	77
Wesleyan University, CT	57
Wesley College, DE	58
Wesley Theological Seminary, DC	61
Westark Community College, AR	18
Westbrook College, ME	134
Westchester Business Institute, NY	231
Westchester Community College, NY	231
West Chester University of Pennsylvania, PA	290
West Coast Christian College, CA	45
West Coast University, CA	45
Western Baptist College, OR	271
Western Bible College, CO	52
Western Carolina University, NC*	244
Western Connecticut State University, CT	57
Western Conservative Baptist Seminary, OR	271
Western Evangelical Seminary, OR	271
Western Illinois University, IL*	99
Western International University, AZ	15
Western Iowa Tech Community College, IA	114
Western Kentucky University, KY	127
Western Maryland College, MD	140
Western Michigan University, MI*	163
Western Montana College, MT	185
Western Nebraska Technical College, NE	189
Western Nevada Community College, NV	190
Western New England College, MA	152
Western New Mexico University, NM	204
Western Oklahoma State College, OK	267
Western Oregon State College, OR	271
Western Piedmont Community College, NC	244
Western State College of Colorado, CO	52
Western State University College of Law of Orange County, CA	45
Western State University College of Law of San Diego, CA	45
Western Texas College, TX	331
Western Washington University, WA	349
Western Wisconsin Technical Institute, WI	361
Western Wyoming Community College, WY	363
Westfield State College, MA	152
West Georgia College, GA*	77
West Hills College, CA	46
West Liberty State College, WV	352
West Los Angeles College, CA	46

Index to Colleges

Westmar College, IA	114
Westminster Choir College, NJ	201
Westminster College, PA	290
Westminster College of Salt Lake City, UT	333
Westminster Theological Seminary, PA	290
Westmoreland County Community College, PA	290
Weston School of Theology, MA	152
West Shore Community College, MI	164
West Texas State University, TX	331
West Valley College, CA	46
West Virginia College of Graduate Studies, WV	352
West Virginia Institute of Technology, WV	352
West Virginia Northern Community College, WV	352
West Virginia State College, WV	352
West Virginia University, WV*	352
West Virginia University, Potomac State College, WV—See Potomac State College of West Virginia University	
West Virginia Wesleyan College, WV	353
Wharton County Junior College, TX	331
Whatcom Community College, WA	349
Wheaton College, IL	100
Wheaton College, MA	152
Wheeling College, WV	353
Wheelock College, MA	152
White Pines College, NH	193
Whittier College, CA	46
Whitworth College, WA	350
Wichita State University, KS*	120
Widener University, PA*	290
Widener University, Delaware Campus, DE	58
Widener University, Pennsylvania Campus, PA	290
Wiley College, TX	332
Wilkes College, PA	290
Wilkes Community College, NC	245
Willamette University, OR	271
William Carey College, MS	174
William Jewell College, MO	183
William Mitchell College of Law, MN	170
William Paterson College of New Jersey, NJ	201
William Penn College, IA	114
William Rainey Harper College, IL	100
Williamsburg Technical College, SC	302
William Smith College, NY	231
Williamsport Area Community College, PA	290
Williamsport School of Commerce, PA	291
William Tyndale College, MI	164
William Woods College, MO	183
Willmar Community College, MN	170
Wilmington College, DE*	59
Wilmington College of Ohio, OH	261
Wilson College, PA	291
Wingate College, NC	245
Winona State University, MN	170
Winston-Salem State University, NC	245
Winthrop College, SC	302
Wisconsin Conservatory of Music, WI	361
Wisconsin Indianhead Technical Institute, Ashland Campus, WI	362
Wisconsin Indianhead Technical Institute, New Richmond Campus, WI	362
Wisconsin Indianhead Technical Institute, Rice Lake Campus, WI	362
Wisconsin Indianhead Technical Institute, Superior Campus, WI	362
Wisconsin Lutheran College, WI	362
Wisconsin School of Professional Psychology, WI	362
Wittenberg University, OH	262
Wofford College, SC	302
Woodbury University, CA	46
Wood Junior College, MS	174
Worcester Polytechnic Institute, MA	153
Worcester State College, MA*	153
Worthington Community College, MN	170
Wor-Wic Tech Community College, MD	140
Wright College, IL—See City Colleges of Chicago, Wilbur Wright College	
Wright State University, OH	262
Wright State University, Western Ohio Branch Campus, OH	262
Xavier University, OH	262
Xavier University of Louisiana, LA	131
Yakima Valley Community College, WA	350
Yale University, CT	58
Yankton College, SD	305
Yavapai College, AZ	15
Yeshiva University of Los Angeles, CA	46
York College, NE	189
York College, NY—See City University of New York, York College	
York College of Pennsylvania, PA	291
York Technical College, SC	303
Young Harris College, GA	78
Youngstown State University, OH*	262
Yuba College, CA	46

*Member of National University Continuing Education Association

Have You Seen These Other Publications from Peterson's Guides?

New Horizons:
The Education and Career Guide for Adults
William C. Haponski, Ph.D., and Charles E. McCabe, M.B.A.

Covers a broad spectrum of options for adults who want to continue their education, including bachelor's and associate degree, external degree, and professional certificate programs, and correspondence courses. Originally published as *Back to School: The College Guide for Adults*, this new edition places heavier emphasis on career-related aspects of adult education. March 1985.

6" x 9", 250 pages (approx.)   Stock no. 3304
ISBN 0-87866-330-4   **$7.95 paperback**

Peterson's Annual Guides/Undergraduate Study
Guide to Four-Year Colleges 1985
FIFTEENTH EDITION
Managing Editor: Kim R. Kaye
Book Editor: Joan H. Hunter

The largest, most up-to-date guide to all 1,900 accredited four-year colleges in the United States and Canada. Contains concise college profiles, a reader guidance section, and two-page "Messages from the Colleges" that are found in no other guide.

8½" x 11", 2,188 pages   Stock no. 2316
ISBN 0-87866-231-6   **$12.95 paperback**

Peterson's Annual Guides/Undergraduate Study
Guide to Two-Year Colleges 1985
FIFTEENTH EDITION
Managing Editor: Kim R. Kaye
Book Editor: Joan H. Hunter

This Guide covers over 1,450 accredited U.S. institutions that grant associate degrees. It contains basic college profiles, 1,800-word college essays written by admissions directors who chose to provide in-depth information, and directories of colleges by geographical area and by major. It serves as a companion volume to the *Guide to Four-Year Colleges 1985*.

8½" x 11", 432 pages   Stock no. 2324
ISBN 0-87866-232-4   **$9.95 paperback**

The College Money Handbook 1985:
The Complete Guide to Expenses, Scholarships, Loans, Jobs, and Special Aid Programs at Four-Year Colleges
SECOND EDITION
Editor: Karen C. Hegener

The only book that describes the complete picture of costs and financial aid at accredited four-year colleges in the United States. The book is divided into three sections: an overview of the financial aid process and ways to make it work for you; cost and aid profiles of each college, showing need-based and merit scholarship programs available; and directories listing colleges by the type of financial aid programs they offer.

8½" x 11", 531 pages   Stock no. 2820
ISBN 0-87866-282-0   **$12.95 paperback**

Peterson's Guide to College Admissions:
Getting into the College of Your Choice
THIRD EDITION
R. Fred Zuker and Karen C. Hegener

This updated edition takes students behind the scenes at college admissions offices and gives current advice from admissions directors all across the country. Contains dozens of campus photos and capsule profiles of 1,700 four-year colleges.

8½" x 11", 366 pages   Stock no. 2243
ISBN 0-87866-224-3   **$9.95 paperback**

SAT Success:
Peterson's Study Guide to English and Math Skills for College Entrance Examinations: SAT, ACT, and PSAT
Joan Davenport Carris and Michael R. Crystal

This brand-new step-by-step text is designed as an effective self-instruction aid to build both the skills and the confidence of students preparing for college entrance examinations. Quiz-filled verbal and math sections plus mock SATs and actual questions from recent tests are included for practice.

8½" x 11", 380 pages   Stock no. 2081
ISBN 0-87866-208-1   **$8.95 paperback**

Corporate Tuition Aid Programs:
A Directory of College Financial Aid for Employees at America's Largest Corporations
Joseph P. O'Neill

Concise charts detail policies and procedures on tuition benefits for 650 *Fortune* 1,000 companies. Explains which employees are eligible, how long they must be employed, what percent of tuition costs are paid by the company, when the employee will be reimbursed, and which types of courses are included.

8½" x 11", 200 pages   Stock no. 6338
ISBN 0-87866-338-X   **$12.95 paperback**

The Independent Study Catalog:
NUCEA's Guide to Independent Study Through Correspondence Instruction 1983–1985
Editor: Joan H. Hunter

A new edition of the ultimate education "wishbook" for people who want to study on their own without the restrictions of regular class attendance. Students can choose from more than 12,000 correspondence courses offered by 72 colleges and universities. Credit and noncredit courses are available at the elementary, high school, undergraduate, and graduate levels.

8½" x 11", 120 pages   Stock no. 1808
ISBN 0-87866-180-8   **$5.95 paperback**

How to Order

These publications are available from all good booksellers, or you may order direct from **Peterson's Guides, Dept. 4629, P.O. Box 2123, Princeton, New Jersey 08540**. Please note that prices are necessarily subject to change without notice.

- Enclose full payment for each book, plus postage and handling charges as follows:

Amount of Order	4th-Class Postage and Handling Charges
$1–$10	$1.25
$10.01–$20	$2.00
$20.01–$40	$3.00
$40.01 +	Add $1.00 shipping and handling for every additional $20 worth of books ordered.

Place your order TOLL-FREE by calling 800-225-0261 between 8:30 A.M. and 4:30 P.M. Eastern time, Monday through Friday. Telephone orders over $15 may be charged to your charge card; institutional and trade orders over $20 may be billed. From New Jersey, Alaska, Hawaii, and outside the United States, call 609-924-5338.

- For faster shipment via United Parcel Service (UPS), add $2.00 over and above the appropriate fourth-class book-rate charges listed.
- Bookstores and tax-exempt organizations should contact us for appropriate discounts.
- You may charge your order to VISA, MasterCard, or American Express. Minimum charge order: $15. Please include the name, account number, and validation and expiration dates for charge orders.
- New Jersey residents should add 6% sales tax to the cost of the books, excluding the postage and handling charge.
- Write for a free catalog describing all of our latest publications.